TREATIES AND OTHER INTERNATIONAL AGREEMENTS OF THE UNITED STATES OF AMERICA 1776–1949

Compiled under the direction of

CHARLES I. BEVANS, LL.B.

Assistant Legal Adviser, Department of State

Volume 2

MULTILATERAL

1918–1930

DEPARTMENT OF STATE PUBLICATION 8441

Released May 1969

CONTENTS[1]

[1] In order to provide a complete chronological list of agreements entered into by the United States during the years covered in this volume, the table of contents includes citations to two agreements which are not printed in this compilation because they entered into force for the United States after 1949 and are therefore contained in the series entitled *United States Treaties and Other International Agreements* (UST). For a more detailed explanation of the scope of these volumes, see the preface at the beginning of volume 1.

ARMISTICE WITH AUSTRIA-HUNGARY

*Protocol and supplement signed at Villa Giusti, near Serravalle, Italy,
November 3, 1918*[1]
Entered into force November 4, 1918[2]

> 1919 For. Rel. (Paris Peace Conference,
> II) 175; Senate Document 147, 66th
> Congress, 1st session

[TRANSLATION]

TERMS OF ARMISTICE WITH AUSTRIA-HUNGARY, NOVEMBER 3, 1918

(A) MILITARY CLAUSES

1. Immediate cessation of hostilities by land and sea and air.

2. Total demobilization of Austro-Hungarian Army and immediate withdrawal of Austro-Hungarian forces operating on front from North Sea to Switzerland.

Within Austro-Hungarian territory limited as in clause 3, below, there shall only be maintained as an organized military force a maximum of 20 divisions reduced to prewar effectives.

Half the divisional corps and army artillery and equipment shall be collected at points to be indicated by Allies and United States of America for delivery to them, beginning with all such material as exists in territories to be evacuated by Austro-Hungarian forces.

3. Evacuation of all territories invaded by Austria-Hungary since the beginning of the war. Withdrawal within such periods as shall be determined by the commander in chief of allied forces on each front, of Austro-Hungarian armies behind a line fixed as follows: From Piz Umbrail to north of Stelvio it will follow crest of Rhetian Alps to sources of the Adige and Eisach, passing thence by the Reschen and Brenner and the heights of Oetz and Ziller.

---

[1] The armistice was signed by representatives of the Supreme Command of the Austro-Hungarian Army and, on behalf of the Allied and Associated Powers, by representatives of the Supreme Command of the Italian Army.

[2] The armistice controlled relations between the contracting parties until the entry into force of the treaty of peace signed at St. Germain-en-Laye Sept. 10, 1919. The United States did not become a party to the treaty of peace but signed a treaty establishing friendly relations with Austria at Vienna Aug. 24, 1921 (TS 659, *post*) and one with Hungary at Budapest Aug. 29, 1921 (TS 660, *post*).

The line thence turns south, crossing Mount Toblach as far as present frontier of Carnic Alps. It follows this line as far as Mount Tarvis, thence to watershed of Julian Alps by Col de Predil, Mount Mangart, the Tricorno (Terglou) and watershed Podberdo, Podlaniscan, and Idria. From this point the line turns southeast toward the Schneeberg, excluding the whole basin of the Save River and its tributaries; from Schneeberg it descends the coast in such a way as to include Castua, Mattuglia, and Volosca in evacuated territories.

It will follow the administrative limits of present Province of Dalmatia, including to the north Lisarica and Tribania and to the south, territory limited by a line from the shore of Cape Planka to the summits of watershed eastward so as to include in evacuated area all the valleys and watercourses flowing toward Sebenico, such as Cicola, Karka, Butisnica, and their tributaries. It will also include all the islands in the north and west of Dalmatia from Premuda, Selve, Uubo, Scherba, Maon, Pago, and Puntadura Islands, in the north, up to Meleda, in the south, embracing Sant' Andrea, Busi, Lissa, Lesina, Tercola, Curzolä, Cazza, and Lagosta as well as neighboring rocks and islets and Pelagosa, only excepting the islands of great and small Zirona, Bua, Solta, and Brazza.

All territories thus evacuated will be occupied by allied and American troops.

All military and railway equipment of all kinds (including coal) within these territories to be left in situ, and surrendered to the Allies and America according to special orders given by commander in chief of forces of associated powers on different fronts.

No new destruction, pillage, or requisition by enemy troops in territories to be evacuated by them and occupied by associated powers.

4. Allied armies shall have the right of free movement over all road and rail and water ways in Austro-Hungarian territory which shall be necessary.

Armies of associated powers shall occupy such strategic points in Austria-Hungary at such times as they may deem necessary to enable them to conduct military operations or to maintain order.

They shall have the right of requisition on payment for troops of associated powers wherever they may be.

5. Complete evacuation of all German troops within 15 days not only from Italian and Balkan fronts but from all Austro-Hungarian territory.

Internment of all German troops which have not left Austria-Hungary before that date.

6. Administration of evacuated territories of Austria-Hungary will provisionally be intrusted to local authorities under control of the allied and associated armies of occupation.

7. Immediate repatriation, without reciprocity, of all prisoners of war and interned allied subjects and of civilian populations evacuated from their

homes on conditions to be laid down by commanders in chief of forces of allied powers on various fronts.

8. Sick and wounded who can not be removed from evacuated territory will be cared for by Austro-Hungarian personnel who will be left on the spot with medical material required.

(B) NAVAL CONDITIONS

1. Immediate cessation of all hostilities at sea and definite information to be given as to location and movements of all Austro-Hungarian ships.

Notification to be made to neutrals that free navigation in all territorial waters is given to the naval and mercantile marines of the allied and associated powers, all questions of neutrality being waived.

2. Surrender to the Allies and United States of America of 15 Austro-Hungarian submarines completed between years 1910 and 1918 and of all German submarines which are in or may hereafter enter Austro-Hungarian territorial waters. All other Austro-Hungarian submarines to be paid off and completely disarmed and to remain under supervision of the Allies.

3. Surrender to the Allies and United States of America, with their complete armament and equipment, of 3 battleships, 3 light cruisers, 9 destroyers, 12 torpedo boats, 1 mine layer, 6 Danube monitors, to be designated by the Allies and United States of America.

All other surface war ships (including river craft) are to be concentrated in Austro-Hungarian naval bases to be designated by the Allies and United States of America, and are to be paid off, completely disarmed, and placed under supervision of Allies and United States of America.

4. Free navigation to all war ships and merchant ships of allied and associated powers to be given in Adriatic, in territorial waters, and up River Danube and its tributaries, and Austro-Hungarian territory.

Allies and associated powers shall have right to sweep up all mine fields and obstructions, and positions of these are to be indicated.

In order to insure free navigation on the Danube, Allies and United States of America shall be empowered to occupy or to dismantle all fortifications or defense works.

5. Existing blockade conditions set up by allied and associated powers are to remain unchanged, and all Austro-Hungarian merchant ships found at sea are to remain liable to capture with the exceptions which may be made by a commission nominated by Allies and United States.

6. All naval aircraft are to be concentrated and immobilized in Austro-Hungarian bases to be designated by Allies and United States of America.

7. Evacuation of all the Italian coast, and of all ports occupied by Austria-Hungary outside their national territory, and abandonment of all floating craft, naval materials, equipment, and materials for inland navigation of all kinds.

8. Occupation by Allies and United States of America of land and sea fortifications and islands which form defenses, and of dockyards and arsenals at Pola.

9. All merchant vessels held by Austria-Hungary belonging to Allies and associated powers to be returned.

10. No destruction of ships or of materials to be permitted before evacuation, surrender, or restoration.

11. All naval and mercantile prisoners of war of allied and associated powers in Austro-Hungarian hands to be returned without reciprocity.

The undersigned plenipotentiaries, duly authorized, signify their approval of above conditions:

November 3, 1918.

Representatives of Austro-Hungarian supreme command	Representatives of Italian supreme command
Victor Weber, Edler von Webenau	Ten. Gen. Pietro Badoglio
Karl Schneller	Magg. Gen. Scipione Scipioni
Y. von Liechtenstein	Colonn. Tullio Marchetti
J. V. Nyékhegyi	Colonn. Pietro Gazzera
Zwierkowski	Colonn. Pietro Maravigna
Victor, Freiherr von Seiller	Colonn. Alberto Pariani
Kamillo Ruggera	Cap. Vasc. Francesco Accinni

Supplement to Protocol

Contains details and executive clauses of certain points of the armistice between the allied and associated powers and Austria-Hungary.

(I) MILITARY CLAUSES

1. Hostilities on land, sea, and air, will cease on all Austro-Hungarian fronts 24 hours after the signing of the armistice, i.e., at 3 o'clock on November 4 (Central European time).

From that hour the Italian and allied troops will not advance beyond the line then reached.

The Austro-Hungarian troops and those of her allies must retire to a distance of at least 3 kilometers (as the crow flies) from the line reached by the Italian troops or by troops of allied countries. Inhabitants of the 3-kilometer zone included between the two lines (above-mentioned) will be able to obtain necessary supplies from their own army or those of the Allies.

All Austro-Hungarian troops who may be at the rear of the fighting lines reached by the Italian troops, on the cessation of hostilities must be regarded as prisoners of war.

2. Regarding the clauses included in articles 2 and 3 concerning artillery equipment and war material to be either collected in places indicated or left in territories which are to be evacuated, the Italian plenipotentiaries repre-

senting all the allied and associated powers, give to the said clauses the following interpretation, which will be carried into execution:

(*a*) Any material or part thereof which may be used for the purpose of war must be given up to the allied and associated powers. The Austro-Hungarian army and the German troops are only authorized to take personal arms and equipment belonging to troops evacuating the territories mentioned in article 3, besides officers' chargers, the transport train, and horses specially allotted to each unit for transport of food supplies, kitchens, officers' luggage, and medical material. This clause applies to the whole army and to all the services.

(*b*) Concerning artillery, it has been arranged that the Austro-Hungarian army and German troops shall abandon all artillery material and equipment in the territory to be evacuated.

The calculations necessary for obtaining a complete and exact total of the artillery divisions and army corps at the disposal of Austro-Hungary on the cessation of hostilities (half of which must be given up to the associated powers) will be made later, in order to arrange, if necessary, for the delivery of other Austro-Hungarian artillery material and for the possible eventual return of material to the Austro-Hungarian army by the allied and associated armies.

All artillery which does not actually form part of the divisional artillery and army corps must be given up, without exception. It will not, however, be necessary to calculate the amount.

(*c*) On the Italian front the delivery of divisional and army corps artillery will be effected at the following places: Trento, Bolzano, Pieve di Cadore, Stazione per la Carnia, Tolmino, Gorizia, and Trieste.

3. Special commissions will be selected by the commanders in chief of allied and associated armies on the various Austro-Hungarian fronts, which will immediately proceed, accompanied by the necessary escorts, to the places they regard as the most suitable from which to control the execution of the provisions established above.

4. It has been determined that the designations M. Toblach and M. Tarvis indicate the groups of mountains dominating the ridge of Toblach Mountains and the Valley of Tarvis.

5. The retirement of Austro-Hungarian troops and those of her allies beyond the lines indicated in article 3 of the protocol of armistice conditions, will take place within 15 days of the cessation of hostilities, as far as the Italian front is concerned.

On the Italian front, Austro-Hungarian troops and those of her allies must have retired beyond the line Tonale—Noce—Lavis—Avisio—Pordoi—Lavinallongo—Falzarego—Pieve di Cadore—Colle Mauria—Alto Tagliamento—Fella—Raccolana—Selle Nevea—Isonzo by the fifth day; they must also have evacuated the Dalmatian territory indicated above.

Austro-Hungarian troops on land and sea, or those of her allies, not having evacuated the territories indicated within the period of 15 days will be regarded as prisoners of war.

6. The payment of any requisitions made by the armies of the allied and associated armies on Austro-Hungarian territory will be carried out according to paragraph 1 of page 227 of "Servizio in Guerra—Part II, Edizone 1915," actually in force in the Italian army.

7. As regards railways and the exercise of the rights confirmed upon the associated powers by article 4 of the armistice agreement between the allied powers and Austria-Hungary, it has been determined that the transport of troops, war material, and supplies for allied and associated powers on the Austro-Hungarian railways system, outside territory evacuated in accordance with the terms of the armistice, and the direction and working of the railways shall be effected by the employees of the Austro-Hungarian railway administration, under the supervision of special commissioners selected by the allied powers, and the military Italian headquarters which it will be considered necessary to establish.

The Austro-Hungarian authorities will give priority to allied military trains and will guarantee their safety.

8. On territory to be evacuated at the cessation of hostilities all mines on roads or railway tracts, all mine fields and other devices for interrupting communication by road or rail must be rendered inactive and harmless.

9. Within a period of eight days from the cessation of hostilities, prisoners and Italian subjects interned in Austria-Hungary must cease all work, except in the case of prisoners and interned who have been employed in agricultural pursuits previous to the day on which the armistice was signed. In any case they must be ready to leave at once on request of the commander in chief of the Italian Army.

10. Austria-Hungary must provide for the protection, safety, and supplies (expenses of these to be repaid) of the various commissions selected by the allied governments to take over war material and to exercise general control, whether in the territory to be evacuated or in any other part of Austria-Hungary.

(II) NAVAL CLAUSES

1. The hour for the cessation of hostilities by sea will be the same as that of the cessation of hostilities by land and air.

Before that time the Austro-Hungarian Government must have furnished the Italian Government, and those of the associated powers, with the necessary information concerning the position and movements of the Austro-Hungarian ships, through the wireless station at Pola, which will transmit the information to Venice.

2. The units referred to in Articles II and III, to be surrendered to the associated powers, must return to Venice between 8 a. m. and 3 p. m. on

November 6; they will take a pilot on board 14 miles from the coast. An exception is made as regards the Danube monitors, which will be required to proceed to a port indicated by the commander in chief of the forces of the associated powers on the Balkan front, under such conditions as he may determine.

3. The following ships will proceed to Venice:

Teghethoff	*Saida*
Prinz Eugen	*Novara*
Ferdinand Max	*Helgoland*

Nine destroyers of the *Tatra* type (at least 800 tons) of most recent construction.

Twelve torpedo boats (200-ton type).

Mine layer *Chamaleon*.

Fifteen submarines built between 1910 and 1918, and all German submarines which are, or may eventually be, in Austro-Hungarian waters.

Premeditated damage, or damage occurring on board the ships to be surrendered will be regarded by the Allied Governments as a grave infringement of the present armistice terms.

The Lago di Garda flotilla will be surrendered to the associated powers in the port of Riva.

All ships to be surrendered to the associated powers will be concentrated in the ports of Buccari and Spalato within 48 hours of the cessation of hostilities.

4. As regards the right of sweeping mine fields and destroying barrages, the Austro-Hungarian Government guarantees to deliver the maps of mine fields and barrages at Pola, Cattaro, and Fiume to the commander of the port of Venice, and to the admiral of the fleet at Brindisi within 48 hours of the cessation of hostilities, and within 96 hours of the cessation of hostilities, maps of mine fields and barrages in the Mediterranean and Italian lakes and rivers, with additional notification of such mine fields or barrages laid by order of the German Government as are within their knowledge.

Within the same period of 96 hours a similar communication concerning the Danube and the Black Sea will be delivered to the commander of the associated forces on the Balkan front.

5. The restitution of merchant ships belonging to the associated powers will take place within 96 hours of the cessation of hostilities, in accordance with the indications determined by each associated power which will be transmitted to the Austro-Hungarian Government. The associated powers reserve to themselves the constitution of the commission referred to in Article 5, and of informing the Austro-Hungarian Government of its functions and of the place in which it will meet.

6. The naval base referred to in Article VI is Spalato.

7. The evacuation referred to in Article VII will be effected within the period fixed for the retirement of the troops beyond the armistice lines. There must be no damage to fixed, mobile, or floating material in the ports.

Evacuations may be effected via the Lagoon canals by means of Austro-Hungarian boats which may be brought in from outside.

8. The occupation referred to in Article VIII will take place within 48 hours of the cessation of hostilities.

The Austro-Hungarian authorities must guarantee the safety of vessels transporting troops for the occupation of Pola and of islands and other places as provided for in the terms of the armistice for the land Army.

The Austro-Hungarian Government will give directions that the ships belonging to associated powers proceeding to Pola should be met 14 miles out by pilots capable of showing them the safest way into port. All damage to the persons or property of the associated powers will be regarded as a grave infringement of the present armistice terms.

The undersigned duly authorized plenipotentiaries have signified their approval of the above conditions.

November 3, 1918.

Representatives of the Supreme Command of the Austro-Hungarian Army	*Representatives of the Supreme Command of the Italian Army*
VICTOR WEBER, EDLER VON WEBENAU	Ten. Gen. PIETRO BADOGLIO
KARL SCHNELLER	Magg. Gen. SCIPIONE SCIPIONI
Y. VON LIECHTENSTEIN	Colonn. TULLIO MARCHETTI
J. V. NYÉKHEGYI	Colonn. PIETRO GAZZERA
ZWIERKOWSKI	Colonn. PIETRO MARAVIGNA
VICTOR, FREIHERR VON SEILLER	Colonn. ALBERTO PARIANI
KAMILLO RUGGERA	Cap. Vasc. FRANCESCO ACCINNI

ARMISTICE WITH GERMANY

Convention, with annexes, addendum, and declaration by German pleni-
potentiaries, signed at Compiègne Forest, near Rethondes, France,
November 11, 1918 [1]
Entered into force November 11, 1918, for a period of 36 days
Prolonged and supplemented by conventions of December 13, 1918, [2]
January 16, 1919, [3] *and February 16, 1919* [4]
Article XVI amended by protocol of April 4, 1919 [5]

> 1919 For. Rel. (Paris Peace Conference,
> II) 1; Senate Document 147, 66th Con-
> gress, 1st session

[TRANSLATION]

TERMS OF ARMISTICE WITH GERMANY, NOVEMBER 11, 1918

Between Marshal Foch, commander in chief of the allied armies, acting
in the name of the allied and associated powers, with Admiral Wemyss, first
sea lord, on the one hand, and Herr Erzberger, secretary of state, president
of the German delegation, Count von Oberndorff, envoy extraordinary and
minister plenipotentiary, Maj. Gen. von Winterfeldt, Capt. Vanselow (German navy), duly empowered and acting with the concurrence of the German
chancellor, on the other hand.

An armistice has been concluded on the following conditions:

Conditions of the Armistice Concluded With Germany

(A) CLAUSES RELATING TO THE WESTERN FRONT

I. Cessation of hostilities by land and in the air six hours after the signing
of the armistice.

---

[1] The armistice controlled relations between the contracting parties until the entry into
force of the treaty of peace signed at Versailles June 28, 1919 (*post*, p. 43). The United
States did not become a party to the treaty of peace but signed a treaty establishing friendly
relations with Germany at Berlin Aug. 25, 1921 (TS 658, *post*).

[2] *Post*, p. 23.
[3] *Post*, p. 24.
[4] *Post*, p. 28.
[5] *Post*, p. 30.

II. Immediate evacuation of the invaded countries—Belgium, France, Luxemburg, as well as Alsace-Lorraine—so ordered as to be completed within 15 days from the signature of the armistice.

German troops which have not left the above-mentioned territories within the period fixed shall be made prisoners of war.

Occupation by the allied and United States forces jointly shall keep pace with the evacuation in these areas.

All movements of evacuation and occupation shall be regulated in accordance with a note (Annexe 1) determined at the time of the signing of the armistice.

III. Repatriation, beginning at once, to be completed within 15 days, of all inhabitants of the countries above enumerated (including hostages, persons under trial, or condemned).

IV. Surrender in good condition by the German armies of the following equipment: 5,000 guns (2,500 heavy, 2,500 field), 25,000 machine guns, 3,000 trench mortars, 1,700 aeroplanes (fighters, bombers—firstly all D. 7's and night-bombing machines).

The above to be delivered in situ to the allied and United States troops in accordance with the detailed conditions laid down in the note (Annexe 1) determined at the time of the signing of the armistice.

V. Evacuation by the German armies of the districts on the left bank of the Rhine. These districts on the left bank of the Rhine shall be administered by the local authorities under the control of the allied and United States armies of occupation.

The occupation of these territories by allied and United States troops shall be assured by garrisons holding the principal crossings of the Rhine (Mainz, Coblenz, Cologne), together with bridgeheads at these points of a 30-kilometer (about 19 miles) radius on the right bank, and by garrisons similarly holding the strategic points of the area.

A neutral zone shall be reserved on the right bank of the Rhine, between the river and a line drawn parallel to the bridgeheads and to the river and 10 kilometers (6¼ miles) distant from them, between the Dutch frontier and the Swiss frontier.

The evacuation by the enemy of the Rhine districts (right and left banks) shall be so ordered as to be completed within a further period of 16 days, in all 31 days after the signing of the armistice.

All movements of evacuation and occupation shall be regulated according to the note (Annexe 1) determined at the time of the signing of the armistice.

VI. In all territories evacuated by the enemy, evacuation of the inhabitants shall be forbidden; no damage or harm shall be done to the persons or property of the inhabitants.

No person shall be prosecuted for having taken part in any military measures previous to the signing of the armistice.

No destruction of any kind to be committed.

Military establishments of all kinds shall be delivered intact, as well as military stores, food, munitions, and equipment, which shall not have been removed during the periods fixed for evacuation.

Stores of food of all kinds for the civil population, cattle, etc., shall be left in situ.

No measure of a general character shall be taken, and no official order shall be given which would have as a consequence the depreciation of industrial establishments or a reduction of their personnel.

VII. Roads and means of communications of every kind, railroads, waterways, roads, bridges, telegraphs, telephones, shall be in no manner impaired.

All civil and military personnel at present employed on them shall remain.

Five thousand locomotives and 150,000 wagons, in good working order, with all necessary spare parts and fittings, shall be delivered to the associated powers within the period fixed in Annexe No. 2 (not exceeding 31 days in all).

Five thousand motor lorries are also to be delivered in good condition within 36 days.

The railways of Alsace-Lorraine shall be handed over within 31 days, together with all personnel and material belonging to the organization of this system.

Further, the necessary working material in the territories on the left bank of the Rhine shall be left in situ.

All stores of coal and material for the upkeep of permanent way, signals, and repair shops, shall be left in situ and kept in an efficient state by Germany, so far as the working of the means of communication on the left bank of the Rhine is concerned.

All lighters taken from the Allies shall be restored to them.

The note attached as Annexe 2 defines the details of these measures.

VIII. The German command shall be responsible for revealing within 48 hours after the signing of the armistice all mines or delay-action fuzes disposed on territories evacuated by the German troops, and shall assist in their discovery and destruction.

The German command shall also reveal all destructive measures that may have been taken (such as poisoning or pollution of wells, springs, etc.).

Breaches of these clauses will involve reprisals.

IX. The right of requisition shall be exercised by the allied and United States armies in all occupied territories, save for settlement of accounts with authorized persons.

The upkeep of the troops of occupation in the Rhine districts (excluding Alsace-Lorraine) shall be charged to the German Government.

X. The immediate repatriation, without reciprocity, according to detailed conditions which shall be fixed, of all allied and United States prisoners of war, including those under trial and condemned. The allied powers and the United States of America shall be able to dispose of these prisoners as they think fit. This condition annuls all other conventions regarding prisoners of war, including that of July, 1918, now being ratified. However, the return of German prisoners of war interned in Holland and Switzerland shall continue as heretofore. The return of German prisoners of war shall be settled at the conclusion of the peace preliminaries.

XI. Sick and wounded who can not be removed from territory evacuated by the German forces shall be cared for by German personnel, who shall be left on the spot with the material required.

(B) CLAUSES RELATING TO THE EASTERN FRONTIERS OF GERMANY

XII. All German troops at present in any territory which before the war formed part of Austria-Hungary, Roumania, or Turkey, shall withdraw within the frontiers of Germany as they existed on August 1, 1914, and all German troops at present in territories which before the war formed part of Russia must likewise return to within the frontiers of Germany as above defined, as soon as the Allies shall think the moment suitable, having regard to the internal situation of these territories.

XIII. Evacuation of German troops to begin at once, and all German instructors, prisoners and agents, civilians as well as military, now on the territory of Russia (frontiers as defined on Aug. 1, 1914), to be recalled.

XIV. German troops to cease at once all requisitions and seizures and any other coercive measures with a view to obtaining supplies intended for Germany in Roumania and Russia (frontiers as defined on Aug. 1, 1914).

XV. Annulment of the treaties of Bucharest and Brest-Litovsk and of the supplementary treaties.

XVI. The Allies shall have free access to the territories evacuated by the Germans on their eastern frontier, either through Danzig or by the Vistula, in order to convey supplies to the populations of these territories or for the purpose of maintaining order.

(C) CLAUSE RELATING TO EAST AFRICA

XVII. Evacuation of all German forces operating in East Africa within a period specified by the Allies.

(D) GENERAL CLAUSES

XVIII. Repatriation without reciprocity, within a maximum period of one month, in accordance with detailed conditions hereafter to be fixed, of all interned civilians, including hostages and persons under trial and condemned, who may be subjects of allied or associated States other than those mentioned in Clause III.

FINANCIAL CLAUSES

XIX. With the reservation that any subsequent concessions and claims by the Allies and United States remain unaffected, the following financial conditions are imposed:

Reparation for damage done.

While the armistice lasts no public securities shall be removed by the enemy which can serve as a pledge to the Allies to cover reparation for war losses.

Immediate restitution of the cash deposit in the National Bank of Belgium and, in general, immediate return of all documents, specie, stocks, shares, paper money, together with plant for the issue thereof, affecting public or private interests in the invaded countries.

Restitution of the Russian and Roumanian gold yielded to Germany or taken by that power.

This gold is to be delivered in trust to the Allies until peace is concluded.

(E) NAVAL CONDITIONS

XX. Immediate cessation of all hostilities at sea and definite information to be given as to the position and movements of all German ships.

Notification to be given to neutrals that freedom of navigation in all territorial waters is given to the navies and mercantile marines of the allied and associated powers, all questions of neutrality being waived.

XXI. All naval and mercantile marine prisoners of war of the allied and associated powers in German hands to be returned without reciprocity.

XXII. To surrender at the ports specified by the Allies and the United States all submarines at present in existence (including all submarine cruisers and mine layers), with armament and equipment complete. Those that can not put to sea shall be deprived of armament and equipment and shall remain under the supervision of the Allies and the United States. Submarines ready to put to sea shall be prepared to leave German ports immediately on receipt of a wireless order to sail to the port of surrender, the remainder to follow as early as possible. The conditions of this article shall be completed within 14 days of the signing of the armistice.

XXIII. The following German surface warships, which shall be designated by the Allies and the United States of America, shall forthwith be disarmed and thereafter interned in neutral ports, or, failing them, allied ports, to be designated by the Allies and the United States of America, and placed under the surveillance of the Allies and the United States of America, only care and maintenance parties being left on board, namely:

  6 battle cruisers.
10 battleships.
  8 light cruisers (including 2 mine layers).
50 destroyers of the most modern type.

All other surface warships (including river craft) are to be concentrated in German naval bases, to be designated by the Allies and the United States of

America, completely disarmed and placed under the supervision of the Allies and the United States of America. All vessels of the auxiliary fleet are to be disarmed. All vessels specified for internment shall be ready to leave German ports seven days after the signing of the armistice. Directions for the voyage shall be given by wireless.

XXIV. The Allies and the United States of America shall have the right to sweep up all mine fields and destroy all obstructions laid by Germany outside German territorial waters, and the positions of these are to be indicated.

XXV. Freedom of access to and from the Baltic to be given to the navies and mercantile marines of the allied and associated powers. This to be secured by the occupation of all German forts, fortifications, batteries, and defense works of all kinds in all the routes from the Cattegat into the Baltic and by the sweeping up and destruction of all mines and obstructions within and without German territorial waters without any questions of neutrality being raised by Germany, and the positions of all such mines and obstructions to be indicated, and the plans relating thereto are to be supplied.

XXVI. The existing blockade conditions set up by the allied and associated powers are to remain unchanged, and all German merchant ships found at sea are to remain liable to capture. The Allies and United States contemplate the provisioning of Germany during the armistice as shall be found necessary.

XXVII. All aerial forces are to be concentrated and immobilized in German bases to be specified by the Allies and the United States of America.

XXVIII. In evacuating the Belgian coasts and ports Germany shall abandon in situ and intact the port material and material for inland waterways, also all merchant ships, tugs and lighters, all naval aircraft and air materials and stores, all arms and armaments and all stores and apparatus of all kinds.

XXIX. All Black Sea ports are to be evacuated by Germany; all Russian warships of all descriptions seized by Germany in the Black Sea are to be handed over to the Allies and the United States of America; all neutral merchant ships seized in the Black Sea are to be released; all warlike and other materials of all kinds seized in those ports are to be returned, and German materials as specified in Clause XXVIII are to be abandoned.

XXX. All merchant ships at present in German hands belonging to the allied and associated powers are to be restored to ports specified by the Allies and the United States of America without reciprocity.

XXXI. No destruction of ships or of materials to be permitted before evacuation, surrender, or restoration.

XXXII. The German Government shall formally notify all the neutral Governments, and particularly the Governments of Norway, Sweden, Denmark, and Holland, that all restrictions placed on the trading of their vessels with the allied and associated countries, whether by the German Government or by private German interests, and whether in return for specific concessions, such as the export of shipbuilding materials, or not, are immediately canceled.

XXXIII. No transfers of German merchant shipping of any description to any neutral flag are to take place after signature of the armistice.

(F) DURATION OF ARMISTICE

XXXIV. The duration of the armistice is to be 36 days, with option to extend. During this period, on failure of execution of any of the above clauses, the armistice may be repudiated by one of the contracting parties on 48 hours' previous notice. It is understood that failure to execute Articles III and XVIII completely in the periods specified is not to give reason for a repudiation of the armistice, save where such failure is due to malice aforethought.

To insure the execution of the present convention under the most favorable conditions, the principle of a permanent international armistice commission is recognized. This commission shall act under the supreme authority of the high command, military and naval, of the allied armies.

The present armistice was signed on the 11th day of November, 1918, at 5 o'clock a. m. (French time).

F. Foch   Erzberger
R. E. Wemyss   Oberndorff
                             Winterfeldt
                             Vanselow

Annex No. 1

I. The evacuation of the invaded territories, Belgium, France, and Luxemburg, and also of Alsace-Lorraine, shall be carried out in three successive stages according to the following conditions:

First stage.—Evacuation of the territories situated between the existing front and line No. 1 on the inclosed map,[6] to be completed within 5 days after the signature of the armistice.

Second stage.—Evacuation of territories situated between line No. 1 and line No. 2, to be carried out within 4 further days (9 days in all after the signing of the armistice).

Third stage.—Evacuation of the territories situated between line No. 2 and line No. 3, to be completed within 6 further days (15 days in all after the signing of the armistice).

Allied and United States troops shall enter these various territories on the expiration of the period allowed to the German troops for the evacuation of each.

In consequence, the allied troops will cross the present German front as from the 6th day following the signing of the armistice, line No. 1 as from the 10th day, and line No. 2 as from the 16th day.

---

[6] Not printed here; see British Command Paper (1918) 9212.

II. *Evacuation of the Rhine district.*—This evacuation shall also be carried out in several successive stages:

(1) Evacuation of territories situated between lines 2 and 3 and line 4, to be completed within 4 further days (19 days in all after the signing of the armistice).

(2) Evacuation of territories situated between lines 4 and 5 to be completed within 4 further days (23 days in all after the signing of the armistice).

(3) Evacuation of territories situated between lines 5 and 6 (line of the Rhine) to be completed within 4 further days (27 days in all after the signing of the armistice).

(4) Evacuation of the bridgeheads and of the neutral zone on the right bank of the Rhine to be completed within 4 further days (31 days in all after the signing of the armistice).

The allied and United States army of occupation shall enter these various territories after the expiration of the period allowed to the German troops for the evacuation of each; consequently the army will cross line No. 3, 20 days after the signing of the armistice. It will cross line No. 4 as from the twenty-fourth day after the signing of the armistice; line No. 5 as from the twenty-eighth day; line No. 6 (Rhine) the thirty-second day, in order to occupy the bridgeheads.

III. *Surrender by the German armies of war material specified by the armistice.*—This war material shall be surrendered according to the following conditions: The first half before the tenth day, the second half before the twentieth day. This material shall be handed over to each of the allied and United States armies by each larger tactical group of the German armies in the proportions which may be fixed by the permanent International Armistice Commission.

Annex No. 2

Conditions regarding communications, railways, waterways, roads, river and sea ports, and telegraphic and telephonic communications:

I. All communications as far as the Rhine, inclusive, or comprised, on the right bank of this river, within the bridgeheads occupied by the allied armies shall be placed under the supreme and absolute authority of the commander in chief of the allied armies, who shall have the right to take any measure he may think necessary to assure their occupation and use. All documents relative to communications shall be held ready for transmission to him.

II. All the material and all the civil and military personnel at present employed in the maintenance and working of all lines of communication are to be maintained in their entirety upon these lines in all territories evacuated by the German troops.

All supplementary material necessary for the upkeep of these lines of communication in the districts on the left bank of the Rhine shall be supplied by the German Government throughout the duration of the armistice.

III. *Personnel.*—The French and Belgian personnel belonging to the services of the lines of communication, whether interned or not, are to be returned to the French and Belgian armies during the 15 days following the signing of the armistice. The personnel belonging to the organization of the Alsace-Lorraine railway system is to be maintained or reinstated in such a way as to insure the working of the system.

The commander in chief of the allied armies shall have the right to make all changes and substitutions that he may desire in the personnel of the lines of communication.

IV. *Material*—(*a*) *Rolling stock.*—The rolling stock handed over to the allied armies in the zone comprised between the present front and line No. 3, not including Alsace-Lorraine, shall amount at least to 5,000 locomotives and 150,000 wagons. This surrender shall be carried out within the period fixed by clause 7 of the armistice, and under conditions the details of which shall be fixed by the permanent International Armistice Commission.

All this material is to be in good condition and in working order, with all the ordinary spare parts and fittings. It may be employed together with the regular personnel, or with any other, upon any part of the railway system of the allied armies.

The material necessary for the working of the Alsace-Lorraine railway system is to be maintained or replaced for the use of the French army.

The material to be left in situ in the territories on the left bank of the Rhine, as well as that on the inner side of the bridgeheads, must permit of the normal working of the railways in these districts.

(*b*) *Permanent way, signals, and workshops.*—The material for signals, machine tools, and tool outfits, taken from the workshops and depots of the French and Belgian lines, are to be replaced under conditions the details of which are to be arranged by the permanent International Armistice Commission.

The allied armies are to be supplied with railroad material, rails, incidental fittings, plant, bridge-building material, and timber necessary for the repair of the lines destroyed beyond the present front.

(*c*) *Fuel and maintenance material.*—The German Government shall be responsible throughout the duration of the armistice for the release of fuel and maintenance material to the depots normally allotted to the railways in the territories on the left bank of the Rhine.

V. *Telegraphic and telephonic communications.*—All telegraphs, telephones, and fixed W/T stations are to be handed over to the allied armies, with all the civil and military personnel and all their material, including all stores on the left bank of the Rhine.

Supplementary stores necessary for the upkeep of the system are to be supplied throughout the duration of the armistice by the German Government according to requirements.

The commander in chief of the allied armies shall place this system under military supervision and shall insure its control, and shall make all changes and substitutions in personnel which he may think necessary.

He will send back to the German Army all the military personnel who are not in his judgment necessary for the working and upkeep of the railway.

All plans of the German telegraphic and telephonic systems shall be handed over to the commander in chief of the allied armies.

Addendum

November 11, 1918.

The representatives of the Allies declare that, in view of fresh events, it appears necessary to them that the following condition shall be added to the clauses of the armistice:

"In case the German ships are not handed over within the periods specified, the Governments of the Allies and of the United States shall have the right to occupy Heligoland to insure their delivery."

F. Foch
R. E. Wemyss,
Admiral

The German delegates declare that they will forward this declaration to the German chancellor, with the recommendation that it be accepted, accompanying it with the reasons by which the Allies have been actuated in making this demand.

Erzberger
Oberndorff
Winterfeldt
Vanselow

Declaration by German Plenipotentiaries

The German Government will naturally endeavor with all its power to take care that the duties imposed upon it shall be carried out.

The undersigned plenipotentiaries recognize that in certain points regard has been paid to their suggestions. They can therefore regard the comments made on November 9, on the conditions of the armistice with Germany and the answer handed to them on November 10, as an essential condition of the whole agreement.

They must, however, allow no doubt to exist on the point that in particular the short time allowed for evacuation, as well as the surrender of indispensable means of transport, threatens to bring about a state of things which, without its being the fault of the German Government and the German people, may render impossible the further fulfillment of the conditions.

The undersigned plenipotentiaries further regard it as their duty with reference to their repeated oral and written declaration once more to point out with all possible emphasis that the carrying out of this agreement must throw the German people into anarchy and famine. According to the declarations which preceded the armistice, conditions were to be expected which, while completely insuring the military situation of our opponents, would have ended the sufferings of women and children who took no part in the war.

The German people, which has held its own for 50 months against a world of enemies, will, in spite of any force that may be brought to bear upon it, preserve its freedom and unity.

A people of 70,000,000 suffers but does not die.

ERZBERGER
OBERNDORFF
WINTERFELDT
VANSELOW

MILITARY ARRANGEMENTS WITH HUNGARY

Convention signed at Belgrade November 13, 1918, regulating conditions for application in Hungary of armistice with Austria-Hungary of November 3, 1918 [1]
Effective from November 13, 1918

1919 For. Rel. (Paris Peace Conference, II) 183; Senate Document 147, 66th Congress, 1st session

[TRANSLATION]

MILITARY CONVENTION REGULATING THE CONDITIONS UNDER WHICH THE ARMISTICE, SIGNED BETWEEN THE ALLIES AND AUSTRIA-HUNGARY, IS TO BE APPLIED IN HUNGARY

1. The Hungarian Government will withdraw all troops north of a line drawn through the upper valley of the Szamos, Bistritz, Maros-Vásárhely, the river Maros to its junction with the Theiss, Maria-Theresiopel, Baja, Fünfkirchen (these places not being occupied by Hungarian troops), course of the Drave, until it coincides with the frontier of Slavonia-Croatia.

The evacuation to be carried out in eight days, the Allies to be entitled to occupy the evacuated territory on the conditions laid down by the general commander in chief of the allied armies. Civil administration will remain in the hands of the Government.

In actual fact only the police and gendarmerie will be retained in the evacuated zone, being indispensable to the maintenance of order, and also such men as are required to insure the safety of the railways.

2. Demobilization of Hungarian naval and military forces. An exception will be made in the case of six infantry divisions and two cavalry divisions, required for the maintenance of internal order and in the case of small sections of police mentioned in paragraph 1.

3. The Allies to have the right of occupying all places and strategic points, which may be permanently fixed by the general commander in chief of the allied armies.

The allied troops to be allowed to pass through or to remain in any part of Hungary.

---

[1] *Ante*, p. 1.

The Allies to have permanent right of use, for military purposes, of all rolling stock and shipping belonging to the State or to private individuals resident in Hungary, also of all draft animals.

4. The rolling stock and railway staff usually employed in the occupied territory will remain (see paragraph 1), and a reserve of 2,000 wagons and 100 locomotives (normal gauge), and 600 wagons and 50 locomotives (narrow gauge), will also be handed over within the month to the general commander in chief. These will be for the use of the allied troops and to compensate for the deficiency of material from Serbia due to the war. Some portion of this material could be levied from Austria. The figures are approximate.

5. The ships and crews, usually employed in the service of the occupied territory, will remain.

In addition, six monitors will be surrendered to the Allies immediately at Belgrade. The rest of the Danube flotilla will be assembled in one of the Danube ports, to be appointed later by the general commander in chief, and will be disarmed there. A levy of 10 passenger vessels, 10 tugs, and 60 lighters will be made on this flotilla as soon as possible for the use of the allied troops, to compensate for the deficiency of material from Serbia due to the war. The figures are approximate.

6. Within 15 days a detachment of 3,000 men from the railway technical troops are to be placed at the disposal of the general commander in chief, supplied with the material necessary to repair the Serbian railways. These figures are approximate.

7. Within 15 days a detachment of sappers of the telegraph branch are to be placed at the disposal of the general commander in chief provided with material necessary for establishing telegraphic and telephone communications with Serbia.

8. Within one month, 25,000 horses are to be placed at the disposal of the general commander in chief, together with such transport material as he may deem necessary. These figures are approximate.

9. Arms and war material to be deposited at places appointed by the general commander in chief. A portion of this material will be levied for the purpose of supplying units to be placed under the orders of the general commander in chief.

10. Immediate liberation of all allied prisoners of war and interned civilians, who will be collected at places convenient for their dispatch by rail. They will there receive directions as to time and place of repatriation, according to the orders issued by the general commander in chief. Hungarian prisoners of war to be provisionally retained.

11. A delay of 15 days is granted for the passage of German troops through Hungary and their quartering meanwhile, dating from the signing of the armistice by Gen. Diaz (Nov. 4, 3 p.m.). Postal and telegraphic communication with Germany will only be permitted under the military control of

the Allies. The Hungarian Government undertakes to allow no military telegraphic communication with Germany.

12. Hungary will facilitate the supplying of the allied troops of occupation; requisitions will be allowed on condition that they are not arbitrary and that they are paid for at current rates.

13. The situation of all Austro-Hungarian mines in the Danube and the Black Sea must be communicated immediately to the general commander in chief. Further, the Hungarian Government undertakes to stop the passage of all floating mines sown in the Danube upstream from the Hungarian and Austrian frontier and to remove all those actually in Hungarian waters.

14. The Hungarian postal service, telegraphs, telephones, and railways will be placed under allied control.

15. An allied representative will be attached to the Hungarian ministry of supplies in order to safeguard allied interests.

16. Hungary is under an obligation to cease all relations with Germany and stringently to forbid the passage of German troops to Roumania.

17. The Allies shall not interfere with the internal administration of affairs in Hungary.

18. Hostilities between Hungary and the Allies are at an end.

Two copies made November 13, 1918, at 11.15 p. m., at Belgrade.

Signed for the Allies by the delegates of the general commander in chief.

Voivode Mishitch
Gen. Henrys

Signed for Hungary by the delegates of the Hungarian Government.

Béla Linder

PROLONGING OF ARMISTICE WITH GERMANY

Convention signed at Trier, Germany, December 13, 1918, prolonging and supplementing armistice convention of November 11, 1918 [1]
Effective from December 17, 1918

1919 For. Rel. (Paris Peace Conference, II) 11; Senate Document 147, 66th Congress, 1st session

[TRANSLATION]

CONVENTION PROLONGING THE ARMISTICE WITH GERMANY, DECEMBER 13, 1918

The undersigned, in virtue of the powers with which they were endowed for the signing of the armistice of the 11th November, 1918, have concluded the following additional agreement:

1. The duration of the armistice signed on the 11th November, 1918, has been prolonged for a month, i.e., till 5 a. m. on the 17th January, 1919.

The one month's extension will be further extended until the conclusion of peace preliminaries, provided this arrangement meets with the approbation of the allied Governments.

2. The clauses of the convention (11th November) which have been incompletely fulfilled will be carried out during the period of extension, according to the conditions laid down by the Permanent International Armistice Commission following the orders given by the allied generalissimo.

3. The following clause is added to the convention of the 11th November, 1918:

"From now onwards the generalissimo reserves to himself the right of occupying (when he deems it advisable), as an additional guarantee, the neutral zone on the right bank of the Rhine, north of the bridgehead of Cologne, and as far as the Dutch frontier.

"Six days' notice will be given by the generalissimo before the occupation comes into effect."

Trier, December 13, 1918.

F. FOCH   ERZBERGER
WEMYSS,   A. OBERNDORFF
Admiral   WINTERFELDT
           VANSELOW

---

[1] *Ante,* p. 9. For further prolongations of the armistice convention, see *post,* pp. 24 and 28.

PROLONGING OF ARMISTICE WITH GERMANY

*Convention signed at Trier, Germany, January 16, 1919, prolonging
and supplementing armistice convention of November 11, 1918* [1]
Effective from January 17, 1919

1919 For. Rel. (Paris Peace Conference,
II) 11; Senate Document 147, 66th
Congress, 1st session

[TRANSLATION]

CONVENTION PROLONGING THE ARMISTICE WITH GERMANY,
JANUARY 16, 1919

The undersigned plenipotentiaries (Admiral Browning taking the place of
Admiral Wemyss), vested with the powers in virtue of which the armistice
agreement of 11th November, 1918, was signed, have concluded the following supplementary agreement:

1. The armistice of the 11th November, 1918, which was prolonged until
the 17th January, 1919, by the agreement of the 13th December, 1918, shall
be again prolonged for one month, that is to say, until the 17th February,
1919, at 5 a.m.

This prolongation of one month shall be extended until the conclusion
of the peace preliminaries, subject to the approval of the allied Governments.

2. The execution of those clauses of the agreement of the 11th November
which have not been entirely carried out shall be proceeded with and completed during the prolongation of the armistice, in accordance with the
detailed conditions fixed by the Permanent International Armistice Commission on the instructions of the allied high command.

3. In substitution of the supplementary railway material specified by
Tables 1 and 2 of the Spa protocol of 17th December,[2] i.e., 500 locomotives
and 19,000 wagons, the German Government shall supply the following
agriculture machinery and instruments:

    400   two-engined steam-plow outfits, complete, with suitable plows.
  6,500   drills.
  6,500   manure distributors.
  6,500   plows.
  6,500   Brabant plows.
 12,500   harrows.

---

[1] *Ante,* p. 9. For a further prolongation of the armistice convention, see *post,* p. 28.
[2] Not printed here.

6,500 scarifiers.
2,500 steel rollers.
2,500 Croskill rollers.
2,500 mowing machines.
2,500 hay-making machines.
3,000 reapers and binders.

or equivalent implements, according to the scale of interchangeability of various kinds of implements considered permissible by the Permanent International Armistice Commission. All this material, which shall be either new or in very good condition, shall be delivered together with all accessories belonging to each implement and with the spare parts required for 18 months' use.

The German Armistice Commission shall, between the present date and the 23d January, supply the Allied Armistice Commission with a list of the material that can be delivered by the 1st March, which must, in principle, constitute not less than one-third of the total quantity. The International Armistice Commission shall, between now and the 23d January, fix the latest dates of delivery, which shall, in principle, not extend beyond the 1st June.

4. The officers in Germany delegated by the allied and associated powers to organize the evacuation of the prisoners of war belonging to the armies of the entente, together with representatives of the relief associations of the United States, France, Great Britain, and Italy shall form a commission charged with the care of Russian prisoners of war in Germany.

This commission, the headquarters of which shall be in Berlin, shall be empowered to deal with the German Government direct, upon instructions from the allied Governments, regarding all questions relating to Russian prisoners of war.

The German Government shall accord the commission all traveling facilities necessary for the purpose of investigating the housing conditions and food supply of such prisoners.

The allied Governments reserve the right to arrange for the repatriation of Russian prisoners of war to any region which they may consider most suitable.

5. *Naval clauses.*—Article XXII, of the armistice agreement of the 11th November, 1918, shall be supplemented as follows:

In order to insure the execution of such clause, the German authorities shall be bound to carry out the following conditions:

All submarines capable of putting to sea, or of being towed, shall be handed over immediately and shall make for allied ports. Such vessels shall include submarine cruisers, mine layers, relief ships, and submarine docks. All submarines which can not be surrendered shall be completely destroyed or dismantled under the supervision of the allied commissioners.

Submarine construction shall cease immediately, and all submarines in course of construction shall be destroyed or dismantled under the supervision of the allied commissioners.

Article XXIII of the armistice agreement of the 11th November, 1918, shall be supplemented as follows:

In order to insure the execution of such clause, the German commission shall furnish the interallied naval armistice commission with a complete list of all surface vessels constructed or in course of construction (launched or on the stocks), specifying probable dates of completion.

Article XXX of the armistice agreement of 11th November, 1918, shall be supplemented as follows:

In order to insure the execution of such clause, the allied high command informs the German high command that all possible measures must be taken immediately for delivery, in allied ports, of all allied merchantmen still detained in German ports.

6. *Restitution of material carried off from Belgian and French territories.*—As restitution of material carried off from French and Belgian territory is indispensable for setting factories once more into working order, the following measures shall be carried out, viz:

(*a*) All machinery, machinery parts, industrial or agricultural plant, accessories of all kinds and, generally, all industrial or agricultural articles carried off by German military or civilian authorities or individuals, under any pretext whatever, from territories formerly occupied by the German armies on the western front, shall be placed at the disposal of the Allies for the purpose of being returned to their places of origin, should the French and Belgian Governments so desire.

These articles shall be returned without further alteration and undamaged.

(*b*) In view of such restitution, the German Government shall immediately furnish the armistice commission with all official or private accounts, agreements for sale or hire, or correspondence relating to such articles, together with all necessary declarations or information regarding their existence, origin, adaptation, present condition and locality.

(*c*) The delegates of the French or Belgian Government shall cause inventories or examinations of such articles to be made on the spot in Germany, should they think fit.

(*d*) The return of such articles shall be effected in accordance with special instructions to be given as required by the French or Belgian authorities.

(*e*) With a view to immediate restitution, declarations shall more particularly be made of all stocks of driving belts, electric motors and parts thereof, or plant removed from France or Belgium and existing in depot parks, railways, ships, and factories.

(*f*) The furnishing of the particulars referred to in articles 3 and 6 hereof shall commence within eight clear days from the 20th January, 1919, and shall be completed in principle before the 1st April, 1919.

7. As a further guarantee, the supreme allied command reserves to itself the right to occupy, whenever it shall consider this desirable, the sector of the fortress of Strassburg formed by the fortifications on the right bank of the Rhine, with a strip of territory extending from 5 to 10 kilometers in front of such fortifications, within the boundaries defined on the map appended hereto.[3]

The supreme allied command shall give six days' notice prior to such occupation, which shall not be preceded by any destruction of material or of buildings.

The limits of the neutral zone will, therefore, be advanced by 10 kilometers.

8. In order to secure the provisioning of Germany and of the rest of Europe, the German Government shall take all necessary steps to place the German fleet, for the duration of the armistice, under the control and the flags of the allied powers and the United States, who shall be assisted by a German delegate.

This arrangement shall in no wise affect the final disposal of such vessels. The Allies and the United States shall, if they consider this necessary, replace the crews either entirely or in part, and the officers and crews so replaced shall be repatriated to Germany.

Suitable compensation, to be fixed by the allied Governments, shall be made for the use of such vessels.

All questions of details, as also any exceptions to be made in the case of certain types of vessel, shall be settled by a special agreement to be concluded immediately.

Trier, January 16, 1919.

FOCH	ERZBERGER
BROWNING	OBERNDORFF
	VON WINTERFELDT
	VANSELOW

---

[3] Not printed here.

PROLONGING OF ARMISTICE WITH GERMANY

Convention signed at Trier, Germany, February 16, 1919, prolonging armistice convention of November 11, 1918 [1]
Effective from February 17, 1919 [2]

> 1919 For. Rel. (Paris Peace Conference, II) 15; Senate Document 147, 66th Congress, 1st session

CONVENTION PROLONGING THE ARMISTICE WITH GERMANY, FEBRUARY 16, 1919

The undersigned plenipotentiaries, possessed of the powers in virtue of which the armistice agreement of November 11, 1918, was signed, have concluded the following additional agreement:

Admiral Wemyss being replaced by Admiral Browning, Gen. von Winterfeldt by Gen. von Hammerstein, and the minister plenipotentiary, Count von Oberndorff, by the minister plenipotentiary, von Haniel.

I. The Germans are to cease all hostilities against the Poles at once, whether in the district of Posen or any other district. With this end in view, they are forbidden to allow their troops to cross the following line: The old frontier between East and West Prussia and Russia as far as Louisenfelde, from thence the line west of Louisenfelde, west of Gr. Neudorff, south of Brzoza, north of Schubin, north of Exin, south of Samotschin, south of Chodziesen, north of Czarnikau, west of Miala, west of Birnbaum, west of Bentschen, west of Wollstein, north of Lissa, north of Rawitsch, south of Krotoschin, west of Adelnau, west of Schildberg, north of Doruchow, to the Silesian frontier.

II. The armistice of November 11, prolonged by the agreements of December 13, 1918, and January 16, 1919, until February 17, 1919, is further

---

[1] *Ante,* p. 9.

[2] The armistice controlled relations between the contracting parties until the entry into force of the treaty of peace signed at Versailles June 28, 1919 (*post,* p. 43). The United States did not become a party to the treaty of peace but signed a treaty establishing friendly relations with Germany at Berlin Aug. 25, 1921 (TS 658, *post*).

prolonged for a short period, the date of expiry not being given, the allied powers and those associated with them reserving to themselves the right to terminate the period at three days' notice.

III. The carrying out of those clauses of the agreement of November 11, 1918, and of the additional agreements of December 13, 1918, and January 16, 1919, the terms of which have not yet been fully carried into effect, will be continued and completed during the prolongation of the armistice, according to detailed arrangements made by the permanent armistice commission, acting on instructions issued by the supreme allied command.

Trier, February 16, 1919.

FOCH   ERZBERGER
BROWNING   FREIHERR V. HAMMERSTEIN
                        VON HANIEL
                        VANSELOW

PASSAGE OF ALLIED FORCES VIA DANZIG

Protocol, with annex, signed at Spa, Germany, April 4, 1919, supplementing article XVI of armistice convention of November 11, 1918 [1]
Entered into force April 4, 1919

III Redmond 3327

PROTOCOL

Article 16 of the armistice of November 11, 1918, imposes on Germany the obligation of allowing the passage of allied forces via Danzig, and, in consequence, according to the view of the Allies, that of General Haller's troops.

The German Government has proposed new means of transportation, viz:

1. From Stettin, via Kreuz toward Posen and Warsaw.
2. From Pillau–Königsberg and Memel, via Korschen–Lyck–Grajewo.
3. By Coblenz–Giessen–Cassel–Halle–Eilenburg and by Frankfort-on-the-Main–Bebra–Erfurt–Leipzig–Eilenburg, thence by Kottbus, Lissa, and Kalisch.

The German Government guarantees the absolute security of these methods of transportation. In addition, measures will be taken to insure that the troops passing through German territory avoid everything which might provoke unrest among the population.

The transportation of the troops will commence about April 15, and will continue for about two months.

The Polish troops which are to be transported are destined for the maintenance of order in accordance with article 16 of the armistice of November 11, 1918.

The execution of the transportation will be carried out as shown in the annex to this protocol.

In the event of the employment of these new methods of transportation proposed by the German Government leading to serious difficulties, which the German Government after having been warned by the allied and associated Governments, was not in a position to overcome, Marshal Foch, com-

---

[1] *Ante*, p. 9.

manding in chief the allied armies, reserves the right of having recourse to the transportation allowed for in article 16 of the armistice of November 11, 1918, under conditions and guaranties to be fixed by the permanent international armistice commission at Spa.

Erzberger
Foch

Spa, *April 4, 1919*

Annex to Protocol

1. The transportation will be carried out by one of the following routes:
   (*a*) Coblenz–Cassel–Halle–Frankfurt–Leipzig.
            Eilenburg–Cottbus–Lissa–Kalisch.
   (*b*) Stettin–Kalisch.
   (*c*) Pillau–Königsberg–Korschen–Lyck–Grajewo.

Six trains ("marches") every 24 hours may be made over each line—in the case of (*a*) above, half on each branch—under the reserve that in the case of the simultaneous use of the lines (*b*) and (*c*), the total number of trains used on both of these lines together does not exceed 10.

The field marshal commanding in chief will first make use of the line (*a*).

The date of the commencement of the movement will be published as soon as possible and at least four days in advance to the German authorities through the medium of the permanent interallied armistice commission, in the case of the employment of one or other of the lines. Particularly, the date of departure of the ships from the ports of embarkation, their size and numbers will immediately be notified to the commission. The transportation will be able to commence from April 15 and will last about two months.

2. The organization of the details of the transportation will be settled by a mixed commission at Spa composed of the French and German Presidents of the subcommission for transportation on the permanent international armistice commission.

This commission must be immediately advised of any incident which arises out of the transportation and particularly of deviations from the route laid down necessitated by force majeure.

Staff officers from the allied army together with the German authorities concerned will control the transportation by routes (*b*) and (*c*) at Stettin and Königsberg. These officers will give the necessary orders to the Polish troops.

3. *Military measures.*—The troops will be transported in complete trains with their ammunition and supplies. The men will not carry ammunition on the person. The ammunition will be stored in one coach on the train and this coach will be sealed.

Liaison between the technical railway personnel, which is solely responsible for technical work on the lines of transportation, and the officers commanding the trains will be carried out through the medium of (*a*) officers from the allied armies accompanying each train; (*b*) officers from the allied armies—two officers with the necessary staff—at the stations where long halts are made.

These officers will also insure the liaison between the troops and the German military authorities.

Standing orders in four languages—French, English, Polish, and German—will be drawn up by Major Courtillet and Major von Boetticher.

All measures will be taken by the allied high command to prevent incidents between the troops and the population. The German authorities on their part will take all the police measures necessary with regard to the population to avoid manifestations and disorder.

Long halts will be made about every six hours—a halt of at least one hour alternating with a halt of at least half an hour—to allow water to be distributed and to allow the troops to leave the train. The troops will not be allowed to leave a certain area which will be fixed by the allied officer in agreement with the German authorities.

The German authorities will have ready the water facilities and the necessary latrines. The food prepared on the train will be distributed at these long halts.

At the ports of Stettin and Pillau–Königsberg a certain area will be kept free around the quays, outside which the fatigue parties employed for the disembarkation will not be allowed to move. The remainder of the troops will be kept on board.

The sick will be attended to by the doctors of the railway if there are no doctors with the troops; in case of need they will be attended to in hospitals on German territory and can be visited there by an officer delegated by the allied military authorities. Transportation of supplies of food and ammunition subsequent to the passage of the divisions will be carried out via Stettin.

Telegraphic and telephonic communications on service matters to and from the allied officers attached to the convoys will be transmitted by the German authorities under the same conditions as German official communications.

4. *Technical measures.*—The transportation will be carried out in principle in trains of a standard type of 50 trucks (100 axles), comprising in particular one first or second class coach for officers and closed trucks with benches, or passenger coaches, for the troops.

These rakes must not be split up or damaged either in course of transportation or when the troops are detrained or when the material is returned empty; they must be returned after the detrainment of the troops as soon as possible and by the same route. The Allies will supply rolling stock for route (*a*), the Germans for routes (*b*) and (*c*).

Every coach forming a part of a loaded train, damaged on the German railways, shall be immediately replaced by the railway system concerned.

The necessary entrainment gear at the ports will be found by Germany; however, the troops must provide themselves with the necessary cordage for the rail journey.

The gear used for transportation on line (a) will, after detrainment, be stored in sealed wagons when the empty material is sent back.

Germany will provide engines on railway systems run by German personnel. Coal and grease will be provided by Germany. Train personnel will be furnished by Germany on the systems worked by German personnel.

5. *Payment.*—Germany will be allowed (i) costs of transportation fixed according to the military tariff in force on the German railways, after deducting the cost of the hire of rolling stock, where the latter is supplied by the Allies.

(ii) The amount of the expenses actually incurred by the transportation through Germany at the express request of the Allies, it being understood that the normal installations along the line of transportation will remain at the charge of Germany.

(iii) The amount of damage caused by the troops proved and agreed by both parties.

The subcommission for transportation of the permanent international armistice commission will be responsible for assessing the above expenses and for carrying out all the necessary investigations for these assessments.

CHINA: EMBARGO ON ARMS

Joint note of Diplomatic Body, Peking, May 5, 1919
Entered into force May 5, 1919
Terminated April 26, 1929 [1]

1919 For. Rel. (I) 670

NOTE FROM DEAN OF DIPLOMATIC BODY TO CHINESE ACTING MINISTER
OF FOREIGN AFFAIRS [2]

[PEKING, *May 5, 1919.*]

SIR: The Diplomatic Body in considering the present state of disunion between North and South in China have been impressed by the fact that the continued possibility of importing military arms and ammunition into the country from abroad could not but exercise a disturbing influence, and as the friendly Powers here represented are firmly determined to discountenance any condition or action which might favour the reversion to hostilities, I am desired by my Colleagues to make the following communication to the Chinese Government.

The Governments of Great Britain, Spain, Portugal, the United States, Russia, Brazil, France and Japan have agreed effectively to restrain their subjects and citizens from exporting to or importing into China arms and munitions of war and material destined exclusively for their manufacture until the establishment of a government whose authority is recognized throughout the whole country and also to prohibit during the above period the delivery of arms and munitions for which contracts have already been made but not executed.

The Representatives of the Netherlands, Denmark, Belgium and Italy are also in full accord with the above policy, but await the instructions of their respective Governments before announcing the adhesion of the latter.

The Foreign Representatives desire to express the earnest hope that the Chinese Government in keeping with this policy will on their part agree to suspend the issue of permits to import military arms, ammunition and munitions of war and will direct the Customs that the introduction of such articles is absolutely prohibited.

[I avail myself, etc.

J. N. JORDAN]

---

[1] For text of a joint note from the Diplomatic Body at Peking informing the Chinese Minister of Foreign Affairs of the cancellation of the agreement, see 1929 For. Rel. (II) 529.
[2] The Chinese Acting Foreign Minister was Ch'en Lu.

DISPOSAL OF TONNAGE FOLLOWING WORLD WAR I (WILSON–LLOYD GEORGE AGREEMENT)

Agreement, with United States memorandum and excerpt from French letter, signed at Paris May 8, 1919
Entered into force May 8, 1919

1919 For. Rel. (Paris Peace Conference, XIII) 845

AGREEMENT

The Allied and Associated Governments whose signatures are hereto affixed, severally agree as regards merchant shipping as follows:

1. The Reparation Commission will as soon as possible compile a list giving fullest particulars available on all enemy ships still in existence, captured, seized or detained by any Allied or Associated Government during the war, and also all other enemy ships or boats which the enemy Powers are required to cede under the Treaty of Peace.[1]

2. The Reparation Commission will take such steps as will secure that each of the Allied and Associated Governments will retain as its own the complete title to and use of all ships captured, seized, or detained during the war as a war measure and prior to November 11, 1918, and will own the same free from any claim of any of the other Allied and Associated Governments.

In all cases where the ships and boats so to be retained by any Allied or Associated Government are in excess of the claims of such Governments respectively for war losses in merchant ships such Governments shall not make any claim for a share in other ships and boats ceded under the Treaty of Peace.

3. In all cases where the ships and boats so to be retained by any such Governments are insufficient to satisfy in full the claims of such Governments respectively for war losses in merchant ships, the enemy ships which remain and which are to be ceded under the Treaty of Peace will be divided into three classes, viz. liners, other merchant ships, and fishing boats, and will be distributed to such Governments on the basis of ton-for-ton and class-for-class of the ships and boats lost and not replaced by the ships and boats retained, but in proportion to the balances due on the claims of such Governments respectively.

---

[1] *Post,* p. 43.

35

4. As the ships and boats so to be retained will, in the case of Brazil, China, Cuba, Siam, and the United States, exceed the total amount of tonnage which would be allocated to those countries were the total enemy tonnage captured, seized, detained or still in existence shared in proportion to losses of ships and boats during the war, in each such case a reasonable value on the excess of ships and boats over the amount which would result from such a division will be determined.

The amount of the value so fixed will be paid over by each such state to the Reparation Commission for the credit of Germany towards the sums due from her for Reparation, in respect to war losses of merchant ships.

5. As soon as the Reparation Commission has collected the necessary information, and is in a position so to do, they will give public notice that after an interval of two months they will proceed to divide the vessels except those captured, seized, or detained by the Allied and Associated Governments which are to be retained by them respectively as hereinbefore provided.

If within one month of the publication of the notice, any Allied, Associated or Neutral Government, person or corporation, a national of such Government and acting through such Government, notifies the Commission that they have an equitable claim against any vessel which has not been, or is not being satisfied by the enemy Governments, that claim will be considered on its merits by the Commission which may adopt any procedure it thinks fit, provided it is expeditious and is calculated to do substantial justice as between the Allied and Associated Governments on the one hand and the claimant on the other.

The Commission will have power to determine claims so presented, and such determination will be conclusive and the Commission will also have power to enforce its findings.

8 May, 1919.

[For the United States:]
    WOODROW WILSON
        Subject to the
        explanation contained
        in the attached
        memorandum.

[For the United Kingdom:]
    D. LLOYD GEORGE

[For France:]
    CLEMENCEAU

UNITED STATES MEMORANDUM

I deem it my duty to state, in signing this document, that, while I feel confident that the Congress of the United States will make the disposal of the funds mentioned in clause four which is there agreed upon, I have no authority to bind it to that action, but must depend upon its taking the same view of the matter that is taken by the joint signatories of this agreement.

W.W.

EXCERPT FROM FRENCH LETTER

[TRANSLATION]

Pending the outcome of the negotiations, which we hope will enable us to accept and sign the general agreement heretofore signed by President Wilson and Mr. Lloyd George in regard to distribution of enemy ships, the French Government agrees with the United States Government:

That in any case the United States, in so far as any interest of the French Government is concerned, shall retain all ships captured, seized or detained by them during the war as a war measure and prior to November 3rd, 1918, the same to be free of any claim of the French Government for reparation.

And that the Reparation Commission will take such steps as will secure that the United States retain as its own the complete title to and the use of all ships, in so far as the interest of the French Government in these particular ships is concerned.

As the tonnage of the ships and boats so to be retained by the United States will exceed the total amount of tonnage which would be allocated to them, were the total enemy tonnage captured, seized, detained or still in existence shared in proportion to the losses of ships and boats during the war, a reasonable value on such excess of ships and boats over the amount which would result from such a division will be determined.

The amount of the value so fixed will be paid over by the United States to the Reparation Commission for the credit of Germany towards the sums due from her for reparation in respect to war losses of merchant ships, subject, however, to the power of the Congress of the United States to make disposal of such funds under the resolution approved May 13 [12], 1917.[2]

8 May, 1919

CLEMENCEAU

[In addition to France, Italy and Japan also became parties to the so-called "Wilson–Lloyd George Agreement." Italy became a party with regard to ultimate disposal of Austro-Hungarian merchant ships by agreements concluded with the United Kingdom September 25 and October 13 and 15, 1919, and June 1, 1921 (*League of Nations Treaty Series,* vol. 6, p. 323). Japan became a party with regard to ultimate disposal of both German and Austro-Hungarian merchant ships by an agreement with the United Kingdom November 10 and 12, 1919 (*ibid.,* p. 333).]

---

[2] 40 Stat. 75.

PRIORITY IN REPARATION PAYMENTS
TO BELGIUM

*Agreement, with initialed annex, approved by the Council of Principal
Allied and Associated Powers at Paris June 24, 1919; notification
to the Government of Belgium approved by the Council June 24,
1919*
Entered into force June 24, 1919

1919 For. Rel. (Paris Peace Conference,
XIII) 849

AGREEMENT

Whereas, Article 237 of the Conditions of Peace with Germany [1] provides,
among other things, that the payments to be made by Germany, by way of
reparation, will be divided by the Allied and Associated Governments in
proportions which have been determined upon by them in advance and on a
basis of general equity and of the rights of each; and

Whereas, it is deemed equitable that after the priority accorded by Article
235, in respect of the expenses of the Armies of Occupation and payments
for the supply of Germany, a certain priority should be granted to Belgium
in respect of the payments made by Germany by way of reparation;

Now, therefore, the undersigned, in the name of their respective Governments, agree that out of the first cash received from Germany, in respect of
reparation, Belgium shall receive, on account of the reparation payments to
which she is entitled the equivalent of 2,500,000,000 gold francs.

For the purposes of the foregoing there shall be reckoned as cash:

(1) Currency received by the Reparation Commission;

(2) The proceeds of the sale by the said Commission of negotiable instruments or securities received from Germany;

---

[1] *Post*, p. 140.

38

(3) The value of deliveries and reparation in kind made by Germany pursuant to the provisions of the Conditions of Peace and debited to the Allied and Associated Governments. This last item shall not be taken into account before May 1, 1921.

It is understood that the restitutions contemplated by Article 238 of the Treaty will not be taken into consideration.

Irrespective of this priority of 2,500,000,000 francs, Belgium will participate in the proportion which will be accorded to her in the division of the first payments and the subsequent divisions contemplated by Article 237 above referred to.

Beginning with May 1, 1921, the above mentioned sum of 2,500,000,000 francs will be amortized at the rate of one-thirtieth per year out of Belgium's share in each of the subsequent payments made by Germany. If, however, Germany should complete payment of its debt in less than thirty years, such amortization will be accelerated so that it will conclude coincidentally with the final settlement of Germany.

The Annex attached hereto will serve as an illustration of the method of applying the foregoing provisions.

[For France:]
    G. CLEMENCEAU

[For the United Kingdom:]
    D. LLOYD GEORGE

[For the United States:]
    WOODROW WILSON

[For Italy:]
    S. SONNINO

ANNEX

Let us assume that Germany pays up to May 1, 1921, in addition to sums which will be applied to its supply of food and raw materials and to the expenses of the Armies of Occupation, the total sum of 13 milliards of francs applicable to reparations. Let us suppose that this sum has been paid as follows:

In cash or securities converted into cash, 1½ milliards.
In different deliveries, 11½ milliards.

Let us further assume that Belgium's share is fixed at 7%, for example. On the foregoing hypothesis Belgium will be entitled:

(1) To receive the cash, that is, 1½ milliards;
(2) On May 1, 1921, each of the interested Powers, having been debited

with the total amount of deliveries in kind received by it, payment will be made to Belgium out of the common fund of 1 milliard of the 11½ milliards mentioned above.

Out of the balance of 10½ milliards, Belgium will be entitled to 7%, that is to say, 735 millions.

If Belgium has received in kind 1,200,000,000, she should pay into the common funds the difference between this sum and the share of the 735 millions to which she is entitled, that is to say, 465 millions.

After 1921, for instance in 1922, if Germany has paid in that year 10 milliards and Belgium has received in kind 300 millions, its account will stand as follows:

Received in kind, 300 millions, ... 300, 000, 000
Amortization payment on the priority of 2½ milliards, ... 83, 330, 000

Total 383, 330, 000

Amount due to Belgium 700 millions, from which are to be deducted the above 383,330,000; balance due from the common fund to Belgium, 316,670,000.

G.C.
W.W.
D.Ll.G.
S.S.

NOTIFICATION TO BELGIUM

M. Clemenceau, President Wilson, and Mr. Lloyd George to the Belgian Minister for Foreign Affairs

PARIS, *June 16, 1919.*

SIR: The Reparation Clauses of the draft Treaty of Peace with Germany obligate Germany to make reimbursement of all sums which Belgium has borrowed from the Allied and Associated Governments up to November 11, 1918, on account of the violation by Germany of the Treaty of 1839. As evidence of such an obligation Germany is to make a special issue of bonds to be delivered to the Reparation Commission.

Each of the undersigned will recommend to the appropriate governmental agency of his Government that, upon the delivery to the Reparation Commission of such bonds, his Government accept an amount thereof corresponding to the sums which Belgium has borrowed from his Government since the war and up to November 11, 1918, together with interest at 5% unless already included in such sums, in satisfaction of Belgium's obligation on account of such loans, which obligation of Belgium's shall thereupon be cancelled.

   We are [etc.]

G. Clemenceau
Woodrow Wilson
D. Lloyd George

Editorial Note

The treaties of peace with Germany, Austria, and Hungary were signed by representatives of the United States in view of the fact that the United States had been in a state of war with each of these countries. The United States representatives signed the treaty of peace with Bulgaria without having been at war with that country, on the theory that article 10 of the Covenant of the League of Nations would obligate the United States to guarantee the settlements. None of these treaties was ratified by the United States. However, in August 1921, the United States concluded bilateral treaties restoring friendly relations with Germany, Austria, and Hungary. Each of these bilateral treaties provides that certain rights and privileges specified in the respective treaties of peace will be accorded to the United States.

The relevant portions of the treaties of peace with Austria and Hungary are printed with the bilateral treaties (Austria: TS 659, *post,* and Hungary: TS 660, *post*). However, because of general interest in the treaty of peace with Germany, commonly referred to as the Treaty of Versailles, the complete text of that treaty (with the exception of Part XIII, the ILO Constitution, which can be found on page 241) is printed here. The specific provisions of the Treaty of Versailles referred to in the bilateral treaty of August 25, 1921, between the United States and Germany (TS 658, *post*), are as follows: Section 1 of Part IV and Parts V, VI, VIII, IX, X, XI, XII, XIV, and XV.

A definitive study of the treaty of peace with Germany was issued in 1947 by the Department of State entitled *The Treaty of Versailles and After: Annotations of the Text of the Treaty* (also incorporated into the *Foreign Relations* series as volume XIII, Paris Peace Conference, 1919). Particular attention is called to pages 29 to 35, which contain status information and references to the texts of the treaties of peace and various other agreements connected with the peace settlement following World War I.

TREATY OF PEACE WITH GERMANY
(TREATY OF VERSAILLES)

*Treaty and protocol signed at Versailles June 28, 1919; protocol signed
by Germany at Paris January 10, 1920*
*Treaty submitted to the Senate by the President of the United States for
advice and consent to ratification July 10, 1919;* [1] *Senate resolutions to advise and consent to ratification failed of adoption November 19, 1919,* [2] *and March 19, 1920;* [3] *treaty returned to the President pursuant to resolution of March 19, 1920* [4]
*Protocol of June 28, 1919, submitted to the Senate by the President of
the United States July 31, 1919;* [5] *considered by the Senate Committee on Foreign Relations and laid aside without action on February 10, 1920;* [6] *returned to the Secretary of State pursuant to
Senate resolution of February 12, 1935* [7]
*Procès-verbal of first deposit of ratifications at Paris dated January 10,
1920*
*Entered into force January 10, 1920, 4:15 p.m., as between contracting
parties (the United States was not a party)* [8]
Revised from time to time by the contracting parties

> 1919 For. Rel. (Paris Peace Conference,
> XIII) 55, 740, 743; Senate document 51,
> 66th Congress, 1st session

THE UNITED STATES OF AMERICA, THE BRITISH EMPIRE, FRANCE, ITALY
and JAPAN,

These Powers being described in the present Treaty as the Principal Allied
and Associated Powers,

BELGIUM, BOLIVIA, BRAZIL, CHINA, CUBA, ECUADOR, GREECE, GUATE-
MALA, HAITI, THE HEDJAZ, HONDURAS, LIBERIA, NICARAGUA, PANAMA,

---

[1] S. Doc. 49, 66th Cong., 1st sess. (text of treaty); S. Doc. 50, 66th Cong., 1st sess.
(address of the President to the Senate delivered on July 10, 1919).

[2] Congressional Record, Nov. 19, 1919 (vol. 58, pt. 9), p. 8786 ff.

[3] *Ibid.,* Mar. 19, 1920 (vol. 59, pt. 5), p. 4598 ff.

[4] *Ibid.,* Mar. 19, 1920 (vol. 59, pt. 5), p. 4600; filed with Unperfected Treaties I–5
(Department of State archives).

[5] S. Ex. A, 66th Cong., 1st sess.; S. Doc. 66, 66th Cong., 1st sess.

[6] Congressional Record, Feb. 10, 1920 (vol. 59, pt. 3), p. 2678.

[7] *Ibid.,* Feb. 12, 1935 (vol. 79, pt. 2), p. 1825; filed with Unperfected Treaties G–9
and I–5 (Department of State archives).

[8] For the treaty of Aug. 25, 1921, restoring friendly relations between the United States
and Germany, see TS 658, *post.*

43

Peru, Poland, Portugal, Roumania, the Serb-Croat-Slovene State, Siam, Czecho-Slovakia, and Uruguay,

These Powers constituting with the Principal Powers mentioned above the Allied and Associated Powers,

of the one part;

And Germany,

of the other part;

Bearing in mind that on the request of the Imperial German Government an Armistice was granted on November 11, 1918,[9] to Germany by the Principal Allied and Associated Powers in order that a Treaty of Peace might be concluded with her, and

The Allied and Associated Powers being equally desirous that the war in which they were successively involved directly or indirectly and which originated in the declaration of war by Austria-Hungary on July 28, 1914, against Serbia, the declaration of war by Germany against Russia on August 1, 1914, and against France on August 3, 1914, and in the invasion of Belgium, should be replaced by a firm, just and durable Peace,

For this purpose the High Contracting Parties represented as follows:

The President of the United States of America, by:
 The Honourable Woodrow Wilson, President of the United States, acting in his own name and by his own proper authority;
 The Honourable Robert Lansing, Secretary of State;
 The Honourable Henry White, formerly Ambassador Extraordinary and Plenipotentiary of the United States at Rome and Paris;
 The Honourable Edward M. House;
 General Tasker H. Bliss, Military Representative of the United States on the Supreme War Council;

His Majesty the King of the United Kingdom of Great Britain and Ireland and of the British Dominions Beyond the Seas, Emperor of India, by:
 The Right Honourable David Lloyd George, M.P., First Lord of His Treasury and Prime Minister;
 The Right Honourable Andrew Bonar Law, M.P., His Lord Privy Seal;
 The Right Honourable Viscount Milner, G.C.B., G.C.M.G., His Secretary of State for the Colonies;
 The Right Honourable Arthur James Balfour, O.M., M.P., His Secretary of State for Foreign Affairs;
 The Right Honourable George Nicoll Barnes, M.P., Minister without portfolio;

And

---

[9] *Ante,* p. 9.

for the Dominion of Canada, by:
  The Honourable Charles Joseph Doherty, Minister of Justice;
  The Honourable Arthur Lewis Sifton, Minister of Customs;

for the Commonwealth of Australia, by:
  The Right Honourable William Morris Hughes, Attorney General and
    Prime Minister;
  The Right Honourable Sir Joseph Cook, G.C.M.G., Minister for the
    Navy;

for the Union of South Africa, by:
  General the Right Honourable Louis Botha, Minister of Native Affairs
    and Prime Minister;
  Lieutenant-General the Right Honourable Jan Christian Smuts, K.C.,
    Minister of Defence;

for the Dominion of New Zealand, by:
  The Right Honourable William Ferguson Massey, Minister of Labour
    and Prime Minister;

for India, by:
  The Right Honourable Edwin Samuel Montagu, M. P., His Secretary of
    State for India;
  Major-General His Highness Maharaja Sir Ganga Singh Bahadur, Ma-
    haraja of Bikaner, G.C.S.I., G.C.I.E., G.C.V.O., K.C.B., A.D.C.;

The President of the French Republic, by:
  Mr. Georges Clemenceau, President of the Council, Minister of War;
  Mr. Stephen Pichon, Minister for Foreign Affairs;
  Mr. Louis-Lucien Klotz, Minister of Finance;
  Mr. André Tardieu, Commissary General for Franco-American Military
    Affairs;
  Mr. Jules Cambon, Ambassador of France;

His Majesty the King of Italy, by:
  Baron S. Sonnino, Deputy;
  Marquis G. Imperiali, Senator, Ambassador of His Majesty the King of
    Italy at London;
  Mr. S. Crespi, Deputy;

His Majesty the Emperor of Japan, by:
  Marquis Saïonzi, formerly President of the Council of Ministers;
  Baron Makino, formerly Minister for Foreign Affairs, Member of the
    Diplomatic Council;
  Viscount Chinda, Ambassador Extraordinary and Plenipotentiary of H.
    M. the Emperor of Japan at London;
  Mr. K. Matsui, Ambassador Extraordinary and Plenipotentiary of H. M.
    the Emperor of Japan at Paris;

Mr. H. IJUIN, Ambassador Extraordinary and Plenipotentiary of H. M. the Emperor of Japan at Rome;

HIS MAJESTY THE KING OF THE BELGIANS, by:
Mr. Paul HYMANS, Minister for Foreign Affairs, Minister of State;
Mr. Jules van den HEUVEL, Envoy Extraordinary and Minister Plenipotentiary, Minister of State;
Mr. Emile VANDERVELDE, Minister of Justice, Minister of State;

THE PRESIDENT OF THE REPUBLIC OF BOLIVIA, by:
Mr. Ismael MONTES, Envoy Extraordinary and Minister Plenipotentiary of Bolivia at Paris;

THE PRESIDENT OF THE REPUBLIC OF BRAZIL, by:
Mr. João Pandiá CALOGERAS, Deputy, formerly Minister of Finance;
Mr. Raul FERNANDES, Deputy;
Mr. Rodrigo Octavio de L. MENEZES, Professor of International Law of Rio de Janeiro;

THE PRESIDENT OF THE CHINESE REPUBLIC, by:
Mr. LOU Tseng-Tsiang, Minister for Foreign Affairs;
Mr. Chengting Thomas WANG, formerly Minister of Agriculture and Commerce;

THE PRESIDENT OF THE CUBAN REPUBLIC, by:
Mr. Antonio Sánchez de BUSTAMANTE, Dean of the Faculty of Law in the University of Havana, President of the Cuban Society of International Law;

THE PRESIDENT OF THE REPUBLIC OF ECUADOR, by:
Mr. Enrique DORN Y DE ALSÚA, Envoy Extraordinary and Minister Plenipotentiary of Ecuador at Paris;

HIS MAJESTY THE KING OF THE HELLENES, by:
Mr. Eleftherios K. VENISÉLOS, President of the Council of Ministers;
Mr. Nicolas POLITIS, Minister for Foreign Affairs;

THE PRESIDENT OF THE REPUBLIC OF GUATEMALA, by:
Mr. Joaquin MÉNDEZ, formerly Minister of State for Public Works and Public Instruction, Envoy Extraordinary and Minister Plenipotentiary of Guatemala at Washington, Envoy Extraordinary and Minister Plenipotentiary on special mission at Paris;

THE PRESIDENT OF THE REPUBLIC OF HAITI, by:
Mr. Tertullien GUILBAUD, Envoy Extraordinary and Minister Plenipotentiary of Haiti at Paris;

HIS MAJESTY THE KING OF THE HEDJAZ, by:
Mr. Rustem HAÏDAR;
Mr. Abdul Hadi AOUNI;

The President of the Republic of Honduras, by:
Dr. Policarpo Bonilla, on special mission to Washington, formerly President of the Republic of Honduras, Envoy Extraordinary and Minister Plenipotentiary;

The President of the Republic of Liberia, by:
The Honourable Charles Dunbar Burgess King, Secretary of State;

The President of the Republic of Nicaragua, by:
Mr. Salvador Chamorro, President of the Chamber of Deputies;

The President of the Republic of Panama, by:
Mr. Antonio Burgos, Envoy Extraordinary and Minister Plenipotentiary of Panama at Madrid;

The President of the Republic of Peru, by:
Mr. Carlos G. Candamo, Envoy Extraordinary and Minister Plenipotentiary of Peru at Paris;

The President of the Polish Republic, by:
Mr. Ignace J. Paderewski, President of the Council of Ministers, Minister for Foreign Affairs;
Mr. Roman Dmowski, President of the Polish National Committee;

The President of the Portuguese Republic, by:
Dr. Affonso Augusto da Costa, formerly President of the Council of Ministers;
Dr. Augusto Luiz Vieira Soares, formerly Minister for Foreign Affairs;

His Majesty the King of Roumania, by:
Mr. Ion I. C. Bratiano, President of the Council of Ministers, Minister for Foreign Affairs;
General Constantin Coanda, Corps Commander, A.D.C. to the King, formerly President of the Council of Ministers;

His Majesty the King of the Serbs, the Croats, and the Slovenes, by:
Mr. Nicholas P. Pachitch, formerly President of the Council of Ministers;
Mr. Ante Trumbic, Minister for Foreign Affairs;
Mr. Milenko Vesnitch, Envoy Extraordinary and Minister Plenipotentiary of H. M. the King of the Serbs, the Croats and the Slovenes at Paris;

His Majesty the King of Siam, by:
His Highness Prince Charoon, Envoy Extraordinary and Minister Plenipotentiary of H. M. the King of Siam at Paris;
His Serene Highness Prince Traidos Prabandhu, Under Secretary of State for Foreign Affairs;

THE PRESIDENT OF THE CZECHO-SLOVAK REPUBLIC, by:

Mr. Karel KRAMÁŘ, President of the Council of Ministers;
Mr. Eduard BENEŠ, Minister for Foreign Affairs;

THE PRESIDENT OF THE REPUBLIC OF URUGUAY, by:

Mr. Juan Antonio BUERO, Minister for Foreign Affairs, formerly Minister
of Industry;

GERMANY, by:

Mr. Hermann MÜLLER, Minister for Foreign Affairs of the Empire;
Dr. BELL, Minister of the Empire;
Acting in the name of the German Empire and of each and every compo-
nent State,

WHO having communicated their full powers found in good and due form
have AGREED AS FOLLOWS:

From the coming into force of the present Treaty the state of war will
terminate. From that moment and subject to the provisions of this Treaty
official relations with Germany, and with any of the German States, will be
resumed by the Allied and Associated Powers.

PART I

THE COVENANT OF THE LEAGUE OF NATIONS

THE HIGH CONTRACTING PARTIES,

In order to promote international co-operation and to achieve international peace and security

by the acceptance of obligations not to resort to war,
by the prescription of open, just and honourable relations between nations,
by the firm establishment of the understandings of international law as the
actual rule of conduct among Governments, and
by the maintenance of justice and a scrupulous respect for all treaty obligations in the dealings of organised peoples with one another,

Agree to this Covenant of the League of Nations.

ARTICLE 1

The original Members of the League of Nations shall be those of the
Signatories which are named in the Annex to this Covenant and also such
of those other States named in the Annex as shall accede without reservation to this Covenant. Such accession shall be effected by a Declaration deposited with the Secretariat within two months of the coming into force of
the Covenant. Notice thereof shall be sent to all other Members of the
League.

Any fully self-governing State, Dominion or Colony not named in the Annex may become a Member of the League if its admission is agreed to by two-thirds of the Assembly, provided that it shall give effective guarantees of its sincere intention to observe its international obligations, and shall accept such regulations as may be prescribed by the League in regard to its military, naval and air forces and armaments.

Any Member of the League may, after two years' notice of its intention so to do, withdraw from the League, provided that all its international obligations and all its obligations under this Covenant shall have been fulfilled at the time of its withdrawal.

ARTICLE 2

The action of the League under this Covenant shall be effected through the instrumentality of an Assembly and of a Council, with a permanent Secretariat.

ARTICLE 3

The Assembly shall consist of Representatives of the Members of the League.

The Assembly shall meet at stated intervals and from time to time as occasion may require at the Seat of the League or at such other place as may be decided upon.

The Assembly may deal at its meetings with any matter within the sphere of action of the League or affecting the peace of the world.

At meetings of the Assembly each Member of the League shall have one vote, and may have not more than three Representatives.

ARTICLE 4

The Council shall consist of Representatives of the Principal Allied and Associated Powers, together with Representatives of four other Members of the League. These four Members of the League shall be selected by the Assembly from time to time in its discretion. Until the appointment of the Representatives of the four Members of the League first selected by the Assembly, Representatives of Belgium, Brazil, Spain and Greece shall be members of the Council.

With the approval of the majority of the Assembly, the Council may name additional Members of the League whose Representatives shall always be members of the Council; the Council with like approval may increase the number of Members of the League to be selected by the Assembly for representation on the Council.

The Council shall meet from time to time as occasion may require, and at least once a year, at the Seat of the League, or at such other place as may be decided upon.

The Council may deal at its meetings with any matter within the sphere of action of the League or affecting the peace of the world.

Any Member of the League not represented on the Council shall be invited to send a Representative to sit as a member at any meeting of the Council during the consideration of matters specially affecting the interests of that Member of the League.

At meetings of the Council, each Member of the League represented on the Council shall have one vote, and may have not more than one Representative.

Article 5

Except where otherwise expressly provided in this Covenant or by the terms of the present Treaty, decisions at any meeting of the Assembly or of the Council shall require the agreement of all the Members of the League represented at the meeting.

All matters of procedure at meetings of the Assembly or of the Council, including the appointment of Committees to investigate particular matters, shall be regulated by the Assembly or by the Council and may be decided by a majority of the Members of the League represented at the meeting.

The first meeting of the Assembly and the first meeting of the Council shall be summoned by the President of the United States of America.

Article 6

The permanent Secretariat shall be established at the Seat of the League. The Secretariat shall comprise a Secretary General and such secretaries and staff as may be required.

The first Secretary General shall be the person named in the Annex; thereafter the Secretary General shall be appointed by the Council with the approval of the majority of the Assembly.

The secretaries and staff of the Secretariat shall be appointed by the Secretary General with the approval of the Council.

The Secretary General shall act in that capacity at all meetings of the Assembly and of the Council.

The expenses of the Secretariat shall be borne by the Members of the League in accordance with the apportionment of the expenses of the International Bureau of the Universal Postal Union.

Article 7

The Seat of the League is established at Geneva.

The Council may at any time decide that the Seat of the League shall be established elsewhere.

All positions under or in connection with the League, including the Secretariat, shall be open equally to men and women.

Representatives of the Members of the League and officials of the League when engaged on the business of the League shall enjoy diplomatic privileges and immunities.

The buildings and other property occupied by the League or its officials or by Representatives attending its meetings shall be inviolable.

ARTICLE 8

The Members of the League recognise that the maintenance of peace requires the reduction of national armaments to the lowest point consistent with national safety and the enforcement by common action of international obligations.

The Council, taking account of the geographical situation and circumstances of each State, shall formulate plans for such reduction for the consideration and action of the several Governments.

Such plans shall be subject to reconsideration and revision at least every ten years.

After these plans shall have been adopted by the several Governments, the limits of armaments therein fixed shall not be exceeded without the concurrence of the Council.

The Members of the League agree that the manufacture by private enterprise of munitions and implements of war is open to grave objections. The Council shall advise how the evil effects attendant upon such manufacture can be prevented, due regard being had to the necessities of those Members of the League which are not able to manufacture the munitions and implements of war necessary for their safety.

The Members of the League undertake to interchange full and frank information as to the scale of their armaments, their military, naval and air programmes and the condition of such of their industries as are adaptable to war-like purposes.

ARTICLE 9

A permanent Commission shall be constituted to advise the Council on the execution of the provisions of Articles 1 and 8 and on military, naval and air questions generally.

ARTICLE 10

The Members of the League undertake to respect and preserve as against external aggression the territorial integrity and existing political independence of all Members of the League. In case of any such aggression or in case of any threat or danger of such aggression the Council shall advise upon the means by which this obligation shall be fulfilled.

ARTICLE 11

Any war or threat of war, whether immediately affecting any of the Members of the League or not, is hereby declared a matter of concern to the whole

League, and the League shall take any action that may be deemed wise and effectual to safeguard the peace of nations. In case any such emergency should arise the Secretary General shall on the request of any Member of the League forthwith summon a meeting of the Council.

It is also declared to be the friendly right of each Member of the League to bring to the attention of the Assembly or of the Council any circumstance whatever affecting international relations which threatens to disturb international peace or the good understanding between nations upon which peace depends.

ARTICLE 12

The Members of the League agree that if there should arise between them any dispute likely to lead to a rupture, they will submit the matter either to arbitration or to inquiry by the Council, and they agree in no case to resort to war until three months after the award by the arbitrators or the report by the Council.

In any case under this Article the award of the arbitrators shall be made within a reasonable time, and the report of the Council shall be made within six months after the submission of the dispute.

ARTICLE 13

The Members of the League agree that whenever any dispute shall arise between them which they recognise to be suitable for submission to arbitration and which cannot be satisfactorily settled by diplomacy, they will submit the whole subject-matter to arbitration.

Disputes as to the interpretation of a treaty, as to any question of international law, as to the existence of any fact which if established would constitute a breach of any international obligation, or as to the extent and nature of the reparation to be made for any such breach, are declared to be among those which are generally suitable for submission to arbitration.

For the consideration of any such dispute the court of arbitration to which the case is referred shall be the Court agreed on by the parties to the dispute or stipulated in any convention existing between them.

The Members of the League agree that they will carry out in full good faith any award that may be rendered, and that they will not resort to war against a Member of the League which complies therewith. In the event of any failure to carry out such an award, the Council shall propose what steps should be taken to give effect thereto.

ARTICLE 14

The Council shall formulate and submit to the Members of the League for adoption plans for the establishment of a Permanent Court of International Justice. The Court shall be competent to hear and determine any dispute of an international character which the parties thereto submit to it. The Court may also give an advisory opinion upon any dispute or question referred to it by the Council or by the Assembly.

ARTICLE 15

If there should arise between Members of the League any dispute likely to lead to a rupture, which is not submitted to arbitration in accordance with Article 13, the Members of the League agree that they will submit the matter to the Council. Any party to the dispute may effect such submission by giving notice of the existence of the dispute to the Secretary General, who will make all necessary arrangements for a full investigation and consideration thereof.

For this purpose the parties to the dispute will communicate to the Secretary General, as promptly as possible, statements of their case with all the relevant facts and papers, and the Council may forthwith direct the publication thereof.

The Council shall endeavour to effect a settlement of the dispute, and if such efforts are successful, a statement shall be made public giving such facts and explanations regarding the dispute and the terms of settlement thereof as the Council may deem appropriate.

If the dispute is not thus settled, the Council either unanimously or by a majority vote shall make and publish a report containing a statement of the facts of the dispute and the recommendations which are deemed just and proper in regard thereto.

Any Member of the League represented on the Council may make public a statement of the facts of the dispute and of its conclusions regarding the same.

If a report by the Council is unanimously agreed to by the members thereof other than the Representatives of one or more of the parties to the dispute, the Members of the League agree that they will not go to war with any party to the dispute which complies with the recommendations of the report.

If the Council fails to reach a report which is unanimously agreed to by the members thereof, other than the Representatives of one or more of the parties to the dispute, the Members of the League reserve to themselves the right to take such action as they shall consider necessary for the maintenance of right and justice.

If the dispute between the parties is claimed by one of them, and is found by the Council, to arise out of a matter which by international law is solely within the domestic jurisdiction of that party, the Council shall so report, and shall make no recommendation as to its settlement.

The Council may in any case under this Article refer the dispute to the Assembly. The dispute shall be so referred at the request of either party to the dispute, provided that such request be made within fourteen days after the submission of the dispute to the Council.

In any case referred to the Assembly, all the provisions of this Article and of Article 12 relating to the action and powers of the Council shall apply to the action and powers of the Assembly, provided that a report made by the Assembly, if concurred in by the Representatives of those Members of the League represented on the Council and of a majority of the other Members of the League, exclusive in each case of the Representatives of the parties to the dispute, shall have the same force as a report by the Council concurred in by all the members thereof other than the Representatives of one or more of the parties to the dispute.

ARTICLE 16

Should any Member of the League resort to war in disregard of its covenants under Articles 12, 13 or 15, it shall *ipso facto* be deemed to have committed an act of war against all other Members of the League, which hereby undertake immediately to subject it to the severance of all trade or financial relations, the prohibition of all intercourse between their nationals and the nationals of the covenant-breaking State, and the prevention of all financial, commercial or personal intercourse between the nationals of the covenant-breaking State and the nationals of any other State, whether a Member of the League or not.

It shall be the duty of the Council in such case to recommend to the several Governments concerned what effective military, naval or air force the Members of the League shall severally contribute to the armed forces to be used to protect the covenants of the League.

The Members of the League agree, further, that they will mutually support one another in the financial and economic measures which are taken under this Article, in order to minimise the loss and inconvenience resulting from the above measures, and that they will mutually support one another in resisting any special measures aimed at one of their number by the covenant-breaking State, and that they will take the necessary steps to afford passage through their territory to the forces of any of the Members of the League which are co-operating to protect the covenants of the League.

Any Member of the League which has violated any covenant of the League may be declared to be no longer a Member of the League by a vote of the Council concurred in by the Representatives of all the other Members of the League represented thereon.

ARTICLE 17

In the event of a dispute between a Member of the League and a State which is not a Member of the League, or between States not Members of the League, the State or States not Members of the League shall be invited to accept the obligations of membership in the League for the purposes of such dispute, upon such conditions as the Council may deem just. If such invitation is accepted, the provisions of Articles 12 to 16 inclusive shall be applied with such modifications as may be deemed necessary by the Council.

Upon such invitation being given the Council shall immediately institute an inquiry into the circumstances of the dispute and recommend such action as may seem best and most effectual in the circumstances.

If a State so invited shall refuse to accept the obligations of membership in the League for the purposes of such dispute, and shall resort to war against a Member of the League, the provisions of Article 16 shall be applicable as against the State taking such action.

If both parties to the dispute when so invited refuse to accept the obligations of membership in the League for the purposes of such dispute, the Council may take such measures and make such recommendations as will prevent hostilities and will result in the settlement of the dispute.

ARTICLE 18

Every treaty or international engagement entered into hereafter by any Member of the League shall be forthwith registered with the Secretariat and shall as soon as possible be published by it. No such treaty or international engagement shall be binding until so registered.

ARTICLE 19

The Assembly may from time to time advise the reconsideration by Members of the League of treaties which have become inapplicable and the consideration of international conditions whose continuance might endanger the peace of the world.

ARTICLE 20

The Members of the League severally agree that this Covenant is accepted as abrogating all obligations or understandings *inter se* which are inconsistent with the terms thereof, and solemnly undertake that they will not hereafter enter into any engagements inconsistent with the terms thereof.

In case any Member of the League shall, before becoming a Member of the League, have undertaken any obligations inconsistent with the terms of this Covenant, it shall be the duty of such Member to take immediate steps to procure its release from such obligations.

ARTICLE 21

Nothing in this Covenant shall be deemed to affect the validity of international engagements, such as treaties of arbitration or regional understandings like the Monroe doctrine, for securing the maintenance of peace.

ARTICLE 22

To those colonies and territories which as a consequence of the late war have ceased to be under the sovereignty of the States which formerly governed them and which are inhabited by peoples not yet able to stand by themselves under the strenuous conditions of the modern world, there should be applied the principle that the well-being and development of such peoples form a sacred trust of civilisation and that securities for the performance of this trust should be embodied in this Covenant.

The best method of giving practical effect to this principle is that the tutelage of such peoples should be entrusted to advanced nations who by reason of their resources, their experience or their geographical position can best undertake this responsibility, and who are willing to accept it, and that this tutelage should be exercised by them as Mandatories on behalf of the League.

The character of the mandate must differ according to the stage of the development of the people, the geographical situation of the territory, its economic conditions and other similar circumstances.

Certain communities formerly belonging to the Turkish Empire have reached a stage of development where their existence as independent nations can be provisionally recognised subject to the rendering of administrative advice and assistance by a Mandatory until such time as they are able to stand alone. The wishes of these communities must be a principal consideration in the selection of the Mandatory.

Other peoples, especially those of Central Africa, are at such a stage that the Mandatory must be responsible for the administration of the territory under conditions which will guarantee freedom of conscience and religion, subject only to the maintenance of public order and morals, the prohibition of abuses such as the slave trade, the arms traffic and the liquor traffic, and the prevention of the establishment of fortifications or military and naval bases and of military training of the natives for other than police purposes and the defence of territory, and will also secure equal opportunities for the trade and commerce of other Members of the League.

There are territories, such as South-West Africa and certain of the South Pacific Islands, which, owing to the sparseness of their population, or their small size, or their remoteness from the centres of civilisation, or their geographical contiguity to the territory of the Mandatory, and other circumstances, can be best administered under the laws of the Mandatory as integral portions of its territory, subject to the safeguards above mentioned in the interests of the indigenous population.

In every case of mandate, the Mandatory shall render to the Council an annual report in reference to the territory committed to its charge.

The degree of authority, control, or administration to be exercised by the Mandatory shall, if not previously agreed upon by the Members of the League, be explicitly defined in each case by the Council.

A permanent Commission shall be constituted to receive and examine the annual reports of the Mandatories and to advise the Council on all matters relating to the observance of the mandates.

ARTICLE 23

Subject to and in accordance with the provisions of international conventions existing or hereafter to be agreed upon, the Members of the League:

(*a*) will endeavour to secure and maintain fair and humane conditions of labour for men, women, and children, both in their own countries and in all countries to which their commercial and industrial relations extend, and for that purpose will establish and maintain the necessary international organisations;

(*b*) undertake to secure just treatment of the native inhabitants of territories under their control;

(*c*) will entrust the League with the general supervision over the execution of agreements with regard to the traffic in women and children, and the traffic in opium and other dangerous drugs;

(*d*) will entrust the League with the general supervision of the trade in arms and ammunition with the countries in which the control of this traffic is necessary in the common interest;

(*e*) will make provision to secure and maintain freedom of communications and of transit and equitable treatment for the commerce of all Members of the League. In this connection, the special necessities of the regions devastated during the war of 1914–1918 shall be borne in mind;

(*f*) will endeavour to take steps in matters of international concern for the prevention and control of disease.

ARTICLE 24

There shall be placed under the direction of the League all international bureaux already established by general treaties if the parties to such treaties consent. All such international bureaux and all commissions for the regulation of matters of international interest hereafter constituted shall be placed under the direction of the League.

In all matters of international interest which are regulated by general conventions but which are not placed under the control of international bureaux or commissions, the Secretariat of the League shall, subject to the consent of the Council and if desired by the parties, collect and distribute all relevant information and shall render any other assistance which may be necessary or desirable.

The Council may include as part of the expenses of the Secretariat the expenses of any bureau or commission which is placed under the direction of the League.

ARTICLE 25

The Members of the League agree to encourage and promote the establishment and co-operation of duly authorised voluntary national Red Cross organizations having as purposes the improvement of health, the prevention of disease and the mitigation of suffering throughout the world.

ARTICLE 26

Amendments to this Covenant will take effect when ratified by the Members of the League whose Representatives compose the Council and by a majority of the Members of the League whose Representatives compose the Assembly.

No such amendment shall bind any Member of the League which signifies its dissent therefrom, but in that case it shall cease to be a Member of the League.

ANNEX

I. ORIGINAL MEMBERS OF THE LEAGUE OF NATIONS SIGNATORIES OF THE TREATY OF PEACE

UNITED STATES OF AMERICA	HAITI
BELGIUM	HEDJAZ
BOLIVIA	HONDURAS
BRAZIL	ITALY
BRITISH EMPIRE	JAPAN
CANADA	LIBERIA
AUSTRALIA	NICARAGUA
SOUTH AFRICA	PANAMA
NEW ZEALAND	PERU
INDIA	POLAND
CHINA	PORTUGAL
CUBA	ROUMANIA
ECUADOR	SERB-CROAT-SLOVENE STATE
FRANCE	SIAM
GREECE	CZECHO-SLOVAKIA
GUATEMALA	URUGUAY

STATES INVITED TO ACCEDE TO THE COVENANT

ARGENTINE REPUBLIC	PERSIA
CHILI	SALVADOR
COLOMBIA	SPAIN
DENMARK	SWEDEN
NETHERLANDS	SWITZERLAND
NORWAY	VENEZUELA
PARAGUAY	

II. FIRST SECRETARY GENERAL OF THE LEAGUE OF NATIONS

The Honourable Sir James Eric DRUMMOND, K.C.M.G., C.B.

PART II

BOUNDARIES OF GERMANY

ARTICLE 27

The boundaries of Germany will be determined as follows:

1. *With Belgium:*

From the point common to the three frontiers of Belgium, Holland and Germany and in a southerly direction:

the north-eastern boundary of the former territory of *neutral Moresnet,* then the eastern boundary of the *Kreis* of Eupen, then the frontier between Belgium and the *Kreis* of Montjoie, then the north-eastern and eastern boundary of the *Kreis* of Malmédy to its junction with the frontier of Luxemburg.

2. *With Luxemburg:*

The frontier of August 3, 1914, to its junction with the frontier of France of the 18th July, 1870.

3. *With France:*

The frontier of July 18, 1870, from Luxemburg to Switzerland with the reservations made in Article 48 of Section IV (Saar Basin) of Part III.

4. *With Switzerland:*

The present frontier.

5. *With Austria:*

The frontier of August 3, 1914, from Switzerland to Czecho-Slovakia as hereinafter defined.

6. *With Czecho-Slovakia:*

The frontier of August 3, 1914, between Germany and Austria from its junction with the old administrative boundary separating Bohemia and the province of Upper Austria to the point north of the salient of the old province of Austrian Silesia situated at about 8 kilometres east of Neustadt.

7. *With Poland:*

From the point defined above to a point to be fixed on the ground about 2 kilometres east of Lorzendorf:

the frontier as it will be fixed in accordance with Article 88 of the present Treaty;

thence in a northerly direction to the point where the administrative boundary of Posnania crosses the river Bartsch:

a line to be fixed on the ground leaving the following places in Poland: Skorischau, Reichthal, Trembatschau, Kunzendorf, Schleise, Gross Kosel, Schreibersdorf, Rippin, Fürstlich-Niefken, Pawelau, Tscheschen, Konradau, Johannisdorf, Modzenowe, Bogdaj, and in Germany: Lorzendorf, Kaulwitz, Glausche, Dalbersdorf, Reesewitz, Stradam, Gross Wartenberg, Kraschen, Neu Mittelwalde, Domaslawitz, Wedelsdorf, Tscheschen Hammer;

thence the administrative boundary of Posnania north-westwards to the point where it cuts the Rawitsch-Herrnstadt railway;

thence to the point where the administrative boundary of Posnania cuts the Reisen-Tschirnau road:

a line to be fixed on the ground passing west of Triebusch and Gabel and east of Saborwitz;

thence the administrative boundary of Posnania to its junction with the eastern administrative boundary of the *Kreis* of Fraustadt;

thence in a north-westerly direction to a point to be chosen on the road between the villages of Unruhstadt and Kopnitz:

a line to be fixed on the ground passing west of Geyersdorf, Brenno, Fehlen, Altkloster, Klebel, and east of Ulbersdorf, Buchwald, Ilgen, Weine, Lupitze, Schwenten;

thence in a northerly direction to the northernmost point of Lake Chlop:

a line to be fixed on the ground following the median line of the lakes; the town and the station of Bentschen however (including the junction of the lines Schwiebus-Bentschen and Züllichau-Bentschen) remaining in Polish territory;

thence in a north-easterly direction to the point of junction of the boundaries of the *Kreise* of Schwerin, Birnbaum and Meseritz:

a line to be fixed on the ground passing east of Betsche;

thence in a northerly direction the boundary separating the *Kreise* of Schwerin and Birnbaum, then in an easterly direction the northern boundary of Posnania to the point where it cuts the river Netze;

thence upstream to its confluence with the Küddow:

the course of the Netze;

thence upstream to a point to be chosen about 6 kilometres southeast of Schneidemühl:

the course of the Küddow;

thence north-eastwards to the most southern point of the re-entrant of the northern boundary of Posnania about 5 kilometres west of Stahren:

a line to be fixed on the ground leaving the Schneidemühl-Konitz railway in this area entirely in German territory;

thence the boundary of Posnania north-eastwards to the point of the salient it makes about 15 kilometres east of Flatow;

thence north-eastwards to the point where the river Kamionka meets the southern boundary of the *Kreis* of Konitz about 3 kilometres north-east of Grunau:

a line to be fixed on the ground leaving the following places to Poland: Jasdrowo, Gr. Lutau, Kl. Lutau, Wittkau, and to Germany: Gr. Butzig, Cziskowo, Battrow, Böck, Grunau;

thence in a northerly direction the boundary between the *Kreise* of Konitz and Schlochau to the point where this boundary cuts the river Brahe;

thence to a point on the boundary of Pomerania 15 kilometres east of Rummelsburg:

a line to be fixed on the ground leaving the following places in Poland: Konarzin, Kelpin, Adl. Briesen, and in Germany: Sampohl, Neuguth, Steinfort, Gr. Peterkau;

then the boundary of Pomerania in an easterly direction to its junction with the boundary between the *Kreis* of Konitz and Schlochau;

thence northwards the boundary between Pomerania and West Prussia to the point on the river Rheda about 3 kilometres north-west of Gohra where that river is joined by a tributary from the north-west;

thence to a point to be selected in the bend of the Piasnitz river about 1½ kilometres north-west of Warschkau:

a line to be fixed on the ground;

thence this river downstream, then the median line of Lake Zarnowitz, then the old boundary of West Prussia to the Baltic Sea.

8. *With Denmark:*

The frontier as it will be fixed in accordance with Articles 109 to 111 of Part III, Section XII (Schleswig).

ARTICLE 28.

The boundaries of East Prussia, with the reservations made in Section IX (East Prussia) of Part III, will be determined as follows:

from a point on the coast of the Baltic Sea about 1½ kilometres north of Pröbbernau church in a direction of about 159° East from true North:

a line to be fixed on the ground for about 2 kilometres;

thence in a straight line to the light at the bend of the Elbing Channel in approximately latitude 54°19½′ North, longitude 19°26′ East of Greenwich;

thence to the easternmost mouth of the Nogat River at a bearing of approximately 209° East from true North;

thence up the course of the Nogat River to the point where the latter leaves the Vistula (Weichsel);

thence up the principal channel of navigation of the Vistula, then the southern boundary of the *Kreis* of Marienwerder, then that of the *Kreis* of Rosenberg eastwards to the point where it meets the old boundary of East Prussia.

thence the old boundary between East and West Prussia, then the boundary between the *Kreise* of Osterode and Neidenburg, then the course of the river Skottau downstream, then the course of the Neide upstream to a point situated about 5 kilometres west of Bialutten being the nearest point to the old frontier of Russia;

thence in an easterly direction to a point immediately south of the intersection of the road Neidenburg-Mlava with the old frontier of Russia:

a line to be fixed on the ground passing north of Bialutten;

thence the old frontier of Russia to a point east of Schmalleningken, then the principal channel of navigation of the Nieman (Memel) downstream, then the Skierwieth arm of the delta to the Kurisches Haff;

thence a straight line to the point where the eastern shore of the Kurische Nehrung meets the administrative boundary about 4 kilometres south-west of Nidden;

thence this administrative boundary to the western shore of the Kurische Nehrung.

ARTICLE 29

The boundaries as described above are drawn in red on a one-in-a-million map which is annexed to the present Treaty (Map No. 1.)[10]

In the case of any discrepancies between the text of the Treaty and this map or any other map which may be annexed, the text will be final.

ARTICLE 30

In the case of boundaries which are defined by a waterway, the terms "course" and "channel" used in the present Treaty signify: in the case of non-navigable rivers, the median line of the waterway or of its principal arm, and, in the case of navigable rivers, the median line of the principal channel of navigation. It will rest with the Boundary Commissions provided by the present Treaty to specify in each case whether the frontier line shall follow any changes of the course or channel which may take place or whether it shall be definitely fixed by the position of the course or channel at the time when the present Treaty comes into force.

PART III

POLITICAL CLAUSES FOR EUROPE

SECTION I

Belgium

ARTICLE 31

Germany, recognizing that the Treaties of April 19, 1839, which established the status of Belgium before the war, no longer conform to the requirements of the situation, consents to the abrogation of the said Treaties and undertakes immediately to recognize and to observe whatever conventions may be entered into by the Principal Allied and Associated Powers, or

---

[10] Printed in S. Doc. 51, 66th Cong., 1st sess., between pp. 52 and 53.

by any of them, in concert with the Governments of Belgium and of the Netherlands, to replace the said Treaties of 1839. If her formal adhesion should be required to such conventions or to any of their stipulations, Germany undertakes immediately to give it.

ARTICLE 32

Germany recognizes the full sovereignty of Belgium over the whole of the contested territory of Moresnet (called *Moresnet neutre*).

ARTICLE 33

Germany renounces in favour of Belgium all rights and title over the territory of Prussian Moresnet situated on the west of the road from Liége to Aix-la-Chapelle; the road will belong to Belgium where it bounds this territory.

ARTICLE 34

Germany renounces in favour of Belgium all rights and title over the territory comprising the whole of the *Kreise* of Eupen and of Malmédy.

During the six months after the coming into force of this Treaty, registers will be opened by the Belgian authority at Eupen and Malmédy in which the inhabitants of the above territory will be entitled to record in writing a desire to see the whole or part of it remain under German sovereignty.

The results of this public expression of opinion will be communicated by the Belgian Government to the League of Nations, and Belgium undertakes to accept the decision of the League.

ARTICLE 35

A Commission of seven persons, five of whom will be appointed by the Principal Allied and Associated Powers, one by Germany and one by Belgium, will be set up fifteen days after the coming into force of the present Treaty to settle on the spot the new frontier line between Belgium and Germany, taking into account the economic factors and the means of communication.

Decisions will be taken by a majority and will be binding on the parties concerned.

ARTICLE 36

When the transfer of the sovereignty over the territories referred to above has become definite, German nationals habitually resident in the territories will definitely acquire Belgian nationality *ipso facto,* and will lose their German nationality.

Nevertheless, German nationals who became resident in the territories after August 1, 1914, shall not obtain Belgian nationality without a permit from the Belgian Government.

ARTICLE 37

Within the two years following the definitive transfer of the sovereignty over the territories assigned to Belgium under the present Treaty, German nationals over 18 years of age habitually resident in those territories will be entitled to opt for German nationality.

Option by a husband will cover his wife, and option by parents will cover their children under 18 years of age.

Persons who have exercised the above right to opt must within the ensuing twelve months transfer their place of residence to Germany.

They will be entitled to retain their immovable property in the territories acquired by Belgium. They may carry with them their movable property of every description. No export or import duties may be imposed upon them in connection with the removal of such property.

ARTICLE 38

The German Government will hand over without delay to the Belgian Government the archives, registers, plans, title deeds and documents of every kind concerning the civil, military, financial, judicial or other administrations in the territory transferred to Belgian sovereignty.

The German Government will likewise restore to the Belgian Government the archives and documents of every kind carried off during the war by the German authorities from the Belgian public administrations, in particular from the Ministry of Foreign Affairs at Brussels.

ARTICLE 39

The proportion and nature of the financial liabilities of Germany and of Prussia which Belgium will have to bear on account of the territories ceded to her shall be fixed in conformity with Articles 254 and 256 of Part IX (Financial Clauses) of the present Treaty.

SECTION II

Luxemburg

ARTICLE 40

With regard to the Grand Duchy of Luxemburg, Germany renounces the benefit of all the provisions inserted in her favour in the Treaties of February 8, 1842, April 2, 1847, October 20–25, 1865, August 18, 1866, February 21 and May 11, 1867, May 10, 1871, June 11, 1872, and November 11, 1902, and in all Conventions consequent upon such Treaties.

Germany recognizes that the Grand Duchy of Luxemburg ceased to form part of the German Zollverein as from January 1, 1919, renounces all rights to the exploitation of the railways, adheres to the termination of the régime of neutrality of the Grand Duchy, and accepts in advance all international arrangements which may be concluded by the Allied and Associated Powers relating to the Grand Duchy.

ARTICLE 41

Germany undertakes to grant to the Grand Duchy of Luxemburg, when a demand to that effect is made to her by the Principal Allied and Associated Powers, the rights and advantages stipulated in favour of such Powers or their nationals in the present Treaty with regard to economic questions, to questions relative to transport and to aerial navigation.

SECTION III

Left Bank of the Rhine

ARTICLE 42

Germany is forbidden to maintain or construct any fortifications either on the left bank of the Rhine or on the right bank to the west of a line drawn 50 kilometres to the East of the Rhine.

ARTICLE 43

In the area defined above the maintenance and the assembly of armed forces, either permanently or temporarily, and military manœuvres of any kind, as well as the upkeep of all permanent works for mobilization, are in the same way forbidden.

ARTICLE 44

In case Germany violates in any manner whatever the provisions of Articles 42 and 43, she shall be regarded as committing a hostile act against the Powers signatory of the present Treaty and as calculated to disturb the peace of the world.

SECTION IV

Saar Basin

ARTICLE 45

As compensation for the destruction of the coal-mines in the north of France and as part payment towards the total reparation due from Germany for the damage resulting from the war, Germany cedes to France in full and absolute possession, with exclusive rights of exploitation, unencumbered and free from all debts and charges of any kind, the coal-mines situated in the Saar Basin as defined in Article 48.

ARTICLE 46

In order to assure the rights and welfare of the population and to guarantee to France complete freedom in working the mines, Germany agrees to the provisions of Chapters I and II of the Annex hereto.

ARTICLE 47

In order to make in due time permanent provision for the government of the Saar Basin in accordance with the wishes of the populations, France and Germany agree to the provisions of Chapter III of the Annex hereto.

ARTICLE 48

The boundaries of the territory of the Saar Basin, as dealt with in the present stipulations, will be fixed as follows:

On the south and south-west: by the frontier of France as fixed by the present Treaty.

On the north-west and north: by a line following the northern administrative boundary of the *Kreis* of Merzig from the point where it leaves the French frontier to the point where it meets the administrative boundary separating the commune of Saarhölzbach from the commune of Britten; following this communal boundary southwards and reaching the administrative boundary of the canton of Merzig so as to include in the territory of the Saar Basin the canton of Mettlach, with the exception of the commune of Britten; following successively the northern administrative boundaries of the cantons of Merzig and Haustadt, which are incorporated in the aforesaid Saar Basin, then successively the administrative boundaries separating the *Kreise* of Sarrelouis, Ottweiler and Saint-Wendel from the *Kreise* of Merzig, Trèves (Trier) and the Principality of Birkenfeld as far as a point situated about 500 metres north of the village of Furschweiler (viz., the highest point of the Metzelberg).

On the north-east and east: from the last point defined above to a point about 3½ kilometres east-north-east of Saint-Wendel:

a line to be fixed on the ground passing east of Furschweiler, west of Roschberg, east of points 418, 329 (south of Roschberg), west of Leitersweiler, north-east of point 464, and following the line of the crest southwards to its junction with the administrative boundary of the *Kreis* of Kusel;

thence in a southerly direction the boundary of the *Kreis* of Kusel, then the boundary of the *Kreis* of Homburg towards the south-south-east to a point situated about 1000 metres west of Dunzweiler;

thence to a point about 1 kilometre south of Hornbach:

a line to be fixed on the ground passing through point 424 (about 1000 metres south-east of Dunzweiler), point 363 (Fuchs-Berg), point 322 (south-west of Waldmohr), then east of Jägersburg and Erbach, then encircling Homburg, passing through the points 361 (about 2½ kilometres north-east by east of that town), 342 (about 2 kilometres south-east of that town), 347 (Schreiners-Berg), 356, 350 (about 1½ kilometres south-east of Schwarzenbach), then passing east of Einöd, south-east of points 322 and 333, about 2 kilometres east of Webenheim, about 2 kilometres east of Mimbach, passing east of the plateau which is traversed by the road from Mimbach to Böckweiler (so as to include this road in the territory of the Saar Basin), passing immediately north of the junction of the roads from Böckweiler and Altheim situated about 2 kilometres north of Altheim, then passing south of Ring-weilerhof and north of point 322, rejoining the frontier of France at the angle which it makes about 1 kilometre south of Hornbach (see Map No. 2 [11] scale 1/100,000 annexed to the present Treaty).

A commission composed of five members, one appointed by France, one by Germany, and three by the Council of the League of Nations, which will select nationals of other Powers, will be constituted within fifteen days from the coming into force of the present Treaty, to trace on the spot the frontier line described above.

In those parts of the preceding line which do not coincide with adminis-trative boundaries, the Commission will endeavour to keep to the line in-dicated, while taking into consideration, so far as is possible, local economic interests and existing communal boundaries.

The decisions of this Commission will be taken by a majority, and will be binding on the parties concerned.

ARTICLE 49

Germany renounces in favour of the League of Nations, in the capacity of trustee, the government of the territory defined above.

At the end of fifteen years from the coming into force of the present Treaty the inhabitants of the said territory shall be called upon to indicate the sovereignty under which they desire to be placed.

ARTICLE 50

The stipulations under which the cession of the mines in the Saar Basin shall be carried out, together with the measures intended to guarantee the rights and the well-being of the inhabitants and the government of the terri-tory, as well as the conditions in accordance with which the plebiscite herein-before provided for is to be made, are laid down in the Annex hereto. This Annex shall be considered as an integral part of the present Treaty, and Ger-many declares her adherence to it.

ANNEX

In accordance with the provisions of Articles 45 to 50 of the present Treaty, the stipulations under which the cession by Germany to France of the mines of the Saar Basin will be effected, as well as the measures intended to ensure respect for the rights and well-being of the population and the government of the territory, and the conditions in which the inhabitants will be called upon to indicate the sovereignty under which they may wish to be placed, have been laid down as follows:

---

[11] Printed in S. Doc. 51, 66th Cong., 1st sess., between pp. 64 and 65.

CHAPTER I

Cession and Exploitation of Mining Property

From the date of the coming into force of the present Treaty, all the deposits of coal situated within the Saar Basin as defined in Article 48 of the said Treaty, become the complete and absolute property of the French State.

The French State will have the right of working or not working the said mines, or of transferring to a third party the right of working them, without having to obtain any previous authorisation or to fulfil any formalities.

The French State may always require that the German mining laws and regulations referred to below shall be applied in order to ensure the determination of its rights.

2

The right of ownership of the French State will apply not only to the deposits which are free and for which concessions have not yet been granted, but also to the deposits for which concessions have already been granted, whoever may be the present proprietors, irrespective of whether they belong to the Prussian State, to the Bavarian State, to other States or bodies, to companies or to individuals, whether they have been worked or not, or whether a right of exploitation distinct from the right of the owners of the surface of the soil has or has not been recognized.

3

As far as concerns the mines which are being worked, the transfer of the ownership to the French State will apply to all the accessories and subsidiaries of the said mines, in particular to their plant and equipment both on and below the surface, to their extracting machinery, their plants for transforming coal into electric power, coke and by-products, their workshops, means of communication, electric lines, plant for catching and distributing water, land, buildings such as offices, managers', employees' and workmen's dwellings, schools, hospitals and dispensaries, their stocks and supplies of every description, their archives and plans, and in general everything which those who own or exploit the mines possess or enjoy for the purpose of exploiting the mines and their accessories and subsidiaries.

The transfer will apply also to the debts owing for products delivered before the entry into possession by the French State, and after the signature of the present Treaty, and to deposits of money made by customers, whose rights will be guaranteed by the French State.

4

The French State will acquire the property free and clear of all debts and charges. Nevertheless, the rights acquired, or in course of being acquired, by the employees of the mines and their accessories and subsidiaries at the date of the coming into force of the present Treaty, in connection with pensions for old age or disability, will not be affected. In return, Germany must pay over to the French State a sum representing the actuarial amounts to which the said employees are entitled.

5

The value of the property thus ceded to the French State will be determined by the Reparation Commission referred to in Article 233 of Part VIII (Reparation) of the present Treaty.

This value shall be credited to Germany in part payment of the amount due for reparation.

It will be for Germany to indemnify the proprietors or parties concerned, whoever they may be.

6

No tariff shall be established on the German railways and canals which may directly or indirectly discriminate to the prejudice of the transport of the personnel or products of the mines and their accessories or subsidiaries, or of the material necessary to their exploitation. Such transport shall enjoy all the rights and privileges which any international railway conventions may guarantee to similar products of French origin.

7

The equipment and personnel necessary to ensure the despatch and transport of the products of the mines and their accessories and subsidiaries, as well as the carriage of workmen and employees, will be provided by the local railway administration of the Basin.

8

No obstacle shall be placed in the way of such improvements of railways or waterways as the French State may judge necessary to assure the despatch and the transport of the products of the mines and their accessories and subsidiaries, such as double trackage, enlargement of stations, and construction of yards and appurtenances. The distribution of expenses will, in the event of disagreement, be submitted to arbitration.

The French State may also establish any new means of communication, such as roads, electric lines and telephone connections which it may consider necessary for the exploitation of the mines.

It may exploit freely and without any restrictions the means of communication of which it may become the owner, particularly those connecting the mines and their accessories and subsidiaries with the means of communication situated in French territory.

9

The French State shall always be entitled to demand the application of the German mining laws and regulations in force on November 11, 1918, excepting provisions adopted exclusively in view of the state of war, with a view to the acquisition of such land as it may judge necessary for the exploitation of the mines and their accessories and subsidiaries.

The payment for damage caused to immovable property by the working of the said mines and their accessories and subsidiaries shall be made in accordance with the German mining laws and regulations above referred to.

10

Every person whom the French State may substitute for itself as regards the whole or part of its rights to the exploitation of the mines and their accessories and subsidiaries shall enjoy the benefit of the privileges provided in this Annex.

11

The mines and other immovable property which become the property of the French State may never be made the subject of measures of forfeiture, forced sale, expropriation or requisition, nor of any other measure affecting the right of property.

The personnel and the plant connected with the exploitation of these mines or their accessories and subsidiaries, as well as the product extracted from the mines or manufactured in their accessories and subsidiaries, may not at any time be made the subject of any measures of requisition.

12

The exploitation of the mines and their accessories and subsidiaries, which become the property of the French State, will continue, subject to the provisions of paragraph 23 below, to be subject to the régime established by the German laws and regulations in force on November 11, 1918, excepting provisions adopted exclusively in view of the state of war.

The rights of the workmen shall similarly be maintained, subject to the provisions of the said paragraph 23, as established on November 11, 1918, by the German laws and regulations above referred to.

No impediment shall be placed in the way of the introduction or employment in the mines and their accessories and subsidiaries of workmen from without the Basin.

The employees and workmen of French nationality shall have the right to belong to French labour unions.

13

The amount contributed by the mines and their accessories and subsidiaries, either to the local budget of the territory of the Saar Basin or to the communal funds, shall be fixed with due regard to the ratio of the value of the mines to the total taxable wealth of the Basin.

14

The French State shall always have the right of establishing and maintaining, as incidental to the mines, primary or technical schools for its employees and their children, and of causing instruction therein to be given in the French language, in accordance with such curriculum and by such teachers as it may select.

It shall also have the right to establish and maintain hospitals, dispensaries, workmen's houses and gardens and other charitable and social institutions.

15

The French State shall enjoy complete liberty with respect to the distribution, despatch and sale prices of the products of the mines and their accessories and subsidiaries.

Nevertheless, whatever may be the total product of the mines, the French Government undertakes that the requirements of local consumption for industrial and domestic purposes shall always be satisfied in the proportion existing in 1913 between the amount consumed locally and the total output of the Saar Basin.

CHAPTER II

Government of the Territory of the Saar Basin

16

The Government of the territory of the Saar Basin shall be entrusted to a Commission representing the League of Nations. This Commission shall sit in the territory of the Saar Basin.

17

The Governing Commission provided for by paragraph 16 shall consist of five members chosen by the Council of the League of Nations, and will include one citizen of France, one native inhabitant of the Saar Basin, not a citizen of France, and three members belonging to three countries other than France or Germany.

The members of the Governing Commission shall be appointed for one year and may be re-appointed. They can be removed by the Council of the League of Nations, which will provide for their replacement.

The members of the Governing Commission will be entitled to a salary which will be fixed by the Council of the League of Nations, and charged on the local revenues.

18

The Chairman of the Governing Commission shall be appointed for one year from among the members of the Commission by the Council of the League of Nations and may be re-appointed.

The Chairman will act as the executive of the Commission.

19

Within the territory of the Saar Basin the Governing Commission shall have all the powers of government hitherto belonging to the German Empire, Prussia, or Bavaria, including the appointment and dismissal of officials, and the creation of such administrative and representative bodies as it may deem necessary.

It shall have full powers to administer and operate the railways, canals and the different public services.

Its decisions shall be taken by a majority.

20

Germany will place at the disposal of the Governing Commission all official documents and archives under the control of Germany, of any German State, or of any local authority, which relate to the territory of the Saar Basin or to the rights of the inhabitants thereof.

21

It will be the duty of the Governing Commission to ensure, by such means and under such conditions as it may deem suitable, the protection abroad of the interests of the inhabitants of the territory of the Saar Basin.

22

The Governing Commission shall have the full right of user of all property, other than mines, belonging, either in public or in private domain, to the Government of the German Empire, or the Government of any German State, in the territory of the Saar Basin.

As regards the railways an equitable apportionment of rolling stock shall be made by a mixed Commission on which the Government of the territory of the Saar Basin and the German railways will be represented.

Persons, goods, vessels, carriages, wagons and mails coming from or going to the Saar Basin shall enjoy all the rights and privileges relating to transit and transport which are specified in the provisions of Part XII (Ports, Waterways and Railways) of the present Treaty.

23

The laws and regulations in force on November 11, 1918, in the territory of the Saar Basin (except those enacted in consequence of the state of war) shall continue to apply.

If, for general reasons or to bring these laws and regulations into accord with the provisions of the present Treaty, it is necessary to introduce modifications, these shall be decided on, and put into effect by the Governing Commission, after consultation with the elected representatives of the inhabitants in such a manner as the Commission may determine.

No modification may be made in the legal régime for the exploitation of the mines, provided for in paragraph 12, without the French State being previously consulted, unless such modification results from a general regulation respecting labour adopted by the League of Nations.

In fixing the conditions and hours of labour for men, women and children, the Governing Commission is to take into consideration the wishes expressed by the local labour organisations, as well as the principles adopted by the League of Nations.

24

Subject to the provisions of paragraph 4, no rights of the inhabitants of the Saar Basin acquired or in process of acquisition at the date of the coming into force of this Treaty, in respect of any insurance system of Germany or in respect of any pension of any kind are affected by any of the provisions of the present Treaty.

Germany and the Government of the territory of the Saar Basin will preserve and continue all of the aforesaid rights.

25

The civil and criminal courts existing in the territory of the Saar Basin shall continue.

A civil and criminal court will be established by the Governing Commission to hear appeals from the decisions of the said courts and to decide matters for which these courts are not competent.

The Governing Commission will be responsible for settling the organisation and jurisdiction of the said court.

Justice will be rendered in the name of the Governing Commission.

26

The Governing Commission will alone have the power of levying taxes and dues in the territory of the Saar Basin.

These taxes and dues will be exclusively applied to the needs of the territory.

The fiscal system existing on November 11, 1918, will be maintained as far as possible, and no new tax except customs duties may be imposed without previously consulting the elected representatives of the inhabitants.

27

The present stipulations will not affect the existing nationality of the inhabitants of the territory of the Saar Basin.

No hindrance shall be placed in the way of those who wish to acquire a different nationality, but in such case the acquisition of the new nationality will involve the loss of any other.

28

Under the control of the Governing Commission the inhabitants will retain their local assemblies, their religious liberties, their schools and their language.

The right of voting will not be exercised for any assemblies other than the local assemblies, and will belong to every inhabitant over the age of twenty years, without distinction of sex.

29

Any of the inhabitants of the Saar Basin who may desire to leave the territory will have full liberty to retain in it their immovable property or to sell it at fair prices, and to remove their movable property free of any charges.

30

There will be no military service, whether compulsory or voluntary, in the territory of the Saar Basin, and the construction of fortifications therein is forbidden.

Only a local gendarmerie for the maintenance of order may be established.

It will be the duty of the Governing Commission to provide in all cases for the protection of persons and property in the Saar Basin.

31

The territory of the Saar Basin as defined by Article 48 of the present Treaty shall be subjected to the French customs régime. The receipts from the customs duties on goods intended for local consumption shall be included in the budget of the said territory after deduction of all costs of collection.

No export tax shall be imposed upon metallurgical products or coal exported from the said territory to Germany, nor upon German exports for the use of the industries of the territory of the Saar Basin.

Natural or manufactured products originating in the Basin in transit over German territory and, similarly, German products in transit over the territory of the Basin shall be free of all customs duties.

Products which both originate in and pass from the Basin into Germany shall be free of import duties for a period of five years from the date of the coming into force of the present Treaty, and during the same period articles imported from Germany into the territory of the Basin for local consumption shall likewise be free of import duties.

During these five years the French Government reserves to itself the right of limiting to the annual average of the quantities imported into Alsace-Lorraine and France in the years 1911 to 1913 the quantities which may be sent into France of all articles coming from the Basin which include raw materials and semi-manufactured goods imported duty free from Germany. Such average shall be determined after reference to all available official information and statistics.

32

No prohibition or restriction shall be imposed upon the circulation of French money in the territory of the Saar Basin.

The French State shall have the right to use French money in all purchases, payments and contracts connected with the exploitation of the mines or their accessories and subsidiaries.

33

The Governing Commission shall have power to decide all questions arising from the interpretation of the preceding provisions.

France and Germany agree that any dispute involving a difference of opinion as to the interpretation of the said provisions shall in the same way be submitted to the Governing Commission, and the decision of a majority of the Commission shall be binding on both countries.

CHAPTER III

Plebiscite

34

At the termination of a period of fifteen years from the coming into force of the present Treaty, the population of the territory of the Saar Basin will be called upon to indicate their desires in the following manner:

A vote will take place by communes or districts, on the three following alternatives: (*a*) maintenance of the régime established by the present Treaty and by this Annex; (*b*) union with France; (*c*) union with Germany.

All persons without distinction of sex, more than twenty years old at the date of the voting, resident in the territory at the date of the signature of the present Treaty, will have the right to vote.

The other conditions, methods and the date of the voting shall be fixed by the Council of the League of Nations in such a way as to secure the freedom, secrecy and trustworthiness of the voting.

35

The League of Nations shall decide on the sovereignty under which the territory is to be placed, taking into account the wishes of the inhabitants as expressed by the voting:

(*a*) If, for the whole or part of the territory, the League of Nations decides in favour of the maintenance of the régime established by the present Treaty and this Annex, Germany hereby agrees to make such renunciation of her sovereignty in favour of the League of Nations as the latter shall deem necessary. It will be the duty of the League of Nations to take appropriate steps to adapt the régime definitively adopted to the permanent welfare of the territory and the general interest;

(*b*) If, for the whole or part of the territory, the League of Nations decides in favour of union with France, Germany hereby agrees to cede to France in accordance with the decision of the League of Nations all rights and title over the territory specified by the League;

(*c*) If, for the whole or part of the territory, the League of Nations decides in favour of union with Germany, it will be the duty of the League of Nations to cause the German Government to be reestablished in the government of the territory specified by the League.

36

If the League of Nations decides in favour of the union of the whole or part of the territory of the Saar Basin with Germany, France's rights of ownership in the mines situated in such part of the territory will be repurchased by Germany in their entirety, at a price payable in gold. The price to be paid will be fixed by three experts, one nominated by Germany, one by France, and one, who shall be neither a Frenchman nor a German, by the Council of the League of Nations; the decision of the experts will be given by a majority.

The obligation of Germany to make such payment shall be taken into account by the Reparation Commission, and for the purpose of this payment Germany may create a prior charge upon her assets or revenues upon such detailed terms as shall be agreed to by the Reparation Commission.

If, nevertheless, Germany after a period of one year from the date on which the payment becomes due shall not have effected the said payment, the Reparation Commission shall do so in accordance with such instructions as may be given by the League of Nations, and, if necessary, by liquidating that part of the mines which is in question.

37

If, in consequence of the repurchase provided for in paragraph 36, the ownership of the mines or any part of them is transferred to Germany, the French State and French nationals shall have the right to purchase such amount of coal of the Saar Basin as their industrial and domestic needs are found at that time to require. An equitable arrangement regarding amounts of coal, duration of contract, and prices will be fixed in due time by the Council of the League of Nations.

38

It is understood that France and Germany may, by special agreements concluded before the time fixed for the payment of the price for the repurchase of the mines, modify the provisions of paragraphs 36 and 37.

39

The Council of the League of Nations shall make such provisions as may be necessary for the establishment of the régime which is to take effect after the decisions of the League of Nations mentioned in paragraph 35 have be-come operative, including an equitable apportionment of any obligations of the Government of the territory of the Saar Basin arising from loans raised by the Commission or from other causes.

From the coming into force of the new régime, the powers of the Govern-ing Commission will terminate, except in the case provided for in paragraph 35 (a).

40

In all matters dealt with in the present Annex, the decisions of the Council of the League of Nations will be taken by a majority.

SECTION V

Alsace-Lorraine

The HIGH CONTRACTING PARTIES, recognising the moral obligation to redress the wrong done by Germany in 1871 both to the rights of France and to the wishes of the population of Alsace and Lorraine, which were separated from their country in spite of the solemn protest of their representatives at the Assembly of Bordeaux,

Agree upon the following Articles:

ARTICLE 51

The territories which were ceded to Germany in accordance with the Preliminaries of Peace signed at Versailles on February 26, 1871, and the Treaty of Frankfort of May 10, 1871, are restored to French sovereignty as from the date of the Armistice of November 11, 1918.

The provisions of the Treaties establishing the delimitation of the frontiers before 1871 shall be restored.

ARTICLE 52

The German Government shall hand over without delay to the French Government all archives, registers, plans, titles and documents of every kind concerning the civil, military, financial, judicial or other administrations of the territories restored to French sovereignty. If any of these documents, archives, registers, titles or plans have been misplaced, they will be restored by the German Government on the demand of the French Government.

ARTICLE 53

Separate agreements shall be made between France and Germany dealing with the interests of the inhabitants of the territories referred to in Article 51, particularly as regards their civil rights, their business and the exercise of their professions, it being understood that Germany undertakes as from the present date to recognise and accept the regulations laid down in the Annex hereto regarding the nationality of the inhabitants or natives of the said territories, not to claim at any time or in any place whatsoever as German nationals those who shall have been declared on any ground to be French, to receive all others in her territory, and to conform, as regards the property of German nationals in the territories indicated in Article 51, with the provisions of Article 297 and the Annex to Section IV of Part X (Economic Clauses) of the present Treaty.

Those German nationals who without acquiring French nationality shall receive permission from the French Government to reside in the said territories shall not be subjected to the provisions of the said Article.

ARTICLE 54

Those persons who have regained French nationality in virtue of paragraph 1 of the Annex hereto will be held to be Alsace-Lorrainers for the purposes of the present Section.

The persons referred to in paragraph 2 of the said Annex will from the day on which they have claimed French nationality be held to be Alsace-Lorrainers with retroactive effect as from November 11, 1918. For those whose application is rejected, the privilege will terminate at the date of the refusal.

Such juridical persons will also have the status of Alsace-Lorrainers as shall have been recognised as possessing this quality, whether by the French administrative authorities or by a judicial decision.

ARTICLE 55

The territories referred to in Article 51 shall return to France free and quit of all public debts under the conditions laid down in Article 255 of Part IX (Financial Clauses) of the present Treaty.

ARTICLE 56

In conformity with the provisions of Article 256 of Part IX (Financial Clauses) of the present Treaty, France shall enter into possession of all property and estate, within the territories referred to in Article 51, which belong to the German Empire or German States, without any payment or credit on this account to any of the States ceding the territories.

This provision applies to all movable or immovable property of public or private domain together with all rights whatsoever belonging to the German Empire or German States or to their administrative areas.

Crown property and the property of the former Emperor or other German sovereigns shall be assimilated to property of the public domain.

ARTICLE 57

Germany shall not take any action, either by means of stamping or by any other legal or administrative measures not applying equally to the rest of her territory, which may be to the detriment of the legal value or redeemability of German monetary instruments or monies which, at the date of the signature of the present Treaty, are legally current, and at that date are in the possession of the French Government.

ARTICLE 58

A special Convention will determine the conditions for repayment in marks of the exceptional war expenditure advanced during the course of the war by Alsace-Lorraine or by the public bodies in Alsace-Lorraine on account of the Empire in accordance with German law, such as payment to the families of persons mobilised, requisitions, billeting of troops, and assistance to persons who have been evacuated.

In fixing the amount of these sums Germany shall be credited with that portion which Alsace-Lorraine would have contributed to the Empire to meet the expenses resulting from these payments, this contribution being calculated according to the proportion of the Imperial revenues derived from Alsace-Lorraine in 1913.

ARTICLE 59

The French Government will collect for its own account the Imperial taxes, duties and dues of every kind leviable in the territories referred to in Article 51 and not collected at the time of the Armistice of November 11, 1918.

ARTICLE 60

The German Government shall without delay restore to Alsace-Lorrainers (individuals, juridical persons and public institutions) all property, rights and interests belonging to them on November 11, 1918, in so far as these are situated in German territory.

ARTICLE 61

The German Government undertakes to continue and complete without delay the execution of the financial clauses regarding Alsace-Lorraine contained in the Armistice Conventions.

ARTICLE 62

The German Government undertakes to bear the expense of all civil and military pensions which had been earned in Alsace-Lorraine on date of November 11, 1918, and the maintenance of which was a charge on the budget of the German Empire.

The German Government shall furnish each year the funds necessary for the payment in francs, at the average rate of exchange for that year, of the sums in marks to which persons resident in Alsace-Lorraine would have been entitled if Alsace-Lorraine had remained under German jurisdiction.

ARTICLE 63

For the purposes of the obligation assumed by Germany in Part VIII (Reparation) of the present Treaty to give compensation for damages caused to the civil populations of the Allied and Associated countries in the form of fines, the inhabitants of the territories referred to in Article 51 shall be assimilated to the above-mentioned populations.

ARTICLE 64

The regulations concerning the control of the Rhine and of the Moselle are laid down in Part XII (Ports, Waterways and Railways) of the present Treaty.

ARTICLE 65

Within a period of three weeks after the coming into force of the present Treaty, the port of Strasburg and the port of Kehl shall be constituted, for a period of seven years, a single unit from the point of view of exploitation.

The administration of this single unit will be carried on by a manager named by the Central Rhine Commission, which shall also have power to remove him.

This manager shall be of French nationality.

He will reside in Strasburg and will be subject to the supervision of the Central Rhine Commission.

There will be established in the two ports free zones in conformity with Part XII (Ports, Waterways and Railways) of the present Treaty.

A special Convention between France and Germany, which shall be submitted to the approval of the Central Rhine Commission, will fix the details of this organisation, particularly as regards finance.

It is understood that for the purpose of the present Article the port of Kehl includes the whole of the area necessary for the movements of the port and the trains which serve it, including the harbour, quays and railroads, platforms, cranes, sheds and warehouses, silos, elevators and hydro-electric plants, which make up the equipment of the port.

The German Government undertakes to carry out all measures which shall be required of it in order to assure that all the making-up and switching of trains arriving at or departing from Kehl, whether for the right bank or the left bank of the Rhine, shall be carried on in the best conditions possible.

All property rights shall be safeguarded. In particular the administration of the ports shall not prejudice any property rights of the French or Baden railroads.

Equality of treatment as respects traffic shall be assured in both ports to the nationals, vessels and goods of every country.

In case at the end of the sixth year France shall consider that the progress made in the improvement of the port of Strasburg still requires a prolongation of this temporary régime, she may ask for such prolongation from the Central Rhine Commission, which may grant an extension for a period not exceeding three years.

Throughout the whole period of any such extension the free zones above provided for shall be maintained.

Pending appointment of the first manager by the Central Rhine Commission a provisional manager who shall be of French nationality may be appointed by the Principal Allied and Associated Powers subject to the foregoing provisions.

For all purposes of the present Article the Central Rhine Commission will decide by a majority of votes.

ARTICLE 66

The railway and other bridges across the Rhine now existing within the limits of Alsace-Lorraine shall, as to all their parts and their whole length, be the property of the French State, which shall ensure their upkeep.

ARTICLE 67

The frontier railway stations shall be established by a subsequent agreement, it being stipulated in advance that on the Rhine frontier they shall be situated on the right bank.

The same shall apply to the rights of the Empire with regard to railway and tramway concessions within the territories referred to in Article 51.

This substitution shall not entail any payment on the part of the French State.

The frontier railway stations shall be established by a subsequent agreement, it being stipulated in advance that on the Rhine frontier they shall be situated on the right bank.

ARTICLE 68

In accordance with the provisions of Article 268 of Chapter I of Section I of Part X (Economic Clauses) of the present Treaty, for a period of five years from the coming into force of the present Treaty, natural or manufactured products originating in and coming from the territories referred to in Article 51 shall, on importation into German customs territory, be exempt from all customs duty.

The French Government may fix each year, by decree communicated to the German Government, the nature and amount of the products which shall enjoy this exemption.

The amount of each product which may be thus sent annually into Germany shall not exceed the average of the amounts sent annually in the years 1911–1913.

Further, during the period of five years above mentioned, the German Government shall allow the free export from Germany and the free reimportation into Germany, exempt from all customs duties and other charges (including internal charges), of yarns, tissues, and other textile materials or textile products of any kind and in any condition, sent from Germany into the territories referred to in Article 51, to be subjected there to any finishing process, such as bleaching, dyeing, printing, mercerization, gassing, twisting or dressing.

ARTICLE 69

During a period of ten years from the coming into force of the present Treaty, central electric supply works situated in German territory and formerly furnishing electric power to the territories referred to in Article 51 or to any establishment the working of which passes permanently or temporarily from Germany to France, shall be required to continue such supply up to the amount of consumption corresponding to the undertakings and contracts current on November 11, 1918.

Such supply shall be furnished according to the contracts in force and at a rate which shall not be higher than that paid to the said works by German nationals.

ARTICLE 70

It is understood that the French Government preserves its right to prohibit in the future in the territories referred to in Article 51 all new German participation:

(1) In the management or exploitation of the public domain and of public services, such as railways, navigable waterways, water works, gas works, electric power, etc.;

(2) In the ownership of mines and quarries of every kind and in enterprises connected therewith;

(3) In metallurgical establishments, even though their working may not be connected with that of any mine.

ARTICLE 71

As regards the territories referred to in Article 51, Germany renounces on behalf of herself and her nationals as from November 11, 1918, all rights under the law of May 25, 1910, regarding the trade in potash salts, and generally under any stipulations for the intervention of German organisations in the working of the potash mines. Similarly, she renounces on behalf of herself and her nationals all rights under any agreements, stipulations or laws which may exist to her benefit with regard to other products of the aforesaid territories.

ARTICLE 72

The settlement of the questions relating to debts contracted before November 11, 1918, between the German Empire and the German States or their nationals residing in Germany on the one part and Alsace-Lorrainers residing in Alsace-Lorraine on the other part shall be effected in accordance with the provisions of Section III of Part X (Economic Clauses) of the present Treaty, the expression "before the war" therein being replaced by the expression "before November 11, 1918". The rate of exchange applicable in the case of such settlement shall be the average rate quoted on the Geneva Exchange during the month preceding November 11, 1918.

There may be established in the territories referred to in Article 51, for the settlement of the aforesaid debts under the conditions laid down in Section III of Part X (Economic Clauses) of the present Treaty, a special clearing office, it being understood that this office shall be regarded as a "central office" under the provisions of paragraph 1 of the Annex to the said Section.

ARTICLE 73

The private property, rights and interests of Alsace-Lorrainers in Germany will be regulated by the stipulations of Section IV of Part X (Economic Clauses) of the present Treaty.

ARTICLE 74

The French Government reserves the right to retain and liquidate all the property, rights and interests which German nationals or societies controlled by Germany possessed in the territories referred to in Article 51 on November 11, 1918, subject to the conditions laid down in the last paragraph of Article 53 above.

Germany will directly compensate her nationals who may have been dispossessed by the aforesaid liquidations.

The product of these liquidations shall be applied in accordance with the stipulations of Sections III and IV of Part X (Economic Clauses) of the present Treaty.

ARTICLE 75

Notwithstanding the stipulations of Section V of Part X (Economic Clauses) of the present Treaty, all contracts made before the date of the promulgation in Alsace-Lorraine of the French decree of November 30, 1918, between Alsace-Lorrainers (whether individuals or juridical persons) or others resident in Alsace-Lorraine on the one part and the German Empire or German States and their nationals resident in Germany on the other part, the execution of which has been suspended by the Armistice or by subsequent French legislation, shall be maintained.

Nevertheless, any contract of which the French Government shall notify the cancellation to Germany in the general interest within a period of six months from the date of the coming into force of the present Treaty, shall be annulled except in respect of any debt or other pecuniary obligation arising out of any act done or money paid thereunder before November 11, 1918. If this dissolution would cause one of the parties substantial prejudice, equitable compensation, calculated solely on the capital employed without taking account of loss of profits, shall be accorded to the prejudiced party.

With regard to prescriptions, limitations and forfeitures in Alsace-Lorraine, the provisions of Articles 300 and 301 of Section V of Part X (Economic Clauses) shall be applied with the substitution for the expression "outbreak of war" of the expression "November 11, 1918", and for the expression "duration of the war" of the expression "period from November 11, 1918, to the date of the coming into force of the present Treaty".

ARTICLE 76

Questions concerning rights in industrial, literary or artistic property of Alsace-Lorrainers shall be regulated in accordance with the general stipulations of Section VII of Part X (Economic Clauses) of the present Treaty, it being understood that Alsace-Lorrainers holding rights of this nature under German legislation will preserve full and entire enjoyment of those rights on German territory.

ARTICLE 77

The German Government undertakes to pay over to the French Government such proportion of all reserves accumulated by the Empire or by public or private bodies dependent upon it, for the purposes of disability and old age insurance, as would fall to the disability and old age insurance fund at Strasburg.

The same shall apply in respect of the capital and reserves accumulated in Germany falling legitimately to other social insurance funds, to miners' superannuation funds, to the fund of the railways of Alsace-Lorraine, to other superannuation organisations established for the benefit of the personnel of public administrations and institutions operating in Alsace-Lorraine, and also in respect of the capital and reserves due by the insurance fund of private employees at Berlin, by reason of engagements entered into for the benefit of insured persons of that category resident in Alsace-Lorraine.

A special Convention shall determine the conditions and procedure of these transfers.

ARTICLE 78

With regard to the execution of judgments, appeals and prosecutions, the following rules shall be applied:

(1) All civil and commercial judgments which shall have been given since August 3, 1914, by the Courts of Alsace-Lorraine between Alsace-Lorrainers, or between Alsace-Lorrainers and foreigners, or between foreigners, and which shall not have been appealed from before November 11, 1918, shall be regarded as final and susceptible of immediate execution without further formality.

When the judgment has been given between Alsace-Lorrainers and Germans or between Alsace-Lorrainers and subjects of the allies of Germany, it shall only be capable of execution after the issue of an *exequatur* by the corresponding new tribunal in the restored territory referred to in Article 51.

(2) All judgments given by German Courts since August 3, 1914, against Alsace-Lorrainers for political crimes or misdemeanors shall be regarded as null and void.

(3) All sentences passed since November 11, 1918, by the Court of the Empire at Leipzig on appeals against the decisions of the Courts of Alsace-Lorraine shall be regarded as null and void and shall be so pronounced. The papers in regard to the cases in which such sentences have been given shall be returned to the Courts of Alsace-Lorraine concerned.

All appeals to the Court of the Empire against decisions of the Courts of Alsace-Lorraine shall be suspended. The papers shall be returned under the aforesaid conditions for transfer without delay to the French Cour de Cassation, which shall be competent to decide them.

(4) All prosecutions in Alsace-Lorraine for offences committed during the period between November 11, 1918, and the coming into force of the present Treaty will be conducted under German law except in so far as this has been modified by decrees duly published on the spot by the French authorities.

(5) All other questions as to competence, procedure or administration of justice shall be determined by a special Convention between France and Germany.

ARTICLE 79

The stipulations as to nationality contained in the Annex hereto shall be considered as of equal force with the provisions of the present Section.

All other questions concerning Alsace-Lorraine which are not regulated by the present Section and the Annex thereto or by the general provisions of the present Treaty will form the subject of further conventions between France and Germany.

ANNEX

I

As from November 11, 1918, the following persons are *ipso facto* reinstated in French nationality:

(1) Persons who lost French nationality by the application of the Franco-German Treaty of May 10, 1871, and who have not since that date acquired any nationality other than German;

(2) The legitimate or natural descendants of the persons referred to in the immediately preceding paragraph, with the exception of those whose ascendants in the paternal line include a German who migrated into Alsace-Lorraine after July 15, 1870;

(3) All persons born in Alsace-Lorraine of unknown parents, or whose nationality is unknown.

2

Within the period of one year from the coming into force of the present Treaty, persons included in any of the following categories may claim French nationality:

(1) All persons not restored to French nationality under paragraph 1 above, whose ascendants include a Frenchman or Frenchwoman who lost French nationality under the conditions referred to in the said paragraph;

(2) All foreigners, not nationals of a German State, who acquired the status of a citizen of Alsace-Lorraine before August 3, 1914;

(3) All Germans domiciled in Alsace-Lorraine, if they have been so domiciled since a date previous to July 15, 1870, or if one of their ascendants was at that date domiciled in Alsace-Lorraine;

(4) All Germans born or domiciled in Alsace-Lorraine who have served in the Allied or Associated armies during the present war, and their descendants;

(5) All persons born in Alsace-Lorraine before May 10, 1871, of foreign parents, and the descendants of such persons;

(6) The husband or wife of any person whose French nationality may have been restored under paragraph 1, or who may have claimed and obtained French nationality in accordance with the preceding provisions.

The legal representative of a minor may exercise, on behalf of that minor, the right to claim French nationality; and if that right has not been exercised, the minor may claim French nationality within the year following his majority.

Except in the cases provided for in No. (6) of the present paragraph, the French authorities reserve to themselves the right, in individual cases, to reject the claim to French nationality.

3

Subject to the provisions of paragraph 2, Germans born or domiciled in Alsace-Lorraine shall not acquire French nationality by reason of the restoration of Alsace-Lorraine to France, even though they may have the status of citizens of Alsace-Lorraine.

They may acquire French nationality only by naturalisation, on condition of having been domiciled in Alsace-Lorraine from a date previous to August 3, 1914, and of submitting proof of unbroken residence within the restored territory for a period of three years from November 11, 1918.

France will be solely responsible for their diplomatic and consular protection from the date of their application for French naturalisation.

The French Government shall determine the procedure by which reinstatement in French nationality as of right shall be effected, and the conditions under which decisions shall be given upon claims to such nationality and applications for naturalisation, as provided by the present Annex.

SECTION VI

Austria

ARTICLE 80

Germany acknowledges and will respect strictly the independence of Austria, within the frontiers which may be fixed in a Treaty between that State and the Principal Allied and Associated Powers; she agrees that this independence shall be inalienable, except with the consent of the Council of the League of Nations.

SECTION VII

Czecho-Slovak State

ARTICLE 81

Germany, in conformity with the action already taken by the Allied and Associated Powers, recognizes the complete independence of the Czecho-Slovak State which will include the autonomous territory of the Ruthenians to the south of the Carpathians. Germany hereby recognizes the frontiers of this State as determined by the Principal Allied and Associated Powers and the other interested States.

ARTICLE 82

The old frontier as it existed on August 3, 1914, between Austria-Hungary and the German Empire will constitute the frontier between Germany and the Czecho-Slovak State.

ARTICLE 83

Germany renounces in favour of the Czecho-Slovak State all rights and title over the portion of Silesian territory defined as follows:

starting from a point about 2 kilometres south-east of Katscher, on the boundary between the *Kreise* of Leobschütz and Ratibor:

the boundary between the two *Kreise;*

then, the former boundary between Germany and Austria-Hungary up to a point on the Oder immediately to the south of the Ratibor-Oderberg railway;

thence, towards the north-west and up to a point about 2 kilometres to the south-east of Katscher:

a line to be fixed on the spot passing to the west of Kranowitz.

A Commission composed of seven members, five nominated by the Principal Allied and Associated Powers, one by Poland and one by the Czecho-Slovak State, will be appointed fifteen days after the coming into force of the present Treaty to trace on the spot the frontier line between Poland and the Czecho-Slovak State.

The decisions of this Commission will be taken by a majority and shall be binding on the parties concerned.

Germany hereby agrees to renounce in favour of the Czecho-Slovak State all rights and title over the part of the *Kreis* of Leobschütz comprised within the following boundaries in case after the determination of the frontier between Germany and Poland the said part of that *Kreis* should become isolated from Germany;

from the south-eastern extremity of the salient of the former Austrian frontier at about 5 kilometres to the west of Leobschütz southwards and up to the point of junction with the boundary between the *Kreise* of Leobschütz and Ratibor:

the former frontier between Germany and Austria-Hungary;

then, northwards, the administrative boundary between the *Kreise* of Leobschütz and Ratibor up to a point situated about 2 kilometres to the south-east of Katscher;

thence, north-westwards and up to the starting-point of this definition;

a line to be fixed on the spot passing to the east of Katscher.

ARTICLE 84

German nationals habitually resident in any of the territories recognized as forming part of the Czecho-Slovak State will obtain Czecho-Slovak nationality *ipso facto* and lose their German nationality.

ARTICLE 85

Within a period of two years from the coming into force of the present Treaty, German nationals over eighteen years of age habitually resident in any of the territories recognized as forming part of the Czecho-Slovak State will be entitled to opt for German nationality. Czecho-Slovaks who are German nationals and are habitually resident in Germany will have a similar right to opt for Czecho-Slovak nationality.

Option by a husband will cover his wife and option by parents will cover their children under eighteen years of age.

Persons who have exercised the above right to opt must within the succeeding twelve months transfer their place of residence to the State for which they have opted.

They will be entitled to retain their landed property in the territory of the other State where they had their place of residence before exercising the right to opt. They may carry with them their moveable property of every description. No export or import duties may be imposed upon them in connection with the removal of such property.

Within the same period Czecho-Slovaks who are German nationals and are in a foreign country will be entitled, in the absence of any provisions to the contrary in the foreign law, and if they have not acquired the foreign nationality, to obtain Czecho-Slovak nationality and lose their German nationality by complying with the requirements laid down by the Czecho-Slovak State.

ARTICLE 86

The Czecho-Slovak State accepts and agrees to embody in a Treaty with the Principal Allied and Associated Powers such provisions as may be deemed necessary by the said Powers to protect the interests of inhabitants of that State who differ from the majority of the population in race, language or religion.

The Czecho-Slovak State further accepts and agrees to embody in a Treaty with the said Powers such provisions as they may deem necessary to protect freedom of transit and equitable treatment of the commerce of other nations.

The proportion and nature of the financial obligations of Germany and Prussia which the Czecho-Slovak State will have to assume on account of the Silesian territory placed under its sovereignty will be determined in accordance with Article 254 of Part IX (Financial Clauses) of the present Treaty.

Subsequent agreements will decide all questions not decided by the present Treaty which may arise in consequence of the cession of the said territory.

SECTION VIII

Poland

ARTICLE 87

Germany, in conformity with the action already taken by the Allied and Associated Powers, recognizes the complete independence of Poland, and renounces in her favour all rights and title over the territory bounded by the Baltic Sea, the eastern frontier of Germany as laid down in Article 27 of Part II (Boundaries of Germany) of the present Treaty up to a point situated about 2 kilometres to the east of Lorzendorf, then a line to the acute angle which the northern boundary of Upper Silesia makes about 3 kilometres north-west of Simmenau, then the boundary of Upper Silesia to its meeting point with the old frontier between Germany and Russia, then this frontier to the point where it crosses the course of the Niemen, and then the northern frontier of East Prussia as laid down in Article 28 of Part II aforesaid.

The provisions of this Article do not, however, apply to the territories of East Prussia and the Free City of Danzig, as defined in Article 28 of Part II (Boundaries of Germany) and in Article 100 of Section XI (Danzig) of this Part.

The boundaries of Poland not laid down in the present Treaty will be subsequently determined by the Principal Allied and Associated Powers.

A Commission consisting of seven members, five of whom shall be nominated by the Principal Allied and Associated Powers, one by Germany and one by Poland, shall be constituted fifteen days after the coming into force of the present Treaty to delimit on the spot the frontier line between Poland and Germany.

The decisions of the Commission will be taken by a majority of votes and shall be binding upon the parties concerned.

ARTICLE 88

In the portion of Upper Silesia included within the boundaries described below, the inhabitants will be called upon to indicate by a vote whether they wish to be attached to Germany or to Poland:

starting from the northern point of the salient of the old province of Austrian Silesia situated about 8 kilometers east of Neustadt, the former frontier between Germany and Austria to its junction with the boundary between the *Kreise* of Leobschütz and Ratibor;

thence in a northerly direction to a point about 2 kilometers southeast of Katscher:

the boundary between the *Kreise* of Leobschütz and Ratibor;

thence in a south-easterly direction to a point on the course of the Oder immediately south of the Ratibor-Oderberg railway:

a line to be fixed on the ground passing south of Kranowitz;

thence the old boundary between Germany and Austria, then the old boundary between Germany and Russia to its junction with the administrative boundary between Posnania and Upper Silesia;

thence this administrative boundary to its junction with the administrative boundary between Upper and Middle Silesia;

thence westwards to the point where the administrative boundary turns in an acute angle to the south-east about 3 kilometres north-west of Simmenau:

the boundary between Upper and Middle Silesia;

then in a westerly direction to a point to be fixed on the ground about 2 kilometres east of Lorzendorf:

a line to be fixed on the ground passing north of Klein Hennersdorf:

thence southwards to the point where the boundary between Upper and Middle Silesia cuts the Städtel-Karlsruhe road:

a line to be fixed on the ground passing west of Hennersdorf, Polkowitz, Noldau, Steinersdorf and Dammer, and east of Strehlitz, Nassadel, Eckersdorf, Schwirz and Städtel;

thence the boundary between Upper and Middle Silesia to its junction with the eastern boundary of the *Kreis* of Falkenberg;

then the eastern boundary of the *Kreis* of Falkenberg to the point of the salient which is 3 kilometres east of Puschine;

thence to the northern point of the salient of the old province of Austrian Silesia situated about 8 kilometres east of Neustadt:

a line to be fixed on the ground passing east of Zülz.

The régime under which this plebiscite will be taken and given effect to is laid down in the Annex hereto.

The Polish and German Governments hereby respectively bind themselves to conduct no prosecutions on any part of their territory and to take no exceptional proceedings for any political action performed in Upper Silesia during the period of the régime laid down in the Annex hereto and up to the settlement of the final status of the country.

Germany hereby renounces in favour of Poland all rights and title over the portion of Upper Silesia lying beyond the frontier line fixed by the Principal Allied and Associated Powers as the result of the plebiscite.

ANNEX

1

Within fifteen days from the coming into force of the present Treaty the German troops and such officials as may be designated by the Commission set up under the provisions of paragraph 2 shall evacuate the plebiscite area. Up to the moment of the completion of the evacuation they shall refrain from any form of requisitioning in money or in kind and from all acts likely to prejudice the material interests of the country.

Within the same period the Workmen's and Soldiers' Councils which have been constituted in this area shall be dissolved. Members of such Councils who are natives of another region and are exercising their functions at the date of the coming into force of the present Treaty, or who have gone out of office since March 1, 1919, shall be evacuated.

All military and semi-military unions formed in the said area by inhabitants of the district shall be immediately disbanded. All members of such military organizations who are not domiciled in the said area shall be required to leave it.

2

The plebiscite area shall be immediately placed under the authority of an International Commission of four members to be designated by the following Powers; the United States of America, France, the British Empire and Italy. It shall be occupied by troops belonging to the Allied and Associated Powers, and the German Government undertakes to give facilities for the transference of these troops to Upper Silesia.

3

The Commission shall enjoy all the powers exercised by the German or the Prussian Government, except those of legislation or taxation. It shall also be substituted for the Government of the province and the *Regierungsbezirk*.

It shall be within the competence of the Commission to interpret the powers hereby conferred upon it and to determine to what extent it shall exercise them, and to what extent they shall be left in the hands of the existing authorities.

Changes in the existing laws and the existing taxation shall only be brought into force with the consent of the Commission.

The Commission will maintain order with the help of the troops which will be at its disposal, and, to the extent which it may deem necessary, by means of gendarmerie recruited among the inhabitants of the country.

The Commission shall provide immediately for the replacement of the evacuated German officials and, if occasion arises, shall itself order the evacuation of such authorities and proceed to the replacement of such local authorities as may be required.

It shall take all steps which it thinks proper to ensure the freedom, fairness and secrecy of the vote. In particular, it shall have the right to order the expulsion of any person who may in any way have attempted to distort the result of the plebiscite by methods of corruption or intimidation.

The Commission shall have full power to settle all questions arising from the execution of the present clauses. It shall be assisted by technical advisers chosen by it from among the local population.

The decisions of the Commission shall be taken by a majority vote.

4

The vote shall take place at such date as may be determined by the Principal Allied and Associated Powers, but not sooner than six months or later than eighteen months after the establishment of the Commission in the area.

The right to vote shall be given to all persons without distinction of sex who:

(a) Have completed their twentieth year on the 1st January of the year in which the plebiscite takes place;

(b) Were born in the plebiscite area or have been domiciled there since a date to be determined by the Commission, which shall not be subsequent to January 1, 1919, or who have been expelled by the German authorities and have not retained their domicile there.

Persons convicted of political offences shall be enabled to exercise their right of voting.

Every person will vote in the commune where he is domiciled or in which he was born, if he has not retained his domicile in the area.

The result of the vote will be determined by communes according to the majority of votes in each commune.

5

On the conclusion of the voting, the number of votes cast in each commune will be communicated by the Commission to the Principal Allied and Associated Powers, with a full report as to the taking of the vote and a recommendation as to the line which ought to be adopted as the frontier of Germany in Upper Silesia. In this recommendation regard will be paid to the wishes of the inhabitants as shown by the vote, and to the geographical and economic conditions of the locality.

6

As soon as the frontier has been fixed by the Principal Allied and Associated Powers, the German authorities will be notified by the International Commission that they are free to take over the administration of the territory which it is recognised should be German; the said authorities must proceed to do so within one month of such notification and in the manner prescribed by the Commission.

Within the same period and in the manner prescribed by the Commission, the Polish Government must proceed to take over the administration of the territory which it is recognised should be Polish.

When the administration of the territory has been provided for by the German and Polish authorities respectively, the powers of the Commission will terminate.

The cost of the army of occupation and expenditure by the Commission, whether in discharge of its own functions or in the administration of the territory, will be a charge on the area.

ARTICLE 89

Poland undertakes to accord freedom of transit to persons, goods, vessels, carriages, wagons and mails in transit between East Prussia and the rest of Germany over Polish territory, including territorial waters, and to treat them at least as favourably as the persons, goods, vessels, carriages, wagons and mails respectively of Polish or of any other more favoured nationality, origin, importation, starting point, or ownership as regards facilities, restrictions and all other matters.

Goods in transit shall be exempt from all customs or other similar duties.

Freedom of transit will extend to telegraphic and telephonic services under the conditions laid down by the conventions referred to in Article 98.

ARTICLE 90

Poland undertakes to permit for a period of fifteen years the exportation to Germany of the products of the mines in any part of Upper Silesia transferred to Poland in accordance with the present Treaty.

Such products shall be free from all export duties or other charges or restrictions on exportation.

Poland agrees to take such steps as may be necessary to secure that any such products shall be available for sale to purchasers in Germany on terms as favourable as are applicable to like products sold under similar conditions to purchasers in Poland or in any other country.

ARTICLE 91

German nationals habitually resident in territories recognised as forming part of Poland will acquire Polish nationality *ipso facto* and will lose their German nationality.

German nationals, however, or their descendants who became resident in these territories after January 1, 1908, will not acquire Polish nationality without a special authorisation from the Polish State.

Within a period of two years after the coming into force of the present Treaty, German nationals over 18 years of age habitually resident in any of the territories recognised as forming part of Poland will be entitled to opt for German nationality.

Poles who are German nationals over 18 years of age and habitually resident in Germany will have a similar right to opt for Polish nationality.

Option by a husband will cover his wife and option by parents will cover their children under 18 years of age.

Persons who have exercised the above right to opt may within the succeeding twelve months transfer their place of residence to the State for which they have opted.

They will be entitled to retain their immovable property in the territory of the other State where they had their place of residence before exercising the right to opt.

They may carry with them their movable property of every description. No export or import duties or charges may be imposed upon them in connection with the removal of such property.

Within the same period Poles who are German nationals and are in a foreign country will be entitled, in the absence of any provisions to the contrary in the foreign law, and if they have not acquired the foreign nationality, to obtain Polish nationality and to lose their German nationality by complying with the requirements laid down by the Polish State.

In the portion of Upper Silesia submitted to a plebiscite the provisions of this Article shall only come into force as from the definitive attribution of the territory.

ARTICLE 92

The proportion and the nature of the financial liabilities of Germany and Prussia which are to be borne by Poland will be determined in accordance with Article 254 of Part IX (Financial Clauses) of the present Treaty.

There shall be excluded from the share of such financial liabilities assumed by Poland that portion of the debt which, according to the finding of the Reparation Commission referred to in the above-mentioned Article, arises from measures adopted by the German and Prussian Governments with a view to German colonisation in Poland.

In fixing under Article 256 of the present Treaty the value of the property and possessions belonging to the German Empire and to the German States which pass to Poland with the territory transferred above, the Reparation Commission shall exclude from the valuation buildings, forests and other State property which belonged to the former Kingdom of Poland; Poland shall acquire these properties free of all costs and charges.

In all the German territory transferred in accordance with the present Treaty and recognised as forming definitively part of Poland, the property, rights and interests of German nationals shall not be liquidated under Article 297 by the Polish Government except in accordance with the following provisions:

(1) The proceeds of the liquidation shall be paid direct to the owner;

(2) If on his application the Mixed Arbitral Tribunal provided for by Section VI of Part X (Economic Clauses) of the present Treaty, or an arbitrator appointed by that Tribunal, is satisfied that the conditions of the sale or measures taken by the Polish Government outside its general legislation were unfairly prejudicial to the price obtained, they shall have discretion to award to the owner equitable compensation to be paid by the Polish Government.

Further agreements will regulate all questions arising out of the cession of the above territory which are not regulated by the present Treaty.

Article 93

Poland accepts and agrees to embody in a Treaty with the Principal Allied and Associated Powers such provisions as may be deemed necessary by the said Powers to protect the interests of inhabitants of Poland who differ from the majority of the population in race, language or religion.

Poland further accepts and agrees to embody in a Treaty with the said Powers such provisions as they may deem necessary to protect freedom of transit and equitable treatment of the commerce of other nations.

SECTION IX

East Prussia

Article 94

In the area between the southern frontier of East Prussia, as described in Article 28 of Part II (Boundaries of Germany) of the present Treaty, and the line described below, the inhabitants will be called upon to indicate by a vote the State to which they wish to belong:

The western and northern boundary of *Regierungsbezirk* Allenstein to its junction with the boundary between the *Kreise* of Oletsko and Angerburg; thence, the northern boundary of the *Kreis* of Oletsko to its junction with the old frontier of East Prussia.

ARTICLE 95

The German troops and authorities will be withdrawn from the area defined above within a period not exceeding fifteen days after the coming into force of the present Treaty. Until the evacuation is completed they will abstain from all requisitions in money or in kind and from all measures injurious to the economic interests of the country.

On the expiration of the above-mentioned period the said area will be placed under the authority of an International Commission of five members appointed by the Principal Allied and Associated Powers. This Commission will have general powers of administration and, in particular, will be charged with the duty of arranging for the vote and of taking such measures as it may deem necessary to ensure its freedom, fairness and secrecy. The Commission will have all necessary authority to decide any questions to which the execution of these provisions may give rise. The Commission will make such arrangements as may be necessary for assistance in the exercise of its functions by officials chosen by itself from the local population. Its decisions will be taken by a majority.

Every person, irrespective of sex, will be entitled to vote who:

(a) Is 20 years of age at the date of the coming into force of the present Treaty, and

(b) Was born within the area where the vote will take place or has been habitually resident there from a date to be fixed by the Commission.

Every person will vote in the commune where he is habitually resident or, if not habitually resident in the area, in the commune where he was born.

The result of the vote will be determined by communes (*Gemeinde*) according to the majority of the votes in each commune.

On the conclusion of the voting the number of votes cast in each commune will be communicated by the Commission to the Principal Allied and Associated Powers, with a full report as to the taking of the vote and a recommendation as to the line which ought to be adopted as the boundary of East Prussia in this region. In this recommendation regard will be paid to the wishes of the inhabitants as shown by the vote and to the geographical and economic conditions of the locality. The Principal Allied and Associated Powers will then fix the frontier between East Prussia and Poland in this region.

If the line fixed by the Principal Allied and Associated Powers is such as to exclude from East Prussia any part of the territory defined in Article 94, the renunciation of its rights by Germany in favour of Poland, as provided in Article 87 above, will extend to the territories so excluded.

As soon as the line has been fixed by the Principal Allied and Associated Powers, the authorities administering East Prussia will be notified by the

International Commission that they are free to take over the administration of the territory to the north of the line so fixed, which they shall proceed to do within one month of such notification and in the manner prescribed by the Commission. Within the same period and as prescribed by the Commission, the Polish Government must proceed to take over the administration of the territory to the south of the line. When the administration of the territory by the East Prussian and Polish authorities respectively has been provided for, the powers of the Commission will terminate.

Expenditure by the Commission, whether in the discharge of its own functions or in the administration of the territory, will be borne by the local revenues. East Prussia will be required to bear such proportion of any deficit as may be fixed by the Principal Allied and Associated Powers.

ARTICLE 96

In the area comprising the *Kreise* of Stuhm and Rosenberg and the portion of the *Kreis* of Marienburg which is situated east of the Nogat and that of Marienwerder east of the Vistula, the inhabitants will be called upon to indicate by a vote, to be taken in each commune (*Gemeinde*), whether they desire the various communes situated in this territory to belong to Poland or to East Prussia.

ARTICLE 97

The German troops and authorities will be withdrawn from the area defined in Article 96 within a period not exceeding fifteen days after the coming into force of the present Treaty. Until the evacuation is completed they will abstain from all requisitions in money or in kind and from all measures injurious to the economic interests of the country.

On the expiration of the above-mentioned period, the said area will be placed under the authority of an International Commission of five members appointed by the Principal Allied and Associated Powers. This Commission, supported if occasion arises by the necessary forces, will have general powers of administration and in particular will be charged with the duty of arranging for the vote and of taking such measures as it may deem necessary to ensure its freedom, fairness and secrecy. The Commission will conform as far as possible to the provisions of the present Treaty relating to the plebiscite in the Allenstein area; its decisions will be taken by a majority.

Expenditure by the Commission, whether in the discharge of its own functions or in the administration of the territory, will be borne by the local revenues.

On the conclusion of the voting the number of votes cast in each commune will be communicated by the Commission to the Principal Allied and Associated Powers with a full report as to the taking of the vote and a recommendation as to the line which ought to be adopted as the boundary of East

Prussia in this region. In this recommendation regard will be paid to the wishes of the inhabitants as shown by the vote and to the geographical and economic conditions of the locality. The Principal Allied and Associated Powers will then fix the frontier between East Prussia and Poland in this region, leaving in any case to Poland for the whole of the section bordering on the Vistula full and complete control of the river including the east bank as far east of the river as may be necessary for its regulation and improvement. Germany agrees that in any portion of the said territory which remains German, no fortifications shall at any time be erected.

The Principal Allied and Associated Powers will at the same time draw up regulations for assuring to the population of East Prussia to the fullest extent and under equitable conditions access to the Vistula and the use of it for themselves, their commerce and their boats.

The determination of the frontier and the foregoing regulations shall be binding upon all the parties concerned.

When the administration of the territory has been taken over by the East Prussian and Polish authorities respectively, the powers of the Commission will terminate.

ARTICLE 98

Germany and Poland undertake, within one year of the coming into force of this Treaty, to enter into conventions of which the terms, in case of difference, shall be settled by the Council of the League of Nations, with the object of securing, on the one hand to Germany full and adequate railroad, telegraphic and telephonic facilities for communication between the rest of Germany and East Prussia over the intervening Polish territory, and on the other hand to Poland full and adequate railroad, telegraphic and telephonic facilities for communication between Poland and the Free City of Danzig over any Germany territory that may, on the right bank of the Vistula, intervene, between Poland and the Free City of Danzig.

SECTION X

Memel

ARTICLE 99

Germany renounces in favour of the Principal Allied and Associated Powers all rights and title over the territories included between the Baltic, the north eastern frontier of East Prussia as defined in Article 28 of Part II (Boundaries of Germany) of the present Treaty and the former frontier between Germany and Russia.

Germany undertakes to accept the settlement made by the Principal Allied and Associated Powers in regard to these territories, particularly in so far as concerns the nationality of the inhabitants.

Free City of Danzig

ARTICLE 100

Germany renounces in favour of the Principal Allied and Associated Powers all rights and title over the territory comprised within the following limits:

from the Baltic Sea southwards to the point where the principal channels of navigation of the Nogat and the Vistula (Weichsel) meet:

the boundary of East Prussia as described in Article 28 of Part II (Boundaries of Germany) of the present Treaty;

thence the principal channel of navigation of the Vistula downstream to a point about 6½ kilometres north of the bridge of Dirschau;

thence north-west to point 5, 1½ kilometres south-east of the church of Güttland:

a line to be fixed on the ground;

thence in a general westerly direction to the salient made by the boundary of the *Kreis* of Berent 8½ kilometres north-east of Schöneck:

a line to be fixed on the ground passing between Mühlbanz on the south and Rambeltsch on the north;

thence the boundary of the *Kreis* of Berent westwards to the re-entrant which it forms 6 kilometres north-north-west of Schöneck;

thence to a point on the median line of Lonkener See:

a line to be fixed on the ground passing north of Neu Fietz and Schatarpi and south of Barenhütte and Lonken;

thence the median line of Lonkener See to its northernmost point;

thence to the southern end of Pollenziner See:

a line to be fixed on the ground;

thence the median line of Pollenziner See to its northernmost point;

thence in a north-easterly direction to a point about 1 kilometre south of Koliebken church, where the Danzig-Neustadt railway crosses a stream:

a line to be fixed on the ground passing south-east of Kamehlen, Krissau, Fidlin, Sulmin (Richthof), Mattern, Schäferei, and to the north-west of Neuendorf, Marschau, Czapielken, Hoch- and Klein-Kelpin, Pulvermühl, Renneberg and the towns of Oliva and Zoppot;

thence the course of the stream mentioned above to the Baltic Sea.

The boundaries described above are drawn on a German map, scale 1/100,000, attached to the present Treaty (Map No. 3).[12]

---

[12] Printed in S. Doc. 51, 66th Cong., 1st sess., between pp. 148 and 149.

Article 101

A Commission composed of three members appointed by the Principal Allied and Associated Powers, including a High Commissioner as President, one member appointed by Germany and one member appointed by Poland, shall be constituted within fifteen days of the coming into force of the present Treaty for the purpose of delimiting on the spot the frontier of the territory as described above, taking into account as far as possible the existing communal boundaries.

Article 102

The Principal Allied and Associated Powers undertake to establish the town of Danzig, together with the rest of the territory described in Article 100, as a Free City. It will be placed under the protection of the League of Nations.

Article 103

A constitution for the Free City of Danzig shall be drawn up by the duly appointed representatives of the Free City in agreement with a High Commissioner to be appointed by the League of Nations. This constitution shall be placed under the guarantee of the League of Nations.

The High Commissioner will also be entrusted with the duty of dealing in the first instance with all differences arising between Poland and the Free City of Danzig in regard to this Treaty or any arrangements or agreements made thereunder.

The High Commissioner shall reside at Danzig.

Article 104

The Principal Allied and Associated Powers undertake to negotiate a Treaty between the Polish Government and the Free City of Danzig, which shall come into force at the same time as the establishment of the said Free City, with the following objects:

(1) To effect the inclusion of the Free City of Danzig within the Polish Customs frontiers, and to establish a free area in the port;

(2) To ensure to Poland without any restriction the free use and service of all waterways, docks, basins, wharves and other works within the territory of the Free City necessary for Polish imports and exports;

(3) To ensure to Poland the control and administration of the Vistula and of the whole railway system within the Free City, except such street and other railways as serve primarily the needs of the Free City, and of postal, telegraphic and telephonic communication between Poland and the port of Danzig;

(4) To ensure to Poland the right to develop and improve the waterways, docks, basins, wharves, railways and other works and means of communica-

tion mentioned in this Article, as well as to lease or purchase through appropriate processes such land and other property as may be necessary for these purposes;

(5) To provide against any discrimination within the Free City of Danzig to the detriment of citizens of Poland and other persons of Polish origin or speech;

(6) To provide that the Polish Government shall undertake the conduct of the foreign relations of the Free City of Danzig as well as the diplomatic protection of citizens of that city when abroad.

ARTICLE 105

On the coming into force of the present Treaty German nationals ordinarily resident in the territory described in Article 100 will *ipso facto* lose their German nationality in order to become nationals of the Free City of Danzig.

ARTICLE 106

Within a period of two years from the coming into force of the present Treaty, German nationals over 18 years of age ordinarily resident in the territory described in Article 100 will have the right to opt for German nationality.

Option by a husband will cover his wife and option by parents will cover their children less than 18 years of age.

All persons who exercise the right of option referred to above must during the ensuing twelve months transfer their place of residence to Germany.

These persons will be entitled to preserve the immovable property possessed by them in the territory of the Free City of Danzig. They may carry with them their movable property of every description. No export or import duties shall be imposed upon them in this connection.

ARTICLE 107

All property situated within the territory of the Free City of Danzig belonging to the German Empire or to any German State shall pass to the Principal Allied and Associated Powers for transfer to the Free City of Danzig or to the Polish State as they may consider equitable.

ARTICLE 108

The proportion and nature of the financial liabilities of Germany and of Prussia to be borne by the Free City of Danzig shall be fixed in accordance with Article 254 of Part IX (Financial Clauses) of the present Treaty.

All other questions which may arise from the cession of the territory referred to in Article 100 shall be settled by further agreements.

SECTION XII

Schleswig

ARTICLE 109

The frontier between Germany and Denmark shall be fixed in conformity with the wishes of the population.

For this purpose, the population inhabiting the territories of the former German Empire situated to the north of a line, from East to West, (shown by a brown line on the map No. 4,[13] annexed to the present Treaty):

leaving the Baltic Sea about 13 kilometres east-north-east of Flensburg, running

south-west so as to pass south-east of: Sygum, Ringsberg, Munkbrarup, Adelby, Tastrup, Jarplund, Oversee, and north-west of: Langballigholz, Langballig, Bönstrup, Rüllschau, Weseby, Kleinwolstrup, Gross-Solt,

thence westwards passing south of Frörup and north of Wanderup,

thence in a south-westerly direction passing south-east of Oxlund, Stieglund and Ostenau and north-west of the villages on the Wanderup-Kollund road,

thence in a north-westerly direction passing south-west of Löwenstedt, Joldelund, Goldelund, and north-east of Kolkerheide and Högel to the bend of the Soholmer Au, about 1 kilometre east of Soholm, where it meets the southern boundary of the *Kreis* of Tondern,

following this boundary to the North Sea,

passing south of the islands of Fohr and Amrum and north of the islands of Oland and Langeness,

shall be called upon to pronounce by a vote which will be taken under the following conditions:

(1) Within a period not exceeding ten days from the coming into force of the present Treaty, the German troops and authorities (including the *Oberpräsidenten, Regierungs-präsidenten, Landräthe, Amtsvorsteher, Ober-bürgermeister*) shall evacuate the zone lying to the north of the line above fixed.

Within the same period the Workmen's and Soldiers' Councils which have been constituted in this zone shall be dissolved; members of such Councils who are natives of another region and are exercising their functions at the date of the coming into force of the present Treaty, or who have gone out of office since March 1, 1919, shall also be evacuated.

The said zone shall immediately be placed under the authority of an International Commission, composed of five members, of whom three will be designated by the Principal Allied and Associated Powers; the Norwegian and Swedish Governments will each be requested to designate a member;

---

[13] Printed in S. Doc. 51, 66th Cong., 1st sess., between pp. 160 and 161.

in the event of their failing to do so, these two members will be chosen by the Principal Allied and Associated Powers.

The Commission, assisted in case of need by the necessary forces, shall have general powers of administration. In particular, it shall at once provide for filling the places of the evacuated German authorities, and if necessary shall itself give orders for their evacuation, and proceed to fill the places of such local authorities as may be required. It shall take all steps which it thinks proper to ensure the freedom, fairness, and secrecy of the vote. It shall be assisted by German and Danish technical advisers chosen by it from among the local population. Its decisions will be taken by a majority.

One half of the expenses of the Commission and of the expenditure occasioned by the plebiscite shall be paid by Germany.

(2) The right to vote shall be given to all persons, without distinction of sex, who:

(a) Have completed their twentieth year at the date of the coming into force of the present Treaty; and

(b) Were born in the zone in which the plebiscite is taken, or have been domiciled there since a date before January 1, 1900, or had been expelled by the German authorities without having retained their domicile there.

Every person will vote in the commune (*Gemeinde*) where he is domiciled or of which he is a native.

Military persons, officers, non-commissioned officers and soldiers of the German army, who are natives of the zone of Schleswig in which the plebiscite is taken, shall be given the opportunity to return to their native place in order to take part in the voting there.

(3) In the section of the evacuated zone lying to the north of a line, from East to West (shown by a red line on map No. 4 which is annexed to the present Treaty):

passing south of the island of Alsen and following the median line of Flensburg Fjord,

leaving the fjord about 6 kilometres north of Flensburg and following the course of the stream flowing past Kupfermühle upstream to a point north of Niehuus,

passing north of Pattburg and Ellund and south of Fröslee to meet the eastern boundary of the *Kreis* of Tondern at its junction with the boundary between the old jurisdictions of Slogs and Kjær (*Slog Herred* and *Kjær Herred*),

following the latter boundary to where it meets the Scheidebek,

following the course of the Scheidebek (Alte Au), Süder Au and Wied Au downstream successively to the point where the latter bends northwards about 1,500 metres west of Ruttebüll, thence, in a west-north-westerly direction to meet the North Sea north of Sieltoft,

thence, passing north of the island of Sylt,

the vote above provided for shall be taken within a period not exceeding three weeks after the evacuation of the country by the German troops and authorities.

The result will be determined by the majority of votes cast in the whole of this section. This result will be immediately communicated by the Commission to the Principal Allied and Associated Powers and proclaimed.

If the vote results in favour of the reincorporation of this territory in the Kingdom of Denmark, the Danish Government in agreement with the Commission will be entitled to effect its occupation with their military and administrative authorities immediately after the proclamation.

(4) In the section of the evacuated zone situated to the south of the preceding section and to the north of the line which starts from the Baltic Sea 13 kilometres from Flensburg and ends north of the islands of Oland and Langeness, the vote will be taken within a period not exceeding five weeks after the plebiscite shall have been held in the first section.

The result will be determined by communes (*Gemeinden*), in accordance with the majority of the votes cast in each commune (*Gemeinde*).

ARTICLE 110

Pending a delimitation on the spot, a frontier line will be fixed by the Principal Allied and Associated Powers according to a line based on the result of the voting, and proposed by the International Commission, and taking into account the particular geographical and economic conditions of the localities in question.

From that time the Danish Government may effect the occupation of these territories with the Danish civil and military authorities, and the German Government may reinstate up to the said frontier line the German civil and military authorities whom it has evacuated.

Germany hereby renounces definitively in favour of the Principal Allied and Associated Powers all rights of sovereignty over the territories situated to the north of the frontier line fixed in accordance with the above provisions. The Principal Allied and Associated Powers will hand over the said territories to Denmark.

ARTICLE 111

A Commission composed of seven members, five of whom shall be nominated by the Principal Allied and Associated Powers, one by Denmark, and one by Germany, shall be constituted within fifteen days from the date when the final result of the vote is known, to trace the frontier line on the spot.

The decisions of the Commission will be taken by a majority of votes and shall be binding on the parties concerned.

ARTICLE 112

All the inhabitants of the territory which is returned to Denmark will acquire Danish nationality *ipso facto,* and will lose their German nationality.

Persons, however, who had become habitually resident in this territory after October 1, 1918, will not be able to acquire Danish nationality without permission from the Danish Government.

ARTICLE 113

Within two years from the date on which the sovereignty over the whole or part of the territory of Schleswig subjected to the plebiscite is restored to Denmark:

Any person over 18 years of age, born in the territory restored to Denmark, not habitually resident in this region, and possessing German nationality, will be entitled to opt for Denmark;

Any person over 18 years of age habitually resident in the territory restored to Denmark will be entitled to opt for Germany.

Option by a husband will cover his wife and option by parents will cover their children less than 18 years of age.

Persons who have exercised the above right to opt must within the ensuing twelve months transfer their place of residence to the State in favour of which they have opted.

They will be entitled to retain the immovable property which they own in the territory of the other State in which they were habitually resident before opting. They may carry with them their movable property of every description. No export or import duties may be imposed upon them in connection with the removal of such property.

ARTICLE 114

The proportion and nature of the financial or other obligations of Germany and Prussia which are to be assumed by Denmark will be fixed in accordance with Article 254 of Part IX (Financial Clauses) of the present Treaty.

Further stipulations will determine any other questions arising out of the transfer to Denmark of the whole or part of the territory of which she was deprived by the Treaty of October 30, 1864.

SECTION XIII

Heligoland

ARTICLE 115

The fortifications, military establishments, and harbours of the Islands of Heligoland and Dune shall be destroyed under the supervision of the Principal Allied Governments by German labour and at the expense of Germany within a period to be determined by the said Governments.

The term "harbours" shall include the north-east mole, the west wall, the outer and inner breakwaters and reclaimed land within them, and all naval and military works, fortifications and buildings, constructed or under construction, between lines connecting the following positions taken from the British Admiralty chart No. 126 of April 19, 1918.

(a) lat. 54° 10′ 49″ N.; long. 7° 53′ 39″ E.;
(b) — 54° 10′ 35″ N.;   —   7° 54′ 18″ E.;
(c) — 54° 10′ 14″ N.;   —   7° 54′ 00″ E.;
(d) — 54° 10′ 17″ N.;   —   7° 53′ 37″ E.;
(e) — 54° 10′ 44″ N.;   —   7° 53′ 26″ E.

These fortifications, military establishments and harbours shall not be reconstructed nor shall any similar works be constructed in future.

SECTION XIV

Russia and Russian States

ARTICLE 116

Germany acknowledges and agrees to respect as permanent and inalienable the independence of all the territories which were part of the former Russian Empire on August 1, 1914.

In accordance with the provisions of Article 259 of Part IX (Financial Clauses) and Article 292 of Part X (Economic Clauses) Germany accepts definitely the abrogation of the Brest-Litovsk Treaties and of all other treaties, conventions and agreements entered into by her with the Maximalist Government in Russia.

The Allied and Associated Powers formally reserve the rights of Russia to obtain from Germany restitution and reparation based on the principles of the present Treaty.

ARTICLE 117

Germany undertakes to recognize the full force of all treaties or agreements which may be entered into by the Allied and Associated Powers with States now existing or coming into existence in future in the whole or part of the former Empire of Russia as it existed on August 1, 1914, and to recognize the frontiers of any such States as determined therein.

PART IV

GERMAN RIGHTS AND INTERESTS OUTSIDE GERMANY

ARTICLE 118

In territory outside her European frontiers as fixed by the present Treaty, Germany renounces all rights, titles and privileges whatever in or over territory which belonged to her or to her allies, and all rights, titles and privileges whatever their origin which she held as against the Allied and Associated Powers.

Germany hereby undertakes to recognise and to conform to the measures which may be taken now or in the future by the Principal Allied and Associated Powers, in agreement where necessary with third Powers, in order to carry the above stipulation into effect.

In particular Germany declares her acceptance of the following Articles relating to certain special subjects.

SECTION I

German Colonies

ARTICLE 119

Germany renounces in favour of the Principal Allied and Associated Powers all her rights and titles over her oversea possessions.

ARTICLE 120

All movable and immovable property in such territories belonging to the German Empire or to any German State shall pass to the Government exercising authority over such territories, on the terms laid down in Article 257 of Part IX (Financial Clauses) of the present Treaty. The decision of the local courts in any dispute as to the nature of such property shall be final.

ARTICLE 121

The provisions of Sections I and IV of Part X (Economic Clauses) of the present Treaty shall apply in the case of these territories whatever be the form of Government adopted for them.

ARTICLE 122

The Government exercising authority over such territories may make such provisions as it thinks fit with reference to the repatriation from them of German nationals and to the conditions upon which German subjects of European origin shall, or shall not, be allowed to reside, hold property, trade or exercise a profession in them.

ARTICLE 123

The provisions of Article 260 of Part IX (Financial Clauses) of the present Treaty shall apply in the case of all agreements concluded with German nationals for the construction or exploitation of public works in the German oversea possessions, as well as any sub-concessions or contracts resulting therefrom which may have been made to or with such nationals.

ARTICLE 124

Germany hereby undertakes to pay, in accordance with the estimate to be presented by the French Government and approved by the Reparation Commission, reparation for damage suffered by French nationals in the Cameroons or the frontier zone by reason of the acts of the German civil and military authorities and of German private individuals during the period from January 1, 1900, to August 1, 1914.

ARTICLE 125

Germany renounces all rights under the Conventions and Agreements with France of November 4, 1911, and September 28, 1912, relating to Equatorial Africa. She undertakes to pay to the French Government, in accordance with the estimate to be presented by that Government and approved by the Reparation Commission, all the deposits, credits, advances, etc., effected by virtue of these instruments in favour of Germany.

ARTICLE 126

Germany undertakes to accept and observe the agreements made or to be made by the Allied and Associated Powers or some of them with any other Power with regard to the trade in arms and spirits, and to the matters dealt with in the General Act of Berlin of February 26, 1885, the General Act of Brussels of July 2, 1890,[14] and the conventions completing or modifying the same.

ARTICLE 127

The native inhabitants of the former German oversea possessions shall be entitled to the diplomatic protection of the Governments exercising authority over those territories.

SECTION II

China

ARTICLE 128

Germany renounces in favour of China all benefits and privileges resulting from the provisions of the final Protocol signed at Peking on September 7, 1901,[15] and from all annexes, notes and documents supplementary thereto. She likewise renounces in favour of China any claim to indemnities accruing thereunder subsequent to March 14, 1917.

ARTICLE 129

From the coming into force of the present Treaty the High Contracting Parties shall apply, in so far as concerns them respectively:

[14] TS 383, *ante*, vol. 1, p. 134.
[15] TS 397, *ante*, vol. 1, p. 302.

(1) The Arrangement of August 29, 1902,[16] regarding the new Chinese customs tariff;

(2) The Arrangement of September 27, 1905,[17] regarding Whang-Poo, and the provisional supplementary Arrangement of April 4[9], 1912.[18]

China, however, will no longer be bound to grant to Germany the advantages or privileges which she allowed Germany under these Arrangements.

ARTICLE 130

Subject to the provisions of Section VIII of this Part, Germany cedes to China all the buildings, wharves and pontoons, barracks, forts, arms and munitions of war, vessels of all kinds, wireless telegraphy installations and other public property belonging to the German Government, which are situated or may be in the German Concessions at Tientsin and Hankow or elsewhere in Chinese territory.

It is understood, however, that premises used as diplomatic or consular residences or offices are not included in the above cession, and, furthermore, that no steps shall be taken by the Chinese Government to dispose of the German public and private property situated within the so-called Legation Quarter at Peking without the consent of the Diplomatic Representatives of the Powers which, on the coming into force of the present Treaty, remain Parties to the Final Protocol of September 7, 1901.

ARTICLE 131

Germany undertakes to restore to China within twelve months from the coming into force of the present Treaty all the astronomical instruments which her troops in 1900–1901 carried away from China, and to defray all expenses which may be incurred in effecting such restoration, including the expenses of dismounting, packing, transporting, insurance and installation in Peking.

ARTICLE 132

Germany agrees to the abrogation of the leases from the Chinese Government under which the German Concessions at Hankow and Tientsin are now held.

China, restored to the full exercise of her sovereign rights in the above areas, declares her intention of opening them to international residence and trade. She further declares that the abrogation of the leases under which these concessions are now held shall not affect the property rights of nationals of Allied and Associated Powers who are holders of lots in these concessions.

---

[16] For the schedule of tariff duties agreed upon by representatives of the several powers at Shanghai Aug. 29, 1902, see annex III of the commercial treaty between the United States and China signed at Shanghai Oct. 8, 1903 (TS 430, *post*).

[17] TS 448, *ante,* vol. 1, p. 446.

[18] *Ante,* vol. 1, p. 879.

ARTICLE 133

Germany waives all claims against the Chinese Government or against any Allied or Associated Government arising out of the internment of German nationals in China and their repatriation. She equally renounces all claims arising out of the capture and condemnation of German ships in China, or the liquidation, sequestration or control of German properties, rights and interests in that country since August 14, 1917. This provision, however, shall not affect the rights of the parties interested in the proceeds of any such liquidation, which shall be governed by the provisions of Part X (Economic Clauses) of the present Treaty.

ARTICLE 134

Germany renounces in favour of the Government of His Britannic Majesty the German State property in the British Concession at Shameen at Canton. She renounces in favour of the French and Chinese Governments conjointly the property of the German school situated in the French Concession at Shanghai.

SECTION III

Siam

ARTICLE 135

Germany recognises that all treaties, conventions and agreements between her and Siam, and all rights, title and privileges derived therefrom, including all rights of extraterritorial jurisdiction, terminated as from July 22, 1917.

ARTICLE 136

All goods and property in Siam belonging to the German Empire or to any German State, with the exception of premises used as diplomatic or consular residences or offices, pass *ipso facto* and without compensation to the Siamese Government.

The goods, property and private rights of German nationals in Siam shall be dealt with in accordance with the provisions of Part X (Economic Clauses) of the present Treaty.

ARTICLE 137

Germany waives all claims against the Siamese Government on behalf of herself or her nationals arising out of the seizure or condemnation of German ships, the liquidation of German property, or the internment of German nationals in Siam. This provision shall not affect the rights of the parties interested in the proceeds of any such liquidation, which shall be governed by the provisions of Part X (Economic Clauses) of the present Treaty.

Liberia

ARTICLE 138

Germany renounces all rights and privileges arising from the arrangements of 1911 and 1912 regarding Liberia, and particularly the right to nominate a German Receiver of Customs in Liberia.

She further renounces all claim to participate in any measures whatsoever which may be adopted for the rehabilitation of Liberia.

ARTICLE 139

Germany recognizes that all treaties and arrangements between her and Liberia terminated as from August 4, 1917.

ARTICLE 140

The property, rights and interests of Germans in Liberia shall be dealt with in accordance with Part X (Economic Clauses) of the present Treaty.

SECTION V

Morocco

ARTICLE 141

Germany renounces all rights, titles and privileges conferred on her by the General Act of Algeciras of April 7, 1906,[19] and by the Franco-German Agreements of February 9, 1909, and November 4, 1911. All treaties, agreements, arrangements and contracts concluded by her with the Sherifian Empire are regarded as abrogated as from August 3, 1914.

In no case can Germany take advantage of these instruments and she undertakes not to intervene in any way in negotiations relating to Morocco which may take place between France and the other Powers.

ARTICLE 142

Germany having recognized the French Protectorate in Morocco, hereby accepts all the consequences of its establishment, and she renounces the régime of the capitulations therein.

This renunciation shall take effect as from August 3, 1914.

ARTICLE 143

The Sherifian Government shall have complete liberty of action in regu-

---

[19] TS 456, *ante,* vol. 1, p. 464.

lating the status of German nationals in Morocco and the conditions in which they may establish themselves there.

German protected persons, semsars and "associés agricoles" shall be considered as having ceased, as from August 3, 1914, to enjoy the privileges attached to their status and shall be subject to the ordinary law.

Article 144

All property and possessions in the Sherifian Empire of the German Empire and the German States pass to the Maghzen without payment.

For this purpose, the property and possessions of the German Empire and States shall be deemed to include all the property of the Crown, the Empire or the States, and the private property of the former German Emperor and other Royal personages.

All movable and immovable property in the Sherifian Empire belonging to German nationals shall be dealt with in accordance with Sections III and IV of Part X (Economic Clauses) of the present Treaty.

Mining rights which may be recognised as belonging to German nationals by the Court of Arbitration set up under the Moroccan Mining Regulations shall form the subject of a valuation, which the arbitrators shall be requested to make, and these rights shall then be treated in the same way as property in Morocco belonging to German nationals.

Article 145

The German Government shall ensure the transfer to a person nominated by the French Government of the shares representing Germany's portion of the capital of the State Bank of Morocco. The value of these shares, as assessed by the Reparation Commission, shall be paid to the Reparation Commission for the credit of Germany on account of the sums due for reparation. The German Government shall be responsible for indemnifying its nationals so dispossessed.

This transfer will take place without prejudice to the repayment of debts which German nationals may have contracted towards the State Bank of Morocco.

Article 146

Moroccan goods entering Germany shall enjoy the treatment accorded to French goods.

SECTION VI

Egypt

Article 147

Germany declares that she recognises the Protectorate proclaimed over Egypt by Great Britain on December 18, 1914, and that she renounces the régime of the Capitulations in Egypt.

This renunciation shall take effect as from August 4, 1914.

ARTICLE 148

All treaties, agreements, arrangements and contracts concluded by Germany with Egypt are regarded as abrogated as from August 4, 1914.

In no case can Germany avail herself of these instruments and she undertakes not to intervene in any way in negotiations relating to Egypt which may take place between Great Britain and the other Powers.

ARTICLE 149

Until an Egyptian law of judicial organization establishing courts with universal jurisdiction comes into force, provision shall be made, by means of decrees issued by His Highness the Sultan, for the exercise of jurisdiction over German nationals and property by the British Consular Tribunals.

ARTICLE 150

The Egyptian Government shall have complete liberty of action in regulating the status of German nationals and the conditions under which they may establish themselves in Egypt.

ARTICLE 151

Germany consents to the abrogation of the decree issued by His Highness the Khedive on November 28, 1904, relating to the Commission of the Egyptian Public Debt, or to such changes as the Egyptian Government may think it desirable to make therein.

ARTICLE 152

Germany consents, in so far as she is concerned, to the transfer to His Britannic Majesty's Government of the powers conferred on His Imperial Majesty the Sultan by the Convention signed at Constantinople on October 29, 1888, relating to the free navigation of the Suez Canal.

She renounces all participation in the Sanitary, Maritime, and Quarantine Board of Egypt and consents, in so far as she is concerned, to the transfer to the Egyptian Authorities of the powers of that Board.

ARTICLE 153

All property and possessions in Egypt of the German Empire and the German States pass to the Egyptian Government without payment.

For this purpose, the property and possessions of the German Empire and States shall be deemed to include all the property of the Crown, the Empire or the States, and the private property of the former German Emperor and other Royal personages.

All movable and immovable property in Egypt belonging to German nationals shall be dealt with in accordance with Sections III and IV of Part X (Economic Clauses) of the present Treaty.

ARTICLE 154

Egyptian goods entering Germany shall enjoy the treatment accorded to British goods.

SECTION VII

Turkey and Bulgaria

ARTICLE 155

Germany undertakes to recognise and accept all arrangements which the Allied and Associated Powers may make with Turkey and Bulgaria with reference to any rights, interests and privileges whatever which might be claimed by Germany or her nationals in Turkey and Bulgaria and which are not dealt with in the provisions of the present Treaty.

SECTION VIII

Shantung

ARTICLE 156

Germany renounces, in favour of Japan, all her rights, title and privileges—particularly those concerning the territory of Kiaochow, railways, mines and submarine cables—which she acquired in virtue of the Treaty concluded by her with China on March 6, 1898, and of all other arrangements relative to the Province of Shantung.

All German rights in the Tsingtao-Tsinanfu Railway, including its branch lines, together with its subsidiary property of all kinds, stations, shops, fixed and rolling stock, mines, plant and material for the exploitation of the mines, are and remain acquired by Japan, together with all rights and privileges attaching thereto.

The German State submarine cables from Tsingtao to Shanghai and from Tsingtao to Chefoo, with all the rights, privileges and properties attaching thereto, are similarly acquired by Japan, free and clear of all charges and encumbrances.

ARTICLE 157

The movable and immovable property owned by the German State in the territory of Kiaochow, as well as all the rights which Germany might claim in consequence of the works or improvements made or of the expenses incurred by her, directly or indirectly, in connection with this territory, are and remain acquired by Japan, free and clear of all charges and encumbrances.

ARTICLE 158

Germany shall hand over to Japan within three months from the coming into force of the present Treaty the archives, registers, plans, title-deeds and documents of every kind, wherever they may be, relating to the administration, whether civil, military, financial, judicial or other, of the territory of Kiaochow.

Within the same period Germany shall give particulars to Japan of all treaties, arrangements or agreements relating to the rights, title or privileges referred to in the two preceding Articles.

PART V

MILITARY, NAVAL AND AIR CLAUSES

In order to render possible the initiation of a general limitation of the armaments of all nations, Germany undertakes strictly to observe the military, naval and air clauses which follow.

SECTION I

Military Clauses

CHAPTER I

EFFECTIVES AND CADRES OF THE GERMAN ARMY

ARTICLE 159

The German military forces shall be demobilized and reduced as prescribed hereinafter.

ARTICLE 160

(1) By a date which must not be later than March 31, 1920, the German Army must not comprise more than seven divisions of infantry and three divisions of cavalry.

After that date the total number of effectives in the Army of the States constituting Germany must not exceed one hundred thousand men, including officers and establishments of depots. The Army shall be devoted exclusively to the maintenance of order within the territory and to the control of the frontiers.

The total effective strength of officers, including the personnel of staffs, whatever their composition, must not exceed four thousand.

(2) Divisions and Army Corps headquarters staffs shall be organised in accordance with Table No. I annexed to this Section.

The number and strengths of the units of infantry, artillery, engineers, technical services and troops laid down in the aforesaid Table constitute maxima which must not be exceeded.

The following units may each have their own depot:

An Infantry regiment;
A Cavalry regiment;
A regiment of Field Artillery;
A battalion of Pioneers.

(3) The divisions must not be grouped under more than two army corps headquarters staffs.

The maintenance or formation of forces differently grouped or of other organisations for the command of troops or for preparation for war is forbidden.

The Great Germany General Staff and all similar organisations shall be dissolved and may not be reconstituted in any form.

The officers, or persons in the position of officers, in the Ministries of War in the different States in Germany and in the Administrations attached to them, must not exceed three hundred in number and are included in the maximum strength of four thousand laid down in the third sub-paragraph of paragraph (1) of this Article.

ARTICLE 161

Army administrative services consisting of civilian personnel not included in the number of effectives prescribed by the present Treaty will have such personnel reduced in each class to one-tenth of that laid down in the Budget of 1913.

ARTICLE 162

The number of employees or officials of the German States, such as customs officers, forest guards and coastguards, shall not exceed that of the employees or officials functioning in these capacities in 1913.

The number of gendarmes and employees or officials of the local or municipal police may only be increased to an extent corresponding to the increase of population since 1913 in the districts or municipalities in which they are employed.

These employees and officials may not be assembled for military training.

ARTICLE 163

The reduction of the strength of the German military forces as provided for in Article 160 may be effected gradually in the following manner:

Within three months from the coming into force of the present Treaty the total number of effectives must be reduced to 200,000 and the number of units must not exceed twice the number of those laid down in Article 160.

At the expiration of this period, and at the end of each subsequent period of three months, a Conference of military experts of the Principal Allied and Associated Powers will fix the reductions to be made in the ensuing three months, so that by March 31, 1920, at the latest the total number of German effectives does not exceed the maximum number of 100,000 men laid down in Article 160. In these successive reductions the same ratio between the number of officers and of men, and between the various kinds of units, shall be maintained as is laid down in that Article.

Chapter II

ARMAMENT, MUNITIONS AND MATERIAL

Article 164

Up till the time at which Germany is admitted as a member of the League of Nations the German Army must not possess an armament greater than the amounts fixed in Table No. II annexed to this Section, with the exception of an optional increase not exceeding one-twenty-fifth part for small arms and one-fiftieth part for guns, which shall be exclusively used to provide for such eventual replacements as may be necessary.

Germany agrees that after she has become a member of the League of Nations the armaments fixed in the said Table shall remain in force until they are modified by the Council of the League. Furthermore she hereby agrees strictly to observe the decisions of the Council of the League on this subject.

Article 165

The maximum number of guns, machine guns, trench-mortars, rifles and the amount of ammunition and equipment which Germany is allowed to maintain during the period between the coming into force of the present Treaty and the date of March 31, 1920, referred to in Article 160, shall bear the same proportion to the amount authorized in Table No. III annexed to this Section as the strength of the German Army as reduced from time to time in accordance with Article 163 bears to the strength permitted under Article 160.

Article 166

At the date of March 31, 1920, the stock of munitions which the German Army may have at its disposal shall not exceed the amounts fixed in Table No. III annexed to this Section.

Within the same period the German Government will store these stocks at points to be notified to the Governments of the Principal Allied and Associated Powers. The German Government is forbidden to establish any other stocks, depots or reserves of munitions.

Article 167

The number and calibre of the guns constituting at the date of the coming into force of the present Treaty the armament of the fortified works, fortresses, and any land or coast forts which Germany is allowed to retain must be notified immediately by the German Government to the Governments of the Principal Allied and Associated Powers, and will constitute maximum amounts which may not be exceeded.

Within two months from the coming into force of the present Treaty, the maximum stock of ammunition for these guns will be reduced to, and maintained at, the following uniform rates:—fifteen hundred rounds per piece for those the calibre of which is 10.5 cm. and under: five hundred rounds per piece for those of higher calibre.

ARTICLE 168

The manufacture of arms, munitions, or any war material, shall only be carried out in factories or works the location of which shall be communicated to and approved by the Governments of the Principal Allied and Associated Powers, and the number of which they retain the right to restrict.

Within three months from the coming into force of the present Treaty, all other establishments for the manufacture, preparation, storage or design of arms, munitions, or any war material whatever shall be closed down. The same applies to all arsenals except those used as depots for the authorised stocks of munitions. Within the same period the personnel of these arsenals will be dismissed.

ARTICLE 169

Within two months from the coming into force of the present Treaty German arms, munitions and war material, including anti-aircraft material, existing in Germany in excess of the quantities allowed, must be surrendered to the Governments of the Principal Allied and Associated Powers to be destroyed or rendered useless. This will also apply to any special plant intended for the manufacture of military material, except such as may be recognised as necessary for equipping the authorised strength of the German army.

The surrender in question will be effected at such points in German territory as may be selected by the said Governments.

Within the same period arms, munitions and war material, including anti-aircraft material, of origin other than German, in whatever state they may be, will be delivered to the said Governments, who will decide as to their disposal.

Arms and munitions which on account of the successive reductions in the strength of the German army become in excess of the amounts authorized by Tables II and III annexed to this Section must be handed over in the manner laid down above within such periods as may be decided by the Conferences referred to in Article 163.

ARTICLE 170

Importation into Germany of arms, munitions and war material of every kind shall be strictly prohibited.

The same applies to the manufacture for, and export to, foreign countries of arms, munitions and war material of every kind.

ARTICLE 171

The use of asphyxiating, poisonous or other gases and all analogous liquids, materials or devices being prohibited, their manufacture and importation are strictly forbidden in Germany.

The same applies to materials specially intended for the manufacture, storage and use of the said products or devices.

The manufacture and the importation into Germany of armoured cars, tanks and all similar constructions suitable for use in war are also prohibited.

ARTICLE 172

Within a period of three months from the coming into force of the present Treaty, the German Government will disclose to the Governments of the Principal Allied and Associated Powers the nature and mode of manufacture of all explosives, toxic substances or other like chemical preparations used by them in the war or prepared by them for the purpose of being so used.

CHAPTER III

RECRUITING AND MILITARY TRAINING

ARTICLE 173

Universal compulsory military service shall be abolished in Germany.

The German Army may only be constituted and recruited by means of voluntary enlistment.

ARTICLE 174

The period of enlistment for non-commissioned officers and privates must be twelve consecutive years.

The number of men discharged for any reason before the expiration of their term of enlistment must not exceed in any year five per cent. of the total effectives fixed by the second sub-paragraph of paragraph (1) of Article 160 of the present Treaty.

ARTICLE 175

The officers who are retained in the Army must undertake the obligation to serve in it up to the age of forty-five years at least.

Officers newly appointed must undertake to serve on the active list for twenty-five consecutive years at least.

Officers who have previously belonged to any formations whatever of the Army, and who are not retained in the units allowed to be maintained, must not take part in any military exercise whether theoretical or practical, and will not be under any military obligations whatever.

The number of officers discharged for any reason before the expiration of their term of service must not exceed in any year five per cent. of the total effectives of officers provided for in the third sub-paragraph of paragraph (1) of Article 160 of the present Treaty.

Article 176

On the expiration of two months from the coming into force of the present Treaty there must only exist in Germany the number of military schools which is absolutely indispensable for the recruitment of the officers of the units allowed. These schools will be exclusively intended for the recruitment of officers of each arm, in the proportion of one school per arm.

The number of students admitted to attend the courses of the said schools will be strictly in proportion to the vacancies to be filled in the cadres of officers. The students and the cadres will be reckoned in the effectives fixed by the second and third sub-paragraphs of paragraph (1) of Article 160 of the present Treaty.

Consequently, and during the period fixed above, all military academies or similar institutions in Germany, as well as the different military schools for officers, student officers (*Aspiranten*), cadets, non-commissioned officers or student non-commissioned officers (*Aspiranten*), other than the schools above provided for, will be abolished.

Article 177

Educational establishments, the universities, societies of discharged soldiers, shooting or touring clubs and, generally speaking, associations of every description, whatever be the age of their members, must not occupy themselves with any military matters.

In particular they will be forbidden to instruct or exercise their members, or to allow them to be instructed or exercised, in the profession or use of arms.

These societies, associations, educational establishments and universities must have no connection with the Ministries of War or any other military authority.

Article 178

All measures of mobilization or appertaining to mobilization are forbidden.

In no case must formations, administrative services or General Staffs include supplementary cadres.

ARTICLE 179

Germany agrees, from the coming into force of the present Treaty, not to accredit nor to send to any foreign country any military, naval or air mission, nor to allow any such mission to leave her territory, and Germany further agrees to take appropriate measures to prevent German nationals from leaving her territory to become enrolled in the Army, Navy or Air service of any foreign Power, or to be attached to such Army, Navy or Air service for the purpose of assisting in the military, naval or air training thereof, or otherwise for the purpose of giving military, naval or air instruction in any foreign country.

The Allied and Associated Powers agree, so far as they are concerned, from the coming into force of the present Treaty, not to enrol in nor to attach to their armies or naval or air forces any German national for the purpose of assisting in the military training of such armies or naval or air forces, or otherwise to employ any such German national as military, naval or aeronautic instructor.

The present provision does not, however, affect the right of France to recruit for the Foreign Legion in accordance with French military laws and regulations.

CHAPTER IV

FORTIFICATIONS

ARTICLE 180

All fortified works, fortresses and field works situated in German territory to the west of a line drawn fifty kilometres to the east of the Rhine shall be disarmed and dismantled.

Within a period of two months from the coming into force of the present Treaty such of the above fortified works, fortresses and field works as are situated in territory not occupied by Allied and Associated troops shall be disarmed, and within a further period of four months they shall be dismantled. Those which are situated in territory occupied by Allied and Associated troops shall be disarmed and dismantled within such periods as may be fixed by the Allied High Command.

The construction of any new fortification, whatever its nature and importance, is forbidden in the zone referred to in the first paragraph above.

The system of fortified works of the southern and eastern frontiers of Germany shall be maintained in its existing state.

TABLE NO. I

STATE AND ESTABLISHMENT OF ARMY CORPS HEADQUARTERS STAFFS AND OF INFANTRY AND CAVALRY DIVISIONS

These tabular statements do not form a fixed establishment to be imposed on Germany, but the figures contained in them (number of units and strengths) represent maximum figures, which should not in any case be exceeded.

I. ARMY CORPS HEADQUARTERS STAFFS

Unit	Maximum No. authorised	Maximum strengths of each unit	
		Officers	N.C.O.'s and men
Army Corps Headquarters Staff...................	2	30	150
Total for Headquarters Staffs.................	....	60	300

II. ESTABLISHMENT OF AN INFANTRY DIVISION

Unit	Maximum No. of such units in a single division	Maximum strengths of each unit	
		Officers	N.C.O.'s and men
Headquarters of an infantry division...............	1	25	70
Headquarters of divisional infantry.................	1	4	30
Headquarters of divisional artillery................	1	4	30
Regiment of infantry...............................	3	70	2,300
(Each regiment comprises 3 battalions of infantry. Each battalion comprises 3 companies of infantry and 1 machine-gun company.)			
Trench mortar company........................	3	6	150
Divisional squadron...........................	1	6	150
Field artillery regiment...........................	1	85	1,300
(Each regiment comprises 3 groups of artillery. Each group comprises 3 batteries.)			
Pioneer battalion.................................	1	12	400
(This battalion comprises 2 companies of pioneers, 1 pontoon detachment, 1 searchlight section.)			
Signal detachment................................	1	12	300
(This detachment comprises 1 telephone detachment, 1 listening section, 1 carrier pigeon section.)			
Divisional medical service.........................	1	20	400
Parks and convoys................................	....	14	800
Total for infantry division......................	....	410	10,830

III. ESTABLISHMENT OF A CAVALRY DIVISION

Unit	Maximum No. of such units in a single division	Maximum strengths of each unit	
		Officers	N.C.O.'s and men
Headquarters of a cavalry division.................	1	15	50
Cavalry regiment...........................	6	40	800
(Each regiment comprises 4 squadrons.)			
Horse artillery group (3 batteries)...............	1	20	400
Total for cavalry division.......................	....	275	5,250

TABLE NO. II

TABULAR STATEMENT OF ARMAMENT ESTABLISHMENT FOR A MAXIMUM OF SEVEN INFANTRY DIVISIONS, THREE CAVALRY DIVISIONS, AND TWO ARMY CORPS HEADQUARTERS STAFFS

Material	Infantry division	For 7 infantry divisions	Cavalry division	For 3 cavalry divisions	Two army corps headquarters staffs	Total of columns 2, 4, and 5
	(1)	(2)	(3)	(4)	(5)	(6)
Rifles.................	12,000	84,000	....	....	This establishment must be drawn from the increased armaments of the divisional infantry.	84,000
Carbines..............	....	....	6,000	18,000		18,000
Heavy machine guns....	108	756	12	36		792
Light machine guns.....	162	1,134	....	....		1,134
Medium trench mortars.	9	63	....	....		63
Light trench mortars....	27	189	....	....		189
7.7 cm. guns..........	24	168	12	36		204
10.5 cm. howitzers......	12	84	....	....		84

TABLE NO. III

MAXIMUM STOCKS AUTHORISED

Material	Maximum number of Arms authorised	Establishment per unit	Maximum totals
		Rounds	*Rounds*
Rifles..	84,000	} 400	40,800,000
Carbines..	18,000	}	
Heavy machine guns.............................	792	} 8,000	15,408,000
Light machine guns..............................	1,134	}	
Medium trench mortars..........................	63	400	25,200
Light trench mortars............................	189	800	151,200
Field artillery:			
7.7 cm. guns................................	204	1,000	204,000
10.5 cm. howitzers...........................	84	800	67,200

Naval Clauses

ARTICLE 181

After the expiration of a period of two months from the coming into force of the present Treaty the German naval forces in commission must not exceed:

  6 battleships of the *Deutschland* or *Lothringen* type,
  6 light cruisers,
12 destroyers,
12 torpedo boats,

or an equal number of ships constructed to replace them as provided in Article 190.

No submarines are to be included.

All other warships, except where there is provision to the contrary in the present Treaty, must be placed in reserve or devoted to commercial purposes.

ARTICLE 182

Until the completion of the minesweeping prescribed by Article 193 Germany will keep in commission such number of minesweeping vessels as may be fixed by the Governments of the Principal Allied and Associated Powers.

ARTICLE 183

After the expiration of a period of two months from the coming into force of the present Treaty the total personnel of the German Navy, including the manning of the fleet, coast defences, signal stations, administration and other land services, must not exceed fifteen thousand, including officers and men of all grades and corps.

The total strength of officers and warrant officers must not exceed fifteen hundred.

Within two months from the coming into force of the present Treaty the personnel in excess of the above strength shall be demobilized.

No naval or military corps or reserve force in connection with the Navy may be organised in Germany without being included in the above strength.

ARTICLE 184

From the date of the coming into force of the present Treaty all the German surface warships which are not in German ports cease to belong to Germany, who renounces all rights over them.

Vessels which, in compliance with the Armistice of November 11, 1918, are now interned in the ports of the Allied and Associated Powers are declared to be finally surrendered.

Vessels which are now interned in neutral ports will be there surrendered to the Governments of the Principal Allied and Associated Powers. The German Government must address a notification to that effect to the neutral Powers on the coming into force of the present Treaty.

ARTICLE 185

Within a period of two months from the coming into force of the present Treaty the German surface warships enumerated below will be surrendered to the Governments of the Principal Allied and Associated Powers in such Allied ports as the said Powers may direct.

These warships will have been disarmed as provided in Article XXIII of the Armistice of November 11, 1918. Nevertheless they must have all their guns on board.

BATTLESHIPS

Oldenburg	*Posen*
Thuringen	*Westfalen*
Ostfriesland	*Rheinland*
Helgoland	*Nassau*

LIGHT CRUISERS

Stettin	*Stralsund*
Danzig	*Augsburg*
München	*Kolberg*
Lübeck	*Stuttgart*

and, in addition, forty-two modern destroyers and fifty modern torpedo boats, as chosen by the Governments of the Principal Allied and Associated Powers.

ARTICLE 186

On the coming into force of the present Treaty the German Government must undertake, under the supervision of the Governments of the Principal Allied and Associated Powers, the breaking-up of all the German surface warships now under construction.

ARTICLE 187

The German auxiliary cruisers and fleet auxiliaries enumerated below will be disarmed and treated as merchant ships.

INTERNED IN NEUTRAL COUNTRIES:

Berlin	*Seydliz*
Santa Fé	*Yorck*

IN GERMANY:

Ammon	*Fürst Bülow*
Answald	*Gertrud*
Bosnia	*Kigoma*
Cordoba	*Rugia*
Cassel	*Santa Elena*
Dania	*Schleswig*
Rio Negro	*Möwe*
Rio Pardo	*Sierra Ventana*
Santa Cruz	*Chemnitz*
Schwaben	*Emil Georg von Strauss*
Solingen	*Habsburg*
Steigerwald	*Meteor*
Franken	*Waltraute*
Gundomar	*Scharnhorst*

ARTICLE 188

On the expiration of one month from the coming into force of the present Treaty all German submarines, submarine salvage vessels and docks for submarines, including the tubular dock, must have been handed over to the Governments of the Principal Allied and Associated Powers.

Such of these submarines, vessels and docks as are considered by the said Governments to be fit to proceed under their own power or to be towed shall be taken by the German Government into such Allied ports as have been indicated.

The remainder, and also those in course of construction, shall be broken up entirely by the German Government under the supervision of the said Governments. The breaking-up must be completed within three months at the most after the coming into force of the present Treaty.

ARTICLE 189

Articles, machinery and material arising from the breaking-up of German warships of all kinds, whether surface vessels or submarines, may not be used except for purely industrial or commercial purposes.

They may not be sold or disposed of to foreign countries.

ARTICLE 190

Germany is forbidden to construct or acquire any warships other than those intended to replace the units in commission provided for in Article 181 of the present Treaty.

The warships intended for replacement purposes as above shall not exceed the following displacement:

Armoured ships	10,000 tons,
Light cruisers	6,000 tons,
Destroyers	800 tons,
Torpedo boats	200 tons.

Except where a ship has been lost, units of the different classes shall only be replaced at the end of a period of twenty years in the case of battleships and cruisers, and fifteen years in the case of destroyers and torpedo boats, counting from the launching of the ship.

Article 191

The construction or acquisition of any submarine, even for commercial purposes, shall be forbidden in Germany.

Article 192

The warships in commission of the German fleet must have on board or in reserve only the allowance of arms, munitions and war material fixed by the Principal Allied and Associated Powers.

Within a month from the fixing of the quantities as above, arms, munitions and war material of all kinds, including mines and torpedoes, now in the hands of the German Government and in excess of the said quantities, shall be surrendered to the Governments of the said Powers at places to be indicated by them. Such arms, munitions and war material will be destroyed or rendered useless.

All other stocks, depots or reserves of arms, munitions or naval war material of all kinds are forbidden.

The manufacture of these articles in German territory for, and their export to, foreign countries shall be forbidden.

Article 193

On the coming into force of the present Treaty Germany will forthwith sweep up the mines in the following areas in the North Sea to the eastward of longitude 4°00′ E. of Greenwich:

(1) Between parallels of latitude 53°00′ N. and 59°00′ N.; (2) To the northward of latitude 60°30′ N.

Germany must keep these areas free from mines.

Germany must also sweep and keep free from mines such areas in the Baltic as may ultimately be notified by the Governments of the Principal Allied and Associated Powers.

Article 194

The personnel of the German Navy shall be recruited entirely by voluntary engagements entered into for a minimum period of twenty-five consecutive years for officers and warrant officers; twelve consecutive years for petty officers and men.

The number engaged to replace those discharged for any reason before the expiration of their term of service must not exceed five per cent. per annum of the totals laid down in this Section (Article 183).

The personnel discharged from the Navy must not receive any kind of naval or military training or undertake any further service in the Navy or Army.

Officers belonging to the German Navy and not demobilised must engage to serve till the age of forty-five, unless discharged for sufficient reasons.

No officer or man of the German mercantile marine shall receive any training in the Navy.

ARTICLE 195

In order to ensure free passage into the Baltic to all nations, Germany shall not erect any fortifications in the area comprised between latitudes 55°27′ N. and 54°00′ N. and longitudes 9°00′ E. and 16°00′ E. of the meridian of Greenwich, nor instal any guns commanding the maritime routes between the North Sea and the Baltic. The fortifications now existing in this area shall be demolished and the guns removed under the supervision of the Allied Governments and in periods to be fixed by them.

The German Government shall place at the disposal of the Governments of the Principal Allied and Associated Powers all hydrographical information now in its possession concerning the channels and adjoining waters between the Baltic and the North Sea.

ARTICLE 196

All fortified works and fortifications, other than those mentioned in Section XIII (Heligoland) of Part III (Political Clauses for Europe) and in Article 195, now established within fifty kilometres of the German coast or on German islands off that coast shall be considered as of a defensive nature and may remain in their existing condition.

No new fortifications shall be constructed within these limits. The armament of these defences shall not exceed, as regards the number and calibre of guns, those in position at the date of the coming into force of the present Treaty. The German Government shall communicate forthwith particulars thereof to all the European Governments.

On the expiration of a period of two months from the coming into force of the present Treaty the stocks of ammunition for these guns shall be reduced to and maintained at a maximum figure of fifteen hundred rounds per piece for calibres of 4.1-inch and under, and five hundred rounds per piece for higher calibres.

ARTICLE 197

During the three months following the coming into force of the present Treaty the German high-power wireless telegraphy stations at Nauen, Hanover and Berlin shall not be used for the transmission of messages concerning naval, military or political questions of interest to Germany or any State which has been allied to Germany in the war, without the assent of the Governments of the Principal Allied and Associated Powers. These stations may be used for commercial purposes, but only under the supervision of the said Governments, who will decide the wave-length to be used.

During the same period Germany shall not build any more high-power wireless telegraphy stations in her own territory or that of Austria, Hungary, Bulgaria or Turkey.

SECTION III

Air Clauses

ARTICLE 198

The armed forces of Germany must not include any military or naval air forces.

Germany may, during a period not extending beyond October 1, 1919, maintain a maximum number of one hundred seaplanes or flying boats, which shall be exclusively employed in searching for submarine mines, shall be furnished with the necessary equipment for this purpose, and shall in no case carry arms, munitions or bombs of any nature whatever.

In addition to the engines installed in the seaplanes or flying boats above mentioned, one spare engine may be provided for each engine of each of these craft.

No dirigible shall be kept.

ARTICLE 199

Within two months from the coming into force of the present Treaty the personnel of air forces on the rolls of the German land and sea forces shall be demobilised. Up to October 1, 1919, however, Germany may keep and maintain a total number of one thousand men, including officers, for the whole of the cadres and personnel, flying and non-flying, of all formations and establishments.

ARTICLE 200

Until the complete evacuation of German territory by the Allied and Associated troops, the aircraft of the Allied and Associated Powers shall enjoy in Germany freedom of passage through the air, freedom of transit and of landing.

ARTICLE 201

During the six months following the coming into force of the present Treaty, the manufacture and importation of aircraft, parts of aircraft, engines for aircraft, and parts of engines for aircraft, shall be forbidden in all German territory.

ARTICLE 202

On the coming into force of the present Treaty, all military and naval aeronautical material, except the machines mentioned in the second and third paragraphs of Article 198, must be delivered to the Governments of the Principal Allied and Associated Powers.

Delivery must be effected at such places as the said Governments may select, and must be completed within three months.

In particular, this material will include all items under the following heads which are or have been in use or were designed for warlike purposes:

Complete aeroplanes and seaplanes, as well as those being manufactured, repaired or assembled.

Dirigibles able to take the air, being manufactured, repaired or assembled.

Plant for the manufacture of hydrogen.

Dirigible sheds and shelters of every kind for aircraft.

Pending their delivery, dirigibles will, at the expense of Germany, be maintained inflated with hydrogen; the plant for the manufacture of hydrogen, as well as the sheds for dirigibles, may, at the discretion of the said Powers, be left to Germany until the time when the dirigibles are handed over.

Engines for aircraft.

Nacelles and fuselages.

Armament (guns, machine guns, light machine guns, bomb-dropping apparatus, torpedo-dropping apparatus, synchronization apparatus, aiming apparatus).

Munitions (cartridges, shells, bombs loaded or unloaded, stocks of explosives or of material for their manufacture).

Instruments for use on aircraft.

Wireless apparatus and photographic or cinematograph apparatus for use on aircraft.

Component parts of any of the items under the preceding heads.

The material referred to above shall not be removed without special permission from the said Governments.

SECTION IV

Inter-Allied Commissions of Control

ARTICLE 203

All the military, naval and air clauses contained in the present Treaty, for the execution of which a time-limit is prescribed, shall be executed by

Germany under the control of Inter-Allied Commissions specially appointed for this purpose by the Principal Allied and Associated Powers.

ARTICLE 204

The Inter-Allied Commissions of Control will be specially charged with the duty of seeing to the complete execution of the delivery, destruction, demolition and rendering things useless to be carried out at the expense of the German Government in accordance with the present Treaty.

They will communicate to the German authorities the decisions which the Principal Allied and Associated Powers have reserved the right to take, or which the execution of the military, naval and air clauses may necessitate.

ARTICLE 205

The Inter-Allied Commissions of Control may establish their organisations at the seat of the central German Government.

They shall be entitled as often as they think desirable to proceed to any point whatever in German territory, or to send sub-commissions, or to authorize one or more of their members to go, to any such point.

ARTICLE 206

The German Government must give all necessary facilities for the accomplishment of their missions to the Inter-Allied Commissions of Control and to their members.

It shall attach a qualified representative to each Inter-Allied Commission of Control for the purpose of receiving the communications which the Commission may have to address to the German Government and of supplying or procuring for the Commission all information or documents which may be required.

The German Government must in all cases furnish at its own cost all labour and material required to effect the deliveries and the works of destruction, dismantling, demolition, and of rendering things useless, provided for in the present Treaty.

ARTICLE 207

The upkeep and cost of the Commissions of Control and the expenses involved by their work shall be borne by Germany.

ARTICLE 208

The Military Inter-Allied Commission of Control will represent the Governments of the Principal Allied and Associated Powers in dealing with the German Government in all matters concerning the execution of the military clauses.

In particular it will be its duty to receive from the German Government the notifications relating to the location of the stocks and depots of munitions, the armament of the fortified works, fortresses and forts which Germany is allowed to retain, and the location of the works or factories for the production of arms, munitions and war material and their operations.

It will take delivery of the arms, munitions and war material, will select the points where such delivery is to be effected, and will supervise the works of destruction, demolition, and of rendering things useless, which are to be carried out in accordance with the present Treaty.

The German Government must furnish to the Military Inter-Allied Commission of Control all such information and documents as the latter may deem necessary to ensure the complete execution of the military clauses, and in particular all legislative and administrative documents and regulations.

ARTICLE 209

The Naval Inter-Allied Commission of Control will represent the Governments of the Principal Allied and Associated Powers in dealing with the German Government in all matters concerning the execution of the naval clauses.

In particular it will be its duty to proceed to the building yards and to supervise the breaking-up of the ships which are under construction there, to take delivery of all surface ships or submarines, salvage ships, docks and the tubular dock, and to supervise the destruction and breaking-up provided for.

The German Government must furnish to the Naval Inter-Allied Commission of Control all such information and documents as the Commission may deem necessary to ensure the complete execution of the naval clauses, in particular the design of the warships, the composition of their armaments, the details and models of the guns, munitions, torpedoes, mines, explosives, wireless telegraphic apparatus and, in general, everything relating to naval war material, as well as all legislative or administrative documents or regulations.

ARTICLE 210

The Aeronautical Inter-Allied Commission of Control will represent the Governments of the Principal Allied and Associate Powers in dealing with the German Government in all matters concerning the execution of the air clauses.

In particular it will be its duty to make an inventory of the aeronautical material existing in German territory, to inspect aeroplane, balloon and motor manufactories, and factories producing arms, munitions and explosives capable of being used by aircraft, to visit all aerodromes, sheds, landing grounds, parks and depots, to authorise, where necessary, a removal of material and to take delivery of such material.

The German Government must furnish to the Aeronautical Inter-Allied Commission of Control all such information and legislative, administrative or other documents which the Commission may consider necessary to ensure the complete execution of the air clauses, and in particular a list of the personnel belonging to all the German Air Services, and of the existing material, as well as of that in process of manufacture or on order, and a list of all establishments working for aviation, of their positions, and of all sheds and landing grounds.

SECTION V

General Articles

ARTICLE 211

After the expiration of a period of three months from the coming into force of the present Treaty, the German laws must have been modified and shall be maintained by the German Government in conformity with this Part of the present Treaty.

Within the same period all the administrative or other measures relating to the execution of this Part of the Treaty must have been taken.

ARTICLE 212

The following portions of the Armistice of November 11, 1918: Article VI, the first two and the sixth and seventh paragraphs of Article VII; Article IX; Clauses I, II and V of Annex n° 2, and the Protocol, dated April 4, 1919,[20] supplementing the Armistice of November 11, 1918, remain in force so far as they are not inconsistent with the above stipulations.

ARTICLE 213

So long as the present Treaty remains in force, Germany undertakes to give every facility for any investigation which the Council of the League of Nations, acting if need be by a majority vote, may consider necessary.

---

[20] *Ante,* p. 30.

PART VI

PRISONERS OF WAR AND GRAVES

SECTION I

Prisoners of War

ARTICLE 214

The repatriation of prisoners of war and interned civilians shall take place as soon as possible after the coming into force of the present Treaty and shall be carried out with the greatest rapidity .

ARTICLE 215

The repatriation of German prisoners of war and interned civilians shall, in accordance with Article 214, be carried out by a Commission composed of representatives of the Allied and Associated Powers on the one part and of the German Government on the other part.

For each of the Allied and Associated Powers a Sub-Commission, composed exclusively of Representatives of the interested Power and of Delegates of the German Government, shall regulate the details of carrying into effect the repatriation of the prisoners of war.

ARTICLE 216

From the time of their delivery into the hands of the German authorities the prisoners of war and interned civilians are to be returned without delay to their homes by the said authorities.

Those amongst them who before the war were habitually resident in territory occupied by the troops of the Allied and Associated Powers are likewise to be sent to their homes, subject to the consent and control of the military authorities of the Allied and Associated armies of occupation.

ARTICLE 217

The whole cost of repatriation from the moment of starting shall be borne by the German Government who shall also provide the land and sea transport and staff considered necessary by the Commission referred to in Article 215.

ARTICLE 218

Prisoners of war and interned civilians awaiting disposal or undergoing sentence for offences against discipline shall be repatriated irrespective of the completion of their sentence or of the proceedings pending against them.

This stipulation shall not apply to prisoners of war and interned civilians punished for offences committed subsequent to May 1, 1919.

During the period pending their repatriation all prisoners of war and interned civilians shall remain subject to the existing regulations, more especially as regards work and discipline.

ARTICLE 219

Prisoners of war and interned civilians who are awaiting disposal or undergoing sentence for offences other than those against discipline may be detained.

ARTICLE 220

The German Government undertakes to admit to its territory without distinction all persons liable to repatriation.

Prisoners of war or other German nationals who do not desire to be repatriated may be excluded from repatriation; but the Allied and Associated Governments reserve to themselves the right either to repatriate them or to take them to a neutral country or to allow them to reside in their own territories.

The German Government undertakes not to institute any exceptional proceedings against these persons or their families nor to take any repressive or vexatious measures of any kind whatsoever against them on this account.

ARTICLE 221

The Allied and Associated Governments reserve the right to make the repatriation of German prisoners of war or German nationals in their hands conditional upon the immediate notification and release by the German Government of any prisoners of war who are nationals of the Allied and Associated Powers and may still be in Germany.

ARTICLE 222

Germany undertakes:

(1) To give every facility to Commissions to enquire into the cases of those who cannot be traced; to furnish such Commissions with all necessary means of transport; to allow them access to camps, prisons, hospitals and all other places; and to place at their disposal all documents, whether public or private, which would facilitate their enquiries;

(2) To impose penalties upon any German officials or private persons who have concealed the presence of any nationals of any of the Allied and Associated Powers or have neglected to reveal the presence of any such after it had come to their knowledge.

ARTICLE 223

Germany undertakes to restore without delay from the date of the coming into force of the present Treaty all articles, money, securities and documents which have belonged to nationals of the Allied and Associated Powers and which have been retained by the German authorities.

ARTICLE 224

The High Contracting Parties waive reciprocally all repayment of sums due for the maintenance of prisoners of war in their respective territories.

SECTION II

Graves

ARTICLE 225

The Allied and Associated Governments and the German Government will cause to be respected and maintained the graves of the soldiers and sailors buried in their respective territories.

They agree to recognise any Commission appointed by an Allied or Associated Government for the purpose of identifying, registering, caring for or erecting suitable memorials over the said graves and to facilitate the discharge of its duties.

Furthermore they agree to afford, so far as the provisions of their laws and the requirements of public health allow, every facility for giving effect to requests that the bodies of their soldiers and sailors may be transferred to their own country.

ARTICLE 226

The graves of prisoners of war and interned civilians who are nationals of the different belligerent States and have died in captivity shall be properly maintained in accordance with Article 225 of the present Treaty.

The Allied and Associated Governments on the one part and the German Government on the other part reciprocally undertake also to furnish to each other:

(1) A complete list of those who have died, together with all information useful for identification;

(2) All information as to the number and position of the graves of all those who have been buried without identification.

PART VII

PENALTIES

ARTICLE 227

The Allied and Associated Powers publicly arraign William II of Hohenzollern, formerly German Emperor, for a supreme offence against international morality and the sanctity of treaties.

A special tribunal will be constituted to try the accused, thereby assuring him the guarantees essential to the right of defence. It will be composed of five judges, one appointed by each of the following Powers: namely, the United States of America, Great Britain, France, Italy and Japan.

In its decision the tribunal will be guided by the highest motives of international policy, with a view to vindicating the solemn obligations of international undertakings and the validity of international morality. It will be its duty to fix the punishment which it considers should be imposed.

The Allied and Associated Powers will address a request to the Government of the Netherlands for the surrender to them of the ex-Emperor in order that he may be put on trial.

ARTICLE 228

The German Government recognises the right of the Allied and Associated Powers to bring before military tribunals persons accused of having committed acts in violation of the laws and customs of war. Such persons shall, if found guilty, be sentenced to punishments laid down by law. This provision will apply notwithstanding any proceedings or prosecution before a tribunal in Germany or in the territory of her allies.

The German Government shall hand over to the Allied and Associated Powers, or to such one of them as shall so request, all persons accused of having committed an act in violation of the laws and customs of war, who are specified either by name or by the rank, office or employment which they held under the German authorities.

ARTICLE 229

Persons guilty of criminal acts against the nationals of one of the Allied and Associated Powers will be brought before the military tribunals of that Power.

Persons guilty of criminal acts against the nationals of more than one of the Allied and Associated Powers will be brought before military tribunals composed of members of the military tribunals of the powers concerned.

In every case the accused will be entitled to name his own counsel.

ARTICLE 230

The German Government undertakes to furnish all documents and information of every kind, the production of which may be considered necessary to ensure the full knowledge of the incriminating acts, the discovery of offenders and the just appreciation of responsibility.

PART VIII

REPARATION

SECTION I

General Provisions

ARTICLE 231

The Allied and Associated Governments affirm and Germany accepts the responsibility of Germany and her allies for causing all the loss and damage to which the Allied and Associated Governments and their nationals have been subjected as a consequence of the war imposed upon them by the aggression of Germany and her allies.

ARTICLE 232

The Allied and Associated Governments recognize that the resources of Germany are not adequate, after taking into account permanent diminutions of such resources which will result from other provisions of the present Treaty, to make complete reparation for all such loss and damage.

The Allied and Associated Governments, however, require, and Germany undertakes, that she will make compensation for all damage done to the civilian population of the Allied and Associated Powers and to their property during the period of the belligerency of each as an Allied or Associated Power against Germany by such aggression by land, by sea and from the air, and in general all damage as defined in Annex I hereto.

In accordance with Germany's pledges, already given, as to complete restoration for Belgium, Germany undertakes, in addition to the compensation for damage elsewhere in this Part provided for, as a consequence of the violation of the Treaty of 1839, to make reimbursement of all sums which Belgium has borrowed from the Allied and Associated Governments up to November 11, 1918, together with interest at the rate of five per cent. (5%) per annum on such sums. This amount shall be determined by the Reparation Commission, and the German Government undertakes thereupon forthwith to make a special issue of bearer bonds to an equivalent amount payable in marks gold, on May 1, 1926, or, at the option of the German Government, on the 1st of May in any year up to 1926. Subject to the foregoing, the form of such bonds shall be determined by the Reparation Commission. Such bonds shall be handed over to the Reparation Commission, which has authority to take and acknowledge receipt thereof on behalf of Belgium.

ARTICLE 233

The amount of the above damage for which compensation is to be made by Germany shall be determined by an Inter-Allied Commission, to be called the *Reparation Commission* and constituted in the form and with the powers set forth hereunder and in Annexes II to VII inclusive hereto.

This Commission shall consider the claims and give to the German Government a just opportunity to be heard.

The findings of the Commission as to the amount of damage defined as above shall be concluded and notified to the German Government on or before May 1, 1921, as representing the extent of that Government's obligations.

The Commission shall concurrently draw up a schedule of payments prescribing the time and manner for securing and discharging the entire obligation within a period of thirty years from May 1, 1921. If, however, within the period mentioned, Germany fails to discharge her obligations, any balance remaining unpaid may, within the discretion of the Commission, be postponed for settlement in subsequent years, or may be handled otherwise in such manner as the Allied and Associated Governments, acting in accordance with the procedure laid down in this Part of the present Treaty, shall determine.

ARTICLE 234

The Reparation Commission shall after May 1, 1921, from time to time, consider the resources and capacity of Germany, and, after giving her representatives a just opportunity to be heard, shall have discretion to extend the date, and to modify the form of payments, such as are to be provided for in accordance with Article 233; but not to cancel any part, except with the specific authority of the several Governments represented upon the Commission.

ARTICLE 235

In order to enable the Allied and Associated Powers to proceed at once to the restoration of their industrial and economic life, pending the full determination of their claims, Germany shall pay in such instalments and in such manner (whether in gold, commodities, ships, securities or otherwise) as the Reparation Commission may fix, during 1919, 1920 and the first four months of 1921, the equivalent of 20,000,000,000 gold marks. Out of this sum the expenses of the armies of occupation subsequent to the Armistice of November 11, 1918, shall first be met, and such supplies of food and raw materials as may be judged by the Governments of the Principal Allied and Associated Powers to be essential to enable Germany to meet her obligations for reparation may also, with the approval of the said Governments, be paid for out of the above sum. The balance shall be reckoned towards liquidation of the amounts due for reparation. Germany shall further deposit bonds as prescribed in paragraph 12 (c) of Annex II hereto.

ARTICLE 236

Germany further agrees to the direct application of her economic resources to reparation as specified in Annexes III, IV, V, and VI, relating respectively to merchant shipping, to physical restoration, to coal and derivatives of coal, and to dyestuffs and other chemical products; provided always that the value of the property transferred and any services rendered by her under these Annexes, assessed in the manner therein prescribed, shall be credited to her towards liquidation of her obligations under the above Articles.

ARTICLE 237

The successive instalments, including the above sum, paid over by Germany in satisfaction of the above claims will be divided by the Allied and Associated Governments in proportions which have been determined upon by them in advance on a basis of general equity and of the rights of each.

For the purposes of this division the value of property transferred and services rendered under Article 243, and under Annexes III, IV, V, VI, and VII, shall be reckoned in the same manner as cash payments effected in that year.

ARTICLE 238

In addition to the payments mentioned above Germany shall effect, in accordance with the procedure laid down by the Reparation Commission, restitution in cash of cash taken away, seized or sequestrated, and also restitution of animals, objects of every nature and securities taken away, seized or sequestrated, in the cases in which it proves possible to identify them in territory belonging to Germany or her allies.

Until this procedure is laid down, restitution will continue in accordance with the provisions of the Armistice of November 11, 1918, and its renewals and the Protocols thereto.

ARTICLE 239

The German Government undertakes to make forthwith the restitution contemplated by Article 238 and to make the payments and deliveries contemplated by Articles 233, 234, 235 and 236.

ARTICLE 240

The German Government recognizes the Commission provided for by Article 233 as the same may be constituted by the Allied and Associated Governments in accordance with Annex II, and agrees irrevocably to the possession and exercise by such Commission of the power and authority given to it under the present Treaty.

The German Government will supply to the Commission all the information which the Commission may require relative to the financial situation and operations and to the property, productive capacity, and stocks and current production of raw materials and manufactured articles of Germany and her nationals, and further any information relative to military operations which in the judgment of the Commission may be necessary for the assessment of Germany's liability for reparation as defined in Annex I.

The German Government will accord to the members of the Commission and its authorised agents the same rights and immunities as are enjoyed in Germany by duly accredited diplomatic agents of friendly Powers.

Germany further agrees to provide for the salaries and expenses of the Commission and of such staff as it may employ.

ARTICLE 241

Germany undertakes to pass, issue and maintain in force any legislation, orders and decrees that may be necessary to give complete effect to these provisions.

ARTICLE 242

The provisions of this Part of the present Treaty do not apply to the property, rights and interests referred to in Sections III and IV of Part X (Economic Clauses) of the present Treaty, nor to the product of their liquidation, except so far as concerns any final balance in favour of Germany under Article 243 (a).

ARTICLE 243

The following shall be reckoned as credits to Germany in respect of her reparation obligations:

(a) Any final balance in favour of Germany under Section V (Alsace-Lorraine) of Part III (Political Clauses for Europe) and Sections III and IV of Part X (Economic Clauses) of the present Treaty;

(b) Amounts due to Germany in respect of transfers under Section IV (Saar Basin) of Part III (Political Clauses for Europe), Part IX (Financial Clauses), and Part XII (Ports, Waterways and Railways);

(c) Amounts which in the judgment of the Reparation Commission should be credited to Germany on account of any other transfers under the present Treaty of property, rights, concessions or other interests.

In no case however shall credit be given for property restored in accordance with Article 238 of the present Part.

ARTICLE 244

The transfer of the German submarine cables which do not form the subject of particular provisions of the present Treaty is regulated by Annex VII hereto.

ANNEX I

Compensation may be claimed from Germany under Article 232 above in respect of the total damage under the following categories:

(1) Damage to injured persons and to surviving dependents by personal injury to or death of civilians caused by acts of war, including bombardments or other attacks on land, on sea, or from the air, and all the direct consequences thereof, and of all operations of war by the two groups of belligerents wherever arising.

(2) Damage caused by Germany or her allies to civilian victims of acts of cruelty, violence or maltreatment (including injuries to life or health as a consequence of imprisonment, deportation, internment or evacuation, of

exposure at sea or of being forced to labour), wherever arising, and to the surviving dependents of such victims.

(3) Damage caused by Germany or her allies in their own territory or in occupied or invaded territory to civilian victims of all acts injurious to health or capacity to work, or to honour, as well as the surviving dependents of such victims.

(4) Damage caused by any kind of maltreatment of prisoners of war.

(5) As damage caused to the peoples of the Allied and Associated Powers, all pensions and compensation in the nature of pensions to naval and military victims of war (including members of the air force), whether mutilated, wounded, sick or invalided, and to the dependents of such victims, the amount due to the Allied and Associated Governments being calculated for each of them as being the capitalised cost of such pensions and compensation at the date of the coming into force of the present Treaty on the basis of the scales in force in France at such date.

(6) The cost of assistance by the Governments of the Allied and Associated Powers to prisoners of war and to their families and dependents.

(7) Allowances by the Governments of the Allied and Associated Powers to the families and dependents of mobilised persons or persons serving with the forces, the amount due to them for each calendar year in which hostilities occurred being calculated for each Government on the basis of the average scale for such payments in force in France during that year.

(8) Damage caused to civilians by being forced by Germany or her allies to labour without just remuneration.

(9) Damage in respect of all property wherever situated belonging to any of the Allied or Associated States or their nationals, with the exception of naval and military works or materials, which has been carried off, seized, injured or destroyed by the acts of Germany or her allies on land, on sea or from the air, or damage directly in consequence of hostilities or of any operations of war.

(10) Damage in the form of levies, fines and other similar exactions imposed by Germany or her allies upon the civilian population.

ANNEX II

1

The Commission referred to in Article 233 shall be called "The Reparation Commission" and is hereinafter referred to as "the Commission".

2

Delegates to this Commission shall be nominated by the United States of America, Great Britain, France, Italy, Japan, Belgium and the Serb-Croat-Slovene State. Each of these Powers will appoint one Delegate and also one Assistant Delegate, who will take his place in case of illness or necessary absence, but at other times will only have the right to be present at proceedings without taking any part therein.

On no occasion shall the Delegates of more than five of the above Powers have the right to take part in the proceedings of the Commission and to record their votes. The Delegates of the United States, Great Britain, France and Italy shall have this right on all occasions. The Delegate of Belgium shall have this right on all occasions other than those referred to below. The Delegate of Japan shall have this right on occasions when questions relating to damage at sea, and questions arising under Article 260 of Part IX (Financial Clauses) in which Japanese interests are concerned, are under consideration. The Delegate of the Serb-Croat-Slovene State shall have this right when questions relating to Austria, Hungary or Bulgaria are under consideration.

Each Government represented on the Commission shall have the right to withdraw therefrom upon twelve months notice filed with the Commission and confirmed in the course of the sixth month after the date of the original notice.

3

Such of the other Allied and Associated Powers as may be interested shall have the right to appoint a Delegate to be present and act as Assessor only while their respective claims and interests are under examination or discussion, but without the right to vote.

4

In case of the death, resignation or recall of any Delegate, Assistant Delegate or Assessor, a successor to him shall be nominated as soon as possible.

5

The Commission will have its principal permanent Bureau in Paris and will hold its first meeting in Paris as soon as practicable after the coming into force of the present Treaty, and thereafter will meet in such place or places and at such time as it may deem convenient and as may be necessary for the most expeditious discharge of its duties.

6

At its first meeting the Commission shall elect, from among the Delegates referred to above, a Chairman and a Vice-Chairman, who shall hold office for one year and shall be eligible for re-election. If a vacancy in the Chairmanship or Vice-Chairmanship should occur during the annual period, the Commission shall proceed to a new election for the remainder of the said period.

7

The Commission is authorised to appoint all necessary officers, agents and employees who may be required for the execution of its functions, and to fix their remuneration; to constitute committees, whose members need not necessarily be members of the Commission, and to take all executive steps necessary for the purpose of discharging its duties; and to delegate authority and discretion to officers, agents and committees.

8

All proceedings of the Commission shall be private, unless, on particular occasions, the Commission shall otherwise determine for special reasons.

9

The Commission shall be required, if the German Government so desire, to hear, within a period which it will fix from time to time, evidence and arguments on the part of Germany on any question connected with her capacity to pay.

10

The Commission shall consider the claims and give to the German Government a just opportunity to be heard, but not to take any part whatever in the decisions of the Commission. The Commission shall afford a similar opportunity to the allies of Germany, when it shall consider that their interests are in question.

11

The Commission shall not be bound by any particular code or rules of law or by any particular rule of evidence or of procedure, but shall be guided by justice, equity and good faith. Its decisions must follow the same principles and rules in all cases where they are applicable. It will establish rules relating to methods of proof of claims. It may act on any trustworthy modes of computation.

12

The Commission shall have all the powers conferred upon it, and shall exercise all the functions assigned to it, by the present Treaty.

The Commission shall in general have wide latitude as to its control and handling of the whole reparation problem as dealt with in this Part of the present Treaty and shall have authority to interpret its provisions. Subject to the provisions of the present Treaty, the Commission is constituted by the several Allied and Associated Governments referred to in paragraphs 2 and 3 above as the exclusive agency of the said Governments respectively for receiving, selling, holding, and distributing the reparation payments to be made by Germany under this Part of the present Treaty. The Commission must comply with the following conditions and provisions:

(a) Whatever part of the full amount of the proved claims is not paid in gold, or in ships, securities and commodities or otherwise, Germany shall be required, under such conditions as the Commission may determine, to cover by way of guarantee by an equivalent issue of bonds, obligations or otherwise, in order to constitute an acknowledgment of the said part of the debt.

(*b*) In periodically estimating Germany's capacity to pay, the Commission shall examine the German system of taxation, first, to the end that the sums for reparation which Germany is required to pay shall become a charge upon all her revenues prior to that for the service or discharge of any domestic loan, and secondly, so as to satisfy itself that, in general, the German scheme of taxation is fully as heavy proportionately as that of any of the Powers represented on the Commission.

(*c*) In order to facilitate and continue the immediate restoration of the economic life of the Allied and Associated countries, the Commission will as provided in Article 235 take from Germany by way of security for and acknowledgment of her debt a first instalment of gold bearer bonds free of all taxes and charges of every description established or to be established by the Government of the German Empire or of the German States, or by any authority subject to them; these bonds will be delivered on account and in three portions, the marks gold being payable in conformity with Article 262 of Part IX (Financial Clauses) of the present Treaty as follows:

(1) To be issued forthwith, 20,000,000,000 Marks gold bearer bonds, payable not later than May 1, 1921, without interest. There shall be specially applied towards the amortisation of these bonds the payments which Germany is pledged to make in conformity with Article 235, after deduction of the sums used for the reimbursement of expenses of the armies of occupation and for payment of foodstuffs and raw materials. Such bonds as have not been redeemed by May 1, 1921, shall then be exchanged for new bonds of the same type as those provided for below (paragraph 12, *c*, (2)).

(2) To be issued forthwith, further 40,000,000,000 Marks gold bearer bonds, bearing interest at $2\frac{1}{2}$ per cent. per annum between 1921 and 1926, and thereafter at 5 per cent. per annum with an additional 1 per cent. for amortisation beginning in 1926 on the whole amount of the issue.

(3) To be delivered forthwith a covering undertaking in writing to issue when, but not until, the Commission is satisfied that Germany can meet such interest and sinking fund obligations, a further instalment of 40,000,000,000 Marks gold 5 per cent. bearer bonds, the time and mode of payment of principal and interest to be determined by the Commission.

The dates for payment of interest, the manner of applying the amortisation fund, and all other questions relating to the issue, management and regulation of the bond issue shall be determined by the Commission from time to time.

Further issues by way of acknowledgment and security may be required as the Commission subsequently determines from time to time.

(*d*) In the event of bonds, obligations or other evidence of indebtedness issued by Germany by way of security for or acknowledgment of her reparation debt being disposed of outright, not by way of pledge, to persons other than the several Governments in whose favour Germany's original reparation indebtedness was created, an amount of such reparation indebtedness shall be deemed to be extinguished corresponding to the nominal value of the bonds, etc., so disposed of outright, and the obligation of Germany in respect of such bonds shall be confined to her liabilities to the holders of the bonds, as expressed upon their face.

(e) The damage for repairing, reconstructing and rebuilding property in the invaded and devastated districts, including reinstallation of furniture, machinery and other equipment, will be calculated according to the cost at the dates when the work is done.

(f) Decisions of the Commission relating to the total or partial cancellation of the capital or interest of any verified debt of Germany must be accompanied by a statement of its reasons.

13

As to voting, the Commission will observe the following rules:

When a decision of the Commission is taken, the votes of all the Delegates entitled to vote, or in the absence of any of them, of their Assistant Delegates, shall be recorded. Abstention from voting is to be treated as a vote against the proposal under discussion. Assessors have no vote.

On the following questions unanimity is necessary:

(a) Questions involving the sovereignty of any of the Allied and Associated Powers, or the cancellation of the whole or any part of the debt or obligations of Germany;

(b) Questions of determining the amount and conditions of bonds or other obligations to be issued by the German Government and of fixing the time and manner for selling, negotiating or distributing such bonds;

(c) Any postponement, total or partial, beyond the end of 1930, of the payment of instalments falling due between May 1, 1921, and the end of 1926 inclusive;

(d) Any postponement, total or partial, of any instalment falling due after 1926 for a period exceeding three years;

(e) Questions of applying in any particular case a method of measuring damages different from that which has been previously applied in a similar case;

(f) Questions of the interpretation of the provisions of this Part of the present Treaty.

All other questions shall be decided by the vote of a majority.

In case of any difference of opinion among the Delegates, which cannot be solved by reference to their Governments, upon the question whether a given case is one which requires a unanimous vote for its decision or not, such difference shall be referred to the immediate arbitration of some impartial person to be agreed upon by their Governments, whose award the Allied and Associated Governments agree to accept.

14

Decisions of the Commission, in accordance with the powers conferred upon it, shall forthwith become binding and may be put into immediate execution without further proceedings.

15

The Commission will issue to each of the interested Powers, in such form as the Commission shall fix:

(1) A certificate stating that it holds for the account of the said Power bonds of the issues mentioned above, the said certificate, on the demand of the Power concerned, being divisible in a number of parts not exceeding five;

(2) From time to time certificates stating the goods delivered by Germany on account of her reparation debt which it holds for the account of the said Power.

The said certificates shall be registered, and upon notice to the Commission, may be transferred by endorsement.

When bonds are issued for sale or negotiation, and when goods are delivered by the Commission, certificates to an equivalent value must be withdrawn.

16

Interest shall be debited to Germany as from May 1, 1921, in respect of her debt as determined by the Commission, after allowing for sums already covered by cash payments or their equivalent, or by bonds issued to the Commission, or under Article 243. The rate of interest shall be 5 per cent. unless the Commission shall determine at some future time that circumstances justify a variation of this rate.

The Commission, in fixing on May 1, 1921, the total amount of the debt of Germany, may take account of interest due on sums arising out of the reparation of material damage as from November 11, 1918, up to May 1, 1921.

17

In case of default by Germany in the performance of any obligation under this Part of the present Treaty, the Commission will forthwith give notice of such default to each of the interested Powers and may make such recommendations as to the action to be taken in consequence of such default as it may think necessary.

18

The measures which the Allied and Associated Powers shall have the right to take, in case of voluntary default by Germany, and which Germany agrees not to regard as acts of war, may include economic and financial prohibitions and reprisals and in general such other measures as the respective Governments may determine to be necessary in the circumstances.

19

Payments required to be made in gold or its equivalent on account of the proved claims of the Allied and Associated Powers may at any time be accepted by the Commission in the form of chattels, properties, commodities, businesses, rights, concessions, within or without German territory, ships, bonds, shares or securities of any kind, or currencies of Germany or other States, the value of such substitutes for gold being fixed at a fair and just amount by the Commission itself.

20

The Commission, in fixing or accepting payment in specified properties or rights, shall have due regard for any legal or equitable interests of the Allied and Associated Powers or of neutral Powers or of their nationals therein.

21

No member of the Commission shall be responsible, except to the Government appointing him, for any action or omission as such member. No one of the Allied or Associated Governments assumes any responsibility in respect of any other Government.

22

Subject to the provisions of the present Treaty this Annex may be amended by the unanimous decision of the Governments represented from time to time upon the Commission.

23

When all the amounts due from Germany and her allies under the present Treaty or the decisions of the Commission have been discharged and all sums received, or their equivalents, shall have been distributed to the Powers interested, the Commission shall be dissolved.

ANNEX III

1

Germany recognises the right of the Allied and Associated Powers to the replacement, ton for ton (gross tonnage) and class for class, of all merchant ships and fishing boats lost or damaged owing to the war.

Nevertheless, and in spite of the fact that the tonnage of German shipping at present in existence is much less than that lost by the Allied and Associated

Powers in consequence of the German aggression, the right thus recognised will be enforced on German ships and boats under the following conditions:

The German Government, on behalf of themselves and so as to bind all other persons interested, cede to the Allied and Associated Governments the property in all the German merchant ships which are of 1,600 tons gross and upwards; in one-half, reckoned in tonnage, of the ships which are between 1,000 tons and 1,600 tons gross; in one-quarter, reckoned in tonnage, of the steam trawlers; and in one-quarter, reckoned in tonnage, of the other fishing boats.

2

The German Government will, within two months of the coming into force of the present Treaty, deliver to the Reparation Commission all the ships and boats mentioned in paragraph 1.

3

The ships and boats mentioned in paragraph 1 include all ships and boats which (a) fly, or may be entitled to fly, the German merchant flag; or (b) are owned by any German national, company or corporation or by any company or corporation belonging to a country other than an Allied or Associated country and under the control or direction of German nationals; or (c) are now under construction (1) in Germany, (2) in other than Allied or Associated countries for the account of any German national, company or corporation.

4

For the purpose of providing documents of title for the ships and boats to be handed over as above mentioned, the German Government will:

(a) Deliver to the Reparation Commission in respect of each vessel a bill of sale or other document of title evidencing the transfer to the Commission of the entire property in the vessel, free from all encumbrances, charges and liens of all kinds, as the Commission may require;

(b) Take all measures that may be indicated by the Reparation Commission for ensuring that the ships themselves shall be placed at its disposal.

5

As an additional part of reparation, Germany agrees to cause merchant ships to be built in German yards for the account of the Allied and Associated Governments as follows:

(a) Within three months of the coming into force of the present Treaty, the Reparation Commission will notify to the German Government the amount of tonnage to be laid down in German shipyards in each of the two years next succeeding the three months mentioned above.

(b) Within two years of the coming into force of the present Treaty the Reparation Commission will notify to the German Government the amount of tonnage to be laid down in each of the three years following the two years mentioned above.

(*c*) The amount of tonnage to be laid down in each year shall not exceed 200,000 tons, gross tonnage.

(*d*) The specifications of the ships to be built, the conditions under which they are to be built and delivered, the price per ton at which they are to be accounted for by the Reparation Commission, and all other questions relating to the accounting, ordering, building and delivery of the ships, shall be determined by the Commission.

6

Germany undertakes to restore in kind and in normal condition of upkeep to the Allied and Associated Powers, within two months of the coming into force of the present Treaty, in accordance with procedure to be laid down by the Reparation Commission, any boats and other movable appliances belonging to inland navigation which since August 1, 1914, have by any means whatever come into her possession or into the possession of her nationals, and which can be identified.

With a view to make good the loss in inland navigation tonnage, from whatever cause arising, which has been incurred during the war by the Allied and Associated Powers, and which cannot be made good by means of the restitution prescribed above, Germany agrees to cede to the Reparation Commission a portion of the German river fleet up to the amount of the loss mentioned above, provided that such cession shall not exceed 20 per cent of the river fleet as it existed on November 11, 1918.

The conditions of this cession shall be settled by the arbitrators referred to in Article 339 of Part XII (Ports, Waterways and Railways) of the present Treaty, who are charged with the settlement of difficulties relating to the apportionment of river tonnage resulting from the new international régime applicable to certain river systems or from the territorial changes affecting those systems.

7

Germany agrees to take any measures that may be indicated to her by the Reparation Commission for obtaining the full title to the property in all ships which have during the war been transferred, or are in process of transfer, to neutral flags, without the consent of the Allied and Associated Governments.

8

Germany waives all claims of any description against the Allied and Associated Governments and their nationals in respect of the detention, employment, loss or damage of any German ships or boats, exception being made of payments due in respect of the employment of ships in conformity with the Armistice Agreement of January 13 [16], 1919,[21] and subsequent Agreements.

The handing over of the ships of the German mercantile marine must be continued without interruption in accordance with the said Agreement.

9

Germany waives all claims to vessels or cargoes sunk by or in consequence of naval action and subsequently salved, in which any of the Allied or Associated Governments or their nationals may have any interest either as owners, charterers, insurers or otherwise, notwithstanding any decree of condemnation which may have been made by a Prize Court of Germany or of her allies.

ANNEX IV

1

The Allied and Associated Powers require, and Germany undertakes, that in part satisfaction of her obligations expressed in the present Part she will, as hereinafter provided, devote her economic resources directly to the physical restoration of the invaded areas of the Allied and Associated Powers, to the extent that these Powers may determine.

2

The Allied and Associated Governments may file with the Reparation Commission lists showing:

(a) Animals, machinery, equipment, tools and like articles of a commercial character, which have been seized, consumed or destroyed by Germany or destroyed in direct consequence of military operations, and which such Governments, for the purpose of meeting immediate and urgent needs, desire to have replaced by animals and articles of the same nature which are in being in German territory at the date of the coming into force of the present Treaty;

(b) Reconstruction materials (stones, bricks, refractory bricks, tiles, wood, window-glass, steel, lime, cement, etc.), machinery, heating apparatus, furniture and like articles of a commercial character which the said Governments desire to have produced and manufactured in Germany and delivered to them to permit of the restoration of the invaded areas.

3

The lists relating to the articles mentioned in 2 (a) above shall be filed within sixty days after the date of the coming into force of the present Treaty.

---

[21] *Ante,* p. 24.

The lists relating to the articles in 2 (*b*) above shall be filed on or before December 31, 1919.

The lists shall contain all such details as are customary in commercial contracts dealing with the subject matter, including specifications, dates of delivery (but not extending over more than four years), and places of delivery, but not price or value, which shall be fixed as hereinafter provided by the Commission.

4

Immediately upon the filing of such lists with the Commission, the Commission shall consider the amount and number of the materials and animals mentioned in the lists provided for above which are to be required of Germany. In reaching a decision on this matter the Commission shall take into account such domestic requirements of Germany as it deems essential for the maintenance of Germany's social and economic life, the prices and dates at which similar articles can be obtained in the Allied and Associated countries as compared with those to be fixed for German articles, and the general interest of the Allied and Associated Governments that the industrial life of Germany be not so disorganised as to affect adversely the ability of Germany to perform the other acts of reparation stipulated for.

Machinery, equipment, tools and like articles of a commercial character in actual industrial use are not, however, to be demanded of Germany unless there is no free stock of such articles respectively which is not in use and is available, and then not in excess of thirty per cent. of the quantity of such articles in use in any one establishment or undertaking.

The Commission shall give representatives of the German Government an opportunity and a time to be heard as to their capacity to furnish the said materials, articles and animals.

The decision of the Commission shall thereupon and at the earliest possible moment be communicated to the German Government and to the several interested Allied and Associated Governments.

The German Government undertakes to deliver the materials, articles and animals as specified in the said communication, and the interested Allied and Associated Governments severally agree to accept the same, provided they conform to the specification given, or are not, in the judgment of the Commission, unfit to be utilized in the work of reparation.

5

The Commission shall determine the value to be attributed to the materials, articles and animals to be delivered in accordance with the foregoing, and the Allied or Associated Power receiving the same agrees to be charged with such value, and the amount thereof shall be treated as a payment by Germany to be divided in accordance with Article 237 of this Part of the present Treaty.

In cases where the right to require physical restoration as above provided is exercised, the Commission shall ensure that the amount to be credited against the reparation obligation of Germany shall be the fair value of work done or materials supplied by Germany, and that the claim made by the interested Power in respect of the damage so repaired by physical restoration shall be discharged to the extent of the proportion which the damage thus repaired bears to the whole of the damage thus claimed for.

6

As an immediate advance on account of the animals referred to in paragraph 2 (*a*) above, Germany undertakes to deliver in equal monthly instalments in the three months following the coming into force of the present Treaty the following quantities of live stock:

(1) *To the French Government*

      500 stallions (3 to 7 years);
   30,000 fillies and mares (18 months to 7 years), type: Ardennais, Boulonnais or
              Belgian;
    2,000 bulls (18 months to 3 years);
   90,000 milch cows (2 to 6 years);
    1,000 rams;
  100,000 sheep;
   10,000 goats.

(2) *To the Belgian Government*

      200 stallions (3 to 7 years), large Belgian type;
    5,000 mares (3 to 7 years), large Belgian type;
    5,000 fillies (18 months to 3 years), large Belgian type;
    2,000 bulls (18 months to 3 years);
   50,000 milch cows (2 to 6 years);
   40,000 heifers;
      200 rams;
   20,000 sheep;
   15,000 sows.

The animals delivered shall be of average health and condition.

To the extent that animals so delivered cannot be identified as animals taken away or seized, the value of such animals shall be credited against the reparation obligations of Germany in accordance with paragraph 5 of this Annex.

7

Without waiting for the decisions of the Commission referred to in paragraph 4 of this Annex to be taken, Germany must continue the delivery to France of the agricultural material referred to in Article III of the renewal dated January 16, 1919, of the Armistice.

ANNEX V

1

Germany accords the following options for the delivery of coal and derivatives of coal to the undermentioned signatories of the present Treaty.

2

Germany undertakes to deliver to France seven million tons of coal per year for ten years. In addition, Germany undertakes to deliver to France annually for a period not exceeding ten years an amount of coal equal to the difference between the annual production before the war of the coal mines of the Nord and Pas de Calais, destroyed as a result of the war, and the production of the mines of the same area during the years in question: such delivery not to exceed twenty million tons in any one year of the first five years, and eight million tons in any one year of the succeeding five years.

It is understood that due diligence will be exercised in the restoration of the destroyed mines in the Nord and the Pas de Calais.

3

Germany undertakes to deliver to Belgium eight million tons of coal annually for ten years.

4

Germany undertakes to deliver to Italy up to the following quantities of coal:

July 1919 to June 1920				4½	million tons,
— 1920 —	1921			6	—
— 1921 —	1922			7½	—
— 1922 —	1923			8	—
— 1923 —	1924			} 8½	—
and each of the following five years					

At least two-thirds of the actual deliveries to be land-borne.

5

Germany further undertakes to deliver annually to Luxemburg, if directed by the Reparation Commission, a quantity of coal equal to the pre-war annual consumption of German coal in Luxemburg.

6

The prices to be paid for coal delivered under these options shall be as follows:

(a) For overland delivery, including delivery by barge, the German pithead price to German nationals, plus the freight to French, Belgian, Italian or Luxemburg frontiers, provided that the pithead price does not exceed the pithead price of British coal for export. In the case of Belgian bunker coal, the price shall not exceed the Dutch bunker price.

Railroad and barge tariffs shall not be higher than the lowest similar rates paid in Germany.

(b) For sea delivery, the German export price f. o. b. German ports, or the British export price f. o. b. British ports, whichever may be lower.

7

The Allied and Associated Governments interested may demand the delivery, in place of coal, of metallurgical coke in the proportion of 3 tons of coke to 4 tons of coal.

8

Germany undertakes to deliver to France, and to transport to the French frontier by rail or by water, the following products, during each of the three years following the coming into force of this Treaty:

Benzol	35, 000 tons
Coal tar	50, 000 tons
Sulphate of ammonia	30, 000 tons

All or part of the coal tar may, at the option of the French Government, be replaced by corresponding quantities of products of distillation, such as light oils, heavy oils, anthracene, naphthalene or pitch.

9

The price paid for coke and for the articles referred to in the preceding paragraph shall be the same as the price paid by German nationals under the same conditions of shipment to the French frontier or to the German ports, and shall be subject to any advantages which may be accorded similar products furnished to German nationals.

10

The foregoing options shall be exercised through the intervention of the Reparation Commission, which, subject to the specific provisions hereof, shall have power to determine all questions relative to procedure and the qualities and quantities of products, the quantity of coke which may be substituted for coal, and the times and modes of delivery and payment. In giving notice to the German Government of the foregoing options the Commission shall give at least 120 days' notice of deliveries to be made after January 1, 1920, and at least 30 days' notice of deliveries to be made between the coming into force of this Treaty and January 1, 1920. Until Germany has received the demands referred to in this paragraph, the provisions of the Protocol of December 25, 1918, (Execution of Article VI of the Armistice of November 11, 1918) remain in force. The notice to be given to the German Government of the exercise of the right of substitution accorded by paragraphs 7 and 8 shall be such as the Reparation Commission may consider sufficient. If the Commission shall determine that the full exercise of the foregoing options would interfere unduly with the industrial requirements of Germany, the Commission is authorised to postpone or to cancel deliveries, and in so doing to settle all questions of priority; but the coal to replace coal from destroyed mines shall receive priority over other deliveries.

ANNEX VI

1

Germany accords to the Reparation Commission an option to require as part of reparation the delivery by Germany of such quantities and kinds of dyestuffs and chemical drugs as the Commission may designate, not exceeding 50 per cent. of the total stock of each and every kind of dyestuff and chemical drug in Germany or under German control at the date of the coming into force of the present Treaty.

This option shall be exercised within sixty days of the receipt by the Commission of such particulars as to stocks as may be considered necessary by the Commission.

2

Germany further accords to the Reparation Commission an option to require delivery during the period from the date of the coming into force of the present Treaty until January 1, 1920, and during each period of six months thereafter until January 1, 1925, of any specified kind of dyestuff and chemical drug up to an amount not exceeding 25 per cent. of the German production of such dyestuffs and chemical drugs during the previous six months period. If in any case the production during such previous six months was, in the opinion of the Commission, less than normal, the amount required may be 25 per cent. of the normal production.

Such option shall be exercised within four weeks after the receipt of such particulars as to production and in such form as may be considered necessary by the Commission; these particulars shall be furnished by the German Government immediately after the expiration of each six months period.

3

For dyestuffs and chemical drugs delivered under paragraph 1, the price shall be fixed by the Commission having regard to pre-war net export prices and to subsequent increases of cost.

For dyestuffs and chemical drugs delivered under paragraph 2, the price shall be fixed by the Commission having regard to pre-war net export prices and subsequent variations of cost, or the lowest net selling price of similar dyestuffs and chemical drugs to any other purchaser.

4

All details, including mode and times of exercising the options, and making delivery, and all other questions arising under this arrangement shall be determined by the Reparation Commission; the German Government will furnish to the Commission all necessary information and other assistance which it may require.

5

The above expression "dyestuffs and chemical drugs" includes all synthetic dyes and drugs and intermediate or other products used in connection with dyeing, so far as they are manufactured for sale. The present arrangement shall also apply to cinchona bark and salts of quinine.

ANNEX VII

Germany renounces on her own behalf and on behalf of her nationals in favour of the Principal Allied and Associated Powers all rights, titles or privileges of whatever nature in the submarine cables set out below, or in any portions thereof:

Emden-Vigo: from the Straits of Dover to off Vigo;
Emden-Brest: from off Cherbourg to Brest;
Emden-Teneriffe: from off Dunkirk to off Teneriffe;
Emden-Azores (1): from the Straits of Dover to Fayal;
Emden-Azores (2): from the Straits of Dover to Fayal;
Azores-New York (1): from Fayal to New York;
Azores-New York (2): from Fayal to the longitude of Halifax;
Teneriffe-Monrovia: from off Teneriffe to off Monrovia;
Monrovia-Lome:

from about . . . . $\begin{cases} \text{lat.} & : 2°30' \text{ N.;} \\ \text{long.} & : 7°40' \text{ W. of Greenwich;} \end{cases}$

to about . . . . $\begin{cases} \text{lat.} & : 2°20' \text{ N.;} \\ \text{long.} & : 5°30' \text{ W. of Greenwich;} \end{cases}$

and from about . . . . $\begin{cases} \text{lat.} & : 3°48' \text{ N.;} \\ \text{long.} & : 0°00', \end{cases}$

to Lome;
Lome-Duala: from Lome to Duala;
Monrovia-Pernambuco: from off Monrovia to off Pernambuco;
Constantinople-Constanza: from Constantinople to Constanza;
Yap-Shanghai, Yap-Guam, and Yap-Menado (Celebes); from Yap Island to Shanghai, from Yap Island to Guam Island, and from Yap Island to Menado.

The value of the above mentioned cables or portions thereof in so far as they are privately owned, calculated on the basis of the original cost less a suitable allowance for depreciation, shall be credited to Germany in the reparation account.

SECTION II

Special Provisions

ARTICLE 245

Within six months after the coming into force of the present Treaty the German Government must restore to the French Government the trophies, archives, historical souvenirs or works of art carried away from France by the German authorities in the course of the war of 1870–1871 and during this last war, in accordance with a list which will be communicated to it by the French Government; particularly the French flags taken in the course of the war of 1870–1871 and all the political papers taken by the German authorities on October 10, 1870, at the chateau of Cerçay, near Brunoy

(Seine-et-Oise) belonging at the time to Mr. Rouher, formerly Minister of State.

ARTICLE 246

Within six months from the coming into force of the present Treaty, Germany will restore to His Majesty the King of the Hedjaz the original Koran of the Caliph Othman, which was removed from Medina by the Turkish authorities and is stated to have been presented to the ex-Emperor William II.

Within the same period Germany will hand over to His Britannic Majesty's Government the skull of the Sultan Mkwawa which was removed from the Protectorate of German East Africa and taken to Germany.

The delivery of the articles above referred to will be effected in such place and in such conditions as may be laid down by the Governments to which they are to be restored.

ARTICLE 247

Germany undertakes to furnish to the University of Louvain, within three months after a request made by it and transmitted through the intervention of the Reparation Commission, manuscripts, incunabula, printed books, maps and objects of collection corresponding in number and value to those destroyed in the burning by Germany of the Library of Louvain. All details regarding such replacement will be determined by the Reparation Commission.

Germany undertakes to deliver to Belgium, through the Reparation Commission, within six months of the coming into force of the present Treaty, in order to enable Belgium to reconstitute two great artistic works:

(1) The leaves of the triptych of the Mystic Lamb painted by the Van Eyck brothers, formerly in the Church of St. Bavon at Ghent, now in the Berlin Museum;

(2) The leaves of the triptych of the Last Supper, painted by Dierick Bouts, formerly in the Church of St. Peter at Louvain, two of which are now in the Berlin Museum and two in the Old Pinakothek at Munich.

PART IX

FINANCIAL CLAUSES

ARTICLE 248

Subject to such exceptions as the Reparation Commission may approve, a first charge upon all the assets and revenues of the German Empire and its constituent States shall be the cost of reparation and all other costs arising under the present Treaty or any treaties or agreements supplementary thereto or under arrangements concluded between Germany and the Allied and Associated Powers during the Armistice or its extensions.

Up to May 1, 1921, the German Government shall not export or dispose of, and shall forbid the export or disposal of, gold without the previous approval of the Allied and Associated Powers acting through the Reparation Commission.

ARTICLE 249

There shall be paid by the German Government the total cost of all armies of the Allied and Associated Governments in occupied German territory from the date of the signature of the Armistice of November 11, 1918, including the keep of men and beasts, lodging and billeting, pay and allowances, salaries and wages, bedding, heating, lighting, clothing, equipment, harness and saddlery, armament and rolling-stock, air services, treatment of sick and wounded, veterinary and remount services, transport service of all sorts (such as by rail, sea or river, motor lorries), communications and correspondence, and in general the cost of all administrative or technical services the working of which is necessary for the training of troops and for keeping their numbers up to strength and preserving their military efficiency.

The cost of such liabilities under the above heads so far as they relate to purchases or requisitions by the Allied and Associated Governments in the occupied territories shall be paid by the German Government to the Allied and Associated Governments in marks at the current or agreed rate of exchange. All other of the above costs shall be paid in gold marks.

ARTICLE 250

Germany confirms the surrender of all material handed over to the Allied and Associated Powers in accordance with the Armistice of November 11, 1918, and subsequent Armistice Agreements, and recognizes the title of the Allied and Associated Powers to such material.

There shall be credited to the German Government, against the sums due from it to the Allied and Associated Powers for reparation, the value, as assessed by the Reparation Commission, referred to in Article 233 of Part VIII (Reparation) of the present Treaty, of the material handed over in accordance with Article VII of the Armistice of November 11, 1918, or Article III of the Armistice Agreement of January 16, 1919, as well as of any other material handed over in accordance with the Armistice of November 11, 1918, and of subsequent Armistice Agreements, for which, as having non-military value, credit should in the judgment of the Reparation Commission be allowed to the German Government.

Property belonging to the Allied and Associated Governments or their nationals restored or surrendered under the Armistice Agreements in specie shall not be credited to the German Government.

Article 251

The priority of the charges established by Article 248 shall, subject to the qualifications made below, be as follows:

(*a*) The cost of the armies of occupation as defined under Article 249 during the Armistice and its extensions;

(*b*) The cost of any armies of occupation as defined under Article 249 after the coming into force of the present Treaty;

(*c*) The cost of reparation arising out of the present Treaty or any treaties or conventions supplementary thereto;

(*d*) The cost of all other obligations incumbent on Germany under the Armistice Conventions or under this Treaty or any treaties or conventions supplementary thereto.

The payment for such supplies of food and raw material for Germany and such other payments as may be judged by the Allied and Associated Powers to be essential to enable Germany to meet her obligations in respect of reparation will have priority to the extent and upon the conditions which have been or may be determined by the Governments of the said Powers.

Article 252

The right of each of the Allied and Associated Powers to dispose of enemy assets and property within its jurisdiction at the date of the coming into force of the present Treaty is not affected by the foregoing provisions.

Article 253

Nothing in the foregoing provisions shall prejudice in any manner charges or mortgages lawfully effected in favour of the Allied or Associated Powers or their nationals respectively, before the date at which a state of war existed between Germany and the Allied or Associated Power concerned, by the German Empire or its constituent States, or by German nationals, on assets in their ownership at that date.

Article 254

The Powers to which German territory is ceded shall, subject to the qualifications made in Article 255, undertake to pay:

(1) A portion of the debt of the German Empire as it stood on August 1, 1914, calculated on the basis of the ratio between the average for the three financial years 1911, 1912, 1913, of such revenues of the ceded territory, and the average for the same years of such revenues of the whole German Empire as in the judgment of the Reparation Commission are best calculated to represent the relative ability of the respective territories to make payment;

(2) A portion of the debt as it stood on August 1, 1914, of the German State to which the ceded territory belonged, to be determined in accordance with the principle stated above.

Such portions shall be determined by the Reparation Commission.

The method of discharging the obligation, both in respect of capital and of interest, so assumed shall be fixed by the Reparation Commission. Such method may take the form, *inter alia*, of the assumption by the Power to which the territory is ceded of Germany's liability for the German debt held by her nationals. But in the event of the method adopted involving any payments to the German Government, such payments shall be transferred to the Reparation Commission on account of the sums due for reparation so long as any balance in respect of such sums remains unpaid.

Article 255

(1) As an exception to the above provision and inasmuch as in 1871 Germany refused to undertake any portion of the burden of the French debt, France shall be, in respect of Alsace-Lorraine, exempt from any payment under Article 254.

(2) In the case of Poland that portion of the debt which, in the opinion of the Reparation Commission, is attributable to the measures taken by the German and Prussian Governments for the German colonisation of Poland shall be excluded from the apportionment to be made under Article 254.

(3) In the case of all ceded territories other than Alsace-Lorraine, that portion of the debt of the German Empire or German States which, in the opinion of the Reparation Commission, represents expenditure by the Governments of the German Empire or States upon the Government properties referred to in Article 256 shall be excluded from the apportionment to be made under Article 254.

Article 256

Powers to which German territory is ceded shall acquire all property and possessions situated therein belonging to the German Empire or to the German States, and the value of such acquisitions shall be fixed by the Reparation Commission, and paid by the State acquiring the territory to the Reparation Commission for the credit of the German Government on account of the sums due for reparation.

For the purposes of this Article the property and possessions of the German Empire and States shall be deemed to include all the property of the Crown, the Empire or the States, and the private property of the former German Emperor and other Royal personages.

In view of the terms on which Alsace-Lorraine was ceded to Germany in 1871, France shall be exempt in respect thereof from making any payment or credit under this Article for any property or possessions of the German Empire or States situated therein.

Belgium also shall be exempt from making any payment or any credit under this Article for any property or possessions of the German Empire or States situated in German territory ceded to Belgium under the present Treaty.

ARTICLE 257

In the case of the former German territories, including colonies, protectorates or dependencies, administered by a Mandatory under Article 22 of Part I (League of Nations) of the present Treaty, neither the territory nor the Mandatory Power shall be charged with any portion of the debt of the German Empire or States.

All property and possessions belonging to the German Empire or to the German States situated in such territories shall be transferred with the territories to the Mandatory Power in its capacity as such and no payment shall be made nor any credit given to those Governments in consideration of this transfer.

For the purposes of this Article the property and possessions of the German Empire and of the German States shall be deemed to include all the property of the Crown, the Empire or the States and the private property of the former German Emperor and other Royal personages.

ARTICLE 258

Germany renounces all rights accorded to her or her nationals by treaties, conventions or agreements, of whatsoever kind, to representation upon or participation in the control or administration of commissions, state banks, agencies or other financial or economic organisations of an international character, exercising powers of control or administration, and operating in any of the Allied or Associated States, or in Austria, Hungary, Bulgaria or Turkey, or in the dependencies of these States, or in the former Russian Empire.

ARTICLE 259

(1) Germany agrees to deliver within one month from the date of the coming into force of the present Treaty, to such authority as the Principal Allied and Associated Powers may designate, the sum in gold which was to be deposited in the Reichsbank in the name of the Council of the Administration of the Ottoman Public Debt as security for the first issue of Turkish Government currency notes.

(2) Germany recognises her obligation to make annually for the period of twelve years the payments in gold for which provision is made in the German Treasury Bonds deposited by her from time to time in the name of the Council of the Administration of the Ottoman Public Debt as security for the second and subsequent issues of Turkish Government currency notes.

(3) Germany undertakes to deliver, within one month from the coming into force of the present Treaty, to such authority as the Principal Allied and Associated Powers may designate, the gold deposit constituted in the Reichsbank or elsewhere, representing the residue of the advance in gold agreed to on May 5, 1915, by the Council of the Administration of the Ottoman Public Debt to the Imperial Ottoman Government.

(4) Germany agrees to transfer to the Principal Allied and Associated Powers any title that she may have to the sum in gold and silver transmitted by her to the Turkish Ministry of Finance in November, 1918, in anticipation of the payment to be made in May, 1919, for the service of the Turkish Internal Loan.

(5) Germany undertakes to transfer to the Principal Allied and Associated Powers, within a period of one month from the coming into force of the present Treaty, any sums in gold transferred as pledge or as collateral security to the German Government or its nationals in connection with loans made by them to the Austro-Hungarian Government.

(6) Without prejudice to Article 292 of Part X (Economic Clauses) of the present Treaty, Germany confirms the renunciation provided for in Article XV of the Armistice of November 11, 1918, of any benefit disclosed by the Treaties of Bucharest and of Brest-Litovsk and by the treaties supplementary thereto.

Germany undertakes to transfer, either to Roumania or to the Principal Allied and Associated Powers as the case may be, all monetary instruments, specie, securities and negotiable instruments, or goods, which she has received under the aforesaid Treaties.

(7) The sums of money and all securities, instruments and goods of whatsoever nature, to be delivered, paid and transferred under the provisions of this Article, shall be disposed of by the Principal Allied and Associated Powers in a manner hereafter to be determined by those Powers.

ARTICLE 260

Without prejudice to the renunciation of any rights by Germany on behalf of herself or of her nationals in the other provisions of the present Treaty, the Reparation Commission may within one year from the coming into force of the present Treaty demand that the German Government become possessed of any rights and interests of German nationals in any public utility undertaking or in any concession operating in Russia, China, Turkey, Austria, Hungary and Bulgaria, or in the possessions or dependencies of these States or in any territory formerly belonging to Germany or her allies, to be ceded by Germany or her allies to any Power or to be administered by a Mandatory under the present Treaty, and may require that the German Government transfer, within six months of the date of demand, all such rights and interests and any similar rights and interests the German Government may itself possess to the Reparation Commission.

Germany shall be responsible for indemnifying her nationals so dispossessed, and the Reparation Commission shall credit Germany, on account of sums due for reparation, with such sums in respect of the value of the transferred rights and interests as may be assessed by the Reparation Commission, and the German Government shall, within six months from the coming into force of the present Treaty, communicate to the Reparation

Commission all such rights and interests, whether already granted, contingent or not yet exercised, and shall renounce on behalf of itself and its nationals in favour of the Allied and Associated Powers all such rights and interests which have not been so communicated.

ARTICLE 261

Germany undertakes to transfer to the Allied and Associated Powers any claims she may have to payment or repayment by the Governments of Austria, Hungary, Bulgaria or Turkey, and, in particular, any claims which may arise, now or hereafter, from the fulfilment of undertakings made by Germany during the war to those Governments.

ARTICLE 262

Any monetary obligation due by Germany arising out of the present Treaty and expressed in terms of gold marks shall be payable at the option of the creditors in pounds sterling payable in London; gold dollars of the United States of America payable in New York; gold francs payable in Paris; or gold lire payable in Rome.

For the purpose of this Article the gold coins mentioned above shall be defined as being of the weight and fineness of gold as enacted by law on January 1, 1914.

ARTICLE 263

Germany gives a guarantee to the Brazilian Government that all sums representing the sale of coffee belonging to the State of Sao Paolo in the ports of Hamburg, Bremen, Antwerp and Trieste, which were deposited with the Bank of Bleichröder at Berlin, shall be reimbursed together with interest at the rate or rates agreed upon. Germany, having prevented the transfer of the sums in question to the State of Sao Paolo at the proper time, guarantees also that the reimbursement shall be effected at the rate of exchange of the day of the deposit.

PART X

ECONOMIC CLAUSES

SECTION I

Commercial Relations

CHAPTER I

CUSTOMS REGULATIONS, DUTIES AND RESTRICTIONS

ARTICLE 264

Germany undertakes that goods the produce or manufacture of any one of the Allied or Associated States imported into German territory, from whatsoever place arriving, shall not be subjected to other or higher duties or charges (including internal charges) than those to which the like goods the produce or manufacture of any other such State or of any other foreign country are subject.

Germany will not maintain or impose any prohibition or restriction on the importation into German territory of any goods the produce or manufacture of the territories of any one of the Allied or Associated States, from whatsoever place arriving, which shall not equally extend to the importation of the like goods the produce or manufacture of any other such State or of any other foreign country.

ARTICLE 265

Germany further undertakes that, in the matter of the régime applicable on importation, no discrimination against the commerce of any of the Allied and Associated States as compared with any other of the said States or any other foreign country shall be made, even by indirect means, such as customs regulations or procedure, methods of verification or analysis, conditions of payment of duties, tariff classification or interpretation, or the operation of monopolies.

ARTICLE 266

In all that concerns exportation Germany undertakes that goods, natural products or manufactured articles, exported from German territory to the territories of any one of the Allied or Associated States shall not be subjected to other or higher duties or charges (including internal charges) than those paid on the like goods exported to any other such State or to any other foreign country.

Germany will not maintain or impose any prohibition or restriction on the exportation of any goods sent from her territory to any one of the Allied or Associated States which shall not equally extend to the exportation of the like goods, natural products or manufactured articles, sent to any other such State or to any other foreign country.

ARTICLE 267

Every favour, immunity or privilege in regard to the importation, exportation or transit of goods granted by Germany to any Allied or Associated State or to any other foreign country whatever shall simultaneously and unconditionally, without request and without compensation, be extended to all the Allied and Associated States.

ARTICLE 268

The provisions of Articles 264 to 267 inclusive of this Chapter and of Article 323 of Part XII (Ports, Waterways and Railways) of the present Treaty are subject to the following exceptions:

(a) For a period of five years from the coming into force of the present Treaty, natural or manufactured products which both originate in and come from the territories of Alsace and Lorraine reunited to France shall, on importation into German customs territory, be exempt from all customs duty.

The French Government shall fix each year, by decree communicated to the German Government, the nature and amount of the products which shall enjoy this exemption.

The amount of each product which may be thus sent annually into Germany shall not exceed the average of the amounts sent annually in the years 1911–1913.

Further, during the period above mentioned the German Government shall allow the free export from Germany, and the free re-importation into Germany, exempt from all customs duties and other charges (including internal charges), of yarns, tissues, and other textile materials or textile products of any kind and in any condition, sent from Germany into the territories of Alsace or Lorraine, to be subjected there to any finishing process, such as bleaching, dyeing, printing, mercerisation, gassing, twisting or dressing.

(*b*) During a period of three years from the coming into force of the present Treaty natural or manufactured products which both originate in and come from Polish territories which before the war were part of Germany shall, on importation into German customs territory, be exempt from all customs duty.

The Polish Government shall fix each year, by decree communicated to the German Government, the nature and amount of the products which shall enjoy this exemption.

The amount of each product which may be thus sent annually into Germany shall not exceed the average of the amounts sent annually in the years 1911–1913.

(*c*) The Allied and Associated Powers reserve the right to require Germany to accord freedom from customs duty, on importation into German customs territory, to natural products and manufactured articles which both originate in and come from the Grand Duchy of Luxemburg, for a period of five years from the coming into force of the present Treaty.

The nature and amount of the products which shall enjoy the benefits of this régime shall be communicated each year to the German Government.

The amount of each product which may be thus sent annually into Germany shall not exceed the average of the amounts sent annually in the years 1911–1913.

Article 269

During the first six months after the coming into force of the present Treaty, the duties imposed by Germany on imports from Allied and Associated States shall not be higher than the most favourable duties which were applied to imports into Germany on July 31, 1914.

During a further period of thirty months after the expiration of the first six months, this provision shall continue to be applied exclusively with regard to products which, being comprised in Section A of the First Category of the German Customs Tariff of December 25, 1902, enjoyed at the above-mentioned date (July 31, 1914) rates conventionalised by treaties with the Allied and Associated Powers, with the addition of all kinds of wine and vegetable oils, of artificial silk and of washed or scoured wool, whether or not they were the subject of special conventions before July 31, 1914.

ARTICLE 270

The Allied and Associated Powers reserve the right to apply to German territory occupied by their troops a special customs régime as regards imports and exports, in the event of such a measure being necessary in their opinion in order to safeguard the economic interests of the population of these territories.

CHAPTER II

SHIPPING

ARTICLE 271

As regards sea fishing, maritime coasting trade, and maritime towage, vessels of the Allied and Associated Powers shall enjoy, in German territorial waters, the treatment accorded to vessels of the most favoured nation.

ARTICLE 272

Germany agrees that, notwithstanding any stipulation to the contrary contained in the Conventions relating to the North Sea fisheries and liquor traffic, all rights of inspection and police shall, in the case of fishing-boats of the Allied Powers, be exercised solely by ships belonging to those Powers.

ARTICLE 273

In the case of vessels of the Allied or Associated Powers, all classes of certificates or documents relating to the vessel, which were recognised as valid by Germany before the war, or which may hereafter be recognised as valid by the principal maritime States, shall be recognised by Germany as valid and as equivalent to the corresponding certificates issued to German vessels.

A similar recognition shall be accorded to the certificates and documents issued to their vessels by the Governments of new States, whether they have a sea-coast or not, provided that such certificates and documents shall be issued in conformity with the general practice observed in the principal maritime States.

The High Contracting Parties agree to recognise the flag flown by the vessels of an Allied or Associated Power having no sea-coast which are registered at some one specified place situated in its territory; such place shall serve as the port of registry of such vessels.

CHAPTER III

UNFAIR COMPETITION

ARTICLE 274

Germany undertakes to adopt all the necessary legislative and administrative measures to protect goods the produce or manufacture of any one of the Allied and Associated Powers from all forms of unfair competition in commercial transactions.

Germany undertakes to prohibit and repress by seizure and by other appropriate remedies the importation, exportation, manufacture, distribution, sale or offering for sale in its territory of all goods bearing upon themselves or their usual get-up or wrappings any marks, names, devices, or description whatsoever which are calculated to convey directly or indirectly a false indication of the origin, type, nature, or special characteristics of such goods.

ARTICLE 275

Germany undertakes on condition that reciprocity is accorded in these matters to respect any law, or any administrative or judicial decision given in conformity with such law, in force in any Allied or Associated State and duly communicated to her by the proper authorities, defining or regulating the right to any regional appellation in respect of wine or spirits produced in the State to which the region belongs, or the conditions under which the use of any such appellation may be permitted; and the importation, exportation, manufacture, distribution, sale or offering for sale of products or articles bearing regional appellations inconsistent with such law or order shall be prohibited by the German Government and repressed by the measures prescribed in the preceding Article.

CHAPTER IV

TREATMENT OF NATIONALS OF ALLIED AND ASSOCIATED POWERS

ARTICLE 276

Germany undertakes:

(a) Not to subject the nationals of the Allied and Associated Powers to any prohibition in regard to the exercise of occupations, professions, trade and industry, which shall not be equally applicable to all aliens without exception;

(b) Not to subject the nationals of the Allied and Associated Powers in regard to the rights referred to in paragraph (a) to any regulation or restriction which might contravene directly or indirectly the stipulations of the said paragraph, or which shall be other or more disadvantageous than those which are applicable to nationals of the most favoured nation;

(c) Not to subject the nationals of the Allied and Associated Powers, their property, rights or interests, including companies and associations in which they are interested, to any charge, tax or impost, direct or indirect, other or higher than those which are or may be imposed on her own nationals or their property, rights or interests;

(*d*) Not to subject the nationals of any one of the Allied and Associated Powers to any restriction which was not applicable on July 1, 1914, to the nationals of such Powers unless such restriction is likewise imposed on her own nationals.

Article 277

The nationals of the Allied and Associated Powers shall enjoy in German territory a constant protection for their persons and for their property, rights and interests, and shall have free access to the courts of law.

Article 278

Germany undertakes to recognise any new nationality which has been or may be acquired by her nationals under the laws of the Allied and Associated Powers and in accordance with the decisions of the competent authorities of these Powers pursuant to naturalisation laws or under treaty stipulations, and to regard such persons as having, in consequence of the acquisition of such new nationality, in all respects severed their allegiance to their country of origin.

Article 279

The Allied and Associated Powers may appoint consuls-general, consuls, vice-consuls, and consular agents in German towns and ports. Germany undertakes to approve the designation of the consuls-general, consuls, vice-consuls, and consular agents, whose names shall be notified to her, and to admit them to the exercise of their functions in conformity with the usual rules and customs.

Chapter V

GENERAL ARTICLES

Article 280

The obligations imposed on Germany by Chapter I and by Articles 271 and 272 of Chapter II above shall cease to have effect five years from the date of the coming into force of the present Treaty, unless otherwise provided in the text, or unless the Council of the League of Nations shall, at least twelve months before the expiration of that period, decide that these obligations shall be maintained for a further period with or without amendment.

Article 276 of Chapter IV shall remain in operation, with or without amendment, after the period of five years for such further period, if any, not exceeding five years, as may be determined by a majority of the Council of the League of Nations.

ARTICLE 281

If the German Government engages in international trade, it shall not in respect thereof have or be deemed to have any rights, privileges or immunities of sovereignty.

SECTION II

Treaties

ARTICLE 282

From the coming into force of the present Treaty and subject to the provisions thereof the multilateral treaties, conventions and agreements of an economic or technical character enumerated below and in the subsequent Articles shall alone be applied as between Germany and those of the Allied and Associated Powers party thereto:

(1) Conventions of March 14, 1884,[22] December 1, 1886,[23] and March 23, 1887,[23] and Final Protocol of July 7, 1887,[24] regarding the protection of submarine cables.

(2) Convention of October 11, 1909, regarding the international circulation of motor-cars.

(3) Agreement of May 15, 1886, regarding the sealing of railway trucks subject to customs inspection, and Protocol of May 18, 1907.

(4) Agreement of May 15, 1886, regarding the technical standardisation of railways.

(5) Convention of July 5, 1890, regarding the publication of customs tariffs and the organisation of an International Union for the publication of customs tariffs.[25]

(6) Convention of December 31, 1913, regarding the unification of commercial statistics.

(7) Convention of April 25, 1907, regarding the raising of the Turkish customs tariff.

(8) Convention of March 14, 1857, for the redemption of toll dues on the Sound and Belts.

(9) Convention of June 22, 1861, for the redemption of the Stade Toll on the Elbe.

(10) Convention of July 16, 1863, for the redemption of the toll dues on the Scheldt.

(11) Convention of October 29, 1888, regarding the establishment of a definite arrangement guaranteeing the free use of the Suez Canal.

---

[22] TS 380, *ante,* vol. 1, p. 89.
[23] TS 380–2, *ante,* vol. 1, p. 112
[24] TS 380–3, *ante,* vol. 1, p. 114.
[25] TS 384, *ante,* vol. 1, p. 172.

(12) Conventions of September 23, 1910, respecting the unification of certain regulations regarding collisions [26] and salvage at sea.[27]

(13) Convention of December 21, 1904, regarding the exemption of hospital ships from dues and charges in ports.[28]

(14) Convention of February 4, 1898, regarding the tonnage measurement of vessels for inland navigation.

(15) Convention of September 26, 1906, for the suppression of night-work for women.

(16) Convention of September 26, 1906, for the suppression of the use of white phosphorus in the manufacture of matches.

(17) Conventions of May 18, 1904,[29] and May 4, 1910, regarding the suppression of the White Slave Traffic.

(18) Convention of May 4, 1910, regarding the suppression of obscene publications.[30]

(19) Sanitary Conventions of January 30, 1892, April 15, 1893, April 3, 1894, March 19, 1897, and December 3, 1903.[31]

(20) Convention of May 20, 1875, regarding the unification and improvement of the metric system.[32]

(21) Convention of November 29, 1906, regarding the unification of pharmacopœial formulae for potent drugs.[33]

(22) Convention of November 16 and 19, 1885, regarding the establishment of a concert pitch.

(23) Convention of June 7, 1905, regarding the creation of an International Agricultural Institute at Rome.[34]

(24) Conventions of November 3, 1881, and April 15, 1889, regarding precautionary measures against phylloxera.

(25) Convention of March 19, 1902, regarding the protection of birds useful to agriculture.

(26) Convention of June 12, 1902, as to the protection of minors.

ARTICLE 283

From the coming into force of the present Treaty the High Contracting Parties shall apply the conventions and agreements hereinafter mentioned, in so far as concerns them, on condition that the special stipulations contained in this Article are fulfilled by Germany.

---

[26] 1911 For. Rel. 19.
[27] TS 576, *ante,* vol. 1, p. 780.
[28] TS 459, *ante,* vol. 1, p. 430.
[29] TS 496, *ante,* vol. 1, p. 424.
[30] TS 559, *ante,* vol. 1, p. 748.
[31] TS 466, *ante,* vol. 1, p. 359.
[32] TS 378, *ante,* vol. 1, p. 39.
[33] TS 510, *ante,* vol. 1, p. 568.
[34] TS 489, *ante,* vol. 1, p. 436.

Postal Conventions:

Conventions and agreements of the Universal Postal Union concluded at Vienna, July 4, 1891.[35]

Conventions and agreements of the Postal Union signed at Washington, June 15, 1897.[36]

Conventions and agreements of the Postal Union signed at Rome, May 26, 1906.[37]

Telegraphic Conventions:

International Telegraphic Conventions signed at St. Petersburg July 10/22, 1875.

Regulations and Tariffs drawn up by the International Telegraphic Conference, Lisbon, June 11, 1908.

Germany undertakes not to refuse her assent to the conclusion by the new States of the special arrangements referred to in the conventions and agreements relating to the Universal Postal Union and to the International Telegraphic Union, to which the said new States have adhered or may adhere.

ARTICLE 284

From the coming into force of the present Treaty the High Contracting Parties shall apply, in so far as concerns them, the International Radio-Telegraphic Convention of July 5, 1912,[38] on condition that Germany fulfils the provisional regulations which will be indicated to her by the Allied and Associated Powers.

If within five years after the coming into force of the present Treaty a new convention regulating international radio-telegraphic communications should have been concluded to take the place of the Convention of July 5, 1912, this new convention shall bind Germany, even if Germany should refuse either to take part in drawing up the convention, or to subscribe thereto.

This new convention will likewise replace the provisional regulations in force.

ARTICLE 285

From the coming into force of the present Treaty, the High Contracting Parties shall apply in so far as concerns them and under the conditions stipulated in Article 272, the conventions hereinafter mentioned:

(1) The Conventions of May 6, 1882, and February 1, 1889, regulating the fisheries in the North Sea outside territorial waters.

(2) The Conventions and Protocols of November 16, 1887, February 14, 1893, and April 11, 1894, regarding the North Sea liquor traffic.

---

[35] *Ante,* vol. 1, p. 188.
[36] *Ante,* vol. 1, p. 206.
[37] *Ante,* vol. 1, p. 492.
[38] TS 581, *ante,* vol. 1, p. 883.

ARTICLE 286

The International Convention of Paris of March 20, 1883,[39] for the protection of industrial property, revised at Washington on June 2, 1911;[40] and the International Convention of Berne of September 9, 1886, for the protection of literary and artistic works, revised at Berlin on November 13, 1908, and completed by the additional Protocol signed at Berne on March 20, 1914, will again come into effect as from the coming into force of the present Treaty, in so far as they are not affected or modified by the exceptions and restrictions resulting therefrom.

ARTICLE 287

From the coming into force of the present Treaty the High Contracting Parties shall apply, in so far as concerns them, the Convention of the Hague of July 17, 1905, relating to civil procedure. This renewal, however, will not apply to France, Portugal and Roumania.

ARTICLE 288

The special rights and privileges granted to Germany by Article 3 of the Convention of December 2, 1899, relating to Samoa [41] shall be considered to have terminated on August 4, 1914.

ARTICLE 289

Each of the Allied or Associated Powers, being guided by the general principles or special provisions of the present Treaty, shall notify to Germany the bilateral treaties or conventions which such Allied or Associated Power wishes to revive with Germany.

The notification referred to in the present Article shall be made either directly or through the intermediary of another Power. Receipt thereof shall be acknowledged in writing by Germany. The date of the revival shall be that of the notification.

The Allied and Associated Powers undertake among themselves not to revive with Germany any conventions or treaties which are not in accordance with the terms of the present Treaty.

The notification shall mention any provisions of the said conventions and treaties which, not being in accordance with the terms of the present Treaty, shall not be considered as revived.

In case of any difference of opinion, the League of Nations will be called on to decide.

A period of six months from the coming into force of the present Treaty is allowed to the Allied and Associated Powers within which to make the notification.

---

[39] TS 379, *ante,* vol. 1, p. 80.
[40] TS 579, *ante,* vol. 1, p. 791.
[41] TS 314, *ante,* vol. 1, p. 276.

Only those bilateral treaties and conventions which have been the subject of such a notification shall be revived between the Allied and Associated Powers and Germany; all the others are and shall remain abrogated.

The above regulations apply to all bilateral treaties or conventions existing between all the Allied and Associated Powers signatories to the present Treaty and Germany, even if the said Allied and Associated Powers have not been in a state of war with Germany.

Article 290

Germany recognises that all the treaties, conventions or agreements which she has concluded with Austria, Hungary, Bulgaria or Turkey since August 1, 1914, until the coming into force of the present Treaty are and remain abrogated by the present Treaty.

Article 291

Germany undertakes to secure to the Allied and Associated Powers, and to the officials and nationals of the said Powers, the enjoyment of all the rights and advantages of any kind which she may have granted to Austria, Hungary, Bulgaria or Turkey, or to the officials and nationals of these States by treaties, conventions or arrangements concluded before August 1, 1914, so long as those treaties, conventions or arrangements remain in force.

The Allied and Associated Powers reserve the right to accept or not the enjoyment of these rights and advantages.

Article 292

Germany recognises that all treaties, conventions or arrangements which she concluded with Russia, or with any State or Government of which the territory previously formed a part of Russia, or with Roumania, before August 1, 1914, or after that date until the coming into force of the present Treaty, are and remain abrogated.

Article 293

Should an Allied or Associated Power, Russia, or a State or Government of which the territory formerly constituted a part of Russia, have been forced since August 1, 1914, by reason of military occupation or by other means or for any other cause, to grant or to allow to be granted by the act of any public authority, concessions, privileges and favours of any kind to Germany or to a German national, such concessions, privileges and favours are *ipso facto* annulled by the present Treaty.

No claims or indemnities which may result from this annulmen. shall be charged against the Allied or Associated Powers or the Powers, States, Governments or public authorities which are released from their engagements by the present Article.

ARTICLE 294

From the coming into force of the present Treaty Germany undertakes to give the Allied and Associated Powers and their nationals the benefit *ipso facto* of the rights and advantages of any kind which she has granted by treaties, conventions, or arrangements to non-belligerent States or their nationals since August 1, 1914, until the coming into force of the present Treaty, so long as those treaties, conventions or arrangements remain in force.

ARTICLE 295

Those of the High Contracting Parties who have not yet signed, or who have signed but not yet ratified, the Opium Convention signed at The Hague on January 23, 1912,[42] agree to bring the said Convention into force, and for this purpose to enact the necessary legislation without delay and in any case within a period of twelve months from the coming into force of the present Treaty.

Furthermore, they agree that ratification of the present Treaty should in the case of Powers which have not yet ratified the Opium Convention be deemed in all respects equivalent to the ratification of that Convention and to the signature of the Special Protocol [43] which was opened at The Hague in accordance with the resolutions adopted by the Third Opium Conference in 1914 for bringing the said Convention into force.

For this purpose the Government of the French Republic will communicate to the Government of the Netherlands a certified copy of the protocol of the deposit of ratifications of the present Treaty, and will invite the Government of the Netherlands to accept and deposit the said certified copy as if it were a deposit of ratifications of the Opium Convention and a signature of the Additional Protocol of 1914.

SECTION III

Debts

ARTICLE 296

There shall be settled through the intervention of Clearing Offices to be established by each of the High Contracting Parties within three months of the notification referred to in paragraph (*e*) hereafter the following classes of pecuniary obligations:

(1) Debts payable before the war and due by a national of one of the Contracting Powers, residing within its territory, to a national of an Opposing Power, residing within its territory;

(2) Debts which became payable during the war to nationals of one

---

[42] TS 612, *ante*, vol. 1, p. 855.
[43] *Ante*, vol. 1, p. 878.

Contracting Power residing within its territory and arose out of transactions or contracts with the nationals of an Opposing Power, resident within its territory, of which the total or partial execution was suspended on account of the declaration of war;

(3) Interest which has accrued due before and during the war to a national of one of the Contracting Powers in respect of securities issued by an Opposing Power, provided that the payment of interest on such securities to the nationals of that Power or to neutrals has not been suspended during the war;

(4) Capital sums which have become payable before and during the war to nationals of one of the Contracting Powers in respect of securities issued by one of the Opposing Powers, provided that the payment of such capital sums to nationals of that Power or to neutrals has not been suspended during the war.

The proceeds of liquidation of enemy property, rights and interests mentioned in Section IV and in the Annex thereto will be accounted for through the Clearing Offices, in the currency and at the rate of exchange hereinafter provided in paragraph (d), and disposed of by them under the conditions provided by the said Section and Annex.

The settlements provided for in this Article shall be effected according to the following principles and in accordance with the Annex to this Section:

(a) Each of the High Contracting Parties shall prohibit, as from the coming into force of the present Treaty, both the payment and the acceptance of payment of such debts, and also all communications between the interested parties with regard to the settlement of the said debts otherwise than through the Clearing Offices;

(b) Each of the High Contracting Parties shall be respectively responsible for the payment of such debts due by its nationals, except in the cases where before the war the debtor was in a state of bankruptcy or failure, or had given formal indication of insolvency or where the debt was due by a company whose business has been liquidated under emergency legislation during the war. Nevertheless, debts due by the inhabitants of territory invaded or occupied by the enemy before the Armistice will not be guaranteed by the States of which those territories form part;

(c) The sums due to the nationals of one of the High Contracting Parties by the nationals of an Opposing State will be debited to the Clearing Office of the country of the debtor, and paid to the creditor by the Clearing Office of the country of the creditor;

(d) Debts shall be paid or credited in the currency of such one of the Allied and Associated Powers, their colonies or protectorates, or the British Dominions or India, as may be concerned. If the debts are payable in some other currency they shall be paid or credited in the currency of the country concerned, whether an Allied or Associated Power, Colony, Protectorate, British Dominion or India, at the pre-war rate of exchange.

For the purpose of this provision the pre-war rate of exchange shall be defined as the average cable transfer rate prevailing in the Allied or Associated country concerned during the month immediately preceding the outbreak of war between the said country concerned and Germany.

If a contract provides for a fixed rate of exchange governing the conversion of the currency in which the debt is stated into the currency of the Allied or Associated country concerned, then the above provisions concerning the rate of exchange shall not apply.

In the case of new States the currency in which and the rate of exchange at which debts shall be paid or credited shall be determined by the Reparation Commission provided for in Part VIII (Reparation);

(e) The provisions of this Article and of the Annex hereto shall not apply as between Germany on the one hand and any one of the Allied and Associated Powers, their colonies or protectorates, or any one of the British Dominions or India on the other hand, unless within a period of one month from the deposit of the ratification of the present Treaty by the Power in question, or of the ratification on behalf of such Dominion or of India, notice to that effect is given to Germany by the Government of such Allied or Associated Power or of such Dominion or of India as the case may be;

(f) The Allied and Associated Powers who have adopted this Article and the Annex hereto may agree between themselves to apply them to their respective nationals established in their territory so far as regards matters between their nationals and German nationals. In this case the payments made by application of this provision will be subject to arrangements between the Allied and Associated Clearing Offices concerned.

ANNEX

1

Each of the High Contracting Parties will, within three months from the notification provided for in Article 296, paragraph (e), establish a Clearing Office for the collection and payment of enemy debts.

Local Clearing Offices may be established for any particular portion of the territories of the High Contracting Parties. Such local Clearing Offices may perform all the functions of a central Clearing Office in their respective districts, except that all transactions with the Clearing Office in the Opposing State must be effected through the central Clearing Office.

2

In this Annex the pecuniary obligations referred to in the first paragraph of Article 296 are described "as enemy debts", the persons from whom the same are due as "enemy debtors", the persons to whom they are due as "enemy creditors", the Clearing Office in the country of the creditor is called the "Creditor Clearing Office", and the Clearing Office in the country of the debtor is called the "Debtor Clearing Office."

3

The High Contracting Parties will subject contraventions of paragraph (a) of Article 296 to the same penalties as are at present provided by their legislation for trading with the enemy. They will similarly prohibit within their territory all legal process relating to payment of enemy debts, except in accordance with the provisions of this Annex.

4

The Government guarantee specified in paragraph (b) of Article 296 shall take effect whenever, for any reason, a debt shall not be recoverable, except in a case where at the date of the outbreak of war the debt was barred by the laws of prescription in force in the country of the debtor, or where the debtor was at that time in a state of bankruptcy or failure or had given formal indication of insolvency, or where the debt was due by a company whose business has been liquidated under emergency legislation during the war. In such case the procedure specified by this Annex shall apply to payment of the dividends.

The terms "bankruptcy" and "failure" refer to the application of legislation providing for such juridical conditions. The expression "formal indication of insolvency" bears the same meaning as it has in English law.

5

Creditors shall give notice to the Creditor Clearing Office within six months of its establishment of debts due to them, and shall furnish the Clearing Office with any documents and information required of them.

The High Contracting Parties will take all suitable measures to trace and punish collusion between enemy creditors and debtors. The Clearing Offices will communicate to one another any evidence and information which might help the discovery and punishment of such collusion.

The High Contracting Parties will facilitate as much as possible postal and telegraphic communication at the expense of the parties concerned and through the intervention of the Clearing Offices between debtors and creditors desirous of coming to an agreement as to the amount of their debt.

The Creditor Clearing Office will notify the Debtor Clearing Office of all debts declared to it. The Debtor Clearing Office will, in due course, inform the Creditor Clearing Office which debts are admitted and which debts are contested. In the latter case, the Debtor Clearing Office will give the grounds for the non-admission of debt.

6

When a debt has been admitted, in whole or in part, the Debtor Clearing Office will at once credit the Creditor Clearing Office with the amount admitted, and at the same time notify it of such credit.

7

The debt shall be deemed to be admitted in full and shall be credited forthwith to the Creditor Clearing Office unless within three months from the receipt of the notification or such longer time as may be agreed to by the Creditor Clearing Office notice has been given by the Debtor Clearing Office that it is not admitted.

8

When the whole or part of a debt is not admitted the two Clearing Offices will examine into the matter jointly and will endeavour to bring the parties to an agreement.

9

The Creditor Clearing Office will pay to the individual creditor the sums credited to it out of the funds placed at its disposal by the Government of its country and in accordance with the conditions fixed by the said Government, retaining any sums considered necessary to cover risks, expenses or commissions.

10

Any person having claimed payment of an enemy debt which is not admitted in whole or in part shall pay to the clearing office, by way of fine, interest at 5 per cent. on the part not admitted. Any person having unduly refused to admit the whole or part of a debt claimed from him shall pay, by way of fine, interest at 5 per cent. on the amount with regard to which his refusal shall be disallowed.

Such interest shall run from the date of expiration of the period provided for in paragraph 7 until the date on which the claim shall have been disallowed or the debt paid.

Each Clearing Office shall in so far as it is concerned take steps to collect the fines above provided for, and will be responsible if such fines cannot be collected.

The fines will be credited to the other Clearing Office, which shall retain them as a contribution towards the cost of carrying out the present provisions.

11

The balance between the Clearing Offices shall be struck monthly and the credit balance paid in cash by the debtor State within a week.

Nevertheless, any credit balances which may be due by one or more of the Allied and Associated Powers shall be retained until complete payment shall have been effected of the sums due to the Allied or Associated Powers or their nationals on account of the war.

12

To facilitate discussion between the Clearing Offices each of them shall have a representative at the place where the other is established.

13

Except for special reasons all discussions in regard to claims will, so far as possible, take place at the Debtor Clearing Office.

14

In conformity with Article 296, paragraph (*b*), the High Contracting Parties are responsible for the payment of the enemy debts owing by their nationals.

The Debtor Clearing Office will therefore credit the Creditor Clearing Office with all debts admitted, even in case of inability to collect them from the individual debtor. The Governments concerned will, nevertheless, invest their respective Clearing Offices with all necessary powers for the recovery of debts which have been admitted.

As an exception, the admitted debts owing by persons having suffered injury from acts of war shall only be credited to the Creditor Clearing Office when the compensation due to the person concerned in respect of such injury shall have been paid.

15

Each Government will defray the expenses of the Clearing Office set up in its territory, including the salaries of the staff.

16

Where the two Clearing Offices are unable to agree whether a debt claimed is due, or in case of a difference between an enemy debtor and an enemy creditor or between the Clearing Offices, the dispute shall either be referred to arbitration if the parties so agree under conditions fixed by agreement between them, or referred to the Mixed Arbitral Tribunal provided for in Section VI hereafter.

At the request of the Creditor Clearing Office the dispute may, however, be submitted to the jurisdiction of the Courts of the place of domicile of the debtor.

17

Recovery of sums found by the Mixed Arbitral Tribunal, the Court, or the Arbitration Tribunal to be due shall be effected through the Clearing Offices as if these sums were debts admitted by the Debtor Clearing Office.

18

Each of the Governments concerned shall appoint an agent who will be responsible for the presentation to the Mixed Arbitral Tribunal of the cases conducted on behalf of its Clearing Office. This agent will exercise a general control over the representatives or counsel employed by its nationals.

Decisions will be arrived at on documentary evidence, but it will be open to the Tribunal to hear the parties in person, or according to their preference by their representatives approved by the two Governments, or by the agent referred to above, who shall be competent to intervene along with the party or to re-open and maintain a claim abandoned by the same.

19

The Clearing Offices concerned will lay before the Mixed Arbitral Tribunal all the information and documents in their possession, so as to enable the Tribunal to decide rapidly on the cases which are brought before it.

20

Where one of the parties concerned appeals against the joint decision of the two Clearing Offices he shall make a deposit against the costs, which deposit shall only be refunded when the first judgment is modified in favour of the appellant and in proportion to the success he may attain, his opponent in case of such a refund being required to pay an equivalent proportion of the costs and expenses. Security accepted by the Tribunal may be substituted for a deposit.

A fee of 5 per cent. of the amount in dispute shall be charged in respect of all cases brought before the Tribunal. This fee shall, unless the Tribunal directs otherwise, be borne by the unsuccessful party. Such fee shall be added to the deposit referred to. It is also independent of their security.

The Tribunal may award to one of the parties a sum in respect of the expenses of the proceedings.

Any sum payable under this paragraph shall be credited to the Clearing Office of the successful party as a separate item.

21

With a view to the rapid settlement of claims, due regard shall be paid in the appointment of all persons connected with the Clearing Offices or with the Mixed Arbitral Tribunal to their knowledge of the language of the other country concerned.

Each of the Clearing Offices will be at liberty to correspond with the other and to forward documents in its own language.

22

Subject to any special agreement to the contrary between the Governments concerned, debts shall carry interest in accordance with the following provisions:

Interest shall not be payable on sums of money due by way of dividend, interest or other periodical payments which themselves represent interest on capital.

The rate of interest shall be 5 per cent. per annum except in cases where, by contract, law or custom, the creditor is entitled to payment of interest at a different rate. In such cases the rate to which he is entitled shall prevail.

Interest shall run from the date of commencement of hostilities (or, if the sum of money to be recovered fell due during the war, from the date at which it fell due) until the sum is credited to the Clearing Office of the creditor.

Sums due by way of interest shall be treated as debts admitted by the Clearing Offices and shall be credited to the Creditor Clearing Office in the same way as such debts.

23

Where by decision of the Clearing Offices or the Mixed Arbitral Tribunal a claim is held not to fall within Article 296, the creditor shall be at liberty to prosecute the claim before the Courts or to take such other proceedings as may be open to him.

The presentation of a claim to the Clearing Office suspends the operation of any period of prescription.

24

The High Contracting Parties agree to regard the decisions of the Mixed Arbitral Tribunal as final and conclusive, and to render them binding upon their nationals.

25

In any case where a Creditor Clearing Office declines to notify a claim to the Debtor Clearing Office, or to take any step provided for in this Annex, intended to make effective in whole or in part a request of which it has received due notice, the enemy creditor shall be entitled to receive from the Clearing Office a certificate setting out the amount of the claim, and shall then be entitled to prosecute the claim before the courts or to take such other proceedings as may be open to him.

SECTION IV

Property, Rights and Interests

ARTICLE 297

The question of private property, rights and interests in an enemy country shall be settled according to the principles laid down in this Section and to the provisions of the Annex hereto.

(a) The exceptional war measures and measures of transfer (defined in paragraph 3 of the Annex hereto) taken by Germany with respect to the property, rights and interests of nationals of Allied or Associated Powers, including companies and associations in which they are interested, when liquidation has not been completed, shall be immediately discontinued or stayed and the property, rights and interests concerned restored to their owners, who shall enjoy full rights therein in accordance with the provisions of Article 298.

(b) Subject to any contrary stipulations which may be provided for in the present Treaty, the Allied and Associated Powers reserve the right to retain and liquidate all property, rights and interests belonging at the date of the coming into force of the present Treaty to German nationals, or companies controlled by them, within their territories, colonies, possessions and protectorates, including territories ceded to them by the present Treaty.

The liquidation shall be carried out in accordance with the laws of the Allied or Associated State concerned, and the German owner shall not be able to dispose of such property, rights or interests nor to subject them to any charge without the consent of that State.

German nationals who acquire *ipso facto* the nationality of an Allied or Associated Power in accordance with the provisions of the present Treaty will not be considered as German nationals within the meaning of this paragraph.

(c) The price or the amount of compensation in respect of the exercise of the right referred to in the preceding paragraph (b) will be fixed in accordance with the methods of sale or valuation adopted by the laws of the country in which the property has been retained or liquidated.

(d) As between the Allied and Associated Powers or their nationals on the one hand and Germany or her nationals on the other hand, all the exceptional war measures, or measures of transfer, or acts done or to be done in execution of such measures as defined in paragraphs 1 and 3 of the Annex hereto shall be considered as final and binding upon all persons except as regards the reservations laid down in the present Treaty.

(e) The nationals of Allied and Associated Powers shall be entitled to compensation in respect of damage or injury inflicted upon their property, rights or interests, including any company or association in which they are interested, in German territory as it existed on August 1, 1914, by the application either of the exceptional war measures or measures of transfer mentioned in paragraphs 1 and 3 of the Annex hereto. The claims made in this respect by such nationals shall be investigated, and the total of the compensation shall be determined by the Mixed Arbitral Tribunal provided for in Section VI or by an Arbitrator appointed by that Tribunal. This compensation shall be borne by Germany, and may be charged upon the property of German nationals within the territory or under the control of the claimant's State. This property may be constituted as a pledge for enemy liabilities under the conditions fixed by paragraph 4 of the Annex hereto. The payment of this compensation may be made by the Allied or Associated State, and the amount will be debited to Germany.

(*f*) Whenever a national of an Allied or Associated Power is entitled to property which has been subjected to a measure of transfer in German territory and expresses a desire for its restitution, his claim for compensation in accordance with paragraph (*e*) shall be satisfied by the restitution of the said property if it still exists in specie.

In such case Germany shall take all necessary steps to restore the evicted owner to the possession of his property, free from all encumbrances or burdens with which it may have been charged after the liquidation, and to indemnify all third parties injured by the restitution.

If the restitution provided for in this paragraph cannot be effected, private agreements arranged by the intermediation of the Powers concerned or the Clearing Offices provided for in the Annex to Section III may be made, in order to secure that the national of the Allied or Associated Power may secure compensation for the injury referred to in paragraph (*e*) by the grant of advantages or equivalents which he agrees to accept in place of the property, rights or interests of which he was deprived.

Through restitution in accordance with this Article, the price or the amount of compensation fixed by the application of paragraph (*e*) will be reduced by the actual value of the property restored, account being taken of compensation in respect of loss of use or deterioration.

(*g*) The rights conferred by paragraph (*f*) are reserved to owners who are nationals of Allied or Associated Powers within whose territory legislative measures prescribing the general liquidation of enemy property, rights or interests were not applied before the signature of the Armistice.

(*h*) Except in cases where, by application of paragraph (*f*), restitutions in specie have been made, the net proceeds of sales of enemy property, rights or interests wherever situated carried out either by virtue of war legislation, or by application of this Article, and in general all cash assets of enemies, shall be dealt with as follows:

(1) As regards Powers adopting Section III and the Annex thereto, the said proceeds and cash assets shall be credited to the Power of which the owner is a national, through the Clearing Office established thereunder; any credit balance in favour of Germany resulting therefrom shall be dealt with as provided in Article 243.

(2) As regards Powers not adopting Section III and the Annex thereto, the proceeds of the property, rights and interests, and the cash assets, of the nationals of Allied or Associated Powers held by Germany shall be paid immediately to the person entitled thereto or to his Government; the proceeds of the property, rights and interests, and the cash assets, of German nationals

received by an Allied or Associated Power shall be subject to disposal by such Power in accordance with its laws and regulations and may be applied in payment of the claims and debts defined by this Article or paragraph 4 of the Annex hereto. Any property, rights and interests or proceeds thereof or cash assets not used as above provided may be retained by the said Allied or Associated Power and if retained the cash value thereof shall be dealt with as provided in Article 243.

In the case of liquidations effected in new States, which are signatories of the present Treaty as Allied and Associated Powers, or in States which are not entitled to share in the reparation payments to be made by Germany, the proceeds of liquidations effected by such States shall, subject to the rights of the Reparation Commission under the present Treaty, particularly under Articles 235 and 260, be paid direct to the owner. If on the application of that owner, the Mixed Arbitral Tribunal, provided for by Section VI of this Part, or an arbitrator appointed by that Tribunal, is satisfied that the conditions of the sale or measures taken by the Government of the State in question outside its general legislation were unfairly prejudicial to the price obtained, they shall have discretion to award to the owner equitable compensation to be paid by that State.

(*i*) Germany undertakes to compensate her nationals in respect of the sale or retention of their property, rights or interests in Allied or Associated States.

(*j*) The amount of all taxes and imposts upon capital levied or to be levied by Germany on the property, rights and interests of the nationals of the Allied or Associated Powers from November 11, 1918, until three months from the coming into force of the present Treaty, or, in the case of property, rights or interests which have been subjected to exceptional measures of war, until restitution in accordance with the present Treaty, shall be restored to the owners.

ARTICLE 298

Germany undertakes, with regard to the property, rights and interests, including companies and associations in which they were interested, restored to nationals of Allied and Associated Powers in accordance with the provisions of Article 297, paragraph (*a*) or (*f*):

(*a*) to restore and maintain, except as expressly provided in the present Treaty, the property, rights and interests of the nationals of Allied or Associated Powers in the legal position obtaining in respect of the property, rights and interests of German nationals under the laws in force before the war;

(*b*) not to subject the property, rights or interests of the nationals of the Allied or Associated Powers to any measures in derogation of property rights which are not applied equally to the property, rights and interests of German nationals, and to pay adequate compensation in the event of the application of these measures.

ANNEX

1

In accordance with the provisions of Article 297, paragraph (d), the validity of vesting orders and of orders for the winding up of businesses or companies, and of any other orders, directions, decisions or instructions of any court or any department of the Government of any of the High Contracting Parties made or given, or purporting to be made or given, in pursuance of war legislation with regard to enemy property, rights and interests is confirmed. The interests of all persons shall be regarded as having been effectively dealt with by any order, direction, decision or instruction dealing with property in which they may be interested, whether or not such interests are specifically mentioned in the order, direction, decision, or instruction. No question shall be raised as to the regularity of a transfer of any property, rights or interests dealt with in pursuance of any such order, direction, decision or instruction. Every action taken with regard to any property, business, or company, whether as regards its investigation, sequestration, compulsory administration, use, requisition, supervision, or winding up, the sale or management of property, rights or interests, the collection or discharge of debts, the payment of costs, charges or expenses, or any other matter whatsoever, in pursuance of orders, directions, decisions, or instructions of any court or of any department of the Government of any of the High Contracting Parties, made or given, or purporting to be made or given, in pursuance of war legislation with regard to enemy property, rights or interests, is confirmed. Provided that the provisions of this paragraph shall not be held to prejudice the titles to property heretofore acquired in good faith and for value and in accordance with the laws of the country in which the property is situated by nationals of the Allied and Associated Powers.

The provisions of this paragraph do not apply to such of the above-mentioned measures as have been taken by the German authorities in invaded or occupied territory, nor to such of the above mentioned measures as have been taken by Germany or the German authorities since November 11, 1918, all of which shall be void.

2

No claim or action shall be made or brought against any Allied or Associated Power or against any person acting on behalf of or under the direction of any legal authority or Department of the Government of such a Power by Germany or by any German national wherever resident in respect of any act or omission with regard to his property, rights or interests during the war or in preparation for the war. Similarly no claim or action shall be made or brought against any person in respect of any act or omission under or in accordance with the exceptional war measures, laws or regulations of any Allied or Associated Power.

3

In Article 297 and this Annex the expression "exceptional war measures" includes measures of all kinds, legislative, administrative, judicial or others, that have been taken or will be taken hereafter with regard to enemy property, and which have had or will have the effect of removing from the proprietors the power of disposition over their property, though without affecting the ownership, such as measures of supervision, of compulsory administration, and of sequestration; or measures which have had or will have as an object the seizure of, the use of, or the interference with enemy assets, for whatsoever motive, under whatsoever form or in whatsoever place. Acts in the execution of these measures include all detentions, instructions, orders or decrees of Government departments or courts applying these measures to enemy property, as well as acts performed by any person connected with the administration or the supervision of enemy property, such as the payment of debts, the collecting of credits, the payment of any costs, charges or expenses, or the collecting of fees.

Measures of transfer are those which have affected or will affect the ownership of enemy property by transferring it in whole or in part to a person other than the enemy owner, and without his consent, such as measures directing the sale, liquidation, or devolution of ownership in enemy property, or the cancelling of titles or securities.

4

All property, rights and interests of German nationals within the territory of any Allied or Associated Power and the net proceeds of their sale, liquidation or other dealing therewith may be charged by that Allied or Associated Power in the first place with payment of amounts due in respect of claims by the nationals of that Allied or Associated Power with regard to their property, rights and interests, including companies and associations in which they are interested, in German territory, or debts owing to them by German nationals, and with payment of claims growing out of acts committed by the German Government or by any German authorities since July 31, 1914, and before that Allied or Associated Power entered into the war. The amount of such claims may be assessed by an arbitrator appointed by Mr. Gustave Ador, if he is willing, or if no such appointment is made by him, by an arbitrator appointed by the Mixed Arbitral Tribunal provided for in Section VI. They may be charged in the second place with payment of the amounts due in respect of claims by the nationals of such Allied or Associated Power with regard to their property, rights and interests in the territory of other enemy Powers, in so far as those claims are otherwise unsatisfied.

5

Notwithstanding the provisions of Article 297, where immediately before the outbreak of war a company incorporated in an Allied or Associated State had rights in common with a company controlled by it and incorporated in Germany to the use of trade-marks in third countries, or enjoyed the use in common with such company of unique means of reproduction of goods or articles for sale in third countries, the former company shall alone have the right to use these trade-marks in third countries to the exclusion of the German company, and these unique means of reproduction shall be handed over to the former company, notwithstanding any action taken under German war legislation with regard to the latter company or its business, industrial property or shares. Nevertheless, the former company, if requested, shall deliver to the latter company derivative copies permitting the continuation of reproduction of articles for use within German territory.

6

Up to the time when restitution is carried out in accordance with Article 297, Germany is responsible for the conservation of property, rights and interests of the nationals of Allied or Associated Powers, including companies and associations in which they are interested, that have been subjected by her to exceptional war measures.

7

Within one year from the coming into force of the present Treaty the Allied or Associated Powers will specify the property, rights and interests over which they intend to exercise the right provided in Article 297, paragraph (f).

8

The restitution provided in Article 297 will be carried out by order of the German Government or of the authorities which have been substituted for it. Detailed accounts of the action of administrators shall be furnished to the interested persons by the German authorities upon request, which may be made at any time after the coming into force of the present Treaty.

9

Until completion of the liquidation provided for by Article 297, paragraph (b), the property, rights and interests of German nationals will continue to be subject to exceptional war measures that have been or will be taken with regard to them.

10

Germany will, within six months from the coming into force of the present Treaty, deliver to each Allied or Associated Power all securities, certificates, deeds, or other documents of title held by its nationals and relating to property, rights or interests situated in the territory of that Allied or Associated Power, including any shares, stock debentures, debenture stock, or other obligations of any company incorporated in accordance with the laws of that Power.

Germany will at any time on demand of any Allied or Associated Power furnish such information as may be required with regard to the property, rights and interests of German nationals within the territory of such Allied or Associated Power, or with regard to any transactions concerning such property, rights or interests effected since July 1, 1914.

11

The expression "cash assets" includes all deposits or funds established before or after the declaration of war, as well as all assets coming from deposits, revenues, or profits collected by administrators, sequestrators, or others from funds placed on deposit or otherwise, but does not include sums belonging to the Allied or Associated Powers or to their component States, Provinces, or Municipalities.

12

All investments wheresoever effected with the cash assets of nationals of the High Contracting Parties, including companies and associations in which such nationals were interested, by persons responsible for the administration of enemy properties or having control over such administration, or by order of such persons or of any authority whatsoever shall be annulled. These cash assets shall be accounted for irrespective of any such investment.

13

Within one month from the coming into force of the present Treaty, or on demand at any time, Germany will deliver to the Allied and Associated Powers all accounts, vouchers, records, documents and information of any kind which may be within German territory, and which concern the property, rights and interests of the nationals of those Powers, including companies and associations in which they are interested, that have been subjected to an exceptional war measure, or to a measure of transfer either in German territory or in territory occupied by Germany or her allies.

The controllers, supervisors, managers, administrators, sequestrators, liquidators and receivers shall be personally responsible under guarantee of the German Government for the immediate delivery in full of those accounts and documents, and for their accuracy.

14

The provisions of Article 297 and this Annex relating to property, rights and interests in an enemy country, and the proceeds of the liquidation thereof, apply to debts, credits and accounts, Section III regulating only the method of payment.

In the settlement of matters provided for in Article 297 between Germany and the Allied or Associated States, their colonies or protectorates, or any one of the British Dominions or India, in respect of any of which a declaration shall not have been made that they adopt Section III, and between their respective nationals, the provisions of Section III respecting the currency in which payment is to be made and the rate of exchange and of interest shall apply unless the Government of the Allied or Associated Power concerned shall within six months of the coming into force of the present Treaty notify Germany that the said provisions are not to be applied.

15

The provisions of Article 297 and this Annex apply to industrial, literary and artistic property which has been or will be dealt with in the liquidation of property, rights, interests, companies or businesses under war legislation by the Allied or Associated Powers, or in accordance with the stipulations of Article 297, paragraph (b).

SECTION V

Contracts, Prescriptions, Judgments

ARTICLE 299

(a) Any contract concluded between enemies shall be regarded as having been dissolved as from the time when any two of the parties became enemies, except in respect of any debt or other pecuniary obligation arising out of any act done or money paid thereunder, and subject to the exceptions and special rules with regard to particular contracts or classes of contracts contained herein or in the Annex hereto.

(b) Any contract of which the execution shall be required in the general interest, within six months from the date of the coming into force of the present Treaty, by the Allied or Associated Governments of which one of the parties is a national, shall be excepted from dissolution under this Article.

When the execution of the contract thus kept alive would, owing to the alteration of trade conditions, cause one of the parties substantial prejudice the Mixed Arbitral Tribunal provided for by Section VI shall be empowered to grant to the prejudiced party equitable compensation.

(c) Having regard to the provisions of the constitution and law of the United States of America, of Brazil, and of Japan, neither the present Article, nor Article 300, nor the Annex hereto shall apply to contracts made between nationals of these States and German nationals; nor shall Article 305 apply to the United States of America or its nationals.

(d) The present Article and the annex hereto shall not apply to contracts the parties to which became enemies by reason of one of them being an inhabitant of territory of which the sovereignty has been transferred, if such party shall acquire under the present Treaty the nationality of an Allied or Associated Power, nor shall they apply to contracts between nationals of the Allied and Associated Powers between whom trading has been prohibited by reason of one of the parties being in Allied or Associated territory in the occupation of the enemy.

(*e*) Nothing in the present Article or the annex hereto shall be deemed to invalidate a transaction lawfully carried out in accordance with a contract between enemies if it has been carried out with the authority of one of the belligerent Powers.

ARTICLE 300

(*a*) All periods of prescription, or limitation of right of action, whether they began to run before or after the outbreak of war, shall be treated in the territory of the High Contracting Parties, so far as regards relations between enemies, as having been suspended for the duration of the war. They shall begin to run again at earliest three months after the coming into force of the present Treaty. This provision shall apply to the period prescribed for the presentation of interest or dividend coupons or for the presentation for repayment of securities drawn for repayment or repayable on any other ground.

(*b*) Where, on account of failure to perform any act or comply with any formality during the war, measures of execution have been taken in German territory to the prejudice of a national of an Allied or Associated Power, the claim of such national shall, if the matter does not fall within the competence of the Courts of an Allied or Associated Power, be heard by the Mixed Arbitral Tribunal provided for by Section VI.

(*c*) Upon the application of any interested person who is a national of an Allied or Associated Power the Mixed Arbitral Tribunal shall order the restoration of the rights which have been prejudiced by the measures of execution referred to in paragraph (*b*), wherever, having regard to the particular circumstances of the case, such restoration is equitable and possible.

If such restoration is inequitable or impossible the Mixed Arbitral Tribunal may grant compensation to the prejudiced party to be paid by the German Government.

(*d*) Where a contract between enemies has been dissolved by reason either of failure on the part of either party to carry out its provisions or of the exercise of a right stipulated in the contract itself the party prejudiced may apply to the Mixed Arbitral Tribunal for relief. The Tribunal will have the powers provided for in paragraph (*c*).

(*e*) The provisions of the preceding paragraphs of this Article shall apply to the nationals of Allied and Associated Powers who have been prejudiced by reason of measures referred to above taken by Germany in invaded or occupied territory, if they have not been otherwise compensated.

(*f*) Germany shall compensate any third party who may be prejudiced by any restitution or restoration ordered by the Mixed Arbitral Tribunal under the provisions of the preceding paragraphs of this Article.

(*g*) As regards negotiable instruments, the period of three months provided under paragraph (*a*) shall commence as from the date on which any exceptional regulations applied in the territories of the interested Power with regard to negotiable instruments shall have definitely ceased to have force.

ARTICLE 301

As between enemies no negotiable instrument made before the war shall be deemed to have become invalid by reason only of failure within the required time to present the instrument for acceptance or payment or to give notice of non-acceptance or non-payment to drawers or indorsers or to protest the instrument, nor by reason of failure to complete any formality during the war.

Where the period within which a negotiable instrument should have been presented for acceptance or for payment, or within which notice of non-acceptance or non-payment should have been given to the drawer or indorser, or within which the instrument should have been protested, has elapsed during the war, and the party who should have presented or protested the instrument or have given notice of non-acceptance or non-payment has failed to do so during the war, a period of not less than three months from the coming into force of the present Treaty shall be allowed within which presentation, notice of non-acceptance or non-payment or protest may be made.

ARTICLE 302

Judgments given by the Courts of an Allied or Associated Power in all cases which, under the present Treaty, they are competent to decide, shall be recognised in Germany as final, and shall be enforced without it being necessary to have them declared executory.

If a judgment in respect to any dispute which may have arisen has been given during the war by a German Court against a national of an Allied or Associated State in a case in which he was not able to make his defence, the Allied and Associated national who has suffered prejudice thereby shall be entitled to recover compensation, to be fixed by the Mixed Arbitral Tribunal provided for in Section VI.

At the instance of the national of the Allied or Associated Power the compensation above-mentioned may, upon order to that effect of the Mixed Arbitral Tribunal, be effected where it is possible by replacing the parties in the situation which they occupied before the judgment was given by the German Court.

The above compensation may likewise be obtained before the Mixed Arbitral Tribunal by the nationals of Allied or Associated Powers who have suffered prejudice by judicial measures taken in invaded or occupied territories, if they have not been otherwise compensated.

ARTICLE 303

For the purpose of Sections III, IV, V and VII, the expression "during the war" means for each Allied or Associated Power the period between the commencement of the state of war between that Power and Germany and the coming into force of the present Treaty.

ANNEX

I. *General Provisions*

1

Within the meaning of Articles 299, 300 and 301, the parties to a contract shall be regarded as enemies when trading between them shall have been prohibited by or otherwise became unlawful under laws, orders or regulations to which one of those parties was subject. They shall be deemed to have become enemies from the date when such trading was prohibited or otherwise became unlawful.

2

The following classes of contracts are excepted from dissolution by Article 299 and, without prejudice to the rights contained in Article 297 (*b*) of Section IV, remain in force subject to the application of domestic laws, orders or regulations made during the war by the Allied and Associated Powers and subject to the terms of the contracts:

(*a*) Contracts having for their object the transfer of estates or of real or personal property where the property therein had passed or the object had been delivered before the parties became enemies;

(*b*) Leases and agreements for leases of land and houses;

(*c*) Contracts of mortgage, pledge or lien;

(*d*) Concessions concerning mines, quarries or deposits;

(*e*) Contracts between individuals or companies and States, provinces, municipalities, or other similar juridical persons charged with administrative functions, and concessions granted by States, provinces, municipalities, or other similar juridical persons charged with administrative functions.

3

If the provisions of a contract are in part dissolved under Article 299, the remaining provisions of that contract shall, subject to the same application of domestic laws as is provided for in paragraph 2, continue in force if they are severable, but where they are not severable the contract shall be deemed to have been dissolved in its entirety.

II. *Provisions relating to certain classes of Contracts*

STOCK EXCHANGE AND COMMERCIAL EXCHANGE CONTRACTS

4

(*a*) Rules made during the war by any recognised Exchange or Commercial Association providing for the closure of contracts entered into before the war by an enemy are confirmed by the High Contracting Parties, as also any action taken thereunder, provided:

(1) That the contract was expressed to be made subject to the rules of the Exchange or Association in question;

(2) That the rules applied to all persons concerned;

(3) That the conditions attaching to the closure were fair and reasonable.

(b) The preceding paragraph shall not apply to rules made during the occupation by Exchanges or Commercial Associations in the districts occupied by the enemy.

(c) The closure of contracts relating to cotton "futures", which were closed as on July 31, 1914, under the decision of the Liverpool Cotton Association, is also confirmed.

SECURITY

5

The sale of a security held for an unpaid debt owing by an enemy shall be deemed to have been valid irrespective of notice to the owner if the creditor acted in good faith and with reasonable care and prudence, and no claim by the debtor on the ground of such sale shall be admitted.

This stipulation shall not apply to any sale of securities effected by an enemy during the occupation in regions invaded or occupied by the enemy.

NEGOTIABLE INSTRUMENTS

6

As regards Powers which adopt Section III and the Annex thereto the pecuniary obligations existing between enemies and resulting from the issue of negotiable instruments shall be adjusted in conformity with the said Annex by the instrumentality of the Clearing Offices, which shall assume the rights of the holder as regards the various remedies open to him.

7

If a person has either before or during the war become liable upon a negotiable instrument in accordance with an undertaking given to him by a person who has subsequently become an enemy, the latter shall remain liable to indemnify the former in respect of his liability notwithstanding the outbreak of war.

III. *Contracts of Insurance*

8

Contracts of insurance entered into by any person with another person who subsequently became an enemy will be dealt with in accordance with the following paragraphs.

FIRE INSURANCE

9

Contracts for the insurance of property against fire entered into by a person interested in such property with another person who subsequently became an enemy shall not be deemed to have been dissolved by the outbreak of war, or by the fact of the person becoming an enemy, or on account of the failure during the war and for a period of three months thereafter to perform his obligations under the contract, but they shall be dissolved at the date when the annual premium becomes payable for the first time after the expiration of a period of three months after the coming into force of the present Treaty.

A settlement shall be effected of unpaid premiums which became due during the war, or of claims for losses which occurred during the war.

10

Where by administrative or legislative action an insurance against fire effected before the war has been transferred during the war from the original to another insurer, the transfer will be recognised and the liability of the original insurer will be deemed to have ceased as from the date of the transfer. The original insurer will, however, be entitled to receive on demand full information as to the terms of the transfer, and if it should appear that these terms were not equitable they shall be amended so far as may be necessary to render them equitable.

Furthermore, the insured shall, subject to the concurrence of the original insurer, be entitled to retransfer the contract to the original insurer as from the date of the demand.

LIFE INSURANCE

11

Contracts of life insurance entered into between an insurer and a person who subsequently became an enemy shall not be deemed to have been dissolved by the outbreak of war, or by the fact of the person becoming an enemy.

Any sum which during the war became due upon a contract deemed not to have been dissolved under the preceding provision shall be recoverable after the war with the addition of interest at five per cent. per annum from the date of its becoming due up to the day of payment.

Where the contract has lapsed during the war owing to non-payment of premiums, or has become void from breach of the conditions of the contract, the assured or his representatives or the person entitled shall have the right at any time within twelve months of the coming into force of the present Treaty to claim from the insurer the surrender value of the policy at the date of its lapse or avoidance.

Where the contract has lapsed during the war owing to non-payment of premiums the payment of which has been prevented by the enforcement of measures of war, the assured or his representative or the persons entitled shall have the right to restore the contract on payment of the premiums with interest at five per cent. per annum within three months from the coming into force of the present Treaty.

12

Any Allied or Associated Power may within three months of the coming into force of the present Treaty cancel all the contracts of insurance running between a German insurance company and its nationals under conditions which shall protect its nationals from any prejudice.

To this end the German insurance company will hand over to the Allied or Associated Government concerned the proportion of its assets attributable to the policies so cancelled and will be relieved from all liability in respect of such policies. The assets to be handed over shall be determined by an actuary appointed by the Mixed Arbitral Tribunal.

13

Where contracts of life insurance have been entered into by a local branch of an insurance company established in a country which subsequently became an enemy country, the contract shall, in the absence of any stipulation to the contrary in the contract itself, be governed by the local law, but the insurer shall be entitled to demand from the insured or his representatives the refund of sums paid on claims made or enforced under measures taken during the war, if the making or enforcement of such claims was not in accordance with the terms of the contract itself or was not consistent with the laws or treaties existing at the time when it was entered into.

14

In any case where by the law applicable to the contract the insurer remains bound by the contract notwithstanding the non-payment of premiums until notice is given to the insured of the termination of the contract, he shall be entitled where the giving of such notice was prevented by the war to recover the unpaid premiums with interest at five per cent. per annum from the insured.

15

Insurance contracts shall be considered as contracts of life assurance for the purpose of paragraphs 11 to 14 when they depend on the probabilities of human life combined with the rate of interest for the calculation of the reciprocal engagements between the two parties.

MARINE INSURANCE

16

Contracts of marine insurance including time policies and voyage policies entered into between an insurer and a person who subsequently became an enemy, shall be deemed to have been dissolved on his becoming an enemy, except in cases where the risk undertaken in the contract had attached before he became an enemy.

Where the risk had not attached, money paid by way of premium or otherwise shall be recoverable from the insurer.

Where the risk had attached effect shall be given to the contract notwithstanding the party becoming an enemy, and sums due under the contract either by way of premiums or in respect of losses shall be recoverable after the coming into force of the present Treaty.

In the event of any agreement being come to for the payment of interest on sums due before the war to or by the nationals of States which have been at war and recovered after the war, such interest shall in the case of losses recoverable under contracts of marine insurance run from the expiration of a period of one year from the date of the loss.

17

No contract of marine insurance with an insured person who subsequently became an enemy shall be deemed to cover losses due to belligerent action by the Power of which the insurer was a national or by the allies or associates of such Power.

18

Where it is shown that a person who had before the war entered into a contract of marine insurance with an insurer who subsequently became an enemy entered after the outbreak of war into a new contract covering the same risk with an insurer who was not an enemy, the new contract shall be deemed to be substituted for the original contract as from the date when it was entered into, and the premiums payable shall be adjusted on the basis of the original insurer having remained liable on the contract only up till the time when the new contract was entered into.

OTHER INSURANCES

19

Contracts of insurance entered into before the war between an insurer and a person who subsequently became an enemy, other than contracts dealt with in paragraphs 9 to 18, shall be treated in all respects on the same footing as contracts of fire insurance between the same persons would be dealt with under the said paragraphs.

RE-INSURANCE

20

All treaties of re-insurance with a person who became an enemy shall be regarded as having been abrogated by the person becoming an enemy, but without prejudice in the case of life or marine risks which had attached before the war to the right to recover payment after the war for sums due in respect of such risks.

Nevertheless if, owing to invasion, it has been impossible for the re-insured to find another re-insurer, the treaty shall remain in force until three months after the coming into force of the present Treaty.

Where a re-insurance treaty becomes void under this paragraph, there shall be an adjustment of accounts between the parties in respect both of premiums paid and payable and of liabilities for losses in respect of life or marine risks which had attached before the war. In the case of risks other than those mentioned in paragraphs 11 to 18 the adjustment of accounts shall be made as at the date of the parties becoming enemies without regard to claims for losses which may have occurred since that date.

21

The provisions of the preceding paragraph will extend equally to re-insurances existing at the date of the parties becoming enemies of particular risks undertaken by the insurer in a contract of insurance against any risks other than life or marine risks.

22

Re-insurance of life risks effected by particular contracts and not under any general treaty remain in force.

The provisions of paragraph 12 apply to treaties of re-insurance of life insurance contracts in which enemy companies are the re-insurers.

23

In case of a re-insurance effected before the war of a contract of marine insurance, the cession of a risk which had been ceded to the re-insurer shall, if it had attached before the outbreak of war, remain valid and effect be given to the contract notwithstanding the outbreak of war; sums due under the contract of re-insurance in respect either of premiums or of losses shall be recoverable after the war.

24

The provisions of paragraphs 17 and 18 and the last part of paragraph 16 shall apply to contracts for the re-insurance of marine risks.

Mixed Arbitral Tribunal

ARTICLE 304

(*a*) Within three months from the date of the coming into force of the present Treaty, a Mixed Arbitral Tribunal shall be established between each of the Allied and Associated Powers on the one hand and Germany on the other hand. Each such Tribunal shall consist of three members. Each of the Governments concerned shall appoint one of these members. The President shall be chosen by agreement between the two Governments concerned.

In case of failure to reach agreement, the President of the Tribunal and two other persons either of whom may in case of need take his place, shall be chosen by the Council of the League of Nations, or, until this is set up, by M. Gustave Ador if he is willing. These persons shall be nationals of Powers that have remained neutral during the war.

If any Government does not proceed within a period of one month in case there is a vacancy to appoint a member of the Tribunal, such member shall be chosen by the other Government from the two persons mentioned above other than the President.

The decision of the majority of the members of the Tribunal shall be the decision of the Tribunal.

(*b*) The Mixed Arbitral Tribunals established pursuant to paragraph (*a*), shall decide all questions within their competence under Sections III, IV, V and VII.

In addition, all questions, whatsoever their nature, relating to contracts concluded before the coming into force of the present Treaty between nationals of the Allied and Associated Powers and German nationals shall be decided by the Mixed Arbitral Tribunal, always excepting questions which, under the laws of the Allied, Associated or Neutral Powers, are within the jurisdiction of the National Courts of those Powers. Such questions shall be decided by the National Courts in question, to the exclusion of the Mixed Arbitral Tribunal. The party who is a national of an Allied or Associated Power may nevertheless bring the case before the Mixed Arbitral Tribunal if this is not prohibited by the laws of his country.

(*c*) If the number of cases justifies it, additional members shall be appointed and each Mixed Arbitral Tribunal shall sit in divisions. Each of these divisions will be constituted as above.

(*d*) Each Mixed Arbitral Tribunal will settle its own procedure except in so far as it is provided in the following Annex, and is empowered to award the sums to be paid by the loser in respect of the costs and expenses of the proceedings.

(*e*) Each Government will pay the remuneration of the member of the Mixed Arbitral Tribunal appointed by it and of any agent whom it may appoint to represent it before the Tribunal. The remuneration of the President will be determined by special agreement between the Governments concerned; and this remuneration and the joint expenses of each Tribunal will be paid by the two Governments in equal moieties.

(*f*) The High Contracting Parties agree that their courts and authorities shall render to the Mixed Arbitral Tribunals direct all the assistance in their power, particularly as regards transmitting notices and collecting evidence.

(*g*) The High Contracting Parties agree to regard the decisions of the Mixed Arbitral Tribunal as final and conclusive, and to render them binding upon their nationals.

ANNEX

1

Should one of the members of the Tribunal either die, retire, or be unable for any reason whatever to discharge his function, the same procedure will be followed for filling the vacancy as was followed for appointing him.

2

The Tribunal may adopt such rules of procedure as shall be in accordance with justice and equity and decide the order and time at which each party must conclude its arguments, and may arrange all formalities required for dealing with the evidence.

3

The agent and counsel of the parties on each side are authorized to present orally and in writing to the Tribunal arguments in support or in defence of each case.

4

The Tribunal shall keep record of the questions and cases submitted and the proceedings thereon, with the dates of such proceedings.

5

Each of the Powers concerned may appoint a secretary. These secretaries shall act together as joint secretaries of the Tribunal and shall be subject to its direction. The Tribunal may appoint and employ any other necessary officer or officers to assist in the performance of its duties.

6

The Tribunal shall decide all questions and matters submitted upon such evidence and information as may be furnished by the parties concerned.

7

Germany agrees to give the Tribunal all facilities and information required by it for carrying out its investigations.

8

The language in which the proceedings shall be conducted shall, unless otherwise agreed, be English, French, Italian or Japanese, as may be determined by the Allied or Associated Power concerned.

9

The place and time for the meetings of each Tribunal shall be determined by the President of the Tribunal.

ARTICLE 305

Whenever a competent court has given or gives a decision in a case covered by Sections III, IV, V or VII, and such decision is inconsistent with the provisions of such Sections, the party who is prejudiced by the decision shall be entitled to obtain redress which shall be fixed by the Mixed Arbitral Tribunal. At the request of the national of an Allied or Associated Power, the redress may, whenever possible, be effected by the Mixed Arbitral Tribunal directing the replacement of the parties in the position occupied by them before the judgment was given by the German court.

SECTION VII

Industrial Property

ARTICLE 306

Subject to the stipulations of the present Treaty, rights of industrial, literary and artistic property, as such property is defined by the International Conventions of Paris and of Berne, mentioned in Article 286, shall be reestablished or restored, as from the coming into force of the present Treaty, in the territories of the High Contracting Parties, in favour of the persons entitled to the benefit of them at the moment when the state of war commenced or their legal representatives. Equally, rights which, except for the war, would have been acquired during the war in consequence of an application made for the protection of industrial property, or the publication of a literary or artistic work, shall be recognised and established in favour of those persons who would have been entitled thereto, from the coming into force of the present Treaty.

Nevertheless, all acts done by virtue of the special measures taken during the war under legislative, executive or administrative authority of any Allied or Associated Power in regard to the rights of German nationals in industrial, literary or artistic property shall remain in force and shall continue to maintain their full effect.

No claim shall be made or action brought by Germany or German nationals in respect of the use during the war by the Government of any Allied or Associated Power, or by any persons acting on behalf or with the assent of such Government, of any rights in industrial, literary or artistic property, nor in respect of the sale, offering for sale, or use of any products, articles or apparatus whatsoever to which such rights applied.

Unless the legislation of any one of the Allied or Associated Powers in force at the moment of the signature of the present Treaty otherwise directs, sums due or paid in virtue of any act or operation resulting from the execution of the special measures mentioned in paragraph I of this Article shall be dealt with in the same way as other sums due to German nationals are directed to be dealt with by the present Treaty; and sums produced by any special measures taken by the German Government in respect of rights in industrial, literary or artistic property belonging to the nationals of the Allied or Associated Powers shall be considered and treated in the same way as other debts due from German nationals.

Each of the Allied and Associated Powers reserves to itself the right to impose such limitations, conditions or restrictions on rights of industrial, literary or artistic property (with the exception of trade-marks) acquired before or during the war, or which may be subsequently acquired in accordance with its legislation, by German nationals, whether by granting licences, or by the working, or by preserving control over their exploitation, or in any other way, as may be considered necessary for national defence, or in the public interest, or for assuring the fair treatment by Germany of the rights of industrial, literary and artistic property held in German territory by its nationals, or for securing the due fulfilment of all the obligations undertaken by Germany in the present Treaty. As regards rights of industrial, literary and artistic property acquired after the coming into force of the present Treaty, the right so reserved by the Allied and Associated Powers shall only be exercised in cases where these limitations, conditions or restrictions may be considered necessary for national defence or in the public interest.

In the event of the application of the provisions of the preceding paragraph by any Allied or Associated Power, there shall be paid reasonable indemnities or royalties, which shall be dealt with in the same way as other sums due to German nationals are directed to be dealt with by the present Treaty.

Each of the Allied or Associated Powers reserves the right to treat as void and of no effect any transfer in whole or in part or other dealing with rights of or in respect of industrial, literary or artistic property effected after August 1, 1914, or in the future, which would have the result of defeating the objects of the provisions of this Article.

The provisions of this Article shall not apply to rights in industrial, literary or artistic property which have been dealt with in the liquidation of businesses or companies under war legislation by the Allied or Associated Powers, or which may be so dealt with by virtue of Article 297, paragraph (*b*).

ARTICLE 307

A minimum of one year after the coming into force of the present Treaty shall be accorded to the nationals of the High Contracting Parties, without extension fees or other penalty, in order to enable such persons to accomplish any act, fulfil any formality, pay any fees, and generally satisfy any obligation prescribed by the laws or regulations of the respective States relating to the obtaining, preserving, or opposing rights to, or in respect of, industrial property either acquired before August 1, 1914, or which, except for the war, might have been acquired since that date as a result of an application made before the war or during its continuance, but nothing in this Article shall give any right to reopen interference proceedings in the United States of America where a final hearing has taken place.

All rights in, or in respect of, such property which may have lapsed by reason of any failure to accomplish any act, fulfil any formality, or make any payment, shall revive, but subject in the case of patents and designs to the imposition of such conditions as each Allied or Associated Power may deem reasonably necessary for the protection of persons who have manufactured or made use of the subject matter of such property while the rights had lapsed. Further, where rights to patents or designs belonging to German nationals are revived under this Article, they shall be subject in respect of the grant of licences to the same provisions as would have been applicable to them during the war, as well as to all the provisions of the present Treaty.

The period from August 1, 1914, until the coming into force of the present Treaty shall be excluded in considering the time within which a patent should be worked or a trade mark or design used, and it is further agreed that no patent, registered trade mark or design in force on August 1, 1914, shall be subject to revocation or cancellation by reason only of the failure to work such patent or use such trade mark or design for two years after the coming into force of the present Treaty.

ARTICLE 308

The rights of priority, provided by Article 4 of the International Convention for the Protection of Industrial Property of Paris, of March 20, 1883, revised at Washington in 1911 or by any other Convention or Statute, for the filing or registration of applications for patents or models of utility, and for the registration of trade marks, designs and models which had not expired on August 1, 1914, and those which have arisen during the war, or would have arisen but for the war, shall be extended by each of the High Contracting Parties in favour of all nationals of the other High Contracting Parties for a period of six months after the coming into force of the present Treaty.

Nevertheless, such extension shall in no way affect the right of any of the High Contracting Parties or of any person who before the coming into force of the present Treaty was *bona fide* in possession of any rights of industrial property conflicting with rights applied for by another who claims rights of priority in respect of them, to exercise such rights by itself or himself personally, or by such agents or licensees as derived their rights from it or him before the coming into force of the present Treaty; and such persons shall not be amenable to any action or other process of law in respect of infringement.

ARTICLE 309

No action shall be brought and no claim made by persons residing or carrying on business within the territories of Germany on the one part and of the Allied or Associated Powers on the other, or persons who are nationals of such Powers respectively, or by any one deriving title during the war from such persons, by reason of any action which has taken place within the territory of the other party between the date of the declaration of war and that of the coming into force of the present Treaty, which might constitute an infringement of the rights of industrial property or rights of literary and artistic property, either existing at any time during the war or revived under the provisions of Articles 307 and 308.

Equally, no action for infringement of industrial, literary or artistic property rights by such persons shall at any time be permissible in respect of the sale or offering for sale for a period of one year after the signature of the present Treaty in the territories of the Allied or Associated Powers on the one hand or Germany on the other, of products or articles manufactured, or of literary or artistic works published, during the period between the declaration of war and the signature of the present Treaty, or against those who have acquired and continue to use them. It is understood, nevertheless, that this provision shall not apply when the possessor of the rights was domiciled or had an industrial or commercial establishment in the districts occupied by Germany during the war.

This Article shall not apply as between the United States of America on the one hand and Germany on the other.

ARTICLE 310

Licences in respect of industrial, literary or artistic property concluded before the war between nationals of the Allied or Associated Powers or persons residing in their territory or carrying on business therein, on the one part, and German nationals, on the other part, shall be considered as cancelled as from the date of the declaration of war between Germany and the Allied or Associated Power. But, in any case, the former beneficiary of a contract of this kind shall have the right, within a period of six months after the coming into force of the present Treaty, to demand from the proprietor of the rights the grant of a new licence, the conditions of which, in default of agreement between the parties, shall be fixed by the duly qualified tribunal in the country under whose legislation the rights had been acquired, except in the case of licences held in respect of rights acquired under German law. In such cases the conditions shall be fixed by the Mixed Arbitral Tribunal referred to in Section VI of this Part. The tribunal may, if necessary, fix also the amount which it may deem just should be paid by reason of the use of the rights during the war.

No licence in respect of industrial, literary or artistic property, granted under the special war legislation of any Allied or Associated Power, shall be affected by the continued existence of any licence entered into before the war, but shall remain valid and of full effect, and a licence so granted to the former beneficiary of a licence entered into before the war shall be considered as substituted for such licence.

Where sums have been paid during the war by virtue of a licence or agreement concluded before the war in respect of rights of industrial property or for the reproduction or the representation of literary, dramatic or artistic works, these sums shall be dealt with in the same manner as other debts or credits of German nationals, as provided by the present Treaty.

This Article shall not apply as between the United States of America on the one hand and Germany on the other.

ARTICLE 311

The inhabitants of territories separated from Germany by virtue of the present Treaty shall, notwithstanding this separation and the change of nationality consequent thereon, continue to enjoy in Germany all the rights in industrial, literary and artistic property to which they were entitled under German legislation at the time of the separation.

Rights of industrial, literary and artistic property which are in force in the territories separated from Germany under the present Treaty at the moment of the separation of these territories from Germany, or which will be re-established or restored in accordance with the provisions of Article 306 of the present Treaty, shall be recognized by the State to which the said territory is transferred and shall remain in force in that territory for the same period of time given them under the German law.

SECTION VIII

Social and State Insurance in Ceded Territory

ARTICLE 312

Without prejudice to the provisions contained in other Articles of the present Treaty, the German Government undertakes to transfer to any Power to which German territory in Europe is ceded, and to any Power administering former German territory as a mandatory under Article 22 of Part I (League of Nations), such portion of the reserves accumulated by the Government of the German Empire or of German States, or by public or private organisations under their control, as is attributable to the carrying on of Social or State Insurance in such territory.

The Powers to which these funds are transferred must apply them to the performance of the obligations arising from such insurances.

The conditions of the transfer will be determined by special conventions to be concluded between the German Government and the Governments concerned.

In case these special conventions are not concluded in accordance with the above paragraph within three months after the coming into force of the present Treaty, the conditions of transfer shall in each case be referred to a Commission of five members, one of whom shall be appointed by the German Government, one by the other interested Government and three by the Governing Body of the International Labour Office from the nationals of other States. This Commission shall by majority vote within three months after appointment adopt recommendations for submission to the Council of the League of Nations, and the decisions of the Council shall forthwith be accepted as final by Germany and the other Government concerned.

PART XI

AERIAL NAVIGATION

Article 313

The aircraft of the Allied and Associated Powers shall have full liberty of passage and landing over and in the territory and territorial waters of Germany, and shall enjoy the same privileges as German aircraft, particularly in case of distress by land or sea.

Article 314

The aircraft of the Allied and Associated Powers shall, while in transit to any foreign country whatever, enjoy the right of flying over the territory and territorial waters of Germany without landing, subject always to any regulations which may be made by Germany, and which shall be applicable equally to the aircraft of Germany and to those of the Allied and Associated countries.

Article 315

All aerodromes in Germany open to national public traffic shall be open for the aircraft of the Allied and Associated Powers, and in any such aerodrome such aircraft shall be treated on a footing of equality with German aircraft as regards charges of every description, including charges for landing and accommodation.

Article 316

Subject to the present provisions, the rights of passage, transit and landing, provided for in Articles 313, 314 and 315, are subject to the observance of such regulations as Germany may consider it necessary to enact, but such regulations shall be applied without distinction to German aircraft and to those of the Allied and Associated countries.

ARTICLE 317

Certificates of nationality, airworthiness, or competency, and licences, issued or recognised as valid by any of the Allied or Associated Powers, shall be recognised in Germany as valid and as equivalent to the certificates and licences issued by Germany.

ARTICLE 318

As regards internal commercial air traffic, the aircraft of the Allied and Associated Powers shall enjoy in Germany most favoured nation treatment.

ARTICLE 319

Germany undertakes to enforce the necessary measures to ensure that all German aircraft flying over her territory shall comply with the Rules as to lights and signals, Rules of the Air and Rules for Air Traffic on and in the neighbourhood of aerodromes, which have been laid down in the Convention relative to Aerial Navigation concluded between the Allied and Associated Powers.

ARTICLE 320

The obligations imposed by the preceding provisions shall remain in force until January 1, 1923, unless before that date Germany shall have been admitted into the League of Nations or shall have been authorised, by consent of the Allied and Associated Powers, to adhere to the Convention relative to Aerial Navigation concluded between those Powers.

PART XII

PORTS, WATERWAYS AND RAILWAYS

SECTION I

General Provisions

ARTICLE 321

Germany undertakes to grant freedom of transit through her territories on the routes most convenient for international transit, either by rail, navigable waterway, or canal, to persons, goods, vessels, carriages, wagons and mails coming from or going to the territories of any of the Allied and Associated Powers (whether contiguous or not); for this purpose the crossing of territorial waters shall be allowed. Such persons, goods, vessels, carriages, wagons and mails shall not be subjected to any transit duty or to any undue delays or restrictions, and shall be entitled in Germany to national treatment as regards charges, facilities, and all other matters.

Goods in transit shall be exempt from all Customs or other similar duties.

All charges imposed on transport in transit shall be reasonable, having regard to the conditions of the traffic. No charge, facility or restriction shall depend directly or indirectly on the ownership or on the nationality of the ship or other means of transport on which any part of the through journey has been, or is to be, accomplished.

ARTICLE 322

Germany undertakes neither to impose nor to maintain any control over transmigration traffic through her territories beyond measures necessary to ensure that passengers are *bona fide* in transit; nor to allow any shipping company or any other private body, corporation or person interested in the traffic to take any part whatever in, or to exercise any direct or indirect influence over, any administrative service that may be necessary for this purpose.

ARTICLE 323

Germany undertakes to make no discrimination or preference, direct or indirect, in the duties, charges and prohibitions relating to importations into or exportations from her territories, or, subject to the special engagements contained in the present Treaty, in the charges and conditions of transport of goods or persons entering or leaving her territories, based on the frontier crossed; or on the kind, ownership or flag of the means of transport (including aircraft) employed; or on the original or immediate place of departure of the vessel, wagon or aircraft of other means of transport employed, or its ultimate or intermediate destination; or on the route of or places of trans-shipment on the journey; or on whether any port through which the goods are imported or exported is a German port or a port belonging to any foreign country or on whether the goods are imported or exported by sea, by land or by air.

Germany particularly undertakes not to establish against the ports and vessels of any of the Allied and Associated Powers any surtax or any direct or indirect bounty for export or import by German ports or vessels, or by those of another Power, for example by means of combined tariffs. She further undertakes that persons or goods passing through a port or using a vessel of any of the Allied and Associated Powers shall not be subjected to any formality or delay whatever to which such persons or goods would not be subjected if they passed through a German port or a port of any other Power, or used a German vessel or a vessel of any other Power.

ARTICLE 324

All necessary administrative and technical measures shall be taken to shorten, as much as possible, the transmission of goods across the German frontiers and to ensure their forwarding and transport from such frontiers, irrespective of whether such goods are coming from or going to the territories of the Allied and Associated Powers or are in transit from or to those territories, under the same material conditions in such matters as rapidity of carriage and care *en route* as are enjoyed by other goods of the same kind carried on German territory under similar conditions of transport.

In particular, the transport of perishable goods shall be promptly and regularly carried out, and the customs formalities shall be effected in such a way as to allow the goods to be carried straight through by trains which make connection.

ARTICLE 325

The seaports of the Allied and Associated Powers are entitled to all favours and to all reduced tariffs granted on German railways or navigable waterways for the benefit of German ports or of any port of another Power.

ARTICLE 326

Germany may not refuse to participate in the tariffs or combinations of tariffs intended to secure for ports of any of the Allied and Associated Powers advantages similar to those granted by Germany to her own ports or the ports of any other Power.

SECTION II

Navigation

CHAPTER I

FREEDOM OF NAVIGATION

ARTICLE 327

The nationals of any of the Allied and Associated Powers as well as their vessels and property shall enjoy in all German ports and on the inland navigation routes of Germany the same treatment in all respects as German nationals, vessels and property.

In particular the vessels of any one of the Allied or Associated Powers shall be entitled to transport goods of any description, and passengers, to or from any ports or places in German territory to which German vessels may have access, under conditions which shall not be more onerous than those applied in the case of national vessels; they shall be treated on a footing of equality with national vessels as regards port and harbour facilities and charges of every description, including facilities for stationing, loading and unloading, and duties and charges of tonnage, harbour, pilotage, lighthouse, quarantine, and all analogous duties and charges of whatsoever nature, levied in the name of or for the profit of the Government, public functionaries, private individuals, corporations or establishments of any kind.

In the event of Germany granting a preferential régime to any of the Allied or Associated Powers or to any other foreign Power, this régime shall be extended immediately and unconditionally to all the Allied and Associated Powers.

There shall be no impediment to the movement of persons or vessels other than those arising from prescriptions concerning customs, police, sanitation, emigration and immigration, and those relating to the import and export of prohibited goods. Such regulations must be reasonable and uniform and must not impede traffic unnecessarily.

CHAPTER II

FREE ZONES IN PORTS

ARTICLE 328

The free zones existing in German ports on August 1, 1914, shall be maintained. These free zones, and any other free zones which may be established in German territory by the present Treaty, shall be subject to the régime provided for in the following Articles.

Goods entering or leaving a free zone shall not be subjected to any import or export duty, other than those provided for in Article 330.

Vessels and goods entering a free zone may be subjected to the charges established to cover expenses of administration, upkeep and improvement of the port, as well as to the charges for the use of various installations, provided that these charges shall be reasonable having regard to the expenditure incurred, and shall be levied in the conditions of equality provided for in Article 327.

Goods shall not be subjected to any other charge except a statistical duty which shall not exceed 1 per mille *ad valorem,* and which shall be devoted exclusively to defraying the expenses of compiling statements of the traffic in the port.

ARTICLE 329

The facilities granted for the erection of warehouses, for packing and for unpacking goods, shall be in accordance with trade requirements for the time being. All goods allowed to be consumed in the free zone shall be exempt from duty, whether of excise or of any other description, apart from the statistical duty provided for in Article 328 above.

There shall be no discrimination in regard to any of the provisions of the present Article between persons belonging to different nationalities or between goods of different origin or destination.

ARTICLE 330

Import duties may be levied on goods leaving the free zone for consumption in the country on the territory of which the port is situated. Conversely, export duties may be levied on goods coming from such country and brought into the free zone. These import and export duties shall be levied on the same basis and at the same rates as similar duties levied at the other Customs frontiers of the country concerned. On the other hand, Germany shall not levy, under any denomination, any import, export or transit duty on goods carried by land or water across her territory to or from the free zone from or to any other State.

Germany shall draw up the necessary regulations to secure and guarantee such freedom of transit over such railways and waterways in her territory as normally give access to the free zone.

CHAPTER III

CLAUSES RELATING TO THE ELBE, THE ODER, THE NIEMEN (RUSSSTROM-MEMEL-NIEMEN) AND THE DANUBE

(1) *General Clauses*

ARTICLE 331

The following rivers are declared international:

the Elbe (*Labe*) from its confluence with the Vltava (*Moldau*), and the Vltava (*Moldau*) from Prague;
the Oder (*Odra*) from its confluence with the Oppa;
the Niemen (*Russstrom-Memel-Niemen*) from Grodno;
the Danube from Ulm;
and all navigable parts of these river systems which naturally provide more than one State with access to the sea, with or without transhipment from one vessel to another; together with lateral canals and channels constructed either to duplicate or to improve naturally navigable sections of the specified river systems, or to connect two naturally navigable sections of the same river.

The same shall apply to the Rhine-Danube navigable waterway, should such a waterway be constructed under the conditions laid down in Article 353.

ARTICLE 332

On the waterways declared to be international in the preceding Article, the nationals, property and flags of all Powers shall be treated on a footing of perfect equality, no distinction being made to the detriment of the nationals, property or flag of any Power between them and the nationals, property or flag of the riparian State itself or of the most favoured nation.

Nevertheless, German vessels shall not be entitled to carry passengers or goods by regular services between the ports of any Allied or Associated Power, without special authority from such Power.

ARTICLE 333

Where such charges are not precluded by any existing conventions, charges varying on different sections of a river may be levied on vessels using the navigable channels or their approaches, provided that they are intended solely to cover equitably the cost of maintaining in a navigable condition, or of improving, the river and its approaches, or to meet expenditure incurred in the interests of navigation. The schedule of such charges shall be calculated on the basis of such expenditure and shall be posted up in the ports. These charges shall be levied in such a manner as to render any detailed examination of cargoes unnecessary, except in cases of suspected fraud or contravention.

ARTICLE 334

The transit of vessels, passengers and goods on these waterways shall be effected in accordance with the general conditions prescribed for transit in Section I above.

When the two banks of an international river are within the same State goods in transit may be placed under seal or in the custody of customs agents. When the river forms a frontier goods and passengers in transit shall be exempt from all customs formalities; the loading and unloading of goods, and the embarkation and disembarkation of passengers, shall only take place in the ports specified by the riparian State.

ARTICLE 335

No dues of any kind other than those provided for in the present Part shall be levied along the course or at the mouth of these rivers.

This provision shall not prevent the fixing by the riparian States of customs, local octroi or consumption duties, or the creation of reasonable and uniform charges levied in the ports, in accordance with public tariffs, for the use of cranes, elevators, quays, warehouses, etc.

ARTICLE 336

In default of any special organisation for carrying out the works connected with the upkeep and improvement of the international portion of a navigable system, each riparian State shall be bound to take suitable measures to remove any obstacle or danger to navigation and to ensure the maintenance of good conditions of navigation.

If a State neglects to comply with this obligation any riparian State, or any State represented on the International Commission, if there is one, may appeal to the tribunal instituted for this purpose by the League of Nations.

ARTICLE 337

The same procedure shall be followed in the case of a riparian State undertaking any works of a nature to impede navigation in the international section. The tribunal mentioned in the preceding Article shall be entitled to enforce the suspension or suppression of such works, making due allowance in its decisions for all rights in connection with irrigation, water-power, fisheries, and other national interests, which, with the consent of all the riparian States or of all the States represented on the International Commission, if there is one, shall be given priority over the requirements of navigation.

Appeal to the tribunal of the League of Nations does not require the suspension of the works.

ARTICLE 338

The régime set out in Articles 332 to 337 above shall be superseded by one to be laid down in a General Convention drawn up by the Allied and Associated Powers, and approved by the League of Nations, relating to the waterways recognised in such Convention as having an international character. This Convention shall apply in particular to the whole or part of the above-mentioned river systems of the Elbe (*Labe*), the Oder (*Odra*), the Niemen (*Russstrom-Memel-Niemen*), and the Danube, and such other parts of these river systems as may be covered by a general definition.

Germany undertakes, in accordance with the provisions of Article 379, to adhere to the said General Convention as well as to all projects prepared in accordance with Article 343 below for the revision of existing international agreements and regulations.

ARTICLE 339

Germany shall cede to the Allied and Associated Powers concerned, within a maximum period of three months from the date on which notification shall be given her, a proportion of the tugs and vessels remaining registered in the ports of the river systems referred to in Article 331 after the deduction of those surrendered by way of restitution or reparation. Germany shall in the same way cede material of all kinds necessary to the Allied and Associated Powers concerned for the utilisation of those river systems.

The number of the tugs and boats, and the amount of the material so ceded, and their distribution, shall be determined by an arbitrator or arbitrators nominated by the United States of America, due regard being had to the legitimate needs of the parties concerned, and particularly to the shipping traffic during the five years preceding the war.

All craft so ceded shall be provided with their fittings and gear, shall be in a good state of repair and in condition to carry goods, and shall be selected from among those most recently built.

The cessions provided for in the present Article shall entail a credit of which the total amount, settled in a lump sum by the arbitrator or arbitrators, shall not in any case exceed the value of the capital expended in the initial establishment of the material ceded, and shall be set off against the total sums due from Germany; in consequence, the indemnification of the proprietors shall be a matter for Germany to deal with.

(2) *Special Clauses relating to the Elbe, the Oder and the Niemen* (*Russstrom-Memel-Niemen*)

ARTICLE 340

The Elbe (*Labe*) shall be placed under the administration of an International Commission which shall comprise:

4 representatives of the German States bordering on the river;
2 representatives of the Czecho-Slovak State;
1 representative of Great Britain;
1 representative of France;
1 representative of Italy;
1 representative of Belgium.

Whatever be the number of members present, each delegation shall have the right to record a number of votes equal to the number of representatives allotted to it.

If certain of these representatives cannot be appointed at the time of the coming into force of the present Treaty, the decisions of the Commission shall nevertheless be valid.

ARTICLE 341

The Oder (*Odra*) shall be placed under the administration of an International Commission, which shall comprise:

1 representative of Poland;
3 representatives of Prussia;
1 representative of the Czecho-Slovak State;
1 representative of Great Britain;
1 representative of France;
1 representative of Denmark;
1 representative of Sweden.

If certain of these representatives cannot be appointed at the time of the coming into force of the present Treaty, the decisions of the Commission shall nevertheless be valid.

ARTICLE 342

On a request being made to the League of Nations by any riparian State, the Niemen (*Russstrom-Memel-Niemen*) shall be placed under the administration of an International Commission, which shall comprise one representative of each riparian State, and three representatives of other States specified by the League of Nations.

ARTICLE 343

The International Commissions referred to in Articles 340 and 341 shall meet within three months of the date of the coming into force of the present Treaty. The International Commission referred to in Article 342 shall meet within three months from the date of the request made by a riparian State. Each of these Commissions shall proceed immediately to prepare a project for the revision of the existing international agreements and regulations, drawn up in conformity with the General Convention referred to in Article 338, should such Convention have been already concluded. In the absence of such Convention, the project for revision shall be in conformity with the principles of Articles 332 to 337 above.

ARTICLE 344

The projects referred to in the preceding Article shall, *inter alia*:

(*a*) designate the headquarters of the International Commission, and prescribe the manner in which its President is to be nominated;

(*b*) specify the extent of the Commission's powers, particularly in regard to the execution of works of maintenance, control, and improvement on the river system, the financial régime, the fixing and collection of charges, and regulations for navigation;

(*c*) define the sections of the river or its tributaries to which the international régime shall be applied.

ARTICLE 345

The international agreements and regulations at present governing the navigation of the Elbe (*Labe*), the Oder (*Odra*), and the Niemen (*Russstrom-Memel-Niemen*) shall be provisionally maintained in force until the ratification of the above-mentioned projects. Nevertheless, in all cases where such agreements and regulations in force are in conflict with the provisions of Articles 332 to 337 above, or of the General Convention to be concluded, the latter provisions shall prevail.

(3) *Special Clauses relating to the Danube*

ARTICLE 346

The European Commission of the Danube reassumes the powers it possessed before the war. Nevertheless, as a provisional measure, only representatives of Great Britain, France, Italy and Roumania shall constitute this Commission.

ARTICLE 347

From the point where the competence of the European Commission ceases, the Danube system referred to in Article 331 shall be placed under the administration of an International Commission composed as follows:

2 representatives of German riparian States;

1 representative of each other riparian State;

1 representative of each non-riparian State represented in the future on the European Commission of the Danube.

If certain of these representatives cannot be appointed at the time of the coming into force of the present Treaty, the decisions of the Commission shall nevertheless be valid.

ARTICLE 348

The International Commission provided for in the preceding Article shall meet as soon as possible after the coming into force of the present Treaty, and shall undertake provisionally the administration of the river in conformity with the provisions of Articles 332 to 337, until such time as a definitive statute regarding the Danube is concluded by the Powers nominated by the Allied and Associated Powers.

ARTICLE 349

Germany agrees to accept the régime which shall be laid down for the Danube by a Conference of the Powers nominated by the Allied and Associated Powers, which shall meet within one year after the coming into force of the present Treaty, and at which German representatives may be present.

ARTICLE 350

The mandate given by Article 57 of the Treaty of Berlin of July 13, 1878, to Austria-Hungary, and transferred by her to Hungary, to carry out works at the Iron Gates, is abrogated. The Commission entrusted with the administration of this part of the river shall lay down provisions for the settlement of accounts subject to the financial provisions of the present Treaty. Charges which may be necessary shall in no case be levied by Hungary.

ARTICLE 351

Should the Czecho-Slovak State, the Serb-Croat-Slovene State or Roumania, with the authorisation of or under mandate from the International Commission, undertake maintenance, improvement, weir, or other works on a part of the river system which forms a frontier, these States shall enjoy on the opposite bank, and also on the part of the bed which is outside their territory, all necessary facilities for the survey, execution and maintenance of such works.

ARTICLE 352

Germany shall be obliged to make to the European Commission of the Danube all restitutions, reparations and indemnities for damages inflicted on the Commission during the war.

ARTICLE 353

Should a deep-draught Rhine-Danube navigable waterway be constructed, Germany undertakes to apply thereto the régime prescribed in Articles 332 to 338.

Chapter IV

CLAUSES RELATING TO THE RHINE AND THE MOSELLE

Article 354

As from the coming into force of the present Treaty, the Convention of Mannheim of October 17, 1868, together with the Final Protocol thereof, shall continue to govern navigation on the Rhine, subject to the conditions hereinafter laid down.

In the event of any provisions of the said Convention being in conflict with those laid down by the General Convention referred to in Article 338 (which shall apply to the Rhine) the provisions of the General Convention shall prevail.

Within a maximum period of six months from the coming into force of the present Treaty, the Central Commission referred to in Article 355 shall meet to draw up a project of revision of the Convention of Mannheim. This project shall be drawn up in harmony with the provisions of the General Convention referred to above, should this have been concluded by that time, and shall be submitted to the Powers represented on the Central Commission. Germany hereby agrees to adhere to the project so drawn up.

Further, the modifications set out in the following Articles shall immediately be made in the Convention of Mannheim.

The Allied and Associated Powers reserve to themselves the right to arrive at an understanding in this connection with Holland, and Germany hereby agrees to accede if required to any such understanding.

Article 355

The Central Commission provided for in the Convention of Mannheim shall consist of nineteen members, viz.:

2 representatives of the Netherlands;
2 representatives of Switzerland;
4 representatives of German riparian States;
4 representatives of France, which in addition shall appoint the President of the Commission;
2 representatives of Great Britain;
2 representatives of Italy;
2 representatives of Belgium.

The headquarters of the Central Commission shall be at Strasburg.

Whatever be the number of members present, each Delegation shall have the right to record a number of votes equal to the number of representatives allotted to it.

If certain of these representatives cannot be appointed at the time of the coming into force of the present Treaty, the decisions of the Commission shall nevertheless be valid.

ARTICLE 356

Vessels of all nations, and their cargoes, shall have the same rights and privileges as those which are granted to vessels belonging to the Rhine navigation, and to their cargoes.

None of the provisions contained in Articles 15 to 20 and 26 of the above-mentioned Convention of Mannheim, in Article 4 of the Final Protocol thereof, or in later Conventions, shall impede the free navigation of vessels and crews of all nations on the Rhine and on waterways to which such Conventions apply, subject to compliance with the regulations concerning pilotage and other police measures drawn up by the Central Commission.

The provisions of Article 22 of the Convention of Mannheim and of Article 5 of the Final Protocol thereof shall be applied only to vessels registered on the Rhine. The Central Commission shall decide on the steps to be taken to ensure that other vessels satisfy the conditions of the general regulations applying to navigation on the Rhine.

ARTICLE 357

Within a maximum period of three months from the date on which notification shall be given Germany shall cede to France tugs and vessels, from among those remaining registered in German Rhine ports after the deduction of those surrendered by way of restitution or reparation, or shares in German Rhine navigation companies.

When vessels and tugs are ceded, such vessels and tugs, together with their fittings and gear, shall be in good state of repair, shall be in condition to carry on commercial traffic on the Rhine, and shall be selected from among those most recently built.

The same procedure shall be followed in the matter of the cession by Germany to France of:

(1) the installations, berthing and anchorage accommodation, platforms, docks, warehouses, plant, etc., which German subjects or German companies owned on August 1, 1914, in the port of Rotterdam, and

(2) the shares or interests which Germany or German nationals possessed in such installations at the same date.

The amount and specifications of such cessions shall be determined within one year of the coming into force of the present Treaty by an arbitrator or arbitrators appointed by the United States of America, due regard being had to the legitimate needs of the parties concerned.

The cessions provided for in the present Article shall entail a credit of which the total amount, settled in a lump sum by the arbitrator or arbitrators mentioned above, shall not in any case exceed the value of the capital expended in the initial establishment of the ceded material and installations, and shall be set off against the total sums due from Germany; in consequence, the indemnification of the proprietors shall be a matter for Germany to deal with.

ARTICLE 358

Subject to the obligation to comply with the provisions of the Convention of Mannheim or of the Convention which may be substituted therefor, and to the stipulations of the present Treaty, France shall have on the whole course of the Rhine included between the two extreme points of the French frontier:

(*a*) the right to take water from the Rhine to feed navigation and irrigation canals (constructed or to be constructed) or for any other purpose, and to execute on the German bank all works necessary for the exercise of this right;

(*b*) the exclusive right to the power derived from works of regulation on the river, subject to the payment to Germany of the value of half the power actually produced, this payment, which will take into account the cost of the works necessary for producing the power, being made either in money or in power and in default of agreement being determined by arbitration. For this purpose France alone shall have the right to carry out in this part of the river all works of regulation (weirs or other works) which she may consider necessary for the production of power. Similarly, the right of taking water from the Rhine is accorded to Belgium to feed the Rhine-Meuse navigable waterway provided for below.

The exercise of the rights mentioned under (*a*) and (*b*) of the present Article shall not interfere with navigability nor reduce the facilities for navigation, either in the bed of the Rhine or in the derivations which may be substituted therefor, nor shall it involve any increase in the tolls formerly levied under the Convention in force. All proposed schemes shall be laid before the Central Commission in order that that Commission may assure itself that these conditions are complied with.

To ensure the proper and faithful execution of the provisions contained in (*a*) and (*b*) above, Germany:

(1) binds herself not to undertake or to allow the construction of any lateral canal or any derivation on the right bank of the river opposite the French frontiers;

(2) recognises the possession by France of the right of support on and the right of way over all lands situated on the right bank which may be required in order to survey, to build, and to operate weirs which France, with the consent of the Central Commission, may subsequently decide to establish. In accordance with such consent, France shall be entitled to decide upon and fix the limits of the necessary sites, and she shall be permitted to occupy such lands after a period of two months after simple notification, subject to the payment by her to Germany of indemnities of which the total amount shall be fixed by the Central Commission. Germany shall make it her business to indemnify the proprietors whose property will be burdened with such servitudes or permanently occupied by the works.

Should Switzerland so demand, and if the Central Commission approves, the same rights shall be accorded to Switzerland for the part of the river forming her frontier with other riparian States;

(3) shall hand over to the French Government, during the month following the coming into force of the present Treaty, all projects, designs, drafts of concessions and of specifications concerning the regulation of the Rhine for any purpose whatever which have been drawn up or received by the Governments of Alsace-Lorraine or of the Grand Duchy of Baden.

ARTICLE 359

Subject to the preceding provisions, no works shall be carried out in the bed or on either bank of the Rhine where it forms the boundary of France and Germany without the previous approval of the Central Commission or of its agents.

ARTICLE 360

France reserves the option of substituting herself as regards the rights and obligations resulting from agreements arrived at between the Government of Alsace-Lorraine and the Grand Duchy of Baden concerning the works to be carried out on the Rhine; she may also denounce such agreements within a term of five years dating from the coming into force of the present Treaty.

France shall also have the option of causing works to be carried out which may be recognised as necessary by the Central Commission for the upkeep or improvement of the navigability of the Rhine above Mannheim.

ARTICLE 361

Should Belgium within a period of 25 years from the coming into force of the present Treaty decide to create a deep-draught Rhine-Meuse navigable waterway, in the region of Ruhrort, Germany shall be bound to construct, in accordance with plans to be communicated to her by the Belgian Government, after agreement with the Central Commission, the portion of this navigable waterway situated within her territory.

The Belgian Government shall, for this purpose, have the right to carry out on the ground all necessary surveys.

Should Germany fail to carry out all or part of these works, the Central Commission shall be entitled to carry them out instead; and, for this purpose, the Commission may decide upon and fix the limits of the necessary sites and occupy the ground after a period of two months after simple notification, subject to the payment of indemnities to be fixed by it and paid by Germany.

This navigable waterway shall be placed under the same administrative régime as the Rhine itself, and the division of the cost of initial construction, including the above indemnities, among the States crossed thereby shall be made by the Central Commission.

ARTICLE 362

Germany hereby agrees to offer no objection to any proposals of the Central Rhine Commission for extending its jurisdiction:

(1) to the Moselle below the Franco-Luxemburg frontier down to the Rhine, subject to the consent of Luxemburg;

(2) to the Rhine above Basle up to the Lake of Constance, subject to the consent of Switzerland;

(3) to the lateral canals and channels which may be established either to duplicate or to improve naturally navigable sections of the Rhine or the Moselle, or to connect two naturally navigable sections of these rivers, and also any other parts of the Rhine river system which may be covered by the General Convention provided for in Article 338 above.

CHAPTER V

CLAUSES GIVING TO THE CZECHO-SLOVAK STATE THE USE OF NORTHERN PORTS

ARTICLE 363

In the ports of Hamburg and Stettin Germany shall lease to the Czecho-Slovak State, for a period of 99 years, areas which shall be placed under the general régime of free zones and shall be used for the direct transit of goods coming from or going to that State.

ARTICLE 364

The delimitation of these areas, and their equipment, their exploitation, and in general all conditions for their utilisation, including the amount of the rental, shall be decided by a Commission consisting of one delegate of Germany, one delegate of the Czecho-Slovak State and one delegate of Great Britain. These conditions shall be susceptible of revision every ten years in the same manner.

Germany declares in advance that she will adhere to the decisions so taken.

SECTION III

Railways

CHAPTER 1

CLAUSES RELATING TO INTERNATIONAL TRANSPORT

ARTICLE 365

Goods coming from the territories of the Allied and Associated Powers, and going to Germany, or in transit through Germany from or to the territories of the Allied and Associated Powers, shall enjoy on the German railways as regards charges to be collected (rebates and drawbacks being taken into account), facilities, and all other matters, the most favourable treatment applied to goods of the same kind carried on any German lines, either in internal traffic, or for export, import or in transit, under similar conditions of transport, for example as regards length of route. The same rule shall be applied, on the request of one or more of the Allied and Associated Powers, to goods specially designated by such Power or Powers coming from Germany and going to their territories.

International tariffs established in accordance with the rates referred to in the preceding paragraph and involving through way-bills shall be established when one of the Allied and Associated Powers shall require it from Germany.

ARTICLE 366

From the coming into force of the present Treaty the High Contracting Parties shall renew, in so far as concerns them and under the reserves indicated in the second paragraph of the present Article, the conventions and arrangements signed at Berne on October 14, 1890, September 20, 1893, July 16, 1895, June 16, 1898, and September 19, 1906, regarding the transportation of goods by rail.

If within five years from the date of the coming into force of the present Treaty a new convention for the transportation of passengers, luggage and goods by rail shall have been concluded to replace the Berne Convention of October 14, 1890, and the subsequent additions referred to above, this new convention and the supplementary provisions for international transport by rail which may be based on it shall bind Germany, even if she shall have refused to take part in the preparation of the convention or to subscribe to it. Until a new convention shall have been concluded, Germany shall conform to the provisions of the Berne Convention and the subsequent additions referred to above, and to the current supplementary provisions.

ARTICLE 367

Germany shall be bound to co-operate in the establishment of through ticket services (for passengers and their luggage) which shall be required by any of the Allied and Associated Powers to ensure their communication by rail with each other and with all other countries by transit across the territories of Germany; in particular Germany shall, for this purpose, accept trains and carriages coming from the territories of the Allied and Associated Powers and shall forward them with a speed at least equal to that of her best long-distance trains on the same lines. The rates applicable to such through services shall not in any case be higher than the rates collected on German internal services for the same distance, under the same conditions of speed and comfort.

The tariffs applicable under the same conditions of speed and comfort to the transportation of emigrants going to or coming from ports of the Allied and Associated Powers and using the German railways shall not be at a higher kilometric rate than the most favourable tariffs (drawbacks and rebates being taken into account) enjoyed on the said railways by emigrants going to or coming from any other ports.

ARTICLE 368

Germany shall not apply specially to such through services, or to the transportation of emigrants going to or coming from the ports of the Allied and Associated Powers, any technical, fiscal or administrative measures, such as measures of customs examination, general police, sanitary police, and control, the result of which would be to impede or delay such services.

ARTICLE 369

In case of transport partly by rail and partly by internal navigation, with or without through way-bill, the preceding Articles shall apply to the part of the journey performed by rail.

CHAPTER II

ROLLING-STOCK

ARTICLE 370

Germany undertakes that German wagons shall be fitted with apparatus allowing:

(1) of their inclusion in goods trains on the lines of such of the Allied and Associated Powers as are parties to the Berne Convention of May 15, 1886, as modified on May 18, 1907, without hampering the action of the continuous brake which may be adopted in such countries within ten years of the coming into force of the present Treaty, and

(2) of the acceptance of wagons of such countries in all goods trains on the German lines.

The rolling stock of the Allied and Associated Powers shall enjoy on the German lines the same treatment as German rolling stock as regards movement, upkeep and repairs.

CHAPTER III

CESSIONS OF RAILWAY LINES

ARTICLE 371

Subject to any special provisions concerning the cession of ports, waterways and railways situated in the territories over which Germany abandons her sovereignty, and to the financial conditions relating to the concessionnaires and the pensioning of the personnel, the cession of railways will take place under the following conditions:

(1) The works and installations of all the railroads shall be handed over complete and in good condition.

(2) When a railway system possessing its own rolling-stock is handed over in its entirety by Germany to one of the Allied and Associated Powers, such stock shall be handed over complete, in accordance with the last inventory before November 11, 1918, and in a normal state of upkeep.

(3) As regards lines without any special rolling-stock, Commissions of experts designated by the Allied and Associated Powers, on which Germany shall be represented, shall fix the proportion of the stock existing on the system to which those lines belong to be handed over. These Commissions shall have regard to the amount of the material registered on these lines in the last inventory before November 11, 1918, the length of track (sidings included), and the nature and amount of the traffic. These Commissions shall also specify the locomotives, carriages and wagons to be handed over in each case; they shall decide upon the conditions of their acceptance, and shall make the provisional arrangements necessary to ensure their repair in German workshops.

(4) Stocks of stores, fittings and plant shall be handed over under the same conditions as the rolling-stock.

The provisions of paragraphs 3 and 4 above shall be applied to the lines of former Russian Poland converted by Germany to the German gauge, such lines being regarded as detached from the Prussian State System.

CHAPTER IV

PROVISIONS RELATING TO CERTAIN RAILWAY LINES

ARTICLE 372

When as a result of the fixing of new frontiers a railway connection between two parts of the same country crosses another country, or a branch line from one country has its terminus in another, the conditions of working, if not specifically provided for in the present Treaty, shall be laid down in a convention between the railway administrations concerned. If the administrations cannot come to an agreement as to the terms of such convention, the points of difference shall be decided by commissions of experts composed as provided in the preceding Article.

ARTICLE 373

Within a period of five years from the coming into force of the present Treaty the Czecho-Slovak State may require the construction of a railway line in German territory between the stations of Schlauney and Nachod. The cost of construction shall be borne by the Czecho-Slovak State.

ARTICLE 374

Germany undertakes to accept, within ten years of the coming into force of the present Treaty, on request being made by the Swiss Government after agreement with the Italian Government, the denunciation of the International Convention of October 13, 1909, relative to the St. Gothard railway. In the absence of agreement as to the conditions of such denunciation, Germany hereby agrees to accept the decision of an arbitrator designated by the United States of America.

CHAPTER V

TRANSITORY PROVISIONS

ARTICLE 375

Germany shall carry out the instructions given her, in regard to transport, by an authorised body acting on behalf of the Allied and Associated Powers:

(1) For the carriage of troops under the provisions of the present Treaty, and of material, ammunition and supplies for army use;

(2) As a temporary measure, for the transportation of supplies for certain regions, as well as for the restoration, as rapidly as possible, of the normal conditions of transport, and for the organisation of postal and telegraphic services.

SECTION IV

Disputes and Revision of Permanent Clauses

ARTICLE 376

Disputes which may arise between interested Powers with regard to the interpretation and application of the preceding Articles shall be settled as provided by the League of Nations.

ARTICLE 377

At any time the League of Nations may recommend the revision of such of these Articles as relate to a permanent administrative régime.

ARTICLE 378

The stipulations in Articles 321 to 330, 332, 365, and 367 to 369 shall be subject to revision by the Council of the League of Nations at any time after five years from the coming into force of the present Treaty.

Failing such revision, no Allied or Associated Power can claim after the expiration of the above period of five years the benefit of any of the stipulations in the Articles enumerated above on behalf of any portion of its territories in which reciprocity is not accorded in respect of such stipulations. The period of five years during which reciprocity cannot be demanded may be prolonged by the Council of the League of Nations.

SECTION V

Special Provision

ARTICLE 379

Without prejudice to the special obligations imposed on her by the present Treaty for the benefit of the Allied and Associated Powers, Germany undertakes to adhere to any General Conventions regarding the international régime of transit, waterways, ports or railways which may be concluded by the Allied and Associated Powers, with the approval of the League of Nations, within five years of the coming into force of the present Treaty.

SECTION VI

Clauses Relating to the Kiel Canal

ARTICLE 380

The Kiel Canal and its approaches shall be maintained free and open to the vessels of commerce and of war of all nations at peace with Germany on terms of entire equality.

ARTICLE 381

The nationals, property and vessels of all Powers shall, in respect of charges, facilities, and in all other respects, be treated on a footing of perfect equality in the use of the Canal, no distinction being made to the detriment of nationals, property and vessels of any Power between them and the nationals, property and vessels of Germany or of the most favoured nation.

No impediment shall be placed on the movement of persons or vessels other than those arising out of police, customs, sanitary, emigration or immigration regulations and those relating to the import or export of prohibited goods. Such regulations must be reasonable and uniform and must not unnecessarily impede traffic.

ARTICLE 382

Only such charges may be levied on vessels using the Canal or its approaches as are intended to cover in an equitable manner the cost of maintaining in a navigable condition, or of improving, the Canal or its approaches, or to meet expenses incurred in the interests of navigation. The schedule of such charges shall be calculated on the basis of such expenses, and shall be posted up in the ports.

These charges shall be levied in such a manner as to render any detailed examination of cargoes unnecessary, except in the case of suspected fraud or contravention.

ARTICLE 383

Goods in transit may be placed under seal or in the custody of customs agents; the loading and unloading of goods, and the embarkation and disembarkation of passengers, shall only take place in the ports specified by Germany.

ARTICLE 384

No charges of any kind other than those provided for in the present Treaty shall be levied along the course or at the approaches of the Kiel Canal.

ARTICLE 385

Germany shall be bound to take suitable measures to remove any obstacle or danger to navigation, and to ensure the maintenance of good conditions of navigation. She shall not undertake any works of a nature to impede navigation on the Canal or its approaches.

ARTICLE 386

In the event of violation of any of the conditions of Articles 380 to 386, or of disputes as to the interpretation of these Articles, any interested Power can appeal to the jurisdiction instituted for the purpose by the League of Nations.

In order to avoid reference of small questions to the League of Nations, Germany will establish a local authority at Kiel qualified to deal with disputes in the first instance and to give satisfaction so far as possible to complaints which may be presented through the consular representatives of the interested Powers.

PART XIII

[LABOUR]

The Constitution of the International Labour Organisation
[44]

PART XIV

GUARANTEES

SECTION I

Western Europe

ARTICLE 428

As a guarantee for the execution of the present Treaty by Germany, the German territory situated to the west of the Rhine, together with the bridge-heads, will be occupied by Allied and Associated troops for a period of fifteen years from the coming into force of the present Treaty.

---

[44] For text, see *post*, p. 241.

ARTICLE 429

If the conditions of the present Treaty are faithfully carried out by Germany, the occupation referred to in Article 428 will be successively restricted as follows:

(1) At the expiration of five years there will be evacuated: the bridgehead of Cologne and the territories north of a line running along the Ruhr, then along the railway Jülich, Duren, Euskirchen, Rheinbach, thence along the road Rheinbach to Sinzig, and reaching the Rhine at the confluence with the Ahr; the roads, railways and places mentioned above being excluded from the area evacuated.

(2) At the expiration of ten years there will be evacuated: the bridgehead of Coblenz and the territories north of a line to be drawn from the intersection between the frontiers of Belgium, Germany and Holland, running about 4 kilometres south of Aix-la-Chapelle, then to and following the crest of Forst Gemünd, then east of the railway of the Urft Valley, then along Blankenheim, Valdorf, Dreis, Ulmen to and following the Moselle from Bremm to Nehren, then passing by Kappel and Simmern, then following the ridge of the heights between Simmern and the Rhine and reaching this river at Bacharach; all the places, valleys, roads and railways mentioned above being excluded from the area evacuated.

(3) At the expiration of fifteen years there will be evacuated: the bridgehead of Mainz, the bridgehead of Kehl and the remainder of the German territory under occupation.

If at that date the guarantees against unprovoked aggression by Germany are not considered sufficient by the Allied and Associated Governments, the evacuation of the occupying troops may be delayed to the extent regarded as necessary for the purpose of obtaining the required guarantees.

ARTICLE 430

In case either during the occupation or after the expiration of the fifteen years referred to above the Reparation Commission finds that Germany refuses to observe the whole or part of her obligations under the present Treaty with regard to reparation, the whole or part of the areas specified in Article 429 will be re-occupied immediately by the Allied and Associated forces.

ARTICLE 431

If before the expiration of the period of fifteen years Germany complies with all the undertakings resulting from the present Treaty, the occupying forces will be withdrawn immediately.

ARTICLE 432

All matters relating to the occupation and not provided for by the present Treaty shall be regulated by subsequent agreements, which Germany hereby undertakes to observe.

SECTION II

Eastern Europe

ARTICLE 433

As a guarantee for the execution of the provisions of the present Treaty, by which Germany accepts definitely the abrogation of the Brest-Litovsk Treaty, and of all treaties, conventions and agreements entered into by her with the Maximalist Government in Russia, and in order to ensure the restoration of peace and good government in the Baltic Provinces and Lithuania, all German troops at present in the said territories shall return to within the frontiers of Germany as soon as the Governments of the Principal Allied and Associated Powers shall think the moment suitable, having regard to the internal situation of these territories. These troops shall abstain from all requisitions and seizures and from any other coercive measures, with a view to obtaining supplies intended for Germany, and shall in no way interfere with such measures for national defence as may be adopted by the Provisional Governments of Esthonia, Latvia and Lithuania.

No other German troops shall, pending the evacuation or after the evacuation is complete, be admitted to the said territories.

PART XV

MISCELLANEOUS PROVISIONS

ARTICLE 434

Germany undertakes to recognise the full force of the Treaties of Peace and Additional Conventions which may be concluded by the Allied and Associated Powers with the Powers who fought on the side of Germany and to recognise whatever dispositions may be made concerning the territories of the former Austro-Hungarian Monarchy, of the Kingdom of Bulgaria and of the Ottoman Empire, and to recognize the new States within their frontiers as there laid down.

ARTICLE 435

The High Contracting Parties, while they recognize the guarantees stipulated by the Treaties of 1815, and especially by the Act of November 20, 1815, in favour of Switzerland, the said guarantees constituting international obligations for the maintenance of peace, declare nevertheless that the provisions of these treaties, conventions, declarations and other supplementary Acts concerning the neutralized zone of Savoy, as laid down in paragraph

1 of Article 92 of the Final Act of the Congress of Vienna and in paragraph 2 of Article 3 of the Treaty of Paris of November 20, 1815, are no longer consistent with present conditions. For this reason the High Contracting Parties take note of the agreement reached between the French Government and the Swiss Government for the abrogation of the stipulations relating to this zone which are and remain abrogated.

The High Contracting Parties also agree that the stipulations of the Treaties of 1815 and of the other supplementary Acts concerning the free zones of Upper Savoy and the Gex district are no longer consistent with present conditions, and that it is for France and Switzerland to come to an agreement together with a view to settling between themselves the status of these territories under such conditions as shall be considered suitable by both countries.

ANNEX

I

The Swiss Federal Council has informed the French Government on May 5, 1919, that after examining the provisions of Article 435 in a like spirit of sincere friendship it has happily reached the conclusion that it was possible to acquiesce in it under the following conditions and reservations:

(1) The neutralized zone of Haute-Savoie:

(a) It will be understood that as long as the Federal Chambers have not ratified the agreement come to between the two Governments concerning the abrogation of the stipulations in respect of the neutralized zone of Savoy, nothing will be definitively settled, on one side or the other, in regard to this subject.

(b) The assent given by the Swiss Government to the abrogation of the above mentioned stipulations presupposes, in conformity with the text adopted, the recognition of the guarantees formulated in favour of Switzerland by the Treaties of 1815 and particularly by the Declaration of November 20, 1815.

(c) The agreement between the Governments of France and Switzerland for the abrogation of the above mentioned stipulations will only be considered as valid if the Treaty of Peace contains this Article in its present wording. In addition the Parties to the Treaty of Peace should endeavour to obtain the assent of the signatory Powers of the Treaties of 1815 and of the Declaration of November 20, 1815, which are not signatories of the present Treaty of Peace.

(2) Free zone of Haute-Savoie and the district of Gex:

(a) The Federal Council makes the most express reservations to the interpretation to be given to the statement mentioned in the last paragraph of the above Article for insertion in the Treaty of Peace, which provides that "the stipulations of the Treaties of 1815 and other supplementary acts concerning the free zones of Haute-Savoie and the Gex district are no longer consistent with present conditions". The Federal Council would not wish that its acceptance of the above wording should lead to the conclusion that it would agree to the suppression of a system intended to give neighbouring territory the benefit of a special régime which is appropriate to the geographical and economical situation and which has been well tested.

In the opinion of the Federal Council the question is not the modification of the customs system of the zones as set up by the Treaties mentioned above, but only the regulation in a manner more appropriate to the economic conditions of the present day of the terms of the exchange of goods between the regions in question. The Federal Council has been led to make the preceding observations by the perusal of the draft Convention concerning the future constitution of the zones which was annexed to the note of April 26 from the French Government. While making the above reservations the Federal Council declares its readiness to examine in the most friendly spirit any proposals which the French Government may deem it convenient to make on the subject.

(b) It is conceded that the stipulations of the Treaties of 1815 and other supplementary acts relative to the free zones will remain in force until a new arrangement is come to between France and Switzerland to regulate matters in this territory.

II

The French Government have addressed to the Swiss Government, on May 18, 1919, the following note in reply to the communication set out in the preceding paragraph:

In a note dated May 5 the Swiss Legation in Paris was good enough to inform the Government of the French Republic that the Federal Government adhered to the proposed Article to be inserted in the Treaty of Peace between the Allied and Associated Governments and Germany.

The French Government have taken note with much pleasure of the agreement thus reached, and, at their request, the proposed Article, which had been accepted by the Allied and Associated Governments, has been inserted under No. 435 in the Peace conditions presented to the German Plenipotentiaries.

The Swiss Government, in their note of May 5 on this subject, have expressed various views and reservations.

Concerning the observations relating to the free zones of Haute-Savoie and the Gex district, the French Government have the honour to observe that the provisions of the last paragraph of Article 435 are so clear that their purport cannot be misapprehended, especially where it implies that no other Power but France and Switzerland will in future be interested in that question.

The French Government, on their part, are anxious to protect the interests of the French territories concerned, and, with that object, having their special situation in view, they bear in mind the desirability of assuring them a suitable customs régime and determining, in a manner better suited to present conditions, the methods of exchanges between these territories and the adjacent Swiss territories, while taking into account the reciprocal interests of both regions.

It is understood that this must in no way prejudice the right of France to adjust her customs line in this region in conformity with her political frontier, as is done on the other portions of her territorial boundaries, and as was done by Switzerland long ago on her own boundaries in this region.

The French Government are pleased to note on this subject in what a friendly disposition the Swiss Government take this opportunity of declaring their willingness to consider any French proposal dealing with the system to be substituted for the present régime of the said free zones, which the French Government intend to formulate in the same friendly spirit.

Moreover, the French Government have no doubt that the provisional maintenance of the régime of 1815 as to the free zones referred to in the above mentioned paragraph of the note from the Swiss Legation of May 5, whose object is to provide for the passage from the present régime to the conventional régime, will cause no delay whatsoever in the establishment of the new situation which has been found necessary by the two Governments. This remark applies also to the ratification by the Federal Chambers, dealt with in paragraph 1 (a), of the Swiss note of May 5, under the heading "Neutralized zone of Haute-Savoie".

ARTICLE 436

The High Contracting Parties declare and place on record that they have taken note of the Treaty signed by the Government of the French Republic on July 17, 1918, with His Serene Highness the Prince of Monaco defining the relations between France and the Principality.

ARTICLE 437

The High Contracting Parties agree that, in the absence of a subsequent agreement to the contrary, the Chairman of any Commission established by the present Treaty shall in the event of an equality of votes be entitled to a second vote.

ARTICLE 438

The Allied and Associated Powers agree that where Christian religious missions were being maintained by German societies or persons in territory belonging to them, or of which the government is entrusted to them in accordance with the present Treaty, the property which these missions or missionary societies possessed, including that of trading societies whose profits were devoted to the support of missions, shall continue to be devoted to missionary purposes. In order to ensure the due execution of this undertaking the Allied and Associated Governments will hand over such property to boards of trustees appointed by or approved by the Governments and composed of persons holding the faith of the Mission whose property is involved.

The Allied and Associated Governments, while continuing to maintain full control as to the individuals by whom the Missions are conducted, will safeguard the interests of such Missions.

Germany, taking note of the above undertaking, agrees to accept all arrangements made or to be made by the Allied or Associated Government concerned for carrying on the work of the said missions or trading societies and waives all claims on their behalf.

ARTICLE 439

Without prejudice to the provisions of the present Treaty, Germany undertakes not to put forward directly or indirectly against any Allied or Associated Power, signatory of the present Treaty, including those which without having declared war, have broken off diplomatic relations with the German Empire, any pecuniary claim based on events which occurred at any time before the coming into force of the present Treaty.

The present stipulation will bar completely and finally all claims of this nature, which will be thenceforward extinguished, whoever may be the parties in interest.

ARTICLE 440

Germany accepts and recognises as valid and binding all decrees and orders concerning German ships and goods and all orders relating to the payment of costs made by any Prize Court of any of the Allied or Associated Powers, and undertakes not to put forward any claim arising out of such decrees or orders on behalf of any German national.

The Allied and Associated Powers reserve the right to examine in such manner as they may determine all decisions and orders of German Prize Courts, whether affecting the property rights of nationals of those Powers or of neutral Powers. Germany agrees to furnish copies of all the documents constituting the record of the cases, including the decisions and orders made, and to accept and give effect to the recommendations made after such examination of the cases.

The present Treaty, of which the French and English texts are both authentic, shall be ratified.

The deposit of ratifications shall be made at Paris as soon as possible.

Powers of which the seat of the Government is outside Europe will be entitled merely to inform the Government of the French Republic through their diplomatic representative at Paris that their ratification has been given; in that case they must transmit the instrument of ratification as soon as possible.

A first procès-verbal of the deposit of ratifications will be drawn up as soon as the Treaty has been ratified by Germany on the one hand, and by three of the Principal Allied and Associated Powers on the other hand.

From the date of this first procès-verbal the Treaty will come into force between the High Contracting Parties who have ratified it. For the determination of all periods of time provided for in the present Treaty this date will be the date of the coming into force of the Treaty.

In all other respects the Treaty will enter into force for each Power at the date of the deposit of its ratification.

The French Government will transmit to all the signatory Powers a certified copy of the procès-verbaux of the deposit of ratifications.

In faith whereof the above-named Plenipotentiaries have signed the present Treaty.

Done at Versailles, the twenty-eighth day of June, one thousand nine hundred and nineteen, in a single copy which will remain deposited in the archives of the French Republic, and of which authenticated copies will be transmitted to each of the Signatory Powers.

[For the United States:]
WOODROW WILSON [SEAL]
ROBERT LANSING [SEAL]
HENRY WHITE [SEAL]
E. M. HOUSE [SEAL]
TASKER H. BLISS [SEAL]

[For the United Kingdom:]
D. LLOYD GEORGE [SEAL]
A. BONAR LAW [SEAL]
MILNER [SEAL]
ARTHUR JAMES BALFOUR [SEAL]
GEORGE N. BARNES [SEAL]

[For the Dominion of Canada:]
CHAS. J. DOHERTY [SEAL]
ARTHUR L. SIFTON [SEAL]

[For the Commonwealth of Australia:]
W. M. HUGHES [SEAL]
JOSEPH COOK [SEAL]

[For the Union of South Africa:]
LOUIS BOTHA [SEAL]
J. CHR. SMUTS [SEAL]

[For the Dominion of New Zealand:]
W. F. MASSEY [SEAL]

[For India:]
ED. S. MONTAGU [SEAL]
GANGA SINGH, MAHARAJA DE
BIKANER [SEAL]

[For France:]
G. CLEMENCEAU [SEAL]
S. PICHON [SEAL]
L. L. KLOTZ [SEAL]
ANDRÉ TARDIEU [SEAL]
JULES CAMBON [SEAL]

[For Italy:]
SIDNEY SONNINO [SEAL]
IMPERIALI [SEAL]
SILVIO CRESPI [SEAL]

[For Japan:]
SAIONJI [SEAL]
N. MAKINO [SEAL]
S. CHINDA [SEAL]
K. MATSUI [SEAL]
H. IJUIN [SEAL]

[For Belgium:]
HYMANS [SEAL]
J. VAN DEN HEUVEL [SEAL]
EMILE VANDERVELDE [SEAL]

[For Bolivia:]
ISMAEL MONTES [SEAL]

[For Brazil:]
CALOGERAS [SEAL]
RODRIGO OCTAVIO [SEAL]

[For China:]

[For Cuba:]
ANTONIO S. DE BUSTAMANTE [SEAL]

[For Ecuador:]
E. DORN Y DE ALSUA [SEAL]

[For Greece:]
ELEFTHERIOS VENISÉLOS [SEAL]
NICOLAS POLITIS [SEAL]

[For Guatemala:]
JOAQUIN MÉNDEZ [SEAL]

[For Haiti:]
TERTULLIEN GUILBAUD [SEAL]

[For the Hedjaz:]
   M. Rustem Haidar [seal]
   Abdul Hadi Aouni [seal]

[For Honduras:]
   P. Bonilla [seal]

[For Liberia:]
   C. D. B. King [seal]

[For Nicaragua:]
   Salvador Chamorro [seal]

[For Panama:]
   Antonio Burgos [seal]

[For Peru:]
   C. G. Candamo [seal]

[For Poland:]
   I. J. Paderewski [seal]
   Roman Dmowski [seal]

[For Portugal:]
   Affonso Costa [seal]
   Augusto Soares [seal]

[For Roumania:]
   Ion I. C. Bratiano [seal]
   General C. Coanda [seal]

[For the Serbs, Croats, and Slovenes:]
   Nik P. Pachitch [seal]
   Dr. Ante Trumbic [seal]
   Mil. R. Vesnitch [seal]

[For Siam:]
   Charoon [seal]
   Traidos Prabandhu [seal]

[For the Czecho-Slovak Republic:]
   Karel Kramar
   Dr. Edward Benes [seal]

[For Uruguay:]
   J. A. Buero [seal]

[For Germany:]
   Hermann Müller [seal]
   Dr. Bell [seal]

Protocol of June 28, 1919

With a view to indicating precisely the conditions in which certain provisions of the Treaty of even date are to be carried out, it is agreed by the High Contracting Parties that:

(1) A Commission will be appointed by the Principal Allied and Associated Powers to supervise the destruction of the fortifications of Heligoland in accordance with the Treaty. This Commission will be authorized to decide what portion of the works protecting the coast from sea erosion are to be maintained and what portion must be destroyed;

(2) Sums reimbursed by Germany to German nationals to indemnify them in respect of the interests which they may be found to possess in the railways and mines referred to in the second paragraph of Article 156 shall be credited to Germany against the sums due by way of reparation;

(3) The list of persons to be handed over to the Allied and Associated Governments by Germany under the second paragraph of Article 228 shall be communicated to the German Government within a month from the coming into force of the Treaty;

(4) The Reparation Commission referred to in Article 240 and paragraphs 2, 3 and 4 of Annex IV cannot require trade secrets or other confidential information to be divulged;

(5) From the signature of the Treaty and within the ensuing four months Germany will be entitled to submit for examination by the Allied and Associated Powers documents and proposals in order to expedite the work connected with reparation, and thus to shorten the investigation and to accelerate the decisions;

(6) Proceedings will be taken against persons who have committed punishable offences in the liquidation of German property, and the Allied and Associated Powers will welcome any information or evidence which the German Government can furnish on this subject.

Done at Versailles, the twenty-eigthth day of June, one thousand nine hundred and nineteen.

[For the United States:]
WOODROW WILSON
ROBERT LANSING
HENRY WHITE
E. M. HOUSE
TASKER H. BLISS

[For the United Kingdom:]
D. LLOYD GEORGE
A. BONAR LAW
MILNER
ARTHUR JAMES BALFOUR
GEORGE N. BARNES

[For the Dominion of Canada:]
CHAS. J. DOHERTY
ARTHUR L. SIFTON

[For the Commonwealth of Australia:]
W. M. HUGHES
JOSEPH COOK

[For the Union of South Africa:]
LOUIS BOTHA
J. C. SMUTS

[For the Dominion of New Zealand:]
W. F. MASSEY

[For India:]
ED. S. MONTAGU
GANGA SINGH, MAHARAJA DE
    BIKANER

[For France:]
G. CLEMENCEAU
S. PICHON
L. L. KLOTZ
ANDRÉ TARDIEU
JULES CAMBON

[For Italy:]
SIDNEY SONNINO
IMPERIALI
SILVIO CRESPI

[For Japan:]
SAIONJI
N. MAKINO
S. CHINDA
K. MATSUI
H. IJUIN

[For Belgium:]
HYMANS
J. VAN DEN HEUVEL
EMILE VANDERVELDE

[For Bolivia:]
ISMAEL MONTES

[For Brazil:]
CALOGERAS
RODRIGO OCTAVIO

[For China:]

[For Cuba:]
ANTONIO S. DE BUSTAMANTE

[For Ecuador:]
E. DORN Y DE ALSUA

[For Greece:]
ELEFTHERIOS VENISELOS
NICOLAS POLITIS

[For Guatemala:]
JOAQUIN MÉNDEZ

[For Haiti:]
TERTULLIEN GUILBAUD

[For the Hedjaz:]
M. RUSTEM HAIDAR
ABDUL HADI AOUNI

[For Honduras:]
P. BONILLA

[For Liberia:]
C. D. B. KING

[For Nicaragua:]
SALVADOR CHAMORRO

[For Panama:]
ANTONIO BURGOS

[For Peru:]
C. G. CANDAMO

[For Poland:]
I. J. PADEREWSKI
ROMAN DMOWSKI

[For Portugal:]
AFFONSO COSTA
AUGUSTO SOARES

[For Roumania:]
   ION I. C. BRATIANO
   GENERAL C. COANDA

[For the Serbs, Croats, and Slovenes:]
   NIK P. PACHITCH
   DR. ANTE TRUMBIC
   MIL. R. VESNITCH

[For Siam:]
   CHAROON
   TRAIDOS PRABANDHU

[For the Czecho-Slovak Republic:]
   KAREL KRAMAR
   DR. EDWARD BENES

[For Uruguay:]
   J. A. BUERO

[For Germany:]
   HERMANN MÜLLER
   DR. BELL

PROTOCOL SIGNED BY GERMANY JANUARY 10, 1920

At the moment of proceeding to the first deposit of ratifications of the Treaty of Peace, it is placed on record that the following obligations, which Germany had undertaken to execute by the Armistice Conventions and supplementary Agreements, have not been executed or have not been completely fulfilled:

(1) Armistice Convention of November 11, 1918,[45] Clause VII; obligation to deliver 5,000 locomotives and 150,000 wagons. 42 locomotives and 4,460 wagons are still to be delivered;

(2) Armistice Convention of November 11, 1918, Clause XII; obligation to withdraw the German troops in Russian territory within the frontiers of Germany, as soon as the Allies shall think the moment suitable. The withdrawal of these troops has not been effected, despite the reiterated instructions of August 27, September 27 and October 10, 1919;

(3) Armistice Convention of November 11, 1918, Clause XIV; obligation to cease at once all requisitions, seizures or coercive measures in Russian territory. The German troops have continued to have recourse to such measures;

(4) Armistice Convention of November 11, 1918, Clause XIX; obligation to return immediately all documents, specie, stocks, shares, paper money, together with plant for the issue thereof, affecting public or private interests in the invaded countries. The complete lists of specie and securities carried off, collected or confiscated by the Germans in the invaded countries have not been supplied;

(5) Armistice Convention of November 11, 1918, Clause XXII; obligation to surrender all German submarines. Destruction of the German submarine *U.C. 48* off Ferrol by order of her German commander, and destruction in the North Sea of certain submarines proceeding to England for surrender;

(6) Armistice Convention of November 11, 1918, Clause XXIII; obligation to maintain in Allied ports the German warships designated by the Allied and Associated Powers, these ships being intended to be ultimately handed

---

[45] *Ante,* p. 9.

over. Clause XXXI; obligation not to destroy any ship before delivery. Destruction of the said ships at Scapa Flow on June 21, 1919;

(7) Protocol of December 17, 1918, Annex to the Armistice Convention of December 13, 1918; obligation to restore the works of art and artistic documents carried off in France and Belgium. All the works of art removed into the unoccupied parts of Germany have not been restored;

(8) Armistice Convention of January 16, 1919,[46] Clause III and Protocol 392/1 Additional Clause III of July 25, 1919; obligation to hand over agricultural machinery in the place of the supplementary railway material provided for in Tables 1 and 2 annexed to the Protocol of Spa of December 17, 1918. The following machines had not been delivered on the stipulated date of October 1, 1919. 40 "Heucke" steam plough outfits; all the cultivators for the outfits; all the spades; 1,500 shovels; 1,130 T.F. 23/26 ploughs; 1,765 T.F. 18/21 ploughs; 1,512 T.F. 23/26 ploughs; 629 T.F. o m. 20 Brabant ploughs; 1,205 T.F. o m. 26 Brabant ploughs; 4,282 harrows of 2 k. 500; 2,157 steel cultivators; 966 2 m. 50 manure distributors; 1,608 3 m. 50 manure distributors;

(9) Armistice Convention of January 16, 1919, Clause VI; obligation to restore the industrial material carried off from French and Belgian territory. All this material has not been restored;

(10) Convention of January 16, 1919, Clause VIII; obligation to place the German merchant fleet under the control of the Allied and Associated Powers. A certain number of ships whose delivery had been demanded under this clause have not yet been handed over;

(11) Protocols of the Conferences of Brussels of March 13 and 14, 1919; obligation not to export war material of all kinds. Exportation of aeronautical material to Sweden, Holland and Denmark.

A certain number of the above provisions which have not been executed or have not been executed in full have been renewed by the Treaty of June 28, 1919, whose coming into force will *ipso facto* render the sanctions there provided applicable. This applies particularly to the various measures to be taken on account of reparation.

Further, the question of the evacuation of the Baltic provinces has been the subject of an exchange of notes and of decisions which are being carried out. The Allied and Associated Powers expressly confirming the contents of their notes, Germany by the present Protocol undertakes to continue to execute them faithfully and strictly.

Finally, as the Allied and Associated Powers could not allow to pass without penalty the other failures to execute the Armistice Conventions and violations so serious as the destruction of the German fleet at Scapa Flow, the destruction of *U.C. 48* off Ferrol and the destruction in the North Sea of

---

[46] *Ante,* p. 24.

certain submarines on their way to England for surrender, Germany undertakes:

(1) A. To hand over as reparation for the destruction of the German fleet at Scapa Flow:

(*a*) Within 60 days from the date of the signature of the present Protocol and in the conditions laid down in the second paragraph of Article 185 of the Treaty of Peace the five following light cruisers:

> *Königsberg,*
> *Pillau,*
> *Graudenz,*
> *Regensburg,*
> *Strassburg.*

(*b*) Within 90 days from the date of the signature of the present Protocol, and in good condition and ready for service in every respect, such a number of floating docks, floating cranes, tugs and dredgers, equivalent to a total displacement of 400,000 tons, as the Principal Allied and Associated Powers may require. As regards the docks, the lifting power will be considered as the displacement. In the number of docks referred to above there will be about 75 per cent. of docks over 10,000 tons. The whole of this material will be handed over on the spot;

B. To deliver within 10 days from the signature of the present Protocol a complete list of all floating docks, floating cranes, tugs and dredgers which are German property. This list, which will be delivered to the Naval Inter-Allied Commission of Control referred to in Article 209 of the Treaty of Peace, will specify the material which on November 11, 1918, belonged to the German Government or in which the German Government had at that date an important interest;

C. The officers and men who formed the crews of the warships sunk at Scapa Flow and who are at present detained by the Principal Allied and Associated Powers will, with the exception of those whose surrender is provided for by Article 228 of the Treaty of Peace, be repatriated at latest when Germany has carried out the provisions of Paragraphs A. and B. above;

D. The destroyer B. 98 will be considered as one of the 42 destroyers whose delivery is provided for by Article 185 of the Treaty of Peace;

(2) To hand over within 10 days from the signature of the present Protocol the engines and motors of the submarines *U. 137* and *U. 138* as compensation for the destruction of *U.C. 48;*

(3) To pay to the Allied and Associated Governments before January 31, 1920, the value of the aeronautical material exported, in accordance with the decision which will be given and the valuation which will be made and

notified by the Aeronautical Inter-Allied Commission of Control referred to in Article 210 of the Treaty of Peace.

In the event of Germany not fulfilling these obligations within the periods laid down above, the Allied and Associated Powers reserve the right to take all military or other measures of coercion which they may consider appropriate.

Done at Paris, the tenth day of January, one thousand nine hundred and twenty, at four o'clock p.m.

[For Germany:]
V. SIMSON
FREIHERR VON LERSNER

INTERNATIONAL LABOR ORGANIZATION

Constitution signed at Versailles June 28, 1919 (part XIII of Treaty of Versailles [1])

Effective January 10, 1920; for the United States August 20, 1934

Joint resolution of Congress providing for United States membership, with a proviso, June 19, 1934 [2]

Resolution of the General Conference of the ILO inviting the United States to accept membership in the Organization adopted June 22, 1934

ILO membership accepted by the President of the United States, with a proviso, effective August 20, 1934 [3]

Proclaimed by the President of the United States September 10, 1934

Amendments adopted by the ILO General Conference on November 2, 1922,[4] and November 5, 1945;[5] revised by instrument of amendment adopted October 9, 1946,[6] as later amended

49 Stat. 2712; Treaty Series 874

THE CONSTITUTION OF THE INTERNATIONAL
LABOUR ORGANISATION

SECTION I

ORGANISATION OF LABOUR

Whereas the League of Nations has for its object the establishment of universal peace, and such a peace can be established only if it is based upon social justice;

---

[1] The ILO Constitution also formed part XIII of the Treaty of Saint-Germain-en-Laye of Sept. 10, 1919; part XII of the Treaty of Neuilly-sur-Seine of Nov. 27, 1919; and part XIII of the Treaty of Trianon of June 4, 1920.

[2] 48 Stat. 1182; TS 874, p. 28. Sec. 2 of the joint resolution reads as follows: ". . . in accepting such membership the President shall assume on behalf of the United States no obligation under the covenant of the League of Nations."

[3] For text of U.S. acceptance, see p. 30 of TS 874.

[4] For text, see footnote 8, p. 244.

[5] 2 UNTS 17; the United States did not become a party.

[6] TIAS 1868, *post*, vol. 4.

And whereas conditions of labour exist involving such injustice, hardship and privation to large numbers of people as to produce unrest so great that the peace and harmony of the world are imperilled; and an improvement of those conditions is urgently required: as, for example, by the regulation of the hours of work, including the establishment of a maximum working day and week, the regulation of the labour supply, the prevention of unemployment, the provision of an adequate living wage, the protection of the worker against sickness, disease and injury arising out of his employment, the protection of children, young persons and women, provision for old age and injury, protection of the interests of workers when employed in countries other than their own, recognition of the principle of freedom of association, the organisation of vocational and technical education and other measures;

Whereas also the failure of any nation to adopt humane conditions of labour is an obstacle in the way of other nations which desire to improve the conditions in their own countries;

The HIGH CONTRACTING PARTIES, moved by sentiments of justice and humanity as well as by the desire to secure the permanent peace of the world, agree to the following:

CHAPTER I

Organisation

ARTICLE 387 [7]

A permanent organisation is hereby established for the promotion of the objects set forth in the Preamble.

The original Members of the League of Nations shall be the original Members of this organisation, and hereafter membership of the League of Nations shall carry with it membership of the said organisation.

ARTICLE 388

The permanent organisation shall consist of:

(1) a General Conference of Representatives of the Members and,

(2) an International Labour Office controlled by the Governing Body described in Article 393.

ARTICLE 389

The meetings of the General Conference of Representatives of the Members shall be held from time to time as occasion may require, and at least once in every year. It shall be composed of four Representatives of each of the Members, of whom two shall be Government Delegates and the two

---

[7] The numbering of the articles in the present text is that of Part XIII of the Treaty of Versailles.

others shall be Delegates representing respectively the employers and the workpeople of each of the Members.

Each Delegate may be accompanied by advisers, who shall not exceed two in number for each item on the agenda of the meeting. When questions specially affecting women are to be considered by the Conference, one at least of the advisers should be a woman.

The Members undertake to nominate non-Government Delegates and advisers chosen in agreement with the industrial organisations, if such organisations exist, which are most representative of employers or workpeople, as the case may be, in their respective countries.

Advisers shall not speak except on a request made by the Delegate whom they accompany and by the special authorization of the President of the Conference, and may not vote.

A Delegate may by notice in writing addressed to the President appoint one of his advisers to act as his deputy, and the adviser, while so acting, shall be allowed to speak and vote.

The names of the Delegates and their advisers will be communicated to the International Labour Office by the Government of each of the Members.

The credentials of Delegates and their advisers shall be subject to scrutiny by the Conference, which may, by two-thirds of the votes cast by the Delegates present, refuse to admit any Delegate or adviser whom it deems not to have been nominated in accordance with this Article.

ARTICLE 390

Every Delegate shall be entitled to vote individually on all matters which are taken into consideration by the Conference.

If one of the Members fails to nominate one of the non-Government Delegates whom it is entitled to nominate, the other non-Government Delegate shall be allowed to sit and speak at the Conference, but not to vote.

If in accordance with Article 389 the Conference refuses admission to a Delegate of one of the Members, the provisions of the present Article shall apply as if that Delegate had not been nominated.

ARTICLE 391

The meetings of the Conference shall be held at the seat of the League of Nations, or at such other place as may be decided by the Conference at a previous meeting by two-thirds of the votes cast by the Delegates present.

ARTICLE 392

The International Labour Office shall be established at the seat of the League of Nations as part of the organisation of the League.

ARTICLE 393 [8]

The International Labour Office shall be under the control of a Governing Body consisting of twenty-four persons, appointed in accordance with the following provisions:

The Governing Body of the International Labour Office shall be constituted as follows:

Twelve persons representing the Governments:
Six persons elected by the Delegates to the Conference representing the employers;
Six persons elected by the Delegates to the Conference representing the workers.

Of the twelve persons representing the Governments eight shall be nominated by the Members which are of the chief industrial importance, and four shall be nominated by the Members selected for the purpose by the Government Delegates to the Conference, excluding the Delegates of the eight Members mentioned above.

Any question as to which are the Members of the chief industrial importance shall be decided by the Council of the League of Nations.

The period of office of the Members of the Governing Body will be three years. The method of filling vacancies and other similar questions may be determined by the Governing Body subject to the approval of the Conference.

---

[8] By an amendment adopted by the International Labor Conference on Nov. 2, 1922 (149 LNTS 35) effective June 4, 1934, the text of art. 393 was revised to read as follows:

ARTICLE 393

The International Labour Office shall be under the control of a Governing Body consisting of thirty-two persons:

Sixteen representing Governments,
Eight representing the Employers, and
Eight representing the Workers.

Of the sixteen persons representing Governments, eight shall be appointed by the Members of chief industrial importance, and eight shall be appointed by the Members selected for that purpose by the Government Delegates to the Conference excluding the Delegates of the eight Members mentioned above. Of the sixteen Members represented six shall be non-European States.

Any question as to which are the Members of chief industrial importance shall be decided by the Council of the League of Nations.

The persons representing the Employers and the persons representing the Workers shall be elected respectively by the Employers' Delegates and the Workers' Delegates to the Conference. Two Employers' representatives and two Workers' representatives shall belong to non-European States.

The period of office of the Governing Body shall be three years.

The method of filling vacancies and of appointing substitutes, and other similar questions, may be decided by the Governing Body subject to the approval of the Conference.

The Governing Body shall, from time to time, elect one of its number to act as its Chairman, shall regulate its own procedure, and shall fix its own times of meeting. A special meeting shall be held if a written request to that effect is made by at least twelve of the representatives on the Governing Body.

The Governing Body shall, from time to time, elect one of its members to act as its Chairman, shall regulate its own procedure and shall fix its own times of meeting. A special meeting shall be held if a written request to that effect is made by at least ten members of the Governing Body.

ARTICLE 394

There shall be a Director of the International Labour Office, who shall be appointed by the Governing Body, and, subject to the instructions of the Governing Body, shall be responsible for the efficient conduct of the International Labour Office and for such other duties as may be assigned to him.

The Director or his deputy shall attend all meetings of the Governing Body.

ARTICLE 395

The staff of the International Labour Office shall be appointed by the Director, who shall, so far as is possible with due regard to the efficiency of the work of the Office, select persons of different nationalities. A certain number of these persons shall be women.

ARTICLE 396

The functions of the International Labour Office shall include the collection and distribution of information on all subjects relating to the international adjustment of conditions of industrial life and labour, and particularly the examination of subjects which it is proposed to bring before the Conference with a view to the conclusion of international conventions, and the conduct of such special investigations as may be ordered by the Conference.

It will prepare the agenda for the meetings of the Conference.

It will carry out the duties required of it by the provisions of this Part of the present Treaty in connection with international disputes.

It will edit and publish in French and English, and in such other languages as the Governing Body may think desirable, a periodical paper dealing with problems of industry and employment of international interest.

Generally, in addition to the functions set out in this Article, it shall have such other powers and duties as may be assigned to it by the Conference.

ARTICLE 397

The Government Departments of any of the Members which deal with questions of industry and employment may communicate directly with the Director through the Representative of their Government on the Governing Body of the International Labour Office, or failing any such Representative, through such other qualified official as the Government may nominate for the purpose.

Article 398

The International Labour Office shall be entitled to the assistance of the Secretary-General of the League of Nations in any matter in which it can be given.

Article 399

Each of the Members will pay the travelling and subsistence expenses of its Delegates and their advisers and of its Representatives attending the meetings of the Conference or Governing Body, as the case may be.

All the other expenses of the International Labour Office and of the meetings of the Conference or Governing Body shall be paid to the Director by the Secretary-General of the League of Nations out of the general funds of the League.

The Director shall be responsible to the Secretary-General of the League for the proper expenditure of all moneys paid to him in pursuance of this Article.

Chapter II

Procedure

Article 400

The agenda for all meetings of the Conference will be settled by the Governing Body, who shall consider any suggestion as to the agenda that may be made by the Government of any of the Members or by any representative organisation recognised for the purpose of Article 389.

Article 401

The Director shall act as the Secretary of the Conference, and shall transmit the agenda so as to reach the Members four months before the meeting of the Conference, and, through them, the non-Government Delegates when appointed.

Article 402

Any of the Governments of the Members may formally object to the inclusion of any item or items in the agenda. The grounds for such objection shall be set forth in a reasoned statement addressed to the Director, who shall circulate it to all the Members of the Permanent Organisation.

Items to which such objection has been made shall not, however, be excluded from the agenda, if at the Conference a majority of two-thirds of the votes cast by the Delegates present is in favour of considering them.

If the Conference decides (otherwise than under the preceding paragraph) by two-thirds of the votes cast by the Delegates present that any subject shall be considered by the Conference, that subject shall be included in the agenda for the following meeting.

ARTICLE 403

The Conference shall regulate its own procedure, shall elect its own President, and may appoint committees to consider and report on any matter.

Except as otherwise expressly provided in this Part of the present Treaty, all matters shall be decided by a simple majority of the votes cast by the Delegates present.

The voting is void unless the total number of votes cast is equal to half the number of the Delegates attending the Conference.

ARTICLE 404

The Conference may add to any committees which it appoints technical experts, who shall be assessors without power to vote.

ARTICLE 405

When the Conference has decided on the adoption of proposals with regard to an item in the agenda, it will rest with the Conference to determine whether these proposals should take the form: (a) of a recommendation to be submitted to the Members for consideration with a view to effect being given to it by national legislation or otherwise, or (b) of a draft international convention for ratification by the Members.

In either case a majority of two-thirds of the votes cast by the Delegates present shall be necessary on the final vote for the adoption of the recommendation or draft convention, as the case may be, by the Conference.

In framing any recommendation or draft convention of general application the Conference shall have due regard to those countries in which climatic conditions, the imperfect development of industrial organisation or other special circumstances make the industrial conditions substantially different and shall suggest the modifications, if any, which it considers may be required to meet the case of such countries.

A copy of the recommendation or draft convention shall be authenticated by the signature of the President of the Conference and of the Director and shall be deposited with the Secretary-General of the League of Nations. The Secretary-General will communicate a certified copy of the recommendation or draft convention to each of the Members.

Each of the Members undertakes that it will, within the period of one year at most from the closing of the session of the Conference, or if it is impossible owing to exceptional circumstances to do so within the period of one year, then at the earliest practicable moment and in no case later than eighteen months from the closing of the session of the Conference, bring the recommendation or draft convention before the authority or authorities within whose competence the matter lies, for the enactment of legislation or other action.

In the case of a recommendation, the Members will inform the Secretary-General of the action taken.

In the case of a draft convention, the Member will, if it obtains the consent of the authority or authorities within whose competence the matter lies, communicate the formal ratification of the convention to the Secretary-General and will take such action as may be necessary to make effective the provisions of such convention.

If on a recommendation no legislative or other action is taken to make a recommendation effective, or if the draft convention fails to obtain the consent of the authority or authorities within whose competence the matter lies, no further obligation shall rest upon the Member.

In the case of a federal State, the power of which to enter into conventions on labour matters is subject to limitations, it shall be in the discretion of that Government to treat a draft convention to which such limitations apply as a recommendation only, and the provisions of this Article with respect to recommendations shall apply in such case.

The above Article shall be interpreted in accordance with the following principle:

In no case shall any Member be asked or required, as a result of the adoption of any recommendation or draft convention by the Conference, to lessen the protection afforded by its existing legislation to the workers concerned.

Article 406

Any convention so ratified shall be registered by the Secretary-General of the League of Nations, but shall only be binding upon the Members which ratify it.

Article 407

If any convention coming before the Conference for final consideration fails to secure the support of two-thirds of the votes cast by the Delegates present, it shall nevertheless be within the right of any of the Members of the Permanent Organisation to agree to such convention among themselves.

Any convention so agreed to shall be communicated by the Governments concerned to the Secretary-General of the League of Nations, who shall register it.

Article 408

Each of the Members agrees to make an annual report to the International Labour Office on the measures which it has taken to give effect to the provisions of conventions to which it is a party. These reports shall be made in such form and shall contain such particulars as the Governing Body may request. The Director shall lay a summary of these reports before the next meeting of the Conference.

Article 409

In the event of any representation being made to the International Labour Office by an industrial association of employers or of workers that any of the Members has failed to secure in any respect the effective observance within its jurisdiction of any convention to which it is a party, the Governing Body may communicate this representation to the Government against which it is made and may invite that Government to make such statement on the subject as it may think fit.

ARTICLE 410

If no statement is received within a reasonable time from the Government in question, or if the statement when received is not deemed to be satisfactory by the Governing Body, the latter shall have the right to publish the representation and the statement, if any, made in reply to it.

ARTICLE 411

Any of the Members shall have the right to file a complaint with the International Labour Office if it is not satisfied that any other Member is securing the effective observance of any convention which both have ratified in accordance with the foregoing Articles.

The Governing Body may, if it thinks fit, before referring such a complaint to a Commission of Enquiry, as hereinafter provided for, communicate with the Government in question in the manner described in Article 409.

If the Governing Body does not think it necessary to communicate the complaint to the Government in question, or if, when they have made such communication, no statement in reply has been received within a reasonable time which the Governing Body considers to be satisfactory, the Governing Body may apply for the appointment of a Commission of Enquiry to consider the complaint and to report thereon.

The Governing Body may adopt the same procedure either of its own motion or on receipt of a complaint from a Delegate to the Conference.

When any matter arising out of Articles 410 or 411 is being considered by the Governing Body, the Government in question shall, if not already represented thereon, be entitled to send a representative to take part in the proceedings of the Governing Body while the matter is under consideration. Adequate notice of the date on which the matter will be considered shall be given to the Government in question.

ARTICLE 412

The Commission of Enquiry shall be constituted in accordance with the following provisions:

Each of the Members agrees to nominate within six months of the date on which the present Treaty comes into force three persons of industrial experience, of whom one shall be a representative of employers, one a representative of workers, and one a person of independent standing, who shall together form a panel from which the Members of the Commission of Enquiry shall be drawn.

The qualifications of the persons so nominated shall be subject to scrutiny by the Governing Body, which may by two-thirds of the votes cast by the representatives present refuse to accept the nomination of any person whose qualifications do not in its opinion comply with the requirements of the present Article.

Upon the application of the Governing Body, the Secretary-General of the League of Nations shall nominate three persons, one from each section of this panel, to constitute the Commission of Enquiry, and shall designate one of them as the President of the Commission. None of these three persons shall be a person nominated to the panel by any Member directly concerned in the complaint.

ARTICLE 413

The Members agree that, in the event of the reference of a complaint to a Commission of Enquiry under Article 411, they will each, whether directly concerned in the complaint or not, place at the disposal of the Commission all the information in their possession which bears upon the subject-matter of the complaint.

ARTICLE 414

When the Commission of Enquiry has fully considered the complaint, it shall prepare a report embodying its findings on all questions of fact relevant to determining the issue between the parties and containing such recommendations as it may think proper as to the steps which should be taken to meet the complaint and the time within which they should be taken.

It shall also indicate in this report the measures, if any, of an economic character against a defaulting Government which it considers to be appropriate, and which it considers other Governments would be justified in adopting.

ARTICLE 415

The Secretary-General of the League of Nations shall communicate the report of the Commission of Enquiry to each of the Governments concerned in the complaint, and shall cause it to be published.

Each of these Governments shall within one month inform the Secretary-General of the League of Nations whether or not it accepts the recommendations contained in the report of the Commission; and if not, whether it proposes to refer the complaint to the Permanent Court of International Justice of the League of Nations.

ARTICLE 416

In the event of any Member failing to take the action required by Article 405, with regard to a recommendation or draft Convention, any other Member shall be entitled to refer the matter to the Permanent Court of International Justice.

ARTICLE 417

The decision of the Permanent Court of International Justice in regard to a complaint or matter which has been referred to it in pursuance of Article 415 or Article 416 shall be final.

ARTICLE 418

The Permanent Court of International Justice may affirm, vary or reverse any of the findings or recommendations of the Commission of Enquiry, if any, and shall in its decision indicate the measures, if any, of an economic character which it considers to be appropriate, and which other Governments would be justified in adopting against a defaulting Government.

ARTICLE 419

In the event of any Member failing to carry out within the time specified the recommendations, if any, contained in the report of the Commission of Enquiry, or in the decision of the Permanent Court of International Justice, as the case may be, any other Member may take against that Member the measures of an economic character indicated in the report of the Commission or in the decision of the Court as appropriate to the case.

ARTICLE 420

The defaulting Government may at any time inform the Governing Body that it has taken the steps necessary to comply with the recommendations of the Commission of Enquiry or with those in the decision of the Permanent Court of International Justice, as the case may be, and may request it to apply to the Secretary-General of the League to constitute a Commission of Enquiry to verify its contention. In this case the provisions of Articles 412, 413, 414, 415, 417 and 418 shall apply, and if the report of the Commission of Enquiry or the decision of the Permanent Court of International Justice is in favour of the defaulting Government, the other Governments shall forthwith discontinue the measures of an economic character that they have taken against the defaulting Government.

CHAPTER III

General

ARTICLE 421

The Members engage to apply conventions which they have ratified in accordance with the provisions of this Part of the present Treaty to their colonies, protectorates and possessions which are not fully self-governing:

(1) Except where owing to the local conditions the convention is inapplicable, or

(2) Subject to such modifications as may be necessary to adapt the convention to local conditions.

And each of the Members shall notify to the International Labour Office the action taken in respect of each of its colonies, protectorates and possessions which are not fully self-governing.

ARTICLE 422

Amendments to this Part of the present Treaty which are adopted by the Conference by a majority of two-thirds of the votes cast by the Delegates present shall take effect when ratified by the States whose representatives compose the Council of the League of Nations and by three-fourths of the Members.

ARTICLE 423

Any question or dispute relating to the interpretation of this Part of the present Treaty or of any subsequent convention concluded by the Members in pursuance of the provisions of this Part of the present Treaty shall be referred for decision to the Permanent Court of International Justice.

CHAPTER IV

Transitory Provisions

ARTICLE 424

The first meeting of the Conference shall take place in October, 1919. The place and agenda for this meeting shall be as specified in the Annex hereto.

Arrangements for the convening and the organisation of the first meeting of the Conference will be made by the Government designated for the purpose in the said Annex. That Government shall be assisted in the preparation of the documents for submission to the Conference by an International Committee constituted as provided in the said Annex.

The expenses of the first meeting and of all subsequent meetings held before the League of Nations has been able to establish a general fund, other than the expenses of Delegates and their advisers, will be borne by the Members in accordance with the apportionment of the expenses of the International Bureau of the Universal Postal Union.

ARTICLE 425

Until the League of Nations has been constituted all communications which under the provisions of the foregoing Articles should be addressed to the Secretary-General of the League will be preserved by the Director of the International Labour Office, who will transmit them to the Secretary-General of the League.

ARTICLE 426

Pending the creation of a Permanent Court of International Justice, disputes which in accordance with this Part of the present Treaty would be submitted to it for decision will be referred to a tribunal of three persons appointed by the Council of the League of Nations.

ANNEX

First Meeting of Annual Labour Conference, 1919

The place of meeting will be Washington.

The Government of the United States of America is requested to convene the Conference.

The International Organising Committee will consist of seven Members, appointed by the United States of America, Great Britain, France, Italy, Japan, Belgium and Switzerland. The Committee may, if it thinks necessary, invite other Members to appoint representatives.

Agenda:

(1) Application of principle of the 8-hours day or of the 48-hours week.
(2) Question of preventing or providing against unemployment.
(3) Women's employment:

(a) Before and after child-birth, including the question of maternity benefit;
(b) During the night;
(c) In unhealthy processes.

(4) Employment of children:

(a) Minimum age of employment;
(b) During the night;
(c) In unhealthy processes.

(5) Extension and application of the International Conventions adopted at Berne in 1906 on the prohibition of night work for women employed in industry and the prohibition of the use of white phosphorus in the manufacture of matches.

SECTION II

GENERAL PRINCIPLES

ARTICLE 427

The High Contracting Parties, recognising that the well-being, physical, moral and intellectual, of industrial wage-earners is of supreme international importance, have framed, in order to further this great end, the permanent machinery provided for in Section I and associated with that of the League of Nations.

They recognise that differences of climate, habits and customs, of economic opportunity and industrial tradition, make strict uniformity in the conditions of labour difficult of immediate attainment. But, holding as they do, that labour should not be regarded merely as an article of commerce, they think that there are methods and principles for regulating labour conditions which all industrial communities should endeavour to apply, so far as their special circumstances will permit.

Among these methods and principles, the following seem to the High Contracting Parties to be of special and urgent importance:

First.—The guiding principle above enunciated that labour should not be regarded merely as a commodity or article of commerce.

Second.—The right of association for all lawful purposes by the employed as well as by the employers.

Third.—The payment to the employed of a wage adequate to maintain a reasonable standard of life as this is understood in their time and country.

Fourth.—The adoption of an eight hours day or a forty-eight hours week as the standard to be aimed at where it has not already been attained.

Fifth.—The adoption of a weekly rest of at least twenty-four hours, which should include Sunday wherever practicable.

Sixth.—The abolition of child labour and the imposition of such limitations on the labour of young persons as shall permit the continuation of their education and assure their proper physical development.

Seventh.—The principle that men and women should receive equal remuneration for work of equal value.

Eighth.—The standard set by law in each country with respect to the conditions of labour should have due regard to the equitable economic treatment of all workers lawfully resident therein.

Ninth.—Each State should make provision for a system of inspection in which women should take part, in order to ensure the enforcement of the laws and regulations for the protection of the employed.

Without claiming that these methods and principles are either complete or final, the High Contracting Parties are of opinion that they are well fitted to guide the policy of the League of Nations; and that, if adopted by the industrial communities who are Members of the League, and safeguarded in practice by an adequate system of such inspection, they will confer lasting benefits upon the wage-earners of the world.

[For signatures to the Treaty of Versailles, see *ante*, p. 234.]

LIQUOR TRAFFIC IN AFRICA

Convention signed at Saint-Germain-en-Laye September 10, 1919
Senate advice and consent to ratification, with a reservation, February 28, 1929 [1]
Ratified by the President of the United States, with a reservation, March 7, 1929 [1]
Ratification of the United States deposited at Paris March 22, 1929
Entered into force July 31, 1920; for the United States March 22, 1929
Proclaimed by the President of the United States March 26, 1929

46 Stat. 2199; Treaty Series 779

[TRANSLATION]

THE UNITED STATES OF AMERICA, BELGIUM, THE BRITISH EMPIRE, FRANCE, ITALY, JAPAN AND PORTUGAL

Whereas it is necessary to continue in the African territories placed under their administration the struggle against the dangers of alcoholism which they have maintained by subjecting spirits to constantly increasing duties;

Whereas, further, it is necessary to prohibit the importation of distilled beverages rendered more especially dangerous to the native populations by the nature of the products entering into their composition or by the opportunities which a low price gives for their extended use;

Whereas, finally, the restrictions placed on the importation of spirits would be of no effect unless the local manufacture of distilled beverages was at the same time strictly controlled;

Have appointed as their plenipotentiaries:

The President of the United States of America:

The Honorable Frank Lyon Polk, Under-Secretary of State;

The Honorable Henry White, formerly Ambassador Extraordinary and Plenipotentiary of the United States at Rome and Paris;

---

[1] The U.S. reservation reads as follows:

"Should any dispute whatever arise between any of the high contracting parties and the United States relative to the application of the present convention which can not be settled by negotiation, such dispute shall be submitted to the Permanent Court of Arbitration at The Hague established by the convention of October 18, 1907 [TS 536, *ante,* vol. 1, p. 577], or to such other arbitral tribunal upon which the parties to the dispute may agree."

255

General Tasker H. Bliss, Military Representative of the United States on the Supreme War Council;

His Majesty the King of the Belgians:
Mr. Paul Hymans, Minister for Foreign Affairs, Minister of State;
Mr. Jules van den Heuvel, Envoy Extraordinary and Minister Plenipotentiary of His Majesty the King of the Belgians, Minister of State;
Mr. Émile Vandervelde, Minister of Justice, Minister of State;

His Majesty the King of the United Kingdom of Great Britain and Ireland and of the British Dominions Beyond the Seas, Emperor of India:
The Right Honorable Arthur James Balfour, O.M., M.P., His Secretary of State for Foreign Affairs;
The Right Honorable Andrew Bonar Law, M. P., His Lord Privy Seal;
The Right Honorable Viscount Milner, G.C.B., G.C.M.G., His Secretary of State for the Colonies;
The Right Honorable George Nicoll Barnes, M.P., Minister without portfolio; and:

for the Dominion of Canada: The Honorable Sir Albert Edward Kemp, K.C.M.G., Minister of the Overseas Forces;
for the Commonwealth of Australia: The Honorable George Foster Pearce, Minister of Defence;
for the Union of South Africa: The Right Honorable Viscount Milner, G. C. B., G. C. M. G.;
for the Dominion of New Zealand: The Honorable Sir Thomas Mackenzie, K.C.M.G., High Commissioner for New Zealand in the United Kingdom;
for India: The Right Honorable Baron Sinha, K.C., Under-Secretary of State for India;

The President of the French Republic:
Mr. Georges Clemenceau, President of the Council, Minister of War;
Mr. Stephen Pichon, Minister for Foreign Affairs;
Mr. Louis-Lucien Klotz, Minister of Finance;
Mr. André Tardieu, Commissary-General for Franco-American Military Affairs;
Mr. Jules Cambon, Ambassador of France;

His Majesty the King of Italy:
The Honorable Tommaso Tittoni, Senator of the Kingdom, Minister for Foreign Affairs;
The Honorable Vittorio Scialoja, Senator of the Kingdom;
The Honorable Maggiorino Ferraris, Senator of the Kingdom;
The Honorable Guglielmo Marconi, Senator of the Kingdom;
The Honorable Silvio Crespi, Deputy;

His Majesty the Emperor of Japan:

Viscount Chinda, Ambassador Extraordinary and Plenipotentiary of H. M. the Emperor of Japan at London;

Mr. K. Matsui, Ambassador Extraordinary and Plenipotentiary of H. M. the Emperor of Japan at Paris;

The President of the Portuguese Republic:

Dr. Affonso da Costa, formerly President of the Council of Ministers;

Dr. Augusto Luiz Vieira Soares, formerly Minister for Foreign Affairs;

Who, having communicated their full powers found in good and due form, Have agreed as follows:

ARTICLE 1

The High Contracting Parties undertake to apply the following measures for the restriction of the liquor traffic in the territories which are or may be subjected to their control throughout the whole of the continent of Africa, with the exception of Algiers, Tunis, Morocco, Libya, Egypt, and the Union of South Africa.

The provisions applicable to the continent of Africa shall also apply to the islands lying within 100 nautical miles of the coast.

ARTICLE 2

The importation, distribution, sale and possession of trade spirits of every kind, and of beverages mixed with these spirits, are prohibited in the area referred to in Article 1. The local Governments concerned will decide respectively which distilled beverages will be regarded in their territories as falling within the category of trade spirits. They will endeavor to establish a nomenclature and measures against fraud as uniform as possible.

ARTICLE 3

The importation, distribution, sale and possession are also forbidden of distilled beverages containing essential oils or chemical products which are recognised as injurious to health, such as thuyone, star anise, benzoic aldehyde, salicylic ethers, hyssop and absinthe.

The local Governments concerned will likewise endeavor to establish by common agreement the nomenclature of those beverages whose importation, distribution, sale and possession according to the terms of this provision should be prohibited.

ARTICLE 4

An import duty of not less than 800 francs per hectolitre of pure alcohol shall be levied upon all distilled beverages, other than those indicated in Articles 2 and 3, which are imported into the area referred to in Article 1, except in so far as the Italian colonies are concerned, where the duty may not be less than 600 francs.

The High Contracting Parties will prohibit the importation, distribution, sale and possession of spirituous liquors in those regions of the area referred to in Article 1 where their use has not been developed.

The above prohibition can be suspended only in the case of limited quantities destined for the consumption of non-native persons, and imported under the system and conditions determined by each Government.

ARTICLE 5

The manufacture of distilled beverages of every kind is forbidden in the area referred to in Article 1.

The importation, distribution, sale and possession of stills and of all apparatus or portions of apparatus suitable for distillation of alcohol and the redistillation of brandies and spirits are forbidden in the same area, subject to the provisions of Article 6.

The provisions of the two preceding paragraphs do not apply to the Italian colonies; the manufacture of distilled beverages, other than those specified in Articles 2 and 3, will continue to be permitted therein, on condition that they are subject to an excise duty equal to the import duty established in Article 4.

ARTICLE 6

The restrictions on the importation, distribution, sale, possession and manufacture of spirituous beverages do not apply to pharmaceutical alcohols intended for medical, surgical or pharmaceutical establishments. The importation, distribution, sale and possession are also permitted of:

(1) Testing stills, that is to say, the small apparatus in general use for laboratory experiments, which are employed intermittently, are not fitted with rectifying heads, and the capacity of whose retort does not exceed one litre;

(2) Apparatus or parts of apparatus intended for experiments in scientific institutions;

(3) Apparatus or parts of apparatus employed for definite purposes, other than the production of alcohol, by pharmacists holding a diploma, and by persons who can show good cause for the possession of such apparatus;

(4) Apparatus necessary for the manufacture of alcohol for industrial purposes, and employed by duly authorized persons, such manufacture being subject to the supervision established by the local administration.

The necessary permission in the foregoing cases will be granted by the local administration of the territory in which the stills, apparatus, or portions of apparatus are to be utilized.

ARTICLE 7

A Central International Office, placed under the control of the League of Nations, shall be established for the purpose of collecting and preserving documents of all kinds exchanged by the High Contracting Parties with regard to the importation and manufacture of spirituous liquors under the conditions referred to in the present Convention.

Each of the High Contracting Parties shall publish an annual report showing the quantities of spirituous beverages imported or manufactured and the duties levied under Articles 4 and 5. A copy of this report shall be sent to the Central International Office and to the Secretary-General of the League of Nations.

ARTICLE 8

The High Contracting Parties agree that if any dispute whatever should arise between them relating to the application of the present Convention which cannot be settled by negotiation, this dispute shall be submitted to an arbitral tribunal in conformity with the Covenant of the League of Nations.

ARTICLE 9

The High Contracting Parties reserve the right of introducing into the present Convention by common agreement after a period of five years such modifications as may prove to be necessary.

ARTICLE 10

The High Contracting Parties will use every effort to obtain the adhesion to the present Convention of the other States exercising authority over territories of the African Continent.

This adhesion shall be notified through the diplomatic channel to the Government of the French Republic, and by it to all the signatory or adhering States. The adhesion will come into effect from the date of the notification to the French Government.

ARTICLE 11

All the provisions of former general international Conventions relating to the matters dealt with in the present Convention shall be considered as abrogated in so far as they are binding between the Powers which are parties to the present Convention.

The present Convention shall be ratified as soon as possible.

Each Power will address its ratification to the French Government, which will inform all the other signatory Powers.

The ratifications will remain deposited in the archives of the French Government.

The present Convention will come into force for each signatory Power from the date of the deposit of its ratification, and from that moment that Power will be bound in respect of other Powers which have already deposited their ratification.

On the coming into force of the present Convention, the French Government will transmit a certified copy to the Powers which under the Treaties of Peace have undertaken to accept and observe it, and are in consequence placed in the same position as the Contracting Parties. The names of these Powers will be notified to the States which adhere.

In faith whereof, the above-named Plenipotentiaries have signed the present Convention.

Done at Saint-Germain-en-Laye, the tenth day of September, one thousand nine hundred and nineteen, in a single copy which will remain deposited in the archives of the Government of the French Republic, and of which authenticated copies will be sent to each of the signatory Powers.

[For the United States:]
FRANK L. POLK   [SEAL]
HENRY WHITE   [SEAL]
TASKER H. BLISS   [SEAL]

[For Belgium:]
HYMANS   [SEAL]
VAN DEN HEUVEL   [SEAL]
E. VANDERVELDE   [SEAL]

[For the United Kingdom:]
ARTHUR JAMES BALFOUR   [SEAL]
MILNER   [SEAL]
GEO. N. BARNES   [SEAL]

[For the Dominion of Canada:]
A. E. KEMP   [SEAL]

[For the Commonwealth of Australia]
G. F. PEARCE   [SEAL]

[For the Union of South Africa:]
MILNER   [SEAL]

[For the Dominion of New Zealand:]
THOS. MACKENZIE   [SEAL]

[For India:]
SINHA OF RAIPUR   [SEAL]

[For France:]
G. CLEMENCEAU   [SEAL]
S. PICHON   [SEAL]
L. L. KLOTZ   [SEAL]
ANDRÉ TARDIEU   [SEAL]
JULES CAMBON   [SEAL]

[For Italy:]
TOM. TITTONI   [SEAL]
VITTORIO SCIALOJA   [SEAL]
MAGGIORINO FERRARIS   [SEAL]
GUGLIELMO MARCONI   [SEAL]

[For Japan:]
S. CHINDA   [SEAL]
K. MATSUI   [SEAL]

[For Portugal:]
AFFONSO COSTA   [SEAL]
AUGUSTO SOARES   [SEAL]

AFRICA: REVISION OF GENERAL ACT OF BERLIN AND GENERAL ACT AND DECLARATION OF BRUSSELS

Convention signed at Saint-Germain-en-Laye September 10, 1919
Senate advice and consent to ratification, with an understanding, April 3, 1930 [1]
Ratified by the President of the United States, with an understanding, April 11, 1930 [1]
Ratification of the United States deposited at Paris October 29, 1934
Entered into force July 31, 1920; for the United States October 29, 1934
Proclaimed by the President of the United States November 3, 1934

49 Stat. 3027; Treaty Series 877

[TRANSLATION]

THE UNITED STATES OF AMERICA, BELGIUM, THE BRITISH EMPIRE, FRANCE, ITALY, JAPAN, AND PORTUGAL,

Whereas the General Act of the African Conference, signed at Berlin on February 26, 1885,[2] was primarily intended to demonstrate the agreement of the Powers with regard to the general principles which should guide their commercial and civilizing action in the little known or inadequately organized regions of a continent where slavery and the slave trade still flourished; and

Whereas by the Brussels Declaration of July 2, 1890,[3] it was found necessary to modify for a provisional period of fifteen years the system of free imports established for twenty years by Article 4 of the said Act, and since

---

[1] The U.S. understanding reads as follows: ". . . in the event of a dispute in which the United States of America may be involved arising under the Convention, such dispute shall, if the United States of America so requests, be submitted to a court of arbitration constituted in accordance with the Convention for the Pacific Settlement of International Disputes, signed at The Hague on October 18, 1907 [TS 536, *ante*, vol. 1, p. 577], or to some other court of arbitration."

[2] For text, in the original French, see *British and Foreign State Papers,* vol. 76, p. 4; for an English translation, see *American Journal of International Law,* Supp. 3, p. 7.

[3] For the General Act of Brussels, see TS 383, *ante,* vol. 1, p. 134; for the Brussels Declaration, see XIX Hertslet 304.

that date no agreement has been entered into, notwithstanding the provisions of the said Act and Declaration; and

Whereas the territories in question are now under the control of recognized authorities, are provided with administrative institutions suitable to the local conditions, and the evolution of the native populations continues to make progress;

Wishing to ensure by arrangements suitable to modern requirements the application of the general principles of civilization established by the Acts of Berlin and Brussels,

Have appointed as their Plenipotentiaries:

The President of the United States of America:

The Honorable Frank Lyon Polk, Under-Secretary of State;

The Honorable Henry White, formerly Ambassador Extraordinary and Plenipotentiary of the United States at Rome and Paris;

General Tasker H. Bliss, Military Representative of the United States on the Supreme War Council;

His Majesty the King of the Belgians:

Mr. Paul Hymans, Minister for Foreign Affairs, Minister of State;

Mr. Jules van den Heuvel, Envoy Extraordinary and Minister Plenipotentiary of His Majesty the King of the Belgians, Minister of State;

Mr. Émile Vandervelde, Minister of Justice, Minister of State;

His Majesty the King of Great Britain and Ireland and of the British Dominions beyond the Seas, Emperor of India:

The Right Honorable Arthur James Balfour, O.M., M.P., His Secretary of State for Foreign Affairs;

The Right Honorable Andrew Bonar Law, M.P., His Lord Privy Seal;

The Right Honorable Viscount Milner, G.C.B., G.C.M.G., His Secretary of State for the Colonies;

The Right Honorable George Nicoll Barnes, M.P., Minister without portfolio; and:

for the Dominion of Canada: The Honorable Sir Albert Edward Kemp, K.C.M.G., Minister of the Overseas Forces;

for the Commonwealth of Australia: The Honorable George Foster Pearce, Minister of Defence;

for the Union of South Africa: The Right Honorable Viscount Milner, G.C.B., G.C.M.G.;

for the Dominion of New Zealand: The Honorable Sir Thomas Mackenzie, K.C.M.G., High Commissioner for New Zealand in the United Kingdom;

for India: The Right Honorable Baron Sinha, K.C., Under-Secretary of State for India;

The President of the French Republic:

Mr. Georges Clemenceau, President of the Council, Minister of War;

Mr. Stephen Pichon, Minister for Foreign Affairs;

Mr. Louis-Lucien Klotz, Minister of Finance;

Mr. André Tardieu, Commissary-General for Franco-American Military Affairs;

Mr. Jules Cambon, Ambassador of France;

His Majesty the King of Italy:

The Honorable Tommaso Tittoni, Senator of the Kingdom, Minister for Foreign Affairs;

The Honorable Vittorio Scialoja, Senator of the Kingdom;

The Honorable Maggiorino Ferraris, Senator of the Kingdom;

The Honorable Guglielmo Marconi, Senator of the Kingdom;

The Honorable Silvio Crespi, Deputy;

His Majesty the Emperor of Japan:

Viscount Chinda, Ambassador Extraordinary and Plenipotentiary of H. M. the Emperor of Japan at London;

Mr. K. Matsui, Ambassador Extraordinary and Plenipotentiary of H. M. the Emperor of Japan at Paris;

Mr. H. Ijuin, Ambassador Extraordinary and Plenipotentiary of H. M. the Emperor of Japan at Rome;

The President of the Portuguese Republic:

Dr. Affonso da Costa, formerly President of the Council of Ministers;

Dr. Augusto Luiz Vieira Soares, formerly Minister for Foreign Affairs;

Who, after having communicated their full powers recognized in good and due form,

Have agreed as follows:

ARTICLE 1

The Signatory Powers undertake to maintain between their respective nationals and those of States, Members of the League of Nations, which may adhere to the present Convention a complete commercial equality in the territories under their authority within the area defined by Article 1 of the General Act of Berlin of February 26, 1885, set out in the Annex hereto, but subject to the reservation specified in the final paragraph of that article.

ANNEX

ARTICLE 1 OF THE GENERAL ACT OF BERLIN OF FEBRUARY 26, 1885

The trade of all nations shall enjoy complete freedom:

1. In all the regions forming the basin of the Congo and its affluents. This basin is bounded by the watersheds (or mountain ridges) of the adjacent basins, namely, in particular, those of the Niari, the Ogowé, the Shari, and the Nile, on the north; by the eastern watershed line of the affluents of Lake Tanganyika on the east; and by the watersheds of the basins of the Zambesi and the Logé on the south. It therefore comprises all the regions watered by the Congo and its affluents, including Lake Tanganyika, with its eastern tributaries.

2. In the maritime zone extending along the Atlantic Ocean from the parallel situated in 2° 30′ of south latitude to the mouth of the Logé.

The northern boundary will follow the parallel situated in 2° 30′ from the coast to the point where it meets the geographical basin of the Congo, avoiding the basin of the Owogé, to which the provisions of the present Act do not apply.

The southern boundary will follow the course of the Logé to its source, and thence pass eastward till it joins the geographical basin of the Congo.

3. In the zone stretching eastward from the Congo Basin as above defined, to the Indian Ocean from 5° of north latitude to the mouth of the Zambesi in the south, from which point the line of demarcation will ascend the Zambesi to 5 miles above its confluence with the Shiré, and then follow the watershed between the affluents of Lake Nyassa and those of the Zambesi, till at last it reaches the watershed between the waters of the Zambesi and the Congo.

It is expressly recognized that in extending the principle of free trade to this eastern zone, the Conference Powers only undertake engagements for themselves, and that in the territories belonging to an independent Sovereign State this principle shall only be applicable in so far as it is approved by such State. But the Powers agree to use their good offices with the Governments established on the African shore of the Indian Ocean for the purpose of obtaining such approval, and in any case of securing the most favorable conditions to the transit of all nations.

ARTICLE 2

Merchandise belonging to the nationals of the Signatory Powers, and to those of States, Members of the League of Nations, which may adhere to the present Convention, shall have free access to the interior of the regions specified in Article 1. No differential treatment shall be imposed upon the said merchandise on importation or exportation, the transit remaining free from all duties, taxes or dues, other than those collected for services rendered.

Vessels flying the flag of any of the said Powers shall also have access to all the coast and to all maritime ports in the territories specified in Article 1; they shall be subject to no differential treatment.

Subject to these provisions, the States concerned reserve to themselves complete liberty of action as to the customs and navigation regulations and tariffs to be applied in their territories.

ARTICLE 3

In the territories specified in Article 1 and placed under the authority of one of the Signatory Powers, the nationals of those Powers, or of States, Members of the League of Nations, which may adhere to the present Convention shall, subject only to the limitations necessary for the maintenance of public security and order, enjoy without distinction the same treatment and the same rights as the nationals of the Power exercising authority in the territory, with regard to the protection of their persons and effects, with regard to the acquisition and transmission of their movable and real property, and with regard to the exercise of their occupations.

ARTICLE 4

Each State reserves the right to dispose freely of its property and to grant concessions for the development of the natural resources of the territory, but no regulations on these matters shall admit of any differential treatment between the nationals of the Signatory Powers and of States, Members of the League of Nations, which may adhere to the present Convention.

ARTICLE 5

Subject to the provisions of the present chapter, the navigation of the Niger, of its branches and outlets, and of all the rivers, and of their branches and outlets, within the territories specified in Article 1, as well as of the lakes situated within those territories, shall be entirely free for merchant vessels and for the transport of goods and passengers.

Craft of every kind belonging to the nationals of the Signatory Powers and of States, Members of the League of Nations, which may adhere to the present Convention shall be treated in all respects on a footing of perfect equality.

ARTICLE 6

The navigation shall not be subject to any restriction or dues based on the mere fact of navigation.

It shall not be held to any obligation in regard to landing, stopping, warehousing, bulk breaking or enforced lay over.

No maritime or river toll, based on the mere fact of navigation, shall be levied on vessels, nor shall any transit duty be levied on goods on board. Only such taxes or duties shall be collected as may be in compensation for services rendered to navigation itself. The tariff of these taxes or duties shall not admit of any differential treatment.

ARTICLE 7

The affluents of the rivers and lakes specified in Article 5 shall in all respects be subject to the same rules as the rivers or lakes of which they are tributaries.

The roads, railways or lateral canals which may be constructed with the special object of obviating the innavigability or correcting the imperfections of the water route on certain sections of the rivers and lakes specified in Article 5, their affluents, branches and outlets, shall be considered, in their quality of means of communication, as dependencies of these rivers and lakes, and shall be equally open to the traffic of the nationals of the Signatory Powers and of the States, Members of the League of Nations, which may adhere to the present Convention.

On these roads, railways and canals only such tolls shall be collected as are calculated on the cost of construction, maintenance and management, and on the profits reasonably accruing to the undertaking. As regards the tariff of these tolls, the nationals of the Signatory Powers and of States, Members of the League of Nations, which may adhere to the present Convention, shall be treated on a footing of perfect equality.

ARTICLE 8

Each of the Signatory Powers shall remain free to establish the rules which it may consider expedient for the purpose of ensuring the safety and supervision of navigation, on the understanding that these rules shall facilitate, as far as possible, the circulation of merchant vessels.

ARTICLE 9

In such sections of the rivers and of their affluents, as well as on such lakes, as are not necessarily utilized by more than one riparian State, the Governments exercising authority shall remain free to establish such systems as may be required for the maintenance of public safety and order, and for other necessities of the work of civilization and colonization; but the regulations shall not admit of any differential treatment between vessels or between nationals of the Signatory Powers and of States, Members of the League of Nations, which may adhere to the present Convention.

ARTICLE 10

The Signatory Powers acknowledge their obligation to maintain in the regions under their control actual authority and police forces sufficient to insure protection for persons and property and, if the case should arise, freedom for commerce and transit.

ARTICLE 11

The Signatory Powers exercising sovereign rights or authority in African territories will continue to see to the preservation of the native populations and the improvement of their moral and material conditions. They will, in particular, endeavor to secure the complete suppression of slavery in all its forms and of the black slave trade by land and sea.

They will protect and favor, without distinction of nationality or of religion, the religious, scientific or charitable institutions and undertakings created and organized by the nationals of the other Signatory Powers and of States, Members of the League of Nations, which may adhere to the present Convention, which aim at leading the natives in the path of progress and civilization. Scientific missions, their outfits and their collections, shall likewise be the objects of special solicitude.

Freedom of conscience and the free exercise of all forms of religion are expressly guaranteed to all nationals of the Signatory Powers and to those of the States, Members of the League of Nations, which may become parties to the present Convention. Accordingly, missionaries shall have the right to enter into, and to travel and reside in, African territory with a view to pursuing their religious work.

The application of the provisions of the two preceding paragraphs shall be subject only to such restrictions as may be necessary for the maintenance of

public security and order, or as may result from the enforcement of the constitutional law of any of the Powers exercising authority in African territories.

ARTICLE 12

The Signatory Powers agree that if any dispute whatever should arise
between them relating to the application of the present Convention which
cannot be settled by negotiation, this dispute shall be submitted to an arbitral
tribunal in conformity with the provisions of the Covenant of the League
of Nations.

ARTICLE 13

Except in so far as the stipulations contained in Article 1 of the present
Convention are concerned, the General Act of Berlin of 26th February, 1885,
and the General Act of Brussels of 2nd July, 1890, with the accompanying
Declaration of equal date, shall be considered as abrogated, in so far as they
are binding between the Powers which are Parties to the present Convention.

ARTICLE 14

States exercising authority over African territories, and other States,
Members of the League of Nations, which were parties either to the Act of
Berlin or to the Act of Brussels or the Declaration annexed thereto, may
adhere to the present Convention. The Signatory Powers will use their best
endeavors to obtain the adhesion of these States.

This adhesion shall be notified through the diplomatic channel to the
Government of the French Republic, and by it to all the Signatory or
adhering States. The adhesion will come into force from the date of its
notification to the French Government.

ARTICLE 15

The Signatory Powers will reassemble at the expiration of ten years from
the coming into force of the present Convention, in order to introduce into it
such modifications as experience may have shown to be necessary.

The present Convention shall be ratified as soon as possible.

Each Power will address its ratification to the French Government, which
will inform all the other Signatory Powers.

The ratifications will remain deposited in the archives of the French
Government.

The present Convention will come into force for each Signatory Power
from the date of the deposit of its ratification, and from that moment that
Power will be bound in respect of other Powers which have already deposited
their ratifications.

On the coming into force of the present Convention, the French Government will transmit a certified copy to the Powers which, under the Treaties

of Peace, have undertaken to accept and observe it. The names of these Powers will be notified to the States which adhere.

In faith whereof the above-named Plenipotentiaries have signed the present Convention.

Done at Saint-Germain-en-Laye, the 10th day of September, 1919, in a single copy, which will remain deposited in the archives of the Government of the French Republic, and of which authenticated copies will be sent to each of the Signatory Powers.

[For the United States:]
FRANK L. POLK   [SEAL]
HENRY WHITE   [SEAL]
TASKER H. BLISS   [SEAL]

[For Belgium:]
HYMANS   [SEAL]
J. VAN DEN HEUVEL   [SEAL]
E. VANDERVELDE   [SEAL]

[For the United Kingdom:]
ARTHUR JAMES BALFOUR   [SEAL]
MILNER   [SEAL]
G. N. BARNES   [SEAL]

[For the Dominion of Canada:]
A. E. KEMP   [SEAL]

[For the Commonwealth of Australia:]
G. F. PEARCE   [SEAL]

[For the Union of South Africa:]
MILNER   [SEAL]

[For the Dominion of New Zealand:]
THOS. MACKENZIE   [SEAL]

[For India:]
SINHA OF RAIPUR   [SEAL]

[For France:]
G. CLEMENCEAU   [SEAL]
S. PICHON   [SEAL]
L. L. KLOTZ   [SEAL]
ANDRÉ TARDIEU   [SEAL]
JULES CAMBON   [SEAL]

[For Italy:]
TOM. TITTONI   [SEAL]
VITTORIO SCIALOJA   [SEAL]
MAGGIORINO FERRARIS   [SEAL]
GUGLIELMO MARCONI   [SEAL]

[For Japan:]
S. CHINDA   [SEAL]
K. MATSUI   [SEAL]
H. IJUIN   [SEAL]

[For Portugal:]
AFFONSO COSTA   [SEAL]
AUGUSTO SOARES   [SEAL]

STATUS OF SPITSBERGEN (SVALBARD)

Treaty signed at Paris February 9, 1920, with annex
Senate advice and consent to ratification February 18, 1924
Ratified by the President of the United States March 4, 1924
Ratification of the United States deposited at Paris April 2, 1924
Proclaimed by the President of the United States June 10, 1924
Entered into force August 14, 1925, in accordance with provisions of
article 10

43 Stat. 1892; Treaty Series 686

The President of the United States of America; His Majesty the King of Great Britain and Ireland and of the British Dominions beyond the Seas, Emperor of India; His Majesty the King of Denmark; the President of the French Republic; His Majesty the King of Italy; His Majesty the Emperor of Japan; His Majesty the King of Norway; Her Majesty the Queen of the Netherlands; His Majesty the King of Sweden,

Desirous, while recognising the sovereignty of Norway over the Archipelago of Spitsbergen, including Bear Island, of seeing these territories provided with an equitable régime, in order to assure their development and peaceful utilisation,

Have appointed as their respective Plenipotentiaries with a view to concluding a Treaty to this effect:

The President of the United States of America:

Mr. Hugh Campbell Wallace, Ambassador Extraordinary and Plenipotentiary of the United States of America at Paris;

His Majesty the King of Great Britain and Ireland and of the British Dominions beyond the Seas, Emperor of India:

The Right Honourable the Earl of Derby, K.G., G.C.V.O., C.B., His Ambassador Extraordinary and Plenipotentiary at Paris; and

for the Dominion of Canada: The Right Honourable Sir George Halsey Perley, K.C.M.G., High Commissioner for Canada in the United Kingdom;

for the Commonwealth of Australia: The Right Honourable Andrew Fisher, High Commissioner for Australia in the United Kingdom;

269

for the Dominion of New Zealand: The Right Honourable Sir Thomas MacKenzie, K.C.M.G., High Commissioner for New Zealand in the United Kingdom;

for the Union of South Africa: Mr. Reginald Andrew Blankenberg, O.B.E., Acting High Commissioner for South Africa in the United Kingdom;

for India: The Right Honourable the Earl of Derby, K.G., G.C.V.O., C.B.;

His Majesty the King of Denmark:
Mr. Herman Anker Bernhoft, Envoy Extraordinary and Minister Plenipotentiary of H. M. the King of Denmark at Paris;

The President of the French Republic:
Mr. Alexandre Millerand, President of the Council, Minister for Foreign Affairs;

His Majesty the King of Italy:
The Honourable Maggiorino Ferraris, Senator of the Kingdom;

His Majesty the Emperor of Japan:
Mr. K. Matsui, Ambassador Extraordinary and Plenipotentiary of H. M. the Emperor of Japan at Paris;

His Majesty the King of Norway:
Baron Wedel Jarlsberg, Envoy Extraordinary and Minister Plenipotentiary of H. M. the King of Norway at Paris;

Her Majesty the Queen of the Netherlands:
Mr. John Loudon, Envoy Extraordinary and Minister Plenipotentiary of H. M. the Queen of the Netherlands at Paris;

His Majesty the King of Sweden:
Count J.-J.-A. Ehrensvärd, Envoy Extraordinary and Minister Plenipotentiary of H. M. the King of Sweden at Paris;

Who, having communicated their full powers, found in good and due form, have agreed as follows:

ARTICLE 1

The High Contracting Parties undertake to recognise, subject to the stipulations of the present Treaty, the full and absolute sovereignty of Norway over the Archipelago of Spitsbergen, comprising, with Bear Island or Beeren-Eiland, all the islands situated between 10° and 35° longitude East of Greenwich and between 74° and 81° latitude North, especially West Spitsbergen, North-East Land, Barents Island, Edge Island, Wiche Islands, Hope Island or Hopen-Eiland, and Prince Charles Foreland, together with all islands great or small and rocks appertaining thereto (see annexed map).[1]

---

[1] Not printed here; see British Treaty Series No. 18 (1924).

ARTICLE 2

Ships and nationals of all the High Contracting Parties shall enjoy equally the rights of fishing and hunting in the territories specified in Article 1 and in their territorial waters.

Norway shall be free to maintain, take or decree suitable measures to insure the preservation and, if necessary, the re-constitution of the fauna and flora of the said regions, and their territorial waters; it being clearly understood that these measures shall always be applicable equally to the nationals of all the High Contracting Parties without any exemption, privilege or favour whatsoever, direct or indirect to the advantage of any one of them.

Occupiers of land whose rights have been recognised in accordance with the terms of Articles 6 and 7 will enjoy the exclusive right of hunting on their own land: (1) in the neighbourhood of their habitations, houses, stores, factories and installations, constructed for the purpose of developing their property, under conditions laid down by the local police regulations; (2) within a radius of 10 kilometres round the headquarters of their place of business or works; and in both cases, subject always to the observance of regulations made by the Norwegian Government in accordance with the conditions laid down in the present Article.

ARTICLE 3

The nationals of all the High Contracting Parties shall have equal liberty of access and entry for any reason or object whatever to the waters, fjords and ports of the territories specified in Article 1; subject to the observance of local laws and regulations, they may carry on there without impediment all maritime, industrial, mining and commercial operations on a footing of absolute equality.

They shall be admitted under the same conditions of equality to the exercise and practice of all maritime, industrial, mining or commercial enterprises both on land and in the territorial waters, and no monopoly shall be established on any account or for any enterprise whatever.

Notwithstanding any rules relating to coasting trade which may be in force in Norway, ships of the High Contracting Parties going to or coming from the territories specified in Article 1 shall have the right to put into Norwegian ports on their outward or homeward voyage for the purpose of taking on board or disembarking passengers or cargo going to or coming from the said territories, or for any other purpose.

It is agreed that in every respect and especially with regard to exports, imports and transit traffic, the nationals of all the High Contracting Parties, their ships and goods shall not be subject to any charges or restrictions whatever which are not borne by the nationals, ships or goods which enjoy in Norway the treatment of the most favoured nation; Norwegian nationals, ships or goods being for this purpose assimilated to those of the other High Contracting Parties, and not treated more favourably in any respect.

No charge or restriction shall be imposed on the exportation of any goods to the territories of any of the Contracting Powers other or more onerous than on the exportation of similar goods to the territory of any other Contracting Power (including Norway) or to any other destination.

ARTICLE 4

All public wireless telegraphy stations established or to be established by, or with the authorisation of, the Norwegian Government within the territories referred to in Article 1 shall always be open on a footing of absolute equality to communications from ships of all flags and from nationals of the High Contracting Parties, under the conditions laid down in the Wireless Telegraphy Convention of July 5, 1912,[2] or in the subsequent International Convention which may be concluded to replace it.

Subject to international obligations arising out of a state of war, owners of landed property shall always be at liberty to establish and use for their own purposes wireless telegraphy installations, which shall be free to communicate on private business with fixed or moving wireless stations, including those on board ships and aircraft.

ARTICLE 5

The High Contracting Parties recognise the utility of establishing an international meteorological station in the territories specified in Article 1, the organisation of which shall form the subject of a subsequent Convention.

Conventions shall also be concluded laying down the conditions under which scientific investigations may be conducted in the said territories.

ARTICLE 6

Subject to the provisions of the present Article, acquired rights of nationals of the High Contracting Parties shall be recognised.

Claims arising from taking possession or from occupation of land before the signature of the present Treaty shall be dealt with in accordance with the Annex hereto, which will have the same force and effect as the present Treaty.

ARTICLE 7

With regard to methods of acquisition, enjoyment and exercise of the right of ownership of property, including mineral rights, in the territories specified in Article 1, Norway undertakes to grant to all nationals of the High Contracting Parties treatment based on complete equality and in conformity with the stipulations of the present Treaty.

Expropriation may be resorted to only on grounds of public utility and on payment of proper compensation.

---

[2] TS 581, *ante,* vol. 1, p. 883.

ARTICLE 8

Norway undertakes to provide for the territories specified in Article 1 mining regulations which, especially from the point of view of imposts, taxes or charges of any kind, and of general or particular labour conditions, shall exclude all privileges, monopolies or favours for the benefit of the State or of the nationals of any one of the High Contracting Parties, including Norway, and shall guarantee to the paid staff of all categories the remuneration and protection necessary for their physical, moral and intellectual welfare.

Taxes, dues and duties levied shall be devoted exclusively to the said territories and shall not exceed what is required for the object in view.

So far, particularly, as the exportation of minerals is concerned, the Norwegian Government shall have the right to levy an export duty which shall not exceed 1% of the maximum value of the minerals exported up to 100,000 tons, and beyond that quantity the duty will be proportionately diminished. The value shall be fixed at the end of the navigation season by calculating the average free on board price obtained.

Three months before the date fixed for their coming into force, the draft mining regulations shall be communicated by the Norwegian Government to the other Contracting Powers. If during this period one or more of the said Powers propose to modify these regulations before they are applied, such proposals shall be communicated by the Norwegian Government to the other Contracting Powers in order that they may be submitted to examination and the decision of a Commission composed of one representative of each of the said Powers. This Commission shall meet at the invitation of the Norwegian Government and shall come to a decision within a period of three months from the date of its first meeting. Its decisions shall be taken by a majority.

ARTICLE 9

Subject to the rights and duties resulting from the admission of Norway to the League of Nations, Norway undertakes not to create nor to allow the establishment of any naval base in the territories specified in Article 1 and not to construct any fortification in the said territories, which may never be used for warlike purposes.

ARTICLE 10

Until the recognition by the High Contracting Parties of a Russian Government shall permit Russia to adhere to the present Treaty, Russian nationals and companies shall enjoy the same rights as nationals of the High Contracting Parties.

Claims in the territories specified in Article 1 which they may have to put forward shall be presented under the conditions laid down in the present Treaty (Article 6 and Annex) through the intermediary of the Danish Government, who declare their willingness to lend their good offices for this purpose.

The present Treaty, of which the French and English texts are both authentic, shall be ratified.

Ratifications shall be deposited at Paris as soon as possible.

Powers of which the seat of the Government is outside Europe may confine their action to informing the Government of the French Republic, through their diplomatic representative at Paris, that their ratification has been given, and in this case, they shall transmit the instrument as soon as possible.

The present Treaty will come into force, in so far as the stipulations of Article 8 are concerned, from the date of its ratification by all the signatory Powers; and in all other respects on the same date as the mining regulations provided for in that Article.

Third Powers will be invited by the Government of the French Republic to adhere to the present Treaty duly ratified. This adhesion shall be effected by a communication addressed to the French Government, which will undertake to notify the other Contracting Parties.

In witness whereof the above-named Plenipotentiaries have signed the present Treaty.

Done at Paris, the ninth day of February, 1920, in duplicate, one copy to be transmitted to the Government of His Majesty the King of Norway, and one deposited in the archives of the French Republic; authenticated copies will be transmitted to the other Signatory Powers.

[For the United States:]		[For Denmark:]	
Hugh C. Wallace	[seal]	H. A. Bernhoft	[seal]
[For the United Kingdom:]		[For France:]	
Derby	[seal]	A. Millerand	[seal]
[For the Dominion of Canada:]		[For Italy:]	
George H. Perley	[seal]	Maggiorino Ferraris	[seal]
[For the Commonwealth of Australia:]		[For Japan:]	
Andrew Fisher	[seal]	K. Matsui	[seal]
[For the Dominion of New Zealand:]		[For Norway:]	
Th. MacKenzie	[seal]	Wedel Jarlsberg	[seal]
[For the Union of South Africa:]		[For the Netherlands:]	
R. A. Blankenberg	[seal]	J. Loudon	[seal]
[For India:]		[For Sweden:]	
Derby	[seal]	J. Ehrensvard	[seal]

Annex

1

(1) Within three months from the coming into force of the present Treaty, notification of all claims to land which had been made to any Government before the signature of the present Treaty must be sent by the Government of the claimant to a Commissioner charged to examine such claims. The Commissioner will be a judge or jurisconsult of Danish nationality possessing

the necessary qualifications for the task, and shall be nominated by the Danish Government.

(2) The notification must include a precise delimitation of the land claimed and be accompanied by a map on a scale of not less than 1/1,000,000 on which the land claimed is clearly marked.

(3) The notification must be accompanied by the deposit of a sum of one penny for each acre (40 ares) of land claimed, to defray the expenses of the examination of the claims.

(4) The Commissioner will be entitled to require from the claimants any further documents or information which he may consider necessary.

(5) The Commissioner will examine the claims so notified. For this purpose he will be entitled to avail himself of such expert assistance as he may consider necessary, and in case of need to cause investigations to be carried out on the spot.

(6) The remuneration of the Commissioner will be fixed by agreement between the Danish Government and the other Governments concerned. The Commissioner will fix the remuneration of such assistants as he considers it necessary to employ.

(7) The Commissioner, after examining the claims, will prepare a report showing precisely the claims which he is of opinion should be recognised at once and those which, either because they are disputed or for any other reason, he is of opinion should be submitted to arbitration as hereinafter provided. Copies of this report will be forwarded by the Commissioner to the Governments concerned.

(8) If the amount of the sums deposited in accordance with clause (3) is insufficient to cover the expenses of the examination of the claims, the Commissioner will, in every case where he is of opinion that a claim should be recognised, at once state what further sum the claimant should be required to pay. This sum will be based on the amount of the land to which the claimant's title is recognised.

If the sums deposited in accordance with clause (3) exceed the expenses of the examination, the balance will be devoted to the cost of the arbitration hereinafter provided for.

(9) Within three months from the date of the report referred to in clause (7) of this paragraph, the Norwegian Government shall take the necessary steps to confer upon claimants whose claims have been recognised by the Commissioner a valid title securing to them the exclusive property in the land in question, in accordance with the laws and regulations in force or to be enforced in the territories specified in Article 1 of the present Treaty, and subject to the mining regulations referred to in Article 8 of the present Treaty.

In the event, however, of a further payment being required in accordance with clause (8) of this paragraph, a provisional title only will be delivered, which title will become definitive on payment by the claimant, within such reasonable period as the Norwegian Government may fix, of the further sum required of him.

2

Claims which for any reason the Commissioner referred to in clause (1) of the preceding paragraph has not recognised as valid will be settled in accordance with the following provisions:

(1) Within three months from the date of the report referred to in clause (7) of the preceding paragraph, each of the Governments whose nationals have been found to possess claims which have not been recognised will appoint an arbitrator.

The Commissioner will be the President of the Tribunal so constituted. In cases of equal division of opinion, he shall have the deciding vote. He will nominate a Secretary to receive the documents referred to in clause (2) of this paragraph and to make the necessary arrangements for the meeting of the Tribunal.

(2) Within one month from the appointment of the Secretary referred to in clause (1) the claimants concerned will send to him through the intermediary of their respective Governments statements indicating precisely their claims and accompanied by such documents and arguments as they may wish to submit in support thereof.

(3) Within two months from the appointment of the Secretary referred to in clause (1) the Tribunal shall meet at Copenhagen for the purpose of dealing with the claims which have been submitted to it.

(4) The language of the Tribunal shall be English. Documents or arguments may be submitted to it by the interested parties in their own language, but in that case must be accompanied by an English translation.

(5) The claimants shall be entitled, if they so desire, to be heard by the Tribunal either in person or by counsel, and the Tribunal shall be entitled to call upon the claimants to present such additional explanations, documents or arguments as it may think necessary.

(6) Before the hearing of any case the Tribunal shall require from the parties a deposit or security for such sum as it may think necessary to cover the share of each party in the expenses of the Tribunal. In fixing the amount of such sum the Tribunal shall base itself principally on the extent of the land claimed. The Tribunal shall also have power to demand a further deposit from the parties in cases where special expense is involved.

(7) The honorarium of the arbitrators shall be calculated per month, and fixed by the Governments concerned. The salary of the Secretary and any other persons employed by the Tribunal shall be fixed by the President.

(8) Subject to the provisions of this Annex the Tribunal shall have full power to regulate its own procedure.

(9) In dealing with the claims the Tribunal shall take into consideration:

(*a*) any applicable rules of International Law;

(*b*) the general principles of justice and equity;

(*c*) the following circumstances:

(i) the date on which the land claimed was first occupied by the claimant or his predecessors in title;

(ii) the date on which the claim was notified to the Government of the claimant;

(iii) the extent to which the claimant or his predecessors in title have developed and exploited the land claimed. In this connection the Tribunal shall take into account the extent to which the claimants may have been prevented from developing their undertakings by conditions or restrictions resulting from the war of 1914–1919.

(10) All the expenses of the Tribunal shall be divided among the claimants in such proportion as the Tribunal shall decide. If the amount of the sums paid in accordance with clause (6) is larger than the expenses of the Tribunal, the balance shall be returned to the parties whose claims have been recognised in such proportion as the Tribunal shall think fit.

(11) The decisions of the Tribunal shall be communicated by it to the Governments concerned, including in every case the Norwegian Government.

The Norwegian Government shall within three months from the receipt of each decision take the necessary steps to confer upon the claimants whose claims have been recognised by the Tribunal a valid title to the land in question, in accordance with the laws and regulations in force or to be enforced in the territories specified in Article 1, and subject to the mining regulations referred to in Article 8 of the present Treaty. Nevertheless, the titles so conferred will only become definitive on the payment by the claimant concerned, within such reasonable period as the Norwegian Government may fix, of his share of the expenses of the Tribunal.

3

Any claims which are not notified to the Commissioner in accordance with clause (1) of paragraph 1, or which not having been recognised by him are not submitted to the Tribunal in accordance with paragraph 2, will be finally extinguished.

SPANISH-AMERICAN POSTAL CONVENTION

Convention and final protocol signed at Madrid November 13, 1920
Ratified and approved by the Postmaster General of the United States
May 3, 1922
Approved by the President of the United States May 8, 1922
Entered into force January 1, 1921
Terminated by convention of September 15, 1921 [1]

42 Stat. 2141; Post Office Department print

SPANISH-AMERICAN POSTAL CONVENTION SIGNED AT MADRID, THE 13TH OF NOVEMBER, 1920, BETWEEN SPAIN, ARGENTINA, BOLIVIA, BRAZIL, COLOMBIA, COSTA RICA, CUBA, CHILE, DOMINICAN REPUBLIC, ECUADOR, EL SALVADOR, THE UNITED STATES, THE PHILIPPINE ISLANDS, GUATEMALA, HAITI, HONDURAS, MEXICO, NICARAGUA, PANAMA, PARAGUAY, PERU, URUGUAY AND VENEZUELA.

The undersigned, assembled in Madrid, duly authorized by their respective governments, and in accordance with Paragraph 2 of Article 21 of the Principal Convention of the Universal Postal Union,[2] have mutually agreed, subject to ratification, on the following provisions for the regulation and improvement of their postal relations.

ARTICLE I

1. All the countries signing this Convention shall constitute a single postal territory.

2. Prepayment of postage is obligatory on all classes of mail to be transmitted from one to another of the countries constituting this Union, letters alone being granted a slight concession relative to insufficient prepayment.

3. Each of the contracting countries agrees to transport freely and gratuitously through its territory and by means of the services maintained by its postal administration or utilized for the direct despatch of its own mails, the mails received from any of these countries destined to any other.

However, the expenses for land or maritime transportation of the mails shall be borne by the country of origin in case there is required for their

---

[1] *Post,* p. 309.
[2] Convention signed at Madrid May 26, 1906, *ante,* vol. 1, p. 505.

278

subsequent forwarding the intermediary of countries other than those adhering to this Convention.

4. It is decreed as a fundamental principle that, in the postal relations between the contracting countries, the rates which each administration has established in its domestic service shall apply.

5. The provisions of this Convention extend to letters; post cards, single and with reply paid; printed matter of all classes; commercial papers; and samples.

ARTICLE II

1. Letters

(a) Every letter which does not bear stamps corresponding to the first postage rate of an ordinary letter shall be considered as not prepaid and shall not be forwarded by the office of origin.

(b) The office of origin alone shall be authorized to determine the rating of letters insufficiently prepaid, which shall be for double the amount of the insufficiency, according to the weight. The office of destination shall collect from the addressee the amount of the rating imposed by the office of origin, which amount shall belong to the office of destination.

2. Post Cards

For post cards, both single and with reply paid, the domestic rates of each country shall apply.

3. Books, Periodicals, Printed Matter and Commercial Papers

The weight of packages containing books, periodicals, printed matter or commercial papers, shall not exceed 4 kilograms, with the exception of works printed in a single volume, the maximum weight of which may not exceed 5 kilograms. The dimensions of these packages shall not exceed 45 centimeters in any direction.

Packages presented in the form of a roll shall be transmitted through the mail provided that their size does not exceed 1 meter in length by 15 centimeters in diameter.

Commercial papers shall be prepaid at the minimum rate fixed by the regulations of the country of origin.

4. Samples

Samples shall be freely transmitted through the mail provided they have no commercial value and their size does not exceed 30 centimeters in length by 20 centimeters in width and 10 centimeters in depth or thickness. If in the form of a roll, the greatest dimensions shall be 30 centimeters in length by 15 in diameter.

Samples shall not bear postage lower than that specified in the regulations of the country of origin.

ARTICLE III

Responsibility for the Loss of Registered Articles

1. In the case of the loss of a registered article, the sender shall have the right to an indemnity equal to that fixed by the domestic regulations of the country of origin for a similar case, but not exceeding 50 francs gold.

2. The payment of the indemnity by the despatching administration shall be made at the latest within a period of 12 months, counting from the day following that on which the claim is first filed. The administration responsible for the loss shall reimburse the administration of origin without delay and within the period indicated, the amount of the indemnity which it may have paid to the sender. This payment shall be made in the money of the creditor country, or the equivalent in the money of another country which may be mutually agreed upon by the administrations concerned.

ARTICLE IV

In everything which does not conflict with the provisions of this Convention, the regulations of the Universal Postal Union shall govern.

ARTICLE V

This Convention shall take effect on the first of January, 1921, for the countries which on that date may have ratified it, and those which have not done so shall participate in its provisions whenever they notify the other contracting parties of their ratification.

This Convention shall have an indefinite duration, but any one of the parties may withdraw from the Convention upon one year's previous notice given to the other signatory administrations.

Done in Madrid, the 13th of November, 1920.

For the Delegation of Spain:
CONDE DE COLOMBÍ
JOSÉ DE GARCÍA TORRES
GUILLERMO CAPDEVILA
JOSÉ DE ESPAÑA
MARTÍN VICENTE
ANTONIO CAMACHO
JUSTO G. HERVÁS
J. ORTEGA MUNILLA
BERNARDO ROLLAND
MANUEL G. ACEBO

For the Delegation of the United States of North America:
OTTO PRAEGER
S. M. WEBER
ELIZABETH LEE WOODS

For the Argentine Republic:
A. BARRERA NICHOLSON
EUGENIO TROISÍ
NATALIO R. FIRPO

For the Delegation of Bolivia:
LUIS RODRÍGUEZ

For the United States of Brazil:
ALCIBIADES PEÇANHA
JOSÉ HENRIQUE ADERNE

For the Delegation of Colombia:
W. MACLELLAN
GABRIEL ROLDÁN

For the Republic of Costa Rica:
MANUEL M. DE PERALTA

For the Republic of Cuba:
JUAN IRURETAGOYENA

For the Delegation of Chile:
FLORENCIO MÁRQUEZ DE LA PLATA
M. COUSIÑO

For the Dominican Republic:
LEOPOLDO LOVELACE

For Ecuador:
LUIS ROBALINO DÁVILA
LEÓNIDAS A. YEROVI

For the Republic of El Salvador:
ISMAEL G. FUENTES

The United States of America—for the
Philippine Islands:
JOSÉ TOPACIO

For the Republic of Guatemala:
JUAN J. ORTEGA
ENRIQUE TRAUMANN

For the Republic of Haiti:
LUIS MA. SOLER

For the Republic of Honduras:
RICARDO BELTRÁN Y RÓZPIDE

For the United Mexican States:
COSME HINOJOSA
JULIO POULAT
ALFONSO REYES

For Nicaragua:
M. IGO. TERÁN

For the Republic of Panama:
J. D. AROSEMENA

For Paraguay:
FERNANDO PIGNET

For Peru:
D. C. URREA
O. BARRENECHEA Y RAIGADA
Chargé d'Affaires of Peru

For Uruguay:
ADOLFO AGORIO

For the United States of Venezuela:
PEDRO EMILIO COLL
S. BARCELÓ

FINAL PROTOCOL

Before signing the foregoing Convention, the signatory delegates have agreed to the following additional protocol:

1. The notices of ratification of this Convention shall be received in Madrid.

2. This protocol shall have the same validity as if it had been inserted in the text of the Convention to which it refers, a copy of the same to be signed and deposited in the Archives of the Spanish Government and a copy to be supplied to each party.

Done in Madrid the 13th day of November, 1920.

CONDE DE COLOMBÍ
LEOPOLDO LOVELACE
JUAN IRURETAGOYENA
FLORENCIO MÁRQUEZ DE LA PLATA
M. COUSIÑO
LUIS ROBALINO DÁVILA
LEÓNIDAS A. YEROVI
J. POULAT
ALFONSO REYES
J. D. AROSEMENA
GABRIEL ROLDÁN
W. MACLELLAN
O. BARRENECHEA Y RAIGADA
BARCELÓ
ENRIQUE TRAUMANN
ALCIBIADES PEÇANHA

JOSÉ HENRIQUE ADERNE
ELIZABETH LEE WOODS
OTTO PRAEGER
JOSÉ TOPACIO
LUIS MA. SOLER
RICARDO BELTRÁN Y RÓZPIDE
EUGENIO TROISÍ
A. DE LA CRUZ
ADOLFO AGORIO
A. BARRERA NICHOLSON
FERNANDO PIGNET
LUIS RODRÍGUEZ
M. IGO. TERÁN
ISMAEL G. FUENTES
D. C. URREA

UNIVERSAL POSTAL UNION

Convention and final protocol signed at Madrid November 30, 1920 [1]
Ratified and approved by the Postmaster General of the United States,
with the exception of certain provisions, December 31, 1921 [2]
Approved by the President of the United States, with the exception of
certain provisions, January 23, 1922 [2]
Ratifications exchanged at Madrid December 1, 1921; ratification of
the United States deposited at Madrid February 24, 1922
Entered into force January 1, 1922
Terminated by convention of August 28, 1924 [3]

42 Stat. 1971; Post Office Department print

[TRANSLATION]

Universal Postal Convention, concluded between Germany, United States of
America, Philippine Islands, the other Island Possessions of the United
States of America, Argentine Republic, Austria, Belgium and the Colony
of the Belgian Congo, Bolivia, Brazil, Bulgaria, Chile, China, Republic of
Colombia, Republic of Costa Rica, Republic of Cuba, Denmark, Do-
minican Republic, Egypt, Ecuador, Spain and the Spanish Colonies,
Ethiopia, Finland, France, Algeria, the French Colonies and Protectorates
of Indo China, the whole of the other French Colonies, Great Britain, and
Various British Dominions, Colonies and Protectorates, British India, the
Commonwealth of Australia, Canada, New Zealand, the Union of South
Africa, Greece, Guatemala, Republic of Haiti, Republic of Honduras,
Hungary, Iceland, Italy and the Italian Colonies, Japan, Chosen (Korea),
the whole of the other Japanese Dependencies, Republic of Liberia, Lux-
emburg, Morocco (except the Spanish Zone), Morocco (Spanish Zone),
Mexico, Nicaragua, Norway, Republic of Panama, Paraguay, Netherlands,
Dutch East Indies, Dutch Colonies in America, Peru, Persia, Poland,
Portugal, Portuguese Colonies in Africa, in Asia and Oceania, Roumania,
Salvador, Territory of the Sarre, Kingdom of the Serbs, Croats and

---

[1] For text of regulations for execution of the convention, see 42 Stat. 2010.
[2] The United States excepted the provisions contained in para. 3 of art. 3 and in the
last sentence of para. 1 of art. 25.
[3] *Post,* p. 443.

Slovenes, Kingdom of Siam, Sweden, Switzerland, Czecho-Slovakia, Tunis, Turkey, Uruguay, and United States of Venezuela.

The undersigned, plenipotentiaries of the Governments of the above-named countries, being assembled in Congress at Madrid, by virtue of Article 25 of the Universal Postal Convention concluded at Rome on the 26th of May, 1906,[4] have by mutual consent and subject to ratification, revised the said Convention to read as follows:

ARTICLE 1

Definition of the Postal Union

The countries between which the present Convention is concluded, as well as those which may adhere to it hereafter, form, under the title of Universal Postal Union, a single postal territory for the reciprocal exchange of correspondence between their post offices.

ARTICLE 2

Articles to Which the Convention Applies

The provisions of this Convention cover letters, post cards, both single and reply-paid, printed papers of every kind, commercial papers, and samples of merchandise originating in one of the countries of the Union and addressed to another of those countries. They also apply to the exchange by post of the articles above mentioned between the countries of the Union and countries outside of the Union, whenever the services of two of the contracting parties at least are used for that exchange.

ARTICLE 3

Conveyance of Mails Between Contiguous Countries; Third Services

1. The Postal Administrations of contiguous countries or countries able to correspond directly with each other without making use of the services of a third Administration settle, by mutual consent, the conditions of conveyance across the frontier or from one frontier to the other of the mails which they exchange.

2. In the absence of any other arrangement, the direct sea conveyance between two countries by means of packets or vessels maintained by one of them is considered as a third service; and this conveyance, as well as conveyance between two offices of the same country, by means of sea or land services maintained by another country, is governed by the terms of the following article.

3. The high contracting parties undertake not to impose, on postal grounds, special obligations on packets employed in regular mail services and

---

[4] *Ante,* vol. 1, p. 492.

maintained by a country of the Union, in exchange for advantages and privileges which may exist or be established in favor of any class of merchant ships, especially as regards the formalities and arrangements on entering or leaving port.

ARTICLE 4

Transit and Warehousing Charges

1. Freedom of transit is guaranteed throughout the entire territory of the Union.

Administrations have the right to suppress the postal service with any country which does not observe the provisions of the preceding paragraph. These Administrations must give previous notice of this measure, by telegraph, to the Administration concerned.

2. The several Postal Administrations of the Union may send reciprocally through the medium of one or of several of them, both closed mails and correspondence *à découvert,* according to the needs of the traffic and the requirements of the postal service.

3. Correspondence exchanged in closed mails between two Administrations of the Union, by means of the services of one or of several other Administrations of the Union is subject to the following transit charges to be paid to each of the countries traversed or whose services participate in the conveyance, viz.:

1) For land transits:

(*a*) 1 franc 50 centimes per kilogram of letters and post cards and 20 centimes per kilogram of other articles, if the distance traversed does not exceed 3,000 kilometers;

(*b*) 3 francs per kilogram of letters and post cards and 40 centimes per kilogram of other articles, if the distance traversed exceeds 3,000 kilometers but does not exceed 6,000 kilometers;

(*c*) 4 francs 50 centimes per kilogram of letters and post cards and 60 centimes per kilogram of other articles, if the distance traversed exceeds 6,000 kilometers but does not exceed 9,000 kilometers;

(*d*) 6 francs per kilogram of letters and post cards and 80 centimes per kilogram of other articles, if the distance traversed exceeds 9,000 kilometers.

2) For sea transits:

(*a*) 1 franc 50 centimes per kilogram of letters and post cards and 20 centimes per kilogram of other articles, if the distance traversed does not exceed 300 nautical miles. Sea conveyance over a distance not exceeding 300 nautical miles is, however, gratuitous if the Administration concerned already receives, on account of the mails conveyed, the remuneration applicable to territorial transit;

(*b*) 4 francs per kilogram of letters and post cards and 50 centimes per kilogram of other articles, exchanged over a distance exceeding 300 nautical miles between European countries, between Europe and ports of Africa and Asia on the Mediterranean and the Black Seas, or between one of these ports and another, and between Europe and North America. The same rates are applicable to conveyance anywhere within the Union, between two ports of a single State, as well as between the ports of two States served by the same line of packets when the sea transit involved does not exceed 1,500 nautical miles;

(*c*) 8 francs per kilogram of letters and post cards and 1 franc per kilogram of other articles, for all transits not included in the categories given above in paragraphs (*a*) and (*b*).

In the case of sea conveyance performed by two or more Administrations, the charges paid for the entire transit may not exceed 8 francs per kilogram of letters and post cards, and 1 franc per kilogram of other articles; these charges are, when occasion arises, shared between the Administrations participating in the service, in proportion to the distances traversed, without prejudice to any other arrangement which may be made between the parties interested.

4. For the warehousing in a port of closed mails, brought by one vessel and intended to be taken on by another, a fixed payment of 50 centimes per bag is made to the Post Office of the place where the mails are warehoused, provided that such Office does not receive payment for a land or sea transit. Simple transshipment, however, from vessel to vessel does not give rise to any payment.

5. Correspondence exchanged *à découvert* between two Administrations of the Union is subject to the following transit charges per article, and irrespective of weight or destination, namely:

Letters 6   centimes each.
Post cards.. 2½ centimes each.
Other articles.. 2½ centimes each.

6. The transit rates specified in the present article do not apply to conveyance within the Union by means of extraordinary services specially established or maintained by one Administration at the request of one or several other Administrations. The conditions of this class of conveyance are regulated by mutual consent between the Administrations concerned.

Moreover, in all cases where the transit, either by land or by sea, is at present gratuitous or subject to more advantageous conditions, such state of things is maintained.

7. The expenses of transit and warehousing are borne by the Administration of the country of origin.

8. The general accounting for these expenses is based on statements pre-

pared once in every three years, during a period of 28 days to be determined in the detailed regulations [5] of the present Convention.

9. The correspondence mentioned in paragraphs 3 and 4 of article 13 hereafter, reply halves of double post cards returned to the country of origin, articles redirected or missent, undelivered articles, advices of delivery, post-office money orders, and all other documents relative to the postal service are exempt from all charges for land or sea transit.

10. When the annual balance of the accounts for transit and warehousing charges between two Administrations does not exceed 1,000 francs, the debtor Administration is relieved of all payment under this heading.

ARTICLE 5

Aerial Services

Aerial services established for the conveyance of correspondence between two or more countries are considered as analogous to the extraordinary services to which article 4, § 6, refers.

The conditions of conveyance are settled by mutual consent between the Administrations concerned. The transit charges applicable to each aerial service are, however, uniform for all Administrations which use the service without sharing in the working expenses.

ARTICLE 6

Rates of Postage, Surcharges, and General Conditions

1. The rates of postage for the conveyance of correspondence throughout the entire extent of the Union, including delivery at the residence of the addressees in the countries of the Union where a delivery is or shall be organized, are fixed as follows in case of prepayment:

1) For letters, 50 centimes for the first 20 grams and 25 centimes for every 20 grams or fraction of 20 grams above the initial weight of 20 grams;

2) For postcards, 30 centimes for single cards or for each of the two halves of reply post cards;

3) For printed papers of every kind, commercial papers, and samples of merchandise, 10 centimes for each article or packet bearing a separate address and for every 50 grams or fraction of 50 grams, provided that such article or packet does not contain any letter or written note having the character of actual personal correspondence, and that it is made up in such a manner as to admit of its being easily examined.

The rate on commercial papers must not be less than 50 centimes per packet, and the rate on samples must not be less than 20 centimes per packet.

---

[5] See footnote 1, p. 282.

Exceptionally, articles printed in relief for the special use of the blind are admitted at the rate of 5 centimes per packet and for every 500 grams or fraction of 500 grams.

2. Over and above the rates fixed by the preceding paragraph a surcharge proportionate to the expenses incurred may be levied on every article forwarded by services maintained by Administrations outside the Union, or by extraordinary services within the Union which involve special payment.

When the rate of prepayment for the single post card comprises the surcharge authorized by the preceding paragraph, the same rate is applicable to each half of the reply-paid post card.

The country of destination is authorized to impose a special surcharge, in accordance with its internal legislation, on articles addressed *poste restante*. If the article is redirected or returned as undelivered, the surcharge is canceled.

3. Correspondence of every kind not prepaid or insufficiently prepaid is liable to a charge equal to double postage or double the amount of the deficiency, to be paid by the addressees; but that charge may not be less than 30 centimes.

4. Articles other than letters and post cards must be prepaid at least partially.

The privilege of not prepaying postage or of prepaying partially does not apply to letters, post cards, or to other articles sent with the evident intention of avoiding payment of postage.

5. Letters may not exceed 2 kilograms in weight, or measure more than 45 centimeters in any direction, or, if they are in the form of a roll, 75 centimeters in length and 10 centimeters in diameter.

6. Packets of samples of merchandise may not contain any article having a saleable value; they must not exceed 500 grams in weight, or measure more than 30 centimeters in length, 20 centimeters in breadth, and 10 centimeters in depth, or, if they are in the form of a roll, 30 centimeters in length and 15 centimeters in diameter.

7. Packets of commercial papers and printed papers may not exceed 2 kilograms in weight, or measure more than 45 centimeters in any direction. Packets in the form of a roll may, however, be allowed to pass through the post so long as they do not exceed 10 centimeters in diameter and 75 centimeters in length.

Packets of printed papers intended for the special use of the blind, and printed volumes sent singly, may weigh as much as 3 kilograms, but may not exceed the dimensions prescribed for other classes of printed papers.

8. Stamps or forms of prepayment, obliterated or not, as well as all printed papers representing a monetary value, save the exceptions authorized by the detailed Regulations of the present Convention are excluded from transmission at the reduced rate.

Article 7

Registered Articles; Advices of Delivery; Requests for Information

1. The articles specified in article 6 may be registered.

The reply halves of reply-paid post cards can not, however, be registered by the original senders.

2. Every registered article is liable, at the charge of the sender:

1) To the ordinary prepaid rate of postage on the article, according to its character;

2) To a fixed registration fee of 50 centimes at most, including the issue of a certificate of posting to the sender.

3. The sender of a registered article may obtain an advice of the delivery of such article by paying, at the time of posting, a fixed fee of 50 centimes at most. Double this fee may be charged for advices of delivery applied for after the posting of the article and for requests for information relating to ordinary or registered articles. In the case of requests for information respecting registered articles, no fee is charged if the sender has already paid the special fee for an advice of delivery.

Article 8

Trade Charges on Packets

1. Registered correspondence marked with trade charges to be collected on delivery may be exchanged between countries of which the Administrations agree to provide this service.

These articles are subject to the same regulations and rates as registered articles.

The sender pays, in addition, a fixed trade charge fee of 10 centimes.

The maximum trade charge is equal to the maximum amount fixed for money orders addressed to the country in which the article originated.

In the absence of any contrary arrangement between the Administrations concerned, the amount of the trade charge is expressed in the money of the country of destination.

2. Subject to the same reservation, the amount collected from the addressee is to be transmitted to the sender by means of a money order, after deducting a collection fee of 15 centimes and the ordinary rate chargeable for money orders calculated on the amount of the balance.

Trade charge money orders which have not been paid to the payees for any reason whatever are not repaid to the office of issue, and their amount accrues definitely to the Administration of the country from which the articles marked with the trade charge were sent, after the expiration of the legal period of validity.

In all other respects, trade charge money orders are subject to the provisions of the Agreement concerning the Money Order Service.

3. For the loss of a registered article marked with a trade charge the responsibility of the postal service toward the sender is fixed under the conditions settled by article 10 hereafter for registered articles.

4. The sums duly collected from the addressee, after deduction of the charge for the money order and the collection fee, are guaranteed to the sender under the conditions laid down by the Agreement concerning the Money Order Service for sums converted into money orders, except in the case provided for in the second paragraph of § 1 of Article 10 below.

5. If the article has been delivered to the addressee without the collection of the trade charge, the sender is entitled to compensation, unless the failure to collect the charge is due to fault or negligence on his part. The compensation may not, in any case, exceed the amount of the trade charge. The same rule applies if the amount collected from the addressee is less than the amount of the trade charge indicated. By paying compensation the Administration takes over the rights of the sender in any action which may be taken against the addressee or third parties.

The responsibility rests with the Office of the country of destination, unless the latter can prove that the failure to collect the trade charge or the collection of a smaller sum is due to a breach of the regulations by the Office of the country of origin.

6. As regards articles marked with trade charges of which the amount has been duly collected from the addressee but not forwarded to the sender, the Office of origin is authorized to pay this amount to the proper person within a year at latest from the day following the date of application. This payment is made on behalf of the Office of destination. Any compensation for articles marked with trade charges delivered to the addressee without collection of the amount indicated or against collection of a smaller amount, as well as for articles of which the amount has been collected fraudulently, must be paid by the Office of origin to the proper person within the same period. The payment is also made on account of the Office of destination, if the responsibility rests with that Office by virtue of the provisions of § 5 above. The same rules apply if the Office of destination, duly informed of the application, has let six months pass without settling the matter. This period is extended to nine months in relations with oversea countries. The periods include the time necessary for the dispatch of the request to the Office of destination and its return to the Office of origin.

The Office of origin may, however, postpone exceptionally the compensation of the sender beyond the period before mentioned, when, at the expiration of this period, it has not been definitely informed as to the disposal of the article with trade charge, or as to the responsibility incurred.

The Office of destination is bound to repay to the Office of dispatch the sums advanced under the conditions prescribed in § 5 above.

ARTICLE 9

Identity Cards

1. Each Administration may issue, to persons who apply for them, identity cards intended to serve as proofs of identity for all kinds of post office business. These cards are valid in all the countries of the Union except those which may notify that they do not adhere to this service.

2. The Administration which issues an identity card is authorized to make, on this account, a charge which must be represented by postage stamps on the card; this charge may not exceed 1 franc.

3. Administrations are relieved from all responsibility when it is established that a postal packet was delivered or a money order was paid on presentation of a proper identity card.

4. The holder of an identity card is responsible for the consequences of the loss, abstraction or fraudulent use of the card.

5. The identity card is valid for two years from the date of issue. If, during the period of validity of the card, the personal appearance of the holder is modified to such an extent that it no longer agrees with the photograph or description, the card must be renewed, even before the expiration of this period.

ARTICLE 10

Responsibility for Registered Articles

1. In case of the loss of a registered article, and except in cases beyond control, the sender is entitled to an indemnity of 50 francs.

Administrations are, however, relieved from all responsibility for the loss of registered articles of which the contents fall within the prohibitions prescribed by article 18, section 2, of the present Convention.

2. Countries prepared to undertake risks arising from causes beyond control are authorized to collect from the sender, on this account, a supplementary charge of 50 centimes at most for each registered article.

3. The payment of the indemnity must be undertaken by the Administration to which the dispatching Office is subordinate. That Administration can make a claim on the Administration responsible, that is to say, against the Administration on the territory or in the service of which the loss took place.

In case of the loss, under circumstances beyond control, on the territory or in the service of a country undertaking the risks mentioned in the preceding paragraph, of a registered article sent from another country, the country in which the loss occurred is responsible for it to the dispatching Office, if the latter undertakes risks in cases beyond control in dealing with its own public.

4. Until the contrary is proved, responsibility rests with the Administration which, having received the article without making any observation, and being furnished with all the particulars for inquiry prescribed by the regulations, cannot establish delivery to the addressee or regular transfer to the following Administration, as the case may be. For articles addressed "Poste Restante," or held at the disposal of the addressees, responsibility ceases on delivery to a person who has proved his identity according to the rules in force in the country of destination, and whose name and description correspond to those indicated in the address.

5. The payment of the indemnity by the dispatching Office must take place as soon as possible, and at the latest within six months of the date of the application. This period is extended to nine months in relations with oversea countries.

The dispatching Office may exceptionally postpone settlement of the indemnity beyond the period mentioned when, on its expiration, it has not been definitely informed as to the disposal of the article inquired for, or when the question whether the loss of the article is due to a cause beyond control is not yet decided.

The Office of origin is, however, authorized to settle with the sender on account of the Office, whether intermediate or of destination, which, duly informed of the application, has let six months (nine months in relations with oversea countries) pass without settling the matter.

The Office responsible or on whose account the payment is made in accordance with the preceding paragraph is bound to repay to the dispatching Office the amount of the indemnity and, if occasion arise, interest, within a period of three months after notice of payment. This repayment is made free of cost to the creditor Office, by means of either a money order or a draft, or in coin current in the creditor country. After the period of three months, the sum due to the dispatching Office bears interest, at the rate of 7 per cent per annum, dating from the day of expiration of the said period.

In case an Office of which the responsibility is duly proved has at first declined to pay the indemnity, it must, in addition, bear all the necessary charges resulting from the unwarranted delay in payment.

6. It is understood that the application for an indemnity is only entertained if made within a year, counting from the day following the posting of the registered article; after this term the applicant has no right to any indemnity.

7. If the loss has occurred in course of conveyance without its being possible to ascertain on the territory or in the service of what country the loss took place, the Administrations concerned bear the loss in equal shares.

8. Administrations cease to be responsible for registered articles for which the owners have given a receipt and accepted delivery, as well as for articles

which they cannot account for in consequence of the destruction of official documents through a cause beyond control.

ARTICLE 11

Withdrawal of Correspondence; Alteration of Address, or of Conditions of Dispatch

1. The sender of an article of mail can have it withdrawn from the post or have its address altered, so long as the article has not been delivered to the addressee.

2. The request to this effect is sent by post or by telegraph at the expense of the sender, who must pay as follows:

1) For every request by post, the charge for a registered single-rate letter;
2) For every request by telegraph, the charge for a telegram according to the ordinary tariff.

3. The sender of a registered article marked with a trade charge can, under the conditions laid down for requests for alteration of address, demand the total or partial cancellation of the amount of the trade charge.

ARTICLE 12

Determination of equivalents with reference to the franc for fixing postage rates and settling accounts

The franc, taken as the basis of postage rates, is the gold franc corresponding in weight and fineness to the gold coins established by the legislation in force in the various countries which have adopted that monetary unit.

In all countries of the Union postage rates are fixed at equivalents corresponding, as exactly as possible, in the actual currency of each country, to the value of the gold franc.

The payments to be made by the Post offices of the various countries under the terms of the present Convention, for the settlement of their accounts with each other, are made on the basis of the gold franc.

ARTICLE 13

Prepayment; Reply Coupons; Exemptions from Postage

1. Prepayment of postage on every description of article can be effected either by means of postage stamps valid in the country of origin for the correspondence of private individuals, or by means of impressions of stamping machines, officially adopted and working under the immediate control of the Administration.

The following are considered as duly prepaid: reply post cards bearing postage stamps of the country of issue, articles properly prepaid for their first transmission and on which complementary postage has been paid before their redirection, as well as newspapers or packets of newspapers with the words "Abonnements-poste," or the equivalent, which are sent in virtue of the special Agreement for newspaper subscriptions, provided for in article 21 of the present Convention.

2. Reply coupons may be sold in those countries of which the Postal Administrations have agreed to issue them. The minimum selling price of a reply coupon is 50 centimes, or the equivalent of this sum in the money of the issuing country.

This coupon is exchangeable in any country of the Union for a stamp or stamps representing the postage on a single-rate letter originating in that country for abroad. The exchange must, however, be made before the end of the second month following the month of issue; this period is increased by four months in relations with oversea countries. The Detailed Regulations of the Convention settle the other conditions of this exchange and in particular the intervention of the International Bureau in manufacturing, supplying, and accounting for the coupons.

3. Official correspondence relative to the Postal Service exchanged between Postal Administrations, between these Administrations and the International Bureau, between Post Offices of Union countries, and between these Offices and the Administrations, is exempt from postage.

4. The same privilege is accorded to correspondence concerning prisoners of war, dispatched or received, either directly or as intermediary, by the Information Bureaus established on behalf of such persons, in belligerent countries or in neutral countries which have received belligerents on their territories.

With the exception of articles marked with a trade charge, correspondence intended for prisoners of war or dispatched by them is also exempt from all postal charges, not only in the countries of origin and destination, but in intermediate countries.

Belligerents received and interned in a neutral country are treated like prisoners of war, properly so-called, in so far as the application of the above-mentioned rules is concerned.

5. Correspondence posted on the high seas in the letter box on board a vessel or handed to postal officials on board or to the commanders of ships may, in the absence of different arrangements between the Administrations concerned, be prepaid by means of the postage stamps, and according to the tariff of the country to which the said vessel belongs or by which it is maintained. If the posting on board takes place during the stay at one of the two terminal points of the voyage or at any intermediate port of call, prepayment is valid only if it is effected by means of the postage stamps and according to the tariff of the country in the waters of which the vessel happens to be.

ARTICLE 14

Retention of Postage Collections

1. Each Administration keeps the whole of the sums which it collects by virtue of the various articles of the present Convention, exceptions being made in the case of the credit due for the money orders referred to in paragraph 2 of article 8, and also in regard to reply coupons (art. 13).

2. Consequently, there is no necessity under this head for any accounts between the several Administrations of the Union, subject to the reservations made in paragraph 1 of the present article.

3. Letters and other postal packets must not be subjected, either in the country of origin or in that of destination, to any postal tax or postal duty at the expense of the senders or addressees other than those prescribed by the present Convention.

ARTICLE 15

Express Packets

1. All classes of correspondence are, at the request of the senders, sent out for delivery by special messenger immediately after arrival, in those countries of the Union which agree to undertake this service.

2. Such correspondence, which is called "express," is subject to a special charge for delivery; this charge is fixed at 1 franc in addition to the ordinary postage, and must be fully paid in advance by the sender. It is retained by the Administration which collects it.

3. When the addressee's house is situated outside the free delivery zone of the office of destination, that Office may collect an additional charge up to the amount of the fee fixed for express delivery in its inland service, less the fixed charge paid by the sender, or its equivalent in the money of the country which levies this additional charge.

The additional charge prescribed above is not canceled in case of redirection or nondelivery and is retained by the Administration which has collected it.

4. "Express" packets, upon which the total amount of the charges payable in advance has not been prepaid, are delivered by the ordinary means, unless they have been treated as express by the office of origin.

ARTICLE 16

Redirection; undelivered correspondence

1. No supplementary postage is charged for the redirection of articles of mail within the Union.

2. Undelivered correspondence does not, when returned, involve the repayment of the transit charges due to intermediate Administrations for the previous conveyance of such correspondence.

3. Unpaid letters and post cards and insufficiently paid articles of every description, which are returned to the country of origin as redirected or as undeliverable, are delivered to the addressees or senders, against payment of the charges due on them on departure or arrival or in course of transmission in consequence of redirection after the first transmission.

ARTICLE 17

Closed mails exchanged with warships

1. Closed mails may be exchanged between the Post Offices of any one of the contracting countries and the commanding officers of naval divisions or ships of war of the same country stationed abroad, or between the commanding officer of one of those naval divisions or ships of war and the commanding officer of another division or ship of the same country, through the medium of the land or sea services maintained by other countries.

2. Correspondence of every description inclosed in these mails must consist exclusively of such as is addressed to or sent by the officers and crews of the ships to or from which the mails are forwarded; the rates and conditions of dispatch applicable to them are settled, according to its internal regulations, by the Postal Administration of the country to which the ships belong.

3. In the absence of any contrary arrangement between the Offices concerned, the Post Office which dispatches or receives the mails in question is accountable to the intermediate Offices for transit charges calculated in accordance with the provisions of article 4.

ARTICLE 18

Prohibitions

1. Apart from the exceptions prescribed by the present Convention and Detailed Regulations, articles which do not fulfill the conditions laid down for each class of correspondence are not to be forwarded.

2. It is forbidden to send by post:

(*a*) Samples and other articles which, from their nature, may expose postal officials to danger, or soil or damage the correspondence;

(*b*) Explosive, inflammable, or dangerous substances; animals and insects, living or dead, except in the cases provided for in the Detailed Regulations of the present Convention;

(*c*) Samples of which the number forwarded by the same sender to the same addressee shows an obvious intention of avoiding the payment of the customs charges due to the country of destination;

(*d*) Articles liable to customs duty;

(*e*) Opium, morphine, cocaine, and other narcotics;

(*f*) Obscene or immoral articles;

(g) Any articles whatever of which the importation or circulation are forbidden in the countries of origin or destination.

3. Packets falling under the prohibitions of the present article, which have been wrongly admitted to the post, must be returned to the Post Office of origin, except in cases where the Administration of the country of destination is authorized by its laws or by its internal regulations to dispose of them otherwise.

Explosive, inflammable, or dangerous substances, and obscene or immoral articles, however, are not returned to the country of origin; they are destroyed on the spot under the direction of the Administration which has found them.

4. The right is, moreover, reserved to the Government of every country of the Union to refuse to convey over its territory, or to deliver, articles admitted at reduced rates in regard to which the laws, ordinances, or decrees which regulate the conditions of their publication or circulation in that country have not been complied with, or correspondence of any kind bearing conspicuously inscriptions, designs, etc., forbidden by the legal enactments or regulations in force in the same country.

5. The high contracting parties undertake to adopt or to propose to their legislatures the measures necessary for preventing and, if necessary, for punishing the insertion of opium, morphine, cocaine, and other narcotics in the mail articles specified in article 2 of the present Convention.

ARTICLE 19

Relations with countries outside the Union

1. Offices of the Union which have relations with countries situated outside the Union are to lend their assistance to all the other Offices of the Union:

1) For the transmission, by their services, either à découvert or in closed mails, if this method of transmission is admitted by mutual consent between the Offices of origin and destination of the mails, of correspondence addressed to or originating in countries outside the Union;

2) For the exchange of correspondence, either à découvert or in closed mails, across the territories or by means of services maintained by the said countries outside the Union;

3) That the correspondence conveyed may be subject outside the Union, as within the Union, to the transit charges fixed by article 4.

2. The total charges for the sea transit, within and without the Union, may not exceed 15 francs per kilogram of letters and post cards and 1 franc per kilogram of other articles. If occasion arise these charges are divided, in the ratio of distances, between the Offices taking part in the conveyance.

3. The charges for transit, by land or sea, without as well as within the limits of the Union, on the correspondence to which the present article applies

are established in the same manner as the transit charges relating to correspondence exchanged between Union countries by means of the services of other countries of the Union.

4. The transit charges on correspondence for countries outside the Postal Union are payable by the office of the country of origin, which fixes the postage rates in its services for the said correspondence, but these rates may not be lower than the normal Union tariff.

5. The transit charges on correspondence originating in countries outside the Union are not payable by the Office of the country of destination. That Office delivers without charge correspondence transmitted to it as fully prepaid; it charges unpaid or insufficiently prepaid correspondence according to the rules applicable in its own service to similar articles addressed to the country where the said correspondence originates.

6. With regard to responsibility in the matter of registered articles, correspondence is treated:

For transmission within the limits of the Union, in accordance with the provisions of the present Convention;

For the transmission outside the limits of the Union, in accordance with the conditions notified by the Office of the Union which serves as the intermediate Office.

Article 20

Counterfeit Impressions and Postage Stamps

The high contracting parties undertake to adopt, or to propose to their respective legislatures, the necessary measures for punishing the fraudulent use, for the prepayment of correspondence, of counterfeit postage stamps or stamps already used, as well as of counterfeit impressions of stamping machines or of impressions already used. They also undertake to adopt or to propose to their respective legislatures, the necessary measures for prohibiting and repressing the fraudulent manufacture, sale, hawking, or distribution of impressed and adhesive stamps in use in the postal service, forged or imitated in such a manner that they could be mistaken for the impressed and adhesive stamps issued by the Administration of any one of the contracting countries.

Article 21

Services Governed By Special Agreements

The arrangements relating to insured letters and boxes, postal money orders, postal parcels, collection of bills and drafts, subscriptions to newspapers, and transfers to and from postal cheque accounts, form the subject of special agreements between the various countries or groups of countries composing the Union.

ARTICLE 22

Detailed Regulations; Special Agreements Between Administrations

1. The Postal Administrations of the various countries composing the Union are empowered to draw up, by mutual agreement, in the form of Detailed Regulations, all the measures of order and detail which are judged necessary.

2. The several Administrations may, moreover, make among themselves the necessary agreements on the subject of questions which do not concern the Union generally, provided that these agreements do not infringe the present Convention.

3. The Administrations concerned are, however, permitted to come to mutual arrangements for the adoption of lower rates of postage within a radius of 30 kilometers.

ARTICLE 23

Internal Laws; Restricted Unions

1. The present Convention involves no alteration in the legislation of any country as regards anything which is not covered by the provisions of this Convention.

2. It does not restrict the right of the contracting parties to maintain and to conclude treaties, as well as to maintain and establish more restricted Unions, with a view to the reduction of postage rates or to any other improvement of postal relations.

ARTICLE 24

International Bureau

1. Under the name of the International Bureau of the Universal Postal Union a central Office is maintained which is conducted under the supervision of the Swiss Postal Administration, and the expenses of which are borne by all the Administrations of the Union.

2. This office is entrusted with the duty of collecting, collating, publishing, and distributing information of every kind which concerns the international postal service; of giving, at the request of the parties concerned, an opinion upon questions in dispute; of making known proposals for modifying the acts of the Congress; of notifying alterations adopted; and, in general, of taking up such studies and duties as may be confided to it in the interest of the Postal Union.

ARTICLE 25

Disputes To Be Settled by Arbitration

1. In case of disagreement between two or more members of the Union as to the interpretation of the present Convention, or as to the responsibility

imposed on an Administration by the application of the said Convention, the question in dispute is decided by arbitration. To that end each of the Administrations concerned chooses another member of the Union not directly interested in the matter.

If one of the Offices concerned does not take any action on a proposal for arbitration within 12 months from the day following the date of the first application, the International Bureau, on a request to that effect, may call on the defaulting Administration to appoint an arbitrator, or may appoint one officially.

2. The decision of the arbitrators is given on an absolute majority of votes.

3. In case of an equality of votes the arbitrators choose, with the view of settling the difference, another Administration with no interest in the question in dispute.

4. The terms of the present article apply equally to all the Agreements concluded by virtue of the foregoing article 21.

ARTICLE 26

Adhesions to the Convention

1. Countries which have not taken part in the present Convention are admitted to adhere to it upon their request.

2. This adhesion is notified diplomatically to the Government of the Swiss Confederation, and by that Government to all the countries of the Union.

3. It implies complete participation in all the clauses and admission to all the advantages given by the present Convention.

4. The Government of the Swiss Confederation settles, by agreement with the Government of the country concerned, the share to be contributed by the Administration of this latter country toward the expenses of the International Bureau, and, if necessary, the rates to be charged by that Administration in accordance with Article 12 above.

ARTICLE 27

Congresses and Conferences

1. Congresses of plenipotentiaries of the contracting countries, or simple administrative Conferences, according to the importance of the questions to be solved, are held when a demand for them is made or approved by two-thirds, at least, of the Governments or Administrations, as the case may be.

2. A Congress shall, in any case, be held not later than five years after the date of the entry into force of the acts settled at the last Congress.

3. Each country may be represented either by one or several delegates, or by the delegation of another country. But it is understood that the delegate or delegates of one country can undertake the representation of two countries only, including the country they represent.

4. In the deliberations each country has one vote only.

5. Each Congress settles the place of meeting of the next Congress.

6. For Conferences, the Administrations settle the places of meeting on the proposal of the International Bureau.

ARTICLE 28

Proposals Made Between Congresses

1. In the interval between meetings, any postal Administration of a country of the Union has the right to address to the other participating Administrations through the medium of the International Bureau, proposals concerning the business of the Union.

In order to be considered, every proposal must be supported by at least two Administrations, not including that which originates the proposal. When the International Bureau does not receive, at the same time as the proposal, the necessary number of declarations of support, the proposal falls.

2. Every proposal is subject to the following procedure:

A period of six months is allowed to the Administrations of the Union to examine the proposals and to communicate their observations, if any, to the International Bureau. Amendments are not admitted. The answers are tabulated by the International Bureau, and communicated to the Administrations, with an invitation to declare themselves for or against. Those who have not furnished their vote within a period of six months from the date of the second circular of the International Bureau notifying to them the observations which have been received, are considered as abstaining.

3. In order to become binding, the proposals must obtain:

1. Unanimity of votes if they involve the addition of new provisions or any modification of the provisions of the present article or of articles 2, 3, 4, 5, 6, 7, 8, 10, 11, 12, 14, 15, 17, 20, 29, 30, and 31;

2. Two-thirds of the votes if they involve a modification of the provisions of the present Convention other than those of the above-mentioned articles;

3. A simple majority, if they affect the interpretation of the provisions of the present Convention, except in the case of dispute provided for by the foregoing article 25.

4. Resolutions duly adopted are sanctioned in the first two cases, by a diplomatic declaration, which the Government of the Swiss Confederation undertakes to prepare and forward to all the Governments of the contracting countries, and in the third case by a simple notification from the International Bureau to all the Administrations of the Union.

5. No modification or resolution adopted comes into force until at least three months after its notification.

ARTICLE 29

Protectorates and Colonies Included in the Union

For the application of the foregoing articles 24, 27, and 28, the following are considered as forming a single country or Administration, as the case may be:

1. The Colony of the Belgian Congo;
2. The Empire of British India;
3. The Dominion of Canada;
4. The Commonwealth of Australia with British New Guinea;
5. The Union of South Africa;
6. The other Dominions and the whole of the British Colonies and Protectorates;
7. The Philippine Islands;
8. The whole of the other island possessions of the United States of America, comprising the islands of Hawaii, Porto Rico, Guam, and the Virgin Islands of the United States of America;
9. The whole of the Spanish Colonies;
10. Algeria;
11. The French Colonies and Protectorates in Indo-China;
12. The whole of the other French Colonies;
13. The whole of the Italian Colonies;
14. Chosen (Korea);
15. The whole of the other Japanese Dependencies;
16. The Dutch East Indies;
17. The Dutch Colonies in America;
18. The Portuguese Colonies of Africa;
19. The Portuguese Colonies in Asia and Oceania.

ARTICLE 30

Duration of the Convention

The present Convention shall come into force on the 1st of January 1922, and shall remain in operation for an indefinite period; but each contracting party has the right to withdraw from the Union by notice given one year in advance by its Government to the Government of the Swiss Confederation.

Each country is, however, authorized to put the postage rates into force before the above-mentioned date, on condition of informing the International Bureau to that effect at least one month in advance, and, if necessary, by telegram.

ARTICLE 31

Previous Conventions Canceled; Ratification

1. From the date on which the present Convention comes into force the provisions of the Convention of the Universal Postal Union concluded at Rome in 1906 are repealed.

2. The present Convention shall be ratified as soon as possible. The acts of ratification shall be exchanged at Madrid.

3. In faith whereof the plenipotentiaries of the above-named countries have signed the present Convention at Madrid on the thirtieth of November, one thousand nine hundred and twenty.

For Germany:
RONGE
SCHENK
ORTH

For the United States of America:
CONDE DE COLOMBI
For Otto Praeger

For the Philippine Islands and the island possessions of the United States of America:
CONDE DE COLOMBI
For S. M. Weber

For the Argentine Republic:
A. BARRERA NICHOLSON

For Austria:
EBERAN

For Belgium:
A. PIRARD
TIXHON
HUB. KRAINS

For the Colony of the Belgian Congo:
M. HALEWYCK
G. TONDEUR

For Bolivia:
LUIS RODRIGUEZ

For Brazil:
ALCIBIADES PEÇANHA
J. HENRIQUE ADERNE

For Bulgaria:
N. STARTCHEFF
N. BOSCHNAKOFF

For Chile:
A. DE LA CRUZ
FLORENCIO MARQUEZ DE LA PLATA
GUS. COUSIÑO

For China:
LIOU FOU-TCHENG

For the Republic of Colombia:
W. MACLELLAN
GABRIEL ROLDAN

For the Republic of Costa Rica:
MANUEL M. DE PERALTA

For the Republic of Cuba:
JUAN IRURETAGOYENA

For Denmark:
HOLLNAGEL JENSEN
HOLMBLAD

For the Dominican Republic:
LEOPOLDO LOVELACE

For Egypt:
N. T. BORTON

For the Republic of Ecuador:
LUIS ROBALINO DÁVILA
LEÓNIDAS A. YEROVI

For Spain:
CONDE DE COLOMBI
JOSÉ DE GARCIA TORRES
GUILLERMO CAPDEVILA
JOSÉ DE ESPAÑA
MARTIN VICENTE
ANTONIO CAMACHO

For the Spanish Colonies:
BERNARDO ROLLAND
MANUEL G. ACEBO

For Ethiopia:
WEULDEU–BERHANE

For Finland:
G. E. F. ALBRECHT

For France:
M. LEBON
P. M. GEORGES BONNET
M. LEBON
G. BLIN
P. BOUILLARD
BARRAIL

For Algeria:
H. Treuillé

For the French Colonies and Protectorates of Indochina:
André Touzet

For the whole of the other French
Colonies:
G. Demartial

For Great Britain and various British Dominions, Colonies and Protectorates:
F. H. Williamson
E. J. Harrington
E. L. Ashley Foakes

For British India:
G. R. Clarke

For the Commonwealth of Australia:
Justinian Oxenham

For Canada:
F. H. Williamson

For New Zealand:
R. B. Morris

For the Union of South Africa:
H. W. S. Twycross
D. J. O'Kelly

For Greece:
P. Scassi
Th. Penthéroudakis

For Guatemala:
Juan J. Ortega
Enrique Traumann

For the Republic of Haiti:
Luis Ma. Solér

For the Republic of Honduras:
Ricardo Beltran y Rózpide

For Hungary:
C. de Fejér
G. Baron Szalay

For Iceland:
Hollnagel Jensen

For Italy and the Italian Colonies:
E. Delmati
T. C. Giannini
S. Ortisi

For Japan:
S. Nakanishi
Arajiro Miura
Y. Hiratsuka

For Chosen:
S. Nakanishi
Arajiro Miura
Y. Hiratsuka

For all the other Japanese Dependencies:
S. Nakanishi
Arajiro Miura
Y. Hiratsuka

For the Republic of Liberia:
Luis Ma. Solér

For Luxemburg:
G. Faber

For Morocco (excluding the Spanish Zone):
Gérard Japy
J. Walter

For Morocco (Spanish Zone):
M. Aguirre de Cárcer
L. López-Ferrer
C. Garcia de Castro

For Mexico:
P. Cosme Hinojosa
Julio Poulat
Alfonso Reyes

For Nicaragua:
M. Igo. Terán

For Norway:
Summerchild
Klaus Helsing

For the Republic of Panama:
J. D. Arosemena

For Paraguay:
Fernando Pignet

For the Netherlands:
A. W. Kymmell
J. S. v. Gelder

For the Netherlands Indies:
Wigman
W. F. Gerdes Oosterbeek
J. van der Werf

For the Netherlands Colonies in
America:
Wigman
W. F. Gerdes Oosterbeek
J. van der Werf

For Peru:
D. C. Urrea
O. Barrenechea y Raigada

For Persia:
Hosséïn Kahn Alaï
C. Molitor

For Poland:
W. Dobrowolski
Maciejewski
Dr. Marjan Blachier

For Portugal:
HENRIQUE MOUSINHO DE ALBUQUER-
QUE

For the Portuguese Colonies in Africa:
JUVENAL ELVAS FLORIADO SANTA
BARBARA

For the Portuguese Colonies in Asia and
Oceania:
JOSÉ EMILIO DOS SANTOS E SILVA

For Roumania:
D. G. MARINESCO
EUG. BOUKMAN

For Salvador:
ISMAEL G. FUENTES

For the Territory of the Saar:
DOUARCHE

For the Kingdom of the Serbs, Croats
and Slovenes:
DRAG. DIMITRIYEVITCH
S. P. TOUTOUNDJITCH
DR. FRANYA PAVLITCH
COSTA ZLATANOVITCH

For the Kingdom of Siam:
PHRA SANPAKITCH PREECHA

For Sweden:
JULIUS JUHLIN
THORE WENNQVIST

For Switzerland:
MENGOTTI
F. BOSS

For Czechoslovakia:
Dr. OTOKAR RUZICKA
VACLAV KUCERA

For Tunis:
GÉRARD JAPY
A. BARBARAT

For Turkey:
MÉHMÉD-ALI

For Uruguay:
ADOLFO AGORIO

For the United States of Venezuela:
PEDRO-EMILIO COLL
BARCELÓ
A. POSSE

FINAL PROTOCOL

At the moment of proceeding to sign the Conventions adopted by the Universal Postal Congress of Madrid, the undersigned Plenipotentiaries have agreed as follows:

I

The provisions of article 11 of the Convention do not apply to Great Britain and to the British Dominions, Colonies, and Protectorates, of which the internal legislation does not permit the withdrawal of correspondence at the request of the sender.

II

Each country of the Union, whether or not it has the franc for its monetary unit, is empowered to fix in its own currency, by agreement with the Swiss Postal Administration, the equivalents of the rates prescribed by the present Convention.

These equivalents must not exceed the rates fixed by the present Convention, or be less than the rates in force on the 1st of October, 1920. They may, however, be modified in accordance with the rise or fall of the value of the legal currency of the country concerned, on condition that they do not fall below the rates adopted when the Convention of Rome came into force.

III

When the rates in force in one country are, when compared with the gold franc, so much lower than those of another country that it becomes advantageous to send articles of mail addressed to the first country unpaid or insufficiently prepaid, the Administration of the second country may declare complete prepayment to be obligatory.

The Administration of the country with regard to which this measure is taken is authorized to apply it, as a reciprocal measure and for the same period, to correspondence addressed to other country.

Each country is empowered not to accept reply-paid post cards in the service with other countries when the difference between the postage rates of the two countries is such that the use of these cards may give rise to abuses on the part of the public.

IV

Countries of the Union are empowered to charge a surtax, which may not exceed 30 centimes per 20 grams or fraction of 20 grams, for each article which, at the request of the sender, is conveyed in a floating safe placed on board a mail vessel. The surtax is retained by the country of origin of the article.

The use of floating safes is regulated by mutual agreement between the Administrations which agree to provide this service in their reciprocal relations.

V

Note is taken of the declaration made by the British delegation in the name of their Government to the effect that it has assigned to New Zealand, with the Cook Islands and other island dependencies, the vote which article 29, par. 6, of the Convention attributes to the other dominions and the whole of the British colonies and protectorates.

VI

The protocol remains open to those countries whose representatives have to-day signed only the principal Convention, or only a certain number of the Conventions settled by the Congress, in order to permit them to adhere to the other Conventions signed this day, or to one or other of them.

VII

If one or more of the contracting parties to the Postal Conventions signed to-day at Madrid should not ratify one or other of those Conventions, this Convention shall be none the less valid for the States which shall have ratified it.

In faith whereof the undermentioned plenipoteniaries have drawn up the present final Protocol, which shall have the same force and validity as if its provisions were inserted in the text itself of the Conventions to which it relates, and they have signed it in a single copy which shall remain in the Archives of the Government of Spain and of which a copy shall be delivered to each party.

Done at Madrid, the 30th of November, one thousand nine hundred and twenty.

For Germany:
  RONGE
  SCHENK
  ORTH

For the United States of America:
  CONDE DE COLOMBI
    For Otto Praeger

For the Philippine Islands and the island possessions of the United States of America:
  CONDE DE COLOMBI
    For S. M. Weber

For the Argentine Republic:
  A. BARRERA NICHOLSON

For Austria:
  EBERAN

For Belgium:
  A. PIRARD
  TIXHON
  HUB. KRAINS

For the Colony of the Belgian Congo:
  M. HALEWYCK
  G. TONDEUR

For Bolivia:
  LUIS RODRIGUEZ

For Brazil:
  ALCIBIADES PEÇANHA
  J. HENRIQUE ADERNE

For Bulgaria:
  N. STARTCHEFF
  N. BOSCHNAKOFF

For Chile:
  A. DE LA CRUZ
  FLORENCIO MARQUEZ DE LA PLATA
  GUS. COUSIÑO

For China:
  LIOU FOU-TCHENG

For the Republic of Colombia:
  W. MACLELLAN
  GABRIEL ROLDAN

For the Republic of Costa Rica:
  MANUEL M. DE PERALTA

For the Republic of Cuba:
  JUAN IRURETAGOYENA

For Denmark:
  HOLLNAGEL JENSEN
  HOLMBLAD

For the Dominican Republic:
  LEOPOLDO LOVELACE

For Egypt:
  N. T. BORTON

For the Republic of Ecuador:
  LUIS ROBALINO DÁVILA
  LEÓNIDAS A. YEROVI

For Spain:
  CONDE DE COLOMBI
  JOSÉ DE GARCIA TORRES
  GUILLERMO CAPDEVILA
  JOSÉ DE ESPAÑA
  MARTIN VICENTE
  ANTONIO CAMACHO

For the Spanish Colonies:
  BERNARDO ROLLAND
  MANUEL G. ACEBO

For Ethiopia:
  WEULDEU-BERHANE

For Finland:
  G. E. F. ALBRECHT

For France:
  M. LEBON
  P. M. GEORGES BONNET
  M. LEBON
  G. BLIN
  P. BOUILLARD
  BARRAIL

For Algeria:
  H. TREUILLÉ

For the French Colonies and Protectorates of Indochina:
  ANDRÉ TOUZET

For all the other French Colonies:
  G. DEMARTIAL

For Great Britain and various British Dominions, Colonies and Protectorates:
  F. H. WILLIAMSON
  E. J. HARRINGTON
  E. L. ASHLEY FOAKES

For British India:
  G. R. CLARKE

For the Commonwealth of Australia:
JUSTINIAN OXENHAM

For Canada:
F. H. WILLIAMSON

For New Zealand:
R. B. MORRIS

For the Union of South Africa:
H. W. S. TWYCROSS
D. J. O'KELLY

For Greece:
P. SCASSI
TH. PENTHEROUDAKIS

For Guatemala:
JUAN J. ORTEGA
ENRIQUE TRAUMANN

For the Republic of Haiti:
LUIS MA. SOLÉR

For the Republic of Honduras:
RICARDO BELTRÁN Y RÓZPIDE

For Hungary:
C. DE FEJÉR
G. BARON SZALAY

For Iceland:
HOLLNAGEL JENSEN

For Italy and the Italian Colonies:
E. DELMATI
T. C. GIANNINI
S. ORTISI

For Japan:
S. NAKANISHI
ARAJIRO MIURA
Y. HIRATSUKA

For Chosen:
S. NAKANISHI
ARAJIRO MIURA
Y. HIRATSUKA

For all the other Japanese Dependencies:
S. NAKANISHI
ARAJIRO MIURA
Y. HIRATSUKA

For the Republic of Liberia:
LUIS MA. SOLÉR

For Luxemburg:
G. FABER

For Morocco (excluding the Spanish Zone):
GÉRARD JAPY
J. WALTER

For Morocco (Spanish Zone):
M. AGUIRRE DE CÁRCER
L. LÓPEZ-FERRER
C. GARCIA DE CASTRO

For Mexico:
P. COSME HINOJOSA
JULIO POULAT
ALFONSO REYES

For Nicaragua:
M. IGO. TERÁN

For Norway:
SUMMERCHILD
KLAUS HELSING

For the Republic of Panama:
J. D. AROSEMENA

For Paraguay:
FERNANDO PIGNET

For the Netherlands:
A. W. KYMMELL
J. S. V. GELDER

For the Netherlands Indies:
WIGMAN
W. F. GERDES OOSTERBEEK
J. VAN DER WERF

For the Netherlands Colonies in America:
WIGMAN
W. F. GERDES OOSTERBEEK
J. VAN DER WERF

For Peru:
D. C. URREA
O. BARRENECHEA Y RAIGADA

For Persia:
HUSSÉIN KHAN ALAÏ
C. MOLITOR

For Poland:
W. DOBROWOLSKI
MACIEJEWSKI
DR. MARJAN BLACHIER

For Portugal:
HENRIQUE MOUSINHO DE ALBUQUER-
QUE

For the Portuguese Colonies in Africa:
JUVENAL ELVAS FLORIADO SANTA
BARBARA

For the Portuguese Colonies in Asia and Oceania:
JOSÉ EMILIO DOS SANTOS E SILVA

For Roumania:
D. G. MARINESCO
EUG. BOUKMAN

For Salvador:
ISMAEL G. FUENTES

For the Territory of the Saar:
DOUARCHE

For the Kingdom of the Serbs, Croats
and Slovenes:
DRAG. DIMITRIYEVITCH
S. P. TOUTOUNDJITCH
DR. FRANYA PAVLITCH
COSTA ZLATANOVITCH

For the Kingdom of Siam:
PHRA SANPAKITCH PREECHA

For Sweden:
JULIUS JUHLIN
THORE WENNQVIST

For Switzerland:
MENGOTTI
F. BOSS

For Czechoslovakia:
DR. OTOKAR RUZICKA
VACLAV KUCERA

For Tunis:
GÉRARD JAPY
A. BARBARAT

For Turkey:
MÉHMÉD-ALI

For Uruguay:
ADOLFO AGORIO

For the United States of Venezuela:
PEDRO-EMILIO COLL
BARCELÓ
A. POSSE

[For text of regulations for execution of the convention, see 42 Stat. 2010.]

PAN AMERICAN POSTAL UNION

Principal convention and final protocol signed at Buenos Aires September 15, 1921 [1]
Ratified and approved by the Postmaster General of the United States February 24, 1922
Approved by the President of the United States February 28, 1922
Ratification of the United States deposited at Buenos Aires June 14, 1922
Entered into force January 1, 1923
Terminated by convention of November 9, 1926 [2]

42 Stat. 2154; Post Office Department print

[TRANSLATION]

PRINCIPAL CONVENTION CONCLUDED BETWEEN ARGENTINA, BOLIVIA, BRAZIL, COLOMBIA, COSTA RICA, CUBA, CHILE, DOMINICAN REPUBLIC, ECUADOR, EL SALVADOR, UNITED STATES OF AMERICA, GUATEMALA, MEXICO, NICARAGUA, PANAMA, PARAGUAY, PERU, URUGUAY, AND VENEZUELA.

The undersigned, plenipotentiaries of the countries above named, assembled in congress in Buenos Aires in exercise of the authority conferred by Article 23 of the Universal Postal Convention of Madrid,[3] actuated by the desire to extend and perfect the Pan American postal services and to establish a solidarity of action which, in the Universal Postal Congresses, may represent effectively the common interests of the American Republics in all that refers to communication by mail, have agreed subject to ratification, upon the following Convention:

ARTICLE 1

Pan American Postal Union

The contracting countries, which, in accordance with the preceding declaration, constitute the Pan American Postal Union, with the object of improving the execution of the Postal services, agree upon the following articles:

---

[1] For text of regulations for execution of the convention, see 42 Stat. 2166.
[2] *Post,* p. 617.
[3] Convention signed at Madrid Nov. 30, 1920, *ante,* p. 282.

ARTICLE 2

Free and gratuitous transit

1. The countries adhering to this Convention shall form a single postal territory.

2. Each of the contracting countries is bound to transport freely and gratuitously through its territory, by means of the services maintained by its postal administration, or which it utilizes for the direct despatch of its own mail, the mail which it receives from any of the other countries destined to any other contracting country, or to any country of the Universal Postal Union.

Nevertheless, the expense of land or sea conveyance of mail will be chargeable to the country of origin when the intervention of countries other than those adhering to this Convention is required for its subsequent transportation, and such transportation is not free but subject to charges.

ARTICLE 3

Liberty of tariffs

1. Liberty of tariffs is established as a fundamental principle. In the postal relations between the contracting countries those tariffs shall rule which each of the postal administrations may establish, within one-half of the equivalent in dollars of the maximum fixed by the Universal Postal Convention of Madrid.

ARTICLE 4

System of control, and special services

1. The provisions of this Convention shall apply to letters, post cards, printed matter of all kinds, commercial papers and samples.

2. Countries which are influenced by proximity, or by common boundaries, or by the importance and volume of their postal exchanges, may establish between themselves, more restricted unions in connection with any of the services instituted by the present Convention and the special regulations effected by this Congress.

ARTICLE 5

Obligatory postage

Prepayment of full postage is obligatory in the contracting countries on every class of correspondence, including sealed packages, with the sole exception of letters in their usual and ordinary form, upon which it is obligatory to prepay at least one rate. On letters insufficiently prepaid only the amount of the unpaid postage may be collected.

ARTICLE 6

Franking privilege

1. The contracting parties agree to grant the franking privilege, in their domestic as well as in the Pan American service, to the correspondence of the International Office of the Pan American Postal Union, and to that of the members of the diplomatic corps of the signatory countries. Consuls shall enjoy the franking privilege for the official correspondence which they direct to their respective countries, for that which they exchange among themselves, and for that which they may direct to the government of the country to which they are accredited, whenever this privilege is reciprocally granted.

2. The dispatch of the correspondence of the diplomatic corps which is exchanged between the Secretaries of State of the respective countries and their Embassies and Legations abroad, shall be through the medium of diplomatic pouches, which shall enjoy the franking privilege and all the safeguards of official dispatches.

3. Similarly the contracting parties agree to extend the franking privilege to one exchange copy, in each direction, of newspapers and other American periodicals, when these publications are of manifest responsibility and treat of affairs of general interest.

ARTICLE 7

Prohibitions

Without prejudice to the provisions of the domestic legislation of each country regarding restrictions on the circulation of correspondence, distribution will not be given to pornographic publications or to those which attack security and public order.

ARTICLE 8

Special services

The contracting countries undertake to adhere as promptly as possible to the special services established by the Universal Postal Convention of Madrid which are not already in operation.

Also they undertake to extend to all the American continent the said postal services which are in operation within their own countries.

ARTICLE 9

Varied provisions

1. The signatory countries will adopt the "Postage paid" service, in furtherance of which they undertake to permit the circulation of newspapers or periodical publications, singly or in packages, except those issued for propaganda or exclusively for commercial advertising.

2. In case any administration not adhering to this Convention—notwithstanding the special measures in force in the contracting countries in the matter of packet or other analogous privileges, granted with the obligation of gratuitous postal transportation—basing its action upon section 3 of Article III [3] of the Universal Postal Convention of Madrid, shall attempt to collect fees for maritime transit from any of the countries which form the Pan American Postal Union, there will be demanded from the navigation companies which enjoy the said privileges reimbursement of the sums which their administration collects on account of maritime transit; and in the event of this being denied the contracting parties may, at the request of the interested administration, withdraw the advantages or privileges accorded.

ARTICLE 10

Official language

Spanish is adopted as the official language for matters relative to the mail service. Those countries whose language is not Spanish may use their own.

ARTICLE 11

Protection to postal agents

The authorities of the contracting countries are obligated to render, when they are requested to do so, such assistance as may be needed by postal agents in charge of the transportation of pouches and mail in transit through such countries.

ARTICLE 12

Arbitration

Every conflict of disagreement that may arise in the postal relations of the American countries shall be settled by arbitration, which shall be effected in the manner established by article 25 of the Universal Postal Convention of Madrid.

Every designation of arbitrators must be from the signatory countries, with the intervention of the International Office of the Pan American Postal Union.

ARTICLE 13

International Office of the Pan American Postal Union

1. The central office now functioning in Montevideo is retained, under the name of International Office of the Pan American Postal Union. It shall be under the supervision of the General Administration of Posts, Telegraphs

and Telephones of the Republic of Uruguay, and its expenses shall be borne by the postal administrations of all the contracting countries.

2. The International Office of the Pan American Postal Union is charged with the duty of

(*a*) collecting, arranging, publishing and distributing data of every kind which specially interest the Pan American International postal service;

(*b*) giving, at the request of the parties concerned, its opinion upon disputed questions that arise by reason of measures pertaining to the relations of the American postal administrations;

(*c*) making known the requests for modification of the acts of the Congress which may be formulated;

(*d*) giving notification of the changes that may be adopted;

(*e*) making known the results obtained from the provisions and regulatory measures of importance which the administrations adopt in their domestic service, and which shall be communicated to it by them as a matter of information;

(*f*) preparing a Pan American Postal Guide;

(*g*) making a Pan American Postal Map;

(*h*) formulating a statistical summary of the Pan American postal movement, in accordance with the data which each administration shall communicate to it annually;

(*i*) compiling a table showing the most rapid routes for the transmission of mail from one to another of the contracting countries;

(*j*) publishing the table of equivalents and the tariff of postage of the domestic service of each one of the interested countries;

(*k*) and, in general, undertaking the studies and investigations that may be requested of it in the interest of the contracting countries.

3. The International Office of the Pan American Postal Union will take charge of the matters which article 13 of the Universal Postal Convention and Article VII of the Regulations for its Execution [4] assign to the International Bureau of Berne in the event that any of the contracting administrations shall adhere to the service of reply coupons.

4. The special expenses incurred in preparing the Pan American Postal Guide, and in making the map of the postal communications of America, and those of the meeting of Congresses or Conferences, will be borne by the administrations of the signatory countries in equal parts.

5. The General Administration of Posts, Telegraphs and Telephones of Uruguay will supervise the expenses of the International Office of the Pan American Postal Union, and will make such advances of funds as it may need.

---

[4] See footnote 1, p. 309.

ARTICLE 14

Application of the Universal Postal Convention and of domestic legislation

1. All matters which relate to the exchange of mail between the contracting countries and which are not provided for by this Convention shall be subject to the provisions of the Universal Postal Convention and the regulations for its execution.

2. Similarly, the domestic legislation of the contracting countries shall apply to any matter not governed by one Convention or the other.

ARTICLE 15

Propositions during the interval between meetings

The present Convention may be modified in the interval which occurs between Congresses or meetings, according to the procedure established by article 28 of the Universal Postal Convention of Madrid. In order to be effective, modifications of this article, and of articles 2, 3, 7, 8, 11, 12, 13, 16 and 18 must obtain an unanimous vote; modifications of articles 5, 6 and 9 must obtain a two-thirds vote and modifications of the remaining articles may be made by a simple majority.

ARTICLE 16

Modifications and amendments

Modifications or resolutions adopted by the contracting parties, even those of domestic regulations which affect the international service, shall become effective four months after the date of the communication transmitted by the International Office of the Pan American Postal Union.

ARTICLE 17

Meetings of Congresses

1. Congresses shall meet at least every five years, counting from the date on which the Convention adopted at the last Congress was put into effect.

2. Each Congress shall fix the place of meetings for the next Congress.

ARTICLE 18

Monetary unit

For the purpose of this Convention the dollar is established as the monetary unit.

ARTICLE 19

Effective date and duration of the Convention and deposit of ratifications

The present Convention shall come into force on January 1, 1923, but countries which have ratified it may put it into execution before that date. It shall remain in force without time limit, each of the contracting countries reserving the right to retire from this Union by means of notice given by its Government to the Government of the Republic of Uruguay one year in advance.

The deposit of ratifications will be made in the city of Buenos Aires as soon as possible. Certification of the deposit of each ratification will be made, and the Government of the Argentine Republic will forward a copy, through diplomatic channels, to the Governments of the other signatory countries.

On the date on which the present Convention comes into force the provisions of the South American Postal Convention, agreed to in Montevideo, February 2, 1911, shall be abrogated.

In the event that this Convention shall not be ratified by one or more of the participating countries, it shall not lose its validity with respect to the States that have ratified it.

In testimony whereof the plenipotentiaries of the countries above named subscribe the present Convention, in Buenos Aires, the fifteenth day of September, 1921.

For Argentina:
  AMADEO E. GRANDI
  EDUARDO F. GIUFFRA

For Brazil:
  LABIENNO SALGADO DOS SANTOS
  HENRIQUE ADERNE

For Bolivia:
  LUIS SANSUSTE

For Colombia:
  CARLOS CUERVO MARQUEZ

For Costa Rica:
  CARLOS F. VALENZUELA

For Chile:
  TULIO MAQUIEIRA
  JORGE SAAVEDRA AGÜERO
  PEDRO A. RIVERA

For Ecuador:
  MANUEL BUSTAMANTE

For the United States of America:
  O. K. DAVIS
  EDWIN SANDS

For Mexico:
  JOSÉ V. CHÁVES
  JULIO JIMENEZ RUEDA

For Panama:
  ESTANISLAO S. ZEBALLOS

For Peru:
  CÉSAR SANCHEZ AIZCORBE
  FRANCISCO ENRIQUE MÁLAGA GRENET

For Cuba:
  ALBERTO DE LA TORRE Y SOUBLETTE

For the Dominican Republic:

For El Salvador:
  GUSTAVO A. RUIZ

For Guatemala:
  ALBERTO DODERO
  JULIO ALVAREZ

For Nicaragua:
  BARTOLOMÉ M. PONS

For Paraguay:
  JUAN B. GAON (HIJO)

For Uruguay:
  DANIEL MUÑOZ
  JUAN RAMPÓN

For Venezuela:
  CARLOS CUERVO MÁRQUEZ

FINAL PROTOCOL OF THE PRINCIPAL CONVENTION

At the moment of proceeding to sign the Convention concluded by the Pan American Postal Congress, the undersigned plenipotentiaries have agreed upon the following:

I

The contracting countries reserve the right to maintain their existing tariffs with the contracting countries until the next Pan American Postal Congress.

II

Upon the establishment of the Pan American Railroad each of the contracting countries will contribute to the maintenance of the service of transportation of mail by train proportionally to the weight of the mail which it dispatches in the event that gratuitous transport is not obtained.

III

The contracting countries undertake to exert their best efforts to obtain from the navigation companies which transport their mail to foreign countries a reduction of existing rates, and that in no case shall such companies charge for a return service a sum greater than that which they receive in the country of origin.

It is understood that the provision of the preceding paragraph does not refer to cases in which, on account of postal or other privilege, the companies are obligated to transport the mail gratuitously.

IV

Panama records the fact that she is not able to accept the provisions of section 2 of article 2 of the Convention relating to gratuitous transit.

V

Although the Bolivian Administration does not consider itself obligated to establish immediately the service of declared value in view of the terms in which Article 8 of the present Convention is conceived, its execution is postponed on account of fundamental reasons, to a more opportune time.

VI

Argentina, Brazil, Chile, Guatemala, Panama, Paraguay and Uruguay reserve the right to fix their rates in gold francs in conformity with the monetary unit of the Universal Postal Convention of Madrid.

VII

The Protocol remains open in favor of those countries whose representatives have not subscribed the Principal Convention today, or have signed only a certain number of the Conventions sanctioned by the Congress, with the object of permitting them to adhere to the other Conventions which they have not subscribed.

VIII

The Congress invites Spain to adhere to this Convention and the regulations for its execution, and with that in view, charges the International Office at Montevideo with formulating the corresponding invitation.

For Argentina:
AMADEO E. GRANDI
EDUARDO F. GIUFFRA

For Brazil:
LABIENNO SALGADO DOS SANTOS
HENRIQUE ADERNE

For Costa Rica:
CARLOS F. VALENZUELA

For Chile:
TULIO MAQUIEIRA
JORGE SAAVEDRA AGÜERO
PEDRO A. RIVERA

For Ecuador:
MANUEL BUSTAMANTE

For the United States of America:
O. K. DAVIS
EDWIN SANDS

For Mexico:
JOSÉ V. CHÁVES
JULIO JIMENEZ RUEDA

For Panama:
ESTANISLAO S. ZEBALLOS

For Peru:
CÉSAR SANCHEZ AIZCORBE

For Bolivia:
LUIS SANSUSTE

For Colombia:
CARLOS CUERVO MARQUEZ

For Cuba:
ALBERTO DE LA TORRE Y SOUBLETTE

For the Dominican Republic:

For El Salvador:
GUSTAVO A. RUIZ

For Guatemala:
ALBERTO DODERO
JULIO ALVAREZ

For Nicaragua:
BARTOLOMÉ M. PONS

For Paraguay:
JUAN B. GAON (HIJO)

For Uruguay:
DANIEL MUÑOZ
JUAN RAMPÓN

For Venezuela:
CARLOS CUERVO MÁRQUEZ

[For text of regulations for execution of the convention, see 42 Stat. 2166.]

PAN AMERICAN POSTAL UNION: PARCEL POST

Convention and final protocol signed at Buenos Aires September 15, 1921 [1]
Ratified and approved by the Postmaster General of the United States February 24, 1922
Approved by the President of the United States February 28, 1922
Ratification of the United States deposited at Buenos Aires June 14, 1922
Entered into force January 1, 1923
Terminated by convention of November 9, 1926 [2]

42 Stat. 2174; Post Office Department print

[TRANSLATION]

PARCEL POST CONVENTION CONCLUDED BETWEEN ARGENTINA, BOLIVIA, BRAZIL, COLOMBIA, COSTA RICA, CUBA, CHILE, DOMINICAN REPUBLIC, ECUADOR, EL SALVADOR, MEXICO, UNITED STATES OF AMERICA, GUATEMALA, NICARAGUA, PARAGUAY, PERU, PANAMA, URUGUAY, AND VENEZUELA.

The undersigned, plenipotentiaries of the Governments of the above named countries, in the exercise of the authority conferred by Article 21 of the Universal Postal Convention of Madrid,[3] agree, under the reservation of ratification, in establishing the service of parcel post, according to the following articles:

1

Object of the Convention

1. Under the denomination of parcel post, parcels with or without declared value may be sent from one of the above named countries to another of them, by the most rapid route.

2. The maximum weight of each parcel will be 10 kilograms, any administration being at liberty to limit it to 5 kilograms, and not to handle bulky packages, or those with declared value, or collect on delivery.

---

[1] For text of regulations for execution of the convention, see 42 Stat. 2180.
[2] *Post,* p. 629.
[3] Convention signed at Madrid Nov. 30, 1920, *ante,* p. 282.

2

Transit

1. Liberty of transit is guaranteed in the territory of each of the signatory countries, and the responsibility of the Administrations which intervene in the transit is pledged, within the limits determined by Article 7. In consequence, the several Administrations which participate in this Convention may reciprocally send parcel post packages through one or several of them as intermediary.

2. Transmission of parcels will be effected through the open or closed mails.

3

Bonifications

1. The Administration of origin will pay to each of the Administrations which may intervene in transit a territorial transit charge fixed at 20 cents gold for each parcel which does not exceed five kilos, and at 40 cents gold for those which exceed that weight.

2. The Office of origin will pay to that of destination 20 cents gold for each parcel that does not exceed five kilos, and 40 cents gold for those which exceed that weight.

3. There are not included in the imposts the charges for maritime transit which must be collected in accordance with the Parcel Post Convention of Madrid.

4

Tariffs and Postage

1. There is established as a fundamental principle the right, which each country reserves, to fix within the maximum of 30 cents gold per kilo, the tariffs on the parcels which it dispatches independently of the bonifications set forth in the preceding article for the offices of intermediation and of destination.

2. The freedom of action which this provision establishes includes the adoption of the system of weight which is legally in force in each country, and the subdivision of the postage by fractions of weight.

3. The system adopted for the application of tariffs does not alter the procedure established in the previous article for the payment of bonifications, which will be effected exclusively in the two divisions of five and ten kilos, whatever may be the actual weight of the parcel.

4. Postage on parcels must be fully prepaid.

5. The conditions governing the handling of parcels with value declared, bulky parcels, or Collect on Delivery will be arranged between the countries which agree to put those services in force.

5

Customs Duties and Delivery Charges

The Administration of destination may collect from the addressees of parcels:

1. The customs duties.

2. A charge fixed at ten cents gold, as a maximum, for the delivery of the parcel to the addressee, and for the fulfillment of all formalities, whether of customs or others not specially provided for.

3. A charge for storage, for holding parcels which have not been withdrawn (by the addressee) within ten days from the date of sending the corresponding notice of arrival to the addressee.

4. A surcharge of ten cents gold, as a maximum, for the delivery of each parcel at the residence of the addressee.

5. The charge provided by the consular tariff when it has not been prepaid by the sender.

6

Prohibitions

The parcels of which the present Convention treats may not be subjected to any other charges than those established in the preceding article.

7

Responsibilities

The indemnities of which Article 16 of the Parcel Post Convention of Madrid treats will be paid in accordance with the details of that provision in the following form: five dollars as a maximum, per parcel up to five kilos in weight, and ten dollars as a maximum for those which exceed five kilos.

8

Propositions in the Interval Between Congresses

For the application of Article 24 of the Parcel Post Convention of Madrid, the following conditions are established:

1. Unanimity of votes for propositions which introduce new provisions or modify those of the present article or those of articles 2, 3, 4, 5 and 6.

2. Two thirds of the votes to modify the other provisions.

9

Monetary Unit

To give effect to the provisions of Section 1, Article 4, it is understood that the unit dollar which is established by the present Convention will have for each contracting country the value of the legal equivalent fixed in that country in its own money.

10

Matters Not Provided for.

All matters not specially provided for by this Convention will be governed by the provisions of the Parcel Post Convention of Madrid.

11

Force and Duration of the Convention

1. This Convention shall come into force on January 1, 1923, but before that date the countries which have ratified it may put it into effect. It will remain in force without limitation of time. Each of the contracting countries reserves the right to retire from the Union by means of notice given by its Government to the Government of the Republic of Uruguay one year in advance.

2. The deposit of ratifications shall be in the city of Buenos Aires as soon as possible. The record of the deposit of ratification by each country will be certified and the Government of the Argentine Republic will send through diplomatic channels one copy of this record to the Governments of the other signatory countries.

3. From the date on which the present Convention comes into force the stipulations of the South American Parcel Post Convention, agreed to in Montevideo on February 2, 1911; and those of the Special Conventions between the signatory countries are abrogated.

4. In case the Convention shall not be ratified by one or more of the contracting countries, it shall not lose its validity for those countries which have ratified it.

In faith of which the plenipotentiaries of the above named countries subscribe the present Convention, in Buenos Aires, September 15, 1921.

For Argentina:
AMADEO E. GRANDI
EDUARDO F. GIUFFRA

For Bolivia:
LUIS SANSUSTE

For Costa Rica:
CARLOS F. VALENZUELA

For Cuba:
ALBERTO DE LA TORRE Y SOUBLETTE

For Chile:
TULIO MAQUIEIRA
JORGE SAAVEDRA AGÜERO
PEDRO A. RIVERA

For the Dominican Republic:

For Ecuador:
MANUEL BUSTAMANTE

For El Salvador:
GUSTAVO A. RUIZ

For the United States of America:
O. K. DAVIS
EDWIN SANDS

For Brazil:
LABIENNO SALGADO DOS SANTOS
JOSÉ HENRIQUE ADERNE

For Colombia:
CARLOS CUERVO MÁRQUEZ

For Guatemala:
ALBERTO DODERO
JULIO ALVAREZ

For Mexico:
JOSÉ V. CHÁVES
JULIO JIMENEZ RUEDA

For Nicaragua:
BARTOLOMÉ M. PONS

For Panama:
ESTANISLAO S. ZEBALLOS

For Paraguay:
JUAN B. GAONA (HIJO)

For Peru:
CÉSAR SANCHEZ AIZCORBE
FRANCISCO ENRIQUE MÁLAGA GRENET

For Uruguay:
DANIEL MUÑOZ
JUAN RAMPÓN

For Venezuela:
CARLOS CUERVO MÁRQUEZ

FINAL PROTOCOL

I

Argentina declares that she is not able to comply with the provision of Section 2, Article 5, until her domestic legislation, which is contrary to this provision, may be modified, which reform will be undertaken.

II

Argentina retains the right to levy a surcharge of one franc fifty centimes per parcel, on account of territorial transit, on parcels which must be transported by the Trans Andes railroad.

For Argentina:
AMADEO E. GRANDI
EDUARDO F. GIUFFRA

For Bolivia:
LUIS SANSUSTE

For Brazil:
LABIENNO SALGADO DOS SANTOS
JOSÉ HENRIQUE ADERNE

For Colombia:
CARLOS CUERVO MÁRQUEZ

For Ecuador:
MANUEL BUSTAMANTE

For El Salvador:
GUSTAVO A. RUIZ

For the United States of America:
O. K. DAVIS
EDWIN SANDS

For Guatemala:
ALBERTO DODERO
JULIO ALVAREZ

For Mexico:
JOSÉ V. CHÁVES
JULIO JIMENEZ RUEDA

For Costa Rica:
CARLOS F. VALENZUELA

For Cuba:
ALBERTO DE LA TORRE Y SOUBLETTE

For Chile:
TULIO MAQUIEIRA
JORGE SAAVEDRA AGÜERO
PEDRO A. RIVERA

For the Dominican Republic:

For Nicaragua:
BARTOLOMÉ M. PONS

For Panama:
ESTANISLAO S. ZEBALLOS

For Paraguay:
JUAN B. GAONA (HIJO)

For Peru:
CÉSAR SANCHEZ AIZCORBE
FRANCISCO ENRIQUE MÁLAGA GRENET

For Uruguay:
DANIEL MUÑOZ
JUAN RAMPÓN

For Venezuela:
CARLOS CUERVO MÁRQUEZ

[For text of regulations for execution of the convention, see 42 Stat. 2180.]

WEIGHTS AND MEASURES

Convention signed at Sèvres October 6, 1921
Senate advice and consent to ratification January 5, 1923
Ratified by the President of the United States September 19, 1923
Ratification of the United States deposited at Paris October 24, 1923
Entered into force June 23, 1922; for the United States October 24,
1923
Proclaimed by the President of the United States October 27, 1923

43 Stat. 1686; Treaty Series 673

[TRANSLATION]

INTERNATIONAL CONVENTION FOR THE AMENDMENT

1st. Of the Convention signed at Paris, May 20, 1875,[1] to insure the international unification and improvement of the metric system;

2nd. Of the regulations annexed to the said convention;

Concluded between: Germany, Argentine Republic, Austria, Belgium, Brazil, Bulgaria, Canada, Chile, Denmark, Spain, the United States of America, Finland, France, Great Britain, Hungary, Italy, Japan, Mexico, Norway, Peru, Portugal, Rumania, The Serbs, Croats and Slovenes State, Siam, Sweden, Switzerland and Uruguay.

The undersigned plenipotentiaries of the countries hereinafter enumerated, having met in conference in Paris, have agreed on the following:

ARTICLE 1

Article 7 and 8 of the Convention of May 20, 1875, are superseded by the following provisions:

ARTICLE 7. After the Committee shall have proceeded with the work of coordinating the measures relative to electric units and when the General Conference shall have so decided by a unanimous vote, the Bureau will have charge of the establishment and keeping of the standards of the electric units and their test copies and also of comparing with those standards, the national or other standards of precision.

---

[1] TS 378, *ante,* vol. 1, p. 39.

The Bureau is also charged with the duty of making the determinations relative to physical constants, a more accurate knowledge of which may be useful in increasing precision and further insuring uniformity in the provinces to which the above mentioned units belong (Article 6 and 1st paragraph of Article 7).

It is finally charged with the duty of coordinating similar determinations effected in other institutions.

ARTICLE 8. The international prototypes and standards and also their test copies shall be deposited in the Bureau; access to the deposit shall be solely reserved for the International Committee.

ARTICLE 2

Articles 6, 8, 9, 10, 11, 12, 15, 17, 18 and 20, of the regulations annexed to the Convention of May 20, 1875, are superseded by the following provisions.

ARTICLE 6. The annual appropriation for the international Bureau consists of two parts, one of which is fixed, the other complementary.

The fixed part is, in principle, 250,000 francs, but on the unanimous vote of the Committee may be raised to 300,000 francs. It is borne by all the states and autonomous colonies that adhered to the meter convention before the sixth General Conference.

The complementary part is made up of contributions from the states and autonomous colonies that joined the Convention after the aforesaid General Conference.

The Committee is charged with the duty of drawing up on the motion of the Director the annual budget, but without exceeding the amount computed in accordance with the provisions of the two paragraphs above. The budget is made known every year by means of a special financial report to the governments of the high contracting parties.

If the Committee find it necessary either to increase beyond 300,000 francs, the fixed part of the annual appropriation or to modify the computation of the contributions as determined by Article 20, of these regulations, it should lay the matter before the governments so as to enable them to issue in good time the needed instructions to their delegates to the next General Conference in order that the said conference may deliberate to good purpose. The decision will stand only in the case that no opposition shall have been expressed before or in the conference by any of the contracting states.

If the state should let three years go without paying its contribution, that contribution shall be divided among the other states proportionally to their own contribution. The additional sum thus paid by the states to make up the whole of the appropriation of the Bureau shall be regarded as an advance to the delinquent state and shall be reimbursed to them if that state should make good its arrears.

The advantages and prerogatives conferred by adhering to the Meter Convention are suspended in the case of states that have been delinquent three years.

After three more years the delinquent state shall be expelled from the Convention and the reckoning of the contributions restored in accordance with the provisions of Article 20, of these regulations.

ARTICLE 8. The International Committee mentioned at Article 3 of the Convention shall be composed of 18 members all from different states.

At the time of the renewal by halves of the International Committee, the outgoing members shall be first those who may have been provisionally elected to fill vacancies between two sessions of the conference; the others will be drawn by lot.

Outgoing members may be reelected.

ARTICLE 9. The International Committee organizes itself by electing by its own secret vote its chairman and secretary. Those appointments are notified to the governments of the high contracting parties.

The chairman and the secretary of the Committee and the Director of the Bureau must belong to different countries.

Once organized, the Committee cannot hold other elections or make other appointments except before three months shall have elapsed after the notice of a vacancy calling for a vote shall have been given to all the members.

ARTICLE 10. The International Committee directs all the metrological works that the high contracting parties shall decide to have carried on jointly.

It is also charged with the duty of seeing to the conservation of the international prototypes and standards.

It may, lastly, institute the cooperation of specialists in questions of metrology and coordinate the results of their work.

ARTICLE 11. The Committee shall meet at least once in two years.

ARTICLE 12. The balloting in the Committee is by a majority vote; in case of a tie vote the chairman has the casting vote.

Decisions are only valid if the members present are at least one half of the elected members forming the Committee.

Subject to that condition absent members have a right to delegate their votes to present members who must prove that they have been so delegated. This also applies to appointments by secret ballot.

The Director of the Bureau is a non-voting member of the Committee.

ARTICLE 15. The International Committee will draw up a detailed set of regulations for the organization and work of the Bureau and will fix the dues to be paid for the extraordinary works provided by Articles 6 and 7 of the Convention.

Those dues will be applied to improving the scientific equipment of the Bureau. A certain amount may be drawn annually for the retirement fund from the total dues collected by the Bureau.

ARTICLE 17. A regulation drawn up by the Committee will determine the maximum staff for each category of the personnel of the Bureau. The Director and his assistants shall be elected by secret ballot by the International Committee. Other appointments shall be notified to the governments of the high contracting parties. The Director will appoint the other members of the personnel within the bounds laid by the regulation mentioned in the first paragraph above.

ARTICLE 18. The Director of the Bureau shall have access to the place where the international prototypes are deposited only in pursuance of a resolution of the Committee and in the presence of at least one of its members.

The place of deposit of the prototypes shall be opened only by means of three keys, one of which shall be in the possession of the Director of Archives of France, the second in that of the chairman of the Committee and the third in that of the Director of the Bureau.

The standards of the class of national prototypes alone shall be used for the ordinary comparing work of the Bureau.

ARTICLE 20. The scale of contributions spoken of in Article 9 of the Convention is established for its fixed part on the basis of the appropriation referred to in Article 6 of the present regulations and of the population; the normal contribution of each state cannot be less than 5 to a thousand nor more than 15% of the whole appropriation, regardless of the population.

In order to establish that scale, it shall first be found which are the states that are in the conditions required for the minimum and maximum and the remainder of the quota shall be distributed among the other states in the direct ratio of their population.

The quota thus reckoned stands for the whole time included between two consecutive General Conferences and can only be modified in the meanwhile in the following cases:

(a) If one of the adhering states allows three successive years to pass without making its payments;

(b) When, on the contrary, a state which had been previously delinquent for more than three years pays up its arrears; and the occasion arises to return to the other governments the advances made by them.

The complementary contribution is computed on the same basis of population and is like that which the states that have long belonged to the Convention pay under the same conditions.

If after adhering to the convention a state declares it would like to extend the benefits thereof to one or more of its colonies that are not autonomous, the number of the population of the said colonies would be added to that of the State in reckoning the scale of contributions.

When a colony that is recognized as autonomous shall desire to adhere to the convention, it will be regarded with respect to its admission into the

Convention and as the mother country may decide, either as a dependency of that mother country or as a contracting state.

ARTICLE 3

Any state may adhere to this convention by giving notice thereof to the French Government which shall notify all the participant states and the chairman of the International Committee of Weights and Measures.

Any new accession to the Convention of May 20, 1875, will necessarily involve adhesion to this Convention.

ARTICLE 4

The present convention shall be ratified. Each power shall within the shortest possible time send its ratification to the French Government which will see to its being notified to the other signatory countries. The ratifications shall remain in deposit in the archives of the French Government. The present Convention will go into effect for each signatory country on the very date of the deposit of its instrument of ratification.

Done at Sèvres, October 6, 1921, in one copy that will be deposited in the Archives of the French Government and of which certified copies shall be forwarded to every one of the signatory countries.

This copy, dated as above, may be signed until March 31, 1922.

In witness whereof the plenipotentiaries hereinbelow named, whose powers have been found to be in good and due form, have signed the present Convention.

For Germany:
  FORSTER
  KÖSTERS

For Argentina:
  M.-T. DE ALVEAR
  LUIS BEMBERG

For Austria:
  MAYRHAUSER

For Belgium:
  ERN. PASQUIER

For Brazil:
  FRANC. RAMOS DE ANDRADE
  NEVES

For Bulgaria:
  SAVOFF

For Canada:
  HARDINGE OF PENSHURST
  J. E. SEARS, Jr.

For Chile:
  M. AMUNATEGUI

For Denmark:
  K. PRYTZ

For Spain:
  SEVERO GOMEZ NUÑEZ

For the United States:
  SHELDON WHITEHOUSE
  SAMUEL W. STRATTON

For Finland:
  G. MELANDER

For France:
  P. APPELL
  PAUL JANET
  A. PEROT
  J. VIOLLE

For Great Britain:
  HARDINGE OF PENSHURST
  J. E. SEARS, Jr.
  P. A. MACMAHON

For Hungary:
  BODOLA LAJOS

For Italy:
VITO VOLTERRA
NAPOLEONE REGGIANI

For Japan:
A. TANAKADATE
SAISHIRO KOSHIDA

For Mexico:
JUAN F. URQUIDI

For Norway:
D. ISAACHSEN

For Peru:
G. TIRADO

For Portugal:
ARMANDO NAVARRO

For Rumania:
ST. HEPITES
C. STATESCU

For the Serbs, Croats, and Slovenes:
M. BOCHKOVITCH
CELESTIN KARGATCHIN

For Siam:
DAMRAS

For Sweden:
K. A. WALLROTH
IVAR FREDHOLM

For Switzerland:
RAOUL GAUTIER

For Uruguay:
J. C. BLANCO

EXTRATERRITORIALITY AND ADMINISTRATION OF JUSTICE IN CHINA

Resolutions adopted by the Conference on the Limitation of Armament at Washington December 10, 1921

Execution of provisions: The Commission on Extraterritoriality in China was constituted in 1926. It made a study of the system and published a report, "Report of the Commission on Extraterritoriality in China" (Washington, 1926), which included findings of fact and recommendations as to steps to be taken preparatory to a general relinquishment by the powers of their extraterritorial rights in China

Conference on the Limitation of Armament, Washington, November 12, 1921–February 6, 1922 (U.S. Government Printing Office, 1922), p. 1642; Senate documents 124 and 125, 67th Congress, 2d session

RESOLUTION REGARDING EXTRATERRITORIALITY IN CHINA

The representatives of the Powers hereinafter named, participating in the discussion of Pacific and Far Eastern questions in the Conference on the Limitation of Armament, to wit, the United States of America, Belgium, the British Empire, France, Italy, Japan, the Netherlands and Portugal:

Having taken note of the fact that in the Treaty between Great Britain and China dated September 5, 1902, in the Treaty between the United States of America and China dated October 8, 1903,[1] and in the Treaty between Japan and China dated October 8, 1903, these several Powers have agreed to give every assistance towards the attainment by the Chinese Government of its expressed desire to reform its judicial system and to bring it into accord with that of Western nations, and have declared that they are also "prepared to relinquish extraterritorial rights when satisfied that the state of the Chinese laws, the arrangements for their administration, and other considerations warrant" them in so doing;

Being sympathetically disposed towards furthering in this regard the aspiration to which the Chinese Delegation gave expression on November 16, 1921,

---

[1] TS 430, *post.*

329

to the effect that "immediately or as soon as circumstances will permit, existing limitations upon China's political, jurisdictional and administrative freedom of action are to be removed";

Considering that any determination in regard to such action as might be appropriate to this end must depend upon the ascertainment and appreciation of complicated states of fact in regard to the laws and the judicial system and the methods of judicial administration of China, which this Conference is not in a position to determine;

Have resolved

That the Governments of the Powers above named shall establish a Commission (to which each of such Governments shall appoint one member) to inquire into the present practice of extraterritorial jurisdiction in China, and into the laws and the judicial system and the methods of judicial administration of China, with a view to reporting to the Governments of the several Powers above named their findings of fact in regard to these matters, and their recommendations as to such means as they may find suitable to improve the existing conditions of the administration of justice in China, and to assist and further the efforts of the Chinese Government to effect such legislation and judicial reforms as would warrant the several Powers in relinquishing, either progressively or otherwise, their respective rights of extraterritoriality;

That the Commission herein contemplated shall be constituted within three months after the adjournment of the Conference in accordance with detailed arrangements to be hereafter agreed upon by the Governments of the Powers above named, and shall be instructed to submit its report and recommendations within one year after the first meeting of the Commission;

That each of the Powers above named shall be deemed free to accept or to reject all or any portion of the recommendations of the Commission herein contemplated, but that in no case shall any of the said Powers make its acceptance of all or any portion of such recommendations either directly or indirectly dependent on the granting by China of any special concession, favor, benefit or immunity, whether political or economic.

ADDITIONAL RESOLUTION REGARDING ACCESSION

That the Non-Signatory Powers, having by treaty extraterritorial rights in China, may accede to the Resolution affecting extraterritoriality and the administration of justice in China by depositing within three months after the adjournment of the Conference a written notice of accession with the Government of the United States for communication by it to each of the Signatory Powers.

ADDITIONAL RESOLUTION REGARDING PARTICIPATION BY CHINA

That China, having taken note of the Resolutions affecting the establishment of a Commission to investigate and report upon extraterritoriality and the administration of justice in China, expresses its satisfaction with the sympathetic disposition of the Powers hereinbefore named in regard to the aspiration of the Chinese Government to secure the abolition of extraterritoriality in China, and declares its intention to appoint a representative who shall have the right to sit as a member of the said Commission, it being understood that China shall be deemed free to accept or to reject any or all of the recommendations of the Commission. Furthermore, China is prepared to cooperate in the work of this Commission and to afford to it every possible facility for the successful accomplishment of its tasks.

[The Conference on the Limitation of Armament held at Washington November 12, 1921–February 6, 1922, concerned itself with two groups of questions: (1) the question of the limitation of armament, and (2) Pacific and Far Eastern questions. In order to deal with both fields, two committees were set up: the first, consisting of delegates of the United States, the British Empire, France, Italy, and Japan, to deal with questions of armament, and the second, consisting of delegates of the United States, Belgium, the British Empire, China, France, Italy, Japan, the Netherlands, and Portugal, to deal with Pacific and Far Eastern questions. The resolutions were adopted in plenary sessions of the Conference.]

INSULAR POSSESSIONS AND DOMINIONS IN THE PACIFIC (FOUR–POWER TREATY)

Treaty and declaration signed at Washington December 13, 1921
Senate advice and consent to ratification, with a reservation and under-
standing, March 24, 1922 [1]
Ratified by the President of the United States, with a reservation and
understanding, June 9, 1923 [1]
Procès-verbal of deposit of ratifications (including that of the United
States) at Washington dated August 17, 1923
Entered into force August 17, 1923
Proclaimed by the President of the United States August 21, 1923
Supplemented by agreement of February 6, 1922 [2]

43 Stat. 1646; Treaty Series 669

The United States of America, the British Empire, France and Japan,

With a view to the preservation of the general peace and the maintenance of their rights in relation to their insular possessions and insular dominions in the region of the Pacific Ocean,

Have determined to conclude a Treaty to this effect and have appointed as their Plenipotentiaries:

The President of the United States of America:
Charles Evans Hughes,
Henry Cabot Lodge,
Oscar W. Underwood and Elihu Root,
citizens of the United States;

His Majesty the King of the United Kingdom of Great Britain and Ireland and of the British Dominions beyond the Seas, Emperor of India:
The Right Honourable Arthur James Balfour, O.M., M.P., Lord President of His Privy Council:
The Right Honourable Baron Lee of Fareham, G.B.E., K.C.B., First Lord of His Admiralty;

---

[1] The U.S. reservation and understanding reads as follows: "The United States understands that under the statement in the preamble and under the terms of this treaty there is no commitment to armed force, no alliance, no obligation to join in any defense."

[2] TS 670, *post*, p. 372.

The Right Honourable Sir Auckland Campbell Geddes, K.C.B., His Ambassador Extraordinary and Plenipotentiary to the United States of America;
and
　for the Dominion of Canada:
　　The Right Honourable Robert Laird Borden, G.C.M.G., K.C.;
　for the Commonwealth of Australia:
　　The Honourable George Foster Pearce, Minister of Defence;
　for the Dominion of New Zealand:
　　Sir John William Salmond, K. C., Judge of the Supreme Court of New Zealand;
　for the Union of South Africa:
　　The Right Honourable Arthur James Balfour, O.M., M.P.;
　for India:
　　The Right Honourable Valingman Sankaranarayana Srinivasa Sastri, Member of the Indian Council of State;

The President of the French Republic:
　Mr. René Viviani, Deputy, Former President of the Council of Ministers;
　Mr. Albert Sarraut, Deputy, Minister of the Colonies;
　Mr. Jules J. Jusserand, Ambassador Extraordinary and Plenipotentiary to the United States of America, Grand Cross of the National Order of the Legion of Honour;

His Majesty the Emperor of Japan:
　Baron Tomosaburo Kato, Minister for the Navy, Junii, a member of the First Class of the Imperial Order of the Grand Cordon of the Rising Sun with the Paulownia Flower;
　Baron Kijuro Shidehara, His Ambassador Extraordinary and Plenipotentiary at Washington, Joshii, a member of the First Class of the Imperial Order of the Rising Sun;
　Prince Iyesato Tokugawa, Junii, a member of the First Class of the Imperial Order of the Rising Sun;
　Mr. Masanao Hanihara, Vice-Minister for Foreign Affairs, Jushii, a member of the Second Class of the Imperial Order of the Rising Sun;

Who, having communicated their Full Powers, found in good and due form, have agreed as follows:

I

The High Contracting Parties agree as between themselves to respect their rights in relation to their insular possessions and insular dominions in the region of the Pacific Ocean.

If there should develop between any of the High Contracting Parties a controversy arising out of any Pacific question and involving their said rights which is not satisfactorily settled by diplomacy and is likely to affect the harmonious accord now happily subsisting between them, they shall invite the other High Contracting Parties to a joint conference to which the whole subject will be referred for consideration and adjustment.

II

If the said rights are threatened by the aggressive action of any other Power, the High Contracting Parties shall communicate with one another fully and frankly in order to arrive at an understanding as to the most efficient measures to be taken, jointly or separately, to meet the exigencies of the particular situation.

III

This Treaty shall remain in force for ten years from the time it shall take effect, and after the expiration of said period it shall continue to be in force subject to the right of any of the High Contracting Parties to terminate it upon twelve months' notice.

IV

This Treaty shall be ratified as soon as possible in accordance with the constitutional methods of the High Contracting Parties and shall take effect on the deposit of ratifications, which shall take place at Washington, and thereupon the agreement between Great Britain and Japan, which was concluded at London on July 13, 1911, shall terminate. The Government of the United States will transmit to all the Signatory Powers a certified copy of the proces-verbal of the deposit of ratifications.

The present Treaty, in French and in English, shall remain deposited in the Archives of the Government of the United States, and duly certified copies thereof will be transmitted by that Government to each of the Signatory Powers.

In faith whereof the above named Plenipotentiaries have signed the present Treaty.

Done at the City of Washington, the thirteenth day of December, One Thousand Nine Hundred and Twenty-One.

[For the United States:]
CHARLES EVANS HUGHES [SEAL]
HENRY CABOT LODGE [SEAL]
OSCAR W. UNDERWOOD [SEAL]
ELIHU ROOT [SEAL]

[For the United Kingdom:]
ARTHUR JAMES BALFOUR [SEAL]
LEE OF FAREHAM [SEAL]
A. C. GEDDES [SEAL]

[For the Dominion of Canada:]
R. L. BORDEN [SEAL]

[For the Commonwealth of Australia:]
G. F. PEARCE [SEAL]

[For the Dominion of New Zealand:]
JOHN W. SALMOND [SEAL]

[For the Union of South Africa:]
ARTHUR JAMES BALFOUR [SEAL]

[For India:]
V. S. SRINIVASA SASTRI [SEAL]

[For France:]
RENÉ VIVIANI   [SEAL]
A. SARRAUT   [SEAL]
JUSSERAND   [SEAL]

[For Japan:]
T. KATO   [SEAL]
K. SHIDEHARA   [SEAL]
TOKUGAWA IYESATO   [SEAL]
M. HANIHARA   [SEAL]

Declaration

In signing the Treaty this day between The United States of America, The British Empire, France and Japan, it is declared to be the understanding and intent of the Signatory Powers:

1. That the Treaty shall apply to the Mandated Islands in the Pacific Ocean; provided, however, that the making of the Treaty shall not be deemed to be an assent on the part of The United States of America to the mandates and shall not preclude agreements between The United States of America and the Mandatory Powers respectively in relation to the mandated islands.

2. That the controversies to which the second paragraph of Article I refers shall not be taken to embrace questions which according to principles of international law lie exclusively within the domestic jurisdiction of the respective Powers.

Washington, D.C., December 13, 1921.

CHARLES EVANS HUGHES
HENRY CABOT LODGE
OSCAR W. UNDERWOOD
ELIHU ROOT
ARTHUR JAMES BALFOUR
LEE OF FAREHAM
A. C. GEDDES
R. L. BORDEN
G. F. PEARCE
JOHN W. SALMOND

ARTHUR JAMES BALFOUR
V. S. SRINIVASA SASTRI
RENÉ VIVIANI
A. SARRAUT
JUSSERAND
T. KATO
K. SHIDEHARA
TOKUGAWA IYESATO
M. HANIHARA

[The following note was delivered by the American Minister at The Hague to the Netherlands Minister for Foreign Affairs on February 4, 1922:

"The United States of America have concluded on December 13, 1921, with the British Empire, France, and Japan, a treaty with a view to the preservation of the general peace and the maintenance of their rights in relation to their insular possessions and the insular dominions in the region of the Pacific Ocean. They have agreed thereby as between themselves to respect their rights in relation to these possessions and dominions.

"The Netherlands not being signatory to the said treaty and the Netherlands possessions in the region of the Pacific Ocean therefore not being included in the agreement referred to, the Government of the United States of America, anxious to forestall any conclusion contrary to the spirit of the treaty, desires to declare that it is firmly resolved to respect the rights of the Netherlands in relation to their insular possessions in the region of the Pacific Ocean."

An identical note, *mutatis mutandis,* was delivered by the American Minister at Lisbon to the Portuguese Minister for Foreign Affairs on the same date. The Ministers of the other three governments parties to the treaty of December 13, 1921 (British, French, and Japanese), also delivered identical notes, *mutatis mutandis,* to the Netherlands and Portuguese governments. (Department of State files: telegram no. 3 of Feb. 3, 1922, to American Minister to the Netherlands and despatch no. 862 of Feb. 13, 1922, from the American Minister at The Hague; telegram no. 9 of Feb. 3, 1922, to the American Minister to Portugal and despatch no. 853 of Feb. 13, 1922, from the American Minister at Lisbon; S. Doc. 128, 67th Cong., 2d sess.)]

FOREIGN POSTAL AGENCIES IN CHINA

Resolution adopted by the Conference on the Limitation of Armament at Washington February 1, 1922

> Conference on the Limitation of Armament, Washington, November 12, 1921–February 6, 1922 (U.S. Government Printing Office, 1922), p. 1646; Senate documents 124 and 125, 67th Congress, 2d session

RESOLUTION REGARDING FOREIGN POSTAL AGENCIES IN CHINA

A. Recognizing the justice of the desire expressed by the Chinese Government to secure the abolition of foreign postal agencies in China, save or except in leased territories or as otherwise specifically provided by treaty, it is resolved:

(1) The four Powers having such postal agencies agree to their abandonment subject to the following conditions:

(*a*) That an efficient Chinese postal service is maintained;
(*b*) That an assurance is given by the Chinese Government that they contemplate no change in the present postal administration so far as the status of the foreign Co-Director General is concerned.

(2) To enable China and the Powers concerned to make the necessary dispositions, this arrangement shall come into force and effect not later than January 1, 1923.

B. Pending the complete withdrawal of foreign postal agencies, the four Powers concerned severally undertake to afford full facilities to the Chinese customs authorities to examine in those agencies all postal matter (excepting ordinary letters, whether registered or not, which upon external examination appear plainly to contain only written matter) passing through them, with a view to ascertaining whether they contain articles which are dutiable or contraband or which otherwise contravene the customs regulations or laws of China.

[For parties, see bracketed note p. 331.]

FOREIGN ARMED FORCES IN CHINA

Resolution adopted by the Conference on the Limitation of Armament at Washington February 1, 1922

> *Conference on the Limitation of Armament, Washington, November 12, 1921–February 6, 1922* (U.S. Government Printing Office, 1922), p. 1648; Senate documents 124 and 125, 67th Congress, 2d session

RESOLUTION REGARDING FOREIGN ARMED FORCES IN CHINA

Whereas

The Powers have from time to time stationed armed forces, including police and railway guards, in China to protect the lives and property of foreigners lawfully in China;

And whereas

It appears that certain of these armed forces are maintained in China without the authority of any treaty or agreement;

And whereas

The Powers have declared their intention to withdraw their armed forces now on duty in China without the authority of any treaty or agreement, whenever China shall assure the protection of the lives and property of foreigners in China;

And whereas

China has declared her intention and capacity to assure the protection of the lives and property of foreigners in China;

Now

To the end that there may be clear understanding of the conditions upon which in each case the practical execution of those intentions must depend; It is resolved:

That the Diplomatic Representatives in Peking of the Powers now in conference at Washington, to wit, the United States of America, Belgium, the British Empire, France, Italy, Japan, the Netherlands and Portugal, will be instructed by their respective Governments whenever China shall so request, to associate themselves with three representatives of the Chinese Government to conduct collectively a full and impartial inquiry into the issues raised by the

338

foregoing declarations of intention made by the Powers and by China and shall thereafter prepare a full and comprehensive report setting out without reservation their findings of fact and their opinions with regard to the matter hereby referred for inquiry, and shall furnish a copy of their report to each of the nine Governments concerned which shall severally make public the report with such comment as each may deem appropriate. The Representatives of any of the Powers may make or join in minority reports stating their differences, if any, from the majority report.

That each of the Powers above named shall be deemed free to accept or reject all or any of the findings of fact or opinions expressed in the report but that in no case shall any of the said Powers make its acceptance of all or any of the findings of fact or opinions either directly or indirectly dependent on the granting by China of any special concession, favor, benefit or immunity, whether political or economic.

[For parties, see bracketed note p. 331.]

FOREIGN RADIO STATIONS IN CHINA

Resolution adopted by the Conference on the Limitation of Armament at Washington February 1, 1922, with accompanying declarations

> Conference on the Limitation of Armament, Washington, November 12, 1921–February 6, 1922 (U.S. Government Printing Office, 1922), p. 1650; Senate documents 124 and 125, 67th Congress, 2d session

RESOLUTION REGARDING RADIO STATIONS IN CHINA, AND ACCOMPANYING DECLARATIONS

The representatives of the Powers hereinafter named participating in the discussion of Pacific and Far Eastern questions in the Conference on the Limitation of Armament, to wit, the United States of America, Belgium, the British Empire, China, France, Italy, Japan, the Netherlands and Portugal,

Have resolved

1. That all radio stations in China, whether maintained under the provisions of the International Protocol of September 7, 1901,[1] or in fact maintained in the grounds of any of the foreign Legations in China, shall be limited in their use to sending and receiving government messages and shall not receive or send commercial or personal or unofficial messages, including press matter: Provided, however, that in case all other telegraphic communication is interrupted, then, upon official notification accompanied by proof of such interruption to the Chinese Ministry of Communications, such stations may afford temporary facilities for commercial, personal or unofficial messages, including press matter, until the Chinese Government has given notice of the termination of the interruption;

2. All radio stations operated within the territory of China by a foreign Government or the citizens or subjects thereof under treaties or concessions of the Government of China, shall limit the messages sent and received by the terms of the treaties or concessions under which the respective stations are maintained;

---

[1] TS 397, *ante,* vol. 1, p. 302.

3. In case there be any radio station maintained in the territory of China by a foreign Government or citizens or subjects thereof without the authority of the Chinese Government, such station and all the plant, apparatus and material thereof shall be transferred to and taken over by the Government of China, to be operated under the direction of the Chinese Ministry of Communications under fair and full compensation to the owners for the value of the installation, as soon as the Chinese Ministry of Communications is prepared to operate the same effectively for the general public benefit;

4. If any questions shall arise as to the radio stations in leased territories, in the South Manchurian Railway Zone or in the French Concession at Shanghai, they shall be regarded as matters for discussion between the Chinese Government and the Government concerned;

5. The owners or managers of all radio stations maintained in the territory of China by foreign Powers or citizens or subjects thereof shall confer with the Chinese Ministry of Communications for the purpose of seeking a common arrangement to avoid interference in the use of wave lengths by wireless stations in China, subject to such general arrangements as may be made by an international conference convened for the revision of the rules established by the International Radio Telegraph Convention, signed at London, July 5, 1912.[2]

[For parties, see bracketed note p. 331.]

Declaration Concerning the Resolution Regarding Radio Stations in China [3]

The Powers other than China declare that nothing in paragraphs 3 or 4 of the Resolution of December 7th, 1921,[4] is to be deemed to be an expression of opinion by the Conference as to whether the stations referred to therein are or are not authorized by China.

They further give notice that the result of any discussion arising under paragraph 4 must, if it is not to be subject to objection by them, conform with the principle of the open door or equality of opportunity approved by the Conference.

Declaration by the Chinese Delegation Concerning Radio Stations in China [3]

The Chinese Delegation takes this occasion formally to declare that the Chinese Government does not recognize or concede the right of any foreign Power or of the nationals thereof to install or operate, without its express consent, radio stations in Legation grounds, settlements, concessions, leased territories, railway areas or other similar areas.

---

[2] TS 581, *ante,* vol. 1, p. 883.

[3] Recorded in the minutes of the plenary session of Feb. 1, 1922.

[4] Dec. 7, 1921, was the date on which the resolution regarding radio stations in China was first submitted to the Committee on Pacific and Far Eastern Questions.

UNIFICATION OF RAILWAYS IN CHINA

Resolution adopted by the Conference on the Limitation of Armament at Washington February 1, 1922, with declaration by China

> Conference on the Limitation of Armament, Washington, November 12, 1921–February 6, 1922 (U.S. Government Printing Office, 1922), p. 1652; Senate documents 124 and 125, 67th Congress, 2d session

RESOLUTION REGARDING THE UNIFICATION OF RAILWAYS IN CHINA, AND ACCOMPANYING DECLARATION BY CHINA

The Powers represented in this Conference record their hope that to the utmost degree consistent with legitimate existing rights, the future development of railways in China shall be so conducted as to enable the Chinese Government to effect the unification of railways into a railway system under Chinese control, with such foreign financial and technical assistance as may prove necessary in the interests of that system.

[For parties, see bracketed note p. 331.]

Declaration by China [1]

The Chinese Delegation notes with sympathetic appreciation the expression of the hope of the Powers that the existing and future railways of China may be unified under the control and operation of the Chinese Government with such foreign financial and technical assistance as may be needed. It is our intention as speedily as possible to bring about this result. It is our purpose to develop existing and future railways in accordance with a general program that will meet the economic, industrial and commercial requirements of China. It will be our policy to obtain such foreign financial and technical assistance as may be needed from the Powers in accordance with the principle of the open door or equal opportunity; and the friendly support of these Powers will be asked for the effort of the Chinese Government to bring all the railways of China, now existing or to be built, under its effective and unified control and operation.

---

[1] Made on Jan. 19, 1922, before the Committee on Pacific and Far Eastern Questions.

342

REDUCTION OF CHINESE MILITARY FORCES

Resolution adopted by the Conference on the Limitation of Armament at Washington February 1, 1922

> Conference on the Limitation of Armament, Washington, November 12, 1921–February 6, 1922 (U.S. Government Printing Office, 1922), p. 1654; Senate documents 124 and 125, 67th Congress, 2d session

RESOLUTION REGARDING THE REDUCTION OF CHINESE MILITARY FORCES

Whereas the Powers attending this Conference have been deeply impressed with the severe drain on the public revenue of China through the maintenance in various parts of the country of military forces, excessive in number and controlled by the military chiefs of the Provinces without coordination;

And whereas the continued maintenance of these forces appears to be mainly responsible for China's present unsettled political conditions;

And whereas it is felt that large and prompt reductions of these forces will not only advance the cause of China's political unity and economic development but will hasten her financial rehabilitation;

Therefore, without any intention to interfere in the internal problems of China, but animated by the sincere desire to see China develop and maintain for herself an effective and stable Government alike in her own interest and in the general interest of trade;

And being inspired by the spirit of this Conference whose aim is to reduce, through the limitation of armament, the enormous disbursements which manifestly constitute the greater part of the encumbrance upon enterprise and national prosperity;

It is resolved:

That this Conference express to China the earnest hope that immediate and effective steps may be taken by the Chinese Government to reduce the aforesaid military forces and expenditures.

[For parties, see bracketed note p. 331.]

NOTIFICATION REGARDING COMMITMENTS OF OR WITH RESPECT TO CHINA

Resolution adopted by the Conference on the Limitation of Armament at Washington February 1, 1922

Conference on the Limitation of Armament, Washington, November 12, 1921–February 6, 1922 (U.S. Government Printing Office, 1922), p. 1654; Senate documents 124 and 125, 67th Congress, 2d session

RESOLUTION REGARDING EXISTING COMMITMENTS OF CHINA OR WITH RESPECT TO CHINA

The Powers represented in this Conference, considering it desirable that there should hereafter be full publicity with respect to all matters affecting the political and other international obligations of China and of the several Powers in relation to China, are agreed as follows:

I. The several Powers other than China will at their earliest convenience file with the Secretariat General of the Conference for transmission to the participating Powers, a list of all treaties, conventions, exchanges of notes, or other international agreements which they may have with China, or with any other Power or Powers in relation to China, which they deem to be still in force and upon which they may desire to reply. In each case, citations will be given to any official or other publication in which an authoritative text of the documents may be found. In any case in which the document may not have been published, a copy of the text (in its original language or languages) will be filed with the Secretariat General of the Conference.

Every treaty or other international agreement of the character described which may be concluded hereafter shall be notified by the Governments concerned within sixty (60) days of its conclusion to the Powers who are signatories of or adherents to this Agreement.

II. The several Powers other than China will file with the Secretariat General of the Conference, at their earliest convenience, for transmission to the participating Powers a list, as nearly complete as may be possible, of all those contracts between their nationals, of the one part, and the Chinese Government or any of its administrative subdivisions or local authorities, of

344

the other part, which involve any concession, franchise, option or preference with respect to railway construction, mining, forestry, navigation, river conservancy, harbor works, reclamation, electrical communications, or other public works or public services, or for the sale of arms or ammunition, or which involve a lien upon any of the public revenues or properties of the Chinese Government or of any of its administrative subdivisions. There shall be, in the case of each document so listed, either a citation to a published text, or a copy of the text itself.

Every contract of the public character described which may be concluded hereafter shall be notified by the Governments concerned within sixty (60) days after the receipt of information of its conclusion to the Powers who are signatories of or adherents to this Agreement.

III. The Chinese Government agrees to notify in the conditions laid down in this Agreement every treaty, agreement or contract of the character indicated herein which has been or may hereafter be concluded by that Government or by any local authority in China with any foreign Power or the nationals of any foreign Power, whether party to this Agreement or not, so far as the information is in its possession.

IV. The Governments of Powers having treaty relations with China, which are not represented at the present Conference, shall be invited to adhere to this Agreement.

The United States Government, as convener of the Conference, undertakes to communicate this Agreement to the Governments of the said Powers, with a view to obtaining their adherence thereto as soon as possible.

[For parties, see bracketed note p. 331.]

COMMISSION OF JURISTS TO CONSIDER LAWS OF WAR

Resolutions adopted by the Conference on the Limitation of Armament at Washington February 4, 1922

> Conference on the Limitation of Armament, Washington, November 12, 1921–February 6, 1922 (U.S. Government Printing Office, 1922), p. 1640; Senate documents 124 and 125, 67th Congress, 2d session

RESOLUTION ESTABLISHING A COMMISSION OF JURISTS TO CONSIDER AMENDMENT OF THE LAWS OF WAR

The United States of America, the British Empire, France, Italy and Japan have agreed:

I. That a Commission composed of not more than two members representing each of the above-mentioned Powers shall be constituted to consider the following questions:

(a) Do existing rules of international law adequately cover new methods of attack or defense resulting from the introduction or development, since the Hague Conference of 1907, of new agencies of warfare?

(b) If not so, what changes in the existing rules ought to be adopted in consequence thereof as a part of the law of nations?

II. That notices of appointment of the members of the Commission shall, within three months after the adjournment of the present Conference, be transmitted to the Government of the United States of America which after consultation with the Powers concerned will fix the day and place for the meeting of the Commission.

III. That the Commission shall be at liberty to request assistance and advice from experts in international law and in land, naval and aerial warfare.

IV. That the Commission shall report its conclusions to each of the Powers represented in its membership.

Those Powers shall thereupon confer as to the acceptance of the report and the course to be followed to secure the consideration of its recommendations by the other civilized Powers.

[For parties, see bracketed note p. 331.]

RESOLUTION LIMITING THE JURISDICTION OF THE COMMISSION
OF JURISTS

Resolved, That it is not the intention of the Powers agreeing to the appointment of a Commission to consider and report upon the rules of international law respecting new agencies of warfare that the Commission shall review or report upon the rules or declarations relating to submarines or to the use of noxious gases and chemicals already adopted by the Powers in this conference.

[For parties, see bracketed note p. 331.]

LIMITATION OF NAVAL ARMAMENT

Resolution adopted by the Conference on the Limitation of Armament
at Washington February 4, 1922
Effective between February 4, 1922, and August 17, 1923

> *Conference on the Limitation of Armament, Washington, November 12, 1921–February 6, 1922* (U.S. Government Printing Office, 1922), p. 1642

Resolution Regarding the Sale of Ships Before the Ratification of the Treaty Limiting Naval Armament

It should therefore be recorded in the minutes of the Subcommittee and of the full Conference that the Powers signatory of the Treaty of Naval Limitation [1] regard themselves in honor bound not to sell any ships between the present date and the ratification of the Treaty, when such a sale would be a breach of Article XVIII.

[For parties, see bracketed note p. 331.]

---

[1] Treaty signed at Washington Feb. 6, 1922 (TS 671), *post*, p. 351.

BOARD OF REFERENCE FOR FAR EASTERN QUESTIONS

Resolution adopted by the Conference on the Limitation of Armament at Washington February 4, 1922

> Conference on the Limitation of Armament, Washington, November 12, 1921–February 6, 1922 (U.S. Government Printing Office, 1922), p. 1642; Senate documents 124 and 125, 67th Congress, 2d session

RESOLUTION ESTABLISHING A BOARD OF REFERENCE FOR FAR EASTERN QUESTIONS

The representatives of the Powers assembled at the present Conference at Washington, to wit, the United States of America, Belgium, the British Empire, China, France, Italy, Japan, the Netherlands and Portugal:

Desiring to provide a procedure for dealing with questions that may arise in connection with the execution of the provisions of Articles III and V of the Treaty to be signed at Washington on February 6th, 1922,[1] with reference to their general policy designed to stabilize conditions in the Far East, to safeguard the rights and interests of China, and to promote intercourse between China and the other Powers upon the basis of equality of opportunity;

Resolve that there shall be established in China a Board of Reference to which any questions arising in connection with the execution of the aforesaid Articles may be referred for investigation and report.

The Special Conference provided for in Article II of the Treaty to be signed at Washington on February 6th, 1922, with reference to the Chinese Customs Tariff,[2] shall formulate for the approval of the Powers concerned a detailed plan for the constitution of the Board.

[For parties, see bracketed note p. 331.]

[1] TS 723, *post*, p. 377.
[2] TS 724, *post*, p. 384.

CHINESE EASTERN RAILWAY

Resolutions adopted by the Conference on the Limitation of Armament at Washington February 4, 1922

> Conference on the Limitation of Armament, Washington, November 12, 1921–February 6, 1922 (U.S. Government Printing Office, 1922), p. 1658

RESOLUTION REGARDING THE CHINESE EASTERN RAILWAY, APPROVED BY THE POWERS INCLUDING CHINA

Resolved, That the preservation of the Chinese Eastern Railway for those in interest requires that better protection be given to the Railway and the persons engaged in its operation and use; a more careful selection of personnel to secure efficiency of service, and a more economical use of funds to prevent waste of the property.

That the subject should immediately be dealt with through the proper diplomatic channels.

[For parties, see bracketed note p. 331.]

RESOLUTION REGARDING THE CHINESE EASTERN RAILWAY, APPROVED BY THE POWERS OTHER THAN CHINA

The powers other than China, in agreeing to the Resolution regarding the Chinese Eastern Railway, reserve the right to insist hereafter upon the responsibility of China for performance or nonperformance of the obligations towards the foreign stockholders, bondholders, and creditors of the Chinese Eastern Railway Company which the Powers deem to result from the contracts under which the Railroad was built and the action of China thereunder and the obligations which they deem to be in the nature of a trust resulting from the exercise of power by the Chinese Government over the possession and administration of the Railroad.

[For parties, see bracketed note p. 331.]

LIMITATION OF NAVAL ARMAMENT (FIVE-POWER TREATY OR WASHINGTON TREATY)

Treaty signed at Washington February 6, 1922; procès-verbal of deposit of ratifications signed at Washington August 17, 1923
Senate advice and consent to ratification March 29, 1922
Ratified by the President of the United States June 9, 1923
Entered into force August 17, 1923
Proclaimed by the President of the United States August 21, 1923
Terminated December 31, 1936, in accordance with terms of article XXIII [1]

43 Stat. 1655; Treaty Series 671

The United States of America, the British Empire, France, Italy and Japan;

Desiring to contribute to the maintenance of the general peace, and to reduce the burdens of competition in armament;

Have resolved, with a view to accomplishing these purposes, to conclude a treaty to limit their respective naval armament, and to that end have appointed as their Plenipotentiaries:

The President of the United States of America:

Mr. Charles Evans Hughes,
Mr. Henry Cabot Lodge,
Mr. Oscar W. Underwood,
Mr. Elihu Root,
    citizens of the United States;

His Majesty the King of the United Kingdom of Great Britain and Ireland and of the British Dominions beyond the Seas, Emperor of India:

The Right Honourable Arthur James Balfour, O.M., M.P., Lord President of His Privy Council;
The Right Honourable Baron Lee of Fareham, G.B.E., K.C.B., First Lord of His Admiralty;
The Right Honourable Sir Auckland Campbell Geddes, K.C.B., His Ambassador Extraordinary and Plenipotentiary to the United States of America;

---

[1] Japan gave notice Dec. 29, 1934, of its intention to terminate the treaty.

and
> for the Dominion of Canada:
> > The Right Honourable Sir Robert Laird Borden, G.C.M.G., K.C.;
> for the Commonwealth of Australia:
> > Senator the Right Honourable George Foster Pearce, Minister for Home
> > and Territories;
> for the Dominion of New Zealand:
> > The Honourable Sir John William Salmond, K.C., Judge of the Su-
> > preme Court of New Zealand;
> for the Union of South Africa:
> > The Right Honourable Arthur James Balfour, O.M., M.P.;
> for India:
> > The Right Honourable Valingman Sankaranarayana Srinivasa Sastri,
> > Member of the Indian Council of State;

The President of the French Republic:
> Mr. Albert Sarraut, Deputy, Minister of the Colonies;
> Mr. Jules J. Jusserand, Ambassador Extraordinary and Plenipotentiary to
> the United States of America, Grand Cross of the National Order of the
> Legion of Honour;

His Majesty the King of Italy:
> The Honourable Carlo Schanzer, Senator of the Kingdom;
> The Honourable Vittorio Rolandi Ricci, Senator of the Kingdom, His
> Ambassador Extraordinary and Plenipotentiary at Washington;
> The Honourable Luigi Albertini, Senator of the Kingdom;

His Majesty the Emperor of Japan:
> Baron Tomosaburo Kato, Minister for the Navy, Junii, a member of the
> First Class of the Imperial Order of the Grand Cordon of the Rising
> Sun with the Paulownia Flower;
> Baron Kijuro Shidehara, His Ambassador Extraordinary and Plenipoten-
> tiary at Washington, Joshii, a member of the First Class of the Imperial
> Order of the Rising Sun;
> Mr. Masanao Hanihara, Vice Minister for Foreign Affairs, Jushii, a mem-
> ber of the Second Class of the Imperial Order of the Rising Sun;

Who, having communicated to each other their respective full powers,
found to be in good and due form, have agreed as follows:

CHAPTER I

GENERAL PROVISIONS RELATING TO THE LIMITATION OF NAVAL ARMAMENT

ARTICLE I

The Contracting Powers agree to limit their respective naval armament as
provided in the present Treaty.

ARTICLE II

The Contracting Powers may retain respectively the capital ships which are specified in Chapter II, Part 1. On the coming into force of the present Treaty, but subject to the following provisions of this Article, all other capital ships, built or building, of the United States, the British Empire and Japan shall be disposed of as prescribed in Chapter II, Part 2.

In addition to the capital ships specified in Chapter II, Part 1, the United States may complete and retain two ships of the *West Virginia* class now under construction. On the completion of these two ships the *North Dakota* and *Delaware* shall be disposed of as prescribed in Chapter II, Part 2.

The British Empire may, in accordance with the replacement table in Chapter II, Part 3, construct two new capital ships not exceeding 35,000 tons (35,560 metric tons) standard displacement each. On the completion of the said two ships the *Thunderer, King George V, Ajax* and *Centurion* shall be disposed of as prescribed in Chapter II, Part 2.

ARTICLE III

Subject to the provisions of Article II, the Contracting Powers shall abandon their respective capital ship building programs, and no new capital ships shall be constructed or acquired by any of the Contracting Powers except replacement tonnage which may be constructed or acquired as specified in Chapter II, Part 3.

Ships which are replaced in accordance with Chapter II, Part 3, shall be disposed of as prescribed in Part 2 of that Chapter.

ARTICLE IV

The total capital ship replacement tonnage of each of the Contracting Powers shall not exceed in standard displacement, for the United States 525,000 tons (533,400 metric tons); for the British Empire 525,000 tons (533,400 metric tons); for France 175,000 tons (177,800 metric tons); for Italy 175,-000 tons (177,800 metric tons); for Japan 315,000 tons (320,040 metric tons).

ARTICLE V

No capital ship exceeding 35,000 tons (35,560 metric tons) standard displacement shall be acquired by, or constructed by, for, or within the jurisdiction of, any of the Contracting Powers.

ARTICLE VI

No capital ship of any of the Contracting Powers shall carry a gun with a calibre in excess of 16 inches (406 millimetres).

Article VII

The total tonnage for aircraft carriers of each of the Contracting Powers shall not exceed in standard displacement, for the United States 135,000 tons (137,160 metric tons); for the British Empire 135,000 tons (137,160 metric tons); for France 60,000 tons (60,960 metric tons); for Italy 60,000 tons (60,960 metric tons); for Japan 81,000 tons (82,296 metric tons).

Article VIII

The replacement of aircraft carriers shall be effected only as prescribed in Chapter II, Part 3, provided, however, that all aircraft carrier tonnage in existence or building on November 12, 1921, shall be considered experimental, and may be replaced, within the total tonnage limit prescribed in Article VII, without regard to its age.

Article IX

No aircraft carrier exceeding 27,000 tons (27,432 metric tons) standard displacement shall be acquired by, or constructed by, for or within the jurisdiction of, any of the Contracting Powers.

However, any of the Contracting Powers may, provided that its total tonnage allowance of aircraft carriers is not thereby exceeded, build not more than two aircraft carriers, each of a tonnage of not more than 33,000 tons (33,528 metric tons) standard displacement, and in order to effect economy any of the Contracting Powers may use for this purpose any two of their ships, whether constructed or in course of construction, which would otherwise be scrapped under the provisions of Article II. The armament of any aircraft carriers exceeding 27,000 tons (27,432 metric tons) standard displacement shall be in accordance with the requirements of Article X, except that the total number of guns to be carried in case any of such guns be of a calibre exceeding 6 inches (152 millimetres), except anti-aircraft guns and guns not exceeding 5 inches (127 millimetres), shall not exceed eight.

Article X

No aircraft carrier of any of the Contracting Powers shall carry a gun with a calibre in excess of 8 inches (203 millimetres). Without prejudice to the provisions of Article IX, if the armament carried includes guns exceeding 6 inches (152 millimetres) in calibre the total number of guns carried, except anti-aircraft guns and guns not exceeding 5 inches (127 millimetres), shall not exceed ten. If alternatively the armament contains no guns exceeding 6 inches (152 millimetres) in calibre, the number of guns is not limited. In either case the number of anti-aircraft guns and of guns not exceeding 5 inches (127 millimetres) is not limited.

ARTICLE XI

No vessel of war exceeding 10,000 tons (10,160 metric tons) standard displacement, other than a capital ship or aircraft carrier, shall be acquired by, or constructed by, for, or within the jurisdiction of, any of the Contracting Powers. Vessels not specifically built as fighting ships nor taken in time of peace under government control for fighting purposes, which are employed on fleet duties or as troop transports or in some other way for the purpose of assisting in the prosecution of hostilities otherwise than as fighting ships, shall not be within the limitations of this Article.

ARTICLE XII

No vessel of war of any of the Contracting Powers, hereafter laid down, other than a capital ship, shall carry a gun with a calibre in excess of 8 inches (203 millimetres).

ARTICLE XIII

Except as provided in Article IX, no ship designated in the present Treaty to be scrapped may be reconverted into a vessel of war.

ARTICLE XIV

No preparations shall be made in merchant ships in time of peace for the installation of warlike armaments for the purpose of converting such ships into vessels of war, other than the necessary stiffening of decks for the mounting of guns not exceeding 6 inch (152 millimetres) calibre.

ARTICLE XV

No vessel of war constructed within the jurisdiction of any of the Contracting Powers for a non-Contracting Power shall exceed the limitations as to displacement and armament prescribed by the present Treaty for vessels of a similar type which may be constructed by or for any of the Contracting Powers; provided, however, that the displacement for aircraft carriers constructed for a non-Contracting Power shall in no case exceed 27,000 tons (27,432 metric tons) standard displacement.

ARTICLE XVI

If the construction of any vessel of war for a non-Contracting Power is undertaken within the jurisdiction of any of the Contracting Powers, such Power shall promptly inform the other Contracting Powers of the date of the signing of the contract and the date on which the keel of the ship is laid; and shall also communicate to them the particulars relating to the ship prescribed in Chapter II, Part 3, Section I (b), (4) and (5).

Article XVII

In the event of a Contracting Power being engaged in war, such Power shall not use as a vessel of war any vessel of war which may be under construction within its jurisdiction for any other Power, or which may have been constructed within its jurisdiction for another Power and not delivered.

Article XVIII [2]

Each of the Contracting Powers undertakes not to dispose by gift, sale or any mode of transfer of any vessel of war in such a manner that such vessel may become a vessel of war in the Navy of any foreign Power.

Article XIX

The United States, the British Empire and Japan agree that the status quo at the time of the signing of the present Treaty, with regard to fortifications and naval bases, shall be maintained in their respective territories and possessions specified hereunder:

(1) The insular possessions which the United States now holds or may hereafter acquire in the Pacific Ocean, except (a) those adjacent to the coast of the United States, Alaska and the Panama Canal Zone, not including the Aleutian Islands, and (b) the Hawaiian Islands;

(2) Hongkong and the insular possessions which the British Empire now holds or may hereafter acquire in the Pacific Ocean, east of the meridian of 110° east longitude, except (a) those adjacent to the coast of Canada, (b) the Commonwealth of Australia and its Territories, and (c) New Zealand;

(3) The following insular territories and possessions of Japan in the Pacific Ocean, to wit: the Kurile Islands, the Bonin Islands, Amami-Oshima, the Loochoo Islands, Formosa and the Pescadores, and any insular territories or possessions in the Pacific Ocean which Japan may hereafter acquire.

The maintenance of the status quo under the foregoing provisions implies that no new fortifications or naval bases shall be established in the territories and possessions specified; that no measures shall be taken to increase the existing naval facilities for the repair and maintenance of naval forces, and that no increase shall be made in the coast defences of the territories and possessions above specified. This restriction, however, does not preclude such repair and

---

[2] For text of a resolution adopted Feb. 4, 1922, relating to this article, see *ante*, p. 348.

replacement of worn-out weapons and equipment as is customary in naval and military establishments in time of peace.

ARTICLE XX

The rules for determining tonnage displacement prescribed in Chapter II, Part 4, shall apply to the ships of each of the Contracting Powers.

CHAPTER II

RULES RELATING TO THE EXECUTION OF THE TREATY—DEFINITION OF TERMS

PART 1

Capital Ships Which May Be Retained by the Contracting Powers

In accordance with Article II ships may be retained by each of the Contracting Powers as specified in this Part.

SHIPS WHICH MAY BE RETAINED BY THE UNITED STATES

Name:	Tonnage
Maryland	32,600
California	32,300
Tennessee	32,300
Idaho	32,000
New Mexico	32,000
Mississippi	32,000
Arizona	31,400
Pennsylvania	31,400
Oklahoma	27,500
Nevada	27,500
New York	27,000
Texas	27,000
Arkansas	26,000
Wyoming	26,000
Florida	21,825
Utah	21,825
North Dakota	20,000
Delaware	20,000
Total tonnage	500,650

On the completion of the two ships of the *West Virginia* class and the scrapping of the *North Dakota* and *Delaware,* as provided in Article II, the total tonnage to be retained by the United States will be 525,850 tons.

SHIPS WHICH MAY BE RETAINED BY THE BRITISH EMPIRE

Name:	Tonnage
Royal Sovereign	25, 750
Royal Oak	25, 750
Revenge	25, 750
Resolution	25, 750
Ramillies	25, 750
Malaya	27, 500
Valiant	27, 500
Barham	27, 500
Queen Elizabeth	27, 500
Warspite	27, 500
Benbow	25, 000
Emperor of India	25, 000
Iron Duke	25, 000
Marlborough	25, 000
Hood	41, 200
Renown	26, 500
Repulse	26, 500
Tiger	28, 500
Thunderer	22, 500
King George V	23, 000
Ajax	23, 000
Centurion	23, 000
Total tonnage	580, 450

On the completion of the two new ships to be constructed and the scrapping of the *Thunderer, King George V, Ajax* and *Centurion*, as provided in Article II, the total tonnage to be retained by the British Empire will be 558,950 tons.

SHIPS WHICH MAY BE RETAINED BY FRANCE

Name:	Tonnage (metric tons)
Bretagne	23, 500
Lorraine	23, 500
Provence	23, 500
Paris	23, 500
France	23, 500
Jean Bart	23, 500
Courbet	23, 500
Condorcet	18, 890
Diderot	18, 890
Voltaire	18, 890
Total tonnage	221, 170

France may lay down new tonnage in the years 1927, 1929, and 1931, as provided in Part 3, Section II.

SHIPS WHICH MAY BE RETAINED BY ITALY

Name:	Tonnage (metric tons)
Andrea Doria	22,700
Caio Duilio	22,700
Conte Di Cavour	22,500
Giulio Cesare	22,500
Leonardo Da Vinci	22,500
Dante Alighieri	19,500
Roma	12,600
Napoli	12,600
Vittorio Emanuele	12,600
Regina Elena	12,600
Total tonnage	182,800

Italy may lay down new tonnage in the years 1927, 1929, and 1931, as provided in Part 3, Section II.

SHIPS WHICH MAY BE RETAINED BY JAPAN

Name:	Tonnage
Mutsu	33,800
Nagato	33,800
Hiuga	31,260
Ise	31,260
Yamashiro	30,600
Fu-So	30,600
Kirishima	27,500
Haruna	27,500
Hiyei	27,500
Kongo	27,500
Total tonnage	301,320

Part 2

Rules for Scrapping Vessels of War

The following rules shall be observed for the scrapping of vessels of war which are to be disposed of in accordance with Articles II and III.

I. A vessel to be scrapped must be placed in such condition that it cannot be put to combatant use.

II. This result must be finally effected in any one of the following ways:

(a) Permanent sinking of the vessel;

(b) Breaking the vessel up. This shall always involve the destruction or removal of all machinery, boilers and armour, and all deck, side and bottom plating;

(c) Converting the vessel to target use exclusively. In such case all the provisions of paragraph III of this Part, except subparagraph (6), in so far as may be necessary to enable the ship to be used as a mobile target, and except sub-paragraph (7), must be previously complied with. Not more than one capital ship may be retained for this purpose at one time by any of the Contracting Powers.

(d) Of the capital ships which would otherwise be scrapped under the present Treaty in or after the year 1931, France and Italy may each retain two sea-going vessels for training purposes exclusively, that is, as gunnery or torpedo schools. The two vessels retained by France shall be of the *Jean Bart* class, and of those retained by Italy one shall be the *Dante Alighieri*, the other of the *Giulio Cesare* class. On retaining these ships for the purpose above stated, France and Italy respectively undertake to remove and destroy their conning-towers, and not to use the said ships as vessels of war.

III. (a) Subject to the special exceptions contained in Article IX, when a vessel is due for scrapping, the first stage of scrapping, which consists in rendering a ship incapable of further warlike service, shall be immediately undertaken.

(b) A vessel shall be considered incapable of further warlike service when there shall have been removed and landed, or else destroyed in the ship:

(1) All guns and essential portions of guns, fire-control tops and revolving parts of all barbettes and turrets;

(2) All machinery for working hydraulic or electric mountings;

(3) All fire-control instruments and range-finders;

(4) All ammunition, explosives and mines;

(5) All torpedoes, war-heads and torpedo tubes;

(6) All wireless telegraphy installations;

(7) The conning tower and all side armour, or alternatively all main propelling machinery; and

(8) All landing and flying-off platforms and all other aviation accessories.

IV. The periods in which scrapping of vessels is to be effected are as follows:

(a) In the case of vessels to be scrapped under the first paragraph of Article II, the work of rendering the vessels incapable of further warlike service, in accordance with paragraph III of this Part, shall be completed within six months from the coming into force of the present Treaty, and the scrapping shall be finally effected within eighteen months from such coming into force.

(b) In the case of vessels to be scrapped under the second and third paragraphs of Article II, or under Article III, the work of rendering the vessel incapable of further warlike service in accordance with paragraph III of this Part shall be commenced not later than the date of completion of its successor, and shall be finished within six months from the date of such completion. The vessel shall be finally scrapped, in accordance with paragraph II of this Part, within eighteen months from the date of completion of its successor. If, however, the completion of the new vessel be delayed, then the work of rendering the old vessel incapable of further warlike service in accordance with paragraph III of this Part shall be commenced within four years from the laying of the keel of the new vessel, and shall be finished within six months from the date on which such work was commenced, and the old vessel shall be finally scrapped in accordance with paragraph II of this Part within eighteen months from the date when the work of rendering it incapable of further warlike service was commenced.

Part 3

Replacement

The replacement of capital ships and aircraft carriers shall take place according to the rules in Section I and the tables in Section II of this Part.

Section I

RULES FOR REPLACEMENT

(a) Capital ships and aircraft carriers twenty years after the date of their completion may, except as otherwise provided in Article VIII and in the tables in Section II of this Part, be replaced by new construction, but within the limits prescribed in Article IV and Article VII. The keels of such new construction may, except as otherwise provided in Article VIII and in the tables in Section II of this Part, be laid down not earlier than seventeen years from the date of completion of the tonnage to be replaced, provided, however, that no capital ship tonnage, with the exception of the ships referred to in the third paragraph of Article II, and the replacement tonnage specifically mentioned in Section II of this Part, shall be laid down until ten years from November 12, 1921.

(b) Each of the Contracting Powers shall communicate promptly to each of the other Contracting Powers the following information:

(1) The names of the capital ships and aircraft carriers to be replaced by new construction;

(2) The date of governmental authorization of replacement tonnage;

(3) The date of laying the keels of replacement tonnage;

(4) The standard displacement in tons and metric tons of each new ship to be laid down, and the principal dimensions, namely, length at waterline, extreme beam at or below waterline, mean draft at standard displacement;

(5) The date of completion of each new ship and its standard displacement in tons and metric tons, and the principal dimensions, namely, length at waterline, extreme beam at or below waterline, mean draft at standard displacement, at time of completion.

(c) In case of loss or accidental destruction of capital ships or aircraft carriers, they may immediately be replaced by new construction subject to the tonnage limits prescribed in Articles IV and VII and in conformity with the other provisions of the present Treaty, the regular replacement program being deemed to be advanced to that extent.

(d) No retained capital ships or aircraft carriers shall be reconstructed except for the purpose of providing means of defense against air and submarine attack, and subject to the following rules: The Contracting Powers may, for that purpose, equip existing tonnage with bulge or blister or anti-air attack deck protection, providing the increase of displacement thus effected does not exceed 3,000 tons (3,048 metric tons) displacement for each ship. No alterations in side armor, in calibre, number or general type of mounting of main armament shall be permitted except:

(1) in the case of France and Italy, which countries within the limits allowed for bulge may increase their armor protection and the calibre of the guns now carried on their existing capital ships so as not to exceed 16 inches (406 millimeters) and

(2) the British Empire shall be permited to complete, in the case of the *Renown*, the alterations to armor that have already been commenced but temporarily suspended.

SECTION II

REPLACEMENT AND SCRAPPING OF CAPITAL SHIPS

United States

Year	Ships laid down	Ships completed	Ships scrapped (age in parentheses)	Ships retained. Summary Pre-Jutland	Post-Jutland
			Maine (20), Missouri (20), Virginia (17), Nebraska (17), Georgia (17), New Jersey (17), Rhode Island (17), Connecticut (17), Louisiana (17), Vermont (16), Kansas (16), Minnesota (16), New Hampshire (15), South Carolina (13), Michigan (13), Washington (0), South Dakota (0), Indiana (0), Montana (0), North Carolina (0), Iowa (0), Massachusetts (0), Lexington (0), Constitution (0), Constellation (0), Saratoga (0), Ranger (0), United States (0).*	17	1
1922....		A, B, #.....	Delaware (12), North Dakota (12).	15	3
1923....				15	3
1924....				15	3
1925....				15	3
1926....				15	3
1927....				15	3
1928....				15	3
1929....				15	3
1930....				15	3
1931....	C, D....			15	3
1932....	E, F....			15	3
1933....	G....			15	3
1934....	H, I....	C, D....	Florida (23), Utah (23), Wyoming (22).	12	5
1935....	J....	E, F....	Arkansas (23), Texas (21), New York (21).	9	7
1936....	K, L....	G....	Nevada (20), Oklahoma (20)......	7	8
1937....	M....	H, I....	Arizona (21), Pennsylvania (21)...	5	10
1938....	N, O....	J....	Mississippi (21)...............	4	11
1939....	P, Q....	K, L....	New Mexico (21), Idaho (20).....	2	13
1940....		M....	Tennessee (20).................	1	14
1941....		N, O....	California (20), Maryland (20)....	0	15
1942....		P, Q....	2 ships West Virginia class........	0	15

* The United States may retain the *Oregon* and *Illinois*, for noncombatant purposes, after complying with the provisions of Part 2, III, (b).
# Two West Virginia class.

NOTE.—A, B, C, D, etc., represent individual capital ships of 35,000 tons standard displacement, laid down and completed in the years specified.

REPLACEMENT AND SCRAPPING OF CAPITAL SHIPS

British Empire

Year	Ships laid down	Ships completed	Ships scrapped (age in parentheses)	Ships retained. Summary	
				Pre-	Post-
				Jutland	
			Commonwealth (16), Agamemnon (13), Dreadnought (15), Bellerophon (12), St. Vincent (11), Inflexible (13), Superb (12), Neptune (10), Hercules (10), Indomitable (13), Temeraire (12), New Zealand (9), Lion (9), Princess Royal (9), Conqueror (9), Monarch (9), Orion (9), Australia (8), Agincourt (7), Erin (7), 4 building or projected.*	21	1
1922.....	A. B#.....	.....	.....	21	1
1923.....	.....	.....	.....	21	1
1924.....	.....	.....	.....	21	1
1925.....	.....	A. B......	King George V (13), Ajax (12), Centurion (12), Thunderer (13).	17	3
1926.....	.....	.....	.....	17	3
1927.....	.....	.....	.....	17	3
1928.....	.....	.....	.....	17	3
1929.....	.....	.....	.....	17	3
1930.....	.....	.....	.....	17	3
1931.....	C. D.....	.....	.....	17	3
1932.....	E. F.....	.....	.....	17	3
1933.....	G......	.....	.....	17	3
1934.....	H. I......	C. D......	Iron Duke (20), Marlborough (20), Emperor of India (20), Benbow (20).	13	5
1935.....	J..........	E. F......	Tiger (21), Queen Elizabeth (20), Warspite (20), Barham (20).	9	7
1936.....	K. L.......	G..........	Malaya (20), Royal Sovereign (20).	7	8
1937.....	M..........	H. I......	Revenge (21), Resolution (21).....	5	10
1938.....	N. O......	J..........	Royal Oak (22)...............	4	11
1939.....	P. Q.......	K. L.......	Valiant (23), Repulse (23)........	2	13
1940.....	.....	M........	Renown (24).................	1	14
1941.....	.....	N. O......	Ramillies (24), Hood (21).........	0	15
1942.....	.....	P. Q.......	A (17), B (17).................	0	15

*The British Empire may retain the *Colossus* and *Collingwood* for noncombatant purposes, after complying with the provisions of Part 2, III, (b).

#Two 35,000-ton ships, standard displacement.

NOTE.—A, B, C, D, etc., represent individual capital ships of 35,000 tons standard displacement laid down and completed in the years specified.

REPLACEMENT AND SCRAPPING OF CAPITAL SHIPS

France

Year	Ships laid down	Ships completed	Ships scrapped (age in parentheses)	Ships retained. Summary	
				Pre-	Post-
				Jutland	
1922....	....	....	....	7	0
1923....	....	....	....	7	0
1924....	....	....	....	7	0
1925....	....	....	....	7	0
1926....	....	....	....	7	0
1927....	35,000 tons.	....	....	7	0
1928....	....	....	....	7	0
1929....	35,000 tons.	....	....	7	0
1930....	....	35,000 tons.	Jean Bart (17), Courbet (17)......	5	(*)
1931....	35,000 tons.	....	....	5	(*)
1932....	35,000 tons.	35,000 tons.	France (18).....................	4	(*)
1933....	35,000 tons.	....	....	4	(*)
1934....	....	35,000 tons.	Paris (20), Bretagne (20)........	2	(*)
1935....	....	35,000 tons.	Provence (20)...................	1	(*)
1936....	....	35,000 tons.	Lorraine (20)...................	0	(*)
1937....	....	....	....	0	(*)
1938....	....	....	....	0	(*)
1939....	....	....	....	0	(*)
1940....	....	....	....	0	(*)
1941....	....	....	....	0	(*)
1942....	....	....	....	0	(*)

*Within tonnage limitations; number not fixed.

NOTE.—France expressly reserves the right of employing the capital ship tonnage allotment as she may consider advisable, subject solely to the limitations that the displacement of individual ships should not surpass 35,000 tons, and that the total capital ship tonnage should keep within the limits imposed by the present Treaty.

REPLACEMENT AND SCRAPPING OF CAPITAL SHIPS

Italy

Year	Ships laid down	Ships completed	Ships scrapped (age in parentheses)	Ships retained. Summary	
				Pre-Jutland	Post-Jutland
1922....	....	....	....	6	0
1923....	....	....	....	6	0
1924....	....	....	....	6	0
1925....	....	....	....	6	0
1926....	....	....	....	6	0
1927....	35,000 tons.	....	....	6	0
1928....	....	....	....	6	0
1929....	35,000 tons.	....	....	6	0
1930....	....	....	....	6	0
1931....	35,000 tons.	35,000 tons.	Dante Alighieri (19)...............	5	(*)
1932....	45,000 tons.	....	....	5	(*)
1933....	25,000 tons.	35,000 tons.	Leonardo da Vinci (19).............	4	(*)
1934....	....	....	....	4	(*)
1935....	....	35,000 tons.	Giulio Cesare (21).................	3	(*)
1936....	....	45,000 tons.	Conte di Cavour (21), Duilio (21).	1	(*)
1937....	....	25,000 tons.	Andrea Doria (21).................	0	(*)

*Within tonnage limitations; number not fixed.

NOTE.—Italy expressly reserves the right of employing the capital ship tonnage allotment as she may consider advisable, subject solely to the limitations that the displacement of individual ships should not surpass 35,000 tons, and the total capital ship tonnage should keep within the limits imposed by the present Treaty.

REPLACEMENT AND SCRAPPING OF CAPITAL SHIPS

Japan

Year	Ships laid down	Ships completed	Ships scrapped (age in parentheses)	Ships retained. Summary	
				Pre-	Post-
				Jutland	
			Hizen (20), Mikasa (20), Kashima (16), Katori (16), Satsuma (12), Aki (11), Settsu (10), Ikoma (14), Ibuki (12), Kurama (11), Amagi (0), Akagi (0), Kaga (0), Tosa (0), Takao (0), Atago (0). Projected program 8 ships not laid down.*	8	2
1922				8	2
1923				8	2
1924				8	2
1925				8	2
1926				8	2
1927				8	2
1928				8	2
1929				8	2
1930				8	2
1931	A			8	2
1932	B			8	2
1933	C			8	2
1934	D	A	Kongo (21)	7	3
1935	E	B	Hiyei (21), Haruna (20)	5	4
1936	F	C	Kirishima (21)	4	5
1937	G	D	Fuso (22)	3	6
1938	H	E	Yamashiro (21)	2	7
1939	I	F	Ise (22)	1	8
1940		G	Hiuga (22)	0	9
1941		H	Nagato (21)	0	9
1942		I	Mutsu (21)	0	9

*Japan may retain the *Shikishima* and *Asahi* for noncombatant purposes, after complying with the provisions of Part 2, III, (b).

NOTE.—A, B, C, D, etc., represent individual capital ships of 35,000 tons standard displacement, laid down and completed in the years specified.

NOTE APPLICABLE TO ALL THE TABLES IN SECTION II

The order above prescribed in which ships are to be scrapped is in accordance with their age. It is understood that when replacement begins according to the above tables the order of scrapping in the case of the ships of each of the Contracting Powers may be varied at its option; provided, however, that such Power shall scrap in each year the number of ships above stated.

PART 4

Definitions

For the purposes of the present Treaty, the following expressions are to be understood in the sense defined in this Part.

CAPITAL SHIP

A capital ship, in the case of ships hereafter built, is defined as a vessel of war, not an aircraft carrier, whose displacement exceeds 10,000 tons (10,160 metric tons) standard displacement, or which carries a gun with a calibre exceeding 8 inches (203 millimetres).

AIRCRAFT CARRIER

An aircraft carrier is defined as a vessel of war with a displacement in excess of 10,000 tons (10,160 metric tons) standard displacement designed for the specific and exclusive purpose of carrying aircraft. It must be so constructed that aircraft can be launched therefrom and landed thereon, and not designed and constructed for carrying a more powerful armament than that allowed to it under Article IX or Article X as the case may be.

STANDARD DISPLACEMENT

The standard displacement of a ship is the displacement of the ship complete, fully manned, engined, and equipped ready for sea, including all armament and ammunition, equipment, outfit, provisions and fresh water for crew, miscellaneous stores and implements of every description that are intended to be carried in war, but without fuel or reserve feed water on board.

The word "ton" in the present Treaty, except in the expression "metric tons", shall be understood to mean the ton of 2240 pounds (1016 kilos).

Vessels now completed shall retain their present ratings of displacement tonnage in accordance with their national system of measurement. However, a Power expressing displacement in metric tons shall be considered for the application of the present Treaty as owning only the equivalent displacement in tons of 2240 pounds.

A vessel completed hereafter shall be rated at its displacement tonnage when in the standard condition defined herein.

CHAPTER III

MISCELLANEOUS PROVISIONS

ARTICLE XXI

If during the term of the present Treaty the requirements of the national security of any Contracting Power in respect of naval defence are, in the opinion of that Power, materially affected by any change of circumstances, the Contracting Powers will, at the request of such Power, meet in conference with a view to the reconsideration of the provisions of the Treaty and its amendment by mutual agreement.

In view of possible technical and scientific developments, the United States, after consultation with the other Contracting Powers, shall arrange for a conference of all the Contracting Powers which shall convene as soon as possible after the expiration of eight years from the coming into force of the present Treaty to consider what changes, if any, in the Treaty may be necessary to meet such developments.

Article XXII

Whenever any Contracting Power shall become engaged in a war which in its opinion affects the naval defence of its national security, such Power may after notice to the other Contracting Powers suspend for the period of hostilities its obligations under the present Treaty other than those under Articles XIII and XVII, provided that such Power shall notify the other Contracting Powers that the emergency is of such a character as to require such suspension.

The remaining Contracting Powers shall in such case consult together with a view to agreement as to what temporary modifications if any should be made in the Treaty as between themselves. Should such consultation not produce agreement, duly made in accordance with the constitutional methods of the respective Powers, any one of said Contracting Powers may, by giving notice to the other Contracting Powers, suspend for the period of hostilities its obligations under the present Treaty, other than those under Articles XIII and XVII.

On the cessation of hostilities the Contracting Powers will meet in conference to consider what modifications, if any, should be made in the provisions of the present Treaty.

Article XXIII

The present Treaty shall remain in force until December 31st, 1936, and in case none of the Contracting Powers shall have given notice two years before that date of its intention to terminate the Treaty, it shall continue in force until the expiration of two years from the date on which notice of termination shall be given by one of the Contracting Powers, whereupon the Treaty shall terminate as regards all the Contracting Powers. Such notice shall be communicated in writing to the Government of the United States, which shall immediately transmit a certified copy of the notification to the other Powers and inform them of the date on which it was received. The notice shall be deemed to have been given and shall take effect on that date. In the event of notice of termination being given by the Government of the United States, such notice shall be given to the diplomatic representatives at

Washington of the other Contracting Powers, and the notice shall be deemed to have been given and shall take effect on the date of the communication made to the said diplomatic representatives.

Within one year of the date on which a notice of termination by any Power has taken effect, all the Contracting Powers shall meet in conference.

ARTICLE XXIV

The present Treaty shall be ratified by the Contracting Powers in accordance with their respective constitutional methods and shall take effect on the date of the deposit of all the ratifications, which shall take place at Washington as soon as possible. The Government of the United States will transmit to the other Contracting Powers a certified copy of the procès-verbal of the deposit of ratifications.

The present Treaty, of which the French and English texts are both authentic, shall remain deposited in the archives of the Government of the United States, and duly certified copies thereof shall be transmitted by that Government to the other Contracting Powers.

In faith whereof the above-named Plenipotentiaries have signed the present Treaty.

Done at the City of Washington the sixth day of February, One Thousand Nine Hundred and Twenty-Two.

[For the United States:]		[For the Union of South Africa:]
CHARLES EVANS HUGHES [SEAL]		ARTHUR JAMES BALFOUR [SEAL]
HENRY CABOT LODGE [SEAL]		[For India:]
OSCAR W. UNDERWOOD [SEAL]		V. S. SRINIVASA SASTRI [SEAL]
ELIHU ROOT [SEAL]		[For France:]
[For the United Kingdom:]		A. SARRAUT [SEAL]
ARTHUR JAMES BALFOUR [SEAL]		JUSSERAND [SEAL]
LEE OF FAREHAM [SEAL]		[For Italy:]
A. C. GEDDES [SEAL]		CARLO SCHANZER [SEAL]
[For the Dominion of Canada:]		V. ROLANDI RICCI [SEAL]
R. L. BORDEN [SEAL]		LUIGI ALBERTINI [SEAL]
[For the Commonwealth of Australia:]		[For Japan:]
G. F. PEARCE [SEAL]		T. KATO [SEAL]
[For the Dominion of New Zealand:]		K. SHIDEHARA [SEAL]
JOHN W. SALMOND [SEAL]		M. HANIHARA [SEAL]

PROCÈS-VERBAL OF DEPOSIT OF RATIFICATIONS OF THE TREATY BETWEEN THE UNITED STATES OF AMERICA, THE BRITISH EMPIRE, FRANCE, ITALY AND JAPAN, TO LIMIT THEIR RESPECTIVE NAVAL ARMAMENT, CONCLUDED AT WASHINGTON, FEBRUARY 6, 1922

In conformity with Article XXIV of the Treaty between the United States of America, the British Empire, France, Italy and Japan to limit their respective naval armament, concluded at Washington on February 6, 1922, the undersigned representatives of the United States of America, the British Empire, France, Italy and Japan, this day met at the Department of State at Washington to proceed with the deposit with the Government of the United States of America of the instruments of ratification of the said Treaty by the governments they represent.

The representative of the Government of the French Republic made the following declaration:

"The French Government considers and always has considered that the ratios of total tonnage in capital ships and aircraft carriers allowed to the several Contracting Powers do not represent the respective importance of the maritime interests of those Powers and cannot be extended to the categories of vessels other than those for which they were expressly stipulated." [Translation.]

The instruments of ratification produced having been found upon examination to be in due form, are entrusted to the Government of the United States of America to be deposited in the archives of the Department of State.

In witness whereof, the present procès-verbal, of which a certified copy will be sent by the Government of the United States of America to each one of the Powers signatory to the said treaty, is signed.

Done at Washington, August 17, 1923, at 12 o'clock.

[For the United States of America:]
CHARLES EVANS HUGHES   [SEAL]

[For the British Empire:]
H. G. CHILTON   [SEAL]

[For France:]
ANDRE DE LABOULAYE   [SEAL]

[For Italy:]
AUGUSTO ROSSO   [SEAL]

[For Japan:]
M. HANIHARA   [SEAL]

INSULAR POSSESSIONS AND DOMINIONS IN THE PACIFIC (SUPPLEMENT TO FOUR–POWER TREATY)

Agreement supplementary to the treaty of December 13, 1921, signed at Washington February 6, 1922; procès-verbal of deposit of ratifications signed at Washington August 17, 1923

Senate advice and consent to ratification, with a reservation and understanding, March 27, 1922 [1]

Ratified by the President of the United States, with a reservation and understanding, June 9, 1923 [1]

Entered into force August 17, 1923

Proclaimed by the President of the United States August 21, 1923

Terminated December 31, 1936, upon termination of treaty of December 13, 1921

43 Stat. 1652; Treaty Series 670

The United States of America, the British Empire, France and Japan have, through their respective Plenipotentiaries, agreed upon the following stipulations supplementary to the Quadruple Treaty signed at Washington on December 13, 1921: [2]

The term "insular possessions and insular dominions" used in the aforesaid Treaty shall, in its application to Japan, include only Karafuto (or the Southern portion of the island of Sakhalin), Formosa and the Pescadores, and the islands under the mandate of Japan.

The present agreement shall have the same force and effect as the said Treaty to which it is supplementary.

The provisions of Article IV of the aforesaid Treaty of December 13, 1921, relating to ratification shall be applicable to the present Agreement, which in French and English shall remain deposited in the Archives of the Government of the United States, and duly certified copies thereof shall be transmitted by that Government to each of the other Contracting Powers.

In faith whereof the respective Plenipotentiaries have signed the present Agreement.

---

[1] For text of U.S. reservation and understanding, see p. 373.

[2] TS 669, *ante*, p. 332.

Done at the City of Washington, the sixth day of February, One Thousand Nine Hundred and Twenty-two.

[For the United States:]
  CHARLES EVANS HUGHES [SEAL]
  HENRY CABOT LODGE [SEAL]
  OSCAR W. UNDERWOOD [SEAL]
  ELIHU ROOT [SEAL]

[For the United Kingdom:]
  ARTHUR JAMES BALFOUR [SEAL]
  LEE OF FAREHAM [SEAL]
  A. C. GEDDES [SEAL]

  [For the Dominion of Canada:]
  R. L. BORDEN [SEAL]

[For the Commonwealth of Australia:]
  G. F. PEARCE [SEAL]

[For the Dominion of New Zealand:]
  JOHN W. SALMOND [SEAL]

[For the Union of South Africa:]
  ARTHUR JAMES BALFOUR [SEAL]

[For India:]
  V. S. SRINIVASA SASTRI [SEAL]

[For France:]
  A. SARRAUT [SEAL]
  JUSSERAND [SEAL]

[For Japan:]
  T. KATO [SEAL]
  K. SHIDEHARA [SEAL]
  M. HANIHARA [SEAL]

PROCÈS-VERBAL OF DEPOSIT OF RATIFICATIONS OF THE AGREEMENT BE-
TWEEN THE UNITED STATES OF AMERICA, THE BRITISH EMPIRE, FRANCE
AND JAPAN, CONCLUDED AT WASHINGTON, FEBRUARY 6, 1922, SUPPLE-
MENTARY TO THE TREATY CONCLUDED BETWEEN THEM ON DECEMBER
13, 1921, RELATING TO THEIR INSULAR POSSESSIONS AND INSULAR
DOMINIONS IN THE REGION OF THE PACIFIC OCEAN

In conformity with the Agreement between the United States of America, the British Empire, France and Japan, concluded at Washington on February 6, 1922, supplementary to the Treaty concluded between the same Four Powers at Washington on December 13, 1921, relating to their insular possessions and insular dominions in the region of the Pacific Ocean, the undersigned representatives of the United States of America, the British Empire, France and Japan this day met at the Department of State at Washington to proceed with the deposit with the Government of the United States of America of the instruments of ratification of the said Agreement by the governments they respectively represent.

The representative of the United States of America declared that the instrument of ratification of the United States is deposited with the reservation and understanding recited in the ratification, and which repeats the declaration of intent and understanding signed on December 13, 1921, by the Plenipotentiaries of the Four Powers Signatories of the Treaty of December 13, 1921, as follows:

"1. That the Four Power Treaty relating to Pacific Possessions shall apply to the Mandated Islands in the Pacific Ocean; provided, however, that the making of the Treaty shall not be deemed to be an assent on the part of the United States of America to the mandates and shall not preclude agreements between the United States of America and the Mandatory Powers respectively in relation to the mandated islands.

"2. That the controversies to which the second paragraph of Article I of the Four Power Treaty relating to Pacific Possessions refers shall not be taken to embrace questions which according to principles of international law lie exclusively within the domestic jurisdiction of the respective Powers."

The instruments of ratification produced, having been found upon examination to be in due form, are entrusted to the Government of the United States of America to be deposited in the archives of the Department of State.

In witness whereof, the present procès-verbal, of which a certified copy will be sent by the Government of the United States of America to each one of the Powers signatory to the said Treaty, is signed.

Done at Washington, August 17, 1923, at 12 o'clock.

For the United States of America:		For France:	
CHARLES EVANS HUGHES	[SEAL]	ANDRÉ DE LABOULAYE	[SEAL]
For the British Empire:		For Japan:	
H. G. CHILTON	[SEAL]	M. HANIHARA	[SEAL]

PRINCIPLES AND POLICIES CONCERNING CHINA (NINE–POWER TREATY)

Treaty signed at Washington February 6, 1922
Senate advice and consent to ratification March 30, 1922
Ratified by the President of the United States June 9, 1923
Procès-verbal of deposit of ratifications (including that of the United States) at Washington dated August 5, 1925
Entered into force August 5, 1925
Proclaimed by the President of the United States August 5, 1925

44 Stat. 2113; Treaty Series 723

The United States of America, Belgium, the British Empire, China, France, Italy, Japan, the Netherlands and Portugal:

Desiring to adopt a policy designed to stabilize conditions in the Far East, to safeguard the rights and interests of China, and to promote intercourse between China and the other Powers upon the basis of equality of opportunity;

Have resolved to conclude a treaty for that purpose and to that end have appointed as their respective Plenipotentiaries;

The President of the United States of America:
Charles Evans Hughes,
Henry Cabot Lodge,
Oscar W. Underwood,
Elihu Root,
    citizens of the United States;

His Majesty the King of the Belgians:
Baron de Cartier de Marchienne, Commander of the Order of Leopold and of the Order of the Crown, His Ambassador Extraordinary and Plenipotentiary at Washington;

His Majesty the King of the United Kingdom of Great Britain and Ireland and of the British Dominions beyond the Seas, Emperor of India:
The Right Honourable Arthur James Balfour, O.M., M.P., Lord President of His Privy Council;

375

The Right Honourable Baron Lee of Fareham, G.B.E., K.C.B., First Lord of His Admiralty;

The Right Honourable Sir Auckland Campbell Geddes, K.C.B., His Ambassador Extraordinary and Plenipotentiary to the United States of America;

and

for the Dominion of Canada:

The Right Honourable Sir Robert Laird Borden, G.C.M.G., K.C.;

for the Commonwealth of Australia:

Senator the Right Honourable George Foster Pearce, Minister for Home and Territories;

for the Dominion of New Zealand:

The Honourable Sir John William Salmond, K.C., Judge of the Supreme Court of New Zealand;

for the Union of South Africa:

The Right Honourable Arthur James Balfour, O.M., M.P.;

for India:

The Right Honourable Valingman Sankaranarayana Srinivasa Sastri, Member of the Indian Council of State;

The President of the Republic of China:

Mr. Sao-Ke Alfred Sze, Envoy Extraordinary and Minister Plenipotentiary at Washington;

Mr. V. K. Wellington Koo, Envoy Extraordinary and Minister Plenipotentiary at London;

Mr. Chung-Hui Wang, former Minister of Justice;

The President of the French Republic:

Mr. Albert Sarraut, Deputy, Minister of the Colonies;

Mr. Jules J. Jusserand, Ambassador Extraordinary and Plenipotentiary to the United States of America, Grand Cross of the National Order of the Legion of Honour;

His Majesty the King of Italy:

The Honourable Carlo Schanzer, Senator of the Kingdom;

The Honourable Vittorio Rolandi Ricci, Senator of the Kingdom, His Ambassador Extraordinary and Plenipotentiary at Washington;

The Honourable Luigi Albertini, Senator of the Kingdom;

His Majesty the Emperor of Japan:

Baron Tomosaburo Kato, Minister for the Navy, Junii, a member of the First Class of the Imperial Order of the Grand Cordon of the Rising Sun with the Paulownia Flower;

Baron Kijuro Shidehara, His Ambassador Extraordinary and Plenipotentiary at Washington, Joshii, a member of the First Class of the Imperial Order of the Rising Sun;

Mr. Masanao Hanihara, Vice Minister for Foreign Affairs, Jushii, a member of the Second Class of the Imperial Order of the Rising Sun;

Her Majesty the Queen of The Netherlands:
Jonkheer Frans Beelaerts van Blokland, Her Envoy Extraordinary and Minister Plenipotentiary;
Jonkheer Willem Hendrik de Beaufort, Minister Plenipotentiary, Chargé d'Affaires at Washington;

The President of the Portuguese Republic:
Mr. José Francisco de Horta Machado da Franca, Viscount d'Alte, Envoy Extraordinary and Minister Plenipotentiary at Washington;
Mr. Ernesto Julio de Carvalho e Vasconcellos, Captain of the Portuguese Navy, Technical Director of the Colonial Office.

Who, having communicated to each other their full powers, found to be in good and due form, have agreed as follows:

ARTICLE I

The Contracting Powers, other than China, agree:

(1) To respect the sovereignty, the independence, and the territorial and administrative integrity of China; [1]

(2) To provide the fullest and most unembarrassed opportunity to China to develop and maintain for herself an effective and stable government;

(3) To use their influence for the purpose of effectually establishing and maintaining the principle of equal opportunity for the commerce and industry of all nations throughout the territory of China;

(4) To refrain from taking advantage of conditions in China in order to seek special rights or privileges which would abridge the rights of subjects or citizens of friendly States, and from countenancing action inimical to the security of such States.

ARTICLE II

The Contracting Powers agree not to enter into any treaty, agreement, arrangement, or understanding, either with one another, or, individually or collectively, with any Power or Powers, which would infringe or impair the principles stated in Article I.

ARTICLE III

With a view to applying more effectually the principles of the Open Door [2] or equality of opportunity in China for the trade and industry of all nations,

---

[1] In accordance with a recommendation of the Committee on Pacific and Far Eastern Questions, the following declaration on the part of China was included in the records of the conference at the sixth plenary meeting Feb. 4:

"China upon her part is prepared to give an undertaking not to alienate or lease any portion of her territory or littoral to any Power."

[2] For background on the "open door" policy, see *ante,* vol. 1, p. 278.

the Contracting Powers, other than China, agree that they will not seek, nor support their respective nationals in seeking—

(a) any arrangement which might purport to establish in favour of their interests any general superiority of rights with respect to commercial or economic development in any designated region of China;

(b) any such monopoly or preference as would deprive the nationals of any other Power of the right of undertaking any legitimate trade or industry in China, or of participating with the Chinese Government, or with any local authority, in any category of public enterprise, or which by reason of its scope, duration or geographical extent is calculated to frustrate the practical application of the principle of equal opportunity.

It is understood that the foregoing stipulations of this Article are not to be so construed as to prohibit the acquisition of such properties or rights as may be necessary to the conduct of a particular commercial, industrial, or financial undertaking or to the encouragement of invention and research.

China undertakes to be guided by the principles stated in the foregoing stipulations of this Article in dealing with applications for economic rights and privileges from Governments and nationals of all foreign countries, whether parties to the present Treaty or not.

ARTICLE IV

The Contracting Powers agree not to support any agreements by their respective nationals with each other designed to create Spheres of Influence or to provide for the enjoyment of mutually exclusive opportunities in designated parts of Chinese territory.

ARTICLE V

China agrees that, throughout the whole of the railways in China, she will not exercise or permit unfair discrimination of any kind. In particular there shall be no discrimination whatever, direct or indirect, in respect of charges or of facilities on the ground of the nationality of passengers or the countries from which or to which they are proceeding, or the origin or ownership of goods or the country from which or to which they are consigned, or the nationality or ownership of the ship or other means of conveying such passengers or goods before or after their transport on the Chinese Railways.

The Contracting Powers, other than China, assume a corresponding obligation in respect of any of the aforesaid railways over which they or their nationals are in a position to exercise any control in virtue of any concession, special agreement or otherwise.

ARTICLE VI

The Contracting Powers, other than China, agree fully to respect China's rights as a neutral in time of war to which China is not a party; and China declares that when she is a neutral she will observe the obligations of neutrality.

ARTICLE VII

The Contracting Powers agree that, whenever a situation arises which in the opinion of any one of them involves the application of the stipulations of the present Treaty, and renders desirable discussion of such application, there shall be full and frank communication between the Contracting Powers concerned.

ARTICLE VIII

Powers not signatory to the present Treaty, which have Governments recognized by the Signatory Powers and which have treaty relations with China, shall be invited to adhere to the present Treaty. To this end the Government of the United States will make the necessary communications to nonsignatory Powers and will inform the Contracting Powers of the replies received. Adherence by any Power shall become effective on receipt of notice thereof by the Government of the United States.

ARTICLE IX

The present Treaty shall be ratified by the Contracting Powers in accordance with their respective constitutional methods and shall take effect on the date of the deposit of all the ratifications, which shall take place at Washington as soon as possible. The Government of the United States will transmit to the other Contracting Powers a certified copy of the procès-verbal of the deposit of ratifications.

The present Treaty, of which the French and English texts are both authentic, shall remain deposited in the archives of the Government of the United States, and duly certified copies thereof shall be transmitted by that Government to the other Contracting Powers.

In faith whereof the above-named Plenipotentiaries have signed the present Treaty.

Done at the City of Washington the Sixth day of February One Thousand Nine Hundred and Twenty-Two.

[For the United States:]
CHARLES EVANS HUGHES   [SEAL]
HENRY CABOT LODGE   [SEAL]
OSCAR W. UNDERWOOD   [SEAL]
ELIHU ROOT   [SEAL]

[For Belgium:]
BARON DE CARTIER DE MAR-
CHIENNE   [SEAL]

[For the United Kingdom:]
ARTHUR JAMES BALFOUR   [SEAL]
LEE OF FAREHAM   [SEAL]
A. C. GEDDES   [SEAL]

[For the Dominion of Canada:]
R. L. BORDEN   [SEAL]

[For the Commonwealth of Australia:]
G. F. PEARCE   [SEAL]

[For the Dominion of New Zealand:]
JOHN W. SALMOND   [SEAL]

[For the Union of South Africa:]
ARTHUR JAMES BALFOUR   [SEAL]

[For India:]
V. S. SRINIVASA SASTRI   [SEAL]

[For China:]
    SAO-KE ALFRED SZE   [SEAL]
    V. K. WELLINGTON KOO   [SEAL]
    CHUNG-HUI WANG   [SEAL]

[For France:]
    A. SARRAUT   [SEAL]
    JUSSERAND   [SEAL]

[For Italy:]
    CARLO SCHANZER   [SEAL]
    V. ROLANDI RICCI   [SEAL]
    LUIGI ALBERTINI   [SEAL]

[For Japan:]
    T. KATO   [SEAL]
    K. SHIDEHARA   [SEAL]
    M. HANIHARA   [SEAL]

[For the Netherlands:]
    BEELAERTS VAN BLOKLAND   [SEAL]
    W. DE BEAUFORT   [SEAL]

[For Portugal:]
    ALTE   [SEAL]
    ERNESTO DE VASCONCELLOS   [SEAL]

REVISION OF CHINESE CUSTOMS TARIFF

Treaty signed at Washington February 6, 1922
Senate advice and consent to ratification March 30, 1922
Ratified by the President of the United States June 9, 1923
Procès-verbal of deposit of ratifications (including that of the United States) at Washington dated August 5, 1925
Entered into force August 5, 1925
Proclaimed by the President of the United States August 5, 1925

44 Stat. 2122; Treaty Series 724

The United States of America, Belgium, the British Empire, China, France, Italy, Japan, The Netherlands and Portugal:

With a view to increasing the revenues of the Chinese Government, have resolved to conclude a treaty relating to the revision of the Chinese customs tariff and cognate matters, and to that end have appointed as their Plenipotentiaries:

The President of the United States of America:
   Charles Evans Hughes,
   Henry Cabot Lodge,
   Oscar W. Underwood,
   Elihu Root,
       citizens of the United States;

His Majesty the King of the Belgians:
   Baron de Cartier de Marchienne, Commander of the Order of Leopold and of the Order of the Crown, His Ambassador Extraordinary and Plenipotentiary at Washington;

His Majesty the King of the United Kingdom of Great Britain and Ireland and of the British Dominions beyond the Seas, Emperor of India:
   The Right Honourable Arthur James Balfour, O.M., M.P., Lord President of His Privy Council;
   The Right Honourable Baron Lee of Fareham, G.B.E., K.C.B., First Lord of His Admiralty;
   The Right Honourable Sir Auckland Campbell Geddes, K.C.B., His Ambassador Extraordinary and Plenipotentiary to the United States of America;

and
  for the Dominion of Canada:
    The Right Honourable Sir Robert Laird Borden, G. C. M. G., K. C.;
  for the Commonwealth of Australia:
    Senator the Right Honourable George Foster Pearce, Minister for Home
      and Territories;
  for the Dominion of New Zealand:
    The Honourable Sir John William Salmond, K.C., Judge of the Su-
      preme Court of New Zealand;
  for the Union of South Africa:
    The Right Honourable Arthur James Balfour, O.M., M.P.;
  for India:
    The Right Honourable Valingman Sankaranarayana Srinivasa Sastri,
      Member of the Indian Council of State;

The President of the Republic of China:
    Mr. Sao-Ke Alfred Sze, Envoy Extraordinary and Minister Plenipotentiary
      at Washington;
    Mr. V. K. Wellington Koo, Envoy Extraordinary and Minister Pleni-
      potentiary at London;
    Mr. Chung-Hui Wang, former Minister of Justice;

The President of the French Republic:
    Mr. Albert Sarraut, Deputy, Minister of the Colonies;
    Mr. Jules J. Jusserand, Ambassador Extraordinary and Plenipotentiary to
      to the United States of America, Grand Cross of the National Order of
      the Legion of Honour;

His Majesty the King of Italy:
    The Honourable Carlo Schanzer, Senator of the Kingdom;
    The Honourable Vittorio Rolandi Ricci, Senator of the Kingdom, His
      Ambassador Extraordinary and Plenipotentiary at Washington;
    The Honourable Luigi Albertini, Senator of the Kingdom;

His Majesty the Emperor of Japan:
    Baron Tomosaburo Kato, Minister for the Navy, Junii, a member of the
      First Class of the Imperial Order of the Grand Cordon of the Rising
      Sun with the Paulownia Flower;
    Baron Kijuro Shidehara, His Ambassador Extraordinary and Plenipo-
      tentiary at Washington, Joshii, a member of the First Class of the Im-
      perial Order of the Rising Sun;
    Mr. Masanao Hanihara, Vice Minister for Foreign Affairs, Jushii, a mem-
      ber of the Second Class of the Imperial Order of the Rising Sun;

Her Majesty the Queen of The Netherlands:
    Jonkheer Frans Beelaerts van Blokland, Her Envoy Extraordinary and
      Minister Plenipotentiary;

Jonkheer Willem Hendrik de Beaufort, Minister Plenipotentiary, Chargé d'Affaires at Washington;

The President of the Portuguese Republic;

Mr. José Francisco de Herta Machado da Franca, Viscount d'Alte, Envoy Extraordinary and Minister Plenipotentiary at Washington;

Mr. Ernesto Julio de Carvalho e Vasconcellos, Captain of the Portuguese Navy, Technical Director of the Colonial Office;

Who, having communicated to each other their full powers, found to be in good and due form, have agreed as follows:

ARTICLE I

The representatives of the Contracting Powers having adopted, on the fourth day of February, 1922, in the City of Washington, a Resolution, which is appended as an Annex to this Article, with respect to the revision of Chinese Customs duties, for the purpose of making such duties equivalent to an effective 5 per centum ad valorem, in accordance with existing treaties concluded by China with other nations, the Contracting Powers hereby confirm the said Resolution and undertake to accept the tariff rates fixed as a result of such revision. The said tariff rates shall become effective as soon as possible but not earlier than two months after publication thereof.

ANNEX

With a view to providing additional revenue to meet the needs of the Chinese Government, the Powers represented at this Conference, namely the United States of America, Belgium, the British Empire, China, France, Italy, Japan, The Netherlands, and Portugal agree:

That the customs schedule of duties on imports into China adopted by the Tariff Revision Commission at Shanghai on December 19, 1918,[1] shall forthwith be revised so that the rates of duty shall be equivalent to 5 per cent. effective, as provided for in the several commercial treaties to which China is a party.

A Revision Commission shall meet at Shanghai, at the earliest practicable date, to effect this revision forthwith and on the general lines of the last revision.

This Commission shall be composed of representatives of the Powers above named and of representatives of any additional Powers having Governments at present recognized by the Powers represented at this Conference and who have treaties with China providing for a tariff on imports and exports not to exceed 5 per cent. ad valorem and who desire to participate therein.

The revision shall proceed as rapidly as possible with a view to its completion within four months from the date of the adoption of this Resolution by the Conference on the Limitation of Armament and Pacific and Far Eastern Questions.

The revised tariff shall become effective as soon as possible but not earlier than two months after its publication by the Revision Commission.

The Government of the United States, as convener of the present Conference, is requested forthwith to communicate the terms of this Resolution to

---

[1] For text, see John V. A. MacMurray, *Treaties and Agreements With and Concerning China, 1894–1919,* vol. II, p. 1456.

the Governments of Powers not represented at this Conference but who participated in the Revision of 1918, aforesaid.

ARTICLE II

Immediate steps shall be taken, through a Special Conference, to prepare the way for the speedy abolition of likin and for the fulfillment of the other conditions laid down in Article VIII of the Treaty of September 5th, 1902, between Great Britain and China, in Articles IV and V of the Treaty of October 8th, 1903, between the United States and China,[2] and in Article I of the Supplementary Treaty of October 8th, 1903, between Japan and China, with a view to levying the surtaxes provided for in those articles.

The Special Conference shall be composed of representatives of the Signatory Powers, and of such other Powers as may desire to participate and may adhere to the present Treaty, in accordance with the provisions of Article VIII, in sufficient time to allow their representatives to take part. It shall meet in China within three months after the coming into force of the present Treaty, on a day and at a place to be designated by the Chinese Government.

ARTICLE III

The Special Conference provided for in Article II shall consider the interim provisions to be applied prior to the abolition of likin and the fulfillment of the other conditions laid down in the articles of the treaties mentioned in Article II; and it shall authorize the levying of a surtax on dutiable imports as from such date, for such purposes, and subject to such conditions as it may determine.

The surtax shall be at a uniform rate of $2\frac{1}{2}$ per centum ad valorem, provided, that in case of certain articles of luxury which, in the opinion of the Special Conference, can bear the greater increase without unduly impeding trade, the total surtax may be increased but may not exceed 5 per centum ad valorem.

ARTICLE IV

Following the immediate revision of the customs schedule of duties on imports into China, mentioned in Article I, there shall be a further revision thereof to take effect at the expiration of four years following the completion of the aforesaid immediate revision, in order to ensure that the customs duties shall correspond to the ad valorem rates fixed by the Special Conference provided for in Article II.

Following this further revision there shall be, for the same purpose, periodical revisions of the customs schedule of duties on imports into China every seven years, in lieu of the decennial revision authorized by existing treaties with China.

---

[2] TS 430, *post.*

In order to prevent delay, any revision made in pursuance of this Article shall be effected in accordance with rules to be prescribed by the Special Conference provided for in Article II.

ARTICLE V

In all matters relating to customs duties there shall be effective equality of treatment and of opportunity for all the Contracting Powers.

ARTICLE VI

The principle of uniformity in the rates of customs duties levied at all the land and maritime frontiers of China is hereby recognized. The Special Conference provided for in Article II shall make arrangements to give practical effect to this principle; and it is authorized to make equitable adjustments in those cases in which a customs privilege to be abolished was granted in return for some local economic advantage.

In the meantime, any increase in the rates of customs duties resulting from tariff revision, or any surtax hereafter imposed in pursuance of the present Treaty, shall be levied at a uniform rate ad valorem at all land and maritime frontiers of China.

ARTICLE VII

The charge for transit passes shall be at the rate of $2\frac{1}{2}$ per centum ad valorem until the arrangements provided for by Article II come into force.

ARTICLE VIII

Powers not signatory to the present Treaty whose Governments are at present recognized by the Signatory Powers, and whose present treaties with China provide for a tariff on imports and exports not to exceed 5 per centum ad valorem, shall be invited to adhere to the present Treaty.

The Government of the United States undertakes to make the necessary communications for this purpose and to inform the Governments of the Contracting Powers of the replies received. Adherence by any Power shall become effective on receipt of notice thereof by the Government of the United States.

ARTICLE IX

The provisions of the present Treaty shall override all stipulations of treaties between China and the respective Contracting Powers which are inconsistent therewith, other than stipulations according most favored nation treatment.

ARTICLE X

The present Treaty shall be ratified by the Contracting Powers in accordance with their respective constitutional methods and shall take effect on the date of the deposit of all the ratifications, which shall take place at Washington as soon as possible. The Government of the United States will transmit to the other Contracting Powers a certified copy of the procès-verbal of the deposit of ratifications.

The present Treaty, of which the French and English texts are both authentic, shall remain deposited in the archives of the Government of the United States, and duly certified copies thereof shall be transmitted by that Government to the other Contracting Powers.

In faith whereof the above-named Plenipotentiaries have signed the present Treaty.

Done at the City of Washington the sixth day of February, One Thousand Nine Hundred and Twenty-two.

[For the United States:]
   CHARLES EVANS HUGHES   [SEAL]
   HENRY CABOT LODGE   [SEAL]
   OSCAR W. UNDERWOOD   [SEAL]
   ELIHU ROOT   [SEAL]

[For Belgium:]
   BARON DE CARTIER DE MARCHIENNE
                                [SEAL]

[For the United Kingdom:]
   ARTHUR JAMES BALFOUR   [SEAL]
   LEE OF FAREHAM   [SEAL]
   A. C. GEDDES   [SEAL]

[For the Dominion of Canada:]
   R. L. BORDEN   [SEAL]

[For the Commonwealth of Australia:]
   G. F. PEARCE   [SEAL]

[For the Dominion of New Zealand:]
   JOHN W. SALMOND   [SEAL]

[For the Union of South Africa:]
   ARTHUR JAMES BALFOUR   [SEAL]

[For India:]
   V. S. SRINIVASA SASTRI   [SEAL]

[For China:]
   SAO-KE ALFRED SZE   [SEAL]
   V. K. WELLINGTON KOO   [SEAL]
   CHUNG-HUI WANG   [SEAL]

[For France:]
   A. SARRAUT   [SEAL]
   JUSSERAND   [SEAL]

[For Italy:]
   CARLO SCHANZER   [SEAL]
   V. ROLANDI RICCI   [SEAL]
   LUIGI ALBERTINI   [SEAL]

[For Japan:]
   T. KATO   [SEAL]
   K. SHIDEHARA   [SEAL]
   M. HANIHARA   [SEAL]

[For the Netherlands:]
   BEELAERTS VAN BLOKLAND   [SEAL]
   W. DE BEAUFORT   [SEAL]

[For Portugal:]
   ALTE   [SEAL]
   ERNESTO DE VASCONCELLOS   [SEAL]

[The following statement on behalf of China was included in the records of the conference at the sixth plenary meeting February 4:

"The Chinese Delegation has the honor to inform the Committee on Far Eastern Questions of the Conference on the Limitation of Armament that the Chinese Government have no intention to effect any change which may disturb the present administration of the Chinese Maritime Customs."]

COMMISSIONS OF INQUIRY FOR SETTLEMENT OF DISPUTES (INTER–AMERICAN)

Convention signed at Washington February 7, 1923
Senate advice and consent to ratification January 28, 1925
Ratified by the President of the United States April 7, 1925
Procès-verbal of deposit of ratifications (including that of the United States) at Washington dated June 13, 1925
Entered into force June 13, 1925
Proclaimed by the President of the United States June 15, 1925

44 Stat. 2070; Treaty Series 717

CONVENTION FOR THE ESTABLISHMENT OF INTERNATIONAL COMMISSIONS OF INQUIRY

The Government of the United States of America and the Governments of the Republics of Guatemala, El Salvador, Honduras, Nicaragua and Costa Rica, desiring to unify and recast in one single convention, the conventions which the Government of the United States concluded with the Government of Guatemala on September 20, 1913,[1] with the Government of El Salvador on August 7, 1913,[2] with the Government of Honduras on November 3, 1913,[3] with the Government of Nicaragua on December 17, 1913,[4] and with the Government of Costa Rica on February 13, 1914,[5] all relating to the Establishment of International Commissions of Inquiry, have for that purpose, named as their Plenipotentiaries:

The President of the United States of America:

The Honorable Charles E. Hughes, Secretary of State of the United States of America.

The Honorable Sumner Welles, Envoy Extraordinary and Minister Plenipotentiary.

---

[1] TS 598, *post.*
[2] S. Ex. K, 63d Cong., 2d sess.; did not enter into force.
[3] TS 625, *post.*
[4] S. Ex. O, 63d Cong., 2d sess.; did not enter into force.
[5] TS 603, *post.*

The President of the Republic of Guatemala:
Señor Don Francisco Sánchez Latour, Envoy Extraordinary and Minister Plenipotentiary to the United States of America.

The President of the Republic of El Salvador:
Señor Doctor Don Francisco Martinez Suárez, President of the Supreme Court.
Señor Doctor Don J. Gustavo Guerrero, Envoy Extraordinary and Minister Plenipotentiary to Italy and Spain.

The President of the Republic of Honduras:
Señor Doctor Don Alberto Uclés, Ex-Minister for Foreign Affairs.
Señor Doctor Don Salvador Córdova, Ex-Minister Resident in El Salvador.
Señor Don Raúl Toledo López, Chargé d'Affaires in France.

The President of the Republic of Nicaragua:
Señor General Don Emiliano Chamorro, Ex-President of the Republic and Envoy Extraordinary and Minister Plenipotentiary to the United States of America.
Señor Don Adolfo Cárdenas, Minister of Finance.
Señor Doctor Don Maximo H. Zépeda, Ex-Minister for Foreign Affairs.

The President of the Republic of Costa Rica:
Señor Licenciado Don Alfredo González Flores, Ex-President of the Republic.
Señor Licenciado Don J. Rafael Oreamuno, Envoy Extraordinary and Minister Plenipotentiary to the United States of America.

Who, after having exhibited to one another their respective full powers which were found to be in good and proper form, have agreed upon the following articles:

ARTICLE I

When two or more of the Contracting Parties shall have failed to adjust satisfactorily through diplomatic channels a controversy originating in some divergence or difference of opinion regarding questions of fact, relative to failure to comply with the provisions of any of the treaties or conventions existing between them and which affect neither the sovereign and independent existence of any of the signatory Republics, nor their honor or vital interests, the Parties bind themselves to institute a Commission of Inquiry with the object of facilitating the settlement of the dispute by means of an impartial inquiry into the facts.

This obligation ceases if the parties in dispute should agree by common accord to submit the question to arbitration or to the decision of another Tribunal.

A Commission of Inquiry shall not be formed except at the request of one of the Parties directly interested in the investigation of the facts which it is sought to elucidate.

ARTICLE II

Once the case contemplated in the preceding article has arisen, the Parties shall by common accord draw up a protocol in which shall be stated the question or questions of fact which it is desired to elucidate.

When, in the judgment of one of the interested Governments, it has been impossible to reach an agreement upon the terms of the Protocol, the Commission will proceed with the investigation, taking as a basis the diplomatic correspondence upon the matter, which has passed between the parties.

ARTICLE III

Within the period of thirty days subsequent to the date on which the exchange of ratifications of the present Treaty has been completed, each of the Parties which have ratified it shall proceed to nominate five of its nationals, to form a permanent list of Commissioners. The Governments shall have the right to change their respective nominations whenever they should deem it advisable, notifying the other Contracting Parties.

ARTICLE IV

When the formation of a Commission of Inquiry may be in order, each of the Parties directly interested in the dispute shall be represented on the Commission by one of its nationals, selected from the permanent list. The Commissioners selected by the Parties shall by common accord, choose a President who shall be one of the persons included in the permanent list by any of the Governments which has no interest in the dispute.

In default of said common agreement, the President shall be designated by lot, but in this case each of the Parties shall have the right to challenge no more than two of the persons selected in the drawing.

Whenever there shall be more than two Governments, directly interested in a dispute and the interests of two or more of them be identical, the Government or Governments, which may be parties to the dispute, shall have the right to increase the number of their Commissioners from among the members of the permanent list nominated by said Government or Governments, as far as it may be necessary, so that both sides in the dispute may always have equal representation on the Commission.

In case of a tie, the President of the Commission shall have two votes.

If for any reason any one of the members appointed to form the Commission should fail to appear, the procedure for his replacement shall be the same as that followed for his appointment. While they may be members of a Commission of Inquiry, the Commissioners shall enjoy the immunities which the laws of the country, where the Commission meets, may confer on members of the National Congress.

The diplomatic representatives of any of the Contracting Parties accredited to any of the Governments which may have an interest in the questions which it is desired to elucidate, shall not be members of a Commission.

ARTICLE V

The Commission shall be empowered to examine all the facts, antecedents, and circumstances relating to the question or questions which may be the object of the investigation, and when it renders its report it shall elucidate said facts, antecedents, and circumstances and shall have the right to recommend any solutions or adjustments which, in its opinion, may be pertinent, just and advisable.

ARTICLE VI

The findings of the Commission will be considered as reports upon the disputes, which were the objects of the investigation, but will not have the value or force of judicial decisions or arbitral awards.

ARTICLE VII

In the case of arbitration or complaint before the Tribunal created by a Convention signed by the five Republics of Central America, on the same date as this Convention,[6] the reports of the Commission of Inquiry may be presented as evidence by any of the litigant Parties.

ARTICLE VIII

The Commission of Inquiry shall meet on the day and in the place designated in the respective protocol and failing this, in the place to be determined by the same Commission, and once installed it shall have the right to go to any localities which it shall deem proper for the discharge of its duties. The Contracting Parties pledge themselves to place at the disposal of the Commission, or of its agents, all the means and facilities necessary for the fulfilment of its mission.

ARTICLE IX

The signatory Governments grant to all the Commissions which may be constituted the power to summon and swear in witnesses and to receive evidence and testimony.

ARTICLE X

During the investigation the Parties shall be heard and may have the right to be represented by one or more agents and counsel.

---

[6] For text, see *Conference on Central American Affairs, Washington, December 4, 1922–February 7, 1923* (U.S. Government Printing Office, 1923), p. 296.

ARTICLE XI

All members of the Commission shall take oath before the highest judicial authority of the place where it may meet, duly and faithfully to discharge their duties.

ARTICLE XII

The Inquiry shall be conducted so that both Parties must be heard. Consequently, the Commission shall notify each Party of the statements of fact submitted by the other, and shall fix periods of time in which to receive evidence.

Once the Parties are notified, the Commission shall proceed to the investigation, even though they fail to appear.

ARTICLE XIII

As soon as the Commission of Inquiry is organized, it shall, at the request of any of the Parties to the dispute, have the right to fix the status in which the Parties must remain, in order that the conditions may not be aggravated and matters may remain in the same state pending the rendering of the report by the Commission.

ARTICLE XIV

The report of the Commission shall be published within three months, to be reckoned from the date of its inauguration unless the Parties directly interested decrease or increase the time by mutual consent.

The report shall be signed by all the members of the Commission. Should one or more of them refuse to sign it, note shall be taken of the fact, and the report shall always be valid provided it obtains a majority vote.

In every case the vote of the minority, if any, shall be published with the report of the Commission.

One copy of the report of the Commission and of the vote of the minority, if any, shall be sent to each of the Ministries of Foreign Affairs of the Contracting Parties.

ARTICLE XV

Each Party shall bear its own expenses and a proportionate share of the general expenses of the Commission.

The President of the Commission shall receive a monthly compensation of not less than 500 dollars, American gold, in addition to his travelling expenses.

ARTICLE XVI

The present Convention, signed in one original, shall be deposited with the Government of the United States of America, which Government shall furnish to each of the other Signatory Governments an authenticated copy thereof. It shall be ratified by the President of the United States of America, by and with the advice and consent of the Senate thereof, and by the Executive and Legislative Powers of the Republics of Guatemala, El Salvador, Honduras, Nicaragua, and Costa Rica, in conformity with their constitutions and laws.

The ratifications shall be deposited with the Government of the United States of America, which will furnish to each of the other Governments an authenticated copy of the procès verbal of the deposit of ratification. It shall take effect for the parties which ratify it immediately after the day on which at least three of the Contracting Governments deposit their ratifications with the Government of the United States of America. It will continue in force for a period of ten years, and shall remain in force thereafter for a period of twelve months from the date on which any one of the Contracting Governments shall have given notification to the others, in proper form, of its desire to denounce it.

The denunciation of this Convention by one or more of the said Contracting Parties shall leave it in force for the Parties which have ratified it but have not denounced it, provided that these be no less than three in number. Should any Central American States bound by this Convention form a single political entity, this Convention shall be considered in force as between the new entity and the Contracting Republics, which may have remained separate, provided that these be no less than two in number. Any of the Signatory Republics, which should fail to ratify this Convention, shall have the right to adhere to it while it is in force.

In witness whereof the above-named Plenipotentiaries have signed the present convention and affixed thereto their respective seals.

Done at the City of Washington, the seventh day of February, one thousand nine hundred and twenty-three.

[For the United States:]
    CHARLES E. HUGHES   [SEAL]
    SUMNER WELLES   [SEAL]

[For Guatemala:]
    FRANCISCO SÁNCHEZ LATOUR   [SEAL]

[For El Salvador:]
    F. MARTÍNEZ SUÁREZ   [SEAL]
    J. GUSTAVO GUERRERO   [SEAL]

[For Honduras:]
    ALBERTO UCLÉS   [SEAL]
    SALVADOR CÓRDOVA   [SEAL]
    RAÚL TOLEDO LÓPEZ   [SEAL]

[For Nicaragua:]
    EMILIANO CHAMORRO   [SEAL]
    ADOLFO CÁRDENAS   [SEAL]
    MÁXIMO H. ZEPEDA   [SEAL]

[For Costa Rica:]
    ALFREDO GONZÁLEZ   [SEAL]
    J. RAFAEL OREAMUNO   [SEAL]

INTERNATIONAL CENTRAL AMERICAN TRIBUNAL

Protocol signed at Washington February 7, 1923
Entered into force February 7, 1923

> *Conference on Central American Affairs,*
> *Washington, December 4, 1922–February*
> *7, 1923* (U.S. Government Printing Office,
> 1923), p. 401; 1923 For. Rel. (I) 327

PROTOCOL OF AN AGREEMENT BETWEEN THE GOVERNMENT OF THE UNITED STATES OF AMERICA AND GUATEMALA, EL SALVADOR, HONDURAS, NICARAGUA AND COSTA RICA, WHEREBY THE FORMER WILL DESIGNATE FIFTEEN OF ITS CITIZENS TO SERVE IN THE TRIBUNAL WHICH MAY BE CREATED IN CONFORMITY WITH THE TERMS OF THE CONVENTION ESTABLISHING AN INTERNATIONAL CENTRAL AMERICAN TRIBUNAL

I

The Governments of Guatemala, El Salvador, Honduras, Nicaragua and Costa Rica have communicated to the Government of the United States of America the Convention signed by them on this date for the establishment of an International Central American Tribunal,[1] and at the same time have requested the Government of the United States to cooperate with them for the realization of the purposes of said Convention in the manner indicated therein.

II

The Government of the United States of America herewith expresses its full sympathy and accord with the purposes of the aforementioned Convention, and desires to state that it will gladly cooperate with the Governments of the Central American Republics in the realization of said purposes. With this end in view, the Government of the United States of America will designate fifteen of its citizens who meet the necessary requirements and may serve

---

[1] For text, see *Conference on Central American Affairs, Washington, December 4, 1922–February 7, 1923* (U.S. Government Printing Office, 1923), p. 296.

in the Tribunals that will be created in conformity with the terms of said Convention.

Washington, February seventh, nineteen hundred and twenty-three.

[For the United States:]		[For Nicaragua:]	
CHARLES E. HUGHES [SEAL]		EMILIANO CHAMORRO [SEAL]	
SUMNER WELLES [SEAL]		ADOLFO CÁRDENAS [SEAL]	
[For Guatemala:]		MÁXIMO H. ZEPEDA [SEAL]	
F. SÁNCHEZ LATOUR [SEAL]		[For Costa Rica:]	
MARCIAL PREM [SEAL]		ALFREDO GONZÁLEZ [SEAL]	
[For El Salvador:]		J. RAFAEL OREAMUNO [SEAL]	
F. MARTÍNEZ SUÁREZ [SEAL]			
J. GUSTAVO GUERRERO [SEAL]			
[For Honduras:]			
ALBERTO UCLÉS [SEAL]			
SALVADOR CÓRDOVA [SEAL]			
RAÚL TOLEDO LÓPEZ [SEAL]			

PROTECTION OF COMMERCIAL, INDUSTRIAL, AND AGRICULTURAL TRADEMARKS AND COMMERCIAL NAMES (INTER–AMERICAN)

Convention signed at Santiago April 28, 1923
Senate advice and consent to ratification, with understandings or conditions, February 24, 1925 [1]
Ratified by the President of the United States, with understandings or conditions, April 7, 1925 [1]
Ratification of the United States deposited at Santiago June 16, 1925
Entered into force September 30, 1926
Proclaimed by the President of the United States January 12, 1927
Replaced by convention and protocol of February 20, 1929, [2] *as between contracting parties to the later convention*

44 Stat. 2494; Treaty Series 751

CONVENTION FOR THE PROTECTION OF COMMERCIAL, INDUSTRIAL AND AGRICULTURAL TRADE MARKS AND COMMERCIAL NAMES

Their Excellencies the Presidents of Venezuela, Panama, United States of America, Uruguay, Ecuador, Chile, Guatemala, Nicaragua, Costa Rica, Brazil, Salvador, Colombia, Cuba, Paraguay, Dominican Republic, Honduras, Argentine Republic and Haití.

Being desirous that their respective countries may be represented at the Fifth International Conference of American States, have sent thereto, the following Delegates, duly authorized to approve the recommendations, resolutions, conventions and treaties which they might deem advantageous to the interest of America:

---

[1] The U.S. understandings or conditions read as follows:

"First, that in section 1 of Article VIII the words 'and to which they give course for the purposes,' the equivalents of which appear in the Spanish, Portuguese, and French texts of the convention, shall be inserted in the English text after the word 'registration,' so that the English text of the section shall read as follows:

" 'Section 1. To keep a detailed record of the applications for the recognition of marks received through the national offices of registration and to which they give course for the purposes of this convention, as well as of all assignments or transfers thereof and of all notices pertaining thereto.'

"Second, that in Article II of the Appendix, subheading C, line 2, the words 'for

395

Venezuela: César Zumeta, José Austria;

Panamá: Narciso Garay, José Lefevre;

United States of America: Henry P. Fletcher, Frank B. Kellogg, Atlee Pomerene, Willard Saulsbury, Frank C. Partridge, George E. Vincent, William Eric Fowler, Leo S. Rowe;

Uruguay: J. Antonio Buero, Eugenio Martínez Thedy;

Ecuador: Rafael M. Arízaga, José Rafael Bustamante, Dr. Alberto Muñoz Vernaza;

Chile: Agustín Edwards, Manuel Rivas Vicuña, Carlos Aldunate Solar, Luis Barros Borgoño, Emilio Bello Codesido, Antonio Huneeus, Alcibíades Roldán, Guillermo Subercaseaux, Alejandro del Río;

Guatemala: Eduardo Poirier, Máximo Soto Hall;

Nicaragua: Carlos Cuadra Pasos, Arturo Elizondo;

Costa Rica: Alejandro Alvarado Quirós;

United States of Brazil: Afranio de Mello Franco, Sylvino Gurgel do Amaral, J. de P. Rodríguez Alves, A. de Ipanema Moreira, Helio Lobo;

El Salvador: Cecilio Bustamante;

Colombia: Guillermo Valencia, Laureano Gómez, Carlos Uribe Echeverri;

Cuba: José C. Vidal y Caro, Carlos García Vélez, Arístides Agüero, Manuel Márquez Sterling;

Paraguay: Manuel Gondra;

Dominican Republic: Tulio M. Cestero;

Honduras: Benjamín Villaseca Mujica;

Footnote continued from p. 395—

registration,' the equivalents of which appear in the Spanish, Portuguese, and French texts, shall be inserted in the English text after the word 'application' so that the English text of the line shall read as follows:

" '2. The date of the application for registration in the State of first registration or deposit.'

"Third, that the expressions in Article I 'Without prejudice to the rights of third parties' and in Article II 'in the absence of other proof of ownership of a mark' are, and shall be, interpreted to protect every user of a trade-mark in the United States having ownership thereof by reason of adoption and use, and with or without subsequent registration, from any claim of priority under this convention based upon an application or a deposit in a signatory State subsequent to the actual date of such adoption and use in the United States.

"Fourth, that the expression 'legal protection for his mark' in Section 2(a) of Article V shall be interpreted to include ownership of the mark in the United States acquired by adoption and use and with or without subsequent registration.

"Fifth, that nothing contained in this convention shall take away or lessen any trade-mark right or any right to use a trade-mark of any person residing or doing business in the United States heretofore or hereafter lawfully acquired under the common law or by virtue of the statutes of the several States or of the United States; . . . ."

² TS 833, *post,* p. 751.

Argentine Republic: Manuel Augusto Montes de Oca, Fernando Saguier, Manuel Malbrán;

Haití: Arturo Rameau.

Who, after having presented their credentials and the same having been found in due and proper form, have agreed upon the following Convention for the Protection of Commercial, Industrial and Agricultural Trade-Marks, and Commercial Names, which shall be regarded as revision of the Convention of Buenos Aires of 1910.[3]

ARTICLE I

Section 1. The High Contracting Parties agree that any commercial, industrial or agricultural trade-mark registered or deposited in any of the States signatory of the Convention, by a person domiciled in any of such States, either directly, or through his duly authorized representative, may obtain in the other signatory States the same protection granted by them to the marks registered or deposited in their own territory, without prejudice to the rights of third parties and provided that the formalities and conditions required by the domestic law of each State, as well as the following requirements, are complied with:

a) Any person interested in the registration or deposit of the mark shall present to the proper Inter American Bureau through the proper office of the State of first registration or deposit, an application for recognition of the rights claimed, in accordance with the requirements prescribed in the Appendix of this Convention, which is declared to be a part hereof.

b) He shall pay, besides the fees of charges established by the domestic legislation of each State in which recognition of rights is desired, and other expenses incident to such recognition, a fee equivalent in value to fifty dollars ($50.00) United States gold, this sum to be paid only once for each period and for a single mark. Such fee shall be used to cover the expenses of the said Inter American Bureau.

Section 2. The period during which protection is granted shall be the same as that accorded by the laws of the particular State.

Section 3. Protection under this Convention may be renewed at the expiration of each period upon fulfillment of the requirements set forth in paragraph (*b*) hereof. Application for renewal may also be made by the interested party directly to the proper Inter American Bureau.

Section 4. Commercial names shall be protected in all the signatory States, without deposit or registration, whether the same form part of a trade mark or not, in accordance with the domestic law of each State.

---

[3] Convention signed at Buenos Aires Aug. 20, 1910 (TS 626), *ante,* vol. 1, p. 772.

ARTICLE II

The date of filing in the State where first application is made for registration or deposit through the proper Inter American Bureau, in the absence of other proof of ownership of a mark, shall determine priority for the registration or deposit of such make in any of the signatory States.

ARTICLE III

Section 1. Each signatory State, upon receipt of an application for recognition communicated by the proper Inter American Bureau, shall determine whether protection can be granted in accordance with its laws, and notify the Inter American Bureau as soon as possible of its decision.

Section 2. In case objection is made to the registration or deposit of a mark under this Convention, the term to answer such objection in the country where it is made shall begin ninety days after the date of sending notice of such objection to the proper Inter American Bureau. This Bureau shall have no other part in the controversy originated by the opposition.

ARTICLE IV

The transfer of a mark registered or deposited in one of the contracting States shall be equally recognized in each one of the other States with the same force and effect as if made in accordance with the respective laws of each one of those States, provided that the mark transferred is a mark registered or deposited in the country where the recognition of transference under this Convention is applied for, and provided that the principles of Article V of this Convention are not impaired. Notification of transfer shall be made through the proper office of the State of first registration or deposit and the proper Inter American Bureau upon payment of the fees corresponding to each State for such transference.

ARTICLE V

Section 1. In any civil, criminal or administrative proceeding arising in a country with respect to a mark, such as opposition, falsification, imitation or unauthorized appropriation, as also the false representation as to the origin of a product, the domestic authorities of the same State alone shall have jurisdiction thereof, and the precepts of law and procedure of that State shall be observed.

Section 2. When refused protection under this Convention in a signatory State because of prior registration or a pending application for registration, the proprietor of a mark claiming recognition of rights under this Convention shall have the right to seek and obtain the cancellation of the previously registered mark, upon proving, according to the procedure by law of the country where cancellation is sought, such refusal, and either:

(a) That he had legal protection for his mark in any of the contracting States before the date of application for the registration which he seeks to cancel; or

(b) That the registrant had no right to the ownership, use or employment of the registered mark at the date of its deposit; or

(c) That the mark covered by the registration which he seeks to cancel has been abandoned.

Section 3. (Transitory). Those who have heretofore sought the benefits of this Convention for their marks and who have been denied protection in certain States, may avail themselves of the right established in this article within two years after the present revision enters into effect. Those who subsequently seek to secure the benefits of the Convention shall have a period of one year, calculated in each instance from the day following that of the receipt by the proper Inter American Bureau of notice of refusal of protection, within which they may avail themselves of this right.

Section 4. This recourse shall not be applicable to trade marks the registration or deposit of which is already beyond question under national legislation; but it shall apply to renewals.

Section 5. The proof that a trade mark conceals or misrepresents the true quality, nature or origin of the merchandise covered by it, shall be cause for cancellation of the registration or deposit effected through the respective Inter American Bureau.

ARTICLE VI

For the purposes indicated in the present Convention, a union of American Nations is hereby constituted which shall act through two international bureaus, established, one in the city of Havana and the other in the city of Rio de Janeiro.

ARTICLE VII

The High Contracting Parties agree to confer the postal frank on the official correspondence of the Bureaus.

ARTICLE VIII

The Inter American Bureaus for the registration of trade-marks shall have the following duties:

Section 1. To keep a detailed record of the applications for the recognition of marks received through the national offices of registration and to which they give course for the purposes of this convention, as well as of all assignments or transfers thereof and of all notices pertaining thereto.

Section 2. To communicate to each of the contracting States, for such action as may be necessary, the application for recognition received.

Section 3. To distribute the fees received, in accordance with the provisions of paragraph (b) Article 1.

The Inter American Bureaus shall remit to the proper governments or, if the governments should so desire, to their local representatives in Havana and Rio de Janeiro, duly authorized therefor, the charges stipulated, at the time when recognition of the alleged rights is requested by the applicant in accordance with this Convention. The cost of remitting the said charges shall be for account of the States to which remittance is made. The Inter American Bureaus shall return to the interested parties any sums returned to such Bureaus.

Section 4. To communicate to the State of first registration or deposit, for the information of the owner of the mark, the notices received from other countries with respect to the granting, opposition to, or denial of protection, or any other circumstance related to the mark.

Section 5. To publish periodical bulletins in which shall appear notices of applications for protection in accordance with this Convention, received from and sent to the various States under the provisions of the Convention, as well as documents, information, studies and articles concerning protection of industrial property.

The High Contracting Parties agree to furnish to the Inter American Bureaus all the official gazettes, reviews and other publications containing notices of the registration of trade marks and commercial names, as well as of judicial proceedings and decisions relative thereto.

Section 6. To carry on any investigation on the subject of trade-marks which the government of any of the signatory States may request, and to encourage the investigation of problems, difficulties or obstacles which may hinder the operation of this Convention.

Section 7. To co operate with the governments of the contracting States in the preparation of material for international conferences on this subject; to present to the said States such suggestions as they may consider useful, and such opinions as may be requested as to what modifications should be introduced in the present Convention, or in the laws concerning industrial property; and in general to facilitate the execution of the purposes of this Convention.

Section 8. To inform the signatory governments at least once a year as to the work which the Bureaus are doing.

Section 9. To maintain relations with similar offices, and scientific and industrial institutions and organizations for the exchange of publications, information and data relative to the progress of the law of industrial property.

Section 10. To establish, in accordance with the provisions of this Convention, the regulations which the Directors may consider necessary for the internal administration of the Bureaus.

Article IX

The Bureau established in the city of Havana shall arrange with the contracting States for the registration or deposit of commercial, industrial and agricultural trade marks coming from the United States of America, Cuba, Haití, Dominican Republic, Guatemala, El Salvador, Honduras, Nicaragua, Costa Rica, Panamá, Colombia, and Ecuador.

The Bureau established in Rio de Janeiro shall arrange for the registration of the marks coming from Brazil, Uruguay, the Argentine Republic, Paraguay, Chile and Venezuela.

Transitory Paragraph. The Inter American Bureau of Rio de Janeiro shall be installed as soon as the present Convention shall have been ratified by one third of the signatory States.

Article X

The two Inter American Bureaus shall be considered as one, and, for the purposes of uniformity in their procedure, it is provided:

(a) That both Bureaus adopt the same system of books and accounts;
(b) That each of them send to the other copies of all applications registrations, communications and other documents relative to the recognition of the rights of owners of marks.

Article XI

The Inter American Bureaus shall both be governed by the same regulations, prepared for the purpose by the governments of the Republics of Cuba and of Brazil.

Article XII

The part of the fees received by each Inter American Bureau which is stipulated for this purpose by the provisions of this Convention, shall be assigned to the maintenance and operation thereof.

The proceeds of the sale of publications by the Inter American Bureaus to individuals shall be assigned to the same purpose; and if both these sums should be insufficient, the deficit shall be paid by the contracting States in the following manner:

80% of the total deficit of the operating budget of both Bureaus shall be paid by the contracting States in proportion to the number of marks which they may have had registered each year through the Inter American Bureaus and the balance of 20% by the same States in proportion to the number of marks they may have registered at the request of the Inter American Bureaus.

Any annual surplus in one of the Bureaus shall be assigned to the reduction of the deficit, if any, of the other.

The Inter American Bureaus shall not incur any expense or obligation which does not appear in their definitive budgets and for which no funds may have been made available at the time of incurring such expense or obligation.

The provisional budget of annual expenditures of each Bureau shall be submitted to the approval of the Government of the State in which such Bureau is established, and shall be communicated to the contracting States for such observations as they may see fit to formulate.

The auditing of the accounts of the Inter American Bureaus shall be done by the officer authorized by the respective government, and the Directors of the Bureaus shall transmit the auditor's report to the contracting States through diplomatic channels.

ARTICLE XIII

Trade-marks which enjoy the protection of the Convention of 1910 shall continue to enjoy this protection without payment of any fees to the contracting States.

The High Contracting Parties agree that the protection accorded by their national legislation to all marks received up to the day on which the revised Convention becomes effective shall continue to be granted in accordance with the Convention of 1910, if they have ratified it.

ARTICLE XIV

The ratifications or adhesions to this Convention shall be communicated to the Government of the Republic of Chile, which shall communicate them to the other signatory or adhering States. These communications shall take the place of an exchange of ratifications.

The revised Convention shall become effective thirty days after the receipt by the Government of Chile of notice of ratification by a number of countries equivalent to one third of the signatory States; and from that moment the Convention signed on August 20, 1910 shall cease to exist, without prejudice to the provisions of Article XIII of this Convention.

The Government of Chile obligates itself to communicate by telegraph and in writing to all the signatory and adhering States the date on which the Convention in its present form becomes effective in accordance with the provisions of this Article.

ARTICLE XV

The American States not represented in this Conference may adhere to this Convention by communicating their decision in due form to the Government of the Republic of Chile, and shall be assigned to the group which each may select.

ARTICLE XVI

Any signatory State that may see fit to withdraw from this Convention, shall so notify the government of the Republic of Chile, which shall communicate the fact to the other signatory States; and one year after the receipt of such notification, this Convention shall cease in respect of the State that shall have withdrawn, but such withdrawal shall not affect the rights previously acquired in accordance with this Convention.

Article XVII

The Inter American Bureaus shall continue so long as not less than one half of the ratifying states adhere to the Convention. If the number of States adhering to the Convention shall become less than half, the Bureaus shall be liquidated under the direction of the Governments of Cuba and Brazil, and their funds shall be distributed among the adhering countries in the same proportion as they would have contributed to their support. The buildings and other tangible property of the Bureaus shall become the property of the Governments of Cuba and Brazil, respectively, in recognition of the services of those Republics in giving effect to the Convention, it being understood that the said Governments shall dedicate such property to purposes preeminently inter American in character.

The High Contracting Parties agree to accept as final any steps which may be taken for the liquidation of the Bureaus.

The termination of the Convention shall not affect rights acquired during the period of its effectiveness.

Article XVIII

Any differences between the contracting States relative to the interpretation or execution of this Convention shall be decided by arbitration.

APPENDIX

Regulations

Article I. Any application to obtain protection under the Convention of which the present appendix is a part shall be made by the owner of the mark or his legal representative to the administration of the State of first registration or deposit, in the manner prescribed by the respective regulations, accompanied by a money order payable to the Director of the proper Inter American Bureau in the sum required by this Convention. His application and money order shall be accompanied by an electrotype of the mark reproducing it as registered in the State of first registration or deposit, and having the dimensions required in the State of first registration or deposit.

Article II. The administration of the State of first registration or deposit, having ascertained that the registration of the mark is regular and in force, shall send to the Inter American Bureau:

A. The money order;

B. The electrotype of the mark;

C. A certificate in duplicate containing the following details:

1. The name and address of the owner of the mark;

2. The date of the application for registration in the State of first registration or deposit;

3. The date of registration of the mark in the State of first registration or deposit;

4. The order number of the registration in the State of first registration or deposit;

5. The date of expiration of the protection of the mark in the State of first registration or deposit;

6. A facsimile of the mark;

7. A statement of the goods on which the mark is used;

8. The date of the application for recognition of the rights claimed under the Convention.

Should the applicant wish to claim color as a distinctive element of his mark, he shall send thirty copies of the mark printed on paper, showing the color, and a brief description of the same.

Article III. The proper Inter American Bureau, upon receipt of the communication of the office of the State of first registration or deposit, mentioned in the foregoing article, shall enter all the information in its books and inform the office of the State of first registration or deposit of the receipt of the application and of the number and date of the entry.

Article IV. Copies of the entry in the books of the respective Inter-American Bureau containing all the details required shall be sent to the administration of the States in which the Convention has been ratified and in which protection is applied for. This data shall also be sent to the other contracting States, for the purposes of information.

Article V. The Inter American Bureaus shall publish in their bulletins reproductions of the marks received and such particulars as are necessary.

Article VI. The notice of acceptance, opposition or refusal of a mark by the contracting States shall be transmitted by the proper Inter American Bureau to the administration of the State of first registration or deposit with a view to its communication to whom it may concern.

Article VII. Changes in ownership of a mark communicated to the respective Inter American Bureau shall be entered in its register and corresponding notice sent to the other contracting States.

Article VIII. The Directors of the Inter American Bureaus, may, in their discretion, appoint or remove the officials or employees of their Bureaus giving notice thereof to the governments of the countries where such offices are established.

In witness whereof, the Delegates sign this Convention, and affix the seal of the Fifth International Conference of American States, in the city of Santiago, Chile, on the twenty eighth day of the month of April in the year one thousand nine hundred and twenty three, in English, Spanish, Portuguese and French.

This Convention shall be filed in the Ministry of Foreign Affairs of the Republic of Chile in order that certified copies may be made and forwarded through appropriate diplomatic channels to each of the Signatory States.

For Venezuela:
C. ZUMETA
JOSÉ AUSTRIA

For Panama:
NARCISO GARAY
J. E. LEFEVRE

For the United States of America:
HENRY P. FLETCHER
FRANK B. KELLOGG
ATLEE POMERENE
WILLARD SAULSBURY
FRANK C. PARTRIDGE
GEORGE E. VINCENT
WILLIAM ERIC FOWLER
L. S. ROWE

For Uruguay:
J. A. BUERO
EUGENIO MARTÍNEZ THEDY

For Ecuador:
RAFAEL M. ARÍZAGA
JOSÉ RAFAEL BUSTAMANTE
A. MUÑOZ VERNAZA

For Chile:
AGUSTÍN EDWARDS
MANUEL RIVAS VICUÑA
CARLOS ALDUNATE S.
L. BARROS B.
EMILIO BELLO C.
ANTONIO HUNEEUS
ALCIBÍADES ROLDÁN
GUILLERMO SUBERCASEAUX
ALEJANDRO DEL RÍO

For Guatemala:
EDUARDO POIRIER
MAXIMO SOTO HALL

For Nicaragua:
CARLOS CUADRA PASOS
ARTURO ELIZONDO

For Costa Rica:
ALEJANDRO ALVARADO QUIRÓS

For the United States of Brazil:
AFRANIO DE MELLO FRANCO
S. GURGEL DO AMARAL
J. DE P. RODRÍGUEZ ALVES
A. DE IPANEMA MOREIRA
HELIO LOBO

For El Salvador:
CECILIO BUSTAMANTE

For Colombia:
GUILLERMO VALENCIA
LAUREANO GÓMEZ
CARLOS URIBE ECHEVERRI

For Cuba:
J. C. VIDAL CARO
CARLOS GARCÍA VÉLEZ
A. DE AGÜERO
M. MÁRQUEZ STERLING

For Paraguay:
M. GONDRA

For the Dominican Republic:
TULIO M. CESTERO

For Honduras:
BENJAMÍN VILLASECA M.

For the Argentine Republic:
M. A. MONTES DE OCA
FERNANDO SAGUIER
MANUEL E. MALBRÁN

For Hayti:
ARTURO RAMEAU

PAN AMERICAN UNION

Resolution adopted by the Fifth International Conference of American States at Santiago May 1, 1923
Amended by resolution of February 20, 1928,[1] of the Sixth International Conference of American States

> Report of the Delegates of the United States of America to the Fifth International Conference of American States, Held at Santiago, Chile, March 25 to May 3, 1923 (U.S. Government Printing Office, 1924), p. 125

ORGANIZATION OF THE PAN AMERICAN UNION

The Fifth International Conference of American States.

RESOLVES:

ARTICLE I. To confirm the existence of the Union of the Republics of the American Continent, which maintains under the name of the "Pan American Union," the institution which serves as its permanent organ and has its seat in the building of the American Republics, in the city of Washington.

ARTICLE II. The functions of the Pan American Union are:

1. To compile and distribute information and reports concerning the commercial, industrial, agricultural, and educational development, as well as the general progress of the American countries.

2. To compile and classify information referring to the Conventions and Treaties concluded among the American Republics and between these and other States, as well as to the legislation of the former.

3. To assist in the development of commercial and cultural relations between the American Republics and of their more intimate mutual acquaintance.

4. To act as a Permanent Commission of the International Conferences of American States; to keep their records and archives; to assist in obtaining ratification of the Treaties and Conventions, as well as compliance with the resolutions adopted; and to prepare the program and regulations of each Conference.

---

[1] *Post,* p. 730.

5. To submit to the various Governments, at the time of the holding of each Conference, a report upon the work of the institution since the adjournment of the last Conference, and also special reports upon any matters which may have been referred to it.

6. To perform such other functions entrusted to it by the Conference, or by the Governing Board by virtue of the powers conferred upon it by this resolution.

To carry out the purposes for which this institution is organized, the Governing Board shall provide for the establishment of such administrative divisions or sections within the Pan American Union as may be deemed necessary.

ARTICLE III. The Pan American Union will have the cooperation of the following Permanent Commissions, to be designated by the Governing Board:

1. For the development of economic and commercial relations between the American Republics.

2. For the study of all matters relating to the international organization of labor in America.

3. For the study of questions relating to hygiene in the countries of the Continent.

4. For the development of intellectual cooperation, with special reference to cooperation between universities.

ARTICLE IV. In the Capital of each of the Republics of America, that form the Pan American Union, there shall be established a Pan American Committee, attached to the Ministry of Foreign Affairs and composed as far as possible of former Delegates to an International Conference of American States, or Pan American offices attached to the Ministry of Foreign Affairs.

The Committees or Offices shall have the following duties:

a) To assist in securing ratification of the Treaties and Conventions, as well as compliance with the resolutions adopted by the Conferences;

b) To furnish the Pan American Union promptly and in a complete manner, all the information it may need in the preparation of its work.

c) To present upon their own initiative, projects which they may consider adapted to the purposes of the Union, and to fulfill such other functions which in view of these purposes may be conferred upon them by the respective Governments.

ARTICLE V. The Governments of the American Republics enjoy, as of right, representation at the International Conferences of American States and in the Pan American Union.

The government of the Pan American Union shall be vested in a Governing Board, composed of the diplomatic representatives of the American Republics accredited to the Government of the United States of America, and the Secretary of State of that country.

An American Republic which for any reason may not have a diplomatic representative accredited to the Government of the United States of America, may appoint a special representative on the Governing Board. In case of the temporary absence, due to official leave or illness, of an Ambassador, Minister or Chargé d'Affaires accredited at Washington, he may be replaced on the Board, by a Special Representative of the respective Government, who may be selected from among the other members of the Governing Board, in which case such Representative shall have as many votes as States represented.

The Governing Board will elect its President and Vice President.

ARTICLE VI. The Governing Board shall appoint the following officers:

A Director General, who shall have charge of the administration of the Pan American Union, with power to promote its most ample development, in accordance with the terms of this resolution, with the regulations and with the resolutions of the Governing Board, to which he shall be responsible. He shall attend in an advisory capacity the meetings of the Governing Board, of the Committees, and of the International Conferences of American States, for the purpose of giving such information as may be required.

An Assistant Director who shall act as Secretary of the Governing Board.

The Governing Board shall determine the manner of appointment of the remainder of the personnel, as well as their duties and all matters affecting their welfare.

The Director General shall prepare, with the approval of the Governing Board and in accordance with this Resolution, the internal regulations by which the various services of the Pan American Union shall be governed.

ARTICLE VII. The Director General of the Pan American Union shall present at the regular session of the Governing Board in November, a detailed budget of the expenses of the next fiscal year. This budget, after being approved by the Governing Board, shall be communicated to the Governments members of the Union, with an indication of the quota, fixed in proportion to population, which each Government shall pay into the Treasury of the Pan American Union not later than the first of July of the following year.

The Governing Board shall elect from among its members a Committee charged with examining, on the dates determined by the Board, the accounts of the expenditures of the Union, in conformity with the financial arrangements established by the Regulations.

ARTICLE VIII. Whenever the Governing Board may so decide, publications shall be issued under the auspices of the Pan American Union relative to matters that may have been submitted to it. In order to assure the greatest possible accuracy in these publications, the Governments of the countries that form the Union, shall transmit directly to the Library of the Pan American Union, two copies of the official documents or publications which may relate to matters connected with the purposes of the Union.

All correspondence and publications of the Pan American Union shall be carried free of charge by the mails of the American Republics.

[The countries which participated in the Fifth International Conference of American States were as follows: Argentina, Brazil, Chile, Colombia, Costa Rica, Cuba, the Dominican Republic, Ecuador, El Salvador, Guatemala, Haiti, Honduras, Nicaragua, Panama, Paraguay, the United States, Uruguay, and Venezuela.]

UNIFORMITY OF NOMENCLATURE
FOR CLASSIFICATION OF MERCHANDISE
(INTER–AMERICAN)

Convention signed at Santiago May 3, 1923
Senate advice and consent to ratification February 18, 1924
Ratified by the President of the United States April 21, 1924
Ratification of the United States deposited at Santiago May 30, 1924
Entered into force May 30, 1924
Proclaimed by the President of the United States January 12, 1927
Terminated for the United States May 24, 1955 [1]

44 Stat. 2559; Treaty Series 754

CONVENTION ON UNIFORMITY OF NOMENCLATURE FOR THE CLASSIFICATION
OF MERCHANDISE

Their Excellencies the Presidents of Venezuela, Panama, United States of America, Uruguay, Ecuador, Chile, Guatemala, Nicaragua, Costa Rica, Brazil, Salvador, Colombia, Cuba, Paraguay, Dominican Republic, Honduras, Argentine Republic, and Hayti:

Being desirous that their respective countries may be represented at the Fifth International Conference of American States, have sent thereto the following Delegates, duly authorized to approve the recommendations, resolutions, conventions and treaties which they might deem advantageous to the interests of America.

Venezuela: Pedro César Dominici, César Zumeta, José Austria;

Panamá: Narciso Garay, José E. LeFevre;

United States of America: Henry P. Fletcher, Frank B. Kellogg, Atlee Pomerene, Willard Saulsbury, George E. Vincent, Frank C. Partridge, William Eric Fowler, Leo S. Rowe;

Uruguay: J. Antonio Buero, Justino Jiménez de Aréchaga, Eugenio Martínez Thedy;

Ecuador: Rafael M. Arízaga, José Rafael Bustamante, Alberto Muñoz Vernaza;

Chile: Agustín Edwards, Manuel Rivas Vicuña, Carlos Aldunate Solar,

---

[1] Pursuant to notice of withdrawal dated May 24, 1954.

Luis Barros Borgoño, Emilio Bello Codesido, Antonio Huneeus, Alcibíades Roldán, Guillermo Subercaseaux, Alejandro del Río;

Guatemala: Eduardo Poirier, Máximo Soto Hall;

Nicaragua: Carlos Cuadra Pasos, Arturo Elizondo;

Costa Rica: Alejandro Alvarado Quirós;

United States of Brazil: Afranio de Mello Franco, Sylvino Gurgel do Amaral, J. de P. Rodríguez Alves, A. de Ipanema Moreira, Helio Lobo;

El Salvador: Cecilio Bustamante;

Colombia: Guillermo Valencia, Laureano Gómez, Carlos Uribe Echeverri;

Cuba: José C. Vidal Caro, Carlos García Vélez, Arístides Agüero, Manuel Márquez Sterling;

Paraguay: Manuel Gondra, Higinio Arbo;

Dominican Republic: Tulio M. Cestero;

Honduras: Benjamín Villaseca Mujica;

Argentine Republic: Manuel Augusto Montes de Oca, Fernando Saguier, Manuel E. Malbrán;

Hayti: Arthur Rameau.

Who, after having presented their credentials and the same having been found in due and proper form, have agreed upon the following Convention:

Article I

The High Contracting Parties agree to employ the Brussels nomenclature of 1913 in their statistics of international commerce, either exclusively or as a supplement to other systems.

Article II

Any controversy which may arise between the High Contracting Parties regarding the interpretation or operation of this Convention shall be settled by arbitration.

Article III

The American States not represented at the Fifth International Conference may adhere to this Convention by communicating their decision in due form to the Government of the Republic of Chile.

Article IV

The deposit of ratifications shall be made in the city of Santiago, Chile. The Chilean Government shall communicate such ratifications to the other Signatory States. This communication shall have the effect of an exchange of ratifications.

Article V

This Convention shall become effective for each Signatory State on the date of the ratification thereof by such State. It shall remain in force without limitation of time, but each Signatory State, upon notification of its intention to the Government of the Republic of Chile, may withdraw from said Convention upon the expiration of the period of one year counting from the date of the notification of such intention.

In witness whereof, the Delegates sign this Convention in English, Spanish, Portuguese, and French and affix the seal of the Fifth International Conference of American States, in the city of Santiago, Chile, on the 3rd day of May in the year one thousand nine hundred and twenty three.

This Convention shall be filed in the Ministry of Foreign Affairs of the Republic of Chile, in order that certified copies may be made and forwarded through appropriate diplomatic channels to each of the Signatory States.

For Venezuela:
  PEDRO CÉSAR DOMINICI
  CÉSAR ZUMETA
  JOSÉ AUSTRIA

For Panama:
  NARCISO GARAY
  J. E. LEFEVRE

For the United States of America:
  HENRY P. FLETCHER
  FRANK B. KELLOGG
  ATLEE POMERENE
  WILLARD SAULSBURY
  GEORGE E. VINCENT
  FRANK C. PARTRIDGE
  WILLIAM ERIC FOWLER
  LEO S. ROWE

For Uruguay:
  J. ANTONIO BUERO
  JUSTINO JIMÉNEZ DE ARÉCHAGA
  EUGENIO MARTÍNEZ THEDY

For Ecuador:
  RAFAEL M. ARÍZAGA
  JOSÉ RAFAEL BUSTAMANTE
  ALBERTO MUÑOZ VERNAZA

For Chile:
  AGUSTÍN EDWARDS
  MANUEL RIVAS VICUÑA
  CARLOS ALDUNATE SOLAR
  LUIS BARROS BORGOÑO
  EMILIO BELLO CODESIDO
  ANTONIO HUNEEUS
  ALCIBÍADES ROLDÁN
  GUILLERMO SUBERCASEAUX
  ALEJANDRO DEL RÍO

For Guatemala:
  EDUARDO POIRIER
  MÁXIMO SOTO HALL

For Nicaragua:
  CARLOS CUADRA PASOS
  ARTURO ELIZONDO

For Costa Rica:
  ALEJANDRO ALVARADO QUIRÓS

For the United States of Brazil:
  AFRANIO DE MELLO FRANCO
  SYLVINO GURGEL DO AMARAL
  J. DE P. RODRÍGUEZ ALVES
  A. DE IPANEMA MOREIRA
  HELIO LOBO

For El Salvador:
  CECILIO BUSTAMANTE

For Colombia:
  GUILLERMO VALENCIA
  LAUREANO GÓMEZ
  CARLOS URIBE ECHEVERRI

For Cuba:
  JOSÉ C. VIDAL CARO
  CARLOS GARCÍA VÉLEZ
  ARÍSTIDES AGÜERO
  MANUEL MÁRQUEZ STERLING

For Paraguay:
  MANUEL GONDRA
  HIGINIO ARBO

For the Dominican Republic:
  TULIO M. CESTERO

For Honduras:
  BENJAMÍN VILLASECA MUJICA

For the Argentine Republic:
  MANUEL A. MONTES DE OCA
  FERNANDO SAGUIER
  MANUEL E. MALBRÁN

For Hayti:
  ARTURO RAMEAU

AVOIDANCE OR PREVENTION OF CONFLICTS BETWEEN AMERICAN STATES (GONDRA TREATY)

Treaty signed at Santiago May 3, 1923
Senate advice and consent to ratification March 18, 1924
Ratified by the President of the United States April 21, 1924
Ratification of the United States deposited at Santiago May 30, 1924
Entered into force October 8, 1924 [1]
Proclaimed by the President of the United States January 12, 1927
Supplemented by convention of January 5, 1929, [2] *and additional protocol of December 26, 1933* [3]

44 Stat. 2527; Treaty Series 752

TREATY TO AVOID OR PREVENT CONFLICTS BETWEEN THE AMERICAN STATES

The Governments represented at the Fifth International Conference of American States, desiring to strengthen progressively the principles of justice and of mutual respect which inspire the policy observed by them in their reciprocal relations, and to quicken in their peoples sentiments of concord and of loyal friendship which may contribute toward the consolidation of such relations,

Confirm their most sincere desire to maintain an immutable peace, not only between themselves but also with all the other nations of the earth;

Condemn armed peace which increases military and naval forces beyond the necessities of domestic security and the sovereignty and independence of States, and,

With the firm purpose of taking all measures which will avoid or prevent the conflicts which may eventually occur between them, agree to the present treaty, negotiated and concluded by the Plenipotentiary Delegates whose full powers were found to be in good and due form by the Conference:

Venezuela: César Zumeta, José Austria.
Panamá: José Lefevre.

---

[1] Date of deposit of second instrument of ratification.
[2] TS 780, *post,* p. 745.
[3] TS 887, *post,* vol. 3.

413

United States of America: Henry P. Fletcher, Frank B. Kellogg, Atlee Pomerene, Willard Saulsbury, George E. Vincent, Frank C. Partridge, William Eric Fowler, Leo S. Rowe.

Uruguay: Eugenio Martínez Thedy.

Ecuador: José Rafael Bustamante.

Chile: Manuel Rivas Vicuña, Cárlos Aldunate Solar, Luis Barros Borgoño, Emilio Bello Codesido, Antonio Huneeus, Alcibiades Roldán, Guillermo Subercaseaux, Alejandro del Rio.

Guatemala: Eduardo Poirier, Máximo Soto Hall.

Nicaragua: Carlos Cuadra Pasos, Arturo Elizondo.

United States of Brazil: Afranio de Mello Franco, Sylvino Gurgel do Amaral, Helio Lobo.

Colombia: Guillermo Valencia.

Cuba: José C. Vidal Caro, Cárlos García Vélez, Arístides Agüero, Manuel Márquez Sterling.

Paraguay: Manuel Gondra.

Dominican Republic: Tulio M. Cestero.

Honduras: Benjamin Villaseca Mujica.

Argentina: Manuel E. Malbrán.

Haiti: Arturo Rameau.

Article I

All controversies which for any cause whatsoever may arise between two or more of the High Contracting Parties and which it has been impossible to settle through diplomatic channels, or to submit to arbitration in accordance with existing treaties, shall be submitted for investigation and report to a Commission to be established in the manner provided for in Article IV. The High Contracting Parties undertake, in case of disputes, not to begin mobilization or concentration of troops on the frontier of the other Party, nor to engage in any hostile acts or preparations for hostilities, from the time steps are taken to convene the Commission until the said Commission has rendered its report or until the expiration of the time provided for in Article VII.

This provision shall not abrogate nor limit the obligations contained in treaties of arbitration in force between two or more of the High Contracting Parties, nor the obligations arising out of them.

It is understood that in disputes arising between Nations which have no general treaties of arbitration, the investigation shall not take place in questions affecting constitutional provisions, nor in questions already settled by the other treaties.

Article II

The controversies referred to in Article I shall be submitted to the Commission of Inquiry whenever it has been impossible to settle them through diplomatic negotiations or procedure or by submission to arbitration, or in cases in which the circumstances of fact render all negotiation impossible and there is imminent danger of an armed conflict between the Parties. Any one of the Governments directly interested in the investigation of the facts giving rise to the controversy may apply for the convocation of the Commission of Inquiry and to this end it shall be necessary only to communicate officially this decision to the other Party and to one of the Permanent Commissions established by Article III.

ARTICLE III

Two Commissions to be designated as permanent shall be established with their seats at Washington (United States of America) and at Montevideo (Uruguay). They shall be composed of the three American diplomatic agents longest accredited in said capitals, and at the call of the Foreign Offices of those States they shall organize, appointing their respective chairmen. Their functions shall be limited to receiving from the interested Parties the request for a convocation of the Commission of Inquiry, and to notifying the other Party thereof immediately. The Government requesting the convocation shall appoint at the same time the persons who shall compose the Commission of Inquiry in representation of that Government, and the other Party shall, likewise, as soon as it receives notification, designate its members.

The Party initiating the procedure established by this Treaty may address itself, in doing so, to the Permanent Commission which it considers most efficacious for a rapid organization of the Commission of Inquiry. Once the request for convocation has been received and the Permanent Commission has made the respective notifications the question or controversy existing between the Parties and as to which no agreement has been reached, will *ipso facto* be suspended.

ARTICLE IV

The Commission of Inquiry shall be composed of five members, all nationals of American States, appointed in the following manner: each Government shall appoint two at the time of convocation, only one of whom may be a national of its country. The fifth shall be chosen by common accord by those already appointed and shall perform the duties of President. However, a citizen of a nation already represented on the Commission may not be elected. Any of the Governments may refuse to accept the elected member, for reasons which it may reserve to itself, and in such event a substitute shall be appointed, with the mutual consent of the Parties, within thirty days following the notification of this refusal. In the failure of such agreement, the designation shall be made by the President of an American Republic not interested in the dispute, who shall be selected by lot by the Commissioners already appointed, from a list of not more than six American Presidents to be formed as follows: each Government party to the controversy, or if there are more than two Governments directly interested in the dispute, the Government or Governments on each side of the controversy, shall designate three Presidents of American States which maintain the same friendly relations with all the Parties to the dispute.

Whenever there are more than two Governments directly interested in a controversy, and the interest of two or more of them are identical, the Government or Governments on each side of the controversy shall have the right to increase the number of their Commissioners, as far as it may be necessary, so that both sides in the dispute may always have equal representation on the Commission.

Once the Commission has been thus organized in the capital city, seat of the Permanent Commission which issued the order of convocation, it shall notify the respective Governments of the date of its inauguration, and it may then determine upon the place or places in which it will function, taking into account the greater facilities for investigation.

The Commission of Inquiry shall itself establish its rules of procedure. In this regard there are recommended for incorporation into said rules of procedure the provisions contained in Articles 9, 10, 11, 12 and 13 of the Convention signed in Washington, February, 1923,[4] between the Government of the United States of America and the Governments of the Republics of Guatemala, El Salvador, Honduras, Nicaragua and Costa Rica, which appear in the appendix to this Treaty.

Its decisions and final report shall be agreed to by the majority of its members.

Each Party shall bear its own expenses and a proportionate share of the general expenses of the Commission.

ARTICLE V

The Parties to the controversy shall furnish the antecedents and data necessary for the investigation. The Commission shall render its report within one year from the date of its inauguration. If it has been impossible to finish the investigation or draft the report within the period agreed upon, it may be extended six months beyond the period established, provided the Parties to the controversy are in agreement upon this point.

ARTICLE VI

The findings of the Commission will be considered as reports upon the disputes, which were the subjects of the investigation, but will not have the value or force of judicial decisions or arbitral awards.

---

[4] Convention signed at Washington Feb. 7, 1923 (TS 717), *ante,* pp. 390–391.

Article VII

Once the report is in possession of the Governments parties to the dispute, six months' time will be available for renewed negotiations in order to bring about a settlement of the difficulty in view of the findings of said report; and if during this new term they should be unable to reach a friendly arrangement, the Parties in dispute shall recover entire liberty of action to proceed as their interests may dictate in the question dealt with in the investigation.

Article VIII

The present Treaty does not abrogate analogous conventions which may exist or may in the future exist between two or more of the High Contracting Parties; neither does it partially abrogate any of their provisions, although they may provide special circumstances or conditions differing from those herein stipulated.

Article IX

The present Treaty shall be ratified by the High Contracting Parties, in conformity with their respective constitutional procedures, and the ratifications shall be deposited in the Ministry for Foreign Affairs of the Republic of Chile, which will communicate them through diplomatic channels to the other Signatory Governments, and it shall enter into effect for the Contracting Parties in the order of ratification.

The Treaty shall remain in force indefinitely; any of the High Contracting Parties may denounce it and the denunciation shall take effect as regards the Party denouncing one year after notification thereof has been given.

Notice of the denunciation shall be sent to the Government of Chile, which will transmit it for appropriate action to the other Signatory Governments.

Article X

The American States which have not been represented in the Fifth Conference may adhere to the present Treaty, transmitting the official document setting forth such adherence to the Ministry for Foreign Affairs of Chile, which will communicate it to the other Contracting Parties.

In witness whereof, the Plenipotentiaries and Delegates sign this Convention in Spanish, English, Portuguese and French and affix the seal of the Fifth International Conference of American States, in the city of Santiago, Chile, on the 3rd day of May in the year one thousand nine hundred and twenty three.

This Convention shall be filed in the Ministry for Foreign Affairs of the Republic of Chile in order that certified copies thereof may be forwarded through diplomatic channels to each of the Signatory States.

For Venezuela:
C. ZUMETA
JOSÉ AUSTRIA

For Panama:
J. E. LEFEVRE

For the United States of America:
HENRY P. FLETCHER
FRANK B. KELLOGG
ATLEE POMERENE
WILLARD SAULSBURY
GEORGE E. VINCENT
FRANK C. PARTRIDGE
WILLIAM ERIC FOWLER
L. S. ROWE

For Uruguay:
EUGENIO MARTÍNEZ THEDY
With reservations relative to the provisions of Article I (first) in so far as they exclude from the investigation questions that affect constitutional provisions.

For Ecuador:
JOSÉ RAFAEL BUSTAMANTE

For Chile:
MANUEL RIVAS VICUÑA
CARLOS ALDUNATE S.
L. BARROS B.
EMILIO BELLO C.
ANTONIO HUNEEUS
ALCIBÍADES ROLDÁN
GUILLERMO SUBERCASEAUX
ALEJANDRO DEL RÍO

For Guatemala:
EDUARDO POIRIER
MÁXIMO SOTO HALL

For Nicaragua:
CARLOS CUADRA PASOS
ARTURO ELIZONDO

For the United States of Brazil:
AFRANIO DE MELLO FRANCO
S. GURGEL DO AMARAL
HELIO LOBO

For Colombia:
GUILLERMO VALENCIA

For Cuba:
J. C. VIDAL CARO
CARLOS GARCÍA VÉLEZ
A. DE AGÜERO
M. MÁRQUEZ STERLING

For Paraguay:
M. GONDRA

For the Dominican Republic:
TULIO M. CESTERO

For Honduras:
BENJAMÍN VILLASECA M.

For the Argentine Republic:
MANUEL E. MALBRÁN

For Hayti:
ARTURO RAMEAU

APPENDIX

ARTICLE I

The Signatory Governments grant to all the Commissions which may be constituted the power to summon witnesses, to administer oaths and to receive evidence and testimony.

ARTICLE II

During the investigation the Parties shall be heard and may have the right to be represented by one or more agents and counsel.

ARTICLE III

All members of the Commission shall take oath duly and faithfully to discharge their duties before the highest judicial authority of the place where it may meet.

ARTICLE IV

The Inquiry shall be conducted so that both Parties shall be heard. Consequently, the Commission shall notify each Party of the statements of facts submitted by the other, and shall fix periods of time in which to receive evidence.

Once the Parties are notified, the Commission shall proceed to the investigation, even though they fail to appear.

Article V

As soon as the Commission of Inquiry is organized, it shall at the request of any of the Parties to the dispute, have the right to fix the status in which the Parties must remain, in order that the situation may not be aggravated and matters may remain in *statu quo* pending the rendering of the report by the Commission.

PUBLICITY OF CUSTOMS DOCUMENTS (INTER–AMERICAN)

Convention signed at Santiago May 3, 1923
Senate advice and consent to ratification February 18, 1924
Ratified by the President of the United States April 21, 1924
Ratification of the United States deposited at Santiago May 30, 1924
Entered into force July 10, 1925
Proclaimed by the President of the United States January 12, 1927

44 Stat. 2547; Treaty Series 753

CONVENTION ON PUBLICITY OF CUSTOMS DOCUMENTS

Their Excellencies the Presidents of Venezuela, Panama, United States of America, Uruguay, Ecuador, Chile, Guatemala, Nicaragua, Costa Rica, Brazil, Salvador, Colombia, Cuba, Paraguay, Dominican Republic, Honduras, Argentine Republic, and Hayti:

Being desirous that their respective countries may be represented at the Fifth International Conference of American States, have sent thereto the following Delegates, duly authorized to approve the recommendations, resolutions, conventions and treaties which they might deem advantageous to the interests of America.

Venezuela: Pedro César Dominici, César Zumeta, José Austria;

Panamá: Narciso Garay, José E. Lefevre;

United States of America: Henry P. Fletcher, Frank B. Kellogg, Atlee Pomerene, Willard Saulsbury, Frank C. Partridge, George E. Vincent, William Eric Fowler, Leo S. Rowe;

Uruguay: J. Antonio Buero, Justino Jiménez de Aréchaga, Eugenio Martínez Thedy;

Ecuador: Rafael M. Arízaga, José Rafael Bustamante, Alberto Muñoz Vernaza;

Chile: Agustín Edwards, Manuel Rivas Vicuña, Carlos Aldunate Solar, Luis Barros Borgoño, Emilio Bello Codesido, Antonio Huneeus, Alcibíades Roldán, Guillermo Subercaseaux, Alejandro del Río;

Guatemala: Eduardo Poirier, Máximo Soto Hall;

Nicaragua: Carlos Cuadro Pasos, Arturo Elizondo;

Costa Rica: Alejandro Alvarado Quirós;

United States of Brazil: Afranio de Mello Franco, Sylvino Gurgel do Amaral, J. de P. Rodríguez Alves, A. de Ipanema Moreira, Helio Lobo;

El Salvador: Cecilio Bustamante;

Colombia: Guillermo Valencia, Laureano Gómez, Carlos Uribe Echeverri;

Cuba: José C. Vidal Caro, Carlos García Vélez, Arístides Agüero, Manuel Márquez Sterling;

Paraguay: Manuel Gondra, Higinio Arbo;

Dominican Republic: Tulio M. Cestero;

Honduras: Benjamín Villaseca Mujica;

Argentine Republic: Manuel Augusto Montes de Oca, Fernando Saguier, Manuel E. Malbrán;

Hayti: Arthur Rameau.

Who, after having presented their credentials and the same having been found in due and proper form, have agreed upon the following Convention on Publicity of Customs Documents:

The High Contracting Parties, considering that it is of the utmost importance to give the greatest publicity to all customs laws, decrees, and regulations, agree as follows:

ARTICLE I

The High Contracting Parties agree to communicate to each other all the laws, decrees and regulations that govern the importation or the exportation of merchandise, as well as all laws, decrees and regulations referring to vessels entering into or sailing from their ports.

ARTICLE II

The High Contracting Parties agree to publish in full or in an abridged form the laws, decrees and regulations mentioned in Art. I, which have been communicated to them by the several American Countries that have ratified this Convention.

ARTICLE III

The High Contracting Parties will communicate to the Central Executive Council of the Inter American High Commission the laws, decrees or regulations to which Art. I refers.

ARTICLE IV

The High Contracting Parties resolve to entrust to the Central Executive Council of the Inter American High Commission the preparation of a handbook as detailed as possible, of the customs laws, decrees, and regulations enforced in the American countries. This handbook will be published in English, Spanish, Portuguese and French.

ARTICLE V

This Convention will become effective as soon as it is ratified by six Signatory States.

ARTICLE VI

The American countries not represented at the Fifth International Conference of American States may adhere to this Convention at any time. The respective protocol will be signed in Santiago, Chile, the original texts of this Convention being filed in the archives of the Government of the Republic of Chile.

ARTICLE VII

The ratifications of this Convention will be deposited with the Ministry of Foreign Affairs of the Republic of Chile.

The Government of the Republic of Chile will notify the Signatory States, through diplomatic channels, of the deposit of these ratifications; this notification will be equivalent to an exchange of ratifications.

ARTICLE VIII

This Convention may be denounced at any time. The denunciation must be made to the Government of the Republic of Chile and will affect the Government making such denouncement, one year after the date of the notification.

ARTICLE IX

Any controversy which may arise between the High Contracting Parties with respect to the execution or interpretation of this Convention, shall be decided by arbitration.

This Convention is issued in Spanish, English, Portuguese and French, each of which texts is authentic.

In witness whereof, the Delegates sign this Convention in English, Spanish, Portuguese and French and affix the seal of the Fifth International Conference of American States, in the city of Santiago, Chile, on the 3rd day of May in the year one thousand nine hundred and twenty three.

This Convention shall be filed in the Ministry of Foreign Affairs of the Republic of Chile, in order that certified copies may be made and forwarded through appropriate diplomatic channels to each of the Signatory States.

For Venezuela:
   PEDRO CÉSAR DOMINICI
   CÉSAR ZUMETA
   JOSÉ AUSTRIA

For Panama:
   NARCISO GARAY
   J. E. LEFEVRE

For the United States of America:
   HENRY P. FLETCHER
   FRANK B. KELLOGG
   ATLEE POMERENE
   WILLARD SAULSBURY
   GEORGE E. VINCENT
   FRANK C. PARTRIDGE
   WILLIAM ERIC FOWLER
   LEO S. ROWE

For Uruguay:
J. Antonio Buero
Justino Jiménez de Aréchaga
Eugenio Martínez Thedy

For Ecuador:
Rafael M. Arízaga
José Rafael Bustamante
Alberto Muñoz Vernaza

For Chile:
Agustín Edwards
Manuel Rivas Vicuña
Carlos Aldunate Solar
Luis Barros Borgoño
Emilio Bello Codesido
Antonio Huneeus
Alcibíades Roldán
Guillermo Subercaseaux
Alejandro del Río

For Guatemala:
Eduardo Poirier
Máximo Soto Hall

For Nicaragua:
Carlos Cuadra Pasos
Arturo Elizondo

For Costa Rica:
Alejandro Alvarado Quirós

For the United States of Brazil:
Afranio de Mello Franco
Sylvino Gurgel do Amaral
J. de P. Rodríguez Alves
A. de Ipanema Moreira
Helio Lobo

For El Salvador:
Cecilio Bustamante

For Colombia:
Guillermo Valencia
Laureano Gómez
Carlos Uribe Echeverri

For Cuba:
José C. Vidal Caro
Carlos García Vélez
Arístides Agüero
Manuel Márquez Sterling

For Paraguay:
Manuel Gondra
Higinio Arbo

For the Dominican Republic:
Tulio M. Cestero

For Honduras:
Benjamín Villaseca Mujica

For the Argentine Republic:
Manuel A. Montes de Oca
Fernando Saguier
Manuel E. Malbrán

For Hayti:
Arturo Rameau

REIMBURSEMENT OF COSTS OF AMERICAN ARMY OF OCCUPATION

Agreement signed at Paris May 25, 1923
Notification of approval by the President of the United States given to the French Government August 24, 1923 [1]
Superseded by agreement of January 14, 1925 [2]

> 1923 For. Rel. (II) 180 and 1919 For. Rel. (Paris Peace Conference, XIII) 880; Treaty Series 671–A

The present Agreement is concluded between the Government of the United States of America, of the one part,

And the Governments of Great Britain, France, Italy, and Belgium of the other part.

The Governments of Great Britain, France, Italy and Belgium undertake to use every effort to secure the adherence to this Agreement of the other Allied Powers who have a right to participate in the payments affected by the said Agreement.

ARTICLE 1

For the purpose of the present Agreement the net amount due to the Government of the United States for the costs of its Army of Occupation will be reckoned as follows:

The total net costs as they are certified by the United States Government and as they will figure in the accounts of the Reparation Commission after deducting the following sums, if they have not already been deducted:

(*a*) Any amount already collected by the United States Government in the form of the requisition of paper marks;

(*b*) The value of the Armistice material and material abandoned by Germany not possessing a military character.

---

[1] The United States considered ratification unnecessary (see art. 6). On Aug. 24, 1923, the Department of State informed the American Chargé d'Affaires at Paris: "Inasmuch as the agreement is not a treaty but rather an executive agreement . . . it is deemed by the Government that the formal approval by the President will suffice . . . ." (1923 For. Rel. (II) 186).

[2] *Post,* p. 504.

The value in gold of the paper marks, of the Armistice material and of the abandoned material not possessing a military character, shall be fixed by the Reparation Commission and the Reparation Commission will agree with the Government of the United States as to the amount thereof to be deducted from the total net costs of the American Army of Occupation.

ARTICLE 2

I. The net amount due to the United States will be paid in twelve equal yearly instalments, the first instalment to be paid on or before the 31st December 1923.

II. No interest will be charged; however, if the Allied Governments should decide at any time to charge interest from a fixed date for the unpaid costs of their Armies of Occupation, the same rate of interest commencing from the same date shall be allowed the Government of the United States for the unpaid balance of its claim.

III. Each of the yearly instalments referred to in paragraph I of the present Article constitutes up to the 31st December 1926 a first charge on the payments of all kinds to be credited to Germany's "Reparation" account [3] excluding those specially excepted by paragraph IV below, and, from the 1st January 1927, if the payments of all kinds to be placed to the credit of the Reparation account are insufficient, a first charge in addition on all the payments to be placed to the credit of Armies of Occupation account, exclusive of paper marks requisitioned to meet the needs of the Armies of Occupation for local currency during the year in the course of which the said yearly instalment should be paid to the Government of the United States. The charges established by the present paragraph are applicable whether these payments are made by Germany or for her account or by or for the account of another country from whom a similar payment may be exacted, to any organization which has been or may be designated to receive such payments and including the payments made directly to the interested Governments.

IV. For the purpose of the execution of the present Agreement, the payments by the German Government subjected to the charges referred to in paragraph III above shall not include:

a) Deliveries in kind intended to be used in the interior of the receiving countries, their colonies and their dominions made by virtue of the various annexes to Part VIII of the Treaty of Versailles [4] or of any other procedure

---

[3] The "Reparation" account of Germany includes all payments in cash or kind which are devoted to making good the damages for which the Allies have claimed compensation from Germany in accordance with the terms of the Treaty of Versailles. Accordingly, there are excluded from the "Reparation" account such items as the costs of the Reparation Commission, the payments made through the Clearing Offices, and the cost of the Armies of Occupation. [Footnote in original.]

[4] *Ante*, p. 137.

approved to date by the Reparation Commission [5] to the Allied countries having a credit on account of reparations;

b) The proceeds of the British Reparation Recovery Act or of any other similar legislation enacted or to be enacted by the other Allied Governments in pursuance of paragraph 2 of the decision of the Allied Governments of 3rd March 1921; [6]

c) The value of transfers and cessions of property, rights and interests made in execution of the Treaty of Versailles, unless such transfers (e. g., under Articles 254 and 256 of the Treaty of Versailles) result in a payment to the credit of Germany's reparation account made by Powers not having a right to reparation, or unless such cessions of property, rights and interests (e. g., under Article 260 of the Treaty of Versailles) are liquidated or sold for cash by the Reparation Commission for the credit of Germany.

V. If, in the course of one calendar year between 1st January 1923 and 31st December 1926, the amount of the sum due to the Government of the United States exceeds 25% of the total of the payments made by or for the account of Germany for the credit of her reparation account as defined above (excluding the sums carried to the account of the Armies of Occupation), the amount of the instalment payable to the Government of the United States shall be reduced to a sum equivalent to 25% of such payments, and ⅛ of the sum deducted shall be added to each of the instalments to be paid in the course of the years 1927 to 1934 inclusive.

VI. Nevertheless, for the purpose of the present Agreement, the European Allied Governments, creditors on account of their Armies of Occupation, undertake to apply during each of the years 1923 to 1926 inclusive by priority to the payment of the current expenses for their respective Armies of Occupation, in so far as these have not been met by the requisition of paper marks, the value of the deliveries in kind referred to in paragraph (*a*) above, the proceeds of any Reparation Recovery Act for the time being in force and referred to in paragraph (*b*) above, and the value of the transfers and cessions of property rights and interests referred to in paragaph (*c*) above, in such a way as to be able to place as far as possible the value of the other payments which Germany will make to her credit on account of reparations.

VII. If, after 1926, the payments to the Government of the United States in the course of any particular year are insufficient to satisfy the amount due to that Government in the course of that year, the arrears shall be carried over to a special account bearing simple interest at 4½%.

This account of arrears shall be liquidated as soon as the payments received from Germany in the course of any year admit.

---

[5] The other procedures approved to date by the Reparation Commission are those of:
　　a) The Wiesbaden Agreements signed on the 6th and 7th October 1921;
　　b) The Bemelmans-Cuntze Agreement of 2nd June, 1922;
　　c) The Gillet-Ruppel Agreement of 2nd June, 1922. [Footnote in original.]
[6] For background, see 1919 For. Rel. (Paris Peace Conference, XIII) 430.

These arrears shall have the same priority as that given under paragraph III of Article 2 of the present Agreement to the equal annual instalments.

VIII. However, if in the course of one of the first four years it should prove necessary to utilise all or a part of the payments in cash made by Germany to cover the costs of the Armies of Occupation of the European Allies in the course of that year, the American priority of 25% shall be calculated on the total of the payments in cash made by Germany in the course of that year on reparation account and on the account of the Armies of Occupation of the European Allied Powers, exclusive of paper marks requisitioned to meet the needs of the Armies of Occupation for local currency. The sum to be remitted to the Government of the United States in the course of any one of the first four years shall not, however, exceed 50% of the total balance of the payments in cash made by Germany in the course of the year in question, which remains for credit to reparation account. If the American priority calculated as above for any particular year cannot be met by the 50% payments calculated as above, the balance of this priority shall be chargeable against the payments in cash made by Germany in the course of the following years up to and including 1926 instead of being spread over the payments of the last eight years. At the beginning of 1927 the total deficit which has accrued shall be spread over the payments of the last eight years.

IX. If at the end of the year 1927 or of any year following, the arrears have reached such an amount as might, in the opinion of the Government of the United States, endanger the complete execution of the payments within the period of twelve years, the Allied Governments will, upon the request of the Government of the United States and in agreement with it, use their best endeavours to make such modifications of the present Agreement as may seem necessary to ensure the complete execution of the payments within the prescribed period of twelve years.

X. The Allied Governments, however, reserve all their rights in respect of the payments in kind and in cash which might be collected in occupied territory through the intervention of any Allied authority.

Article 3

The present Agreement has been drawn up in contemplation of annual payments to be made by Germany and with the recognition of the impossibility of foreseeing and determining at this moment the distribution of any extraordinary payment which may be made by Germany in any particular year.

If, however, a loan is floated or an anticipatory payment effected by Germany in any manner, the Allied Governments will put themselves in communication with the Government of the United States for the purpose of discussing the participation of the United States in such extraordinary payments.

If, as a consequence of a loan floated either in America or elsewhere, or of any anticipatory payment made by Germany by any means whatever, a moratorium were granted to Germany, the Allied Governments will put themselves into communication with the Government of the United States for the purpose of reaching an agreement which would not cause any prejudice to the Government of United States.

No discount shall be allowed for any anticipatory payments.

ARTICLE 4

The Allied Governments which have approved the agreement of 11th March 1922,[7] declare that the charge upon the payments in cash to be received from Germany and set up by the last part of Article 8 of the Inter-allied Agreement of March 11th 1922, in favour of the unpaid balance of the costs of the British and French Armies of Occupation up to 1st May 1921, shall only apply to the balance, if such there be, of the German payments after payment of the sums due to the United States in execution of the present Agreement. The fact that the Government of the United States has taken note of this declaration cannot, however, be interpreted as an expression of opinion of the Government of the United States with regard to the Agreement of 11th March 1922.

ARTICLE 5

If the Government of the United States should come to an agreement with the Reparation Commission to receive, in accordance with the provisions of the Treaty of Versailles or any supplementary Agreement, German dye-stuffs, the value of these dye-stuffs determined by agreement between the Government of the United States and the Reparation Commission, shall be deducted from the annual payment due to the Government of the United States under the present Agreement in the course of the calendar year in which these dye-stuffs shall have been received.

If, in the course of any calendar year, the value of the dye-stuffs thus supplied to the United States exceeds the annual sum due to the Government of the United States, the excess shall be utilised:

(a) During the years from 1923 to 1926 to supplement, as far as necessary, the payments already made, so as to bring them, for each year, up to $\frac{1}{12}$ of the American claim;

(b) During 1927 and the years following, to liquidate the account of arrears.

If, when these operations have been completed, there still remains a balance, this shall be regarded as an anticipatory payment of the annual instalments fixed in accordance with Article 2 of the present Agreement.

No discount shall be allowed on these anticipatory payments.

---

[7] 1919 For. Rel. (Paris Peace Conference, XIII) 870.

ARTICLE 6

If at any time the arrears due to the United States reach a total such that the Government of the United States considers that there is a risk of its not being paid within the prescribed period of 12 years, the Government of the United States shall have the right to abrogate the present Agreement, if within a period of three months from the date of a notification to that effect, the Agreement has not been modified to its satisfaction.

In negotiating the present Agreement, the respective Governments, with a view to arriving at an arrangement for the payment of the costs of the American Army of Occupation, have voluntarily avoided raising any question of right or interpretation.

The respective Governments desire, nevertheless, to state that, in case the present Agreement should be abrogated for any reason whatsoever, each of them reserves the right to maintain all its rights whatsoever may be their extent, such as each deems them to exist at this date.

The present Agreement shall take effect after such ratifications as may be required in accordance with the constitutional methods of the High Contracting Parties.

Ratifications shall be exchanged at Paris as soon as possible.

In faith whereof the undersigned, duly authorized, have signed the present Agreement.

Done at Paris, the twenty-fifth day of May one thousand nine hundred and twenty-three, in a single copy which will remain deposited in the archives of the French Republic, and of which authenticated copies will be transmitted to each of the Signatory Powers.

For the United States of America:
ELIOT WADSWORTH

For Great Britain:
JOHN BRADBURY

For France:
JEAN TANNERY

For Italy:
M. D'AMELIO

For Belgium:
A. BEMELMANS

BILLS OF LADING FOR CARRIAGE OF GOODS BY SEA

Convention and protocol of signature concluded at Brussels August 25, 1924, with declarations and reservations; signed for the United States June 23, 1925

Senate advice and consent to ratification, subject to two understandings, May 6, 1937 [1]

Ratified by the President of the United States, subject to two understandings, May 26, 1937 [1]

Procès-verbal of first deposit of ratifications at Brussels dated June 2, 1930; ratification of the United States deposited at Brussels June 29, 1937

Entered into force June 2, 1931; for the United States December 29, 1937

Proclaimed by the President of the United States November 6, 1937

Amended by protocol of February 23, 1968 [2]

51 Stat. 233; Treaty Series 931

[TRANSLATION]

INTERNATIONAL CONVENTION FOR THE UNIFICATION OF CERTAIN RULES RELATING TO BILLS OF LADING, SIGNED AT BRUSSELS, AUGUST 25, 1924

The President of the German Republic, the President of the Argentine Republic, His Majesty the King of the Belgians, the President of the Republic of Chile, the President of the Republic of Cuba, His Majesty the King of Denmark and Iceland, His Majesty the King of Spain, the Chief of the Estonian State, the President of the United States of America, the President of the Republic of Finland, the President of the French Republic, His Majesty the King of the United Kingdom of Great Britain and Ireland and of the

---

[1] The U.S. understandings read as follows:

". . . notwithstanding the provisions of Article 4, Section 5, and the first paragraph of Article 9 of the convention, neither the carrier nor the ship shall in any event be or become liable within the jurisdiction of the United States of America for any loss or damage to or in connection with goods in an amount exceeding $500.00, lawful money of the United States of America, per package or unit unless the nature and value of such goods have been declared by the shipper before shipment and inserted in the bill of lading"; and

". . . should any conflict arise between the provisions of the convention and the provisions of the Act of April 16, 1936, known as the 'Carriage of Goods by Sea Act' [49 Stat. 1207], the provisions of said Act shall prevail."

[2] Not in force as of Mar. 31, 1969.

British Possessions Beyond the Seas, Emperor of India, His Serene Highness the Regent of the Kingdom of Hungary, His Majesty the King of Italy, His Majesty the Emperor of Japan, the President of the Republic of Latvia, the President of the Republic of Mexico, His Majesty the King of Norway, Her Majesty the Queen of the Netherlands, the President of the Republic of Peru, the President of the Republic of Poland, the President of the Portuguese Republic, His Majesty the King of Rumania, His Majesty the King of the Serbs, Croats and Slovenes, His Majesty the King of Sweden, and the President of the Republic of Uruguay,

Having recognized the utility of laying down in common accord certain uniform rules relating to bills of lading, have decided to conclude a Convention to that effect and have designated as their Plenipotentiaries namely:

The President of the German Republic:
His Excellency Mr. von Keller, Minister of Germany at Brussels.

The President of the Argentine Republic:

His Majesty the King of the Belgians:
Mr. L. Franck, Minister of Colonies, President of the International Maritime Committee;
Mr. A. Le Jeune, Senator, Vice President of the International Maritime Committee;
Mr. F. Sohr, Doctor of Law, Secretary General of the International Maritime Committee, Professor at the University of Brussels.

The President of the Republic of Chile:
His Excellency Mr. Armando Quezada, Minister of Chile at Brussels.

The President of the Republic of Cuba:

His Majesty the King of Denmark and Iceland:

His Majesty the King of Spain:
His Excellency the Marquis of Villalobar and Guimarey, Ambassador of Spain at Brussels.

Chief of the Estonian State:
His Excellency Mr. Pusta, Minister of Estonia at Brussels.

The President of the United States of America:
His Excellency Mr. William Phillips, Ambassador of the United States of America at Brussels.

The President of the Republic of Finland:

The President of the French Republic:
His Excellency Mr. M. Herbette, Ambassador of France at Brussels.

His Majesty the King of the United Kingdom of Great Britain and Ireland and of the British Possessions Beyond the Seas, Emperor of India:
  His Excellency the Right Honorable Sir George Grahame, G.C.V.O., K.C.M.G., Ambassador of His Britannic Majesty at Brussels.

His Serene Highness the Regent of the Kingdom of Hungary:
  Count Oliver Woracziczky, Baron of Pabienitz, Chargé d'Affaires of Hungary at Brussels.

His Majesty the King of Italy:
  Mr. J. Daneo, Chargé d'Affaires ad interim of Italy at Brussels.

His Majesty the Emperor of Japan:
  His Excellency Mr. M. Adatci, Ambassador of Japan at Brussels.

The President of the Republic of Latvia:

The President of the Republic of Mexico:

His Majesty the King of Norway:

Her Majesty the Queen of the Netherlands:

The President of the Republic of Peru:

The President of the Republic of Poland and the Free City of Danzig:
  His Excellency Count Jean Szembek, Minister of Poland at Brussels.

The President of the Portuguese Republic:

His Majesty the King of Rumania:
  His Excellency Mr. Henry Catargi, Minister of Rumania at Brussels.

His Majesty the King of the Serbs, Croats, and Slovenes:
  Messrs. Straznicky and Verona.

His Majesty the King of Sweden:

The President of the Republic of Uruguay:

Who, duly authorized therefor, have agreed on the following:

ARTICLE 1

In this convention the following words are employed with the meanings set out below:

(a) "Carrier" includes the owner of the vessel or the charterer who enters into a contract of carriage with a shipper.

(b) "Contract of carriage" applies only to contracts of carriage covered by a bill of lading or any similar document of title, insofar as such document relates to the carriage of goods by sea; it also applies to any bill of lading or any similar document as aforesaid issued under or pursuant to a charter party from the moment at which such instrument regulates the relations between a carrier and a holder of the same.

(c) "Goods" includes goods, wares, merchandise, and articles of every kind whatsoever except live animals and cargo which by the contract of carriage is stated as being carried on deck and is so carried.

(d) "Ship" means any vessel used for the carriage of goods by sea.

(e) "Carriage of goods" covers the period from the time when the goods are loaded on to the time they are discharged from the ship.

ARTICLE 2

Subject to the provisions of Article 6 under every contract of carriage of goods by sea the carrier, in relation to the loading, handling, stowage, carriage, custody, care, and discharge of such goods, shall be subject to the responsibilities and liabilities, and entitled to the rights and immunities hereinafter set forth.

ARTICLE 3

1. The carrier shall be bound before and at the beginning of the voyage to exercise due diligence to:

(a) Make the ship seaworthy;

(b) Properly man, equip, and supply the ship;

(c) Make the holds, refrigerating and cool chambers, and all other parts of the ship in which goods are carried, fit and safe for their reception, carriage, and preservation.

2. Subject to the provisions of Article 4 the carrier shall properly and carefully load, handle, stow, carry, keep, care for, and discharge the goods carried.

3. After receiving the goods into his charge the carrier or the master or agent of the carrier shall, on demand of the shipper, issue to the shipper a bill of lading showing among other things:

(a) The leading marks necessary for identification of the goods as the same are furnished in writing by the shipper before the loading of such goods starts, provided such marks are stamped or otherwise shown clearly upon the goods if uncovered, or on the cases or coverings in which such goods are contained, in such a manner as should ordinarily remain legible until the end of the voyage;

(b) Either the number of packages or pieces, or the quantity, or weight, as the case may be, as furnished in writing by the shipper;

(c) The apparent order and condition of the goods;

Provided that no carrier, master, or agent of the carrier shall be bound to state or show in the bill of lading any marks, number, quantity, or weight which he has reasonable grounds for suspecting not accurately to represent the goods actually received or which he has had no reasonable means of checking.

4. Such a bill of lading shall be prima facie evidence of the receipt by the carrier of the goods as therein described in accordance with paragraph 3 (a), (b), and (c).

5. The shipper shall be deemed to have guaranteed to the carrier the accuracy at the time of shipment of the marks, number, quantity, and weight, as furnished by him, and the shipper shall indemnify the carrier against all loss, damages, and expenses arising or resulting from inaccuracies in such particulars. The right of the carrier to such indemnity shall in no way limit his responsibility and liability under the contract of carriage to any person other than the shipper.

6. Unless notice of loss or damage and the general nature of such loss or damage be given in writing to the carrier or his agent at the port of discharge before or at the time of the removal of the goods into the custody of the person entitled to delivery thereof under the contract of carriage, such removal shall be prima facie evidence of the delivery by the carrier of the goods as described in the bill of lading.

If the loss or damage is not apparent, the notice must be given within three days of the delivery.

The notice in writing need not be given if the state of the goods has at the time of their receipt been the subject of joint survey or inspection.

In any event the carrier and the ship shall be discharged from all liability in respect of loss or damage unless suit is brought within one year after delivery of the goods or the date when the goods should have been delivered.

In the case of any actual or apprehended loss or damage the carrier and the receiver shall give all reasonable facilities to each other for inspecting and tallying the goods.

7. After the goods are loaded the bill of lading to be issued by the carrier, master, or agent of the carrier to the shipper shall, if the shipper so demands, be a "shipped" bill of lading, provided that if the shipper shall have previously taken up any document of title to such goods, he shall surrender the same as against the issue of the "shipped" bill of lading. At the option of the carrier such document of title may be noted at the port of shipment by the carrier, master, or agent with the name or names of the ship or ships upon which the goods have been shipped and the date or dates of shipment, and when so noted, if it shows the particulars mentioned in paragraph 3 of Article 3, it shall for the purpose of this article be deemed to constitute a "shipped" bill of lading.

8. Any clause, covenant, or agreement in a contract of carriage relieving the carrier or the ship from liability for loss or damage to or in connection with goods arising from negligence, fault, or failure in the duties and obligations provided in this article, or lessening such liability otherwise than as

provided in this convention, shall be null and void and of no effect. A benefit of insurance in favor of the carrier or similar clause shall be deemed to be a clause relieving the carrier from liability.

ARTICLE 4

1. Neither the carrier nor the ship shall be liable for loss or damage arising or resulting from unseaworthiness unless caused by want of due diligence on the part of the carrier to make the ship seaworthy and to secure that the ship is properly manned, equipped, and supplied and to make the holds, refrigerating and cool chambers, and all other parts of the ship in which goods are carried fit and safe for their reception, carriage, and preservation in accordance with the provisions of paragraph 1 of Article 3. Whenever loss or damage has resulted from unseaworthiness, the burden of proving the exercise of due diligence shall be on the carrier or other person claiming exemption under this article.

2. Neither the carrier nor the ship shall be responsible for loss or damage arising or resulting from:

(a) Act, neglect, or default of the master, mariner, pilot, or the servants of the carrier in the navigation or in the management of the ship;

(b) Fire, unless caused by the actual fault or privity of the carrier;

(c) Perils, dangers, and accidents of the sea or other navigable waters;

(d) Act of God;

(e) Act of war;

(f) Act of public enemies;

(g) Arrest or restraint of princes, rulers, or people, or seizure under legal process;

(h) Quarantine restrictions;

(i) Act or omission of the shipper or owner of the goods, his agent, or representative;

(j) Strikes or lockouts or stoppage or restraint of labor from whatever cause, whether partial or general;

(k) Riots and civil commotions;

(l) Saving or attempting to save life or property at sea;

(m) Wastage in bulk or weight or any other loss or damage arising from inherent defect, quality, or vice of the goods;

(n) Insufficiency of packing;

(o) Insufficiency or inadequacy of marks;

(p) Latent defects not discoverable by due diligence;

(q) Any other cause arising without the actual fault or privity of the carrier, or without the fault or neglect of the agents or servants of the carrier, but the burden of proof shall be on the person claiming the benefit of this exception to show that neither the actual fault or privity of the carrier nor the fault or neglect of the agents or servants of the carrier contributed to the loss or damage.

3. The shipper shall not be responsible for loss or damage sustained by the carrier or the ship arising or resulting from any cause without the act, fault, or neglect of the shipper, his agents, or his servants.

4. Any deviation in saving or attempting to save life or property at sea or any reasonable deviation shall not be deemed to be an infringement or breach of this convention or of the contract of carriage, and the carrier shall not be liable for any loss or damage resulting therefrom.

5. Neither the carrier nor the ship shall in any event be or become liable for any loss or damage to or in connection with goods in an amount exceeding 100 pounds sterling per package or unit or the equivalent of that sum in other currency unless the nature and value of such goods have been declared by the shipper before shipment and inserted in the bill of lading.

This declaration if embodied in the bill of lading shall be prima facie evidence but shall not be binding or conclusive on the carrier.

By agreement between the carrier, master, or agent of the carrier and the shipper another maximum amount than that mentioned in this paragraph may be fixed, provided that such maximum shall not be less than the figure above named.

Neither the carrier nor the ship shall be responsible in any event for loss or damage to, or in connection with, goods if the nature or value thereof has been knowingly misstated by the shipper in the bill of lading.

6. Goods of an inflammable, explosive, or dangerous nature to the shipment whereof the carrier, master, or agent of the carrier has not consented with knowledge of their nature and character may at any time before discharge be landed at any place or destroyed or rendered innocuous by the carrier without compensation, and the shipper of such goods shall be liable for all damages and expenses directly or indirectly arising out of or resulting from such shipment. If any such goods shipped with such knowledge and consent shall become a danger to the ship or cargo, they may in like manner be landed at any place or destroyed or rendered innocuous by the carrier without liability on the part of the carrier except to general average, if any.

Article 5

A carrier shall be at liberty to surrender in whole or in part all or any of his rights and immunities, or to increase any of his responsibilities and liabilities under this convention provided such surrender or increase shall be embodied in the bill of lading issued to the shipper.

The provisions of this convention shall not be applicable to charter parties, but if bills of lading are issued in the case of a ship under a charter-party they shall comply with the terms of this convention. Nothing in these rules shall be held to prevent the insertion in a bill of lading of any lawful provision regarding general average.

ARTICLE 6

Notwithstanding the provisions of the preceding articles, a carrier, master, or agent of the carrier and a shipper shall in regard to any particular goods be at liberty to enter into any agreement in any terms as to the responsibility and liability of the carrier for such goods, and as to the rights and immunities of the carrier in respect of such goods, or concerning his obligation as to seaworthiness so far as this stipulation is not contrary to public policy, or concerning the care or diligence of his servants or agents in regard to the loading, handling, stowage, carriage, custody, care, and discharge of the goods carried by sea, provided that in this case no bill of lading has been or shall be issued and that the terms agreed shall be embodied in a receipt which shall be a nonnegotiable document and shall be marked as such.

Any agreement so entered into shall have full legal effect:

Provided that this article shall not apply to ordinary commercial shipments made in the ordinary course of trade, but only to other shipments where the character or condition of the property to be carried or the circumstances, terms, and conditions under which the carriage is to be performed are such as reasonably to justify a special agreement.

ARTICLE 7

Nothing herein contained shall prevent a carrier or a shipper from entering into any agreement, stipulation, condition, reservation, or exemption as to the responsibility and liability of the carrier or the ship for the loss or damage to, or in connection with, the custody and care and handling of goods prior to the loading on, and subsequent to the discharge from, the ship on which the goods are carried by sea.

ARTICLE 8

The provisions of this convention shall not affect the rights and obligations of the carrier under any statute for the time being in force relating to the limitation of the liability of owners of seagoing vessels.

ARTICLE 9

The monetary units mentioned in this convention are to be taken to be gold value.

Those contracting states in which the pound sterling is not a monetary unit reserve to themselves the right of translating the sums indicated in this convention in terms of pound sterling into terms of their own monetary system in round figures.

The national laws may reserve to the debtor the right of discharging his debt in national currency according to the rate of exchange prevailing on the day of the arrival of the ship at the port of discharge of the goods concerned.

ARTICLE 10

The provisions of this convention shall apply to all bills of lading issued in any of the contracting States.

ARTICLE 11

After an interval of not more than two years from the day on which the convention is signed, the Belgian Government shall place itself in communication with the governments of the high contracting parties which have declared themselves prepared to ratify the convention, with a view to deciding whether it shall be put into force. The ratifications shall be deposited at Brussels at a date to be fixed by agreement among the said governments. The first deposit of ratifications shall be recorded in a procès-verbal signed by the representatives of the powers which take part therein and by the Belgian Minister for Foreign Affairs.

The subsequent deposits of ratifications shall be made by means of a written notification, addressed to the Belgian Government and accompanied by the instrument of ratification.

A duly certified copy of the procès-verbal relating to the first deposit of ratifications, of the notifications referred to in the previous paragraph, and also of the instruments of ratification accompanying them, shall be immediately sent by the Belgian Government through the diplomatic channel to the powers who have signed this convention or who have acceded to it. In the cases contemplated in the preceding paragraph the said Government shall inform them at the same time of the date on which it received the notification.

ARTICLE 12

Nonsignatory States may accede to the present convention whether or not they have been represented at the International Conference at Brussels.

A State which desires to accede shall notify its intention in writing to the Belgian Government, forwarding to it the document of accession, which shall be deposited in the archives of the said Government.

The Belgian Government shall immediately forward to all the States which have signed or acceded to the convention a duly certified copy of the notification and the act of accession, mentioning the date on which it received the notification.

ARTICLE 13

The high contracting parties may at the time of signature, ratification, or accession declare that their acceptance of the present convention does not include any or all of the self-governing dominions, or of the colonies, over-seas possessions, protectorates, or territories under their sovereignty or authority, and they may subsequently accede separately on behalf of any self-governing dominion, colony, overseas possession, protectorate, or territory excluded in their declaration. They may also denounce the convention sepa-rately in accordance with its provisions in respect of any self-governing domin-ion, or any colony, overseas possession, protectorate, or territory under their sovereignty or authority.

ARTICLE 14

The present convention shall take effect, in the case of the States which have taken part in the first deposit of ratifications, one year after the date of the procès-verbal recording such deposit. As respects the States which ratify subsequently or which accede, and also in cases in which the convention is subsequently put into effect in accordance with Article 13, it shall take effect six months after the notifications specified in paragraph 2 of Article 11, and paragraph 2 of Article 12, have been received by the Belgian Government.

ARTICLE 15

In the event of one of the contracting States wishing to denounce the present convention, the denunciation shall be notified in writing to the Belgian Government, which shall immediately communicate a duly certified copy of the notification to all the other States informing them of the date on which it was received.

The denunciation shall only operate in respect of the State which made the notification, and on the expiry of one year after the notification has reached the Belgian Government.

ARTICLE 16

Any one of the contracting States shall have the right to call for a fresh conference with a view to considering possible amendments.

A State which would exercise this right should notify its intention to the other States through the Belgian Government, which would make arrange-ments for convening the conference.

Done at Brussels, in a single copy, August 25, 1924.

For Germany:
    KELLER

For the Argentine Republic:

For Belgium:
    LOUIS FRANCK
    ALBERT LE JEUNE
    SOHR

For Chile:
    ARMANDO QUEZADA

For the Republic of Cuba:

For Denmark:

For Spain:
    THE MARQUIS OF VILLALOBAR

For Estonia:
    PUSTA

For the United States of America:
    WILLIAM PHILLIPS

For Finland:

For France:
  MAURICE HERBETTE

For Great Britain:
  GEORGE GRAHAME

For Hungary:
  WORACZICZKY

For Italy:
  GIULIO DANEO

For Japan:
  M. ADATCI
    Subject to the reservations formulated in the note relative to this treaty and appended to my letter dated August 25, 1925, to His Excellency Mr. Emile Vandervelde, Minister for Foreign Affairs of Belgium.

For Latvia:

For Mexico:

For Norway:

For the Netherlands:

For Peru:

For Poland and the Free City of Danzig:
  SZEMBEK

For Portugal:

For Rumania:
  HENRY CATARGI

For the Kingdom of the Serbs, Croats and Slovenes:
  Dr. MILORAD STRAZNICKY
  Dr. VERONA

For Sweden:

For Uruguay:

PROTOCOL OF SIGNATURE

In proceeding to the signature of the international convention for the unification of certain rules relating to bills of lading, the undersigned plenipotentiaries have adopted the present protocol which will have the same validity as if the provisions thereof were inserted in the very text of the convention to which it refers.

The high contracting parties may give effect to this convention either by giving it the force of law or by including in their national legislation in a form appropriate to that legislation, the rules adopted under this convention.

They may reserve the right:

1. To prescribe that in the cases referred to in paragraph 2 (c) to (p) of Article 4, the holder of a bill of lading shall be entitled to establish responsibility for loss or damage arising from the personal fault of the carrier or the fault of his servants which are not covered by paragraph (a);

2. To apply Article 6 insofar as the national coasting trade is concerned to all classes of goods without taking account of the restriction set out in the last paragraph of that article.

Done at Brussels, in a single copy, August 25, 1924.

For Germany:
  KELLER

For the Argentine Republic:

For Belgium:
  LOUIS FRANCK
  ALBERT LE JEUNE
  SOHR

For Chile:
  ARMANDO QUEZADA

For the Republic of Cuba:

For Denmark:

For Spain:
  THE MARQUIS OF VILLALOBAR

For Estonia:
  PUSTA

For the United States of America:
  WILLIAM PHILLIPS

For Finland:

For France:
  MAURICE HERBETTE

For Great Britain:
  GEORGE GRAHAME

  In proceeding to the signature of the present Convention, His Excellency made, in the name of his Government, the declaration of which the terms are reproduced in an annex to the present Procès-Verbal.

For Hungary:
  WORACZICZKY

For Italy:
  GIULIO DANEO

For Japan:

For Latvia:

For Mexico:

For Norway:

For the Netherlands:

For Peru:

For Poland and the Free City of Danzig:
  SZEMBEK

For Portugal:

For Rumania:
  HENRY CATARGI

For the Kingdom of the Serbs, Croats and Slovenes:
  DR. MILORAD STRAZNICKY
  DR. VERONA

For Sweden:

For Uruguay:

British Declarations

I, the Undersigned, His Britannic Majesty's Ambassador at Brussels, on affixing my signature to the Protocol of Signature of the International Convention for the unification of certain rules relating to Bills of Lading, on this 15th day of November 1924, hereby make the following Declarations by direction of my Government:

I declare that His Britannic Majesty's Government adopt the last reservation in the additional Protocol of the Bills of Lading Convention.

I further declare that my signature applies only to Great Britain and Northern Ireland. I reserve the right of each of the British Dominions, Colonies, Overseas Possessions and Protectorates, and of each of the territories over which His Britannic Majesty exercises a mandate to accede to this Convention under Article 13.

GEORGE GRAHAME

His Britannic Majesty's Ambassador at Brussels

Brussels, this 15th day of November 1924.

Note annexed to a letter of His Excellency the Ambassador of Japan to the Minister of Foreign Affairs of Belgium, on August 25, 1925

At the moment of proceeding to the signature of the International Convention for the unification of certain rules relating to Bills of Lading, the undersigned, Plenipotentiary of Japan, makes the following reservations:

a) *To Article 4:*

Japan reserves to itself until further notice the acceptance of the provisions in (a) of paragraph 2 of Article 4.

b) Japan is of the opinion that the Convention does not in any part apply to national coasting trade: consequently, there should be no occasion to make it the object of provisions in the Protocol. However, if it be not so, Japan reserves to itself the right freely to regulate the national coasting trade by its own law.

M. Adatci

Brussels, August 25, 1925

UNIVERSAL POSTAL UNION

Convention and final protocol of convention signed at Stockholm August 28, 1924 [1]
Ratified and approved by the Postmaster General of the United States March 19, 1925
Approved by the President of the United States March 24, 1925
Entered into force October 1, 1925
Terminated by convention of June 28, 1929 [2]

44 Stat. 2221; Post Office Department print

[TRANSLATION]

UNIVERSAL POSTAL CONVENTION

TABLE OF CONTENTS

TITLE I

THE UNIVERSAL POSTAL UNION

CHAPTER I

Organization and jurisdiction of the Union

---

[1] For text of regulations for execution of the convention, see 44 Stat. 2273.
[2] *Post,* p. 873.

CHAPTER III

Collect on delivery articles

58. Rates and conditions. Settlement.
59. Cancellation of the amount to be collected.
60. Responsibility in case of loss of articles.
61. Guarantee of the sums regularly collected.
62. Indemnity in case of noncollection, insufficient collection or fraudulent collection.
63. Sums regularly collected. Indemnity. Payment and recourse.
64. Period for payment.
65. Fixing of responsibility.
66. Reimbursement of sums advanced.
67. C.O.D. money orders.
68. Sharing of C.O.D. charges and fees.

CHAPTER IV

Retention of postage. Transit and warehousing charges

69. Retention of postage.
70. Transit charges.
71. Warehousing charges.
72. Freedom from transit charges.
73. Extraordinary services.
74. Airplane services.
75. Payments and accounts.
76. Transit charges in relations with countries outside of the Union.
77. Exchange of closed mails with warships.

Various provisions

78. Failure to observe liberty of transit.
79. Obligations.

Final provisions

80. Effective date and duration of the Convention.

FINAL PROTOCOL

   I. Withdrawal of correspondence.
  II. Equivalents. Maximum and minimum limits.
 III. Option of requiring prepayment.
  IV. Mailing of correspondence in another country.
   V. Avoirdupois ounce.
  VI. Reply coupons.
 VII. Registration fee.
VIII. Warehousing charges.
  IX. Protocol left open to countries not represented.
   X. Protocol left open to countries represented for signatures and adhesions.
  XI. Period for notification of adhesion of countries not represented.
 XII. Research Committee.

UNIVERSAL POSTAL CONVENTION

Concluded between the Union of South Africa, Albania, Germany, the United States of America, the whole of the Insular Possessions of the United States of America other than the Philippine Islands, the Philippine Islands, the Argentine Republic, the Commonwealth of Australia, Austria, Belgium, the Colony of the Belgian Congo, Bolivia, Brazil, Bulgaria, Canada, Chile, China, the Republic of Colombia, the Republic of Costa Rica, the Republic of Cuba, Denmark, the Free City of Danzig, the Dominican

Republic, Egypt, Ecuador, Spain, the Spanish Colonies, Esthonia, Abyssinia, Finland, France, Algeria, the French Colonies and Protectorates of Indo-China, the whole of the other French Colonies, Great Britain and various British Colonies and Protectorates, Greece, Guatemala, the Republic of Haiti, the Republic of Honduras, Hungary, British India, the Irish Free State, Iceland, Italy, the whole of the Italian Colonies, Japan, Korea, the whole of the other Japanese Dependencies, Latvia, the Republic of Liberia, Lithuania, Luxemburg, Morocco (except the Spanish Zone), Morocco (Spanish Zone), Mexico, Nicaragua, Norway, New Zealand, the Republic of Panama, Paraguay, the Netherlands, the Dutch East Indies, the Dutch Colonies in America, Peru, Persia, Poland, Portugal, the Portuguese Colonies of Africa, the Portuguese Colonies of Asia and Oceania, Rumania, the Republic of San Marino, El Salvador, the Saar Territory, the Kingdom of the Serbs, Croats, and Slovenes, the Kingdom of Siam, Sweden, Switzerland, Czechoslovakia, Tunis, Turkey, the Union of the Socialistic Soviet Republics, Uruguay and the United States of Venezuela.

The undersigned plenipotentiaries of the countries above enumerated, being assembled in congress at Stockholm by virtue of Article 27 of the Universal Postal Convention concluded at Madrid on November 30, 1920,[3] have, by common consent and subject to ratification, revised the said Convention in accordance with the following provisions:

TITLE I

THE UNIVERSAL POSTAL UNION

CHAPTER I

ORGANIZATION AND JURISDICTION OF THE UNION

ARTICLE 1

Composition of the Union

The countries between which the present Convention is concluded form, under the denomination of Universal Postal Union, a single postal territory for the reciprocal exchange of correspondence. The purpose of the Postal Union is also to assure the organization and perfection of the various international postal services.

ARTICLE 2

New adhesions. Procedure

Countries which do not form part of the Union are permitted to adhere to the Convention at any time.

---

[3] *Ante,* p. 282.

Notice of their request for adhesion must be given, through diplomatic channels, to the Government of the Swiss Confederation, and by the latter to the Governments of all of the countries of the Union.

ARTICLE 3

Convention and Agreements of the Union

The regular mail service is governed by the provisions of the Convention.

Other services, especially such as those of insured letters and boxes, parcel post, money orders, postal checks, collections by mail, and subscriptions to newspapers and periodicals, form the subject of Agreements among countries of the Union.

Such Agreements are obligatory only for the countries which have adhered to them.

Adhesion to one or more of those Agreements is subject to the provisions of the preceding Article.

ARTICLE 4

Regulations of execution

The Administrations of the Union draw up, by mutual consent, in the Regulations of Execution,[4] the measures of order and detail necessary for the execution of the Convention and the Agreements.

ARTICLE 5

Special treaties and restricted Unions. Frontier Zones

1. The countries of the Union have the right to maintain and conclude treaties, as well as to maintain and establish restricted unions, with a view to the reduction of rates or to any other improvement of postal relations.

2. For their part, the Administrations are authorized to make the necessary agreements among themselves relative to questions which do not interest the whole of the Union, on the condition that they do not introduce any provisions less favorable than those provided by the Acts of the Union. They may, in particular, with regard to articles of correspondence, make agreements among themselves for the adoption of reduced postage rates within a radius of 30 kilometers.

ARTICLE 6

Domestic legislation

The provisions of the Convention and Agreements of the Union do not affect the legislation of each country in anything which is not expressly provided for by those Acts.

---

[4] See footnote 1, p. 443.

ARTICLE 7

Relations with countries foreign to the Union

Administrations of the Union which maintain relations with countries foreign to the Union are bound to place those relations at the disposal of the other Administrations for the exchange of correspondence.

The provisions of the Convention apply to the exchange of articles of correspondence between countries of the Union and countries foreign to the Union whenever such exchange employs the services of at least two of the contracting parties.

ARTICLE 8

Colonies, Protectorates, etc.

In the sense of the Convention and the Agreements, particularly in regard to their right to vote in Congresses and Conferences and in the interval between meetings, as well as to their share in the expenses of the International Bureau of the Universal Postal Union, the following are considered as forming a single country or a single Administration of the Union, as the case may be:

1° The Colony of the Belgian Congo;

2° The whole of the Insular Possessions of the United States of America other than the Philippine Islands, and comprising Hawaii, Porto Rico, Guam, and the Virgin Islands of the United States of America;

3° The Philippine Islands;

4° The whole of the Spanish Colonies;

5° Algeria;

6° The French Colonies and Protectorates of Indo-China;

7° The whole of the other French Colonies;

8° The whole of the Italian Colonies;

9° Korea;

10° The whole of the other Japanese Dependencies;

11° The Dutch East Indies;

12° The Dutch Colonies in America;

13° The Portuguese Colonies of Africa;

14° The Portuguese Colonies of Asia and Oceania.

ARTICLE 9

Extent of the Union

The following are considered as belonging to the Universal Postal Union:

(a) Post Offices established by countries of the Union in countries foreign to the Union;

(b) The Principality of Liechtenstein, as belonging to the Postal Administration of Switzerland;

(c) The Faroe Islands and Greenland as forming part of Denmark;

(d) The Spanish possessions on the north coast of Africa, as forming part of Spain; the Republic of Andorra, as belonging to the Spanish Postal Administration;

(e) The Principality of Monaco, as belonging to the Postal Administration of France;

(f) Walfish Bay, as forming part of the Union of South Africa; Basutoland, as belonging to the Postal Administration of the Union of South Africa;

(g) The Norwegian post offices established on the islands of Spitzbergen, as belonging to the Postal Administration of Norway.

ARTICLE 10

Arbitration

1. In case of disagreement between two or more members of the Union as to the interpretation of the Convention and Agreements, or as to the responsibility imposed upon an Administration by the application of those Acts, the question in dispute is decided by arbitration. To that end, each of the Administrations concerned chooses another member of the Union which is not directly interested in the matter.

If one of the Administrations involved in the dispute does not take any action on a proposal for arbitration within a period of six months, or nine months in the case of oversea countries, the International Bureau, upon a request made of it to that effect, may call upon the defaulting Administration to appoint an arbitrator, or may appoint one itself officially.

2. The decision of the arbitrators is made on an absolute majority of votes.

3. In case of equality of votes, the arbitrators, for the purpose of settling the difference, choose another Administration which likewise has no interest in the dispute. In case of disagreement on a choice, that Administration shall be designated by the International Bureau from among the members of the Union not proposed by the arbitrators.

4. Only such Administrations as are executing the Agreement under litigation may be designated as arbitrators.

ARTICLE 11

Withdrawal from the Union. Termination of participation in the Agreements

Each contracting party has the option of withdrawing from the Union or of ceasing to participate in the Agreements by notice given one year in advance by its Government to the Government of the Swiss Confederation.

CHAPTER II

CONGRESSES, CONFERENCES, COMMITTEES

ARTICLE 12

Congresses

1. Delegates from the countries of the Union meet in Congress not later than five years after the effective date of the Acts of the preceding Congress, with a view to revising or completing them, if necessary.

Each country is represented at the Congress by one or more plenipotentiary delegates, provided with the necessary credentials by their Government. It may, if necessary, be represented by the delegation of another country. However, it is understood that a delegation may be charged with representing only two countries, including the one by which it was first accredited.

In the deliberations each country has only one vote.

2. Each Congress fixes the place of meeting of the next Congress. The Congress is called together by the Government of the country in which it is to take place, after agreement with the International Bureau. That Government is likewise charged with notifying all the Governments and Countries of the Union of the decisions made by the Congress.

ARTICLE 13

Ratifications. Effective date and duration of the Acts of the Congress

The Acts of the Congresses are ratified as soon as possible, and the ratifications are communicated to the Government of the country in which the Congress was held.

In case that one or more of the contracting parties do not ratify one or the other of the Acts signed by them, the Acts will be none the less valid for the countries which have ratified them.

Those Acts are put into effect simultaneously and have the same duration.

From the date fixed for the entry into force of the Acts adopted by a Congress, all the Acts of the preceding Congress are abrogated, barring contrary agreement.

ARTICLE 14

Extraordinary Congresses

An extraordinary Congress is called together after agreement with the International Bureau when a request to that effect is made or approved by at least two-thirds of the contracting countries.

The rules set forth in Articles 12 and 13 are applicable to the delegations in the deliberations and Acts of the extraordinary Congresses.

ARTICLE 15

Regulations of Congresses

Each Congress draws up the necessary regulations for its work and its deliberations.

ARTICLE 16

Conferences

Conferences charged with the examination of purely administrative questions may be called together at the request of at least two-thirds of the Administrations of the Union.

They are called together after agreement with the International Bureau.

The Conferences draw up their regulations.

ARTICLE 17

Committees

The Committees charged by a Congress or a Conference with the study of one or more determined questions are called together by the International Bureau, if necessary after agreement with the Administration of the country where such Committees are to meet.

CHAPTER III

PROPOSITIONS DURING THE INTERVAL BETWEEN MEETINGS

ARTICLE 18

Introduction of the propositions

During the interval between meetings, every Administration has the right to address propositions concerning the Convention and its Regulations to the Administrations through the intermediary of the International Bureau.

The same right is accorded to the Administrations of the countries participating in the Agreements in regard to those Agreements and their Regulations.

In order to be considered, all propositions introduced during the interval between meetings must be supported by at least two Administrations, without counting the one from which they come. Such propositions are ignored when the International Bureau does not receive, at the same time, the necessary number of declarations of support.

ARTICLE 19

Examination of the Propositions

Every proposition is submitted to the following procedure:

A period of six months is allowed to the Administrations, in order to examine the propositions and send their observations, if any, to the International Bureau. Amendments are not admitted. The replies are assembled by the International Bureau and communicated to the Administrations, with an invitation to pronounce themselves for or against. Those which have not sent in their votes within a period of six months, counting from the date of the second circular of the International Bureau notifying them of the observations made, are considered as abstaining.

If the proposition concerns an Agreement or the Regulations relative thereto, only the Administrations which have adhered to that Agreement can take part in the procedure indicated above.

ARTICLE 20

Conditions of Approval

1. In order to become effective, the propositions must obtain:

(a) Unanimity of votes if it is a question of adding new provisions or modifying the provisions of Titles I and II and of Articles 33 to 36, 38, 48 to 53, 55, 56, 58, 60 to 63, 65 to 75, 77 to 80 of the Convention, and of Articles 1, 4, 17, 53, 66, and 86 of the Regulations.

(b) Two-thirds of the votes if it is a question of modifying provisions other than those mentioned in the preceding paragraph.

(c) Absolute majority if it is a question of interpreting the provisions of the Convention and its Regulations, except the case of disagreement to be submitted to arbitration contemplated by Article 10.

2. The Agreements fix the conditions to which the approval of propositions concerning them is subject.

ARTICLE 21

Notification of the Resolutions

The additions to and modifications of the Convention and Agreements are sanctioned by a diplomatic declaration which the Government of the Swiss Confederation is charged with making up and transmitting, at the request of the International Bureau, to the Governments of the contracting countries.

The additions to and modifications of the Regulations are established and communicated to the Administrations by the International Bureau. The same applies to the interpretations contemplated under letter (c) of the preceding Article.

ARTICLE 22

Execution of the Resolutions

No addition or modification adopted is effective until at least three months after its notification.

CHAPTER IV

THE INTERNATIONAL BUREAU

ARTICLE 23

General Attributions

1. A central Office, functioning at Berne under the name of International Bureau of the Universal Postal Union and placed under the supervision of the Swiss Postal Administration, serves as an organ of liaison, information, and consultation for the countries of the Union.

This Bureau is charged, principally, with assembling, coordinating, publishing, and distributing information of all kinds which concerns the international postal service; with giving, at the request of the interested parties an opinion on questions in dispute; with making known requests for modification of the Acts of the Congress; with notifying the changes adopted; and, in general, with undertaking the studies and works of editing and documentation which the Convention, the Agreements, and their Regulations attribute to it, or which may be intrusted to it in the interest of the Union.

2. It intervenes, as a disbursing office, in the settlement of accounts of all kinds relative to the international postal service between Administrations requesting such intervention.

ARTICLE 24

Expenses of the International Bureau

1. Each Congress fixes the maximum figure which the ordinary annual expenses of the International Bureau may amount to.

Those expenses, as well as the extraordinary expenses arising from the meeting of a Congress, a Conference or a Committee and the expenses incurred in connection with special work confided to the Bureau, are shared by all of the countries of the Union.

2. The countries of the Union are divided, for that purpose, into seven classes, each of which contributes to the expenses in the following proportion:

First class	25 units
Second class	20 units
Third class	15 units
Fourth class	10 units
Fifth class	5 units
Sixth class	3 units
Seventh class	1 unit

3. In case of a new adhesion, the Government of the Swiss Confederation determines, by mutual agreement with the Government of the country concerned, the class in which it is to be placed in view of the division of the expenses of the International Bureau.

TITLE II

RULES OF GENERAL ORDER

SOLE CHAPTER

ARTICLE 25

Liberty of Transit

1. Liberty of transit is guaranteed throughout the entire territory of the Union.

2. Liberty of transit of parcel post is limited to the territory of the countries participating in that service. Insured articles may be transported in closed mails over the territory of countries which do not adhere to the Agreement relative to that service, but the responsibility of those countries is limited to that prescribed for registered articles.

ARTICLE 26

Right To Utilize the Services of the Union

The countries of the Union recognize the right of all persons to utilize the services which form the subject of the Convention and Agreements.

ARTICLE 27

Prohibition Against Unauthorized Charges

It is forbidden to collect postage charges of any nature whatever, other than those provided by the Convention and the Agreements.

ARTICLE 28

Temporary Suspension of Service

When, as a result of exceptional circumstances, an Administration finds itself obliged to suspend, temporarily, and in a general or partial manner, either the dispatch of articles of correspondence delivered to it by another Administration, or the execution of one or of several special services, it is bound to give notice thereof immediately, if necessary by telegraph, to the Administration or Administrations concerned.

ARTICLE 29

Monetary Standard

The franc used as the monetary unit in the provisions of the Convention and the Agreements is the gold franc of 100 centimes weighing $10/31$ of a gram and having a fineness of 0.900.

ARTICLE 30

Equivalents

In each country of the Union, the rates are fixed according to equivalents corresponding, as exactly as possible, to the value of the franc in the current money of that country.

ARTICLE 31

Forms. Language

1. The forms used by the Administrations in their reciprocal relations shall be edited in the French language, with or without an interlinear translation in another language, unless the Administrations concerned arrange otherwise by direct agreement.

2. The forms used by the public which are not printed in the French language must bear an interlinear translation in that language.

3. The forms covered by Sections 1 and 2 shall have dimensions as near as possible to those prescribed by the Regulations of the Convention and of the Agreements.

4. The Administrations may come to agreements as to the language to be employed for official correspondence in their reciprocal relations.

ARTICLE 32

Identity Cards

1. Each Administration may issue, to persons who apply for them, identity cards valid as proof of identity in all transactions effected by the post offices of the countries which do not give notice of their refusal to admit them.

2. The Administration which issues an identity card is authorized to collect, on that account, a charge not exceeding 1 franc.

3. Administrations are relieved from all responsibility when it is proved that a mail article was delivered or a money order was paid upon presentation of a regular identity card.

Neither are they responsible for the consequences of loss, theft or fraudulent use of a regular identity card.

4. An identity card is valid for a period of three years, counting from the date of issue.

TITLE III

PROVISIONS CONCERNING POSTAL CORRESPONDENCE

CHAPTER I

GENERAL PROVISIONS

ARTICLE 33

Articles of Correspondence

The denomination "articles of correspondence" applies to letters, single and reply-paid post cards, commercial papers, samples of merchandise, and prints of all kinds, including prints in relief for the use of the blind.

ARTICLE 34

Rates of Postage and General Conditions

1. The rates of postage for the transportation of articles of correspondence throughout the whole extent of the Union, including delivery at the residence of the addressee in countries where the delivery service is or may be established, are fixed in accordance with the indications of the following table:

Articles	Units of weight	Rates	Limits	
			Of weight	Of dimensions
	Grams	*Centimes*		
Letters, first unit of weight.....	20	25	} 2 kg...	⎰45 cm. on each side. In the form of a roll: 75 cm. in length and 10 cm. in diameter.
Letters, each additional unit...	....	15		
Post cards, single...............	....	15	....	Maximum: 15 cm. in length and 10.5 cm. in width.
Post cards, with reply paid....	....	30	....	Minimum: 10 cm. in length and 7 cm. in diameter.
Prints......................	50	5	2 kg[1]...	As for letters.
Prints, raised, for the blind....	1,000	5	3 kg...	
Commercial papers..........	50	5	2 kg...	
Commercial papers, minimum charge.	....	25	....	
Samples of merchandise.......	50	5	500 g..	⎰45 cm. in length; 20 cm. in width; 10 cm. in thickness. In the form of a roll: 45 cm. in length and 15 cm. in diameter.
Samples of merchandise, minimum charge.	....	10	....	

[1] That weight is increased to 3 kilograms for single volumes.

The Administrations have the option of granting, in their reciprocal relations, to newspapers and periodicals mailed directly by the publishers, a reduction of 50 per cent from the regular rate for printed matter.

The same option is accorded to them in regard to stitched or bound books, with the exception of all price lists and catalogs.

The same also applies to literary and scientific editions exchanged between institutions of learning.

2. Each country of the Union shall fix the rates to be charged for articles of correspondence in accordance with the indications of the foregoing table.

3. Letters shall not contain any letter, note or document addressed to persons other than the addressee or to persons making their domicile with the latter.

4. Commercial papers, samples of merchandise and prints of any kind shall not contain any letter or note having the character of actual and personal correspondence; they shall be so prepared as to facilitate verification, except as provided by the Regulations.

5. The limits of weight and dimensions fixed by Section 1 of this Article shall not apply to the correspondence relative to the postal service mentioned in Section 1 of Article 43.

6. Packages containing samples of merchandise shall not contain any article having a salable value.

7. The inclusion in a single package of different classes of mail matter (grouped articles) is authorized under the conditions set forth in the Regulations.

8. Except as provided by the Convention and the Regulations, articles which do not comply with the requirements shall not be dispatched.

Articles which have been accepted contrary to the requirements may be returned to the country of origin. If the country of destination effects delivery to the addressee, it shall collect such postage and surcharges as are provided for the class of correspondence to which the article actually belongs.

9. Articles bearing letter postage may contain dutiable articles, in the event that the importation of such articles in the form of letters is permitted by the country of destination.

These articles should bear, on the address side, a label conforming to the requirements of the Regulations.

The Administrations of destination are authorized to turn such articles over to the customs service, open them officially and collect the import duties in the manner prescribed by their legislation.

ARTICLE 35

Prepayment

Articles other than letters and post cards shall be entirely prepaid.

Reply post cards on both halves of which the postage is not fully prepaid at the time of mailing shall not be dispatched.

ARTICLE 36

Charge in Case of Absence or Insufficiency of Prepayment

In case of absence or insufficiency of prepayment, and with the exceptions provided by Article 39 of the Regulations for certain classes of reforwarded mail, articles of correspondence of all classes are subject, at the expense of the addressees, to a charge double the amount of the deficient postage or the insufficiency; but that charge shall not be lower than 10 centimes.

ARTICLE 37

Correspondence Outside of the Union

1. The rates for correspondence addressed to countries outside of the Union must not be lower than the normal Union rates.

2. Correspondence originating in countries outside of the Union which is delivered to a Union country unprepaid or insufficiently prepaid is charged with the amount of the deficient postage by the delivering Administration in accordance with the rules applicable in its own service to similar articles addressed to the countries from which the said correspondence comes.

ARTICLE 38

Surtaxes

There may be collected, in addition to the rates fixed by Articles 34 and 37, for every article transported by services maintained by Administrations foreign to the Union, or by extraordinary services within the Union giving rise to special expenses, a surtax proportionate to those expenses.

When the rate of prepayment of the single post card includes the surtax authorized by the preceding paragraph, the same rate is applicable to each half of the reply-paid post card.

ARTICLE 39

Special Charges

1. The Administrations are authorized to charge late fees in accordance with the provisions of their own legislation for articles mailed in their services for dispatch at the last moment.

2. Countries of destination which are authorized by their own legislation to deliver articles liable to customs duty may collect a charge of 50 centimes at most per piece for customs service.

3. Countries of destination are authorized to collect a special charge in accordance with their own legislation on articles addressed to general delivery.

ARTICLE 40

Special Delivery Articles

1. Articles of correspondence are, at the request of the senders, delivered to the addressee by special messenger immediately after their arrival in countries whose Administrations undertake that service in their reciprocal relations.

2. Such articles, known as "special delivery articles," are subject, besides the regular postage, to a special charge the minimum of which shall be double the postage on an ordinary letter and the maximum 1 franc. This postage must be completely prepaid by the sender.

3. In the event that the addressee's residence is situated outside of the free delivery zone of the office of destination, delivery by special messenger may give rise to the collection of supplementary postage corresponding to that collected in the domestic service.

Special delivery is not obligatory in such cases.

4. Special delivery articles upon which the total amount of the charges payable in advance has not been prepaid are delivered by the ordinary means, unless they have been treated as special delivery articles by the office of origin.

ARTICLE 41

Prohibitions

1. It is forbidden to send by mail:

(a) Articles which, by their nature or wrapping, may expose postal employees to danger, or soil or damage the mails.

(b) Explosive, inflammable, or dangerous substances.

(c) Live animals, with the exception of bees and silkworms.

(d) Articles liable to customs duty, including samples of merchandise sent in quantities with a view to avoiding the payment of duty; subject, however, to the provisions of Article 34, Section 9.

(e) Opium, morphine, cocaine, and other narcotics.

(f) Obscene or immoral articles.

(g) Any articles whatever whose circulation is prohibited in the country of origin or that of destination.

It is also forbidden to send in the unregistered mails coins, bank notes, paper money, articles of gold or silver, precious stones, jewelry, and other precious articles.

2. Articles which have been wrongly admitted to the mails must be returned to the country of origin, except in cases where the Administration of the country of destination is authorized by its legislation or domestic regulations to dispose of them otherwise.

However, explosive, inflammable, or dangerous substances, and obscene or immoral articles, are not returned to the country of origin; they are destroyed on the spot by the services of the Administration which has detected their presence.

In cases where articles wrongly accepted for mailing are neither returned to the country of origin nor delivered to the addressee, the dispatching Administration should be informed so that it may take the necessary measures.

3. The right is, moreover, reserved for every country of the Union to refuse to convey in transit in open mail over its territory or to deliver articles admitted at reduced rates in regard to which the laws, ordinances, or decrees regulating the conditions of their publication or circulation or in that country have not been observed.

These articles should be returned to the country of origin.

ARTICLE 42

Forms of prepayment

1. Prepayment is effected either by means of postage stamps valid in the country of origin for the correspondence of private individuals or by means of impressions of stamping machines, officially adopted and operating under the immediate control of the Administration.

2. The following are considered as duly prepaid: Reply post cards bearing printed or adhesive postage stamps of the country of issue of the cards; articles regularly prepaid for their first transmission and on which the additional postage has been paid before their redirection; as well as newspapers or packages of newspapers and periodicals whose address bears the words "abonnement-poste" (subscription by mail) or an equivalent notation sent under the Agreement concerning subscriptions to newspapers and periodicals.

3. Correspondence mailed on the high seas, in the box on board ship, or handed to postal agents on board or to the commanders of ships, may be prepaid, barring contrary agreement between the Administrations concerned, by means of the postage stamps and according to the postage rates of the country to which the said vessel belongs or by which it is maintained. If the mailing on board takes place during the stay at one of the two terminal points of the voyage or at one of the ports of call, the prepayment is valid only if it is effected by means of the postage stamps and according to the postage rates of the country in whose waters the vessel is stationed.

ARTICLE 43

Franking privilege

1. Correspondence relating to the postal service exchanged between the Postal Administrations, between those Administrations and the International Bureau, between the post offices of countries of the Union, and between

those offices and the Administrations, as well as that for which the franking privilege is expressly provided by the provisions of the Convention and Agreements and their Regulations, is admitted free of postage.

2. Correspondence (except collect on delivery articles) addressed to prisoners of war or mailed by them is likewise free of all postal charges, not only in the countries of origin and destination but also in the intermediary countries.

The same is true of correspondence concerning prisoners of war, sent or received either direct or as intermediary by the information offices which may be established on behalf of such persons in belligerent countries or in neutral countries which have received belligerents on their territory.

Belligerents received and interned in a neutral country are assimilated to prisoners of war properly so called insofar as concerns the application of the above provisions.

ARTICLE 44

Reply coupons

Reply coupons are placed on sale in the countries of the Union.

The selling price is determined by the interested Administrations, but may not be less than 40 gold centimes or the equivalent of that sum in the money of the issuing country.

Each coupon is exchangeable in any country of the Union for a postage stamp or postage stamps representing the postage on a single-rate letter originating in that country and addressed to a foreign country. However, the exchange must be made before the expiration of the sixth month following that of issue.

Moreover, the right is reserved for each country to require that the articles of correspondence for the prepayment of which the reply coupons are exchanged be mailed at the time of presentation of the coupons.

ARTICLE 45

Withdrawal. Change of address

1. The sender of an article of correspondence may cause it to be withdrawn from the mails or have its address changed, provided that such article has not been delivered to the addressee.

2. The request to be made to that effect is sent by mail or by telegraph at the expense of the sender, who must pay, for every request by mail, the charge applicable to a single-rate registered letter; and, for every request by telegraph, the charge for a telegram, increased by the postage charge in case of change of address.

Article 46

Forwarding. Undelivered correspondence

1. The forwarding of articles of correspondence within the Union does not give rise to the collection of any additional charge, with the exceptions provided by the Regulations.

The same applies to the return to the sender of undelivered correspondence.

2. Forwarded or returned articles of correspondence are delivered to the addressees or senders upon payment of the charges due on them on departure, on arrival or in the course of transmission, as a result of redirection beyond the first transmission.

3. Correspondence which is undeliverable for any reason whatsoever must be returned immediately to the country of origin.

The period of retention of correspondence held at the disposal of the addressees or addressed "general delivery" is governed by the laws of the country of destination. However, such period may not exceed six months in relations with oversea countries and two months in other relations. The return to the country of origin must take place within a shorter period, if the sender has so requested by a notation in the address in a language known in the country of destination.

4. Prints without value are not returned, unless the sender, by a notation on the outside of the article, requests the return.

5. The "general delivery" charge provided by Article 39 does not follow the article in case of redirection or return as undeliverable.

6. The additional charge stipulated by Article 40, Section 3, remains collectible in case of redirection or return as undeliverable of a special delivery article.

Article 47

Inquiries

1. An inquiry as to the disposal made of any article may give rise to the collection of a fee fixed at 1 franc maximum.

As for registered articles, no fee is collected if the sender has already paid the special fee for a return receipt.

2. Inquiries are admitted only within the period of one year, counting from the day following that of mailing.

Chapter II

REGISTERED ARTICLES

Article 48

Charges

1. The articles of correspondence designated in Article 33 may be sent under registration.

However, the reply halves of post cards may not be registered by the original senders of such articles.

2. The postage for all registered articles shall be paid in advance. It consists of:

(*a*) The ordinary cost of prepayment of the article, according to its nature.

(*b*) A fixed registration fee of 40 centimes maximum.

3. A receipt shall be delivered without charge to the sender of a registered article at the time of mailing.

4. The countries disposed to undertake risks which may arise from cases of force majeure (causes beyond control) are authorized to collect a special charge of 40 centimes at most for each registered article.

ARTICLE 49

Return receipts

The sender of a registered article may obtain a return receipt by paying, at the time of mailing, a fixed charge of 40 centimes at most.

The return receipt may be requested after mailing the article, within the period fixed by Article 47 for inquiries, and by means of the payment of a fee which must not exceed double that provided by the preceding paragraph.

ARTICLE 50

Extent of responsibility

With the exceptions provided in the following Article, the Administrations are responsible for the loss of registered articles.

The sender is entitled, under that head, to an indemnity, the amount of which is fixed at 50 francs for each article.

If he has paid the fee for an inquiry, and if such inquiry was rendered necessary by a fault of the service, that fee is likewise returned to him.

ARTICLE 51

Exceptions to the principle of responsibility

The Administrations are released from all responsibility for the loss of registered articles:

(*a*) In case of force majeure; however, the responsibility is maintained in regard to an Administration of origin which has undertaken to cover the risks of force majeure (Article 48, Section 4);

(*b*) When they cannot account for the articles as a result of the destruction of the records of the service resulting from a case of force majeure;

(*c*) When it is a question of articles whose contents fall within the scope of the prohibitions provided by Article 41, Section 1;

(*d*) When the sender has not made any application within the period contemplated by Article 47.

ARTICLE 52

Termination of responsibility

The Administrations cease to be responsible for registered articles the delivery of which they have effected under the conditions prescribed by their domestic regulations.

For articles addressed to general delivery or held at the disposal of th(addressees, responsibility ceases upon delivery to a person who has proved his identity in accordance with the rules in force in the country of destination, whose names and description are in conformity with the indications of the address.

ARTICLE 53

Payment of indemnity

The obligation of paying indemnity falls upon the Administration to which the office of origin of the article belongs, with the reservation of its right to make a claim against the responsible Administration.

ARTICLE 54

Period for payment

1. The payment of the indemnity must take place as soon as possible, and, at the latest, within the period of six months, counting from the day following the date of the inquiry (application). That period is extended to nine months in relations with oversea countries.

2. The Administration of origin is authorized to settle with the sender on account of the Administration of intermediation or of destination which, duly advised of the application, has let six months pass without settling the matter; that period is extended to nine months in relations with oversea countries.

The dispatching Administration may exceptionally postpone the settlement of the indemnity beyond the period provided by the preceding Section when the question of knowing whether the loss of the article was due to a case of force majeure has not yet been settled.

ARTICLE 55

Fixing of Responsibility

1. Until the contrary is proved, the responsibility for the loss of a registered article falls on the Administration which, having received the article without making any observations, and, being put in possession of all the particulars of inquiry prescribed by regulations, can not establish either delivery to the addressee or regular transmission to the next Administration if any.

If the loss has taken place in the course of conveyance and it is impossible to establish on the territory or in the service of which country the loss occurred the Administrations concerned bear the loss in equal shares. However, the whole of the indemnity due must be turned over to the Administration of origin by the first Administration which can not establish the regular transmission of the article in question to the corresponding service. It is incumbent upon the latter Administration to recover from the other responsible Administrations the share of each of them in the indemnity paid to the sender.

2. When a registered article has been lost under circumstances of force majeure, the Administration on whose territory or in whose service the loss took place is not responsible to the dispatching Administration unless both countries undertake risks arising from cases of force majeure.

3. By the fact of the payment of the indemnity, the responsible Administration is subrogated up to the amount of that indemnity in the rights of the person who has received it for all eventual recourse against the addressee, the sender, or a third person.

Article 56

Repayment of the Indemnity to the Administration of Origin

The Administration which is responsible, or on whose account the payment is made in accordance with Article 54, is bound to reimburse the dispatching Administration for the amount of the indemnity within a period of three months following notification of the payment.

That reimbursement is made without expense for the creditor Administration by means of either a money order or a draft or in money valid in the creditor country. At the expiration of the period of three months the sum due to the dispatching Administration bears interest at the rate of 7 percent per annum, counting from the date of expiration of the said period.

The Administration whose responsibility is duly established and which has at first declined to pay the indemnity must bear all the additional expenses resulting from the unjustified delay in making the payment.

However, the Administrations may agree among themselves to settle periodically the indemnities which they have paid to the senders and the justness of which they have recognized.

Article 57

Responsibility for Registered Articles Outside of the Limits of the Union

Responsibility for registered articles addressed to or coming from countries foreign to the Union or passing in transit through such countries is governed by the following provisions:

(a) For the conveyance within the jurisdiction of the Union, in accordance with the provisions of the Convention;

(b) For conveyance outside of the limits of the Union, in accordance with the conditions made known by the Administration of the Union which serves as intermediary.

Chapter III

COLLECT ON DELIVERY ARTICLES

Article 58

Rates and Conditions. Settlement

1. Registered articles may be sent collect on delivery in relations between countries whose Administrations agree to conduct that service.

Barring contrary agreement, the amount to be collected is expressed in the money of the country of origin of the article.

The maximum C.O.D. charge is equal to the maximum amount fixed for money orders addressed to the country of origin of the article.

Collect on delivery articles are subject to the formalities and rates applicable to registered articles.

The sender also pays a fixed charge, which may not be lower than 20 centimes nor higher than 50 centimes, and a proportional fee of $\frac{1}{2}$ percent of the amount of the C.O.D. charge. The Administration of origin has the option of rounding off those charges, in accordance with the conveniences of its monetary system.

2. The amount collected from the addressee is transmitted to the sender by means of a C.O.D. money order, which is issued free of charge.

The Administrations may agree upon another procedure for the settlement of the sums collected. They may, in particular, undertake, under conditions to be agreed upon, to turn them over to a postal account-current in the country of destination of the article.

Article 59

Cancellation of the Amount To Be Collected

The sender of a registered C.O.D. article may request total or partial cancellation of the amount to be collected.

Requests of this nature are subject to the same provisions as requests for withdrawal or change of address (Article 45).

Article 60

Responsibility in Case of Loss of Articles

The loss of a registered C.O.D. article involves the responsibility of the postal service under the conditions laid down by Articles 50 and 51.

ARTICLE 61

Guarantee of Sums Regularly Collected

The sums regularly collected from the addressee, whether or not they have been converted into money orders or turned over to a postal account-current are guaranteed to the sender, under the conditions laid down by the Agreement concerning Money Orders, or by the provisions governing the Postal Check service.

ARTICLE 62

Indemnity in Case of Noncollection, Insufficient Collection or Fraudulent Collection

1. If the article has been delivered to the addressee without collecting the amount indicated, the sender is entitled to indemnity, provided that an application has been made within the the period provided by Article 47, Section 2, and unless the noncollection is due to fault or negligence on his part, or unless the contents of the article come under the prohibitions contemplated in Article 41.

The same applies if the sum collected from the addressee is less than the amount indicated, or if the collection has been fraudulently made.

In any case the indemnity may not exceed the amount to be collected on delivery.

2. By the fact of the payment of the indemnity, the responsible Administration is subrogated in the rights of the sender for all eventual recourse against the addressee or third parties.

ARTICLE 63

Sums Regularly Collected. Indemnity. Payment and Recourse

The obligation of paying the amounts regularly collected, as well as the indemnity referred to in the preceding Article, falls upon the Administration to which the office of origin of the article belongs, with the reservation of its right to recourse against the responsible Administration.

ARTICLE 64

Period for Payment

The provisions of Article 54 concerning the periods for payment of indemnity for the loss of a registered article are applied to the payment of the sums collected or the indemnity for C.O.D. articles.

ARTICLE 65

Fixing of Responsibility

The payment by the dispatching Administration of sums regularly collected, as well as of the indemnity provided for by Article 62, is made for the account of the Administration of destination. The latter is responsible, unless it can prove that the fault is due to the failure of the dispatching Administration to observe a provision of the Regulations.

In the case of fraudulent collection as a result of the disappearance in the service of a C.O.D. article, the responsibility of the Administrations involved is determined in accordance with the rules provided in Article 55 for the loss of registered articles in general.

ARTICLE 66

Reimbursement of Sums Advanced

The Administration of destination is bound to reimburse the Administration of origin, under the conditions provided by Article 56, for the sums which have been advanced on its account.

ARTICLE 67

C.O.D. Money Orders

The amount of a C.O.D. money order which, for any reason, has not been paid to the payee, is not repaid to the Administration of issue. It is held at the disposal of the payee by the Administration of origin of the C.O.D. article, and finally reverts to that Administration, after the expiration of the period prescribed by law.

In all other respects, and with the reservations provided by the Regulations, C.O.D. money orders are subject to the provisions fixed by the Agreement concerning Money Orders.

ARTICLE 68

Sharing of C.O.D. Charges and Fees

The charges fixed in the last paragraph of Section 1 of Article 58 are divided equally between the Administration of origin and that of the country of destination, under the conditions prescribed by the Regulations.

In the event that two Administrations do not collect a fixed charge for collect on delivery service of the same amount, the pro-rata share to be paid to the corresponding Administration is calculated on the basis of the lower rate.

CHAPTER IV

RETENTION OF POSTAGE. TRANSIT AND WAREHOUSING CHARGES

ARTICLE 69

Retention of postage

Except in cases expressly provided for by the Convention, each Administration retains the whole of the sums which it has collected.

ARTICLE 70

Transit Charges

1. Correspondence exchanged in closed mails between two Administrations of the Union, by means of the services of one or several other Administrations (third services), is subject to the payment, to each of the countries traversed or whose services participate in the conveyance, of the transit charges indicated in the following table:

	Per kilogram	
	Of letters and post cards	Of other articles
1°. Territorial transit:	*Fr. C.*	*Fr. C.*
Up to 1,000 km.	0. 75	0. 10
From 1,000 to 2,000 km.	1. 00	. 15
From 2,000 to 3,000 km.	1. 50	. 20
From 3,000 to 6,000 km.	2. 50	. 30
From 6,000 to 9,000 km.	3. 50	. 40
Over 9,000 km.	4. 50	. 50
2°. Maritime transit:		
Up to 300 nautical miles.	. 75	. 10
From 300 to 1,500 nautical miles.	2. 00	. 25
Between Europe and North America.	3. 00	. 40
From 1,500 to 6,000 nautical miles.	4. 00	. 50
Over 6,000 nautical miles.	6. 00	. 75

2. The transit charges for maritime service on a route not exceeding 300 nautical miles are fixed at one-third the sums provided by the preceding Section, if the Administration concerned already receives, on account of the mails conveyed, compensation for territorial transit.

3. In the case of maritime transit effected by two or more Administrations, the total transit charges may not exceed 6 francs per kilogram of letters and post cards and 0.75 francs per kilogram of other articles. When the totals of such charges exceed 6 francs and 0.75 francs respectively, they are divided among the Administrations participating in the transportation in proportion to the distances traversed, without prejudice to different agreements which may be made between the parties concerned.

4. Barring contrary agreement, maritime conveyances effected directly between two countries, by means of ships belonging to one of them, as well as conveyances effected between two offices of the same country through the intermediary of services belonging to another country, are considered as third services.

5. Correspondence exchanged in open mail between two Administrations of the Union is subject, without regard to weight or destination, to the following transit charges, namely:

Letters	6	centimes each
Post cards	2½	centimes each
Other articles	2½	centimes each

However, the Administrations are authorized to consider as closed mails articles sent in open mail which exceed the weight of 250 grams.

6. Newspapers or packets of newspapers and periodicals sent under the Agreement concerning Subscriptions to Newspapers and Periodicals, as well as boxes with declared value sent under the Agreement concerning Letters and Boxes with Declared Value, are considered as other articles in regard to transit charges.

7. An Administration is authorized to submit to the deliberation of a Commission of arbiters the results of statistics which, in its opinion, differ too greatly from reality. Such arbitration is effected in accordance with the provisions of Article 10.

ARTICLE 71

Warehousing Charges

The warehousing in a port of closed mails brought by one steamship and intended to be taken up again by another steamship gives rise to the payment of a charge fixed at 50 centimes per sack to the profit of the Administration to which the place of warehousing belongs, unless that Administration already receives payment for territorial or maritime transit.

ARTICLE 72

Freedom From Transit Charges

The following are exempt from all maritime or territorial transit charges: The correspondence sent free of postage mentioned in Article 43; reply post cards returned to the country of origin; redirected articles; undeliverable articles; return receipts; money orders and all other documents relative to the Postal Service, especially the correspondence relative to postal checks.

Missent dispatches are considered, insofar as the payment of transit and warehousing charges is concerned, as though they had followed their normal route.

ARTICLE 73

Extraordinary Services

The transit charges specified under Article 70 do not apply to transit within the Union by means of extraordinary services specially created or maintained by one Administration at the request of one or more other Administrations. The conditions for this class of conveyance are fixed from time to time among the Administrations concerned.

ARTICLE 74

Airplane Service

1. The transit charges provided by Article 70 are not applicable to the airplane services established for the transportation of correspondence between two or more countries.

2. The transit charges relative to each trip made by the airplane are uniform for all the Administrations which make use of them without participating in the operating expenses.

3. The Postal Administrations of the countries served directly by airplane services determine, by agreement with the Companies concerned, the transit charges for the mails loaded at landing fields on their respective territories for the trips made by means of the planes of those companies. However, each Administration which controls an airplane service reserves the right to collect direct from each Administration which makes use of it the transit charges for the entire trip by that service.

4. The transfer en route of the mails which successively use several separate airplane services must be effected through the intermediary of the Postal Administration of the country in which the transfer takes place. This rule is not applicable when such transfer takes place between airplanes performing the successive sections of one and the same service.

If the dispatches must be stored before their reforwarding by another airplane service, the interested Postal Administration is entitled to warehousing charges under the conditions provided by Article 71.

In addition to those eventual warehousing charges, the Administrations of the countries traversed have no right to any compensation for the mails carried by airplane over their territories.

ARTICLE 75

Payments and Accounts

1. The transit and warehousing charges are borne by the Administration of the country of origin.

2. The general accounting for such charges is based upon statistics taken once every five years, during a period of 28 days, to be determined in the Regulations.

3. When the annual balance of the accounts of transit and warehousing charges between two Administrations does not exceed 1,000 francs, the debtor Administration is relieved of all payment on that account.

ARTICLE 76

Transit Charges in Relations With Countries Foreign to the Union

1. The Administrations which have relations with countries situated outside the Union must lend their assistance to all the other Administrations of

the Union in order that the mails may be subject, outside of the Union, as within its limits, to the transit charges fixed by Article 70.

2. The total maritime transit charges within the Union and outside of the Union must not, however, exceed 15 francs per kilogram of letters and post cards and 1 franc per kilogram of other articles. In such cases, those charges are shared among the Administrations participating in the conveyance in proportion to the distances.

3. The transit charges, territorial or maritime, outside of the limits of the Union as well as within the territory of the Union, for correspondence to which the present Article applies, are fixed in the same way as the transit charges relating to correspondence exchanged between Union countries by means of the services of other countries of the Union.

ARTICLE 77

Exchange of Closed Mails With Warships

1. Closed mails may be exchanged between the post offices of any one of the contracting countries and the commanding officers of naval divisions or warships of the same country stationed abroad or between the commanding officer of another division or ship of the same country, through the intermediary of land or sea services maintained by other countries.

2. Correspondence of all kinds contained in such mails shall consist only of such as is addressed to or sent by the officers and crews of the ships to or from which the mails are sent; the rates and conditions of dispatch applicable to them are determined, according to its domestic regulations, by the Postal Administration of the country to which the ships belong.

3. Barring contrary agreement between the Administrations concerned, the dispatching or receiving Administration of the mails in question is indebted to the intermediary Administrations for transit charges calculated in accordance with the provisions of Article 70.

VARIOUS PROVISIONS

ARTICLE 78

Failure To Observe Liberty Transit

When a country does not observe the provisions of Article 25 concerning liberty of transit, the Administrations have the right to discontinue postal service with it. They must give advance notice of that measure by telegram to the Administrations concerned.

ARTICLE 79

Obligations

The contracting countries undertake to adopt, or to propose to their respective legislative bodies, the necessary measures:

(a) For punishing both the counterfeiting and the fraudulent use of international reply coupons and the fraudulent use, for the prepayment of mail articles, of counterfeit or used postage stamps, as well as of counterfeit or used impressions of stamping machines;

(b) For prohibiting or repressing the fraudulent manufacture, sale, peddling, or distribution of embossed or adhesive stamps in use in the postal service which are counterfeited or imitated in such a way that they might be mistaken for the embossed or adhesive stamps issued by the Administration of one of the contracting countries;

(c) For punishing the fraudulent manufacture or circulating of postal identity cards, as well as the fraudulent use of such cards;

(d) For preventing, and, if necessary, punishing the insertion of opium, morphine, cocaine and other narcotics in the mail articles in favor of which such insertion is not expressly authorized by the Convention and Agreements of the Union.

FINAL PROVISIONS

ARTICLE 80

Effective Date and Duration of the Convention

The present Convention shall become effective on October 1, 1925, and shall remain effective indefinitely.

In faith of which, the Plenipotentiaries of the countries enumerated below have signed the present Convention in one copy, which shall be filed in the Archives of the Government of Sweden, and one copy of which shall be delivered to each Party.

Done at Stockholm, August 28, 1924.

For the Union of South Africa:
   For E. A. Sturman:
      D. J. O'KELLY
      D. J. O'KELLY

For Albania:
   DAVID BJURSTRÖM

For Germany:
   W. SCHENK
   K. ORTH

For the United States of America:
   JOSEPH STEWART
   EUGENE R. WHITE
   EDWIN SANDS

For the whole of the insular possessions of the United States of America other than the Philippine Islands:
   JOSEPH STEWART
   EUGENE R. WHITE
   EDWIN SANDS

219–916—69——31

For the Philippine Islands:
   JUAN RUIZ

For the Argentine Republic:
   M. RODRIGUEZ OCAMPO

For the Commonwealth of Australia:

For Austria:
   JULIUS JUHLIN
   GUSTAF KIHLMARK
   GUNNAR LAGER
   THORE WENNQVIST

For Belgium:
   A. PIRARD
   HUB. KRAINS
   O. SCHOCKAERT

For the Colony of the Belgian Congo:
   M. HALEWYCK
   G. TONDEUR

For Bolivia:
Mto. Urriolagoitia H

For Brazil:
A. de Almeida-Brandão
J. Henrique Aderne

For Bulgaria:
N. Boschnacoff
St. Ivanoff

For Canada:
Peter T. Coolican

For Chile:
Cesar Leon
L. Tagle Salinas
C. Verneuil

For China:
Tai Tch'enne Linne

For the Republic of Colombia:
Luis Serrano-Blanco

For the Republic of Costa Rica:
V. Andersson

For the Republic of Cuba:
José D. Morales Diaz
César Carvallo

For Denmark:
C. Mondrup
Holmblad

For the Free City of Danzig:
Dr. Alfred Wysocki
Dr. Marjan Blachier

For the Dominican Republic:
C. F. G. Hagström

For Egypt:
H. Mazloum
E. Maggiar
Wahbé Ibrahim

For Ecuador:

For Spain:
El Conde de San Esteban de
Cañongo
José Moreno Pineda
A. Camacho

For the Spanish Colonies:
Martin Vicente Salto

For Esthonia:
Edward Wirgo

For Ethiopia:
B. Marcos
A. Bousson

For Finland:
G. E. F. Albrecht

For France:
M. Lebon
Robert Hicguet
A. Body
Douarche
G. Béchel

For Algeria:
H. Treuillé

For the French Colonies and Protectorates of Indochina:
André Touzet

For the whole of the other French Colonies:
G. Pillias
Ginestou

For Great Britain and divers British Colonies and Protectorates:
F. H. Williamson
E. L. Ashley Foakes
W. G. Gilbert

For Greece:
Pentheroudakis
J. Lachnidakis

For Guatemala:

For the Republic of Haiti:
Carl Schlyter

For the Republic of Honduras:

For Hungary:
O. de Fejér
G. Baron Szalay

For British India:
Geoffrey Clarke
Hemanta Kumar Raha

For the Irish Free State:
For P. S. O'Heigeartaigh:
P. S. MacCathmhaoil
P. S. MacCathmhaoil
D. O'Hiarlatha

For Iceland:
C. Mondrup
Holmblad

For Italy:
Luigi Picarelli
Paolo Riello
Giovanni Bartoli

For the whole of the Italian Colonies:
Luigi Picarelli
Paolo Riello
Giovanni Bartoli

For Japan:
S. Komori
H. Kawai
H. Makino

For Korea:
S. Komori
R. Takahashi

For the whole of the other Japanese Dependencies:
K. Sugino
H. Kawai

For Latvia:
Ed. Kadikis
Louis Rudans

For the Republic of Liberia:
Gustaf W. de Horn de Rantzien

For Lithuania:
I. Jurkunas-Scheynius
Adolfas Sruoga

For Luxemburg:
Jaaques

For Morocco (with the exception of the Spanish Zone):
F. Gentil
Walter

For Morocco (Spanish Zone):
El Conde de San Esteban de Cañongo
José Moreno Pineda
A. Camacho

For Mexico:
R. Nieto
José V. Chávez

For Nicaragua:

For Norway:
Klaus Helsing
Oskar Homme

For New Zealand:
A. T. Markman

For the Republic of Panama:
José D. Morales
César Carvallo

For Paraguay:
Gunnar Langborg

For the Netherlands:
Schreuder
J. S. v. Gelder
J. M. Lamers

For the Netherlands Indies:
I. J. Milborn
For M. W. F. Gerdes Oosterbeek:
I. J. Milborn

For the Netherlands Colonies in America:
I. J. Milborn
For M. W. F. Gerdes Oosterbeek:
I. J. Milborn

For Peru:
Emil Hector

For Persia:
Fahimed Dowleh
E. Pire

For Poland:
Dr. Alfred Wysocki
Dr. Marjan Blachier

For Portugal:
Henrique Mousinho d'Albuquerque
Adalberto da Costa Veiga

For the Portuguese Colonies of Africa:
Juvenal Elvas Floriado Santa Barbara

For the Portuguese Colonies of Asia and Oceania:
Joaquim Pires Ferreira Chaves

For Rumania:
George Lecca

For the Republic of San Marino:
Percival Kalling

For El Salvador:

For the Territory of the Saar:
P. Courtilet

For the Kingdom of the Serbs, Croats and Slovenes:
Dragutin Dimitrijevic
Sava Tutundzic
Milos Kovacevic
Stojsa Krbavac

For the Kingdom of Siam:
Phya Sanpakitch Preecha

For Sweden:
Julius Juhlin
Gustaf Kihlmark
Gunnar Lager
Thore Wennqvist

For Switzerland:
P. Dubois
C. Roches

For Czechoslovakia:
Judr Otokar Ruzicka
Joseph Zabrodsky

For Tunisia:
F. Gentil
Barbarat

For Turkey:
  For Mehmed Sabry:
    BÉHA TALY
    BÉHA TALY

For the Union of Soviet Socialist Republics:
  V. OSSINSKY
  V. DOVGOLEVSKI
  E. HIRSCHFELD
  E. SYREVITCH
  KATISS
  V. TCHITCHINADSE

For Uruguay:
  ADOLFO AGORIO

For the United States of Venezuela:
  LUIS ALEJANDRO AGUILAR

FINAL PROTOCOL OF THE CONVENTION

At the moment of signing the Universal Postal Convention concluded on the present date, the undersigned Plenipotentiaries have agreed as follows:

I

Withdrawal of correspondence

The provisions of Article 45 of the Convention do not apply to Great Britain, or to the British dominions, colonies, and protectorates, whose domestic legislation does not permit the withdrawal of correspondence upon the request of the sender.

II

Equivalents, maximum and minimum limits

1. Each country has the option of increasing by as much as 60 per cent, or of decreasing by 20 per cent, the postage rates fixed by Article 34, Section 1, in accordance with the following table:

	Minimum limits	Maximum limits
	Gold centimes	*Gold centimes*
Letters:		
First unit	20	40
Each additional unit	12	24
Post cards:		
Single	12	24
Reply	24	48
Prints, for each 50 grams	4	8
Prints in relief for the blind, for each 1,000 grams	4	8
Commercial papers, for each 50 grams	4	8
Minimum rate	20	....
Samples, for each 50 grams	4	8
Minimum rate	8	....

The rates chosen shall, as far as possible, be in the same proportion as the basic rates, each Administration having the option of rounding off the rates to suit the conveniences of its own monetary system.

2. It is permissible for each country to reduce the postage on single post cards to 10 centimes, and that on reply post cards to 20 centimes.

3. The print rate may, by exception, be reduced to 3 centimes per unit of 50 grams.

4. It is permissible for each country to fix, at its option, the amount of indemnity to be paid to its inhabitants under Article 50.

However, the adjustment of accounts between the interested Administrations shall be effected on the basis of the amount of 50 francs.

5. The rates of postage adopted by a country are applicable to the charges to be collected upon arrival as a result of absence or insufficiency of prepayment.

III

Option of Requiring Prepayment

When a country allows its postage rate to fall below 20 centimes for the first unit of weight of letters, and below the proportional amount for post cards and other articles, the other countries are authorized to apply obligatory prepayment in regard to it, and may distribute, without collecting the postage due, the short-paid or unprepaid correspondence originating in that country. It is understood that the latter country also has the right to prescribe obligatory prepayment.

The option is also reserved for each country of not admitting post cards in relations with another country when the difference between the rates in the two countries is such that the use of the cards in question may give rise to abuses on the part of the public.

IV

Mailing of Correspondence in Another Country

Each country is authorized to take all the measures deemed appropriate to prevent correspondence originating on its territory from being transported across the border to be mailed in another country. In particular, it has the right to charge with its domestic postage or to return to origin articles which persons or firms located in that country mail or cause to be mailed in another country in order to profit by lower rates, addressed to persons or firms of the interior of that same country. The means of collecting the charges are left to the choice of that country.

V

Avoirdupois Ounce

It is admitted, as an exceptional measure, that the countries which, on account of their domestic legislation, can not adopt the decimal metric system as a standard, have the option of substituting for it the avoirdupois ounce (28.3465 grams) by assimilating 1 ounce to 20 grams for letters and 2 ounces to 50 grams for prints, commercial papers, and samples.

VI

Reply Coupons

The Administrations have the option of not undertaking the sale of reply coupons.

They are authorized to restrict the number of reply coupons to be sold to or exchanged by the same person in one day.

In such a case, they advise the International Bureau of their decision, which Bureau communicates it to the Administrations of the Union.

The Postal Administrations of Persia and Uruguay have the option of not undertaking the service of exchanging reply coupons, temporarily.

VII

Registration Fee

The countries which can not fix at 40 centimes the registration fee contemplated by Article 48, Section 2, of the Convention, are, however, authorized to collect a fee which may amount to as much as 50 centimes at most.

VIII

Warehousing Charges

Exceptionally, the Portuguese Administration is authorized to collect, for all mails transferred at the port of Lisbon, the warehousing charges provided by Article 71.

IX

Protocol Left Open to the Countries Not Represented

Ecuador, Guatemala, the Republic of Honduras, Nicaragua, and El Salvador, which form part of the Postal Union, not having been represented at the Congress, the Protocol remains open to them in order that they may adhere to the Convention and the Agreements concluded there, or merely to one or another of them.

The Protocol also remains open for the same purpose to the Commonwealth of Australia, whose delegate was obliged to be absent at the moment of signing the Acts.

X

Protocol Left Open to the Countries Represented for Signatures and Adhesions

The Protocol remains open in favor of the countries whose representatives have to-day signed only the Convention or a certain number of the Agreements drawn up by the Congress, for the purpose of permitting them to adhere to the other Agreements signed on this date, or to one or another of them.

XI

Period for Notification of Adhesion of Countries Not Represented

The adhesions contemplated in Article IX above shall be communicated to the Government of the Kingdom of Sweden by the respective Governments, through diplomatic channels, and by the latter to the countries of the Union. The period which is allowed to them to make such notification will expire on September 1, 1925.

XII

Research Committee

A Committee composed of representatives of 14 Administrations is intrusted with the task of investigating and studying ways and means for simplifying and accelerating the labors of the Congresses.

The result of these investigations shall be submitted to the decision of the Administrations early enough to permit of them being applied to the next Congress.

With this end in view the said Committee is authorized to make whatever proposals it may consider suitable; and should they obtain a majority of votes they will come into force.

The International Bureau will undertake the secretarial work of the Committee thus formed, and its Director will take part in the deliberations.

In faith of which the undersigned Plenipotentiaries have drawn up the present Protocol, which shall have the same force and validity as if the provisions which it contains were inserted in the text of the Convention to which it belongs, and they have signed it in a single copy which shall remain deposited in the Archives of the Government of Sweden and a copy thereof shall be delivered to each Party.

Done at Stockholm, August 28, 1924.

For the Union of South Africa:
  For E. A. Sturman:
    D. J. O'KELLY
    D. J. O'KELLY

For Albania:
  DAVID BJURSTRÖM

For Germany:
  W. SCHENK
  K. ORTH

For the United States of America:
  JOSEPH STEWART
  EUGENE R. WHITE
  EDWIN SANDS

For the whole of the insular possessions of the United States of America other than the Philippine Islands:
  JOSEPH STEWART
  EUGENE R. WHITE
  EDWIN SANDS

For the Philippine Islands:
  JUAN RUIZ

For the Argentine Republic:
  M. RODRIGUEZ OCAMPO

For the Commonwealth of Australia:

For Austria:
JULIUS JUHLIN
GUSTAF KIHLMARK
GUNNAR LAGER
THORE WENNQVIST

For Belgium:
A. PIRARD
HUB. KRAINS
O. SCHOCKAERT

For the Colony of the Belgian Congo:
M. HALEWYCK
G. TONDEUR

For Bolivia:
MTO. URRIOLAGOITIA H

For Brazil:
A. DE ALMEIDA-BRANDÃO
J. HENRIQUE ADERNE

For Bulgaria:
N. BOSCHNACOFF
ST. IVANOFF

For Canada:
PETER T. COOLICAN

For Chile:
CESAR LEON
L. TAGLE SALINAS
C. VERNEUIL

For China:
TAI TCH'ENNE LINNE

For the Republic of Colombia:
LUIS SERRANO-BLANCO

For the Republic of Costa Rica:
V. ANDERSSON

For the Republic of Cuba:
JOSE D. MORALES DIAZ
CESAR CARVALLO

For Denmark:
C. MONDRUP
HOLMBLAD

For the Free City of Danzig:
DR. ALFRED WYSOCKI
DR. MARJAN BLACHIER

For the Dominican Republic:
C. F. G. HAGSTRÖM

For Egypt:
H. MAZLOUM
E. MAGGIAR
WAHBÉ IBRAHIM

For Ecuador:

For Spain:
EL CONDE SAN ESTEBAN DE CAÑONGO
JOSÉ MORENO PINEDA
A. CAMACHO

For the Spanish Colonies:
MARTIN VICENTE SALTO

For Esthonia:
EDWARD WIRGO

For Ethiopia:
B. MARCOS
A. BOUSSON

For Finland:
G. E. F. ALBRECHT

For France:
M. LEBON
ROBERT HICGUET
A. BODY
DOUARCHE
G. BÉCHEL

For Algeria:
H. TREUILLÉ

For the French Colonies and Protectorates of Indochina:
ANDRÉ TOUZET

For the whole of the other French Colonies:
G. PILLIAS
GINESTOU

For Great Britain and divers British Colonies and Protectorates:
F. H. WILLIAMSON
E. L. ASHLEY FOAKES
W. G. GILBERT

For Greece:
PENTHEROUDAKIS
J. LACHNIDAKIS

For Guatemala:

For the Republic of Haiti:
CARL SCHLYTER

For the Republic of Honduras:

For Hungary:
O. DE FEJÉR
G. BARON SZALAY

For British India:
GEOFFREY CLARKE
HEMANTA KUMAR RAHA

For the Irish Free State:
For P. S. O'Heigeartaigh:
P. S. MACCATHMHAOIL
P. S. MACCATHMHAOIL
D. O'HIARLATHA

For Iceland:
C. MONDRUP
HOLMBLAD

For Italy:
LUIGI PICARELLI
PAOLO RIELLO
GIOVANNI BARTOLI

For the whole of the Italian Colonies:
LUIGI PICARELLI
PAOLO RIELLO
GIOVANNI BARTOLI

For Japan:
S. KOMORI
H. KAWAI
H. MAKINO

For Korea:
S. KOMORI
R. TAKAHASHI

For the whole of the other Japanese Dependencies:
K. SUGINO
H. KAWAI

For Latvia:
ED. KADIKIS
LOUIS RUDANS

For the Republic of Liberia:
GUSTAF W. DE HORN DE RANTZIEN

For Lithuania:
I. JURKUNAS-SCHEYNIUS
ADOLFAS SRUOGA

For Luxemburg:
JAAQUES

For Morocco (with the exception of the Spanish Zone):
F. GENTIL
WALTER

For Morocco (Spanish Zone):
EL CONDE DE SAN ESTEBAN DE CANAÑGO
JOSÉ MORENO PINEDA
A. CAMACHO

For Mexico:
R. NIETO
JOSÉ V. CHÁVEZ

For Nicaragua:

For Norway:
KLAUS HELSING
OSKAR HOMME

For New Zealand:
A. T. MARKMAN

For the Republic of Panama:
JOSÉ D. MORALES
CÉSAR CARVALLO

For Paraguay:
GUNNAR LANGBORG

For the Netherlands:
SCHREUDER
J. S. v. GELDER
J. M. LAMERS

For the Netherlands Indies:
I. J. MILBORN
For M. W. F. Gerdes Oosterbeek:
I. J. MILBORN

For the Netherlands Colonies in America:
I. J. MILBORN
For M. W. F. Gerdes Oosterbeek:
I. J. MILBORN

For Peru:
EMIL HECTOR

For Persia:
FAHIMED DOWLEH
E. PIRE

For Poland:
DR. ALFRED WYSOCKI
DR. MARJAN BLACHIER

For Portugal:
HENRIQUE MOUSINHO D'ALBUQUERQUE
ADALBERTO DA COSTA VEIGA

For the Portuguese Colonies of Africa:
JUVENAL ELVAS FLORIADO SANTA BARBARA

For the Portuguese Colonies of Asia and Oceania:
JOAQUIM PIRES FERREIRA CHAVES

For Rumania:
GEORGE LECCA

For the Republic of San Marino:
PERCIVAL KALLING

For El Salvador:

For the Territory of the Saar:
P. COURTILET

For the Kingdom of the Serbs, Croats and Slovenes:
DRAGUTIN DIMITRIJEVIC
SAVA TUTUNDZIC
MILOS KOVACEVIC
STOJSA KRBAVAC

For the Kingdom of Siam:
PHYA SANPAKITCH PREECHA

For Sweden:
JULIUS JUHLIN
GUSTAF KIHLMARK
GUNNAR LAGER
THORE WENNQVIST

For Switzerland:
  P. Dubois
  C. Roches

For Czechoslovakia:
  Judr Otokar Ruzicka
  Joseph Zabrodsky

For Tunisia:
  F. Gentil
  Barbarat

For Turkey:
  For Mehmed Sabry:
    Béha Taly
  Béha Taly

For the Union of Soviet Socialist Republics:
  V. Ossinsky
  V. Dovgolevski
  E. Hirschfeld
  E. Syrevitch
  Katiss
  V. Tchitchinadse

For Uruguay:
  Adolfo Agorio

For the United States of Venezuela:
  Luis Alejandro Aguilar

[For text of regulations for execution of the convention, see 44 Stat. 2273.]

PAN AMERICAN SANITARY CODE

Convention signed at Havana November 14, 1924, with appendix
Senate advice and consent to ratification February 23, 1925
Ratified by the President of the United States March 28, 1925
Ratification of the United States deposited at Havana April 13, 1925
Proclaimed by the President of the United States April 28, 1925
Entered into force June 26, 1925 [1]
Amended by additional protocol of October 19, 1927; [2] *replaced in*
part (arts. 2, 9–11, 16–53, 61, and 62) by International Sanitary
Regulations (World Health Organization Regulations No. 2) of
May 25, 1951, [3] *as between states bound by the regulations*

44 Stat. 2031; Treaty Series 714

PAN AMERICAN SANITARY CODE

The Presidents of Argentine, Brazil, Chile, Colombia, Costa Rica, Cuba, Dominican Republic, Guatemala, Haiti, Honduras, Mexico, Salvador, Panama, Paraguay, Peru, United States of America, Uruguay and Venezuela, being desirous of entering into a sanitary convention for the purpose of better promoting and protecting the public health of their respective nations, and particularly to the end that effective cooperative international measures may be applied for the prevention of the international spread of the communicable infections of human beings and to facilitate international commerce and communication, have appointed as their plenipotentiaries, to-wit:

The Republic of Argentine
  Dr. Gregorio Araoz Alfaro
  Dr. Joaquín Llambías

The United States of Brazil
  Dr. Nascimento Gurgel
  Dr. Raúl Almeida Magalhaes

The Republic of Chile
  Dr. Carlos Graf

The Republic of Colombia
  Dr. R. Gutiérrez Lee

The Republic of Costa Rica
  Dr. José Varela Zequeira

---

[1] Date of deposit of second instrument of ratification.
[2] TS 763, *post,* p. 648.
[3] 7 UST 2255; TIAS 3625.

The Republic of Cuba
  Dr. Mario G. Lebredo
  Dr. José A. López del Valle
  Dr. Hugo Roberts
  Dr. Diego Tamayo
  Dr. Francisco M. Fernández
  Dr. Domingo F. Ramos

The Republic of El Salvador
  Dr. Leopoldo Paz

The United States of America
  Dr. Hugh S. Cumming
  Dr. Richard Creel
  Mr. P. D. Cronin
  Dr. Francis D. Patterson

The Republic of Guatemala
  Dr. José de Cubas y Serrate

The Republic of Haiti
  Dr. Charles Mathon

The Republic of Honduras
  Dr. Arístides Agramonte

The Republic of Mexico
  Dr. Alfonso Pruneda

The Republic of Panama
  Dr. Jaime de la Guardia

The Republic of Paraguay
  Dr. Andrés Gubetich

The Republic of Peru
  Dr. Carlos E. Paz Soldán

The Dominican Republic
  Dr. R. Pérez Cabral

The Republic of Uruguay
  Dr. Justo F. González

The United States of Venezuela
  Dr. Enrique Tejera
  Dr. Antonio Smith

Who, having exchanged their full powers, found in good and due form, have agreed to adopt, ad referendum, the following

PAN AMERICAN SANITARY CODE

Chapter I

OBJECTS OF THE CODE AND DEFINITIONS OF TERMS USED THEREIN

ARTICLE 1. The objects of this code are:

(a) The prevention of the international spread of communicable infections of human beings.

(b) The promotion of cooperative measures for the prevention of the introduction and spread of disease into and from the territories of the signatory Governments.

(c) The standardization of the collection of morbidity and mortality statistics by the signatory Governments.

(d) The stimulation of the mutual interchange of information which may be of value in improving the public health, and combating the diseases of man.

(e) The standardization of the measures employed at places of entry, for the prevention of the introduction and spread of the communicable diseases of man, so that greater protection against them shall be achieved and unnecessary hindrance to international commerce and communication eliminated.

ART. 2. DEFINITIONS. As herein used, the following words and phrases shall be taken in the sense hereinbelow indicated, except as a different meaning for the word or phrase in question may be given in a particular article, or is plainly to be collected from the context or connection where the term is used.

AIRCRAFT. Any vehicle which is capable of transporting persons or things through the air, including aeroplanes, seaplanes, gliders, helecopters, air ships, balloons and captive balloons.

AREA. A well determined portion of territory.

DISINFECTION. The act of rendering free from the causal agencies of disease.

FUMIGATION. A standard process by which the organisms of disease or their potential carriers are exposed to a gas in lethal concentrations.

INDEX, AEDES AEGYPTI. The percentage ratio determined after examination between the number of houses in a given area and the number in which larvae or mosquitoes of the Aedes aegypti are found, in a fixed period of time.

INSPECTION. The act of examining persons, buildings, areas, or things which may be capable of harboring, transmitting or transporting the infectious agents of disease, or of propagating or favoring the propagation of such agents. Also the act of studying and observing measures put in force for the suppression or prevention of disease.

INCUBATION, PERIOD OF. For plague, cholera and yellow fever, each 6 days, for smallpox, 14 days, and for typhus fever 12 days.

ISOLATION. The separation of human beings or animals from other human beings or animals in such manner as to prevent the interchange of disease.

PLAGUE. Bubonic, septicemic, pneumonic or rodent plague.

PORT. Any place or area where a vessel or aircraft may seek harbor, discharge or receive passengers, crew, cargo or supplies.

RODENTS. Rats, domestic and wild, and other rodents.

CHAPTER II

SECTION 1.   NOTIFICATION AND SUBSEQUENT COMMUNICATIONS TO OTHER COUNTRIES

ART. 3. Each of the signatory Governments agrees to transmit to each of the other signatory Governments and to the Pan American Sanitary Bureau, at intervals of not more than two weeks, a statement containing information as to the state of its public health, particularly that of its ports.

The following diseases are obligatorily reportable:

Plague, cholera, yellow fever, smallpox, typhus, epidemic cerebrospinal meningitis, acute epidemic poliomyelitis, epidemic lethargic encephalitis, influenza or epidemic la grippe, typhoid and paratyphoid fevers, and such other diseases as the Pan American Sanitary Bureau may, by resolution, add to the above list.

ART. 4. Each signatory Government agrees to notify adjacent countries and the Pan American Sanitary Bureau immediately by the most rapid available means of communication, of the appearance in its territory of an authentic or officially suspected case or cases of plague, cholera, yellow fever, smallpox, typhus or any other dangerous contagion liable to be spread through the intermediary agency of international commerce.

ART. 5. This notification is to be accompanied, or very promptly followed, by the following additional information:

1. The area where the disease has appeared.
2. The date of its appearance, its origin, and its form.
3. The probable source or country from which introduced and manner of introduction.
4. The number of confirmed cases, and number of deaths.
5. The number of suspected cases and deaths.
6. In addition, for plague, the existence among rodents of plague, or of an unusual mortality among rodents; for yellow fever, the Aedes aegypti index of the locality.
7. The measures which have been applied for the prevention of the spread of the disease, and its eradication.

ART. 6. The notification and information prescribed in Articles 4 and 5 are to be addressed to diplomatic or consular representatives in the capital of the infected country, and to the Pan American Sanitary Bureau at Washington, which shall immediately transmit the information to all countries concerned.

ART. 7. The notification and the information prescribed in Articles 3, 4, 5, and 6 are to be followed by further communications in order to keep other Governments informed as to the progress of the disease or diseases. These communications will be made at least once weekly, and will be as complete as possible, indicating in detail the measures employed to prevent the extension of the disease. The telegraph, the cable, and the radio will be employed for this purpose, except in those instances in which the data may be transmitted rapidly by mail. Reports by telegraph, cable or radio will be confirmed by letter. Neighboring countries will endeavor to make special arrangements for the solution of local problems that do not involve widespread international interest.

ART. 8. The signatory Governments agree that in the event of the appearance of any of the following diseases, namely: cholera, yellow fever, plague, typhus fever or other pestilential diseases in severe epidemic form, in their territory, they will immediately put in force appropriate sanitary measures for the prevention of the international carriage of any of the said diseases therefrom by passengers, crew, cargo and vessels, and mosquitoes, rats and vermin that may be carried thereon, and will promptly notify each of the other signatory Governments and the Pan American Sanitary Bureau as to the nature and extent of the sanitary measures which they have applied for the accomplishment of the requirements of this article.

SECTION 2.   PUBLICATION OF PRESCRIBED MEASURES

ART. 9. Information of the first non-imported case of plague, cholera, or yellow fever justifies the application of sanitary measures against an area where said disease may have appeared.

ART. 10. The Government of each country obligates itself to publish immediately the preventive measures which will be considered necessary to be taken by vessels or other means of transport, passengers and crew at any port of departure or place located in the infected area. The said publication is to be communicated at once to the accredited diplomatic or consular representatives of the infected country, and to the Pan American Sanitary Bureau. The signatory Government also obligate themselves to make known in the same manner the revocation of these measures, or of modifications thereof that may be made.

ART. 11. In order that an area may be considered to be no longer infected, it must be officially established:

1. That there has neither been a death nor a new case as regards plague or cholera for ten days; and as regards yellow fever for twenty days, either since the isolation, or since the death or recovery of the last patient.

2. That all means for the eradication of the disease have been applied and, in the case of plague, that effective measures against rats have been continuously carried out, and that the disease has not been discovered among them within six months; in the case of yellow fever, that Aedes aegypti index of the infected area has been maintained at an average of not more than 2 per cent for the 30-day period immediately preceding, and that no portion of the infected area has had an index in excess of 5 per cent for the same period of time.

SECTION 3.   MORBIDITY AND MORTALITY STATISTICS

ART. 12. The international classification of the causes of death is adopted as the Pan American Classification of the Causes of Death, and shall be used by the signatory nations in the interchange of mortality and morbidity reports.

ART. 13. The Pan American Sanitary Bureau is hereby authorized and directed to re-publish from time to time the Pan American Classification of the Causes of Death.

ART. 14. Each of the signatory Governments agrees to put in operation at the earliest practicable date a system for the collection and tabulation of vital statistics which shall include:

1. A central statistical office presided over by a competent official.

2. The establishment of regional statistical offices.

3. The enactment of laws, decrees or regulations requiring the prompt reporting of births, deaths and communicable diseases, by health officers, physicians, midwives and hospitals, and providing penalties for failure to make such reports.

ART. 15. The Pan American Sanitary Bureau shall prepare and publish standard forms for the reporting of deaths and cases of communicable disease, and all other vital statistics.

CHAPTER III

Sanitary Documents

SECTION 1.   BILLS OF HEALTH

ART. 16. The master of any vessel or aircraft which proceeds to a port of any of the signatory Governments, is required to obtain at the port of departure and ports of call, a bill of health, in duplicate, issued in accordance with the information set forth in the appendix and adopted as the standard bill of health.

ART. 17. The bill of health will be accompanied by a list of the passengers, and stowaways if any, which shall indicate the port where they embarked and the port to which they are destined, and a list of the crew.

ART. 18. Consuls and other officials signing or countersigning bills of health should keep themselves accurately informed with respect to the sanitary conditions of their ports, and the manner in which this code is obeyed by vessels and their passengers and crews while therein. They should have accurate knowledge of local mortality and morbidity, and of sanitary conditions which may affect vessels in port. To this end, they shall be furnished with information they request pertaining to sanitary records, harbors and vessels.

ART. 19. The signatory Governments may assign medical or sanitary officers as public health attaches to embassies or legations, and as representatives to international conferences.

ART. 20. If at the port of departure there be no consul or consular agent of the country of destination, the bill of health may be issued by the consul or consular agent of a friendly Government authorized to issue such bill of health.

ART. 21. The bill of health should be issued not to exceed forty eight hours before the departure of the ship to which it is issued. The sanitary visa should not be given more than twenty-four hours before departure.

ART. 22. Any erasure or alteration of a bill of health shall invalidate the document, unless such alteration or erasure shall be made by competent authority, and notation thereof appropriately made.

ART. 23. A clean bill of health is one which shows the complete absence in the port of departure of cholera, yellow fever, plague, typhus fever, or of other pestilential disease in severe epidemic form, liable to be transported by international commerce. Provided, that the presence only of bona fide imported cases of such disease, when properly isolated, shall not compel the issuance of a foul bill of health, but notation of the presence of such cases will be made under the heading of "Remarks" on the Bill of health.

ART. 24. A foul bill of health is one which shows the presence of nonimported cases of any of the diseases referred to in Art. 23.

ART. 25. Specific bills of health are not required of vessels which, by reason of accident, storm or other emergency condition, including wireless change of itinerary, are obliged to put into ports other than their original destinations but such vessels shall be required to exhibit such bills of health as they possess.

ART. 26. It shall be the duty of the Pan American Sanitary Bureau to publish appropriate information which may be distributed by port health officers, for the purpose of instructing owners, agents and masters of vessels as to the methods which should be put in force by them for the prevention of the international spread of disease.

SECTION 2.   OTHER SANITARY DOCUMENTS

ART. 27. Every vessel carrying a medical officer will maintain a sanitary log which will be kept by him, and he will record therein daily: the sanitary condition of the vessel, and its passengers and crew; a record showing the names of passengers and crew which have been vaccinated by him; name, age, nationality, home address, occupation and nature of illness or injury of all passengers and crew treated during the voyage; the source and sanitary quality of the drinking water of the vessel, the place where taken on board, and the method in use on board for its purification; sanitary conditions, observed in ports visited during the voyage; the measures taken to prevent the ingress and egress of rodents to and from the vessel; the measures which have been taken to protect the passengers and crew against mosquitoes, other insects, and vermin. The sanitary log will be signed by the master and medical officer of the vessel, and will be exhibited upon the request of any sanitary or consular officer. In the absence of a medical officer, the master shall record the above information in the log of the vessel, in so far as possible.

ART. 28. Equal or similar forms for Quarantine Declarations, Certificate of Fumigation, and Certificate of Vaccination, set forth in the appendix, are hereby adopted as standard forms.

Chapter IV

CLASSIFICATION OF PORTS

ART. 29. An infected port is one in which any of the following diseases exist, namely, plague, cholera, yellow fever, or other pestilential disease in severe epidemic form.

ART. 30. A suspected port is a port in which, or in the areas contiguous thereto, a non imported case or cases of any of the diseases referred to in Art. 23, have occurred within sixty days, or which has not taken adequate measures to protect itself against such diseases, but which is not known to be an infected port.

ART. 31. A clean port, Class A, is one in which the following conditions are fulfilled:

1. The absence of non-imported cases of any of the diseases referred to in Art. 23, in the port itself and in the areas contiguous thereto.

2. (a) The presence of a qualified and adequate health staff.

(b) Adequate means of fumigation.

(c) Adequate personnel and material for the capture or destruction of rodents.

(d) An adequate bacteriological and pathological laboratory;

(e) A safe water supply.

(f) Adequate means for the collection of mortality and morbidity data;

(g) Adequate facilities for the isolation of suspects and the treatment of infectious diseases.

(h) Signatory Governments shall register in the Pan-American Sanitary Bureau those places that comply with these conditions.

ART. 32. A clean port, Class B, is one in which the conditions described in Art. 31, 1 and 2 (a) above, are fulfilled, but in which one or more of the other requirements of Art. 31, 2 are not fulfilled.

ART. 33. An unclassified port is one with regard to which the information concerning the existence or non-existence of any of the diseases referred to in Art. 23, and the measures which are being applied for the control of such diseases, is not sufficient to classify such port.

An unclassified port shall be provisionally considered as a suspected or infected port, as the information available in each case may determine, until definitely classified.

ART. 34. The Pan American Sanitary Bureau shall prepare and publish, at intervals, a tabulation of the most commonly used ports of the Western Hemisphere, giving information as to sanitary conditions.

Chapter V

CLASSIFICATION OF VESSELS

Art. 35. A clean vessel is one coming from a clean port, Class A or B, which has had no case of plague, cholera, yellow fever, small pox or typhus aboard during the voyage, and which has complied with the requirements of this code.

Art. 36. An infected or suspected vessel is:

1. One which has had on board during the voyage a case or cases of any of the diseases mentioned in Art. 35.
2. One which is from an infected or suspected port.
3. One which is from a port where plague or yellow fever exists.
4. Any vessel on which there has been mortality among rats.
5. A vessel which has violated any of the provisions of this code.

Provided that the sanitary authorities should give due consideration in applying sanitary measures to a vessel that has not docked.

Art. 37. Any master or owner of any vessel, or any person violating any provisions of this Code or violating any rule or regulation made in accordance with this Code, relating to the inspection of vessels, the entry or departure from any quarantine station, grounds or anchorages, or trespass thereon, or to the prevention of the introduction of contagious or infectious disease into any of the signatory countries, or any master, owner, or agent of a vessel making a false statement relative to the sanitary condition of a vessel, or its contents, or as to the health of any passenger, or person thereon, or who interferes with a quarantine or health officer in the proper discharge of his duty, or fails or refuses to present bills of health, or other sanitary document, or pertinent information to a quarantine or health officer, shall be punished in accordance with the provisions of such laws, rules or regulations, as may be or may have been enacted, or promulgated, in accordance with the provisions of this Code, by the Government of the country within whose jurisdiction the offense is committed.

Chapter VI

THE TREATMENT OF VESSELS

Art. 38. Clean vessels will be granted pratique by the port health authority upon acceptable evidence that they properly fulfill the requirements of Art. 35.

Art. 39. Suspected vessels will be subjected to necessary sanitary measures to determine their actual condition.

Art. 40. Vessels infected with any of the diseases referred to in Art. 23 shall be subjected to such sanitary measures as will prevent the continuance thereon, and the spread therefrom, of any of said diseases to other or ports. The disinfection of cargo, stores and personal effects shall be limited to the destruction of the vectors of disease which may be contained therein, provided that things which have been freshly soiled with human excretions capable of transmitting disease, shall always be disinfected. Vessels on which there is undue prevalence of rats, mosquitoes, lice, or any other potential vector of communicable disease, may be disinfected irrespective of the classification of the vessel.

ART. 41. Vessels infected with plague shall be subjected to the following treatment.

1. The vessel shall be held for observation and necessary treatment.

2. The sick, if any, shall be removed and placed under appropriate treatment in isolation.

3. The vessel shall be simultaneously fumigated throughout for the destruction of rats. In order to render fumigation more effective, cargo may be wholly or partially discharged prior to such fumigation, but care will be taken to discharge no cargo which might harbor rats,[4] except for fumigation.

4. All rats recovered after fumigation should be examined bacteriologically.

5. Healthy contacts, except those actually exposed to cases of pneumonic plague, will not be detained in quarantine.

6. The vessel will not be granted pratique until it is reasonably certain that it is free from rats and vermin.

ART. 42. Vessels infected with cholera shall be subjected to the following treatment.

1. The vessels shall be held for observation and necessary treatment.

2. The sick, if any, shall be removed and placed under appropriate treatment in isolation.

3. All persons on board shall be subjected to bacteriological examination, and shall not be admitted to entry until demonstrated free from cholera vibrios.

4. Appropriate disinfection shall be performed.

ART. 43. Vessels infected with yellow fever shall be subjected to the following treatment.

1. The vessel shall be held for observation and necessary treatment.

---

[4] Explanatory Footnote:—The nature of the goods or merchandise likely to harbor rats (plague suspicious cargo), shall, for purpose of this section, be deemed to be the following, namely; rice or other grain (exclusive of flour); oilcake in sacks; beans in mats or sacks; goods packed in crates with straw or similar packing material; matting in bundles; dried vegetables in baskets or cases; dried and salted fish; peanuts in sacks; dry ginger; curios, etc., in fragile cases; copra, loose hemp in bundles; coiled rope in sacking; kapok; maize in bags; sea grass in bales; tiles, large pipes and similar articles; and bamboo poles in bundles. [Footnote in original.]

2. The sick, if any, shall be removed and placed under appropriate treatment in isolation from Aedes aegypti mosquitoes.

3. All persons on board non immune to yellow fever shall be placed under observation to complete six days from the last possible exposure to Aedes aegypti mosquitoes.

4. The vessel shall be freed from Aedes aegypti mosquitoes.

ART. 44. Vessels infected with smallpox shall be subjected to the following treatment.

1. The vessels shall be held for observation and necessary treatment.

2. The sick, if any, shall be removed and placed under appropriate treatment in isolation.

3. All persons on board shall be vaccinated. As an option the passenger may elect to undergo isolation to complete fourteen days from the last possible exposure to the disease.

4. All living quarters of the vessels shall be rendered mechanically clean, and used clothing and bedding of the patient disinfected.

ART. 45. Vessels infected with typhus shall be subjected to the following treatment.

1. The vessel shall be held for observation and necessary treatment.

2. The sick, if any, shall be removed and placed under appropriate treatment in isolation from lice.

3. All persons on board and their personal effects shall be deloused.

4. All persons on board who have been exposed to the infection shall be placed under observation to complete twelve days from the last possible exposure to the infection.

5. The vessel shall be deloused.

ART. 46. The time of detention of vessels for inspection or treatment shall be the least consistent with public safety and scientific knowledge. It is the duty of port health officers to facilitate the speedy movement of vessels to the utmost compatible with the foregoing.

ART. 47. The power and authority of quarantine will not be utilized for financial gain, and no charges for quarantine services will exceed actual cost plus a reasonable surcharge for administrative expenses and fluctuations in the market prices of materials used.

CHAPTER VII

FUMIGATION STANDARDS

ART. 48. Sulphur dioxide, hydrocyanic acid and cyanogen chloride gas mixture shall be considered as standard fumigants when used in accordance with the table set forth in the appendix, as regards hours of exposure and of quantities of fumigants per 1,000 cubic feet.

ART. 49. Fumigation of ships to be most effective should be performed periodically and preferably at six months intervals, and should include the entire vessel and its lifeboats. The vessels should be free of cargo.

ART. 50. Before the liberation of hydrogen cyanide or cyanogen chloride, all personnel of the vessel will be removed, and care will be observed that all compartments are rendered as nearly gas tight as possible.

CHAPTER VIII

MEDICAL OFFICERS OF VESSELS

ART. 51. In order to better protect the health of travelers by sea, to aid in the prevention of the international spread of disease and to facilitate the movement of international commerce and communication, the signatory Governments are authorized in their discretion to license physicians employed on vessels.

ART. 52. It is recommended that license not be issued unless the applicant therefor is a graduate in medicine from a duly chartered and recognized school of medicine, is the holder of an unrepealed license to practice medicine, and has successfully passed an examination as to his moral and mental fitness to be the surgeon or medical officer of a vessel. Said examination shall be set by the directing head of the national health service, and shall require of the applicant a competent knowledge of medicine and surgery. Said directing head of the national health service may issue a license to an applicant who successfully passes the examination, and may revoke said license upon conviction of malpractice, unprofessional conduct, offenses involving moral turpitude or infraction of any of the sanitary laws or regulations of any of the signatory Governments based upon the provisions of this code.

ART. 53. When duly licensed as aforesaid, said surgeons or medical officers of vessels may be utilized in aid of inspection as defined in this code.

CHAPTER IX

THE PAN AMERICAN SANITARY BUREAU

Functions and Duties

ART. 54. The organization, functions and duties of the Pan American Sanitary Bureau shall include those heretofore determined for the International Sanitary Bureau by the various International Sanitary and other Conferences of American Republics, and such additional administrative functions and duties as may be hereafter determined by Pan American Sanitary Conferences.

ART. 55. The Pan American Sanitary Bureau shall be the central coordinating sanitary agency of the various member Republics of the Pan American Union, and the general collection and distribution center of sanitary information to and from said Republics. For this purpose it shall, from time to time, designate representatives to visit and confer with the sanitary authorities of the various signatory Governments on public health matters, and such representatives shall be given all available sanitary information in the countries visited by them in the course of their official visits and conferences.

ART. 56. In addition, the Pan American Sanitary Bureau shall perform the following specific functions:

To supply to the sanitary authorities of the signatory Governments through its publications, or in other appropriate manner, all available information relative to the actual status of the communicable diseases of man, new invasions of such diseases, the sanitary measures undertaken, and the progress effected in the control or eradication of such diseases; new methods for combating disease; morbidity and mortality statistics; public health organization and administration; progress in any of the branches of preventive medicine, and other pertinent information relative to sanitation and public health in any of its phases, including a bibliography of books and periodicals on public hygiene.

In order to more efficiently discharge its functions, it may undertake cooperative epidemiological and other studies; may employ at headquarters and elsewhere, experts for this purpose; may stimulate and facilitate scientific researches and the practical application of the results therefrom; and may accept gifts, benefactions and bequests, which shall be accounted for in the manner now provided for the maintenance funds of the Bureau.

ART. 57. The Pan American Sanitary Bureau shall advise and consult with the sanitary authorities of the various signatory Governments relative to public health problems, and the manner of interpreting and applying the provisions of this Code.

ART. 58. Officials of the National Health Services may be designated as representatives, ex-officio, of the Pan American Sanitary Bureau, in addition to their regular duties, and when so designated they may be empowered to act as sanitary representatives of one or more of the signatory Governments when properly designated and accredited to so serve.

ART. 59. Upon request of the sanitary authorities of any of the signatory Governments, the Pan American Sanitary Bureau is authorized to take the necessary preparatory steps to bring about an exchange of professors, medical and health officers, experts or advisers in public health or any of the sanitary sciences, for the purpose of mutual aid and advancement in the protection of the public health of the signatory Governments.

ART. 60. For the purpose of discharging the functions and duties imposed upon the Pan American Sanitary Bureau, a fund of not less than $50,000 shall be collected by the Pan American Union, apportioned among the signatory Governments on the same basis as are the expenses of the Pan American Union.

Chapter X

AIRCRAFT

ART. 61. The provisions of this Convention shall apply to aircraft, and the signatory Governments agree to designate landing places for aircraft which shall have the same status as quarantine anchorages.

Chapter XI

SANITARY CONVENTION OF WASHINGTON

ART. 62. The provisions of Articles 5, 6, 13, 14, 15, 16, 17, 18, 25, 30, 32, 33, 34, 37, 38, 39, 40, 41, 42, 43, 44, 45, 49, and 50, of the Pan American Sanitary Convention concluded in Washington on October 14, 1905,[5] are hereby continued in full force and effect, except in so far as they may be in conflict with the provisions of this Convention.

Chapter XII

Be it understood that this Code does not in any way abrogate or impair the validity or force of any existing treaty convention or agreement between any of the signatory governments and any other government.

Chapter XIII

TRANSITORY DISPOSITION

ART. 63. The Governments which may not have signed the present Convention are to be admitted to adherence thereto upon demand, notice of this adherence to be given through diplomatic channels to the Government of the Republic of Cuba.

Made and signed in the city of Havana, on the fourteenth day of the month of November, 1924, in two copies, in English and Spanish, respectively, which shall be deposited with the Department of Foreign Relations of the Republic of Cuba, in order that certified copies thereof, in both English and Spanish, may be made for transmission through diplomatic channels to each of the signatory Governments.

By the Republic of Argentine:
GREGORIO ARAOZ ALFARO
JOAQUIN LLAMBIAS

By the United States of Brazil:
NASCIMENTO GURGEL
RAUL ALMEIDA MAGALHAES

By the Republic of Chile:
CARLOS GRAF

By the Republic of Colombia:
R. GUTIERREZ LEE

By the Republic of Costa Rica:
JOSE VARELA ZEQUEIRA

---

[5] TS 518, *ante*, vol. 1, p. 450.

By the Republic of Cuba:
  MARIO G. LEBREDO
  JOSE A. LOPEZ DEL VALLE
  HUGO ROBERTS
  DIEGO TAMAYO
  FRANCISCO M. FERNANDEZ
  DOMINGO F. RAMOS

By the Republic of El Salvador:
  LEOPOLDO PAZ

By the United States of America:
  HUGH S. CUMMING
  RICHARD CREEL
  P. D. CRONIN

By the Republic of Guatemala:
  JOSE DE CUBAS Y SERRATE

By the Republic of Haiti:
  CHARLES MATHON

By the Republic of Honduras:
  ARISTIDES AGRAMONTE

By the Republic of Mexico:
  ALFONSO PRUNEDA

By the Republic of Panama:
  JAIME DE LA GUARDIA

By the Republic of Paraguay:
  ANDRES GUBETICH

By the Republic of Peru:
  CARLOS E. PAZ SOLDAN

By the Dominican Republic:
  R. PEREZ CABRAL

By the Republic of Uruguay:
  JUSTO F. GONZALEZ

By the United States of Venezuela:
  ENRIQUE TEJERA
  ANTONIO SMITH

APPENDIX

TABLE I

Quantities per 1,000 Cubic Feet

Chemicals	Sulphur Dioxide				Hydrocyanic Acid				Cyanogen Chloride Mixture			
	Mosquitoes	Rats	Lice	Bedbugs	Mosquitoes	Rats	Lice	Bedbugs	Mosquitoes	Rats	Lice	Bedbugs
Sulphur...........	2 lbs.	3 lbs.	4 lbs.	3 lbs.								
Sodium Cyanide....					½ oz.	5 oz.	10 oz.	5 oz.	½ oz.	4 oz.	8 oz.	4 oz.
Sulphuric Acid......					½ oz.	5 oz.	10 oz.	5 oz.				
Sodium Chlorate....									¼ oz.	2 oz.	4 oz.	2 oz.
Hydrochloric Acid...									2⅛ oz.	17 oz.	34 oz.	17 oz.
Water.............					1¼ oz.	12½ oz.	25 oz.	12½ oz.	2⅛ oz.	17 oz.	34 oz.	17 oz.

TABLE II

Hours of Exposure

Mosquitoes	Rats	Lice	Bedbugs	Mosquitoes	Rats	Lice	Bedbugs	Mosquitoes	Rats	Lice	Bedbugs
1 hr.	6 hrs.	6 hrs.	6 hrs.	½ hr.	2 hrs.	2 hrs.	2 hrs.	½ hr.	1½ hrs.	1½ hrs.	1½ hrs.

Serial No.

....

....Health Service

.............Quarantine Station.............

CERTIFICATE OF VACCINATION AGAINST SMALLPOX

Name...Sex...................

Age...............................Date of Vaccination........................

Height.............................Date of Reaction........................

Result:
  Immune Reaction
  Vaccinoid
  Successful Vaccination

Signed

....

Signature   *Medical Officer in Charge*

...............................Health Service

CERTIFICATE OF DISCHARGE FROM NATIONAL QUARANTINE

.... Quarantine Station

Port of ....
........................, 192

I CERTIFY that the ....
of ...., from ....
bound for ...., has in all respects complied with the
quarantine regulations prescribed under the authority of the laws of ....
...., and the Pan American Sanitary
(country)
Code, and that the vessel, cargo, crew, and passengers are, to the best of my knowledge and
belief, free from quarantinable diseases or danger of conveying the same. Said vessel is this
day granted   **free**   pratique.
     provisional

1. Rat guards of an accepted design to be placed on all lines leading from the vessels.
2. Gangways to be raised at night, or lighted and watched.
3. Vessels to be fumigated after discharge of cargo.

....
Quarantine Officer

.... Health Service

CERTIFICATE OF FUMIGATION

(Not to be taken up by port authorities)

Port of ....
........................, 192

THIS IS TO CERTIFY that the ....
from ....has been fumigated at this station
for the destruction of ...., as follows:

		Cubic Capacity	Kilos or Pounds Sulphur	Grams or Ounces Cyanide	Grams or Ounces Cyanide and Sodium Chlorate	
Holds	1	......	......	......	......	Date..................
	2	......	......	......	......	Duration of exposure...
	3	......	......	......	......	....
	4	......	......	......	......	Evidence of rats before
	5	......	......	......	......	fumigation............
Engine-room & shaft alley.		......	......	......	......	Rats after fumigation:
Bunkers..................		......	......	......	......	living...., dead.......
Forepeak.................		......	......	......	......	....
Forecastle................		......	......	......	......	Inspection made by
Steerage.................		......	......	......	......	....
Dining saloon (1st cabin)...		......	......	......	......	Opened by...........
Pantry (1st cabin).........		......	......	......	......	Dunnage or other pro-
Galley....................		......	......	......	......	tection to rats; how
Second Cabin.............		......	......	......	......	treated prior to fumi-
Second Cabin Pantry......		......	......	......	......	gation................
Provision storeroom.......		......	......	......	......	....
Living quarters...........		......	......	......	......	....
Staterooms...............		......	......	......	......	....
Smoking Room...........		......	......	......	......	....
Total...............		......	......	....	......	

....
Quarantine Officer

On the reverse side make a report of all compartments which were not fumigated, why
they were not, and give treatment. Also report any other pertinent information.

QUARANTINE DECLARATION

...................Quarantine Station

.............................., 192

Name of vessel........ ....; destination.......................;
nationality....................; rig....................; tonnage..................;
date of arrival.......................; port of departure.....................;
intermediate ports..;
days from port of departure................; days from last port....................;
previous ports of departure and call.....................................;
officers and crew................; cabin passengers.......................; steerage
passengers...................; total number of persons on board...................;
cargo.........................; ballast (tons)...........................; character
of.........................; source...................... If water
ballast, were tanks filled at the port of departure or at sea?.........................
In ports of departure and call, did vessel lie at wharf or at moorings in harbor or roadstead?
.... If vessel lay at
moorings, how far from shore?...
Was there communication with the shore?........................... What changes
in the personnel of the crew, if any?.......................................
....

Sickness, cases of, in port of departure.   No.............; result.....................
in intermediate ports. No.............; result.....................
at sea.   . . . . . No.............; result.....................
Were the sick sent to hospital or allowed to remain on board?......................
Was the bedding and clothing of those sick at sea frequently aired and washed?...........

....
Do you know of any circumstance affecting the health of the crew, or which renders the
ship dangerous to the health of any part of..................................
(Country)
.... If so, state them......................................
....

---

*I certify that the foregoing statements, and the answers to the questions, are true to the best of my knowledge
and belief.*

Master...
Ship's Surgeon...
Vessel...

Treatment of vessel..;
(Inspected and passed or detained)
disinfection of hold...................; cabin and forecastle.......................;
(Method)   (Method)
bedding, clothing, etc...
(Method)
Detained.............days; sickness in quarantine................................;
(Number of cases, and nature)
discharged in free pratique.. Port named in
certificate of discharge...

....
Quarantine Officer

INTERNATIONAL STANDARD FORM BILL OF HEALTH

Information Concerning the Vessel

I..............................(Official title)...........................
(the person authorized to issue the bill, at the port of............................)
do hereby state that the vessel hereinafter named clears (or leaves) from the port of
...............................under the following circumstances: Name of
vessel.................................; nationality...........................
Master.................................; tonnage, gross...................;
net......................... Name of medical officer.......................
Number of officers.............; of crew, including petty officers.....................;

officers' families................ Passengers destined for............................
(Country of destination)
Embarking at this port................... First cabin......................; second
cabin......................; steerage..................... Total number of passen-
gers on board...................................
Ports visited within preceding four months.....................................
....
....
Location of vessel while in port—wharf......................................; open
bay........................; distance from shore......................
If any passengers or members of crew disembarked on account of sickness, state disease..
....
Time vessel was in port (date and hour of arrival)..................................;
(date and hour of departure).......................................
Character of communication with shore....................................
Sanitary condition of vessel.....................................
Sanitary measures, if any, adopted while in port...................................
Date of last fumigation for the destruction of rodents...............................
Number of rodents obtained.......................................
Port where fumigated............................and officials supervising the
fumigation......................................
Method of fumigation used (for rodents).....................................;
for mosquitoes)..

Information Concerning the Port

Sanitary conditions of port and vicinity......................................
Prevailing diseases at port and vicinity......................................

Number of Cases and Deaths from the Following Named Diseases During the Two
Weeks Ending.....................

Diseases	Number of Cases [1]	Number of Deaths [1]	REMARKS (Any conditions affecting the public health existing in the port or vicinity to be here stated)
Yellow Fever..................	....	....	
Asiatic Cholera...............	....	....	
Cholera nostras or cholerine....	....	....	
Smallpox.....................	....	....	
Typhus Fever.................	....	....	
Plague.......................	....	....	
Leprosy......................	....	....	

([1] When there are no cases or deaths, entry to that effect must be made.)

Health Office of the Port of... (When
practicable this certificate should be signed by the Health Officer of the Port)
Date of last case of:
    Cholera..
    Yellow Fever...
    Human Plague..
    Typhus..
    Rodent Plague..
Measures, if any, imposed by the municipality against rats during the last six months....
....

Signature of Port Health Officer

I certify that the vessel has complied with the rules and regulations made under the terms of the Pan American Sanitary Code, and with the laws and regulations of the country of destination. The vessel leaves this port bound for............................, via.....................

    Given under my hand and seal this....................................day of
........................, 192....
(Signature of consular officer)....................................
   [SEAL]
Countersigned by
....
Medical Officer

CLAIMS AGAINST AUSTRIA AND HUNGARY

Agreement signed at Washington November 26, 1924
Ratified by the President of the United States August 4, 1925; by
Austria August 25, 1925; by Hungary November 5, 1925
Ratifications exchanged at Washington December 12, 1925
Entered into force December 12, 1925

44 Stat. 2213; Treaty Series 730

The United States of America and the Republic of Austria, hereafter described as Austria, and the Kingdom of Hungary, hereafter described as Hungary, being desirous of determining the amounts to be paid by Austria and by Hungary in satisfaction of their obligations under the treaties concluded by the United States with Austria on August 24, 1921,[1] and with Hungary on August 29, 1921,[2] which secure to the United States and its nationals rights specified under a Joint Resolution of the Congress of the United States of July 2, 1921,[3] including rights under the Treaties of St. Germain-en-Laye [4] and Trianon,[5] respectively, have resolved to submit the questions for decision to a commissioner and have appointed as their plenipotentiaries to sign an agreement for that purpose:

The President of the United States of America, Charles Evans Hughes, Secretary of State of the United States of America,

The President of the Federal Republic of Austria, Mr. Edgar L. G. Prochnik, Chargé d'Affaires of Austria in Washington, and

The Governor of Hungary, Count László Széchényi, Envoy Extraordinary and Minister Plenipotenitary of Hungary to the United States,

Who, having communicated their full powers, found to be in good and due form, have agreed as follows:

ARTICLE I

The three governments shall agree upon the selection of a Commissioner who shall pass upon all claims for losses, damages or injuries suffered by the

---

[1] TS 659, *post.*
[2] TS 660, *post.*
[3] 42 Stat. 105.
[4] For relevant portions of the Treaty of St. Germain-en-Laye, see TS 659, *post.*
[5] For relevant portions of the Treaty of Trianon, see TS 660, *post.*

United States or its nationals embraced within the terms of the Treaty of August 24, 1921, between the United States and Austria and/or the Treaty of August 29, 1921, between the United States and Hungary, and/or the Treaties of St. Germain-en-Laye and/or Trianon, and shall determine the amounts to be paid to the United States by Austria and by Hungary in satisfaction of all such claims (excluding those falling within paragraphs 5, 6 and 7 of Annex I to Section I of Part VIII of both the Treaty of St. Germain-en-Laye and the Treaty of Trianon) and including the following categories:

(1) Claims of American citizens arising since July 31, 1914, in respect of damage to or seizure of their property, rights and interests, including any company or association in which they are interested, within the territories of either the former Austrian Empire or the former Kingdom of Hungary as they respectively existed on August 1, 1914;

(2) Other claims for loss or damage to which the United States or its nationals have been subjected with respect to injuries to or death of persons, or with respect to property, rights and interests, including any company or association in which American nationals are interested, since July 31, 1914, as a consequence of the war;

(3) Debts owing to American citizens by the Austrian and/or the Hungarian Governments or by their nationals.

ARTICLE II

Should the Commissioner for any cause be unable to discharge his functions, a successor shall be chosen in the same manner that he was selected. The Commissioner shall hold a session at Washington within two months after the coming into force of the present agreement. He may fix the time and the place of subsequent sessions according to convenience. All claims shall be presented to the Commissioner within one year from the date on which he holds the first session required by the foregoing provision.

ARTICLE III

The Commissioner shall cause to be kept an accurate record of the questions and cases submitted and correct minutes of proceedings. To this end each of the Governments may appoint a secretary, and these secretaries shall act together as joint secretaries and shall be subject to the direction of the Commissioner.

ARTICLE IV

The three Governments may designate agents and counsel who may present oral or written arguments to the Commissioner under such conditions as he may prescribe.

The Commissioner shall receive and consider all written statements or documents which may be presented to him, in accordance with rules which he may prescribe, by or on behalf of the respective Governments in support of or in answer to any claim.

The Governments of Austria and Hungary shall be notified of all claims filed with the Commissioner and shall be given such period of time as the Commissioner shall by rule determine in which to answer any claim filed.

The decisions of the Commissioner shall be accepted as final and binding upon the three Governments.

ARTICLE V

Each Government shall pay its own expenses, including the compensation of the secretary appointed by it and that of its agent and counsel. All other expenses which by their nature are a charge on the three Governments, including the compensation of the Commissioner and such employees as he may appoint to assist him in the performance of his duties, shall be borne one-half by the Government of the United States and one-half by the Governments of Austria and Hungary in equal moieties.

ARTICLE VI

This agreement shall be ratified in accordance with the constitutional forms of the contracting parties and shall come into force on the date of the exchange of ratifications.

In faith whereof, the above named plenipotentiaries have signed the present agreement and have hereunto affixed their seals.

Done in triplicate at the City of Washington this twenty-sixth day of November, one thousand nine hundred and twenty-four.

[For the United States:]   CHARLES EVANS HUGHES [SEAL]
[For Austria:]   EDGAR PROCHNIK   [SEAL]
[For Hungary:]   LÁSZLÓ SZÉCHÉNYI   [SEAL]

DISTRIBUTION OF DAWES ANNUITIES (FINANCE MINISTERS' AGREEMENT, 1925)

Final protocol and agreement signed at Paris January 14, 1925
Entered into force January 14, 1925
Extended and amended by agreements of September 21, 1925,[1] and
January 13, 1927 [2]
Supplanted by New (Young) Plan of January 20, 1930 [3]

1925 For. Rel. (II) 145 and 1919 For. Rel. (Paris Peace Conference, XIII) 902

FINAL PROTOCOL

The representatives of the Governments of Belgium, France, Great Britain, the United States of America, Italy, Japan, Brazil, Greece, Poland, Portugal, Roumania, Serb-Croat-Slovene State, Czechoslovakia, assembled at Paris from the 7th to the 14th January 1925 with a view to settling as between their respective Governments questions which arise out of the distribution of the receipts already entered, or to be entered, in the accounts of the Reparation Commission, in particular after the 1st January 1923 to 1st September 1924, and also in the first years of the application of the Dawes Plan [4] which formed the subject of the Agreements concluded in London on 31st [30th] August 1924,

Have agreed on the provisions contained in the Agreement of today's date of which a copy is attached to the present Protocol.

Done at Paris, *14th January 1925.*

[For Belgium:]
CLEMENTEL

[For France:]
G. THEUNIS

[For the United Kingdom:]
WINSTON S. CHURCHILL

[For the United States of America:]
MYRON T. HERRICK
FRANK B. KELLOGG
JAMES A. LOGAN JR.

[For Italy:]
ALBERTO DE' STEFANI

---

[1] *Post,* p. 521.
[2] *Post,* p. 644.
[3] 1919 For. Rel. (Paris Peace Conference, XIII) 902. The United States did not become a party to the New (Young) Plan; for background, see *ibid.,* p. 388.
[4] For background, see *ibid.,* p. 382.

504

[For Japan:]
K. Ishii

[For Brazil:]
L. M. de Souza Dantas

[For Greece:]
Em. J. Tsouderos

[For Poland:]
J. Mrozowski
J. Karsnicki

[For Portugal:]
Antonio da Fonseca
Vintila Bratiano

[For Romania:]
N. Titulescu

[For the Serb-Croat-Slovene State:]
Stoyadinovitch

[For Czechoslovakia:]
Stefan Osusky

Agreement

The Governments of Belgium, France, Great Britain, Italy, Japan, the United States of America, Brazil, Greece, Poland, Portugal, Roumania, the Serb-Croat-Slovene State and Czechoslovakia, respectively represented by the undersigned, have agreed as follows.

Agreement Regarding the Distribution of the Dawes Annuities

SUMMARY

CHAPTER   V.—MISCELLANEOUS QUESTIONS

CHAPTER I—ALLOCATION OF THE DAWES ANNUITIES

ARTICLE 1

COSTS OF THE COMMISSIONS

A) The maximum normal charge on the Dawes Annuities of the Reparation Commission, including the organisations set up under the Dawes Plan, shall be:

For the year from 1st September 1924 . . . . . . 9¼ million gold marks.
For the later years . . . . 7½   —   —   —

(to be taken partly in foreign currencies or in German currency as required).

Of these sums not more than 3,700,000 gold marks a year shall be attributable to the organisations set up under the Dawes Plan. If necessary this sum may be increased in order to meet the costs of the arbitral bodies provided for by the Dawes Plan and the London Protocol.

B) The maximum charge for the Interallied Rhineland High Commission (including deliveries under Articles 8–12 of the Rhineland Agreement [5]) shall not exceed 10 million gold marks (to be taken in foreign currencies or in German currency as required) for the year from 1st September 1924, this sum being allocated between the French, British and Belgian High Commissariats in the proportion of 62:16:22, after providing for the other expenses of the Commission. The amount for any later year will be settled at a later date.

C) The charge of the Military Commission of Control shall not exceed a maximum of 8 million gold marks (to be taken in German currency) in the year from 1st September 1924. The amount of any later year will be settled at a later date. This figure does not include the Commission's expenses in national currencies, which shall continue to be paid by the Governments concerned, the amounts so paid being credited to their respective accounts by the Reparation Commission.

ARTICLE 2

COSTS OF ARMIES OF OCCUPATION 1924/1925

A) The sums to be allowed as a prior charge on payments by Germany during the year 1st September 1924 to 31st August 1925 in respect of the

---

[5] Agreement signed at Versailles June 28, 1919, *ibid.*, p. 762.

costs of the Armies of Occupation of Belgium, Great Britain and France, shall be fixed at the following amounts:

Belgian Army	25, 000, 000 gold marks
British Army	25, 000, 000 — —
French Army	110, 000, 000 — —

B) Belgium, Great Britain and France will meet their additional Army costs during the period mentioned out of their respective shares in German reparation payments, but shall not be debited on reparation account therewith, that is to say, their respective reparation arrears will be increased by corresponding sums.

C) The additional Army costs shall be calculated as follows. Each Power will be entitled to receive:

1. The sums payable under the Finance Ministers' Agreement of 11th March 1922,[6] calculated in the case of Great Britain on the basis of the French capitation rate with a special allowance of 2 gold marks a man, converted into sterling on the basis of the mean rates of exchange of the respective currencies during the month of December 1921. The value of German marks supplied to the Armies of Occupation and the value of any requisitions under Article 6 of the Rhineland Agreement shall, as heretofore, be included in these sums, and

2. The value of the requisitions and services under Articles 8–12 of the Rhineland Agreement, which are credited to Germany in the accounts of the Agent General for Reparations.

For each Power the additional Army costs shall be the difference between the total sum so calculated and the amount of the prior charge set out in paragraph (A) above.

D) It is agreed that the Powers concerned in the occupation shall not charge for effectives in excess of the strength authorised for each respectively by Article 1 (2) and (3) of the Agreement of 11th March 1922.

E) The provisions of this Article for the year to 31st August 1925 are accepted without prejudice to any question of principle, and the Allied Governments and the Government of the United States of America will discuss, before the 1st September 1925, the arrangement for Army Costs in the future.[7]

ARTICLE 3

SHARE OF THE UNITED STATES OF AMERICA IN THE DAWES ANNUITIES

A) Out of the amount received from Germany on account of the Dawes annuities, there shall be paid to the United States of America the following sums in reimbursement of the costs of the United States Army of Occupation and for the purpose of satisfying the awards of the Mixed Claims Commis-

---

[6] *Ibid.*, p. 870.
[7] See agreement of Sept. 21, 1925, *post*, p. 521.

sion established in pursuance of the Agreement between the United States and Germany of August 10th, 1922.[8]

1. Fifty-five million gold marks per annum beginning September 1st, 1926, and continuing until the principal sums outstanding on account of the costs of the United States Army of Occupation, as already reported to the Reparation Commission, shall be extinguished. These annual payments constitute a first charge on cash made available for transfer by the Transfer Committee out of the Dawes Annuities, after the provision of the sums necessary for the service of the 800 million gold mark German external loan, 1924, and for the costs of the Reparation Commission, the organisations established pursuant to the Dawes Plan, the Interallied Rhineland High Commission, the Military Control Commissions, and the payment to the Danube Commission provided for in Article 9 below, and for any other prior charges which may hereafter with the assent of the United States of America be admitted. If in any year the total sum of fifty-five million gold marks be not transferred to the United States of America the arrears shall be carried forward to the next succeeding annual instalment payable to the United States of America, which shall be *pro tanto* increased. Arrears shall be cumulative and shall bear simple interest at $4\frac{1}{2}\%$ from the end of the year in which the said arrears accumulated until they are satisfied.

2. Two and one quarter per cent $(2\frac{1}{4}\%)$ of all receipts from Germany on account of the Dawes Annuities available for distribution as reparations, provided that the annuity resulting from this percentage shall not in any year exceed the sum of forty-five million gold marks.

B) Subject to the provisions of Paragraph A above, the United States of America agree:

1. To waive any claim under the Army Cost Agreement of May 25th, 1923,[9] on cash receipts obtained since 1st January 1923 beyond the sum of $14,725,154.40 now deposited by Belgium to the account of the Treasury of the United States in a blocked account in the Federal Reserve Bank of New-York, which sum shall forthwith be released to the United States Treasury.

2. That the Agreement of May 25th 1923 does not apply to payments on account of reparations by any ex-enemy Powers other than Germany.

3. That the Agreement of May 25th 1923, is deemed to be superseded by the present Agreement.

C) The provisions of this Agreement relating to the admission against the Dawes Annuities of charges other than reparations, and the allotments provided for such charges shall not be modified by the Allied Governments,

---

[8] TS 665, *post.*
[9] TS 671–A, *ante,* p. 424.

so as to reduce the sums to be distributed as reparations save in agreement with the United States of America.

D) The United States of America is recognised as having an interest, proportionate to its 2¼% interest in the part of the annuities available for reparation, in any distribution of railway bonds, industrial debentures or other bonds issued under the Dawes Plan, or in the proceeds of any sale of undistributed bonds or debentures and as having the right also to share in any distribution or in the proceeds of any sale, of such bonds or debentures for any arrears that may be due to it in respect of the repayment of its army costs as provided in the present Agreement. The United States of America is also recognised as having an interest in any other disposition that may be made of the bonds if not sold or distributed.

Article 4

BELGIAN WAR DEBT

A) As from the 1st September 1924 5% of the total sum available in any year after meeting the charges for the service of the German External Loan, 1924, and the charges for Costs of Commissions; Costs of U.S. Army of Occupation; Annuity for Arrears of pre-1st May 1921 Army Costs; Prior charge for current Army Costs; and any other prior charges which may hereafter be agreed, shall be applied to the reimbursement of the Belgian War Debt as defined in the last paragraph of Article 232 of the Treaty of Versailles.[10]

B) The amounts so applied in any year shall be distributed between the Powers concerned in proportion to the amount of the debts due to them respectively as of 1st May 1921. Pending the final settlement of the accounts, France shall receive 46% Great Britain 42% and Belgium (by reason of her debt to U.S.A.) 12%.

Article 5

RESTITUTION

A) There shall be applied to the satisfaction of claims for restitution:

a) During the first four years 1% of the total sum available in any year after meeting the charges for the service of the German External Loan, 1924, and the charges for Costs of Commissions: Costs of U.S. Army of occupation; annuity for arrears of pre-1st May 1921 Army Costs; prior charge for current Army Costs; and any other prior charge which may hereafter be agreed;

b) During subsequent years 1% of the balance of the first milliard after meeting the charges enumerated above and 2% of the surplus of the annuity.

---

[10] *Ante,* p. 138.

B) The amount so applied shall be distributed between the Powers having a claim for restitution proportionately to their respective claims under this head as accepted by the Reparation Commission.

C) The French and Italian Governments reserve their rights to claim restitution of certain objects of art by the application of article 238 [11] of the Treaty of Versailles. The other Allied Governments will support their efforts to secure the execution by Germany of such restitution. Nevertheless, if the fulfilment of this obligation involves a charge on the Dawes annuities the value will be charged against the share in the annuity of the Power interested.

ARTICLE 6

BELGIAN PRIORITY

A) It is agreed that the determination of the exact position as regards the satisfaction of the Belgian priority depends on the settlement of the distribution account which the Reparation Commission has been requested to draw up.

B) Out of the part of the annuities received from Germany and available for distribution as reparations among the Allied Powers after 1st September 1924, Belgium will receive:

a) During the year commencing 1st September 1924 : 8%.

b) During the year commencing 1st September 1925, so long as Belgian priority is not extinguished 8% of each monthly payment. As soon as the priority is extinguished, the percentage of all further payments during the year in question will be reduced to 4.5%.

c) During the year commencing 1st September 1926 and during each succeeding year : 4.5%.

This reduction in percentage is accepted as fully discharging Belgium from her obligations to repay her priority.

C) As from the date at which Belgian priority is extinguished or at the latest from 1st September 1926, the 3½% released by the above arrangements for the repayment of the Belgian priority will be payable to France and Great Britain in the proportion 52 : 22, in addition to their Spa percentages.

The sums debited to Belgium in respect of the period to 1st September 1924, will not be regarded as creating for her either excess payments or arrears, provided that this shall be without prejudice to the liability of Belgium to account for any final balance under the Economic Clauses of the Treaty.

D) The right accruing to Belgium as a result of previous Agreements on payments received or to be received from or on account of Austria, Hungary and Bulgaria remain unaltered.

---

[11] *Ante,* p. 140.

ARTICLE 7

GREEK AND ROUMANIAN REPARATION PERCENTAGES

A) The percentage of reparation payments available for distribution between the Allied Powers to be allotted to Greece is fixed at 0.4 percent of payments by Germany and of the first half of payments by Austria, Hungary and Bulgaria and 25 percent of the second half of payments by Austria, Hungary and Bulgaria.

B) The percentage of reparation payments available for distribution between the Allied Powers to be allotted to Roumania is fixed at 1.1 percent of payments made by Germany and of the first half of payments by Austria, Hungary and Bulgaria, and 20 percent of the second half of payments made by Austria, Hungary and Bulgaria.

ARTICLE 8

MISCELLANEOUS CLAIMS

A) The following claims namely:

a) Costs of military occupation of the Plebiscite zones (Annex to Article 88 of Treaty [12]);

b) Costs of repatriation of German prisoners of war (Article 217 of the Treaty [13]);

c) Repayment of exceptional war expenses advanced by Alsace-Lorraine during the war, or by public bodies in Alsace-Lorraine, on account of the Empire (Article 58 of the Treaty [14]);

d) Payment of certain indemnities in the Cameroons and French Equatorial Africa (Articles 124 and 125 of the Treaty [15]).

shall be submitted for valuation to the Reparation Commission which shall be at liberty to use for this purpose all the means at its disposal including reference to arbitration as proposed in Article 11 below.

The amounts of these claims when established shall be credited to the interested Powers in their Reparation accounts as at the 1st September 1924, and the credits treated as arrears at that date in accordance with the provisions of Article 19 below.

B) The following claims would appear to be payable apart from and in addition to the Dawes annuities namely:

a) The costs of the civil and military pensions in Alsace-Lorraine earned at the date of the Armistice (Article 62 of the Treaty [16]);

---

[12] *Ante,* p. 91.
[13] *Ante,* p. 134.
[14] *Ante,* p. 79.
[15] *Ante,* p. 108.
[16] *Ante,* p. 79.

b) The transfer of the reserves of social insurance funds in Alsace-Lorraine (Article 77 of the Treaty[17]). Should, however, the German Government succeed in establishing that these claims must be met out of the Dawes Annuities the Allied Governments will concert together as to the manner in which they should be dealt with.

ARTICLE 9

COMPENSATION DUE TO THE EUROPEAN COMMISSION OF THE DANUBE

There shall be paid forthwith to the European Commission of the Danube out of the Annuities the sum of 266,800 gold francs, being the amount agreed to be due from Germany to the Commission in respect of compensation for damages.

ARTICLE 10

CLEARING OFFICE BALANCES

No special charge shall be admitted against the Dawes annuities in respect of Clearing Offices balances of pre-war debts or other claims under the Economic Clauses of the Treaty unless it is shown that any Allied Power claiming the benefit of such charge has a net credit balance due for payment, after applying, to meet its claims under the Economic Clauses, the German properties and other assets which it has the power to liquidate under the same articles. No provision shall be made for such net credit balances during the first four years of the Dawes Plan.

CHAPTER II—SETTLEMENT OF PAST ACCOUNTS

ARTICLE 11

DISTRIBUTION ACCOUNTS—PROVISION AS TO ARBITRATION

The Allied Governments request the Reparation Commission to draw up as soon as possible definite distribution accounts as at 1st September 1924.

They will give authority to their respective Delegates on the Reparation Commission, to submit to arbitration all questions of fact or of figures arising on the accounts and to the fullest possible extent, questions of interpretation, on which they are not unanimous, in so far as is not already provided for in any existing arrangement.

The above provisions will apply in particular to the settlement of the Ruhr accounts in accordance with the principles set out below and to questions which may arise in regard to the amounts due under the heads of restitutions or other non-reparation claims.

---

[17] *Ante*, p. 84.

ARTICLE 12

RUHR ACCOUNTS

A) The Reparation Commission shall fix in accordance with the provisions of the Treaty of Versailles and the practice hitherto in force the value in gold marks of the receipts of every nature obtained by the French, Belgian, and Italian Governments from Germany since 11th January 1923, in so far as such receipts have not already been accounted for to it. The Reparation Commission shall similarly determine the amounts to be set against such receipts with a view to securing that the Powers concerned receive credit for expenditure actually incurred by them, subject, however, to the detailed provisions below with respect to Army Costs.

B) Separate accounts will be drawn up for deliveries in kind and cash receipts.

C) The account of deliveries in kind shall include the value as determined by the Reparation Commission of:

1. Deliveries in kind not yet accounted for to the Commission including deliveries paid for from the "fonds commun" and the "fonds special".

2. All requisitions under or on the analogy of Article 6 of the Rhineland Agreement and all paper marks seized and fines imposed by the Armies of Occupation during the period 1st January 1923, up to the 31st August 1924, in so far as they have not already been reported to the Reparation Commission.

Against these receipts will be allowed as deductions the extra costs incurred by the French and Belgian Governments during the period 1st January 1923, to the 31st August 1924, through the maintenance of military forces in German territory not occupied on the 1st January 1923, after setting off the normal costs of the maintenance of these forces in their home garrisons.

The net value of the deliveries in kind so determined shall be debited in the reparation accounts against the Powers which have received them.

The value of coal and coke sold to Luxemburg during the same period shall be treated as a delivery in kind to France.

D) The account of cash receipts shall include cash receipts of all kinds obtained by the Occupying Powers including the gross amounts obtained from taxes or duties, licences, derogations, etc., and the net receipts of the Railway Regie, as ascertained by the Reparation Commission after verification of the accounts.

From these receipts will be allowed as deductions the civil costs of collection and expenses of administration incurred before the 31st August 1924, and the costs of loading coal and exploitation of mines and cokeries up to the same date.

The balance of the account shall, with the exception of the sum mentioned in sub-paragraph 1 of parag. B of Art. 3, be paid over to the Belgian Government which shall be debited on account of the priority for the period before 1st

September 1924, with the full amount so received less the interest due on the German Treasury Bills transferred to Belgium in 1922.

E) In accordance with Annexe III to the London Protocol no claim will be made for payment out of the Dawes annuities of any costs in respect of military forces in German territory not occupied on the 1st January, 1923, other than the value of requisitions effected by, or services rendered to these forces after 1st September, 1924. The value of such requisitions or services will be accounted for as deliveries on Reparation Account to the Allied Powers concerned.

Chapter III—Special Questions Arising Out of Previous Agreements

Article 13

EXTENSION BEYOND JANUARY 1ST, 1923 OF THE PROVISIONS OF ARTICLE 2 OF THE AGREEMENT OF MARCH 11, 1922: APPROPRIATION OF DELIVERIES IN KIND TO THE COST OF ARMIES OF OCCUPATION

The French, British and Belgian Governments agree that the *forfaits* fixed, or to be fixed, for their respective armies of occupation from the 1st January, 1923, and until the 31st August, 1928, in so far as they are not met out of requisitions of paper marks and services, etc., under Article 6 of the Rhineland Agreement, should be charged on the deliveries in kind (including receipts under the British Reparation Recovery Act and any similar levy established by any other Government) received by them respectively, and the Reparation Commission is requested to give effect to this decision in its accounts.

Article 14

EXTENSION BEYOND JANUARY 1ST, 1923, OF THE PROVISIONS OF ARTICLE 6 OF THE AGREEMENT OF MARCH 11, 1922: RETENTION BY EACH POWER OF THE DELIVERIES IN KIND RECEIVED BY IT

Each of the Allied Governments having a credit due to it on reparation account shall be entitled to retain, without being required to make payment in cash for the value thereof, the deliveries in kind (including Reparation Recovery Act Receipts) received and retained by them between the 31st December 1922, and the 1st September 1924. The receipts of each Power, however, up to the 1st September 1924, shall be taken into account in determining the adjustments provided for in Article 19.

Article 15

COSTS OF ARMIES OF OCCUPATION FOR THE PERIOD 1ST MAY 1922 TO 31ST AUGUST 1924

A) The credits to be given in respect of the costs of occupation for the period 1st May 1922 to 1st May 1924, are as follows:

	French share of *forfait*	Belgian share of *forfait*	British share of *forfait*
	Gold marks	*Gold marks*	*Gold marks*
May 1st, 1922 to April 30th, 1923...........	155, 526, 693	30, 680, 158	21, 092, 922
May 1st, 1923 to April 30th, 1924...........	117, 195, 330	23, 284, 922	22, 369, 567

B) As regards the costs of occupation for the period 1st May 1924 to 31st August 1924, the Allied Governments will authorise their representatives on the Reparation Commission to make the necessary adjustment on the basis of the principles on which the above figures were calculated.

C) The Reparation Commission is requested to introduce those figures into its accounts for the years in question.

ARTICLE 16

DEBITS FOR THE VESSELS ALLOTTED OR TRANSFERRED TO BELGIUM UNDER ARTICLE 6 (4) OF THE SPA PROTOCOL

The debits in the Interallied accounts for the vessels allotted or transferred to Belgium under Article 6 (4) of the Spa Protocol [18] shall be dealt with under Article 12 of the Finance Ministers' Agreement of the 11th March 1922 instead of as provided for in the Spa Protocol.

ARTICLE 17

DEBIT FOR SHANTUNG RAILWAYS AND MINES

In respect of the Railways and Mines referred to in the second paragraph of Article 156 of the Treaty of Versailles,[19] Japan will be debited by the Reparation Commission in the Interallied accounts only with the equivalent of compensation which has been or may be in fact paid by the German Government to its nationals for their interests. Pending the establishment of the amounts in question Japan will be regarded as entitled to her full percentage of reparations as from 1st September 1924.

CHAPTER IV—INTEREST AND ARREARS

ARTICLE 18

INTEREST ACCOUNT

The Allied Governments agree that all interest charges on reparation receipts up to 1st September 1924, should be waived as between the Allied

---

[18] Agreement signed at Spa July 16, 1920, 1919 For. Rel. (Paris Peace Conference, XIII) 851; for an informal U.S. reservation of Aug. 27, 1920, see *ibid.*, p. 860.

[19] *Ante,* p. 114.

Powers and all provisions in existing agreements requiring interest accounts to be kept to that date are cancelled. Interest at 5% shall, however, be charged as from 1st September, 1924, on the excess receipts shown in the account to be drawn up under Article 19 below as due at that date by any Allied Power to the Reparation Pool as well as on any further excess receipts which may accrue after that date until they are repaid.

ARTICLE 19

EXCESSES AND ARREARS

A) The Reparation Commission shall as soon as possible draw up an account showing, as at 1st September, 1924, for each Power entitled to a share in the reparation payments of Germany, but not including the United States of America.

a) The net receipts of that Power on reparation account as at 1st September, 1924, which shall be calculated by deducting from its total gross receipts as valued for the purpose of Interallied distribution, the credits due to it in respect of Spa coal advances, of costs of Armies of Occupation (excluding the arrears as at 1st May, 1921, provided for in Article 21), costs of Commissions of Control not paid in German currency, profits on exchange, and of any other approved claims such as the claims referred to in Article 8 A) of this Agreement;

b) The amount that Power should have received had the total net reparation receipts of all the Powers been distributed in accordance with the Spa percentages.

By deducting from the amount due to each Power its actual debit, the Reparation Commission will determine the arrears due to that power or the excess payments due from that Power as at 1st September, 1924.

B) A similar calculation shall be made by the Reparation Commission on the 1st September in each succeeding year.

C) For the purpose of the above calculations the figures relating to Belgium shall be included on the same footing as those relating to other Powers but, save as provided elsewhere in this Agreement, Belgium shall be free of any obligation to repay reparation receipts obtained before 1st September 1924.

Belgium shall, however, if the case arises, be required to account with interest for any excess of reparation receipts obtained by her after 1st September 1924, over her due proportion, as laid down elsewhere in this Agreement, of the total receipts effectively debited to all the Powers after that date. In the contrary case Belgium will be regarded as having a claim in respect of arrears.

D) The provisions of the second paragraph of Article 7 of the Agreement of 11th March 1922 relating to the debits to be entered in the account to be drawn up under Article 235 of the Treaty [20] in respect of coal received by

---

[20] *Ante*, p. 139.

Italy before 1st May 1921, shall apply also to the debits for coal received by Italy between 1st May 1921 and 31st December 1922.

ARTICLE 20

RECOVERY OF ARREARS

Except as otherwise provided for in this Agreement:

(A) The excess receipts of any Power as fixed at the end of each year under Article 19 shall be repaid by the deduction of a certain percentage from the share of that Power in each succeeding annuity until the debt is extinguished with interest at 5%, provided that no repayments under this sub-section shall be required out of the annuities for the years commencing 1st September 1924 and 1st September 1925.

(B) In the case of Italy and the S. H. S. [Serb-Croat-Slovene] State this deduction shall be fixed at 10%. In the case of other countries the deduction shall be calculated by the Reparation Commission on a similar basis.

(C) The repayments made by the Debtor Powers shall be distributed between the Powers in credit to the Reparation Pool in proportion to their respective arrears.

ARTICLE 21

COSTS OF THE ARMIES OF OCCUPATION TO 1ST MAY 1921

The arrears due to France and Great Britain on account of pre-1st May 1921 Army Costs shall be excluded from the general account of arrears and shall be discharged by a special allotment out of the Dawes annuities (ranking immediately after the charge in favour of U.S. Army Costs) of the following amounts namely:

1st year	15 million gold marks.
2nd year	20 — — —
3rd year	25 — — —
4th year	30 — — —

and thereafter an annuity of 30 million gold marks till the arrears are extinguished.

This allotment shall be divided between France and Great Britain in the proportions France 57%, Great Britain 43%. The allotment shall be taken in deliveries in kind during the first two years of the Dawes Plan and thereafter may be transferred either in deliveries in kind or cash. This arrangement will not affect the distribution of any cash receipts now in the hands of the Reparation Commission available for the liquidation of Army Costs arrears, which receipts will be dealt with in accordance with Article 8 of the Agreement of 11th March 1922 and credited against the capital arrears. Further, the annuity above provided for will retain a prior charge up to 25% of its amount on any cash receipts not arising out of the Dawes Plan which may accrue to the Reparation Commission in the future on account of Germany.

Chapter V—Miscellaneous Questions

Article 22

PAYMENT BY CZECHOSLOVAKIA FOR DELIVERIES IN KIND

The sums due by Czechoslovakia to the Reparation Commission in respect of the deliveries in kind received by her from Germany and Hungary since 1st May 1921, shall be placed in a suspense account and carry interest at 5% from the 1st September, 1924.

Article 23

BULGARIAN PAYMENTS

Without prejudice to any question of principle, the payments made or to be made up to 31st December 1926, by Bulgaria under the Protocol of Sofia dated 21st March 1923,[21] will be distributed between the Allied Powers in the proportions laid down in Article 2 of the Spa Protocol. The Allied Governments will agree together as to the method of distribution of these payments to be adopted after 31st December 1926.

Article 24

PROPERTIES CEDED TO THE FREE CITY OF DANZIG

The Allied Governments give full powers to their respective representatives on the Reparation Commission to settle all questions connected with the debt due by the Free City of Danzig in respect of the value of the public properties ceded to the Free City by Germany, including such adjustments of the payments to be made by the Free City as may be necessitated by its financial situation.

Article 25

RECOMMENDATIONS WITH REGARD TO DISTRIBUTION OF PAYMENTS THROUGHOUT THE YEAR

The Finance Ministers draw the attention of the Reparation Commission to the fact that the operation of the Dawes Plan would be greatly facilitated if the Agent General for Reparation Payments could so arrange that the annual payments to be made during the operation of the Dawes Plan may be distributed throughout the course of each year, and they request the Reparation Commission and the Agent General to consider what steps can be taken to secure this result, which is of particular importance during the second and third years of the Plan.

---

[21] For text, in the orginal French, see *British and Foreign State Papers,* vol. 117, p. 534.

With a view to accomplishing this result the Allied Governments, so far as they are concerned, authorise the Reparation Commission and the Agent General for Reparation Payments in cooperation with the Trustees for Railway Bonds and Industrial Debentures to take all action that may be necessary to arrange the due dates of the payments to be made on the Railway and Industrial Bonds so as to provide for a gradual and even flow of payments throughout each annuity year.

Furthermore, the Finance Ministers authorise the Reparation Commission to make arrangements, so far as may be practicable without prejudicing the requirements of other Powers, to enable the Portuguese Government to obtain during the earlier months of the second year of the Dawes Plan (within the limit of its share in the second annuity) the sums necessary to complete certain outstanding orders for deliveries in kind of special importance to it.

ARTICLE 26

INTERPRETATION AND ARBITRATION

This Agreement shall be transmitted to the Reparation Commission, and the Commission will be requested to give effect thereto and to adjust the payments during the remainder of the year to 31st August 1925, and during subsequent years, so that the total receipts of each Allied Power during each year shall not exceed its share under this Agreement. The Reparation Commission shall have authority by unanimous resolution to interpret the provisions of the Agreement, in so far as the Allied Powers are concerned. If any difference or dispute shall arise on the Reparation Commission or between the Allied Powers in respect of the interpretation of any provisions of this Agreement or as to anything to be done hereunder whether by the Commission or otherwise, the same shall be referred to the arbitration of a single arbitrator to be agreed unanimously by the members of the Reparation Commission, or, failing agreement, to be appointed by the President for the time being of the Permanent Court of International Justice.

Any difference or dispute that may arise with the United States of America regarding the interpretation of this Agreement affecting American claims or the rights of the United States of America under this Agreement shall be referred to an arbitrator to be agreed upon between the United States of America and the Reparation Commission acting unanimously.

ARTICLE 27

RESERVATION AS TO THE RIGHTS AND OBLIGATIONS OF GERMANY

The provisions of the present Arrangement concluded between the Powers interested in reparations do not prejudice any rights or obligations of Germany under the Treaties, Conventions and Arrangements at present in force.

The present agreement, done in English and French in a Single Copy will be deposited in the Archives of the Government of the French Republic which will supply certified copies thereof to each of the Signatory Powers.

In the interpretation of this Agreement, the English and French texts shall be both authentic.

PARIS, *January 14th, 1925.*

[For Belgium:]
CLEMENTEL

[For France:]
G. THEUNIS

[For the United Kingdom:]
WINSTON S. CHURCHILL

[For the United States of America:]
MYRON T. HERRICK
FRANK B. KELLOGG
JAMES A. LOGAN JR

[For Italy:]
ALBERTO DE' STEFANI

[For Japan:]
K. ISHII

[For Brazil:]
L. M. DE SOUZA DANTAS

[For Greece:]
EM. J. TSOUDEROS

[For Poland:]
J. MROZOWSKI
J. KARSNICKI

[For Portugal:]
ANTONIO DA FONSECA
VINTILA BRATIANO

[For Romania:]
N. TITULESCU

[For the Serb-Croat-Slovene State:]
STOYADINOVITCH

[For Czechoslovakia:]
STEFAN OSUSKY

ALLOCATION OF DAWES ANNUITIES

Agreement signed at Paris September 21, 1925
Extended and amended by agreement of January 13, 1927 [1]

1925 For. Rel. (II) 163 and 1919 For.
Rel. (Paris Peace Conference, XIII) 919

The Governments of Belgium, the United States of America, France, Great Britain, Italy, Japan, Brazil, Greece, Poland, Portugal, Roumania, the Serb-Croat-Slovene State and Czechoslovakia, respectively represented by the undersigned, have agreed as follows:

ARTICLE 1

ARMIES OF OCCUPATION

The provisions of paragraphs A, B, C, D of Article 2 of the Financial Agreement of the 14th January, 1925,[2] relative to the costs of the armies of occupation shall remain in force during the second year of the Dawes Plan.[3]

One-twelfth of the credits therein provided for shall be allocated monthly.

The Allied Governments and the Government of the United States of America will discuss before the 1st September, 1926, under the conditions laid down in paragraph E of the above-mentioned Article, the arrangements for army costs in the future.

Nevertheless, if during the course of the second Dawes year the Allied Governments decide to evacuate or modify any of the zones of occupation, this discussion will take place within the two months following such evacuation or modification.

ARTICLE 2

INTER–ALLIED RHINELAND HIGH COMMISSION

The maximum charge for the Inter-Allied Rhineland High Commission (including deliveries under Articles 8 to 12 of the Rhineland Agreement [4]) shall not exceed 9,000,000 gold marks (to be taken in foreign currency or in

---

[1] *Post*, p. 644.
[2] *Ante*, p. 506.
[3] For background, see 1919 For. Rel. (Paris Peace Conference, XIII) 382.
[4] Agreement signed at Versailles June 28, 1919, *ibid.*, p. 762.

German currency as required) during the second year of the Dawes Plan, this sum being allocated between the French, British and Belgian Commissariats as follows:—

French High Commissariat	5, 580, 000
British High Commissariat	1, 440, 000
Belgian High Commissariat	1, 980, 000

This provision is only to be drawn upon as and to the extent required, and at the end of every three months the Inter-Allied Rhineland High Commission shall transmit to the Reparation Commission a certified statement of the expenditure actually incurred by each Delegation in the execution of its duties under the Rhineland Agreement.

A similar statement covering the expenditure of the first Dawes year will be transmitted to the Reparation Commission as soon as possible after the 31st August, 1925.

Any savings at the end of the year will be paid into the common reparation fund for distribution in accordance with the provisions of the Financial Agreement of the 14th January, 1925, to the Powers having the right under that Agreement to participate in the receipts from Germany on account of the Dawes annuities available for distribution as reparations.

The Allied Governments and the Government of the United States of America will discuss before the 1st September, 1926, the arrangements for the costs of the Inter-Allied Rhineland High Commission in the future.

Nevertheless, if during the course of the second Dawes year the Allied Governments decide to evacuate or modify any of the zones of occupation, this discussion will take place within the two months following such evacuation or modification.

ARTICLE 3

INTER-ALLIED MILITARY COMMISSION OF CONTROL

The charge of the Military Commission of Control shall not exceed a maximum of 6,800,000 gold marks (to be taken in German currency) in the second year of the Dawes Plan.

This provision is only to be drawn upon as and to the extent required, and in the event of the Governments deciding upon any modification of the functions of the commission a fresh estimate of its expenditure shall be at once drawn up.

At the end of every three months the Conference of Ambassadors will transmit to the Reparation Commission a certified statement of the expenditure incurred by the Inter-Allied Commission of Control.

A similar statement covering the expenditure of the first Dawes year will be transmitted to the Reparation Commission as soon as possible after the 31st August, 1925.

This figure does not include the commission's expenses in national currencies, which shall continue to be paid by the Governments concerned, the amounts so paid being credited to their respective accounts by the Reparation Commission.

Any savings at the end of the year will be paid into the common reparation fund for distribution in accordance with the provisions of the Financial Agreement of the 14th January, 1925, to the Powers having the right under that Agreement to participate in the receipts from Germany on account of the Dawes Annuities available for distribution as reparation.

The present Agreement, done in English and French in a single copy, will be deposited in the archives of the Government of the French Republic, which will supply certified copies thereof to each of the Signatory Powers.

In the interpretation of this Agreement, the English and French texts shall be both authentic.

PARIS, *September 21, 1925.*

[For Belgium:]
MAUCLÈRE

[For France:]
ROBERT PERIER

[For the United States of America:]
RALPH W. S. HILL

[For the United Kingdom:]
BASIL KEMBALL COOK

[For Italy:]
CORSI

[For Japan:]
SHIZUO YAMAJI

[For Brazil:]
L. M. DE SOUZA DANTAS

[For Greece:]
LÉON V. MELAS

[For Poland:]
J. MROZOWSKI

[For Portugal:]
J. BARRETO

[For Romania:]
AL. ZEUCEANU

[For the Serb-Croat-Slovene State:]
DR. PLOJ

[For Czechoslovakia:]
STEFAN OSUSKY

PROTECTION OF INDUSTRIAL PROPERTY

Convention signed at The Hague November 6, 1925
Senate advice and consent to ratification December 16, 1930
Ratified by the President of the United States December 27, 1930
Ratification of the United States deposited at Bern January 22, 1931
Notification of United States deposit given by Switzerland to other parties February 6, 1931
Entered into force June 1, 1928; for the United States March 6, 1931
Proclaimed by the President of the United States March 6, 1931
Replaced by conventions of June 2, 1934,[1] and October 31, 1958,[2] as between contracting parties to the later conventions[3]

47 Stat. 1789; Treaty Series 834

[TRANSLATION]

CONVENTION OF UNION OF PARIS OF MARCH 20, 1883, FOR THE PROTECTION OF INDUSTRIAL PROPERTY REVISED AT BRUSSELS DECEMBER 14, 1900, AT WASHINGTON JUNE 2, 1911, AND AT THE HAGUE NOVEMBER 6, 1925

The President of the German Reich; the President of the Republic of Austria; His Majesty the King of the Belgians; the President of the United States of Brazil; the President of the Republic of Cuba; His Majesty the King of Denmark; the President of the Dominican Republic; His Majesty the King of Spain; the President of the Republic of Estonia; the President of the United States of America; the President of the Republic of Finland; the President of the French Republic; His Majesty the King of the United Kingdom of Great Britain and Ireland and of the British Dominions beyond the Seas, Emperor of India; His Serene Highness the Governor of Hungary; His Majesty the King of Italy; His Majesty the Emperor of Japan; His Majesty the Sultan of Morocco; the President of the United Mexican States;

---

[1] TS 941, *post*, vol. 3.
[2] 13 UST 1; TIAS 4931.
[3] The Stockholm Act of the Paris Convention for the Protection of Industrial Property was signed July 14, 1967, by 39 countries, including the United States; it was not in force as of Jan. 1, 1969. The act replaces the 1883 convention, as revised, as regards the relations between the countries to which it applies and to the extent that it applies.

524

His Majesty the King of Norway; Her Majesty the Queen of the Netherlands; the President of the Polish Republic, in the name of Poland and the Free City of Danzig; the President of the Portuguese Republic; His Majesty the King of the Serbs, Croats and Slovenes; His Majesty the King of Sweden; the Federal Council of the Swiss Confederation; the States of Syria and Greater Lebanon; the President of the Czechoslovak Republic; His Highness the Bey of Tunis; the President of the Turkish Republic,

Having deemed it expedient to make certain modifications and additions in the international convention of March 20, 1883,[4] for the creation of an international union for the protection of industrial property, revised at Brussels on December 14, 1900,[5] and at Washington on June 2, 1911,[6] have appointed as their plenipotentiaries, to wit:

The President of the German Reich:

Mr. W. F. von Vietinghoff, Counselor of the German Legation at The Hague;

Mr. von Specht, Privy Councilor, President of the Patent Office;

Mr. Klauer, Ministerial Councilor at the Ministry of Justice;

Prof. Dr. Albert Osterrieth, Counselor of Justice;

The President of the Republic of Austria:

Dr. Carl Duschanek, Ministerial Councilor, Vice President of the Austrian Patent Office;

Dr. Hans Fortwängler, Ministerial Councilor at that Office;

His Majesty the King of the Belgians:

Mr. Octave Mavaut, Director General of Industry at the Ministry of Industry, Labor, and Social Service;

Mr. Albert Capitaine, Advocate at the Liége Court of Appeal, former President of the Bar, Belgian Delegate at the Washington Conference;

Mr. Louis André, Advocate at the Brussels Court of Appeal;

Mr. Thomas Braun, Advocate at the Brussels Court of Appeal;

Mr. Daniel Coppieters, Advocate at the Brussels Court of Appeal;

The President of the United States of Brazil:

Dr. Julio Augusto Barboza Carneiro, Member of the Economic Committee of the League of Nations;

Prof. Dr. Carlos Americo Barbosa de Oliveira, Professor at the Polytechnic School, Director of the Wenceslau Braz Normal School of Arts and Crafts;

---

[4] TS 379, *ante*, vol. 1, p. 80.
[5] TS 411, *ante*, vol. 1, p. 296.
[6] TS 579, *ante*, vol. 1, p. 791.

The President of the Republic of Cuba:
  Dr. Raphael Martinez Ortiz, Envoy Extraordinary and Minister Plenipotentiary of Cuba at Paris;
  Dr. Raphael de la Torre, Chargé d'Affaires of Cuba at The Hague;

His Majesty the King of Denmark:
  Dr. N. J. Ehrenreich Hansen, Assistant Bureau Chief at the Ministry of Industry, Commerce, and Navigation;

The President of the Dominican Republic:
  Mr. C. G. de Haseth Cz., Consul of the Dominican Republic at The Hague;

His Majesty the King of Spain:
  His Excellency Mr. Santiago Mendez de Vigo, Envoy Extraordinary and Minister Plenipotentiary of His Majesty the King of Spain at The Hague:
  Mr. Fernando Cabello y Lapiedra, Chief of the Spanish Bureau of Industrial and Commercial Property;
  Mr. José Garcia-Monge y de Vera, Secretary of the Spanish Bureau of Industrial and Commercial Property;

The President of the Republic of Estonia:
  Mr. O. Aarmann, Engineer, Director of the Patent Office;

The President of the United States of America:
  Mr. Thomas E. Robertson, Commissioner of Patents, Member of the Bar of the Supreme Court of the United States;
  Mr. Wallace R. Lane, former President of the American and Chicago Patent Law Associations, Member of the Bar of the Supreme Court of the United States and the Supreme Court of Illinois;
  Mr. Jo. Baily Brown, Pittsburgh, Member of the Bar of the Supreme Court of the United States and the Supreme Court of Pennsylvania;

The President of the Republic of Finland:
  Mr. Yrjö Saastamoinen, Chargé d'Affaires of Finland at The Hague;

The President of the French Republic:
  His Excellency Mr. Chassain de Marcilly, Envoy Extraordinary and Minister Plenipotentiary of France at The Hague;
  Mr. Marcel Plaisant, Deputy, Advocate at the Paris Court of Appeal;
  Mr. Charles Drouets, Director of Industrial Property at the Ministry of Commerce;
  Mr. Georges Maillard, Advocate at the Paris Court of Appeal, Vice President of the Technical Committee on Industrial Property;

His Majesty the King of the United Kingdom of Great Britain and Ireland and of the British Dominions beyond the Seas, Emperor of India:

For Great Britain and Northern Ireland:

Sir Hubert Llewellyn Smith, G.C.B., Chief Economic Adviser to His Britannic Majesty's Government;

Mr. Alfred James Martin, O.E.B., Assistant Comptroller of the Patent Office and Industrial Property Department of the Board of Trade;

Sir Arthur Balfour, K.B.E., one of His Majesty's Justices of the Peace; Chairman of the Committee on Trade and Industry;

For the Dominion of Canada:

Mr. Frederick Herbert Palmer, M.C., Canadian Government Trade Commissioner;

For the Commonwealth of Australia:

Lieut. Col. Charles Vincent Watson, D.S.O., V.D., Commissioner of Patents and Registrar of Trade Marks and Designs;

For the Irish Free State:

Count Gerald O'Kelly de Gallagh, Representative of the Irish Free State;

His Serene Highness the Governor of Hungary:

Mr. Elemér de Pompéry, President of the Court of Patents;

His Majesty the King of Italy:

Mr. Domenico Barone, Councilor of State;

Mr. Gustavo de Sanctis, Director of the Bureau of Industrial Property;

Mr. Letterio Laboccetta, Engineer;

Mr. Gino Olivetti, Deputy, Secretary General of the Confederation of Italian Industry;

Prof. Mario Ghiron, Professor of Industrial Law at the University of Rome;

His Majesty the Emperor of Japan:

Mr. Saichiro Sakikawa, President of the Patent Office;

Mr. Nobumbi Ito;

His Majesty the Sultan of Morocco:

His Excellency Mr. Chassain de Marcilly, Envoy Extraordinary and Minister Plenipotentiary of France at The Hague;

The President of the United Mexican States:

Mr. Julio Poulat, Commercial Attaché to the Mexican Legation at Paris;

His Majesty the King of Norway:

Mr. Birger Gabriel Wyller, Director General of the Norwegian Bureau of Industrial Property;

Her Majesty the Queen of the Netherlands:
Dr. J. Alingh Prins, President of the Council for Patents, Director of the Office of Industrial Property;
Dr. H. Bijleveld, former Minister, Member of the Chamber of Deputies, former President of the Council for Patents, former Director of the Office of Industrial Property;
Dr. J. W. Dijckmeester, Member of the Council for Patents;

The President of the Polish Republic:
For Poland:
His Excellency Dr. Stanislas Kozminski, Envoy Extraordinary and Minister Plenipotentiary of Poland at The Hague;
Dr. Frédéric Zoll, Professor at the University of Cracow;
For the Free City of Danzig:
His Excellency Dr. Stanislas Kozminski, Envoy Extraordinary and Minister Plenipotentiary of Poland at The Hague;

The President of the Portuguese Republic:
His Excellency Mr. A. C. De Sousa Santos Bandeira, Envoy Extraordinary and Minister Plenipotentiary of Portugal at The Hague;

His Majesty the King of the Serbs, Croats and Slovenes:
Dr. Yanko Choumane, President of the Office for the Protection of Industrial Property at the Ministry of Commerce and Industry;
Mr. Mihailo Preditch, Secretary of that Office;

His Majesty the King of Sweden:
Director General E. O. J. Björklund, Chief of the Administration of Patents and Registration;
Mr. K. H. R. Hjertén, Counselor of the Court of Appeal of Göta;
Mr. A. E. Hasselrot, former Bureau Director at the above Administration, Adviser in matters of industrial property;

The Federal Council of the Swiss Confederation:
His Excellency Mr. Arthur de Pury, Envoy Extraordinary and Minister Plenipotentiary of Switzerland at The Hague;
Mr. Walther Kraft, Director of the Federal Bureau of Intellectual Property;

The President of the French Republic:
For the States of Syria and Greater Lebanon:
His Excellency Mr. Chassain de Marcilly, Envoy Extraordinary and Minister Plenipotentiary of France at The Hague;

The President of the Czechoslovak Republic:
His Excellency Mr. P. Baráček, Engineer, Envoy Extraordinary and Minister Plenipotentiary of Czechoslovakia at The Hague;

Dr. Karel Hermann-Otavský, Professor at the University of Prague;
Mr. Bohuslav Pavlousek, Engineer, Vice President of the Patent Office
at Prague;

His Highness the Bey of Tunis:
His Excellency Mr. Chassain de Marcilly, Envoy Extraordinary and
Minister Plenipotentiary of France at The Hague;

The President of the Turkish Republic:
Mehmed Essad Bey, Chargé d'Affaires of Turkey at The Hague.

Who, having communicated to each other their respective full powers,
which were found to be in good and due form, have agreed upon the
following articles:

Article 1

The contracting countries constitute themselves into a union for the protection of industrial property.

The scope of the protection of industrial property includes patents, utility models, industrial designs and models, trade-marks, commercial names and indications of origin, or appellations of origin, as well as the repression of unfair competition.

Industrial property is to be understood in the broadest meaning and is to be applied not only to industry and commerce as such, but likewise to agricultural industries (wines, grain, tobacco leaves, fruit, cattle, etc.) and extractive industries (minerals, mineral waters, etc.).

The term "patents" includes the various types of industrial patents granted by the laws of the contracting countries, such as patents of importation, improvement patents, patents and certificates of addition, etc.

Article 2

Nationals of each of the contracting countries shall, in all other countries of the Union, as regards the protection of industrial property, enjoy the advantages that their respective laws now grant, or may hereafter grant, to their own nationals, without any prejudice of the rights specially provided by the present convention. Consequently they shall have the same protection as the latter, and the same legal remedy against any infringement of their rights, provided they observe the conditions and formalities imposed on subjects or citizens.

Nevertheless no condition as to the possession of a domicile or establishment in the country where protection is claimed can be required of those who enjoy the benefits of the Union for the enjoyment of any industrial-property rights.

The provisions of the legislation of each of the contracting countries relative to judicial and administrative proceedings and to competent authority, as well as to the choice of domicile or the appointment of an authorized agent, which may be required by the laws on industrial property are expressly reserved.

ARTICLE 3

Nationals of countries not forming part of the Union who are domiciled or who have real and effective industrial or commercial establishments in the territory of any of the countries of the Union, shall be assimilated to the nationals of the contracting countries.

ARTICLE 4

(a) Any person who has duly applied for a patent, the registration of a utility model, industrial design or model, or trade-mark in one of the contracting countries, or his legal representative or assignee, shall enjoy, subject to the rights of third parties, for the purposes of registration in other countries, a right of priority during the periods hereinafter stated.

(b) Consequently, subsequent filing in any of the other countries of the Union before the expiration of these periods shall not be invalidated through any acts accomplished in the interval, either, particularly, by another filing, by publication of the invention, or by the working of it, by the sale of copies of the design or model, or by use of the trade-mark.

(c) The above-mentioned periods of priority shall be twelve months for patents and utility models, and six months for industrial designs and models and trade-marks.

These periods shall start from the date of filing of the first application in a country of the Union; the day of filing is not counted in this period.

If the last day of the period is a *dies non* in the country where protection is claimed, the period shall be extended until the next working day.

(d) Any person desiring to take advantage of the priority of a previous application must make a declaration giving particulars as to the date of such application and the country in which it was made. Each country will determine for itself the latest date at which such declaration must be made.

The particulars referred to shall be stated in the publications issued by the competent authority, and in particular in the patents issued and the specifications relating thereto.

The contracting countries may require any person making a declaration of priority to produce a copy of the application (with the specification, drawings, etc.) previously made. The copy, certified as correct by the authority receiving this demand, shall not require any legal authentication, and in any circumstances can be filed at any time within the period of three months from the lodging of the last application. They may also require that the declaration shall be accompanied by a certificate by the proper authority showing the date of application, and also by a translation.

No other formalities may be required for the declaration of priority at the time of application. Each of the contracting countries shall decide for itself what consequences shall follow the omission of the formalities prescribed by the present article, but such consequence shall in no case be more serious than the loss of the right of priority.

At later stages, further proof in support of the application may be required.

(e) Where an application is filed in a country for the registration of an industrial design or model by virtue of a right of priority based on the registration of a utility model, the period of priority shall not exceed that fixed for industrial designs and models.

Furthermore, it is allowable to deposit in a country a utility model by virtue of rights of priority based on a patent application, and vice versa.

(f) If an application for a patent contains claims for multiple priority, or if examination discloses that the application contains more than one invention, the competent authorities must at least allow the applicant to divide it, subject to the conditions of internal legislation, reserving as date of each divisional application the date of the initial application and, if there is occasion for it, the benefits of the right of priority.

ARTICLE 4 *bis*

Patents applied for in the various contracting countries by nationals of the Union shall be independent of the patents obtained for the same invention in other countries, whether such countries be or be not parties to the Union.

This stipulation must receive a strict interpretation; in particular, it shall be understood to mean that patents applied for during the period of priority are independent, both as regards the grounds for refusal and for revocation, and also as regards their normal duration.

This stipulation shall apply to all patents already existing at the time when it shall come into effect.

The same stipulation shall apply, in the case of the accession of new countries, to patents in existence, either on one side or the other, at the time of accession.

ARTICLE 5

The introduction by the patentee into the country where the patent has been granted of objects manufactured in any of the countries of the Union shall not entail forfeiture.

Nevertheless, each of the contracting countries shall have the right to take the necessary legislative measures to prevent the abuses which might result from the exercise of the exclusive rights conferred by the patent; for example, failure to use.

These measures will only provide for the revocation of the patent if the granting of compulsory licenses shall not suffice to prevent such abuses.

In all cases the patent will not be subject to such measures before the expiration of at least three years from the date of its grant and if the patentee produces just excuses.

The protection of designs and industrial models cannot be liable to cancellation by reason of the introduction of objects corresponding to those protected.

Articles shall not be required to bear any indication of registration for recognition of this right.

If in a country the use of a registered trade-mark is compulsory, the registration cannot be canceled until after a reasonable period, and only then if those interested cannot justify the causes of their inaction.

ARTICLE 5 *bis*

A period of grace of at least three months will be granted for the payment of taxes prescribed for the maintenance of industrial-property rights, together with a surcharge if the internal legislation of a country so provides.

For patents of invention the contracting countries undertake moreover either to prolong that extended period to six months at least, or to provide for the restoration of a patent which has lapsed owing to the nonpayment of fees, it being understood that these provisions are subject to the conditions prescribed by internal legislation.

ARTICLE 5 *ter*

In each of the contracting countries the following shall not be considered as infringing the rights of the patentee:

(1) The use on board ships of other countries of the Union of anything the subject matter of his patent in the body of the ship, in the machinery, tackle, apparatus, and other accessories when such ships enter temporarily or accidentally the waters of the country, provided that such thing is employed there exclusively for the needs of the vessel.

(2) The use of anything the subject matter of the patent in the construction of or functioning of the engines of locomotion for air or land of the other countries of the Union, or the accessories of these engines, when these enter the country temporarily or accidentally.

ARTICLE 6

Every trade-mark duly registered in the country of origin shall be admitted for registration and protected in the form originally registered in the other countries of the Union.

Nevertheless, the following marks may be refused or canceled:

(1) Those which are of such a nature as to prejudice rights acquired by third parties in the country in which protection is applied for.

(2) Those which have no distinctive character, or which consist exclusively of signs or indications which serve in trade to designate the kind, quality, quantity, destination, value, place of origin, or date of production, or which have become customary in the current language, or in the bona fide and unquestioned usages of the trade of the country in which protection is sought.

In arriving at a decision as to the distinctiveness of the character of a mark, all the circumstances of the case must be taken into account, and in particular the length of time that such a mark has been in use.

(3) Those which are contrary to morality or public order.

It is to be understood that a mark cannot be considered as contrary to public order for the sole reason that it does not conform to some legislative requirement concerning trade-marks, except in circumstances where this requirement itself relates to public order.

The following shall be deemed the country of origin:

The country of the Union where the applicant has an actual and genuine industrial or commercial establishment; and if he has not such an establishment, the country of the Union where he has his domicile; and if he has not a domicile in the Union, the country of his nationality in the case where he is under the jurisdiction of a country of the Union.

In no case shall the renewal of the registration of a trade-mark in the country of origin involve the obligation of renewal of the registration of the mark in other countries of the Union in which the mark has been registered.

The benefits of priority shall subsist in trade-mark applications filed in the period allowed by article 4, even when the registration in the country of origin is only completed after the expiration of such period.

The provisions of paragraph 1 do not preclude the right of requiring from an applicant a certificate, in due form, as to the registration of his mark, issued by the competent authority of the country of origin, but no legal authentication of such certificate shall be required.

ARTICLE 6 *bis*

The contracting countries undertake to refuse or invalidate, either administratively if their legislation so permits, or at the request of an interested party, the registration of a trade-mark which constitutes a reproduction or imitation liable to create confusion with a trade-mark considered by the competent authority of the country of registration to be well known there as being already a mark of a national of another contracting country and used for products of the same or a similar kind.

A period of at least three years must be granted in order to claim the cancellation of these marks. The period shall start from the date of registration of the mark.

No period shall be established to claim the cancellation of fraudulently registered marks.

ARTICLE 6 *ter*

The contracting countries undertake to refuse or invalidate registration, and to prohibit by appropriate means the use, failing authorization from the competent authority, whether as trade-mark or as components of such, of all coats of arms, flags, and other state emblems of contracting countries, official control and guarantee signs and stamps adopted by them, and all imitation from an heraldic point of view.

The prohibition of official control and guarantee signs and stamps shall apply only in cases where marks which comprise them are intended to be used on merchandise of the same or a similar nature.

For the application of these provisions the contracting countries agree to communicate reciprocally, through the intermediary of the International Bureau of Bern, the list of state emblems and official control and guarantee signs and stamps which they desire, or will desire, to place, wholly or with certain reservations, under the protection of the present article, as well as all subsequent modifications added to the list. Each contracting country shall place the communicated list at the disposal of the public in due course.

Each contracting country may, within a period of twelve months from the receipt of the notification, and through the intermediary of the International Bureau of Bern, transmit its possible objections to any other country concerned.

For state emblems which are well known the provisions of paragraph 1 shall be applicable only to marks registered after the signature of this convention.

For state emblems which are not well known, and for official signs and stamps, these provisions shall be applicable only to marks registered more than two months after the receipt of the notification provided for in paragraph 3.

In the case of bad faith, countries shall have the right to cancel even the marks registered before the signature of the present convention and embodying state emblems, signs, and stamps.

Nationals of each country who are authorized to make use of state emblems, and signs and stamps of their country, may use them even if there be a similarity with those of another country.

The contracting countries undertake to prohibit the unauthorized use in trade of state coats of arms of other contracting countries when such use would be liable to cause confusion as to the origin of the product.

The preceding provisions will not prevent the countries' exercising the right to refuse or to invalidate, by the application of No. 3 of paragraph 2 of article 6, marks containing without authority coats of arms, flags, decorations, and other state emblems or official signs and stamps adopted by a country of the Union.

ARTICLE 7

The nature of the goods on which the trade-mark is to be used can in no case form an obstacle to the registration of the trade-mark.

ARTICLE 7 *bis*

The contracting countries undertake to allow the filing of, and to protect, trade-marks belonging to associations the existence of which is not contrary to the law of the country of origin, even if such associations do not possess an industrial or commercial establishment.

Nevertheless, each country shall be the sole judge of the particular conditions on which an association may be allowed to obtain protection for its marks.

ARTICLE 8

A trade name shall be protected in all the countries of the Union without the obligation of filing or registration, whether or not it form part of a trade-mark.

ARTICLE 9

All goods illegally bearing a trade-mark or trade name shall be seized on importation into those countries of the Union where this mark or name has a right to legal protection.

Seizure shall be effected equally in the country where the mark or name was illegally applied, or in the country to which the article bearing it has been imported.

The seizure shall take place at the request either of the proper Government department or of any other competent authority, or of any interested party or actual or legal person, in conformity with the domestic law of each country.

The authorities are not bound to effect the seizure in transit.

If the law of a country does not admit of seizure on importation, such seizure shall be replaced by prohibition of importation or by seizure within such country.

If the law of any country does not admit either of seizure upon importation, or of prohibition of importation, or of seizure within the country, and until such time as this legislation shall be accordingly modified, these measures will be replaced by the remedies assured in such cases to nationals by the law of such country.

ARTICLE 10

The stipulations of the preceding article shall be applicable to every product which may falsely bear as indication of origin the name of a specified locality or country when such indication shall be joined to a trade name of a fictitious character or used with the intent to defraud.

Any producer, manufacturer, or trader engaged in the production, manufacture, or trade of such goods and established either in the locality falsely designated as the place of origin, or in the district where the locality is situated, or in the country falsely designated, shall be deemed in all cases a party concerned, whether such person be actual or legal.

Article 10 *bis*

The contracting countries are bound to assure to nationals of the Union an effective protection against unfair competition.

Every act of competition contrary to honest practice in industrial or commercial matters constitutes an act of unfair competition.

The following particularly are to be forbidden:

(1) All acts whatsoever of a nature to create confusion by no matter what means with the goods of a competitor.

(2) False allegations, in the course of trade, of a nature to discredit the goods of a competitor.

Article 10 *ter*

The contracting countries undertake to assure to the nationals of other countries of the Union appropriate legal remedies to repress effectively all acts set forth in articles 9, 10, and 10 *bis*.

They undertake, moreover, to provide measures to permit syndicates and associations representing the industry or the trade interested, and of which the existence is not contrary to the laws of their country, to take action in justice or before the administrative authorities, in view of the repression of the acts set forth in articles 9, 10, and 10 *bis*, so far as the law of the country in which protection is claimed permits it to the syndicates and associations of that country.

Article 11

The contracting countries shall, in conformity with the legislation of each country, accord temporary protection to patentable inventions, to utility models, and to industrial designs or models, as well as to trade-marks in respect of products which shall be exhibited at official, or officially recognized, international exhibitions held in the territory of one of them.

This temporary protection shall not prolong the periods provided by article 4. If later the right of priority is sought, the competent authority of each country may date the period from the date of the introduction of the product into the exhibition.

Each country may require, as proof of the identity of the object exhibited, and of the date of the introduction, such proofs as it may consider necessary.

Article 12

Each of the contracting countries agrees to establish a special Government service for industrial property, and a central office for communication to the public of patents, utility models, industrial designs or models, and trade-marks.

This service shall publish an official periodical paper.

ARTICLE 13

The international office, established at Berne under the name of International Bureau for the Protection of Industrial Property, is placed under the high authority of the Government of the Swiss Confederation, which is to regulate its organization and supervise its working.

The official language of the International Bureau is French.

The International Bureau centralizes information of every kind relating to the protection of industrial property and collates and publishes it. It interests itself in all matters of common utility to the Union and edits, with the help of documents supplied to it by the various Administrations, a periodical paper in the French language, dealing with questions regarding the object of the Union.

The numbers of this paper, as well as the documents published by the International Bureau, are circulated among the Administrations of the countries of the Union in the proportion of the number of contributing units as mentioned below. Such further copies as may be desired, either by the said Administrations or by societies or private persons, will be paid for separately.

The International Bureau shall at all times hold itself at the service of members of the Union, in order to supply them with any special information they may need on questions relating to the international system of industrial property. The Director of the International Bureau will furnish an annual report on its working, which shall be communicated to all the members of the Union.

The expenses of the International Bureau will be borne by the contracting countries in common. Unless fresh sanction is given, they must not exceed the sum of 120,000 Swiss francs per annum. This sum may be increased in cases of necessity by a unanimous decision of one of the conferences provided for by article 14.

To determine the part which each country should contribute to this total of expenses the contracting countries and those which may afterwards join the Union shall be divided into six classes, each contributing in the proportion of a certain number of units, namely:

First class	25 units
Second class	20 units
Third class	15 units
Fourth class	10 units
Fifth class	5 units
Sixth class	3 units

These coefficients will be multiplied by the number of countries in each class, and the sum of the result thus obtained will supply the number of units by which the total expense has to be divided. The quotient will give the amount of the unit of expense.

Each of the contracting countries will designate, at the time of its accession, the class in which it wishes to be placed.

The Government of the Swiss Confederation is to superintend the expenses of the International Bureau, to advance the necessary funds, and to render an annual account which will be communicated to all the other Administrations.

ARTICLE 14

The present convention shall be submitted to periodical revisions with a view to the introduction of amendments calculated to improve the system of the Union.

For this purpose, conferences shall be held successively in one of the contracting countries between the delegates of the said countries.

The Administration of the country in which the conference is to be held will make preparation for the transaction of that conference, with the assistance of the International Bureau.

The Director of the International Bureau will be present at the meetings of the conferences, and will take part in the discussions, but without the privilege of voting.

ARTICLE 15

It is agreed that the contracting countries respectively reserve to themselves the right to make separately, as between themselves, special arrangements for the protection of industrial property, in so far as such arrangements do not contravene the provisions of the present convention.

ARTICLE 16

The countries which have not taken part in the present convention shall be permitted to adhere to it upon their request.

The accession shall be notified through the diplomatic channel to the Government of the Swiss Confederation, and by the latter to all the other Governments.

It shall entail, as a matter of right, accession to all the classes, as well as admission to all the advantages, stipulated in the present convention, and shall take effect one month after the dispatch of the notification by the Government of the Swiss Confederation to the other countries of the Union, unless a subsequent date has been indicated by the acceding country.

ARTICLE 16 *bis*

The contracting countries have the right of acceding to the present convention at any time on behalf of their colonies, possessions, dependencies, and protectorates, or territories administrated by virtue of a mandate from the League of Nations, or any of them.

For this purpose they may either make a general declaration, including all their colonies, possessions, dependencies, and protectorates, and the territories referred to in paragraph 1, in the accession, or may expressly name those included, or may confine themselves to indicating those which are excluded therefrom.

This declaration shall be notified in writing to the Government of the Swiss Confederation and by the latter to all the other Governments.

Under the same conditions, the contracting countries may denounce the convention on behalf of their colonies, possessions, dependencies, and protectorates, or for the territories referred to in paragraph 1, or for any of them.

ARTICLE 17

The execution of the reciprocal engagements contained in the present convention is subordinated, in so far as necessary, to the observance of the formalities and rules established by the constitutional laws of those of the contracting countries which are bound to procure the application of the same, which they engage to do with as little delay as possible.

ARTICLE 17 *bis*

The convention shall remain in force for an unlimited time, till the expiration of one year from the date of its denunciation.

This denunciation shall be addressed to the Government of the Swiss Confederation. It shall affect only the denouncing country, the convention remaining in operation as regards the other contracting countries.

ARTICLE 18

The present act shall be ratified and the ratifications deposited at The Hague not later than the 1st of May, 1928. It shall come into force, between the countries which will have ratified it, one month after such date. However, if before May 1, 1928, it should be ratified by at least six countries, it will come into force between those countries one month after the Government of the Swiss Confederation has notified them of the filing of the sixth ratification, and for the countries which should subsequently ratify, one month after the notification of each of these ratifications.

This act shall replace, as regards relations between the countries which ratify it, the convention of the Union of Paris of 1883, revised at Washington June 2, 1911, and its final protocol, which shall remain in force as regards relations with countries which have not ratified the present act.

ARTICLE 19

The present act shall be signed in a single copy, which shall be deposited in the archives of the Government of the Netherlands. A certified copy shall be forwarded by the latter to each of the Governments of the contracting countries.

In witness whereof, the respective plenipotentiaries have signed the present act.

Done at The Hague, in a single copy, the 6th day of November, 1925.

For Germany:
VIETINGHOFF
V. SPECHT
KLAUER
ALBERT OSTERRIETH

For Australia:
C. V. WATSON

For Austria:
Dr. CARL DUSCHANEK
Dr. HANS FORTWÄNGLER

For Belgium:
CAPITAINE
LOUIS ANDRÉ
THOMAS BRAUN
D. COPPIETERS

For the United States of Brazil:
J. A. BARBOZA CARNEIRO
CARLOS AMERICO BARBOSA DE
OLIVEIRA

For Canada:
FREDERICK H. PALMER

For Cuba:
R. DE LA TORRE

For Denmark:
N. J. EHRENREICH HANSEN

For the Free City of Danzig:
ST. KOZMINSKI

For the Dominican Republic:
C. G. DE HASETH Cz.

For Spain:
SANTIAGO MENDEZ DE VIGO
FERNANDO CABELLO LAPIEDRA
JOSÉ GARCIA MONGE

For Estonia:
O. AARMANN

For the United States of America:
THOMAS E. ROBERTSON
WALLACE R. LANE
JO. BAILY BROWN

For Finland:
YRJÖ SAASTAMOINEN

For France:
CH. DE MARCILLY
MARCEL PLAISANT
CH. DROUETS
GEORGES MAILLARD

For Great Britain and Northern Ireland:
H. LLEWELLYN SMITH
A. J. MARTIN
A. BALFOUR

For Hungary:
ELEMÉR DE POMPÉRY

For the Irish Free State:
G. O'KELLY DE GALLAGH

For Italy:
DOMENICO BARONE
LETTERIO LABOCCETTA
MARIO GHIRON

For Japan:
S. SAKIKAWA
N. ITO

For Morocco:
CH. DE MARCILLY

For the United Mexican States:
JULIO POULAT

For Norway:
B. WYLLER

For the Netherlands:
J. ALINGH PRINS
BIJLEVELD
DIJCKMEESTER

For Poland:
ST. KOZMINSKI
FRÉDÉRIC ZOLL

For Portugal:
BANDEIRA

For the Kingdom of the Serbs, Croats and Slovenes:
Dr. YANKO CHOUMANE
MIHAILO PRÉDITCH

For Sweden:
  E. O. J. BJÖRKLUND
  H. HJERTÉN
  AXEL HASSELROT

For Switzerland:
  A. DE PURY
  W. KRAFT

For Syria and Greater Lebanon:
  CH. DE MARCILLY

For Czechoslovakia:
  BARÁČEK
  Prof. DR. KAREL HERMANN-OTAVSKY
  Engineer BOHUSLAV PAVLOUSEK

For Tunis:
  CH. DE MARCILLY

For Turkey:

INTERNATIONAL INSTITUTE OF AGRICULTURE

Protocol signed at Rome April 21, 1926
Senate advice and consent to adherence May 1, 1934
Adherence declared by the President of the United States August 25, 1934
Declaration of United States adherence deposited at Rome January 15, 1936 [1]
Entered into force January 1, 1927; for the United States August 25, 1934
Proclaimed by the President of the United States January 24, 1936
Terminated February 27, 1948, [2] *in accordance with terms of article III of protocol of March 30, 1946,* [3] *providing for dissolution of the Institute and transfer of its functions and assets to the Food and Agriculture Organization of the United Nations*

49 Stat. 3350; Treaty Series 903

[TRANSLATION]

PROTOCOL RELATIVE TO THE INTERNATIONAL CONVENTION OF JUNE 7, 1905

The undersigned, duly authorized by their respective Governments, have agreed as follows:

Paragraphs 3 and 4 of article 10 of the International Convention of June 7, 1905,[4] for the creation of the International Institute of Agriculture, are replaced by the following text:

"The amount of the contribution is fixed each year as follows: The number of the units of subscription is multiplied by the number of countries in each group; the total thus calculated gives the number of units by which the

---

[1] In depositing the instrument of adherence by the United States, the American Ambassador at Rome, in a note of Jan. 15, 1936, to the Italian Undersecretary of State for Foreign Affairs, stated that the adherence of the United States to the protocol "extends to and embraces Hawaii, the Philippines, Puerto Rico and the Virgin Islands, which at its request, made in 1924, were admitted to form part of the International Institute of Agriculture, in conformity with the last paragraph of Article 10 of the Convention of June 7, 1905."

[2] For explanation of termination date, see footnote 1, p. 4, of TIAS 1719. For text of Final Act of the Permanent Committee of the Institute, dated Feb. 27, 1948, see *Department of State Bulletin*, June 27, 1948, p. 828.

[3] TIAS 1719, *post*, vol. 4.

[4] TS 489, *ante*, vol. 1, p. 439.

total expenditure authorized by the General Assembly shall be divided, reckoned in the currency of Italy, where the Institute has its headquarters, and after deducting the receipts other than the contributions of the states; the quotient gives the amount of the unit of subscription.

"In no case shall the contribution corresponding to each unit of subscription exceed the sum of 4,000 gold francs as a maximum.

"Contributions paid after the close of the financial year shall be deducted from the expenditure of the following year."

The present protocol shall take effect on January 1, 1927.
ROME, *April 21, 1926.*

Germany:
  C. VON NEURATH   [SEAL]

Argentina:
  CARLOS BREBBIA   [SEAL]

Austria:
  LOTHAR EGGER   [SEAL]
  Subject to ratification.

Belgium:
  OS. BOLLE   [SEAL]

Belgian Congo:
  P. DE VUYST   [SEAL]

Brazil:
  OSCAR DE TEFFÉ   [SEAL]

Bulgaria:
  G. RADEFF   [SEAL]

Chile:
  E. VILLEGAS   [SEAL]

Denmark:
  HARALD SCAVENIUS   [SEAL]

Egypt:
  M. M. GAZAERLY   [SEAL]

Ecuador:
  LUIS ANTONIO PEÑAHERRERA   [SEAL]

Spain:
  THE COUNT OF VIÑAZA   [SEAL]

Estonia:
  A. JÜRGENSON   [SEAL]

Finland:
  ROLF THESLEFF   [SEAL]

France:
  RENÉ BESNARD   [SEAL]
  A. MASSÉ   [SEAL]

French West Africa:
  RENÉ BESNARD   [SEAL]
  LOUIS DOP   [SEAL]

Algeria:
  RENÉ BESNARD   [SEAL]
  LOUIS DOP   [SEAL]

Indochina:
  RENÉ BESNARD   [SEAL]
  LOUIS DOP   [SEAL]

Madagascar:
  RENÉ BESNARD   [SEAL]
  LOUIS DOP   [SEAL]

Morocco (French zone):
  RENÉ BESNARD   [SEAL]
  LOUIS DOP   [SEAL]

Regency of Tunis:
  RENÉ BESNARD   [SEAL]
  LOUIS DOP   [SEAL]

Great Britain and Northern Ireland:
  RONALD GRAHAM   [SEAL]

Australia:
  RONALD GRAHAM   [SEAL]

Canada:
  RONALD GRAHAM   [SEAL]

British-Indian Empire:
  RONALD GRAHAM   [SEAL]
  Subject to reservation indicated below.

Irish Free State:
  RONALD GRAHAM   [SEAL]

New Zealand:
  RONALD GRAHAM   [SEAL]

Union of South Africa:
  J. S. SMIT   [SEAL]

Greece:
  N. MAVROUDIS   [SEAL]

Hungary:
  R. MÁRFFY MANTUANO   [SEAL]

Italy:
  BENITO MUSSOLINI   [SEAL]

Eritrea:
BENITO MUSSOLINI   [SEAL]

Cirenaica:
BENITO MUSSOLINI   [SEAL]

Italian Somaliland:
BENITO MUSSOLINI   [SEAL]

Tripolitania:
BENITO MUSSOLINI   [SEAL]

Japan:
M. MATSUDA   [SEAL]

Latvia:
PIERRE LEYA   [SEAL]

Lithuania:
VALDEMARAS ČARNECKIS   [SEAL]

Luxemburg:
P. DE VUYST   [SEAL]

Mexico:
M. Y. DE NEGRI   [SEAL]

Norway:
OVE P. L. VANGENSTEN   [SEAL]

Netherlands:
A. VAN DER GOES   [SEAL]

Netherland India:
A. VAN DER GOES   [SEAL]

Peru:
G. CISNEROS Y RAYGADA   [SEAL]

Persia:
F. PAKREVAN   [SEAL]

Poland:
S. PRZEZDZIECKI   [SEAL]

Portugal:
HENRIQUE TRINDADE COELHO   [SEAL]

Rumania:
With the specification that Rumania
adheres to the contribution of states
of the second category.
N. M. VLADESCO   [SEAL]

Sweden:
BILDT   [SEAL]

Switzerland:
WAGNIÈRE   [SEAL]

Czechoslovakia:
MILOS ČERMÁK   [SEAL]

I hereby declare that my signature is given for India on the understanding that the Government of India accept the new method of fixing the contribution of the states acceding to the International Institute of Agriculture at Rome and agree to the amendments to paragraphs 3 and 4 of article 10 of the convention of June 7, 1905, subject to the reservation that if in any year their liability as a member of group II under the new system exceeds 11,000 rupees per annum in terms of Indian currency, they reserve to themselves the liberty of withdrawing to a lower group.

RONALD GRAHAM

INTERNATIONAL SANITARY CONVENTION

*Convention signed at Paris June 21, 1926, with annexes; protocol of
  signature signed at Paris June 21, 1926*
*Senate advice and consent to ratification, with understandings and con-
  ditions, March 22, 1928* [1]
*Ratified by the President of the United States, with understandings and
  conditions, April 7, 1928* [1]
Ratification of the United States deposited at Paris May 22, 1928
*Entered into force March 28, 1928; for the United States May 22,
  1928*
Proclaimed by the President of the United States June 21, 1928
Supplemented and amended by convention of December 15, 1944, [2] *as
  between contracting parties to the later convention; replaced by
  International Sanitary Regulations (World Health Organization
  Regulations No. 2) of May 25, 1951,* [3] *as amended, as between
  states bound by the regulations*

45 Stat. 2492; Treaty Series 762

[TRANSLATION]

INTERNATIONAL SANITARY CONVENTION

His Majesty the King of Afghanistan; the President of the Republic of
Albania; the President of the German Empire; the President of the Argentine
Nation; the Federal President of the Austrian Republic; His Majesty the
King of the Belgians; the President of the Republic of the United States of
Brazil; His Majesty the King of the Bulgarians; the President of the Republic
of Chile; the President of the Republic of China; the President of the Re-
public of Colombia; the President of the Republic of Cuba; His Majesty
the King of Denmark; the President of the Dominican Republic; His Majesty
the King of Egypt; the President of the Republic of Ecuador; His Majesty the
King of Spain; the President of the United States of America; Her Majesty
the Queen of Ethiopia and His Imperial and Royal Highness the Prince
Hereditary and Regent of the Empire; the President of the Republic of

---

[1] For test of U.S. understandings and conditions, see p. 601.
[2] TS 991, *post*, vol. 3.
[3] 7 UST 2255; TIAS 3625.

545

Finland; the President of the Republic of France; His Majesty the King of the United Kingdom of Great Britain and Ireland and of the British Possessions beyond the Seas, Emperor of India; the President of the Republic of Greece; the President of the Republic of Guatemala; the President of the Republic of Haiti; His Majesty the King of the Hedjaz; the President of the Republic of Honduras; His Serene Highness the Regent of the Kingdom of Hungary; His Majesty the King of Italy; His Majesty the Emperor of Japan; the President of the Republic of Liberia; the President of the Republic of Lithuania; Her Royal Highness Madame the Grand Duchess of Luxembourg; His Majesty the Sultan of Morocco; the President of the Republic of Mexico; His Serene Highness the Prince of Monaco; His Majesty the King of Norway; the President of the Republic of Paraguay; Her Majesty the Queen of the Netherlands; the President of the Republic of Peru; His Majesty the Shah of Persia; the President of the Republic of Poland; the President of the Portuguese Republic; His Majesty the King of Rumania; the Captains Regents of San-Marino; His Majesty the King of the Serbs, Croats and Slovenes; the President of the Republic of Salvador; the Governor General Representing the Sovereign Authority of the Soudan; the Swiss Federal Council; the President of the Republic of Czechoslovakia; His Highness the Bey of Tunis; the President of the Turkish Republic; the Central Executive Committee of the Union of the Soviet Socialist Republics; the President of the Republic of Uruguay and the President of the Republic of Venezuela,

Having decided to make in the provisions of the Sanitary Convention signed at Paris on January 17, 1912,[4] the changes that are called for by the new data of prophylactic science and experience to set up an international set of regulations relative to exanthematous typhus and smallpox and to broaden, as far as possible, the field of application of the principles which inspired the international health regulations, have decided to conclude a convention to that effect and have appointed as their plenipotentiaries, to wit:

His Majesty the King of Afghanistan:

Mr. Islambek Khoudoiar Khan, Secretary of the Legation of Afghanistan at Paris.

The President of the Republic of Albania:

Dr. Osman, Director of Tirana Hospital.

The President of the German Empire:

Mr. Franoux, Privy Councilor of Legation of the Embassy of Germany at Paris.

Dr. Hamel, Counselor to the Imperial Ministry of the Interior.

---

[4] TS 649, *ante*, vol. 1, p. 814.

The President of the Argentine Republic:
  Mr. Federico Alvarez de Toledo, Minister of Argentina at Paris.
  Dr. Araoz Alfaro, Chairman of the Department of Hygiene.
  Mr. Manuel Carbonnel, Professor of Hygiene at the Faculty of Medicine of Buenos Aires.

The Federal President of the Republic of Austria:
  Mr. Alfred Grünberger, Minister of Austria at Paris.

His Majesty the King of the Belgians:
  Mr. Velghe, Secretary General of the Ministry of the Interior and Hygiene.

The President of the Republic of the United States of Brazil:
  Dr. Carlos Chagas, Director General of the National Department of Public Health, Director of the Oswaldo Cruz Institute.
  Dr. Gilberto Moura Costa.

His Majesty the King of the Bulgarians:
  Mr. Morfoff, Minister of Bulgaria at Paris.
  Dr. Tochko Petroff, Professor at the Faculty of Medicine of Sofia.

The President of the Republic of Chile:
  Mr. Armando Quezada, Minister of Chile at Paris.
  Dr. Emilio Aldunate, Professor at the Faculty of Medicine of Chile.
  Dr. J. Rodríguez Barros, Professor at the Faculty of Medicine of Chile.

The President of the Republic of China:
  General Yao Si-kiou, Military Attaché at Paris.
  Dr. Scie Ton-fa, Special Secretary of the Legation of China at Paris.

The President of the Republic of Colombia:
  Dr. Miguel Jiménez López, Professor at the Faculty of Medicine of Bogota, Minister Plenipotentiary of Colombia at Berlin.

The President of the Republic of Cuba:
  Mr. Ramiro Hernández Portela, Counselor of the Legation of Cuba at Paris.
  Dr. Mario Lebredo, Director of Las Animas Hospital.

His Majesty the King of Denmark:
  Dr. Th. Madsen, Director of the State Institute of Serology.
  Mr. I. A. Korbing, Director of the Amalgamated Shipowners Association.

The President of the Republic of Poland, for the Free City of Danzig:
  Dr. Witold Chodzko, former Minister of Health.
  Dr. Carl Stade, Councilor of State of the Senate of the Free City of Danzig.

The President of the Dominican Republic:
Dr. Betances, Professor at the Faculty of Medicine of Santo Domingo.

His Majesty the King of Egypt:
Fakhry Pasha, Minister of Egypt at Paris.
Major Charles P. Thomson, D.S.O., President of the Sanitary, Maritime, and Quarantine Board of Egypt.
Dr. Mohammed Abd El Salam, El Guindy Bey, Second Secretary of the Legation of Egypt at Brussels, Representative of the Government of Egypt to the Committee of the International Bureau of Public Health.

The President of the Republic of Ecuador:
Dr. J. Illingourth Ycaza.

His Majesty the King of Spain:
The Marquis de Faura, Minister-Counselor of the Embassy of Spain at Paris.
Dr. Francisco Murillo y Palacios, Director General of Health of Spain.

The President of the United States of America:
Dr. H. S. Cumming, Surgeon General, Public Health Service.
Dr. Taliaferro Clerk, Senior Surgeon, Public Health Service.
Dr. W. W. King, Surgeon, Public Health Service.

Her Majesty the Queen of Ethiopia and His Imperial and Royal Highness the Prince Hereditary and Regent of the Empire:
Count Lagarde, Duke of Entotto, Minister Plenpotentiary.

The President of the Republic of Finland:
Mr. Charles Enckell, Minister of Finland at Paris.
Dr. Oswald Streng, Professor at the University of Helsingfors.

The President of the French Republic:
His Excellency Camille Barrère, Ambassador of France.
Mr. Harismendy, Minister Plenipotentiary, Assistant Director in the Ministry of Foreign Affairs.
Mr. de Navailles, Assistant Director in the Ministry of Foreign Affairs.
Dr. Calmette, Assistant Director of the *Institut Pasteur*.
Dr. Léon Bernard, Professor at the Faculty of Medicine of Paris.

For Algeria:
Dr. Lucien Raynaud, Inspector General of the Division of Hygiene of Algeria.

For French West Africa:
Dr. Paul Gouzien, Physician, Inspector General of the Colonial Forces.

For French East Africa:
Dr. Thiroux, Physician-Inspector of the Colonial Forces.

For French Indo-China
> Dr. L'Herminier, Representative of Indo-China to the Advisory Committee of the Oriental Bureau of the League of Nations.
> Dr. Noel Bernard, Director of the *Instituts Pasteur* of Indo-China.

For the States of Syria, Greater Lebanon, the Alaouites and Jebel ed Druz:
> Mr. Harismendy, Minister Plenipotentiary, Assistant Director in the Ministry of Foreign Affairs.
> Dr. Delmas.

For all other colonies, protectorates, possessions and territories under French mandate:
> Dr. Audibert, Inspector General of the Health Service in the Ministry of the Colonies.

His Majesty the King of the United Kingdom of Great Britain and Ireland and of the British Dominions beyond the Seas, Emperor of India:
> Sir George Seaton Buchanan, Kt., C.B., M.D., Chief Physician in the Ministry of Health.
> Mr. John Murray, C.M.G., Counselor in the Foreign Office.

For the Dominion of Canada:
> Dr. John Andrew Amyot, C.M.G., M.B., Director General of the Ministry of Health of the Dominion of Canada.

For the Commonwealth of Australia:
> Dr. William Campbell Sawers, D.S.O., M.B., Physician in the Ministry of Health.

For the Dominion of New Zealand:
> Lt. Col. Sydney Price James, M.D.

For India:
> Mr. David Thomas Chadwick, C.S.I., C.I.E., Secretary to the Government of India in the Ministry of Commerce.

For the Union of South Africa:
> Dr. Philip Stock, C.B., C.B.E., Representative to the Committee of the International Bureau of Public Health.

The President of the Republic of Greece:
> Mr. Al C. Carapanos, Minister of Greece at Paris.
> Dr. Matarangas Gerassimos.

The President of the Republic of Guatemala:
> Dr. Francisco A. Figueroa, Chargé d'Affaires at Paris.

The President of the Republic of Haiti:
> Dr. Georges Audain.

His Majesty the King of Hejaz:
  Dr. Mahmoud Hamoudé, Director General of Public Health.

The President of the Republic of Honduras:
  Dr. Rubén Audino-Aguilar, Chargé d'Affaires at Paris.

His Serene Highness the Regent of the Kingdom of Hungary:
  Dr. Charles Grosch, Counselor in the Ministry of Social Security.

His Majesty the King of Italy:
  Dr. Albert Lutrario, Prefect, First Class.
  Dr. Giovanni Vittorio Repetti, Physician General of the Royal Italian
    Navy, Sanitary Director of the General Emigration Commission.
  Col. Odoardo Huetter, Harbor Master of Venice.
  Mr. Guido Rocco, First Secretary of the Embassy of Italy at Paris.
  Dr. Cancelleiere, Vice-Prefect, First Class.
  Dr. Druetti, Sanitary Representative abroad.

His Majesty the Emperor of Japan:
  Mr. Hajime Matsushima, Counselor of Embassy.
  Dr. Mitsuzo Tsurumi, Representative of Japan on the Committee of the
    International Bureau of Public Health.

The President of the Republic of Liberia:
  Baron R. A. L. Lehmann, Minister of Liberia at Paris.
  Mr. N. Ooms, First Secretary of the Legation.

The President of the Republic of Lithuania:
  Dr. Pranas Vaiciuska, Lieutenant General for Health, reserve, Instructor
    at the University of Kaunas, Chief Physician of the City of Kaunas.

Her Royal Highness the Grand Duchess of Luxembourg:
  Dr. Praum, Director of the Bacteriology Laboratory of Luxembourg.

His Majesty the Sultan of Morocco:
  Mr. Harismendy, Minister Plenipotentiary, Assistant Director in the
    Ministry of Foreign Affairs.
  Dr. Lucien Raynaud, Inspector General of the Division of Health of
    Algeria.

The President of the Republic of Mexico:
  Dr. Raphael Cabrera, Minister of Mexico at Brussels.

His Serene Highness the Prince of Monaco:
  Mr. Roussel-Despierres, Secretary of State to H. S. H. The Prince of
    Monaco.
  Dr. Marsan, Director of the Division of Hygiene of the Principality.

His Majesty the King of Norway:
Mr. Sigurd Bentzon, Counselor of the Legation of Norway at Paris.
Dr. H. Mathias Gram, Director General of the Sanitary Administration.

The President of the Republic of Paraguay:
Dr. R. V. Caballero, Chargé d'Affaires of Paraguay in France.

Her Majesty the Queen of the Netherlands:
Mr. Doude van Troostwyk, Minister of the Netherlands at Berne.
Dr. N. M. Josephus Jitta, President of the Health Board.
Dr. de Vogel, former Chief Inspector of the Sanitary Service in the Netherlands Indies.
Mr. van der Plas, Consul of the Netherlands at Jidda.

The President of the Republic of Peru:
Dr. Pablo S. Mimbela, Minister Plenipotentiary of Peru at Berne.

His Majesty the Shah of Persia:
Dr. Ali-Khan Partow-Aazam, former Assistant Secretary in the Ministry of Public Education, Vice President of the Health Board, and Director of the Imperial Hospital.
Dr. Mansour-Charif, former physician to the Royal Family.

The President of the Republic of Poland:
Dr. Witold Chodzko, former Minister of Health.
Mr. Taylor, Assistant Chief of the Treaty Section.

The President of the Portuguese Republic:
Professor Ricardo Jorge, Director General of Public Health.

His Majesty the King of Rumania:
Dr. Jean Cantacuzene, Professor at the Faculty of Medicine of Bucharest.

The Regents of San Marino:
Dr. Guelpa.

The President of the Republic of El Salvador:
Professor Lardé-Arthés.

His Majesty the King of the Serbs, Croats, and Slovenes:
Mr. Miroslav Spalaikovitch, Minister Plenipotentiary at Paris.

The Governor-General representing the sovereign authority of the Soudan:
Dr. Oliver Francis Haynes Atkey, M.B., F.R.C.S., Director of the Medical Service of the Soudan.

The Swiss Federal Council:
Mr. Alphonse Dunant, Minister of Switzerland at Paris.
Dr. Carrière, Director of the Federal Public Health Service.

The President of the Czechoslovak Republic:
  Dr. Ladislav Prochazka, Chief of the Sanitary Service of the City of Praha.

His Highness the Bey of Tunis:
  Mr. de Navailles, Assistant Director in the Ministry of Foreign Affairs.

The President of the Turkish Republic:
  His Excellency Aly Féthy Bey, Ambassador of Turkey at Paris.

The Supreme Soviet of the Union of Soviet Socialist Republics:
  Professor Nikolai Semachko, Member of the Supreme Soviet of the U.S.S.R., People's Commissar for Public Health of the R.S.F.S.R.
  Mr. Jacques Davtian, Counselor of Embassy of the Union of Soviet Socialist Republics at Paris.
  Mr. Vladimir Egoriew, Assistant Director of the People's Commission for Foreign Affairs.
  Dr. Ilia Mammoulia, Member of the Supreme Soviet of the Georgian Soviet Socialist Republic.
  Dr. Leon Bronstein, People's Commissar for Public Health of the Ukrainian Soviet Socialist Republic.
  Dr. Oganes Meburnoutoff, Member of the College of the People's Commission for Public Health of the Uzbek Soviet Socialist Republic.
  Dr. Nikolas Freyberg, Counselor to the People's Commission for Public Health of the R.S.F.S.R.
  Dr. Alexis Syssine, Chief of the Sanitary and Epidemiological Department of the People's Commission for Public Health of the R.S.F.S.R., University Professor.

The President of the Oriental Republic of Uruguay:
  Mr. A. Herosa, former Chargé d'Affaires of Uruguay at Paris.

The President of the Republic of Venezuela:
  Mr. José Ignacio Cárdenas, Minister of Venezuela at Madrid and The Hague.

Who, after depositing their full powers, found to be in good and due form, have agreed to the following provisions:

PRELIMINARY PROVISION

For the purposes of this Convention, the high contracting parties adopt the following definitions:

1. The word *circonscription* designates a fully defined part of territory, for example: a province, a government, a district, a department, a canton, an island, a commune, a city, a city district, a village, a port, a community, et cetera, regardless of the area and population of those parts of territory.

2. The word *observation* means isolation of the persons either on board a ship or in a sanitary station before they are given free pratique.

The word *surveillance* means that the persons are not isolated, are immediately given free pratique, but are reported to the health authorities in the several places they are to visit and subjected to a medical examination by which their health condition is ascertained.

3. The word *équipage* includes all persons who are not on board for the mere purpose of being carried from one country to another, but who are employed in any capacity whatsoever in the service of the ship or persons on board, or of the cargo.

4. The word *jour* means an interval of twenty-four hours.

Title I. General Provisions

Chapter I. *Provisions to be observed by the Governments of the countries participating in the present convention on the appearance of plague, cholera, yellow fever, or certain other infectious diseases in their territory*

Section I. Notification and Subsequent Communications to Other Countries

Article 1

Each Government shall immediately notify the other Governments and, at the same time the International Office of Public Hygiene:

(1) The first authentic case of plague, cholera, or yellow fever discovered in its territory;

(2) The first authentic case of plague, cholera, or yellow fever which occurs outside the limits of local areas already affected;

(3) The existence of an epidemic of typhus or of smallpox.

Article 2

Every notification prescribed in Article 1 shall be accompanied, or very promptly followed, by detailed information as to—

(1) Where the disease has appeared;

(2) The date of its appearance, its source and its type;

(3) The number of established cases and the number of deaths;

(4) The extent of the area or areas affected;

(5) In the case of plague, the existence of that disease or of an unusual mortality among rats;

(6) In the case of cholera, the number of germ carriers when these have been discovered;

(7) In the case of yellow fever, the presence and relative prevalence (index) of *Stegomyia calopus* (*Aedes Egypti*);

(8) The measures taken.

ARTICLE 3

The notifications contemplated in Articles 1 and 2 are to be addressed to the Diplomatic Missions or failing them to consular offices in the capital of the infected country and shall be held at the disposition of consular officers established in its territory.

These notifications shall also be addressed to the International Office of Public Hygiene which shall communicate them immediately to all diplomatic missions, or failing them, to the Consulates, in Paris, as well as to the principal public health authorities of the participating countries. Those prescribed under Article 1 shall be addressed by telegram.

The telegram addressed by the International Office of Public Hygiene to the Governments of countries participating in the present Convention or to the principal public health authorities of these countries, and the telegrams transmitted by these Governments and by these authorities under this Convention, are treated like State telegrams and enjoy the priority accorded to such telegrams by Article 5 of the International Telegraphic Convention of July 10/22, 1875.

ARTICLE 4

The notification and the information contemplated in Articles 1 and 2 shall be followed by subsequent communications sent regularly to the International Office of Public Hygiene so as to keep the Governments informed of the progress of the epidemic.

These communications, which shall be as frequent and as complete as possible and shall take place at least once a week with regard to the number of cases and deaths, shall indicate in particular the precautions adopted with a view to preventing the spread of the disease. They shall specify the measures enforced upon the departure of vessels to prevent exportation of the disease, and especially the measures taken with regard to rats or insects.

ARTICLE 5

The Governments undertake to reply to any request for information which is made to them by the International Office of Public Hygiene in regard to epidemic diseases mentioned in the Convention, which occur in their territory, and in regard to circumstances likely to affect the transmission of these diseases from one country to another.

ARTICLE 6

Since rats [5] are the principal agents by which bubonic plague is spread, the Governments undertake to make use of all means in their power to

---

[5] The provisions of this Convention regarding rats are applicable to the case of other rodents, and in general to other animals known to be the means of spreading plague. [Footnote in original.]

diminish this danger and constantly to keep themselves informed of the condition of the rats in their ports as regards plague infection, by frequent and periodical examinations; and in particular to carry out the systematic collection and the bacteriological examination of rats in every plague-infected area, during a period of not less than six months from the finding of the last plague-infected rat.

The methods and the results of these examinations shall be communicated in ordinary circumstances at regular intervals, and in the case of plague every month, to the International Office of Public Hygiene in order that Governments may be kept uninterruptedly informed by that Office of the condition of ports in regard to plague amongst rats.

On the first discovery of plague among rats on land, in a port free from infection during the previous six months, the communications shall be sent by the most rapid ways.

ARTICLE 7

In order to facilitate the fulfilment of duties put upon it by this Convention, and having regard to the benefits derived from the information furnished by the epidemiological intelligence service of the League of Nations, including its Eastern Bureau at Singapore, and of other analogous bureaus, as well as by the Pan-American Sanitary Bureau, the International Office of Public Hygiene is empowered to make the needful arrangements with the Health Committee of the League of Nations, as well as with the Pan-American Sanitary Bureau and other similar organizations.

It stands understood that the relations established under the arrangements above indicated will not involve any derogation from the provisions of the Convention of Rome of December 9, 1907,[6] and cannot work the effect of substituting any other sanitary body for the International Office of Public Hygiene.

ARTICLE 8

As it is of primary importance that the foregoing provisions be promptly and scrupulously complied with, the Governments recognize the necessity of giving instructions to the appropriate services in regard to the application of these provisions.

As notification is of no value unless every Government be itself informed, in good time, of cases of plague, cholera, yellow fever, typhus, or smallpox, and also of suspected cases of these diseases which occur in its territory, countries participating in the Convention undertake to make it compulsory to declare such cases.

ARTICLE 9

It is recommended that neighboring countries should make special arrangements, with the object of organizing direct exchange of information between

---

[6] TS 511, *ante*, vol. 1, p. 742.

the head of the department concerned as regards territories that are contiguous or have close commercial relations. These arrangements shall be communicated to the International Office of Public Hygiene.

SECTION II. CONDITIONS WHICH WARRANT CONSIDERING THAT THE MEASURES PRESCRIBED BY THE CONVENTION ARE OR HAVE CEASED TO BE APPLICABLE TO ARRIVALS FROM PARTICULAR AREAS

ARTICLE 10

The notification of imported cases of plague, cholera or yellow fever shall not lead to the adoption of the measures prescribed in the following Chapter II in regard to arrivals from the area in which they occurred.

But the measures may be adopted when a first case of plague or yellow fever has occurred which is recognized as a case not imported, or when the cases of cholera form a *foyer*,[7] or when exanthematous typhus or smallpox exists in epidemic form.

ARTICLE 11

In order that the measures prescribed in Chapter II may be limited to places which are actually stricken, Governments must restrict their application to arrivals from defined local areas in which the diseases coming under the present Convention have appeared under the conditions indicated in the second paragraph of Article 10.

But this limitation of an infected local area must be accepted only on the express condition that the Government of the country in which this area is comprised shall take the measures necessary (1) for checking the spread of the epidemic and (2) for applying the measures prescribed by Article 13 below.

ARTICLE 12

The Government of a country in which an infected area is situated will inform other Governments and the International Office of Public Hygiene in the manner specified in Article 3, when the danger of infection from that area has ceased, and when all the preventive measures have been taken. From the time of this information the measures prescribed in Chapter II will no longer be applicable to arrivals from the area in question, except in exceptional circumstances, which must be established.

---

[7] A *"foyer"* exists when the occurrence of new cases outside the immediate surroundings of the first cases proves that the spread of the disease has not been limited to the place where it began. [Footnote in original.]

SECTION III. MEASURES AT THE PORTS AND ON THE DEPARTURE OF VESSELS

ARTICLE 13

The competent authority shall be obliged to take effectual measures—

(1) To prevent the embarkation of persons showing symptoms of plague, cholera, yellow fever, exanthematous typhus or smallpox, and of persons in such relations with the sick as to render them liable to transmit the infection of these diseases;

(2) In the case of plague, to prevent rats gaining access to ships;

(3) In the case of cholera, to see that the drinking water and foodstuffs taken on board is wholesome, and that water taken in as ballast is disinfected if necessary;

(4) In the case of yellow fever, to prevent mosquitoes gaining access to ships;

(5) In the case of exanthematous typhus, to secure the delousing of all suspects before their embarkation;

(6) In the case of smallpox, to subject to disinfection worn garments and rags before they are compressed.

ARTICLE 14

Governments undertake to maintain in and around their large ports and, as far as possible, in and around their other ports, a sanitary service possessing an organization and equipment capable of carrying out the application of the prophylactic measures in the case of the diseases coming under this Convention and especially the measures laid down in Articles 6, 8 and 13.

The said Governments will supply at least once a year to the International Office of Public Hygiene a statement showing in the case of each of their ports the condition of its sanitary organization commensurate with the provisions of the preceding paragraph. The Office will forward such information through the proper channels to the principal health authorities of the participating countries either directly or through some other international sanitary organization in accordance with the arrangements concluded under Article 7.

CHAPTER II. *Measures of defence against the diseases mentioned in Chapter I*

ARTICLE 15

Any ship, whatever port it comes from, may be subjected by the sanitary authority to a medical inspection, and if circumstances require it, to a thorough examination.

The sanitary measures and actions to which a ship may be subjected on arrival shall be determined by the actual condition found to exist on board and the sanitary particulars of the voyage.

It rests with each Government, taking into account the information furnished under the provisions of Section I, Chapter I, and of Article 14 of this Convention, as well as the obligations placed upon it by Section II, Chapter I, to determine what procedure is applicable in its own ports to arrivals from any foreign port, and in particular to decide whether, from the point of view of the procedure to be applied, a particular foreign port should be considered as infected.

The measures as provided in this Chapter must be regarded as constituting a maximum within the limits of which Governments may regulate the procedure to be applied to ships on their arrival.

SECTION I. NOTIFICATION OF MEASURES PRESCRIBED

ARTICLE 16

Every Government is bound to communicate immediately to the Diplomatic Mission or, failing that, to the Consul of the infected country, residing in its capital, as well as to the International Office of Public Hygiene which shall immediately make them known to the other Governments, the measures which it considers necessary to prescribe with regard to arrivals from that country. Such information will in like manner be held at the disposition of other diplomatic or consular representatives established in its territory.

It also is bound to communicate, through the same channels, the withdrawal of these measures or any modifications thereof.

In the absence of a Diplomatic Mission or a Consulate in the capital, the communications shall be made direct to the Government of the country concerned.

SECTION II. MERCHANDISE AND BAGGAGE—IMPORTATION AND TRANSIT

ARTICLE 17

Subject to the provisions of the last paragraph of Article 50, the entry of merchandise and baggage arriving by land or by sea for import or for transit may not be prohibited nor may merchandise or baggage be detained at land frontiers or in ports. The only measures which may be prescribed with regard to such merchandise and baggage are specified in the following paragraphs:

(a) In the case of plague, body linen, wearing apparel and bedding which have been in recent use may be subjected to disinsectisation, and, if necessary, to disinfection.

Merchandise coming from an infected local area and likely to harbor plague-infected rats may be unloaded only on condition that the precautions necessary to prevent the escape of rats and to ensure their destruction are taken as far as practicable.

(b) In the case of cholera, body linen, wearing apparel and bedding which have been in recent use may be subjected to disinfection.

In derogation of the provisions of this Article, the importation of fresh fish, shellfish and vegetables may be prohibited unless they have undergone a treatment calculated to destroy cholera vibrios.

(c) In the case of exanthematous typhus, body linen, wearing apparel and bedding which have been in recent use, as well as rags not carried as merchandise in large quantities, may be subjected to disinsectisation.

(d) In the case of smallpox, body linen, wearing apparel and bedding which have been in recent use, as well as rags not carried as merchandise in large quantities, may be subjected to disinfection.

ARTICLE 18

It rests with the authority of the country to which the merchandise and things are consigned to decide in what manner and at what place disinfection shall be carried out and what shall be the methods adopted to secure the destruction of rats and insects (fleas, lice, mosquitoes, et cetera). These operations must be performed in such a fashion as to injure articles as little as possible. Clothes and other articles of small value, including rags not carried in merchandise in large quantities, may be destroyed by fire.

It rests with each State to settle questions of compensation for damage caused by disinfection, deratisation or disinsectisation, or by the destruction of the things referred to above.

If, on account of these measures, charges are levied by the sanitary authority, either directly or indirectly through a company or an individual, the rates of these charges must be in accordance with a tariff made public beforehand and so drawn up that the State and the sanitary authority shall, on the whole, derive no profit from its application.

ARTICLE 19

Letters and correspondence, printed matter, books, newspapers, business documents, et cetera, shall not be subject to any sanitary measure. Post parcels shall be subjected to restriction only if their contents include articles on which the measures provided by Article 17 of the present Convention may be enforced.

ARTICLE 20

When merchandise or baggage has been subjected to the operations prescribed in Article 17, any interested party can require the sanitary authorities to issue a free certificate showing the measures that have been taken.

SECTION III. PROVISIONS RELATING TO EMIGRANTS

ARTICLE 21

The sanitary authorities in a country of emigration must subject its emigrants to a medical examination before their departure.

It is recommended that special arrangements be made between the countries of emigration, immigration and transit, with a view to laying down the conditions under which this examination shall be considered satisfactory by them, so that rejections on medical grounds at the frontier of the countries of transit and destination may be reduced to a minimum.

It is also recommended that these arrangements should determine what preventive measures against infectious diseases shall be applied to emigrants in the country of departure.

ARTICLE 22

It is recommended that, at the towns or ports of embarkation for emigrants, there should be an adequate health and sanitary administration having especially (1) a service for medical examination and treatment, as well as the necessary medical and prophylactic equipment; (2) an establishment supervised by the State where emigrants may be subjected to the health formalities, temporarily housed, and undergo all necessary medical examinations and have their food and drinking supplies examined; (3) premises situated at the port where medical examinations shall be made at the time of the final embarkation.

ARTICLE 23

It is recommended that emigrant ships be provided with a sufficient quantity of vaccines (anti-smallpox, anti-cholera, et cetera), in order to permit, if necessary, of vaccinations during the voyage.

SECTION IV. MEASURES AT PORTS AND MARINE FRONTIERS

A. Plague

ARTICLE 24

A ship shall be regarded as *infected:*

(1) if it has a case of human plague on board;

(2) or if a case of human plague broke out more than six days after embarkation;

(3) or if plague-infected rats are found on board.

A ship shall be regarded as *suspected:*

(1) If a case of human plague broke out in the first six days after embarkation;

(2) or if investigations regarding rats have shown the existence of an unusual mortality without determining the cause thereof.

The ship shall continue to be regarded as suspicious until it has been subjected to the measures prescribed by this Convention at a suitably equipped port.

A ship shall be regarded as *uninfected,* notwithstanding its having come from an infected port, if there has been no human or rat plague on board either at the time of departure, or during the voyage, or at the time of arrival, and the investigations regarding rats have not shown the existence of an unusual mortality.

ARTICLE 25

Plague-infected ships shall undergo the following measures:

(1) Medical inspection;

(2) The patients shall immediately be landed and isolated;

(3) All persons who have been in contact with the patients and those whom the health authority of the port has reason to consider suspect shall be disembarked if possible. They may be subjected to observation or surveillance, or to a period of observation followed by surveillance,[8] provided that the total duration of these measures does not exceed six days from the time of arrival of the ship.

It rests with the sanitary authority of the port, after taking into consideration the date of the last case, the condition of the ship and the local possibilities, to take that one of these measures which seems to it preferable. During the same period the crew may be prevented from going ashore except on duty made known to the sanitary authority;

(4) Bedding which has been used, and such soiled linen, wearing apparel and other articles as are, in the opinion of the sanitary authority, infected shall be disinsectised and, if there be occasion, disinfected;

(5) The parts of the ship which have been occupied by persons suffering from plague or which, in the opinion of the sanitary authority, are infected, shall be disinsectised and, if there be occasion, disinfected;

(6) The sanitary authority may order deratisation before the discharge of cargo, if it is of opinion, having regard to the nature of the cargo, and the way in which it is loaded, that it is possible to effect a total destruction of rats without removing it. In this case, the ship cannot be subjected to a new deratisation after discharge. In other cases the complete destruction of rats on board must

---

[8] In all cases where the present Convention refers to "surveillance" the sanitary authority may substitute "observation" as an exceptional measure in the case of persons who do not offer adequate sanitary guarantees.

Persons under observation or surveillance must submit to all clinical or bacteriological investigations which are considered necessary by the sanitary authority. [Footnote in original.]

be effected when the holds are empty. In the cases of ships in ballast, this shall be done as soon as possible before taking cargo.

Destruction of rats shall be carried out so as to avoid, as far as possible, damage to the ship and cargo (if any). The operation must not last longer than twenty-four hours. All charges made in respect to these operations of deratisation as also all contingent indemnity claims, shall be settled in accordance with the principles laid down in Article 18.

If a ship is only to discharge a part of its cargo, and if the port authorities consider that it is impossible to undertake complete deratisation, the said ship shall be allowed to remain in the port for the time required to discharge that part of its cargo, provided that all precautions, including isolation, are taken to the satisfaction of the sanitary authority to prevent rats from passing from ship to shore, either with unladen goods or otherwise.

The discharge of cargo shall be carried out under the supervision of the sanitary authority, who shall take all measures necessary to prevent the men employed on this duty from becoming infected. The men shall be subjected to observation or to surveillance for a period not exceeding six days from the time when they have ceased to work at the unloading of the ship.

ARTICLE 26

Plague-suspected ships shall undergo the measures indicated in Nos. 1, 4, 5 and 6 of Article 25.

In addition, the crew and passengers may be subjected to surveillance which shall not exceed six days, reckoned from the date of the ship's arrival. The crew may be prevented during the same period from going ashore except on duty made known to the sanitary authority.

ARTICLE 27

Ships uninfected with plague shall be given free pratique immediately, with the reservation that the sanitary authority of the port of arrival may prescribe the following measures with regard to them:

(1) Medical inspection to determine whether the condition of the ship corresponds to the definition of a healthy ship;

(2) Destruction of rats on board under the conditions specified in 6 of Article 25 in exceptional cases and for well-founded reasons which will be communicated in writing to the captain of the ship;

(3) The crew and passengers may be subjected to surveillance during a period which shall not exceed six days reckoned from the date on which the ship left the contaminated port. The crew may be prevented during the same period from going ashore except on duty made known to the sanitary authority.

ARTICLE 28

All ships, except those employed in national coastwise service, must be periodically deratised, or be permanently kept in such a condition that rat population is reduced to the minimum. In the first case they receive Deratisation Certificates, and in the second Deratisation Exemption Certificates.

Governments shall make known through the International Office of Public Hygiene those of their ports possessing the equipment and personnel necessary for the deratisation of ships.

A deratisation certificate or a deratisation exemption certificate shall be issued only by the sanitary authority of the aforesaid ports. The certificate shall be valid for six months. One additional month however may be allowed in the case of a ship proceeding to its home port.

If no valid certificate is produced, the sanitary authority at the ports mentioned in the second paragraph of this Article may after inquiry and inspection:

(a) Directly perform the deratisation of the vessel, or cause it to be done under its direction and supervision. When completed to its satisfaction it shall issue a dated *Deratisation Certificate*. It shall decide on each case what process shall be employed practically to exterminate the rats on board; particulars of the mode of deratising applied and of the number of rats destroyed must be entered on the Certificate. Destruction of rats must be accomplished in a manner that will as far as possible save the ship and cargo (if any) from injury. The operation must not last longer than 24 hours. In the case of vessels in ballast, it must be done before loading. All charges on account of these operations of deratisation and all claims, if any, for damages shall be settled according to the terms of Article 18.

(b) Issue a Deratisation Exemption Certificate stating the date and grounds if it is satisfied that the ship is maintained in such a condition that the rat population is reduced to a minimum.

The deratisation and deratisation exemption certificates shall be drawn up as far as possible in a uniform manner. Forms of such certificates will be prepared by the International Office of Public Hygiene.

The competent authority of each country undertakes each year to furnish the International Office of Public Hygiene with a statement of the measures taken under this article and the number of ships which have been subjected to deratisation, or which have been granted deratisation exemption certificates, at the ports referred to in the second paragraph of this Article.

The International Office of Public Hygiene is requested to take in accordance with Article 14 all steps for the interchange of information as to the action taken under this Article and the results obtained.

The provisions of this Article do not affect the rights accorded to sanitary authorities by Articles 24–27 of this Convention.

The Governments shall see that all requisite and practicable measures are taken by the competent authorities to accomplish the destruction of rats in ports and the dependent and neighboring parts as well as on lighters and coastwise vessels.

B. *Cholera*

ARTICLE 29

A ship shall be regarded as *infected* if there is a case of cholera on board, or if there has been a case of cholera during the five days previous to the arrival of the ship in port.

A ship shall be regarded as *suspected* if there has been a case of cholera at the time of departure or during the voyage, but no fresh case in the five days previous to arrival. The ship shall continue to be regarded as suspect until it has been subjected to the measures prescribed by the present Convention.

A ship shall be considered *uninfected* notwithstanding that it came from an infected port or that it may have on board persons proceeding from an infected area if there has been no case of cholera at the time of departure, during the voyage, or on arrival.

Cases presenting the clinical symptoms of cholera in which no cholera vibrios have been found or in which vibrios not strictly showing the characteristics of cholera vibrio have been found, shall be subject to all measures required in the case of cholera.

Germ carriers discovered on the arrival of the ship shall be submitted after disembarkation to all the obligations which may be imposed on such a case by the laws of the country of arrival on its own nationals.

ARTICLE 30

Cholera infected ships shall be subjected to the following measures:

(1) Medical inspection;

(2) The patients shall be immediately landed and isolated;

(3) The crew and passengers may also be landed and either be kept under observation or subjected to surveillance during a period not exceeding five days reckoned from the date of arrival.

However, persons who can show that they have been immunized from cholera by vaccination effected less than six months, and more than six days before, may be subjected to surveillance but not to observation.

(4) Bedding which has been used, soiled linen, wearing apparel and other articles, including foodstuffs, which in the opinion of the sanitary authority of the port have been recently contaminated, shall be disinfected;

(5) The parts of the vessel which have been occupied by cholera patients or which are considered by the health authorities as being contaminated, shall be disinfected;

(6) Unloading shall be carried out under the supervision of the sanitary authority, who will take all measures necessary to prevent the infection of the men engaged in unloading. They shall be subjected to observation or to surveillance which shall not exceed five days from the time when they cease unloading;

(7) When the drinking water stored on board is considered suspicious it shall be turned off after being disinfected and replaced after disinfection of the tanks by a supply of water of good quality;

(8) The health authority may prohibit the turning off without previous disinfection of water ballast if it has been taken in at an infected port;

(9) It may be forbidden to let run or throw human dejections or the residuary waters of the vessel into the waters of the port, unless they are first disinfected.

ARTICLE 31

Vessels suspected of cholera shall be subjected to the measures prescribed under Nos. (1), (4), (5), (7), (8) and (9) of Article 30.

The crew and passengers may be subjected to a surveillance not to exceed five days from the arrival of the vessel. It is recommended that the landing of the crew be prevented during the same period except for purposes connected with the service and made known to the sanitary authority of the port.

ARTICLE 32

If the ship has been declared infected or suspected only because of cases on board presenting the clinical features of cholera, and two bacteriological examinations, made with an interval of not less than 24 hours between them, have not revealed the presence of cholera or any other suspicious vibrios, it shall be classed as uninfected.

ARTICLE 33

Vessels uninfected with cholera shall be granted pratique, immediately.

The health authority of the port of arrival may order in their case the measures provided under Nos. (1), (7), (8) and (9) of Article 30.

The crew and the passengers may be subjected to a surveillance not to exceed five days from the date of arrival of the ship. The landing of the crew may be forbidden during the same period except for purposes connected with the service and made known to the sanitary authority of the port.

ARTICLE 34

Since anti-cholera vaccination is a method of proved efficacy in checking cholera epidemics, and consequently in lessening the likelihood of the spread of the disease, it is recommended, that sanitary administrations will, in the largest measure possible, and as often as practicable, apply specific vaccination in cholera hotbeds and grant certain advantages as regards restrictive measures to persons who agree to be vaccinated.

C. Yellow fever

ARTICLE 35

A ship shall be regarded as *infected* if there is a case of yellow fever on board, or if there was one at the time of departure or during the voyage.

A ship shall be regarded as *suspected* if it had no case of yellow fever but arrives after a voyage of less than six days from an infected port or from an uninfected port in close relation with endemic centers of yellow fever, or if when it arrived having been more than six days out there is reason to believe that it may carry winged *Stegomyia* (*Aedes Egypti*) from the said port.

A ship shall be regarded as *uninfected,* notwithstanding its having come from a yellow fever infected port, if having had no case of yellow fever on board and arrived after more than six days on the way there is no reason to believe that it carries winged *Stegomyia,* or when it proves to the satisfaction of the sanitary authority of the port of arrival:

(a) That during its stay in the port of departure it kept at a distance of more than 200 metres from the inhabited land and at such a distance from the pontoons as to make the access of *Stegomyia* improbable;

(b) Or that at the time of departure it was subjected to effective fumigation in order to destroy mosquitoes.

ARTICLE 36

Ships infected with yellow fever shall undergo the following measures:

(1) Medical inspection;

(2) The patients shall be landed, and those of them who are in the first five days of the disease shall be isolated so as to prevent contamination by mosquitoes;

(3) The other persons who land shall be subjected to observation or surveillance not exceeding six days reckoned from the time of landing;

(4) The ship will be moored at least 200 metres from the inhabited land and at such a distance from the pontoons as will render the access of *Stegomyia* improbable;

(5) Mosquitoes at all stages of evolution shall be destroyed on board as far as possible before discharge of cargo. If unloading takes place before the destruction of mosquitoes, the personnel in charge of that work will be subjected to observation or to surveillance for not more than six days from the time when they ceased unloading.

ARTICLE 37

Ships suspected of yellow fever may be subjected to the measures specified in (1), (3), (4) and (5) of Article 36.

Nevertheless, if the voyage has lasted less than six days if the ship meets the conditions specified under letters (a) and (b) in the subsection of Article 35 relating to uninfected ships, it shall only be subjected to the measures prescribed by Article 36, (1) and (3) and to fumigation.

When 30 days have elapsed after the departure of the ship from the infected port, and no case has occurred during its voyage, the ship may be granted free pratique subject to preliminary fumigation should the sanitary authority deem it necessary.

ARTICLE 38

Ships uninfected with yellow fever shall be granted free pratique after medical inspection.

ARTICLE 39

The measures prescribed in Articles 36 and 37 concern only those regions in which the *Stegomyia* exists, and they shall be applied with due consideration to the climatic conditions prevailing in the countries concerned and also the Stegomyian index.

In other regions they shall be applied to the extent considered necessary by the sanitary authority.

ARTICLE 40

The masters of ships which have touched at ports infected with yellow fever are specially advised to cause a search to be made for mosquitoes and their larvae during the voyage and to secure their systematic destruction in all accessible parts of the ship, particularly in the store rooms, galleys, boiler rooms, water tanks and other places specially likely to harbor *Stegomyia*.

D. Exanthematous typhus

ARTICLE 41

Ships which, during the voyage have had or at the time of their arrival, have a case of typhus on board, may be subjected to the following measures:

(1) Medical inspection;

(2) The patients shall immediately be landed, isolated and deloused;

(3) Other persons reasonably suspected to harbor lice, or to have been exposed to infection, shall also be deloused, and may be subjected to surveillance for a time to be specified, but which shall never be more than 12 days, reckoned from the date of delousing;

(4) Bedding which has been used, and such linen, wearing apparel, and other articles as the sanitary authority, of the port considers to be infected shall be disinfected;

(5) The parts of the ship which have been occupied by persons ill with typhus, and that the sanitary authority regard as infected, shall be disinfected.

The ship shall immediately be given free pratique.

It rests with each Government to take after disembarkation the measures which it considers appropriate to secure the surveillance of persons who arrive on a ship which had no case of exanthematous typhus on board, but who left an area where typhus is epidemic less than 12 days before.

E. Smallpox

Article 42

Ships which have had a case of smallpox on board either during the voyage, or at the time of arrival, may be subjected to the following measures:

(1) Medical inspection;

(2) The patients shall immediately be landed and isolated;

(3) Other persons reasonably suspected to have been exposed to infection on board, and who, in the opinion of the sanitary authority, are not sufficiently protected by recent vaccination, or by a previous attack of smallpox, may be subjected to vaccination followed by surveillance, the period of surveillance being specified in each case according to the circumstances, but never to exceed 14 days, reckoned from the date of arrival;

(4) Bedding which has been used, soiled linen, wearing apparel, and other articles which the sanitary authority of the port considers to be infected, shall be disinfected;

(5) Only those parts of the ship which have been occupied by persons ill with smallpox and which the sanitary authority regards as infected shall be disinfected.

The ship shall immediately be given free pratique.

It rests with each Government to take after disembarkation the measures which it considers appropriate to secure the surveillance of persons who are not protected by vaccination and arrive on a ship that had no smallpox on board, but left an area where smallpox is epidemic less than 14 days before.

Article 43

It is recommended that ships calling in countries where smallpox is epidemic, shall take all precautions possible to secure the vaccination or revaccination of the crew.

It is also recommended that governments should make vaccination and revaccination as general as possible, especially in ports and border regions.

F. Common provisions

Article 44

The captain and the ship's physician must answer all questions that are put to them by the sanitary authority with regard to the health of the ship during the voyage.

When the captain and the physician declare that there has not been any case of plague, cholera, yellow fever, exanthematous typhus or smallpox, and no unusual mortality among rats on the ship since the time of its departure, the sanitary authority may require them to make a solemn or sworn declaration.

ARTICLE 45

In applying the measures set forth in the preceding subsections A., B., C., D. and E, the sanitary authority will take into account the presence of a physician on board and the actual preventive measures taken in the course of the voyage, especially for the destruction of rats.

The sanitary authorities of the countries that find it convenient to come to an agreement on the matter may exempt from medical inspection and other measures uninfected ships carrying a physician specially commissioned by their country.

ARTICLE 46

It is recommended that Governments take into account, as to the treatment to be applied to arrivals from another country, measures taken in the latter country to combat infectious diseases and to prevent their transmission to other countries.

Ships arriving from ports which fulfill the conditions set out in Articles 14 and 51, do not derive from that alone any right to special advantages at the port of arrival, but the Governments agree to take into the fullest consideration the measures already taken in those ports, so that all the measures taken at the port of arrival with regard to ships coming from those ports shall be reduced to a minimum. To that end and in order to put shipping, commerce and traffic to as little inconvenience as possible, it is recommended that special arrangements in accordance with Article 57 of this Convention be made in all cases where it would seem advantageous to do so.

ARTICLE 47

Ships arriving from an infected area which have been submitted to sufficient sanitary measures to the satisfaction of the sanitary authority, shall not undergo those measures again on their arrival at another port, whether or not the latter belongs to the same country, provided nothing has happened since which would call for the application of the sanitary measures above referred to and the ships have not called at an infected port, except for coaling.

A ship shall not be considered as having stopped at a port, when without having been in communication with the shore it has landed passengers only and their luggage and the mail, or has taken on board only mail or passengers, with or without their luggage, who have not communicated with the port or with a contaminated area. In the case of yellow fever the vessel must, in addition, have kept wherever possible not less than two hundred metres from inhabited land and at such a distance from the pontoons as to make access of *Stegomyia* improbable.

ARTICLE 48

The port authority who imposes sanitary measures shall, whenever requested, deliver to the captain, or any other interested person, a certificate specifying the nature of the measures and the methods employed, the parts of the ship treated, and the reasons why the measures have been applied.

It may also in the same way, on demand, issue free of charge to passengers who have arrived by an infected ship a certificate stating the date of their arrival and the measures to which they and their luggage have been subjected.

SECTION V. GENERAL PROVISIONS

ARTICLE 49

It is recommended—

(1) That bills of health be issued free in all ports;

(2) That fees for consular visas be reduced by way of reciprocity, so as not to represent more than the cost of the service rendered;

(3) That the bill of health be made out in at least one of the languages known to the maritime world, in addition to that of the country where it is issued;

(4) That special agreements in the spirit of Article 57 of this Convention be made with a view to doing away gradually with consular visas and bills of health.

ARTICLE 50

It is desirable that the number of ports furnished with an organization and equipment sufficient for the reception of a ship, whatever its health conditions may be, should be in each country commensurate with the importance of the trade and shipping. However, without prejudice to the right of Governments to make agreements for the establishment of common sanitary stations, every country must provide at least one port on each of its seacoasts with the above-mentioned organization and equipment.

Furthermore, it is recommended that all large seaports should be so equipped that uninfected ships at least may undergo immediately upon their arrival, the prescribed sanitary measures without being sent to another port for this purpose.

Every infected or suspected ship which arrives in a port not equipped for its reception must proceed, at its own risk and peril, to one of the ports opened to ships of the category to which it belongs.

Governments shall make known to the International Office of Public Hygiene what ports are open to arrivals from ports infected with plague, cholera, or yellow fever, and in particular those open to infected or suspected ships.

ARTICLE 51

It is recommended that there be set up in large seaports:

(a) A regular port medical service, and permanent medical surveillance of the health condition of crews and of the inhabitants of the port;

(b) An outfit for the transport of the sick and suitable premises for their isolation, and for keeping suspected persons under observation;

(c) Installations necessary for efficient disinfection and disinsectisation; a bacteriological laboratory, and a force prepared to attend to urgent vaccination against smallpox or against other diseases;

(d) A supply of drinking water of quality beyond suspicion for the use of the port, and a system affording all possible security for the removal of waste, filth and waste water;

(e) A competent and adequate staff and necessary equipment for the deratisation of ships, yards, docks and warehouses;

(f) A permanent organization for the detection and examination of rats.

It is also recommended that warehouses and docks should as far as possible be rat proof, and that the sewer system of the port be separate from that of the town.

ARTICLE 52

Governments will refrain from making any sanitary inspection of ships passing through their territorial waters [9] without stopping at the ports or on the coasts of their respective countries.

If the ship, for any reason whatever, should stop at a port or on the coast, it would be subjected to the sanitary laws and regulations of the country to which the port or coast belongs as far as permitted by international conventions.

ARTICLE 53

Special measures may be prescribed regarding any ship in an exceptionally bad sanitary condition likely to facilitate the spread of the diseases mentioned in this Convention, especially crowded ships.

ARTICLE 54

Ships unwilling to comply with obligations imposed by the port authority, in virtue of the provisions of this Convention, shall be at liberty to put out to sea.

Such ships may, however, be permitted to land goods if the ship is isolated and if the goods are subjected to the measures provided by Chapter II., Section II., of this Convention.

---

[9] The expression "territorial waters" must be understood in its strictly juridical sense. It does not include Suez, Panama and Kiel Canals. [Footnote in original.]

Such ships may also be authorized to disembark passengers at their request, on the condition that such passengers submit to the measures prescribed by the sanitary authority.

The ship, while kept isolated, may also take on fuel, stores and water.

Article 55

Each Government undertakes to have a single sanitary tariff only, which shall be published, and the charges therein shall be moderate. This tariff will be applied in ports to all ships, without distinction being made between the national and foreign flags, and to foreigners in the same conditions as to the country's own nationals.

Article 56

International coasting traffic will come under special regulations, to be agreed upon by the countries concerned. Nevertheless the provisions of Article 28 of the present Convention shall be applicable to them in all cases.

Article 57

The Governments, taking into account their peculiar situation, may conclude special agreements amongst themselves, in order to make the sanitary measures prescribed by this Convention more efficacious and less cumbersome. The text of such agreements shall be communicated to the International Office of Public Hygiene.

SECTION VI. MEASURES AT LAND FRONTIERS—TRAVELLERS—RAILWAYS—FRONTIER ZONES—RIVER-WAYS

Article 58

Observations shall not be established at land frontiers.

Persons showing symptoms of the diseases mentioned in this Convention alone may be detained at frontiers.

This principle does not deprive a State of the right to close a portion of its frontiers if need be. The places through which border traffic will exclusively be allowed shall be designated, and in such cases duly equipped sanitary stations shall be set up at the places thus designated. Notice of these measures shall immediately be given to the neighboring country concerned.

Notwithstanding the provisions of the present Article, persons having been in contact with a person ill with pulmonary plague, may be retained at land frontiers under observation for not more than seven days reckoned from the time of arrival.

Persons who have been in contact with a person ill with exanthematous typhus may be submitted to delousing.

ARTICLE 59

In trains coming from infected areas it is important that the railway crew keep watch on the way over the state of health of the travellers.

Medical intervention shall be limited to inspection of travellers and care of the sick and the latter's companions if there be occasion. When this inspection is resorted to, it shall, as far as possible, be combined with the custom examination in order that travellers may suffer as little delay as possible.

ARTICLE 60

Railway cars running in countries where yellow fever exists must be so arranged as to be as little suited as possible for the transport of *Stegomyia*.

ARTICLE 61

Travellers coming from an area which lies under the conditions coming under the second paragraph of Article 10 of this Convention may be subjected on arrival at their destination to surveillance for not more than six days reckoned from the date of their arrival in the case of plague, five days in the case of cholera, six days in the case of yellow fever, twelve days in the case of exanthematous typhus, or fourteen days in the case of smallpox.

ARTICLE 62

With respect to diseases coming under this Convention, Governments, notwithstanding the foregoing provisions, reserve the right in exceptional cases to take special measures in regard to certain classes of persons who do not offer satisfactory sanitary guarantees, especially persons travelling or crossing the frontier in bands. The provisions of this paragraph are not applicable to emigrants save the provisions of Article 21.

These measures may include the establishment at frontiers of sanitary stations, sufficiently equipped, to ensure the surveillance, and the observation if necessary, of the persons concerned, as well as for their medical examination, disinfection, disinsectisation and vaccination.

As far as possible, these exceptional measures should be made the subject of special arrangements between adjoining States.

ARTICLE 63

Railway cars for passengers, mails or luggage and freight cars may not be detained at the frontier.

If, however, one of the carriages is infected or has been occupied by any person suffering from plague, cholera, exanthematous typhus, or smallpox, it shall be detained all the time required to undergo the prophylactic measures indicated for each case.

ARTICLE 64

The measures concerning the crossing of frontiers by railroad and postal employees are within the province of the administrations concerned. They shall be combined so as not to hinder the service.

ARTICLE 65

The regulation of frontier traffic and questions pertaining thereto, shall be left to special arrangements between the contiguous countries in accordance with the provisions of this Convention.

ARTICLE 66

It shall be the province of the Government of the riparian Nations to regulate the sanitary régime of lakes and river routes by means of special arrangements.

TITLE II. SPECIAL PROVISIONS FOR THE SUEZ CANAL AND NEIGHBORING COUNTRIES

SECTION I. MEASURES WITH RESPECT TO ORDINARY VESSELS HAILING FROM CONTAMINATED NORTHERN PORTS AND APPEARING AT THE ENTRANCE OF THE SUEZ CANAL OR IN EGYPTIAN PORTS

ARTICLE 67

Ordinary *uninfected* vessels hailing from a plague or cholera infected port of Europe or the basin of the Mediterranean and presenting themselves for passage through the Suez Canal shall be allowed to pass through in quarantine.

ARTICLE 68

Ordinary *uninfected* vessels wishing to make a landing in Egypt may stop at Alexandria or Port Said.

If the port of departure is contaminated by plague, Article 37 will be applicable.

If the port of departure is contaminated by cholera, Article 33 will be applicable.

The sanitary authority of the port may substitute for surveillance observation either on board or in a quarantine station.

ARTICLE 69

The measures to which *infected* or *suspected* vessels shall be subjected which hail from a plague or cholera infected port of Europe or the shores of the Mediterranean or the Black Sea, and which desire to effect a landing in one of the Egyptian ports or to pass through the Suez Canal, shall be determined by the Sanitary, Maritime and Quarantine Board of Egypt in conformity with the stipulations of the present Convention.

ARTICLE 70

The regulations of the Sanitary, Maritime and Quarantine Board of Egypt shall be revised with the least possible delay to conform with the stipulations of this Convention. In order to become effective, they must be accepted by the several Powers represented on the Board. They shall establish the régime to which ships, passengers and merchandise are to be subjected. They shall decide the minimum number of medical officers to be attached to each station, the method of recruitment, the salaries, and duties of such medical officers and all officials appointed to carry out under the orders of the Sanitary, Maritime and Quarantine Board of Egypt the supervision and the execution of preventive measures.

The names of the physicians and officials shall be proposed to the Egyptian Government by the Sanitary, Maritime and Quarantine Board of Egypt, through its President.

SECTION II. MEASURES IN THE RED SEA

A. Measures with respect to ordinary vessels hailing from the south and appearing in ports of the Red Sea or bound toward the Mediterranean

ARTICLE 71

Independently of the general provisions in Title I, concerning the classification of and the régime of infected, suspected, or uninfected vessels, the special provisions contained in the ensuing articles are applicable to ordinary vessels coming from the south and entering the Red Sea.

ARTICLE 72

Uninfected ships. Uninfected ships may pass through the Suez Canal in quarantine. When the ship is to touch at an Egyptian port:

(a) If the port of departure is infected by plague, the ship must have been six full days on the way else the passengers who land and the crews shall be kept under surveillance until the six days are completed.

Loading and unloading of cargo will be allowed with due observance of the necessary measures to prevent the landing of rats;

(b) If the port of departure is infected by cholera, the ship may receive free pratique, but every passenger or member of the crew who disembarks when five days have not elapsed since the date of departure from the infected port, will be subjected to surveillance until the completion of that time.

The sanitary authority of the port may in all cases where that authority considers it necessary, substitute observation on board or in a quarantine station for surveillance. In all cases the sanitary authority may make the bacteriological examinations which it considers necessary.

ARTICLE 73

Suspected ships. Suspected ships having a physician on board may, if regarded by the sanitary authority as presenting sufficient guarantees, be allowed to pass through the Suez Canal in quarantine under the regulations provided for in Article 70.

When the ship is to stop at an Egyptian port:

(a) In the case of plague, the provisions of Article 6 are applicable, but surveillance may be replaced by observation;

(b) In the case of cholera, the provisions of Article 31 are applicable with the same reservation as to observation instead of surveillance.

ARTICLE 74

Infected ships. (a) *Plague.* The measures laid down in Article 25 are applicable. Where danger of infection exists, the ship may be required to moor at Moses Spring or any other place named by the sanitary authority of the port.

Passage in quarantine may be granted before the expiration of the six days required by the regulations, if the sanitary authority of the port considers it possible.

(b) *Cholera.* The measures laid down in Article 30 are applicable. The ship may be required to moor at Moses Spring or any other place, and in case of a serious outbreak on board, may be sent off to Tor so that vaccination and, if occasion demands, the treatment of the patients may take place.

The ship cannot be authorized to pass through the Suez Canal until the sanitary authority is satisfied that the ship, passengers and crew no longer present any danger.

B. Measures with respect to ordinary vessels hailing from the infected ports of Hedjaz during the pilgrimage season

ARTICLE 75

If plague or cholera prevails in Hedjaz during the time of the Mecca pilgrimage, vessels coming from the Hedjaz or from any other part of the Arabian coast of the Red Sea without having embarked there any pilgrims or similar groups of persons, and which have not had any suspicious occurrence on board during the voyage, shall be placed in the category of ordinary suspected vessels. They shall be subjected to the preventive measures and to the treatment imposed on such vessels.

If they are bound for Egypt they may undergo, in a sanitary establishment designated by the Sanitary, Maritime and Quarantine Board, an observation of five days for cholera and six days for the plague from the date of their embarkation. They shall be subjected, moreover, to all the measures prescribed for suspected vessels (disinfection, et cetera), and shall not be granted pratique until they have passed a favorable medical examination.

It shall be understood that if the vessels have had suspicious occurrences during the voyage they shall pass the observation period at Moses Spring, which shall last five days for cholera and six days for the plague.

SECTION III. ORGANIZATION SURVEILLANCE

ARTICLE 76

The medical inspection prescribed by the Regulations may take place at night on ships that come up to pass through the canal if lighted by electricity, and whenever the sanitary authority of the port is satisfied that the lighting facilities are adequate.

The supervision and performance of the prophylactic measures applied in the Suez Canal, and at the quarantine establishments, shall be entrusted to a corps of sanitary guards. These guards shall have the status of police officers with the right to make requisitions in cases where the sanitary regulations are infringed.

SECTION IV. PASSAGE THROUGH THE SUEZ CANAL IN QUARANTINE

ARTICLE 77

The health authority of the port of Suez shall grant the passage through in quarantine, and the Sanitary, Maritime and Quarantine Board shall be immediately informed thereof. Doubtful cases shall be decided by that Board.

ARTICLE 78

As soon as the permit provided for in the preceding article is granted, a telegram shall be sent to the authority of the port named by the captain as his next port of call and also to the port of final destination. The despatch of the telegram is at the expense of the vessel.

ARTICLE 79

Each country shall establish penalties against vessels which abandon the route indicated by the captain and unduly approach one of the ports within its territory, cases of vis major and enforced sojourn being excepted.

ARTICLE 80

Upon a vessel's being spoken, the captain shall be obliged to declare whether he has on board any gangs of native stokers or of wage-earning employees of any description who are not inscribed on the crew list or the register kept for this purpose.

The following questions in particular shall be asked the captains of all vessels arriving at Suez from the south, and shall be answered under oath or solemn declaration:

Have you any helpers: stokers or other workmen, not inscribed on your crew list or on the special register? What is their nationality? Where did you embark them?

The sanitary physicians shall ascertain the presence of these helpers and if they discover that any of them are missing they should carefully seek the cause of their absence.

ARTICLE 81

A health officer and at least two guards of the sanitary service shall board the vessel and accompany her to Port Said. Their duty shall be to prevent communications and see to the execution of the prescribed measures during the passage through the canal.

ARTICLE 82

All embarkations, landings, and transshipments of passengers or cargo are forbidden during the passage through the Suez Canal.

However, passengers may embark at Suez or Port Said in quarantine.

ARTICLE 83

Vessels passing through in quarantine shall make the trip from Suez to Port Said or *vice versa,* without lying up.

In case of stranding or of being compelled to lie up, the necessary operations shall be performed by the personnel on board, all communications with the employees of the Suez Canal Company being avoided.

ARTICLE 84

When troops are conveyed through the canal on suspicious or infected vessels passing through in quarantine, the trip shall be made in the daytime only. If it is necessary to stop at night in the canal, the vessels shall anchor in Lake Timsah or the Great Lake.

ARTICLE 85

Vessels passing through in quarantine are forbidden to stop in the harbor of Port Said except in the cases contemplated in articles 82 and 86.

The supply and preparation of food on board vessels shall be effected with the means at hand on the vessels.

Stevedores or any other persons who may have gone on board shall be isolated on the quarantine barge. They shall undergo the regulation measures.

ARTICLE 86

When it is absolutely necessary for vessels passing through in quarantine to take on coal or oil at Suez or Port Said, they shall perform this operation under the necessary guarantee for isolation and sanitary surveillance that may be ordered by the Sanitary, Maritime and Quarantine Board of Egypt. When it is possible to maintain a strict supervision of coaling on board the vessel and to prevent all contact with the persons on board, the coaling of the vessels by the workmen of the port may be permitted. At night the place where the coaling is done should be efficiently illuminated by electric lights.

ARTICLE 87

The pilots, electricians, agents of the Company, and sanitary guards must leave the vessel at Port Said outside of the port between the jetties, and thence conducted directly to the quarantine barge where they shall undergo the measures that may be deemed necessary.

ARTICLE 88

The war vessels hereinafter specified shall enjoy the benefits of the following provisions when passing through the Suez Canal:

They shall be recognized by the quarantine authority as uninfected upon the production of a certificate issued by the physicians on board, countersigned by the commanding officer, and affirming under oath or solemn declaration:

(a) That there has not been any case of plague or cholera on board either at the time of departure or during the passage;

(b) That a careful examination of all persons on board, without any exception, has been made less than twelve hours before the arrival in the Egyptian port, and that it revealed no case of these diseases.

These vessels shall be exempted from the medical examination and immediately receive pratique.

The quarantine authorities shall nevertheless have a right to cause their agents to perform the medical examination on board war vessels whenever they deem it necessary.

Suspicious or infected war vessels shall be subjected to the regulations in force.

Only fighting units shall be considered as war vessels, transports and hospital ships falling under the category of ordinary vessels.

ARTICLE 89

The Sanitary, Maritime and Quarantine Board of Egypt is authorized to organize through Egypt territory, by rail, in quarantine trains the transit of the mails and ordinary passengers coming from infected countries.

SECTION V. SANITARY MEASURES APPLICABLE TO THE PERSIAN GULF

ARTICLE 90

The sanitary régime established by Title I of the present Convention shall be applied, as regards vessels navigating the Persian Gulf, by the health authorities of the ports both of departure and arrival.

TITLE III. PROVISIONS SPECIALLY APPLICABLE TO PILGRIMAGES

CHAPTER I. *General provisions*

ARTICLE 91

The provisions of Article 13 are applicable to persons and objects bound for Hedjaz or the Kingdom of Irak and who are to be embarked on a pilgrim ship, even if the port of embarkation is not infected.

ARTICLE 92

When cases of plague or cholera or other epidemic disease exist in the port, no embarkation shall be made on pilgrim ships until after the persons, assembled in groups have been subjected to an observation for the purpose of ascertaining that none of them is stricken with those diseases.

It shall be understood that, in executing this measure, each Government may take into account the local circumstances and possibilities.

In the case of cholera the persons agreeing to being vaccinated there and then by the physician of the sanitary authority shall be submitted to the medical inspection only at the time of the vaccination. They shall not be required to submit to the observation provided for in this article.

ARTICLE 93

Pilgrims must be provided with a round trip ticket or have deposited sufficient money for the return journey, and, if circumstances permit, prove that they command the means necessary for the accomplishment of the pilgrimage.

ARTICLE 94

Only mechanically propelled ships shall be permitted to carry pilgrims on long voyages.

ARTICLE 95

Pilgrim ships that are Red Sea coasters intended for short passages known as "coasting voyages" shall be subject to the provisions in the special regulations published by the Sanitary, Maritime and Quarantine Board of Egypt.

ARTICLE 96

A ship, which, in addition to ordinary passengers, among whom pilgrims of the upper classes may be included, carries pilgrims in less proportion than one pilgrim per 100 tons gross, shall not be considered a pilgrim-ship.

This exemption applies only to the ship, and the pilgrims carried therein, irrespective of class, shall remain subject to all measures prescribed for them in this Convention.

ARTICLE 97

The captain or the agent of the shipping company, as the sanitary authority may elect, must pay all sanitary taxes that may be levied on pilgrims. These taxes must be included in the price of the ticket.

ARTICLE 98

As far as possible, pilgrims who embark or disembark at sanitary stations must have no contact with one another at the landing-places.

Pilgrims who are landed must be distributed at the camp in as small groups as possible.

They must be supplied with good drinking water, obtained either from local sources or by distillation.

ARTICLE 99

Victuals brought by pilgrims shall be destroyed if the sanitary authority considers it necessary.

CHAPTER II. *Pilgrim ships—Sanitary stations*

SECTION I. GENERAL CONDITIONS APPLYING TO SHIPS

ARTICLE 100

The ships must be capable of accommodating the pilgrims in the between-decks. Outside of the space reserved for the crew, it must provide for each person, irrespective of age, an area of 1.50 square metres, i.e. 16 English square feet, and a height between decks of at least 1.80 metres, i.e. about 6 English feet.

It is forbidden to accommodate pilgrims under the first between-deck, that is below the water line.

Satisfactory ventilation must be ensured and below the upper between-deck must be supplemented by mechanical ventilation.

In addition to the space reserved for pilgrims, the ship must provide, on the upper deck, for each person, irrespective of age, a free area of not less than 0.56 square metres, i.e. about 6 English square feet, in addition to the area upon the upper deck, reserved for temporary hospital, the crew, shower baths, and latrines, and for the working of the ship.

ARTICLE 101

On deck places must be set apart, screened from view, of which a sufficient number must be for the exclusive use of women.

These places shall be provided with water pipes under pressure, and provided with taps or douches in such a way as to furnish at all times sea water for the use of the pilgrims even if the ship is lying at anchor.

There shall be one tap or douche for every hundred or fraction of 100 pilgrims.

ARTICLE 102

The vessel must be provided, in addition to closets for the crew, with latrines, fitted with a flushing apparatus or with a water tap.

Some of these latrines shall be reserved exclusively for women.

Latrines must be in the proportion of two per 100 pilgrims, or fraction of 100.

There must be no water closets in the hold.

ARTICLE 103

The vessel must have two places for cooking set apart for the use of the pilgrims.

ARTICLE 104

Infirmaries meeting proper conditions of safety and wholesomeness must be reserved for the accommodation of the sick. They must be on the main deck unless in the opinion of the sanitary authority equally healthy accommodations can be provided elsewhere.

They must be constructed so as to allow persons suffering from infectious diseases and persons who have been in contact with them, to be isolated according to the nature of their illness.

The infirmaries, including temporary infirmaries, must be capable of accommodating at the rate of 3 square metres, i.e. about 32 English square feet per patient, not less than 4 per 100 or fraction of 100 of the pilgrims taken on board.

The infirmaries must be provided with special latrines.

ARTICLE 105

Every vessel shall have on board the medicines, disinfectants, and articles necessary for the care of the sick. The regulations made for this kind of vessels by each Government shall determine the nature and quantity of the medicines. Every vessel must also carry the needful immunizing agents, especially cholera and smallpox vaccines. The care and the remedies shall be furnished free of charge to the pilgrims.

ARTICLE 106

Every vessel embarking pilgrims shall have on board a physician holding a regular diploma who must be acceptable to the Government of the country of the first port in which pilgrims embarked on the outward journey. A second physician meeting the same conditions shall be embarked as soon as the number of pilgrims carried by the vessel exceeds one thousand.

ARTICLE 107

The captain shall be obliged to have handbills posted on board in a position which is conspicuous and accessible to those interested. They shall be in the principal languages of the countries inhabited by the pilgrims embarked, and show:

1. The destination of the vessel;
2. The price of the tickets;
3. The daily ration of water and food allowed to each pilgrim according to the regulations of the country of origin;
4. A price list of victuals not comprised in the daily ration and to be paid for extra.

ARTICLE 108

The heavy baggage of the pilgrims shall be registered and numbered. The pilgrims will be allowed to keep with them only such articles as are absolutely necessary. The regulations made by each Government for its vessels will determine the nature, quantity, and dimensions of the said articles.

ARTICLE 109

Extracts from the provisions of Chapters I, II (sections I, II and III), and III of the present Title shall be posted, in the form of regulations, in the language of the nationality of the vessel as well as in the principal languages of the countries inhabited by the pilgrims embarked, in a conspicuous and accessible place on each deck and between decks on every vessel carrying pilgrims.

SECTION II. MEASURES TO BE TAKEN BEFORE DEPARTURE

ARTICLE 110

At least three days before departure the captain, or in the absence of the captain the owner or agent, of every pilgrim ship must declare his intention to embark pilgrims to the competent authority of the port of departure. In ports of call the captain, or in the absence of the captain the owner or agent, of every pilgrim ship must make this same declaration twelve hours before the departure of the vessel. This declaration must indicate the intended day of sailing and the destination of the vessel.

ARTICLE 111

Upon the declaration prescribed by the preceding article being made, the competent authority shall proceed to the inspection and measurement of the vessel at the expense of the captain.

The inspection only shall be made if the captain is already provided with a certificate of measurement issued by the competent authority of his country, unless it is suspected that the document no longer corresponds to the actual state of the vessel.

ARTICLE 112

The competent authority shall not permit the departure of a pilgrim ship until he has ascertained:

(a) That the vessel has been put in a state of perfect cleanliness and, if necessary, disinfected;

(b) That the vessel is in a condition to undertake the voyage without danger; that she is provided with the necessary plant and appliances for use in case of shipwreck, accident or fire, particularly a wireless apparatus for sending and receiving messages, that may be operated independently of the main engine-room; that she carries a sufficient number of life-saving devices; that she is properly outfitted, appointed, ventilated, and provided with awnings of sufficient thickness and size to shelter the decks, and that there is nothing on board that is or may become injurious to the health or safety of the passengers;

(c) That, in addition to the stores for the vessel and the crew, there are provisions and fuel of good quality on board in places where they can be suitably stored and in sufficient quantity for all the pilgrims and for the entire duration of the voyage;

(d) That the drinking water taken on board is of good quality; that there is a sufficient quantity thereof; that the tanks of drinking water on board are protected against all tainting and closed in such a way that the water can only be let out through the stop cocks or pumps. The devices for letting water out called "suckers" are absolutely forbidden;

(e) That the vessel has a distilling apparatus capable of producing at least 5 liters of water per head each day for every person embarked, including the crew;

(f) That the vessel has a disinfecting chamber whose safety and efficiency have been ascertained by the health authority of the port of embarkation of the pilgrims;

(g) That the crew comprises a physician holding a diploma and as well informed as possible on questions of maritime health and exotic pathology, and who must be acceptable to the Government of the first port where pilgrims embarked on the outward journey, and that the vessel has a supply of medicines in accordance with Article 105;

(h) That the deck of the vessel is free from all cargo and other incumbrances;

(i) That the arrangements of the vessel are such that the measures prescribed by Section III hereinafter may be executed.

ARTICLE 113

The captain shall not sail until he has in his possession:

1. A list viséed by the competent authority and showing the name and sex, of the pilgrims who have been taken on board, and total number of the pilgrims whom he is authorized to embark;

2. A document stating the name, nationality, and tonnage of the vessel, the name of the captain and of the physician, the exact number of persons embarked (crew, pilgrims, and other passengers), the nature of the cargo, and the port of departure.

The competent authority shall indicate on the bill of health whether the number of pilgrims allowed by the regulations is reached or not, and, in case it is not reached, the additional number of passengers which the vessel is authorized to embark in subsequent ports of call.

SECTION III. MEASURES TO BE TAKEN DURING THE PASSAGE

ARTICLE 114

The deck intended for the pilgrims shall remain free from encumbering objects during the voyage and shall be reserved day and night for the persons on board and be placed gratuitously at their service.

ARTICLE 115

Every day the space between decks shall be cleaned carefully and scrubbed with sand while the pilgrims are on deck.

ARTICLE 116

The latrines intended for the passengers as well as those for the crew shall be kept neat and be cleansed and disinfected three times a day, and oftener if needed.

ARTICLE 117

The excretions and dejections of persons showing symptoms of plague or cholera, dysentery or any other disease preventing their using the infirmary latrines shall be collected in vessels containing a disinfecting solution. These vessels shall be emptied into the infirmary latrines which shall be thoroughly disinfected after each projection of matter.

ARTICLE 118

Articles of bedding, carpets, and clothing which have been in contact with the patients mentioned in the preceding article shall be immediately disinfected. The observance of this rule is especially recommended with regard to the clothing of persons who come near to these patients and which may have become soiled.

Such of the articles mentioned above as have no value shall be thrown overboard, if the vessel is neither in a port nor a canal, or else destroyed by fire. The others shall be disinfected as directed by the ship physician.

ARTICLE 119

The quarters occupied by the patients and referred to in Article 104 shall be thoroughly and regularly disinfected.

ARTICLE 120

The quantity of drinking water allowed daily to each pilgrim free of charge, whatever be his age, shall be at least 5 liters.

ARTICLE 121

If there is any doubt about the quality of the drinking water or any possibility of its contamination either at the place of its origin or during the course of the voyage, the water shall be boiled or otherwise sterilized, and the captain shall be obliged to throw it overboard at the first port in which a stop is made and in which he is able to procure a better supply. He may only take it on board after the tanks shall have been disinfected.

ARTICLE 122

The physician shall examine the pilgrims, attend the patients, and see that the rules of hygiene are observed on board. He shall especially:

1. Satisfy himself that the provisions dealt out to the pilgrims are of good quality, that their quantity is in conformity with the obligations assumed, and that they are suitably prepared;

2. Satisfy himself that the requirements of article 120 relative to the distribution of water are observed;

3. If there is any doubt about the quality of the drinking water, remind the captain in writing of the provisions of Article 121;

4. Satisfy himself that the vessel is maintained in a constant state of cleanliness, and especially that the latrines are cleaned in accordance with the provisions of Article 116;

5. Satisfy himself that the lodgings of the pilgrims are maintained in a healthful condition, and that, in case of transmissible disease, they are disinfected in conformity with Article 119;

6. Keep a diary of all the sanitary incidents occurring during the course of the voyage and present on request this diary to the competent authority of the port of call or arrival.

ARTICLE 123

The persons intrusted with the care of patients suffering with the plague, cholera or other diseases shall alone have access to them and shall have no contact with the other persons on board.

ARTICLE 124

In case of a death occurring during the voyage, the captain shall make note of the death opposite the name on the list viséed by the authority of the port of departure, besides entering on his journal the name of the deceased person, his age, where he comes from, the presumable cause of his death according to the physician's certificate, and the date of the death.

In case of death by a transmissible disease, the body shall be wrapped in a shroud saturated with a disinfecting solution and thrown overboard.

ARTICLE 125

The captain shall see that the prophylactic measures executed during the voyage are recorded in the ship's journal. This journal shall be presented by him to the competent authority of the port of arrival.

In each port of call the captain shall have the list prepared in accordance with Article 113 viséed by the competent authority.

In case a pilgrim is landed during the course of the voyage, the captain shall note the fact on the list opposite the name of the pilgrim.

In case of an embarkation, the persons embarked shall be mentioned on this list in conformity with the aforementioned Article 113 and before it is viséed again by the competent authority.

ARTICLE 126

The bill of health delivered at the port of departure shall not be changed during the course of the voyage. If this requirement is not complied with, the vessel may be treated as an infected vessel.

It shall be viséed by the health authority of each port of call, who shall note thereon:

1. The number of passengers landed or embarked in that port;

2. The incidents occurring at sea and affecting the health or life of the persons on board;

3. The sanitary condition of the port of call.

SECTION IV. MEASURES TO BE TAKEN ON THE ARRIVAL OF PILGRIMS IN THE RED SEA

A. Sanitary measures applicable to pilgrim ships bound from the south toward Hedjaz

ARTICLE 127

Pilgrim ships hailing from the south and bound for Hedjaz shall first stop at the sanitary station of Camaran, where they shall be subjected to the measures prescribed in the following articles.

ARTICLE 128

Vessels recognized as *uninfected* after a medical inspection shall obtain pratique when the following operations are completed:

The pilgrims shall be landed; take a shower or sea bath; and their soiled linen and the part of their wearing apparel and baggage which appears suspicious in the opinion of the health authority shall be disinfected. The duration of these operations, including debarkation and embarkation, shall not exceed forty-eight hours. Provided the time limit be not exceeded, the sanitary authority may perform such bacteriological examinations as may be deemed necessary.

If no real or suspected case of plague or cholera is discovered during these operations, the pilgrims shall be reembarked immediately and the vessel shall proceed toward Jeddah.

Vessels found, on medical inspection, to be uninfected shall not undergo the measures prescribed hereinabove, if the following conditions are fulfilled:

(1) All pilgrims on board have been immunized against cholera and smallpox;

(2) The requirements of this Convention have been strictly followed;

(3) There is no reason to doubt the declaration of the captain and doctor of the ship to the effect that no case of plague, cholera or smallpox has occurred on board, either at the time of departure or during the voyage.

For plague, the provisions of Article 27 shall be applied with regard to the rats which may be found on board the vessels.

ARTICLE 129

Suspicious vessels on board of which there were cases of plague in the six days following the embarkation and on board of which an unusual mortality of rats is discovered or cases of cholera at the time of departure but no new case in the last five days, shall be treated in the following manner:

The pilgrims shall be landed; take a shower or sea bath; and their soiled linen and the part of their wearing apparel and baggage which appears suspicious in the opinion of the health authority shall be disinfected; the parts of the vessel that have been occupied by the patients shall be disinfected. The duration of these operations, including debarkation and embarkation, shall not exceed forty-eight hours. Provided this period is not exceeded, such bacteriological examination as may be considered necessary by the sanitary authority may be made.

If no real or suspected case of plague or cholera is discovered during these operations, the pilgrims shall be reembarked immediately and the vessel shall proceed to Jeddah.

For plague, the provisions of Article 26 shall be applicable with regard to the rats which may be found on board.

ARTICLE 130

Infected vessels, that is, those having cases of plague or cholera on board or having had cases of plague more than six days after embarkation, or cholera on board within five days, or on board of which rats infected by plague have been discovered, shall undergo the following treatment:

The persons stricken with plague or cholera shall be landed and isolated at the hospital. The other passengers shall be landed and isolated in groups comprising as few persons as possible, so that the whole number may not suffer with and for a particular group in which plague or cholera should develop.

The soiled linen, wearing apparel, and clothing of the crew and passengers, as well as the vessel, shall be disinfected.

However the local health authority may decide that the unloading of the heavy baggage and the cargo is not necessary, and that only a part of the vessel need be disinfected.

The passengers shall remain in the Camaran establishment five or six days according as whether the case is plague or cholera. If a new case should occur after disembarkation, the period of observation shall be extended by five days for cholera and six days for plague, to date from the isolation of the last case.

For plague, the measures prescribed by Article 25 shall be applied with regard to the rats which may be found on board the vessels.

When these operations have been completed, the ship, having reembarked its pilgrims, shall be sent on to Jeddah.

ARTICLE 131

Ships, to which Articles 128, 129 and 130 apply, will be subject to medical inspection on board on arrival at Jeddah.

If the result is favorable, the ship shall receive free pratique.

If, on the other hand, well established cases of plague or cholera have occurred on board during the voyage, or at the time of arrival at Jeddah, the sanitary authority of the Hedjaz may take all necessary measures subject to the provisions of Article 54.

ARTICLE 132

Every sanitary station designed to receive pilgrims should be provided with a trained, experienced, and sufficiently numerous staff, as well as with all the buildings and apparatus necessary to insure the application, in their entirety, of the measures to which said pilgrims are subject.

B. Sanitary measures applicable to pilgrim ships hailing from north of Port Said and bound toward Hedjaz

ARTICLE 133

If plague or cholera is not found to exist in the port of departure or its neighborhood, and if no case of plague or cholera has occurred during the passage, the vessel shall be immediately granted pratique.

ARTICLE 134

If plague or cholera is known to exist in the port of departure or its vicinity, or if a case of plague or cholera has occurred during the voyage, the vessel shall be subjected at Tor to the rules established for vessels coming from the south and stopping at Camaran. The vessels shall thereupon be granted pratique.

SECTION V. MEASURES TO BE TAKEN UPON THE RETURN OF PILGRIMS

A. Pilgrim ships returning northward

ARTICLE 135

Every vessel bound for Suez or for a Mediterranean port, having on board pilgrims or similar masses of persons, and hailing from a port of Hedjaz or from any other port on the Arabian coast of the Red Sea, must repair to Tor in order to undergo there the observation and the sanitary measures indicated in Articles 140 to 142.

ARTICLE 136

Pending the creation at the port of Akaba of a quarantine station meeting the requirements, pilgrims going from the Hedjaz to Akaba by sea shall undergo the necessary quarantine measures at Tor before landing at Akaba.

ARTICLE 137

Vessels bringing pilgrims back toward the Mediterranean shall pass through the canal in quarantine only.

ARTICLE 138

The agents of navigation companies and captains are warned that, after completing their observation period at the sanitary station of Tor, the

Egyptian pilgrims will alone be permitted to leave the vessel permanently in order to return thereupon to their homes.

Only those pilgrims will be recognized as Egyptians or as residents of Egypt who are provided with a certificate of residence issued by an Egyptian authority and conforming to the established model.

Pilgrims other than Egyptians, can not be landed in an Egyptian port after leaving Tor, except by special permit under special conditions imposed by the Egyptian health authority, in accord with the Sanitary, Maritime and Quarantine Board of Egypt. Consequently, navigation agents and captains are warned that the transshipment of pilgrims not residents of Egypt at Tor, Suez, Port Said, or Alexandria is forbidden except under a special permit for each case.

Vessels having pilgrims on board who are not Egyptian nationals shall be subject to the rules applicable to these pilgrims and shall not be received in any Egyptian port of the Mediterranean.

Article 139

Egyptian pilgrims shall undergo an observation of three days and a medical examination and if there be occasion, disinfection and disinsectisation at Tor, or any other station designated by the Sanitary, Maritime and Quarantine Board of Egypt.

Article 140

If plague or cholera is found to exist in Hedjaz or in the port from which the vessel hails, or if it has existed in Hedjaz during the course of the pilgrimage, the vessel shall be subjected at Tor to the rules adopted at Camaran for infected vessels.

The persons stricken with plague or cholera shall be landed and isolated in the hospitals. The other passengers shall be landed and isolated in groups composed of as few persons as possible, so that the whole number may not suffer with any particular group in which the plague or cholera should develop.

The soiled linen, wearing apparel, and clothing of the crew and passengers, as well as the baggage and cargo suspected of contamination shall be landed and disinfected. Their disinfection as well as that of the vessel shall be thorough.

However, the local health authority may decide that the unloading of the heavy baggage and the cargo is not necessary, and that only a part of the vessel need undergo disinfection.

The measures provided in Article 25 shall be applied with regard to the rats which may be found on board.

All the pilgrims shall be subjected to an observation of six full days from the day on which the disinfecting operations are completed, in the case of plague and five days in the case of cholera. If a case of plague or cholera has appeared in one section, the period of six or five days shall not begin for this section until the day on which the last case was discovered.

ARTICLE 141

In the case contemplated in the preceding article, the Egyptian pilgrims shall be subjected, besides, to an additional observation of three days.

ARTICLE 142

If plague or cholera is not found to exist either in Hedjaz or in the port from which the vessel hails, and has not been known to exist in Hedjaz during the course of the pilgrimage, the vessel shall be subjected at Tor to the rules adopted at Camaran for uninfected vessels.

The pilgrims shall be landed and take a shower or sea bath, and their soiled linen or the part of their wearing apparel and baggage which may appear suspicious in the opinion of the health authority shall be disinfected. The duration of these operations shall not exceed seventy-two hours.

However, a pilgrim ship, if it has had no plague or cholera patients during the course of the voyage from Djeddah to Yambo or Tor and if the individual medical examination made at Tor after debarkation establishes the fact that it contains no such patients, may be authorized by the Sanitary, Maritime and Quarantine Board of Egypt to pass through the Suez Canal in quarantine even at night when the following four conditions are fulfilled:

1. Medical attendance shall be given on board by one or several physicians graduated and duly accepted;
2. The vessel shall be provided with disinfecting chambers in good working order;
3. It shall be shown that the number of pilgrims does not exceed that authorized by the pilgrimage regulations;
4. The captain shall bind himself to repair directly to the port which he names as his next call port.

The sanitary tax to be paid to the quarantine administration shall be the same as the pilgrims would have paid had they remained in quarantine three days.

ARTICLE 143

A vessel which has had a suspicious case on board during the voyage from Tor to Suez may be sent back to Tor.

ARTICLE 144

The transshipment of pilgrims is strictly forbidden in Egyptian ports except by special permit and on the conditions laid by the Egyptian sanitary authority in accord with the Sanitary, Maritime and Quarantine Board of Egypt.

ARTICLE 145

Vessels leaving Hedjaz and having on board pilgrims who are bound for a port on the African shore of the Red Sea shall proceed directly to the quarantine station named by the territorial authority to which that port belongs, where they shall submit to the same quarantine procedure as at Tor.

ARTICLE 146

Vessels sailing from Hedjaz or from a port on the Arabian coast of the Red Sea, in which neither the plague nor cholera prevails, which have no pilgrims or similar groups of people on board, and have had no suspicious occurrence during the voyage, shall be granted pratique at Suez after a favorable medical inspection.

ARTICLE 147

Passengers coming from the Hedjaz who have accompanied the pilgrimage shall be subject to the same measures as pilgrims. The appellation of merchant or any other will not exempt them from the measures applicable to the pilgrims.

B. Returning pilgrims going north by caravan

ARTICLE 148

Whatever the sanitary condition in the Hedjaz may be, pilgrims travelling by caravan must repair to one of the quarantine stations upon their route, there to undergo according to circumstances the measures prescribed by Articles 140 or 142 for pilgrims who have been landed.

C. Pilgrims returning southward

ARTICLE 149

In the event of the pilgrimage being infected, pilgrim ships, returning to places south of the Straits of Bab-el-Mandeb, may be required, by direction of the consular authority of the countries to which the pilgrims are going to stop at Camaran and there undergo medical inspection.

SECTION VI. MEASURES APPLICABLE TO PILGRIMS TRAVELLING BY THE HEDJAZ RAILWAY

ARTICLE 150

The Governments of the countries through which the Hedjaz railway passes shall make all necessary arrangements to organize the sanitary supervision of pilgrims during their journey to the Holy Places, and the application of prophylactic measures in order to prevent the dissemination of infectious diseases presenting epidemic features bearing in mind the principles of the present Convention.

SECTION VII. SANITARY INFORMATION CONCERNING THE PILGRIMAGE

ARTICLE 151

The Sanitary, Maritime and Quarantine Board of Egypt will transmit periodically, and if occasion arises, by the speediest route, to the sanitary authorities of all the countries interested, and concurrently, to the International Office of Public Hygiene under the conditions provided by this convention, all sanitary information and reports that may come to its knowledge during the pilgrimage concerning the sanitary condition of the Hedjaz and the countries through which the pilgrims pass. It will also get up an annual report which shall be sent to the said authorities and the International Office of Public Hygiene.

CHAPTER III. *Sanctions*

ARTICLE 152

Every captain convicted of not having conformed, in the distribution of water, provisions, or fuel, to the obligations assumed by or for him, shall be liable to a fine of not more than fifty francs (gold) for every failure. This fine shall be collected for the benefit of the pilgrim who shall have been the victim of the default, and who shall prove that he has vainly demanded the execution of the agreement made.

ARTICLE 153

Every infraction of Article 107 shall be punished by a fine of not more than 750 francs (gold).

ARTICLE 154

Every captain who has committed or knowingly permitted any fraud whatever concerning the list of pilgrims or the bill of health provided for in Article 113 shall be liable to a fine of not more than 1,250 francs (gold).

ARTICLE 155

Every captain of a vessel arriving without a bill of health of the port of departure, or without a visé of the ports of call, or who is not provided with the list required by the regulations and regularly kept in accordance with Article 113 and Articles 125 and 126, shall be liable in each case to a fine of not more than three hundred francs (gold).

ARTICLE 156

Every captain convicted of having or having had on board more than 100 pilgrims without the presence of a graduated physician according to the provisions of Article 106 shall be liable to a fine of not more than 7,500 francs (gold).

ARTICLE 157

Every captain convicted of having or having had on board a greater number of pilgrims than that which he is authorized to embark according to the provisions of subsection 1 of Article 113 shall be liable to a fine of not more than 125 francs (gold) for each pilgrim in excess.

The pilgrims in excess of the regular number shall be landed at the first station at which a competent authority resides, and the captain shall be obliged to furnish the landed pilgrims with the money necessary to pursue their voyage to their destination.

ARTICLE 158

Every captain convicted of having landed pilgrims at a place other than their destination, except with their consent, or excepting cases of *vis major*, shall be liable to a fine of not more than 500 francs (gold) for each pilgrim wrongfully landed.

ARTICLE 159

All other infractions of the provisions relative to pilgrim ships are punishable by a fine of not less than 250 nor more than 2,500 francs (gold).

ARTICLE 160

Every violation proven in the course of a voyage shall be noted on the ship's papers as well as on the list of pilgrims. The competent authority shall draw up a report thereof and deliver it to the proper party.

ARTICLE 161

Contraventions of Articles 152 to 159 inclusive will be certified by the sanitary authority of the port at which the ship has called.

Penalties will be imposed by the competent authority.

ARTICLE 162

All agents called upon to assist in the execution of the provisions of the present Convention with regard to pilgrim ships are liable to punishment in conformity with the laws of their respective countries in case of faults committed by them in the application of the said provisions.

TITLE IV. SURVEILLANCE AND EXECUTION

I. SANITARY, MARITIME AND QUARANTINE BOARD OF EGYPT

ARTICLE 163

The stipulations of Appendix III of the Sanitary Convention of Venice of January 30, 1892, concerning the composition, powers and duties, and operation of the Sanitary, Maritime and Quarantine Board of Egypt, are confirmed as they appear in the khedival decrees under date of June 19, 1893, and December 25, 1894, as well as in the ministerial decision of June 19, 1893.[10]

The said decrees and decisions are annexed to the present convention.

Notwithstanding the provisions of the said decrees and decisions the high contracting parties agree that—

I. The number of Egyptian delegates on the Egyptian Sanitary, Maritime and Quarantine Board shall be increased to five:

(1) The President of the Board, appointed by the Egyptian Government, and who will only have a casting vote;

(2) A European doctor of medicine, Inspector-General of the Sanitary, Maritime and Quarantine Service;

(3) Three delegates appointed by the Egyptian Government.

II. The Veterinary Service of the Sanitary, Maritime and Quarantine Board shall be transferred to the Egyptian Government.

The following conditions shall be observed:

(1) The Egyptian Government will collect sanitary taxes on imported cattle not to exceed those now collected by the Egyptian Sanitary, Maritime and Quarantine Board;

(2) The Egyptian Government undertakes in consequence to pay annually to the Sanitary, Maritime and Quarantine Board a sum representing the average of the excess of receipts over the expenditures of the said service during the three budgetary years preceding the date on which the present Convention is put into force.

(3) The measures to be taken for the disinfection of cattle ships, of skins, and of other animals' derivatives, shall be as in the past in charge of the Sanitary, Maritime, and Quarantine Board.

(4) The foreign personnel now in the veterinary service of the Sanitary, Maritime and Quarantine Board will be granted the benefit of the salaries appropriated by Law No. 28 of 1923, regarding the conditions of service and the retirement or discharge of officials, employees or agents of foreign nationality.

Grading of salaries shall be as provided by the above-mentioned law. The other details will be fixed by an agreement between the Egyptian Government and the Sanitary, Maritime and Quarantine Board.

III. On account of the great distance between the Port of Suakim and the headquarters of the Egyptian Sanitary, Maritime and Quarantine Board at Alexandria, and the fact that the pilgrims and passengers who disembark in this port of Suakim concern from the sanitary point of view only the territory

---

[10] For text, see *ante*, vol. 1, pp. 404, 409, and 410.

of the Soudan, the sanitary administration of this port will be detached from the said Board.

ARTICLE 164

The ordinary expenses resulting from the provisions of the present Convention, especially those relating to the increase of the personnel belonging to the Sanitary, Maritime and Quarantine Board of Egypt, shall be covered by means of an annual supplementary payment by the Egyptian Government of the sum of 4,000 Egyptian pounds, which may be taken from the surplus revenues from the lighthouse service remaining at the disposal of said Government.

However, the proceeds of a supplementary quarantine tax of ten tariff dollars per pilgrim to be collected at Tor shall be deducted from this sum.

In case the Egyptian Government should find difficulty in bearing this share of the expenses, the Powers represented in the Sanitary, Maritime and Quarantine Board shall reach an understanding with that Government in order to insure the participation of the latter in the expenses contemplated.

ARTICLE 165

The Sanitary, Maritime and Quarantine Board of Egypt shall undertake the task of bringing the provisions of the present Convention into conformity with the regulations at present enforced by it in regard to the plague, cholera, and yellow fever, as well as with the regulations relative to arrivals from the Arabian ports of the Red Sea during the pilgrim season.

To the same end it shall, if occasion arises, revise the general regulations of the sanitary, maritime, and quarantine police at present in force.

These regulations, in order to become effective must be accepted by the various powers represented on the Board.

II. MISCELLANEOUS PROVISIONS

ARTICLE 166

The proceeds from the sanitary taxes and fines collected by the Sanitary, Maritime and Quarantine Board shall in no case be employed for objects other than those within the province of the said Board.

ARTICLE 167

The High Contracting Parties agree to have a set of instructions prepared by their health departments for the purpose of enabling captains of vessels, especially when there is no physician on board, to enforce the provisions contained in the present convention with regard to plague, cholera, and yellow fever.

TITLE V. FINAL PROVISIONS

ARTICLE 168

The present Convention supersedes, as between the High Contracting Parties, the provisions of the Convention signed at Paris on January 17th, 1912, and also, the case arising, those of the Convention signed at Paris on December 3rd, 1903.[11] These two last named Conventions will remain in force as between the High Contracting Parties and any State which is a party thereto and is not a party to the present Convention.

ARTICLE 169

The present Convention will bear to-day's date and may be signed up to October 1st of the current year.

ARTICLE 170

The present Convention shall be ratified and the ratifications shall be deposited at Paris as soon as possible. It shall not come into force until it has been ratified by ten of the High Contracting Parties. Thereafter it will take effect as regards each High Contracting Party from the date of the deposit of its ratification.

ARTICLE 171

The States which have not signed the present Convention shall be permitted to adhere thereto upon request. Notice of this adhesion shall be given through diplomatic channels to the Government of the French Republic and by the latter to the other Contracting Parties.

ARTICLE 172

Any of the High Contracting Parties may declare, at the moment either of its signature, ratification or accession, that its acceptance of the present Convention does not include either all or any of its protectorates, colonies, possessions or mandated territories, and may subsequently accede, in accordance with the preceding Article, on behalf of any one of its protectorates, colonies, possessions or mandated territories excluded by such declaration.

In faith whereof the respective Plenipotentiaries have signed the present Convention.

Done at Paris the twenty-first day of June, nineteen hundred and twenty-six, in a single copy, which will remain deposited in the archives of the Government of the French Republic, and of which certified copies will be transmitted through the diplomatic channel to the other Contracting Parties.

---

[11] TS 466, *ante*, vol. 1, p. 359.

For Afghanistan:
ISLAMBEK KHOUDOIAR KHAN

For Albania:
DR. OSMAN

For Germany:
FRANOUX
HAMEL

For Argentina:
F. A. DE TOLEDO

For Austria:
DR. ALFRED GRUNBERGER

For Belgium:
VELCHE

For Brazil:
CARLOS CHAGAS
GILBERTO MOURA COSTA

For Bulgaria:
B. MORFOFF
TOCHKO PÉTROFF

For Chile:
ARMANDO QUEZADA

For China:
S. K. YAO
SCIE TON FA

For Colombia:
MIGUEL JIMÉNEZ LOPEZ

For Cuba:
R. HERNANDEZ PORTELA

For Denmark:
TH. MADSEN

For Danzig:
CHODZKO
STADE

For the Dominican Republic:
BETANCES

For Egypt:
FAKHRY
DR. M. EL GUINDY

For Ecuador:
J. ILLINGOURTH

For Spain:
MARQUIS DE FAURA
DR. F. MURILLO

For the United States of America:
H. S. CUMMING
W. W. KING

For Ethiopia:
LAGARDE, DUC D'ENTOTTO

For Finland:
ENCKELL

For France:
CAMILLE BARRÈRE
HARISMENDY
NAVAILLES
DR. A. CALMETTE
LÉON BERNARD

For Algeria:
DR. RAYNAUD

For West Africa:
DR. PAUL GOUZIEN

For East Africa:
THIROUX

For Indo-China:
DR. L'HERMINIER
DR. N. BERNARD

For the States of Syria, Greater Lebanon, the Alaouïtes and Jebel ed Druz:
HARISMENDY

For all other colonies, protectorates, possessions and territories under French mandate:
AUDIBERT

For the British Empire:
G. S. BUCHANAN
JOHN MURRAY

For Canada:
J. A. AMYOT

For Australia:
W. C. SAWERS

For New Zealand:
SYDNEY PRICE JAMES

For India:
D. T. CHADWICK

For the Union of South Africa:
PHILIP STOCK

For Greece:
AL. C. CARAPANOS
D. MATARANGAS

For Guatemala:
FRANCISCO A. FIGUEROA

For Haiti:
GEORGES AUDAIN

For the Hedjaz:
DR. MAHMOUD HAMOUDÉ

For Honduras:
RUBÉN AUDINO AGUILAR

For Hungary:
DR. CH. GROSCH

For Italy:
ALBERT LUTRARIO
GIOVANNI VITTORIO REPETTI
ODOARDO HUETTER
G. ROCCO
GUISEPPE DRUETTI

For Japan:
H. MATSUSHIMA
MITSUZO TSURUMI

For the Republic of Liberia:
R. LEHMANN
N. OOMS

For Lithuania:
DR. PR. VAICIUSKA

For Luxembourg:
DR. PRAUM

For Morocco:
HARISMENDY
DR. RAYNAUD

For Mexico:
R. CABRERA

For Monaco:
F. ROUSSEL
DR. MARSAN

For Norway:
SIGURD BENTZON

For Paraguay:
R. V. CABALLERO

For the Netherlands:
DOUDE VAN TROOSTWYK
N. M. JOSEPHUS JITTA
DE VOGEL
VAN DER PLAS

For Peru:
P. MIMBELA

For Persia, ad referendum:
DR. ALI KAHN PARTOW AAZAM
MANSOUR CHARIF

For Poland:
CHODZKO

For Portugal:
RICARDO JORGE

For Rumania:
DR. J. CANTACUZÈNE

For San Marino:
DR. GUELPA

For the Kingdom of the Serbs, Croats
and Slovenes:
M. SPALAIKOVITCH

For Salvador:
CARLOS R. LARDÉ-ARTHÉS

For the Soudan:
OLIVER FRANCIS HAYNES ATKEY

For Switzerland:
DUNANT
CARRIÈRE

For Czechoslovakia:
DR. LADISLAV PROCHAZKA

For Tunis:
NAVAILLES

For Turkey:
A. FÉTHY

For the Union of the Soviet Socialist
Republics:
J. DAVTIAN
J. MAMMOULIA
L. BRONSTEIN
O. MEBOURNOUTOFF
N. FREYBERG
AL. SYSSINE
V. EGORIEW

For Uruguay:
A. HEROSA

For Venezuela, ad referendum:
JOSÉ IG. CARDENAS

ANNEXES

[For text of Khedival decrees of June 19, 1893, and December 25, 1894, and ministerial decision of June 19, 1893, concerning the operation of the Sanitary, Maritime, and Quarantine Service, see *ante,* volume 1, pages 404, 409, and 410.]

PROTOCOL OF SIGNATURE

The undersigned Plenipotentiaries met on the date of this day for the purpose of signing the International Sanitary Convention.

The Plenipotentiaries of the German Empire referring to Article 25 make express reservations as to the power granted by the Convention to several governments to enforce the observation in case of bubonic plague.

The Plenipotentiaries of Brazil declare they are empowered to sign the Convention ad referendum under the reservations entered in the minutes of the last plenary session.

The Plenipotentiaries of Chile declare that they join in the reservations made by the Plenipotentiaries of Brazil and Portugal.

The Plenipotentiaries of China express reservations in the name of their Government concerning the engagement appearing in Article 8, 2nd Section, that it would be compulsory to declare the diseases coming under the Convention.

In the name of their Government the Plenipotentiaries of Egypt renew the express reservations made by them concerning the presence at the Convention of a delegate representing the Soudan. They furthermore declare that the said presence could not in any way affect the rights of sovereignty of Egypt.

The Plenipotentiaries of Spain declare they make in the name of their Government a reservation identical with that of the Plenipotentiaries of the United States of America concerning article 12.

The Plenipotentiaries of the United States of America formally declare that their signing the International Sanitary Convention of this date is not to be construed to mean that the United States of America recognizes a régime or entity acting as Government of a signatory or adhering Power when that régime or entity is not recognized by the United States as the Government of that Power. They further declare that the participation of the United States of America in the International Sanitary Convention of this date does not involve any contractual obligation on the part of the United States to a signatory or adhering Power represented by a régime or entity which the United States does not recognize as representing the Government of that Power, until it is represented by a Government recognized by the United States.

The Plenipotentiaries of the United States of America declare, furthermore, that their Government reserves to itself the right to decide whether from the standpoint of the measures to be applied a foreign district is to be considered as infected and to decide what measures shall be applied to arrival in its own ports under special circumstances.

The great work accomplished by the International Sanitary Convention and the many new provisions carried could not be referred by telegraph to Her Majesty the Queen of Ethiopia and to His Imperial and Royal Highness Prince Tafari Makonnen, Heir to and Regent of the Empire, and the Delegate of the Ethiopian Empire declares that he must refrain from signing the Convention before he receives the necessary instructions.

The British Plenipotentiaries declare that their signing does not bind any part of the British Empire that is a distinct member of the League of Nations and would not sign separately or adhere to the Convention.

They further declare that they reserve the right not to apply the provisions of the 2nd subsection of article 8 to all the Protectorates, Colonies, Possessions or Countries under the British mandate which might be parties to the Convention and which on practical grounds might be unable to give full effect to those provisions relative to the compulsory declaration of the diseases referred to in the said article.

The Delegate of Canada reserves for his Government the right to decide whether from the viewpoint of the measures to be applied a foreign district is to be considered as infected and to decide what measures shall be applied to arrivals in Canadian ports under special circumstances. Subject to that reservation the Delegate from Canada declares that his Government is ready to take into consideration the obligations of article 12 of the Convention and the official information it may receive concerning the existence of the diseases in foreign countries.

The Delegate of India declares that he is authorized to sign the International Sanitary Convention under the reservation that on grounds of a practical nature India is not in a position to assume the obligations resulting from article 8 in so far as it has to do with the obligatory declaration of the diseases named in said article, except in large cities or in cases of epidemic.

The British Plenipotentiaries declare and wish to have it made a record that the reservation of the Plenipotentiaries of Persia about article 90 cannot in any way modify the present status quo pending an agreement to be arrived at between the Persian and British Governments.

The Plenipotentiaries of the Finnish Republic declare that immunization from cholera does not constitute a sufficient guarantee and that their Government reserves to itself notwithstanding the provisions of article 30, the right to make, if the occasion arises, immune persons undergo observation.

On the other hand, considering that the traffic of the Finnish border could only go over two railways in the east very close to each other and a single railway in the west which does not make it permissible to contemplate a partial closing of the frontier, Finland in order to avoid the complete closing in case of epidemic reserves to itself the right to set up observation if occasion arises notwithstanding the provisions in article 58.

The Plenipotentiaries of Japan declare that their Government reserves to itself the right: 1. To forward through the Eastern bureau of Singapore the notices and information, the mailing of which to the International Office of Public Hygiene is required by the Convention; 2. To take such measures as the sanitary authorities may deem necessary with regard to carriers of cholera vibrios.

The Plenipotentiaries of Lithuania declare that though adhering to the Convention, they make special reservations as to its being put into practice between Lithuania and Poland as long as normal relations between the two countries shall not have been restored.

These reservations are of particular importance with respect to the provisions in articles 9, 16, 57 and 66.

The Plenipotentiaries of The Netherlands declare in the name of their Government that it reserves to itself with regard to the Dutch East Indies to enforce the measures provided in article 10, sub-section 2 in the same degree to arrivals from districts afflicted with *murine plague*.

They further declare that their Government reserves to itself with respect to the Dutch East Indies the right to put on article 27–2 a construction to the effect that the destruction of rats referred to in that article may be applied to vessels taking a cargo from a district afflicted with murine plague when the sanitary authority believes that the cargo is likely to carry rats and is stowed in such a way as to make it imposssible to effect the search provided in the last sub-section of article 24.

The Plenipotentiaries of Persia declare that there is nothing warranting any special provision concerning the Persian Gulf being retained in the Convention. The fact that there is in the Convention article 90 constituting Section V of Title II, prevents their signing without making the most express reservations. The Plenipotentiaries of Persia further declare that the status quo could not in any way bind their Government. Again they reserve for their Government the right not to apply the provisions of article 8 relative to the obligatory declaration of the diseases coming under the said article.

The Plenipotentiary of Portugal declares that he is authorized by his Government to sign the Convention *ad referendum* with the reservations entered in the minutes of the last plenary session.

The Plenipotentiary of Turkey declares that Turkey would not relinquish by any treaty the right of being represented in the Sanitary, Maritime and Quarantine Board of Egypt. On the other hand taking into consideration the stipulations in the Convention of the Straits signed at Lausanne and the special conditions of the Straits of Bosphorus and Dardanelles, he reserves the right for the Sanitary Administration of Turkey to put a sanitary guard on board any merchant vessel going through the Straits without a physician and coming from an infected port so as to prevent that vessel from calling at any Turkish port. It is understood, however, that the delay and expenses that such a guard may entail will be very slight.

The Plenipotentiaries of the Union of the Soviet Socialist Republics, calling to mind the declarations made by them on May 26, at the session of the first Commission concerning article 7 of the draft of Convention declare they have no objection to offer to the provisions relative to the right of the International Office of Public Hygiene to make arrangements with other sanitary agencies; but they are of the opinion that that right flows from the arrangement of

Rome of 1907 which defines the functions of the Office. They therefore believe that the provision hereinabove referred to is but a confirmation of that right and should only appear in the minutes and not be made an article of the Convention itself.

The Plenipotentiaries of the Union of Soviet Socialist Republics call to mind that at the time article 12 of the Convention was under consideration they cast their votes against the provision granting the Governments the right to prolong in exceptional cases the application of sanitary measures notwithstanding the declaration of the State concerned that there is no longer any danger of the disease.

They hold that that provision may infringe upon one of the fundamental principles of the previous conventions and become a cause of misunderstanding that could arise from its application.

They therefore declare that in the spirit of the Convention that provision can only be considered in exceptional cases when the Government to which the afflicted district belongs does not meet the obligations laid down by the Convention in that respect.

The Plenipotentiaries of the Soviet Socialist Republics call to mind the reservations already made by them in second Commission concerning the functions, duties and powers of the sanitary, maritime and quarantine board of Egypt. They particularly wish to emphasize the fact that articles 70 and 164 in particular confer upon that board the right to set up different sanitary, maritime and quarantine police regulations on condition that those regulations in order to be capable of execution must be accepted by the different Powers represented in the Council. Inasmuch as the Union of the Soviet Socialist Republics is not yet represented in the sanitary, maritime and quarantine board of Egypt, the Delegation of the Union wishes to reserve the rights of its Government to accept or not to accept the measures worked out by that board.

The undersigned make a formal acknowledgment of the reservations hereinabove set forth and declare that their own countries reserve to themselves the right to invoke the benefit thereof as against the countries in whose name they were made.

In witness whereof, the Plenipotentiaries have signed this Protocol.
Done in Paris, June 21, 1926.

For Afghanistan:
ISLAMBEK KHOUDOIAR KHAN

For Albania:
DR. OSMAN

For the German Empire:
FRANOUX
HAMEL

For the Argentine Republic:
F. A. DE TOLEDO

For Austria:
DR. ALFRED GRUNBERGER

For Belgium:
VELCHE

For Brazil:
CARLOS CHAGAS
GILBERTO MOURA COSTA

For Bulgaria:
B. MORFOFF
TOCHKO PETROFF

For Chile:
ARMANDO QUEZADA

For China:
S. K. YAO
SCIE TON FA

For Colombia:
MIGUEL JIMÉMEZ LOPEZ

For Cuba:
R. HERNANDEZ PORTELA

For Denmark:
TH. MADSEN

For Danzig:
CHODZKO
STADE

For the Dominican Republic:
BETANCES

For Egypt:
FAKHRY
DR. M. EL GUINDY

For Ecuador:
J. ILLINGOURTH

For Spain:
MARQUIS DE FAURA
DR. F. MURILLO

For the United States of America:
H. S. CUMMING
W. W. KING

For Ethiopia:
LAGARDE, DUC D'ENTOTTO

For Finland:
ENCKELL

For France:
CAMILLE BARRÈRE
HARISMENDY
NAVAILLES
DR. A. CALMETTE
LÉON BERNARD

For Algeria:
DR. RAYNAUD

For West Africa:
DR. PAUL GOUZIEN

For East Africa:
THIROUX

For Indo-China:
DR. L'HERMINIER
DR. N. BERNARD

For the States of Syria, Greater Lebanon, the Alaouïtes and Jebel ed Druz:
HARISMENDY

For all other colonies, protectorates, possessions and territories under French mandate:
AUDIBERT

For the British Empire:
G. S. BUCHANAN
JOHN MURRAY

For Canada:
J. A. AMYOT

For Australia:
W. C. SAWERS

For New Zealand:
SYDNEY PRICE JAMES

For India:
D. T. CHADWICK

For the Union of South Africa:
PHILIP STOCK

For Greece:
AL. C. CARAPANOS
D. MATARAMGAS

For Guatemala:
FRANCISCO A. FIGUEROA

For Haiti:
GEORGES AUDAIN

For the Hedjaz:
DR. MAHMOUD HAMOUDE

For Honduras:
RUBÉN AUDINO AGUILAR

For Hungary:
DR. CH. GROSCH

For Italy:
ALBERT LUTRARIO
GIOVANNI VITTORIO REPETTI
ODOARDO HUETTER
G. ROCCO
GUISEPPE DRUETTI

For Japan:
H. MATSUSHIMA
MITSUZO TSURUMI

For the Republic of Liberia:
R. LEHMANN
N. OOMS

For Lithuania:
DR. PR. VAICIUSKA

For Luxembourg:
DR. PRAUM

For Morocco:
HARISMENDY
DR. RAYNAUD

For Mexico:
R. CABRERA

For Monaco:
F. ROUSSEL
DR. MARSAN

For Norway:
SIGURD BENTZON

For Paraguay:
R. V. CABALLERO

For the Netherlands:
DOUDE VAN TROOSTWYK
N. M. JOSEPHUS JITTA
DE VOGEL
VAN DER PLAS

For Peru:
P. MIMBELA

For Persia, ad referendum:
DR. ALI KHAN PARTOW AAZAM
MANSOUR CHARIF

For Poland:
CHODZKO

For Portugal:
RICARDO JORGE

For Rumania:
DR. J. CANTACUZÈNE

For San Marino:
DR. GUELPA

For the Kingdom of the Serbs, Croats
and Slovenes:
M. SPALAIKOVITCH

For Salvador:
CARLOS R. LARDÉ-ARTHÉS

For the Soudan:
OLIVER FRANCIS HAYNES ATKEY

For Switzerland:
DUNANT
CARRIÈRE

For Czechoslovakia:
DR. LADISLAV PROCHAZKA

For Tunis:
NAVAILLES

For Turkey:
A. FÉTHY

For the Union of the Soviet Socialist
Republics:
J. DAVTIAN
J. MAMMOULIA
L. BRONSTEIN
O. MEBOURNOUTOFF
N. FREYBERG
AL. SYSSINE
V. EGORIEW

For Uruguay:
A. HEROSA

For Venezuela, ad referendum:
JOSÉ IG. CARDENAS

SUPPRESSION OF SLAVE TRADE AND SLAVERY

Convention signed at Geneva September 25, 1926
Senate advice and consent to adherence, with a reservation, February 25, 1929 [1]
Adherence declared by the President of the United States, with a reservation, March 1, 1929 [1]
Adherence of the United States deposited with the Secretary-General of the League of Nations March 21, 1929
Entered into force March 9, 1927; for the United States March 21, 1929
Proclaimed by the President of the United States March 23, 1929
Amended by protocol of December 7, 1953, [2] *as between contracting parties to the protocol; supplemented by convention of September 7, 1956,* [3] *as between contracting parties to the later convention*

46 Stat. 2183; Treaty Series 778

SLAVERY CONVENTION

Albania, Germany, Austria, Belgium, the British Empire, Canada, the Commonwealth of Australia, the Union of South Africa, the Dominion of New Zealand, and India, Bulgaria, China, Colombia, Cuba, Denmark, Spain, Estonia, Abyssinia, Finland, France, Greece, Italy, Latvia, Liberia, Lithuania, Norway, Panama, the Netherlands, Persia, Poland, Portugal, Roumania, the Kingdom of the Serbs, Croats and Slovenes, Sweden, Czechoslovakia and Uruguay,

Whereas the signatories of the General Act of the Brussels Conference of 1889–90 [4] declared that they were equally animated by the firm intention of putting an end to the traffic in African slaves;

---

[1] The U.S. reservation reads as follows:

"That the Government of the United States, adhering to its policy of opposition to forced or compulsory labor except as a punishment for crime of which the person concerned has been duly convicted, adheres to the Convention except as to the first subdivision of the second paragraph of article five, which reads as follows:

" '(1) Subject to the transitional provisions laid down in paragraph (2) below, compulsory or forced labor may only be exacted for public purposes.' "

[2] 7 UST 479; TIAS 3532.
[3] 18 UST 3201; TIAS 6418.
[4] TS 383, *ante*, vol. 1, p. 134.

607

Whereas the signatories of the Convention of Saint-Germain-en-Laye of 1919 [5] to revise the General Act of Berlin of 1885 and the General Act and Declaration of Brussels of 1890 affirmed their intention of securing the complete suppression of slavery in all its forms and of the slave trade by land and sea;

Taking into consideration the report of the Temporary Slavery Commission appointed by the Council of the League of Nations on June 12th, 1924;

Desiring to complete and extend the work accomplished under the Brussels Act and to find a means of giving practical effect throughout the world to such intentions as were expressed in regard to slave trade and slavery by the signatories of the Convention of Saint-Germain-en-Laye, and recognising that it is necessary to conclude to that end more detailed arrangements than are contained in that Convention;

Considering, moreover, that it is necessary to prevent forced labour from developing into conditions analogous to slavery,

Have decided to conclude a Convention and have accordingly appointed as their Plenipotentiaries:

The President of the Supreme Council of Albania:
Dr. D. Dino, Envoy Extraordinary and Minister Plenipotentiary to His Majesty the King of Italy.

The President of the German Reich:
Dr. Carl von Schubert, Secretary of State for Foreign Affairs.

The President of the Federal Austrian Republic:
M. Emerich von Pflügl, Envoy Extraordinary and Minister Plenipotentiary, Representative of the Federal Government accredited to the League of Nations.

His Majesty the King of the Belgians:
M. L. de Brouckère, Member of the Senate, First Delegate of Belgium to the Seventh Ordinary Session of the Assembly of the League of Nations.

His Majesty the King of the United Kingdom of Great Britain and Ireland and of the British Dominions beyond the Seas, Emperor of India:
The Right Honourable Viscount Cecil of Chelwood, K.C., Chancellor of the Duchy of Lancaster.
For the Dominion of Canada:
The Right Honourable Sir George E. Foster, G.C.M.G., P.C., L.L.D., Senator, Member of the King's Privy Council for Canada.
For the Commonwealth of Australia:
The Honourable J. G. Latham, C.M.G., K.C., M.P., Attorney-General of the Commonwealth.

---

[5] Convention signed at Saint-Germain-en-Laye Sept. 10, 1919 (TS 877), *ante,* p. 261.

For the Union of South Africa:
  Mr. Jacobus Stephanus Smit, High Commissioner of the Union in London.
For the Dominion of New Zealand:
  The Honourable Sir James Parr, K.C.M.G., High Commissioner in London.
and
For India:
  Sir William Henry Hoare Vincent, G.C.I.E., K.C.S.I., Member of the Council of the Secretary of State for India, former Member of the Executive Council of the Governor-General of India.

His Majesty the King of the Bulgarians:
  M. D. Mikoff, Chargé d'Affaires at Berne, Permanent representative of the Bulgarian Government accredited to the League of Nations.

The Chief Executive of the Chinese Republic:
  M. Chao-Hsin Chu, Envoy Extraordinary and Minister Plenipotentiary at Rome.

The President of the Republic of Colombia:
  Dr. Francisco José Urrutia, Envoy Extraordinary and Minister Plenipotentiary to the Swiss Federal Council, Representative of Colombia on the Council of the League of Nations.

The President of the Republic of Cuba:
  M. A. de Agüero y Bethancourt, Envoy Extraordinary and Minister Plenipotentiary to the President of the German Reich and to the President of the Austrian Federal Republic.

His Majesty the King of Denmark and Iceland:
  M. Herluf Zahle, Envoy Extraordinary and Minister Plenipotentiary to the President of the German Reich.

His Majesty the King of Spain:
  M. M. Lopez Roberts, Marquis de la Torrehermosa, Envoy Extraordinary and Minister Plenipotentiary to the Swiss Federal Council.

The President of the Estonian Republic:
  General Johan Laidoner, Member of Parliament, President of the Committee for Foreign Affairs and National Defence.

Her Majesty the Empress and Queen of the Kings of Abyssinia and His Imperial and Royal Highness the Prince Regent and Heir to the Throne:
  Dedjazmatch Guetatchou, Minister of the Interior;
  Lidj Makonnen Endelkatchou;
  Kentiba Gebrou;

Ato Tasfae, Secretary of the Imperial League of Nations Department at Addis-Abeba.

The President of the Republic of Finland:
M. Rafael W. Erich, Envoy Extraordinary and Minister Plenipotentiary to the Swiss Federal Council, Permanent Delegate of Finland accredited to the League of Nations.

The President of the French Republic:
Count B. Clauzel, Minister Plenipotentiary, Head of the French League of Nations Department.

The President of the Hellenic Republic:
M. D. Caclamanos, Envoy Extraordinary and Minister Plenipotentiary to His Britannic Majesty.
M. V. Dendramis, Chargé d'Affaires at Berne, Permanent Delegate accredited to the League of Nations.

His Majesty the King of Italy:
Professor Vittorio Scialoja, Minister of State, Senator, Representative of Italy on the Council of the League of Nations.

The President of the Republic of Latvia:
M. Charles Duzmans, Permanent Representative accredited to the League of Nations.

The President of the Republic of Liberia:
Baron Rodolphe A. Lehmann, Envoy Extraordinary and Minister Plenipotentiary to the President of the French Republic, Permanent Delegate accredited to the League of Nations.

The President of the Republic of Lithuania:
M. V. Sidzikauskas, Envoy Extraordinary and Minister Plenipotentiary to the President of the German Reich.

His Majesty the King of Norway:
Dr. Fridtjof Nansen, Professor at the University of Oslo.

The President of the Republic of Panama:
Dr. Eusebio A. Morales, Professor of Law at the Panama National Faculty, Finance Minister.

Her Majesty the Queen of the Netherlands:
Jonkheer W. F. van Lennep, Chargé d'Affaires a. i. of the Netherlands at Berne.

His Majesty the Emperor of Persia:
His Highness Prince Arfa, Ambassador, Delegate of Persia accredited to the League of Nations.

The President of the Polish Republic:
M. Auguste Zaleski, Minister for Foreign Affairs.

The President of the Republic of Portugal:
Dr. A. de Vasconcellos, Minister Plenipotentiary, in charge of the League of Nations Department at the Ministry for Foreign Affairs.

His Majesty the King of Roumania:
M. N. Titulesco, Professor at the University of Bucharest, Envoy Extraordinary and Minister Plenipotentiary to His Britannic Majesty, Representative of Roumania on the Council of the League of Nations.

His Majesty the King of the Serbs, Croats and Slovenes:
Dr. M. Jovanovitch, Envoy Extraordinary and Minister Plenipotentiary to the Swiss Federal Council, Permanent Delegate accredited to the League of Nations.

His Majesty the King of Sweden:
M. Einar Hennings, Envoy Extraordinary and Minister Plenipotentiary to the Swiss Federal Council.

The President of the Czechoslovak Republic:
M. Ferdinand Veverka, Envoy Extraordinary and Minister Plenipotentiary to the Swiss Federal Council.

The President of the Republic of Uruguay:
M. B. Fernandez y Medina, Envoy Extraordinary and Minister Plenipotentiary to His Majesty the King of Spain.

Who, having communicated their full powers, have agreed as follows:

ARTICLE 1

For the purpose of the present Convention, the following definitions are agreed upon:

(1) Slavery is the status or condition of a person over whom any or all of the powers attaching to the right of ownership are exercised.

(2) The slave trade includes all acts involved in the capture, acquisition or disposal of a person with intent to reduce him to slavery; all acts involved in the acquisition of a slave with a view to selling or exchanging him; all acts of disposal by sale or exchange of a slave acquired with a view to being sold or exchanged, and, in general, every act of trade or transport in slaves.

ARTICLE 2

The High Contracting Parties undertake, each in respect of the territories placed under its sovereignty, jurisdiction, protection, suzerainty or tutelage, so far as they have not already taken the necessary steps:

(a) To prevent and suppress the slave trade;

(*b*) To bring about, progressively and as soon as possible, the complete abolition of slavery in all its forms.

ARTICLE 3

The High Contracting Parties undertake to adopt all appropriate measures with a view to preventing and suppressing the embarkation, disembarkation and transport of slaves in their territorial waters and upon all vessels flying their respective flags.

The High Contracting Parties undertake to negotiate as soon as possible a general Convention with regard to the slave trade which will give them rights and impose upon them duties of the same nature as those provided for in the Convention of June 17th, 1925, relative to the International Trade in Arms (Articles 12, 20, 21, 22, 23, 24, and paragraphs 3, 4 and 5 of Section II of Annex II), with the necessary adaptations, it being understood that this general Convention will not place the ships (even of small tonnage) of any High Contracting Parties in a position different from that of the other High Contracting Parties.

It is also understood that, before or after the coming into force of this general Convention, the High Contracting Parties are entirely free to conclude between themselves, without, however, derogating from the principles laid down in the preceding paragraph, such special agreements as, by reason of their pecular situation, might appear to be suitable in order to bring about as soon as possible the complete disappearance of the slave trade.

ARTICLE 4

The High Contracting Parties shall give to one another every assistance with the object of securing the abolition of slavery and the slave trade.

ARTICLE 5

The High Contracting Parties recognise that recourse to compulsory or forced labour may have grave consequences and undertake, each in respect of the territories placed under its sovereignty, jurisdiction, protection, suzerainty or tutelage, to take all necessary measures to prevent compulsory or forced labour from developing into conditions analogous to slavery.

It is agreed that:

(1) Subject to the transitional provisions laid down in paragraph (2) below, compulsory or forced labour may only be exacted for public purposes.

(2) In territories in which compulsory or forced labour for other than public purposes still survives, the High Contracting Parties shall endeavour progressively and as soon as possible to put an end to the practice. So long as such forced or compulsory labour exists, this labour shall invariably be of an exceptional character, shall always receive adequate remuneration, and shall not involve the removal of the labourers from their usual place of residence.

(3) In all cases, the responsibility for any recourse to compulsory or forced labour shall rest with the competent central authorities of the territory concerned.

ARTICLE 6

Those of the High Contracting Parties whose laws do not at present make adequate provision for the punishment of infractions of laws and regulations enacted with a view to giving effect to the purposes of the present Convention undertake to adopt the necessary measures in order that severe penalties may be imposed in respect of such infractions.

ARTICLE 7

The High Contracting Parties undertake to communicate to each other and to the Secretary-General of the League of Nations any laws and regulations which they may enact with a view to the application of the provisions of the present Convention.

ARTICLE 8

The High Contracting Parties agree that disputes arising between them relating to the interpretation or application of this Convention shall, if they cannot be settled by direct negotiation, be referred for decision to the Permanent Court of International Justice. In case either or both of the States Parties to such a dispute should not be parties to the Protocol of December 16th, 1920, relating to the Permanent Court of International Justice, the dispute shall be referred, at the choice of the Parties and in accordance with the constitutional procedure of each State, either to the Permanent Court of International Justice or to a court of arbitration constituted in accordance with the Convention of October 18th, 1907,[6] for the Pacific Settlement of International Disputes, or to some other court of arbitration.

ARTICLE 9

At the time of signature or of ratification or of accession, any High Contracting Party may declare that its acceptance of the present Convention does not bind some or all of the territories placed under its sovereignty, jurisdiction, protection, suzerainty or tutelage in respect of all or any provisions of the Convention; it may subsequently accede separately on behalf of any one of them or in respect of any provision to which any one of them is not a party.

ARTICLE 10

In the event of a High Contracting Party wishing to denounce the present Convention, the denunciation shall be notified in writing to the Secretary-General of the League of Nations, who will at once communicate a certified

---

[6] TS 536, *ante*, vol. 1, p. 577.

true copy of the notification to all the other High Contracting Parties, informing them of the date on which it was received.

The denunciation shall only have effect in regard to the notifying State, and one year after the notification has reached the Secretary-General of the League of Nations.

Denunciation may also be made separately in respect of any territory placed under its sovereignty, jurisdiction, protection, suzerainty or tutelage.

ARTICLE 11

The present Convention, which will bear this day's date and of which the French and English texts are both authentic, will remain open for signature by the States Members of the League of Nations until April 1st, 1927.

The Secretary-General of the League of Nations will subsequently bring the present Convention to the notice of States which have not signed it, including States which are not Members of the League of Nations, and invite them to accede thereto.

A State desiring to accede to the Convention shall notify its intention in writing to the Secretary-General of the League of Nations and transmit to him the instrument of accession, which shall be deposited in the archives of the League.

The Secretary-General shall immediately transmit to all the other High Contracting Parties a certified true copy of the notification and of the instrument of accession, informing them of the date on which he received them.

ARTICLE 12

The present Convention will be ratified and the instruments of ratification shall be deposited in the office of the Secretary-General of the League of Nations. The Secretary-General will inform all the High Contracting Parties of such deposit.

The Convention will come into operation for each State on the date of the deposit of its ratification or its accession.

In faith whereof the Plenipotentiaries have signed the present Convention.

Done at Geneva the twenty-fifth day of September, one thousand nine hundred and twenty-six, in one copy, which will be deposited in the archives of the League of Nations. A certified copy shall be forwarded to each signatory State.

Albania
  D. Dino
Germany
  Dr. Carl von Schubert
Austria
  Emerich Pflügl
Belgium
  L. de Brouckère

British Empire
  I declare that my signature does not bind India or any British Dominion which is a separate member of the League of Nations and does not separately sign or accede to the Convention.

  Cecil

Canada
GEORGE EULAS FOSTER

Australia
J. G. LATHAM

Union of South Africa [7]
J. S. SMIT

New Zealand
J. C. PARR

India

Under the terms of Article 9 of this Convention I declare that my signature is not binding as regards the enforcement of the provisions of Article 2, subsection (b), Articles 5, 6 and 7 of this Convention upon the following territories; namely, in Burma: the Naga tracts lying West and South of the Hukawng Valley, bounded on the North and West by the Assam boundary, on the East by the Nanphuk River and on the South by the Singaling Hkamti and the Somra Tracts; in Assam, the Sadiya and Balipara Frontier Tracts, the tribal area to the East of the Naga Hills District, up to the Burma boundary, and a small tract in the South of the Lushai Hills District; nor on the territories in India of any Prince or Chief under the *suzerainty* of His Majesty.[8]

I also declare that my signature to the Convention is not binding in respect of Article 3 in so far as that Article may require India to enter into any Convention whereby vessels, by reason of the fact that they are owned, fitted out or commanded by Indians, or of the fact that one half of the crew is Indian, are classified as native vessels, or are denied any privilege, right or immunity enjoyed by similar vessels of other States Signatories of the Covenant or are made subject to any liability or disability to which similar ships of such other States are not subject.

W. H. VINCENT

Bulgaria
D. MIKOFF

China
CHAO-HSIN CHU

Colombia
FRANCISCO JOSÉ URRUTIA

Cuba
ARISTIDES DE AGÜERO BETHANCOURT

Denmark
HERLUF ZAHLE

Spain

For Spain and the Spanish Colonies, with the exception of the Spanish Protectorate of Morocco [translation].
MARQUIS DE LA TORREHERMOSA

Estonia
J. LAIDONER

Abyssinia
GUETATCHOU
MAKONNEN
KENTIBA GEBROU
ATO TASFAE

Finland
RAFAEL ERICH

France
B. CLAUZEL

Greece
D. CACLAMANOS
V. DENDRAMIS

Italy
VITTORIO SCIALOJA

Latvia
CHARLES DUZMANS

Liberia

Subject to ratification by the Liberian Senate
Bon R. LEHMANN

Lithuania
VENCESLAS SIDZIKAUSKAS

Norway
FRIDTJOF NANSEN

Panama
EUSEBIO A. MORALES

Netherlands
W. F. VAN LENNEP

---

[7] This signature applies to South-West Africa. [Footnote in original.]

[8] In a communication dated May 30, 1938, the Government of India notified the League of Nations that it was withdrawing the first paragraph of its reservation.

Persia

Ad referendum and interpreting Article 3 as without power to compel Persia to bind herself by any arrangement or convention which would place her ships of whatever tonnage in the category of native vessels provided for by the Convention on the Trade in Arms [translation].

PRINCE ARFA

Poland

AUGUSTE ZALESKI

219–916—69——40

Portugal

AUGUSTO DE VASCONCELLOS

Roumania

N. TITULESCO

Kingdom of the Serbs, Croats and Slovenes

M. JOVANOVITCH

Sweden

EINAR HENNINGS

Czechoslovakia

FERDINAND VEVERKA

Uruguay

B. FERNANDEZ Y MEDINA

PAN AMERICAN POSTAL UNION

Principal convention and final protocol, signed at México November 9, 1926, with resolutions of the Second Pan American Postal Congress [1]
Ratified and approved by the Postmaster General May 3, 1927
Approved by the President of the United States May 5, 1927
Ratification of the United States deposited at México May 28, 1927
Entered into force July 1, 1927
Terminated by convention of November 10, 1931 [2]

45 Stat. 2409; Post Office Department print

Principal Convention

Concluded between Argentina, Bolivia, Brazil, Colombia, Costa Rica, Cuba, Chile, the Dominican Republic, Ecuador, El Salvador, Spain, the United States of America, Guatemala, Honduras, Mexico, Panama, Paraguay, Peru and Uruguay.

The undersigned, Plenipotentiaries of the countries above mentioned, assembled in Congress in Mexico, making use of the right granted them by Article 5 of the Universal Postal Convention of Stockholm,[3] and inspired by the desire to extend and perfect their postal relations and establish a solidarity of action capable of representing effectively in the Universal Postal Congresses the common interests of the American Republics and Spain in regard to communications by mail, have agreed to conclude, subject to ratification, the following Convention:

Article 1

Pan-American Postal Union

The contracting countries, in accordance with the foregoing declaration, constitute, under the name of Pan-American Postal Union, a single postal territory.

---

[1] For text of regulations for execution of the convention, see 45 Stat. 2424.
[2] *Post*, vol. 3.
[3] Convention signed at Stockholm Aug. 28, 1924, *ante*, p. 443.

ARTICLE 2

Free and Gratuitous Transit

The contracting countries are bound to transport freely and gratuitously, by means of the territorial and maritime transportation services which they utilize for their own correspondence, that which they may receive from any of these countries destined for any of them or for any country of the Universal Postal Union.

However, the country of origin will be charged with the expenses of territorial or maritime transportation of the correspondence, when it requires, for its subsequent transmission, the intermediary of countries or services other than those adhering to the present Convention, and when such transportation is subject to charges.

ARTICLE 3

Tariffs

The tariff of the domestic service of each country will govern in the relations of the countries which constitute the Pan-American Postal Union, except when the said domestic tariff is higher than that applicable to correspondence destined for the countries of the Universal Postal Union, in which case the latter will govern.

ARTICLE 4

Scope of the Convention, and Special Services

1. The provisions of this Convention will be applied to letters, post cards, prints of all kinds, commercial papers and samples.

2. The contracting countries, either by reason of their proximity or adjacency or by reason of the intensity of their postal relations, may establish among themselves more restricted unions in connection with any of the services referred to by the present Convention and other special Conventions concluded by this Congress.

ARTICLE 5

Registered Correspondence. Responsibility

1. The objects mentioned in the preceding Article may be sent under registration upon payment in advance of a fee equal to that which the Administration of origin has established in its domestic service.

2. Save in cases of force majeure, the contracting Administrations will be responsible for the loss of every registered article. The sender will have the right to indemnity in a sum which in no case may be higher than 3 dollars 85 cents.

ARTICLE 6

Obligatory Prepayment

1. The complete prepayment of all classes of correspondence is declared obligatory, including sealed packages, with the exception of letters in their usual and ordinary form, which will be forwarded whenever they bear at least the postage corresponding to a single-weight-unit.

2. Other articles not prepaid or insufficiently prepaid will be held in the Office of origin, which will proceed with them in the manner determined by its domestic legislation.

3. For insufficiently prepaid letters, only the difference in postage not paid by the sender will be collected from the addressee.

ARTICLE 7

Weight and Volume

The limits of weight and dimensions of the various articles of correspondence will conform to those fixed for the same in the domestic service of each country.

ARTICLE 8

Undelivered Post Cards

Ordinary post cards which have not been delivered for any reason will be destroyed in the country of destination, unless they bear a request for return and the name and address of the sender, in which case they will be returned to the country of origin.

ARTICLE 9

Franking Privilege

1. The contracting parties agree to grant the franking privilege, both in their domestic service and in the Pan-American service, to the correspondence of the International Office of the Pan-American Postal Union, and to that of the members of the Diplomatic Corps of the signatory countries. Consuls will enjoy the franking privilege for the official correspondence which they direct to their respective countries, for that which they exchange among themselves, and for that which they direct to the Government of the country in which they are accredited, whenever reciprocity exists. Vice-Consuls will enjoy the same franking privilege when they are discharging the functions of Consuls.

2. The exchange of correspondence of the Diplomatic Corps between the Secretaries of State of the respective countries and their Embassies and Legations will have a reciprocal character among the contracting countries, and will be effected in open mail or by means of diplomatic pouches, in accordance

with the provisions of Article 5 of the Regulations of Execution.[4] These pouches will enjoy the franking privilege and all the safeguards of the official dispatches.

3. The correspondence referred to in the two preceding paragraphs may be sent free of postage under registration, but without any right to indemnity in case of loss.

ARTICLE 10

Prohibitions

1. Without prejudice to the provisions of the domestic legislation of each country regarding restrictions on the circulation of correspondence, pornographic publications will not be forwarded nor those endangering public safety and order.

2. The contracting Administrations will have the option of not forwarding correspondence of any class having for its object the commission of frauds, swindles or any other offense against property or persons, in accordance with its domestic laws.

3. It is also prohibited to send by mail articles of any classification which, by their text, form, mechanism or application, are immoral or contrary to good morals.

4. Barring contrary arrangements between the Administrations concerned, it is prohibted to inclose money in cash or values payable to the bearer in ordinary or registered correspondence.

The Administrations will not accept pecuniary responsibility for the loss, or for the partial or total rifling, of the contents of the said correspondence.

ARTICLE 11

Special Services

The contracting countries obligate themselves to make extensive to the other countries of the Pan-American Postal Union, on the basis of special agreements, all of the postal services which they realize in the interior of their countries.

ARTICLE 12

Various Provisions

The signatory countries will have the option of accepting the "postage paid" service, under which they are bound to permit the circulation of newspapers or periodical publications, single or in packages, with the exception of those for propaganda or exclusively commercial advertising.

---

[4] See footnote 1, p. 617.

ARTICLE 13

Official Language

Spanish is adopted as the official language for matters relative to the mail service, but countries whose language is not Spanish may use their own.

ARTICLE 14

Protection to Postal Agents

The authorities of the contracting countries will be obliged to lend, when it is requested of them, the co-operation required by the Postal Agents charged with the transportation of pouches and correspondence in transit thru the said countries, and likewise those other functionaries which one Administration agrees to send to any of these countries to carry on studies regarding the development and perfection of its postal services.

For the purpose of the most efficient rendering of such trips, the Administrations may make an agreement to organize an exchange of postal functionaries.

ARTICLE 15

International Transfer Office

1. There is created in Panama a Postal Office charged with receiving and forwarding to its destination all the correspondence which crosses the Isthmus, originating in any of the contracting countries, when it gives rise to transfer operations.

2. For its postal operations, it will be governed by the Regulations formulated by the International Office of the Pan-American Postal Union, after agreement with the Administration of Posts of Panama and the other interested Administrations.

3. The personnel assigned to the service of the said Office will be designated by the Administration of Panama.

4. The cost of maintaining this Office will be charged to the countries which utilize the services thereof, in proportion to the amount of correspondence which they exchange thru its intermediary. The Administration of Panama will advance the necessary funds for the purpose, which shall be reimbursed to it quarterly.

ARTICLE 16

Arbitration

Every conflict or disagreement which may arise in the postal relations of the contracting countries will be settled by arbitration, which will be effected in the manner established by Article 10 of the Universal Postal Convention of Stockholm.

Every designation of arbiters shall be incumbent upon the signatory countries, with the intervention of the International Office of the Pan-American Postal Union if necessary.

ARTICLE 17

International Office of the Pan-American Postal Union

1. With the name of International Office of the Pan-American Postal Union, there will function in Montevideo, under the supervision of the Administration of Posts, Telegraphs and Telephones of the Republic of Uruguay, a Central Office which will serve as an organ of liaison, information and consultation for the countries of this Union.

2. This Office will be charged with:

a) Assembling, co-ordinating, publishing and distributing information of all kinds which specially concerns the Pan-American Postal Service.

b) Giving, at the request of the parties concerned, its opinion on disputed questions which arise in connection with the provisions relative to the relations of the contracting Administrations.

c) Making known the requests for modifications of the Acts of the Congress which may be formulated.

d) Giving notice of the changes which may be adopted.

e) Making known the results obtained from the regulatory provisions and measures of importance which the Administrations may adopt in their domestic service, which will be communicated to it by the same Administrations as information.

f) Preparing a Pan-American Postal Guide.

g) Preparing a Pan-American Postal Atlas.

h) Making up the summary of the Pan-American postal statistics, in accordance with the data which will be communicated to it annually by each Administration.

i) Preparing a table showing the most rapid routes for the transmission of correspondence from one contracting country to another.

j) Publishing the tariff of postage rates of the domestic service of each one of the countries concerned, and the table of equivalents.

k) Publishing and distributing among the countries of the Pan-American Postal Union, annually, a report of the work which it performs.

l) And, in general, carrying out the studies and labors requested of it in the interest of the contracting countries.

3. The special expenses arising from the preparation of the Annual Report, the Pan-American Postal Guide, the Pan-American Postal Atlas, and the Table of Postal Communications of the contracting countries; and those arising on account of the meeting of congresses or conferences, will be proportionately shared by the Administrations of the said countries in conformity with the categories established in Article 8 of the Regulations of Execution.

4. The Administration of Posts, Telegraphs and Telephones of Uruguay will supervise the expenses of the International Office of the Pan-American Postal Union, and will make to it the advances which it requires.

5. The sums advanced by the Postal Administration of Uruguay in accordance with the foregoing Section will be repaid by the debtor Administrations as soon as possible, and, at the latest, before six months from the date on which the country concerned receives the account formulated by the Administration of Posts, Telegraphs and Telephones of Uruguay. After this date, the sums due will bear interest at the rate of seven percent a year, counting from the date of expiration of the said period.

6. The contracting countries are bound to include in their budgets an annual amount destined to take care promptly of the payment of the quota which they are to contribute.

ARTICLE 18

Monetary Unit

For the purposes of this Convention, the dollar is established as the monetary unit.

ARTICLE 19

Congresses

1. Congresses will meet at least every five years, counting from the date on which the Convention concluded by the last one becomes effective.

2. Each Congress will fix the place and year in which the next one shall convene.

ARTICLE 20

Propositions in the Interval Between Meetings

The present Convention may be modified in the interval between Congresses, following the procedure established in Chapter III of the Universal Postal Convention of Stockholm. In order to become effective, the modifications must obtain unanimity of votes for the present Article and Articles 1, 2, 3, 4, 5, 6, 9, 13, 16, 17, 18, 20, 22, 24 and 25; two-thirds of the votes for Articles 7, 10, 11 and 19; and a simple majority for the rest.

ARTICLE 21

Modifications and Amendments

The modifications or resolutions adopted by the contracting parties, even those of a domestic order which affect the international service, will become effective four months after the date of the relative notice from the International Office of the Pan-American Postal Union.

ARTICLE 22

Application of the Universal Postal Convention and Domestic Legislation

1. All matters in connection with the exchange of correspondence among the contracting countries which are not provided for in this Convention will be subject to the stipulations of the Universal Postal Convention and its Regulations.

2. Likewise, the domestic legislation of the said countries will apply in everything that has not been provided for by either Convention.

ARTICLE 23

Propositions for Universal Congresses

All countries forming the Pan-American Postal Union will advise one another, thru the intermediary of the International Office of Montevideo, of the propositions which they may formulate for Universal Postal Congresses, one year in advance of the date on which the particular Congress in question is to be held, in order that, once that they have come to an understanding, they may unanimously support the propositions of a general character, excepting only those which concern the proposing countries alone.

ARTICLE 24

New Adherences

In case of a new adherence, the Government of the Republic of Uruguay, by common consent with the Government of the country concerned, will determine the class in which the said country is to be included, for purposes of sharing the expenses of the International Office.

ARTICLE 25

Effective Date and Duration of the Convention and Deposit of Ratifications

1. The present Convention will become effective July 1, 1927, and will remain in force without time-limit, each one of the contracting parties reserving the right to withdraw from this Union by means of notice given by its Government to that of the Republic of Uruguay one year in advance.

2. The deposit of ratifications will be effected in the City of Mexico as soon as possible, preferably before the effective date of the Conventions in question, and the relative certificate will be made up for each of them, a copy of which will be sent by the Government of Mexico, thru diplomatic channels, to the Governments of the other signatory countries.

3. The stipulations of the Pan-American Postal Convention sanctioned in Buenos Aires September 15, 1921,[5] are abrogated, beginning with the date on which the present Convention enters into force.

---

[5] *Ante,* p. 309.

4. In case that the Convention is not ratified by one or more of the contracting countries, it will none the less be valid for those which have ratified it.

5. In faith of which, the Plenipotentiaries of the countries above named sign the present Convention in Mexico, D. F., on the 9th day of the month of November, 1926.

For Argentina:
  RAÚL D. LÓPEZ

For Bolivia:
  GABRIEL A. PARRODI
  LUIS ARCE LACAZE

For Brazil:
  OCTAVIO DE TEFFÉ

For Colombia:
  CARLOS ALBERTO RODRÍGUEZ

For Costa Rica:
  ÁNGEL J. LAGARDA
  LINO B. ROCHÍN

For Cuba:
  JOSÉ D. MORALES DÍAZ
  PEDRO I. PÉREZ Y GIL
  CÉSAR CARVALLO Y MIYERES

For Chile:
  ENRIQUE BERMÚDEZ

For the Dominican Republic:
  FRANCISCO GARCÍA DE CASTAÑEDA

For Ecuador:
  ARMANDO E. ASPIAZU
  RODOLFO BECERRA SOTO

For El Salvador:
  HÉCTOR REYES
  EUDORO URDANETA

For Spain:
  PEDRO DE IGUAL Y MARTÍNEZ DABÁN
  ANTONIO CAMACHO SANJURJO

For the United States of America:
  JOSEPH STEWART
  EUGENE R. WHITE

For Guatemala:
  EMILIO ARROYAVE L.

For Honduras:
  MIGUEL CARIAS ANDINO
  OTTO REINBECK

For Mexico:
  EDUARDO ORTIZ
  COSME HINOJOSA
  JOSÉ V. CHÁVEZ

For Panama:
  JOSÉ IGNACIO ICAZA

For Paraguay:
  CARLOS MELÉNDEZ

For Peru:
  AUGUSTO S. SALAZAR
  WALTER F. FORD

For Uruguay:
  CÉSAR MIRANDA

FINAL PROTOCOL OF THE PRINCIPAL CONVENTION

At the moment of signing the Principal Convention concluded by the Second Pan-American Postal Congress, the undersigned Plenipotentiaries have agreed upon the following:

I

When the Pan-American Railway is established, each one of the contracting countries will contribute to the maintenance of the mail transportation service thereby, in proportion to the weight of the correspondence which it dispatches, in case that gratuitous transportation is not obtained.

II

The contracting countries are bound to negotiate with the steamship companies transporting their correspondence to foreign countries for a reduction in the present rates, and in order that they may in no case collect, for the return service, an amount greater than that which they collect from the country of origin.

It is understood that the foregoing clause does not affect cases where, on account of packet or other privileges, they are obliged to effect the transportation gratuitously.

III

Panama records the fact that it can not accept the provisions of the first paragraph of Article 2 of the Convention relative to gratuity of transit.

IV

Argentina, Bolivia, Brazil, Chile, Ecuador, Spain, Guatemala, Paraguay and Uruguay reserve the right to fix the equivalents of their rates in gold francs, in accordance with the monetary unit of the Universal Postal Convention of Stockholm.

V

The Protocol remains open in favor of the countries of America whose representatives have not signed the Principal Convention, or which, having signed that Convention, desire to adhere to the other Conventions sanctioned by the Congress.

VI

The United States of America records the fact that, until that country enacts legislation on the subject, it can not accept the provisions of Article 9 of the Convention relative to the franking privilege in the domestic service for diplomatic correspondence and official correspondence of Consulates.

VII

Chile, Ecuador and Peru, as a temporary measure, reserve the right to maintain the rates now applicable in their relations with the Pan-American Postal Union, for both ordinary and registered correspondence.

VIII

Despite the provisions of Article 5, the contracting countries will have the option of establishing, by means of a reduced rate, a special class of registered articles available for prints, the senders of which will not enjoy the right to indemnity in case of loss.

Transitory Article

1. For the purpose of complying with the provisions of Article 15 of the Principal Convention, relative to the creation in Panama of the International Office, the Director of the International Office of the Pan-American Postal

Union will proceed immediately to the Canal Zone, in order to study the best means for organizing that Office and to agree with the Panamanian Administration on the details of installation and the regulations to govern it; and also to draw up the tentative budget for the Office.

2. The Administration of Panama will advance to the Director of the International Office of the Pan-American Postal Union the necessary funds for the expenses made necessary by the mission which is entrusted to him, which funds will be reimbursed in proportional shares as soon as possible, and at the latest within a period of three months, by the Administrations of the countries which will utilize the services of the Office of Panama.

For Argentina:
RAÚL D. LÓPEZ

For Bolivia:
GABRIEL A. PARRODI
LUIS ARCE LACAZE

For Brazil:
OCTAVIO DE TEFFÉ

For Colombia:
CARLOS ALBERTO RODRÍGUEZ

For Costa Rica:
ÁNGEL J. LAGARDA
LINO B. ROCHÍN

For Cuba:
JOSE D. MORALES DÍAZ
PEDRO I. PÉREZ Y GIL
CÉSAR CARVALLO Y MIYERES

For Chile:
ENRIQUE BERMÚDEZ

For the Dominican Republic:
FRANCISCO GARCÍA DE CASTAÑEDA

For Ecuador:
ARMANDO E. ASPIAZU
RODOLFO BECERRA SOTO

For El Salvador:
HÉCTOR REYES
EUDORO URDANETA

For Spain:
PEDRO DE IGUAL Y MARTÍNEZ DABÁN
ANTONIO CAMACHO SANJURJO

For the United States of America:
JOSEPH STEWART
EUGENE R. WHITE

For Guatemala:
EMILIO ARROYAVE L.

For Honduras:
MIGUEL CARIAS ANDINO
OTTO REINBECK

For Mexico:
EDUARDO ORTIZ
COSME HINOJOSA
JOSÉ V. CHÁVEZ

For Panama:
JOSÉ IGNACIO ICAZA

For Paraguay:
CARLOS MELÉNDEZ

For Peru:
AUGUSTO S. SALAZAR
WALTER F. FORD

For Uruguay:
CÉSAR MIRANDA

[For text of regulations for execution of the convention, see 45 Stat. 2424.]

RESOLUTIONS OF THE CONGRESS

The second Pan-American Postal Congress recommends, to all the countries which forms this Union:

I. That they take steps, as far as possible, for the prompt establishment of an air-mail service, as an effective means of obtaining a rapid exchange of correspondence, thus taking another step toward spiritual harmony, which is one of the aims of the Pan-American Postal Union.

II. That, since the parcel-post service constitutes a means which facilitates commercial relations among the contracting countries, it would be convenient to abolish as many requirements as signify a restriction for the effectiveness of the said service; and to abolish the requirement of consular invoices and visas, as well as certificates of origin for parcels whose value does not exceed 150 gold francs or their equivalent in dollars.

III. In view of the fact that advertisements constitute a useful and convenient means of spreading information which tends to increase the knowledge of the peoples, the Congress is of the opinion that articles of this kind should be transported in the international postal service without being subject to customs duties or requirements which tend to limit their aims.

IV. That the Administrations of the Pan-American Postal Union should create, if possible, an Information Office in the Central Post Offices, with a reading room in which will be placed, at the disposal of the public, newspapers, magazines, and publications in general of the various countries of the Union furnished gratuitously by the Governments, publishers or authors.

Mexico, D. F., November 9, 1926.

PAN AMERICAN POSTAL UNION: PARCEL POST

Convention signed at México November 9, 1926
Ratified and approved by the Postmaster General May 3, 1927
Approved by the President of the United States May 5, 1927
Ratification of the United States deposited at México May 28, 1927
Entered into force July 1, 1927
Terminated by agreement of November 10, 1931 [1]

45 Stat. 2434; Post Office Department print

PARCEL POST CONVENTION

Concluded between Argentina, Bolivia, Brazil, Colombia, Costa Rica, Chile, the Dominican Republic, Ecuador, El Salvador, Spain, the United States of America, Guatemala, Honduras, Mexico, Panama, Paraguay, Peru and Uruguay.

The undersigned Plenipotentiaries of the Governments of the countries above mentioned, in exercise of the option conferred by Article 5 of the Universal Postal Convention of Stockholm,[2] agree, subject to ratification, to the establishment of the parcel post service in accordance with the following provisions:

ARTICLE 1

Object of the Convention

Under the denomination of "parcel post", parcels may be sent from one of the above-mentioned countries to another by the most rapid route, it being obligatory to send them in duly sealed receptacles.

Countries which agree to do so may extend the service to include registered, collect-on-delivery and insured parcels.

ARTICLE 2

Transit

Liberty of transit is guaranteed over the territory of each one of the contracting countries, and the responsibility of the Administrations taking

---

[1] *Post,* vol. 3.
[2] Convention signed at Stockholm Aug. 28, 1924, *ante,* p. 443.

part in the transportation is comprised within the limits fixed by Article 7. As a result, the various Administrations may use the intermediary of one or several countries for the reciprocal exchange of parcels.

Parcels will be sent in closed dispatches, the dispatching Administrations being obliged to send a copy of every parcel bill to each one of the intermediary Administrations.

ARTICLE 3

Weight and Dimensions

The maximum weight of each parcel will be 10 kilograms, the Administrations remaining at liberty to limit it to 5, and not to undertake to handle parcels which they consider bulky. It is understood that no country may send parcels with dimensions greater than those fixed by the Regulations of the Convention of Stockholm.

However, the Administrations of the contracting countries may, after obtaining the consent of the intermediary countries, accept parcels with other limits of weight and dimensions.

ARTICLE 4

Postage Rates and Payments

1. The postage on parcels exchanged under this Convention will be composed only of the sum of the rates of origin, territorial transit and destination. If necessary, the maritime rates provided by the Stockholm Agreement will be added.

2. The rates of origin, transit and destination are fixed, for each country, at 50 centimes of a gold franc or their equivalent in dollars for each parcel up to 5 kilograms, and 1 gold franc or its equivalent in dollars for each parcel whose weight exceeds 5 kilograms but not 10 kilograms.

3. However, the contracting Administrations will have the option of increasing these rates up to double their amount, and of applying a fixed surcharge of 25 centimes of a gold franc or their equivalent in dollars to each parcel which they dispatch or receive.

4. Administrations which, in the Universal service, enjoy special authorizations to increase the rates set forth in Section 2, may also make use of the said authorizations in the Pan-American service.

5. Notwithstanding the provisions of the foregoing Sections, no contracting Administration will be obliged to fix a rate lower than that established for this class of articles in its domestic service.

6. The Administration of origin will pay to each one of the Administrations taking part in the transportation, as well as to that of destination, the corresponding charges in accordance with the provisions of the foregoing Sections.

ARTICLE 5

Delivery, Customs, Storage and Other Charges

The Administrations of destination may collect from the addressees of parcels:

a) A fixed charge of 50 centimes of a gold franc or their equivalent in dollars at most for the conveyance of the parcel to the residence of the addressee or its delivery in the office, and for the fulfilment before the customs authorities of the necessary formalities or transactions.

b) A daily charge for storage, for the holding of parcels which have not been withdrawn within a period of 5 days, counting from the date of mailing the relative notice to the addressee. It is optional for the Administrations to increase this period to 15 days.

c) The customs duties and fees in general, and other nonpostal charges established by their domestic legislation.

d) The consular fee, when it has not been prepaid by the sender.

ARTICLE 6

Prohibition Against Other Charges

The parcels of which the present Convention treats may not be subjected to other charges than those established in the foregoing Articles.

ARTICLE 7

Indemnity

1. The indemnity mentioned in Article 36 of the Convention of Stockholm will be paid in accordance with the provisions of that Article, as follows:

a) For parcels up to 5 kilograms, 25 gold francs or their equivalent in dollars at most.

b) For parcels from 5 to 10 kilograms, 50 gold francs or their equivalent in dollars at most.

2. For the payment of the indemnity, account will be taken of the value of the parcel stated by the sender in the customs declaration unless the customs officers, upon appraising the parcel, amend the sender's declaration.

In no case may the indemnity exceed the maximum fixed in the preceding Section.

ARTICLE 8

Parcels Pending Delivery

The period during which parcels must be held at the disposal of the addressees in the offices of destination is fixed at 30 days. The said period may be increased to 90 days by agreement among the Administrations concerned, it being understood that in every case the return will be made without previously consulting the sender.

ARTICLE 9

Fraudulent Declarations

In cases where it is proved that the sender of a parcel, by himself or by agreement with the addressee, has falsely declared the quality, weight or measure of the contents, or in any other way has tried to defraud the fiscal interests of the country of destination, avoiding the payment of import duties by concealing articles or declaring them in such a way as to show the evident intention of nullifying or reducing the amount of those duties, the Administration concerned is authorized to dispose of those articles in accordance with its domestic laws, and neither the sender nor the addressee will have any right to delivery, return or indemnity.

ARTICLE 10

Parcels for Second Addressees

The senders of parcels addressed to Banks or other organizations for delivery to second addressees will be obliged to state, on the labels or wrappers thereof, the exact names and addresses of the persons for whom such parcels are intended.

ARTICLE 11

Abandoned or Returned Parcels

Abandoned parcels, or those returned to origin which can not be delivered to the senders, will be sold by the Administration concerned. If the proceeds of the sale are lower than the charges due on the parcel, the deficit will be divided in equal shares between the Administrations of origin and destination.

ARTICLE 12

Propositions in the Interval Between Meetings

The present Convention may be modified in the interval which transpires between Congresses, following the procedure established in Chapter III of the Postal Convention of Stockholm. In order to become effective, the modifications must obtain:

1. Unanimity of votes, if it is a question of introducing new provisions or modifying the present Article or Articles 1, 2, 3, 4, 5, 6 and 7.

2. Two-thirds of the votes in order to modify the other provisions.

ARTICLE 13

Equivalents

For the application of the provisions of Article 4, Section 2, it is established in the present Convention that each contracting country will determine the legal equivalent of its money with respect to the dollar or the gold franc.

ARTICLE 14

Matters Not Provided for

1. All matters not provided for by this Convention will be governed by the stipulations of the Parcel Post Convention of Stockholm and its Regulations of Execution.

2. However, the contracting Administrations may agree to fix other details for the carrying out of the service.

3. The right of the contracting countries to retain the regulatory procedure adopted for the fulfilment of conventions among themselves is recognized, provided that such procedure is not contrary to the provisions of this Convention.

ARTICLE 15

Effective Date and Duration of the Convention

1. The present Convention will become effective on July 1, 1927, and will remain in force without time-limit, each one of the contracting parties reserving the right to abrogate it by means of notice given by its Government to that of the Republic of Uruguay one year in advance.

2. The deposit of ratifications will be effected in the city of Mexico as soon as possible; the relative certificate will be made up in regard to the ratification by each country, and the Government of Mexico will send a copy of the said certificate, thru diplomatic channels, to the Governments of the other signatory countries.

3. The stipulations of the Parcel Post Convention sanctioned in Buenos Aires on September 15, 1921,[3] are abrogated, beginning with the date on which the present Convention becomes effective.

4. In case that the Convention is not ratified by one or several of the contracting countries, it will none the less be valid for the countries which have ratified it.

In faith of which, the Plenipotentiaries of the countries enumerated sign the present Convention in Mexico, D. F., on the 9th day of November, 1926.

---

[3] *Ante* p. 318.

For Argentina:
RAÚL D. LÓPEZ

For Bolivia:
GABRIEL A. PARRODI
LUIS ARCE LACAZE

For Brazil:
OCTAVIO DE TEFFÉ

For Colombia:
CARLOS ALBERTO RODRÍGUEZ

For Costa Rica:
ÁNGEL J. LAGARDA
LINO B. ROCHÍN

For Chile:
ENRIQUE BERMÚDEZ

For the Dominican Republic:
FRANCISCO GARCÍA DE CASTAÑEDA

For Ecuador:
ARMANDO E. ASPIAZU
RODOLFO BECERRA SOTO

For El Salvador:
HÉCTOR REYES
EUDORO URDANETA

For Spain:
PEDRO DE IGUAL Y MARTÍNEZ DABÁN
ANTONIO CAMACHO SANJURJO

For the United States of America:
JOSEPH STEWART
EUGENE R. WHITE

For Guatemala:
EMILIO ARROYAVE L.

For Honduras:
MIGUEL CARIAS ANDINO
OTTO REINBECK

For Mexico:
EDUARDO ORTIZ
COSME HINOJOSA
JOSÉ V. CHÁVEZ

For Panama:
JOSÉ IGNACIO ICAZA

For Paraguay:
CARLOS MELÉNDEZ

For Peru:
AUGUSTO S. SALAZAR
WALTER F. FORD

For Uruguay:
CÉSAR MIRANDA

PAN AMERICAN POSTAL UNION: MONEY ORDERS

Convention signed at México November 9, 1926
Ratified and approved by the Postmaster General, excluding articles 8,
*   11, 20, and 21, May 3, 1927*
Approved by the President of the United States, excluding articles 8,
*   11, 20, and 21, May 5, 1927*
Ratification of the United States deposited at México June 20, 1927 [1]
Entered into force July 1, 1927
Terminated by agreement of November 10, 1931 [2]

Post Office Department print

CONVENTION FOR THE EXCHANGE OF MONEY ORDERS

Between Argentina, Bolivia, Colombia, Costa Rica, Cuba, Chile, Dominica, Ecuador, El Salvador, Spain, United States, Guatemala, Honduras, Mexico, Panama, Paraguay, Peru and Uruguay.

The undersigned, Plenipotentiaries of the Governments of the countries mentioned above, in the exercise of the authority conferred by article 5 of the Universal Postal Convention of Stockholm,[3] convened, and subject to ratification have established Money Order Service in accordance with the following clauses:

ARTICLE 1

Object of the Convention

The exchange of money orders between the contracting countries, whose Administrations agree to the establishment of this service, to be governed by the provisions of this present convention.

ARTICLE 2

Money

The amount of the orders will be expressed in the money of the country of destination; nevertheless, the Administrations have authority to adopt by mutual consent, other money which is more convenient to their uses.

---

[1] For notice of U.S. ratification, see p. 642.
[2] *Post*, vol. 3.
[3] Convention signed at Stockholm Aug. 28, 1924, *ante*, p. 443.

ARTICLE 3

Conditions for the Exchange of Money Orders

The exchange of money orders between the contracting countries will be carried on by means of lists, conforming to form "A" attached.[4]

Each Administration will designate an office of its country which will be in charge of the making up of said lists and forwarding them to the offices designated for that purpose by the other Administrations.

ARTICLE 4

Maximum Amount

The Administrations of the contracting countries which agree to the establishment of this service, are authorized upon agreement to fix the maximum amount of the money orders exchanged between them.

Nevertheless, orders relative to the Postal Service, sent under frank, free of postage, under the provisions of Article 8 following, may exceed the maximum amount fixed by each Administration.

ARTICLE 5

Fees or Commissions

Each Administration will have the authority to fix, whenever their interests demand it, the schedule of commissions (or fees) which will be collected for the issue of money orders under the terms of this Convention, but will be obliged to communicate said schedule to the other Administrations, as well as any modification made therein.

Barring agreement to the contrary, the fees or commissions collected shall belong in their entirety to the remitting Administration, not allowing, therefore, any sum to the paying Administration as a fee for payment.

ARTICLE 6

Endorsement

Each of the contracting countries is authorized to permit in its territory and in accordance with its domestic regulations, endorsement of money orders originating in any of the other countries.

ARTICLE 7

Responsibility

Subject to the provisions of the foregoing article, there will be responsibility to the remitter for the sum sent by means of money order until it is paid to the payee or endorsee.

---

[4] Not printed here.

ARTICLE 8

Exemption from Charges

Those money orders pertaining to the Postal Service, exchanged between the Postal Administrations or between the offices dependent upon these Administrations, as well as the orders from Postal Administrations to the International Office at Montevideo and reciprocally, will be exempt from all charges.

ARTICLE 9

Period of Validity of Orders

Barring agreement to the contrary, a money order will be paid in the country of destination during the twelve months following its issue.

The amount of all the orders that have not been paid during that period of time, will be credited in the first account to the Administration of the country of origin, which will proceed in accordance with the regulations of that country.

ARTICLE 10

Change of Address and Repayment of Orders

1. When the remitter desires to correct an error in the address of the payee, or that the amount of a money order be returned, he should apply to the Central Administration of the country in which the order was issued.

2. In no case is a money order to be repaid without obtaining from the Central Administration of the country to which it was sent, assurance that payment has not been effected and that the said Administration expressly authorizes repayment.

ARTICLE 11

Advice of Payment

The remitter of an order will be able to obtain an advice of payment officially given by the Administration of destination, by means of a provision similar to that by which a return receipt is obtained for registered letter, which shall be accepted by the issuing postmaster. This advice will be transmitted directly to the issuing postmaster for delivery to the applicant.

ARTICLE 12

Reissue

The orders are not to be reissued in any other country than the one to which they shall first have been certified.

ARTICLE 13

Domestic Regulations

The money orders which are exchanged between two countries will be subject as regards issue and payment to the regulations in force in the country of origin or the country of payment as the case may be, covering the issue and payment of domestic money orders.

ARTICLE 14

Preparation of the Lists

1. Each Exchange Office will forward to the corresponding Exchange Office, daily or on the date mutually agreed upon, the amounts received in its country for payment in the other, using for that purpose form "A" attached.

2. Any money order noted in these lists shall carry a number, which will be called the international number, commencing each year with No. 1. These lists will likewise be numbered in order commencing with No. 1 the first of each year.

3. The Exchange Offices will acknowledge mutually the receipt of each list by means of the first list following, sent in the opposite direction.

4. Any list that is lacking should be asked for immediately by the office that should have received it. The remitting Exchange Office in that case will send as soon as possible to the office making request a duplicate of the list asked for, duly authenticated.

ARTICLE 15

Verification and Correction of Lists

These lists should be carefully examined by the receiving Exchange Office and corrected when they contain minor errors.

These corrections should be communicated to the remitting Exchange Office upon acknowledgment of receipt of the list on which corrections have been made.

When these lists contain other irregularities, the receiving Exchange Office should ask for an explanation from the dispatching Exchange Office, which should give this information with the least possible delay. In the meantime, the reissue of inland orders corresponding to those about which irregularities have been noted, will be suspended.

ARTICLE 16

Conversion of International Orders to Inland Orders

1. Upon receipt in an Exchange Office of a list of orders, in accordance with the provisions of the foregoing article, said office shall proceed to issue

in favor of the payees inland orders in the money of the country of payment, for the amounts which appear in the list, sending immediately these money orders (inland) to the payees or to the paying offices in accordance with the regulations governing the payment of orders in each country.

2. Duplicates of money orders shall be issued only by the Postal Administration of the paying country, in accordance with its internal regulations and previous proof that the order has not been nor will be paid to the payee or returned to the office of origin.

ARTICLE 17

Rendering and Settling Accounts

1. Barring agreement to the contrary, at the end of each quarter one of the two corresponding Administrations, designated by mutual agreement, shall render an account in which shall be entered in detail: (a) the totals of the lists that contained the particulars of the orders issued in both countries during the quarter; (b) the totals of the orders which have been returned to the remitter, and (c) the totals of those orders which have become invalid during the quarter.

2. The credit of each Administration will be expressed in its own money.

3. The smaller amount will be converted into the money of the creditor country, at the average rate of exchange prevailing during the quarter covered by the account.

4. These accounts are to be rendered in duplicate and forwarded by the accounting Administration to the corresponding Administration.

If a balance appears in favor of this Administration, it shall be paid by means of a sight draft in favor of the creditor country attached to the account.

If a balance appears in favor of the Administration which renders the account, payment will be made by the head of the debtor Administration in the manner indicated in the preceding paragraph, upon return of the accepted account.

5. Forms "B," "C," "D" and "E" attached to this Convention [5] will be used in rendering these quarterly accounts.

6. Also the Administrations may agree not to effect conversions, but to make settlements unilaterally, that is to say, for each Administration to credit to the other the total amount of the orders paid on its account. In this case each Administration would have to render a quarterly account.

ARTICLE 18

Advance Payments on Account

When it is ascertained that one of the corresponding Administrations owes the other on money order account a balance in excess of $5000.00 or the

---

[5] Not printed here.

approximate equivalent of that amount in its own money, the debtor Administration will send with as little delay as possible to the other, and as an advance payment on account, an amount approximating the balance of the accounts for the quarterly settlement referred to in the article above.

ARTICLE 19

Suspension of the Service

The Administrations of the contracting countries may under extraordinary circumstances suspend temporarily the issue of money orders, and may adopt such provisions as may be deemed necessary to safeguard the interests of the Administrations and to avoid speculation through the money order service by commercial institutions.

The Administration that adopts any of the measures referred to in the foregoing paragraph, should communicate that fact immediately to the Administrations with which it exchanges money orders.

ARTICLE 20

Telegraphic Orders

The contracting Administrations may establish the exchange of orders by telegraph in accordance with the provisions of the Stockholm Agreement relating to money order service.

ARTICLE 21

Application of the Provisions of the Agreement of the Universal Postal Union

The provisions of the Agreement of the Universal Postal Union relating to the exchange of money orders, as well as its rules of execution, will be applicable to the exchange of money orders under this convention, in so far as their stipulations do not conflict.

ARTICLE 22

Proposals During the Interval Between Assemblies

This Convention may be modified during the interval between Congresses, in the manner provided for in Chapter III of the Stockholm Postal Convention. In order to give these modifications executory strength it will be necessary to procure:

1. Unanimous vote if it is desired to introduce a new provision or to modify this article or articles 1, 2, 4, 5, 7, 8, 13, 17, 18, 19, 21, and 23.

2. Two thirds of the votes to modify the other provisions.

ARTICLE 23

Standing and Duration of the Convention

1. This Convention will become effective on July 1, 1927, and will remain in force without limitation of time, reserving to each of the contracting parties the right of withdrawal by giving notice thereof through its Government to that of the Oriental Republic of Uruguay one year in advance.

2. The ratifications should be deposited in the City of Mexico in the shortest time possible; a resolution was adopted relative to the deposit of the ratifications of each country, and the Government of Mexico will remit through diplomatic channels a copy of the said resolution to the Governments of the other countries signing.

3. The stipulations of the Money Order Convention adopted at Buenos Aires on September 15, 1921, will be repealed from the date this Convention goes into effect.

4. In case one of the contracting countries fails to ratify this Convention, that fact will not affect the validity for those that shall ratify it.

In testimony whereof, the Plenipotentiaries of the countries named, have signed this Convention at Mexico, D. F., on the ninth day of November 1926.

For Argentina:
  RAÚL D. LÓPEZ

For Bolivia:
  GABRIEL A. PARRODI
  LUIS ARCE LACAZE

For Colombia:
  CARLOS ALBERTO RODRÍGUEZ

For Costa Rica:
  ANGEL J. LAGARDA
  LINO B. ROCHÍN

For Cuba:
  JOSÉ D. MORALES DÍAZ
  PEDRO I. PÉREZ Y GIL
  CÉSAR CARVALLO Y MIYERES

For Chile:
  ENRIQUE BERMÚDEZ

For the Dominican Republic:
  FRANCISCO GARCÍA DE CASTAÑEDA

For Ecuador:
  ARMANDO E. ASPIAZU
  RODOLFO BECERRA SOTO

For El Salvador:
  HÉCTOR REYES
  EUDORO URDANETA

For Spain:
  PEDRO DE IGUAL Y MARTÍNEZ DABÁN
  ANTONIO CAMACHO SANJURJO

For the United States of America:
  JOSEPH STEWART
  EUGENE R. WHITE

For Guatemala:
  EMILIO ARROYAVE L.

For Honduras:
  MIGUEL CARIAS ANDINO
  OTTO REINBECK

For Mexico:
  EDUARDO ORTIZ
  COSME HINOJOSA
  JOSÉ V. CHÁVEZ

For Panama:
  JOSÉ IGNACIO ICAZA

For Paraguay:
  CARLOS MELÉNDEZ

For Peru:
  AUGUSTO S. SALAZAR
  WALTER F. FORD

For Uruguay:
  CÉSAR MIRANDA

NOTICE OF U.S. RATIFICATION

JUNE 20, 1927.

The Honorable,

The DIRECTOR GENERAL OF POSTS,

Mexico, D. F., Mexico.

SIR: I have the honor hereby to give formal notice of the ratification by this Postal Administration of the Pan-American Money Order Convention formulated and signed November 9, 1926, during the sessions of the Pan-American Postal Congress held in Mexico City.

Because of the laws and regulations governing postal money order business in the United States, this Department is forced to exclude from its ratification of the instrument, Articles VIII, XI, XX and XXI.

With reference to Article VIII, I am pleased to say that while there is no authority of law by which money orders pertaining to the Postal Service may be issued in the United States without exaction of a fee, this Administration will be very glad to honor promptly such orders issued in other countries for payment in this without making any charge for the service.

This Postal Service has no provision by which the remitter, on the payment of a fee when the order is issued, may be notified of its payment as contemplated by Article XI, and cannot therefore ratify that article of the convention. In any instance where an allegation of non-payment or wrong payment is made, however, this Department will gladly conduct an investigation, and, if possible, satisfactorily adjust the dispute, informing the issuing Postal Administration fully of the result of the inquiry, and for this service no fee is exacted.

As the telegraph service in this Republic is not controlled by the Federal Government, it is not possible to arrange for the exchange of orders by telegraph as provided by Article XX, and therefore ratification of that article by this Administration cannot be made.

The provisions of the agreement of the Universal Postal Union relating to the exchange of money orders in certain details are so entirely different from the principles on which the money order system of the United States is based that this Administration has never found it practicable or desirable to adhere to that portion of the Universal Postal Union Agreement. We cannot therefore ratify Article XXI of the Pan-American Money Order Convention.

With reference to the various postal administrations signatory to the convention this Department is entirely willing to begin the exchange of money orders at once with those countries with which it does not now transact such business. Of course, before the actual transaction of business may begin, it will be necessary to determine through correspondence, the post offices, to be designated as Exchange Offices, the maximum amount of orders, which administration shall render accounts, the manner of effecting conversions and whether the alternative provided in Article II, relative to the use of money other than that of the country of destination shall be adopted.

For the countries with which an exchange is now conducted under the terms of existing conventions, it is to be definitely understood that business shall continue to be transacted in accordance with the terms of such conventions until satisfactory agreements are made under the terms of Articles II and XVII relative to the currency to be used.

The Republic of Cuba and the United States of America now have a money order convention which permits either country to pay money orders issued in the other on the ordinary domestic form. The advantages of this plan to the patrons and the respective postal administrations are so great that it is thought best to continue as heretofore, the two countries, being at liberty by mutual agreement to avail themselves of the procedure prescribed by the Pan-American Convention at a later date should they so desire.

It will be very much appreciated if you will be good enough to cause the postal administrations of the countries whose representatives signed this money order convention to be informed of its ratification by the United States of America, and of the Articles which this Department has found it necessary to except from ratification.

Respectfully,

HARRY S. NEW,
Postmaster General.

ALLOCATION OF DAWES ANNUITIES

Agreement done at Paris January 13, 1927; signed for the United States February 1, 1927

Entered into force January 13, 1927; for the United States February 1, 1927

> 1927 For. Rel. (II) 724 and 1919 For. Rel. (Paris Peace Conference, XIII) 924

The Governments of Belgium, the United States of America, France, Great Britain, Italy, Japan, Brazil, Greece, Poland, Portugal, Roumania, the Serb-Croat-Slovene State and Czechoslovakia, respectively represented by the under-signed have agreed as follows.

AGREEMENT

regulating the amounts to be allocated out of the Annuities of the Experts' Plan for the Armies of Occupation, the Rhineland High Commission and the Military Commission of Control for the period 1st April 1926 to 10th January 1930.

ARTICLE 1

Armies of Occupation

I. For the period 1st April 1926 to 10th January 1930 or until a modification in the zones of military occupation, the amounts to be admitted as a prior charge on the Annuities of the Experts' Plan in respect of the total costs of the Armies of Occupation inclusive of the costs of supplies and services of all kinds under the Rhineland Agreement [1] shall be calculated on a yearly basis of 141,000,000 gold marks divided as follows:—

French Army	100,000,000 gold marks
British Army	25,000,000 " "
Belgian Army	16,000,000 " "

These figures correspond to the following effective strengths:

French Army	60,000
British Army	7,900
Belgian Army	8,900

and constitute maximum amounts.

---

[1] 1919 For. Rel. (Paris Peace Conference, XIII) 762.

II. For the period from the 1st April to the 31st August 1926 and thereafter at six-monthly intervals the allocation to each occupying Power shall be fixed within the limits of its maximum allocation and at the choice of the Power concerned.

a) either in accordance with the proportion between the actual effective strength during the period in question and the basic strength above, or

b) as regards costs other than those of supplies and services under Articles 8–12 of the Rhineland Agreement by application of the provisions of paragraphs I and IV of Article I of the Financial Agreement of the 11th March 1922,[2] and as regards costs of supplies and services under Articles 8–12 of the Rhineland Agreement on the basis of the final debits in respect of such supplies and services.

III. For the application of formula *a*) the Power concerned will furnish certified statements of average monthly strengths.

For the application of formula *b*) the Power concerned will furnish in accordance with the rules now in force for the application of the Agreement of the 11th March 1922, certified statements of effective strengths and of average monthly costs.

IV. Supplies and services furnished under Articles 8–12 of the Rhineland Agreement before the 1st April 1926 will continue to be brought to account as provided for in the Agreement of the 21st September 1925.[3]

V. Provisional allocations shall be fixed on the basis of the maximum figures in paragraph I for the period 1st April to 31st August 1926 and for the first six months of the third Annuity year.

Thereafter the provisional allocations shall be fixed by unanimous decision of the Reparation Commission. The Commission will in principle determine the allocations by the application of formula *a*). Nevertheless in the event of an increase in the retail prices in one of the countries interested between the period 1st April–31st August 1926 and the period under consideration, the Commission will apply a coefficient of increase to the figure obtained by the application of formula *a*) which shall take as exact account as possible of the effects of the increase in retail prices.

The necessary adjustments between the provisional allocations and the amounts actually due shall be made as soon as they are known.

ARTICLE 2

Interallied Rhineland High Commission

The maximum annual charge for the Interallied Rhineland High Commission, inclusive of the costs of supplies and services of all kinds under the

---

[2] *Ibid.,* p. 870.
[3] *Ante,* p. 521.

Rhineland Agreement, shall not exceed 3,335,000 gold marks (to be taken in foreign currency or in German currency as required) as from the 1st April, 1926, this sum being allocated between the French, British and Belgian High Commissariats as follows:

French High Commissariat_____	1, 535, 000 g.m.
British High Commissariat_____	900, 000 "
Belgian High Commissariat_____	900, 000 "

Not more than $\frac{5}{12}$ths of the annual amounts above mentioned shall be allowed in respect of the period April to August 1926 inclusive.

This provision is only to be drawn upon as and to the extent required, and at the end of every six months the Interallied Rhineland High Commission will transmit to the Reparation Commission a certified statement of the expenditure actually incurred by each High Commissariat in the execution of its duties under the Rhineland Agreement.

Any savings at the end of each year will be paid into the Common Reparation fund for distribution in accordance with the provisions of the Financial Agreement of the 14th January 1925 [4] to the Powers having the right under that Agreement to participate in the receipts from Germany on account of the Annuities of the Experts' Plan available for distribution as reparation.

In addition to the above amounts the Allied and Associated Governments interested will at the request of the High Commission, place at its disposal out of the Annuity an amount not exceeding the savings made by it during the first year of the Experts' Plan (in round figures 550,000 gold marks) to meet, in so far as they may be justified, any outstanding claims presented by the German Government in respect of Article 6 of the Rhineland Agreement for the period 1st September 1924–31st August 1925.

The provisions of the present Article will remain in force until the 10th January 1930, or until a modification in the present zones of occupation.

ARTICLE 3

Interallied Military Commission of Control

The provisions of Article 3 of the Agreement of the 21st September 1925 are extended until the end of the third year of the Experts' Plan. Nevertheless, for this third year the maximum fixed by the first paragraph of the above Article is reduced to 350,000 gold marks a month.

The present agreement, done in English and French in a Single Copy will be deposited in the Archives of the Government of the French Republic which will supply certified copies thereof to each of the Signatory Powers.

---

[4] *Ante,* p. 504.

In the interpretation of this Agreement, the English and French texts shall be both authentic.

PARIS, *January 13th, 1927.*

[For Belgium:]
MAUCLÈRE

[For France:]
GUTT

[For the United States of America:]
R. W. S. HILL

[For Great Britain:]
W. A. GOODCHILD

[For Italy:]
CORSI

[For Japan:]
YAMAJI

[For Brazil:]
MONIZ DE ARAGAO

[For Greece:]
CARAPANOS

[For Portugal:]
FERNANDES

[For Romania:]
CONDURAKI

[For the Serb-Croat-Slovene State:]
Dr. PLOJ

[For Czechoslovakia:]
STEFAN OSUSKY

PAN AMERICAN SANITARY CONVENTION

Additional protocol signed at Lima October 19, 1927
Senate advice and consent to ratification February 24, 1928
Ratified by the President of the United States March 14, 1928
Ratification of the United States deposited at Lima July 3, 1928
Proclaimed by the President of the United States July 5, 1928
Entered into force July 3, 1928

45 Stat. 2613; Treaty Series 763

[TRANSLATION]

ADDITION TO THE PAN AMERICAN SANITARY CODE

The Presidents of the Argentine Republic, Bolivia, the United States of Brazil, Colombia, Costa Rica, Cuba, Ecuador, the United States of America, Guatemala, Haiti, Honduras, Nicaragua, Panama, Paraguay, Peru, the Dominican Republic, Uruguay and the United States of Venezuela, desirous of adding to the Sanitary Convention signed at Habana on November 14, 1924,[1] have appointed as their plenipotentiaries, to wit:

Argentine Republic:	Dr. LAURENTINO OLASCOAGA
	Dr. NICOLÁS LOZANO
	Dr. ALFREDO SORDELLI
Bolivia:	Dr. ADOLFO FLORES
	Dr. ADOLFO DURÁN
United States of Brazil:	Dr. JOÃO PEDRO DE ALBUQUERQUE
	Dr. BENTO OSWALDO CRUZ
Colombia:	Dr. JULIO APARACIO
Costa Rica:	Dr. SOLÓN NÚÑEZ F.
	Mr. JAIME G. BENNETT
Cuba:	Dr. FERNANDO RENSOLI
	Dr. MARIO G. LEBREDO
Ecuador:	Dr. LUIS M. CUEVA

---

[1] TS 714, *ante*, p. 483.

648

United States of America:	Dr. HUGH S. CUMMING
	Dr. BOLIVAR J. LLOYD
	Dr. JOHN D. LONG
Guatemala:	Mr. PABLO EMILIO GUEDES
Haiti:	Mr. VÍCTOR KIEFFER MARCHAND
	Dr. GUILLERMO ANGULO P. A.
Honduras:	Dr. JOSÉ JORGE CALLEJAS
Nicaragua:	Mr. JULIO C. GASTIABURÚ
Panama:	Dr. JOSÉ GUILLERMO LEWIS
Paraguay:	Dr. ISIDRO RAMIREZ
Peru:	Dr. CARLOS ENRIQUE PAZ SOLDÁN
	Dr. SEBASTIÁN LORENTE
	Dr. BALTAZAR CARAVEDO
	Dr. DANIEL E. LAVORERÍA
	Dr. JULIO C. GASTIABURÚ
Dominican Republic:	Dr. RAMÓN BAEZ SOLER
	Dr. ALEJANDRO BUSSALLEU
Uruguay:	Dr. JUSTO F. GONZALEZ
United States of Venezuela:	Dr. EMILIO OCHOA

Who, after communicating to one another their full powers and finding them in due form, have agreed to adopt, ad referendum, the following:

ADDITIONAL PROTOCOL TO THE PAN AMERICAN SANITARY CODE

The ratification of the Pan American Sanitary Code shall be deposited in the Office of the Secretary of State of the Republic of Cuba and the Cuban Government shall communicate these ratifications to the other signatory States, which communication shall constitute exchange of ratifications. The Convention shall become effective in each of the signatory States on the date of ratification thereof by said State, and shall remain in force without limitation of time, each one of the signatory or adherent States reserving the right to withdraw from the Convention by giving in due form a year's notice in advance to the Government of the Republic of Cuba.

Done and signed in the City of Lima on the nineteenth day of October, nineteen hundred and twenty-seven, in duplicate, one of which shall be sent to the Ministry of Foreign Relations of Peru and the other to the Pan American Sanitary Office, so that copies thereof may be distributed through the diplomatic channel, to the signatory and adhering Governments.

For the Argentine Republic:
LAURENTINO OLASCOAGA
NICOLÁS LOZANO
A. SORDELLI

For Bolivia:
A. FLORES
ADOLFO F. DURÁN

For the United States of Brazil:
JOAO PEDRO DE ALBUQUERQUE
BENTO OSWALDO CRUZ

For Colombia:
JULIO APARICIO

For Costa Rica:
SOLÓN NÚÑEZ
JAIME G. BENNETT

For Cuba:
D. F. RENSOLI
Dr. MARIO G. LEBREDO

For Ecuador:
LUIS M. CUEVA

For the United States of America:
HUGH S. CUMMING
BOLIVAR J. LLOYD
JOHN D. LONG

For Guatemala:
PABLO EMILIO GUEDES

For Haiti:
V. KIEFER MARCHAND
GMO. ANGULO P. A.

For Honduras:
JOSÉ J. CALLEJAS

For Nicaragua:
J. C. GASTIABURÚ

For Panama:
JOSÉ G. LEWIS

For Paraguay:
ISIDRO RAMÍREZ

For Peru:
CARLOS ENRIQUE PAZ SOLDÁN
SEBASTIÁN LORENTE
BALTAZAR CARAVEDO
D. E. LAVORERÍA
J. C. GASTIABURÚ

For Dominican Republic:
R. BAEZ SOLER
A. BUSSALLEU

For Uruguay:
JUSTO F. GONZALEZ

For the United States of Venezuela:
E. OCHOA

ABOLITION OF IMPORT AND EXPORT PROHIBITIONS AND RESTRICTIONS

*Convention with annex opened for signature at Geneva November 8,
1927, and signed for the United States, with a declaration,
January 30, 1928;[1] protocol signed at Geneva November 8, 1927,
with annexed declaration; supplementary agreement and protocol
done at Geneva July 11, 1928, and signed for the United States
July 31, 1928; protocol concerning entry into force signed at Paris
December 20, 1929*

*Senate advice and consent to ratification, with a declaration and an
understanding, September 19, 1929[2]*

*Ratified by the President of the United States, with a declaration and an
understanding, September 20, 1929[2]*

*Ratification of the United States deposited with the Secretary-General
of the League of Nations September 30, 1929*

*Entered into force January 1, 1930, as between signatories to protocol
of December 20, 1929*

Proclaimed by the President of the United States March 6, 1930

Terminated as to the United States June 30, 1933;[3] terminated definitively June 30, 1934

46 Stat. 2461; Treaty Series 811

Convention

The President of the German Reich; the President of the United States of
America; the President of the Austrian Federal Republic; His Majesty the
King of the Belgians; His Majesty the King of Great Britain and Ireland and
of the British Dominions beyond the Seas, Emperor of India; His Majesty
the King of the Bulgarians; the President of the Chilian Republic; His
Majesty the King of Denmark; His Majesty the King of Egypt; the President

---

[1] For text of U.S. declaration made at time of signing, see p. 663.

[2] The Senate gave its advice and consent to ratification, and the President ratified the
convention, subject to the declaration made at time of signing and with the understanding
that "the provision of Section VI of the protocol to the convention, excepting from the
scope of the convention prohibitions or restrictions applying to prison-made goods, includes
goods the products of forced or slave labor however employed."

[3] Pursuant to notice of denunciation given in accordance with provisions of para. 6 of
protocol of Dec. 20, 1929 (p. 679).

651

of the Estonian Republic; the President of the Republic of Finland; the President of the French Republic; His Serene Highness the Governor of Hungary; His Majesty the King of Italy; His Majesty the Emperor of Japan; the President of the Latvian Republic; Her Royal Highness the Grand-Duchess of Luxemburg; His Majesty the King of Norway; Her Majesty the Queen of the Netherlands; the President of the Polish Republic; the President of the Portuguese Republic; His Majesty the King of Roumania; His Majesty the King of the Serbs, Croats and Slovenes; His Majesty the King of Siam; His Majesty the King of Sweden; the Swiss Federal Council; the President of the Czechoslovak Republic; the President of the Turkish Republic:

Having regard to the resolution of the Assembly of the League of Nations dated September 25th [29th], 1924;

Being guided by the conclusions of the International Economic Conference held at Geneva in May 1927, and agreeing with the latter that import and export prohibitions, and the arbitrary practices and disguised discriminations to which they give rise, have had deplorable results, without the grave drawbacks of these measures being counterbalanced by the financial advantages or social benefits which were anticipated by the countries which had recourse to them;

Being persuaded that it is important for the recovery and future development of world trade that Governments should abandon a policy which is equally injurious to their own and to the general interest;

Being convinced that a return to the effective liberty of international commerce is one of the primary conditions of world prosperity; and

Considering that this object may best be achieved by resort to simultaneous and concerted action in the form of an international convention;

Have appointed their plenipotentiaries, namely:

The President of the German Reich:

Dr. E. Trendelenburg, Secretary of State to the Ministry of National Economy;

The President of the United States of America:

Mr. Hugh R. Wilson, Envoy Extraordinary and Minister Plenipotentiary to the Swiss Federal Council;

The President of the Austrian Federal Republic:

M. Emerich Pflügl, Minister Plenipotentiary, Representative of the Austrian Federal Government accredited to the League of Nations;

His Majesty the King of the Belgians:

M. J. Brunet, Envoy Extraordinary and Minister Plenipotentiary;

M. F. van Langenhove, Chef du Cabinet and General Director for Foreign Commerce in the Ministry of Foreign Affairs;

His Majesty the King of Great Britain and Ireland and of the British Dominions beyond the Seas, Emperor of India:

For Great Britain and Northern Ireland and all parts of the British Empire which are not separate Members of the League of Nations: Sir Sydney Chapman, K.C.B., C.B.E., Economic Adviser to His Britannic Majesty's Government;

For India: Sir Atul C. Chatterjee, High Commissioner for the Empire of India in London;

His Majesty the King of the Bulgarians: M. Georges Danaïllow, Professor at the University of Sofia, M. P.;

The President of the Chilian Republic: M. E. Villegas, Chilian Representative on the Council of the League of Nations;

His Majesty the King of Denmark: M. J. Clan, Envoy Extraordinary and Minister Plenipotentiary, Chairman of the Danish Commission for the Conclusion of Commercial Treaties;

His Majesty the King of Egypt: Sadik Henein Pasha, Envoy Extraordinary and Minister Plenipotentiary to His Majesty the King of Italy;

The President of the Estonian Republic: M. C. R. Pusta, Envoy Extraordinary and Minister Plenipotentiary to His Majesty the King of Spain and to the President of the French Republic;

The President of the Republic of Finland: M. Rafael Waldemar Erich, Envoy Extraordinary and Minister Plenipotentiary to the Swiss Federal Council, Permanent Delegate accredited to the League of Nations;

The President of the French Republic: M. Daniel Serruys, Director of Commercial Agreements in the Ministry of Commerce;

His Serene Highness the Governor of Hungary: M. Baranyai Zoltán, Chargé d'Affaires *a. i.* of the Royal Hungarian Delegation accredited to the League of Nations;

His Majesty the King of Italy: M. A. Di Nola, Director-General of Commerce and of Economic Policy;

His Majesty the Emperor of Japan:
> M. N. Ito, Counsellor of Embassy, Acting Director of the Imperial Japanese League of Nations Office;
> M. J. Tsushima, Financial Commissioner of the Japanese Government in London, Paris and New York;

The President of the Latvian Republic:
> M. Charles Duzmans, Minister Plenipotentiary, Permanent Representative accredited to the League of Nations;

Her Royal Highness the Grand-Duchess of Luxemburg:
> M. Albert Calmes, Member of the Superior Council of the Economic Union of Belgium and Luxemburg;

His Majesty the King of Norway:
> M. Georg Wettstein, Consul-General at Zurich;

Her Majesty the Queen of the Netherlands:
> Dr. F. E. Posthuma, former Minister of Agriculture, Industry and Commerce;
> M. de Graaff, former Minister of the Colonies;
> M. F. M. Wibaut, Member of the Netherlands Senate;

The President of the Polish Republic:
> M. F. Sokal, Minister Plenipotentiary, Permanent Delegate of the Polish Republic accredited to the League of Nations;

The President of the Portuguese Republic:
> M. F. de Calheiros e Menezes, First Secretary of Legation, Chief of the Portuguese Office accredited to the League of Nations;

His Majesty the King of Roumania:
> M. D. Gheorghiu, Director of the Roumanian National Bank;
> M. C. Popescu, Director-General of Industry in the Ministry of Industry and Commerce;

His Majesty the King of the Serbs, Croats and Slovenes:
> M. Constantin Fotitch, Permanent Delegate accredited to the League of Nations;

His Majesty the King of Siam:
> His Highness Prince Charoon, Envoy Extraordinary and Minister Plenipotentiary to the President of the French Republic;

His Majesty the King of Sweden:
> M. Einar Hennings, Envoy Extraordinary and Minister Plenipotentiary to the Swiss Federal Council;

The Swiss Federal Council:

    M. Walter Stucki, Head of the Commerce Division in the Federal Department of Public Economy;

The President of the Czechoslovak Republic:

    Dr. Vincent Ibl, Counsellor of Legation in the Ministry of Foreign Affairs;

The President of the Turkish Republic:

    Mehmed Kemal Bey, Consul at Geneva;

Who, having communicated their full powers, found in good and due form, have agreed to the following provisions:

ARTICLE 1

The provisions of the present Convention shall apply to prohibitions and restrictions imposed on the importation into the territories of any High Contracting Party of goods the produce or manufacture of the territories of any other High Contracting Party, and to prohibitions and restrictions imposed on the exportation of goods from the territories of any High Contracting Party to the territories of any other High Contracting Party.

ARTICLE 2

Subject to the exceptions provided for in the following articles, the High Contracting Parties undertake to abolish within a period of six months from the date of the coming into force of the present Convention, in so far as the respective territories of each of them are concerned, all import and export prohibitions or restrictions, and not thereafter to impose any such prohibitions or restrictions. During this period each of the High Contracting Parties will adopt all appropriate measures in order to reduce existing prohibitions and restrictions to a minimum and will refrain from imposing any new prohibitions or restrictions.

Further, the High Contracting Parties undertake to adopt the necessary measures to ensure that the provisions of the present Convention are strictly observed by all authorities, central or local, and that no regulation is issued in contravention thereof.

ARTICLE 3

Should the High Contracting Parties, in pursuance of their legislation, subject the importation or exportation of goods to certain regulations in respect of the manner, form or place of importation or exportation, or the imposition of marks, or to other formalities or conditions, they undertake that such regulations shall not be made a means of disguised prohibition or arbitrary restriction.

ARTICLE 4

The following classes of prohibitions and restrictions are not prohibited by the present Convention, on condition, however, that they are not applied in such a manner as to constitute a means of arbitrary discrimination between foreign countries where the same conditions prevail, or a disguised restriction on international trade:

1. Prohibitions or restrictions relating to public security.
2. Prohibitions or restrictions imposed on moral or humanitarian grounds.
3. Prohibitions or restrictions regarding traffic in arms, ammunition and implements of war, or, in exceptional circumstances, all other military supplies.
4. Prohibitions or restrictions imposed for the protection of public health or for the protection of animals or plants against disease, insects and harmful parasites.
5. Export prohibitions or restrictions issued for the protection of national treasures of artistic, historic or archaeological value.
6. Prohibitions or restrictions applicable to gold, silver, coins, currency notes, banknotes or securities.
7. Prohibitions or restrictions designed to extend to foreign products the regime established within the country in respect of the production of, trade in, and transport and consumption of native products of the same kind.
8. Prohibitions or restrictions applied to products which, as regards production or trade, are or may in future be subject within the country to State monopoly or to monopolies exercised under State control.

ARTICLE 5

Nothing in this Convention shall affect the right of any High Contracting Party to adopt measures prohibiting or restricting importation or exportation for the purpose of protecting, in extraordinary and abnormal circumstances, the vital interests of the country.

Should measures of this character be adopted, they shall be applied in such a manner as not to lead to any arbitrary discrimination against any other High Contracting Party. Their duration shall be restricted to that of the causes or circumstances from which they arise.

ARTICLE 6

1. The High Contracting Parties, recognising that there exist in the case of certain of them situations of fact or of law which prevent the latter from immediately undertaking, as regards certain specified products, the engagements entered into under the previous articles, have deemed it equitable to authorise these High Contracting Parties to make a reservation in regard to certain temporary exceptions, which the latter undertake to withdraw as soon as the circumstances from which they arise cease to exist.

2. Moreover, the High Contracting Parties, recognising that the abolition of certain import or export prohibitions or restrictions applied by some of them would involve the latter in grave difficulties, and that, moreover, these prohibitions or restrictions do not prejudicially affect the trade of other countries, have also deemed it equitable to authorise these High Contracting Parties to make a reservation in regard to these exceptions.

3. The Annex to the present Convention sets forth the exceptions coming within the provisions of the two preceding paragraphs, which have been agreed to on this day's date in favour of the High Contracting Parties who are mentioned by name in the Annex and who have signed the Convention on that date.

4. Exceptions which the High Contracting Parties may desire to claim subsequently to that date shall be dealt with in accordance with the procedure laid down in the Protocol to the present Convention.

ARTICLE 7

Should one of the High Contracting Parties be obliged to adopt any measure of prohibition or restriction against products of any foreign country, whether the Convention be applicable to that country or not, he shall frame the measure in such a way as to cause the least possible injury to the trade of the other High Contracting Parties.

ARTICLE 8

If a dispute arises between two or more High Contracting Parties as to the interpretation or application of the provisions of the present Convention—with the exception of Articles 4, 5 and 6, and of the provisions of the Protocol relating to these articles—and if such dispute cannot be settled either directly between the parties or by the employment of any other means of reaching agreement, the parties to the dispute may, provided they all so agree, before resorting to any arbitral or judicial procedure, submit the dispute with a view to an amicable settlement to such technical body as the Council of the League of Nations or the parties concerned may appoint. This body will give an advisory opinion after hearing the parties and, if necessary, effecting a meeting between them.

The advisory opinion given by the said body will not be binding upon the parties to the dispute unless it is accepted by all of them, and the parties, if they all so agree, may either after resort to such procedure, or in lieu thereof, have recourse to any arbitral or judicial procedure which they may select, including reference to the Permanent Court of International Justice as regards any matters which are within the competence of that Court under its Statute.

If a dispute of a legal nature arises as to the interpretation or application of the provisions of the present Convention—with the exception of Articles 4, 5 and 6, and of the provisions of the Protocol relating to these articles—

the parties shall, at the request of any of them, refer the matter to the decision of the Permanent Court of International Justice or of an arbitral tribunal selected by them, whether or not there has previously been recourse to the procedure laid down in the first paragraph.

In the event of any difference of opinion as to whether a dispute is of a legal nature or not, the question shall be referred for decision to the Permanent Court of International Justice or to the arbitral tribunal selected by the parties.

The procedure before the body referred to in the first paragraph above or the opinion given by it will in no case involve the suspension of the measures to which the dispute refers; the same will apply in the event of proceedings being taken before the Permanent Court of International Justice—unless the Court decides otherwise under Article 41 of its Statute—or before the arbitral tribunal selected by the parties.

Nothing in the present Convention shall be construed as prejudicing the rights and obligations derived by the High Contracting Parties from the engagements into which they have entered with reference to the jurisdiction of the Permanent Court of International Justice, or from any bilateral conciliation or arbitration conventions between them.

ARTICLE 9

Any High Contracting Party may, either upon ratifying the present Convention or thereafter, declare that he undertakes, in regard to any other High Contracting Party accepting the same obligation, to extend the application of the provisions of paragraph 3 of Article 8 to any dispute which may arise in connection with the interpretation or application of the provisions of the present Convention, including all or part of Articles 4, 5 and 6, and whether or not the dispute is of a legal nature.

Any High Contracting Parties who do not give the undertaking referred to in paragraph 1 as regards Articles 4, 5, and 6, or certain parts of these Articles, and as regards the provisions of the Protocol relating thereto, may make the provisions of paragraphs 1 and 2 of Article 8 applicable to these matters as between themselves.

ARTICLE 10 [4]

Any High Contracting Party may at the time of signature, ratification or accession declare that, in accepting the present Convention, he does not assume any obligations in respect of all or any of his colonies, protectorates or territories under suzerainty or mandate; and the present Convention shall not apply to any territories named in such declaration.

Any High Contracting Party may give notice to the Secretary-General of the League of Nations at any time subsequently that he desires that the Convention shall apply to all or any of his territories which have been made the

[4] For U.S. declaration, see p. 663.

subject of a declaration under the preceding paragraph, and the Convention shall apply to all the territories named in such notice ninety days after its receipt by the Secretary-General of the League of Nations.

Any High Contracting Party may at any time declare that he desires that the present Convention shall cease to apply to all or any of his colonies, protectorates or territories under suzerainty or mandate, and the Convention shall cease to apply to the territories named in such declaration one year after its receipt by the Secretary-General of the League of Nations.

ARTICLE 11

Nothing in the present Convention shall prejudice the rights and obligations which the High Contracting Parties may derive from international Conventions in force to which they are parties.

The present Convention shall not prejudice the provisions of any bilateral agreements in force at the present date between the High Contracting Parties which establish, in regard to import and export prohibitions or restrictions, a more liberal regime than that established by the provisions of the present Convention.

ARTICLE 12

The present Convention shall not in any way affect rights and obligations arising from the Covenant of the League of Nations.

ARTICLE 13

The High Contracting Parties shall, within twelve months after the coming into force of the present Convention in their territories, communicate to one another through the Secretary-General of the League of Nations a report on the steps taken to give effect to the provisions of the Convention.

ARTICLE 14

The present Convention, of which the French and English texts are both authentic, shall bear this day's date.

It shall be open for signature until January 1st, 1929, on behalf of any Member of the League of Nations or of any non-Member State represented at the Conference which drew up this Convention or to which the Council of the League of Nations shall, for this purpose, have communicated a copy of the present Convention.

Members of the League of Nations and non-Member States on whose behalf the Convention has been signed prior to February 1st, 1928, may avail themselves of the procedure referred to in Article 6, paragraph 4.

ARTICLE 15

The present Convention shall be ratified.

The instruments of ratification shall be deposited with the Secretary-General of the League of Nations, who shall notify the receipt thereof to all

Members of the League and to the non-Member States referred to in the previous article.

ARTICLE 16

On and after January 1st, 1929, any Member of the League of Nations or any State referred to in Article 14 may accede to the present Convention.

This accession shall be effected by a notification made to the Secretary-General of the League of Nations, to be deposited in the archives of the Secretariat. The Secretary-General shall at once notify such deposit to all who have signed or acceded to the Convention.

ARTICLE 17

The present Convention shall come into force under the conditions and on the date to be determined at the meeting provided for hereinafter.

Between June 15th and July 15th, 1928, the Secretary-General of the League of Nations shall invite the duly accredited representatives of the Members of the League of Nations and non-Member States on whose behalf the Convention shall have been signed on or before June 15th, 1928, to attend a meeting at which they shall determine:

(a) The reservations which, having been communicated to the High Contracting Parties in accordance with Article 6, paragraph 4, may, with their consent, be made at the time of ratification;

(b) The conditions required for the coming into force of the Convention and, in particular, the number and, if necessary, the names of the Members of the League and of non-Member States, whether they are signatories or not, whose ratification or accession must first be secured;

(c) The last date on which the ratifications may be deposited and the date on which the Convention shall come into force if the conditions required under the preceding paragraph are fulfilled.

If, on the expiration of this period, the ratifications upon which the coming into force of the Convention will be conditional have not been secured, the Secretary-General of the League of Nations shall consult the Members of the League of Nations and non-Member States on whose behalf the Convention has been ratified and ascertain whether they desire nevertheless to bring it into force.

ARTICLE 18

The present Convention may be denounced by a notification in writing addressed to the Secretary-General of the League of Nations on behalf of any Member of the League of Nations or of any non-Member State after the expiration of a period of five years reckoned from the date on which the Convention shall have entered into force.

Such denunciation shall take effect twelve months after the date on which it is received by the Secretary-General of the League of Nations, and shall operate only in respect of the Member of the League of Nations or the non-Member State on whose behalf it is made.

Nevertheless, the Convention may be denounced on behalf of any Member of the League of Nations or any non-Member State after the expiration of the third year from the date of the present Convention, if, after that period, any one of the exceptions allowed in virtue of Article 6, paragraph 1, still exists. This denunciation shall take effect six months after the date on which it is received by the Secretary-General, and shall operate only in respect of the Member of the League of Nations or the non-Member State on whose behalf it its made.

Furthermore, the Convention may be denounced on behalf of any Member of the League of Nations or of any non-Member State after the expiration of the fifth year from the date of the present Convention, if, after that period, such Member of the League of Nations or non-Member State considers that any one of the exceptions allowed by the High Contracting Parties at the meeting provided for in Article 17 has impaired the effects of the present Convention.

This denunciation shall take effect six months after the date on which it is received by the Secretary-General and shall operate only in respect of the Member of the League of Nations or the non-Member State on whose behalf it is made.

Any denunciation made in accordance with the foregoing provisions shall be notified immediately by the Secretary-General of the League of Nations to all the other High Contracting Parties.

If, as a result of denunciations, the conditions for the coming into force of the Convention which the High Contracting Parties may lay down at the meeting provided for in Article 17 should no longer be fulfilled, any High Contracting Party may request the Secretary-General of the League of Nations to summon a Conference to consider the situation created thereby. Failing agreement to maintain the Convention, each of the High Contracting Parties shall be discharged from his obligations from the date on which the denunciation which led to the summoning of this Conference shall take effect.

ARTICLE 19

If, before the expiration of the period of five years mentioned in paragraph 1 of Article 18, notifications should be addressed to the Secretary-General of the League of Nations on behalf of one-third of the Members of the League of Nations and of non-Member States to which the present Convention applies, informing him that they desire the Convention to be revised, all the Members of the League of Nations and all non-Member States to which the Convention applies agree to take part in any consultation which may be held for this purpose.

If the revision has taken place before the end of the fifth year from the date of the coming into force of the present Convention, any Member of the League of Nations or non-Member State who has not accepted the revised Convention shall have the right to denounce the present Convention, without regard to the period of five years provided for in paragraph 4 of Article 18. Such denunciation shall take effect on the date on which the revised Convention comes into force.

If the revision has taken place in the course of the fifth year from the date of the coming into force of the present Convention, the period of denunciation referred to in paragraph 1 of Article 18 will be prolonged by one year.

ANNEX TO ARTICLE 6

In accordance with Article 6, paragraph 3, and with Section IV (d) of the Protocol, each of the exceptions maintained in favour of the countries mentioned below is only admitted under the terms of the present Convention if the country concerned appends its signature thereto on this day's date,[5] and if, on that same date, the prohibition or restriction which it seeks to maintain is still in force.

I

Exceptions agreed to under Paragraph 1

Germany	Coal, coke, peat, lignite, briquettes	import and export
	Scrap iron and scrap of other metals and alloys	export
Austria	Scrap iron and scrap of other metals and alloys	export
Belgium	Scrap iron and scrap of other metals and alloys	export
Great Britain	Synthetic organic dyestuffs and colours or colouring matter containing them, as well as organic intermediate products used in the manufacture of such dyestuffs, colours and colouring matter	import
France	Scrap iron and scrap of other metals and alloys	export
Hungary	Scrap iron and scrap of other metals and alloys	export
Italy	Scrap iron and scrap of other metals and alloys	export
Japan	Synthetic organic dyestuffs and colours or colouring matter containing them, as well as organic intermediate products used in the manufacture of such dyestuffs, colours and colouring matter	import
	Rice	import and export
Luxemburg	Scrap iron and scrap of other metals and alloys	export
Roumania	Scrap iron and scrap of other metals and alloys	export
	Used machinery for industrial installations	import
Czechoslovakia	Coal, coke, peat, lignite, briquettes	import and export
	Scrap iron and scrap of other metals and alloys	export

---

[5] Among the countries referred to in this Annex, the following signed the Convention on November 8th, 1927: Germany, Austria, Belgium, Great Britain, etc., Egypt, France, Hungary, Italy, Japan, Luxemburg, Roumania and Czechoslovakia. [Footnote in original.]

II

Exceptions agreed to under Paragraph 2

Egypt	Live-stock (exportation subject to licence)	export
	Eggs, during certain months of the year	export
	Organic fertilisers, including pigeon-manure, slaughter-house offal and dried blood	export
United States of America	Helium gas	export
Italy	Iron ores	export
	Corn	export
Roumania	Ores of iron, copper and manganese	export
	Crude oil	export

In faith whereof the delegates have signed the present Convention.

Done at Geneva, the eighth day of November, one thousand nine hundred and twenty-seven, in a single copy, which shall be deposited in the archives of the Secretariat of the League of Nations, and of which authenticated copies shall be delivered to all Members of the League of Nations and non-Member States represented at the Conference.

Germany:
DR. TRENDELENBURG
8–XI–27

United States of America:

At the moment of signing the International Convention for the Abolition of Import and Export Prohibitions and Restrictions, and the Protocol to the Convention, I, the undersigned, Envoy Extraordinary and Minister Plenipotentiary of the United States of America to Switzerland, duly empowered to sign the said Convention and Protocol, declare, pursuant to instructions from my Government, that the United States, in accordance with Article 10 of the Convention, does not assume any obligation in respect of the Philippine Islands and that I sign the Convention and Protocol subject to the following reservations and conditions with respect to the United States of America:

(*a*) That prohibitions or restrictions designed to extend to exported products the regime established within the country in respect of the production of, trade in, and transport and consumption of such products in domestic commerce are not prohibited by the said Convention, provided, however, that such prohibitions or restrictions shall not be applied in such a manner as to constitute a means of arbitrary discrimination between foreign countries or a disguised restriction on international trade.

(*b*) That the said Convention affects neither the tariff systems nor the treaty-making methods of the participating countries nor the measures taken to ensure the application thereof, including measures to counteract dumping, bounties, subsidies, unfair methods or acts in foreign trade, undervaluation or discrimination.

HUGH R. WILSON
30–I–28

Austria:
E. PFLÜGL
8–XI–27

Belgium:
J. BRUNET
F. VAN LANGENHOVE
8–XI–27

Great Britain and Northern Ireland and those Parts of the British Empire which are not separate Members of the League of Nations:

I declare that my signature does not include any of His Britannic Majesty's colonies, protectorates or territories under suzerainty or mandate.

S. J. CHAPMAN
8–XI–27

India:

Under the terms of Article 10 I declare that my signature does not include the territories in India of any Prince or Chief under the suzerainty of His Majesty.

ATUL C. CHATTERJEE
26–IV–28

Bulgaria:
PROF. GEORGES DANAÏLLOW
8–XI–27

Chile:

At the moment of signing the present Convention, the undersigned declares, on behalf of his Government:

(a) That he is fully convinced that Nos. 1 and 3 of Article 4 cannot be invoked by the other High Contracting Parties to prohibit or restrict the importation into their territories of Chilean nitrate of soda, principally employed in agriculture.

(b) That, in the Chilean Government's opinion, the Convention affects neither the tariff system nor the treaty-making methods of the participating countries, nor the measures taken to ensure their application, including the measures intended to counteract the effects of dumping [translation].

E. VILLEGAS
14–VI–28

Denmark:

Subject to reservation as regards Greenland [translation].

J. CLAN
8–XI–27

Egypt:
SADIK E. HENEIN
8–XI–27

Estonia:
C. R. PUSTA
30–I–28

Finland:
RAFAEL ERICH
8–XI–27

France:

On signing the present Convention, France declares that by its acceptance it does not intend to assume any obligation in regard to any of its Colonies, Protectorates and territories under its suzerainty or mandate [translation].

D. SERRUYS
8–XI–27

Hungary:
BARANYAI ZOLTÁN
8–XI–27

Italy:
A. DI NOLA
8–XI–27

Japan:

In signing the International Convention for the Abolition of Import and Export Prohibitions and Restrictions we, the undersigned, declare that the provisions of Article 8 of the present Convention are in no way derogatory to the acts of the Japanese judicial authorities in the application of Japanese laws and decrees [translation].

N. ITO
J. TSUSHIMA
8–XI–27

Latvia:
CHARLES DUZMANS
31–I–28

Luxemburg:
ALBERT CALMES
8–XI–27

Norway:
GEORG WETTSTEIN
31–I–28

The Netherlands:
POSTHUMA
DE GRAAFF
F. M. WIBAUT
8–XI–27

Poland:
F. SOKAL
31–I–28

Portugal:
FRANCISCO DE CALHEIROS E MENEZES
31–I–28

Roumania:
D. J. GHEORGHIU
CÉSAR POPESCU

Subject to ratification by the Roumanian Government and Parliament [translation].

8–XI–27

Kingdom of the Serbs, Croats and Slovenes:
CONST. FOTITCH
24–I–28

Siam:
CHAROON
8–XI–27

Sweden:
 Einar Hennings
  2–XII–27

Switzerland:
 W. Stucki
  8–XI–27

Czechoslovakia:
 Dr. Ibl
  8–XI–27

Turkey:
 M. Kemal
  14–V–28

Protocol to the Convention

At the moment of signing the Convention of to-day's date for the Abolition of Import and Export Prohibitions and Restrictions, the undersigned, duly authorised, have agreed on the following provisions, which are intended to ensure the application of the Convention:

Section I

AD ARTICLE 1

(*a*) The words "territories of the High Contracting Parties" employed in the Convention refer only to territories to which it is made applicable.

(*b*) Should the Customs territory of any High Contracting Party include territories which are not placed under his sovereignty, these territories are also to be regarded as "territories" within the meaning of the Convention.

(*c*) In view of the fact that within or immediately adjacent to the territory of India there are areas or enclaves, small in extent and population in comparison with such territory, and that these areas or enclaves form detached portions or settlements of other parent States, and that it is impracticable for administrative reasons to apply to them the provisions of the Convention, it is agreed that these provisions shall not apply to them.

India, however, will apply as regards the areas or enclaves in question a regime which will respect the principles of the Convention and facilitate imports and exports as far as practicable, and will refrain from imposing in regard to them any new measures of prohibition or restriction which would not be authorised by the provisions of the Convention, unless there should be no other means of ensuring the collection of customs and excise duties.

Section II

AD ARTICLE 2

As regards the application of Article 2, the obligation accepted by Canada binds only the Federal Government and not the Provincial Governments, which, under the Constitution, possess the power of prohibiting or restricting the importation and exportation of certain products into or from their territories.

SECTION III

AD ARTICLE 4

(a) *ad No. 4*

The protection of animals and plants against disease also refers to measures taken to preserve them from degeneration or extinction and to measures taken against harmful seeds, plants, parasites and animals.

(b) *ad No. 7*

The High Contracting Parties, although they have refrained from making any reference to measures relating to "standard" products and definitions of products, declare that this paragraph must be interpreted as in no way interfering with the practice followed by certain countries of subjecting the exportation of their products to certain conditions as to quality with the object of preserving the reputation of those products and at the same time of offering a guarantee to the foreign purchaser. They declare, on the other hand, that they interpret the paragraph in question as prohibiting recourse to any system of classifying or defining products which is employed as an indirect means of restricting the importation of foreign products or of subjecting importation to a regime of unfair discrimination.

(c) *ad No. 7*

The High Contracting Parties declare that prohibitions or restrictions the sole object of which is either to prevent imported goods from escaping the payment of the customs duties applicable thereto, or in exceptional cases to prevent the importation of certain goods which would reduce the revenue from the duties imposed on certain other goods, may only be established or maintained, if no other effective means exist of securing the said revenue.

(d) *ad No. 7*

The High Contracting Parties declare that if, on account of the constitution of certain States and the different methods of internal control which they employ, it should prove impossible to secure complete similarity of treatment between native and imported products, any such difference in treatment must not have the object or effect of establishing an unfair discrimination against the latter.

(e) *ad No. 8*

The High Contracting Parties declare that they have solely in view monopolies each of which applies only to one or more specific articles.

SECTION IV

AD ARTICLE 6

(a) *ad No. 1*

The High Contracting Parties who have made the reservations referred to in paragraph 1 of Article 6 declare that they do not regard their acceptance of the provisions of Article 18, paragraph 3, as an undertaking on their part that the circumstances which compelled them to make these reservations will have ceased to exist at the end of three years, but as entitling any High Contracting Party to resume his freedom of action if, in the event of these circumstances not having changed within the said period, he considered that his economic conditions were detrimentally affected by the maintenance of any of the prohibitions or restrictions to which the aforesaid reservations refer.

(b) ad No. 2

By allowing the exceptions referred to in Article 6, paragraph 2, the High Contracting Parties have not intended to give perpetual recognition to their existence, but merely to indicate that the necessity of abolishing these exceptions is not so imperative, in view of their slight importance in international trade.

(c) ad No. 2

The High Contracting Parties declare that, by accepting in the case of Roumania, in consideration of her exceptional situation of fact and of law, the reservation concerning crude oil in accordance with Article 6, paragraph 2, they have not in any way agreed to measures of prohibition or restriction for this product, which they regard as being of very great importance for the world market. The High Contracting Parties feel confident that, as soon as circumstances allow her to do so, Roumania herself, acting in the spirit of the preceding paragraph (b) above, will abolish this prohibition, and, in the meantime, that she will take into account the interests of the neighbouring contracting countries.

The Roumanian Delegation fully associates itself with this declaration.

(d) ad No. 4

(i) Scope of the Provision

As regards paragraph 4, it is understood that any claims for exceptions which may be put forward after the date of the present Convention shall refer only to prohibitions or restrictions in force on that same date.

(ii) Procedure

1. Any High Contracting Party may make known by a communication addressed to the Secretary-General of the League of Nations any prohibitions or restrictions which he desires to be able to maintain in virtue of paragraphs 1 and 2 of Article 6. Such communication must reach the Secretary-General before February 1st, 1928. It shall state the conditions, if any, on which the High Contracting Party in question would be prepared to abandon such prohibitions or restrictions.

2. As soon as possible after February 1st, 1928, the Secretary-General of the League of Nations shall notify the High Contracting Parties of all applications which he has received under the preceding paragraph.

3. Any High Contracting Party wishing to make observations on any applications so communicated may forward such observations to the Secretary-General of the League of Nations not later than May 1st, 1928. As soon as possible after that date, the Secretary-General will inform the High Contracting Parties of all observations received.

4. Any applications and observations made by the High Contracting Parties shall be examined at the meeting provided for in Article 17 of the Convention.

SECTION V

AD ARTICLE 7

The expression "trade of the High Contracting Parties" signifies the trade of their territories to which the Convention applies.

SECTION VI [6]

Prohibitions or restrictions applying to prison made goods are not within the scope of the Convention.

SECTION VII

Should any prohibitions or restrictions be imposed within the limits laid down by the Convention, the High Contracting Parties shall strictly adhere to the following provisions as regards licences:

(a) The conditions to be fulfilled and the formalities to be observed in order to obtain licences shall be brought immediately in the clearest and most definite form to the notice of the public;

(b) The method of issue of the certificates of licences shall be as simple and stable as possible;

(c) The examination of applications and the issue of licences to the applicants shall be carried out with the least possible delay;

(d) The system of issuing licences shall be such as to prevent the traffic in licences. With this object, licences, when issued to individuals, shall state the name of the holder and shall not be capable of being used by any other person.

As regards the allocation of quotas, the High Contracting Parties, without pronouncing upon the method to be adopted, consider that an equitable allocation of such quotas is one of the essential conditions for the equitable treatment of international trade.

In faith whereof the Plenipotentiaries have signed the present Protocol.

Done at Geneva the eighth day of November, one thousand nine hundred and twenty-seven, in a single copy, which shall be deposited in the archives of the Secretariat of the League of Nations, and of which authenticated

---

[6] For U.S. understanding, see footnote 2, p. 651.

copies shall be delivered to all Members of the League of Nations and non-Member States represented at the Conference.

Germany:
DR. TRENDELENBURG

United States of America:
HUGH R. WILSON

Austria:
E. PFLÜGL

Belgium:
J. BRUNET
F. VAN LANGENHOVE

Great Britain and Northern Ireland, and those Parts of the British Empire which are not separate Members of the League of Nations:

I declare that my signature does not include any of His Britannic Majesty's colonies, protectorates or territories under suzerainty or mandate.
S. J. CHAPMAN

India:
Under the terms of Article 10 of the Convention I declare that my signature does not include the territories in India of any Prince or Chief under Suzerainty of His Majesty.
ATUL C. CHATTERJEE

Bulgaria:
PROF. GEORGES DANAÏLLOW

Chile:
E. VILLEGAS

Denmark:
Subject to reservation as regards Greenland [translation].
J. CLAN

Egypt:
SADIK E. HENEIN

Estonia:
C. R. PUSTA

Finland:
RAFAEL ERICH

France:
Subject to the reservations made on signing the Convention [translation].
D. SERRUYS

Hungary:
BARANYAI ZOLTÁN

Italy:
A. DI NOLA

Japan:
Subject to the reservations made on signing the Convention [translation].
N. ITO
J. TSUSHIMA

Latvia:
CHARLES DUZMANS

Luxemburg:
ALBERT CALMES

Norway:
GEORG WETTSTEIN

The Netherlands:
POSTHUMA
DE GRAAFF
F. M. WIBAUT

Poland:
F. SOKAL

Portugal:
FRANCISCO DE CALHEIROS E MENEZES

Roumania:
D. J. GHEORGHIU
CÉSAR POPESCU
Subject to ratification by the Roumanian Government and Parliament [translation].

Kingdom of the Serbs,
  Croats and Slovenes:
CONST. FOTITCH

Siam:
CHAROON

Sweden:
EINAR HENNINGS

Switzerland:
W. STUCKI

Czechoslovakia:
DR. IBL

Turkey:
M. KEMAL

ANNEXED DECLARATION

The delegations of France, Greece, Hungary, Italy, Portugal, the Kingdom of the Serbs, Croats and Slovenes and Switzerland, present at the International Conference for the Abolition of Import and Export Prohibitions and Restrictions, desire to place it on record that, though they have abstained, in the desire not to place any obstacle in the way of the success of the Conference and not to raise between the participating States a controversy on a question of principle which could lead to no definite conclusion, they are nevertheless fully convinced that the prohibition of viticultural products cannot be justified on the ground of the provisions of Article 4, No. 4, of the Convention.

Geneva, November 8th, 1927.

France:
  D. SERRUYS

Greece:
  VASSILI DENDRAMIS

Hungary:
  BARANYAI ZOLTÁN

Italy:
  A. DI NOLA

Portugal:
  F. DE CALHEIROS E MENEZES

Kingdom of the Serbs, Croats and
  Slovenes:
  CONST. FOTITCH

Switzerland:
  W. STUCKI

Chile:
  The Government of the Chilian Republic accedes to the Declaration annexed to the Convention and, like the
  delegations of France, Greece, Hungary,
  Italy, Portugal, the Kingdom of the
  Serbs, Croats and Slovenes and Switzerland, it is convinced that the prohibition
  of viticultural products cannot be justified on the ground of the provisions of
  Article 4, No. 4, of the Convention
  [translation].
  E. VILLEGAS

SUPPLEMENTARY AGREEMENT TO THE CONVENTION OF NOVEMBER 8TH, 1927, FOR THE ABOLITION OF IMPORT AND EXPORT PROHIBITIONS AND RESTRICTIONS

The President of the German Reich; the President of the United States of America; the President of the Austrian Federal Republic; His Majesty the King of the Belgians; His Majesty the King of Great Britain and Ireland and of the British Dominions Beyond the Seas, Emperor of India; His Majesty the King of the Bulgarians; the President of the Chilian Republic; His Majesty the King of Denmark; His Majesty the King of Egypt; the President of the Estonian Republic; the President of the Republic of Finland; the President of the French Republic; His Serene Highness the Governor of Hungary; His Majesty the King of Italy; His Majesty the Emperor of Japan; the President of the Latvian Republic; Her Royal Highness the Grand Duchess of Luxemburg; His Majesty the King of Norway; Her Majesty the Queen of the Netherlands; the President of the Polish Republic; the President of the Portuguese Republic; His Majesty the King of Roumania; His Majesty the King of the Serbs, Croats and Slovenes; His Majesty the King of Siam; His Majesty the King of Sweden; the Swiss Federal Council; the President of the Czechoslovak Republic; the President of the Turkish Republic.

Having regard to the Convention signed at Geneva on November 8th, 1927, for the Abolition of Import and Export Prohibitions and Restrictions;

Having regard to the provisions of Article 17 of the said Convention;

Have appointed as their Plenipotentiaries for the meeting provided for in the said Article, namely:

The President of the German Reich:
  Dr. Ernst Trendelenburg, Secretary of State to the Ministry of National Economy;

The President of the United States of America:
  Mr. Hugh R. Wilson, Envoy Extraordinary and Minister Plenipotentiary to the Swiss Federal Council;

The President of the Austrian Federal Republic:
  Dr. Richard Schüller, Head of Section at the Federal Chancellery;

His Majesty the King of the Belgians:
  M. J. Brunet, Envoy Extraordinary and Minister Plenipotentiary;
  M. F. van Langenhove, Chef du Cabinet and General Director for Foreign Commerce in the Ministry of Foreign Affairs;

His Majesty the King of Great Britain and Ireland and of the British Dominions Beyond the Seas, Emperor of India:
  For Great Britain and Northern Ireland and all parts of the British Empire which are not separate Members of the League of Nations:
    Sir Sydney Chapman, K.C.B., C.B.E., Economic Adviser to His Britannic Majesty's Government;
  For India:
    Mr H. A. F. Lindsay, C.I.E., C.B.E., Indian Trade Commissioner;

His Majesty the King of the Bulgarians:
  M. D. Mikoff, Chargé d'Affaires at Berne;

The President of the Chilian Republic:
  M. Tomás Ramirez Frias, Deputy, former Minister of State, Professor of Political Economy and Civil Law at the University of Santiago;

His Majesty the King of Denmark:
  M. J. Clan, Envoy Extraordinary and Minister Plenipotentiary, Chairman of the Danish Commission for the Conclusion of Commercial Treaties;
  M. William Borberg, Permanent Danish Representative accredited to the League of Nations;

His Majesty the King of Egypt:
  Sadik Henein Pasha, Envoy Extraordinary and Minister Plenipotentiary to His Majesty the King of Italy;

The President of the Estonian Republic:
  M. A. Schmidt, Assistant Minister for Foreign Affairs;

The President of the Republic of Finland:
   M. Rudolf Holsti, Envoy Extraordinary and Minister Plenipotentiary, Permanent Delegate accredited to the League of Nations;
   M. Gunnar Kihlman, Director of Political and Commercial Affairs at the Ministry for Foreign Affairs;

The President of the French Republic:
   M. Daniel Serruys, Director of Commercial Agreements in the Ministry of Commerce;

His Serene Highness the Governor of Hungary:
   M. Alfred Nickl, Counsellor of Legation;

His Majesty the King of Italy:
   M. A. Di Nola, Director-General of Commerce and of Economic Policy;
   M. Pasquale Troise, Director-General of Customs;

His Majesty the Emperor of Japan:
   M. N. Ito, Counsellor of Embassy, Acting Director of the Imperial Japanese League of Nations Office;
   M. J. Tsushima, Financial Commissioner of the Japanese Government in London, Paris and New York;

The President of the Latvian Republic:
   M. Charles Duzmans, Minister Plenipotentiary, Permanent Representative accredited to the League of Nations;

Her Royal Highness the Grand Duchess of Luxemburg:
   M. Albert Calmes, Member of the Superior Council of the Economic Union of Belgium and Luxemburg;

His Majesty the King of Norway:
   M. Gunnar Jahn, Director of the Norwegian Central Bureau of Statistics;

Her Majesty the Queen of the Netherlands:
   Dr. F. E. Posthuma, Former Minister of Agriculture, Industry and Commerce;
   M. de Graaff, Former Minister of the Colonies;
   M. F. M. Wibaut, Member of the Netherlands Senate;

The President of the Polish Republic:
   M. François Dolezal, Under-Secretary of State at the Ministry of Industry and Commerce, member of the Economic Committee of the League of Nations;

The President of the Portuguese Republic:

    M. A. d'Oliveira, Envoy Extraordinary and Minister Plenipotentiary accredited to the Swiss Federal Council and to His Majesty the King of the Belgians, permanent Delegate accredited to the League of Nations;

    M. F. de Calheiros e Menezes, First Secretary of Legation, Chief of the Portuguese Office accredited to the League of Nations;

His Majesty the King of Roumania:

    M. Constantin Antoniade, Envoy Extraordinary and Minister Plenipotentiary accredited to the League of Nations;

    M. D. Gheorghiu, Director of the Roumanian National Bank;

    M. C. Popescu, Director-General of Industry in the Ministry of Industry and Commerce;

His Majesty the King of the Serbs, Croats and Slovenes:

    M. Constantin Fotitch, Permanent Delegate accredited to the League of Nations;

    M. Georges Curcin, Secretary-General of the Serb-Croat-Slovene Confederation of Industrial Corporations;

His Majesty the King of Siam:

    His Highness Prince Charoon, Envoy Extraordinary and Minister Plenipotentiary to the President of the French Republic;

His Majesty the King of Sweden:

    M. Einar Modig, Under-Secretary of State at the Ministry of Commerce;

The President of the Swiss Federal Council:

    M. Walter Stucki, Head of the Commerce Division in the Federal Department of Public Economy;

The President of the Czechoslovak Republic:

    Dr. Vincent Ibl, Counsellor of Legation in the Ministry of Foreign Affairs;

The President of the Turkish Republic:

    Hassan bey, Vice-President of the Grand National Assembly of Turkey;

Who, having communicated their full powers, found in good and due form, have agreed on the following provisions, intended to supplement the provisions of the aforesaid Convention, of which they shall form an integral part.

Article A

The Annex to Article 6 of the Convention of November 8th, 1927, is supplemented as follows for the benefit of the countries named hereafter:

Exceptions agreed to under Paragraph 1

Bulgaria.............	Rose trees and roots and shoots....................	Export
Chile................	Scrap iron and scrap zinc........................	Export
	Mares..	Export
Czechoslovakia.......	Hop shoots......................................	Export
Portugal.............	Fine wool.......................................	Export
	Cork in the raw state...........................	Export
Sweden..............	Scrap iron......................................	Export

Exceptions agreed to under Paragraph 2

Czechoslovakia........	Quartzite.......................................	Export
Estonia..............	Platinum, precious stones, pearls and corals (in a rough state or finished, loose or mounted)...............	Export
Portugal.............	Pine resin......................................	Export
United States.........	Helium gas.....................................	Export

Article B

The High Contracting Parties agree that, in the event of the Agreements concluded on this day's date relating to the Exportation of Hides and Skins and Bones not coming into force in default of the necessary ratifications, each of them shall be authorised to submit subsequent requests for exceptions which they were entitled to submit under the provisions of Article 6 of the Convention and the annexed Protocol, and which they have not submitted in view of the aforesaid Agreements.

Such requests for exception shall be addressed to the Secretary-General of the League of Nations before September 30th, 1929, and shall be notified by him to the High Contracting Parties before October 31st, 1929.

The High Contracting Parties undertake to meet without delay upon receiving an invitation from the Secretary-General in order to examine the requests for exceptions referred to above.

Article C

The High Contracting Parties agree that the Convention in order to be brought into force, must have secured either ratification as provided for in Article 15 or accession as provided for in Article 16 of the said Convention on behalf of at least eighteen members of the League of Nations or non-Member States.

The ratifications must be deposited before September 30th, 1929.

Each of the High Contracting Parties shall have the right to inform the Secretary-General of the League of Nations at the moment of the deposit of his ratification or of the notification of his accession that he makes the entry into force of the Convention, in so far as he is concerned, conditional on ratification or accession on behalf of certain countries, without, however, being entitled to specify countries other than those named below:

Austria	Poland
Czechoslovakia	Roumania
France	Kingdom of the Serbs, Croats and
Germany	Slovenes
Great Britain	Switzerland
Hungary	Turkey
Italy	United States of America
Japan	

The Secretary-General of the League of Nations shall immediately inform each of the High Contracting Parties of each ratification or accession received and of any observations by which it may be accompanied in conformity with the preceding paragraph.

On October 31st, 1929, the Secretary-General of the League of Nations shall notify all the Members of the League and non-Member States on behalf of which the Convention has been signed or acceded to under Article 16 of the Convention of the ratifications deposited and accessions notified before September 30th, 1929.

ARTICLE D

If it appears from the communication of the Secretary-General of the League of Nations, which is referred to in the last paragraph of the preceding Article, that the conditions required in virtue of the first three paragraphs of the said Article and of the annexed Protocol have been fulfilled by September 30th, 1929, the Convention shall come into force on January 1st, 1930.

In the contrary event, the procedure laid down in the last paragraph of Article 17 of the Convention shall be followed.

In faith whereof the above-mentioned Plenipotentiaries have signed the present Agreement.

Done at Geneva on the eleventh day of July, one thousand nine hundred and twenty-eight, in a single copy, which shall be deposited in the archives of the Secretariat of the League of Nations; certified true copies shall be forwarded to all the Members of the League of Nations and all the non-Member States represented at the Conference.

Germany:
    DR. ERNST TRENDELENBURG

United States of America:
    HUGH R. WILSON

Austria:
    DR. RICHARD SCHULLER

Belgium:
    J. BRUNET
    F. VAN LANGENHOVE

Great Britain and Northern Ireland and all parts of the British Empire which are not separate Members of the League of Nations.
    I declare that my signature does not include any of His Britannic Majesty's Colonies, Protectorates or territories under suzerainty or mandate.
    S. J. CHAPMAN

India:
    H. A. F. LINDSAY

Bulgaria:

On signing the present Supplementary Agreement, Bulgaria declares that it shall be ratified and put into force as soon as the national currency shall be re-established in gold [translation].

D. MIKOFF

Chile:
TOMÁS RAMIREZ FRIAS

Denmark:
J. CLAN
WILLIAM BORBERG

Egypt:
SADIK E. HENEIN

Estonia:
A. SCHMIDT

Finland:
RUDOLF HOLSTI
GUNNAR KIHLMAN

France:

On signing the present Supplementary Agreement France declares that by its acceptance it does not intend to assume any obligation in regard to any of its Colonies, Protectorates and territories under its suzerainty or mandate [translation].

D. SERRUYS

Hungary:
NICKL

Italy:
A. DI NOLA
P. TROISE

Japan:
ITO
J. TSUSHIMA

Latvia:
CHARLES DUZMANS

Luxemburg
ALBERT CALMES

Norway:
GUNNAR JAHN

Netherlands:
POSTHUMA
F. M. WIBAUT
S. DE GRAAFF

Poland:
FRANÇOIS DOLEZAL

Portugal:
A. D'OLIVEIRA
F. DE CALHEIROS E MENEZES

Roumania:
ANTONIADE
D. T. GHEORGHIU
CESAR POPESCU

Kingdom of the Serbs,
    Croats and Slovenes:
CONST. FOTITCH
GEORGES CURCIN

Siam:
CHAROON

Sweden:
EINAR MODIG

Switzerland:
W. STUCKI

Czechoslovakia:
IBL

Turkey:
Subject to reservation as regards Article B [translation].
HASSAN

PROTOCOL TO THE SUPPLEMENTARY AGREEMENT

At the moment of proceeding to the signature of the Supplementary Agreement to the International Convention for the Abolition of Import and Export Prohibitions and Restrictions signed on this day's date, the undersigned, duly authorised, have agreed on the following provisions, which are intended to ensure the application of the Supplementary Agreement:

SECTION I

The High Contracting Parties declare that, in the text of the Supplementary Agreement of this day's date, the expression "the Convention" shall be taken to mean both the International Convention for the Abolition of Import and Export Prohibitions and Restrictions dated November 8th, 1927, and the Supplementary Agreement of this day's date.

Section II

Ad Article A

(*a*) Cork in the raw state, in respect of which an exception has been allowed for Portugal, does not include scrap cork, or cork in agglomerated form, in shavings, or in sheets.

(*b*) Although the exceptions set out in Article A, like those appearing in the Annex to Article 6 of the Convention, have been allowed on the condition that the countries benefiting thereby shall sign the present Supplementary Agreement on the day of the general signature, it has appeared equitable to grant an extension of time up to August 31st, 1928, inclusive, to Bulgaria, Portugal and the United States of America.

(*c*) As regards the exception of hop shoots which has been agreed to in favour of Czechoslovakia under paragraph 1 of Article 6 of the Convention, the High Contracting Parties declare that their consent has been given in return for the written undertaking entered into by the Czechoslovak delegation to allow the free export of this product to all countries which now or in the future guarantee Czechoslovakia by legislative or contractual measures the protection of the appellation of origin of Czechoslovak hops.

Section III

Ad Article B

The High Contracting Parties agree to recognise in the case of Italy the application of the provision of the Protocol to the International Agreement relating to the Exportation of Bones (Section 1, *ad* Article 1 (*a*)), in the event of the said Agreement coming into force.

Section IV

Ad Article C

(*a*) Owing to the position of the United States in consequence of a short Session of Congress in the year 1928–29, the High Contracting Parties agree that, if the ratification of the United States has been asked for under paragraph 3 of Article C and has not been deposited by September 30th, 1929, the Convention shall come into force on January 1st, 1930, provided that all the other countries on which the entry into force of the Convention depends and the total number of which would in this case be reduced to seventeen shall have notified the Secretary-General of the League of Nations of their ratifications or accessions before September 30th, 1929, and provided no objection is raised before November 15th, 1929, by any of the countries which, at the time of the deposit of their ratification or accession, made the entry into force of the Convention, in so far as they were concerned conditional upon the ratification or accession of the United States. If any objection is raised, the last paragraph of Article 17 of the Convention shall apply.

(*b*) The High Contracting Parties declare that in drawing up the list of countries which appears in Article C, they have been chiefly guided by the interdependence of certain interests emphasised in the course of the proceedings of the Conference.

They have thought it unnecessary to mention countries the inclusion of which would be justified only by the importance of economic interests or considerations of geographical situation.

If they have not mentioned certain countries, it is because those countries at present impose no prohibitions of any importance. The High Contracting Parties think they can rely upon their ratification or adhesion.

In faith whereof the above-mentioned plenipotentiaries have signed the present Protocol.

Done at Geneva on the eleventh day of July, one thousand nine hundred and twenty-eight, in a single copy, which shall be deposited in the archives of the Secretariat of the League of Nations; certified true copies shall be forwarded to all the Members of the League of Nations and to all the non-Member States represented at the Conference.

Germany:
DR. ERNST TRENDELENBURG

United States of America:
HUGH R. WILSON

Austria:
DR. RICHARD SCHULLER

Belgium:
J. BRUNET
F. VAN LANGENHOVE

Great Britain and Northern Ireland and all parts of the British Empire which are not separate Members of the League of Nations:

I declare that my signature does not include any of His Britannic Majesty's Colonies, Protectorates or territories under suzerainty or mandate.
S. J. CHAPMAN

India:
H. A. F. LINDSAY

Bulgaria:
Subject to the reservation made on signing the Supplementary Agreement [translation].
D. MIKOFF

Chile:
TOMÁS RAMIREZ FRIAS

Denmark:
J. CLAN
WILLIAM BORBERG

Egypt:
SADIK E. HENEIN

Estonia:
A. SCHMIDT

Finland:
RUDOLF HOLSTI
GUNNAR KIHLMAN

France:
Subject to the reservations made on signing the Supplementary Agreement [translation].
D. SERRUYS

Hungary:
NICKL

Italy:
A. DI NOLA
P. TROISE

Japan:
N. ITO
J. TSUSHIMA

Latvia:
CHARLES DUZMANS

Luxemburg:
ALBERT CALMES

Norway:
GUNNAR JAHN

Netherlands:
POSTHUMA
F. M. WIBAUT
S. DE GRAAFF

Poland:
FRANÇOIS DOLEZAL

Portugal:
A. D'OLIVEIRA
F. DE CALHEIROS E MENEZES

Roumania:
ANTONIADE
D. T. GHEORGHIU
CESAR POPESCU

Kingdom of the Serbs, Croats and
Slovenes:
CONST. FOTITCH
GEORGES CURCIN

Siam:
CHAROON

Sweden:
EINAR MODIG

Switzerland:
W. STUCKI

Czechoslovakia:
IBL

Turkey:
Subject to reservation as regards Article B [translation].
HASSAN

ANNEXED DECLARATION

The Austrian, German and Hungarian delegations, in accepting in favour of Czechoslovakia the exception of *quartzite* under paragraph 2 of Article 6 of the Convention, declare that their consent has only been given in return for an undertaking on the part of Czechoslovakia to maintain, as long as the Convention remains in force, the export quotas and conditions provided for in special treaties or arrangements.

Germany:
DR. ERNST TRENDELENBURG

Austria:
DR. RICHARD SCHULLER

Hungary:
NICKL

Czechoslovakia:
IBL

PROTOCOL CONCERNING THE ENTRY INTO FORCE OF THE INTERNATIONAL CONVENTION OF NOVEMBER 8TH, 1927, FOR THE ABOLITION OF IMPORT AND EXPORT PROHIBITIONS AND RESTRICTIONS AND OF THE SUPPLEMENTARY AGREEMENT TO THE SAID CONVENTION OF JULY 11TH, 1928

The undersigned, being duly authorised and met at Paris at the invitation of the Secretary-General of the League of Nations, in conformity with the provisions of Article 17 of the International Convention for the Abolition of Import and Export Prohibitions and Restrictions signed at Geneva on November 8th, 1927, and of Articles C and D of the Supplementary Agreement to the said Convention signed at Geneva on July 11th, 1928;

Having noted that the instruments of ratification were deposited by their respective Governments within the time-limit provided for in the aforesaid Article C of the Supplementary Agreement, except in the case of Germany, on behalf of whom this deposit was not effected until November 23rd, 1929, and except in the case of Norway who has not yet carried out this formality;

Taking note of the annexed declaration made by the delegate of Norway;

Noting that certain of the conditions for the entry into force of the Convention and of the Supplementary Agreement mentioned above as defined in Article 17 of the Convention have not been fulfilled;

Noting furthermore that it is not possible at the moment to fulfil these conditions;

Being anxious nevertheless that the above-mentioned Convention and Supplementary Agreement should be put into force between the countries they represent, and hoping that the said conditions will be realised in the near future;

Have agreed to the following provisions:

1. The German Government's ratification shall be regarded, exceptionally, as having the same effect as if it had been deposited before September 30th, 1929.

2. The forthcoming ratification announced by the Norwegian Government shall be regarded, exceptionally, as having the same effect as if it had been deposited before September 30th, 1929.

3. If ratifications on behalf of Czechoslovakia and Poland are deposited before May 31st, 1930, they shall be regarded, exceptionally, as having the same effect as if they had been deposited before September 30th, 1929.

4. The Convention shall be put into force on January 1st, 1930, by the countries on whose behalf the present Protocol is signed.

In the case of Hungary, the Convention will be put into force in the manner stated in the annexed declaration by the Hungarian delegate.

5. Those of the countries referred to above which have made the putting into force of the Convention conditional on its ratification by Czechoslovakia and Poland or either of these countries, shall not be bound by its provisions after July 1st, 1930, unless both or either of these countries, as the case may be, ratified the Convention before May 31st, 1930, and complies with the obligations arising out of the putting into force of the Convention on January 1st, 1930. Similarly, a country which made the putting into force of the Convention conditional, as far as it is concerned, upon its ratification for any country or countries other than Czechoslovakia or Poland shall not be bound by its provisions after July 1st, 1930, unless such other country or countries are themselves bound after that date.

If any countries waive the benefits of the provisions of the preceding sub-paragraph, they shall inform the Secretary-General of the League of Nations of this fact by a declaration addressed to him before June 20th, 1930.

6. Any of the countries referred to in paragraph 4 shall be relieved of the obligations accepted by it in virtue of the present Protocol on June 30th, 1931, or the same date in 1932, 1933 or 1934, on forwarding a declaration to that effect on any of these dates to the Secretary-General of the League of Nations. This possibility, however, will cease if and when the number of countries for which, before the signature of the present Protocol, the Convention has been ratified without its entry into force being made subject to conditions or with its entry into force being made subject to conditions which are fulfilled, is not less than eighteen.

It is understood that, when a country maintains the Convention in force under the provisions of the second sub-paragraph of No. 5 of this Protocol, in spite of the fact that its conditions have not been fulfilled, those conditions shall not thereby be considered to have been fulfilled for the purpose of the application of the second sentence of the preceding sub-paragraph.

The provisions of the preceding two sub-paragraphs shall apply to Czecho-slovakia and Poland in the event of the Convention being ratified on their behalf within the period mentioned in paragraph 5.

7. The provisions contained in paragraph 6 above shall be extended to any Member of the League of Nations or any non-Member State acceding to the Convention after this day's date.

In faith whereof the undersigned have signed the present Protocol.

Done at Paris, on December twentieth one thousand nine hundred and twenty-nine in a single copy the French and English texts of which are both authoritative and which shall be deposited in the archives of the Secretariat of the League of Nations. Certified true copies shall be transmitted to all of the Members of the League of Nations and to any non-Member States to which the Council of the League of Nations shall have communicated a copy of the Convention of November 8th, 1927.

Germany:
ADOLPH REINSHAGEN

Austria:
DR. GRÜNBERGER

Belgium:
J. BRUNET

Great Britain:
I declare that my signature does not include any of His Britannic Majesty's Colonies, Protectorates or territories under suzerainty or mandate.
S. J. CHAPMAN

Denmark:
BOECK

United States of America:
CHARLES E. LYON

France:
P. ELBEL

Hungary:
NICKL

Italy:
G. MANZONI [7]

Japan:
(Ad referendum)
N. ITO

Luxemburg:
ALBERT CALMES

Norway:
SIGURD BENTZON

The Netherlands:
POSTHUMA

Portugal:
F. DE CALHEIROS E MENEZES

Roumania:
E. G. NEGULCEA

Switzerland:
W. STUCKI

Yugoslavia:
I. CHOUMENKOVITCH

[7] At the time of signing the Protocol, His Excellency the Royal Italian Ambassador in Paris deposited with the Secretariat of the League of Nations the following declaration which must be considered as accompanying the signature affixed by him on the said Protocol:

"In thus affixing its signature, the Royal Italian Government undertakes to put the Convention into force provided the conditions laid down in the present Protocol are fulfilled, as well as the condition specified in Article C of the Supplementary Agreement, namely that eighteen States at least which have ratified the Convention should apply it effectively as from July 1st, 1930" [translation]. [Footnote in original.]

Declaration of the Norwegian Delegation

[TRANSLATION]

The undersigned, being duly authorised by the Norwegian Government, declares that the said Government undertakes to put into force by administrative measures as from January 1st, 1930, and pending the deposit of the formal ratification of the Convention, the provisions of the Convention of November 8, 1927, and of the Supplementary Agreement of July 11, 1928.

Paris, December the twentieth, one thousand nine hundred and twenty-nine.

SIGURD BENTZON

Declaration of the Hungarian Delegation

[TRANSLATION]

The undersigned, being duly authorised by the Hungarian Government,

In consideration of the fact that the special conditions of Hungarian legislation prevent him from appending his signature to paragraphs 4 and 5 of the annexed Protocol,

Declares that, whilst accepting the other provisions of the aforesaid Protocol, his Government will, for its part, regard the Convention as having been put into force by Hungary on January 1, 1930, provided always:

(1) That Austria, Germany, Italy, Roumania, Switzerland, and Yugoslavia are as from July 1, 1930, bound by the provisions of the Convention;

(2) That Poland and Czechoslovakia have ratified the Convention before May 31, 1930, and that they conform with the obligations involved by the coming into force of the Convention on January 1st, 1930.

Paris, December the twentieth, one thousand nine hundred and twenty-nine.

NICKL

TELECOMMUNICATION: RADIOTELEGRAPH

Convention signed at Washington November 25, 1927 [1]
Senate advice and consent to ratification March 21, 1928
Ratified by the President of the United States October 8, 1928
Ratification of the United States deposited at Washington October 8, 1928
Entered into force January 1, 1929
Proclaimed by the President of the United States January 1, 1929
Supplemented by safety-of-life-at-sea convention of May 31, 1929 [2]
Replaced by conventions of December 9, 1932, [3] *October 2, 1947,* [4] *December 22, 1952,* [5] *December 21, 1959,* [6] *and November 12, 1965,* [7] *as between contracting parties to the later conventions*

45 Stat. 2760; Treaty Series 767

[TRANSLATION]

INTERNATIONAL RADIOTELEGRAPH CONVENTION

Concluded among the Governments of:

Union of South Africa, French Equatorial Africa and other colonies, French West Africa, Portuguese West Africa, Portuguese East Africa and the Portuguese Asiatic possessions, Germany, Argentine Republic, Commonwealth of Australia, Austria, Belgium, Bolivia, Brazil, Bulgaria, Canada, Chile, China, Republic of Colombia, Spanish Colony of the Gulf of Guinea, Belgian Congo, Costa Rica, Cuba, Curacao, Cyrenaica, Denmark, Dominican Republic, Egypt, Republic of El Salvador, Eritrea, Spain, Estonia, United States of America, Finland, France, Great Britain, Greece, Guatemala, Republic of Haiti, Republic of Honduras, Hungary, British India, Dutch East Indies, French Indo-China, Irish Free State, Italy, Japan, Chosen, Taiwan, Japanese Sakhalin, the Leased Territory of Kwan-

---

[1] For text of general and supplementary regulations annexed to the convention, see 45 Stat. 2848 or TS 767, p. 13. The United States did not become a party to the supplementary regulations.

[2] TS 910, *post,* p. 782.

[3] TS 867, *post,* vol. 3.

[4] TIAS 1901, *post,* vol. 4.

[5] 6 UST 1213; TIAS 3266.

[6] 12 UST 1761; TIAS 4892.

[7] 18 UST 575; TIAS 6267.

tung and the South Sea Islands under Japanese Mandate, Republic of Liberia, Madagascar, Morocco (with the exception of the Spanish Zone), Mexico, Monaco, Nicaragua, Norway, New Zealand, Republic of Panama, Paraguay, the Netherlands, Peru, Poland, Portugal, Rumania, Kingdom of the Serbs, Croats, and Slovenes, Siam, Italian Somaliland, Sweden, Switzerland, Surinam, Syro-Lebanese Territories, Republic of San Marino, Czechoslovakia, Tripolitania, Tunis, Turkey, Uruguay, and Venezuela.

The undersigned, plenipotentiaries of the Governments of the countries enumerated above, having met in conference at Washington, have, by common accord and subject to ratification, concluded the following Convention:

ARTICLE 1

Definitions

In the present Convention:

The term "radio communication" applies to the transmission by radio of writing, signs, signals, pictures, and sounds of all kinds by means of Hertzian waves.

The term "radio communication station" or simply "station" means a station equipped to carry on radio communications.

The term "fixed station" means a station permanently located and communicating with one or more stations similarly located.

The term "mobile station" means a station capable of moving and which ordinarily does move.

The term "land station" means a station other than a mobile station used for radio communication with mobile stations.

The term "mobile service" means the radio communication service carried on between mobile stations and land stations, and by mobile stations communicating among themselves.

The term "international service" means a radio communication service between a station in one country and a station in another country, or between a land station and a mobile station located outside the limits of the country in which the land station is situated, or between two or more mobile stations on or over the high seas. An internal or national radio communication service which is likely to cause interference with other services outside the limits of the country in which it operates is considered as an international service from the viewpoint of interference.

The term "general communication system" means all the existing telegraph and telephone channels of communication, wire and radio, open to public service, but excluding the radio communication channels of the mobile service.

The term "public service" means a service for the use of the general public.

The term "limited service" means a service which may be used only by specified persons or for specific purposes.

The term "public correspondence" means all radio communications which a station, by reason of being open to public service, must accept from the public for transmission.

The term "private enterprise" means any person, company, or corporation which operates one or more stations for radio communication.

The term "radiotelegram" means a telegram originating in or destined to a mobile station, transmitted by radio over all or part of its route.

ARTICLE 2

Scope of the Convention

§ 1. The contracting Governments undertake to apply the provisions of the present Convention to all radio communication stations established, or operated by the contracting Governments, and open to the international service of public correspondence. They undertake likewise, to apply these provisions to the special services covered by the Regulations annexed to the present Convention.[8]

§ 2. They agree, moreover, to take or to propose to their respective legislatures the necessary measures to impose the observance of the provisions of the present Convention and the Regulations annexed thereto upon individuals and private enterprises authorized to establish and operate radio communication stations in the international service, whether or not open to public correspondence.

§ 3. The contracting Governments recognize the right of two contracting Governments to organize radio communications, between themselves, provided only that they conform to all provisions of the present Convention and the Regulations annexed thereto.

ARTICLE 3

Intercommunication

§ 1. (1) So far as international communications between fixed stations are concerned, each contracting Government reserves entire freedom with relation to the organization of the service and the determination of the correspondence to be exchanged by the stations carrying on these communications.

(2) When, however, these fixed stations carry on an international service of public correspondence, either from country to country or with stations in the mobile service, they must conform, respectively, for each of these two classes of communications, to the provisions of the present Convention and of the Regulations annexed thereto.

§ 2. With regard to communications between stations participating in the mobile service, stations carrying on such communications must, within

---

[8] See footnote 1, p. 683.

the limits of their normal operations, exchange radiotelegrams reciprocally without regard to the radio system adopted by them.

§ 3. In order not to impede scientific progress, however, the provisions of the preceding paragraph shall not prevent the eventual use of a radio system incapable of communicating with other systems, provided that this incapacity be due to the specific nature of that system and it be not the result of devices adopted solely for the purpose of preventing intercommunication.

ARTICLE 4

Limited service

Notwithstanding the provisions of Article 3, a radio communication station may be assigned to a limited international service of public correspondence determined by the purpose of the correspondence or by other circumstances independent of the system employed.

ARTICLE 5

Secrecy of correspondence. False or deceptive signals

The contracting Governments agree to take or to propose to their respective legislatures the necessary measures to prevent:

(a) The unauthorized transmission and reception by means of radio installations of correspondence of a private nature.

(b) The unauthorized divulging of the contents, or simply of the existence, of correspondence which may have been intercepted by means of radio installations.

(c) The unauthorized publication or use of correspondence received by means of radio installations.

(d) The transmission or the placing in circulation of false or deceptive distress signals or distress calls.

ARTICLE 6

Investigation of violations

The contracting Governments undertake to aid each other by supplying information concerning violations of the provisions of the present Convention and of the Regulations annexed thereto, as well as, if necessary, in the prosecution of persons violating these provisions.

ARTICLE 7

Connection with the general communication system

Each of the contracting Governments agrees to take the necessary measures in order that land stations established on its territory and open to the international service of public correspondence shall be connected with the general communication system or at least to take steps to assure rapid and direct exchanges between these stations and the general communication system.

ARTICLE 8

Exchange of information regarding stations and service

The contracting Governments shall notify each other, through the intermediary of the International Bureau of the Telegraph Union, of the names of stations open to the international service of public correspondence and of stations carrying on special services covered by the Regulations annexed to the present Convention, as well as of all data for facilitating and expediting radio communication.

ARTICLE 9

Special devices

Each of the contracting Governments reserves the right to prescribe or permit, in the stations covered by Article 8, independent of the installation, the data relating to which shall be published in accordance with that Article, other devices to be established and operated for special radio transmission, without publishing the details of such devices.

ARTICLE 10

Conditions to be observed by stations.   Interference

§ 1. The stations covered by Article 2 must, so far as practicable, be established and operated under the best conditions known to the practice of the service and must be maintained abreast of scientific and technical progress.

§ 2. All stations, whatever their purpose, must, so far as practicable, be established and operated so as not to interfere with the radio communications or services of other contracting Governments and of individuals or of private enterprises authorized by these contracting Governments to carry on public radio communication service.

ARTICLE 11

Priority for distress calls

Stations participating in the mobile service shall be obliged to give absolute priority to distress calls, regardless of their origin, to answer such calls, and to take such action with regard thereto as may be required.

ARTICLE 12

Charges

Charges applicable to radiotelegrams and the various cases in which these are allowed radio franking privileges shall be established in accordance with the provisions of the Regulations annexed to the present Convention.

ARTICLE 13

Regulations. Conferences

§ 1. The provisions of the present Convention are completed by:

(1) General Regulations which have the same force and become effective at the same time as the Convention.

(2) Supplementary Regulations which bind only the Governments which have signed them.

§ 2. The provisions of the present Convention and of the Regulations annexed thereto shall be revised by conferences of Plenipotentiaries of the contracting Governments, each conference fixing the place and the time of the following meeting.

§ 3. Before any deliberation each Conference shall establish Rules of Procedure setting forth the conditions under which debate shall be organized and carried on.

ARTICLE 14

Special arrangements

The contracting Governments reserve for themselves and for private enterprises duly authorized by them the right to make special arrangements on matters of service which do not interest the Governments generally. These arrangements, however, must be in conformity with the Convention and the Regulations annexed thereto so far as concerns the interference which their execution might produce with the services of other countries.

ARTICLE 15

Suspension of the service

Each government reserves the right to suspend international radio communication service for an indefinite period, if deemed necessary either generally or only for certain connections and/or for certain kinds of radio communication, provided that it shall immediately so advise each of the other contracting Governments through the intermediary of the International Bureau of the Telegraph Union.

ARTICLE 16

International Bureau

§ 1. The International Bureau of the Telegraph Union shall be charged with collecting, coordinating, and publishing information of all kinds relative to radio services, with examining the requests for changes in the Convention and the Regulations annexed thereto, with promulgating the amendments adopted, and generally with performing all administrative tasks with which it shall have been charged in the interest of international radio services.

§ 2. The expense resulting from these activities shall be borne by all the contracting Governments in the proportion fixed by the General Regulations.

ARTICLE 17

International technical consulting committee on radio communications

§ 1. An International Technical Consulting Committee on Radio Communications shall be established for the purpose of studying technical and related questions pertaining to these communications.

§ 2. Its composition, activities, and operations shall be defined in the General Regulations annexed to the present Convention.

ARTICLE 18

Relations with stations of non-contracting countries

§ 1. Each of the contracting governments reserves the right to determine the conditions under which it will accept telegrams or radiotelegrams originating in or destined to a station not subject to the provisions of the present Convention.

§ 2. If a telegram or a radiotelegram is accepted, it must be transmitted, and the usual charges must be applied to it.

ARTICLE 19

Adherences

§ 1. (1) Governments which are not parties to the present Convention shall be permitted to adhere to it upon their request.

(2) Such adherence shall be communicated through diplomatic channels to the contracting Government within whose territory the last Conference shall have been held and by the latter to the remaining Governments.

(3) The adherence shall carry with it to the fullest extent acceptance of of all the clauses of the present Convention and admission to all the advantages stipulated therein.

§ 2. (1) The adherence to the Convention by the Government of a country having colonies, protectorates, or territories under sovereignty or mandate shall not carry with it the adherence of these colonies, protectorates, or territories under sovereignty or mandate, unless a declaration to that effect is made by that Government.

(2) Such colonies, protectorates, or territories under sovereignty or mandate as a whole, or each of them separately, may form the subject of a separate adherence or of a separate denunciation within the provisions of the present Article and of Article 23.

ARTICLE 20

Arbitration

§ 1. In case of disagreement between two contracting Governments, regarding the interpretation or execution of the present Convention or of the Regulations provided for in Article 13, the question must, at the request of one of these governments, be submitted to arbitration. For that purpose each of the Governments involved shall choose another Government not interested in the question at issue.

§ 2. If agreement between the two arbitrators can not be reached the latter shall appoint another contracting Government equally disinterested in the question at issue. If the two arbitrators can not agree upon the choice of this third Government, each arbitrator shall propose a contracting Government not interested in the dispute; and lots shall be drawn between the Governments proposed. The drawing shall devolve upon the Government within whose territory the International Bureau mentioned in Article 16 operates. The decision of the arbitrators shall be by majority vote.

ARTICLE 21

Exchange of laws and regulations

The contracting Governments shall communicate to one another, if they deem it useful, through the intermediary of the International Bureau of the Telegraph Union, the laws and regulations which have been or which may be promulgated in their countries relative to the object of the present Convention.

ARTICLE 22

Naval and military installations

§ 1. The contracting Governments retain their entire liberty regarding radio installations not covered in Article 2, and especially with reference to naval and military installations.

§ 2. All these installations and stations must, so far as practicable, comply with the provisions of the regulations regarding help to be given in case of distress and measures to be taken to prevent interference. They must also, so far as practicable, observe such provisions of the regulations as concern the types of waves and the frequencies to be used, according to the kind of service which these stations carry on.

§ 3. When, however, these installations and stations are used for public correspondence or participate in the special services governed by the Regulations annexed to the present Convention, they must, in general, conform to the provisions of the Regulations for the conduct of these services.

ARTICLE 23

Execution, duration and denunciation

§ 1. The present Convention shall go into effect on January 1, 1929; it shall remain in force for an indeterminate period and until one year from the day on which a denunciation thereof shall have been made.

§ 2. The denunciation shall affect only the Government in whose name it has been made. The Convention shall remain in force for the other contracting Governments.

ARTICLE 24

Ratification

§ 1. The present Convention shall be ratified and the ratifications thereof shall be deposited in Washington with the least practicable delay.

§ 2. In case one or more of the Contracting Governments should not ratify the Convention it shall be none the less binding upon the Governments which shall have ratified it.

In witness whereof, the respective Plenipotentiaries have signed the Convention in a single copy, which shall remain in the archives of the Government of the United States of America and one copy of which shall be sent to each Government.

Done at Washington, November 25, 1927.

For the Union of South Africa:
H. J. LENTON
W. F. C. MORTON

For French Equatorial Africa and other Colonies:
CASSAGNAC

For French West Africa:
CASSAGNAC

For Portuguese West Africa:
ARNALDO DE PAIVA CARVALHO

For Portuguese East Africa and the Portuguese Asiatic Possessions:
MARIO CORRÊA BARATA DA CRUZ

For Germany:
OTTO ARENDT
HERMANN GIESS
H. HARBICH
ARTHUR WERNER
GÜNTHER SUADICANI
E. L. BAER

For the Argentine Republic:
FELIPE A. ESPIL
LUIS F. ORLANDINI
FRANCISCO LAJOUS

For the Commonwealth of Australia:
H. P. BROWN

For Austria:
DR. MAXIMILIAN HARTWICH
ENG. HANS PFEUFFER

For Belgium:
J. PIERART
GOLDSCHMIDT
G. VINCENT

For Bolivia:
GEO. DE LA BARRA

For Brazil:
P. COELHO DE ALMEIDA
FREDERICO VILLAR
MANUEL F. SIMÕES AYRES

For Bulgaria:
ST. BISSEROFF

For Canada:
A. JOHNSTON
LAURENT BEAUDRY
C. P. EDWARDS
W. ARTHUR STEEL

For Chile:
I. HOLGER

For China:
CHIN CHUN WANG
CHANG-HSUAN
HING GING Y. LEE
TI-CHING WU

For the Republic of Colombia:
ENRIQUE OLAYA H.

For the Spanish Colony of the Gulf of
   Guinea:
ADOLFO H. DE SOLÁS

For the Belgian Congo:
J. PIERART
G. VINCENT
ROBERT GOLDSCHMIDT

For Costa Rica:
J. RAFAEL OREAMUNO

For Cuba:
L. ALBURQUERQUE
GONZALO GÜELL
LUIS MARINO PÉREZ

For Curacao:
G. SCHOTEL

For Cyrenaica:
PAOLO ZONTA

For Denmark:
T. G. KRARUP
C. WAMBERG

For the Dominican Republic:
M. L. VASQUEZ G.

For Egypt:
HORACE MAYNE
ALY IBRAHIM

For Eritrea:
CESARE BARDELONI

For Spain:
MARIANO AMOEDO
ANTONIO NIETO
ADOLFO H. DE SOLAS
JOSE SASTRE

For Estonia:
G. JALLAJAS

For the United States of America:
HERBERT HOOVER
STEPHEN DAVIS
JAMES E. WATSON
E. D. SMITH
WALLACE H. WHITE, JR.
W. R. CASTLE, JR.

WILLIAM ROY VALLANCE
C. McK. SALTZMAN
THOS. T. CRAVEN
W. D. TERRELL
OWEN D. YOUNG
SAMUEL REBER
J. BEAVER WHITE
ARTHUR E. KENNELLY

For Finland:
L. ÅSTRÖM

For France:
L. BOULANGER

For Great Britain:
T. F. PURVES
J. JOYCE BRODERICK
F. W. PHILLIPS
F. W. HOME
L. F. BLANDY, AIR COMMODORE
C. H. BOYD
A. LESLIE HARRIS

For Greece:
TH. PENTHEROUDAKIS

For Guatemala:
J. MONTANO N.

For the Republic of Haiti:
RAOUL LIZAIRE

For the Republic of Honduras:
LUIS BOGRÁN

For Hungary:
BERNARD DE PASKAY

For British India:
P. J. EDMUNDS
P. N. MITRA

For the Dutch East Indies:
G. C. HOLTZAPPEL
WARNSINCK
G. SCHOTEL
VAN DOOREN

For French Indo-China:
G. JULLIEN

For the Irish Free State:
P. S. MACCATHMHAOIL
T. S. O'MUINEACHAIN

For Italy:
GUISEPPE GNEME
GIACOMO BARBERA
GINO MONTEFINALE

For Japan:
For Chosen, Taiwan, Japanese Sakhalin, the Leased Territory of Kwantung and the South Sea Islands under Japanese Mandate:
S. SAWADA
N. MORITA
K. NISHIZAKI
I. YAMAMOTO
SANNOSUKE INADA
T. USHIZAWA
T. NAKAGAMI

For the Republic of Liberia:
ERNEST LYON, Subj. to the ratification of the Senate

For Madagascar:
G. JULLIEN

For Morocco (with the exception of the Spanish Zone):
FREDERIC KNOBEL

For Mexico:
PEDRO N. COTA
JUAN B. SALDAÑA

For Nicaragua:
MANUEL ZAVALA

For Norway:
N. NICKELSEN
HARMOD PETERSON
P. TENNFJORD
J. J. LARSEN

For New Zealand:
A. GIBBS

For the Republic of Panama:
R. J. ALFARO

For Paraguay:
JUAN VICENTE RAMÍRIZ

For the Netherlands:
G. J. HOFKER
J. A. BLAND VAN DEN BERG
W. KRUIJT
E. F. W. VÖLTER
WARNSINCK

For Peru:
A. GONZÁLES-PRADA

For Persia:
D. MEFTAH
en referendum

For Poland:
EUGÈNE STALLINGER

For Portugal:
JOSÉ DE LIZ FERREIRA JUNIOR

For Rumania:
G. CRETZIANO (ad referendum)

For the Republic of El Salvador:
FRANCISCO A. LIMA

For the Kingdom of the Serbs, Croats and Slovenes:
V. ANTONIÉVICH

For Siam:
NIDES VIRAJAKICH

For Italian Somaliland:
VALERIO DELLA CAMPANA

For Sweden:
HAMILTON
LITSTRÖM
LEMOINE

For Switzerland:
E. NUSSBAUM

For Surinam:
G. SCHOTEL

For the Syro-Lebanese Territories:
FREDERIC KNOBEL

For the Republic of San Marino:
FRN. FERRARI

For Czechoslovakia:
DR. OTTO KUČERA
ENG. STRNAD

For Tripolitania:
SETTIMIO AURINI

For Tunis:
FREDERIC KNOBEL

For Turkey:
J. A. BLAND VAN DEN BERG

For Uruguay:
VARELA

For Venezuela:
LUIS CHURION

[For text of general and supplementary regulations annexed to the convention, see 45 Stat. 2848 or TS 767, p. 13.]

RIGHTS AND DUTIES OF STATES IN EVENT OF CIVIL STRIFE (INTER-AMERICAN)

Convention signed at Habana February 20, 1928
Senate advice and consent to ratification, with an understanding, April 15, 1930 [1]
Ratified by the President of the United States, with an understanding, May 7, 1930 [1]
Ratification of the United States deposited with the Pan American Union May 21, 1930
Entered into force May 21, 1929; for the United States May 21, 1930
Proclaimed by the President of the United States June 6, 1930
Amended by protocol of May 1, 1957 [2]

46 Stat. 2749; Treaty Series 814

CONVENTION

The Governments of the Republics represented at the Sixth International Conference of American States, held in the city of Habana, Republic of Cuba, in the year 1928, desirous of reaching an agreement as to the duties and rights of states in the event of civil strife, have appointed the following plenipotentiaries:

Perú: Jesús Melquiades Salazar, Víctor Maúrtua, Enrique Castro Oyanguren, Luis Ernesto Denegri.

Uruguay: Jacobo Varela Acevedo, Juan José Amézaga, Leonel Aguirre, Pedro Erasmo Callorda.

Panamá: Ricardo J. Alfaro, Eduardo Chiari.

Ecuador: Gonzalo Zaldumbide, Victor Zevallos, Colón Eloy Alfaro.

Mexico: Julio García, Fernando González Roa, Salvador Urbina, Aquiles Elorduy.

Salvador: Gustavo Guerrero, Héctor David Castro, Eduardo Alvarez.

---

[1] The Senate gave its advice and consent to ratification and the President ratified the convention with the understanding that the provisions of art. 3 shall not apply where a state of belligerency has been recognized.

[2] 284 UNTS 201; S. Ex. F, 86th Cong., 1st sess. The United States has not become a party.

Guatemala: Carlos Salazar, Bernardo Alvarado Tello, Luis Beltranena, José Azurdia.

Nicaragua: Carlos Cuadra Pazos, Joaquín Gómez, Máximo H. Zepeda.

Bolivia: José Antezana, Adolfo Costa du Rels.

Venezuela: Santiago Key Ayala, Francisco Gerardo Yanes, Rafael Angel Arraiz.

Colombia: Enrique Olaya Herrera, Jesús M. Yepes, Roberto Urdaneta Arbeláez, Ricardo Gutiérrez Lee.

Honduras: Fausto Dávila, Mariano Vázquez.

Costa Rica: Ricardo Castro Beeche, J. Rafael Oreamuno, Arturo Tinoco.

Chile: Alejandro Lira, Alejandro Alvarez, Carlos Silva Vildósola, Manuel Bianchi.

Brazil: Raúl Fernandes, Lindolfo Collor, Alarico da Silveira, Sampaio Correa, Eduardo Espínola.

Argentina: Honorio Pueyrredón, (Later resigned), Laurentino Olascoaga, Felipe A. Espil.

Paraguay: Lisandro Díaz León.

Haiti: Fernando Dennis, Charles Riboul.

Dominican Republic: Francisco J. Peynado, Gustavo A. Díaz, Elías Brache, Angel Morales, Tulio M. Cestero, Ricardo Pérez Alfonseca, Jacinto R. de Castro, Federico C. Alvarez.

United States of America: Charles Evans Hughes, Noble Brandon Judah, Henry P. Fletcher, Oscar W. Underwood, Dwight W. Morrow, Morgan J. O'Brien, James Brown Scott, Ray Lyman Wilbur, Leo S. Rowe.

Cuba: Antonio S. de Bustamante, Orestes Ferrara, Enrique Hernández Cartaya, José Manuel Cortina, Arístides Agüero, José B. Alemán, Manuel Márquez Sterling, Fernando Ortiz, Néstor Carbonell, Jesús María Barraqué.

Who, after exchanging their respective full powers, which were found to be in good and due form, have agreed upon the following:

ARTICLE 1

The contracting states bind themselves to observe the following rules with regard to civil strife in another one of them:

1. To use all means at their disposal to prevent the inhabitants of their territory, nationals or aliens, from participating in, gathering elements, cross-

ing the boundary or sailing from their territory for the purpose of starting or promoting civil strife.

2. To disarm and intern every rebel force crossing their boundaries, the expenses of internment to be borne by the state where public order may have been disturbed. The arms found in the hands of the rebels may be seized and withdrawn by the government of the country granting asylum, to be returned, once the struggle has ended, to the state in civil strife.

3. To forbid the traffic in arms and war material, except when intended for the government, while the belligerency of the rebels has not been recognized, in which latter case the rules of neutrality shall be applied.

4. To prevent that within their jurisdiction there be equipped, armed or adapted for warlike purposes any vessel intended to operate in favor of the rebellion.

ARTICLE 2

The declaration of piracy against vessels which have risen in arms, emanating from a government, is not binding upon the other states.

The state that may be injured by depredations originating from insurgent vessels is entitled to adopt the following punitive measures against them: Should the authors of the damages be warships, it may capture and return them to the government of the state to which they belong, for their trial; should the damage originate with merchantmen, the injured state may capture and subject them to the appropriate penal laws.

The insurgent vessel, whether a warship or a merchantman, which flies the flag of a foreign country to shield its actions, may also be captured and tried by the state of said flag.

ARTICLE 3 [3]

The insurgent vessel, whether a warship or a merchantman, equipped by the rebels, which arrives at a foreign country or seeks refuge therein, shall be delivered by the government of the latter to the constituted government of the state in civil strife, and the members of the crew shall be considered as political refugees.

ARTICLE 4

The present convention does not affect obligations previously undertaken by the contracting parties through international agreements.

ARTICLE 5

After being signed, the present convention shall be submitted to the ratification of the signatory states. The Government of Cuba is charged with transmitting authentic certified copies to the governments for the aforementioned purpose of ratification. The instrument of ratification shall be deposited in the archives of the Pan American Union in Washington, the

---

[3] For U.S. understanding, see footnote 1, p. 694.

Union to notify the signatory governments of said deposit. Such notification shall be considered as an exchange of ratifications. This convention shall remain open to the adherence of non-signatory states.

In witness whereof the aforenamed plenipotentiaries sign the present convention in Spanish, English, French, and Portuguese, in the city of Habana, the 20th day of February, 1928.

Peru:
JESÚS M. SALAZAR
VÍCTOR M. MAÚRTUA
LUIS ERNESTO DENEGRI
E. CASTRO OYANGUREN

Uruguay:
VARELA
PEDRO ERASMO CALLORDA

Panama:
R. J. ALFARO
EDUARDO CHIARI

Ecuador:
GONZALO ZALDUMBIDE
VÍCTOR ZEVALLOS
C. E. ALFARO

Mexico:
JULIO GARCÍA
FERNANDO GONZÁLEZ ROA
SALVADOR URBINA
AQUILES ELORDUY

Salvador:
J. GUSTAVO GUERRERO
HÉCTOR DAVID CASTRO
ED. ALVAREZ

Guatemala:
CARLOS SALAZAR
B. ALVARADO
LUIS BELTRANENA
J. AZURDIA

Nicaragua:
CARLOS CUADRA PAZOS
MÁXIMO H. ZEPEDA
JOAQUÍN GÓMEZ

Bolivia:
JOSÉ ANTEZANA
A. COSTA DU R.

Venezuela:
SANTIAGO KEY AYALA
FRANCISCO G. YANES
RAFAEL ANGEL ARRAIZ

Colombia:
ENRIQUE OLAYA HERRERA
R. GUTIÉRREZ LEE
J. M. YEPES

Honduras:
F. DÁVILA
MARIANO VÁZQUEZ

Costa Rica:
RICARDO CASTRO BEECHE
J. RAFAEL OREAMUNO
A. TINOCO JIMÉNEZ

Chile:
ALEJANDRO LIRA
ALEJANDRO ALVAREZ
C. SILVA VILDÓSOLA
MANUEL BIANCHI

Brazil:
RAÚL FERNANDES
LINDOLFO COLLOR

Argentina:
LAURENTINO OLASCOAGA
FELIPE A. ESPIL
CARLOS ALBERTO ALCORTA

Paraguay:
LISANDRO DÍAZ LEÓN
JUAN VICENTE RAMÍREZ

Haiti:
FERNANDO DENNIS

Dominican Republic:
FRACO. J. PEYNADO
TULIO M. CESTERO
JACINTO R. DE CASTRO
ELÍAS BRACHE
R. PÉREZ ALFONSECA

United States of America:
CHARLES EVANS HUGHES
NOBLE BRANDON JUDAH
HENRY P. FLETCHER
OSCAR W. UNDERWOOD
MORGAN J. O'BRIEN
JAMES BROWN SCOTT
RAY LYMAN WILBUR
LEO S. ROWE

Cuba:
ANTONIO S. DE BUSTAMANTE
ORESTES FERRARA
E. HERNÁNDEZ CARTAYA
ARÍSTIDES DE AGÜERO BETHENCOURT
M. MÁRQUEZ STERLING
NÉSTOR CARBONELL

COMMERCIAL AVIATION (INTER-AMERICAN)

Convention signed at Havana February 20, 1928
Senate advice and consent to ratification February 20, 1931
Ratified by the President of the United States March 6, 1931
Ratification of the United States deposited at Havana July 17, 1931
Entered into force June 13, 1929; for the United States August 26, 1931
Proclaimed by the President of the United States July 27, 1931
Terminated as to the United States November 29, 1947 [1]

47 Stat. 1901; Treaty Series 840

CONVENTION

The Governments of the American Republics, desirous of establishing the rules they should observe among themselves for aerial traffic, have decided to lay them down in a convention, and to that effect have appointed as their plenipotentiaries:

Perú: Jesús Melquiades Salazar, Víctor Maúrtua, Enrique Castro Oyanguren, Luis Ernesto Denegri.

Uruguay: Jacobo Varela Acevedo, Juan José Amézaga, Leonel Aguirre, Pedro Erasmo Callorda.

Panamá: Ricardo J. Alfaro, Eduardo Chiari.

Ecuador: Gonzalo Zaldumbide, Víctor Zevallos, Colón Eloy Alfaro.

Mexico: Julio García, Fernando González Roa, Salvador Urbina, Aquiles Elorduy.

Salvador: Gustavo Guerrero, Héctor David Castro, Eduardo Alvarez.

Guatemala: Carlos Salazar, Bernardo Alvarado Tello, Luis Beltranena, José Azurdia.

Nicaragua: Carlos Cuadra Pazos, Joaquín Gómez, Máximo H. Zepeda.

Bolivia: José Antezana, Adolfo Costa du Rels.

---

[1] Pursuant to notice of denunciation given by the United States May 29, 1947, in accordance with terms of art. 37.

Venezuela: Santiago Key Ayala, Francisco Gerardo Yanes, Rafael Angel Arraiz.

Colombia: Enrique Olaya Herrera, Jesús M. Yepes, Roberto Urdaneta Arbeláez, Ricardo Gutiérrez Lee.

Honduras: Fausto Dávila, Mariano Vázquez.

Costa Rica: Ricardo Castro Beeche, J. Rafael Oreamuno, Arturo Tinoco.

Chile: Alejandro Lira, Alejandro Alvarez, Carlos Silva Vildósola, Manuel Bianchi.

Brazil: Raúl Fernandes, Lindolfo Collor, Alarico da Silveira, Sampaio Correa, Eduardo Espínola.

Argentina: Honorio Pueyrredón, (Later resigned), Laurentino Olascoaga, Felipe A. Espil.

Paraguay: Lisandro Díaz León.

Haiti: Fernando Dennis, Charles Riboul.

Dominican Republic: Francisco J. Peynado, Gustavo A. Díaz, Elías Brache, Angel Morales, Tulio M. Cestero, Ricardo Pérez Alfonseca, Jacinto R. de Castro, Federico C. Alvarez.

United States of America: Charles Evans Hughes, Noble Brandon Judah, Henry P. Fletcher, Oscar W. Underwood, Dwight W. Morrow, Morgan J. O'Brien, James Brown Scott, Ray Lyman Wilbur, Leo S. Rowe.

Cuba: Antonio S. de Bustamante, Orestes Ferrara, Enrique Hernández Cartaya, José Manuel Cortina, Arístides Agüero, José B. Alemán, Manuel Márquez Sterling, Fernando Ortiz, Néstor Carbonell, Jesús María Barraqué.

Who, after having exchanged their respective full powers, which have been found to be in good and due form, have agreed upon the following:

ARTICLE 1

The high contracting parties recognize that every state has complete and exclusive sovereignty over the air space above its territory and territorial waters.

ARTICLE 2

The present convention applies exclusively to private aircraft.

ARTICLE 3

The following shall be deemed to be state aircraft:

   a) Military and naval aircraft;

b) Aircraft exclusively employed in state service, such as posts, customs, and police.

Every other aircraft shall be deemed to be a private aircraft.

All state aircraft other than military, naval, customs and police aircraft shall be treated as private aircraft and as such shall be subject to all the provisions of the present convention.

ARTICLE 4

Each contracting state undertakes in time of peace to accord freedom of innocent passage above its territory to the private aircraft of the other contracting states, provided that the conditions laid down in the present convention are observed. The regulations established by a contracting state with regard to admission over its territory of aircraft of other contracting states shall be applied without distinction of nationality.

ARTICLE 5

Each contracting state has the right to prohibit, for reasons which it deems convenient in the public interest, the flight over fixed zones of its territory by the aircraft of the other contracting states and privately owned national aircraft employed in the service of international commercial aviation, with the reservation that no distinction shall be made in this respect between its own private aircraft engaged in international commerce and those of the other contracting states likewise engaged. Each contracting state may furthermore prescribe the route to be followed over its territory by the aircraft of the other states, except in cases of *force majeure* which shall be governed in accordance with the stipulations of Article 18 of this convention. Each state shall publish in advance and notify the other contracting states of the fixation of the authorized routes and the situation and extension of the prohibited zones.

ARTICLE 6

Every aircraft over a prohibited area shall be obliged, as soon as this fact is realized or upon being so notified by the signals agreed upon, to land as soon as possible outside of said area in the airdrome nearest the prohibited area over which it was improperly flying and which is considered as an international airport by the subjacent state.

ARTICLE 7

Aircraft shall have the nationality of the state in which they are registered and can not be validly registered in more than one state.

The registration entry and the certificate of registration shall contain a description of the aircraft and state, the number or other mark of identification given by the constructor of the machine, the registry marks and nationality, the name of the airdrome or airport usually used by the aircraft, and the full name, nationality and domicile of the owner, as well as the date of registration.

ARTICLE 8

The registration of aircraft referred to in the preceding article shall be made in accordance with the laws and special provisions of each contracting state.

ARTICLE 9

Every aircraft engaged in international navigation must carry a distinctive mark of its nationality, the nature of such distinctive mark to be agreed upon by the several contracting states. The distinctive marks adopted will be communicated to the Pan American Union and to the other contracting states.

ARTICLE 10

Every aircraft engaged in international navigation shall carry with it in the custody of the aircraft commander:

a) A certificate of registration, duly certified to according to the laws of the state in which it is registered;

b) A certificate of airworthiness, as provided for in Article 12;

c) The certificates of competency of the commander, pilots, engineers, and crew, as provided for in Article 13;

d) If carrying passengers, a list of their names, addresses and nationality;

e) If carrying merchandise, the bills of lading and manifests, and all other documents required by customs laws and regulations of each country;

f) Log books;

g) If equipped with radiotelegraph apparatus, the corresponding license.

ARTICLE 11

Each contracting state shall every month file with every other state party to this convention and with the Pan American Union, a copy of all registrations and cancellations of registrations of aircraft engaged in international navigation as between the several contracting states.

ARTICLE 12

Every aircraft engaged in international navigation (between the several contracting states) shall be provided with a certificate of airworthiness issued by the state whose nationality it possesses.

This document shall certify to the state in which the aircraft is to operate, that, according to the opinion of the authority that issues it, such aircraft complies with the airworthiness requirements of each of the states named in said certificate.

The aircraft commander shall at all times hold the certificate in his custody and shall deliver it for inspection and verification to the authorized representatives of the state which said aircraft visits.

Each contracting state shall communicate to the other states parties to this convention and to the Pan American Union its regulations governing the rating of its aircraft as to airworthiness and shall similarly communicate any changes made therein.

While the states affirm the principle that the aircraft of each contracting state shall have the liberty of engaging in air commerce with the other contracting states without being subjected to the licensing system of any state with which such commerce is carried on, each and every contracting state mentioned in the certificate of airworthiness reserves the right to refuse to recognize as valid the certificate of airworthiness of any foreign aircraft where inspection by a duly authorized commission of such state shows that the aircraft is not, at the time of inspection, reasonably airworthy in accordance with the normal requirements of the laws and regulations of such state concerning the public safety.

In such cases said state may refuse to permit further transit by the aircraft through its air space until such time as it, with due regard to the public safety, is satisfied as to the airworthiness of the aircraft, and shall immediately notify the state whose nationality the aircraft possesses and the Pan American Union of the action taken.

ARTICLE 13

The aircraft commander, pilots, engineers, and other members of the operating crew of every aircraft engaged in international navigation between the several contracting states shall, in accordance with the laws of each state, be provided with a certificate of competency by the contracting state whose nationality the aircraft possesses.

Such certificate or certificates shall set forth that each pilot, in addition to having fulfilled the requirements of the state issuing the same, has passed a satisfactory examination with regard to the traffic rules existing in the other contracting states over which he desires to fly. The requirements of form of said documents shall be uniform throughout all the contracting states and shall be drafted in the language of all of them, and for this purpose the Pan American Union is charged with making the necessary arrangements amongst the contracting states.

Such certificate or certificates shall be held in the possession of the aircraft commander as long as the pilots, engineers and other members of the operating crew concerned continue to be employed on the aircraft. Upon the return of such certificate an authenticated copy thereof shall be retained in the files of the aircraft.

Such certificate or certificates shall be open at all times to the inspection of the duly authorized representatives of any state visited.

Each contracting state shall communicate to the other states parties to this convention and to the Pan American Union its regulations governing the issuance of such certificates and shall from time to time communicate any changes made therein.

ARTICLE 14

Each and every contracting state shall recognize as valid, certificates of competency of the aircraft commander, pilots, engineers and other members of the operating crew of an aircraft, issued in accordance with the laws and regulations of other contracting states.

ARTICLE 15

The carriage by aircraft of explosives, arms and munitions of war is prohibited in international aerial navigation. Therefore, no foreign or native aircraft authorized for international traffic shall be permitted to transport articles of this nature, either between points situated within the territory of any of the contracting states or through the same even though simply in transit.

ARTICLE 16

Each state may prohbit or regulate the carriage or use, by aircraft possessing the nationality of other contracting states, of photographic apparatus. Such regulations as may be adopted by each state concerning this matter shall be communicated to each other contracting state and to the Pan American Union.

ARTICLE 17

As a measure of public safety or because of lawful prohibitions, the transportation of articles in international navigation other than those mentioned in Articles 15 and 16 may be restricted by any contracting state. Such restrictions shall be immediately communicated to the other contracting states and to the Pan American Union.

All restrictions mentioned in this article shall apply equally to foreign and national aircraft employed in international traffic.

ARTICLE 18

Every aircraft engaged in international traffic which enters the air space of a contracting state with the intention of landing in said state shall do so in the corresponding customs airdrome, except in the cases mentioned in Article 19 and in case of *force majeure,* which must be proved.

Every aircraft engaged in international navigation, prior to its departure from the territorial jurisdiction of a contracting state in which it has landed, shall obtain such clearance as is required by the laws of such state at a port designated as point of departure by such state.

Each and every contracting state shall notify every other state party to this convention and the Pan American Union of such airports as shall be designated by such state as ports of entry and departure.

When the laws or regulations of any contracting state so require, no aircraft shall legally enter into or depart from its territory through places other than those previously authorized by such state as international airports, and the landing therein shall be obligatory unless a special permit, which has been previously communicated to the authorities of said airport, is obtained from the competent authorities of said state, in which permit shall be clearly expressed the distinctive marks which the aircraft is obliged to make visible whenever requested to do so in the manner previously agreed upon in said permit.

In the event that for any reason, after entering the territorial jurisdiction of a contracting state, aircraft of another contracting state should land at a point other than an airport designated as a port of entry in that state the aircraft commander shall immediately notify the nearest competent authority and hold himself, crew, passengers and cargo at the point of landing until proper entry has been granted by such competent authority, unless communication therewith is impracticable within twenty-four hours.

Aircraft of one of the contracting states which flies over the territory of another contracting state shall be obliged to land as soon as ordered to do so by means of the regulation signals, when for any reason this may be necessary.

In the cases provided for in this article, the aircraft, aircraft commander, crew, passengers and cargo shall be subject to such immigration, emigration, customs, police, quarantine or sanitary inspection as the duly authorized representatives of the subjacent state may make in accordance with its laws.

ARTICLE 19

As an exception to the general rules, postal aircraft and aircraft belonging to aerial transport companies regularly constituted and authorized may be exempted, at the option of the subjacent state, from the obligation of landing at an airdrome designated as a port of entry and authorized to land at certain inland airdromes, designated by the customs and police administration of such state, at which customs formalities shall be complied with. The departure of such aircraft from the state visited may be regulated in a similar manner.

However, such aircraft shall follow the normal air route, and make their identity known by signals agreed upon as they fly across the frontier.

ARTICLE 20

From the time of landing of a foreign aircraft at any point whatever until its departure the authorities of the state visited shall have, in all cases, the right to visit and examine the aircraft and to verify all documents with which it must be provided, in order to determine that all the laws, rules and regulations of such states and all the provisions of this convention are complied with.

ARTICLE 21

The aircraft of a contracting state engaged in international air commerce shall be permitted to discharge passengers and a part of its cargo at one of the airports designated as a port of entry of any other contracting state, and to proceed to any other airport or airports in such state for the purpose of discharging the remaining passengers and portions of such cargo and in like manner to take on passengers and load cargo destined for a foreign state or states, provided that they comply with the legal requirements of the country over which they fly, which legal requirements shall be the same for native and foreign aircraft engaged in international traffic and shall be communicated in due course to the contracting states and to the Pan American Union.

ARTICLE 22

Each contracting state shall have the right to establish reservations and restrictions in favor of its own national aircraft in regard to the commercial transportation of passengers and merchandise between two or more points in its territory, and to other remunerated aeronautical operations wholly within its territory. Such reservations and restrictions shall be immediately published and communicated to the other contracting states and to the Pan American Union.

ARTICLE 23

The establishment and operation of airdromes will be regulated by the legislation of each country, equality of treatment being observed.

ARTICLE 24

The aircraft of one contracting state engaged in international commerce with another contracting state shall not be compelled to pay other or higher charges in airports or airdromes open to the public than would be paid by national aircraft of the state visited, likewise engaged in international commerce.

ARTICLE 25

So long as a contracting state shall not have established appropriate regulations, the commander of an aircraft shall have rights and duties analogous to those of the captain of a merchant steamer, according to the respective laws of each state.

ARTICLE 26

The salvage of aircraft lost at sea shall be regulated, in the absence of any agreement to the contrary, by the principles of maritime law.

ARTICLE 27

The aircraft of all states shall have the right, in cases of danger, to all possible aid.

ARTICLE 28

Reparations for damages caused to persons or property located in the subjacent territory shall be governed by the laws of each state.

ARTICLE 29

In case of war the stipulations of the present convention shall not affect the freedom of action of the contracting states either as belligerents or as neutrals.

ARTICLE 30

The right of any of the contracting states to enter into any convention or special agreement with any other state or states concerning international aerial navigation is recognized, so long as such convention or special agreement shall not impair the rights or obligations of any of the states parties to this convention, acquired or imposed herein; provided, however, that two or more states, for reasons of reciprocal convenience and interest may agree upon appropriate regulations pertaining to the operation of aircraft and the fixing of specified routes. These regulations shall in no case prevent the establishment and operation of practicable inter-American aerial lines and terminals. These regulations shall guarantee equality of treatment of the aircraft of each and every one of the contracting states and shall be subject to the same conditions as are set forth in Article 5 of this convention with respect to prohibited areas within the territory of a particular state.

Nothing contained in this convention shall affect the rights and obligations established by existing treaties.

ARTICLE 31

The contracting states obligate themselves in so far as possible to cooperate in inter-American measures relative to:

a) The centralization and distribution of meteorological information, whether statistical, current or special;

b) The publication of uniform aeronautical charts, as well as the establishment of a uniform system of signals;

c) The use of radiotelegraph in aerial navigation, the establishment of the necessary radiotelegraph stations and the observance of the inter-American and international radiotelegraph regulations or conventions at present existing or which may come into existence.

ARTICLE 32

The contracting states shall procure as far as possible uniformity of laws and regulations governing aerial navigation. The Pan American Union shall cooperate with the governments of the contracting states to attain the desired uniformity of laws and regulations for aerial navigation in the states parties to this convention.

Each contracting state shall exchange with every other contracting state within three months after the date of ratification of this convention copies of its air-traffic rules and requirements as to competency for aircraft commanders, pilots, engineers, and other members of the operating crew, and the requirements for airworthiness of aircraft intended to engage in international commerce.

Each contracting state shall deposit with every other state party to this convention and with the Pan American Union three months prior to the date proposed for their enforcement any additions to or amendments of the regulations referred to in the last preceding paragraph.

ARTICLE 33

Each contracting state shall deposit its ratification with the Cuban Government, which shall thereupon inform the other contracting states. Such ratification shall remain deposited in the archives of the Cuban Government.

ARTICLE 34

The present convention will come into force for each signatory state ratifying it in respect to other states which have already ratified, forty days from the date of deposit of its ratification.

ARTICLE 35

Any state may adhere to this convention by giving notice thereof to the Cuban Government, and such adherence shall be effective forty days thereafter. The Cuban Government shall inform the other signatory states of such adherence.

ARTICLE 36

In case of disagreement between two contracting states regarding the interpretation or execution of the present convention the question shall, on the request of one of the governments in disagreement, be submitted to arbitration as hereinafter provided. Each of the governments involved in the disagreement shall choose another government not interested in the question at issue and the government so chosen shall arbitrate the dispute. In the event the two arbitrators cannot reach an agreement they shall appoint another disinterested government as additional arbitrator. If the two arbitrators cannot agree upon the choice of this third government, each arbitrator shall propose a government not interested in the dispute and lots shall be drawn between the two governments proposed. The drawing shall devolve upon the Governing Board of the Pan American Union.

The decision of the arbitrators shall be by majority vote.

ARTICLE 37

Any contracting state may denounce this convention at any time by transmitting notification thereof to the Cuban Government, which shall communicate it to the other states parties to this convention. Such denunciation shall not take effect until six months after notification thereof to the Cuban Government, and shall take effect only with respect to the state making the denunciation.

In witness whereof, the above-named plenipotentiaries have signed this convention and the seal of the Sixth International Conference of American States has been hereto affixed.

Peru:
JESÚS M. SALAZAR
VÍCTOR M. MAÚRTUA
LUIS ERNESTO DENEGRI
E. CASTRO OYANGUREN

Uruguay:
VARELA
PEDRO ERASMO CALLORDA

Panama:
R. J. ALFARO
EDUARDO CHIARI

Ecuador:
GONZALO ZALDUMBIDE
VÍCTOR ZEVALLOS
C. E. ALFARO

Mexico:
JULIO GARCÍA
FERNANDO GONZÁLEZ ROA
SALVADOR URBINA
AQUILES ELORDUY

Salvador:
J. GUSTAVO GUERRERO
HÉCTOR DAVID CASTRO
ED. ALVAREZ

Guatemala:
CARLOS SALAZAR
B. ALVARADO
LUIS BELTRANENA
J. AZURDIA

Nicaragua:
CARLOS CUADRA PAZOS
MÁXIMO H. ZEPEDA
JOAQUÍN GÓMEZ

Bolivia:
JOSÉ ANTEZANA
A. COSTA DU R.

Venezuela:
SANTIAGO KEY AYALA
FRANCISCO G. YANES
RAFAEL ANGEL ARRAIZ

Colombia:
ENRIQUE OLAYA HERRERA
R. GUTIÉRREZ LEE
J. M. YEPES

Honduras:
F. DÁVILA
MARIANO VÁZQUEZ

Costa Rica:
RICARDO CASTRO BEECHE
J. RAFAEL OREAMUNO
A. TINOCO JIMÉNEZ

Chile:
ALEJANDRO LIRA
ALEJANDRO ALVAREZ
C. SILVA VILDÓSOLA
MANUEL BIANCHI

Brazil:
RAÚL FERNANDES
LINDOLFO COLLOR

Argentina:
LAURENTINO OLASCOAGA
FELIPE A. ESPIL
CARLOS ALBERTO ALCORTA

Paraguay:
LISANDRO DÍAZ LEÓN
JUAN VICENTE RAMÍREZ

Haiti:
FERNANDO DENNIS

Dominican Republic:
FRACO. J. PEYNADO
TULIO M. CESTERO
JACINTO R. DE CASTRO
ELÍAS BRACHE
R. PÉREZ ALFONSECA

United States of America:
  CHARLES EVANS HUGHES
  NOBLE BRANDON JUDAH
  HENRY P. FLETCHER
  OSCAR W. UNDERWOOD
  MORGAN J. O'BRIEN
  JAMES BROWN SCOTT
  RAY LYMAN WILBUR
  LEO S. ROWE

Cuba:
  ANTONIO S. DE BUSTAMANTE
  ORESTES FERRARA
  E. HERNÁNDEZ CARTAYA
  ARÍSTIDES DE AGÜERO BETHENCOURT
  M. MÁRQUEZ STERLING
  NÉSTOR CARBONELL

Reservation of the Dominican Republic

The delegation of the Dominican Republic records, as an explanation of its vote, that upon signing the present convention it does not understand that the Dominican Republic dissociates itself from conventions it has already ratified and which are in force.

STATUS OF ALIENS (INTER–AMERICAN)

Convention signed at Havana February 20, 1928
Senate advice and consent to ratification, with exception of articles 3 and
  4, April 16, 1930
Ratified by the President of the United States, with exception of articles
  3 and 4, May 7, 1930
Ratification of the United States deposited with the Pan American
  Union May 21, 1930
Entered into force September 3, 1929; for the United States May 21,
  1930
Proclaimed by the President of the United States June 6, 1930

46 Stat. 2753; Treaty Series 815

CONVENTION

The Governments of the Republics represented at the Sixth International Conference of American States, held in the city of Havana, Republic of Cuba, in the year 1928;

Have decided to conclude a convention for the purpose of determining the status of aliens within their respective territories and to that end have appointed the following plenipotentiaries:

Perú: Jesús Melquiades Salazar, Víctor Maúrtua, Enrique Castro Oyanguren, Luis Ernesto Denegri.

Uruguay: Jacobo Varela Acevedo, Juan José Amézaga, Leonel Aguirre, Pedro Erasmo Callorda.

Panamá: Ricardo J. Alfaro, Eduardo Chiari.

Ecuador: Gonzalo Zaldumbide, Víctor Zevallos, Colón Eloy Alfaro.

Mexico: Julio García, Fernando González Roa, Salvador Urbina, Aquiles Elorduy.

Salvador: Gustavo Guerrero, Héctor David Castro, Eduardo Alvarez.

Guatemala: Carlos Salazar, Bernardo Alvarado Tello, Luis Beltranena, José Azurdia.

Nicaragua: Carlos Cuadra Pazos, Joaquín Gómez, Máximo H. Zepeda.

Bolivia: José Antezana, Adolfo Costa du Rels.

Venezuela: Santiago Key Ayala, Francisco Gerardo Yanes, Rafael Angel Arraiz.

Colombia: Enrique Olaya Herrera, Jesús M. Yepes, Roberto Urdaneta Arbeláez, Ricardo Gutiérrez Lee.

Honduras: Fausto Dávila, Mariano Vázquez.

Costa Rica: Ricardo Castro Beeche, J. Rafael Oreamuno, Arturo Tinoco.

Chile: Alejandro Lira, Alejandro Alvarez, Carlos Silva Vildósola, Manuel Bianchi.

Brazil: Raúl Fernandes, Lindolfo Collor, Alarico da Silveira, Sampaio Correa, Eduardo Espínola.

Argentina: Honorio Pueyrredón, (Later resigned), Laurentino Olascoaga, Felipe A. Espil.

Paraguay: Lisandro Díaz León.

Haiti: Fernando Dennis, Charles Riboul.

Dominican Republic: Francisco J. Peynado, Gustavo A. Díaz, Elías Brache, Angel Morales, Tulio M. Cestero, Ricardo Pérez Alfonseca, Jacinto R. de Castro, Federico C. Alvarez.

United States of America: Charles Evans Hughes, Noble Brandon Judah, Henry P. Fletcher, Oscar W. Underwood, Dwight W. Morrow, Morgan J. O'Brien, James Brown Scott, Ray Lyman Wilbur, Leo S. Rowe.

Cuba: Antonio S. de Bustamante, Orestes Ferrara, Enrique Hernández Cartaya, José Manuel Cortina, Arístides Agüero, José B. Alemán, Manuel Márquez Sterling, Fernando Ortiz, Néstor Carbonell, Jesús María Barraqué.

Who, after depositing their full powers, which were found to be in good and due form, have agreed upon the following provisions:

Article 1

States have the right to establish by means of laws the conditions under which foreigners may enter and reside in their territory.

Article 2

Foreigners are subject as are nationals to local jurisdiction and laws, due consideration being given to the limitations expressed in conventions and treaties.

ARTICLE 3 [1]

Foreigners may not be obliged to perform military service; but those foreigners who are domiciled, unless they prefer to leave the country, may be compelled, under the same conditions as nationals, to perform police, fire-protection, or militia duty for the protection of the place of their domicile against natural catastrophes or dangers not resulting from war.

ARTICLE 4 [1]

Foreigners are obliged to make ordinary or extraordinary contributions, as well as forced loans, always provided that such measures apply to the population generally.

ARTICLE 5

States should extend to foreigners, domiciled or in transit through their territory, all individual guaranties extended to their own nationals, and the enjoyment of essential civil rights without detriment, as regards foreigners, to legal provisions governing the scope of and usages for the exercise of said rights and guaranties.

ARTICLE 6

For reasons of public order or safety, states may expel foreigners domiciled, resident, or merely in transit through their territory.

States are required to receive their nationals expelled from foreign soil who seek to enter their territory.

ARTICLE 7

Foreigners must not mix in political activities, which are the exclusive province of citizens of the country in which they happen to be; in cases of such interference, they shall be liable to the penalties established by local law.

ARTICLE 8

The present convention does not affect obligations previously undertaken by the contracting parties through international agreements.

ARTICLE 9

After being signed, the present convention shall be submitted to the ratification of the signatory states. The Government of Cuba is charged with transmitting authentic certified copies to the governments for the aforementioned purpose of ratification. The instrument of ratification shall be deposited in the archives of the Pan American Union in Washington, the Union to notify the signatory governments of said deposit. Such notification shall be considered as an exchange of ratifications. This convention shall remain open to the adherence of nonsignatory states.

---

[1] Excepted from ratification by the United States.

In witness whereof, the aforenamed plenipotentiaries sign the present convention in Spanish, English, French, and Portuguese, in the city of Habana, the 20th day of February, 1928.

Peru:
JESÚS M. SALAZAR
VÍCTOR M. MAÚRTUA
LUIS ERNESTO DENEGRI
E. CASTRO OYANGUREN

Uruguay:
VARELA
PEDRO ERASMO CALLORDA

Panama:
R. J. ALFARO
EDUARDO CHIARI

Ecuador:
GONZALO ZALDUMBIDE
VÍCTOR ZEVALLOS
C. E. ALFARO

Mexico:
JULIO GARCIA
FERNANDO GONZÁLEZ ROA
SALVADOR URBINA
AQUILES ELORDUY

Salvador:
J. GUSTAVO GUERRERO
HÉCTOR DAVID CASTRO
ED. ALVAREZ

Guatemala:
CARLOS SALAZAR
B. ALVARADO
LUIS BELTRANENA
J. AZURDIA

Nicaragua:
CARLOS CUADRA PAZOS
MÁXIMO H. ZEPEDA
JOAQUIN GÓMEZ

Bolivia:
JOSÉ ANTEZANA
A. COSTA DU R.

Venezuela:
SANTIAGO KEY AYALA
FRANCISCO G. YANES
RAFAEL ANGEL ARRAIZ

Colombia:
ENRIQUE OLAYA HERRERA
R. GUTIÉRREZ LEE
J. M. YEPES

Honduras:
F. DÁVILA
MARIANO VÁZQUEZ

Costa Rica:
RICARDO CASTRO BEECHE
J. RAFAEL OREAMUNO
A. TINOCO JIMÉNEZ

Chile:
ALEJANDRO LIRA
ALEJANDRO ALVAREZ
C. SILVA VILDÓSOLA
MANUEL BIANCHI

Brazil:
RAÚL FERNANDES
LINDOLFO COLLOR

Argentina:
LAURENTINO OLASCOAGA
FELIPE A. ESPIL
CARLOS ALBERTO ALCORTA

Paraguay:
LISANDRO DIAZ LEÓN
JUAN VICENTE RAMIREZ

Haiti:
FERNANDO DENNIS

Dominican Republic:
FRACO. J. PEYNADO
TULIO M. CESTERO
JACINTO R. DE CASTRO
ELÍAS BRACHE
R. PÉREZ ALFONSECA

United States of America:
CHARLES EVANS HUGHES
NOBLE BRANDON JUDAH
HENRY P. FLETCHER
OSCAR W. UNDERWOOD
MORGAN J. O'BRIEN
JAMES BROWN SCOTT
RAY LYMAN WILBUR
LEO S. ROWE

Cuba:
ANTONIO S. DE BUSTAMANTE
ORESTES FERRARA
E. HERNÁNDEZ CARTAYA
ARISTIDESDE AGÜERO BETHENCOURT
M. MÁRQUEZ STERLING
NÉSTOR CARBONELL

Reservation of the Delegation of the United States of America

The delegation of the United States of America signs the present convention making express reservation to Article 3 of the same, which refers to military service of foreigners in case of war.

CONSULAR AGENTS: DUTIES, RIGHTS, PREROGATIVES, AND IMMUNITIES (INTER-AMERICAN)

Convention signed at Havana February 20, 1928
Senate advice and consent to ratification January 22, 1932
Ratified by the President of the United States February 1, 1932
Ratification of the United States deposited with the Pan American Union February 8, 1932
Entered into force September 3, 1929; for the United States February 8, 1932
Proclaimed by the President of the United States February 11, 1932

47 Stat. 1976; Treaty Series 843

CONVENTION

The governments of the Republics represented at the Sixth International Conference of American States, held in the city of Habana, Republic of Cuba, in the year nineteen hundred and twenty-eight, desirous of defining the duties, rights, prerogatives and immunities of consular agents, in accordance with the usages and agreements on the matter;

Have decided to conclude a convention to that end and have appointed the following plenipotentiaries:

Perú: Jesús Melquiades Salazar, Víctor Maúrtua, Enrique Castro Oyanguren, Luis Ernesto Denegri.

Uruguay: Jacobo Varela Acevedo, Juan José Amézaga, Leonel Aguirre, Pedro Erasmo Callorda.

Panamá: Ricardo J. Alfaro, Eduardo Chiari.

Ecuador: Gonzalo Zaldumbide, Víctor Zevallos, Colón Eloy Alfaro.

Mexico: Julio García, Fernando González Roa, Salvador Urbina, Aquiles Elorduy.

Salvador: Gustavo Guerrero, Héctor David Castro, Eduardo Alvarez.

Guatemala: Carlos Salazar, Bernardo Alvarado Tello, Luis Beltranena, José Azurdia.

714

Nicaragua: Carlos Cuadra Pazos, Joaquín Gómez, Máximo H. Zepeda.

Bolivia: José Antezana, Adolfo Costa du Rels.

Venezuela: Santiago Key Ayala, Francisco Gerardo Yanes, Rafael Angel Arraiz.

Colombia: Enrique Olaya Herrera, Jesús M. Yepes, Roberto Urdaneta Arbeláez, Ricardo Gutiérrez Lee.

Honduras: Fausto Dávila, Mariano Vázquez.

Costa Rica: Ricardo Castro Beeche, J. Rafael Oreamuno, Arturo Tinoco.

Chile: Alejandro Lira, Alejandro Alvarez, Carlos Silva Vildósola, Manuel Bianchi.

Brazil: Raúl Fernandes, Lindolfo Collor, Alarico da Silveira, Sampaio Correa, Eduardo Espínola.

Argentina: Honorio Pueyrredón, (Later resigned), Laurentino Olascoaga, Felipe A. Espil.

Paraguay: Lisandro Díaz León.

Haiti: Fernando Dennis, Charles Riboul.

Dominican Republic: Francisco J. Peynado, Gustavo A. Díaz, Elías Brache, Angel Morales, Tulio M. Cestero, Ricardo Pérez Alfonseca, Jacinto R. de Castro, Federico C. Alvarez.

United States of America: Charles Evans Hughes, Noble Brandon Judah, Henry P. Fletcher, Oscar W. Underwood, Dwight W. Morrow, Morgan J. O'Brien, James Brown Scott, Ray Lyman Wilbur, Leo S. Rowe.

Cuba: Antonio S. de Bustamante, Orestes Ferrara, Enrique Hernández Cartaya, José Manuel Cortina, Arístides Agüero, José B. Alemán, Manuel Márquez Sterling, Fernando Ortiz, Néstor Carbonell, Jesús María Barraqué.

Who, after having deposited their full powers found to be in good and due form, have agreed to the following provisions:

Section I. Appointments and functions

ARTICLE 1

States may appoint in the territory of others, with the express or tacit consent of the latter, consuls who shall there represent and defend their commercial and industrial interests and render to their nationals such assistance and protection as they may need.

ARTICLE 2

The form and requirements for appointment, the classes and the rank of the consuls, shall be regulated by the domestic laws of the respective state.

ARTICLE 3

Unless consented to by the state where he is to serve, one of its nationals may not act as consul. The granting of an exequatur implies such consent.

ARTICLE 4

The consul having been appointed, the state shall forward through diplomatic channels to the other state the respective commission which shall contain the name, category and authority of the appointee.

As to a vice consul or commercial agent appointed by the respective consul, where there is authorization by law, the commission shall be issued and communicated to the latter.

ARTICLE 5

States may refuse to accept consuls appointed in their territory or subject the exercise of consular functions to certain special obligations.

ARTICLE 6

The consul can be recognized as such only after having presented his commission and obtained the exequatur of the state in whose territory he is to serve. Provisional recognition can be granted upon the request of the legation of the consul pending the delivery in due form of the exequatur.

Officials appointed under the terms of Article 4 are likewise subject to this formality and in such case it rests with the respective consul to request the exequatur.

ARTICLE 7

The exequatur having been obtained, it shall be presented to the authorities of the consular district, who shall protect the consul in the exercise of his functions and guarantee to him the immunities to which he is entitled.

ARTICLE 8

The territorial government may at any time withdraw the consul's exequatur, but, except in urgent cases, it shall not have recourse to this measure without previously attempting to obtain from the consul's government his recall.

ARTICLE 9

In case of the death, disability or absence of consular agents any of the assistant employees whose official position has been previously made known to the ministry of foreign affairs or the department of state, may temporarily assume the consular functions; while thus engaged he shall enjoy all the rights and prerogatives corresponding to the permanent official.

ARTICLE 10

Consuls shall exercise the functions that the law of their state confers upon them, without prejudice to the legislation of the country where they are serving.

ARTICLE 11

In the exercise of their functions, consuls shall deal directly with the authorities of their district. Should their representations not be heeded, they may then pursue them before the government of the state through the intermediary of their diplomatic representative, but should not communicate directly with the government except in the absence or non-existence of a diplomatic representative.

ARTICLE 12

In case of the absence of a diplomatic representative of the consul's state, the consul may undertake such diplomatic actions as the government of the state in which he functions may permit in such cases.

ARTICLE 13

A person duly accredited for the purpose may combine diplomatic representation and the consular function provided the state before which he is accredited consents to it.

Section II. Prerogatives of consuls

ARTICLE 14

In the absence of a special agreement between two nations, the consular agents who are nationals of the state appointing them, shall neither be arrested nor prosecuted except in the cases when they are accused of committing an act classed as a crime by local legislation.

ARTICLE 15

In criminal cases, the prosecution or the defense may request attendance of consular agents at the trial, as witnesses. This request must be made with all possible consideration to consular dignity and to the duties of the consular office and shall be complied with by the consular official.

Consular agents shall be subject to the jurisdiction of the courts in civil cases, although with the limitation that when the consul is a national of his state and is not engaged in any private business with purposes of gain, his testimony shall be taken either verbally or in writing, at his residence or office, with all the consideration to which he is entitled.

The consul may, nevertheless, of his own free will appear as a witness when such appearance does not seriously hinder the discharge of his official duties.

ARTICLE 16

Consuls are not subject to local jurisdiction for acts done in their official character and within the scope of their authority. In case a private individual deems himself injured by the consul's action, he must submit his complaint to the government, which, if it considers the claim to be relevant, shall make it valid through diplomatic channels.

ARTICLE 17

In respect to unofficial acts, consuls are subject, in civil as well as in criminal matters, to the jurisdiction of the state where they exercise their functions.

ARTICLE 18

The official residence of the consuls and places used for the consulate's offices and archives are inviolable and in no case may the local authorities enter them without the permission of the consular agents; neither shall they examine nor seize, under any pretext whatsoever, documents or other objects found in a consular office. No consular officer shall be required to present his official files before the courts or to make declaration with respect to their contents.

When consular agents are engaged in business within the territory of the state where they are exercising their duties, the files and documents of the consulate shall be kept in a place entirely separate from the one where private or business papers are kept.

ARTICLE 19

Consuls are obliged to deliver, upon the simple request of the local authorities, persons accused or condemned for crimes who may have sought refuge in the consulate.

ARTICLE 20

Consular agents, as well as the employees of the consulate who are nationals of the state appointing them, not engaged in business with purposes of gain, in the state where they perform their functions, shall be exempt from all national, state, provincial, or municipal taxes levied upon their person or property, except such taxes as may apply to the possession or ownership of real estate located in the state where discharging their duties or to the proceeds of the same. Consular agents and employees who are nationals of the state they represent, are exempt from tax on the salaries, honorariums, or wages which they receive in return for their consular services.

ARTICLE 21

The employee who substitutes for the consular agent in his absence, or for another cause, shall enjoy during his temporary term of office the same immunities and prerogatives as the latter.

ARTICLE 22

Consuls engaged in business or exercising other functions apart from those pertaining to their consular duties are subject to local jurisdiction in all their activities not pertaining to the consular service.

Section III. Suspension and termination of consular functions

ARTICLE 23

Consular agents suspend their functions because of illness or leave of absence, and terminate their office:

a) By death;

b) By retirement, resignation, or dismissal; and

c) By the cancellation of the exequatur.

ARTICLE 24

The present convention does not affect obligations previously undertaken by the contracting parties through international agreements.

ARTICLE 25

After being signed, the present convention shall be submitted to the ratification of the signatory states. The Government of Cuba is charged with transmitting authentic certified copies to the governments for the aforementioned purpose of ratification. The instrument of ratification shall be deposited in the archives of the Pan American Union in Washington, the Union to notify the signatory governments of said deposit. Such notification shall be considered as an exchange of ratifications. This convention shall remain open to the adherence of non-signatory states.

In witness whereof, the aforenamed plenipotentiaries sign the present convention in Spanish, English, French, and Portuguese, in the city of Habana, the 20th day of February, 1928.

Peru:
JESÚS M. SALAZAR
VÍCTOR M. MAÚRTUA
LUIS ERNESTO DENEGRI
E. CASTRO OYANGUREN

Uruguay:
VARELA
PEDRO ERASMO CALLORDA

Panama:
R. J. ALFARO
EDUARDO CHIARI

Ecuador:
GONZALO ZALDUMBIDE
VÍCTOR ZEVALLOS
C. E. ALFARO

Mexico:
Julio García
Fernando González Roa
Salvador Urbina
Aquiles Elorduy

Salvador:
J. Gustavo Guerrero
Héctor David Castro
Ed. Alvarez

Guatemala:
Carlos Salazar
B. Alvarado
Luis Beltranena
J. Azurdia

Nicaragua:
Carlos Cuadra Pazos
Máximo H. Zepeda
Joaquín Gómez

Bolivia:
José Antezana
A. Costa du R.

Venezuela:
Santiago Key Ayala
Francisco G. Yanes
Rafael Angel Arraiz

Colombia:
Enrique Olaya Herrera
R. Gutiérrez Lee
J. M. Yepes

Honduras:
F. Dávila
Mariano Vázquez

Costa Rica:
Ricardo Castro Beeche
J. Rafael Oreamuno
A. Tinoco Jiménez

Chile:
Alejandro Lira
Alejandro Alvarez
C. Silva Vildósola
Manuel Bianchi

Brazil:
Raúl Fernandes
Lindolfo Collor

Argentina:
Laurentino Olascoaga
Felipe A. Espil
Carlos Alberto Alcorta

Paraguay:
Lisandro Díaz León
Juan Vicente Ramírez

Haiti:
Fernando Dennis

Dominican Republic:
Fraco. J. Peynado
Tulio M. Cestero
Jacinto R. de Castro
Elías Brache
R. Pérez Alfonseca

United States of America:
Charles Evans Hughes
Noble Brandon Judah
Henry P. Fletcher
Oscar W. Underwood
Morgan J. O'Brien
James Brown Scott
Ray Lyman Wilbur
Leo S. Rowe

Cuba:
Antonio S. de Bustamante
Orestes Ferrara
E. Hernández Cartaya
Arístides de Agüero Bethencourt
M. Márquez Sterling
Néstor Carbonell

Reservation of the Delegation of Venezuela

On behalf of the Government that I represent, I make a reservation with respect to the coincidence of diplomatic and consular functions in the same person, because it is totally opposed to our tradition, maintained since it was established until the present time, in a way that admits of no change.

MARITIME NEUTRALITY (INTER-AMERICAN)

Convention signed at Havana February 20, 1928
Senate advice and consent to ratification, with a reservation, January 28, 1932 [1]
Ratified by the President of the United States, with a reservation, February 6, 1932 [1]
Ratification of the United States deposited with the Pan American Union March 22, 1932
Entered into force January 12, 1931; for the United States March 22, 1932
Proclaimed by the President of the United States May 26, 1932

47 Stat. 1989; Treaty Series 845

CONVENTION

The Governments of the Republics represented at the Sixth International Conference of American States, held in the city of Habana, Republic of Cuba, in the year 1928;

Desiring that, in case war breaks out between two or more states the other states may, in the service of peace, offer their good offices or mediation to bring the conflict to an end, without such an action being considered as an unfriendly act;

Convinced that, in case this aim cannot be attained, neutral states have equal interest in having their rights respected by the belligerents;

Considering that neutrality is the juridical situation of states which do not take part in the hostilities, and that it creates rights and imposes obligations of impartiality, which should be regulated;

Recognizing that international solidarity requires that the liberty of commerce should be always respected, avoiding as far as possible unnecessary burdens for the neutrals;

It being convenient, that as long as this object is not reached, to reduce those burdens as much as possible; and

In the hope that it will be possible to regulate the matter so that all interests concerned may have every desired guaranty;

---

[1] For text of U.S. reservation made at time of signing and maintained in the Senate's resolution of advice and consent and in the President's ratification, see p. 729.

Have resolved to formulate a convention to that effect and have appointed the following plenipotentiaries:

Perú: Jesús Melquiades Salazar, Víctor Maúrtua, Enrique Castro Oyanguren, Luis Ernesto Denegri.

Uruguay: Jacobo Varela Acevedo, Juan José Amézaga, Leonel Aguirre, Pedro Erasmo Callorda.

Panamá: Ricardo J. Alfaro, Eduardo Chiari.

Ecuador: Gonzalo Zaldumbide, Víctor Zevallos, Colón Eloy Alfaro.

Mexico: Julio García, Fernando González Roa, Salvador Urbina, Aquiles Elorduy.

Salvador: Gustavo Guerrero, Héctor David Castro, Eduardo Alvarez.

Guatemala: Carlos Salazar, Bernardo Alvarado Tello, Luis Beltranena, José Azurdia.

Nicaragua: Carlos Cuadra Pazos, Joaquín Gómez, Máximo H. Zepeda.

Bolivia: José Antezana, Adolfo Costa du Rels.

Venezuela: Santiago Key Ayala, Francisco Gerardo Yanes, Rafael Angel Arraiz.

Colombia: Enrique Olaya Herrera, Jesús M. Yepes, Roberto Urdaneta Arbeláez, Ricardo Gutiérrez Lee.

Honduras: Fausto Dávila, Mariano Vázquez.

Costa Rica: Ricardo Castro Beeche, J. Rafael Oreamuno, Arturo Tinoco.

Chile: Alejandro Lira, Alejandro Alvarez, Carlos Silva Vildósola, Manuel Bianchi.

Brazil: Raúl Fernandes, Lindolfo Collor, Alarico da Silveira, Sampaio Correa, Eduardo Espínola.

Argentina: Honorio Pueyrredón, (Later resigned), Laurentino Olascoaga, Felipe A. Espil.

Paraguay: Lisandro Díaz León.

Haiti: Fernando Dennis, Charles Riboul.

Dominican Republic: Francisco J. Peynado, Gustavo A. Díaz, Elías Brache, Angel Morales, Tulio M. Cestero, Ricardo Pérez Alfonseca, Jacinto R. de Castro, Federico C. Alvarez.

United States of America: Charles Evans Hughes, Noble Brandon Judah, Henry P. Fletcher, Oscar W. Underwood, Dwight W. Morrow, Morgan J. O'Brien, James Brown Scott, Ray Lyman Wilbur, Leo S. Rowe.

Cuba: Antonio S. de Bustamante, Orestes Ferrara, Enrique Hernández Cartaya, José Manuel Cortina, Arístides Agüero, José B. Alemán, Manuel Márquez Sterling, Fernando Ortiz, Néstor Carbonell, Jesús María Barraqué.

Who, after having presented their credentials, which were found in good and correct form, have agreed upon the following provisions:

Section I. Freedom of commerce in time of war

ARTICLE 1

The following rules shall govern commerce in time of war:

1. Warships of the belligerents have the right to stop and visit on the high seas and in territorial waters that are not neutral any merchant ship with the object of ascertaining its character and nationality and of verifying whether it conveys cargo prohibited by international law or has committed any violation of blockade. If the merchant ship does not heed the signal to stop, it may be pursued by the warship and stopped by force; outside of such a case the ship cannot be attacked unless, after being hailed, it fails to observe the instructions given it.

The ship shall not be rendered incapable of navigation before the crew and passengers have been placed in safety.

2. Belligerent submarines are subject to the foregoing rules. If the submarine cannot capture the ship while observing these rules, it shall not have the right to continue to attack or to destroy the ship.

ARTICLE 2

Both the detention of the vessel and its crew for violation of neutrality shall be made in accordance with the procedure which best suits the state effecting it and at the expense of the transgressing ship. Said state, except in the case of grave fault on its part, is not responsible for damages which the vessel may suffer.

Section II. Duties and rights of belligerents

ARTICLE 3

Belligerent states are obligated to refrain from performing acts of war in neutral waters or other acts which may constitute on the part of the state that tolerates them, a violation of neutrality.

ARTICLE 4

Under the terms of the preceding article, a belligerent state is forbidden:

a) To make use of neutral waters as a base of naval operations against the enemy, or to renew or augment military supplies or the armament of its ships, or to complete the equipment of the latter;

b) To install in neutral waters radio-telegraph stations or any other apparatus which may serve as a means of communication with its military forces, or to make use of installations of this kind it may have established before the war and which may not have been opened to the public.

ARTICLE 5

Belligerent warships are forbidden to remain in the ports or waters of a neutral state more than twenty-four hours. This provision will be communicated to the ship as soon as it arrives in port or in the territorial waters, and if already there at the time of the declaration of war, as soon as the neutral state becomes aware of this declaration.

Vessels used exclusively for scientific, religious, or philanthropic purposes are exempted from the foregoing provisions.

A ship may extend its stay in port more than twenty-four hours in case of damage or bad conditions at sea, but must depart as soon as the cause of the delay has ceased.

When, according to the domestic law of the neutral state, the ship may not receive fuel until twenty-four hours after its arrival in port, the period of its stay may be extended an equal length of time.

ARTICLE 6

The ship which does not conform to the foregoing rules may be interned by order of the neutral government.

A ship shall be considered as interned from the moment it receives notice to that effect from the local neutral authority, even though a petition for reconsideration of the order has been interposed by the transgressing vessel, which shall remain under custody from the moment it receives the order.

ARTICLE 7

In the absence of a special provision of the local legislation, the maximum number of ships of war of a belligerent which may be in a neutral port at the same time shall be three.

ARTICLE 8

A ship of war may not depart from a neutral port within less than twenty-four hours after the departure of an enemy warship. The one entering first shall depart first, unless it is in such condition as to warrant extending its stay. In any case the ship which arrived later has the right to notify the other through the competent local authority that within twenty-four hours it will leave the port, the one first entering, however, having the right to depart within that time. If it leaves, the notifying ship must observe the interval which is above stipulated.

ARTICLE 9

Damaged belligerent ships shall not be permitted to make repairs in neutral ports beyond those that are essential to the continuance of the voyage and which in no degree constitute an increase in its military strength.

Damages which are found to have been produced by the enemy's fire shall in no case be repaired.

The neutral state shall ascertain the nature of the repairs to be made and will see that they are made as rapidly as possible.

ARTICLE 10

Belligerent warships may supply themselves with fuel and stores in neutral ports, under the conditions especially established by the local authority and in case there are no special provisions to that effect, they may supply themselves in the manner prescribed for provisioning in time of peace.

ARTICLE 11

Warships which obtain fuel in a neutral port cannot renew their supply in the same state until a period of three months has elapsed.

ARTICLE 12

Where the sojourn, supplying, and provisioning of belligerent ships in the ports and jurisdictional waters of neutrals are concerned, the provisions relative to ships of war shall apply equally:

1. To ordinary auxiliary ships;
2. To merchant ships transformed into warships, in accordance with Convention VII of The Hague of 1907.

The neutral vessel shall be seized and in general subjected to the same treatment as enemy merchantmen:

a) When taking a direct part in the hostilities;
b) When at the orders or under the direction of an agent placed on board by an enemy government;
c) When entirely freight-loaded by an enemy government;
d) When actually and exclusively destined for transporting enemy troops or for the transmission of information on behalf of the enemy.

In the cases dealt with in this article, merchandise belonging to the owner of the vessel or ship shall also be liable to seizure.

3. To armed merchantmen.[2]

---

[2] Not accepted by the United States.

Article 13

Auxiliary ships of belligerents, converted anew into merchantmen, shall be admitted as such in neutral ports subject to the following conditions:

1. That the transformed vessel has not violated the neutrality of the country where it arrives;
2. That the transformation has been made in the ports or jurisdictional waters of the country to which the vessel belongs, or in the ports of its allies;
3. That the transformation be genuine, namely, that the vessel show neither in its crew nor in its equipment that it can serve the armed fleet of its country as an auxiliary, as it did before;
4. That the government of the country to which the ship belongs communicate to the state the names of auxiliary craft which have lost such character in order to recover that of merchantmen; and
5. That the same government obligate itself that said ships shall not again be used as auxiliaries to the war fleet.

Article 14

The airships of belligerents shall not fly above the territory or the territorial waters of neutrals if it is not in conformity with the regulations of the latter.

Section III. Rights and duties of neutrals

Article 15

Of the acts of assistance coming from the neutral states, and the acts of commerce on the part of individuals, only the first are contrary to neutrality.

Article 16

The neutral state is forbidden:

a) To deliver to the belligerent, directly or indirectly, or for any reason whatever, ships of war, munitions or any other war material;
b) To grant it loans, or to open credits for it during the duration of war.

Credits that a neutral state may give to facilitate the sale or exportation of its food products and raw materials are not included in this prohibition.

Article 17

Prizes cannot be taken to a neutral port except in case of unseaworthiness, stress of weather, or want of fuel or provisions. When the cause has disappeared, the prizes must leave immediately; if none of the indicated conditions exist, the state shall suggest to them that they depart, and if not obeyed shall have recourse to the means at its disposal to disarm them with their officers and crew, or to intern the prize crew placed on board by the captor.

ARTICLE 18

Outside of the cases provided for in Article 17, the neutral state must release the prizes which may have been brought into its territorial waters.

ARTICLE 19

When a ship transporting merchandise is to be interned in a neutral state, cargo intended for said country shall be unloaded and that destined for others shall be transhipped.

ARTICLE 20

The merchantman supplied with fuel or other stores in a neutral state which repeatedly delivers the whole or part of its supplies to a belligerent vessel, shall not again receive stores and fuel in the same state.

ARTICLE 21

Should it be found that a merchantman flying a belligerent flag, by its preparations or other circumstances, can supply to warships of a state the stores which they need, the local authority may refuse it supplies or demand of the agent of the company a guaranty that the said ship will not aid or assist any belligerent vessel.

ARTICLE 22

Neutral states are not obligated to prevent the export or transit at the expense of any one of the belligerents of arms, munitions and in general of anything which may be useful to their military forces.

Transit shall be permitted when, in the event of a war between two American nations, one of the belligerents is a mediterranean country, having no other means of supplying itself, provided the vital interests of the country through which transit is requested do not suffer by the granting thereof.

ARTICLE 23

Neutral states shall not oppose the voluntary departure of nationals of belligerent states even though they leave simultaneously in great numbers; but they may oppose the voluntary departure of their own nationals going to enlist in the armed forces.

ARTICLE 24

The use by the belligerents of the means of communication of neutral states or which cross or touch their territory is subject to the measures dictated by the local authority.

ARTICLE 25

If as the result of naval operations beyond the territorial waters of neutral states there should be dead or wounded on board belligerent vessels, said states may send hospital ships under the vigilance of the neutral government to the scene of the disaster. These ships shall enjoy complete immunity during the discharge of their mission.

ARTICLE 26

Neutral states are bound to exert all the vigilance within their power in order to prevent in their ports or territorial waters any violation of the foregoing provisions.

Section IV. Fulfilment and observance of the laws of neutrality

ARTICLE 27

A belligerent shall indemnify the damage caused by its violation of the foregoing provisions. It shall likewise be responsible for the acts of persons who may belong to its armed forces.

ARTICLE 28

The present convention does not affect obligations previously undertaken by the contracting parties through international agreements.

ARTICLE 29

After being signed, the present convention shall be submitted to the ratification of the signatory states. The Government of Cuba is charged with transmitting authentic certified copies to the governments for the aforementioned purpose of ratification. The instrument of ratification shall be deposited in the archives of the Pan American Union in Washington, the Union to notify the signatory governments of said deposit. Such notifications shall be considered as an exchange of ratifications. This convention shall remain open to the adherence of nonsignatory states.

In witness whereof, the aforenamed plenipotentiaries sign the present convention in Spanish, English, French, and Portuguese, in the city of Habana, the 20th day of February, 1928.

Peru:
 JESÚS M. SALAZAR
 VICTOR M. MAÚRTUA
 LUIS ERNESTO DENEGRI
 E. CASTRO OYANGUREN

Uruguay:
 VARELA
 PEDRO ERASMO CALLORDA

Panama:
 R. J. ALFARO
 EDUARDO CHIARI

Ecuador:
 GONZALO ZALDUMBIDE
 VICTOR ZEVALLOS
 C. E. ALFARO

Mexico:
 JULIO GARCÍA
 FERNANDO GONZÁLEZ ROA
 SALVADOR URBINA
 AQUILES ELORDUY

Salvador:
 J. GUSTAVO GUERRERO
 HÉCTOR DAVID CASTRO
 ED. ALVAREZ

Guatemala:
 CARLOS SALAZAR
 B. ALVARADO
 LUIS BELTRANENA
 J. AZURDIA

Nicaragua:
  CARLOS CUADRA PAZOS
  MÁXIMO H. ZEPEDA
  JOAQUÍN GÓMEZ

Bolivia:
  JOSÉ ANTEZANA
  A. COSTA DU R.

Venezuela:
  SANTIAGO KEY AYALA
  FRANCISCO G. YANES
  RAFAEL ANGEL ARRAIZ

Colombia:
  ENRIQUE OLAYA HERRERA
  R. GUTIÉRREZ LEE
  J. M. YEPES

Honduras:
  F. DÁVILA
  MARIANO VÁZQUEZ

Costa Rica:
  RICARDO CASTRO BEECHE
  J. RAFAEL OREAMUNO
  A. TINOCO JIMÉNEZ

Chile:
  ALEJANDRO LIRA
  ALEJANDRO ALVAREZ
  C. SILVA VILDÓSOLA
  MANUEL BIANCHI

Brazil:
  RAÚL FERNANDES
  LINDOLFO COLLOR

Argentina:
  LAURENTINO OLASCOAGA
  FELIPE A. ESPIL
  CARLOS ALBERTO ALCORTA

Paraguay:
  LISANDRO DÍAZ LEÓN
  JUAN VICENTE RAMÍREZ

Haiti:
  FERNANDO DENNIS

Dominican Republic:
  FRACO. J. PEYNADO
  TULIO M. CESTERO
  JACINTO R. DE CASTRO
  ELÍAS BRACHE
  R. PÉREZ ALFONSECA

United States of America:
  CHARLES EVANS HUGHES
  NOBLE BRANDON JUDAH
  HENRY P. FLETCHER
  OSCAR W. UNDERWOOD
  MORGAN J. O'BRIEN
  JAMES BROWN SCOTT
  RAY LYMAN WILBUR
  LEO S. ROWE

Cuba:
  ANTONIO S. DE BUSTAMANTE
  ORESTES FERRARA
  E. HERNÁNDEZ CARTAYA
  ARÍSTIDES DE AGÜERO BETHENCOURT
  M. MÁRQUEZ STERLING
  NÉSTOR CARBONELL

Reservation of the Delegation of Chile

The delegation of Chile signs the present convention with a reservation concerning Article 22, paragraph 2.

Reservation of the Delegation of the United States of America

The delegation of the United States of America signs the present convention with a reservation regarding Article 12, section 3.

Reservation of the Delegation of Cuba

The delegation of the Republic of Cuba signs with a reservation in reference to Article 12, section 3.

PAN AMERICAN UNION

Resolution adopted by the Sixth International Conference of American States at Havana February 20, 1928 [1]

> *Report of the Delegates of the United States of America to the Sixth International Conference of American States, Held at Habana, Cuba, January 16 to February 20, 1928* (U.S. Government Printing Office, 1928), p. 239

The Sixth International Conference of American States,

RESOLVES:

That the Pan American Union continue to be governed by the resolutions in force, until the states members of the Union resolve otherwise, with the following modifications:

1. The government of the Pan American Union shall be vested in a Governing Board composed of the representatives that the American Governments may appoint. The appointment may devolve upon the diplomatic representatives of the respective countries at Washington.

2. The Director General shall appoint, with the approval of the Governing Board, the personnel necessary to the work of the Pan American Union, endeavoring as far as possible to distribute the positions among the nationals of the countries members of the Union.

3. Neither the Governing Board nor the Pan American Union shall exercise functions of a political character.

4. The Governing Board of the Pan American Union shall prepare the regulations and fix the status of the members of the staff, determining their salaries and conditions of retirement.

---

[1] In addition to the resolution on the structure and functions of the Pan American Union printed herewith, the Sixth Conference also adopted a convention relating to the organization of the Union which was ratified by the United States but which did not enter into force (for text, see the report of the American delegation, p. 231, or Senate Executive II, 70th Cong., 2d sess.). For text of an earlier resolution, adopted at the Fourth Conference (Buenos Aires, 1910), containing a draft convention, and for other resolutions relating to the Pan American Union adopted at the various Conferences of American States, see the reports of the American delegations to the Conferences, including the Seventh (Montevideo, 1933) and the Eighth (Lima, 1938).

5. The states members of the Union may withdraw from the Union at any time, but shall pay their respective quotas for the period of the current fiscal year.

[The above resolution was incorporated in the final act of the Sixth International Conference of American States, which was signed on February 20, 1928, by delegates representing Argentina, Bolivia, Brazil, Chile, Colombia, Costa Rica, Cuba, the Dominican Republic, Ecuador, El Salvador, Guatemala, Haiti, Honduras, Mexico, Nicaragua, Panama, Paraguay, Peru, the United States, Uruguay, and Venezuela.]

RENUNCIATION OF WAR AS AN INSTRUMENT OF NATIONAL POLICY (KELLOGG-BRIAND PEACE PACT OR PACT OF PARIS)

Treaty signed at Paris August 27, 1928
Senate advice and consent to ratification January 15, 1929
Ratified by the President of the United States January 17, 1929
Ratifications deposited at Washington March 2, 1929
Entered into force July 24, 1929
Proclaimed by the President of the United States July 24, 1929

46 Stat. 2343; Treaty Series 796

The President of the German Reich, The President of the United States of America, His Majesty the King of The Belgians, the President of The French Republic, His Majesty the King of Great Britain, Ireland and The British Dominions Beyond the Seas, Emperor of India, His Majesty the King of Italy, His Majesty the Emperor of Japan, the President of the Republic of Poland, the President of the Czechoslovak Republic,

Deeply sensible of their solemn duty to promote the welfare of mankind;

Persuaded that the time has come when a frank renunciation of war as an instrument of national policy should be made to the end that the peaceful and friendly relations now existing between their peoples may be perpetuated;

Convinced that all changes in their relations with one another should be sought only by pacific means and be the result of a peaceful and orderly process, and that any signatory Power which shall hereafter seek to promote its national interests by resort to war should be denied the benefits furnished by this Treaty;

Hopeful that, encouraged by their example, all the other nations of the world will join in this humane endeavor and by adhering to the present Treaty as soon as it comes into force bring their peoples within the scope of its beneficent provisions, thus uniting the civilized nations of the world in a common renunciation of war as an instrument of their national policy;

Have decided to conclude a Treaty and for that purpose have appointed as their respective Plenipotentiaries:

The President of the German Reich:
Dr. Gustav Stresemann, Minister for Foreign Affairs;

The President of the United States of America:
The Honorable Frank B. Kellogg, Secretary of State;

His Majesty the King of the Belgians:
Mr. Paul Hymans, Minister for Foreign Affairs, Minister of State;

The President of the French Republic:
Mr. Aristide Briand, Minister for Foreign Affairs;

His Majesty the King of Great Britain, Ireland and the British Dominions Beyond the Seas, Emperor of India:

For Great Britain and Northern Ireland and all parts of the British Empire which are not separate Members of the League of Nations:
The Right Honourable Lord Cushendun, Chancellor of the Duchy of Lancaster, Acting Secretary of State for Foreign Affairs;

For the Dominion of Canada:
The Right Honourable William Lyon Mackenzie King, Prime Minister and Minister for External Affairs;

For the Commonwealth of Australia:
The Honourable Alexander John McLachlan, Member of the Executive Federal Council;

For the Dominion of New Zealand:
The Honourable Sir Christopher James Parr, High Commissioner for New Zealand in Great Britain;

For the Union of South Africa:
The Honourable Jacobus Stephanus Smit, High Commissioner for the Union of South Africa in Great Britain;

For the Irish Free State:
Mr. William Thomas Cosgrave, President of the Executive Council;

For India:
The Right Honourable Lord Cushendun, Chancellor of the Duchy of Lancaster, Acting Secretary of State for Foreign Affairs;

His Majesty the King of Italy:
Count Gaetano Manzoni, his Ambassador Extraordinary and Plenipotentiary at Paris.

His Majesty the Emperor of Japan:
Count Uchida, Privy Councillor;

The President of the Republic of Poland:
Mr. A. Zaleski, Minister for Foreign Affairs;

The President of the Czechoslovak Republic:
Dr. Eduard Beneš, Minister for Foreign Affairs;

who, having communicated to one another their full powers found in good and due form have agreed upon the following articles:

ARTICLE I

The High Contracting Parties solemnly declare in the names of their respective peoples that they condemn recourse to war for the solution of international controversies, and renounce it as an instrument of national policy in their relations with one another.

ARTICLE II

The High Contracting Parties agree that the settlement or solution of all disputes or conflicts of whatever nature or of whatever origin they may be, which may arise among them, shall never be sought except by pacific means.

ARTICLE III

The present Treaty shall be ratified by the High Contracting Parties named in the Preamble in accordance with their respective constitutional requirements, and shall take effect as between them as soon as all their several instruments of ratification shall have been deposited at Washington.

This Treaty shall, when it has come into effect as prescribed in the preceding paragraph, remain open as long as may be necessary for adherence by all the other Powers of the world. Every instrument evidencing the adherence of a Power shall be deposited at Washington and the Treaty shall immediately upon such deposit become effective as between the Power thus adhering and the other Powers parties hereto.

It shall be the duty of the Government of the United States to furnish each Government named in the Preamble and every Government subsequently adhering to this Treaty with a certified copy of the Treaty and of every instrument of ratification or adherence. It shall also be the duty of the Government of the United States telegraphically to notify such Governments immediately upon the deposit with it of each instrument of ratification or adherence.

In faith whereof the respective Plenipotentiaries have signed this Treaty in the French and English languages both texts having equal force, and hereunto affix their seals.

Done at Paris, the twenty-seventh day of August in the year one thousand nine hundred and twenty-eight.

[For Germany:]		[For Belgium:]	
GUSTAV STRESEMANN	[SEAL]	PAUL HYMANS	[SEAL]
[For the United States:]		[For France:]	
FRANK B. KELLOGG	[SEAL]	ARI BRIAND	[SEAL]

[For the United Kingdom:]
CUSHENDUN   [SEAL]

[For the Dominion of Canada:]
W. L. MACKENZIE KING   [SEAL]

[For the Commonwealth of Australia:]
A. J. McLACHLAN   [SEAL]

[For the Dominion of New Zealand:]
C. J. PARR   [SEAL]

[For the Union of South Africa:]
J. S. SMIT   [SEAL]

[For the Irish Free State:]
LIAM T. MacCOSGAIR   [SEAL]

[For India:]
CUSHENDUN   [SEAL]

[For Italy:]
G. MANZONI   [SEAL]

[For Japan:]
UCHIDA   [SEAL]

[For Poland:]
AUGUST ZALESKI   [SEAL]

[For Czechoslovakia:]
DR. EDUARD BENES   [SEAL]

INTERNATIONAL EXHIBITIONS

Convention signed at Paris November 22, 1928
Procès-verbal of first deposit of ratifications at Paris dated December 17,
  1930
Senate advice and consent to accession April 30, 1968
Accession signed by the President of the United States May 6, 1968
Proclaimed by the President of the United States August 17, 1968
Entered into force January 17, 1931; for the United States June 24,
  1968
Amended by protocols of May 10, 1948, and November 16, 1966

[For texts of convention and protocols, see 19 UST 5927, 5974; TIAS 6548, 6549.]

INTER-AMERICAN ARBITRATION

Treaty and protocol signed at Washington January 5, 1929
Senate advice and consent to ratification of treaty, with an understanding, April 1, 1935 [1]
Treaty ratified by the President of the United States, with an understanding, April 16, 1935 [1]
Ratification of the United States deposited at Washington April 16, 1935
Entered into force October 28, 1929; for the United States April 16, 1935
Proclaimed by the President of the United States April 16, 1935

49 Stat. 3152; Treaty Series 886

General Treaty of Inter-American Arbitration

The Governments of Venezuela, Chile, Bolivia, Uruguay, Costa Rica, Perú, Honduras, Guatemala, Haiti, Ecuador, Colombia, Brazil, Panamá, Paraguay, Nicaragua, Mexico, El Salvador, the Dominican Republic, Cuba, and the United States of America, represented at the Conference on Conciliation and Arbitration, assembled at Washington, pursuant to the Resolution adopted on February 18, 1928,[2] by the Sixth International Conference of American States held in the City of Habana;

In accordance with the solemn declarations made at said Conference to the effect that the American Republics condemn war as an instrument of national policy and adopt obligatory arbitration as the means for the settlement of their international differences of a juridical character;

Being convinced that the Republics of the New World, governed by the principles, institutions and practices of democracy and bound furthermore by mutual interests, which are increasing each day, have not only the necessity but also the duty of avoiding the disturbance of continental harmony whenever differences which are susceptible of judicial decision arise among them;

---

[1] The U.S. understanding reads as follows: ". . . that the special agreement in each case shall be made only by the President, and then only by and with the advice and consent of the Senate, provided two-thirds of the Senators present concur."

[2] *Report of the Delegates of the United States of America to the Sixth International Conference of American States held at Habana, Cuba, January 16 to February 20, 1928* (U.S. Government Printing Office, 1928), p. 310.

737

Conscious of the great moral and material benefits which peace offers to humanity and that the sentiment and opinion of America demand, without delay, the organization of an arbitral system which shall strengthen the permanent reign of justice and law;

And animated by the purpose of giving conventional form to these postulates and aspirations with the minimum exceptions which they have considered indispensable to safeguard the independence and sovereignty of the States and in the most ample manner possible under present international conditions, have resolved to effect the present treaty, and for that purpose have designated the Plenipotentiaries hereinafter named:

Venezuela:
Carlos F. Grisanti
Francisco Arroyo Parejo

Chile:
Manuel Foster Recabarren
Antonio Planet

Bolivia:
Eduardo Diez de Medina

Uruguay:
José Pedro Varela

Costa Rica:
Manuel Castro Quesada
José Tible-Machado

Peru:
Hernán Velarde
Victor M. Maúrtua

Honduras:
Rómulo Durón
Marcos López Ponce

Guatemala:
Adrián Recinos
José Falla

Haiti:
Auguste Bonamy
Raoul Lizaire

Ecuador:
Gonzalo Zaldumbide

Colombia:
Enrique Olaya Herrera
Carlos Escallón

Brazil:
S. Gurgel do Amaral
A. G. de Araujo-Jorge

Panamá:
Ricardo J. Alfaro
Carlos L. López

Paraguay:
Eligio Ayala

Nicaragua:
Maximo H. Zepeda
Adrián Recinos
J. Lisandro Medina

Mexico:
Fernando González Roa
Benito Flores

El Salvador:
Cayetano Ochoa
David Rosales, Jr.

Dominican Republic:
Angel Morales
Gustavo A. Díaz

Cuba:
Orestes Ferrara
Gustavo Gutiérrez

United States of America:
Frank B. Kellogg
Charles Evans Hughes

Who, after having deposited their full powers, found in good and due form by the Conference, have agreed upon the following:

ARTICLE 1

The High Contracting Parties bind themselves to submit to arbitration all differences of an international character which have arisen or may arise between them by virtue of a claim of right made by one against the other under treaty or otherwise, which it has not been possible to adjust by diplomacy and which are juridical in their nature by reason of being susceptible of decision by the application of the principles of law.

There shall be considered as included among the questions of juridical character:

(a) The interpretation of a treaty;

(b) Any question of international law;

(c) The existence of any fact which, if established, would constitute a breach of an international obligation;

(d) The nature and extent of the reparation to be made for the breach of an international obligation.

The provisions of this treaty shall not preclude any of the Parties, before resorting to arbitration, from having recourse to procedures of investigation and conciliation established in conventions then in force between them.

ARTICLE 2

There are excepted from the stipulations of this treaty the following controversies:

(a) Those which are within the domestic jurisdiction of any of the Parties to the dispute and are not controlled by international law; and

(b) Those which affect the interest or refer to the action of a State not a Party to this treaty.

ARTICLE 3

The arbitrator or tribunal who shall decide the controversy shall be designated by agreement of the Parties.

In the absence of an agreement the following procedure shall be adopted:

Each Party shall nominate two arbitrators, of whom only one may be a national of said Party or selected from the persons whom said Party has designated as members of the Permanent Court of Arbitration at The Hague. The other member may be of any other American nationality. These arbitrators shall in turn select a fifth arbitrator who shall be the president of the court.

Should the arbitrators be unable to reach an agreement among themselves for the selection of a fifth American arbitrator, or in lieu thereof, of another who is not, each Party shall designate a non-American member of the Permanent Court of Arbitration at The Hague, and the two persons so designated shall select the fifth arbitrator, who may be of any nationality other than that of a Party to the dispute.

ARTICLE 4

The Parties to the dispute shall formulate by common accord, in each case, a special agreement which shall clearly define the particular subject-matter of the controversy, the seat of the court, the rules which will be observed in the proceedings, and the other conditions to which the Parties may agree.

If an accord has not been reached with regard to the agreement within three months reckoned from the date of the installation of the court, the agreement shall be formulated by the court.

ARTICLE 5

In case of death, resignation or incapacity of one or more of the arbitrators the vacancy shall be filled in the same manner as the original appointment.

ARTICLE 6

When there are more than two States directly interested in the same controversy and the interests of two or more of them are similar, the State or States who are on the same side of the question may increase the number of arbitrators on the court provided that in all cases the Parties on each side of the controversy shall appoint an equal number of arbitrators. There shall also be a presiding arbitrator selected in the same manner as that provided in the last paragraph of Article 3, the Parties on each side of the controversy being regarded as a single Party for the purpose of making the designation therein described.

ARTICLE 7

The award, duly pronounced and notified to the Parties, settles the dispute definitively and without appeal.

Differences which arise with regard to its interpretation or execution shall be submitted to the decision of the court which rendered the award.

ARTICLE 8

The reservations made by one of the High Contracting Parties shall have the effect that the other Contracting Parties are not bound with respect to the Party making the reservations except to the same extent as that expressed therein.

ARTICLE 9

The present treaty shall be ratified by the High Contracting Parties in conformity with their respective constitutional procedures.

The original treaty and the instruments of ratification shall be deposited in the Department of State of the United States of America which shall give notice of the ratifications through diplomatic channels to the other signatory

Governments and the treaty shall enter into effect for the High Contracting Parties in the order that they deposit their ratifications.

This treaty shall remain in force indefinitely, but it may be denounced by means of one year's previous notice at the expiration of which it shall cease to be in force as regards the Party denouncing the same, but shall remain in force as regards the other signatories. Notice of the denunciation shall be addressed to the Department of State of the United States of America which will transmit it for appropriate action to the other signatory Governments.

Any American State not a signatory of this treaty may adhere to the same by transmitting the official instrument setting forth such adherence to the Department of State of the United States of America which will notify the other High Contracting Parties thereof in the manner heretofore mentioned.

In witness whereof the above mentioned Plenipotentiaries have signed this treaty in English, Spanish, Portuguese, and French and hereunto affix their respective seals.

Done at the city of Washington, on this fifth day of January, 1929.

[For Venezuela:]
The Delegation of Venezuela signs the present treaty of arbitration with the following reservations:

First. There shall be excepted from this Treaty those matters which, according to the Constitution or the laws of Venezuela, are under the jurisdiction of its courts; and especially those matters relating to pecuniary claims of foreigners. In such matters arbitration shall not be resorted to except when legal remedies having been exhausted by the claimant it shall appear that there has been a denial of justice.

Second. There shall also be excepted those matters controlled by international agreements now in force [translation].

CARLOS F. GRISANTI   [SEAL]
FR. ARROYO PAREJO   [SEAL]

[For Chile:]
Chile does not accept obligatory arbitration for questions which have their origin in situations or acts antedating the present treaty nor does it accept obligatory arbitration for those questions which, being under the exclusive competency of the national jurisdiction, the interested parties claim the right to withdraw from the cognizance of the established judicial authorities, unless said authorities decline to pass judgment on any action or exception which any natural or juridical foreign person may

present to them in the form established by the laws of the country [translation].

MANUEL FOSTER   [SEAL]
A. PLANET   [SEAL]

[For Bolivia:]
The Delegation of Bolivia, in accordance with the doctrine and policy invariably maintained by Bolivia in the field of international jurisprudence, gives full adherence to and signs the General Treaty of Inter-American Arbitration which the Republics of America are to sanction, formulating the following express reservations:

First. There may be excepted from the provisions of the present agreement, questions arising from acts occurring or conventions concluded before the said treaty goes into effect, as well as those which, in conformity with international law, are under the exclusive jurisdiction of the state.

Second. It is also understood that, for the submission to arbitration of a territorial controversy or dispute, the zone to which the said arbitration is to apply must be previously determined in the arbitral agreement [translation].

E. DIEZ DE MEDINA   [SEAL]

[For Uruguay:]
I vote in favor of the Treaty of Arbitration, with the reservation formulated by the Delegation of Uruguay at the

Fifth Pan American Conference, favoring broad arbitration; and with the understanding that arbitration will be resorted to only in case of denial of justice, when the national tribunals have jurisdiction, according to the legislation of their own country [translation].

José Pedro Varela   [seal]

[For Costa Rica:]
Reservations of Costa Rica:
(a) The obligations contracted under this Treaty do not annul, abrogate, or restrict the arbitration conventions which are now in force between Costa Rica and another or others of the high contracting parties and do not involve arbitration, disavowal, or renewed discussion of questions which may have already been settled by arbitral awards.

(b) The obligations contracted under this Treaty do not involve the arbitration of judgments handed down by the courts of Costa Rica in civil cases which may be submitted to them and with regard to which the interested parties have recognized the jurisdiction of said courts [translation].

Manuel Castro Quesada   [seal]
José Tible-Machado   [seal]

[For Peru:]
Hernán Velarde   [seal]
Victor M. Maurtua   [seal]

[For Honduras:]
The Delegation of Honduras, in signing the present Treaty, formulates an express reservation making it a matter of record that the provisions thereof shall not be applicable to pending international questions or controversies or to those which may arise in the future relative to acts prior to the date on which the said Treaty goes into effect [translation].

Rómulo E. Durón   [seal]
M. López Ponce   [seal]

[For Guatemala:]
The Delegation of Guatemala makes the following reservations:
1. In order to submit to arbitration any questions relating to the boundaries of the nation, the approval of the Legislative Assembly must first be given, in

each case, in conformity with the Constitution of the Republic.
2. The provisions of the present Convention do not alter or modify the conventions and treaties previously entered into by the Republic of Guatemala [translation].

Adrián Recinos   [seal]
José Falla   [seal]

[For Haiti:]
A. Bonamy   [seal]
Raoul Lizaire   [seal]

[For Ecuador:]
The Delegation of Ecuador, pursuant to instructions of its Government, reserves from the jurisdiction of the obligatory arbitration agreed upon in the present Treaty:
1. Questions at present governed by conventions or treaties now in effect;
2. Those which may arise from previous causes or may result from acts preceding the signature of this treaty;
3. Pecuniary claims of foreigners who may not have previously exhausted all legal remedies before the courts of justice of the country, it being understood that such is the interpretation and the extent of the application which the Government of Ecuador has always given to the Bueno Aires Convention of August 11, 1910 [3] [translation].

Gonzalo Zaldumbide   [seal]

[For Colombia:]
The Delegation of Colombia signs the foregoing Convention with the following two declarations or reservations:
First. The obligations which the Republic of Colombia may contract thereby refer to the differences which may arise from acts subsequent to the ratification of the Convention;
Second. Except in the case of a denial of justice, the arbitration provided for in this convention is not applicable to the questions which may have arisen or which may arise between a citizen, an association or a corporation of one of the parties and the other contracting state when the judges or courts of the latter state are, in accordance with its legislation, competent to settle the controversy [translation].

Enrique Olaya Herrera   [seal]
C Escallón   [seal]

[3] TS 594, ante, vol. 1, p. 763.

[For Brazil:]
S. GURGEL DO AMARAL   [SEAL]
A. ARAUJO JORGE   [SEAL]

[For Panama:]
R. J. ALFARO   [SEAL]
CARLOS L. LÓPEZ   [SEAL]

[For Paraguay:]
Reservation of the Delegation of Paraguay:
I sign this treaty with the reservation that Paraguay excludes from its application questions which directly or indirectly affect the integrity of the national territory and are not merely questions of frontiers or boundaries [translation].
ELIGIO AYALA   [SEAL]

[For Nicaragua:]
MÁXIMO H. ZEPEDA
ADRIÁN RECINOS   [SEAL]
J. LISANDRO MEDINA

[For Mexico:]
Mexican Reservation:
Mexico makes the reservation that differences, which fall under the jurisdiction of the courts, shall not form a subject of the procedure provided for by the Convention, except in case of denial of justice, and until after the judgment passed by the competent national authority has been placed in the class of *res judicata* [translation].
FERDO GONZÁLEZ ROA   [SEAL]
BENITO FLORES

[For El Salvador:]
The Delegation of El Salvador to the Conference on Conciliation and Arbitration assembled in Washington accepts and signs the General Treaty of Inter-American Arbitration concluded this day by said Conference, with the following reservations or restrictions:
1. After the words of paragraph 1 of Article 1 reading: "under treaty or other-

wise", the following words are to be added: "subsequent to the present Convention." The article continues without any other modification.
2. Paragraph (a) of Article 2 is accepted by the Delegation without the final words which read: "and are not controlled by international law", which should be considered as eliminated.
3. This Treaty does not include controversies or differences with regard to points or questions which, according to the Political Constitution of El Salvador, must not be submitted to arbitration, and
4. Pecuniary claims against the nation shall be decided by its judges and courts, since they have jurisdiction thereof, and recourse shall be had to international arbitration only in the cases provided in the Constitution and laws of El Salvador, that is in cases of denial of justice or unusual delay in the administration thereof [translation].
DAVID ROSALES, HIJO   [SEAL]
CAYETANO OCHOA   [SEAL]

[For the Dominican Republic:]
The Dominican Republic, in signing the General Treaty of Inter-American Arbitration, does so with the understanding that controversies relating to questions which are under the jurisdiction of its courts shall not be referred to arbitral jurisdiction except in accordance with the principles of international law [translation].
A. MORALES   [SEAL]
G. A. DÍAZ   [SEAL]

[For Cuba:]
ORESTES FERRARA   [SEAL]
GUSTAVO GUTIÉRREZ   [SEAL]

[For the United States:]
FRANK B. KELLOGG   [SEAL]
CHARLES EVANS HUGHES   [SEAL]

PROTOCOL OF PROGRESSIVE ARBITRATION

Whereas, a General Treaty of Inter-American Arbitration has this day been signed at Washington by Plenipotentiaries of the Governments of Venezuela, Chile, Bolivia, Uruguay, Costa Rica, Perú, Honduras, Guatemala, Haiti, Ecuador, Colombia, Brazil, Panama, Paraguay, Nicaragua, Mexico, El Salvador, the Dominican Republic, Cuba, and the United States of America;

Whereas, that treaty by its terms excepts certain controversies from the stipulations thereof;

Whereas, by means of reservations attached to the treaty at the time of signing, ratifying or adhering, certain other controversies have been or may be also excepted from the stipulations of the treaty or reserved from the operation thereof;

Whereas, it is deemed desirable to establish a procedure whereby such exceptions or reservations may from time to time be abandoned in whole or in part by the Parties to said treaty, thus progressively extending the field of arbitration;

The Governments named above have agreed as follows:

ARTICLE 1

Any Party to the General Treaty of Inter-American Arbitration signed at Washington the fifth day of January, 1929, may at any time deposit with the Department of State of the United States of America an appropriate instrument evidencing that it has abandoned in whole or in part the exceptions from arbitration stipulated in the said treaty or the reservation or reservations attached by it thereto.

ARTICLE 2

A certified copy of each instrument deposited with the Department of State of the United States of America pursuant to the provisions of Article 1 of this protocol shall be transmitted by the said Department through diplomatic channels to every other Party to the above-mentioned General Treaty of Inter-American Arbitration.

In witness whereof the above-mentioned Plenipotentiaries have signed this protocol in English, Spanish, Portuguese and French and hereunto affix their respective seals.

Done at the city of Washington, on this fifth day of January, 1929.

CARLOS F. GRISANTI	[SEAL]	S. GURGEL DO AMARAL	[SEAL]
FR. ARROYO PAREJO	[SEAL]	A. ARAUJO JORGE	[SEAL]
MANUEL FOSTER	[SEAL]	R. J. ALFARO	[SEAL]
A. PLANET	[SEAL]	CARLOS L. LÓPEZ	[SEAL]
E. DIEZ DE MEDINA	[SEAL]	ELIGIO AYALA	[SEAL]
JOSÉ PEDRO VARELA	[SEAL]	MÁXIMO H. ZEPEDA	
MANUEL CASTRO QUESADA	[SEAL]	ADRIÁN RECINOS	[SEAL]
JOSÉ TIBLE MACHADO	[SEAL]	J. LISANDRO MEDINA	
HERNÁN VELARDE	[SEAL]	FERDO GONZÁLEZ ROA	[SEAL]
VICTOR M. MAURTUA	[SEAL]	BENITO FLORES	
RÓMULO E. DURÓN	[SEAL]	CAYETANO OCHOA	[SEAL]
M. LÓPEZ PONCE	[SEAL]	DAVID ROSALES, HIJO	
ADRIÁN RECINOS	[SEAL]	A. MORALES	[SEAL]
JOSÉ FALLA	[SEAL]	G. A. DÍAZ	[SEAL]
A. BONAMY	[SEAL]	ORESTES FERRARA	[SEAL]
RAOUL LIZAIRE		GUSTAVO GUTIÉRREZ	[SEAL]
GONZALO ZALDUMBIDE	[SEAL]	FRANK B. KELLOGG	[SEAL]
ENRIQUE OLAYA HERRERA	[SEAL]	CHARLES EVANS HUGHES	[SEAL]
C. ESCALLÓN	[SEAL]		

INTER-AMERICAN CONCILIATION

Convention signed at Washington January 5, 1929
Senate advice and consent to ratification February 20, 1929
Ratified by the President of the United States February 26, 1929
Ratification of the United States deposited at Santiago March 27, 1929
Proclaimed by the President of the United States April 4, 1929
Entered into force November 15, 1929
Supplemented by additional protocol of December 26, 1933 [1]

46 Stat. 2209; Treaty Series 780

GENERAL CONVENTION OF INTER-AMERICAN CONCILIATION

The Governments of Venezuela, Chile, Bolivia, Uruguay, Costa Rica, Perú, Honduras, Guatemala, Haiti, Ecuador, Colombia, Brazil, Panamá, Paraguay, Nicaragua, Mexico, El Salvador, the Dominican Republic, Cuba, and the United States of America, represented at the Conference on Conciliation and Arbitration, assembled at Washington, pursuant to the Resolution adopted on February 18, 1928,[2] by the Sixth International Conference of American States held in the City of Habana:

Desiring to demonstrate that the condemnation of war as an instrument of national policy in their mutual relations, set forth in the above mentioned resolution, constitutes one of the fundamental bases of Inter-American relations;

Animated by the purpose of promoting, in every possible way, the development of international methods for the pacific settlement of differences between the States;

Being convinced that the "Treaty to Avoid or Prevent Conflicts between the American States", signed at Santiago de Chile, May 3, 1923,[3] constitutes a notable achievement in inter-American relations, which it is necessary to maintain by giving additional prestige and strength to the action of the commissions established by Articles III and IV of the aforementioned treaty;

---

[1] TS 887, *post*, vol. 3.
[2] *Report of the Delegates of the United States of America to the Sixth International Conference of American States held at Habana, Cuba, January 16 to February 20, 1928* (U.S. Government Printing Office, 1928), p. 310.
[3] TS 752, *ante*, p. 413.

Acknowledging the need of giving conventional form to these purposes have agreed to enter into the present Convention, for which purpose they have appointed Plenipotentiaries as follows:

Venezuela:
Carlos F. Grisanti
Francisco Arroyo Parejo

Chile:
Manuel Foster Recabarren
Antonio Planet

Bolivia:
Eduardo Diez de Medina

Uruguay:
José Pedro Varela

Costa Rica:
Manuel Castro Quesada
José Tible-Machado

Perú:
Hernán Velarde
Victor M. Maúrtua

Honduras:
Rómulo Durón
Marcos López Ponce

Guatemala:
Adrián Recinos
José Falla

Haiti:
Auguste Bonamy
Raoul Lizaire

Ecuador:
Gonzalo Zaldumbide

Colombia:
Enrique Olaya Herrera
Carlos Escallón

Brazil:
S. Gurgel do Amaral
A. G. de Araujo-Jorge

Panamá:
Ricardo J. Alfaro
Carlos L. López

Paraguay:
Eligio Ayala

Nicaragua:
Máximo H. Zepeda
Adrián Recinos
J. Lisandro Medina

México:
Fernando González Roa
Benito Flores

El Salvador:
Cayetano Ochoa
David Rosales, Jr.

Dominican Republic:
Angel Morales
Gustavo A. Díaz

Cuba:
Orestes Ferrara
Gustavo Gutiérrez

United States of America:
Frank B. Kellogg
Charles Evans Hughes

Who, after having deposited their full powers, which were found to be in good and due form by the Conference, have agreed as follows:

ARTICLE 1

The High Contracting Parties agree to submit to the procedure of conciliation established by this convention all controversies of any kind which have arisen or may arise between them for any reason and which it may not have been possible to settle through diplomatic channels.

ARTICLE 2

The Commission of Inquiry to be established pursuant to the provisions of Article IV of the Treaty signed in Santiago de Chile on May 3, 1923, shall likewise have the character of Commission of Conciliation.

ARTICLE 3

The Permanent Commissions which have been established by virtue of Article III of the Treaty of Santiago de Chile of May 3, 1923, shall be bound to exercise conciliatory functions, either on their own motion when it appears that there is a prospect of disturbance of peaceful relations, or at the request of a Party to the dispute, until the Commission referred to in the preceding article is organized.

ARTICLE 4

The conciliatory functions of the Commission described in Article 2 shall be exercised on the occasions hereinafter set forth:

(1) The Commission shall be at liberty to begin its work with an effort to conciliate the differences submitted to its examination with a view to arriving at a settlement between the Parties.

(2) Likewise the same Commission shall be at liberty to endeavor to conciliate the Parties at any time which in the opinion of the Commission may be considered to be favorable in the course of the investigation and within the period of time fixed therefor in Article V of the Treaty of Santiago de Chile of May 3, 1923.

(3) Finally, the Commission shall be bound to carry out its conciliatory function within the period of six months which is referred to in Article VII of the Treaty of Santiago de Chile of May 3, 1923.

The Parties to the controversy may, however, extend this time, if they so agree and notify the Commission in due time.

ARTICLE 5

The present convention does not preclude the High Contracting Parties, or one or more of them, from tendering their good offices or their mediation, jointly or severally, on their own motion or at the request of one or more of the Parties to the controversy; but the High Contracting Parties agree not to make use of those means of pacific settlement from the moment that the Commission described in Article 2 is organized until the final act referred to in Article 11 of this convention is signed.

ARTICLE 6

The function of the Commission, as an organ of conciliation, in all cases specified in Article 2 of this convention is to procure the conciliation of the differences subject to its examination by endeavoring to effect a settlement between the Parties.

When the Commission finds itself to be within the case foreseen in paragraph 3 of Article 4 of this convention, it shall undertake a conscientious and impartial examination of the questions which are the subject of the controversy, shall set forth in a report the results of its proceedings, and shall propose to the Parties the bases of a settlement for the equitable solution of the controversy.

ARTICLE 7

Except when the Parties agree otherwise, the decisions and recommendations of any Commission of Conciliation shall be made by a majority vote.

ARTICLE 8

The Commission described in Article 2 of this convention shall establish its rules of procedure. In the absence of agreement to the contrary, the procedure indicated in Article IV of the Treaty of Santiago de Chile of May 3, 1923, shall be followed.

Each party shall bear its own expenses and a proportionate share of the general expenses of the Commission.

ARTICLE 9

The report and the recommendations of the Commission, insofar as it may be acting as an organ of conciliation, shall not have the character of a decision nor an arbitral award, and shall not be binding on the Parties either as regards the exposition or interpretation of the facts or as regards questions of law.

ARTICLE 10

As soon as possible after the termination of its labors the Commission shall transmit to the Parties a certified copy of the report and of the bases of settlement which it may propose.

The Commission in transmitting the report and the recommendations to the Parties shall fix a period of time, which shall not exceed six months, within which the Parties shall pass upon the bases of settlement above referred to.

ARTICLE 11

Once the period of time fixed by the Commission for the Parties to make their decisions has expired, the Commission shall set forth in a final act the decision of the Parties, and if the conciliation has been effected, the terms of the settlement.

ARTICLE 12

The obligations set forth in the second sentence of the first paragraph of Article I of the Treaty of Santiago de Chile of May 3, 1923, shall extend to the time when the final act referred to in the preceding article is signed.

ARTICLE 13

Once the procedure of conciliation is under way it shall be interrupted only by a direct settlement between the Parties or by their agreement to accept absolutely the decision *ex aequo et bono* of an American Chief of State or to submit the controversy to arbitration or to an international court.

ARTICLE 14

Whenever for any reason the Treaty of Santiago de Chile of May 3, 1923, does not apply, the Commission referred to in Article 2 of this convention shall be organized to the end that it may exercise the conciliatory functions stipulated in this convention; the Commission shall be organized in the same manner as that prescribed in Article IV of said treaty.

In such cases, the Commission thus organized shall be governed in its operation by the provisions, relative to conciliation, of this convention.

ARTICLE 15

The provisions of the preceding article shall also apply with regard to the Permanent Commissions constituted by the aforementioned Treaty of Santiago de Chile, to the end that said Commissions may exercise the conciliatory functions prescribed in Article 3 of this convention.

ARTICLE 16

The present convention shall be ratified by the High Contracting Parties in conformity with their respective constitutional procedures, provided that they have previously ratified the Treaty of Santiago, Chile, of May 3, 1923.

The original convention and the instruments of ratification shall be deposited in the Ministry for Foreign Affairs of the Republic of Chile which shall give notice of the ratifications through diplomatic channels to the other signatory Governments and the convention shall enter into effect for the High Contracting Parties in the order that they deposit their ratifications.

This convention shall remain in force indefinitely, but it may be denounced by means of notice given one year in advance at the expiration of which it shall cease to be in force as regards the Party denouncing the same, but shall remain in force as regards the other signatories. Notice of the denunciation shall be addressed to the Ministry for Foreign Affairs of the Republic of Chile which will transmit it for appropriate action to the other signatory Governments.

Any American State not a signatory of this convention may adhere to the same by transmitting the official instrument setting forth such adherence, to the Ministry for Foreign Affairs of the Republic of Chile which will notify the other High Contracting Parties thereof in the manner heretofore mentioned.

In witness whereof the above mentioned Plenipotentiaries have signed this convention in English, Spanish, Portuguese and French and hereunto affix their respective seals.

Done at the city of Washington, on this fifth day of January, 1929.

[For Venezuela:]
CARLOS F. GRISANTI   [SEAL]
FR. ARROYO PAREJO

[For Chile:]
Chile makes exception in this convention of questions which may arise from situations or acts prior thereto [translation].
A. PLANET
MANUEL FOSTER   [SEAL]

[For Bolivia:]
E. DIEZ DE MEDINA   [SEAL]

[For Uruguay:]
JOSÉ PEDRO VARELA   [SEAL]

[For Costa Rica:]
MANUEL CASTRO QUESADA   [SEAL]
JOSÉ TIBLE-MACHADO   [SEAL]

[For Peru:]
HERNÁN VELARDE   [SEAL]
VICTOR M. MAÚRTUA   [SEAL]

[For Honduras:]
RÓMULO E. DURÓN   [SEAL]
M. LÓPEZ PONCE   [SEAL]

[For Guatemala:]
ADRIÁN RECINOS   [SEAL]
JOSÉ FALLA   [SEAL]

[For Haiti:]
A. BONAMY   [SEAL]
RAOUL LIZAIRE   [SEAL]

[For Ecuador:]
GONZALO ZALDUMBIDE   [SEAL]

[For Colombia:]
ENRIQUE OLAYA HERRERA   [SEAL]
C. ESCALLÓN   [SEAL]

[For Brazil:]
S. GURGEL DO AMARAL   [SEAL]
A. ARAUJO-JORGE   [SEAL]

[For Panama:]
R. J. ALFARO   [SEAL]
CARLOS L. LÓPEZ   [SEAL]

[For Paraguay:]
ELIGIO AYALA   [SEAL]

[For Nicaragua:]
MAXIMO H. ZEPEDA   [SEAL]
ADRIAN RECINOS
J. LISANDRO MEDINA

[For Mexico:]
FERNANDO GONZÁLEZ ROA   [SEAL]
BENITO FLORES   [SEAL]

[For El Salvador:]
CAYETANO OCHOA   [SEAL]
DAVID ROSALES, HIJO

[For the Dominican Republic:]
A. MORALES   [SEAL]
G. A. DÍAZ   [SEAL]

[For Cuba:]
ORESTES FERRARA   [SEAL]
GUSTAVO GUTIÉRREZ   [SEAL]

[For the United States:]
FRANK B. KELLOGG   [SEAL]
CHARLES EVANS HUGHES   [SEAL]

TRADEMARK AND COMMERCIAL PROTECTION; REGISTRATION OF TRADEMARKS (INTER-AMERICAN)

Convention, protocol, and regulations signed at Washington February 20, 1929
Senate advice and consent to ratification December 16, 1930
Ratified by the President of the United States February 11, 1931
Ratification of the United States deposited with the Pan American Union February 17, 1931
Convention entered into force April 2, 1930;[1] for the United States February 17, 1931
Protocol entered into force February 17, 1931
Proclaimed by the President of the United States February 27, 1931
Protocol terminated as to the United States September 29, 1945[2]

46 Stat. 2907; Treaty Series 833

GENERAL INTER-AMERICAN CONVENTION FOR TRADE MARK AND COMMERCIAL PROTECTION

The Governments of Peru, Bolivia, Paraguay, Ecuador, Uruguay, Dominican Republic, Chile, Panama, Venezuela, Costa Rica, Cuba, Guatemala, Haiti, Colombia, Brazil, Mexico, Nicaragua, Honduras and the United States of America, represented at the Pan American Trade Mark Conference at Washington in accordance with the terms of the resolution adopted on February 15, 1928,[3] at the Sixth International Conference of American States at Habana, and the resolution of May 2, 1928, adopted by the Governing Board of the Pan American Union at Washington,

Considering it necessary to revise the "Convention for the Protection of Commercial, Industrial, and Agricultural Trade Marks and Commercial Names," signed at Santiago, Chile, on April 28, 1923,[4] which replaced the

---

[1] Date of deposit of second instrument of ratification.
[2] Pursuant to notice of denunciation given by the United States Sept. 29, 1944, in accordance with terms of art. 19.
[3] *Report of the Delegates of the United States of America to the Sixth International Conference of Americn States held at Habana, Cuba, January 16 to February 20, 1928* (U.S. Government Printing Office, 1928), p. 265.
[4] TS 751, *ante*, p. 395.

"Convention for the Protection of Trade Marks" signed at Buenos Aires on on August 20, 1910,[5] with a view of introducing therein the reforms which the development of law and practice have made advisable;

Animated by the desire to reconcile the different juridical systems which prevail in the several American Republics; and

Convinced of the necessity of undertaking this work in its broadest scope, with due regard for the respective national legislations,

Have resolved to negotiate the present Convention for the protection of trade marks, trade names and for the repression of unfair competition and false indications of geographical origin, and for this purpose have appointed as their respective delegates,

Peru:
Alfredo Gonzalez-Prada

Bolivia:
Emeterio Cano de la Vega

Paraguay:
Juan V. Ramirez

Ecuador:
Gonzalo Zaldumbide

Uruguay:
J. Varela Acevedo

Dominican Republic:
Francisco de Moya

Chile:
Oscar Blanco Viel

Panama:
Ricardo J. Alfaro
Juan B. Chevalier

Venezuela:
Pedro R. Rincones

Costa Rica:
Manuel Castro Quesada
Fernando E. Piza

Cuba:
Gustavo Gutierrez
Alfredo Bufill

Guatemala:
Adrian Recinos
Ramiro Fernandez

Haiti:
Raoul Lizaire

Colombia:
Roberto Botero Escobar
Pablo Garcia de la Parra

Brazil:
Carlos Delgado de Carvalho

Mexico:
Francisco Suastegui

Nicaragua:
Vicente Vita

Honduras:
Carlos Izaguirre V.

United States of America:
Francis White
Thomas E. Robertson
Edward S. Rogers

Who, after having deposited their credentials, which were found to be in good and due form by the Conference, have agreed as follows:

---

[5] TS 595, *ante,* vol. 1, p. 772.

Chapter I

EQUALITY OF CITIZENS AND ALIENS AS TO TRADE MARK AND COMMERCIAL PROTECTION

Article 1

The Contracting States bind themselves to grant to the nationals of the other Contracting States and to domiciled foreigners who own a manufacturing or commercial establishment or an agricultural development in any of the States which have ratified or adhered to the present Convention the same rights and remedies which their laws extend to their own nationals or domiciled persons with respect to trade marks, trade names, and the repression of unfair competition and false indications of geographical origin or source.

Chapter II

TRADE MARK PROTECTION

Article 2

The person who desires to obtain protection for his marks in a country other than his own, in which this Convention is in force, can obtain protection either by applying directly to the proper office of the State in which he desires to obtain protection, or through the Inter-American Trade Mark Bureau referred to in the Protocol on the Inter-American Registration of Trade Marks,[6] if this Protocol has been accepted by his country and the country in which he seeks protection.

Article 3

Every mark duly registered or legally protected in one of the Contracting States shall be admitted to registration or deposit and legally protected in the other Contracting States, upon compliance with the formal provisions of the domestic law of such States.

Registration or deposit may be refused or cancelled of marks:

1. The distinguishing elements of which infringe rights already acquired by another person in the country where registration or deposit is claimed.

2. Which lack any distinctive character or consist exclusively of words, symbols, or signs which serve in trade to designate the class, kind, quality, quantity, use, value, place of origin of the products, time of production, or which are or have become at the time registration or deposit is sought, generic or usual terms in current language or in the commercial usage of the country where registration or deposit is sought, when the owner of the marks seeks to appropriate them as a distinguishing element of his mark.

In determining the distinctive character of a mark, all the circumstances existing should be taken into account, particularly the duration of the use

---

[6] For text, see p. 764.

of the mark and if in fact it has acquired in the country where deposit, registration or protection is sought, a significance distinctive of the applicant's goods.

3. Which offend public morals or which may be contrary to public order.

4. Which tend to expose persons, institutions, beliefs, national symbols or those of associations of public interest, to ridicule or contempt.

5. Which contain representations of racial types or scenes typical or characteristic of any of the Contracting States, other than that of the origin of the mark.

6. Which have as a principal distinguishing element, phrases, names or slogans which constitute the trade name or an essential or characteristic part thereof, belonging to some person engaged in any of the other Contracting States in the manufacture, trade or production of articles or merchandise of the same class as that to which the mark is applied.

Article 4

The Contracting States agree to refuse to register or to cancel the registration and to prohibit the use, without authorization by competent authority, of marks which include national and state flags and coats-of-arms, national or state seals, designs on public coins and postage stamps, official labels, certificates or guarantees, or any national or state official insignia or simulations of any of the foregoing.

Article 5

Labels, industrial designs, slogans, prints, catalogues or advertisements used to identify or to advertise goods, shall receive the same protection accorded to trade marks in countries where they are considered as such, upon complying with the requirements of the domestic trade mark law.

Article 6

The Contracting States agree to admit to registration or deposit and to protect collective marks and marks of associations, the existence of which is not contrary to the laws of the country of origin, even when such associations do not own a manufacturing, industrial, commercial or agricultural establishment.

Each country shall determine the particular conditions under which such marks may be protected.

States, Provinces or Municipalities, in their character of corporations, may own, use, register or deposit marks and shall in that sense enjoy the benefits of this Convention.

Article 7

Any owner of a mark protected in one of the Contracting States in accordance with its domestic law, who may know that some other person is using or applying to register or deposit an interfering mark in any other of the Contracting States, shall have the right to oppose such use, registration or deposit and shall have the right to employ all legal means, procedure or recourse provided in the country in which such interfering mark is being used or where its registration or deposit is being sought, and upon proof that the person who is using such mark or applying to register or deposit it, had knowledge of the existence and continuous use in any of the Contracting States of the mark on which opposition is based upon goods of the same class, the opposer may claim for himself the preferential right to use such mark in the country where the opposition is made or priority to register or deposit it in such country, upon compliance with the requirements established by the domestic legislation in such country and by this Convention.

Article 8

When the owner of a mark seeks the registration or deposit of the mark in a Contracting State other than that of origin of the mark and such registration or deposit is refused because of the previous registration or deposit of an interfering mark, he shall have the right to apply for and obtain the cancellation or annulment of the interfering mark upon proving, in accordance with the legal procedure of the country in which cancellation is sought, the stipulations in Paragraph (a) and those of either Paragraph (b) or (c) below:

(a) That he enjoyed legal protection for his mark in another of the Contracting States prior to the date of the application for the registration or deposit which he seeks to cancel; and

(b) that the claimant of the interfering mark, the cancellation of which is sought, had knowledge of the use, employment, registration or deposit in any of the Contracting States of the mark for the specific goods to which said interfering mark is applied, prior to adoption and use thereof or prior to the filing of the application or deposit of the mark which is sought to be cancelled; or

(c) that the owner of the mark who seeks cancellation based on a prior right to the ownership and use of such mark, has traded or trades with or in the country in which cancellation is sought, and that goods designated by his mark have circulated and circulate in said country from a date prior to the filing of the application for registration or deposit for the mark, the cancellation which is claimed, or prior to the adoption and use of the same.

Article 9

When the refusal of registration or deposit of a mark is based on a registration previously effected in accordance with this Convention, the owner of the refused mark shall have the right to request and obtain the cancellation of the mark previously registered or deposited, by proving, in accordance with the legal procedure of the country in which he is endeavoring to obtain registration or deposit of his mark, that the registrant of the mark which he desires to cancel, has abandoned it. The period within which a mark may be declared abandoned for lack of use shall be determined by the internal law of each country, and if there is no provision in the internal law, the period shall be two years and one day beginning from the date of registration or deposit if the mark has never been used, or one year and one day if the abandonment or lack of use took place after the mark has been used.

Article 10

The period of protection granted to marks registered, deposited or renewed under this Convention, shall be the period fixed by the laws of the State in which registration, deposit or renewal is made at the time when made.

Once the registration or deposit of a mark in any Contracting State has been effected, each such registration or deposit shall exist independently of every other and shall not be affected by changes that may occur in the registration or deposit of such mark in the other Contracting States, unless otherwise provided by domestic law.

Article 11

The transfer of the ownership of a registered or deposited mark in the country of its original registration shall be effective and shall be recognized in the other Contracting States, provided that reliable proof be furnished that such transfer has been executed and registered in accordance with the internal law of the State in which such transfer took place. Such transfer shall be recorded in accordance with the legislation of the country in which it is to be effective.

The use and exploitation of trade marks may be transferred separately for each country, and such transfer shall be recorded upon the production of reliable proof that such transfer has been executed in accordance with the internal law of the State in which such transfer took place. Such transfer shall be recorded in accordance with the legislation of the country in which it is to be effective.

Article 12

Any registration or deposit which has been effected in one of the Contracting States, or any pending application for registration or deposit, made by an agent, representative or customer of the owner of a mark in which a right has been acquired in another Contracting State through its registration, prior application or use, shall give to the original owner the right to demand its cancellation or refusal in accordance with the provisions of this Convention and to request and obtain the protection for himself, it being considered that such protection shall revert to the date of the application of the mark so denied or cancelled.

Article 13

The use of a trade mark by its owner in a form different in minor or non-substantial elements from the form in which the mark has been registered in any of the Contracting States, shall not entail forfeiture of the registration or impair the protection of the mark.

In case the form or distinctive elements of the mark are substantially changed, or the list of goods to which it is to be applied is modified or increased, the proprietor of the mark may be required to apply for a new registration, without prejudice to the protection of the original mark or in respect to the original list of goods.

The requirements of the laws of the Contracting States with respect to the legend which indicates the authority for the use of trade marks, shall be deemed fulfilled in respect to goods of foreign origin if such marks carry the words or indications legally used or required to be used in the country of origin of the goods.

CHAPTER III

PROTECTION OF COMMERCIAL NAMES

Article 14

Trade names or commercial names of persons entitled to the benefits of this Convention shall be protected in all the Contracting States. Such protection shall be enjoyed without necessity of deposit or registration, whether or not the name forms part of a trade mark.

Article 15

The names of an individual, surnames and trade names used by manufacturers, industrialists, merchants or agriculturists to denote their trade or calling, as well as the firm's name, the name or title legally adopted and used by associations, corporations, companies or manufacturing, industrial, commercial or agricultural entities, in accordance with the provisions of the respective national laws, shall be understood to be commercial names.

Article 16

The protection which this Convention affords to commercial names shall be:

(a) to prohibit the use or adoption of a commercial name identical with or deceptively similar to one legally adopted and previously used by another engaged in the same business in any of the Contracting States; and

(b) to prohibit the use, registration or filing of a trade mark the distinguishing elements of which consist of the whole or an essential part of a commercial name legally adopted and previously used by another owner domiciled or established in any of the Contracting States, engaged in the manufacture, sale or production of products or merchandise of the same kind as those for which the trade mark is intended.

Article 17

Any manufacturer, industrialist, merchant or agriculturist domiciled or established in any of the Contracting States, may, in accordance with the law and the legal procedure of such countries, oppose the adoption, use, registration or deposit of a trade mark for products or merchandise of the same class as those sold under his commercial name, when he believes that such trade mark or the inclusion in it of the trade or commercial name or a simulation thereof may lead to error or confusion in the mind of the consumer with respect to such commercial name legally adopted and previously in use.

Article 18

Any manufacturer, industrialist, merchant or agriculturist domiciled or established in any of the Contracting States may, in accordance with the law and procedure of the country where the proceeding is brought, apply for and obtain an injunction against the use of any commercial name or the cancellation of the registration or deposit of any trade mark, when such name or mark is intended for use in the manufacture, sale or production of articles or merchandise of the same class, by proving:

(a) that the commercial name or trade mark, the enjoining or cancellation of which is desired, is identical with or deceptively similar to his commercial name already legally adopted and previously used in any of the Contracting States, in the manufacture, sale or production of articles of the same class, and

(b) that prior to the adoption and use of the commercial name, or to the adoption and use or application for registration or deposit of the trade mark, the cancellation of which is sought, or the use of which is sought to be enjoined, he used and continues to use for the manufacture, sale or production of the same products or merchandise his commercial name adopted and previously used in any of the Contracting States or in the State in which cancellation or injunction is sought.

Article 19

The protection of commercial names shall be given in accordance with the internal legislation and by the terms of this Convention, and in all cases where the internal legislation permits, by the competent governmental or administrative authorities whenever they have knowledge or reliable proof of their legal existence and use, or otherwise upon the motion of any interested party.

Chapter IV

REPRESSION OF UNFAIR COMPETITION

Article 20

Every act or deed contrary to commercial good faith or to the normal and honorable development of industrial or business activities shall be considered as unfair competition and, therefore, unjust and prohibited.

Article 21

The following are declared to be acts of unfair competition and unless otherwise effectively dealt with under the domestic laws of the Contracting States shall be repressed under the provisions of this Convention:

(*a*) Acts calculated directly or indirectly to represent that the goods or business of a manufacturer, industrialist, merchant or agriculturist are the goods or business of another manufacturer, industrialist, merchant or agriculturist of any of the other Contracting States, whether such representation be made by the appropriation or simulation of trade marks, symbols, distinctive names, the imitation of labels, wrappers, containers, commercial names, or other means of identification;

(*b*) The use of false descriptions of goods, by words, symbols or other means tending to deceive the public in the country where the acts occur, with respect to the nature, quality, or utility of the goods;

(*c*) The use of false indications of geographical origin or source of goods, by words, symbols, or other means which tend in that respect to deceive the public in the country in which these acts occur;

(*d*) To sell, or offer for sale to the public an article, product or merchandise of such form or appearance that even though it does not bear directly or indirectly an indication of origin or source, gives or produces, either by pictures, ornaments, or language employed in the text, the impression of being a product, article or commodity originating, manufactured or produced in one of the other Contracting States;

(*e*) Any other act or deed contrary to good faith in industrial, commercial or agricultural matters which, because of its nature or purpose, may be considered analogous or similar to those above mentioned.

Article 22

The Contracting States which may not yet have enacted legislation repressing the acts of unfair competition mentioned in this chapter, shall apply to such acts the penalties contained in their legislation on trade marks or in any other statutes, and shall grant relief by way of injunction against the continuance of said acts at the request of any party injured; those causing such injury shall also be answerable in damages to the injured party.

CHAPTER V

REPRESSION OF FALSE INDICATIONS OF GEOGRAPHICAL ORIGIN OR SOURCE

Article 23

Every indication of geographical origin or source which does not actually correspond to the place in which the article, product or merchandise was fabricated, manufactured, produced or harvested, shall be considered fraudulent and illegal, and therefore prohibited.

Article 24

For the purposes of this Convention the place of geographical origin or source shall be considered as indicated when the geographical name of a definite locality, region, country or nation, either expressly and directly, or indirectly, appears on any trade mark, label, cover, packing or wrapping, of any article, product or merchandise, directly or indirectly thereon, provided that said geographical name serves as a basis for or is the dominant element of the sentences, words or expressions used.

Article 25

Geographical names indicating geographical origin or source are not susceptible of individual appropriation, and may be freely used to indicate the origin or source of the products or merchandise or his commercial domicile, by any manufacturer, industrialist, merchant or agriculturist established in the place indicated or dealing in the products there originating.

Article 26

The indication of the place of geographical origin or source, affixed to or stamped upon the product or merchandise, must correspond exactly to the place in which the product or merchandise has been fabricated, manufactured or harvested.

Article 27

Names, phrases or words, constituting in whole or in part geographical terms which through constant, general and reputable use in commerce have come to form the name or designation itself of the article, product or merchandise to which they are applied, are exempt from the provisions of the preceding articles; this exception, however, does not include regional indications of origin of industrial or agricultural products the quality and reputation of which to the consuming public depend on the place of production or origin.

Article 28

In the absence of any special remedies insuring the repression of false indications of geographical origin or source, remedies provided by the domestic sanitary laws, laws dealing with misbranding and the laws relating to trade marks or trade names, shall be applicable in the Contracting States.

Chapter VI

REMEDIES

Article 29

The manufacture, exportation, importation, distribution, or sale is forbidden of articles or products which directly or indirectly infringe any of the provisions of this Convention with respect to trade mark protection; protection and safeguard of commercial names; repression of unfair competition; and repression of false indications of geographical origin or source.

Article 30

Any act prohibited by this Convention will be repressed by the competent administrative or judicial authorities of the government of the state in which the offense was committed, by the legal methods and procedure existing in said country, either by official action, or at the request of interested parties, who may avail themselves of the rights and remedies afforded by the laws to secure indemnification for the damage and loss suffered; the articles, products or merchandise or their marks, which are the instrumentality of the acts of unfair competition, shall be liable to seizure or destruction, or the offending markings obliterated, as the case may be.

Article 31

Any manufacturer, industrialist, merchant or agriculturist, interested in the production, manufacture, or trade in the merchandise or articles affected by any prohibited act or deed, as well as his agents or representatives in any of the Contracting States and the consular officers of the state to which the locality or region falsely indicated as the place to which belongs the geographical origin or source, shall have sufficient legal authority to take and prosecute the necessary actions and proceedings before the administrative authorities and the courts of the Contracting States.

The same authority shall be enjoyed by official commissions or institutions and by syndicates or associations which represent the interests of industry, agriculture or commerce and which have been legally established for the defense of honest and fair trade methods.

Chapter VII

GENERAL PROVISIONS

Article 32

The administrative authorities and the courts shall have sole jurisdiction over administrative proceedings and administrative judgments, civil or criminal, arising in matters relating to the application of the national law.

Any differences which may arise with respect to the interpretation or application of the principles of this Convention shall be settled by the Courts of justice of each State, and only in case of the denial of justice shall they be submitted to arbitration.

Article 33

Each of the Contracting States, in which it does not yet exist, hereby agrees to establish a protective service, for the suppression of unfair competition and false indication of geographic origin or source, and to publish for opposition in the official publication of the government, or in some other periodical, the trade marks solicited and granted as well as the administrative decisions made in the matter.

Article 34

The present Convention shall be subject to periodic revision with the object of introducing therein such improvements as experience may indicate, taking advantage of any international conferences held by the American States, to which each country shall send a delegation in which it is recommended that there be included experts in the subject of trade marks, in order that effective results may be achieved.

The national administration of the country in which such conferences are held shall prepare, with the assistance of the Pan American Union and the Inter-American Trade Mark Bureau, the work of the respective conference.

The Director of the Inter-American Trade Mark Bureau may attend the sessions of such conferences and may take part in the discussions, but shall have no vote.

Article 35

The provisions of this Convention shall have the force of law in those States in which international treaties possess that character, as soon as they are ratified by their constitutional organs.

The Contracting States in which the fulfillment of international agreements is dependent upon the enactment of appropriate laws, on accepting in principle this Convention, agree to request of their legislative bodies the enactment of the necessary legislation in the shortest possible period of time and in accordance with their constitutional provisions.

Article 36

The Contracting States agree that, as soon as this Convention becomes effective, the Trade Mark Conventions of 1910 and 1923 shall automatically cease to have effect; but any rights which have been acquired, or which may be acquired thereunder, up to the time of the coming into effect of this Convention, shall continue to be valid until their due expiration.

Article 37

The present Convention shall be ratified by the Contracting States in conformity with their respective constitutional procedures.

The original Convention and the instruments of ratification shall be deposited with the Pan American Union which shall transmit certified copies of the former and shall communicate notice of such ratifications to the other signatory Governments, and the Convention shall enter into effect for the Contracting States in the order that they deposit their ratifications.

This Convention shall remain in force indefinitely, but it may be denounced by means of notice given one year in advance, at the expiration of which it shall cease to be in force as regards the Party denouncing the same, but shall remain in force as regards the other States. All denunciations shall be sent to the Pan American Union which will thereupon transmit notice thereof to the other Contracting States.

The American States which have not subscribed to this Convention may adhere thereto by sending the respective official instrument to the Pan American Union which, in turn, will notify the governments of the remaining Contracting States in the manner previously indicated.

In witness whereof the above named delegates have signed this Convention in English, Spanish, Portuguese and French, and thereto have affixed their respective seals.

Done in the City of Washington, on the twentieth day of February in the year one thousand nine hundred and twenty-nine.

[For Peru:]
A. GONZÁLEZ PRADA   [SEAL]

[For Bolivia:]
EMETERIO CANO DE LA VEGA   [SEAL]

[For Paraguay:]
JUAN VICENTE RAMÍREZ   [SEAL]

[For Ecuador:]
GONZALO ZALDUMBIDE   [SEAL]

[For Uruguay:]
VARELA   [SEAL]

[For the Dominican Republic:]
FRANCISCO DE MOYA   [SEAL]

[For Chile:]
OSCAR BLANCO VIEL   [SEAL]
I hereby subcribe to this Convention insofar as its provisions are not contrary to the national legislation of my country, with express reservations concerning the provisions of this Convention on which there is no legislation in Chile [translation].

[For Panama:]
R. J. ALFARO   [SEAL]
JUAN B. CHEVALIER   [SEAL]

[For Venezuela:]
P. R. RINCONES   [SEAL]

[For Costa Rica:]
MANUEL CASTRO QUESADA   [SEAL]
F. E. PIZA   [SEAL]

[For Cuba:]
GUSTAVO GUTIÉRREZ   [SEAL]
A. L. BUFILL   [SEAL]

[For Guatemala:]
ADRIÁN RECINOS   [SEAL]
RAMIRO FERNÁNDEZ   [SEAL]

[For Haiti:]
RAOUL LIZAIRE   [SEAL]

[For Colombia:]
PABLO GARCÍA DE LA PARRA   [SEAL]

[For Brazil:]
CARLOS DELGADO DE CAR-
VALHO   [SEAL]

[For Mexico:]
F. SUÁSTEGUI   [SEAL]

[For Nicaragua:]
VICENTE VITA   [SEAL]

[For Honduras:]
CARLOS IZAGUIRRE V.   [SEAL]

[For the United States:]
EDWARD S. ROGERS   [SEAL]
THOMAS E. ROBERTSON   [SEAL]
FRANCIS WHITE   [SEAL]

Protocol on the Inter-American Registration of Trade Marks

Whereas, The Governments of Peru, Bolivia, Paraguay, Ecuador, Uruguay, Dominican Republic, Chile, Panama, Venezuela, Costa Rica, Cuba, Guatemala, Haiti, Colombia, Brazil, Mexico, Nicaragua, Honduras and the United States of America have this day signed at Washington through their respective delegates a General Inter-American Convention for Trade Mark and Commercial Protection;

Whereas, the maintenance of an international American agency is considered desirable that manufacturers, industrialists, merchants and agriculturists may enjoy the trade mark and commercial protection which that Convention grants them, and that it may serve as a center of information, and cooperate in the fulfillment and improvement of the provisions of the Convention;

Whereas, the adoption of a general convention and a protocol may facilitate ratification among the Contracting States and adherence among the American Republics which have not taken part in the negotiations, since acceptance of the Convention does not imply acceptance of this instrument,

The above mentioned governments have agreed as follows:

Article 1

Natural or juridical persons domiciled in or those who possess a manufacturing or commercial establishment or an agricultural enterprise in any of the States that may have ratified or adhered to the present Protocol, may obtain the protection of their trade marks through the registration of such marks in the Inter-American Trade Mark Bureau.

Article 2

The owner of a mark registered or deposited in one of the Contracting States who desires to register it in any of the other Contracting States, shall file an application to this effect in the office of the country of original registration which office shall transmit it to the Inter-American Trade Mark Bureau, complying with the Regulations. A postal money order or draft on a bank of recognized standing, in the amount of $50.00, as a fee for the Inter-American Trade Mark Bureau, plus the amount of the fees required by the national law of each of the countries in which he desires to obtain protection for his mark, shall accompany such application.

Article 3

Immediately on receipt of the application for the registration of a mark, and on determining that it fulfills all the requirements, the Inter-American Trade Mark Bureau shall issue a certificate and shall transmit by registered mail copies of the same accompanied by a money order for the amount required by the respective Offices of the States in which protection is desired. In the case of adhesions or ratifications of additional states after the registration of a mark, the Inter-American Bureau shall, through the respective offices of their countries, inform the proprietors of marks registered through the Bureau, of said adhesions or ratifications, informing them of the right that they have to register their marks in the new adhering or ratifying States, in which registration shall be effected in the manner above mentioned.

Article 4

Each of the Contracting States, through its Trade Mark Office, shall immediately acknowledge to the Inter-American Bureau, the receipt of the application for registration of each mark, and shall proceed to carry through the proceedings with every possible dispatch, directing that the application be published at the expense of the applicant in the usual official papers, and at the proper time shall notify the Inter-American Bureau of the action that it may have taken in accordance with its internal legislation and the provisions of this Convention.

In case protection is granted to the mark, it shall issue a certificate of registration in which shall be indicated the legal period of registration; which certificate shall be issued with the same formalities as national certificates and shall have the same effect in so far as ownership of the mark is concerned. This certificate of registration shall be sent to the Inter-American Trade Mark Bureau, which shall transmit it to the proprietor of the mark through the proper office of the country of origin.

If, within seven months after the receipt by a Contracting State of an application for the protection of a trade mark transmitted by the Inter-American Trade Mark Bureau, the administration of such State does not communicate to the Bureau notice or refusal of protection based on the provisions of its domestic legislation or on the provisions of the General Inter-American Convention for Trade Mark and Commercial Protection such mark shall be considered as registered and the Inter-American Trade Mark Bureau shall so communicate to the applicant through the country of origin, and shall issue a special certificate which shall have the same force and legal value as a national certificate.

In case protection of a mark is refused in accordance with the provisions of the internal legislation of a State or of the General Inter-American Convention for Trade Mark and Commercial Protection, the applicant may have the same recourse which the respective laws grant to the citizens of the state refusing protection. The period within which the recourse and actions granted by national laws may be exercised shall begin four months after receipt by the Inter-American Trade Mark Bureau of the notice of refusal.

The Inter-American registration of a trade mark communicated to the Contracting States, which may already enjoy protection in such States shall replace any other registration of the same mark effected previously by any other means, without prejudice to the rights already acquired by national registration.

Article 5

In order to effect the transfer of ownership of a trade mark or the assignment of the use of the same, the same procedure as that set forth in the foregoing articles shall be followed, except that in this case there shall only be remitted to the Inter-American Bureau $10.00, to be retained by said Bureau, plus the fees fixed by the domestic legislation of each one of the countries in which it is desired to register the transfer or assignment of the mark, it being understood that the use of trade marks may be transferred separately in each country.

Article 6

If the applicant claims color as a distinctive element of his mark he shall be required to:

1. Send a statement attached to the application for registration declaring the color or the combination of colors which he claims; and

2. Attach to the application for registration copies or specimens of the mark as actually used, showing the colors claimed, which shall be attached to the notifications sent by the Inter-American Bureau. The number of copies to be sent shall be fixed by the Regulations.

Article 7

Trade marks shall be published in a bulletin edited by the Inter-American Bureau, wherein shall appear the matter contained in the application for registration and an electrotype of the mark supplied by the applicant.

Each administration of the Contracting States shall receive free of charge from the Inter-American Bureau as many copies of the above mentioned publication as it may ask for.

The publication of a mark in the bulletin of the Inter-American Bureau shall have the same effect as publication in the official journals or bulletins of the Contracting States.

Article 8

The Inter-American Bureau, on receipt of payment of a fee to be fixed by the Regulations, shall furnish to any person who may so request, copies of the entries made in the register with reference to any particular mark.

Article 9

The Inter-American Trade Mark Bureau shall keep a record of renewals which have been effected in compliance with the requirements of the domestic laws of the Contracting States, and after payment of a fee of $10.00 to the Inter-American Trade Mark Bureau and the customary fees required by the States where said renewal is effected.

Six months prior to the expiration of the period of protection, the Inter-American Bureau shall communicate this information to the administration of the country of origin and to the owner of the mark.

Article 10

The owner of a trade mark may at any time relinquish protection in one or several of the Contracting States, by means of a notice sent to the administration of the country of origin of the mark, to be communicated to the Inter-American Bureau, which in turn shall notify the countries concerned.

Article 11

An applicant for registration or deposit, transfer or renewal of a trade mark through the Inter-American Bureau, may appoint by a proper power of attorney at any time, an agent or attorney to represent him in any procedure, administrative, judicial or otherwise, arising in connection with such trade marks or application in any Contracting State.

Such agents or attorneys shall be entitled to notice of all the proceedings and to receive and present all documents that may be required by the Trade Mark Bureau of each country under the provisions of this Protocol.

Article 12

The administration in the country of origin shall notify the Inter-American Bureau of all annulments, cancellations, renunciations, transfers and all other changes in the ownership or use of the mark.

The Inter-American Bureau shall record these changes, notify the administrations of the Contracting States and publish them immediately in its bulletin.

The same procedure shall be followed when the proprietor of the mark requests a reduction in the list of products to which the trade mark is applied.

The subsequent addition of a new product to the list may not be obtained except by a new registration of the mark according to the provisions of Article 2 of this Protocol. The same procedure shall be followed in the case of the substitution of one product for another.

Article 13

The Contracting States bind themselves to send through their respective national trade mark offices, as soon as they are published, two copies of the official bulletins or publications in which judicial or administrative decisions or resolutions, laws, decrees, regulations, circulars, or any other provisions emanating from the executive, legislative or judicial authorities may appear and which refer to the protection of trade marks, the protection of commercial names, the repression of unfair competition and of false indications of origin, whether of an administrative, civil or penal nature.

Article 14

In order to comply with this Protocol, and to facilitate the inter-American registration of trade marks, the Contracting States establish as their international agency the Bureau located in Habana, Republic of Cuba, referred to as the "Inter-American Trade Mark Bureau," and confer upon its official correspondence the postal frank.

Article 15

The Inter-American Trade Mark Bureau shall perform the duties specified in this Protocol and in the Regulations appended hereto, and shall be supported in part by the fees received for handling trade marks and in part by the quotas assigned to the Contracting States. These quotas shall be paid directly and in advance to the Bureau in yearly installments and shall be determined in the following manner:

The population of each Contracting State ratifying this Protocol shall be determined by its latest official census, the number of inhabitants to be divided into units of 100,000 each, fractions above 50,000 to be considered as a full unit, and those under to be disregarded. The annual budget shall be divided by the total number of units, thereby determining the quota per unit. The contribution of each State to the Inter-American Bureau shall be determined by multiplying the quota per unit by the number of units allotted to each State.

Upon receipt of new ratifications and adhesions to this Protocol, the same procedure shall be followed with respect to such States, the quota of each to be determined by adding these additional units and thus determining the quota per unit.

It is expressly agreed that this annual contribution will continue to be paid only so long as the other revenues of the Bureau are not sufficient to cover the expenses of its maintenance. So long as this situation exists, the latest census of population will be used each year and, on the basis of official data furnished by each Contracting State, the changes in population shall be made and the quotas determined anew before fixing the contributions to be paid by those States. Once the Bureau becomes self-supporting through its own receipts, the balance remaining from the quotas shall be returned to the States in proportion to the amounts received from them.

At the end of each year the Inter-American Bureau shall prepare a statement of fees and contributions received and after making provision for its budgetary requirements for the following year and setting aside a reserve fund, shall return the balance to the Contracting States in proportion to the quotas paid by them.

The budget of the Bureau and the reserve fund to be maintained shall be submitted by the Director of the Bureau and approved by the Chief Executive of the State in which the Bureau is established. The Director of the Bureau shall also submit an annual report to all ratifying States, for their information.

Article 16

In case the Bureau should cease to exist, it shall be liquidated under the supervision of the Government of Cuba, the balance of the funds remaining to be distributed among the Contracting States in the same proportion as they contributed to its support. The buildings and other tangible property of the Bureau shall become the property of the Government of Cuba in recognition of the services of that Republic in giving effect to this Protocol; the Government of Cuba agreeing to dedicate such property to purposes essentially inter-American in character.

The Contracting States agree to accept as final any steps that may be taken for the liquidation of the Bureau.

Article 17

The provisions of this Protocol shall have the force of law in those States in which international treaties possess that character, as soon as they are ratified by their constitutional organs.

The Contracting States in which the fulfillment of international agreements is dependent upon the enactment of appropriate laws, on accepting in principle this Protocol, agree to request of their legislative bodies the enactment of the necessary legislation in the shortest possible period of time and in accordance with their constitutional provisions.

Article 18

The Contracting States agree that, as soon as this Protocol becomes effective, the Trade Mark Conventions of 1910 and 1923 shall automatically cease to have effect in so far as they relate to the organization of the Inter-American Bureau; but any rights which have been or which may be acquired in accordance with the provisions of said Conventions, up to the time of the coming into effect of this Protocol, shall continue to be valid until their due expiration.

Article 19

The present Protocol shall be ratified by the Contracting States, in accordance with their respective constitutional procedure, after they shall have ratified the "General Inter-American Convention for Trade Mark and Commercial Protection."

The original Protocol and the instruments of ratification shall be deposited with the Pan American Union, which shall transmit certified copies of the former and shall communicate notice of such ratifications to the Governments of the other signatory States and the Protocol shall become effective for the Contracting States in the order in which they deposit their ratifications.

This Protocol shall remain in force indefinitely, but it may be denounced by means of notice given one year in advance, at the expiration of which it shall cease to be in force as regards the State denouncing the same, but shall remain in force as regards the other States. All denunciations shall be sent to the Pan American Union which will thereupon transmit notice thereof to the other States.

The American States which have not signed this Protocol may adhere thereto by sending the respective official instrument to the Pan American Union which, in turn, will thereupon notify the Governments of the remaining Contracting States in the manner previously indicated.

ANNEX

REGULATIONS

Article 1

The application to obtain protection under the Protocol of which the present Annex is a part shall be made by the owner of the mark or his legal representative to the administration of the State in which the mark has been originally registered or deposited in accordance with the provisions in force in that State, accompanied by a money order or draft payable to the Director of the Inter-American Trade Mark Bureau in the sum required by this Protocol. The application and money order shall be accompanied by an electrotype (10 x 10 centimeters) of the mark reproducing it as registered in the State of original registration.

Article 2

The National Bureau of such State having ascertained that the registration of the mark is legal and valid shall send to the Inter-American Trade Mark Bureau, as soon as possible:

A. The money order;
B. The electrotype of the mark;
C. A certificate in duplicate containing the following details:

1. The name and address of the owner of the mark;
2. The date of the application for registration in the State of original registration;
3. The date of registration of the mark in such State;
4. The order number of the registration in such State;
5. The date of expiration of the protection of the mark in such State;
6. A facsimile of the mark as used;
7. A statement of the goods on which the mark is used;

8. The date of the application to the National Bureau of the State of the original registration to obtain protection under the Convention and this Protocol.

D. When the applicant wishes to claim color as a distinctive element of his mark, thirty copies of the mark printed on paper, showing the color, and a brief description of the same.

Article 3

Within ten days after receipt from such administration of the matter required by Article 2, the Inter-American Trade Mark Bureau shall enter all information in its books and inform the National Bureau of such State of the receipt of the application and of the number and date of the inter-American registration.

Article 4

Within thirty days after such receipt, detailed copies of the inter-American registration shall be sent to the National Bureaus of those States which have ratified the Protocol.

Article 5

The Inter-American Trade Mark Bureau shall publish a periodic bulletin wherein shall appear the data included in the certificate provided for by Section C of Article 2 of these Regulations and also all other information which may be appropriate concerning registration of such marks in the various States.

The Inter-American Trade Mark Bureau may also publish in its bulletin or separately, books, documents, information, studies, and articles concerning the protection of industrial property.

Article 6

The acceptance, opposition, or refusal of a mark by the National Bureau of any one of the Contracting States shall be transmitted within ten days following the date of its receipt by the Inter-American Trade Mark Bureau to the administration of the State of origin of the application with a view to its communication to whom it may concern.

Article 7

Changes in ownership of a mark communicated by the Bureau of the country of origin to the Inter-American Trade Mark Bureau and accompanied by the required fees shall be examined, entered in the register, and corresponding notice sent to the Bureaus of the other Contracting States in which the transfer is to take place, accompanied by the proper fees, all within the time herein fixed with respect to application.

Article 8

The Director of the Inter-American Trade Mark Bureau shall be appointed by the Executive Power of the State in which the Bureau is located, from among lawyers of experience in the subject matter and of recognized moral standing. The Director, at his discretion, may appoint or remove the officials or employees of his Bureau, giving notice thereof to the Government of Cuba; adopt and promulgate such other rules, regulations and circulars as he may deem convenient for the proper functioning of the Bureau and which are not inconsistent with this Protocol.

Article 9

The Inter-American Trade Mark Bureau may carry on any investigation on the subject of trade marks which the Government of any of the Contracting States may request, and encourage the investigation of all problems, difficulties or obstacles which may hinder the operation of the General Inter-American Convention for Trade Mark and Commercial Protection, or of this Protocol.

Article 10

The Inter-American Trade Mark Bureau shall cooperate with the Governments of the Contracting States in the preparation of material for international conferences on this subject; submit to those States such suggestions as it may consider useful, and such opinions as may be requested as to the modifications which should be introduced in the inter-American pacts or in the laws concerning these subjects and in general facilitate the execution of the purposes of this Protocol.

Article 11

The Inter-American Trade Mark Bureau shall inform the signatory Governments at least once a year as to the work which the Bureau has done or is doing.

Article 12

The Inter-American Trade Mark Bureau shall maintain as far as possible relations with similar offices and scientific and industrial institutions and organizations for the exchange of publications, information, and data relative to the progress of the law on the subject of the protection of trade marks, defense and protection of commercial names and suppression of unfair competition and false indications of origin.

Article 13

These Regulations may be modified at any time at the request of any of the Contracting States or the Director of the Bureau, provided that the modification does not violate the General Convention or the Protocol of which the Regulations form a part, and that the modification is approved by the Governing Board of the Pan American Union, after having been circulated among the Contracting States for a period of six months before submission for the approval of the Pan American Union.

In witness whereof the above named delegates have signed this Protocol in English, Spanish, Portuguese and French, and thereto have affixed their respective seals.

Done in the City of Washington on the twentieth day of February in the year one thousand nine hundred and twenty-nine.

[For Peru:]
A. GONZÁLEZ PRADA   [SEAL]

[For Bolivia:]
EMETERIO CANO DE LA VEGA   [SEAL]

[For Paraguay:]
JUAN VICENTE RAMÍREZ   [SEAL]

[For Ecuador:]
GONZALO ZALDUMBIDE   [SEAL]

[For the Dominican Republic:]
FRANCISCO DE MOYA   [SEAL]

[For Panama:]
R. J. ALFARO   [SEAL]
JUAN B. CHEVALIER   [SEAL]

[For Venezuela:]
P. R. RINCONES   [SEAL]

[For Costa Rica:]
MANUEL CASTRO QUESADA   [SEAL]
F. E. PIZA   [SEAL]

[For Cuba:]
GUSTAVO GUTIÉRREZ   [SEAL]
A. L. BUFILL   [SEAL]

[For Haiti:]
RAOUL LIZAIRE   [SEAL]

[For Colombia:]
PABLO GARCÍA DE LA PARRA   [SEAL]

[For Brazil:]
CARLOS DELGADO DE CAR-   [SEAL]
VALHO

[For Mexico:]
F. SUÁSTEGUI   [SEAL]

[For Nicaragua:]
VICENTE VITA   [SEAL]

[For Honduras:]
CARLOS IZAGUIRRE V.   [SEAL]

[For the United States:]
FRANCIS WHITE   [SEAL]
THOMAS E. ROBERTSON   [SEAL]
EDWARD S. ROGERS   [SEAL]

GLOSSARY [7]

Resolved, That the following glossary be followed in the interpretation of terms contained in the General Inter-American Convention on Trade Mark and Commercial Protection, and in the Protocol on the Inter-American Registration of Trade Marks, approved by the Conference:

Nationals: persons; partnerships; firms; corporations; associations; syndicates, unions and all other natural and juridical persons entitled to the benefit of nationality of the contracting countries.

Persons: include not only natural persons but all juridical persons such as partnerships, firms, corporations, associations, syndicates and unions.

Marks or *Trade marks:* include manufacturing, industrial, commercial, agricultural marks, collective marks, and the marks of syndicates, unions and associations.

Collective marks: mean marks lawfully used by two or more owners.

---

[7] Eighth resolution adopted by conference on Feb. 19, 1929.

Commercial names: include trade names, names of individuals, surnames, partnership firm and corporate names, and the names of syndicates, associations, unions and other entities recognized by the laws of the Contracting States, and which are used in manufacturing, industry, commerce and agriculture to identify or distinguish the user's trade, calling or purpose.

Ownership: as applied to trade marks means the right acquired by registration in countries where the right to a trade mark is so acquired, and the right acquired by adoption and use in countries where the right to a trade mark is so acquired.

Owner or *Proprietor:* means the natural or juridical person entitled to ownership as above defined.

Deposit: means the filing of a trade mark in any Contracting Country other than the country of original registration.

Interfering mark or *Infringing mark:* means a mark which so resembles one previously registered, deposited, or used by another person as to be likely, when applied to goods, to cause confusion or mistake or to deceive purchasers as to their commercial source or origin.

Country of origin: means the country of original registration of the mark and not the country of the citizenship or domicile of the registrant or depositor.

Injunction: means a judicial order or process, operating upon the person, requiring the party to whom it is directed to do or (usually) refrain from doing some designated thing.

$: Wherever this sign is used it shall be understood to mean money which is legal currency in Cuba and which has a value equivalent to that of the dollar.

TELECOMMUNICATION: HIGH FREQUENCY RADIO STATIONS ON NORTH AMERICAN CONTINENT

Arrangement between Canada, Cuba, Newfoundland, and the United States drawn up at a shortwave radio conference at Ottawa January 21–25, 1929; related notes of February 1, 26, and 28 and March 6 and 15, 1929
Entered into force March 1, 1929
Terminated as to Cuba October 5, 1933 [1]

Treaty Series 777–A

AN ARRANGEMENT BETWEEN UNITED STATES, CANADA, CUBA, AND OTHER NORTH AMERICAN NATIONS RELATIVE TO THE ASSIGNMENT OF FREQUENCIES ON THE NORTH AMERICAN CONTINENT

(1) The sovereign right of all nations to the use of every radio channel is recognized.

Nevertheless, until technical development progresses to the stage where radio interference can be eliminated, it is agreed that special administrative arrangements are essential in order to promote standardization and to minimize radio interference.

(2) The Governments agree that each country shall be free to assign any frequency to any radio station within its jurisdiction upon the sole condition that no interference with any service of another country will result therefrom.

(3) It is agreed that each Government shall use Appendix I attached hereto, as a general guide in allocating channels to the various services specified therein.

(4) Channels are divided into two classes (1) common channels which are primarily assigned to particular services in all countries, and (2) general communication channels which are assigned for use in specific areas.

(5) With regard to the general communication channels, it is considered that at the present stage of the art, the use of radio channels below 3500 K/C will not normally cause interference at distances greater than 1000 miles and such channels may, therefore, be used with freedom from interference by stations separated by such distance. It is further recognized that stations operating on frequencies above 3500 K/C may become sources of interference at distances in excess of 100 miles, particularly at night.

(6) The Governments agree to take advantage of the physical facts just explained, and by suitable geographical distribution of these two classes of

---

[1] Pursuant to notice of denunciation given by Cuba Oct. 5, 1932, in accordance with terms of para. 17. By an exchange of notes between the United States and Canada dated Feb. 6 and Apr. 1, 1933, it was agreed that the arrangement would continue in force for the United States, Canada, and Newfoundland.

channels throughout North America and the West Indies, to make available for general communication services, the total number of channels set forth in Appendix 2 attached hereto.

(7) Each Government shall have the right to assign to stations under its jurisdiction, in the manner it deems best, such general communication channels as are allocated to that Government under this agreement, as set forth in Appendix No. 2. The Governments agree not to assign to stations within their respective jurisdiction any of the general communication channels allocated to other Governments, unless it can be accomplished without causing interference.

(8) The marine calling frequency of 5525 K/C shall be used until superseded by an international assignment.

(9) In addition to the frequencies assigned specially for experiments (1604, 2398 and 4596 K/C) the Governments agree that experimentation by particularly qualified experimenters, may be authorized on any other channel provided no interference is caused with established services, as provided in Regulation No. 11 of the International Radio Convention of Washington 1927.[2]

(10) The Governments agree to adopt a radio frequency standard based on the unit of time, and to compare at least once every six months, the actual radio frequency measuring standards.

(11) The Governments agree to require all stations, other than mobile and amateur stations, under their jurisdiction, to tune their transmitters with an accuracy of 0.025 percent, or better, of their national frequency standard.

(12) The Governments agree to require all stations likely to cause international interference, other than mobile and amateur stations, to maintain their frequency with an accuracy of 0.05 percent, or better, at all times.

(13) For the purpose of this agreement a channel shall be regarded as a band of frequencies the width of which varies with its position in the range of frequencies under consideration, but which progresses numerically from the lower to the higher frequencies, as shown in the following table:—

Frequency (K/C)	Channel Width (K/C)
1500–2198	4
2200–3313	6
3316–4400	8
4405–5490	10
5495–6000	15

(14) The Governments agree to adopt for the present in their national plan of allocation a separation of 0.2 percent between radio frequency channels; and to permit stations under their respective jurisdiction to occupy the assigned frequency and the adjacent frequencies to the limit permitted by the frequency maintenance tolerances and necessitated by the type of emission the station may be authorized to use. For commercial telephony a band width of six kilocycles shall be permitted. For the present, a 100 kilocycle band width shall be considered standard for television.

---

[2] Convention signed at Washington Nov. 25, 1927 (TS 767), *ante*, p. 683.

(15) The Governments agree to require stations under their jurisdiction to use transmitters which are as free as practicable from all emissions (such as those due to harmonics, decrement, spacing waves, frequency modulation, key clicks, type of keying, mush, etc.) not essential to the type of communication carried on, and which would be detrimental to communication being carried on by stations in other countries.

(16) Appendices Numbers 1 and 2, together with the chart showing graphically the distribution of the frequencies, which are attached hereto, shall constitute a part of this agreement. [Chart not printed here; see separate print of TS 777–A.]

(17) This agreement shall go into effect on March 1st, 1929, and shall remain in force until January 1st, 1932, and thereafter for an indeterminate period and until one year from the day on which a denunciation thereof shall have been made by any one of the contracting parties.

APPENDIX No. 1

Allocation of Channels to Services
(Arranged in order of kilocycles)

Channels [1]	Service	No. of channels
1504 to 1600	Maritime Mobile Services [2]	25
1600 to 1648	Air Mobile Services [3]	12
1648 to 1712	Mobile Services	16
1712 to 2000	Amateurs	72
2000 to 2200	Experimental Visual Broadcasting	50
2200 to 2296	General Communication Services [4]	16 (32)
2296 to 2398	Maritime and Air Mobile Services [3]	17
2398 to 2470	Mobile Services	12
2470 to 2506	Air Mobile Services	6
2506 to 2602	Maritime Mobile Services	16
2602 to 2650	Air Mobile Services	8
2650 to 2746	Maritime and Air Mobile Services	16
2746 to 2950	Experimental Visual Broadcasting	34
2950 to 3004	Maritime and Air Mobile Services	9
3004 to 3058	General Communication Services [4]	9 (18)
3058 to 3106	Air Mobile Services	8
3106 to 3148	Maritime Mobile Services	7
3148 to 3412	General Communication Services [4]	40 (80)
3412 to 3500	Maritime and Air Mobile Services	11
3500 to 3996	Amateurs	62
3996 to 4100	General Communication Services [4]	13
4100 to 4196	Maritime and Air Mobile Services	12
4196 to 4745	General Communication Services [4]	60
4745 to 4795	Maritime and Air Mobile Services [3]	5
4795 to 5495	General Communication Services [4]	70
5495 to 5690	Maritime and Air Mobile Services	13
5690 to 6000	General Communication Services [4]	20
		[5] 639 (704)

NOTES:
[1] The last channel in each group is assigned to the service indicated immediately abreast the group except as specially noted to the contrary.
[2] The channel 1600 Kc/s is assigned to Mobile Services.
[3] The channels 1604, 2398 and 4795 Kc/s are assigned to Experimental Services.
[4] For details regarding General Communication Services, see Appendix 2.
[5] Taking into account Articles 5 and 6 of the Agreement, this total is increased by 65.

Appendix No. 2

Distribution of General Communication Channels

UNITED STATES

3154	3348	4260	4585	4995	5235
3160	3356	4268	4595	5005	5245
3166	3364	4276	4605	5015	5255
3172	3372	4284	4615	5025	5265
3178	3380	4292	4625	5035	5275
3184	3388	4300	4635	5045	5285
3190	3396	4308	4645	5055	5295
3232	3404	4316	4655	5065	5305
3238	3412	4364	4665	5075	5315
3244	4012	4372	4675	5085	5325
3250	4020	4380	4685	5095	5335
3256	4028	4388	4695	5105	5345
3262	4036	4396	4705	5115	5355
3268	4044	4405	4715	5125	5365
3274	4052	4415	4725	5135	5855
3280	4060	4425	4735	5145	5870
3286	4068	4435	4745	5155	5885
3292	4076	4445	4925	5165	5900
3298	4084	4525	4935	5175	5915
3304	4092	4535	4945	5185	5930
3310	4100	4545	4955	5195	5945
3316	4204	4555	4965	5205	5960
3324	4236	4565	4975	5215	5975
3332	4244	4575	4985	5225	5990
3340	4252				

146

CANADA AND NEWFOUNDLAND

2206	3022	3214	3316	4465	5415
2212	3028	3220	3324	4475	5425
2218	3034	3226	3332	4485	5435
2224	3040	3232	x3340	4495	5445
2230	3046	3238	x3348	4815	5455
2236	3052	3244	x3356	4825	5465
2242	3058	3250	x3364	4835	5475
2248	x3154	3256	x3372	4845	5485
2254	x3160	3262	x3380	4855	5495
2260	x3166	3268	x3388	4865	5705
2266	x3172	3274	x3396	4875	5720
2272	x3178	3280	x3404	4885	5735
2278	x3184	3286	x3412	4895	5750
2284	x3190	3292	4324	4905	5765
2290	3196	3298	4332	5385	5780
2296	3202	3304	4340	5395	5795
3010	3208	3310	4348	5405	5810
3016					

103

x Used by Newfoundland.

CUBA

2206	2230	3010	3028	3208	4505
2212	2236	3016	3196	4004	5375
2218	2242	3022	3202	4212	5825
2224	2248				

20

OTHER NATIONS

2254	2278	3034	3058	4220	4515
2260	2284	3040	3214	4228	4805
2266	2290	3046	3220	4356	4915
2272	2296	3052	3226	4455	5840

24

Services	No. of channels
Maritime Mobile Services Exclusively...................................	47
Air Mobile Services Exclusively...	33
Amateurs...	134
Experimental Visual Broadcasting......................................	84
Air and Maritime Mobile Services......................................	81
Experimental...	3
Mobile Services..	29
General Communication Services.......................................	228
Total...	639
Grand total...	704

NOTE: The grand total is obtained by adding on 65 channels made available through the application of articles 5 and 6 of the Agreement.

RELATED NOTES

The Chairman of the Canadian Delegation to the Chairman of the American Delegation

[Telegram]

Ottawa, 1st. February, 1929.

Judge E. O. SYKES,
Federal Radio Commission, Washington, D.C.

"In accordance with the undertaking given by the Canadian delegation at the closing session of the Conference on Friday last, I now have the honour to advise that the proposals for the distribution of channels as set forth in detail in appendices Numbers One and Two and graphic chart attached to draft of document headed "Suggestions for an agreement between United States, Canada, Cuba, Mexico and other North American nations relative to the assignment of frequencies on the North American continent", as per copy transmitted to you by Commander Craven, are approved and accepted by the Canadian delegation. stop. The United States delegation, having already by majority vote approved of these proposals as generally outlined at the final session of the Conference, it is our understanding that there but remains for approval the Articles of Agreement as suggested in draft document in question. stop. As soon as we are advised that this is confirmed by the United States delegation and that these Articles of Agreement are approved and accepted by them, the whole may be considered as approved and accepted by the Canadian authorities."

A. JOHNSTON.

The American Minister to the Canadian Secretary of State
for External Affairs

Ottawa, Canada,

No. 314.   *February 26, 1929.*

SIR:

With regard to the recent short wave length radio conference at Ottawa, I am instructed by my Government to inform you that it approves the recommendations of the delegates at the conference and will announce the agreement effective March 1, 1929.

I avail myself of the occasion to renew to you, Sir, the assurances of my highest consideration.

WILLIAM PHILLIPS

The Right Honorable
WILLIAM LYON MACKENZIE KING, C.M.G., LL.B., LL.D.,
Secretary of State for External Affairs, Ottawa

The Canadian Secretary of State for External Affairs
to the American Minister

DEPARTMENT OF EXTERNAL AFFAIRS
CANADA

No. 16   *Ottawa, 28th February, 1929.*

SIR,

I have the honour to acknowledge your Note of February 26th, 1929, regarding the recent Short Wave Radio Conference at Ottawa.

It is gratifying to the Government of the Dominion of Canada to learn that the Government of the United States approve the recommendations of the delegates at the Conference. The Canadian Government have pleasure in stating that they also accept these recommendations.

It is noted that your Government will announce the agreement effective March 1st, 1929. I have the honour to request that you be good enough to inform them that we will accordingly announce the agreement as effective on the same day.

Accept, Sir, the renewed assurances of my highest consideration,

O. D. SKELTON
For the Secretary of State for External Affairs

The Honourable WILLIAM PHILLIPS,
Minister of the United States of America,
United States Legation, Ottawa

The Canadian Secretary of State for External Affairs
to the American Minister

DEPARTMENT OF EXTERNAL AFFAIRS
CANADA

No. 21. Ottawa, 6th March, 1929.

SIR,

With reference to my Note of February 28th, 1929, regarding the recent Short Wave Radio Conference at Ottawa, I have the honour to state that according to a telegraphic communication received from the Newfoundland delegate, the Government of Newfoundland accept the recommendations of the delegates at the Conference and consider the agreement to be effective as from March 1st, 1929.

I may add that we have not yet received any information from the Governments of Cuba and Mexico as to their views on the same subject.

Accept, Sir, the renewed assurances of my highest consideration.

O. D. SKELTON
For the Secretary of State for External Affairs

The Honourable WILLIAM PHILLIPS,
Minister of the United States of America,
United States Legation, Ottawa

The Canadian Secretary of State for External Affairs
to the American Chargé d'Affaires ad interim

DEPARTMENT OF EXTERNAL AFFAIRS
CANADA

No. 23 Ottawa, 15th March, 1929.

SIR,

With reference to my Note of March 6th, 1929, regarding the recent Short Wave Radio Conference at Ottawa, I have the honour to state that, according to a Note received from the Consul General of Cuba, the agreement on this subject is accepted by the Government of the Republic of Cuba.

Accept, Sir, the renewed assurances of my highest consideration,

O. D. SKELTON
For the Secretary of State for External Affairs

FERDINAND L. MAYER, Esquire,
Chargé d'Affaires ad interim,
United States Legation, Ottawa

SAFETY OF LIFE AT SEA

Convention signed at London May 31, 1929, with annexes of regulations
Senate advice and consent to ratification of convention, with understandings, June 19, 1936 [1]
Convention ratified by the President of the United States, with understandings, July 7, 1936 [1]
Ratification of the United States deposited at London August 7, 1936
Entered into force January 1, 1933; for the United States November 7, 1936
Proclaimed by the President of the United States September 30, 1936
Regulation XIX of annex I amended January 17, 1933 [2]
Replaced by convention of June 10, 1948, [3] *as amended, as between contracting parties to the later convention*
Terminated as to the United States November 19, 1953 [4]

50 Stat. 1121; Treaty Series 910

INTERNATIONAL CONVENTION FOR THE SAFETY OF LIFE AT SEA

PREAMBLE

The Governments of Germany, the Commonwealth of Australia, Belgium, Canada, Denmark, Spain, the Irish Free State, the United States of America,

---

[1] The U.S. understandings read as follows:

"(1) That nothing in this convention shall be so construed as to authorize any person to hold any seaman, whether a citizen of the United States of America or an alien, on board any merchant vessel, domestic or foreign, against his will in a safe harbor within the jurisdiction of the United States of America, when such seaman has been officially admitted thereto as a member of the crew of such vessel or to compel such seaman to proceed to sea on such vessel against his will;

"(2) That nothing in this convention shall be so construed as to nullify or modify Section 4 of the Seaman's Act approved March 4, 1915, 38 Stat. 1164, as interpreted by the Supreme Court of the United States in Strathearn vs. Dillon, 252 U.S. 348, and

"(3) That nothing in this convention shall be so construed as to prevent the officers of the United States of America who exercise the control over vessels provided for in Article 54 from making such inspection of any vessel within the jurisdiction of the United States as may be necessary to determine that the condition of the vessel's seaworthiness corresponds substantially with the particulars set forth in its certificate, that the vessel is sufficiently and efficiently manned, and that it may proceed to sea without danger to either passengers or crew, or to prevent such officers from withholding clearance to any vessel which they find may not proceed to sea with safety, until such time as any such vessel shall be put in condition so that it can proceed to sea without danger to the passengers or crew."

[2] See footnote 10, p. 831.

[3] 3 UST 3450; TIAS 2495.

[4] Pursuant to notice of denunciation given by the United States on Nov. 19, 1952.

Finland, France, the United Kingdom of Great Britain and Northern Ireland, India, Italy, Japan, Norway, the Netherlands, Sweden, the Union of Socialist Soviet Republics; being desirous of promoting safety of life at sea by establishing in common agreement uniform principles and rules directed thereto;

Considering that this end may best be achieved by the conclusion of a Convention;

Have appointed their Plenipotentiaries, namely:

The Government of Germany:

Dr. Friedrich Sthamer, Ambassador Extraordinary and Plenipotentiary of the German Reich in London.

Mr. Gustav Koenigs, Ministerialdirigent in the Reichsverkehrsministerium, Geheimer Regierungsrat, Berlin.

Mr. Arthur Werner, Oberregierungsrat in the Reichsverkehrsministerium, Geheimer Justizrat, Berlin.

Mr. Walter Laas, Professor, Director of the "Germanischer Lloyd" Classification Society, Berlin.

Dr. Otto Riess, Director ret. of the Reichsschiffsvermessungsamt, Geheimer Regierungsrat, Neubrandenburg.

Mr. Hermann Giess, Ministerialrat in the Reichspostministerium, Berlin.

Vice-Admiral Hugo Dominik, President of the "Deutsche Seewarte, Hamburg."

The Government of the Commonwealth of Australia:

Captain Henry James Feakes, Royal Australian Navy, Commonwealth Naval Representative in London.

Lieut.-Commander Thomas Free, Royal Naval Reserve, (Retired).

Captain J. K. Davis, Commonwealth Director of Navigation.

The Government of Belgium:

Baron de Gerlache de Gomery, Director-General of the Marine Department

Mr. Gustave de Winne, Ingénieur en Chef, Director of the Marine Department.

Mr. Georges Goor, Adviser to the Marine Department.

The Government of Canada:

Mr. Alexander Johnston, Deputy Minister of Marine.

Mr. Lucien Pacaud, Secretary in the Office of the Canadian High Commissioner in London.

The Government of Denmark:

Mr. Emil Krogh, Assistant-Secretary in the Marine Department, Ministry of Industry, Commerce and Shipping.

Mr. V. Topsöe-Jensen, Judge of the Supreme Court of Appeal.

Captain V. Lorck, Chief Examiner of Masters and Mates.

Mr. J. A. Körbing, Technical Managing Director of the United Steam Ship Company, Copenhagen.

Mr. Aage H. Larsen, Engineer in Chief of the Ministry of Industry, Commerce and Shipping.

Mr. Arnold Poulsen, Engineer Commissioner to the Ministry of Industry, Commerce and Shipping.

The Government of Spain:

Rear-Admiral Don Francisco Javier de Salas y Gonzalez, Head of the Naval Commission in Europe.

The Government of the Irish Free State:

Mr. J. W. Dulanty, Commissioner for Trade for the Irish Free State in Great Britain.

Mr. E. C. Foster, Chief Surveyor in the Marine Branch, Department of Industry and Commerce.

The Government of the United States of America:

The Honourable Wallace H. White, Junior, Member of Congress, Chairman of the Committee on Merchant Marine and Fisheries.

Mr. Arthur J. Tyrer, Commissioner of Navigation, Department of Commerce.

Mr. Charles M. Barnes, Chief of the Treaty Division, Department of State.

Rear-Admiral George H. Rock, Construction Corps, United States Navy, Assistant Chief of the Bureau of Construction and Repair, Navy Department.

Captain Clarence S. Kempff, United States Navy, Hydrographer, Navy Department.

Mr. Dickerson N. Hoover, Supervising Inspector-General of the Steamboat Inspection Service, Department of Commerce.

Mr. William D. Terrell, Chief of the Radio Division, Department of Commerce.

Rear-Admiral John G. Tawresey, Construction Corps, United States Navy (Retired), United States Shipping Board.

Mr. Herbert B. Walker, President of the American Steamship Owners' Association.

Mr. Henry G. Smith, President of the National Council of American Shipbuilders.

Captain Charles A. McAllister, President of the American Bureau of Shipping.

The Government of Finland:

Baron Gustaf Wrede, President of the Shipping Board.

Captain Väinö Bergman, Inspector of Shipping.

Consul Karl Kurten, Manager of the Finnish Shipowners' Association.

The Government of France:

Mr. Rio, Senator and former Minister.

Captain Haarbleicher, Naval Construction Corps, Director of Mercantile Shipping Service, Department of Public Works.

Commander Marie, Naval Construction Corps, Direction of Mercantile Shipping.

Captain Thouroude, Naval Attaché to the French Embassy in London.

The Government of the United Kingdom of Great Britain and Northern Ireland:

Sir Herbert W. Richmond, Vice-Admiral, Royal Navy.

Sir Westcott Abell, Professor of Naval Architecture, Armstrong College, Newcastle-on-Tyne.

Mr. A. L. Ayre, Vice-President of the Shipbuilding Employers' Federation.

Captain F. W. Bate, Professional Officer, Mercantile Marine Department, Board of Trade.

Mr. C. H. Boyd, Mercantile Marine Department, Board of Trade.

Sir William C. Currie, President of the Chamber of Shipping of the United Kingdom.

Mr. A. J. Daniel, Principal Ship Surveyor, Board of Trade.

Sir Norman Hill, Chairman of the Merchant Shipping Advisory Committee.

Sir Charles Hipwood, Principal Assistant Secretary, Mercantile Marine Department, Board of Trade.

Captain A. R. H. Morrell, Trinity House.

The Government of India:

Sir Geoffrey L. Corbett, Commerce Department, Government of India.

Captain E. V. Whish, Port Officer, Bombay.

Mr. M. A. Master, General Manager of the Scindia Steam Navigation Company.

The Government of Italy:

Lieut.-General of Port G. Ingianni, General Director of the Mercantile Marine.

Vice-Admiral A. Alessio, Chief of the Technical Inspectorate of the Mercantile Marine.

Count D. Rogeri di Villanova, Counsellor to the Italian Embassy in London.

Dr. T. C. Giannini, Counsellor of Emigration.

Major-General of Port F. Marena, Vice-Inspector of Harbour Master Offices.

Engineer-General E. Ferretti, Chief of the Technical Office of the Italian Naval and Aeronautical Register.

Mr. G. Gneme, Chief of the Telegraph Service of the General Direction of Postal and Telegraphic Services.

Commander L. Biancheri, Royal Italian Navy.

The Government of Japan:

Mr. Yukio Yamamoto, Inspector-General of the Mercantile Marine Bureau, Expert in the Department of Communications.

Captain Shichihei Ota, Imperial Japanese Navy.

Mr. Itaro Ishii, First Class Secretary of Embassy.

The Government of Norway:

Mr. B. Vogt, Norwegian Minister in London.

Mr. L. T. Hansen, Director of the Department of Shipping, Ministry of Commerce and Navigation.

Mr. J. Schönheyder, Surveyor-in-Chief of the Ship and Engineer Division, Ministry of Commerce and Navigation.

Mr. Arth H. Mathiesen, Vice-President of the Norwegian Shipowners' Association.

Captain N. Marstrander, Chairman of the Board of the Norwegian Masters' Association.

Mr. A. Birkeland, Manager of the Norwegian Seamen's and Firemen's Union.

The Government of the Netherlands:

Vice-Admiral C. Fock, Inspector-General of Navigation.

Mr. C. H. de Goeje, Ex-Inspector-General of Navigation, Netherland East Indies.

Mr. A. van Driel, Adviser on Naval Architecture, Shipping Inspection Service.

Mr. J. A. Bland van den Berg, Inspector of Coastal and Ships' Radio-telegraphy.

Mr. Phs. van Ommeren, Junior, Chairman of Phs. van Ommeren, Ltd.

Mr. H. G. J. Uilkens, Ex-Commodore of the Netherland Steamship Company.

The Government of Sweden:

Baron Palmstierna, Swedish Minister in London.

Mr. Nils Gustaf Nilsson, Assistant Under-Secretary in the Board of Trade.

Captain Erik Axel Fredrik Eggert, Maritime Expert to the Social Board.

The Government of the Union of Socialist Soviet Republics:

Mr. Jan Lvovitch Arens, Counsellor to the U.S.S.R. Embassy in Paris.

Captain Karl Pavlovitch Eggi, Commander of the Icebreaker "Lenin," Soviet Merchant Fleet (Sovtorgflot).

Who, having communicated their full powers, found in good and due form, have agreed as follows:—

CHAPTER I. PRELIMINARY

ARTICLE 1

THE Contracting Governments undertake to give effect to the provisions of the present Convention for the purpose of promoting safety of life at sea, to promulgate all regulations and to take all other steps which may be necessary to give the present Convention full and complete effect.

The provisions of the present Convention are completed by regulations contained in Annex I, which have the same force and take effect at the same time as the present Convention. Every reference to the present Convention implies at the same time a reference to the Regulations annexed thereto.

ARTICLE 2

Applications and Definitions

1. The provisions of the present Convention shall apply to ships belonging to countries the Governments of which are Contracting Governments, and to ships belonging to territories to which the present Convention is applied under Article 62, as follows:—

Chapter II.—(*Construction*) to passenger ships (mechanically propelled) on international voyages.

Chapter III.—(*Life-saving Appliances*) to passenger ships (mechanically propelled) on international voyages.

Chapter IV.—(*Radiotelegraphy*) to all ships engaged on international voyages except cargo ships of less than 1,600 tons gross tonnage.

Chapter V.—(*Safety of Navigation*) to all ships on all voyages.

Chapter VI.—(*Certificates*) to all the ships to which Chapters II, III and IV apply.

2. The classes of ships to which each Chapter applies are more precisely defined, and the extent of the application is shown, in each Chapter.

3. In the present Convention, unless expressly provided otherwise—

(*a*) a ship is regarded as belonging to a country if it is registered at a port of that country;

(*b*) the expression "Administration" means the Government of the country in which the ship is registered;

(*c*) an international voyage is a voyage from a country to which the present Convention applies to a port outside such country, or conversely; and for this purpose every colony, overseas territory, protectorate or territory under suzerainty or mandate is regarded as a separate country;

(*d*) a ship is a passenger ship if it carries more than 12 passengers;

(*e*) the expression "Regulations" means the Regulations contained in Annex I.

4. The present Convention, unless expressly provided otherwise, does not apply to ships of war.

ARTICLE 3

Cases of "Force Majeure"

No ship, which is not subject to the provisions of the present Convention at the time of its departure on any voyage, shall become subject to the provisions of the present Convention on account of any deviation from its intended voyage due to stress of weather or any other cause of *force majeure*.

Persons who are on board a ship by reason of *force majeure* or in consequence of the obligation laid upon the master to carry shipwrecked or other persons shall not be taken into account for the purpose of ascertaining the application to a ship of any provisions of the present Convention.

CHAPTER II. CONSTRUCTION

ARTICLE 4

Application

1. This Chapter, except where it is otherwise expressly provided, applies to new passenger ships engaged on international voyages.

2. A new passenger ship is a ship the keel of which is laid on or after the 1st July, 1931, or a ship which is converted to passenger service on or after that date, all other passenger ships being described as existing passenger ships.

3. Each Administration may, if it considers that the route and the conditions of the voyage are such as to render the application of the requirements of this Chapter unreasonable or unnecessary, exempt from the requirements of this Chapter individual ships or classes of ships belonging to its country which, in the course of their voyage, do not proceed more than 20 miles from the nearest land.

4. In the case of a passenger ship which, in the course of its voyage, does not proceed more than 200 miles from the nearest land, the Administration of the country to which the ship belongs may allow relaxations from such of the requirements of Regulations IX, X, XV and XIX as may be proved to the satisfaction of the Administration to be neither reasonable nor practicable.

5. In the case of existing passenger ships engaged on international voyages which do not already comply with the provisions of this Chapter relating to new passenger ships, the arrangements on each ship shall be considered by the Administration of the country to which the ship belongs, with a view to improvements being made to provide increased safety where practicable and reasonable.

6. In the case of passenger ships engaged on international voyages which are employed in the carriage of large numbers of unberthed passengers in special trades, such, for example, as the pilgrim trade, an Administration, if satisfied that it is impracticable to enforce compliance with the requirements of this Chapter, may exempt such ships, when they belong to its country, from those requirements on the following conditions:—

(a.) That the fullest provision which the circumstances of the trade will permit shall be made in the matter of construction.

(b.) That steps shall be taken to formulate general rules which shall be applicable to the particular circumstances of these trades. Such rules shall be formulated in concert with such other Contracting Governments, if any, as may be directly interested in the carriage of such passengers.

7. This Chapter does not apply to ships which are not mechanically propelled or to wooden ships of primitive build, such as dhows, junks, &c.

Article 5

Watertight Subdivision of Ships

1. Ships shall be as efficiently subdivided as is possible having regard to the nature of the service for which they are intended. The requirements respecting subdivision are given in the following Articles and in the Regulations.

2. The degree of subdivision provided for by these requirements varies with the length of the ship and with the service, in such manner that the highest degree of subdivision corresponds with the ships of greatest length primarily engaged in the carriage of passengers.

3. Regulations I to V indicate the method to be followed in order to determine the degree of subdivision applicable to a ship.

4. In order that the required degree of subdivision shall be maintained, a loadline corresponding to the approved subdivision draft shall be assigned and marked on the ship's sides. A ship having spaces which are specially adapted for the accommodation of passengers and the carriage of cargo alternatively may, if the owners desire, have one or more additional loadlines assigned and marked to correspond with the subdivision drafts which the Administration may approve for the alternative service conditions. The freeboard corresponding to each approved subdivision loadline, and the conditions of service for which it is approved, shall be clearly indicated on the Safety Certificate. Subdivision loadlines shall be marked and recorded in the manner provided in Regulation VII.

Article 6

Peak and Machinery Space Bulkheads, Shaft Tunnels, &c.

All ships shall be fitted with watertight forward and after peak bulkheads and with watertight bulkheads at the extremities of the machinery space, and, in screw ships, with watertight shaft tunnels or equivalent subdivision in accordance with the provisions of Regulation VI.

ARTICLE 7

Construction, Testing, &c.

Regulations VIII to XIII and XV to XXI prescribe rules for—

(*a*) the construction and testing of subdivision bulkheads, inner bottoms, watertight decks, trunks, ventilators, fire-resisting bulkheads, &c.;

(*b*) the conditions governing openings in bulkheads, in the ship's sides and in the weather deck, and the character and use of means which shall be provided for closing these openings;

(*c*) the tests and the periodical inspections and operation of the means of closing openings in bulkheads and in the ship's side;

(*d*) exits from watertight compartments;

(*e*) pumping arrangements; and

(*f*) power for going astern and auxiliary steering apparatus.

ARTICLE 8

Stability Test

Every new passenger ship shall be inclined upon its completion and the elements of its stability determined. The operating personnel shall be supplied with such information on this subject as is necessary to permit efficient handling of the ship.

ARTICLE 9

Entries in the Official Log Book

A record of the closing and opening of watertight doors, &c., and of all inspections and drills, shall be entered in the official log book as required by Regulation XIV.

ARTICLE 10

Initial and Subsequent Surveys of Ships

The general principles which shall govern the survey of ships, whether new or existing, as regards hull, main and auxiliary boilers and machinery, and equipments, are stated in Regulation XXII. Each Contracting Government undertakes—

(1) to draw up detailed regulations in accordance with these general principles, or to bring its existing regulations into agreement with these principles;

(2) to secure that these regulations shall be enforced.

The detailed regulations referred to in the preceding paragraph shall be in all respects such as to secure that, from the point of view of safety of life, the ship is fit for the service for which it is intended.

CHAPTER III. LIFE-SAVING APPLIANCES, &c.

ARTICLE 11

Interpretation

For the purposes of this Chapter—

(*a*) the expression "new ship" means a ship the keel of which is laid on or after the 1st July, 1931, all other ships being described as existing ships;

(*b*) the expression "short international voyage" means an international voyage in the course of which a ship is not more than 200 miles from the nearest land;

(*c*) the expression "buoyant apparatus" means buoyant deck seats, or buoyant deck chairs, or any other buoyant apparatus excepting boats, life-buoys and life-jackets.

ARTICLE 12

Application

1. This Chapter, except where it is otherwise expressly provided, applies to new passenger ships which are mechanically propelled and engaged on international voyages.

2. Special provisions are laid down in Articles 13, 14, 19 and 25 with regard to new passenger ships engaged on short international voyages.

3. Each Administration, if it considers that the route and the conditions of the voyage are such as to render the application of the full requirements of this Chapter unreasonable or unnecessary, may to that extent exempt from the requirements of this Chapter individual ships or classes of ships belonging to its country which, in the course of their voyage, do not go more than 20 miles from the nearest land.

4. In the case of existing passenger ships which are mechanically propelled and engaged on international voyages and which do not already comply with the provisions of this Chapter relating to new passenger ships, the arrangements on each ship shall be considered by the Administration of the country to which the ship belongs, with a view to securing, so far as this is practicable and reasonable, compliance with the general principles set out in Article 13 not later than the 1st July, 1931, and substantial compliance with the other requirements of this Chapter.

5. In the case of passenger ships which are mechanically propelled and engaged on international voyages and which are employed in the carriage of large numbers of unberthed passengers in special trades, such, for example, as the pilgrim trade, an Administration, if satisfied that it is impracticable to

enforce compliance with the requirements of this Chapter, may exempt such ships, when they belong to its country, from those requirements on the following conditions:

(*a.*) That the fullest provision which the circumstances of the trade will permit shall be made in the matter of lifeboats and other lifesaving appliances and fire protection.

(*b.*) That all such boats and apparatus shall be readily available within the meaning of Article 13.

(*c.*) That a life-jacket shall be provided for every person on board.

(*d.*) That steps shall be taken to formulate general rules which shall be applicable to the particular circumstances of these trades. Such rules shall be formulated in concert with such other Contracting Governments, if any, as may be directly interested in the carriage of such passengers.

Article 13

Lifeboats and Buoyant Apparatus

The general principles governing the provision of lifeboats and buoyant apparatus in a ship to which this Chapter applies are that they shall be readily available in case of emergency and shall be adequate.

1. To be readily available, the lifeboats and buoyant apparatus must comply with the following conditions:—

(*a.*) They must be capable of being got into the water safely and rapidly even under unfavourable conditions of list and trim.

(*b.*) It must be possible to embark the passengers in the boats rapidly and in good order.

(*c.*) The arrangement of each boat and article of buoyant apparatus must be such that it will not interfere with the operation of other boats and buoyant apparatus.

2. To be adequate, the provision of lifeboats and buoyant apparatus must satisfy the following conditions:—

(*a.*) Subject to the provisions of sub-paragraph (*b*) of this paragraph there must be accommodation in boats for all persons on board, and there must, in addition, be buoyant apparatus for 25 per cent. of the persons on board.

(*b.*) In the case of passenger ships engaged on short international voyages, the boats must be provided in accordance with the requirements set out in the table in Regulation XXXIX, and there must be, in addition, buoyant apparatus so that the boats and buoyant apparatus together provide accommodation for all on board as set out in Regulation XXXVIII. There must, in addition, be buoyant apparatus for 10 per cent. of the persons on board.

(*c.*) No more boats shall be required on any passenger ship than are sufficient to accommodate all persons on board.

ARTICLE 14

Ready Availability and Adequacy

The arrangements for securing the principles of ready availability and adequacy mentioned in Article 13 shall be in accordance with the provisions of Regulations XXXVII, XXXVIII and XXXIX.

ARTICLE 15

Standard types of Boats. Life Rafts. Buoyant Apparatus

All the lifeboats, life rafts and buoyant apparatus shall comply with the conditions fixed by the Convention and Regulations XXIV to XXIX .

ARTICLE 16

Construction of Boats

All boats must be properly constructed, and shall be of such form and proportion that they shall have ample stability in a seaway, and sufficient freeboard when loaded with their full complement of persons and equipment.

Each boat must be of sufficient strength to enable it to be safely lowered into the water when loaded with its full complement of persons and equipment.

ARTICLE 17

Embarkation of the Passengers in the Boats

Suitable arrangements shall be made for embarking the passengers in the boats at an embarkation deck. There shall also be a suitable ladder provided at each set of davits.

ARTICLE 18

Capacity of Boats and Life Rafts

The number of persons that a boat of one of the standard types or an approved life raft or buoyant apparatus can accommodate and the conditions of approval of life rafts and buoyant apparatus shall be ascertained in accordance with the provisions of Regulations XXX to XXXV inclusive.

ARTICLE 19

Equipment of Boats and Life Rafts

Regulation XXXVI prescribes the equipment for boats and life rafts.

ARTICLE 20

Life-jackets and Life-buoys

1. Every ship to which this Chapter applies shall carry for every person on board a life-jacket of a type approved by the Administration, and in addition, unless these life-jackets can be adapted for use by children, a sufficient number of life-jackets suitable for children.

2. Every such ship shall also carry life-buoys of a type approved as aforesaid to the number required by Regulation XL.

3. A life-jacket or life-buoy shall not be approved by an Administration unless it satisfies the requirements of Regulation XL applicable to life-jackets and life-buoys respectively.

4. In this Article the expression "life-jacket" includes any appliance capable of being fitted on the body, having the same buoyancy as a life-jacket.

ARTICLE 21

Means of Ingress and Egress. Emergency Lighting

1. Proper arrangements shall be made for ingress to and egress from the different compartments, decks, &c.

2. Provision shall be made for an electric or other system of lighting, sufficient for all requirements of safety, in the different parts of the ship, and particularly upon the decks on which the lifeboats are stowed. On ships in which the boat deck is more than 9·15 metres (30 feet) above the waterline at the lightest seagoing draught, provision shall be made for the illumination from the ship of the lifeboats when alongside and in process of or immediately after being launched. There must be a self-contained source capable of supplying, when necessary, this safety lighting system, and placed in the upper parts of the ship above the bulkhead deck.

3. The exit from every main compartment occupied by passengers or crew shall be continuously lighted by an emergency lamp. The power for these emergency lamps shall be so arranged that they will be supplied from the independent installation referred to in the preceding paragraph in the event of failure of the main generating plant.

ARTICLE 22

Certificated Lifeboatmen. Manning of the Boats

1. In every ship to which this Chapter applies there must be, for any boat or life raft carried in order to comply with this Chapter, such number of certificated lifeboatmen as is required by Regulation XLI for that boat.

2. The allocation of the certificated lifeboatmen to each boat and life raft remains within the discretion of the master, according to the circumstances.

3. By "certificated lifeboatman" is meant any member of the crew who holds a certificate of efficiency issued under the authority of the Administration in accordance with the conditions laid down in the afore-mentioned Regulation.

4. The manning of the boats shall be as prescribed in Regulation XLII.

ARTICLE 23

Line-Throwing Appliances

Every ship to which this Chapter applies shall carry a line-throwing appliance of a type approved by the Administration.

ARTICLE 24

Dangerous Goods. Fire Protection

1. The carriage, either as cargo or ballast, of goods which by reason of their nature, quantity, or mode of stowage, are, either singly or collectively, liable to endanger the lives of the passengers or the safety of the ship, is forbidden.

This provision does not apply to the ship's distress signals, nor to the carriage of naval or military stores for the public service of the State under conditions authorised by the Administration.

Each Administration shall, from time to time by official notice, determine what goods are to be considered dangerous goods, and shall indicate the precautions which must be taken in the packing and stowage thereof.

2. The arrangements to be made for the detection and extinction of fire shall be as prescribed in Regulation XLIII.

ARTICLE 25

Muster Roll and Drills

Special duties for the event of an emergency shall be allotted to each member of the crew.

The muster list shall show all these special duties and shall indicate, in particular, the station to which each man must go, and the duties that he has to perform.

Before the vessel sails, the muster list shall be drawn up and exhibited, and the proper authority shall be satisfied that the muster list has been prepared for the ship. It shall be posted in several parts of the ship, and in particular in the crew's quarters.

Regulations XLIV and XLV prescribe the conditions under which musters of the crew and drills shall take place.

CHAPTER IV. RADIOTELEGRAPHY

ARTICLE 26

Application and Definition

1. This Chapter applies to all ships engaged on international voyages except cargo ships of less than 1,600 tons gross tonnage.

2. For the purposes of this Chapter a cargo ship means any ship not being a passenger ship.

ARTICLE 27

Fitting of Radio Installation

1. All ships to which this Chapter applies shall, unless exempted under Article 28, be fitted with a radiotelegraph installation complying with the provisions of Article 31, as follows:—

(a.) All passenger ships, irrespective of size.
(b.) All cargo ships of 1,600 tons gross tonnage and upwards.

2. Each Administration may delay the application of the provisions of paragraph 1 (b) to cargo ships belonging to its country of less than 2,000 tons gross tonnage for a period not exceeding five years from the date of the coming into force of the present Convention.

ARTICLE 28

Exemptions from the Requirements of Article 27

1. Each Administration may, if it considers that the route and the conditions of the voyage are such as to render a radiotelegraph installation unreasonable or unnecessary, exempt ships belonging to its country from the requirements of Article 27 as follows:—

I. *Passenger Ships.*
(a.) Individual passenger ships or classes of passenger ships which, in the course of their voyage, do not go more than—

(i) 20 miles from the nearest land;
or
(ii) 200 miles in the open sea between two consecutive ports.

(b.) Passenger ships which make voyages entirely within the restricted areas specified in the Annex to this Article.

II. *Cargo Ships.*
Individual cargo ships or classes of cargo ships which, in the course of their voyage, do not go more than 150 miles from the nearest land.

2. Each Administration may, in addition, exempt ships belonging to its country of the following classes:—

I.—Barges in tow and existing sailing ships.

An existing sailing ship is one the keel of which is laid before the 1st July, 1931.

II.—Ships of primitive build, such as dhows, junks, &c., if it is practically impossible to fit them with a radiotelegraph installation.

III.—Ships which are not normally engaged on international voyages, but which in exceptional circumstances are required to undertake a single voyage of that kind.

ANNEX TO ARTICLE 28

1. The Baltic Sea and approaches thereto East of a line drawn from Utsire (Norway) in the North to Texel (Netherlands) in the South, outside the territorial jurisdiction of the Union of Socialist Soviet Republics.

2. The portions of the Gulf of Tartary and the Sea of Okhotsk covered in voyages between ports in Hokkaido and ports in Japanese Sakhalin.

3. The Chosen (Tyosen) Strait between a line in the North drawn from Kawajiri Misaki (Cape Natsungu) to Fusan, and a line in the South drawn from Nagasaki to Giffard Island (off the South-West point of Quelpart Island) and thence to Tin To (Amherst Island).

4. The Yellow Sea North of Parallel 37° North.

5. The Formosa Strait between a line in the North drawn from Fuki Kaku (Syauki Point) to Foochow and a line in the South drawn from South Cape (the South point of Formosa) to Hong Kong.

6. The area within the following limits:—

Parallel 10° N. from long. 94° E. to the coast of Asia, coast of Asia to Saigon (Cape Tiwan), straight lines between Cape Tiwan, lat. 4°30' N. long. 110° E., south point of Palawan Island, Palmas (Miangas) Island, lat. 0° long. 140° E., lat. 0° long. 148° E., lat. 10° S. long. 148° E., Cape York, north coast of Australia from Cape York to Port Darwin (Cape Charles), straight lines between Cape Charles, Ashmore Reef (East Island), lat. 10° S. long. 109° E., Christmas Island, lat. 2° N. long. 94° E., lat. 10° N. long. 94° E., outside the territorial jurisdiction of Australia and of the United States of America.

7. The Caribbean Sea, outside the territorial jurisdiction of the United States of America, in relation to voyages made by sailing ships only.

8. The area of the South Pacific Ocean bounded by the Equator, Meridian 130° W., Parallel 34° S., and the coast of Australia, outside the territorial jurisdiction of Australia.

9. The Tong King Gulf and portions of the China Sea lying to the West of a line drawn from Hong Kong to Lat. 17° N. Long. 110° E., thence due South to Latitude 10° N., and thence West to Saigon.

10. The portions of the Indian Ocean covered in voyages between ports in Madagascar, Reunion and the Mauritius Islands.

11. The portions of the North Atlantic Ocean and Mediterranean Sea covered in voyages between Casablanca (Morocco) and Oran (Algeria) and intermediate ports.

ARTICLE 29
Watches

1. Passenger Ships.

Each passenger ship which, in accordance with Article 27, is required to be fitted with a radiotelegraph installation, shall, for safety purposes, carry a qualified operator, and, if not fitted with an auto-alarm, shall, whilst at sea, keep watches by means of a qualified operator or a certified watcher, as under:—

(*a.*) All passenger ships under 3,000 tons gross tonnage, as determined by the Administration concerned;

(*b.*) All passenger ships of 3,000 tons gross tonnage and over, continuous watch.

Each Administration is authorised to exempt passenger ships belonging to its country from 3,000 tons to 5,500 tons gross tonnage, both included, from the requirement of a continuous watch for a period not exceeding one year from the date of the coming into force of the present Convention, provided that during the period of such exemption they shall maintain a watch of at least 8 hours per day.

2. Cargo Ships.

Each cargo ship which, in accordance with Article 27, is required to be fitted with a radiotelegraph installation, shall, for safety purposes, carry a qualified operator, and, if not fitted with an auto-alarm, shall, whilst at sea, keep watches by means of a qualified operator or a certified watcher, as under:—

(*a.*) All cargo ships under 3,000 tons gross tonnage, as determined by the Administration concerned;

(*b.*) Cargo ships from 3,000 to 5,500 tons gross tonnage, both included, at least 8 hours' watch per day;

(*c.*) Cargo ships over 5,500 tons gross tonnage, continuous watch.

Each Administration is authorised to exempt ships belonging to its country included in (*c*) above from the requirement of a continuous watch for a period not exceeding one year from the date of the coming into force of the present Convention, provided that during the period of such exemption they shall maintain a watch of at least 8 hours per day.

Each Administration is also authorised to exempt ships belonging to its country from 5,500 tons to 8,000 tons gross tonnage from the requirement of a continuous watch for a further period of one year, provided that during this further period of exemption they shall maintain a watch of at least 16 hours per day.

3. On all ships fitted with an auto-alarm this auto-alarm shall, whilst the ship is at sea, always be in operation when the operator or watcher is not on watch.

On ships for which the hours of watch are to be determined by the Administration concerned, such watch should be maintained preferably at hours prescribed for radiotelegraph service by the International Radiotelegraph Convention in force.

On ships which are required to keep 8 hours' or 16 hours' watch per day, such watch shall be maintained at the hours prescribed for radiotelegraph service by the International Radiotelegraph Convention in force.

4. By *auto-alarm* is meant an automatic alarm receiver which complies with the requirements of Article 19, § 21, of the General Regulations annexed to the International Radiotelegraph Convention, 1927.[5]

5. By *qualified operator* is meant a person holding a certificate complying with the provisions of the General Regulations annexed to the International Radiotelegraph Convention in force.

6. By *certified watcher* is meant any person holding a watcher's certificate issued under the authority of the Administration.

ARTICLE 30

Watchers

1. A watcher's certificate shall not be granted by a Contracting Government unless the applicant proves that he is capable—

(a) of receiving and understanding the alarm, distress, safety and urgency signals when these signals occur among a series of other signals;

(b) of correct reception by ear of code groups (mixed letters, figures and punctuation marks) at a speed of sixteen groups per minute, each group being composed of five characters and each figure or punctuation mark counting as two characters;

(c) of regulating the receivers used in the ship's radiotelegraph installation.

2. The Contracting Governments undertake to take steps to ensure that certified watchers observe the secrecy of correspondence.

ARTICLE 31

Technical Requirements

The radiotelegraph installations required by Article 27 above and the direction-finding apparatus required by Article 47 shall comply with the following requirements:—

1. The ship's station must be placed in accordance with the detailed Regulations of the Government of the country to which the ship belongs, in the

---

[5] For text of convention signed at Washington Nov. 25, 1927 (TS 767), see *ante,* p. 683; for text of general and supplementary regulations annexed to the convention, see 45 Stat. 2848 or TS 767, p. 13.

upper part of the ship in a position of the greatest possible safety, as high as practicable above the deepest load water line.

2. There shall be provided, between the bridge of the ship and the wireless telegraph room, means of communication either by voice pipe or by telephone or in some other manner equally efficient.

3. A reliable clock with a seconds hand must be provided in the wireless telegraph room.

4. A reliable emergency light must be provided in the wireless telegraph room.

5. The installation shall comprise a main installation and an emergency (reserve) installation. If, however, the main installation complies with all the requirements of an emergency (reserve) installation the latter is not then obligatory.

6. The main and emergency (reserve) installations must be capable of transmitting and receiving on the frequencies (wave lengths) and types of waves assigned by the International Radiotelegraph Convention in force for the purpose of distress and safety of navigation to ships compulsorily fitted with radiotelegraph installations in accordance with the present Convention.

7. The main and emergency (reserve) transmitters shall have a note frequency of at least 100.

8. The main transmitter shall have a *normal range* of 100 nautical miles, that is to say, it must be capable of transmitting clearly perceptible signals from ship to ship over a range of at least 100 nautical miles by day under normal conditions and circumstances, the receiver being assumed to be one employing a rectifier of the crystal type without amplification.[6]

9. Sufficient power must be available in a ship station at all times to operate the main radiotelegraph installation efficiently under normal conditions over the above range.

10. All parts of the emergency (reserve) installation shall be placed in the upper part of the ship, in a position of the greatest possible safety, as high above the deepest load water line as practicable. The emergency (reserve) installation must be provided with a source of energy independent of the propelling power of the ship and of the main electricity system and must be capable of being put into operation rapidly and of working for at least six continuous hours.

---

[6] Unless a more precise and practical method is available to determine the range of transmitters it is recommended that, as a guide, the following relations between the range in nautical miles (from ship to ship under normal conditions in daytime) and the power of the ship transmitter in metre ampères for 500 kilocycles per second (600 m) be used:—

100 nautical miles	60 M A
80 nautical miles	45 M A
50 nautical miles	25 M A

M being the actual height in metres of the aerial from its highest point to the load line.

A being the current in ampères measured at the base of the aerial in case of B, or fully modulated A 2, transmitters. [Footnote in original.]

For the emergency (reserve) installation, the normal range as defined in paragraph 8 above must be at least 80 nautical miles for ships required to maintain a continuous watch and at least 50 nautical miles for all other ships.[6]

11. The receiving installation must permit of the reception of such of the waves used for the transmission of time signals and meteorological messages as may be considered necessary by the Administration.

12. The receiver must be so arranged as to be capable of maintaining reception by means of a rectifier of the crystal type.

13. In ships in which watch is kept by means of an automatic alarm receiver a means of giving audible warning shall be provided in the wireless telegraph room, in the wireless operator's cabin, and on the bridge, which shall operate continuously after the receiver has been operated by the alarm signal or distress call until stopped. Only one switch for stopping the warning shall be provided and this shall be situated in the wireless telegraph room.

14. In such ships the wireless operator, when going off watch, shall connect the automatic alarm receiver to the aerial and test its efficiency. He shall report to the master or the officer on watch on the bridge whether it is in working order.

15. Whilst the ship is at sea the emergency source of power shall be maintained at its full efficiency and the automatic alarm receiver shall be tested at least once every 24 hours. A statement that both these requirements have been fulfilled must be inserted in the ship's official log daily.

16. A wireless log shall be carried by every ship compulsorily equipped with wireless transmitting apparatus. This document shall be kept in the wireless telegraph room, and in it shall be inserted the names of the operators and watchers as well as all incidents and occurrences connected with the wireless service which may appear to be of importance to safety of life at sea, and in particular all distress messages and distress traffic in full.

17. The direction-finding apparatus required by Article 47 shall be efficient and capable of receiving clearly perceptible signals and of taking bearings from which the true bearing and direction may be determined. It shall be capable of receiving signals on the frequencies prescribed for distress, direction finding and wireless telegraph beacons by the International Radiotelegraph Convention in force.

Efficient communication shall be provided between the apparatus and the bridge.

ARTICLE 32

Competence

The matters governed by the International Radiotelegraph Convention, Washington, 1927, and the Regulations annexed thereto remain, and will continue, subject to the provisions:—

(1.) Of that Convention and of the Regulations annexed thereto, and of any Convention and Regulations which may in the future be substituted therefor;

(2.) Of the present Convention in regard to all the points in which it supplements the aforementioned documents.

CHAPTER V. SAFETY OF NAVIGATION

ARTICLE 33

Application

The provisions of this Chapter referring to ships, unless otherwise expressly provided, apply to all ships on all voyages.

ARTICLE 34

Danger Messages

The master of every ship which meets with dangerous ice, a dangerous derelict, a dangerous tropical storm or any other direct danger to navigation is bound to communicate the information, by all the means of communication at his disposal, to the ships in the vicinity, and also to the competent authorities at the first point of the coast with which he can communicate. It is desirable that the said information be sent in the manner set out in Regulaion XLVI.

Each Administration will take all steps which it thinks necessary to ensure that when intelligence of any of the dangers specified in the previous paragraph is received, it will be promptly brought to the knowledge of those concerned and communicated to other Administrations interested.

The transmission of messages respecting the dangers specified is free of cost to the ships concerned.

ARTICLE 35

Meteorological Services

The Contracting Governments undertake to encourage the collection of meteorological data by ships at sea, and to arrange for their examination, dissemination and exchange in the manner most suitable for the purpose of aiding navigation.

In particular, the Contracting Governments undertake to co-operate in carrying out, as far as practicable, the following meteorological arrangements:—

(*a*) to warn ships of gales, storms and tropical storms, both by the issue of wireless messages and by the display of appropriate signals at coastal points;

(*b*) to issue daily, by radio, weather bulletins suitable for shipping, containing data of existing weather conditions and forecasts;

(*c*) to arrange for certain selected ships to take meteorological observations at specified hours, and to transmit such observations by wireless telegraphy for the benefit of other ships and of the various official meteorological services; and to provide coast stations for the reception of the messages transmitted;

(*d*) to encourage all ship-masters to inform surrounding ships whenever they experience wind force of 10 or above on the Beaufort scale (force 8 or above on the decimal scale).

The information provided for in paragraphs (*a*) and (*b*) of this article will be furnished in form for transmission in accordance with Article 31, §§ 1, 3 and 5, and Article 19, § 25, of the General Regulations annexed to the International Radiotelegraph Convention, Washington, 1927, and during transmission "to all stations" of meteorological information, forecasts and warnings, all ship stations must conform to the provisions of Article 31, § 2, of those General Regulations.

Weather observations from ships addressed to national meteorological services will be transmitted with the priority specified in Article 3, Additional Regulations, International Radiotelegraph Convention, Washington, 1927.

Forecasts, warnings, synoptic and other meteorological reports intended for ships shall be issued and disseminated by the national service in the best position to serve various zones and areas, in accordance with mutual arrangements made by the countries concerned.

Every endeavour will be made to obtain a uniform procedure in regard to the international meteorological services specified in this Article, and, as far as is practicable, to conform to the recommendations made by the International Meteorological Organization, to which organization the Contracting Governments may refer for study and advice any meteorological questions which may arise in carrying out the present Convention.

ARTICLE 36

Ice Patrol. Derelicts

The Contracting Governments undertake to continue a service of ice patrol and a service for study and observation of ice conditions in the North Atlantic. Further, they undertake to take all practicable steps to ensure the destruction or removal of derelicts in the northern part of the Atlantic Ocean east of the line drawn from Cape Sable to a point in latitude 34° N. longitude 70° W. if this destruction or removal is considered necessary at the time.

The Contracting Governments undertake to provide not more than three vessels for these three services. During the whole of the ice season they shall be employed in guarding the south-eastern, southern and south-western limits of the regions of icebergs in the vicinity of the Great Bank of Newfoundland for the purpose of informing trans-Atlantic and other passing vessels of the extent of this dangerous region; for the observation and study of ice conditions in general; for the destruction or removal of derelicts; and for the purpose of affording assistance to vessels and crews requiring aid within the limits of operation of the patrol vessels.

During the rest of the year the study and observation of ice conditions shall be maintained as advisable, and one vessel shall always be available for the search for, and destruction or removal of derelicts.

ARTICLE 37

Ice Patrol. Management and Cost

The Government of the United States is invited to continue the management of these services of ice patrol, study and observation of ice conditions, and derelict destruction and removal. The Contracting Governments specially interested in these services, whose names are given below, undertake to contribute to the expense of maintaining and operating these services in the following proportions:—

	Per cent		Per cent
Belgium	2	Netherlands	5
Canada	3	Norway	3
Denmark	2	Spain	1
France	6	Sweden	2
Germany	10	Union of Socialist Soviet Republics	1
Great Britain and Northern Ireland	40	United States of America	18
Italy	6		
Japan	1		

Each of the Contracting Governments has the right to discontinue its contribution to the expense of maintaining and operating these services after the 1st September, 1932. Nevertheless, the Contracting Government which avails itself of this right will continue responsible for the expense of working up to the 1st September following the date of giving notice of intention to discontinue its contribution. To take advantage of the said right it must give notice to the other Contracting Governments at least six months before the said 1st September; so that, to be free from this obligation on the 1st September, 1932, it must give notice on the 1st March, 1932, at the latest, and similarly for each subsequent year.

If, at any time, the United States Government should not desire to continue these services, or if one of the Contracting Governments should express a wish to relinquish responsibility for the pecuniary contribution defined above, or to have its percentage of obligation altered, the Contracting Governments shall settle the question in accordance with their mutual interests.

The Contracting Governments which contribute to the cost of the three above-mentioned services shall have the right by common consent to make from time to time such alterations in the provisions of this Article and of Article 36 as appear desirable.

ARTICLE 38

Speed near Ice

When ice is reported on, or near, his course, the master of every ship at night is bound to proceed at a moderate speed or to alter his course so as to go well clear of the danger zone.

ARTICLE 39

North Atlantic Routes

The practice of following recognised routes across the North Atlantic in both directions has contributed to safety of life at sea, but the working of these routes should be further investigated and studied with a view to the introduction of such variations as experience may show to be necessary.

The selection of the routes and the initiation of action with regard to them is left to the responsibility of the steamship companies concerned. The Contracting Governments will assist the companies, when requested to do so, by placing at their disposal any information bearing on the routes which may be in the possession of the Governments.

The Contracting Governments undertake to impose on the companies the obligation to give public notice of the regular routes which they propose their vessels should follow, and of any changes made in these routes; they will also use their influence to induce the owners of all vessels crossing the Atlantic to follow, so far as circumstances will permit, the recognised routes, and to induce the owners of all vessels crossing the Atlantic bound to or from ports of the United States via the vicinity of the Great Bank of Newfoundland to avoid as far as practicable, the fishing banks of Newfoundland north of latitude 43° N. during the fishing season, and to pass outside regions known or believed to be endangered by ice.

The Administration managing the ice patrol service is requested to report to the Administration concerned any ship which is observed not to be on any regular, recognised or advertised route, or which crosses the above-mentioned fishing banks during the fishing season, or which, when proceeding to or from ports of the United States, passes through regions known or believed to be endangered by ice.

ARTICLE 40

Collision Regulations

The Contracting Governments agree that the alterations in the International Regulations for Preventing Collisions at Sea shown in Annex II are desirable and ought to be made. The Government of the United Kingdom of Great Britain and Northern Ireland is requested to forward full particulars of the alterations to the other Governments who have accepted the International Regulations for Preventing Collisions at Sea, and ascertain whether they will adopt these alterations; to report the result to the Governments represented at this Conference, and to endeavour to arrange that the revised regulations shall come in force on the 1st July, 1931.

ARTICLE 41

Helm Orders

The Contracting Governments agree that after midnight on the 30th June, 1931, helm or steering orders, *i. e.,* orders to the steersman, shall on all their ships be given in the direct sense, *e. g.,* when the ship is going ahead an order containing the word "starboard" or "right" or any equivalent of "starboard" or "right" shall only be used when it is intended, on ships as at present generally constructed and arranged, that the wheel, the rudder-blade and the head of the ship, shall all move to the right.

ARTICLE 42

Misuse of Distress Signals

The use of an international distress signal, except for the purpose of indicating that a vessel is in distress, and the use of any signal which may be confused with an international distress signal, are prohibited on every ship.

ARTICLE 43

Alarm, Distress and Urgency Signals

The alarm signal and the distress signal may only be used by ships in serious and imminent danger which require immediate assistance. In all other cases in which assistance is required, or in which a vessel desires to issue a warning that it may become necessary to send out the alarm signal or the distress signal at a later stage, use must be made of the urgency signal (XXX) established by the International Radiotelegraph Convention, Washington, 1927.

If a ship has sent out the alarm or distress signal and subsequently finds that assistance is no longer required such ship shall immediately notify all stations concerned as provided for by the Radiotelegraph Convention in force.

ARTICLE 44

Speed of Distress Messages

The speed of transmission of messages in connection with cases of distress, urgency or safety, shall not exceed 16 words per minute.

ARTICLE 45

Distress Messages. Procedure

1. The master of a ship on receiving on his ship a wireless distress signal from any other ship, is bound to proceed with all speed to the assistance of the persons in distress, unless he is unable, or in the special circumstances of the case, considers it unreasonable or unnecessary to do so, or unless he is released under the provisions of paragraphs 3 and 4 of this Article.

2. The master of a ship in distress, after consultation, so far as may be possible, with the masters of the ships which answer his call for assistance, has the right to requisition such one or more of those ships as he considers best able to render assistance, and it shall be the duty of the master or masters of the ship or ships requisitioned to comply with the requisition by continuing to proceed with all speed to the assistance of the persons in distress.

3. A master shall be released from the obligation imposed by paragraph 1 of this Article as soon as he is informed by the master of the ship requisitioned, or, where more ships than one are requisitioned, all the masters of the ships requisitioned, that he or they are complying with the requisition.

4. A master shall be released from the obligation imposed by paragraph 1 of this Article, and, if his ship has been requisitioned, from the obligation imposed by paragraph 2 of this Article, if he is informed by a ship which has reached the persons in distress, that assistance is no longer necessary.

5. If a master of a ship, on receiving a wireless distress call from another ship, is unable, or in the special circumstances of the case considers it unreasonable or unnecessary to go to the assistance of that other ship, he must immediately inform the master of that other ship accordingly, and enter in his log-book his reasons for failing to proceed to the assistance of the persons in distress.

6. The provisions of this Article do not prejudice the International Convention for the unification of certain rules with respect to Assistance and Salvage at Sea, signed at Brussels on the 23rd September, 1910,[7] particularly the obligation to render assistance imposed by Article 11 of that Convention.

ARTICLE 46

Signalling Lamp

All ships of over 150 tons gross tonnage, when engaged on international voyages, shall have on board an efficient signalling lamp.

---

[7] TS 576, *ante*, vol. 1, p. 780.

ARTICLE 47

Direction-Finding Apparatus

Every passenger ship of 5,000 tons gross tonnage and upwards shall, within two years from the date on which the present Convention comes in force, be provided with an approved direction-finding apparatus (radio compass), complying with the provisions of Article 31 (17) of the present Convention.

ARTICLE 48

Manning

The Contracting Governments undertake, each for its national ships, to maintain, or, if it is necessary, to adopt, measures for the purpose of ensuring that, from the point of view of safety of life at sea, all ships shall be sufficiently and efficiently manned.

CHAPTER VI. CERTIFICATES

ARTICLE 49

Issue of Certificates

A certificate called a *Safety Certificate* shall be issued, after inspection and survey, to every passenger ship which complies in an efficient manner with the requirements of Chapters II, III and IV of the Convention.

A certificate called a *Safety Radiotelegraphy Certificate* shall be issued after inspection to every ship other than a passenger ship which complies in an efficient manner with the requirements of Chapter IV of the present Convention.

A certificate called an *Exemption Certificate* shall be issued to every ship to which exemption is granted by a Contracting Government under, and in accordance with, the provisions of Chapters II, III and IV of the present Convention.

The inspection and survey of ships, so far as regards the enforcement of the provisions of the present Convention and the annexed Regulations applicable to such ships and the granting of exemptions therefrom, shall be carried out by officers of the country in which the ship is registered, provided that the Government of each country may entrust the inspection and survey of its ships either to Surveyors nominated for this purpose or to organisations recognised by it. In every case the Government concerned fully guarantees the completeness and efficiency of the inspection and survey.

A Safety Certificate, Safety Radiotelegraphy Certificate, and Exemption Certificate shall be issued either by the Government of the country in which the ship is registered or by any person or organisation duly authorised by that Government. In every case that Government assumes full responsibility for the certificate.

ARTICLE 50

Issue of Certificate by Another Government

A Contracting Government may, at the request of the Government of a country in which a ship coming under the present Convention is registered, cause that ship to be surveyed, and, if satisfied that the requirements of the present Convention are complied with, issue a Safety Certificate or Safety Radiotelegraphy Certificate to such ship, under its own responsibility. Any certificate so issued must contain a statement to the effect that it has been issued at the request of the Government of the country in which the ship is registered, and it shall have the same force and receive the same recognition as a certificate issued under Article 49 of the present Convention.

ARTICLE 51

Form of Certificates

All certificates shall be drawn up in the official language or languages of the country by which they are issued.

The form of the certificates shall be that of the models given in Regulation XLVII. The arrangement of the printed part of the standard certificates shall be exactly reproduced in the certificates issued, or in certified copies thereof, and the particulars inserted by hand shall in the certificates issued, or in certified copies thereof, be inserted in Roman characters and Arabic figures.

The Contracting Governments undertake to communicate one to another a sufficient number of specimens of their certificates for the information of their officers. This exchange shall be made, so far as possible, before the 1st January, 1932.

ARTICLE 52

Duration of Certificates

Certificates shall not be issued for a period of more than twelve months.

If a ship at the time when its certificate expires is not in a port of the country in which it is registered the certificate may be extended by a duly authorised officer of the country to which the ship belongs; but such extension shall be granted only for the purpose of allowing the ship to complete its return voyage to its own country, and then only in cases in which it appears proper and reasonable so to do.

No certificate shall be extended for a longer period than five months, and a ship to which such extension is granted shall not, on returning to its own country, be entitled by virtue of such extension to leave that country again without having obtained a new certificate.

ARTICLE 53

Acceptance of Certificates

Certificates issued under the authority of a Contracting Government shall be accepted by the other Contracting Governments for all purposes covered by the present Convention. They shall be regarded by the other Contracting Governments as having the same force as the certificates issued by them to their own ships.

ARTICLE 54 [8]

Control

Every ship holding a certificate issued under Article 49 or Article 50 is subject, in the ports of the other Contracting Governments, to control by officers duly authorised by such Governments in so far as this control is directed towards verifying that there is on board a valid certificate, and if necessary, that the conditions of the vessel's seaworthiness correspond substantially with the particulars of that certificate; that is to say, so that the ship can proceed to sea without danger to the passengers and the crew.

In the event of this control giving rise to intervention of any kind, the officer carrying out the control shall forthwith inform the Consul of the country in which the ship is registered of all the circumstances in which intervention is deemed to be necessary.

ARTICLE 55

Privileges

The privileges of the present Convention may not be claimed in favour of any ship unless it holds a proper valid certificate.

ARTICLE 56

Qualification of Certificate

If in the course of a particular voyage the ship has on board a number of crew and passengers less than the maximum number which the ship is licensed to carry, and is in consequence, in accordance with the provisions of the present Convention, free to carry a smaller number of life-boats and other life-saving appliances than that stated in the certificate, a memorandum may be issued by the officers or other authorised persons referred to in Articles 49 and 52 above.

This memorandum shall state that in the circumstances there is no infringement of the provisions of the present Convention. It shall be annexed to the certificate and shall be substituted for it in so far as the life-saving appliances are concerned. It shall be valid only for the particular voyage in regard to which it is issued.

---

[8] For U.S. understandings, see footnote 1, p. 782.

CHAPTER VII. GENERAL PROVISIONS

ARTICLE 57

Equivalents

Where in the present Convention it is provided that a particular fitting, appliance or apparatus, or type thereof, shall be fitted or carried in a ship, or that any particular arrangement shall be adopted, any Administration may accept in substitution therefor any other fitting, appliance or apparatus, or type thereof, or any other arrangement, provided that such Administration shall have been satisfied by suitable trials that the fitting, appliance or apparatus, or type thereof, or the arrangement substituted is at least as effective as that specified in the present Convention.

Any Administration which so accepts a new fitting, appliance or apparatus, or type thereof, or new arrangement, shall communicate the fact to the other Administrations, and, upon request, the particulars thereof, together with a report on the trials made.

ARTICLE 58

Laws, Regulations, Reports

The Contracting Governments undertake to communicate to each other—

(1) the text of laws, decrees and regulations which shall have been promulgated on the various matters within the scope of the present Convention;

(2) all available official reports or official summaries of reports in so far as they show the results of the provisions of the present Convention, provided always that such reports or summaries are not of a confidential nature.

The Government of the United Kingdom of Great Britain and Northern Ireland is invited to serve as an intermediary for collecting all this information and for bringing it to the knowledge of the other Contracting Governments.

ARTICLE 59

Measures taken after Agreement

Where the present Convention provides that a measure may be taken after agreement between all or some of the Contracting Governments, the Government of the United Kingdom of Great Britain and Northern Ireland is invited to approach the other Contracting Governments with a view to ascertaining whether they accept such proposals as may be made by any Contracting Government for effecting such a measure, and to inform the other Contracting Governments of the results of the enquiries thus made.

ARTICLE 60

Prior Treaties and Conventions

1. The present Convention replaces and abrogates the Convention for the Safety of Life at Sea, which was signed at London on the 20th January, 1914.[9]

2. All other treaties, conventions and arrangements relating to safety of life at sea, or matters appertaining thereto, at present in force between Governments parties to the present Convention, shall continue to have full and complete effect during the terms thereof as regards—

(a) ships to which the present Convention does not apply;

(b) ships to which the present Convention applies, in respect of subjects for which it has not expressly provided.

To the extent, however, that such treaties, conventions or arrangements conflict with the provisions of the present Convention, the provisions of the present Convention shall prevail.

3. All subjects which are not expressly provided for in the present Convention remain subject to the legislation of the Contracting Governments.

ARTICLE 61

Modifications. Future Conferences

1. Modifications of the present Convention which may be deemed useful or necessary improvements may be at any time proposed by any Contracting Government to the Government of the United Kingdom of Great Britain and Northern Ireland, and such proposals shall be communicated by the latter to all the other Contracting Governments, and if any such modifications are accepted by all the Contracting Governments (including Governments which have deposited ratifications or accessions which have not yet become effective) the present Convention shall be modified accordingly.

2. Conferences for the purpose of revising the present Convention shall be held at such times and places as may be agreed upon by the Contracting Governments.

A Conference for this purpose shall be convoked by the Government of the United Kingdom of Great Britain and Northern Ireland whenever, after the present Convention has been in force for five years, one-third of the Contracting Governments express a desire to that effect.

CHAPTER VIII. FINAL PROVISIONS

ARTICLE 62

Application to Colonies, &c.

1. A Contracting Government may, at the time of signature, ratification, accession or thereafter, by a declaration in writing addressed to the Govern-

---

[9] S. Ex. B, 63d Cong., 2d sess. The United States did not become a party.

ment of the United Kingdom of Great Britain and Northern Ireland, declare its desire that the present Convention shall apply to all or any of its colonies, overseas territories, protectorates or territories under suzerainty or mandate, and the present Convention shall apply to all the territories named in such declaration, two months after the date of the receipt thereof, but failing such declaration, the present Convention will not apply to any such territories.

2. A Contracting Government may at any time by a notification in writing addressed to the Government of the United Kingdom of Great Britain and Northern Ireland express its desire that the present Convention shall cease to apply to all or any of its colonies, overseas territories, protectorates or territories under suzerainty or mandate to which the present Convention shall have, under the provisions of the preceding paragraph, been applicable for a period of not less than five years, and in such case the present Convention shall cease to apply one year after the date of the receipt of such notification by the Government of the United Kingdom of Great Britain and Northern Ireland to all territories mentioned therein.

3. The Government of the United Kingdom of Great Britain and Northern Ireland shall inform all the other Contracting Governments of the application of the present Convention to any colony, overseas territory, protectorate or territory under suzerainty or mandate under the provisions of paragraph 1 of this Article, and of the cessation of any such application under the provisions of paragraph 2, stating in each case the date from which the present Convention has become or will cease to be applicable.

ARTICLE 63

Authentic Texts. Ratification

The present Convention of which both the English and French texts shall be authentic shall bear this day's date.

The present Convention shall be ratified.

The instruments of ratification shall be deposited in the archives of the Government of the United Kingdom of Great Britain and Northern Ireland which will notify all the other signatory or acceding Governments of all ratifications deposited and the date of their deposit.

ARTICLE 64

Accession

A Government (other than the Government of a territory to which Article 62 applies) on behalf of which the present Convention has not been signed shall be allowed to accede thereto at any time after the Convention has come into force. Accessions may be effected by means of notifications in writing addressed to the Government of the United Kingdom of Great Britain and Northern Ireland, and shall take effect three months after their receipt.

The Government of the United Kingdom of Great Britain and Northern Ireland shall inform all signatory and acceding Governments of all accessions received and of the date of their receipt.

A Government which intends to accede to the present Convention but desires to add an area to those specified in the Annex to Article 28 shall, before notifying its accession, inform the Government of the United Kingdom of Great Britain and Northern Ireland of its desire for communication to all the other Contracting Governments. If all the Contracting Governments signify their assent thereto, the area shall be added to those mentioned in the aforesaid Annex when such Government notifies its accession.

ARTICLE 65

Date of coming in Force

The present Convention shall come into force on the 1st July, 1931, as between the Governments which have deposited their ratifications by that date, and provided that at least five ratifications have been deposited with the Government of the United Kingdom of Great Britain and Northern Ireland. Should five ratifications not have been deposited on that date, the present Convention shall come into force three months after the date on which the fifth ratification is deposited. Ratifications deposited after the date on which the present Convention has come into force shall take effect three months after the date of their deposit.

ARTICLE 66

Denunciation

The present Convention may be denounced on behalf of any Contracting Government at any time after the expiration of five years from the date on which the Convention comes into force in so far as that Government is concerned. Denunciation shall be effected by a notification in writing addressed to the Government of the United Kingdom of Great Britain and Northern Ireland, which will notify all the other Contracting Governments of all denunciations received and of the date of their receipt.

A denunciation shall take effect twelve months after the date on which notification thereof is received by the Government of the United Kingdom of Great Britain and Northern Ireland.

In faith whereof, the Plenipotentiaries have signed hereafter.

Done at London this thirty-first day of May, 1929, in a single copy, which shall remain deposited in the archives of the Government of the United Kingdom of Great Britain and Northern Ireland, which shall transmit certified true copies thereof to all signatory Governments.

[For Germany:]
STHAMER
GUSTAV KOENIGS
ARTHUR WERNER
WALTER LAAS
OTTO RIESS
HERMANN GIESS
HUGO DOMINIK

[For Australia:]
HENRY JAMES FEAKES
THOMAS FREE

[For Belgium:]
A. DE GERLACHE DE GOMERY
G. DE WINNE

[For Canada:]
A. JOHNSTON
LUCIEN PACAUD

[For Denmark:]
EMIL KROGH
V. LORCK

[For Spain:]
JAVIER DE SALAS

[For the Irish Free State:]
JOHN WHELAN DULANTY
E. C. FOSTER

[For the United States:]
WALLACE H. WHITE
ARTHUR J. TYRER
CHARLES M. BARNES
GEO. H. ROCK
CLARENCE S. KEMPFF
DICKERSON N. HOOVER
W. D. TERRELL
JOHN G. TAWRESEY
HERBERT B. WALKER
CHARLES A. MCALLISTER

[For Finland:]
GUSTAF WREDE
V. BERGMAN
KARL KURTEN

[For France:]
RIO
A. HAARBLEICHER
JEAN MARIE
F. THOUROUDE

[For the United Kingdom:]
H. W. RICHMOND
WESTCOTT ABELL
A. L. AYRE
F. W. BATE
C. H. BOYD
WILLIAM C. CURRIE
A. J. DANIEL
NORMAN HILL
C. HIPWOOD
A. MORRELL

[For India:]
G. L. CORBETT
E. V. WHISH
MANSUKHLAL ATMARAM MASTER

[For Italy:]
GIULIO INGIANNI
ALBERTO ALESSIO
DELFINO ROGERI DI VILLANOVA
TORQUATO C. GIANNINI
FRANCESCO MARENA
ERNESTO FERRETTI
G. GNEME
LUIGI BIANCHERI

[For Japan:]
YUKIO YAMAMOTO
SHICHIHEI OTA
ITARO ISHII

[For Norway:]
B. VOGT
L. T. HANSEN
ARTH H. MATHIESEN

[For the Netherlands:]
C. FOCK
C. H. DE GOEJE
A. VAN DRIEL
J. A. BLAND-V.-D.-BERG
PHS. VAN OMMEREN
H. G. J. UILKENS

[For Sweden:]
ERIK PALMSTIERNA
NILS GUSTAF NILSSON

[For the Union of Soviet Socialist Republics:]
J. ARENS
K. EGGI

Annex I

REGULATIONS

CONSTRUCTION

Regulation I

Definitions

(1.) The *subdivision loadline* is the waterline used in determining the subdivision of the ship.

The *deepest subdivision loadline* is that which corresponds to the greatest draught.

(2.) The *length of the ship* is the length measured between perpendiculars taken at the extremities of the deepest subdivision loadline.

(3.) The *breadth of the ship* is the extreme width from outside of frame to outside of frame at or below the deepest subdivision loadline.

(4.) The *bulkhead deck* is the uppermost deck up to which the transverse watertight bulkheads are carried.

(5.) The *margin line* is a line drawn parallel to the bulkhead deck at side and 3 inches (76 millimetres) below the upper surface of that deck at side.

(6.) The *draught* is the vertical distance from the top of keel amidships to the subdivision loadline in question.

(7.) The *permeability* of a space is the percentage of that space which can be occupied by water.

The volume of a space which extends above the margin line shall be measured only to the height of that line.

(8.) The *machinery space* is to be taken as extending from the top of keel to the margin line and between the extreme main transverse watertight bulkheads bounding the spaces devoted to the main and auxiliary propelling machinery, boilers when installed, and all permanent coal bunkers.

(9.) *Passenger spaces* are those which are provided for the accommodation and use of passengers, excluding baggage, store, provision and mail rooms.

For the purposes of Regulations III and IV, spaces provided below the margin line for the accommodation and use of the crew shall be regarded as passenger spaces.

(10.) In all cases *volumes* shall be calculated to moulded lines.

Regulation II

Floodable Length

(1.) The floodable length at any point of the length of a ship shall be determined by a method of calculation which takes into consideration the form, draught and other characteristics of the ship in question.

(2.) In a ship with a continuous bulkhead deck, the floodable length at a given point is the maximum portion of the length of the ship, having its centre at the point in question, which can be flooded under the definite assumptions hereafter set forth in Regulation III without the ship being submerged beyond the margin line.

(3.) In the case of a ship not having a continuous bulkhead deck, the floodable length at any point may be determined to an assumed continuous margin line, up to which, having regard to sinkage and trim after damage, the sides of the ship and the bulkheads concerned are carried watertight.

REGULATION III

Permeability

(1.) The definite assumptions referred to in Regulation II relate to the permeabilities of the spaces below the margin line.

In determining the floodable length, a uniform average permeability shall be used throughout the whole length of each of the following portions of the ship below the margin line:—

(*a*) the machinery space as defined in Regulation I (8);
(*b*) the portion forward of the machinery space; and
(*c*) the portion abaft the machinery space.

(2.)—(*a.*) For steamships the uniform average permeability throughout the machinery space shall be determined from the formula—

$$80 + 12 \cdot 5 \left(\frac{a-c}{v} \right), \text{ where}$$

a = volume of the passenger spaces, as defined in Regulation I(9), which are situated below the margin line within the limits of the machinery space.
c = volume of between deck spaces below the margin line within the limits of the machinery space which are appropriated to cargo, coal or stores.
v = whole volume of the machinery space below the margin line.

(*b.*) For ships propelled by internal combustion engines, the uniform average permeability shall be taken as 5 greater than that given by the above formula.

(*c.*) Where it is shown to the satisfaction of the Administration that the average permeability, as determined by detail calculation, is less than that given by the formula, the calculated value may be substituted. For the purposes of such calculation, the permeabilities of passenger spaces, as defined in Regulation I (9), shall be taken as 95, that of all cargo, coal and store spaces as 60, and that of double bottom, oil fuel and other tanks at such values as may be approved in each case by the Administration.

(3.) The uniform average permeability throughout the portion of the ship before (or abaft) the machinery space shall be determined from the formula—

$$63 + 35 \frac{a}{v}, \text{ where}$$

a = volume of the passenger spaces, as defined in Regulation I(9), which are situated below the margin line, before (or abaft) the machinery space, and

v = whole volume of the portion of the ship below the margin line before (or abaft) the machinery space.

(4.) If a between deck compartment between two watertight transverse bulkheads contains any passenger or crew space, the whole of that compartment, less any space completely enclosed within permanent steel bulkheads and appropriated to other purposes, shall be regarded as passenger space. If, however, the passenger or crew space in question is completely enclosed within permanent steel bulkheads, only the space so enclosed need be considered as passenger space.

REGULATION IV

Permissible Length of Compartments

(1.) *Factor of Subdivision.* The maximum permissible length of a compartment having its centre at any point in the ship's length is obtained from the floodable length by multiplying the latter by an appropriate factor called the *factor of subdivision.*

The factor of subdivision shall depend on the length of the ship, and for a given length shall vary according to the nature of the service for which the ship is intended. It shall decrease in a regular and continuous manner—

(*a*) as the length of the ship increases, and

(*b*) from a factor A, applicable to ships primarily engaged in the carriage of cargo, to a factor B, applicable to ships primarily engaged in the carriage of passengers.

The variations of the factors A and B shall be expressed by the following formulae (i) and (ii) where L is the length of the ship as defined in Regulation I(2):—

L in feet.

$$A = \frac{190}{L-198} + .18 \quad \text{(L=430 and upwards).}$$

$$B = \frac{100}{L-138} + .18 \quad \text{(L=260 and upwards).}$$

L in metres.

$$A = \frac{58.2}{L-60} + .18 \quad \text{(L=131 and upwards)} \ \ldots \ldots \ldots \text{(i)}$$

$$B = \frac{30.3}{L-42} + .18 \quad \text{(L=79 and upwards)} \ \ldots \ldots \ldots \text{(ii)}$$

(2.) *Criterion of Service.* For a ship of given length the appropriate factor of subdivision shall be determined by the Criterion of Service

Numeral (hereinafter called the Criterion Numeral) as given by the following formulae (iii) and (iv) where:—

C_s = the Criterion Numeral;

L = length of the ship, as defined in Regulation I(2);

M = the volume of the machinery space, as defined in Regulation I(8); with the addition thereto of the volume of any permanent oil fuel bunkers which may be situated above the inner bottom and before or abaft the machinery space;

P = the whole volume of the passenger spaces below the margin line, as defined in Regulation I(9);

V = the whole volume of the ship below the margin line;

P_1 = KN where:—

N = number of passengers for which the ship is to be certified, and

K has the following values:—

Value of K.

Length in feet and volumes in cubic feet . . . . .6 L.

Length in metres and volumes in cubic metres . . . . .056 L.

Where the value of KN is greater than the sum of P and the whole volume of the actual passenger spaces above the margin line the lower figure may be taken provided that the value of P_1 used is not less than ⅔ KN.

When P_1 is greater than P

$$C_s = 72 \frac{M+2P_1}{V+P_1-P} \quad \text{.................................. (iii)}$$

and in other cases

$$C_s = 72 \frac{M+2P}{V} \quad \text{........................... (iv)}$$

For ships not having a continuous bulkhead deck the volumes are to be taken up to the actual margin lines used in determining the floodable lengths.

(3.) *Rules for Subdivision.*—(a.) *The subdivision abaft the fore peak* of ships 430 feet (131 metres) in length and upwards having a criterion numeral of 23 or less shall be governed by the factor A given by formula (i); of those having a criterion numeral of 123 or more by the factor B given by formula (ii); and of those having a criterion numeral between 23 and 123 by the factor F obtained by linear interpolation between the factors A and B, using the formula:—

$$F = A - \frac{(A-B)(C_s-23)}{100} \quad \text{................... (v)}$$

Where the factor F is less than ·40 and it is shown to the satisfaction of the Administration to be impracticable to comply with the factor F in a machinery compartment of the ship, the subdivision of such compartment may be governed by an increased factor, which, however, shall not exceed ·40.

(*b.*) *The subdivision abaft the fore peak* of ships less than 430 feet (131 metres) but not less than 260 feet (79 metres) in length having a criterion numeral equal to S, where $S = \dfrac{9382 - 20L}{34}$ (L in feet) $= \dfrac{3574 - 25L}{13}$ (L in metres) shall be governed by the factor unity; of those having a criterion numeral of 123 or more by the factor B given by the formula (ii); of those having a criterion numeral between S and 123 by the factor F obtained by linear interpolation between unity and the factor B, using the formula:—

$$F = 1 - \frac{(1-B)\,(C_s - S)}{123 - S} \quad \dotfill \quad \text{(vi)}$$

(*c.*) *The subdivision abaft the fore peak* of ships less than 430 feet (131 metres) but not less than 260 feet (79 metres) in length and having a criterion numeral less than S, and of all ships less than 260 feet (79 metres) in length shall be governed by the factor unity, unless it is shown to the satisfaction of the Administration to be impracticable to comply with this factor in any part of the ship, in which case, the Administration may allow such relaxation as may appear to be justified, having regard to all the circumstances.

(*d.*) The provisions of sub-paragraph (*c*) shall apply also to ships of whatever length, which are to be certified to carry a number of passengers exceeding 12 but not exceeding $\dfrac{L^2(\text{in feet})}{7000} \left(\dfrac{L^2(\text{in metres})}{650} \right)$ or 50, whichever is the less.

REGULATION V

Special Rules concerning Subdivision

(1.) A compartment may exceed the permissible length determined by the rules of Regulation IV provided the combined length of each pair of adjacent compartments to which the compartment in question is common does not exceed either the floodable length or twice the permissible length, whichever is the less.

If one of the two adjacent compartments is situated inside the machinery space, and the second is situated outside the machinery space, and the average permeability of the portion of the ship in which the second is situated differs from that of the machinery space, the combined length of the two compartments shall be adjusted to the mean average permeability of the two portions of the ship in which the compartments are situated.

Where the two adjacent compartments have different factors of subdivision, the combined length of the two compartments shall be determined proportionately.

(2.) In ships 430 feet (131 metres) in length and upwards, one of the main transverse bulkheads abaft the fore peak shall be fitted at a distance from the forward perpendicular which is not greater than the permissible length.

(3.) A main transverse bulkhead may be recessed provided that all parts of the recess lie inboard of vertical surfaces on both sides of the ship, situated at a distance from the shell plating equal to one-fifth the breadth of the ship, as defined in Regulation I (3), and measured at right angles to the centreline at the level of the deepest subdivision loadline.

Any part of a recess which lies outside these limits shall be dealt with as a step in accordance with the following paragraph.

(4.) A main transverse bulkhead may be stepped provided that—

(a) the combined length of the two compartments, separated by the bulkhead in question, does not exceed 90 per cent. of the floodable length, or

(b) additional subdivision is provided in way of the step to maintain the same measure of safety as that secured by a plane bulkhead.

(5.) Where a main transverse bulkhead is recessed or stepped, an equivalent plane bulkhead shall be used in determining the subdivision.

(6.) If the distance between two adjacent main transverse bulkheads, or their equivalent plane bulkheads, or the distance between the transverse planes passing through the nearest stepped portions of the bulkheads, is less than 10 feet (3·05 metres) plus 2 per cent. of the length of the ship, only one of these bulkheads shall be regarded as forming part of the subdivision of the ship in accordance with the provisions of Regulation IV.

(7.) Where a main transverse watertight compartment contains local subdivision and it can be shown to the satisfaction of the Administration that, after any assumed side damage extending over a length of 10 feet (3·05 metres) plus 2 per cent. of the length of the ship, the whole volume of the main compartment will not be flooded, a proportionate allowance may be made in the permissible length otherwise required for such compartment.

In such a case the volume of effective buoyancy assumed on the undamaged side shall not be greater than that assumed on the damaged side.

(8.) Where it is proposed to fit watertight decks, inner skins or longitudinal bulkheads, watertight or non-watertight, the Administration shall be satisfied that the safety of the ship will not be diminished in any respect, particularly having in view the possible listing effect of flooding in way of such structural arrangements.

Regulation VI

Peak and Machinery Space Bulkheads, Shaft Tunnels, &c.

(1.) Every ship shall have a forepeak or collision bulkhead, which shall be watertight up to the bulkhead deck. This bulkhead shall be fitted not less than 5 per cent. of the length of the ship, and not more than 10 feet (3·05 metres) plus 5 per cent. of the length of the ship from the forward perpendicular.

If the ship has a long forward superstructure, the forepeak bulkhead shall be extended weathertight to the deck next above the bulkhead deck. The extension need not be fitted directly over the bulkhead below, provided it is at least 5 per cent. of the length of the ship from the forward perpendicular, and the part of the bulkhead deck which forms the step is made effectively weathertight.

(2.) An afterpeak bulkhead, and bulkheads dividing the machinery space, as defined in Regulation I (8), from the cargo and passenger spaces forward and aft, shall also be fitted and made watertight up to the bulkhead deck. The afterpeak bulkhead may, however, be stopped below the bulkhead deck, provided the degree of safety of the ship as regards subdivision is not thereby diminished.

(3.) In all cases stern tubes shall be enclosed in watertight spaces. The stern gland shall be situated within a watertight shaft tunnel or other space of such volume that if flooded by leakage through the stern gland the margin line will not be submerged.

Regulation VII

Assigning, Marking and Recording of Subdivision Loadlines

(1.) The subdivision loadlines assigned and marked under the provisions of Article 5 of the Convention shall be recorded in the Safety Certificate, and shall be distinguished by the notation C.1 for the principal passenger condition, and C.2, C.3, &c., for the alternative conditions.

(2.) The freeboard corresponding to each of these loadlines inserted in the Safety Certificate shall be measured at the same position and from the same deck line as the freeboards determined by recognised national Freeboard Regulations.

(3.) In no case shall any subdivision loadline mark be placed above the deepest loadline in salt water as determined by the strength of the ship and/or recognised national Freeboard Regulations.

(4.) Whatever may be the position of the subdivision loadline marks, a ship shall in no case be loaded so as to submerge the loadline mark appropriate to the season and locality as determined by the recognised national Freeboard Regulations.

Regulation VIII

Construction and Initial Testing of Watertight Bulkheads, &c.

(1.) Watertight subdivision bulkheads, whether transverse or longitudinal, shall be constructed in such a manner that they shall be capable of supporting with a proper margin of resistance, the pressure due to a head of water up to the margin line in way of each bulkhead. The construction of these bulkheads shall be to the satisfaction of the Administration.

(2.) Steps and recesses in bulkheads shall be watertight and as strong as the bulkhead at the place where each occurs.

Where frames or beams pass through a watertight deck or bulkhead, such deck or bulkhead shall be made structurally watertight without the use of wood or cement.

(3.) Testing main compartments by filling them with water is not compulsory. A complete examination of the bulkheads shall be made by a surveyor; and, in addition, a hose test shall be made in all cases.

(4.) The forepeak shall be tested with water to a head up to the deepest subdivision loadline.

(5.) Double bottoms, including duct keels, and inner skins are to be subjected to a head of water up to the margin line.

(6.) Tanks which are intended to hold liquids, and which form part of the subdivision of the ship, shall be tested for tightness with water to a head up to the deepest subdivision loadline or to a head corresponding to two-thirds of the depth from the top of keel to the margin line in way of the tanks, whichever is the greater; provided that in no case shall the test head be less than 3 feet ($\cdot$92 metre) above the top of the tank.

Regulation IX

Openings in Watertight Bulkheads

(1.) The number of openings in watertight bulkheads shall be reduced to the minimum compatible with the design and proper working of the ship; satisfactory means shall be provided for closing these openings.

(2.)—(*a*.) Where pipes, scuppers, electric-light cables, &c., are carried through watertight subdivision bulkheads, arrangements shall be made to ensure the integrity of the watertightness of the bulkheads.

(*b*.) Sluice valves shall not be permitted in the watertight subdivision bulkheads.

(3.)—(*a*.) No doors, manholes, or access openings are permitted—

(i) in the collision bulkhead below the margin line;

(ii) in watertight transverse bulkheads dividing a cargo space from an adjoining cargo space or from a permanent or reserve bunker, except as provided in paragraph (7).

(*b.*) The collision bulkhead may be pierced below the margin line by not more than one pipe for dealing with fluid in the fore peak tank, provided that the pipe is fitted with a screwdown valve capable of being operated from above the bulkhead deck, the valve chest being secured inside the fore peak to the collision bulkhead.

(4.)—(*a.*) Watertight doors fitted in bulkheads between permanent and reserve bunkers, shall be always accessible, except as provided in sub-paragraph 9 (*b*) for between deck bunker doors.

(*b.*) Satisfactory arrangements shall be made by means of screens or otherwise, to prevent the coal from interfering with the closing of watertight bunker doors.

(5.) Within the machinery space and apart from bunker and shaft tunnel doors, not more than one door may be fitted in each main transverse bulkhead for intercommunication. These doors shall be located so as to have the sills as high as practicable.

(6.)—(*a.*) The only types of watertight doors permissible are hinged doors, sliding doors, and doors of other equivalent patterns, excluding plate doors secured only by bolts.

(*b.*) A hinged door shall be fitted with catches workable from each side of the bulkhead.

(*c.*) A sliding door may have a horizontal or vertical motion. If required to be hand operated only, the gearing shall be capable of being worked at the door itself and also at an accessible position above the bulkhead deck.

(*d.*) If a door is required to be closed by dropping or by the action of a dropping weight, it shall be fitted with a suitable arrangement to regulate the closing movement, and the gearing shall be so arranged that the door can be released both at the door itself and at an accessible position above the bulkhead deck. Hand gear shall also be provided, so arranged as to operate at the door itself and above the bulkhead deck, and also, so that after being disengaged for dropping, it can be quickly re-engaged from either the upper or the lower position.

(*e.*) If a door is required to be power operated from a central control, the gearing shall be so arranged that the door can be operated by power also at the door itself. The arrangements shall be such that the door will close automatically if opened by the local control after being closed from the central control, and also such that any door can be kept closed by local arrangements, which will prevent that door from being opened from the central control. Such power operated doors shall be provided with hand gear, workable both at the door itself and from an accessible position above the bulkhead deck.

(*f.*) In all classes of doors indicators shall be fitted at all operating stations other than at the door itself, showing whether the door is opened or closed.

(7.)—(*a.*) Hinged watertight doors in passenger, crew, and working spaces are only permitted above a deck, the underside of which, at its lowest point at side, is at least 7 feet (2·13 metres) above the deepest subdivision loadline, and they are not permitted in those spaces below such deck.

(b.) Hinged watertight doors of satisfactory construction may be fitted in bulkheads dividing cargo between deck spaces, in levels in which side cargo doors would be permitted under the provisions of Regulation X (11). These doors shall be closed before the voyage commences and shall be kept closed during the voyage, and the time of opening such doors in port and of closing them before the ship leaves port shall be entered in the official log book. Where it is proposed to fit such doors, the number and arrangements shall receive the special consideration of the Administration, and a statement shall be required from the owners certifying as to the absolute necessity of such doors.

(8.) All other watertight doors shall be sliding doors.

(9.)—(a.) When any watertight doors which may be sometimes opened at sea, excluding those at the entrances of tunnels, are fitted in the main transverse watertight bulkheads at such a height that their sills are below the deepest subdivision loadline, the following rules shall apply:—

(I.) When the number of such doors exceeds 5 all the watertight sliding doors shall be power operated and shall be capable of being simultaneously closed from a station situated on the bridge, simultaneous closing of these doors being preceded by a warning sound signal.

(II.) When the number of such doors does not exceed 5—

(i) if the criterion numeral does not exceed 30, all the watertight sliding doors may be operated by hand only;

(ii) if the criterion numeral exceeds 30, but does not exceed 60, all the watertight sliding doors may be either dropping doors fitted with releasing and hand gear operated at the door and from above the bulkhead deck or doors operated by power.

(iii) if the criterion numeral exceeds 60, all the watertight sliding doors shall be operated by power.

(b.) If watertight doors which have sometimes to be open at sea for the purpose of trimming coal are fitted between bunkers in the between-decks below the bulkhead deck, these doors shall be operated by power. The opening and closing of these doors shall be recorded in the official log book.

(c.) When trunkways in connection with refrigerated cargo are carried through more than one main transverse watertight bulkhead, and the sills of the openings are less than 7 feet (2·13 metres) above the deepest subdivision loadline, the watertight doors at such openings shall be operated by power.

(10.) Portable plates on bulkheads shall not be permitted except in machinery spaces. Such plates shall always be in place before the ship leaves port, and shall not be removed at sea except in case of urgent necessity. The necessary precautions shall be taken in replacing them to ensure that the joints shall be watertight.

(11.) All watertight doors shall be kept closed during navigation except when necessarily opened for the working of the ship, and shall always be ready to be immediately closed.

(12.) Where trunkways or tunnels for access from crew's accommodation to the stokehold, for piping, or for any other purpose are carried through main transverse watertight bulkheads, they shall be watertight and in accordance with the requirements of Regulation XII. The access to at least one end of each such tunnel or trunkway, if used as a passage at sea, shall be through a trunk extending watertight to a height sufficient to permit access above the margin line. The access to the other end of the trunkway or tunnel may be through a watertight door of the type required by its location in the ship. Such trunkways or tunnels shall not extend through the first subdivision bulkhead abaft the collision bulkhead.

Where it is proposed to fit tunnels or trunkways for forced draft, piercing main transverse watertight bulkheads, these shall receive the special consideration of the Administration.

REGULATION X

Openings in Ship's Sides below the Margin Line

(1.) The arrangement and efficiency of the means for closing any opening in the ship's sides shall be consistent with its intended purpose and the position in which it is fitted and generally to the satisfaction of the Administration.

(2.)—(a.) If in a between decks, the sills of any sidescuttles are below a line drawn parallel to the bulkhead deck at side and having its lowest point 2½ per cent. of the breadth of the ship above the deepest subdivision loadline, all sidescuttles in that between deck shall be of a non-opening type.

(b.) If in a between decks, the sills of any sidescuttles other than those required to be of a non-opening type by sub-paragraph (a) are below a line drawn parallel to the bulkhead deck at side and having its lowest point at a height of 12 feet (3·66 metres) plus 2½ per cent. of the breadth of the ship above the deepest subdivision loadline, all sidescuttles in that between decks shall be of such construction as will effectively prevent any person opening them without the consent of the master of the ship.

(c.) Other sidescuttles may be of an ordinary opening type.

(d.) If in a between decks, the sills of any of the sidescuttles referred to in sub-paragraph (b) are below a line drawn parallel to the bulkhead deck at side and having its lowest point 4½ feet (1·37 metres), plus 2½ per cent. of the breadth of the ship above the loadline at which the ship is floating on her departure from any port, all the sidescuttles in that between decks shall be closed watertight and locked before the ship leaves port and they shall not be opened during navigation.

The time of opening such sidescuttles in port and of closing and locking them before the ship leaves port shall be entered in the official log book.

The Administration may indicate the limiting mean draught at which these sidescuttles will have their sills above the line defined in this paragraph and at which it will be permissible to open them at sea on the responsibility of the master. In tropical waters in fair weather this limiting draught may be increased by 1 foot (·305 metres).

(3.) Efficient hinged inside deadlights arranged so that they can be easily and effectively closed and secured watertight shall be fitted to all sidescuttles—

(a) which are required to be of a non-opening type;

(b) which are to be fitted within one-eighth of the ship's length of the forward perpendicular;

(c) which are to be fitted in positions defined in sub-paragraph (2) (b);

(d) which will not be accessible during navigation;

(e) which are to be fitted in spaces intended for the accommodation of sailors and firemen;

(f) which are to be fitted in spaces intended for the accommodation of steerage passengers.

(4.) Sidescuttles fitted below the bulkhead deck, other than those referred to in the preceding paragraph, shall be fitted with efficient inside deadlights which may be portable and stowed adjacent to the sidescuttles.

(5.) Sidescuttles and their deadlights, which will not be accessible during navigation, shall be closed and secured before the ship proceeds to sea.

(6.) No sidescuttles shall be fitted in any spaces which are appropriated exclusively to the carriage of cargo or coal.

(7.) Automatic ventilating sidescuttles shall not be fitted in the ship's sides below the margin line without the special sanction of the Administration.

(8.) All machinery and other inlets and discharges in the ship's sides shall be arranged so as to prevent the accidental admission of water into the ship.

(9.) The number of scuppers, sanitary discharges and other similar openings in the ship's sides shall be reduced to the minimum either by making each discharge serve for as many as possible of the sanitary and other pipes, or in any other satisfactory manner.

(10.) Discharges led through the ship's sides from spaces below the margin line shall be fitted with efficient and accessible means for preventing water from passing inboard. It is permissible to have for each separate discharge either one automatic non-return valve fitted with a positive means of closing it from above the bulkhead deck, or, alternatively, two automatic non-return valves without such means, the upper of which valves is so situated above the deepest subdivision loadline as to be always accessible for examination under service conditions.

Where a positive action valve is fitted, the operating position above the bulkhead deck shall always be readily accessible and means shall be provided for indicating whether the valve is open or closed.

(11.) Gangway, cargo and coaling ports fitted below the margin line shall be of sufficient strength. They shall be effectively closed and secured watertight before the ship leaves port, and shall be kept closed during navigation.

Cargo and coaling ports which are to be fitted partly or entirely below the deepest subdivision loadline shall receive the special consideration of the Administration.

(12.) The inboard opening of each ash-shoot, rubbish-shoot, &c., shall be fitted with an efficient cover.

If the inboard opening is situated below the margin line, the cover shall be watertight, and in addition an automatic non-return valve shall be fitted in the shoot in an easily accessible position above the deepest subdivision loadline. When the shoot is not in use both the cover and the valve shall be kept closed and secured.

REGULATION XI

Construction and Initial Tests of Watertight Doors, Sidescuttles, &c.

(1.) The design, materials and construction of all watertight doors, sidescuttles, gangway, cargo and coaling ports, valves, pipes, ash-shoots and rubbish-shoots referred to in these Regulations shall be to the satisfaction of the Administration.

(2.) Each watertight door shall be tested by water pressure to a head up to the margin line. The test shall be made before the ship is put in service, either before or after the door is fitted.

REGULATION XII

Construction and Initial Tests of Watertight Decks, Trunks, &c.

(1.) Watertight decks, trunks, tunnels, duct keels and ventilators shall be of the same strength as watertight bulkheads at corresponding levels. The means used for making them watertight, and the arrangements adopted for closing openings in them, shall be to the satisfaction of the Administration. Watertight ventilators and trunks shall be carried at least up to the margin line.

(2.) After completion a hose or flooding test shall be applied to watertight decks and a hose test to watertight trunks, tunnels and ventilators.

REGULATION XIII

Periodical Operation and Inspection of Watertight Doors, &c.

In all new and existing ships drills for the operating of watertight doors, sidescuttles, valves, and closing mechanisms of scuppers, ash-shoots and rubbish-shoots, shall take place weekly. In ships in which the voyage exceeds one week in duration a complete drill shall be held before leaving port, and others thereafter at least once a week during the voyage, provided that all watertight power doors and hinged doors, in main transverse bulkheads, in use at sea shall be operated daily.

The watertight doors and all mechanisms and indicators connected therewith, and all valves the closing of which is necessary to make a compartment watertight, shall be periodically inspected at sea, at least once a week.

REGULATION XIV

Entries in the Official Log Book

In all new and existing ships hinged doors, portable plates, sidescuttles, gangway, cargo and coaling ports and other openings, which are required by these Regulations to be kept closed during navigation, shall be closed before the ship leaves port. The time of closing, and the time of opening (if permissible under these Regulations), shall be recorded in the official log book.

A record of all drills and inspections required by Regulation XIII shall be entered in the official log book with an explicit record of any defects which may be disclosed.

REGULATION XV

Double Bottoms

(1.) In ships 200 feet (61 metres) and under 249 feet (76 metres) in length a double bottom shall be fitted at least from the machinery space to the fore peak bulkhead, or as near thereto as practicable.

(2.) In ships 249 feet (76 metres) and under 330 feet (100 metres) in length a double bottom shall be fitted at least outside the machinery space, and shall extend to the fore and after peak bulkheads, or as near thereto as practicable.

(3.) In ships 330 feet (100 metres) in length and upwards a double bottom shall be fitted amidships, and shall extend to the fore and after peak bulkheads, or as near thereto as practicable.

(4.) Where a double bottom is required to be fitted the inner bottom shall be continued out to the ship's sides in such a manner as to protect the bottom to the turn of bilge.

Such protection will be deemed satisfactory if the line of intersection of the outer edge of the margin plate with the bilge plating is not lower at any part than a horizontal plane passing through the point of intersection with the frame line amidships of a transverse diagonal line inclined at 25 degrees to the base line and cutting it at a point one-half the ship's moulded breadth from the middle line.

(5.) Wells constructed in the double bottom in connection with the drainage arrangements shall not extend downwards more than necessary, nor shall they be less than 18 inches (457 millimetres) from the outer bottom or from the inner edge of the margin plate. A well extending to the outer bottom is, however, permitted at the after end of the shaft tunnel of screw ships.

REGULATION XVI

Fire-resisting Bulkheads

Ships shall be fitted above the bulkhead deck with fire-resisting bulkheads which shall be continuous from side to side of the ship and arranged to the satisfaction of the Administration.

They shall be constructed of metal or other fire-resisting material, effective to prevent for one hour, under the conditions for which the bulkheads are to be fitted in the ship, the spread of fire generating a temperature of 1,500° F. (815° C.) at the bulkhead.

Steps and recesses and the means for closing all openings in these bulkheads shall be fire-resisting and flametight.

The mean distance between any two adjacent fire-resisting bulkheads in any superstructure shall in general not exceed 131 feet (40 metres).

REGULATION XVII

Side and other Openings, &c., above the Margin Line

(1.) Sidescuttles, gangway, cargo and coaling ports, and other means for closing openings in the ship's sides above the margin line shall be of efficient design and construction and of sufficient strength having regard to the spaces in which they are fitted and their positions relative to the deepest subdivision loadline.

(2.) The bulkhead deck or a deck above it shall be weathertight in the sense that in ordinary sea conditions water will not penetrate in a downward direction. All openings in the exposed weather deck shall have coamings of ample height and strength, and shall be provided with efficient means for expeditiously closing them weathertight.

(3.) Freeing ports and/or scuppers shall be fitted as necessary for rapidly clearing the weather deck of water under all weather conditions.

REGULATION XVIII

Exits from Watertight Compartments

(1.) In passenger and crew spaces, practicable means of exit to the open deck shall be provided for the occupants from each watertight compartment.

(2.) Practicable means of escape for the crew shall be provided from each engine room, shaft tunnel, stokehold compartment, and other working spaces, independent of watertight doors.

REGULATION XIX

Pumping Arrangements

Steamships.

(1.) Ships shall be provided with an efficient pumping plant capable of pumping from and draining any watertight compartment under all practicable conditions after a casualty whether the ship is upright or listed. For this purpose wing suctions will generally be necessary except in narrow compartments at the ends of the ship. Where close ceiling is fitted over the bilges, arrangements shall be made whereby water in the compartment may find its way to the suction pipes. Efficient means shall be provided for draining water from insulated holds.

(2.) In addition to the ordinary bilge pump, worked by the main engines, or its equivalent engine room pump, two independent power bilge pumps shall be provided, except that in ships less than 300 feet (91 · 5 metres) in length, having a criterion numeral less than 30, either two efficient hand pumps of the crank type fitted one forward and one aft, or a portable power pump, may be substituted for one of the additional independent power bilge pumps.

In all cases an additional independent power pump shall be fitted when the criterion numeral exceeds 30.[10]

Sanitary, ballast and general service pumps may be accepted as independent power bilge pumps if fitted with the necessary connections to the bilge pumping system.

(3.) Where two or more independent power pumps are required, the arrangement shall be such that at least one power pump will be available for use in all ordinary circumstances in which a vessel may be flooded at sea. One of the power pumps shall, therefore, be an emergency pump of a reliable submersible type. A source of power situated above the bulkhead deck shall be available for this pump in any case of emergency.

(4.) Where practicable, the power bilge pumps shall be placed in separate watertight compartments so arranged or situated that these compartments

---

[10] This paragraph was inadvertently omitted from the regulations annexed to the original convention. In a note dated Dec. 31, 1930, the British Ambassador at Washington inquired whether the United States would concur in a proposal made by the British Board of Trade that the convention be amended by inserting this paragraph. A statement by the British Secretary of State for Foreign Affairs dated Jan. 17, 1933, certified that the proposed insertion had been accepted by the contracting governments and declared that the convention was regarded as modified accordingly. The President submitted the amendment to the Senate Apr. 15, 1937 (S. Ex. I, 75th Cong., 1st sess.); the Senate gave its advice and consent to ratification May 28, 1937; it was ratified by the President June 9, 1937, and proclaimed Sept. 3, 1937 (51 Stat. 13; TS 921).

will not readily be flooded by the same damage. If the engines and boilers are in two or more watertight compartments, the pumps available for bilge service shall be distributed through these compartments as far as is possible.

(5.) With the exception of pumps which may be provided for peak compartments only, each bilge pump, whether operated by hand or by power, shall be arranged to draw water from any hold or machinery compartment in the ship.

(6.) Each independent power bilge pump shall be capable of giving a speed of water through the main bilge pipe of not less than 400 feet (122 metres) per minute, and it shall have a separate direct suction, to the compartment in which it is situated, of a diameter not less than that of the bilge main. The direct suctions from each independent power bilge pump shall be arranged to pump from either side of the ship.

(7.) Main circulating pumps shall have direct suction connections, provided with non-return valves, to the lowest drainage level in the machinery space, and of a diameter at least two-thirds that of the main sea inlet. Where the fuel is, or may be, coal, and there is no watertight bulkhead between the engines and boilers, a direct discharge overboard shall be fitted from at least one circulating pump, or, alternatively, a bye-pass may be fitted to the circulating discharge.

(8.)—(a.) All pipes from the pumps which are required for draining cargo or machinery spaces shall be entirely distinct from pipes which may be used for filling or emptying spaces where water or oil is carried.

(b.) Lead pipes shall not be used under coal bunkers or oil fuel storage tanks, nor in boiler or machinery spaces, including motor rooms in which oil settling tanks or oil fuel pump units are situated.

(9.) The Administration shall make rules relating to the diameters of the bilge main and branch pipes which shall be proportioned respectively in relation to the size of the ship and the sizes of the compartments to be drained.

(10.) The arrangement of the bilge and ballast pumping system shall be such as to prevent the possibility of water passing from the sea and from water ballast spaces into the cargo and machinery spaces, or from one compartment to another. Special provision shall be made to prevent any deep tank having bilge and ballast connections being inadvertently run up from the sea when containing cargo, or pumped out through a bilge pipe when containing water ballast.

(11.) Provision shall be made to prevent the compartment served by any bilge suction pipe being flooded, in the event of the pipe being severed or otherwise damaged, by collision or grounding, in any other compartment. For this purpose, where the pipe is at any part situated near the side of the ship or in a duct keel, there shall be fitted to the pipe in the compartment containing the open end either a non-return valve, or a screw-down valve which can be operated from a position above the bulkhead deck.

(12.) All distribution boxes, cocks and valves in connection with the bilge pumping arrangement shall be in positions which are accessible at all times under ordinary circumstances. They shall be so arranged that in the event of flooding the emergency bilge pump may be operative on any compartment. If there is only one system of pipes common to all the pumps, the necessary cocks or valves for controlling the bilge suctions must be workable from above the bulkhead deck. If in addition to the main bilge pumping system an emergency bilge pumping system is provided, it shall be independent of the main system and so arranged that the emergency pump is capable of operating on any compartment under flooding conditions.

Motor Ships.

(13.) The bilge pumping arrangements in motor ships shall, so far as practicable, be equivalent to those required for steamships of similar size, except as regards main circulating pumps.

REGULATION XX

Power for Going Astern

Ships shall have sufficient power for going astern to secure proper control of the ship in all circumstances.

REGULATION XXI

Auxiliary Steering Apparatus

Ships shall be provided with an auxiliary steering apparatus which, however, may be of less power than the main apparatus, and need not be worked by steam or other mechanical power, provided adequate arrangements for manual operation are practicable. A duplicate main steering power plant shall be considered as an auxiliary steering apparatus within the meaning of this Regulation.

REGULATION XXII

Initial and Subsequent Surveys of Ships

(1.) Every new or existing ship shall be subjected to the surveys specified below:—

(a.) A survey before the ship is put in service.

(b.) A periodical survey once every twelve months.

(c.) Additional surveys, as occasion arises.

219-916—69——54

(2.) The surveys referred to above shall be carried out as follows:—

(a.) *The survey before the ship is put in service* shall include a complete inspection of the hull, machinery and equipments, including the outside of the ship's bottom and the inside and outside of the boilers. This survey shall be such as to ensure that the arrangements, material, and scantlings of the hull, boilers, and their appurtenances, main and auxiliary machinery-life-saving appliances, and other equipments, fully comply with the requirements of the present Convention and of the detailed regulations promulgated as a result thereof by the Government of the country to which the ship belongs for ships of the service for which it is intended. The survey shall also be such as to ensure that the workmanship of all parts of the ship and its equipments is in all respects satisfactory.

(b.) *The periodical survey* shall include an inspection of the whole of the hull, boilers, machinery, and equipments, including the outside of the ship's bottom. The survey shall be such as to ensure that the ship, as regards the hull, boilers, and their appurtenances, main and auxiliary machinery, life-saving appliances, and other equipments, is in satisfactory condition and fit for the service for which it is intended, and that it complies with the requirements of the present Convention, and of the detailed regulations promulgated as a result thereof by the Government of the country to which the ship belongs.

(c.) *A survey, either general or partial,* according to the circumstances, shall be made every time an accident occurs or a defect is discovered which affects the safety of the ship or the efficiency or completeness of its life-saving appliances or other equipments, or whenever any important repairs or renewals are made. The survey shall be such as to ensure that the necessary repairs or renewals have been effectively made, that the material and workmanship of such repairs or renewals are in all respects satisfactory, and that the ship complies in all respects with the provisions of the present Convention and of the detailed regulations promulgated as a result thereof by the Government of the country to which the ship belongs.

(3.) The detailed regulations referred to in sub-paragraph (2) shall prescribe the requirements to be observed as to the initial and subsequent hydraulic tests to which the main and auxiliary boilers, connections, steam-pipes, high-pressure receivers, and fuel tanks for oil motors are to be submitted, including the test pressure to be applied, and the intervals between two consecutive tests.

Main and auxiliary boilers, connections, tanks and receivers, also steam-piping of more than 3 inches (76 millimetres) internal diameter shall be satisfactorily tested by hydraulic pressure when new. Steam pipes of more than 3 inches (76 millimetres) internal diameter shall be tested by hydraulic pressure periodically.

Regulation XXIII

Maintenance of Conditions after Survey

After the survey of the ship as provided in Regulation XXII has been completed no change shall be made in the structural arrangements, machinery, equipments, &c., covered by the survey, without the sanction of the Administration.

LIFE SAVING APPLIANCES, &C

Regulation XXIV

Standard Types of Boats

The standard types of boats are classified as follows:—

Class I.—Open boats with rigid sides having either (a) internal buoyancy only, or (b) internal and external buoyancy.

Class II.—(a) Open boats with internal and external buoyancy—upper parts of sides collapsible, and (b) decked boats with either fixed or collapsible watertight bulwarks.

No boat may be approved the buoyancy of which depends upon the previous adjustment of one of the principal parts of the hull, or which has not a cubic capacity of at least 3.5 cubic metres (equivalent to 125 cubic feet).

No boat may be approved the weight of which when fully laden with persons and equipment exceeds 20,300 kilogrammes (equivalent to 20 tons).

Regulation XXV

Lifeboats of Class I

Lifeboats of Class I must have a mean sheer at least equal to four per cent. of their length.

The air cases of lifeboats of Class I shall be so placed as to secure stability when fully laden under adverse weather conditions.

In boats certified to carry 100 or more persons the volume of the buoyancy shall be increased to the satisfaction of the Administration.

Lifeboats of Class I must also satisfy the following conditions:—

(a.) Lifeboats with Internal Buoyancy only.

The buoyancy of a wooden boat of this type shall be provided by watertight air-cases, the total volume of which shall be at least equal to one-tenth of the cubic capacity of the boat.

The buoyancy of a metal boat of this type shall not be less than that required above for a wooden boat of the same cubic capacity, the volume of watertight air-cases being increased accordingly.

(b.) Lifeboats with Internal and External Buoyancy.

The internal buoyancy of a wooden boat of this type shall be provided by watertight air-cases, the total volume of which is at least equal to seven and a half per cent. of the cubic capacity of the boat.

The external buoyancy may be of cork or of any other equally efficient material, but such buoyancy shall not be obtained by the use of rushes, cork shavings, loose granulated cork or any other loose granulated substance, or by any means dependent upon inflation by air.

If the buoyancy is of cork, its volume, for a wooden boat, shall not be less than thirty-three thousandths of the cubic capacity of the boat; if of any material other than cork, its volume and distribution shall be such that the buoyancy and stability of the boat are not less than that of a similar boat provided with buoyancy of cork.

The buoyancy of a metal boat shall be not less than that required above for a wooden boat of the same cubic capacity, the volume of the watertight air-cases and that of the external buoyancy being increased accordingly.

REGULATION XXVI

Boats of Class II

Boats of Class II must satisfy the following conditions:—

(a.) Open Boats with Internal and External Buoyancy—Upper Part of Sides collapsible.

A boat of this type shall be fitted both with watertight air-cases and with external buoyancy the aggregate volume of which, for each person which the boat is able to accommodate, shall be at least equal to the following amounts:—

	Cubic Decimetres	Cubic Feet
Air-cases	43	1. 5
External buoyancy (if of cork)	6	0. 2

The external buoyancy may be of cork or of any other equally efficient material, but such buoyancy shall not be obtained by the use of rushes, cork shavings, loose granulated cork, or any other loose granulated substance, or by any means dependent upon inflation by air.

If of any material other than cork, its volume and distribution shall be such that the buoyancy and stability of the boat are not less than that of a similar boat provided with buoyancy of cork.

A metal boat of this type shall be provided with internal and external buoyancy to ensure that the buoyancy of the boat shall be at least equal to that of a wooden boat.

The minimum freeboard of boats of this type shall be fixed in relation to their length; and it shall be measured vertically to the top of the solid hull at the side amidships, from the water-level, when the boat is loaded.

The freeboard in fresh water shall not be less than the following amounts:—

Length of Lifeboat		Minimum Freeboard	
Metres	Equivalent in Feet to—	Millimetres	Equivalent in Inches to—
7.90	26	200	8
8.50	28	225	9
9.15	30	250	10

The freeboard of boats of intermediate lengths is to be found by interpolation.

The collapsible sides must be watertight.

(b.) Decked Boats with either Fixed or Collapsible Watertight Bulwarks.

(i.) *Decked Boats having a Well Deck.*—The area of the well deck of a boat of this type shall be at least 30 per cent. of the total deck area. The height of the well deck above the water-line at all points shall be at least equal to one-half per cent. of the length of the boat, this height being increased to one-and-a-half per cent. of the length of the boat at the ends of the well.

The freeboard of a boat of this type shall be such as to provide for a reserve buoyancy of at least 35 per cent.

(ii.) *Decked Boats Having a Flush Deck.*—The minimum freeboard of boats of this type is independent of their lengths and depends only upon their depths. The depth of the boat is to be measured vertically from the underside of the garboard strake to the top of the deck at the side amidships and the freeboard is to be measured from the top of the deck at the side amidships to the water-level when the boat is loaded.

The freeboard in fresh water shall not be less than the following amounts, which are applicable without correction to boats having a mean sheer equal to three per cent. of their length:—

Depth of Lifeboat		Minimum Freeboard	
Millimetres	Equivalent in Inches to—	Millimetres	Equivalent in Inches to—
310	12	70	$2\frac{3}{4}$
460	18	95	$3\frac{3}{4}$
610	24	130	$5\frac{1}{8}$
760	30	165	$6\frac{1}{2}$

For intermediate depths the freeboard is obtained by interpolation.

If the sheer is less than the standard sheer defined above, the minimum freeboard is obtained by adding to the figures in the table one-seventh of the difference between the standard sheer and the actual mean sheer measured at the stem and stern post; no deduction is to be made from the freeboard on account of the sheer being greater than the standard sheer or on account of the camber of the deck.

(iii.) All decked lifeboats shall be fitted with efficient means for clearing the deck of water.

Regulation XXVII

Motor Boats

A motor boat carried as part of the lifesaving appliances of a vessel, whether required by Regulation XXXVI (2) or not, shall comply with the following conditions:—

(*a.*) It shall comply with the requirements for a lifeboat of Class I, and proper appliances shall be provided for putting it into the water speedily.

(*b.*) It shall be adequately provided with fuel, and kept so as to be at all times ready for use.

(*c.*) The motor and its accessories shall be suitably enclosed to ensure operation under adverse weather conditions, and provision shall be made for going astern.

(*d.*) The speed shall be at least six knots when fully loaded in smooth water.

The volume of the internal buoyancy and, where fitted, the external buoyancy shall be increased in sufficient proportion to compensate for the difference between the weight of the motor, the searchlight, and the wireless telegraph installation and their accessories, and the weight of the additional persons which the boat could accommodate if the motor, the searchlight and the wireless telegraph installation and their accessories were removed.

Regulation XXVIII

Life Rafts

No type of life raft may be approved unless it satifies the following conditions:—

(*a.*) It shall be of approved material and construction;

(*b.*) It shall be effective and stable when floating either way up;

(*c.*) It shall be fitted with fixed or collapsible bulwarks of wood, canvas or other suitable material on both sides;

(*d.*) It shall have a line securely becketed round the outside;

(*e.*) It shall be of such strength that it can be launched or thrown from the vessel's deck without being damaged, and if to be thrown it shall be of such size and weight that it can be easily handled;

(*f.*) It shall have not less than 85 cubic decimetres (equivalent to three cubic feet) of air-cases or equivalent buoyancy for each person to be carried thereon;

(*g.*) It shall have a deck area of not less than 3,720 square centimetres (equivalent to four square feet) for each person to be carried thereon, and it shall effectively support the occupants out of the water;

(*h.*) The air-cases or equivalent buoyancy shall be placed as near as possible to the sides of the life raft, and such buoyancy shall not be by any means dependent on inflation by air.

REGULATION XXIX

Buoyant Apparatus

Buoyant apparatus, whether buoyant deck seats, buoyant deck chairs or other buoyant apparatus, shall be deemed sufficient, so far as buoyancy is concerned, for a person or number of persons to be ascertained by dividing the number of kilogrammes of iron which it is capable of supporting in fresh water by 14·5 (equivalent to the number of pounds divided by 32), and if the apparatus depends for its buoyancy on air it shall not require to be inflated before use in an emergency.

The number of persons for whom the apparatus is deemed suitable shall be determined by the least of the numbers ascertained either as above or by the number of 30·5 centimetres (equivalent to one foot) in the perimeter.

Such approved buoyant apparatus shall comply with the following conditions:—

1. It shall be constructed with proper workmanship and materials.

2. It shall be effective and stable when floating either way up.

3. It shall be of such size, strength and weight that it can be handled without mechanical appliances and, if necessary, thrown without damage from the vessel's deck on which it is stowed.

4. The air-cases or equivalent buoyancy shall be placed as near as possible to the sides of the apparatus.

5. It shall have a line securely becketed round the outside of the apparatus.

REGULATION XXX

Cubic Capacity of Lifeboats of Class I

1. The cubic capacity of a lifeboat of Class I shall be determined by Stirling's (Simpson's) Rule or by any other method giving the same degree of accuracy. The capacity of a square-sterned boat shall be calculated as if the boat had a pointed stern.

2. For example, the capacity in cubic metres (or cubic feet) of a boat, calculated by the aid of Stirling's Rule, may be considered as given by the following formula:—

$$\text{Capacity} = \frac{l}{12}(4A + 2B + 4C)$$

l being the length of the boat in metres (or feet) from the inside of the planking or plating at the stem to the corresponding point at the stern post; in the case of a boat with a square stern, the length is measured to the inside of the transom.

A, B, C denote respectively the areas of the cross-sections at the quarter length forward, amidships, and the quarter length aft, which correspond to the three points obtained by dividing l into four equal parts (the areas corresponding to the two ends of the boat are considered negligible).

The areas A, B, C shall be deemed to be given in square metres (or square feet) by the successive application of the following formula to each of the three cross-sections:—

$$\text{Area} = \frac{h}{12}(a+4b+2c+4d+e)$$

h being the depth measured in metres (or in feet) inside the planking or plating from the keel to the level of the gunwale, or, in certain cases, to a lower level, as determined hereafter.

a, b, c, d, e denote the horizontal breadths of the boat measured in metres (or in feet) at the upper and lower points of the depth and at the three points obtained by dividing h into four equal parts (a and e being the breadths at the extreme points, and c at the middle point, of h).

3. If the sheer of the gunwale, measured at the two points situated at a quarter of the length of the boat from the ends, exceeds 1 per cent. of the length of the boat, the depth employed in calculating the area of the cross-sections A or C shall be deemed to be the depth amidships plus 1 per cent. of the length of the boat.

4. If the depth of the boat amidships exceeds 45 per cent. of the breadth, the depth employed in calculating the area of the midship cross-section B shall be deemed to be equal to 45 per cent. of the breadth, and the depth employed in calculating the areas of the quarter length sections A and C is obtained by increasing this last figure by an amount equal to 1 per cent. of the length of the boat, provided that in no case shall the depths employed in the calculation exceed the actual depths at these points.

5. If the depth of the boat is greater than 122 centimetres (equivalent to 4 feet) the number of persons given by the application of this rule shall be reduced in proportion to the ratio of 122 centimetres to the actual depth, until the boat has been satisfactorily tested afloat with that number of persons on board, all wearing lifejackets.

6. Each Administration shall impose, by suitable formulæ, a limit for the number of persons allowed in boats with very fine ends and in boats very full in form.

7. Each Administration reserves the right to assign to a boat a capacity equal to the product of the length, the breadth and the depth multiplied by 0·6 if it is evident that this formula does not give a greater capacity than that obtained by the above method. The dimensions shall then be measured in the following manner:—

Length.—From the intersection of the outside of the planking with the stem to the corresponding point at the stern post or, in the case of a square sterned boat, to the after side of the transom.

Breadth.—From the outside of the planking at the point where the breadth of the boat is greatest.

Depth.—Amidships inside the planking from the keel to the level of the gunwale, but the depth used in calculating the cubic capacity may not in any case exceed 45 per cent. of the breadth.

In all cases the shipowner has the right to require that the cubic capacity of the boat shall be determined by exact measurement.

8. The cubic capacity of a motorboat is obtained from the gross capacity by deducting a volume equal to that occupied by the motor and its accessories, and, when carried, the wireless telegraphy installation and the searchlight with their accessories.

Regulation XXXI

Deck Area of Boats of Class II

1. The area of the deck of a decked boat shall be determined by the method indicated below or by any other method giving the same degree of accuracy. The same rule is to be applied in determining the area within the fixed bulwarks of a boat of Class II (*a*).

2. For example, the surface in square metres (or square feet) of a boat may be deemed to be given by the following formula:—

$$\text{Area} = \frac{l}{12}(2a + 1\cdot5b + 4c + 1\cdot5d + 2e)$$

l being the length in metres (or in feet) from the intersection of the outside of the planking with the stem to the corresponding point at the stern post.

a, b, c, d, e denote the horizontal breadths in metres (or in feet) outside the planking at the points obtained by dividing *l* into four equal parts and sub-dividing the foremost and aftermost parts into two equal parts (a and e being the breadths at the extreme sub-divisions, c at the middle point of the length, and b and d at the intermediate points).

Regulation XXXII

Marking of Boats, Life Rafts and Buoyant Apparatus

The dimensions of the boat and the number of persons which it is authorised to carry, shall be marked on it in clear permanent characters. These marks shall be specifically approved by the officers appointed to inspect the ship.

Life rafts and buoyant apparatus shall be marked with the number of persons in the same manner.

Regulation XXXIII

Carrying Capacity of Boats

1. The number of persons which a boat of one of the standard types can accommodate is equal to the greatest whole number obtained by divid-

ing the capacity in cubic metres (or cubic feet), or the surface in square metres (or square feet), of the boat by the standard unit of capacity, or unit of surface (according to circumstances), defined below for each type.

2. The standard units of capacity and surface for determining the number of persons are as follows:—

	Cubic Metres	Equivalent in Cubic Feet
Unit of Capacity		
Open boats, Class I(a)........................	0.283	10
Open boats, Class I(b)........................	0.255	9
	Square Metres	Equivalent in Square Feet
Unit of Surface		
Class II....................................	0·325	3½

3. The Administration may accept, in place of $0·325$ or $3\frac{1}{2}$, as the case may be, a smaller divisor, if it is satisfied after trial that the number of persons for whom there is seating accommodation in the decked boat in question is greater than the number obtained by applying the above divisor, provided always that the divisor adopted in place of $0·325$ or $3\frac{1}{2}$, as the case may be, may never be less than $0·280$ or 3, as the case may be.

The Administration which accepts a lower divisor in this way shall communicate to the other Administrations particulars of the trial and drawings of the decked boat in question.

REGULATION XXXIV

Capacity Limits

No boat shall be marked for a greater number of persons than that obtained in the manner specified in these Regulations.

This number shall be reduced—

(1) when it is greater than the number of persons for which there is proper seating accommodation; the latter number shall be determined in such a way that the persons when seated do not interfere in any way with the use of the oars;

(2) when, in the case of boats other than those of Class I, the freeboard when the boat is fully loaded is less than the freeboard laid down for each type respectively; the number shall be reduced until the freeboard when the boat is fully loaded is at least equal to the standard freeboard laid down above.

In boats of Class II (b) (i), the raised part of the deck at the sides may be regarded as affording seating accommodation.

REGULATION XXXV

Equivalents for and Weight of the Persons

In the tests for determining the number of persons which a boat or life raft can accommodate, each person shall be assumed to be an adult person wearing a life-jacket.

In verifications of freeboard the decked boats shall be loaded with a weight of at least 75 kilogrammes (165 lbs.) for each adult person that the decked boat is authorised to carry.

In all cases two children under 12 years of age shall be reckoned as one person.

Regulation XXXVI

Equipment of Boats and Life Rafts

1. The normal equipment of every boat shall consist of:—

(a.) A single banked complement of oars, two spare oars and a steering oar; one set and a half of thole pins or crutches; a boat hook.

(b.) Two plugs for each plug hole (plugs are not required when proper automatic valves are fitted); a bailer and a galvanised iron bucket.

(c.) A rudder and a tiller or yoke and yoke lines.

(d.) Two hatchets.

(e.) A lamp filled with oil and trimmed.

(f.) A mast or masts with one good sail at least, and proper gear for each.

(g.) An efficient compass.

(h.) A life-line becketed round the outside.

(i.) A sea-anchor.

(j.) A painter.

(k.) A vessel containing four and a half litres (equivalent to one gallon) of vegetable or animal oil. The vessel shall be so constructed that the oil can be easily distributed on the water, and so arranged that it can be attached to the sea-anchor.

(l.) An airtight receptacle containing one kilogramme (equivalent to two pounds) of provisions for each person.

(m.) A watertight receptacle provided with a dipper with lanyard containing one litre (equivalent to one quart) of fresh water for each person.

(n.) At least one dozen self-igniting "red lights" and a box of matches in watertight containers.

(o.) Half a kilogramme (equivalent to one pound) of condensed milk for each person.

(p.) A suitable locker for the stowage of the small items of the equipment.

(q.) Any boat which is certified to carry 100 or more persons shall be fitted with a motor and shall comply with the requirements of Regulation XXVII.

A motor lifeboat need not carry a mast or sails or more than half the complement of oars, but it shall carry two boathooks.

Decked lifeboats shall have no plug-hole, but shall be provided with at least two bilge-pumps.

In the case of a ship which carries passengers in the North Atlantic north of 35° North Latitude, only a proportion of the boats, to be fixed by the

Administration, need be equipped with masts and sails, and only one-half the quantity of condensed milk need be carried.

2. Where the number of lifeboats carried on a ship is more than 13, one shall be a motor boat, and where the number is more than 19, two shall be motor boats. These motor lifeboats shall be fitted with a wireless telegraph installation and a searchlight.

The wireless telegraph installation shall comply with conditions as to range and efficiency to be decided by each Administration.

The searchlight shall include a lamp of at least 80 watts, an efficient reflector and a source of power which will give effective illumination of a light coloured object over a width of about 18 metres (60 feet) at a distance of 180 metres (200 yards) for a total period of six hours, and it shall be capable of working for three hours continuously.

Where the power for the wireless equipment and the searchlight are derived from the same source, this shall be sufficient to provide for the adequate working of both appliances.

3. The normal equipment of every approved life raft shall consist of—

(*a.*) Four oars.

(*b.*) Five rowlocks.

(*c.*) A self-igniting lifebuoy light.

(*d.*) A sea-anchor.

(*e.*) A painter.

(*f.*) A vessel containing four and a half litres (equivalent to one gallon) of vegetable or animal oil. The vessel shall be so constructed that the oil can be easily distributed on the water, and so arranged that it can be attached to the sea-anchor.

(*g.*) An airtight receptacle containing one kilogramme (equivalent to two pounds) of provisions for each person.

(*h.*) A watertight receptacle provided with a dipper with lanyard containing one litre (equivalent to one quart) of fresh water for each person.

(*i.*) At least one dozen self-igniting red lights and a box of matches in watertight containers.

4. In the case of a ship which is engaged in short international voyages, the Administration may exempt the boats from carrying the equipment specified under sub-paragraphs (*f*), (*l*) and (*o*) of paragraph 1 and from the requirements of paragraph 2, and may also exempt the life rafts from carrying the equipment specified in paragraph 3 (*g*).

REGULATION XXXVII

Stowage and Handling of Boats and Life Rafts

1. Subject to the conditions of Regulation XXXVIII, the lifeboats may be stowed one above the other, or they may, subject to such conditions as the

Administration may impose, be fitted one within another, but where boats so fitted require lifting before being launched they shall only be permitted if mechanical power appliances for lifting are provided.

2. The lifeboats and life rafts additional to boats stowed under boats attached to davits may be stowed across a deck, bridge or poop and so secured that they will have the best chance of floating free of the ship if there is no time to launch them.

3. As large a number as possible of the additional boats referred to in paragraph 2 shall be capable of being launched on either side of the ship by means of approved appliances for transferring them from one side of the deck to the other.

4. Boats may only be stowed on more than one deck on condition that proper measures are taken to prevent boats on a lower deck being fouled by those stowed on a deck above.

5. Boats shall not be placed in the bows of the ship or in any positions in which they would be brought into dangerous proximity to the propellers at the time of launching.

6. Davits shall be of approved form and so disposed on one or more decks that the boats placed under them can be safely lowered without interference from the operation of any other davits.

7. The davits, blocks, falls and all other gear shall be of such strength that the boats can be safely lowered with the full complement of persons and equipment, with the ship listed to 15 degrees either way. The falls shall be long enough to reach the water with the vessel at her lightest seagoing draught and with a list of 15 degrees.

8. The davits shall be fitted with gear of sufficient power to ensure that the boats, fully equipped and manned, but not otherwise loaded with passengers, can be turned out against the maximum list at which the lowering of the boats is possible.

9. The boats attached to the davits shall have the falls ready for service, and means shall be provided for speedily, but not necessarily simultaneously, detaching the boats from the falls.

10. Where more than one boat is served by the same set of davits, if the falls are of rope, separate falls shall be provided to serve each boat, but where wire falls are used with mechanical appliances for recovering them, separate falls need not be provided. The appliances used must be such as to ensure lowering the boats in turn and rapidly.

Where mechanical appliances are fitted for the recovery of the falls efficient hand gear shall also be provided.

11. On short international voyages where the height of the boat deck above the water line when the vessel is at her lightest sea-going draught does not exceed 4·5 metres (15 feet), the requirements as to strength of davits and turning-out gear in sub-paragraphs 7, 8 and 10 shall not apply.

Regulation XXXVIII

Number and Capacity of Boats, Life Rafts, &c., and Davits

1. A ship shall be provided with sets of davits in accordance with its length as provided in Column A of the Table in Regulation XXXIX, provided that a number of sets of davits greater than the number of boats necessary for the accommodation of all the persons on board shall not be required.

Each set of davits shall have a boat of Class I attached to it. If the lifeboats attached to davits do not provide sufficient accommodation for all the persons on board, additional lifeboats of one of the standard types shall be provided. One additional lifeboat shall, in the first place, be stowed under each of the boats attached to davits. After these have been fitted other boats shall be carried inboard, but an Administration may, if it is of opinion that life rafts will be more readily available and otherwise more satisfactory than these lifeboats in a case of emergency, allow life rafts to be carried provided that the total capacity of the boats on the ship will be at least up to the minimum capacity required by Column C of the Table in Regulation XXXIX.

When in the opinion of the Administration it is neither practicable nor reasonable to place on a ship the number of sets of davits required by Column A of the Table in Regulation XXXIX, the Administration may authorise, under exceptional conditions, a smaller number of sets of davits, provided always that this number shall never be less than the minimum number fixed by Column B of the Table and that the total capacity of the boats on the ship will be at least up to the minimum capacity required by Column C.

2. A ship engaged on short international voyages shall be provided with sets of davits in accordance with its length as provided in Column A of the Table in Regulation XXXIX. Each set of davits shall have a boat of Class I attached to it. If the lifeboats attached to davits do not provide the minimum cubic capacity specified in Column D of the Table in Regulation XXXIX or provide accommodation for all persons on board, additional lifeboats of one of the standard types, approved life rafts or other approved buoyant apparatus shall be provided, and the accommodation thus provided shall be sufficient for all on board.

When in the opinion of the Administration it is neither practicable nor reasonable to place on a ship engaged in short international voyages, the number of sets of davits required by Column A of the Table in Regulation XXXIX, the Administration may authorise, under exceptional conditions, a smaller number of sets of davits, provided always that this number shall never be less than the minimum number fixed by Column B of the Table, and that the total capacity of the boats on the ship will be at least up to the minimum capacity required by Column D.

REGULATION XXXIX

Table relating to davits and lifeboat capacity

The following table fixes, according to the length of the ship—

(A.) *The minimum number of sets of davits* to be provided to each of which must be attached a boat of Class I in accordance with Regulation XXXVIII above.

(B.) *The smaller number of sets of davits which may be authorised exceptionally* under Regulation XXXVIII.

(C.) *The minimum life-boat capacity required*, including the life-boats attached to davits and the additional boats, in accordance with Regulation XXXVIII.

(D.) *The minimum life-boat capacity* required for a ship engaged in short international voyages.

Registered Length of the Ship		(A.) Minimum Number of Sets of Davits	(B.) Smaller Number of Sets of Davits authorised exceptionally	(C.) Minimum Capacity of Lifeboats		(D.) Minimum Capacity of Lifeboats	
Metres	Feet			Cubic Metres	Cubic Feet	Cubic Metres	Cubic Feet
31 and under 37	100 and under 120	2	2	28	980	11	400
37 " 43	120 " 140	2	2	35	1,220	17	600
43 " 49	140 " 160	2	2	44	1,550	24	850
49 " 53	160 " 175	3	3	53	1,880	33	1,150
53 " 58	175 " 190	3	3	68	2,390	37	1,300
58 " 63	190 " 205	4	4	78	2,740	41	1,450
63 " 67	205 " 220	4	4	94	3,330	45	1,600
67 " 70	220 " 230	5	4	110	3,900	48	1,700
70 " 75	230 " 245	5	4	129	4,560	52	1,850
75 " 78	245 " 255	6	5	144	5,100	60	2,100
78 " 82	255 " 270	6	5	160	5,640	68	2,400
82 " 87	270 " 285	7	5	175	6,190	76	2,700
87 " 91	285 " 300	7	5	196	6,930	85	3,000
91 " 96	300 " 315	8	6	214	7,550	94	3,300
96 " 101	315 " 330	8	6	235	8,290	105	3,700
101 " 107	330 " 350	9	7	255	9,000	116	4,100
107 " 113	350 " 370	9	7	273	9,630	125	4,400
113 " 119	370 " 390	10	7	301	10,650	133	4,700
119 " 125	390 " 410	10	7	331	11,700	144	5,100
125 " 133	410 " 435	12	9	370	13,060	156	5,500
133 " 140	435 " 460	12	9	408	14,430	170	6,000
140 " 149	460 " 490	14	10	451	15,920	185	6,550
149 " 159	490 " 520	14	10	490	17,310	201	7,100
159 " 168	520 " 550	16	12	530	18,720	217	7,650
168 " 177	550 " 580	16	12	576	20,350		
177 " 186	580 " 610	18	13	620	21,900		
186 " 195	610 " 640	18	13	671	23,700		
195 " 204	640 " 670	20	14	717	25,350		
204 " 213	670 " 700	20	14	766	27,050		
213 " 223	700 " 730	22	15	808	28,560		
223 " 232	730 " 760	22	15	854	30,180		
232 " 241	760 " 790	24	17	908	32,100		
241 " 250	790 " 820	24	17	972	34,350		
250 " 261	820 " 855	26	18	1,031	36,450		
261 " 271	855 " 890	26	18	1,097	38,750		
271 " 282	890 " 925	28	19	1,160	41,000		
282 " 293	925 " 960	28	19	1,242	43,880		
293 " 303	960 " 995	30	20	1,312	46,350		
303 " 314	995 " 1,030	30	20	1,380	48,750		

Note on (A) and (B).—When the length of the ship exceeds 314 metres (equivalent to 1,030 feet) the Administration shall determine the minimum number of sets of davits for that ship; full particulars of its decision shall be communicated to the other Administrations.

Note on (C) and (D).—For the purposes of this table the capacity of a boat of Class II is obtained by multiplying the number of persons for which the boat is certified by 0·283 to obtain the capacity in cubic metres and by 10 to obtain the capacity in cubic feet.

Note on (D).—When the length of a ship is under 31 metres (equivalent to 100 feet) or over 168 metres (equivalent to 550 feet) the cubic capacity of the lifeboats shall be prescribed by the Administration.

REGULATION XL

Life-Jackets and Life-Buoys

1. A life-jacket shall satisfy the following requirements:—

(*a.*) It shall be constructed with proper workmanship and materials.

(*b.*) It shall be capable of supporting in fresh water for 24 hours 7·5 kilogrammes of iron (equivalent to 16½ pounds);

(*c.*) It shall be reversible.

Life-jackets the buoyancy of which depends on air compartments are prohibited.

2. A lifebuoy shall satisfy the following requirements:—

(*a.*) It shall be of solid cork or any other equivalent material;

(*b.*) It shall be capable of supporting in fresh water for 24 hours at least 14·5 kilogrammes (equivalent to 32 pounds) of iron.

Life-buoys filled with rushes, cork shavings or granulated cork, or any other loose granulated material, or whose buoyancy depends upon air compartments which require to be inflated, are prohibited.

3. The minimum number of life-buoys with which ships are to be provided is fixed by the following table:—

Length of the Ship		Minimum Number of Buoys
Metres	Equivalent in Feet	
Under 61	Under 200	8
61 and under 122	200 and under 400	12
122 and under 183	400 and under 600	18
183 and under 244	600 and under 800	24
244 and over	800 and over	30

4. All the buoys shall be fitted with beckets securely seized. At least one buoy on each side shall be fitted with a life-line of at least 27·5 metres (15 fathoms) in length. Not less than one-half of the total number of life-buoys, and in no case less than six, shall be provided with efficient self-igniting lights which cannot be extinguished in water, and these shall be kept near the buoys to which they belong, with the necessary means of attachment.

5. All the life-buoys and life-jackets shall be so placed as to be readily accessible to the persons on board; their position shall be plainly indicated so as to be known to the persons concerned.

The life-buoys shall always be capable of being rapidly cast loose and shall not be permanently secured in any way.

REGULATION XLI

Certificated Lifeboatmen

In order to obtain the special lifeboatman's certificate provided for in Article 22 of the present Convention, the applicant must prove that he has been trained in all the operations connected with launching lifeboats and the use of oars; that he is acquainted with the practical handling of the boats themselves; and, further, that he is capable of understanding and answering the orders relative to lifeboat service.

There shall be for each boat or life-raft a number of lifeboatmen at least equal to that specified in the following table:—

If the Prescribed Complement is—	The Minimum Number of Certificated Lifeboatmen shall be—
Less than 41 persons	2
From 41 to 61 persons	3
From 62 to 85 persons	4
Above 85 persons	5

REGULATION XLII

Manning of Boats

A deck officer or certificated lifeboatman shall be placed in charge of each boat or life-raft and a second in command shall also be nominated. The person in charge shall have a list of its crew, and shall see that the men placed under his orders are acquainted with their several duties.

A man capable of working the motor shall be assigned to each motor boat.

A man capable of working the wireless and searchlight installations shall be assigned to boats carrying this equipment.

The duty of seeing that the boats, life-rafts and buoyant apparatus and other lifesaving apparatus are at all times ready for use shall be assigned to one or more officers.

REGULATION XLIII

Fire Detection and Extinction

1. An efficient patrol system shall be maintained, so that any outbreak of fire may be promptly detected. In addition, a fire alarm or fire detecting system shall be provided, which will automatically indicate or register at one or more points or stations, where it can be most quickly observed by officers and crew, the presence or indication of fire in any part of the ship not accessible to the patrol system.

2. Every ship shall be provided with powerful pumps, operated by steam or other means. On ships of less than 4,000 tons gross there shall be two, and on larger ships three of these pumps. Each of the pumps shall be capable of delivering a sufficient quantity of water in two powerful jets simultaneously in any given part of the ship, and shall be available for immediate use before the ship leaves port.

3. The service pipes shall permit of two powerful jets of water being simultaneously directed on any given part of a deck occupied by passengers and crew, when the watertight and fire-resisting doors are closed. The service

pipes and hoses shall be of ample size and made of suitable material. The branches of the pipes shall be so placed on each deck that the fire hose can be easily coupled to them.

4. Provision shall be made whereby at least two powerful jets of water can be rapidly and simultaneously directed into any space containing cargo. In addition, arrangements shall be made whereby smothering gas sufficient to give a minimum volume of free gas equal to 30 per cent. of the gross volume of the largest hold in the ship can be promptly conveyed by a permanent piping system into each compartment in which cargo is carried. Steam in adequately equivalent proportion may be accepted in place of smothering gas on steam-driven ships. Provision for the supply of smothering gas or steam need not be required in ships of less than 1,000 tons gross.

5. A sufficient number of portable fluid fire extinguishers shall be provided, at least two being carried in each machinery space.

6. Two equipments, consisting of a smoke helmet or breathing apparatus and a safety lamp, shall be carried on board, and kept in two widely separated places.

7. In steamships in which the main boilers are oil fired, there shall be provided in addition to means whereby two powerful jets of water may be rapidly and simultaneously directed into any part of the machinery spaces—

(a.) Suitable conductors for spraying water on oil without undue disturbance of the surface.

(b.) In each firing space, a receptacle containing 283 cubic decimetres (10 cubic feet) of sand, sawdust impregnated with soda, or other approved dry materials, and scoops for distributing the same.

(c.) In each boiler room, and in each of the machinery spaces in which a part of the oil fuel installation is situated, two approved portable extinguishers of a type discharging froth or other approved medium suitable for quenching oil fires.

(d.) Means whereby froth may be rapidly discharged and distributed over the whole of the lower part of the boiler room or of any one boiler room, if there are more than one, or of any machinery space in which oil fuel units or settling tanks are situated. The quantity of froth which can be discharged shall be ample to cover to a depth of 15·24 centimetres (6 inches) the whole area of the plating formed in any one compartment by the inner bottom plating, or by the shell plating of the vessel, if there is no double-bottom tank. If the engine and boiler rooms are not entirely separate, and fuel can drain from the boiler room bilges into the engine room, the combined engine and boiler rooms shall be considered as one compartment. The apparatus shall be operated and controlled from outside the compartment in which the fire may occur.

(e.) In addition to the foregoing, one extinguisher of the froth type of at least 136 litres (30 gallons) capacity in steamships having one boiler room and two such extinguishers in steamships with more than one boiler room. These extinguishers shall be provided with hoses on reels suitable for reaching any part of the boiler rooms and spaces containing oil-fuel pumping units. Equally efficient apparatus may be accepted in place of the 136 litres (30-gallons) extinguishers.

(*f.*) All containers and valves by which they are operated shall be easily accessible and so placed that they will not readily be cut off from use by an outbreak of fire.

8. In vessels propelled by internal combustion engines there shall be provided in each of the machinery spaces, in addition to means whereby two powerful jets of water may be rapidly and simultaneously directed into any part of the machinery spaces, together with suitable spraying conductors, froth extinguishers as follows:—

(*a.*) At least one approved 45 litres (10-gallons) extinguisher with an addition of one approved 9 litres (2-gallons) extinguisher for each 1,000 B.H.P. of the engines, but the total number of 9 litres (2-gallons) extinguishers so supplied shall be not less than two and need not exceed six.

(*b.*) When a donkey boiler is situated in the machinery space there shall be provided, in place of the 45 litres (10-gallons) extinguisher mentioned above, one of 136 litres (30 gallons) capacity, fitted with suitable hose attachments or other approved methods for distributing the froth.

9. In steamships using oil fuel, if the engine and boiler rooms are not entirely separated by a steel bulkhead, and if fuel oil can drain from the boiler-room bilges into the engine room, one of the fire pumps shall be situated in the tunnel or other space outside the machinery compartment. When more than two pumps are required they shall not all be fitted in the same space.

10. Where any special type of appliance, extinguishing medium or arrangement is specified, any other type of appliance, &c., may be allowed, provided that it is not less effective than the specified one. For example—a Carbon Dioxide system may be accepted in place of a froth installation (paragraph (7), sub-paragraphs (*d*) and (*e*)), provided that the quantity of carbon dioxide carried is sufficient to give a gas saturation of about 25 per cent. for the gross volume of the stokehold to about the top of the boilers.

11. All the fire-extinguishing appliances shall be thoroughly examined at least once each year by a surveyor appointed by the Administration.

Regulation XLIV

Muster List

The muster list shall assign duties to the different members of the crew in connexion with—

(*a.*) The closing of the watertight doors, valves, &c.

(b.) The equipment of the boats, life rafts and buoyant apparatus generally.

(c.) The launching of the boats attached to davits.

(d.) The general preparation of the other boats, the life rafts, and buoyant apparatus.

(e.) The muster of the passengers.

(f.) The extinction of fire.

The muster list shall assign to the members of the stewards' department their several duties in relation to the passengers at a time of emergency. These duties shall include:—

(a.) Warning the passengers.

(b.) Seeing that they are dressed and have put on their lifejackets in a proper manner.

(c.) Assembling the passengers at muster stations.

(d.) Keeping order in the passages and on the stairways, and, generally, controlling the movements of the passengers.

The muster list shall specify definite signals for calling all the crew to their boat and fire stations, and shall give full particulars of these signals.

REGULATION XLV

Musters and Drills

Musters of the crew for boat drill shall take place weekly when practicable, and in vessels in which the voyage exceeds one week, before leaving port. The dates upon which musters are held shall be recorded in the Official Log Book and, if in any week a muster is not held, an entry shall be made stating why a muster was not practicable.

In ships in which the voyage exceeds one week practice musters of passengers should be held at an early period of each voyage.

Different groups of boats shall be used in turn at successive boat drills. The drills and inspections shall be so arranged that the crew thoroughly understand and are practised in the duties they have to perform, and that all lifesaving appliances with the gear appertaining to them are always ready for immediate use.

The emergency signal for summoning passengers to muster stations shall be a succession of more than six short blasts followed by one long blast on the whistle or syren. This shall be supplemented on all ships except those engaged in short international voyages by other electrically operated signals throughout the ship controlled from the bridge. The meaning of all signals affecting passengers shall be clearly stated in different languages on cards posted in their cabins and in other passenger quarters.

SAFETY OF NAVIGATION

Regulation XLVI

Transmission of Information

The transmission of information regarding ice, derelicts, tropical storms or any other direct danger to navigation is obligatory. The form in which the information is sent is not obligatory. It may be transmitted either in plain language (preferably English) or by means of the International Code of Signals (Wireless Telegraphy Section). It should be issued CQ to all ships, and should also be sent to the first point of the coast to which communication can be made with a request that it be transmitted to the appropriate authority.

All messages issued under Article 34 of the present Convention will be preceded by the safety signal TTT followed by an indication of the nature of the danger, thus: TTT Ice; TTT Derelict; TTT Storm; TTT Navigation.

Information Required

The following information is desired, the time in all cases being Greenwich Mean Time:—

(*a.*) *Ice, Derelicts and other Direct Dangers to Navigation.*

(1) the kind of ice, derelict or danger observed;

(2) the position of the ice, derelict or danger when last observed;

(3) the time and date when the observation was made.

(*b.*) *Tropical Storms.*—(Hurricanes in the West Indies, Typhoons in the China Seas, Cyclones in Indian waters, and storms of a similar nature in other regions.)

(1.) *A Statement that a Tropical Storm has been Encountered.*—This obligation should be interpreted in a broad spirit, and information transmitted whenever the master has good reason to believe that a tropical storm exists in his neighbourhood.

(2.) *Meteorological Information.*—In view of the great assistance given by accurate meteorological data in fixing the position and movement of storm centres, each shipmaster should add to his warning message as much of the following meteorological information as he finds practicable:—

(*a*) barometric pressure (millibars, inches or millimetres);

(*b*) change in barometric pressure (the change during the previous two to four hours);

(*c*) wind direction (true not magnetic);

(*d*) wind force (Beaufort or decimal scale);

(*e*) state of the sea (smooth, moderate, rough, high);

(*f*) swell (slight, medium, heavy) and the direction from which it comes.

When barometric pressure is given the word "millibars," "inches" or "millimetres," as the case may be, should be added to the reading, and *it should always be stated whether the reading is corrected or uncorrected.*

When changes of the barometer are reported the course and speed of the ship should also be given.

All directions should be true, not magnetic.

(3.) *Time and Date and Position of the Ship.*—These should be for the time and position when the meteorological observations reported were made and not when the message was prepared or despatched. The time used in all cases should be Greenwich Mean Time.

(4.) *Subsequent Observations.*—When a master has reported a tropical storm it is desirable, but not obligatory, that other observations be made and transmitted at intervals of three hours, so long as the ship remains under the influence of the storm.

Examples

Ice.

TTT Ice. Large berg sighted in 4605 N., 4410 W., at 0800 GMT. May 15.

Derelict.

TTT Derelict. Observed derelict almost submerged in 4006 N., 1243 W., at 1630 GMT. April 21.

Danger to Navigation.

TTT Navigation. Alpha lightship not on station. 1800 GMT. January 3.

Tropical Storm.

TTT Storm. Experiencing tropical storm. Barometer corrected 994 millibars, falling rapidly. Wind NW., force 9, heavy squalls. Swell E. Course ENE., 5 knots. 2204 N., 11354 E. 0030 GMT. August 18.

TTT Storm. Appearances indicate approach of hurricane. Barometer corrected 29·64 inches falling. Wind NE., force 8. Swell medium from NE. Frequent rain squalls. Course 35°, 9 knots. 2200 N., 7236 W. 1300 GMT. September 14.

TTT Storm. Conditions indicate intense cyclone has formed. Wind S. by W. force 5. Barometer uncorrected 753 millimetres, fell 5 millimetres last three hours. Course N. 60 W., 8 knots. 1620 N., 9302 E. 0200 GMT. May 4.

TTT Storm. Typhoon to south-east. Wind increasing from N. and barometer falling rapidly. Position 1812 N., 12605 E. 0300 GMT. June 12.

CERTIFICATES

Regulation XLVII

Form of Safety Certificate for Passenger Ships

SAFETY CERTIFICATE

(*Official Seal*)   (*Country*)

for $\dfrac{\text{an}}{\text{a short}}$ international voyage

Issued under the provisions of the

INTERNATIONAL CONVENTION FOR SAFETY OF LIFE AT SEA, 1929

Name of Ship	Distinctive Number or Letters	Port of Registry	Gross Tonnage

The _____ (*Name*) Government certifies

I, the undersigned, _____ (*Name*) certify

I. That the above-mentioned ship has been duly surveyed in accordance with the provisions of the International Convention referred to above.

II. That the survey showed that the ship complied with the requirements of the said Convention as regards—

(1) the hull, main and auxiliary boilers and machinery;
(2) the watertight subdivision arrangements and details;
(3) the following subdivision loadlines:—

Subdivision loadlines assigned and marked on the ship's side at amidships (Convention Article 5)	Freeboard	To apply when the spaces in which passengers are carried include the following alternative spaces
C. 1	....	....
C. 2	....	....
C. 3	....	....

(4) the boats, life-rafts and life-saving appliances which provide for a total number (crew and passengers) of.............persons, and no more, viz:—

...............boats capable of accommodating.....................persons.
...............life-rafts   "   "   ....   "
...............buoyant apparatus capable of supporting.....................
                persons.
...............life-buoys.
...............life-jackets.
...............certificated lifeboatmen.

(5) the radiotelegraph installations:—

	Requirements of Articles........of the said Convention	Actual provision
Hours of watch.............................	....	....
Whether approved auto-alarm fitted.........	....	....
Whether separate emergency installation fitted.	....	....
Minimum number of operators...............	....	....
Additional operators or watchers............	....	....
Whether direction-finding apparatus fitted....	....	....

III. That in all other respects the ship complies with the requirements of the said Convention, so far as those requirements apply thereto.

This certificate is issued under the authority of the   Government. It will remain in force until

Issued at   the   day of

Here follows the seal or signature of the authority entitled to issue this certificate.

(*Seal.*)

If signed, the following paragraph is to be added:—

The undersigned declares that he is duly authorised by the said Government to issue this certificate.

(*Signature.*)

Form of Safety Radiotelegraphy Certificate

SAFETY RADIOTELEGRAPHY CERTIFICATE

(*Official Seal*)   (*Country*)

Issued under the provisions of the

INTERNATIONAL CONVENTION FOR SAFETY OF LIFE AT SEA, 1929

Name of Ship	Distinctive Number or Letters	Port of Registry	Gross Tonnage

The   (*Name*)   Government certify

I, the undersigned,   (*Name*)   certify

That the above-mentioned ship complies with the provisions of the International Convention referred to above as regards Radiotelegraphy:—

———————	Requirements of Articles.........of the said Convention	Actual Provision
Hours of watch............................	....	....
Whether approved auto-alarm fitted.........	....	....
Whether separate emergency installation fitted.	....	....
Minimum number of operators...............	....	....
Additional operators or watchers...........	....	....
Whether direction-finding apparatus fitted....	....	....

This certificate is issued under the authority of the   Government.
It will remain in force until

Issued at   the   day of

Here follows the seal or signature of the authority entitled to issue this certificate.

                                               (*Seal*)

If signed, the following paragraph is to be added:—

The undersigned declares that he is duly authorised by the said Government to issue this certificate.

                                               (*Signature*)

Form of Exemption Certificate

EXEMPTION CERTIFICATE

(*Official Seal*)   (*Country*)

Issued under the provisions of the

INTERNATIONAL CONVENTION FOR SAFETY OF LIFE AT SEA, 1929

Name of Ship	Distinctive Number or Letters	Port of Registry	Gross Tonnage

<table>
<tr><td>The</td><td>(Name) Government certify</td></tr>
</table>

I, the undersigned,   (*Name*) certify

That the above-mentioned ship is under the authority conferred by Article .... of the
International Convention referred to above exempted from the requirements of†..........
of the Convention on the voyages ....
to...

* Insert here⎫ *
the conditions, if⎪
any, on which⎪
the exemption⎬
certificate   is⎪
granted.   ⎭

This certificate is issued under the authority of the   Government.
It will remain in force until
Issued at   the   day of
Here follows the seal or signature of the authority entitled to issue this certificate.

(*Seal.*)

If signed, the following paragraph is to be added:—
The undersigned declares that he is duly authorised by the said Government to issue this
certificate.

(*Signature.*)

---

† Insert here references to Articles and Regulations, specifying particular paragraphs.

Annex II

INTERNATIONAL REGULATIONS FOR PREVENTING COLLISIONS AT SEA [11]

PRELIMINARY

These Rules shall be followed by all vessels upon the high seas and in all waters connected therewith, navigable by sea-going vessels.

In the following Rules every steam vessel which is under sail and not under steam is to be considered a sailing vessel, and every vessel under steam, whether under sail or not, is to be considered a steam vessel.

The words "steam vessel" shall include any vessel propelled by machinery.

The term "under steam" shall mean under any mechanical power.

A vessel is "under way" within the meaning of these Rules when she is not at anchor or made fast to the shore or aground.

The length of a vessel shall be deemed to be the length appearing in her certificate of registry.

---

[11] This revision of the International Regulations for Preventing Collisions at Sea, recommended by the 1929 London conference for adoption by individual states, was based on "rules of the road" in general use at the time. It was set up to indicate the addition of new material in italics and the deletion of previous material by cancelled lettering. For text of the regulations as promulgated by a British Order in Council of Oct. 13, 1910, see R. G. Marsden, *A Treatise on the Law of Collisions at Sea* (London, 1919), p. 491. For regulations adopted by the United States Congress on Aug. 19, 1890, under which the United States operated until 1952, which were very similar to the British rules, see 26 Stat. 320.

RULES CONCERNING LIGHTS, &C.

The word "visible" in these Rules, when applied to lights, shall mean visible on a dark night with a clear atmosphere.

ARTICLE 1

The Rules concerning lights shall be complied with in all weathers from sunset to sunrise, and during such time no other lights which may be mistaken for the prescribed lights *or impair their visibility* shall be exhibited.

ARTICLE 2

A steam vessel when under way shall carry:—

(*a.*) On or in front of the foremast, or if a vessel without a foremast, then in the fore part of the vessel, ~~at a height above the hull of not less than 20 feet, and if the breadth of the vessel exceeds 20 feet, then at a height above the hull not less than such breadth, so, however, that the light need not be carried at a greater height above the hull than 40 feet~~, a bright white light, so constructed as to show an unbroken light over an arc of the horizon of 20 points of the compass, so fixed as to throw the light 10 points on each side of the vessel, viz., from right ahead to 2 points abaft the beam on either side, and of such a character as to be visible at a distance of at least 5 miles.

(*b.*) *Either forward or aft of the white light mentioned in sub-division (a) a second white light similar in construction and character to that light.*

Vessels of less than 150 feet in length shall not be required to carry this second white light, but may do so.

(*c.*) *These two white lights shall be so placed in a line with the keel that one shall be at least 15 feet higher than the other and in such a position that the lower light shall be forward of the upper one, and higher than the lights mentioned in Article 2 (d) and (e). The vertical distance between the two white lights shall be less than the horizontal distance. The lower of these two white lights, or if only one is carried, then that light, shall be placed at a height above the hull of not less than 20 feet, and, if the breadth of the vessel exceeds 20 feet, then at a height above the hull not less than such breadth, so, however, that the light need not be carried at a greater height above the hull than 40 feet.*

(~~b.~~) (*d.*) On the starboard side a green light so constructed as to show an unbroken light over an arc of the horizon of 10 points of the compass, so fixed as to throw the light from right ahead to 2 points abaft the beam on the starboard side, and of such a character as to be visible at a distance of at least 2 miles.

(~~e.~~) (*e.*) On the port side a red light so constructed as to show an unbroken light over an arc of the horizon of 10 points of the compass, so fixed as to throw the light from right ahead to 2 points abaft the beam on the port side, and of such a character as to be visible at a distance of at least 2 miles.

(d.) (f.) The said green and red side lights shall be fitted with inboard screens projecting at least 3 feet forward from the light, so as to prevent these lights from being seen across the bow.

(e.) A steam vessel when under way may carry an additional white light similar in construction to the light mentioned in sub-division (a). These two lights shall be so placed in line with the keel that one shall be at least 15 feet higher than the other, and in such a position with reference to each other that the lower light shall be forward of the upper one. The vertical distance between these lights shall be less than the horizontal distance.

In naval vessels of special construction in which it is not possible to comply fully with the provisions of this Article as to the position of lights or their range of visibility, those provisions shall be followed as closely as circumstances will permit.

ARTICLE 3

A steam vessel when towing another vessel shall, in addition to her side lights, carry two bright white lights in a vertical line one over the other, not less than 6 feet apart, and when towing more than one vessel shall carry an additional bright white light 6 feet above or below such lights, if the length of the tow, measuring from the stern of the towing vessel to the stern of the last vessel towed, exceeds 600 feet. Each of these lights shall be of the same construction and character, and *one of them* shall be carried in the same position as the white light mentioned in Article 2 (*a*), except the additional light which may *and the lowest light shall* be carried at a height of not less than 14 feet above the hull.

Such steam vessel *The vessel towing and the vessels towed, except the last vessel of the tow,* may carry *in lieu of the light required in Article 10,* a small white light abaft the funnel or aftermast, for the vessel towed *tow* to steer by, but such light shall not be visible forward of the beam.

ARTICLE 4

(*a.*) A vessel which from any accident is not under command shall carry at the same height as the white light mentioned in Article 2 (a), where they can best be seen, and, if a steam vessel, in lieu of that light *the lights required in Article 2 (a) and (b),* two red lights, in a vertical line one over the other, not less than 6 feet apart, *so placed that the lower light shall not be less than 14 feet above the hull,* and of such a character as to be visible all round the horizon at a distance of at least 2 miles; and shall by day carry a vertical line, one over the other not less than 6 feet apart, where they can best be seen, two black balls or shapes each 2 feet in diameter.

(*b.*) A vessel employed in laying or in picking up a telegraph *submarine* cable shall carry in the same position as the white light mentioned in Article 2 (a), and if a steam vessel, in lieu of that light *the lights required in Article 2 (a) and (b),* three lights in a vertical line, one over the other, not less than

6 feet apart, *so placed that the lowest of these lights shall be not less than 14 feet above the hull.* The highest and lowest of these lights shall be red, and the middle light shall be white, and they shall be of such a character as to be visible all around the horizon, at a distance of at least 2 miles. By day she shall carry in a vertical line, one over the other, not less than 6 feet apart, where they can best be seen, three shapes not less than 2 feet in diameter, of which the highest and lowest shall be globular in shape and red in colour, and the middle one diamond in shape and white.

(*c.*) The vessels referred to in this Article, when not making way through the water, shall not carry the side-lights, but when making way shall carry them.

(*d.*) The lights and shapes required to be shown by this Article are to be taken by other vessels as signals that the vessel showing them is not under command and cannot therefore get out of the way.

These signals are not signals of vessels in distress and requiring assistance. Such signals are contained in Article 31.

ARTICLE 5

A sailing vessel under way, and any vessel being towed, shall carry the same lights as are prescribed by Article 2 for a steam vessel under way, with the exception of the white lights mentioned therein, which they shall never carry.

ARTICLE 6

Whenever, as in the case of small vessels under way during bad weather, the green and red side lights cannot be fixed, these lights shall be kept at hand lighted and ready for use; and shall, on the approach of or to other vessels, be exhibited on their respective sides in sufficient time to prevent collision, in such manner as to make them most visible, and so that the green light shall not be seen on the port side nor the red light on the starboard side, nor, if practicable, more than 2 points abaft the beam on their respective sides.

To make the use of these portable lights more certain and easy, the lanterns containing them shall each be painted outside with the colour of the light they respectively contain, and shall be provided with proper screens.

ARTICLE 7

Steam vessels of less than 40, and vessels under oars or sails of less than 20, tons gross tonnage, respectively, and rowing boats, when under way, shall not be ~~obliged~~ *required* to carry the lights mentioned in Article 2 ~~(a), (b) and (c),~~ but if they do not carry them they shall be provided with the following lights:—

1. Steam vessels of less than 40 tons shall carry:

(*a.*) In the fore part of the vessel, ~~or~~ on or in front of the funnel, where it can best be seen, and at a height above the gunwale of not less than 9 feet, a bright white light constructed and fixed as prescribed in Article 2 (*a*), and of such a character as to be visible at a distance of at least ~~2~~ *3* miles.

(*b.*) Green and red side-lights constructed and fixed as prescribed in Article 2 ~~(b) and (c),~~ (*d*) and (*e*), and of such a character as to be visible at a distance of at least 1 mile, or a combined lantern showing a green light and a red light from right ahead to 2 points abaft the beam on their respective sides. Such lantern shall be carried not less than 3 feet below the white light.

2. Small steamboats, such as are carried by sea-going vessels, may carry the white light at a less height than 9 feet above the gunwale, but it shall be carried above *the side-lights or* the combined lantern, mentioned in sub-division 1 (*b*).

3. Vessels under oars or sails, of less than 20 tons, shall ~~have ready at hand~~ *if they do not carry the side-lights, carry, where it can best be seen,* a lantern ~~with~~ *showing* a green ~~glass~~ *light* on one side and a red ~~glass~~ *light* on the other, ~~which, on the approach of or to other vessels, shall be exhibited in sufficient time to prevent collision,~~ *of such a character as to be visible at a distance of at least 1 mile* so that the green light shall not be seen on the port side nor the red light on the starboard side; *provided that, where it is not possible to fix this light, it shall be kept lighted and ready for use, and shall be exhibited in sufficient time to prevent collision.*

4. *Small* rowing boats, whether under oars or sail, shall *only be required to* have ready at hand a *lighted* lantern showing a white light, which shall be temporarily exhibited in sufficient time to prevent collision.

The vessels referred to in this Article shall not be obliged to carry the lights prescribed by Article 4 (*a*), and Article 11, last paragraph.

ARTICLE 8

Sailing pilot-vessels, when engaged on their station on pilotage duty, *and not at anchor,* shall not show the lights required for other vessels, but shall carry a white light at the masthead, visible all around the horizon, *at a distance of at least 3 miles,* and shall also exhibit a flare-up light or flare-up lights at short intervals, which shall never exceed ~~fifteen~~ *ten* minutes.

On the near approach of or to other vessels they shall have their side-lights lighted, ready for use, and shall flash or show them at short intervals, to indicate the direction in which they are heading, but the green light shall not be shown on the port side, nor the red light on the starboard side.

A *sailing* pilot-vessel of such a class as to be obliged to go alongside of a vessel to put a pilot on board may show the white light instead of carrying it at the masthead, and may, instead of the ~~coloured~~ *side*-lights above mentioned, have at hand, ready for use, a lantern with a green glass on the one side and a red glass on the other, to be used as prescribed above.

A steam pilot-vessel ~~exclusively employed for the service of pilots licensed or certified by any pilotage authority or the Committee of any pilotage dis-~~

~~trict,~~ when engaged on her station on pilotage duty and not at anchor, shall, in addition to the lights *and flares* required for ~~all pilot boats~~ *sailing pilot-vessels,* carry at a distance of eight feet below her white mast head light, a red light, visible all round the horizon ~~and of such a character as to be visible on a dark night with a clear atmosphere~~ at a distance of at least ~~two~~ *three* miles, and also the ~~coloured~~ side-lights required to be carried by vessels when under way.

All pilot-vessels, when engaged on their stations on pilotage duty and at anchor, shall carry the lights and show the flares prescribed above, except that the side-lights shall not be shown.

When not engaged on their stations on pilotage duty, they shall carry the same lights as other vessels of their class and tonnage.

~~When engaged on her station on pilotage duty and at anchor she shall carry, in addition to the lights required for all pilot boats, the red light above mentioned, but not the coloured side lights.~~

~~Pilot vessels, when not engaged on their station on pilotage duty, shall carry lights similar to those of other vessels of their tonnage.~~

Article 9 [12] [13]

Fishing-vessels and fishing-boats, when under way and when not required by this Article to carry or show the lights hereinafter specified, shall carry or show the lights prescribed for vessels of their tonnage under way.

(*a.*) Open boats, by which it is to be understood boats not protected from the entry of sea water by means of a continuous deck, when engaged in any fishing at night with outlying tackle extending not more than 150 feet horizontally from the boat into the seaway, shall carry one all-round white light.

Open boats, when fishing at night, with outlying tackle extending more than 150 feet horizontally from the boat into the seaway, shall carry one all-round white light, and, in addition, on approaching or being approached by other vessels, shall show a second white light at least 3 feet below the first light and at a horizontal distance of at least 5 feet away from it in the direction in which the outlying tackle is attached.

The lights mentioned in this sub-division shall be of such a character as to be visible at a distance of at least 2 miles.

[14](*b.*) Vessels and boats, except open boats as defined in sub-division (*a*), when fishing with drift-nets, shall, so long as the nets are wholly or partly in the water, carry two white lights where they can best be seen. Such lights shall be placed so that the vertical distance between them shall be not less

---

[12] This article does not apply to Chinese or Siamese vessels. [Footnote in original.]

[13] The expression "Mediterranean Sea" contained in sub-sections (*b*) and (*c*) of this Article includes the Black Sea and the other adjacent inland seas in communication with it. [Footnote in original.]

[14] Dutch vessels and boats when engaged in the "kol," or hand-line, fishing will carry the lights prescribed for vessels fishing with drift-nets. [Footnote in original.]

than 6 feet and not more than 15 feet, and so that the horizontal distance between them, measured in a line with the keel, shall be not less than 5 feet and not more than 10 feet. The lower of these two lights shall be in the direction of the nets, and both of them shall be of such a character as to show all round the horizon, and to be visible at a distance of not less than 3 miles.

Within the Mediterranean Sea and in the seas bordering the coasts of Japan and Korea,[15] sailing fishing-vessels of less than 20 tons gross tonnage shall not be obliged to carry the lower of these two lights; should they, however, not carry it, they shall show in the same position (in the direction of the net or gear) a white light visible at a distance of not less than one sea mile on the approach of or to other vessels.

(c.) Vessels and boats, except open boats as defined in sub-division (a), when line-fishing with their lines out and attached to or hauling their lines, and when not at anchor or stationary within the meaning of sub-division (h), shall carry the same lights as vessels fishing with drift-nets. When shooting lines, or fishing with towing lines, they shall carry the lights prescribed for a steam or sailing vessel under way respectively.

Within the Mediterranean Sea and in the seas bordering the coasts of Japan and Korea,[15] sailing fishing vessels of less than 20 tons gross tonnage shall not be obliged to carry the lower of these two lights; should they, however, not carry it, they shall show in the same position (in the direction of the lines) a white light, visible at a distance of not less than one sea mile on the approach of or to other vessels.

(d.) Vessels, when engaged in trawling, by which is meant the dragging of an apparatus along the bottom of the sea—

1. If steam vessels, shall carry in the same position as the white light mentioned in Article 2 (a), a tri-coloured lantern so constructed and fixed as to show a white light from right ahead to two points on each bow, and a green light and a red light over an arc of the horizon from two points on each bow to two points abaft the beam on the starboard and port sides respectively; and not less than 6 nor more than 12 feet below the tri-coloured lantern a white light in a lantern, so constructed as to show a clear, uniform and unbroken light all round the horizon.

2. If sailing vessels, shall carry a white light in a lantern, so constructed as to show a clear, uniform and unbroken light all round the horizon, and shall also, on the approach of or to other vessels, show where it can best be seen a white flare-up light or torch in sufficient time to prevent collision.

All lights mentioned in sub-division (d), 1 and 2, shall be visible at a distance of at least 2 miles.

---

[15] Also, as regards Russian vessels, in the seas (excluding the Baltic) bordering the coasts of Russia. [Footnote in original.]

(*e.*) Oyster dredgers and other vessels fishing with dredge-nets shall carry and show the same lights as trawlers.

(*f.*) Fishing-vessels and fishing-boats may at any time use a flare-up light in addition to the lights which they are by this Article required to carry and show, and they may also use working lights.

(*g.*) Every fishing-vessel and every fishing-boat under 150 feet in length, when at anchor, shall exhibit a white light visible all round the horizon at a distance of at least ~~one~~ 2 mile*s*.

Every fishing-vessel of 150 feet in length or upwards, when at anchor, shall exhibit a white light visible all round the horizon at a distance of at least ~~one~~ 2 mile*s* and shall exhibit a second light as provided for vessels of such length by Article 11.

Should any such vessel, whether under 150 feet in length, or of 150 feet in length or upwards, be attached to a net or other fishing gear, she shall, on the approach of other vessels, show an additional white light at least 3 feet below the anchor light, and at a horizontal distance of at least 5 feet away from it in the direction of the net or gear.

(*h.*) If a vessel or boat when fishing becomes stationary in consequence of her gear getting fast to a rock or other obstruction, she shall in day-time haul down the day-signal required by sub-division (*k*); at night show the light or lights prescribed for a vessel at anchor; and, during fog, mist, falling snow, or heavy rain-storms, make the signal prescribed for a vessel at anchor. (See sub-division (*d*), and the last paragraph of Article 15.)

(*i.*) In fog, mist, falling snow, or heavy rain-storms, drift-net vessels attached to their nets, and vessels when trawling, dredging, or fishing with any kind of drag-net, and vessels line fishing with their lines out, shall, if of 20 tons gross tonnage or upwards, respectively, at intervals of not more than one minute, make a blast; if steam vessels, with the whistle or siren, and, if sailing vessels, with the foghorn; each blast to be followed by ringing the bell. Fishing vessels and boats of less than 20 tons gross tonnage shall not be obliged to give the above-mentioned signals; but, if they do not, they shall make some other efficient sound signal at intervals of not more than one minute.

(*k.*) All vessels or boats fishing with nets or lines or trawls, when under way, shall in daytime indicate their occupation ~~to an approaching vessel~~ by displaying a basket ~~or other efficient signal~~ where it can best be seen. If vessels or boats at anchor have their gear out, they shall, on the approach of other vessels, show the same signal on the side on which those vessels can pass.

The vessels required by this Article to carry or show the lights hereinbefore specified shall not be obliged to carry the lights prescribed by Article 4 (*a*) and the last paragraph of Article 11.

ARTICLE 10

~~A vessel which is being overtaken by another shall show from her stern to such last mentioned vessel a white light or a flare-up light.~~

~~The white light required to be shown by this Article may be fixed and carried in a lantern, but in such case the lantern shall be~~ *A vessel when under way shall carry at her stern, a white light* so constructed, fitted, and screened, that it shall throw an unbroken light over an arc of the horizon of 12 points of the compass, viz., for 6 points from right aft on each side of the vessel, *and of such a character* ~~so~~ as to be visible at a distance of at least ~~1 mile~~ *2 miles.* Such light shall be carried as nearly as practicable on the same level as the side lights.

In small vessels, if it is not possible on account of bad weather or other sufficient cause for this light to be fixed, a light shall be kept at hand lighted and ready for use, and shall, on the approach of an overtaking vessel, be shown in sufficient time to prevent collision.

For vessels engaged in towing, see Article 3, last paragraph.

ARTICLE 11

A vessel under 150 feet in length, when at anchor, shall carry forward, where it can best be seen, but at a height not exceeding 20 feet above the hull, a white light in a lantern so constructed as to show a clear, uniform, and unbroken light visible all round the horizon at a distance of at least ~~1~~ *2* miles.

A vessel of 150 feet or upwards in length, when at anchor, shall carry in the forward part of the vessel, at a height of not less than 20, and not exceeding 40, feet above the hull, one such light, and at or near the stern of the vessel, and at such a height that it shall be not less than 15 feet lower than the forward light, another such light.

Between sunrise and sunset all vessels when at anchor in or near a fairway shall carry, forward, where it can best be seen, one black ball, 2 feet in diameter. ~~The length of a vessel shall be deemed to be the length appearing in her certificate of registry.~~

A vessel aground in or near a fairway shall carry *by night* the above light or lights and the two red lights prescribed by Article 4 (*a*), *and by day, where they can best be seen, 3 black balls, each 2 feet in diameter, placed in a vertical line one over the other.*

ARTICLE 12

Every vessel may, if necessary, in order to attract attention, in addition to the lights which she is by these Rules required to carry, show a flare-up light or use any detonating *or other efficient sound* signal that cannot be mistaken for *a prescribed* distress *or fog* signal.

Article 13

Nothing in these Rules shall interfere with the operation of any special rules made by the Government of any nation with respect to additional station and signal lights for two or more ships of war or for vessels sailing under convoy, or with the exhibition of recognition signals adopted by shipowners, which have been authorised by their respective Governments and duly registered and published.

Article 14

A ~~steam~~ vessel proceeding under sail ~~only, but having her funnel up,~~ *when also under steam or other mechanical power* shall carry in *the* daytime, forward, where it can best be seen, one ~~black ball~~ *black cone, point upwards,* 2 feet in diameter *at its base.*

SOUND SIGNALS FOR FOG, &C.

Article 15

All signals prescribed by this Article for vessels under way shall be given—

1. By "steam vessels" on the whistle or siren.
2. By "sailing vessels and vessels towed" on the fog horn.

The words "prolonged blast" used in this Article, shall mean a blast of from 4 to 6 seconds' duration.

A steam vessel shall be provided with an efficient whistle or siren, sounded by steam or some substitute for steam, so placed that the sound may not be intercepted by any obstruction, and with an efficient fog-horn, to be sounded by mechanical means, and also with an efficient bell.[16] A sailing vessel of 20 tons gross tonnage or upwards shall be provided with a similar fog-horn and bell.

In fog, mist, falling snow or heavy rain-storms, whether by day or night, the signals described in this Article shall be used as follows, viz.:—

(*a.*) A steam vessel having way upon her, shall sound, at intervals of not more than 2 minutes, a prolonged blast.

(*b.*) A steam vessel under way, but stopped and having no way upon her, shall sound, at intervals of not more than 2 minutes, 2 prolonged blasts, with an interval of about 1 second between them.

(*c.*) A sailing vessel under way shall sound, at intervals of not more than 1 minute, when on the starboard tack, 1 blast, when on the port tack, 2 blasts in succession, and when with the wind abaft the beam, 3 blasts in succession.

---

[16] In all cases where the rules require a bell to be used a drum may be substituted on board Turkish vessels, or a gong where such articles are used on board small sea-going vessels. [Footnote in original.]

(*d.*) A vessel, when at anchor, shall, at intervals of not more than 1 minute, ring the bell rapidly for about 5 seconds.

In vessels of more than 350 feet in length the bell shall be sounded in the forepart of the vessel, and, in addition, there shall be sounded in the afterpart of the vessel, at intervals of not more than 1 minute, a gong or other instrument, the tone of which cannot be confused with the ringing of the bell.

(*e.*) A vessel, when towing, a vessel employed in laying or in picking up a ~~telegraph~~ *submarine* cable, and a vessel under way, which is unable to get out of the way of an approaching vessel through being not under command, or unable to manœuvre as required by these Rules shall, instead of the signals prescribed in subdivisions (*a*), (*b*) and (*c*) of this Article, at intervals of not more than 2 minutes, sound 3 blasts in succession, viz., 1 prolonged blast followed by 2 short blasts. ~~A vessel towed may give this signal and she shall not give any other.~~

A vessel towed, or if more than one vessel is towed, the last vessel of the tow, shall, at intervals of not more than 2 minutes, sound 4 blasts in succession, viz., 1 prolonged blast followed by 3 short blasts, provided that this signal is not required when it is impossible to keep the vessel manned.

When practicable, the vessel towed shall make this signal immediately after the signal made by the towing vessel.

(*f.*) *A vessel aground in or near a fairway shall give the signal prescribed in paragraph (d), and shall, in addition, give 3 separate and distinct strokes on the bell immediately preceding and following each such signal.*

Sailing vessels and boats of less than 20 tons gross tonnage shall not be obliged to give the above-mentioned signals, but, if they do not, they shall make some other efficient sound-signal at intervals of not more than 1 minute.[17]

SPEED OF SHIPS TO BE MODERATE IN FOG, &C.

ARTICLE 16

Every vessel shall, in a fog, mist, falling snow, or heavy rain-storms, go at a moderate speed, having careful regard to the existing circumstances and conditions.

A steam vessel hearing, apparently forward of her beam, the fog-signal of a vessel the position of which is not ascertained, shall, so far as the circumstances of the case admit, stop her engines, and then navigate with caution until danger of collision is over.

---

[17] Dutch steam pilot-vessels, when engaged on their station on pilotage duty in fog, mist, falling snow, or heavy rain-storms are required to make at intervals of 2 minutes at most one long blast with the siren, followed after 1 second by a long blast with the steam whistle and again after 1 second by a long blast on the siren. When not engaged on their station on pilotage duty, they make the same signals as other steamships. [Footnote in original.]

Steering and Sailing Rules

Preliminary—Risk of Collision

Risk of collision can, when circumstances permit, be ascertained by carefully watching the compass bearing of an approaching vessel. If the bearing does not appreciably change, such risk should be deemed to exist.

ARTICLE 17

When two sailing vessels are approaching one another, so as to involve risk of collision, one of them shall keep out of the way of the other, as follows, viz.:—

(*a.*) A vessel which is running free shall keep out of the way of a vessel which is close-hauled.

(*b.*) A vessel which is closed-hauled on the port tack shall keep out of the way of a vessel which is close-hauled on the starboard tack.

(*c.*) When both are running free, with the wind on different sides, the vessel which has the wind on the port side shall keep out of the way of the other.

(*d.*) When both are running free, with the wind on the same side, the vessel which is to windward shall keep out of the way of the vessel which is to leeward.

(*e.*) A vessel which has the wind aft shall keep out of the way of the other vessel.

ARTICLE 18

When two steam vessels are meeting end on, or nearly end on, so as to involve risk of collision, each shall alter her course to starboard, so that each may pass on the port side of the other.

This Article only applies to cases where vessels are meeting end on, or nearly end on, in such a manner as to involve risk of collision, and does not apply to two vessels which must, if both keep on their respective courses, pass clear of each other.

The only cases to which it does apply are when each of the two vessels is end on, or nearly end on, to the other; in other words, to cases in which, by day, each vessel sees the masts of the other in a line, or nearly in a line, with her own; and, by night, to cases in which each vessel is in such a position as to see both the side-lights of the other.

It does not apply, by day, to cases in which a vessel sees another ahead crossing her own course; or by night, to cases where the red light of one vessel is opposed to the red light of the other, or where the green light of one vessel is opposed to the green light of the other, or where a red light without a green light, or a green light without a red light, is seen ahead, or where both green and red lights are seen anywhere but ahead.

Article 19

When two steam vessels are crossing, so as to involve risk of collision, the vessel which has the other on her own starboard side shall keep out of the way of the other.

Article 20

When a steam vessel and a sailing vessel are proceeding in such directions as to involve risk of collision, the steam vessel shall keep out of the way of the sailing vessel.

Article 21

Where by way of these Rules one of two vessels is to keep out of the way, the other shall keep her course and speed.

Note.—When, in consequence of thick weather or other causes, such vessel finds herself so close that collision cannot be avoided by the action of the giving-way vessel alone, she also shall take such action as will best aid to avert collision. (See Articles 27 and 29.)

Article 22

Every vessel which is directed by these Rules to keep out of the way of another vessel shall, if the circumstances of the case admit, avoid crossing ahead of the other.

Article 23

Every steam vessel which is directed by these Rules to keep out of the way of another vessel shall, on approaching her, if necessary, slacken her speed or stop or reverse.

Article 24

Notwithstanding anything contained in these Rules, every vessel, overtaking any other, shall keep out of the way of the overtaken vessel.

Every vessel coming up with another vessel from any direction more than two points abaft her beam, i. e., in such a position, with reference to the vessel which she is overtaking, that at night she would be unable to see either of that vessel's side-lights, shall be deemed to be an overtaking vessel; and no subsequent alteration of the bearing between the two vessels shall make the overtaking vessel a crossing vessel within the meaning of these Rules, or relieve her of the duty of keeping clear of the overtaken vessel until she is finally past and clear.

As by day the overtaking vessel cannot always know with certainty whether she is forward or abaft this direction from the other vessel, she should, if in doubt, assume that she is an overtaking vessel and keep out of the way.

Article 25

In narrow channels every steam vessel shall, when it is safe and practicable, keep to that side of the fairway or mid-channel which lies on the starboard side of such vessel.

ARTICLE 26

Sailing vessels under way shall keep out of the way of sailing vessels or boats fishing with nets, or lines, or trawls. This Rule shall not give to any vessel or boat engaged in fishing the right of obstructing a fair-way used by vessels other than fishing-vessels or boats.

ARTICLE 27

In obeying and construing these Rules, due regard shall be had to all dangers of navigation and collision, and to any special circumstances which may render a departure from the above Rules necessary in order to avoid immediate danger.

SOUND-SIGNALS FOR VESSELS IN SIGHT OF ONE ANOTHER

ARTICLE 28

The words "short blast" used in this Article shall mean a blast of about one second's duration.

When vessels are in sight of one another, a steam vessel under way, in taking any course authorized or required by these Rules, shall indicate that course by the following signals on her whistle or siren, viz.: —

One short blast to mean, "I am directing my course to starboard."
Two short blasts to mean, "I am directing my course to port."
Three short blasts to mean, "My engines are going full speed astern."

NO VESSEL UNDER ANY CIRCUMSTANCES TO NEGLECT PROPER PRECAUTIONS

ARTICLE 29

Nothing in these Rules shall exonerate any vessel, or the owner, or master, or crew thereof, from the consequences of any neglect to carry lights or signals, or of any neglect to keep a proper look-out, or of the neglect of any precaution which may be required by the ordinary practice of seamen, or by the special circumstances of the case.

RESERVATION OF RULES FOR HARBOURS AND INLAND NAVIGATION

ARTICLE 30

Nothing in these Rules shall interfere with the operation of a special rule, duly made by local authority, relative to the navigation of any harbour, river, or inland waters.

DISTRESS SIGNALS

Article 31

When a vessel is in distress and requires assistance from other vessels or from the shore, the following shall be the signals to be used or displayed by her, either together or separately, viz.: —

In the daytime—

1. A gun or other explosive signal fired at intervals of about a minute;
2. The International Code signal of distress; ~~indicated by N.C.~~
3. The ~~distant~~ *distance* signal, consisting of a square flag, having either above or below it a ball or anything resembling a ball;
4. A continuous sounding with any fog-signal apparatus;
5. *The international distress signal made by radiotelegraphy or radiotelephony, or by any other distance signalling method.*

At night—

1. A gun or other explosive signal fired at intervals of about a minute;
2. Flames on the vessel (as from a burning tar-barrel, oil-barrel, &c.);
3. Rockets or shells, throwing stars of any colour or description, fired one at a time, at short intervals;
4. A continuous sounding with any fog-signal apparatus;
5. *The international distress signal made by radiotelegraphy or radiotelephony, or by any other distance signalling method.*

The use of any of the above signals, except for the purpose of indicating that a vessel is in distress, and the use of any signals which may be confused with any of the above signals, is prohibited.

UNIVERSAL POSTAL UNION

Convention, with final protocol, and provisions concerning the transportation of regular mails by air, with final protocol, signed at London June 28, 1929 [1]
Ratified and approved by the Postmaster General of the United States March 8, 1930
Approved by the President of the United States March 13, 1930
Entered into force July 1, 1930
Terminated by convention of March 20, 1934 [2]

46 Stat. 2523; Post Office Department print

[TRANSLATION]

UNIVERSAL POSTAL CONVENTION

TABLE OF CONTENTS

TITLE I

THE UNIVERSAL POSTAL UNION

CHAPTER I

Organization and extent of the Union

CHAPTER II

Congresses. Conferences. Committees

---

[1] For text of regulations for execution of the convention, with final protocol of the regulations, see 46 Stat. 2579; for postal forms annexed to the provisions concerning transportation of regular mails by air, see 46 Stat. 2728.

[2] *Post,* vol. 3.

concluded between Afghanistan, the Union of South Africa, Albania, Germany, the United States of America, the whole of the Insular Possessions of the United States of America other than the Philippine Islands, the Philippine Islands, the Argentine Republic, the Commonwealth of Australia, Austria, Belgium, the Colony of the Belgian Congo, Bolivia, Brazil, Bulgaria, Canada, Chile, China, the Republic of Colombia, the Republic of Costa Rica, the Republic of Cuba, Denmark, the Free City of Danzig, the Dominican Republic, Egypt, Ecuador, Spain, the whole of the Spanish Colonies, Estonia, Ethiopia (Abyssinia), Finland, France, Algeria, the French Colonies and Protectorates in Indo-China, the whole of the other French Colonies, the United Kingdom of Great Britain and Northern Ireland, Greece, Guatemala, the Republic of Haiti, the Kingdom of Hejaz and Nejd and Dependencies, the Republic of Honduras, Hungary, British India, Iraq, the Irish Free State, Iceland, Italy, the whole of the Italian Colonies, Japan, Chosen (Korea), the whole of the other Japanese Dependencies, Latvia, the Republic of Liberia, Lithuania, Luxemburg, Morocco (except the Spanish zone), Morocco (Spanish zone), Mexico, Nicaragua, Norway, New Zealand, the Republic of Panama, Paraguay, the Netherlands, the Dutch East Indies, the Dutch Colonies in America, Peru, Persia, Poland, Portugal, the Portuguese Colonies in Africa, the Portuguese Colonies in Asia and Oceania, Rumania, the Republic of San Marino, the Republic of El Salvador, the Saar Territory, the Kingdom of Serbs, Croats and Slovenes (Yugoslavia), Siam, Sweden, Switzerland, Czechoslovakia, Tunis, Turkey, the Union of Socialistic Soviet Republics, Uruguay, the Vatican City State, the United States of Venezuela, and Yemen.

The undersigned, plenipotentiaries of the Governments of the countries above enumerated, being assembled in Congress at London by virtue of Article 12 of the Universal Postal Convention concluded at Stockholm on August 28, 1924,[3] have, by common consent and subject to ratification, revised the said Convention to read as follows:

---

[3] *Ante,* p. 443.

Title I

THE UNIVERSAL POSTAL UNION

Chapter I

ORGANIZATION AND EXTENT OF THE UNION

Article 1

Constitution of the Union

The countries between which the present Convention is concluded form, under the name of "Universal Postal Union", a single postal territory for the reciprocal exchange of correspondence. The purpose of the Postal Union is also to assure the organization and perfection of the various international postal services.

Article 2

New adhesions. Procedure

Any country is permitted to adhere to the Convention at any time.

Notice of the request for adhesion must be given, thru diplomatic channels, to the Government of the Swiss Confederation, and by the latter to the Governments of all the countries of the Union.

Article 3

Convention and Agreements of the Union

The regular-mail service is governed by the provisions of the Convention.

Other services, especially such as those of insured letters and boxes, parcel post, postal money orders, postal checks, collection of bills, drafts, etc., by mail, and subscriptions to newspapers and periodicals, form the subject of Agreements between countries of the Union.

These Agreements are binding only upon the countries which have adhered to them.

Adhesion to one or more of these Agreements is subject to the provisions of the preceding Article.

Article 4

Regulations of Execution

The Administrations of the Union draw up, by mutual agreement, in the Regulations of Execution,[4] the measures of order and detail necessary for the execution of the Convention and the Agreements.

---

[4] See footnote 1, p. 873.

ARTICLE 5

Special treaties and agreements. Restricted Unions

1. The countries of the Union have the right to maintain and conclude treaties, as well as to maintain and establish restricted Unions, with a view to the reduction of postage rates or to any other improvement of postal relations.

2. Moreover, the Administrations are authorized to make the necessary agreements among themselves relative to questions which do not interest the whole of the Union, provided that they do not introduce any provisions less favorable than those laid down by the Acts of the Union. They may, in particular, with regard to articles of correspondence, make agreements among themselves for the adoption of reduced postage rates within a frontier zone.

ARTICLE 6

Domestic legislation

The provisions of the Convention and Agreements of the Union do not affect the legislation of any country concerning anything which is not expressly provided for by those Acts.

ARTICLE 7

Exceptional relations

The Administrations which serve certain territories not included in the Union will be bound to act as intermediary for the other Administrations. The provisions of the Convention and its Regulations are applicable to these exceptional relations.

ARTICLE 8

Colonies, Protectorates, etc.

In the sense of the Convention and the Agreements, particularly in regard to their right to vote in Congresses and Conferences and in the interval between meetings, as well as to their contribution to the expenses of the International Bureau of the Universal Postal Union, the following are considered as forming a single country or a single Administration of the Union, as the case may be:

1° The whole of the Insular Possessions of the United States of America other than the Philippine Islands, and comprising Hawaii, Porto Rico, Guam, and the Virgin Islands of the United States of America;

2° The Philippine Islands;

3° The Colony of the Belgian Congo;

4° The whole of the Spanish Colonies;

5° Algeria;

6° The French Colonies and Protectorates in Indo-China;

7° The whole of the other French Colonies;
8° The whole of the Italian Colonies;
9° Chosen (Korea);
10° The whole of the other Japanese Dependencies;
11° The Dutch East Indies;
12° The Dutch Colonies in America;
13° The Portuguese Colonies in Africa;
14° The Portuguese Colonies in Asia and Oceania.

ARTICLE 9

Extent of the Union

The following are considered as belonging to the Universal Postal Union:

(a) The post offices established by countries of the Union in countries foreign to the Union;

(b) The Principality of Liechtenstein, as belonging to the Postal Administration of Switzerland;

(c) The Faroe Islands and Greenland, as forming part of Denmark;

(d) The Spanish possessions on the north coast of Africa, as forming part of Spain;

(e) The Valleys of Andorra, as served by the Spanish and French Postal Administrations;

(f) The Principality of Monaco, as belonging to the Postal Administration of France;

(g) Walfish Bay, as forming part of the Union of South Africa; Basutoland, as belonging to the Postal Administration of the Union of South Africa.

ARTICLE 10

Arbitration

1. In case of disagreement between two or more members of the Union as to the interpretation of the Convention and Agreements, or as to the responsibility imposed upon an Administration by the application of those Acts, the question in dispute is decided by arbitration. To that end, each of the Administrations concerned chooses another member of the Union which is not directly interested in the matter.

If one of the Administrations involved in the dispute does not take any action on a proposal for arbitration within a period of six months, or nine months in the case of distant countries, the International Bureau, upon a request made of it to that effect, may call upon the defaulting Administration to appoint an arbitrator, or may appoint one itself officially.

2. The decision of the arbitrators is made on an absolute majority of votes.

3. In case of equality of votes, the arbitrators, for the purpose of settling the difference, choose another Administration which likewise has no interest in the dispute.

In case of disagreement as to a choice, that Administration is designated by the International Bureau from among the members of the Union not proposed by the arbitrators.

4. Only such Administrations as are executing the Agreement under litigation may be designated as arbitrators.

ARTICLE 11

Withdrawal from the Union. Termination of participation in the Agreements

Each contracting party has the option of withdrawing from the Union or of ceasing to participate in the Agreements by notice given one year in advance by its Government to the Government of the Swiss Confederation.

CHAPTER II

CONGRESSES, CONFERENCES, COMMITTEES

ARTICLE 12

Congresses

1. Delegates from the countries of the Union meet in Congress not later than five years after the effective date of the Acts of the preceding Congress, with a view to revising or completing them as necessary.

Each country is represented at the Congress by one or more plenipotentiary delegates, provided with the necessary credentials by their Government. It may, if necessary, be represented by the delegation of another country. However, it is understood that a delegation may be charged with representing only two countries, including the one by which it was first accredited.

In the deliberations, each country has but one vote.

2. Each Congress fixes the meeting-place of the next Congress. The Congress is called together by the Government of the country in which it is to be held, in consultation with the International Bureau. That Government is likewise charged with notifying all the Governments of the countries of the Union of the decisions made by the Congress.

ARTICLE 13

Ratifications. Entry into force and duration of the Acts of Congresses

The Acts of Congresses are ratified as soon as possible, and the ratifications are communicated to the Government of the country in which the Congress was held, and by that Government to the Governments of the contracting countries.

In case that one or more of the contracting parties do not ratify one or another of the Acts signed by them, the Acts will nevertheless be valid for the countries which have ratified them.

Those Acts are put into effect simultaneously and have the same duration.

From the date fixed for the entry into force of the Acts adopted by a Congress, all the Acts of the preceding Congress are abrogated.

ARTICLE 14

Extraordinary Congresses

An extraordinary Congress is called together by agreement with the International Bureau when a request to that effect is made or approved by at least two-thirds of the contracting countries.

The rules laid down by Articles 12 and 13 are applicable to the delegations, the deliberations, and the Acts of extraordinary Congresses.

ARTICLE 15

Regulations for Congresses

Each Congress draws up the necessary regulations for its work and deliberations.

ARTICLE 16

Conferences

Conferences charged with the examination of purely administrative questions may be called together at the request of at least two-thirds of the Administrations of the Union.

They are called together by agreement with the International Bureau.

Conferences draw up their own regulations.

ARTICLE 17

Committees

Committees charged by a Congress or a Conference with the study of one or more definite questions are called together by the International Bureau, in consultation, if necessary, with the Administration of the country where such Committees are to meet.

CHAPTER III

PROPOSITIONS IN THE INTERVAL BETWEEN MEETINGS

ARTICLE 18

Introduction of propositions

In the interval between meetings, any Administration has the right to address to the other Administrations, thru the intermediary of the International Bureau, propositions concerning the Convention, its Regulations, and their Final Protocols.

The same right is accorded to the Administrations of the countries participating in the Agreements in regard to those Agreements, their Regulations, and their Final Protocols.

In order to be considered, all propositions introduced by an Administration in the interval between meetings must be supported by at least two other Administrations. Such propositions are ignored when the International Bureau does not receive, at the same time, the necessary number of declarations of support.

ARTICLE 19

Examination of propositions

Every proposition is submitted to the following procedure:

A period of six months is allowed to Administrations, in order to examine the propositions and send their observations, if any, to the International Bureau. Amendments are not admitted. The replies are assembled by the International Bureau and communicated to the Administrations, with an invitation to pronounce themselves for or against. Those which have not sent in their votes within a period of six months are considered as abstaining. The periods above mentioned are counted from the dates of the circulars of the International Bureau.

If the proposition concerns an Agreement, its Regulations, or their Final Protocols, only the Administrations which have adhered to that Agreement may take part in the procedure indicated above.

ARTICLE 20

Conditions of approval

1. In order to become effective, the propositions must obtain:

a) Unanimity of votes, if it is a question of adding new provisions or modifying the provisions of Titles I and II and of Articles 32 to 36, 52 to 57, 59 to 61, 63 to 66, 68 to 81 of the Convention, of any of the Articles of its Final Protocol, of Articles 1, 5, 16, 60, 72 and 93 of its Regulations, and of all those of its Final Protocol;

b) Two-thirds of the votes, if it is a question of modifying provisions other than those mentioned in the preceding paragraph;

c) A simple majority, if it is a question of interpreting the provisions of the Convention, its Regulations, and their Final Protocols except in the case of disputes to be submitted to arbitration contemplated by Article 10.

2. The Agreements fix the conditions to which the approval of propositions concerning them is subject.

ARTICLE 21

Notification of decisions

Additions to and modifications of the Convention, the Agreements, and the Final Protocols of those Acts, are sanctioned by a diplomatic declaration which the Government of the Swiss Confederation is charged with making up and transmitting, at the request of the International Bureau, to the Governments of the contracting countries.

Additions to and modifications of the Regulations and their Final Protocols are drawn up and communicated to the Administrations by the International Bureau. The same applies to the interpretations contemplated under letter (c) of the preceding Article.

ARTICLE 22

Effective date of decisions

No addition or modification adopted is effective until at least three months after its notification.

CHAPTER IV

INTERNATIONAL BUREAU

ARTICLE 23

General Functions

1. A central Office functioning at Berne under the name of "International Bureau of the Universal Postal Union" and placed under the supervision of the Swiss Postal Administration, serves as an organ of liaison, information and consultation for the countries of the Union.

This Bureau is charged, principally, with assembling, coordinating, publishing and distributing information of all kinds which concerns the international postal service; with giving, at the request of the interested parties, an opinion on questions in dispute; with making known requests for modification of the Acts of the Congress; with notifying the changes adopted; and, in general, with undertaking the studies and works of editing and documentation which the Convention, the Agreements, and their Regulations attribute to it, or which may be entrusted to it in the interests of the Union.

2. It acts as a clearing-house for the settlement of accounts of all kinds relative to the international postal service between Administrations requesting such intervention.

ARTICLE 24

Expenses of the International Bureau

1. Each Congress fixes the maximum figure for the ordinary annual expenses of the International Bureau.

Those expenses, as well as the extraordinary expenses arising from the meeting of a Congress, a Conference, or a Committee, and the expenses incurred in connection with special work entrusted to the Bureau, are shared by all the countries of the Union.

2. The latter are divided, for that purpose, into seven classes, each of which contributes to the payment of the expenses in the following proportion:

1st class	25 units
2d class	20 units
3d class	15 units
4th class	10 units
5th class	5 units
6th class	3 units
7th class	1 unit

3. In the case of a new adhesion, the Government of the Swiss Confederation determines, by mutual agreement with the Government of the country concerned, the class in which it is to be placed for the apportionment of the expenses of the International Bureau.

TITLE II

GENERAL REGULATIONS

SOLE CHAPTER

ARTICLE 25

Liberty of transit

1. Liberty of transit is guaranteed thruout the entire territory of the Union.

2. Liberty of transit for parcel post is limited to the territory of the countries participating in that service.

Insured articles may be sent in transit in closed mails thru the territory of countries which do not execute that service, or by maritime services on which responsibility for insured articles is not accepted by the countries, but the responsibility of those countries is limited to that prescribed for registered articles.

The transit of small packets thru the territory of countries which do not admit articles of this kind is optional.

ARTICLE 26

Prohibition against unauthorized charges

It is forbidden to collect postal charges of any nature whatever other than those prescribed by the Convention and the Agreements.

ARTICLE 27

Temporary suspension of service

When, as a result of exceptional circumstances, an Administration finds itself obliged to suspend the execution of services temporarily, in whole or in part, it is bound to give notice thereof immediately, by telegraph if necessary, to the Administration or Administrations concerned.

ARTICLE 28

Monetary standard

The franc used as the monetary unit in the provisions of the Convention and the Agreements is the gold franc of 100 centimes weighing $^{10}\!/_{31}$ of a gram and having a fineness of 0.900.

ARTICLE 29

Equivalents

In each country of the Union, the postage rates are fixed according to equivalents corresponding as exactly as possible to the value of the franc in the current money of that country.

ARTICLE 30

Forms. Language

1. The forms used by the Administrations in their reciprocal relations shall be drawn up in the French language, with or without an interlinear translation in another language, unless the Administrations concerned arrange otherwise by direct agreement.

2. The forms used by the public which are not printed in the French language must bear an interlinear translation in that language.

3. The forms mentioned in Sections 1 and 2 shall have the texts, the colors, and, as far as possible, the dimensions prescribed by the Regulations of the Convention and of the Agreements.

4. The Administrations may come to agreements as to the language to be employed for official correspondence in their reciprocal relations.

ARTICLE 31

Identity cards

1. Each Administration may issue, to persons who apply for them, identity cards valid as proof of identity in all transactions effected by the post offices of the countries which do not give notice of their refusal to admit them.

2. The Administration which issues an identity card is authorized to collect, on that account, a charge not exceeding 1 franc.

3. Administrations are relieved from all responsibility when it is proved that a mail article was delivered or a money order paid upon presentation of a regular identity card.

Neither are they responsible for the consequences of loss, theft, or fraudulent use of a regular identity card.

4. An identity card is valid for a period of three years, counting from the date of issue.

Title III

PROVISIONS CONCERNING CORRESPONDENCE

Chapter I

GENERAL PROVISIONS

Article 32

Articles of correspondence

The term "articles of correspondence" applies to letters, single and reply-paid post cards, commercial papers, prints of all kinds including raised print for the blind, samples of merchandise, and small packets.

The service of small packets is limited to the countries which agree to execute it in their reciprocal relations or in one direction only.

Article 33 (See Protocol II and IV)

Postage rates and general conditions

1. The postage rates for the transportation of articles of correspondence thruout the entire extent of the Union, including their delivery at the residence of the addressee in countries where the delivery service is or may be established, and the limits of weight and dimensions, are fixed in accordance with the indications of the following table:

Articles	Units of weight	Rates	Limits — Of weight	Limits — Of dimensions
1	2	3	4	5
	Grams	*Ctms.*		
LETTERS {1st unit of weight........	20	25	}2 kg	45 cm. in each direction; in form of roll: 75 cm. in length and 10 cm. in diameter.
each additional unit......	....	15		
POST CARDS {single......	....	15	....	Maximum: 15 cm. in length. 10.5 cm. in width. Minimum: 10 cm. in length. 7 cm. in width.
with reply paid........	....	30	....	
COMMERCIAL PAPERS..............	50	5	2 kg............	45 cm. on each side; In form of roll: 75 cm. in length; 10 cm. in diameter.
Minimum charge..............	....	25	....	
PRINTS......................	50	5	2 kg. (3 kg. for single volumes).	Prints sent open in the form of folded or unfolded cards are subject to the same minimum limits as post cards.
RAISED PRINT FOR THE BLIND......	1,000	5	5 kg............	45 cm. in length; 20 cm. in width; 10 cm. in thickness. In form of roll: 45 cm. in length; 15 cm. in diameter.
SAMPLES OF MERCHANDISE........	50	5	500 g...........	
Minimum charge...............	....	10	....	
SMALL PACKETS....................	50	15	1 kg............	
Minimum charge...............	....	50	....	

By exception to the provisions of the 1st paragraph above, the Administrations may collect, for the delivery of small packets to the addressees, a special fee for delivery which may not exceed 25 centimes per article.

2. The limits of weight and dimensions fixed by Section 1 of the present Article do not apply to the correspondence relative to the postal service mentioned in Section 1 of Article 47.

3. Each Administration has the option of granting, in its relations with Administrations which have given their consent, to newspapers and periodicals sent directly by the publishers or their representatives, a reduction of 50 per cent in the general print rate. There are excluded from this reduction, regardless of the regularity of their publication, commercial prints such as catalogs, prospectuses, price lists, etc.

The Administrations may grant the same reduction, and in the same relations, irrespective of the senders, to books and pamphlets or sheet music, with the exception of all publicity or advertising matter other than that appearing on the covers or fly leaves of the volumes.

4. Letters shall not contain any letter, note or document having the character of actual personal correspondence addressed to persons other than the addressee or persons residing with the latter.

5. Commercial papers, prints of any kind, samples of merchandise, and small packets shall not contain any letter, note or document having the character of actual personal correspondence; they shall be so prepared as to be easily verified, except as provided by the Regulations.

It is permissible to include in small packets an open invoice reduced to its essential terms, as well as a simple copy of the address of the article with mention of the address of the sender.

6. The inclusion in a single package of different classes of mail matter (grouped articles) is authorized under the conditions fixed by the Regulations.

7. Packages of samples of merchandise may not contain any article having a salable value.

8. With the exceptions provided for by the Convention and its Regulations, articles which do not fulfill the conditions prescribed by the present Article and the corresponding Articles of the Regulations are not forwarded.

Articles which have been wrongly admitted may be returned to the country of origin. However, an Administration of destination whose domestic regulations do not oppose it is authorized to deliver such articles to the addressees. In such a case, it shall, if need be, apply to them the rates and surcharges prescribed for the class of correspondence to which they actually belong. As for articles exceeding the maximum weight-limits fixed by Section 1 of the present Article they may be rated in accordance with their actual weight.

ARTICLE 34

Prepayment

As a general rule, all the articles designated in Article 32 must be fully prepaid by the sender.

Articles other than letters and single post cards which are unprepaid or insufficiently prepaid, or reply post cards both halves of which are not fully prepaid at the time of mailing, are not dispatched.

ARTICLE 35

Charge on unprepaid or insufficiently prepaid correspondence

With the exceptions provided by Article 45, Sections 3, 4 and 5 of the Regulations for certain classes of redirected articles, letters and single post cards not prepaid or insufficiently prepaid are liable to a charge equal to double postage or double the deficiency, to be paid by the addressees; but that charge may not be lower than 10 centimes.

The same treatment may be applied, in the cases above contemplated, to other articles of correspondence which have been erroneously sent to the country of destination.

ARTICLE 36

Surcharges

There may be collected, in addition to the rates fixed by Article 33, for every article transported by extraordinary services involving special payment, a surcharge proportionate to the expenses incurred.

When the rate of prepayment of the single post card includes the surcharge authorized by the preceding paragraph, the same rate is applicable to each half of the reply-paid post card.

ARTICLE 37

Special charges

1. The Administrations are authorized to charge late fees in accordance with the provisions of their own legislation for articles posted in their services for dispatch after the mails have closed.

2. The Administration of the country of destination is authorized to collect a special charge in accordance with its own legislation on articles addressed "General Delivery".

ARTICLE 38

Dutiable articles

Small packets may contain articles liable to customs duty.

The same applies to letters when the country of destination permits the importation of dutiable articles in that form.

ARTICLE 39

Customs inspection

The Administration of the country of destination is authorized to submit the correspondence mentioned in the preceding Article to customs inspection, and, if necessary, to open them officially.

ARTICLE 40

Customs-clearance fee

Articles submitted to customs inspection in the country of destination may be charged on that account, by the postal service, with a customs-clearance fee of 50 centimes at most per article.

ARTICLE 41

Customs duties and other non-postal charges

The Administrations are authorized to collect from the addressees of mail articles, in addition to the postal charges, the customs duties and all other charges which may be due.

ARTICLE 42

Prepayment of customs duty, etc.

1. In relations between countries which have come to an agreement to that effect, the senders may assume, by means of a previous declaration at the office of mailing, payment of the whole of the postal and non-postal charges with which the articles are assessed on delivery.

In such a case, the senders must promise to pay such amounts as may be claimed by the office of destination, and, if need be, post sufficient surety.

The Administration which advances the charges on behalf of the sender is authorized to collect a commission therefor which may not exceed 50 centimes per article. This charge is independent of the one provided for by Article 40 preceding for customs clearance.

2. Every Administration has the right to limit this prepayment service to registered articles.

ARTICLE 43

Cancelation of customs duty

The Administrations undertake to make representations to the respective Customs Administrations with a view to having the customs duties annulled on articles returned to the country of origin, destroyed because of complete deterioration of the contents, or forwarded to a third country.

ARTICLE 44

Special-delivery articles

1. Articles of correspondence are, at the request of the senders, delivered to the addressees by special messenger immediately after their arrival, in countries whose Administrations undertake that service in their reciprocal relations.

2. Such articles, known as "special-delivery articles," are liable, in addition to the regular postage, to a special charge of at least double the postage on an ordinary single-rate letter, and at most one franc. This charge must be fully prepaid by the sender.

3. When the addressee's residence is situated outside the local delivery zone of the office of destination, delivery by special messenger may give rise to the collection of a supplementary charge not exceeding that collected in the domestic service.

However, special delivery is not obligatory in such cases.

4. Special-delivery articles upon which the total amount of the charges payable in advance has not been prepaid are delivered by the ordinary means, unless they have been treated as special-delivery articles by the office of origin. In the latter case, the articles are rated in accordance with the provisions of Article 35.

ARTICLE 45

Prohibitions

1. It is forbidden to send by mail:

(a) Articles which, by their nature or packing, may expose postal employees to danger, or soil or damage the mails.

(b) Explosive, inflammable or dangerous substances.

(c) Live animals, with the exception of bees, leeches and silkworms.

(d) Articles liable to customs duty, with the exceptions provided for by Article 38, as well as samples sent in quantities for the purpose of avoiding the collection of such duty.

However, this prohibition does not apply to dutiable printed matter.

(e) Opium, morphine, cocaine and other narcotics.

(f) Obscene or immoral articles.

(g) Any articles whatever whose entry or circulation is prohibited in the country of origin or that of destination.

It is also forbidden to send, either in the unregistered mails or in registered or unregistered small packets, coins, banknotes, paper money or any values payable to the bearer; platinum, gold or silver, manufactured or unmanufactured; precious stones, jewelry and other precious articles.

The sending of canceled or uncanceled stamps in unsealed envelopes is prohibited.

2. Articles coming under the above prohibitions which have been wrongly accepted for mailing must be treated as follows:

(a) The articles enumerated under letters (a), (d), (e) and (g) of Section 1 above are treated in accordance with the domestic regulations of the Administration which discovers their presence. However, articles containing opium, morphine, cocaine and other narcotics are in no case either delivered to the addressee or returned to origin;

(b) The articles enumerated under (b) and (f) shall be destroyed on the spot by the first Administration which discovers their presence;

(c) The articles enumerated under (c), as well as in the last two paragraphs of Section 1, shall be returned to the country of origin, unless the Administration of the country of destination is disposed to deliver them as an exceptional measure to the addressees.

In cases where articles wrongly accepted for mailing are neither returned to origin nor delivered to the addressee, the dispatching Administration shall be notified, in a precise manner, of the disposal made of such articles, so that it may take the necessary action.

3. Moreover, the right is reserved for every country to refuse to convey in transit in open mail over its territory articles other than letters and post cards in regard to which the laws, ordinances or decrees regulating the conditions of their publication or circulation in that country have not been observed.

These articles shall be returned to the country of origin.

ARTICLE 46

Methods of prepayment

1. Prepayment of postage is effected either by means of postage stamps valid in the country of origin for the correspondence of private individuals, or by means of impressions of stamping machines officially adopted and operating under the immediate control of the Administration; or, in the case of prints, by means of impressions, printed or otherwise obtained, when such a system is authorized by the domestic regulations of the country of origin.

2. The following are considered as duly prepaid: Reply post cards bearing printed or adhesive postage stamps of the country of issue of the cards; articles regularly prepaid for their first transmission and on which the additional postage has been paid before their redirection; as well as newspapers and packages of newspapers and periodicals whose address bears the words "Abonnement-poste" (Subscription by mail) sent under the Agreement concerning subscriptions to newspapers and periodicals.

3. Correspondence mailed on the high seas, in the box on board a vessel, or handed to postal agents on board or to the commanders of vessels, may be prepaid, barring contrary agreement between the Administrations concerned,

by means of the postage stamps and according to the postage rates of the country to which the said vessel belongs or by which it is maintained. If the mailing on board takes place during the stay at one of the two terminal points of the voyage or at one of the ports of call, the prepayment is valid only if it is effected by means of the postage stamps and according to the postage rates of the country in whose waters the vessel happens to be.

Article 47

Franking privilege

1. Correspondence relating to the postal service exchanged between Postal Administrations, between those Administrations and the International Bureau, between post offices of countries of the Union, and between those offices and Administrations, as well as that for which the franking privilege is expressly provided by the provisions of the Convention and Agreements and their Regulations, is exempt from all postal charges.

2. Correspondence, with the exception of collect-on-delivery articles, addressed to prisoners of war or mailed by them, is likewise exempt from all postal charges, not only in the countries of origin and destination but also in intermediate countries.

The same is true of correspondence concerning prisoners of war, sent or received either directly or as intermediary by the information offices which may be established on behalf of such persons in belligerent countries or in neutral countries which have received belligerents on their territory.

Belligerents received and interned in a neutral country are assimilated to prisoners of war properly so-called, insofar as the application of the above provisions is concerned.

Article 48 (See Protocol V)

Reply Coupons

Reply coupons are placed on sale in the countries of the Union.

The selling price thereof is determined by the interested Administrations, but may not be less than 37½ centimes or the equivalent of that sum in money of the country selling them.

Each coupon is exchangeable in any country for a stamp or stamps representing the postage on a single-rate letter originating in that country and addressed to a foreign country.

Moreover, the right is reserved for each country to require that the reply coupons and the articles of correspondence for the prepayment of which they are to be exchanged be presented at the same time.

ARTICLE 49 (See Protocol I)

Withdrawal. Change of address

1. The sender of an article of correspondence may cause it to be withdrawn from the mails or have its address changed, provided that such article has not been delivered to the addressee.

2. The request to be made to that effect is sent by mail or by telegraph at the expense of the sender, who must pay, for every request by mail, the charge applicable to a single-rate registered letter; and, for every request by telegraph, the charge for the telegram.

ARTICLE 50

Forwarding. Undelivered correspondence

1. In case of change of residence of the addressee, articles of correspondence are forwarded to him, unless the sender has forbidden the forwarding by an appropriate notation on the address side.

2. Correspondence which is undeliverable for any reason must be returned immediately to the country of origin.

3. The period of retention for correspondence held at the disposal of the addressees or addressed "general delivery" is fixed by the regulations of the country of destination. However, such period may not exceed two months as a general rule, except in particular cases where the Administration of destination deems it necessary to extend it, as an exceptional measure, up to four months at most. The return to the country of origin must take place within a shorter period, if the sender has so requested by a notation on the address side in a language known in the country of destination.

4. Prints without value are not returned, unless the sender, by a notation on the outside of the article, requests its return. Registered prints must always be returned.

5. The forwarding of articles of correspondence from country to country, or their return to the country of origin, does not give rise to the collection of any additional charge, apart from the exceptions provided for by the Regulations.

6. Forwarded or returned articles of correspondence are delivered to the addressees or senders upon payment of the charges due on them on departure, on arrival, or in the course of transmission, as a result of redirection after the first transmission, without prejudice to the repayment of the customs duties or other special charges which the country of destination does not agree to cancel.

7. In the case of forwarding to another country, or of non-delivery, the general-delivery fee, the customs-clearance fee, the additional special-delivery fee, and the special fee for the delivery of small packets to the addressees, are canceled.

ARTICLE 51

Inquiries

1. An inquiry as to the disposal made of any article may give rise to the collection of a fee fixed at 1 franc maximum.

As for registered articles, no fee is collected if the sender has already paid the special fee for a return receipt.

2. Inquiries are accepted only within the period of one year, counting from the day following that of mailing of the article.

3. Every Administration is obliged to accept inquiries concerning articles mailed on the territory of other Administrations. The inquiry fee is retained in its entirety by the Administration accepting the inquiry.

4. When an inquiry has been made necessary thru a fault of the service the inquiry fee is returned.

CHAPTER II

REGISTERED ARTICLES

ARTICLE 52 (See Protocol VI)

Charges

1. The articles of correspondence designated in Article 32 may be sent under registration.

However, the registration fee applicable to the reply half of a post card can not be legally paid by the original sender of the article.

2. The postage on all registered articles must be paid in advance. It consists of:

(a) The ordinary postage on the article, according to its class;

(b) A fixed registration fee of 40 centimes at most.

3. A receipt shall be delivered without charge to the sender of a registered article at the time of mailing.

4. Countries disposed to undertake risks arising from force majeure (causes beyond control) are authorized to collect a special charge of 40 centimes at most for each registered article.

5. Unprepaid or insufficiently prepaid registered articles which have been wrongly sent to the country of destination are, if delivered, rated in accordance with the provisions laid down for unprepaid or insufficiently prepaid ordinary articles.

ARTICLE 53

Return receipts

The sender of a registered article may obtain a return receipt by paying, at the time of mailing, a fixed charge of 40 centimes at most.

The return receipt may be requested after mailing the article, within the period and upon payment of the charge fixed by Article 51 for inquiries.

ARTICLE 54

Extent of responsibility

With the exceptions provided for by the following Article, the Administrations are responsible for the loss of registered articles.

The sender is entitled, on that account, to indemnity, the amount of which is fixed at 50 francs for each article.

ARTICLE 55

Exceptions to the principle of responsibility

The Administrations are released from all responsibility for the loss of registered articles:

(a) In case of force majeure; however, the responsibility is maintained in regard to an Administration of origin which has undertaken to cover the risks of force majeure (Art. 52, Sec. 4). The country responsible for the loss must, in accordance with its domestic legislation, decide whether such loss is due to circumstances constituting force majeure;

(b) When they can not account for the articles as a result of the destruction of the service records due to a case of force majeure;

(c) When it is a question of an article whose contents fall within the scope of the prohibitions laid down by Article 45, Section 1;

(d) When the sender has not made any inquiry within the period contemplated by Article 51.

ARTICLE 56

Termination of responsibility

Administrations cease to be responsible for registered articles the delivery of which they have effected under the conditions prescribed by their domestic regulations.

For articles addressed "general delivery" or held at the disposal of the addressees, responsibility ceases upon delivery to a person who has proved his identity in accordance with the regulations in force in the country of destination, and whose name and description are in conformity with the indications of the address.

ARTICLE 57

Payment of indemnity

The obligation of paying indemnity falls upon the Administration to which the office of origin of the article belongs, subject to its right to make a claim against the responsible Administration.

Article 58

Period for payment

1. The payment of the indemnity must take place as soon as possible, and, at the latest, within the period of six months, counting from the day following the date of the inquiry. That period is extended to nine months in relations with distant countries.

The dispatching Administration may exceptionally postpone settlement of the indemnity beyond the period prescribed by the preceding paragraph when the question of knowing whether the loss of the article was due to a case of force majeure has not yet been settled.

2. The Administration of origin is authorized to settle with the sender on behalf of the Administration of intermediation or of destination which, duly advised of the application, has let three months pass without settling the matter; that period is extended to six months in relations with distant countries.

Article 59

Fixing of responsibility

1. Until the contrary is proved, responsibility for the loss of a registered article falls on the Administration which, having received the article without making any observations, and, being furnished all particulars of inquiry prescribed by the regulations, can not establish either delivery to the addressee or regular transmission to the next Administration, as the case may be.

However, an Administration of intermediation or destination is released from all responsibility when it can prove that it has not received any inquiry until after the destruction of the service records relative to the article sought, the retention-period prescribed by Article 78 of the Regulations having expired. This reservation does not affect the rights of the claimant.

If the loss has taken place in the course of conveyance, without its being possible to determine on the territory or in the service of which country the loss occurred, the Administrations concerned bear the loss in equal shares. However, the whole of the indemnity due must be turned over to the Administration of origin by the first Administration which can not establish the regular transmission of the article in question to the corresponding service. It is incumbent upon the latter Administration to recover from the other responsible Administrations the share of each of them in the indemnity paid to the sender.

2. When a registered article has been lost under circumstances of force majeure, the Administration on whose territory or in whose service the loss took place is not responsible to the dispatching Administration unless both countries undertake risks arising from cases of force majeure.

3. The customs duties and other charges whose cancelation it has been impossible to obtain are charged to the Administrations responsible for the loss.

4. By the fact of the payment of the indemnity, the responsible Administration is subrogated up to the amount of that indemnity in the rights of the person who has received it for all eventual recourse against the addressee, the sender, or a third party.

5. In case of subsequent recovery of a registered article considered as lost, the person to whom the indemnity has been paid shall be advised that he may obtain possession of the article by repaying the amount of the indemnity.

ARTICLE 60

Repayments of the indemnity to the Administration of origin

1. The Administration which is responsible, or on whose behalf the payment is made in accordance with Article 58, is bound to reimburse the dispatching Administration, within a period of three months following notification of the payment, for the amount of the indemnity actually paid to the sender.

That reimbursement is effected without expense for the creditor Administration by means of either a money order, a check or a draft payable at sight on the capital or on a commercial city of the creditor country, or in coin current in the creditor country. At the expiration of the period of three months the sum due to the dispatching Administration bears interest at the rate of 7 per cent a year, counting from the date of expiration of the said period.

2. The Administration of origin may claim the repayment of the indemnity from the responsible Administration only within the period of two years, counting from the date of notification of the loss; or, if occasion arises, from the date of expiration of the period contemplated by Article 58, Sec. 2.

3. The Administration whose responsibility is duly established and which has at first declined to pay the indemnity must bear all the additional expenses resulting from the unjustified delay in making the payment.

4. Administrations may agree among themselves to make periodical settlements of the indemnities which they have paid to the senders and the justness of which they have recognized.

CHAPTER III

COLLECT-ON-DELIVERY ARTICLES

ARTICLE 61

Rates and conditions.   Settlement

1. Registered articles may be sent C.O.D. in relations between countries whose Administrations agree to conduct that service.

Barring contrary agreement, the amount to be collected is expressed in the money of the country of origin of the article.

The maximum C.O.D. charge is equal to the maximum amount fixed for money orders addressed to the country of origin of the article.

C.O.D. articles are subject to the conditions and rates applicable to registered articles.

The sender also pays a fixed fee, which may not exceed 50 centimes per article, and a proportional fee of ½ percent at most of the amount of the C.O.D. charge.

Each Administration has the option of adopting, for the collection of the proportional fee, the scale which is most convenient for its service.

2. The amount collected from the addressee is transmitted to the sender by means of a C.O.D. money order, which is issued free of charge.

3. Administrations may agree upon some other procedure for the settlement of the sums collected. They may, in particular, undertake to turn them over to a current postal account in the country of destination of the article.

In this case, in the absence of contrary arrangements, the amount of the C.O.D. charge shall be indicated in money of the country of destination. There is collected from the sender, in addition to the postage for a registered article, a fixed fee of 25 centimes at most. The Administration of destination turns over to the current account, by means of a domestic transfer bulletin, the amount collected from the addressee, after deducting a fixed fee of 25 centimes at most and the ordinary transfer charge applicable in its domestic service.

ARTICLE 62

Cancelation or reduction of the amount to be collected

The sender of a registered C.O.D. article may request total or partial cancelation of the amount to be collected.

Requests of this nature are subject to the same provisions as requests for withdrawal or change of address.

If the request for total or partial cancelation of the C.O.D. charge must be sent by telegram, the charge for the telegram is increased by the rate applicable to a single-rate registered letter.

ARTICLE 63

Responsibility in case of loss of articles

The loss of a registered C.O.D. article involves the responsibility of the postal service under the conditions laid down by Articles 54 and 55.

ARTICLE 64

Guarantee of sums regularly collected

The sums regularly collected from the addressee, whether or not they have been converted into money orders or turned over to a current postal account, are guaranteed to the sender under the conditions laid down by the Agreement concerning Money Orders, or by the provisions governing the postal-check service.

ARTICLE 65

Indemnity in case of non-collection, insufficient or fraudulent collection

1. If the article has been delivered to the addressee without collecting the amount of the C.O.D. charge, the sender is entitled to indemnity, provided that an application has been made within the period prescribed by Article 51, Section 2, and unless the non-collection is due to fault or negligence on his part, or unless the contents of the article come under the prohibitions laid down by Article 45.

The same applies if the sum collected from the addressee is lower than the amount of the C.O.D. charge or if the collection has been made fraudulently.

In any case, the indemnity may not exceed the amount to be collected on delivery.

2. By the fact of the payment of the indemnity, the responsible Administration is subrogated, up to the amount of such indemnity, in the rights of the person who has received it, for all eventual recourse against the addressee, the sender, or third parties.

ARTICLE 66

Sums regularly collected. Indemnity. Payment and recourse

The obligation of paying the amounts regularly collected, as well as the indemnity referred to in the preceding Article, falls upon the Administration to which the office of origin of the article belongs, subject to its right to recourse against the responsible Administration.

ARTICLE 67

Period for payment

The provisions of Article 58 concerning the periods for payment of indemnity for the loss of a registered article are applicable to the payment of the sums collected or the indemnity for C.O.D. articles.

ARTICLE 68

Fixing of responsibility

The payment by the dispatching Administration of the sums regularly collected, as well as of the indemnity provided for by Article 65, is effected on behalf of the Administration of destination. The latter is responsible, unless it can prove that the irregularity was due to the failure of the dispatching Administration to observe a provision of the regulations.

In the case of fraudulent collection as a result of the loss of a C.O.D. article in the service, the responsibility of the Administrations involved is determined in accordance with the rules laid down by Article 59 for the loss of registered articles in general.

However, the responsibility of an intermediate Administration which does not participate in the C.O.D. service is limited to that prescribed by Articles 54 and 55 for registered articles.

The other Administrations shall pay the amount not covered by that Administration in equal shares.

ARTICLE 69

Repayment of sums advanced

The Administration of destination is bound to reimburse the Administration of origin, under the conditions prescribed by Article 60, for the sums which have been advanced on its behalf.

ARTICLE 70

C.O.D. money orders and transfer bulletins

1. The amount of a C.O.D. money order which, for any reason, has not been paid to the payee, is not repaid to the Administration of issue. It is held at the disposal of the payee by the Administration of origin of the C.O.D. article, and finally reverts to that Administration, after the expiration of the period prescribed by law.

In all other respects, and apart from the exceptions laid down by the Regulations, C.O.D. money orders are subject to the provisions of the Agreement concerning Money Orders.

2. When, for any reason, a transfer bulletin, issued in accordance with the provisions of Article 61, Section 3, can not be entered to the credit of the payee indicated by the sender of the C.O.D. article, the amount of this bulletin shall be placed, by the Administration which has cashed it, at the disposal of the Administration of origin, to be paid to the sender of the article.

If this payment can not be effected, the procedure outlined in Section 1 of the present Article is followed.

ARTICLE 71

Sharing of C.O.D. charges and fees

The Administration of origin credits the Administration of destination, under the conditions fixed by the Regulations, with a fixed quota of 20 centimes per C.O.D. article, plus $\frac{1}{4}$ percent of the total amount of C.O.D. money orders paid.

The charges fixed by Section 3 of Article 61 are retained in their entirety by the Administration which has collected them.

CHAPTER IV

RETENTION OF POSTAGE. TRANSIT AND WAREHOUSING CHARGES

ARTICLE 72

Retention of postage

Except in cases expressly provided for by the Convention, each Administration retains the whole of the sums which it has collected.

ARTICLE 73

Transit charges

1. Articles of correspondence exchanged in closed mails between two Administrations, by means of the services of one or more other Administrations (third services), are liable, for the benefit of each of the countries traversed or whose services participate in the conveyance, to the transit charges indicated in the following table:

	Per kilogram	
	Of letters and post cards	Of other articles
1°. Territorial transit:	*Fr. c.*	*Fr. c.*
Up to 1,000 km	0.75	0.10
From 1,000 to 2,000 km	1.00	.15
From 2,000 to 3,000 km	1.50	.20
From 3,000 to 6,000 km	2.50	.30
From 6,000 to 9,000 km	3.50	.40
Over 9,000 km	4.50	.50
2°. Maritime transit:		
Up to 300 nautical miles	0.75	.10
From 300 to 1,500 nautical miles	2.00	.25
Between Europe and North America	3.00	.40
From 1,500 to 6,000 nautical miles	4.00	.50
Over 6,000 nautical miles	6.00	.75

2. The transit charges for maritime conveyance on a route not exceeding 300 nautical miles are fixed at one-third the amounts set forth in the preceding Section if the Administration concerned already receives, on account of the mails transported, compensation for territorial transit.

3. In the case of maritime transit effected by two or more Administrations, the total transit charges may not exceed 6 francs per kilogram of letters

and post cards or 0.75 francs per kilogram of other articles. When the totals of such charges exceed 6 francs and 0.75 francs respectively, they are divided between the Administrations taking part in the conveyance in proportion to the distances traversed, without prejudice to different arrangements which may be made between the parties concerned.

4. Barring contrary agreement, maritime transportation effected directly between two countries by means of ships belonging to one of them, as well as conveyances effected between two offices of the same country through the intermediary of services belonging to another country, are considered as third services.

5. The transit charges for correspondence exchanged in open mail between two Administrations are fixed, regardless of the weight or destination, at 5 centimes per article, irrespective of the classification thereof.

6. Small packets, newspapers or packets of newspapers and periodicals sent by virtue of the Agreement concerning Subscriptions to Newspapers and Periodicals, as well as insured boxes sent by virtue of the Agreement concerning Insured Letters and Boxes, are considered as "other articles" in regard to transit in closed mails, and as units in regard to open-mail transit.

ARTICLE 74 (See Protocol X)

Warehousing charges

The warehousing in a port of closed mails brought by one steamship and intended to be taken away by another steamship gives rise to the payment of a charge fixed at 50 centimes per sack, for the profit of the Postal Administration to which the place of warehousing belongs, unless that Administration already receives payment for territorial or maritime transit.

ARTICLE 75

Freedom from transit charges

The following are exempt from all maritime or territorial transit charges: The correspondence sent free of postage mentioned in Article 47; reply post cards returned to the country of origin; redirected articles; returned undeliverable articles; return receipts; money orders; and all other documents relating to the postal service, especially correspondence relative to postal checks.

Missent dispatches are considered, insofar as the payment of transit and warehousing charges is concerned, as tho they had followed their normal route.

ARTICLE 76

Extraordinary services

The transit charges specified under Article 73 do not apply to transportation by means of extraordinary services specially created or maintained by one Administration at the request of one or more other Administrations. The conditions for this class of conveyance are fixed from time to time among the Administrations concerned.

ARTICLE 77

Payments and accounts

1. The transit and warehousing charges are borne by the Administration of the country of origin.

2. The general accounting for such charges is effected on the basis of statistics taken once every three years, during a period of fourteen days. That period is extended to twenty-eight days for dispatches exchanged less than six times a week by the services of any country.

The Regulations determine the period and length of application of the statistics.

3. An Administration is authorized to submit to a Commission of arbiters for consideration the results of statistics which, in its opinon, differ too greatly from reality. Such arbitration is effected in accordance with the provisions of Article 10.

The arbitrators have the right to fix the just amount of the transit charges to be paid.

ARTICLE 78

Exchange of closed mails with warships

1. Closed mails may be exchanged between the post offices of any one of the contracting countries and the commanding officers of naval divisions or warships of the same country stationed abroad, or between the commanding officer of one of those naval divisions or warships and the commanding officer of another division or ship of the same country, thru the intermediary of land or sea services maintained by other countries.

2. Correspondence of all kinds comprised in such dispatches shall be exclusively addressed to or sent by the officers and crews of the ships of destination or origin of the mails; the rates and conditions of dispatch applicable to them are determined, according to its domestic regulations, by the Postal Administration of the country to which the ships belong.

3. Barring contrary agreement between the Administrations concerned, the Postal Administration dispatching or receiving the mails in question is indebted to the intermediate Administrations for transit charges calculated in accordance with the provisions of Article 73.

VARIOUS PROVISIONS

ARTICLE 79

Failure to observe liberty of transit

When a country does not observe the provisions of Article 25 concerning liberty of transit, the Administrations have the right to discontinue postal service with it. They must give advance notice of that measure by telegram to the Administrations concerned.

ARTICLE 80

Obligations

The contracting countries undertake to adopt or to propose to their respective legislative bodies the necessary measures:

(a) For punishing both the counterfeiting and the fraudulent employment of international reply coupons and the fraudulent use, for the prepayment of mail articles, of counterfeit or used postage stamps, as well as of counterfeit or used impressions of stamping machines or printed indicia;

(b) For prohibiting and suppressing the fraudulent manufacture, sale, peddling or distribution of embossed or adhesive stamps in use in the postal service which are counterfeited or imitated in such a way that they might be mistaken for embossed or adhesive stamps issued by the Administration of one of the contracting countries;

(c) For punishing the fraudulent manufacture and circulation of postal identity cards, as well as the fraudulent employment of such cards;

(d) For preventing, and, if occasion arises, punishing the insertion of opium, morphine, cocaine and other narcotics in mail articles in favor of which such insertion is not expressly authorized by the Convention and Agreements of the Union.

FINAL PROVISIONS

ARTICLE 81

Effective date and duration of the Convention

The present Convention will become effective on July 1, 1930, and will remain in force for an indefinite period.

In faith of which, the Plenipotentiaries of the Governments of the Countries above enumerated have signed the present Convention in one copy, which will be filed in the Archives of the Government of the United Kingdom of Great Britian and Northern Ireland, and a copy of which will be delivered to each Party.

Done at London, June 28, 1929.

For Afghanistan:

For the Union of South Africa:
  J. N. REDELINGHUYS
  D. J. O'KELLY

For Albania:
  M. LIBOHOVA

For Germany:
  Dr. K. SAUTTER
  Dr. W. KÜSGEN
  K. ZIEGLER

For the United States of America:
  For Joseph Stewart:
    E. R. WHITE
  EUGENE R. WHITE

For the whole of the insular possessions of the United States of America other than the Philippine Islands:
  EUGENE R. WHITE

For the Philippine Islands:
  C. E. UNSON
  JOSÉ TOPACIO

For the Argentine Republic:

For the Commonwealth of Australia:
M. B. HARRY

For Austria:
WALTHER STOECKL

For Belgium:
O. SCHOCKAERT
HUB. KRAINS

For the Colony of the Belgian Congo:
HALEWYCK DE HEUSCH
F. G. TONDEUR
JAMAR

For Bolivia:
ZAC. BENAVIDES

For Brazil:
JM EULALIO

For Bulgaria:
M. SAVOFF
N. BOSCHNACOFF

For Canada:
L. J. GABOURY
ARTHUR WEBSTER

For Chile:
ANTONIO HUNEEUS
MIGUEL A. PARRA
C. VERNEUIL

For China:
LIU SHU-FAN

For the Republic of Colombia:
JORGE GARCÉS B.

For the Republic of Costa Rica:
PERCY G. HARRISON

For the Republic of Cuba:
GUILLERMO PATTERSON

For Denmark:
V. HOLMBLAD

For the Free City of Danzig:
STANISLAW ŁOŚ
VICTOR ZANDER
ALFRED NORDMANN

For the Dominican Republic:
Dr. E. R. LLUBERES

For Egypt:
H. MAZLOUM
R. SIDHOM

For Ecuador:
E. CHACÓN Q.
E. L. ANDRADE

For Spain:
A. CAMACHO

For the whole of the Spanish colonies:
A. RAMOS GARCIA

For Estonia:
G. JALLAJAS

For Ethiopia:
B. MARCOS
A. BOUSSON

For Finland:
G. E. F. ALBRECHT

For France:
M. LEBON
L. GENTHON
BOUSQUIÉ
MAINGUET
GRANDSIMON
DUSSERRE

For Algeria:
E. HUGUENIN

For the French colonies and protectorates in Indo-China:
For M. Régismanset:
J. CASSAGNAC

For the whole of the other French colonies:
J. CASSAGNAC

For the United Kingdom of Great Britain and Northern Ireland:
F. H. WILLIAMSON
W. G. GILBERT
F. C. G. TWINN
F. R. RADICE
D. O. LUMLEY

For Greece:
TH. PENTHÉROUDAKIS
D. BERNARDOS

For Guatemala:
JOSÉ MATOS

For the Republic of Haiti:
J. G. DALZELL

For the Kingdom of the Hejaz and Nejd and dependencies:
CHEIK HAFIZ WAHBA

For the Republic of Honduras:
HUMBERTO BLANCO-FOMBONA

For Hungary:
G. BARON SZALAY
CHARLES DE FORSTER

For British India:
H. A. SAMS
G. V. BEWOOR
L. P. KULKARNI
P. N. MUKERJI

For Iraq:
DOUGLAS W. GUMBLEY

For the Irish Free State:
P. S. Óh-Éigeartaigh
R. S. O'Cruimín
S. S. Puirséal

For Iceland:
V. Holmblad

For Italy:
Biagio Borriello
Pietro Tosti
Michele Galdi

For the whole of the Italian colonies:
Riccardo Astuto

For Japan:
H. Kawai
Naotaro Yamamoto
J. Shimidzu

For Chosen:
Naotaro Yamamoto
Jingoro Hirao

For the whole of the other Japanese
dependencies:
H. Kawai
Noboru Tomizu

For Latvia:
A. Auzinš

For the Republic of Liberia:
C. W. Dresselhuys

For Lithuania:
A. Sruoga
G. Krolis

For Luxemburg:
Jaaques

For Morocco (except the Spanish
Zone):
Jacques Truelle

For Morocco (Spanish Zone):
A. Camacho

For Mexico:
Lino B. Rochín
José V. Chávez

For Nicaragua:
Eduardo Pérez-Triana

For Norway:
Klaus Helsing
Oskar Homme

For New Zealand:
G. McNamara

For the Republic of Panama:
Carlos A. López G.

For Paraguay:

For the Netherlands:
Damme
Duynstee

For the Netherlands Indies:
J. van der Werf
W. F. Gerdes Oosterbeek
Dommisse
Hoogewooning

For the Netherlands colonies in America:
W. F. Gerdes Oosterbeek
Hoogewooning

For Peru:
M. de Freyre y S.
A. S. Salazar

For Persia:
Hovhannès Khan Mossaed
R. Ardjomende

For Poland:
Łoś
Dr. Marjan Blachier

For Portugal:
Jose Vasco de Carvalho
Adalberto da Costa Veiga

For the Portuguese colonies in Africa:
Mario Corrêa Barata da Cruz

For the Portuguese colonies of Asia and
Oceania:
Luciano Botelho da Costa Mar-
tins

For Rumania:
Général Mihail
I. Manea

For the Republic of San Marino:
M. A. Jamieson
Giovanni Sovrani

For the Republic of Salvador:
Antonio Reyes-Guerra

For the Saar Territory:
P. Courtilet
A. Arend

For the Kingdom of the Serbs, Croats
and Slovenes:
G. Diouritch

For Siam:
Phya Prakit Kolasastra
Luang Bahiddha Nukara

For Sweden:
Anders Örne
Gunnar Lager
Fr. Sandberg

For Switzerland:
  P. Dubois
  C. Roches
  L. Roulet

For Czechoslovakia:
  Dr. Otokar Růžička
  Josef Zabrodsky

For Tunisia:
  Jacques Dumaine
  Dupont

For Turkey:
  Ali Raana
  Yusuf Arifi

For the Union of Soviet Socialist Republics:
  Dr. Eugène Hirschfeld
  M. Khodeeff
  E. Syrevitch

For Uruguay:
  F. A. Costanzo

For the Vatican City State:
  W. A. S. Hewins

For the United States of Venezuela:
  Luis Alejandro Aguilar
  E. Arroyo Lameda

Final Protocol of the Convention

At the moment of proceeding to sign the Universal Postal Convention concluded on the present date, the undersigned Plenipotentiaries have agreed as follows:

I

Withdrawal. Change of address

The provisions of Article 49 of the Convention do not apply to Great Britain, nor to the British Dominions, Colonies and Protectorates, whose domestic legislation does not permit the withdrawal or change of address of correspondence upon the request of the sender.

II

Equivalents. Maximum and minimum limits

1. Each country has the option of increasing by 50 percent, or of decreasing by 20 percent, at most, the postage rates fixed by Article 33, Section 1, in accordance with the indications of the following table:

	Minimum limits	Maximum limits
	Centimes	Centimes
Letters:		
First unit	20	37. 5
Each additional unit	12	22. 5
Post cards:		
Single	12	22. 5
With reply paid	24	45
Commercial papers, each 50 grams	4	7. 5
Minimum charge	20	37. 5
Prints, each 50 grams	4	7. 5
Raised print for the blind, each 1000 grams	4	7. 5
Samples, each 50 grams	4	7. 5
Minimum charge	8	15
Small packets, each 50 grams	12	22. 5
Minimum charge	40	75

The rates chosen shall, as far as possible, be in the same proportion as the basic rates, each Administration having the option of rounding off its rates to suit the conveniences of its monetary system.

2. It is permissible for each country to reduce the postage on single post cards to 10 centimes, and that on reply post cards to 20 centimes.

3. The rates of postage adopted by a country are applicable to the charges to be collected upon arrival as a result of absence or insufficiency of prepayment.

III

Mailing of correspondence in another country

No country is bound to dispatch or deliver to addressees articles which any senders domiciled on its territory mail or cause to be mailed in a foreign country with a view to profiting by lower rates which are established there. The rule applies, without distinction, either to articles prepared in the country inhabited by the sender and transported subsequently across the border, or to articles prepared in a foreign country. The Administration concerned has the right either to return the articles in question to origin or to charge them with its domestic postage rates. The methods of collecting the charges are left to its discretion.

IV

Avoirdupois ounce

It is admitted, as an exceptional measure, that countries which, on account of their domestic legislation, can not adopt the decimal metric system as a standard of weight, have the option of substituting for the avoirdupois ounce (28.3465 it grams), assimilating one ounce to 20 grams for letters and 2 ounces to 50 grams for commercial papers, prints, samples and small packets.

V

Reply coupons

Administrations have the option of not undertaking the sale of reply coupons.

VI

Registration fee

Countries which can not fix at 40 centimes the registration fee contemplated by Article 52, Section 2, of the Convention, are authorized to collect a fee which may amount to as much as 50 centimes, or their domestic registration fee if this is higher.

VII

Air services

The provisions concerning the transportation of regular mails by air are appended to the Universal Postal Convention and are considered as forming an integral part of it and its Regulations.

However, by exception to the general provisions of the Convention, the modification of those provisions may be undertaken from time to time by a Conference comprising the representatives of the Administrations directly interested.

That Conference may be called together thru the intermediary of the International Bureau, at the request of three at least of those Administrations.

All the provisions proposed by that Conference shall be submitted, thru the medium of the International Bureau, to the other Countries of the Union, to be voted upon. The decision will be made on a majority of the votes cast.

VIII

Special transit charges for the Trans-Siberian route

By exception to the provisions of Article 73, Section 1 (Table), the Postal Administration of the Union of Socialist Soviet Republics is authorized to collect transit charges for the Trans-Siberian Railway for both routes (Manchuria or Vladivostok) at the rate of 4.50 francs for L. C. [lettres, cartes] and 0.50 francs for A. O. [autres objets] per kilogram, respectively, for distances exceeding 6000 km.

IX

Special transit charges for Uruguay

As an exceptional measure, Uruguay is authorized to collect, for all oversea dispatches unloaded at Montevideo which it forwards by its own services to countries beyond, the land-transit charges contemplated by Article 73 of the Convention, or 75 centimes per kilogram of letters and post cards and 10 centimes per kilogram of other articles.

X

Warehousing charges

As an exceptional measure, the Portuguese Administration is authorized to collect, for all mails transshipped at the port of Lisbon, the warehousing charges prescribed by Article 74 of the Convention.

XI

Protocol left open to the Countries not represented

As Afghanistan and the Argentine Republic, which form part of the Postal Union, were not represented at the Congress, the Protocol remains open to them in order that they may adhere to the Convention and the Agreements concluded there, or merely to one or another of them.

The Protocol also remains open for the same purpose to Paraguay, whose delegate was obliged to leave before signing the Acts.

XII

Protocol left open to the Countries represented for signatures and adhesions

The Protocol remains open to those Countries whose representatives have signed today only the Convention or a certain number of the Agreements drawn up by the Congress, for the purpose of permitting them to adhere to the other Agreements signed on this date, or to one or another of them.

XIII

Period for notification of adhesions

The adhesions contemplated in Articles XI and XII above shall be communicated by the respective Governments, thru diplomatic channels, to the Government of the United Kingdom of Great Britain and Northern Ireland, and by the latter to the States of the Union. The period which is allowed to them to make such notification will expire on July 1, 1930.

XIV

Preparatory committee

1. A Committee composed of fourteen members, representing the Administrations designated by a majority of votes of the Congress, and of the Director of the International Bureau, is charged with preparing for the following Congress, and in particular with studying the propositions made in view of that Congress, with comparing and coordinating them, giving its opinion on all questions, and finally with presenting a draft and a report which may serve as the basis for the deliberations of the Congress.

2. The Preparatory Committee is called together at the proper time by the International Bureau, prior to the opening of the following Congress, and the draft and report mentioned in the preceding Section are distributed among the Administrations four months at least before the opening of the Congress.

3. The International Bureau undertakes the secretarial work of the Committee.

In faith of which, the undersigned Plenipotentiaries have drawn up the present Protocol, which will have the same force and validity as if the provisions which it contains were included in the text of the Convention to which it belongs, and they have signed it in a single copy which will remain filed in the Archives of the Government of the United Kingdom of Great Britain and Northern Ireland, and a copy of which will be delivered to each Party.

Done at London, June 28, 1929.

For Afghanistan:

For the Union of South Africa:
J. N. REDELINGHUYS
D. J. O'KELLY

For Albania: •
M. LIBOHOVA

For Germany:
Dr. K. SAUTTER
Dr. W. KÜSGEN
K. ZIEGLER

For the United States of America:
For Joseph Stewart:
E. R. WHITE
EUGENE R. WHITE

For the whole of the insular possessions
of the United States of America
other than the Philippine Islands:
EUGENE R. WHITE

For the Philippine Islands:
C. E. UNSON
JOSÉ TOPACIO

For the Argentine Republic:

For the Commonwealth of Australia:
M. B. HARRY

For Austria:
WALTHER STOECKL

For Belgium:
O. SCHOCKAERT
HUB. KRAINS

For the Colony of the Belgian Congo:
HALEWYCK DE HEUSCH
F. G. TONDEUR
JAMAR

For Bolivia:
ZAC. BENAVIDES

For Brazil:
JM EULALIO

For Bulgaria:
M. SAVOFF
N. BOSCHNACOFF

For Canada:
L. J. GABOURY
ARTHUR WEBSTER

For Chile:
ANTONIO HUNEEUS
MIGUEL A. PARRA
C. VERNEUIL

For China:
LIU SHU-FAN

For the Republic of Colombia:
JORGE GARCÉS B.

For the Republic of Costa Rica:
PERCY G. HARRISON

For the Republic of Cuba:
GUILLERMO PATTERSON

For Denmark:
V. HOLMBLAD

For the Free City of Danzig:
STANISŁAW ŁOŚ
VICTOR ZANDER
ALFRED NORDMANN

For the Dominican Republic:
Dr. E. R. LLUBERES

For Egypt:
H. MAZLOUM
R. SIDHOM

For Ecuador:
E. CHACÓN Q.
E. L. ANDRADE

For Spain:
A. CAMACHO

For the whole of the Spanish colonies:
A. RAMOS GARCIA

For Estonia:
G. JALLAJAS

For Ethiopia:
B. MARCOS
A. BOUSSON

For Finland:
G. E. F. ALBRECHT

For France:
M. LEBON
L. GENTHON
BOUSQUIÉ
MAINGUET
GRANDSIMON
DUSSERRE

For Algeria:
E. HUGUENIN

For the French colonies and protector-
ates in Indo-China:
For M. Régismanset:
J. CASSAGNAC

For the whole of the other French
colonies:
J. CASSAGNAC

For the United Kingdom of Great Brit-
ain and Northern Ireland:
F. H. WILLIAMSON
W. G. GILBERT
F. C. G. TWINN
F. R. RADICE
D. O. LUMLEY

For Greece:
TH. PENTHÉROUDAKIS
D. BERNARDOS

For Guatemala:
JOSÉ MATOS

For the Republic of Haiti:
J. G. DALZELL

For the Kingdom of the Hejaz and Nejd
and dependencies:
CHEIK HAFIZ WAHBA

For the Republic of Honduras:
HUMBERTO BLANCO-FOMBONA

For Hungary:
G. BARON SZALAY
CHARLES DE FORSTER

For British India:
H. A. SAMS
G. V. BEWOOR
L. P. KULKARNI
P. N. MUKERJI

For Iraq:
DOUGLAS W. GUMBLEY

For the Irish Free State:
P. S. ÓH–ÉIGEARTAIGH
R. S. O'CRUIMÍN
S. S. PUIRSÉAL

For Iceland:
V. HOLMBLAD

For Italy:
BIAGIO BORRIELLO
PIETRO TOSTI
MICHELE GALDI

For the whole of the Italian colonies:
RICCARDO ASTUTO

For Japan:
H. KAWAI
NAOTARO YAMAMOTO
J. SHIMIDZU

For Chosen:
NAOTARO YAMAMOTO
JINGORO HIRAO

For the whole of the other Japanese
dependencies:
H. KAWAI
NOBORU TOMIZU

For Latvia:
A. AUZINŠ

For the Republic of Liberia:
C. W. DRESSELHUYS

For Lithuania:
A. SRUOGA
G. KROLIS

For Luxemburg:
JAAQUES

For Morocco (except the Spanish
Zone):
JACQUES TRUELLE

For Morocco (Spanish Zone):
A. CAMACHO

For Mexico:
LINO B. ROCHÍN
JOSÉ V. CHÁVEZ

For Nicaragua:
EDUARDO PÉREZ-TRIANA

For Norway:
KLAUS HELSING
OSKAR HOMME

For New Zealand:
G. McNAMARA

For the Republic of Panama:
CARLOS A. LÓPEZ G.

For Paraguay:

For the Netherlands:
DAMME
DUYNSTEE

For the Netherlands Indies:
J. VAN DER WERF
W. F. GERDES OOSTERBEEK
DOMMISSE
HOOGEWOONING

For the Netherlands colonies in America:
W. F. GERDES OOSTERBEEK
HOOGEWOONING

For Peru:
M. DE FREYRE Y S.
A. S. SALAZAR

For Persia:
HOVHANNÈS KHAN MOSSAED
R. ARDJOMENDE

For Poland:
ŁOŚ
Dr. MARJAN BLACHIER

For Portugal:
JOSE VASCO DE CARVALHO
ADALBERTO DA COSTA VEIGA

For the Portuguese colonies in Africa:
MARIO CORRÊA BARATA DA CRUZ

For the Portuguese colonies of Asia and
Oceania:
LUCIANO BOTELHO DA COSTA MARTINS

For Rumania:
GÉNÉRAL MIHAIL
I. MANEA

For the Republic of San Marino:
M. A. JAMIESON
GIOVANNI SOVRANI

For the Republic of Salvador:
ANTONIO REYES-GUERRA

For the Saar Territory:
P. COURTILET
A. AREND

For the Kingdom of the Serbs, Croats
and Slovenes:
G. DIOURITCH

For Siam:
PHYA PRAKIT KOLASASTRA
LUANG BAHIDDHA NUKARA

For Sweden:
ANDERS ÖRNE
GUNNAR LAGER
FR. SANDBERG

For Switzerland:
P. DUBOIS
C. ROCHES
L. ROULET

For Czechoslovakia:
Dr. OTOKAR RŮŽIČKA
JOSEF ZABRODSKY

For Tunisia:
JACQUES DUMAINE
DUPONT

For Turkey:
ALI RAANA
YUSUF ARIFI

For the Union of Soviet Socialist Repub-
lics:
Dr. EUGÈNE HIRSCHFELD
M. KHODEEFF
E. SYREVITCH

For Uruguay:
F. A. COSTANZO

For the Vatican City State:
W. A. S. HEWINS

For the United States of Venezuela:
LUIS ALEJANDRO AGUILAR
E. ARROYO LAMEDA

[For text of regulations for execution of the convention, see 46 Stat. 2579.]

PROVISIONS CONCERNING THE TRANSPORTATION OF REGULAR MAILS BY AIR

TABLE OF CONTENTS

CHAPTER I

General provisions

CHAPTER II

Registered or insured articles

I. REGISTERED ARTICLES

II. INSURED ARTICLES

CHAPTER III

Retention of aerial surcharges. Transportation charges

PROVISIONS CONCERNING THE TRANSPORTATION OF REGULAR MAILS BY AIR

CHAPTER I

GENERAL PROVISIONS

ARTICLE 1

Articles of correspondence admitted to aerial transportation

1. There are admitted to aerial transportation, over all or part of the route, all the articles designated in Article 32 of the Universal Postal Convention, namely: letters, post cards (single or with reply paid), commercial papers, prints of all kinds (including raised print for the blind), samples of merchandise, small packets as well as money orders and subscriptions by mail. These articles take, in this case, the name of "air-mail correspondence."

2. The articles mentioned in Article 32 of the Convention may be subjected to the formality of registration.

3. Insured articles (letters and boxes) may also be admitted to aerial transportation in relations between countries which agree to exchange articles of this kind by air.

ARTICLE 2

Liberty of transit

The liberty of transit provided for in Article 25, of the Universal Postal Convention is guaranteed to air-mail correspondence thruout the entire territory of the Union, whether or not the intermediate Administrations take part in the reforwarding of the correspondence.

ARTICLE 3

Rates and general conditions for admission of air-mail correspondence

1. Articles to be sent by air mail are liable, in addition to the regular postage rates, to a special surcharge for aerial transportation, the amount of which shall be fixed by the Administration of the country of origin; this surcharge must not exceed 25 gold centimes for each 20 grams for each 1,000 kilometers of the air route.

2. As for post cards and money orders, the surcharge is 25 gold centimes at most per piece for each 1,000 kilometers of the air route.

3. The surcharge for reply post cards is collected separately for each half at the point of departure of each of those parts.

4. The surcharges mentioned in Sections 1, 2 and 3 of the present Article apply solely to the services to which the tariff provided for by Article 11, Section 10, is applicable. They must be uniform for every country of destination.

5. The surcharge for air-mail correspondence transported by extraordinary services (Article 11, Section 11) may be increased to take account of the extraordinary expenses which the use of those services occasions.

6. The surcharges must be prepaid at the point of departure. Except in the cases contemplated by Article 6, they may not be collected from the addressee.

7. Air-mail correspondence is prepaid under the conditions fixed by Article 46 of the Universal Postal Convention. However, regardless of the nature of such correspondence, the prepayment may be represented by a handwritten notation, in figures, of the sum collected, expressed in money of the country of origin, in the following form:

"Affranchissement perçu: Fr.____c.____"
(Postage collected: Fr.____c.____)

This notation may appear either in a special hand-stamp impression or on a special adhesive stamp or label, or, finally, it may be simply written on the envelope of the article by any process whatever. In all cases, the notation must be supported by the date-stamp of the office of origin

ARTICLE 4

Unprepaid or insufficiently prepaid air-mail correspondence

1. In case of total lack of prepayment, air-mail correspondence is treated in accordance with the provisions of Articles 34 and 35 of the Universal Postal Convention. Articles whose prepayment at the time of mailing is not obligatory are sent by the ordinary means.

2. In case of insufficient prepayment, air-mail correspondence is sent by the air route when the charges paid represent at least the amount of the aerial surcharge. The provisions of Article 35 of the Universal Postal Convention are applicable in regard to the collection of postage charges not paid at the time of mailing.

3. When such articles are sent by the ordinary means, the office of mailing or the exchange office must strike out every annotation relative to the air transportation.

ARTICLE 5

Delivery of air-mail correspondence

1. Air-mail correspondence is delivered as rapidly as possible, and must at least be included in the first delivery following its arrival at the office of destination.

2. Senders have the option of requesting delivery at the addressee's residence by special carrier, immediately after arrival, by paying the special-delivery fee provided for by Article 44 of the Universal Postal Convention. This option exists only in relations between countries which have organized the special-delivery service in their reciprocal relations.

3. For additional compensation, Administrations may, after agreeing among themselves, undertake delivery at the residence of the addressee by special means; for example, by pneumatic tubes.

ARTICLE 6

Redirection and return of air-mail correspondence

1. Air-mail correspondence addressed to persons who have changed their residence is forwarded to the new destination by the ordinary means, unless the addressee has expressly requested redirection by air mail and has paid in advance, to the forwarding office, the aerial surcharge for the new route. Undeliverable correspondence is returned to origin by the ordinary means.

2. If redirection or return is effected by the ordinary means, the "Par avion" label and every notation relative to the transmission by the air route must be canceled officially by means of two heavy transverse lines.

Chapter II

REGISTERED OR INSURED ARTICLES

I. REGISTERED ARTICLES

Article 7

Registered articles

Registered articles are subject to the postage rates and general conditions for admission provided for by the Universal Postal Convention. They are also liable to the same aerial surcharges as ordinary articles.

Article 8

Responsibility

Postal Administrations assume, in regard to registered articles sent by the air route, the same responsibility as for other registered articles.

II. INSURED ARTICLES

Article 9

Insured articles

1. Administrations which admit insured articles to transportation by air mail are authorized to collect, on account of such articles, a special insurance fee, the amount of which they are to fix.

The sum of the ordinary insurance fee and the special fee must remain within the limits fixed by Article 3, Letter c), of the Agreement concerning Insured Letters and Boxes.

2. As for insured articles passing in transit in closed mails thru the territory of countries not adhering to the aforesaid Agreement, or passing in transit thru air services for which the countries concerned do not accept responsibility for insured articles, the responsibility of those countries is limited to that provided for registered articles.

Chapter III

RETENTION OF AERIAL SURCHARGES. TRANSPORTATION CHARGES

Article 10

Retention of surcharges

Each Administration retains the whole of the sums which it has collected as aerial surcharges of any kind.

Article 11

Aerial transportation charges for closed mails

1. The transit charges contemplated by Article 73 of the Universal Postal Convention do not apply to aerial services.

2. By exception to the provisions of the Convention, countries of destination which assure the reforwarding of air-mail correspondence by the air route in their domestic services are entitled to payment of the internal transportation charges. This payment must be uniform for all routes in the domestic service of one and the same country.

3. The transportation charges relative to one and the same air route are uniform for all Administrations using that service without participating in the operating costs.

4. With the exceptions provided for in Sections 5 and 6 below, the aerial transportation charges are payable to the Postal Administration of the country in which the airport where the correspondence has been taken in charge by the air service is located.

5. The Administration which delivers to an air-transport enterprise mails destined to employ several separate air services in succession may, if it has agreed with the intermediate Administrations, settle directly with that enterprise for the transportation charges for the whole route. The intermediate Administrations, for their part, have the right to demand the application pure and simple of the provisions of Section 4.

6. By exception to the provisions of Sections 4 and 5 above, each Administration controlling an air service retains the right to collect directly from each Administration utilizing that service the transportation charges relative to the whole route.

7. The air-transportation charges for air-mail correspondence sent in closed mails are chargeable to the Administration of the country of origin; the air-transportation charges for correspondence sent in open mail are chargeable to the Administration which delivers them in open mail to another Administration.

8. Barring contrary agreement among the Postal Administrations concerned, the transfer en route, in one and the same airport, of mails which employ several separate air services in succession, must be performed by the Postal Administration of the country where the transshipment is effected. This rule does not apply when the transfer is made between machines performing successive sections of one and the same service.

9. No warehousing charges are collected for air-mail dispatches.

However, in cases where, thru exceptional circumstances, considerable expense must be borne because of such warehousing, Administrations are authorized to collect the warehousing charges contemplated by Article 74 of the Convention.

10. As a temporary measure, the basic rate to be applied in the settlement of accounts among the Administrations for aerial transportation is fixed at 6 centimes of a gold franc for each indivisible fraction of 100 grams of gross weight and of 100 kilometers. All fractions of 100 grams and 100 kilometers are rounded off to the next highest 100 grams and 100 kilometers respectively,

and separately for each dispatch which forms the subject of the aerial statistics. Air-mail dispatches carried in the domestic service are subject to the same rules.

11. The transportation charges specified above do not apply to long-distance transportation by means of services whose creation and upkeep give rise to extraordinary expenses. The conditions for using such services are settled from time to time among the Administrations concerned; they must be uniform for all Administrations using such services.

12. The transportation charges above mentioned are also due on correspondence exempt from transit charges, as well as for missent dispatches or correspondence, in case that they are transmitted by the air route.

13. In addition to the eventual warehousing charges (Section 9 above), Administrations of countries flown over have no right to any remuneration for dispatches transported by air over their territory.

ARTICLE 12

Transportation charges for aerial correspondence in open mail

1. Air-mail correspondence may be exchanged in open mail between two Administrations by the air route.

2. The aerial transportation charges are paid in their entirety to the Postal Administration of the country to which the correspondence is addressed in open mail for reforwarding by the air route; this Administration may require the formation of separate bundles for destinations which it may indicate.

3. In order to determine the transportation charges, the net weight of the aerial correspondence transmitted in open mail is increased by 25 per cent, in order to take account of the expenses of the work of sorting. However, the increase in aerial transportation charges resulting therefrom in favor of one transit country may not exceed 1 franc 50 centimes per 100 grams of net weight.

ARTICLE 13

Calculation of the distance between two countries connected by several air lines

If two countries are connected by several air lines, the transportation charges are calculated in accordance with the average length of those routes and their importance for the international service.

CHAPTER IV

INTERNATIONAL BUREAU

ARTICLE 14

Communications to be addressed to the International Bureau

1. The Administrations shall communicate to one another, thru the intermediary of the International Bureau:

(a) Information as to the aerial surcharges which they collect for air-mail correspondence, in the domestic service as well as when destined for other countries;

(b) Information as to whether or not they admit insured letters and boxes to aerial transportation;

(c) A list of the national or foreign air lines which they utilize for the transportation of air-mail correspondence, whether those lines operate within the country or start from its airports and run to foreign countries; these latter lines should figure in the list with the part of the route for which the Administration utilizing them assumes responsibility on account of the correspondence which it entrusts to them. The list should indicate, in particular, for each line, the distance and transit time from the port of departure to the different ports of call, the frequency of the service, the country to which the aerial transportation charges for the line should be paid, and the special conditions or restrictions to which the utilization of the line is subject. At the end of the information concerning the domestic lines, each Administration shall indicate the average distance which it has adopted for the payment of charges for aerial transportation of air-mail correspondence destined for the interior of its country;

(d) A list of countries of destination to which they undertake the reforwarding of air-mail correspondence by the air route all or part of the way, with indication of the routes by which the reforwarding is effected, the distances on the air routes, and the transportation charges therefor.

This information is given on a form like Model A V 1 hereto appended.[5]

2. The communications under (c) and (d) shall be sent in regularly twice a year; one month before the commencement of the summer service, and one month before that of the winter service. Notice of any modification made subsequently shall be given without delay.

3. The International Bureau prepares, on the basis of the communications which it receives, a Digest of information concerning the air-mail service, including the exchange of insured letters and boxes, a general list of air-mail lines, and a general list of countries served by air lines. These documents are distributed without delay among the Administrations. The general list to be prepared by the International Bureau must correspond to Model A V 1 hereto appended.

The International Bureau is also charged with making up a world map indicating the lines of international air-mail communications, as well as supplementary maps giving the internal lines of each Continent.

4. For temporary information, a copy of each communication mentioned under (c) and (d) will be sent directly by each Administration to all other Administrations which express their desire to receive them.

---

[5] For postal forms annexed to provisions concerning transportation of regular mails by air, see 46 Stat. 2728.

5. Administrations will also communicate regularly, to all Administrations requesting them, the schedules of the air lines of their domestic and international services, with indication of the hours of arrival and departure of the planes from each port of call.

CHAPTER V

SETTLEMENT OF ACCOUNTS

ARTICLE 15

Accounting statistics

1. The general accounting for aerial transportation charges is effected in accordance with statistical tables made up during the seven days following the 14th of June and the 14th of November of each year. The results of the June statistics form the basis for the payments due for the summer service; those of November being used for the winter service.

2. Statistics concerning services which do not operate during the months of June and November will be made up after agreement among the Administrations concerned.

3. As a temporary measure, every Administration has the option of requesting that the settlements of accounts be made quarterly on the basis of the gross weight of the articles actually transported during the preceding quarter. In such a case, an agreement is made among the Administrations concerned as to the procedure to be followed.

ARTICLE 16

Preparation of ordinary or aerial dispatches during the statistical periods for air-mail transportation charges

The provisions of Article 61 of the Regulations of Execution of the Universal Postal Convention do not apply to the semi-annual statistics for the fixing of the aerial transportation charges. However, during such statistical periods, the tags or labels of the dispatches containing air-mail correspondence should bear the conspicuous notation "Statistique-avion" (Air-mail statistics).

ARTICLE 17

Fixing the weight of air-mail correspondence

1. During the statistical periods, the date of dispatch and the gross weight of the dispatch are indicated on the label or outside address of the dispatch. The inclusion of air-mail dispatches in another dispatch of the same kind is prohibited.

2. In case that open-mail correspondence intended to be redispatched by the air route is included in an ordinary or air-mail dispatch, the weight shall

be indicated separately on the letter bill for each country to which the air-mail correspondence is addressed. If necessary, the indications of the weight may be made in a special list conforming to Model A V 2 hereto appended, which is attached to the letter bill.

3. These indications are verified by the exchange office of destination. If that office finds that the actual weight indicated differs by more than 20 grams from the weight announced, it corrects the letter bill or label and immediately points out the error to the dispatching office by bulletin of verification; a copy of that bulletin is sent to each intermediate Adminis-tration, if occasion arises. If the differences of weight detected remain within the limits above mentioned, the indications of the dispatching office are considered as valid.

ARTICLE 18

List of closed air mails

As soon as possible, and in any case within a period of 15 days after each statistical period, the Administrations which have dispatched closed air mails send a list of such dispatches to the different Administrations whose air services they have used, including that of destination, if occasion arises.

ARTICLE 19

Preparation of Forms A V 3 and A V 4 for air-mail dispatches

1. During the statistical periods, the intermediate Administrations take note, on a form agreeing with Model A V 3 hereto appended, of the weights indicated on the labels or outside addresses of the air-mail dispatches which they have reforwarded by the air route beyond the frontiers of their countries. A statement is made up for each exchange office dispatching air mails.

2. Administrations receiving air mails, which assure the reforwarding of the air-mail correspondence which they contain by the air route, either in their domestic service or beyond the frontiers of their countries, prepare a state-ment conforming to Model A V 4 hereto appended, in accordance with the indications figuring in the letter bills. The same procedure is followed in regard to air-mail correspondence contained in ordinary dispatches.

3. As soon as possible, and at the latest one month after the close of statistical operations, the Forms A V 3 and A V 4 are sent to the dispatching exchange offices for acceptance. These offices, after accepting the statements, send them in turn to their Central Administration, which forwards them to the Central Administration of the creditor country.

4. If the creditor Administration has not received any corrective observa-tion within an interval of 3 months, counting from the date of transmittal, the statements are considered as fully accepted. In case of extraordinary circumstances (long distance, etc.), those periods may be extended by com-mon consent between the Administrations concerned.

ARTICLE 20

Aerial transportation account

1. The gross or net weights of the air-mail correspondence figuring in the Forms A V 3 or A V 4 are multiplied by a figure determined by the frequency of the summer and winter services, and the products thus obtained serve as the basis for individual accounts showing, in francs, the charges for transportation due to each Administration for the current six-month period.

2. The duty of preparing these accounts is incumbent upon the creditor Administration, which transmits them to the debtor Administration.

3. The individual accounts are prepared in duplicate and transmitted as soon as possible to the debtor Administration. If the creditor Administration has not received any corrective observation within a period of 3 months from the transmittal of an account, such account is considered as fully accepted.

ARTICLE 21

General account

In the absence of contrary agreement among the Administrations concerned, the general account of aerial transportation charges is made up twice a year by the International Bureau, in accordance with the rules fixed for the transit-charge account.

CHAPTER VI

VARIOUS PROVISIONS

ARTICLE 22

Designation of air-mail correspondence

Air-mail correspondence is provided, at the time of mailing, with a special blue label or imprint bearing the words "Par avion" (By air mail), with a translation into the language of the country of origin.

ARTICLE 23

Aerial transportation over part of the route only

If the sender desires his correspondence dispatched by air mail over a part of the air route only, he should indicate that fact. At the end of the aerial transmission of such correspondence, the note and the "Par avion" label, as well as the special annotation, should be crossed out officially by means of two heavy transverse lines.

ARTICLE 24

Mode of dispatch of air-mail correspondence in ordinary dispatches

The mode of dispatch prescribed by Article 55 of the Regulations of Execution of the Universal Postal Convention for special-delivery articles is also applicable to air-mail correspondence included in ordinary dispatches, except that the word "Exprès" (Special delivery) on the labels of the bundles and in the "Observations" column of the letter bills is to be replaced by the words "Par avion" (By air mail).

ARTICLE 25

Annotations to be made on the letter bills, on the insured bills, and on the labels of dispatches containing air-mail correspondence

1. The presence of air-mail correspondence in ordinary dispatches is indicated by the words "Par avion" in Table No. 1 of the letter bill and in the insured bill, the text of which will be modified accordingly.

2. The letter bills accompanying air-mail dispatches should be provided, in their heading, with the "Par avion" label. The same "Par avion" label is applied to the labels or addresses of such dispatches.

ARTICLE 26

Dispatch of air-mail correspondence

1. Administrations which make use of aerial communications for the transportation of their own correspondence are bound to forward by those same routes the air-mail correspondence received by them from other Administrations.

2. Administrations having no air service forward air-mail correspondence by the most rapid routes utilized by the mails.

The same applies, if for any reason, the dispatch by such other means offers advantages over an existing air route.

ARTICLE 27

Customs clearance of dutiable articles

The Administrations take steps to accelerate, as far as possible, the customs clearance of air-mail correspondence liable to customs duty.

ARTICLE 28

Application of the provisions of the Convention and Agreements

The provisions of the Convention and Agreements, as well as of their respective Regulations, with the exception of the Parcel-Post Agreement and and its Regulations, are applicable in everything which is not expressly regulated by the foregoing Articles.

ARTICLE 29

Effective date and duration of the Provisions adopted

The present Provisions will be effective from the effective date of the Universal Postal Convention. They will have the same duration as that Convention, unless they are renewed by mutual agreement among the Parties concerned.

Done at London, June 28, 1929.

For Afghanistan:

For the Union of South Africa:
J. N. REDELINGHUYS
D. J. O'KELLY

For Albania:
M. LIBOHOVA

For Germany:
Dr. K. SAUTTER
Dr. W. KÜSGEN
K. ZIEGLER

For the United States of America:
For Joseph Stewart:
E. R. WHITE
EUGENE R. WHITE

For the whole of the insular possessions of the United States of America other than the Philippine Islands:
EUGENE R. WHITE

For the Philippine Islands:
C. E. UNSON
JOSÉ TOPACIO

For the Argentine Republic:

For the Commonwealth of Australia:
M. B. HARRY

For Austria:
WALTHER STOECKL

For Belgium:
O. SCHOCKAERT
HUB. KRAINS

For the Colony of the Belgian Congo:
HALEWYCK DE HEUSCH
F. G. TONDEUR
JAMAR

For Bolivia:
ZAC. BENAVIDES

For Brazil:
JM EULALIO

For Bulgaria:
M. SAVOFF
N. BOSCHNACOFF

For Canada:
L. J. GABOURY
ARTHUR WEBSTER

For Chile:
ANTONIO HUNEEUS
MIGUEL A. PARRA
C. VERNEUIL

For China:
LIU SHU-FAN

For the Republic of Colombia:
JORGE GARCÉS B.

For the Republic of Costa Rica:
PERCY G. HARRISON

For the Republic of Cuba:
GUILLERMO PATTERSON

For Denmark:
V. HOLMBLAD

For the Free City of Danzig:
STANISŁAW ŁOŚ
VICTOR ZANDER
ALFRED NORDMANN

For the Dominican Republic:
Dr. E. R. LLUBERES

For Egypt:
H. MAZLOUM
R. SIDHOM

For Ecuador:
E. CHACÓN Q.
E. L. ANDRADE

For Spain:
A. CAMACHO

For the whole of the Spanish colonies:
A. RAMOS GARCIA

For Estonia:
G. JALLAJAS

For Ethiopia:
B. MARCOS
A. BOUSSON

For Finland:
G. E. F. ALBRECHT

For France:
M. LEBON
L. GENTHON
BOUSQUIÉ
MAINGUET
GRANDSIMON
DUSSERRE

For Algeria:
E. HUGUENIN

For the French colonies and protectorates in Indo-China:
For M. Régismanset:
J. CASSAGNAC

For the whole of the other French colonies:
J. CASSAGNAC

For the United Kingdom of Great Britain and Northern Ireland:
F. H. WILLIAMSON
W. G. GILBERT
F. C. G. TWINN
F. R. RADICE
D. O. LUMLEY

For Greece:
TH. PENTHÉROUDAKIS
D. BERNARDOS

For Guatemala:
JOSÉ MATOS

For the Republic of Haiti:
J. G. DALZELL

For the Kingdom of the Hejaz and Nejd and dependencies:
CHEIK HAFIZ WAHBA

For the Republic of Honduras:
HUMBERTO BLANCO-FOMBONA

For Hungary:
G. BARON SZALAY
CHARLES DE FORSTER

For British India:
H. A. SAMS
G. V. BEWOOR
L. P. KULKARNI
P. N. MUKERJI

For Iraq:
DOUGLAS W. GUMBLEY

For the Irish Free State:
P. S. ÓH-ÉIGEARTAIGH
R. S. O'CRUIMÍN
S. S. PUIRSÉAL

For Iceland:
V. HOLMBLAD

For Italy:
BIAGIO BORRIELLO
PIETRO TOSTI
MICHELE GALDI

For the whole of the Italian colonies:
RICCARDO ASTUTO

For Japan:
H. KAWAI
NAOTARO YAMAMOTO
J. SHIMIDZU

For Chosen:
NAOTARO YAMAMOTO
JINGORO HIRAO

For the whole of the other Japanese dependencies:
H. KAWAI
NOBORU TOMIZU

For Latvia:
A. AUZINŠ

For the Republic of Liberia:
C. W. DRESSELHUYS

For Lithuania:
A. SRUOGA
G. KROLIS

For Luxemburg:
JAAQUES

For Morocco (except the Spanish Zone):
JACQUES TRUELLE

For Morocco (Spanish Zone):
A. CAMACHO

For Mexico:
LINO B. ROCHÍN
JOSÉ V. CHÁVEZ

For Nicaragua:
EDUARDO PÉREZ-TRIANA

For Norway:
KLAUS HELSING
OSKAR HOMME

For New Zealand:
G. McNAMARA

For the Republic of Panama:
CARLOS A. LÓPEZ G.

For Paraguay:

For the Netherlands:
DAMME
DUYNSTEE

For the Netherlands Indies:
J. VAN DER WERF
W. F. GERDES OOSTERBEEK
DOMMISSE
HOOGEWOONING

For the Netherlands colonies in America:
W. F. GERDES OOSTERBEEK
HOOGEWOONING

For Peru:
M. DE FREYRE Y S.
A. S. SALAZAR

For Persia:
HOVHANNÈS KHAN MOSSAED
R. ARDJOMENDE

For Poland:
ŁOŚ
Dr. MARJAN BLACHIER

For Portugal:
> JOSE VASCO DE CARVALHO
> ADALBERTO DA COSTA VEIGA

For the Portuguese colonies in Africa:
> MARIO CORRÊA BARATA DA CRUZ

For the Portuguese colonies of Asia and Oceania:
> LUCIANO BOTELHO DA COSTA MARTINS

For Rumania:
> GÉNÉRAL MIHAIL
> I. MANEA

For the Republic of San Marino:
> M. A. JAMIESON
> GIOVANNI SOVRANI

For the Republic of Salvador:
> ANTONIO REYES-GUERRA

For the Saar Territory:
> P. COURTILET
> A. AREND

For the Kingdom of the Serbs, Croats and Slovenes:
> G. DIOURITCH

For Siam:
> PHYA PRAKIT KOLASASTRA
> LUANG BAHIDDHA NUKARA

For Sweden:
> ANDERS ÖRNE
> GUNNAR LAGER
> FR. SANDBERG

For Switzerland:
> P. DUBOIS
> C. ROCHES
> L. ROULET

For Czechoslovakia:
> Dr. OTOKAR RŮŽIČKA
> JOSEF ZÁBRODSKY

For Tunisia:
> JACQUES DUMAINE
> DUPONT

For Turkey:
> ALI RAANA
> YUSUF ARIFI

For the Union of Soviet Socialist Republics:
> Dr. EUGÈNE HIRSCHFELD
> M. KHODEEFF
> E. SYREVITCH

For Uruguay:
> F. A. COSTANZO

For the Vatican City State:
> W. A. S. HEWINS

For the United States of Venezuela:
> LUIS ALEJANDRO AGUILAR
> E. ARROYO LAMEDA

FINAL PROTOCOL OF THE PROVISIONS CONCERNING THE TRANSPORTATION OF REGULAR MAILS BY AIR

Sole Article

Aerial transportation charges for closed mails

The Administrations of British India and the Union of Soviet Socialist Republics have the option of collecting the transportation charges provided for by Article 11 of the Provisions concerning the transportation of regular mails by air for each section of their domestic air systems.

Done at London, June 28, 1929.

For Afghanistan:

For the Union of South Africa:
> J. N. REDELINGHUYS
> D. J. O'KELLY

For Albania:
> M. LIBOHOVA

For Germany:
> Dr. K. SAUTTER
> Dr. W. KÜSGEN
> K. ZIEGLER

For the United States of America:
> For Joseph Stewart:
> E. R. WHITE
> EUGENE R. WHITE

For the whole of the insular possessions of the United States of America other than the Philippine Islands:
> EUGENE R. WHITE

For the Philippine Islands:
> C. E. UNSON
> JOSÉ TOPACIO

For the Argentine Republic:

For the Commonwealth of Australia:
M. B. Harry

For Austria:
Walther Stoeckl

For Belgium:
O. Schockaert
Hub. Krains

For the Colony of the Belgian Congo:
Halewyck de Heusch
F. G. Tondeur
Jamar

For Bolivia:
Zac. Benavides

For Brazil:
Jm Eulalio

For Bulgaria:
M. Savoff
N. Boschnacoff

For Canada:
L. J. Gaboury
Arthur Webster

For Chile:
Antonio Huneeus
Miguel A. Parra
C. Verneuil

For China:
Liu Shu-fan

For the Republic of Colombia:
Jorge Garcés B.

For the Republic of Costa Rica:
Percy G. Harrison

For the Republic of Cuba:
Guillermo Patterson

For Denmark:
V. Holmblad

For the Free City of Danzig:
Stanisław Łoś
Victor Zander
Alfred Nordmann

For the Dominican Republic:
Dr. E. R. Lluberes

For Egypt:
H. Mazloum
R. Sidhom

For Ecuador:
E. Chacón Q.
E. L. Andrade

For Spain:
A. Camacho

For the whole of the Spanish colonies:
A. Ramos Garcia

For Estonia:
G. Jallajas

For Ethiopia:
B. Marcos
A. Bousson

For Finland:
G. E. F. Albrecht

For France:
M. Lebon
L. Genthon
Bousquié
Mainguet
Grandsimon
Dusserre

For Algeria:
E. Huguenin

For the French colonies and protectorates in Indo-China:
For M. Régismanset:
J. Cassagnac

For the whole of the other French colonies:
J. Cassagnac

For the United Kingdom of Great Britain and Northern Ireland:
F. H. Williamson
W. G. Gilbert
F. C. G. Twinn
F. R. Radice
D. O. Lumley

For Greece:
Th. Penthéroudakis
D. Bernardos

For Guatemala:
José Matos

For the Republic of Haiti:
J. G. Dalzell

For the Kingdom of the Hejaz and Nejd and dependencies:
Cheik Hafiz Wahba

For the Republic of Honduras:
Humberto Blanco-Fombona

For Hungary:
G. Baron Szalay
Charles de Forster

For British India:
H. A. Sams
G. V. Bewoor
L. P. Kulkarni
P. N. Mukerji

For Iraq:
Douglas W. Gumbley

For the Irish Free State:
P. S. Óh-Éigeartaigh
R. S. O'Cruimín
S. S. Puirséal

For Iceland:
V. Holmblad

For Italy:
Biagio Borriello
Pietro Tosti
Michele Galdi

For the whole of the Italian colonies:
Riccardo Astuto

For Japan:
H. Kawai
Naotaro Yamamoto
J. Shimidzu

For Chosen:
Naotaro Yamamoto
Jingoro Harao

For the whole of the other Japanese dependencies:
H. Kawai
Noboru Tomizu

For Latvia:
A. Auzinš

For the Republic of Liberia:
C. W. Dresselhuys

For Lithuania:
A. Sruoga
G. Krolis

For Luxemburg:
Jaaques

For Morocco (except the Spanish Zone):
Jacques Truelle

For Morocco (Spanish Zone):
A. Camacho

For Mexico:
Lino B. Rochín
José V. Chávez

For Nicaragua:
Eduardo Pérez-Triana

For Norway:
Klaus Helsing
Oskar Homme

For New Zealand:
G. McNamara

For the Republic of Panama:
Carlos A. López G.

For Paraguay:

219—916—69——60

For the Netherlands:
Damme
Duynstee

For the Netherlands Indies:
J. van der Werf
W. F. Gerdes Oosterbeek
Dommisse
Hoogewooning

For the Netherlands colonies in America:
W. F. Gerdes Oosterbeek
Hoogewooning

For Peru:
M. de Freyre y S.
A. S. Salazar

For Persia:
Hovhannès Khan Mossaed
R. Ardjomende

For Poland:
Łoś
Dr. Marjan Blachier

For Portugal:
Jose Vasco de Carvalho
Adalberto da Costa Veiga

For the Portuguese colonies in Africa:
Mario Corrêa Barata da Cruz

For the Portuguese colonies of Asia and Oceania:
Luciano Botelho da Costa Martins

For Rumania:
Général Mihail
I. Manea

For the Republic of San Marino:
M. A. Jamieson
Giovanni Sovrani

For the Republic of Salvador:
Antonio Reyes-Guerra

For the Saar Territory:
P. Courtilet
A. Arend

For the Kingdom of the Serbs, Croats and Slovenes:
G. Diouritch

For Siam:
Phya Prakit Kolasastra
Luang Bahiddha Nukara

For Sweden:
Anders Örne
Gunnar Lager
Fr. Sandberg

For Switzerland:
  P. Dubois
  C. Roches
  L. Roulet

For Czechoslovakia:
  Dr. Otokar Růžička
  Josef Zabrodsky

For Tunisia:
  Jacques Dumaine
  Dupont

For Turkey:
  Ali Raana
  Yusuf Arifi

For the Union of Soviet Socialist
    Republics:
  Dr. Eugène Hirschfeld
  M. Khodeeff
  E. Syrevitch

For Uruguay:
  F. A. Costanzo

For the Vatican City State:
  W. A. S. Hewins

For the United States of Venezuela:
  Luis Alejandro Aguilar
  E. Arroyo Lameda

[For postal forms annexed to provisions concerning transportation of regular mails by air, see 46 Stat. 2728.]

INTERNATIONAL BUREAU OF EDUCATION

Statutes adopted at Geneva July 25, 1929
United States application for membership, with a declaration, June 17,
*   1958*
United States membership approved by the IBE Council July 12, 1958
Entered into force July 25, 1929; for the United States July 12, 1958

[For text, see 14 UST 311; TIAS 5312.]

PRISONERS OF WAR

Convention signed at Geneva July 27, 1929, with annex
Senate advice and consent to ratification January 7, 1932
Ratified by the President of the United States January 16, 1932
Ratification of the United States deposited at Bern February 4, 1932
Entered into force June 19, 1931; for the United States August 4, 1932
Proclaimed by the President of the United States August 4, 1932
Replaced by convention of August 12, 1949,[1] as between contracting parties to the later convention

47 Stat. 2021; Treaty Series 846

[TRANSLATION]

CONVENTION OF JULY 27, 1929, RELATIVE TO THE TREATMENT OF PRISONERS OF WAR

The President of the German Reich, the President of the United States of America, the Federal President of the Republic of Austria, His Majesty the King of the Belgians, the President of the Republic of Bolivia, the President of the Republic of the United States of Brazil, His Majesty the King of Great Britain, Ireland, and the British Dominions beyond the Seas, Emperor of India, His Majesty the King of the Bulgarians, the President of the Republic of Chile, the President of the Republic of China, the President of the Republic of Colombia, the President of the Republic of Cuba, His Majesty the King of Denmark and Iceland, the President of the Dominican Republic, His Majesty the King of Egypt, His Majesty the King of Spain, the President of the Republic of Estonia, the President of the Republic of Finland, the President of the French Republic, the President of the Hellenic Republic, His Serene Highness the Regent of Hungary, His Majesty the King of Italy, His Majesty the Emperor of Japan, the President of the Republic of Latvia, Her Royal Highness the Grand Duchess of Luxembourg, the President of the United States of Mexico, the President of the Republic of Nicaragua, His Majesty the King of Norway, Her Majesty the Queen of the Netherlands, His Imperial Majesty the Shah of Persia, the President of the Republic of Poland, the President of the Portuguese Republic, His Majesty the King of Rumania, His Majesty the King of the Serbs, Croats, and Slovenes, His

---

[1] 6 UST 3316; TIAS 3364.

Majesty the King of Siam, His Majesty the King of Sweden, the Swiss Federal Council, the President of the Czechoslovak Republic, the President of the Turkish Republic, the President of the Oriental Republic of Uruguay, the President of the Republic of the United States of Venezuela,

recognizing that, in the extreme case of a war, it will be the duty of every Power to diminish, so far as possible, the unavoidable rigors thereof and to mitigate the fate of prisoners of war;

desirous of developing the principles which inspired the international conventions of The Hague, in particular the Convention relative to the laws and customs of war and the Regulations annexed thereto;

have decided to conclude a Convention to that end, and have appointed the following as their Plenipotentiaries, namely:

The President of the German Reich:
His Excellency Herr Edmund Rhomberg, Doctor of Laws, Minister unassigned;

The President of the United States of America:
The Honorable Eliot Wadsworth, former Assistant Secretary of the Treasury,
His Excellency the Honorable Hugh R. Wilson, Envoy Extraordinary and Minister Plenipotentiary of the United States of America at Berne;

The Federal President of the Republic of Austria:
Herr Marc Leitmaier, Doctor of Laws, Ministerial Counselor at the Federal Chancellery, Department of Foreign Affairs;

His Majesty the King of the Belgians:
M. Paul Demolder, Surgeon General, Chief of the Medical Corps of the First Military District,
M. Joseph de Ruelle, Counselor of the Ministry of Foreign Affairs;

The President of the Republic of Bolivia:
His Excellency Sr. Alberto Cortadellas, Minister Resident of Bolivia at Berne;

The President of the Republic of the United States of Brazil:
His Excellency Sr. Raoul de Rio-Branco, Envoy Extraordinary and Minister Plenipotentiary of Brazil at Berne;

His Majesty the King of Great Britain, Ireland and the British Dominions beyond the Seas, Emperor of India:
For Great Britain and Northern Ireland and All Parts of the British Empire Which Are Not Separate Members of the League of Nations:
The Right Honorable Sir Horace Rumbold, G.C.M.G., M.V.O., Ambassador of His Britannic Majesty at Berlin;

For the Dominion of Canada:
Mr. Walter Alexander Riddell, Permanent Counselor of the Canadian Government to the League of Nations;

For the Commonwealth of Australia:
His Excellency Mr. Claud Russell, Envoy Extraordinary and Minister Plenipotentiary of His Britannic Majesty at Berne;

For the Dominion of New Zealand:
His Excellency Mr. Claud Russell, Envoy Extraordinary and Minister Plenipotentiary of His Britannic Majesty at Berne;

For the Union of South Africa:
Mr. Eric Hendrik Louw, High Commissioner of the Union of South Africa at London;

For the Irish Free State:
Mr. Sean Lester, Representative of the Irish Free State to the League of Nations;

For India:
His Excellency Mr. Claud Russell, Envoy Extraordinary and Minister Plenipotentiary of His Britannic Majesty at Berne;

His Majesty the King of the Bulgarians:
M. Dimitri Mikoff, Chargé d'Affaires of Bulgaria at Berne, Permanent Representative of the Bulgarian Government to the League of Nations,
M. Stéphane N. Laftchieff, Member of the Administrative Council of the Bulgarian Red Cross;

The President of the Republic of Chile:
Colonel Guillermo Novoa-Sepulveda, Military Attaché to the Legation of Chile at Berlin,
Captain Dario Pulgar-Arriagada, Medical Corps;

The President of the Republic of China:
Mr. Chi Yung Hsiao, Chargé d'Affaires *ad interim* of China at Berne;

The President of the Republic of Colombia:
His Excellency Sr. Francisco José de Urrutia, Envoy Extraordinary and Minister Plenipotentiary of Colombia at Berne;

The President of the Republic of Cuba:
His Excellency Sr. Carlos de Armenteros y de Cardenas, Envoy Extraordinary and Minister Plenipotentiary of Cuba at Berne,
Sr. Carlos Blanco y Sanchez, Secretary of Legation, attached to the Delegation of Cuba to the League of Nations;

His Majesty the King of Denmark and Iceland:
For Denmark:
His Excellency Mr. Harald de Scavenius, Chamberlain, Envoy Extraordinary and Minister Plenipotentiary of Denmark in Switzerland and in the Netherlands, former Minister of Foreign Affairs,
Mr. Gustave M. Rasmussen, Charge d'Affaires *ad interim* of Denmark at Berne;

The President of the Dominican Republic:
Sr. Charles Ackermann, Consul of the Dominican Republic at Geneva;

His Majesty the King of Egypt:
M. Mohammed Abdel Moneim Riad, Counselor of the State Legal Department, Professor of International Law at the Military School of Cairo,
M. Henri Wassif Simaika, Attaché of the Royal Legation of Egypt at Rome;

His Majesty the King of Spain:
His Excellency the Marquis de la Torrehermosa, Envoy Extraordinary and Minister Plenipotentiary of Spain at Berne;

The President of the Republic of Estonia:
Mr. Hans Leesment, Doctor of Medicine, President of the Estonian Red Cross;

The President of the Republic of Finland:
Lieutenant-Colonel A. E. Martola, Military Attaché to the Legation of Finland at Paris;

The President of the French Republic:
His Excellency M. Henri Chassain de Marcilly, Ambassador of France at Berne,
M. Jean du Sault, Counselor of the Embassy of France at Berne;

The President of the Hellenic Republic:
M. Raphael Raphael, Chargé d'Affaires *ad interim* of Greece at Berne,
Lieutenant-Colonel Sophocles Veniselos, Military Attaché to the Legation of Greece at Paris;

His Serene Highness the Regent of Hungary:
His Excellency M. Paul de Hevesy, Minister Resident, Permanent Delegate of the Royal Government to the League of Nations;

His Majesty the King of Italy:
Sig. Giovanni Ciraolo, Senator of the Kingdom;

His Majesty the Emperor of Japan:
His Excellency Mr. Isaburo Yoshida, Envoy Extraordinary and Minister Plenipotentiary of Japan at Berne,
Lieutenant-Colonel Sadamu Shimomura,
Captain Seizo Miura, Naval Attaché to the Embassy of Japan at Paris;

The President of the Republic of Latvia:

His Excellency Mr. Charles Duzmans, Envoy Extraordinary and Minister Plenipotentiary of Latvia to His Majesty the King of the Serbs, Croats and Slovens, Permanent Delegate to the League of Nations,

His Excellency Mr. Oskar Voit, Envoy Extraordinary and Minister Plenipotentiary of Latvia in Switzerland, Germany, Hungary, and the Netherlands;

Her Royal Highness the Grand Duchess of Luxembourg:

M. Charles Vermaire, Consul of the Grand Duchy at Geneva;

The President of the United States of Mexico:

His Excellency Sr. Francisco Castillo Nájera, Surgeon General, Envoy Extraordinary and Minister Plenipotentiary of Mexico at Brussels;

The President of the Republic of Nicaragua:

Sr. Antoine Sottile, Doctor of Laws, Permanent Delegate of Nicaragua to the League of Nations;

His Majesty the King of Norway:

His Excellency Mr. Johannes Irgens, Envoy Extraordinary and Minister Plenipotentiary of Norway at Berne, Rome, and Athens,

Mr. Jens Christian Meinich, Commandant of Infantry, Secretary General of the Norwegian Red Cross;

Her Majesty the Queen of the Netherlands:

His Excellency Mr. Willem Isaac Doude van Troostwijk, Envoy Extraordinary and Minister Plenipotentiary of the Netherlands at Berne,

Major-General Johan Carl Diehl, Inspector-General of the Medical Corps of the Army, Vice President of the Netherland Red Cross,

Mr. Jacob Harberts, Commandant of the General Staff, Professor at the War College;

His Imperial Majesty the Shah of Persia:

His Excellency M. Anouchirevan Khan Sepahbodi, Envoy Extraordinary and Minister Plenipotentiary of Persia at Berne;

The President of the Republic of Poland:

Colonel Joseph Gabriel Pracki, Medical Corps,
Lieutenant-Colonel W. Jerzy Babecki;

The President of the Portuguese Republic:

His Excellency Sr. Vasco de Quevedo, Envoy Extraordinary and Minister Plenipotentiary of Portugal at Berne,

Sr. Francisco de Calheiros e Menezes, First Secretary of Legation;

His Majesty the King of Rumania:

His Excellency M. Michel B. Boeresco, Envoy Extraordinary and Minister Plenipotentiary of Rumania at Berne,

Colonel Eugene Vertejano, Officer of the General Staff;

His Majesty the King of the Serbs, Croats and Slovenes:

His Excellency M. Ilija Choumenkovitch, Envoy Extraordinary and Minister Plenipotentiary of the Kingdom of the Serbs, Croats and Slovenes at Berne, Permanent Delegate to the League of Nations;

His Majesty the King of Siam:

His Serene Highness, Prince Varnvaidya, Envoy Extraordinary and Minister Plenipotentiary of Siam at London;

His Majesty the King of Sweden:

His Excellency Mr. Karl Ivan Westman, Envoy Extraordinary and Minister Plenipotentiary of Sweden at Berne;

The Swiss Federal Council:

M. Paul Dinichert, Minister Plenipotentiary, Chief of the Division of Foreign Affairs of the Federal Political Department,

Colonel Carl Hauser, Medical Corps, Surgeon General of the Army,

M. Anton Züblin, Infantry Colonel unassigned, Attorney,

Lieutenant-Colonel Roger de la Harpe, Medical Corps, Surgeon,

Major Dietrich Schindler, Judge Advocate General's Department, Professor of International Law at the University of Zürich;

The President of the Czechoslovak Republic:

His Excellency M. Zdeněk Fierlinger, Envoy Extraordinary and Minister Plenipotentiary of Czechoslovakia at Berne;

The President of the Turkish Republic:

His Excellency Hassan Bey, Vice President of the Grand National Assembly of Turkey, Vice President of the Turkish Red Crescent,

His Excellency Nusret Bey, President of the Council of State of the Republic,

Professor Akil Moukhtar Bey, Doctor of Medicine,

Lieutenant-Colonel Abdulkadir Bey, Military Surgeon, Professor at the Military Academy and at the Hospital of Gulhane;

The President of the Oriental Republic of Uruguay:

His Excellency Sr. Alfredo de Castro, Envoy Extraordinary and Minister Plenipotentiary of Uruguay at Berne;

The President of the Republic of the United States of Venezuela:

His Excellency Sr. Caracciolo Parra-Pérez, Envoy Extraordinary and Minister Plenipotentiary of Venezuela at Rome,

Sr. Ivan Manuel Hurtado-Machado, Chargé d'Affaires *ad interim* of Venezuela at Berne;

Who, after having communicated to each other their full powers, found to be in good and due form, have agreed as follows:

TITLE I. GENERAL PROVISIONS

ARTICLE 1

The present Convention shall apply, without prejudice to the stipulations of Title VII:

1) To all persons mentioned in Articles 1, 2 and 3 of the Regulations annexed to the Hague Convention respecting the laws and customs of war on land, of October 18, 1907,[2] and captured by the enemy.[3]

2) To all persons belonging to the armed forces of belligerent parties, captured by the enemy in the course of military operations at sea or in the air, except for such derogations as might be rendered inevitable by the conditions of capture. However, such derogations shall not infringe upon the fundamental principles of the present Convention; they shall cease from the moment when the persons captured have rejoined a prisoners-of-war camp.

ARTICLE 2

Prisoners of war are in the power of the hostile Power, but not of the individuals or corps who have captured them.

They must at all times be humanely treated and protected, particularly against acts of violence, insults and public curiosity.

Measures of reprisal against them are prohibited.

ARTICLE 3

Prisoners of war have the right to have their person and their honor respected. Women shall be treated with all the regard due to their sex.

Prisoners retain their full status.

ARTICLE 4

The Power detaining prisoners of war is bound to provide for their maintenance.

---

[2] TS 539, *ante*, vol. 1, p. 631.

[3] *Annexed Regulations:*

ART. 1. The laws, rights, and duties of war apply not only to armies, but also to militia and volunteer corps fulfilling the following conditions:

1. To be commanded by a person responsible for his subordinates;
2. To have a fixed distinctive emblem recognizable at a distance;
3. To carry arms openly; and
4. To conduct their operations in accordance with the laws and customs of war.

In countries where militia or volunteer corps constitute the army, or form part of it, they are included under the denomination "army."

ART. 2. The inhabitants of a territory which has not been occupied, who, on the approach of the enemy, spontaneously take up arms to resist the invading troops without having had time to organize themselves in accordance with Article 1, shall be regarded as belligerents if they carry arms openly and if they respect the laws and customs of war.

ART. 3. The armed forces of the belligerent parties may consist of combatants and noncombatants. In the case of capture by the enemy, both have a right to be treated as prisoners of war. [Footnote in original.]

Difference in treatment among prisoners is lawful only when it is based on the military rank, state of physical or mental health, professional qualifications or sex of those who profit thereby.

TITLE II. CAPTURE

ARTICLE 5

Every prisoner of war is bound to give, if he is questioned on the subject, his true name and rank, or else his regimental number.

If he infringes this rule, he is liable to have the advantages given to prisoners of his class curtailed.

No coercion may be used on prisoners to secure information relative to the condition of their army or country. Prisoners who refuse to answer may not be threatened, insulted, or exposed to unpleasant or disadvantageous treatment of any kind whatever.

If, because of his physical or mental condition, a prisoner is unable to identify himself, he shall be turned over to the medical corps.

ARTICLE 6

All effects and objects of personal use—except arms, horses, military equipment and military papers—shall remain in the possession of prisoners of war, as well as metal helmets and gas masks.

Money in the possession of prisoners may not be taken away from them except by order of an officer and after the amount is determined. A receipt shall be given. Money thus taken away shall be entered to the account of each prisoner.

Identification documents, insignia of rank, decorations and objects of value may not be taken from prisoners.

TITLE III. CAPTIVITY

SECTION I. EVACUATION OF PRISONERS OF WAR

ARTICLE 7

Prisoners of war shall be evacuated within the shortest possible period after their capture, to depots located in a region far enough from the zone of combat for them to be out of danger.

Only prisoners who, because of wounds or sickness, would run greater risks by being evacuated than by remaining where they are may be temporarily kept in a dangerous zone.

Prisoners shall not be needlessly exposed to danger while awaiting their evacuation from the combat zone.

Evacuation of prisoners on foot may normally be effected only by stages of 20 kilometers a day, unless the necessity of reaching water and food depots requires longer stages.

ARTICLE 8

Belligerents are bound mutually to notify each other of their capture of prisoners within the shortest period possible, through the intermediary of the information bureaus, such as are organized according to Article 77. They are likewise bound to inform each other of the official addresses to which the correspondence of their families may be sent to prisoners of war.

As soon as possible, every prisoner must be enabled to correspond with his family himself, under the conditions provided in Articles 36 *et seq.*

As regards prisoners captured at sea, the provisions of the present article shall be observed as soon as possible after arrival at port.

SECTION II. PRISONERS-OF-WAR CAMPS

ARTICLE 9

Prisoners of war may be interned in a town, fortress, or other place, and bound not to go beyond certain fixed limits. They may also be interned in enclosed camps; they may not be confined or imprisoned except as an indispensable measure of safety or sanitation, and only while the circumstances which necessitate the measure continue to exist.

Prisoners captured in unhealthful regions or where the climate is injurious tor persons coming from temperate regions, shall be transported, as soon as possible, to a more favorable climate.

Belligerents shall, so far as possible, avoid assembling in a single camp prisoners of different races or nationalities.

No prisoner may, at any time, be sent into a region where he might be exposed to the fire of the combat zone, nor used to give protection from bombardment to certain points or certain regions by his presence.

CHAPTER I. *Installation of Camps*

ARTICLE 10

Prisoners of war shall be lodged in buildings or in barracks affording all possible guarantees of hygiene and healthfulness.

The quarters must be fully protected from dampness, sufficiently heated and lighted. All precautions must be taken against danger of fire.

With regard to dormitories—the total surface, minimum cubic amount of air, arrangement and material of bedding—the conditions shall be the same as for the troops at base camps of the detaining Power.

CHAPTER 2. *Food and Clothing of Prisoners of War*

ARTICLE 11

The food ration of prisoners of war shall be equal in quantity and quality to that of troops at base camps.

Furthermore, prisoners shall receive facilities for preparing, themselves, additional food which they might have.

A sufficiency of potable water shall be furnished them. The use of tobacco shall be permitted. Prisoners may be employed in the kitchens.

All collective disciplinary measures affecting the food are prohibited.

ARTICLE 12

Clothing, linen and footwear shall be furnished prisoners of war by the detaining Power. Replacement and repairing of these effects must be assured regularly. In addition, laborers must receive work clothes wherever the nature of the work requires it.

Canteens shall be installed in all camps where prisoners may obtain, at the local market price, food products and ordinary objects.

Profits made by the canteens for camp administrations shall be used for the benefit of prisoners.

CHAPTER 3. *Sanitary Service in Camps*

ARTICLE 13

Belligerents shall be bound to take all sanitary measures necessary to assure the cleanliness and healthfulness of camps and to prevent epidemics.

Prisoners of war shall have at their disposal, day and night, installations conforming to sanitary rules and constantly maintained in a state of cleanliness.

Furthermore, and without prejudice to baths and showers with which the camp shall be as well provided as possible, prisoners shall be furnished a sufficient quantity of water for the care of their own bodily cleanliness.

It shall be possible for them to take physical exercise and enjoy the open air.

ARTICLE 14

Every camp shall have an infirmary, where prisoners of war shall receive every kind of attention they need. If necessary, isolated quarters shall be reserved for the sick affected with contagious diseases.

Expenses of treatment, including therein those of temporary prosthetic equipment, shall be borne by the detaining Power.

Upon request, belligerents shall be bound to deliver to every prisoner treated an official statement showing the nature and duration of his illness as well as the attention received.

It shall be lawful for belligerents reciprocally to authorize, by means of private arrangements, the retention in the camps of physicians and attendants to care for prisoners of their own country.

Prisoners affected with a serious illness or whose condition necessitates an important surgical operation, must be admitted, at the expense of the detaining Power, to any military or civil medical unit qualified to treat them.

ARTICLE 15

Medical inspections of prisoners of war shall be arranged at least once a month. Their purpose shall be the supervision of the general state of health and cleanliness, and the detection of contagious diseases, particularly tuberculosis and venereal diseases.

CHAPTER 4. *Intellectual and Moral Needs of Prisoners of War*

ARTICLE 16

Prisoners of war shall enjoy complete liberty in the exercise of their religion, including attendance at the services of their faith, on the sole condition that they comply with the measures of order and police issued by the military authorities.

Ministers of a religion, prisoners of war, whatever their religious denomination, shall be allowed to minister fully to members of the same religion.

ARTICLE 17

So far as possible, belligerents shall encourage intellectual diversions and sports organized by prisoners of war.

CHAPTER 5. *Internal Discipline of Camps*

ARTICLE 18

Every camp of prisoners of war shall be placed under the command of a responsible officer.

Besides the external marks of respect provided by the regulations in force in their armies with regard to their nationals, prisoners of war must salute all officers of the detaining Power.

Officers who are prisoners of war are bound to salute only officers of a higher or equal rank of that Power.

ARTICLE 19

The wearing of insignia of rank and of decorations shall be permitted.

ARTICLE 20

Regulations, orders, notices and proclamations of every kind must be communicated to prisoners of war in a language which they understand. The same principle shall be applied in examinations.

CHAPTER 6. *Special Provisions Regarding Officers and Persons of Equivalent Status*

ARTICLE 21

Upon the beginning of hostilities, belligerents shall be bound to communicate to one another the titles and ranks in use in their respective armies, with a view to assuring equality of treatment between corresponding ranks of officers and persons of equivalent status.

Officers and persons of equivalent status who are prisoners of war shall be treated with the regard due their rank and age.

ARTICLE 22

In order to assure service in officers' camps, soldiers of the same army who are prisoners of war and, wherever possible, who speak the same language, shall be assigned thereto, in sufficient numbers, considering the rank of the officers and persons of equivalent status.

The latter shall secure their food and clothing from the pay which shall be granted them by the detaining Power. Administration of the mess-fund by the officers themselves must be facilitated in every way.

CHAPTER 7. *Financial Resources of Prisoners of War*

ARTICLE 23

Subject to private arrangements between belligerent Powers, and particularly those provided in Article 24, officers and persons of equivalent status who are prisoners of war shall receive from the detaining Power the same pay as officers of corresponding rank in the armies of that Power, on the condition, however, that this pay does not exceed that to which they are entitled in the armies of the country which they have served. This pay shall be granted them in full, once a month if possible, and without being liable to any deduction for expenses incumbent on the detaining Power, even when they are in favor of the prisoners.

An agreement between the belligerents shall fix the rate of exchange applicable to this payment; in the absence of such an agreement, the rate adopted shall be that in force at the opening of hostilities.

All payments made to prisoners of war as pay must be reimbursed at the end of hostilities, by the Power which they have served.

ARTICLE 24

Upon the outbreak of hostilities, the belligerents shall, by common agreement, fix the maximum amount of ready money which prisoners of war of various ranks and classes shall be allowed to keep in their possession. Any surplus taken or withheld from a prisoner shall be entered to his account, the same as any deposit of money effected by him, and may not be converted into another currency without his consent.

Pay to the credit of their accounts shall be given to prisoners of war at the end of their captivity.

During their imprisonment, facilities shall be granted them for the transfer of these amounts, in whole or in part, to banks or private persons in their country of origin.

CHAPTER 8. *Transfer of Prisoners of War*

ARTICLE 25

Unless the conduct of military operations so requires, sick and wounded prisoners of war shall not be transferred as long as their recovery might be endangered by the trip.

ARTICLE 26

In case of transfer, prisoners of war shall be officially notified of their new destination in advance; they shall be allowed to take with them their personal effects, their correspondence and packages which have arrived for them.

All due measures shall be taken that correspondence and packages addressed to their former camp may be forwarded to them without delay.

Money deposited to the account of transferred prisoners shall be transmitted to the competent authority of their new place of residence.

The expenses occasioned by the transfer shall be charged to the detaining Power.

SECTION III. LABOR OF PRISONERS OF WAR

CHAPTER 1. *Generalities*

ARTICLE 27

Belligerents may utilize the labor of able prisoners of war, according to their rank and aptitude, officers and persons of equivalent status excepted.

However, if officers or persons of equivalent status request suitable work, it shall be secured for them so far as is possible.

Noncommissioned officers who are prisoners of war shall only be required to do supervisory work, unless they expressly request a remunerative occupation.

Belligerents shall be bound, during the whole period of captivity, to allow to prisoners of war who are victims of accidents in connection with their work the enjoyment of the benefit of the provisions applicable to laborers of the same class according to the legislation of the detaining Power. With regard to prisoners of war to whom these legal provisions might not be applied by reason of the legislation of that Power, the latter undertakes to recommend to its legislative body all proper measures equitably to indemnify the victims.

CHAPTER 2. *Organization of the Labor*

ARTICLE 28

The detaining Power shall assume entire responsibility for the maintenance, care, treatment and payment of wages of prisoners of war working for the account of private persons.

ARTICLE 29

No prisoner of war may be employed at labors for which he is physically unfit.

ARTICLE 30

The length of the day's work of prisoners of war, including therein the trip going and returning, shall not be excessive and must not, in any case, exceed that allowed for the civil workers in the region employed at the same work. Every prisoner shall be allowed a rest of twenty-four consecutive hours every week, preferably on Sunday.

CHAPTER 3. *Prohibited Labor*

ARTICLE 31

Labor furnished by prisoners of war shall have no direct relation with war operations. It is especially prohibited to use prisoners for manufacturing and transporting arms or munitions of any kind, or for transporting material intended for combatant units.

In case of violation of the provisions of the preceding paragraph, prisoners, after executing or beginning to execute the order, shall be free to have their protests presented through the mediation of the agents whose functions are set forth in Articles 43 and 44, or, in the absence of an agent, through the mediation of representatives of the protecting Power.

ARTICLE 32

It is forbidden to use prisoners of war at unhealthful or dangerous work.

Any aggravation of the conditions of labor by disciplinary measures is forbidden.

CHAPTER 4. *Labor Detachments*

ARTICLE 33

The system of labor detachments must be similar to that of prisoners-of-war camps, particularly with regard to sanitary conditions, food, attention in case of accident or sickness, correspondence and the receipt of packages.

Every labor detachment shall be dependent on a prisoners' camp. The commander of this camp shall be responsible for the observation, in the labor detachment, of the provisions of the present Convention.

CHAPTER 5. *Wages*

ARTICLE 34

Prisoners of war shall not receive wages for work connected with the administration, management and maintenance of the camps.

Prisoners utilized for other work shall be entitled to wages to be fixed by agreements between the belligerents.

These agreements shall also specify the part which the camp administration may retain, the amount which shall belong to the prisoner of war and the manner in which that amount shall be put at his disposal during the period of his captivity.

While awaiting the conclusion of the said agreements, payment for labor of prisoners shall be settled according to the rules given below:

a) Work done for the State shall be paid for in accordance with the rates in force for soldiers of the national army doing the same work, or, if none exists, according to a rate in harmony with the work performed.

b) When the work is done for the account of other public administrations or for private persons, conditions shall be regulated by agreement with the military authority.

The pay remaining to the credit of the prisoner shall be delivered to him at the end of his captivity. In case of death, it shall be forwarded through the diplomatic channel to the heirs of the deceased.

SECTION IV. EXTERNAL RELATIONS OF PRISONERS OF WAR

ARTICLE 35

Upon the outbreak of hostilities, belligerents shall publish the measures provided for the execution of the provisions of this section.

ARTICLE 36

Each of the belligerents shall periodically determine the number of letters and postal cards per month which prisoners of war of the various classes shall be allowed to send, and shall inform the other belligerent of this number. These letters and cards shall be transmitted by post by the shortest route. They may not be delayed or retained for disciplinary reasons.

Within a period of not more than one week after his arrival at the camp, and likewise in case of sickness, every prisoner shall be enabled to write his family a postal card informing it of his capture and of the state of his health. The said postal cards shall be forwarded as rapidly as possible and may not be delayed in any manner.

As a general rule, correspondence of prisoners shall be written in their native language. Belligerents may allow correspondence in other languages.

ARTICLE 37

Prisoners of war shall be allowed individually to receive parcels by mail, containing foods and other articles intended to supply them with food or clothing. Packages shall be delivered to the addressees and a receipt given.

ARTICLE 38

Letters and consignments of money or valuables, as well as parcels by post intended for prisoners of war or dispatched by them, either directly, or by the mediation of the information bureaus provided for in Article 77, shall be exempt from all postal duties in the countries of origin and destination, as well as in the countries they pass through.

Presents and relief in kind for prisoners shall be likewise exempt from all import and other duties, as well as of payments for carriage by the State railways.

Prisoners may, in cases of acknowledged urgency, be allowed to send telegrams, paying the usual charges.

ARTICLE 39

Prisoners of war shall be allowed to receive shipments of books individually, which may be subject to censorship.

Representatives of the protecting Powers and duly recognized and authorized aid societies may send books and collections of books to the libraries of prisoners' camps. The transmission of these shipments to libraries may not be delayed under the pretext of censorship difficulties.

ARTICLE 40

Censorship of correspondence must be effected within the shortest possible time. Furthermore, inspection of parcels post must be effected under proper conditions to guarantee the preservation of the products which they may contain and, if possible, in the presence of the addressee or an agent duly recognized by him.

Prohibitions of correspondence promulgated by the belligerents for military or political reasons, must be transient in character and as short as possible.

ARTICLE 41

Belligerents shall assure all facilities for the transmission of instruments, papers or documents intended for prisoners of war or signed by them, particularly of powers of attorney and wills.

They shall take the necessary measures to assure, in case of necessity, the authentication of signatures made by prisoners.

SECTION V. PRISONERS' RELATIONS WITH THE AUTHORITIES

CHAPTER 1. *Complaints of Prisoners of War because of the Conditions of Captivity*

ARTICLE 42

Prisoners of war shall have the right to inform the military authorities in whose power they are of their requests with regard to the conditions of captivity to which they are subjected.

They shall also have the right to address themselves to representatives of the protecting Powers to indicate to them the points on which they have complaints to formulate with regard to the conditions of captivity.

These requests and complaints must be transmitted immediately.

Even if they are recognized to be unfounded, they may not occasion any punishment.

CHAPTER 2. *Representatives of Prisoners of War*

ARTICLE 43

In every place where there are prisoners of war, they shall be allowed to appoint agents entrusted with representing them directly with military authorities and protecting Powers.

This appointment shall be subject to the approval of the military authority.

The agents shall be entrusted with the reception and distribution of collective shipments. Likewise, in case the prisoners should decide to organize a mutual assistance system among themselves, this organization would be in the sphere of the agents. Further, they may lend their offices to prisoners to facilitate their relations with the aid societies mentioned in Article 78.

In camps of officers and persons of equivalent status, the senior officer prisoner of the highest rank shall be recognized as intermediary between the camp authorities and the officers and persons of equivalent status who are prisoners. For this purpose, he shall have the power to appoint a prisoner officer to assist him as an interpreter during the conferences with the camp authorities.

ARTICLE 44

When the agents are employed as laborers, their activity as representatives of prisoners of war must be counted in the compulsory period of labor.

All facilities shall be accorded the agents for their intercourse with the military authorities and with the protecting Power. This intercourse shall not be limited.

No representative of the prisoners may be transferred without the necessary time being allowed him to inform his successors about affairs under consideration.

CHAPTER 3. *Penalties Applicable to Prisoners of War*

1. GENERAL PROVISIONS

ARTICLE 45

Prisoners of war shall be subject to the laws, regulations, and orders in force in the armies of the detaining Power.

An act of insubordination shall justify the adoption towards them of the measures provided by such laws, regulations and orders.

The provisions of the present chapter, however, are reserved.

ARTICLE 46

Punishments other than those provided for the same acts for soldiers of the national armies may not be imposed upon prisoners of war by the military authorities and courts of the detaining Power.

Rank being identical, officers, noncommissioned officers or soldiers who are prisoners of war undergoing a disciplinary punishment, shall not be subject to less favorable treatment than that provided in the armies of the detaining Power with regard to the same punishment.

Any corporal punishment, any imprisonment in quarters without daylight and, in general, any form of cruelty, is forbidden.

Collective punishment for individual acts is also forbidden.

ARTICLE 47

Acts constituting an offense against discipline, and particularly attempted escape, shall be verified immediately; for all prisoners of war, commissioned or not, preventive arrest shall be reduced to the absolute minimum.

Judicial proceedings against prisoners of war shall be conducted as rapidly as the circumstances permit; preventive imprisonment shall be limited as much as possible.

In all cases, the duration of preventive imprisonment shall be deducted from the disciplinary or judicial punishment inflicted, provided that this deduction is allowed for national soldiers.

ARTICLE 48

Prisoners of war may not be treated differently from other prisoners after having suffered the judicial or disciplinary punishment which has been imposed on them.

However, prisoners punished as a result of attempted escape may be subjected to special surveillance, which, however, may not entail the suppression of guarantees granted prisoners by the present Convention.

ARTICLE 49

No prisoner of war may be deprived of his rank by the detaining Power.

Prisoners given disciplinary punishment may not be deprived of the prerogatives attached to their rank. In particular, officers and persons of equivalent status who suffer punishment involving deprivation of liberty shall not be placed in the same quarters as non-commissioned officers or privates being punished.

ARTICLE 50

Escaped prisoners of war who are retaken before being able to rejoin their own army or to leave the territory occupied by the army which captured them shall be liable only to disciplinary punishment.

Prisoners who, after having succeeded in rejoining their army or in leaving the territory occupied by the army which captured them, may again be taken prisoners, shall not be liable to any punishment on account of their previous flight.

ARTICLE 51

Attempted escape, even if it is a repetition of the offense, shall not be considered as an aggravating circumstance in case the prisoner of war should be given over to the courts on account of crimes or offenses against persons or property committed in the course of that attempt.

After an attempted or accomplished escape, the comrades of the person escaping who assisted in the escape, may incur only disciplinary punishment on this account.

Article 52

Belligerents shall see that the competent authorities exercise the greatest leniency in deciding the question of whether an infraction committed by a prisoner of war should be punished by disciplinary or judicial measures.

This shall be the case especially when it is a question of deciding on acts in connection with escape or attempted escape.

A prisoner may not be punished more than once because of the same act or the same count.

Article 53

No prisoner of war on whom a disciplinary punishment has been imposed, who might be eligible for repatriation, may be kept back because he has not undergone the punishment.

Prisoners to be repatriated who might be threatened with a penal prosecution may be excluded from repatriation until the end of the proceedings and, if necessary, until the completion of the punishment; those who might already be imprisoned by reason of a sentence may be detained until the end of their imprisonment.

Belligerents shall communicate to each other the lists of those who may not be repatriated for the reasons given in the preceding paragraph.

2. Disciplinary Punishments

Article 54

Arrest is the most severe disciplinary punishment which may be imposed on a prisoner of war.

The duration of a single punishment may not exceed thirty days.

This maximum of thirty days may not, further, be exceeded in the case of several acts for which the prisoner has to undergo discipline at the time when it is ordered for him, whether or not these acts are connected.

When, during or after the end of a period of arrest, a prisoner shall have a new disciplinary punishment imposed upon him, a space of at least three days shall separate each of the periods of arrest, if one of them is ten days or more.

Article 55

Subject to the provisions given in the last paragraph of Article 11, food restrictions allowed in the armies of the detaining Power are applicable, as an increase in punishment, to prisoners of war given disciplinary punishment.

However, these restrictions may be ordered only if the state of health of the prisoners punished permits it.

ARTICLE 56

In no case may prisoners of war be transferred to penitentiary establishments (prisons, penitentiaries, convict prisons, etc.) there to undergo disciplinary punishment.

The quarters in which they undergo disciplinary punishment shall conform to sanitary requirements.

Prisoners punished shall be enabled to keep themselves in a state of cleanliness.

These prisoners shall every day be allowed to exercise or to stay in the open air at least two hours.

ARTICLE 57

Prisoners of war given disciplinary punishment shall be allowed to read and write, as well as to send and receive letters.

On the other hand, packages and money sent may be not delivered to the addressees until the expiration of the punishment. If the packages not distributed contain perishable products, these shall be turned over to the camp infirmary or kitchen.

ARTICLE 58

Prisoners of war given disciplinary punishment shall be allowed, on their request, to be present at the daily medical inspection. They shall receive the care considered necessary by the doctors and, if necessary, shall be removed to the camp infirmary or to hospitals.

ARTICLE 59

Excepting the competence of courts and higher military authorities, disciplinary punishment may be ordered only by an officer provided with disciplinary powers in his capacity as commander of a camp or detachment, or by the responsible officer replacing him.

3. JUDICIAL SUITS

ARTICLE 60

At the opening of a judicial proceeding directed against a prisoner of war, the detaining Power shall advise the representative of the protecting Power thereof as soon as possible, and always before the date set for the opening of the trial.

This advice shall contain the following information:

a) Civil state and rank of prisoner;

b) Place of sojourn or imprisonment;

c) Specification of the count or counts of the indictment, giving the legal provisions applicable.

If it is not possible to mention in that advice the court which will pass upon the matter, the date of opening the trial and the place where it will take place, this information must be furnished to the representative of the protecting Power later, as soon as possible, and at all events, at least three weeks before the opening of the trial.

ARTICLE 61

No prisoner of war may be sentenced without having had an opportunity to defend himself.

No prisoner may be obliged to admit himself guilty of the act of which he is accused.

ARTICLE 62

The prisoner of war shall be entitled to assistance by a qualified counsel of his choice, and, if necessary, to have recourse to the services of a competent interpreter. He shall be advised of his right by the detaining Power, in due time before the trial.

In default of a choice by the prisoner, the protecting Power may obtain a counsel for him. The detaining Power shall deliver to the protecting Power, on its request, a list of persons qualified to present the defense.

Representatives of the protecting Power shall be entitled to attend the trial of the case.

The only exception to this rule is the case where the trial of the case must be secret in the interest of the safety of the State. The detaining Power should so advise the protecting Power.

ARTICLE 63

Sentence may be pronounced against a prisoner of war only by the same courts and according to the same procedure as in the case of persons belonging to the armed forces of the detaining Power.

ARTICLE 64

Every prisoner of war shall have the right of appeal against any sentence rendered with regard to him, in the same way as individuals belonging to the armed forces of the detaining Power.

ARTICLE 65

Sentences pronounced against prisoners of war shall be communicated to the protecting Power immediately.

ARTICLE 66

If the death penalty is pronounced against a prisoner of war, a communication setting forth in detail the nature and circumstances of the offense shall be sent as soon as possible to the representative of the protecting Power, for transmission to the Power in whose armies the prisoner served.

The sentence shall not be executed before the expiration of a period of at least three months after this communication.

ARTICLE 67

No prisoner of war may be deprived of the benefit of the provisions of Article 42 of the present Convention as a result of a sentence or otherwise.

TITLE IV. TERMINATION OF CAPTIVITY

SECTION I. DIRECT REPATRIATION AND HOSPITALIZATION IN A NEUTRAL COUNTRY

ARTICLE 68

Belligerents are bound to send back to their own country, regardless of rank or number, seriously sick and seriously injured prisoners of war, after having brought them to a condition where they can be transported.

Agreements between belligerents shall accordingly settle as soon as possible the cases of invalidity or of sickness, entailing direct repatriation, as well as the cases entailing possible hospitalization in a neutral country. While awaiting the conclusion of these agreements, belligerents may have reference to the model agreement annexed, for documentary purposes, to the present Convention.

ARTICLE 69

Upon the outbreak of hostilities, belligerents shall come to an agreement to name mixed medical commissions. These commissions shall be composed of three members, two of them belonging to a neutral country and one appointed by the detaining Power; one of the physicians of the neutral country shall preside. These mixed medical commissions shall proceed to the examination of sick or wounded prisoners and shall make all due decisions regarding them.

Decisions of these commissions shall be by majority and carried out with the least possible delay.

ARTICLE 70

Besides those who are designated by the camp physician, the following prisoners of war shall be inspected by the mixed medical Commission mentioned in Article 69, with a view to their direct repatriation or their hospitalization in a neutral country:

a) Prisoners who make such a request directly of the camp physician;

b) Prisoners who are presented by the agents provided for in Article 43, acting on their own initiative or at the request of the prisoners themselves;

c) Prisoners who have been proposed by the Power in whose armies they have served or by an aid society duly recognized and authorized by that Power.

ARTICLE 71

Prisoners of war who are victims of accidents in connection with work, except those voluntarily injured, shall enjoy the benefit of the same provisions, as far as repatriation or possible hospitalization in a neutral country are concerned.

ARTICLE 72

Throughout the duration of hostilities and for humane considerations, belligerents may conclude agreements with a view to the direct repatriation or hospitalization in a neutral country of able-bodied prisoners of war who have undergone a long period of captivity.

ARTICLE 73

The expenses of repatriation or of transportation to a neutral country of prisoners of war shall be borne, from the frontiers of the detaining Power, by the Power in whose armies the prisoners have served.

ARTICLE 74

No repatriated person may be utilized in active military service.

SECTION II. RELEASE AND REPATRIATION UPON CESSATION OF HOSTILITIES

ARTICLE 75

When belligerents conclude a convention of armistice, they must, in principle, have appear therein stipulations regarding the repatriation of prisoners of war. If it has not been possible to insert stipulations in this regard in such convention, belligerents shall nevertheless come to an agreement in this regard as soon as possible. In any case, repatriation of prisoners shall be effected with the least possible delay after the conclusion of peace.

Prisoners of war against whom a penal prosecution might be pending for a crime or an offense of municipal law may, however, be detained until the end of the proceedings and, if necessary, until the expiration of the punishment. The same shall be true of those sentenced for a crime or offense of municipal law.

On agreement between the belligerents, commissions may be established for the purpose of searching for dispersed prisoners and assuring their repatriation.

TITLE V. DEATH OF PRISONERS OF WAR

ARTICLE 76

Wills of prisoners of war shall be received and drawn up in the same way as for soldiers of the national army.

The same rules shall be observed regarding death certificates.

Belligerents shall see that prisoners of war dying in captivity are honorably buried and that the graves bear all due information, are respected and properly maintained.

TITLE VI. BUREAUS OF RELIEF AND INFORMATION CONCERNING PRISONERS OF WAR

Article 77

Upon the outbreak of hostilities, each of the belligerent Powers, as well as the neutral Powers which have received belligerents, shall institute an official information bureau for prisoners of war who are within their territory.

Within the shortest possible period, each of the belligerent Powers shall inform its information bureau of every capture of prisoners effected by its armies, giving it all the information regarding identity which it has, allowing it quickly to advise the families concerned, and informing it of the official addresses to which families may write to prisoners.

The information bureau shall immediately forward all this information to the interested Powers, through the intervention, on one hand, of the protecting Powers and, on the other, of the central agency provided for in Article 79.

The information bureau, being charged with replying to all inquiries about prisoners of war, shall receive from the various services concerned full information respecting internments, and transfers, releases on parole, repatriations, escapes, stays in hospitals, deaths, as well as other information necessary to enable it to make out and keep up to date an individual return for each prisoner of war.

The bureau shall state in this return, in so far as is possible and subject to the provisions of Article 5: the regimental number, given names and surname, date and place of birth, rank and unit of the interested party, the given name of the father and the name of the mother, the address of the person to be advised in case of accident, wounds, date and place of capture, internment, wounding and death, as well as any other important information.

Weekly lists containing all new information likely to facilitate the identification of each prisoner shall be transmitted to the interested Powers.

At the conclusion of peace the individual return of the prisoner of war shall be delivered to the Power which he served.

The information bureau shall further be bound to receive all objects of personal use, valuables, letters, pay vouchers, identification marks, etc., which are left by prisoners of war who have been repatriated, released on parole, escaped or died, and to transmit them to the countries interested.

Article 78

Relief societies for prisoners of war, which are properly constituted in accordance with the laws of their country and with the object of serving as the channel for charitable effort, shall receive from the belligerents, for themselves and their duly accredited agents, every facility for the efficient performance of their humane task within the bounds imposed by military necessities. Agents of these societies may be admitted to the camps for the purpose of distributing relief, as also to the halting places of repatriated prisoners, if furnished with a personal permit by the military authorities, and on giving an undertaking in writing to comply with all measures of order and police which the latter may issue.

ARTICLE 79

A central information agency for prisoners of war shall be created in a neutral country. The International Committee of the Red Cross shall propose the organization of such an agency to the interested Powers, if it considers it necessary.

The function of that agency shall be to centralize all information respecting prisoners, which it may obtain through official or private channels; it shall transmit it as quickly as possible to the country of origin of the prisoners or to the Power which they have served.

These provisions must not be interpreted as restricting the humanitarian activity of the International Committee of the Red Cross.

ARTICLE 80

Information bureaus shall enjoy the privilege of free postage on postal matter, as well as all exemptions provided in Article 38.

TITLE VII. APPLICATION OF THE CONVENTION TO CERTAIN CLASSES OF CIVILIANS

ARTICLE 81

Individuals who follow armed forces without directly belonging thereto, such as newspaper correspondents and reporters, sutlers, contractors, who fall into the enemy's hands and whom the latter thinks expedient to detain, shall be entitled to be treated as prisoners of war, provided they are in possession of a certificate from the military authorities of the armed forces which they were accompanying.

TITLE VIII. EXECUTION OF THE CONVENTION

SECTION I. GENERAL PROVISIONS

ARTICLE 82

The provisions of the present Convention must be respected by the High Contracting Parties under all circumstances.

In case, in time of war, one of the belligerents is not a party to the Convention, its provisions shall nevertheless remain in force as between the belligerents who are parties thereto.

ARTICLE 83

The High Contracting Parties reserve the right to conclude special conventions on all questions relative to prisoners of war, on which it seems to them expedient to have particular regulations.

Prisoners of war shall receive the benefit of these agreements until the completion of repatriation, except in the case of express stipulations to the contrary contained in the above-mentioned agreements or in later agreements, or also except in the case of more favorable measures taken by one or the other of the belligerent Powers respecting the prisoners which they hold.

In order to assure the reciprocal application of the stipulations of the present Convention, and to facilitate the conclusion of the special conventions provided for above, belligerents may, upon the commencement of hostilities, authorize meetings of representatives of the respective authorities charged with the administration of prisoners of war.

ARTICLE 84

The text of the present Convention and of the special conventions provided for in the foregoing article, shall be posted, wherever possible in the native language of the prisoners of war, in places where it may be consulted by all the prisoners.

The text of these conventions shall be communicated to prisoners who find it impossible to get the information from the posted text, upon their request.

ARTICLE 85

The High Contracting Parties shall communicate to one another through the Swiss Federal Council, the official translations of the present Convention, as well as of the laws and regulations which they may come to adopt to assure the application of the present Convention.

SECTION II. ORGANIZATION OF CONTROL

ARTICLE 86

The High Contracting Parties recognize that the regular application of the present Convention will find a guaranty in the possibility of collaboration of the protecting Powers charged with safeguarding the interests of belligerents; in this respect, the protecting Powers may, besides their diplomatic personnel, appoint delegates from among their own nationals or from among the nationals of other neutral Powers. These delegates must be subject to the approval of the belligerent near which they exercise their mission.

Representatives of the protecting Power or its accepted delegates shall be permitted to go to any place, without exception, where prisoners of war are interned. They shall have access to all places occupied by prisoners and may interview them, as a general rule without witnesses, personally or through interpreters.

Belligerents shall so far as possible facilitate the task of representatives or accepted delegates of the protecting Power. The military authorities shall be informed of their visit.

Belligerents may come to an agreement to allow persons of the same nationality as the prisoners to be permitted to take part in inspection trips.

ARTICLE 87

In case of disagreement between the belligerents as to the application of the provisions of the present Convention, the protecting Powers must, in so far as possible, lend their good offices for the purpose of settling the difference.

For this purpose, each of the protecting Powers may, in particular, suggest to the interested belligerents a meeting of representatives thereof, possibly upon a neutral territory suitably chosen. Belligerents shall be bound to accede to proposals in this sense which are made to them. The protecting Power may, if occasion arises, submit for the approval of the Powers concerned a person belonging to a neutral Power or a person delegated by the International Committee of the Red Cross, who shall be summoned to take part in this meeting.

ARTICLE 88

The foregoing provisions are not an obstacle to the humanitarian activity which the International Committee of the Red Cross may use for the protection of prisoners of war, with the consent of the interested belligerents.

SECTION III. FINAL PROVISIONS

ARTICLE 89

In the relations between Powers bound by the Hague Convention respecting the Laws and Customs of War on Land, whether it is a question of that of July 29, 1899,[4] or that of October 18, 1907, and who participate in the present Convention, this latter shall complete Chapter II of the Regulations annexed to the said Hague Conventions.

ARTICLE 90

The present Convention, which will bear this day's date, may be signed up to February 1, 1930, on behalf of all the countries represented at the Conference which opened at Geneva July 1, 1929.

ARTICLE 91

The present Convention shall be ratified as soon as possible.

The ratifications shall be deposited at Berne.

A record of the deposit of each instrument of ratification shall be prepared, a duly certified copy of which shall be forwarded by the Swiss Federal Council to the Governments of all the countries on whose behalf the Convention has been signed or notification of adherence made.

ARTICLE 92

The present Convention shall become effective six months after the deposit of at least two instruments of ratification.

---

[4] TS 403, *ante*, vol. 1, p. 247.

Subsequently, it shall become effective for each High Contracting Party six months after the deposit of its instrument of ratification.

ARTICLE 93

From the date on which it becomes effective, the present Convention shall be open for adherences given on behalf of any country in whose name this Convention was not signed.

ARTICLE 94

Adherences shall be given by written notification addressed to the Swiss Federal Council and shall take effect six months after the date of their receipt.

The Swiss Federal Council shall communicate adherences to the Governments of all the countries on whose behalf the Convention was signed or notification of adherence made.

ARTICLE 95

A state of war shall give immediate effect to ratifications deposited and to adherences notified by belligerent Powers prior to or after the outbreak of hostilities. The communication of ratifications or adherences received from Powers at war shall be made by the Swiss Federal Council by the most rapid method.

ARTICLE 96

Each of the High Contracting Parties shall have the right to denounce the present Convention. The denunciation shall not take effect until one year after notification has been made in writing to the Swiss Federal Council. The latter shall communicate such notification to the Governments of all the High Contracting Parties.

The denunciation shall have effect only with respect to the High Contracting Party which gave notification thereof.

Moreover, such denunciation shall not take effect during a war in which the denouncing Power is involved. In this case, the present Convention shall continue in effect, beyond the period of one year, until the conclusion of peace, and, in any event, until the processes of repatriation are completed.

ARTICLE 97

A duly certified copy of the present Convention shall be deposited in the archives of the League of Nations by the Swiss Federal Council. Likewise, ratifications, adherences, and denunciations of which the Swiss Federal Council shall be notified, shall be communicated by it to the League of Nations.

In faith whereof, the Plenipotentiaries named above have signed the present Convention.

Done at Geneva, the twenty-seventh of July, one thousand nine hundred and twenty-nine, in a single copy, which shall remain in the archives of the

Swiss Confederation and duly certified copies of which shall be forwarded to the Governments of all the countries invited to the Conference.

For Germany:
EDMUND RHOMBERG

For the United States of America:
ELIOT WADSWORTH
HUGH R. WILSON

For Austria:
LEITMAIER

For Belgium:
Dr. DEMOLDER
J. DE RUELLE

For Bolivia:
A. CORTADELLAS

For Brazil:
RAUL DO RIO-BRANCO

For Great Britain and Northern Ireland
and all parts of the British Empire
which are not separate members of
the League of Nations:
HORACE RUMBOLD

For Canada:
W. A. RIDDELL

For Australia:
CLAUD RUSSELL

For New Zealand:
CLAUD RUSSELL

For South Africa:
ERIC H. LOUW

For the Irish Free State:
SEAN LESTER

For India:
CLAUD RUSSELL

For Bulgaria:
D. MIKOFF
STEPHAN N. LAFTCHIEFF

For Chile:
GMO NOVOA
D. PULGAR

For China:
C. Y. HSIAO

For Colombia:
FRANCISCO JOSÉ URRUTIA

For Cuba:
CARLOS DE ARMENTEROS
CARLOS BLANCO

For Denmark:
HARALD SCAVENIUS
GUSTAV RASMUSSEN

For the Dominican Republic:
CH. ACKERMANN

For Egypt:
MOHAMMED ABDEL MONEIM RIAD

For Spain:
Ad Referendum
MAURICIO LOPEZ ROBERTS Y TERRY,
MARQUÉS DE LA TORREHERMOSA

For Estonia:
Dr. LEESMENT

For Finland:
A. E. MARTOLA

For France:
H. DE MARCILLY
J. DU SAULT

For Greece:
R. RAPHAËL
S. VENISELOS

For Hungary:
PAUL DE HEVESY

For Italy:
GIOVANNI CIRAOLO

For Japan:
ISABURO YOSHIDA
S. SHIMOMURA
S. MIURA

For Latvia:
CHARLES DUZMANS
Dr. OSKAR VOIT

For Luxembourg:
CH. G. VERMAIRE

For Mexico:
FR. CASTILLO NÁJERA

For Nicaragua:
A. SOTTILE

For Norway:
J. IRGENS
JENS MEINICH

For the Netherlands:
W. DOUDE VAN TROOSTWIJK
Dr. DIEHL
J. HARBERTS

For Persia:
ANOUCHIREVAN SEPAHBODI

For Poland:
JÓZEF G. PRACKI
W. JERZY BABECKI

For Portugal:
VASCO DE QUEVEDO
F. DE CALHEIROS E MENEZES

For Rumania:
M. B. BOERESCO
Colonel E. VERTEJANO

For the Kingdom of the Serbs, Croats
and Slovenes:
I. CHOUMENKOVITCH

For Siam:
VARNVAIDYA

For Sweden:
K. I. WESTMAN

For Switzerland:
PAUL DINICHERT
HAUSER
ZÜBLIN
DE LA HARPE
SCHINDLER

For Czechoslovakia:
ZD. FIERLINGER

For Turkey:
HASSAN
Dr. ABDULKADIR
M. NUSRET
Dr. AKIL MOUKHTAR

For Uruguay:
ALFREDO DE CASTRO

For Venezuela:
C. PARRA-PÉREZ
I. M. HURTADO-MACHADO

ANNEX TO THE CONVENTION OF JULY 27, 1929, RELATIVE TO THE TREATMENT OF PRISONERS OF WAR

MODEL AGREEMENT CONCERNING DIRECT REPATRIATION AND HOSPITALIZA-
TION IN A NEUTRAL COUNTRY OF PRISONERS OF WAR FOR REASONS OF
HEALTH

I. Governing Principles for Direct Repatriation and Hospitalization in a Neutral Country

A. DIRECT REPATRIATION

There shall be repatriated directly:

1. Sick and wounded who, according to medical opinion, are not likely to recover in one year, their condition requiring treatment and their mental or physical fitness appearing to have suffered considerable diminution;

2. Incurable sick and wounded whose mental or physical fitness appears to have suffered considerable diminution;

3. Cured sick and wounded whose mental or physical fitness appears to have suffered considerable diminution.

B. HOSPITALIZATION IN A NEUTRAL COUNTRY

There shall be placed in hospitals:

1. Sick and wounded whose cure within a period of one year is to be expected, such cure appearing more certain and more rapid if the sick and wounded are given the benefit of the resources offered by the neutral country than if their captivity properly so-called is prolonged;

2. Prisoners of war whose mental or physical health appears, according to medical opinion, to be seriously menaced by continuance in captivity, while hospitalization in a neutral country would probably remove this danger.

C. REPATRIATION OF THOSE HOSPITALIZED IN A NEUTRAL COUNTRY

There shall be repatriated the prisoners of war hospitalized in a neutral country who belong to the following categories:

1. Those whose state of health appears to be or to be becoming such that they fall within the categories of persons eligible to repatriation for reasons of health;

2. The recovered whose mental or physical fitness seems to have suffered a considerable diminution.

II. Special Principles for Direct Repatriation or Hospitalization in a Neutral Country

A. REPATRIATION

There shall be repatriated:

1. All prisoners of war who, as the result of organic injuries, have the following impairments, actual or functional: loss of a member, paralysis, articular or other defects, provided that the loss is at least a foot or a hand, or is equivalent to the loss of a foot or a hand;

2. All wounded or injured prisoners of war whose condition is such that it renders them invalids whose cure, within a period of one year, can not be anticipated from a medical standpoint;

3. All the sick whose condition is such that it renders them invalids whose cure, within a period of one year, can not be anticipated from a medical standpoint;

The following, in particular, belong to this category:

a) Progressive tuberculosis of any organs which, according to medical opinion, can no longer be cured or at least considerably improved by a course of treatment in a neutral country.

b) Nontubercular affections of the respiratory organs presumed incurable (such as, above all, strongly developed pulmonary emphysema, with or without bronchitis, bronchiectasis, serious asthma, gas poisoning, etc.);

c) Serious chronic affections of the organs of circulation (for example: valvular affections with tendencies to disorders of compensation, relatively serious affections of the myocardium, pericardium of the vessels, especially inoperable aneurisms of the large vessels, etc.);

d) Serious chronic affections of the digestive organs;

e) Serious chronic affections of the urinary and sexual organs (particularly, for example: all cases of confirmed chronic nephritis with complete semeiology, and most especially when cardiac and vascular impairments already exist; likewise, pyelites and chronic cystitis, etc.);

f) Serious chronic diseases of the central and peripheral nervous system (such as, particularly, serious neurasthenia and hysteria, all unquestionable cases of epilepsy, serious cases of Basedow's disease, etc.);

g) Blindness in both eyes, or in one eye when the vision of the other remains below 1 in spite of the use of corrective glasses; reduction in acuteness of vision in case it is impossible to restore it by correction to the acuteness of ½ for one eye at least; other ocular affections coming in the present class (glaucoma, iritis, choroiditis, etc.);

h) Total deafness in both ears, as well as total deafness in one ear in case the partially deaf ear does not discern the ordinary spoken voice at a distance of one meter;

i) All unquestionable cases of mental affections;

k) All serious cases of chronic poisoning by metals or other causes (lead poisoning, mercury poisoning, morphinism, cocainism, alcoholism, gas poisoning, etc.);

l) Chronic affections of the organs of locomotion (arthritis deformans, gout, rheumatism with impairments clinically discoverable), provided they are serious;

m) All malignant growths, if they are not amenable to relatively minor operations without endangering the life of the patient;

n) All cases of malaria with noticeable organic changes (important chronic increases in size of the liver, of the spleen, cachexia, etc.);

o) Serious chronic cutaneous affections, in so far as their nature does not constitute a medical indication for hospitalization in a neutral country;

p) Serious avitaminoses (beri-beri, pellagra, chronic scurvy).

B. Hospitalization

Prisoners of war must be hospitalized if they have the following affections:

1. All forms of tuberculosis of any organs whatever if, according to present medical knowledge, they may be cured, or at least considerably improved by methods applicable in a neutral country (altitude, treatment in sanatoria, etc.);

2. All forms—necessitating treatment—of affections of the respiratory, circulatory, digestive, genito-urinary, and nervous organs, of organs of the senses, of the locomotor and cutaneous apparatus provided, however, that the forms of these affections do not belong to the categories requiring direct repatriation, or are not acute diseases properly so-called susceptible to a complete cure. The affections contemplated in this paragraph are those which offer really better chances of cure for the patient by the application of means of treatment available in a neutral country than if he were treated in captivity.

Nervous troubles, the efficient or determinant causes of which are the events of the war or even of the captivity itself, such as the psychasthenia of prisoners of war and other analogous cases, should be given special consideration.

All duly verified cases of this kind should be hospitalized, provided that the seriousness or constitutional character thereof does not make them cases for direct repatriation.

Cases of psychasthenia of prisoners of war which are not cured after three months of hospitalization in a neutral country or which, after this period has expired, are not obviously on the road to final recovery, should be repatriated.

3. All cases of wounds or lesions and their consequences which offer better chances of cure in a neutral country than in captivity, provided that these cases are not either eligible for direct repatriation or else are insignificant;

4. All cases of malaria, duly verified and not presenting organic changes clinically discoverable (chronic enlargement of the liver, of the spleen, cachexia, etc.), if the stay in a neutral country offers particularly favorable prospects of final cure;

5. All cases of poisoning (particularly by gases, metals, alkaloids) for which the prospects of cure in a neutral country are especially favorable.

There shall be excluded from hospitalization:

1. All duly verified cases of mental affections;

2. All organic or functional nervous affections reputed to be incurable; (These two categories belong to those giving a right to direct repatriation.)

3. Serious chronic alcoholism;

4. All contagious affections during the period in which they are transmissible (acute infectious diseases, primary and secondary syphilis, trachoma, leprosy, etc.).

III. General Observations

The conditions given above should, generally speaking, be interpreted and applied in as broad a spirit as possible.

This breadth of interpretation should be especially applied to neuropathic or psychopathic conditions caused or brought to a head by the events of the war or even of the captivity itself (psychasthenia of prisoners of war), and also to cases of tuberculosis in all degrees.

It is needless to state that camp physicians and the mixed medical commissions may find themselves confronted with a great number of cases not mentioned among the examples given under Section II, or cases not fitting in with these examples. The examples mentioned above are given only as typical examples; an analogous list of examples of surgical alterations has not been drawn up because, with the exception of cases incontestable by their very nature (amputations), it is difficult to make a list of particular types; experience has shown that a recital of these particular cases was not without disadvantages in practice.

All cases not fitting exactly into the examples cited shall be decided by invoking the spirit of the above governing principles.

AMELIORATION OF THE CONDITION OF THE WOUNDED AND SICK OF ARMIES IN THE FIELD (RED CROSS CONVENTION)

Convention signed at Geneva July 27, 1929
Senate advice and consent to ratification January 7, 1932
Ratified by the President of the United States January 16, 1932
Ratification of the United States deposited at Bern February 4, 1932
Entered into force June 19, 1931; for the United States August 4, 1932
Proclaimed by the President of the United States August 4, 1932
Replaced by convention of August 12, 1949,[1] as between contracting parties to the later convention

47 Stat. 2074; Treaty Series 847

[TRANSLATION]

CONVENTION OF GENEVA OF JULY 27, 1929, FOR THE AMELIORATION OF THE CONDITION OF THE WOUNDED AND SICK OF ARMIES IN THE FIELD

The President of the German Reich, the President of the United States of America, the Federal President of the Republic of Austria, His Majesty the King of the Belgians, the President of the Republic of Bolivia, the President of the Republic of the United States of Brazil, His Majesty the King of Great Britain, Ireland and the British Dominions beyond the Seas, Emperor of India, His Majesty the King of the Bulgarians, the President of the Republic of Chile, the President of the Republic of China, the President of the Republic of Colombia, the President of the Republic of Cuba, His Majesty the King of Denmark and Iceland, the President of the Dominican Republic, His Majesty the King of Egypt, His Majesty the King of Spain, the President of the Republic of Estonia, the President of the Republic of Finland, the President of the French Republic, the President of the Hellenic Republic, His Serene Highness the Regent of Hungary, His Majesty the King of Italy, His Majesty the Emperor of Japan, the President of the Republic of Latvia, Her Royal Highness the Grand Duchess of Luxembourg, the President of the United States of Mexico, the President of the Republic of Nicaragua, His Majesty the King of Norway, Her Majesty the Queen of the Netherlands, His Imperial Majesty the Shah of Persia, the President of the

---

[1] 6 UST 3114; TIAS 3362.

965

Republic of Poland, the President of the Portuguese Republic, His Majesty the King of Rumania, His Majesty the King of the Serbs, Croats and Slovenes, His Majesty the King of Siam, His Majesty the King of Sweden, the Swiss Federal Council, the President of the Czechoslovak Republic, the President of the Turkish Republic, the President of the Oriental Republic of Uruguay, the President of the Republic of the United States of Venezuela, equally desirous of diminishing, so far as lies within their power, the evils inseparable from war, and wishing to perfect and complete, for this purpose, the provisions agreed upon at Geneva, August 22, 1864,[2] and July 6, 1906,[3] to ameliorate the condition of the wounded and the sick of armies in the field, have decided to conclude a new Convention for this purpose, and have appointed the following as their plenipotentiaries, namely:

The President of the German Reich:
   His Excellency Herr Edmund Rhomberg, Doctor of Laws, Minister unassigned;

The President of the United States of America:
   The Honorable Eliot Wadsworth, former Assistant Secretary of the Treasury,
   His Excellency the Honorable Hugh R. Wilson, Envoy Extraordinary and Minister Plenipotentiary of the United States of America at Berne;

The Federal President of the Republic of Austria:
   Herr Marc Leitmaier, Doctor of Laws, Ministerial Counselor at the Federal Chancellery, Department of Foreign Affairs;

His Majesty the King of the Belgians:
   M. Paul Demolder, Surgeon General, Chief of the Medical Corps of the First Military District,
   M. Joseph de Ruelle, Counselor of the Ministry of Foreign Affairs;

The President of the Republic of Bolivia:
   His Excellency Sr. Alberto Cortadellas, Minister Resident of Bolivia at Berne;

The President of the Republic of the United States of Brazil:
   His Excellency Sr. Raoul de Rio-Branco, Envoy Extraordinary and Minister Plenipotentiary of Brazil at Berne;

His Majesty the King of Great Britain, Ireland and the British Dominions beyond the Seas, Emperor of India:
   For Great Britain and Northern Ireland and All Parts of the British Empire Which Are Not Separate Members of the League of Nations:
   The Right Honorable Sir Horace Rumbold, G.C.M.G., M.V.O., Ambassador of His Britannic Majesty at Berlin;

---

[2] TS 377, *ante*, vol. 1, p. 7.
[3] TS 464, *ante*, vol. 1, p. 516.

For the Dominion of Canada:

Mr. Walter Alexander Riddell, Permanent Counselor of the Canadian Government to the League of Nations;

For the Commonwealth of Australia:

His Excellency Mr. Claud Russell, Envoy Extraordinary and Minister Plenipotentiary of His Britannic Majesty at Berne;

For the Dominion of New Zealand:

His Excellency Mr. Claud Russell, Envoy Extraordinary and Minister Plenipotentiary of His Britannic Majesty at Berne;

For the Union of South Africa:

Mr. Eric Hendrik Louw, High Commissioner of the Union of South Africa at London;

For the Irish Free State:

Mr. Sean Lester, Representative of the Irish Free State to the League of Nations;

For India:

His Excellency Mr. Claud Russell, Envoy Extraordinary and Minister Plenipotentiary of His Britannic Majesty at Berne;

His Majesty the King of the Bulgarians:

M. Dimitri Mikoff, Chargé d'Affaires of Bulgaria at Berne, Permanent Representative of the Bulgarian Government to the League of Nations,

M. Stéphane M. Laftchieff, Member of the Administrative Council of the Bulgarian Red Cross;

The President of the Republic of Chile:

Colonel Guillermo Novoa-Sepulveda, Military Attaché to the Legation of Chile at Berlin,

Captain Dario Pulgar-Arriagada, Medical Corps;

The President of the Republic of China:

Mr. Chi Yung Hsiao, Chargé d'Affaires *ad interim* of China at Berne;

The President of the Republic of Colombia:

His Excellency Sr. Francisco José de Urrutia, Envoy Extraordinary and Minister Plenipotentiary of Colombia at Berne;

The President of the Republic of Cuba:

His Excellency Sr. Carlos de Armenteros y de Cardenas, Envoy Extraordinary and Minister Plenipotentiary of Cuba at Berne,

Sr. Carlos Blanco y Sanchez, Secretary of Legation, attached to the Delegation of Cuba to the League of Nations;

His Majesty the King of Denmark and Iceland:

For Denmark:

His Excellency Mr. Harald de Scavenius, Chamberlain, Envoy Extraordinary and Minister Plenipotentiary of Denmark in Switzerland and in the Netherlands, former Minister of Foreign Affairs,

Mr. Gustave M. Rasmussen, Chargé d'Affaires *ad interim* of Denmark at Berne;

The President of the Dominican Republic:

Sr. Charles Ackermann, Consul of the Dominican Republic at Geneva;

His Majesty the King of Egypt:

M. Mohammed Abdel Moneim Riad, Counselor of the State Legal Department, Professor of International Law at the Military School of Cairo,

M. Henri Wassif Simaika, Attaché of the Royal Legation of Egypt at Rome;

His Majesty the King of Spain:

His Excellency the Marquis de la Torrehermosa, Envoy Extraordinary and Minister Plenipotentiary of Spain at Berne;

The President of the Republic of Estonia:

Mr. Hans Leesment, Doctor of Medicine, President of the Estonian Red Cross;

The President of the Republic of Finland:

Lieutenant-Colonel A. E. Martola, Military Attaché to the Legation of Finland at Paris;

The President of the French Republic:

His Excellency M. Henri Chassain de Marcilly, Ambassador of France at Berne,

M. Jean du Sault, Counselor of the Embassy of France at Berne;

The President of the Hellenic Republic:

M. Raphael Raphael, Chargé d'Affaires *ad interim* of Greece at Berne,

Lieutenant-Colonel Sophocles Veniselos, Military Attaché to the Legation of Greece at Paris;

His Serene Highness the Regent of Hungary:

His Excellency M. Paul de Hevesy, Minister Resident, Permanent Delegate of the Royal Government to the League of Nations;

His Majesty the King of Italy:

Sig. Giovanni Ciraolo, Senator of the Kingdom;

His Majesty the Emperor of Japan:

His Excellency Mr. Isaburo Yoshida, Envoy Extraordinary and Minister Plenipotentiary of Japan at Berne,

Lieutenant-Colonel Sadamu Shimomura,

Captain Seizo Miura, Naval Attaché to the Embassy of Japan at Paris;

The President of the Republic of Latvia:

His Excellency Mr. Charles Duzmans, Envoy Extraordinary and Minister Plenipotentiary of Latvia to His Majesty the King of the Serbs, Croats and Slovenes, Permanent Delegate to the League of Nations,

His Excellency Mr. Oskar Voit, Envoy Extraordinary and Minister Plenipotentiary of Latvia in Switzerland, Germany, Hungary, and the Netherlands;

Her Royal Highness the Grand Duchess of Luxembourg:

M. Charles Vermaire, Consul of the Grand Duchy at Geneva;

The President of the United States of Mexico:

His Excellency Sr. Francisco Castillo Nájera, Surgeon General, Envoy Extraordinary and Minister Plenipotentiary of Mexico at Brussels;

The President of the Republic of Nicaragua:

Sr. Antoine Sottile, Doctor of Laws, Permanent Delegate of Nicaragua to the League of Nations;

His Majesty the King of Norway:

His Excellency Mr. Johannes Irgens, Envoy Extraordinary and Minister Plenipotentiary of Norway at Berne, Rome, and Athens,

Mr. Jens Christian Meinich, Commandant of Infantry, Secretary General of the Norwegian Red Cross;

Her Majesty the Queen of the Netherlands:

His Excellency Mr. Willem Isaac Doude van Troostwijk, Envoy Extraordinary and Minister Plenipotentiary of the Netherlands at Berne,

Major-General Johan Carl Diehl, Inspector-General of the Medical Corps of the Army, Vice President of the Netherland Red Cross,

Mr. Jacob Harberts, Commandant of the General Staff, Professor at the War College;

His Imperial Majesty the Shah of Persia:

His Excellency M. Anouchirevan Khan Sepahbodi, Envoy Extraordinary and Minister Plenipotentiary of Persia at Berne;

The President of the Republic of Poland:

Colonel Joseph Gabriel Pracki, Medical Corps,
Lieutenant-Colonel W. Jerzy Babecki;

The President of the Portuguese Republic:

His Excellency Sr. Vasco de Quevedo, Envoy Extraordinary and Minister Plenipotentiary of Portugal at Berne,

Sr. Francisco de Calheiros e Menezes, First Secretary of Legation;

His Majesty the King of Rumania:

His Excellency M. Michel B. Boeresco, Envoy Extraordinary and Minister Plenipotentiary of Rumania at Berne,

Colonel Eugene Vertejano, Officer of the General Staff;

His Majesty the King of the Serbs, Croats and Slovenes:

His Excellency M. Ilija Choumenkovitch, Envoy Extraordinary and Minister Plenipotentiary of the Kingdom of the Serbs, Croats and Slovenes at Berne, Permanent Delegate to the League of Nations;

His Majesty the King of Siam:

His Serene Highness, Prince Varnvaidya, Envoy Extraordinary and Minister Plenipotentiary of Siam at London;

His Majesty the King of Sweden:

His Excellency Mr. Karl Ivan Westman, Envoy Extraordinary and Minister Plenipotentiary of Sweden at Berne;

The Swiss Federal Council:

M. Paul Dinichert, Minister Plenipotentiary, Chief of the Division of Foreign Affairs of the Federal Political Department,

Colonel Carl Hauser, Medical Corps, Surgeon General of the Army,

M. Anton Züblin, Infantry Colonel unassigned, Attorney,

Lieutenant-Colonel Roger de la Harpe, Medical Corps, Surgeon,

Major Dietrich Schindler, Judge Advocate General's Department, Professor of International Law at the University of Zürich;

The President of the Czechoslovak Republic:

His Excellency M. Zdeněk Fierlinger, Envoy Extraordinary and Minister Plenipotentiary of Czechoslovakia at Berne;

The President of the Turkish Republic:

His Excellency Hassan Bey, Vice President of the Grand National Assembly of Turkey, Vice President of the Turkish Red Crescent,

His Excellency Nusret Bey, President of the Council of State of the Republic,

Professor Akil Moukhtar Bey, Doctor of Medicine,

Lieutenant-Colonel Abdulkadir Bey, Military Surgeon, Professor at the Military Academy and at the Hospital of Gulhane;

The President of the Oriental Republic of Uruguay:

His Excellency Sr. Alfredo de Castro, Envoy Extraordinary and Minister Plenipotentiary of Uruguay at Berne;

The President of the Republic of the United States of Venezuela:

His Excellency Sr. Caracciolo Parra-Pérez, Envoy Extraordinary and Minister Plenipotentiary of Venezuela at Rome,

Sr. Ivan Manuel Hurtado-Machado, Chargé d'Affaires *ad interim* of Venezuela at Berne;

Who, after having communicated to each other their full powers, found to be in good and due form, have agreed as follows:

CHAPTER I. *The Wounded and Sick*

ARTICLE 1

Officers, soldiers, and other persons officially attached to the armies who are wounded or sick shall be respected and protected in all circumstances; they shall be humanely treated and cared for without distinction of nationality by the belligerent in whose power they are.

A belligerent, however, when compelled to leave his wounded or sick in the hands of his adversary, shall leave with them, so far as military exigencies permit, a portion of the personnel and matériel of his sanitary service to assist in caring for them.

ARTICLE 2

Subject to the care that must be taken of them under the preceding article, the wounded and sick of an army who fall into the power of the other belligerent shall become prisoners of war, and the general rules of international law in respect to prisoners of war shall become applicable to them.

The belligerents shall remain free, however, to agree upon such clauses to the benefit of the wounded and sick prisoners as they may deem of value over and above already existing obligations.

ARTICLE 3

After every engagement, the belligerent who remains in possession of the field of battle shall take measures to search for the wounded and the dead and to protect them from robbery and ill-treatment.

A local armistice or cessation of fire to enable the removal of wounded left between the lines shall be arranged whenever circumstances permit.

ARTICLE 4

Belligerents shall mutually forward to each other as soon as possible the names of the wounded, sick and dead taken in charge or discovered by them, as well as all indications which may serve for their identification.

They shall draw up and forward to each other death certificates.

They shall collect and likewise forward to each other all objects of personal use found on the field of battle or on the dead, especially one-half of their identity plaque, the other half remaining attached to the body.

They shall see that a careful examination, if possible, medical, is made of the bodies of the dead prior to their interment or cremation, with a view to verifying their death, establishing their identity, and in order to be able to furnish a report thereon.

They shall further see that they are honorably buried and that the graves are treated with respect and may always be found again.

For this purpose, and at the outbreak of hostilities, they shall officially organize a service of graves in order to render any later exhumation possible and to make certain of the identity of bodies even though they may have been moved from grave to grave.

Upon the termination of hostilities, they shall exchange lists of graves and of dead buried in their cemeteries and elsewhere.

ARTICLE 5

The military authority may make an appeal to the charitable zeal of the inhabitants to receive and, under its supervision, to care for, the wounded or sick of the armies, granting to persons responding to such appeals special protection and certain facilities.

CHAPTER II. *Sanitary Formations and Establishments*

ARTICLE 6

Mobile sanitary formations, i. e., those which are intended to accompany armies in the field, and the fixed establishments belonging to the sanitary service shall be protected and respected by the belligerents.

ARTICLE 7

The protection due to sanitary formations and establishments shall cease if they are used to commit acts injurious to the enemy.

ARTICLE 8

A sanitary formation or establishment shall not be deprived of the protection accorded by Article 6 by the fact:

1) that the personnel of the formation or establishment is armed and uses its arms in self-defense or in defense of its wounded and sick;

2) that in the absence of armed hospital attendants the formation is guarded by an armed detachment or by sentinels;

3) that hand firearms or ammunition taken from the wounded and sick and not yet turned over to the proper authorities are found in the formation or establishment;

4) that there is found in the formation or establishment personnel or matériel of the veterinary service which does not integrally belong to it.

CHAPTER III. *Personnel*

ARTICLE 9

The personnel charged exclusively with the removal, transportation, and treatment of the wounded and sick, as well as with the administration of sanitary formations and establishments, and the chaplains attached to armies, shall be respected and protected under all circumstances. If they fall into the hands of the enemy they shall not be treated as prisoners of war.

Military personnel which has received special instructions to be used when necessary as auxiliary attendants or litter bearers in the removal, transportation and treatment of the wounded and sick, and bearing an identification document, shall benefit by the same conditions as the permanent sanitary personnel if they are captured at the moment when they are fulfilling these functions.

ARTICLE 10

The personnel of volunteer aid societies, duly recognized and authorized by their Government, who are employed in the same functions as the personnel contemplated in Article 9, paragraph 1, are assimilated to that personnel upon condition that the said societies shall be subject to military laws and regulations.

Each High Contracting Party shall make known to the other, either in time of peace or at the opening or during the progress of hostilities, and in any case before actual employment, the names of the societies which it has authorized to render assistance, under its responsibility, in the official sanitary service of its armies.

ARTICLE 11

A recognized society of a neutral country may only lend the services of its sanitary personnel and formations to a belligerent with the prior consent of its own Government and the authority of such belligerent.

The belligerent who has accepted such assistance shall be required to notify the enemy before making any use thereof.

ARTICLE 12

The persons described in Articles 9, 10 and 11 may not be detained after they have fallen into the power of the adversary.

Unless there is an agreement to the contrary, they shall be sent back to the belligerent to whose service they are attached as soon as a way is open for their return and military exigencies permit.

While waiting to be returned, they shall continue in the exercise of their functions under the direction of the adversary; they shall be assigned preferably to the care of the wounded and sick of the belligerent to whose service they are attached.

At the time of their departure they may carry with them such effects, instruments, arms and means of transport as belong to them.

ARTICLE 13

While they remain in their power, belligerents shall secure to the personnel mentioned in Articles 9, 10 and 11, the same maintenance and quarters, pay and allowances, as to persons of corresponding rank in their own armies.

At the outbreak of hostilities the belligerents shall reach an understanding on the corresponding ranks of their sanitary personnel.

CHAPTER IV. *Buildings and Matériel*

ARTICLE 14

If mobile sanitary formations, whatever may be their nature, fall into the power of the adversary, they shall retain their matériel, their means of transportation, and their conducting personnel.

The competent military authority, however, shall have the right to employ them in caring for the wounded and sick; restitution shall take place in accordance with the conditions prescribed for the sanitary personnel and as far as possible at the same time.

ARTICLE 15

Buildings and matériel of the fixed sanitary establishments of the army shall remain subject to the laws of war, but may not be diverted from their use so long as they are necessary for the wounded and sick.

However, commanders of troops engaged in operations may use them in case of urgent military necessity if, before such use, the wounded and sick treated there have been provided for.

ARTICLE 16

The buildings of aid societies admitted to the benefits of the Convention shall be regarded as private property.

The matériel of these societies, irrespective of its location, shall likewise be regarded as private property.

The right of requisition recognized to belligerents by the laws and customs of war shall be exercised only in case of urgent necessity and after the wounded and sick have been provided for.

CHAPTER V. *Sanitary Transports*

ARTICLE 17

Vehicles equipped for sanitary evacuation traveling singly or in convoy shall be treated as mobile sanitary formations subject to the following special provisions:

A belligerent intercepting sanitary transportation vehicles, traveling either singly or in convoy, may, if required by military necessity, stop them and break up the convoy, charging himself in all cases with the care of the wounded and sick whom it contains. He may only utilize such vehicles in the sector wherein they were intercepted and exclusively for sanitary needs. When their local mission is at an end, these vehicles must be returned under the conditions stipulated in Article 14.

Military personnel assigned by competent orders for sanitary transportation purposes shall be returned under the conditions stipulated in Article 12 for sanitary personnel, and subject to the provisions of the last paragraph of Article 18.

All means of transportation especially organized for evacuation purposes, as well as their appurtenances attached to the sanitary service, shall be returned in conformity with the provisions of Chapter IV.

Military means of transportation and their teams, other than those belonging to the sanitary service, may be captured.

The civil personnel and all means of transportation obtained by requisition shall be subject to the general rules of international law.

ARTICLE 18

Aircraft used as a means of sanitary transportation shall enjoy the protection of the Convention during such time as they are exclusively reserved for the evacuation of wounded and sick and for the transportation of sanitary personnel and matériel.

They shall be painted in white and shall bear clearly visible the distinctive sign mentioned in Article 19 alongside of the national colors on their upper and lower surfaces.

Excepting with special and express permission, a flight over the firing-line, as well as over the zone situated in front of the major medical dressing stations, and in general over any territory under the control of or occupied by the enemy shall be forbidden.

Sanitary aircraft must comply with all summons to land.

In the case of a landing thus required or made accidentally upon territory occupied by the enemy, the wounded and sick, as well as the sanitary personnel and matériel, including the aircraft, shall benefit by the provisions of the present Convention.

The pilot, mechanics, and wireless operators who have been captured shall be returned on condition of only being utilized in the sanitary service until the termination of hostilities.

CHAPTER VI. *The Distinctive Sign*

ARTICLE 19

Out of respect to Switzerland the heraldic emblem of the red cross on a white ground, formed by the reversal of the Federal colors, is continued as the emblem and distinctive sign of the sanitary service of armies.

However, for countries which already use, as a distinctive sign, in place of the red cross, the red crescent or the red lion and sun on a white field, these emblems shall likewise be recognized within the meaning of the present Convention.

ARTICLE 20

The emblem shall appear on flags and brassards, as well as upon all matériel, appertaining to the sanitary service, with the permission of the competent military authority.

Article 21

The personnel protected in virtue of the first paragraph of Article 9 and Articles 10 and 11 shall wear attached to the left arm a brassard bearing the distinctive sign, issued and stamped by a competent military authority.

The personnel mentioned in Article 9, paragraphs 1 and 2, shall be furnished with an identification document consisting either of an inscription in their military booklet or a special document.

Persons mentioned in Articles 10 and 11 who do not wear military uniform shall be furnished by competent military authority with a certificate of identity containing their photograph and attesting to their sanitary status.

Identification documents must be uniform and of the same type in each army.

The sanitary personnel may in no case be deprived of their insignia nor of their own identification papers.

In case of loss they shall have the right to obtain duplicates.

Article 22

The distinctive flag of the Convention may only be displayed over the sanitary formations and establishments which the Convention provides shall be respected, and with the consent of the military authorities. In fixed establishments it shall, and in mobile formations it may, be accompanied by the national flag of the belligerent to whose service the formation or establishment is attached.

Sanitary formations which have fallen into the power of the enemy, however, shall fly no other flag than that of the Convention as long as they continue in that situation.

The belligerents, in so far as military exigencies allow, shall take such measures as may be necessary to render the distinctive emblems marking sanitary formations and establishments plainly visible to the land, air and sea forces of the enemy, with a view to preventing the possibility of any aggressive action.

Article 23

The sanitary formations of neutral countries which, under the conditions set forth in Article 11, have been authorized to render their services, shall fly, with the flag of the Convention, the national flag of the belligerent to which they are attached.

They shall have the right during such time as they are rendering service to a belligerent to fly their own national flag also.

The provisions of the second paragraph of the preceding article are applicable to them.

Article 24

The emblem of the red cross on a white ground and the words *Red Cross* or *Geneva Cross* may be used, whether in time of peace or war, only to protect or designate sanitary formations and establishments, the personnel and matériel protected by the Convention.

The same shall apply with respect to the emblems mentioned in the second paragraph of Article 19 for such countries as use them.

Moreover, the volunteer aid societies provided for under Article 10 may, in conformity with their national legislation, employ the distinctive emblem for their humanitarian activities in time of peace.

As an exceptional measure and with the specific authorization of one of the national Red Cross Societies (Red Crescent, Red Lion and Sun), the use of the emblem of the Convention may be allowed in peace time to designate the location of relief stations reserved exclusively to giving free assistance to wounded or sick.

CHAPTER VII. *The Application and Execution of the Convention*

ARTICLE 25

The provisions of the present Convention shall be respected by the High Contracting Parties under all circumstances.

If, in time of war, a belligerent is not a party to the Convention, its provisions shall nevertheless remain in force as between all the belligerents who are parties to the Convention.

ARTICLE 26

It shall be the duty of the commanders-in-chief of the belligerent armies to provide for the details of execution of the foregoing articles, as well as for unforeseen cases, in accordance with the instructions of their respective Governments, and conformably to the general principles of this Convention.

ARTICLE 27

The High Contracting Parties shall take the necessary steps to acquaint their troops, and particularly the protected personnel, with the provisions of this Convention, and to make them known to the people at large.

CHAPTER VIII. *The Repression of Abuses and Infractions*

ARTICLE 28

The Governments of the High Contracting Parties whose legislation may not now be adequate shall take or shall recommend to their legislatures such measures as may be necessary at all times:

a) to prevent the use by private persons or by societies other than those upon which this Convention confers the right thereto, of the emblem or of the name of the *Red Cross* or *Geneva Cross*, as well as any other sign or designation constituting an imitation thereof, whether for commercial or other purposes;

b) by reason of the homage rendered to Switzerland as a result of the adoption of the inverted Federal colors, to prevent the use, by private persons or by organizations, of the arms of the Swiss Confederation or of signs constituting an imitation thereof, whether as trade-marks, commercial labels, or portions thereof, or in any way contrary to commercial ethics, or under conditions wounding Swiss national pride.

The prohibition mentioned in subparagraph *a*) of the use of signs or designations constituting an imitation of the emblem or designation of the *Red Cross* or *Geneva Cross*, as well as the prohibition mentioned in subparagraph *b*) of the use of the arms of the Swiss Confederation or signs constituting an imitation thereof, shall take effect from the time set in each act of legislation and at the latest five years after this Convention goes into effect. After such going into effect it shall be unlawful to take out a trade-mark or commercial label contrary to such prohibitions.

ARTICLE 29

The Governments of the High Contracting Parties whose penal laws may not be adequate, shall likewise take or recommend to their legislatures the necessary measures to repress in time of war all acts in contravention of the provisions of the present Convention.

They shall communicate to one another through the Swiss Federal Council the measures taken with a view to such repression, not later than five years from the date of the ratification of the present Convention.

ARTICLE 30

At the request of a belligerent, an investigation must be held, in such manner as shall be agreed upon by the interested parties, concerning any alleged violation of the Convention; whenever such a violation is proved, the belligerents shall put an end to it and repress it as promptly as possible.

Final Provisions

ARTICLE 31

The present Convention, which will bear the date of this day, may be signed up to February 1, 1930, on behalf of all the countries represented at the Conference which opened at Geneva on July 1, 1929, as well as by the countries not represented at the Conference which are parties to the Geneva Conventions of 1864 or of 1906.

ARTICLE 32

The present Convention shall be ratified as soon as possible.

The ratifications shall be deposited at Berne.

A record of the deposit of each instrument of ratification shall be prepared, a duly certified copy of which shall be forwarded by the Swiss Federal

Council to the Governments of all the countries on whose behalf the Convention has been signed or notification of adhesion made.

ARTICLE 33

The present Convention shall become effective six months after the deposit of at least two instruments of ratification.

Subsequently, it shall become effective for each High Contracting Party six months after the deposit of its instrument of ratification.

ARTICLE 34

The present Convention shall replace the Conventions of August 22, 1864, and of July 6, 1906, in the relations between the High Contracting Parties.

ARTICLE 35

From the date on which it becomes effective, the present Convention shall be open for adhesions given on behalf of any country in whose name this Convention was not signed.

ARTICLE 36

Adhesions shall be given by written notification addressed to the Swiss Federal Council and shall take effect six months after the date of their receipt.

The Swiss Federal Council shall communicate adhesions to the Governments of all the countries on whose behalf the Convention was signed or notification of adhesion made.

ARTICLE 37

A state of war shall give immediate effect to ratifications deposited or adhesions notified by belligerent Powers prior to or after the outbreak of hostilities. The communication of ratifications or adhesions received from Powers at war shall be made by the Swiss Federal Council by the most rapid method.

ARTICLE 38

Each of the High Contracting Parties shall have the right to denounce the present Convention. The denunciation shall not take effect until one year after notification has been made in writing to the Swiss Federal Council. The latter shall communicate such notification to the Governments of all the High Contracting Parties.

The denunciation shall have effect only with respect to the High Contracting Party which gave notification of it.

Moreover, such denunciation shall not take effect during a war in which the denouncing Power is involved. In this case, the present Convention shall continue in effect, beyond the period of one year, until the conclusion of peace.

Article 39

A duly certified copy of the present Convention shall be deposited in the archives of the League of Nations by the Swiss Federal Council. Likewise, ratifications, adhesions, and denunciations of which the Swiss Federal Council has been notified shall be communicated by it to the League of Nations.

In faith whereof, the Plenipotentiaries named above have signed the present Convention.

Done at Geneva, the twenty-seventh of July, one thousand nine hundred and twenty-nine, in a single copy, which shall remain in the archives of the Swiss Confederation and duly certified copies of which shall be forwarded to the Governments of all the countries invited to the Conference.

For Germany:
EDMUND RHOMBERG

For the United States of America:
ELIOT WADSWORTH
HUGH R. WILSON

For Austria:
LEITMAIER

For Belgium:
Dr. DEMOLDER
J. DE RUELLE

For Bolivia:
A. CORTADELLAS

For Brazil:
RAUL DO RIO-BRANCO

For Great Britain and Northern Ireland, and all parts of the British Empire which are not separate members of the League of Nations:

I declare that the signature which I affix to this Convention for Great Britain and Northern Ireland, and all parts of the British Empire which are not separate members of the League of Nations is given with the reservation that His Britannic Majesty interprets Article 28 of the Convention as meaning that the legislative provisions contemplated in this article may provide that the individuals, associations, firms or societies that shall, before the present Convention goes into effect, have used the arms of the Swiss Confederation, or signs constituting an imitation of the said arms, for any legal purpose, shall not be prevented from continuing to employ such arms or signs for the same purpose.

HORACE RUMBOLD

For Canada:

I declare that the signature which I affix to this Convention for Canada is given with the reservation that the Government of the Dominion of Canada interprets Article 28 of the Convention as meaning that the legislative provisions contemplated in this article may provide that the individuals, associations, firms and societies that shall, before the present Convention goes into effect, have used the arms of the Swiss Confederation, or signs constituting an imitation of the said arms, for any legal purpose, shall not be prevented from continuing to employ such arms or signs for the same purpose.

W. A. RIDDELL

For Australia:

I declare that the signature which I affix to this Convention for Australia is given with the reservation that the Government of the Commonwealth of Australia interprets Article 28 of the Convention as meaning that the legislative provisions contemplated in this article may provide that the individuals, associations, firms and societies that shall, before the present Convention goes into effect, have used the arms of the Swiss Confederation, or signs constituting an imitation of the said arms, for any legal purpose, shall not be prevented from continuing to employ such arms or signs for the same purpose.

CLAUD RUSSELL

For New Zealand:

I declare that the signature which I affix to this Convention for New Zealand is given with the reservation that the Government of New Zealand interprets Article 28 of the Convention as meaning that the legislative provisions contemplated in this article may provide that the individuals, associations, firms or societies that shall, before the present Convention goes into effect, have used the arms of the Swiss Confederation, or signs constituting an imitation of the said arms, for any legal purpose, shall not be prevented from continuing to employ such arms or signs for the same purpose.

CLAUD RUSSELL

For South Africa:
ERIC H. LOUW

For the Irish Free State:
I declare that the signature which I affix to this Convention for the Irish Free State is given with the reservation that it interprets Article 28 of the Convention as meaning that the legislative provisions contemplated in this article may provide that the individuals, associations, firms or societies that shall, before the present Convention goes into effect, have used the arms of the Swiss Confederation, or signs constituting an imitation of the said arms, for any legal purpose, shall not be prevented from continuing to employ such arms or signs for the same purpose.

SEAN LESTER

For India:
I declare that the signature which I affix to this Convention for the Government of India is given with the reservation that the Government of India interprets Article 28 of the Convention as meaning that the legislative provisions contemplated in this article may provide that the individuals, associations, firms or societies that shall, before the present Convention goes into effect, have used the arms of the Swiss Confederation, or signs constituting an imitation of the said arms, for any legal purpose, shall not be prevented from continuing to employ such arms or signs for the same purpose.

CLAUD RUSSELL

For Bulgaria:
D. MIKOFF
STEPHEN N. LAFTCHIEFF

For Chile:
GMO NOVOA
D. PULGAR

For China:
C. Y. HSIAO

For Colombia:
FRANCISCO JOSÉ URRUTIA

For Cuba:
CARLOS DE ARMENTEROS
CARLOS BLANCO

For Denmark:
HARALD SCAVENIUS
GUSTAV RASMUSSEN

For the Dominican Republic:
CH. ACKERMANN

For Egypt:
MOHAMMED ABDEL MONEIM RIAD
H. W. M. SIMAIKA

For Spain:
Ad Referendum
MAURICIO LOPEZ ROBERTS Y TERRY, MARQUÉS DE LA TORREHERMOSA

For Estonia:
Dr. LEESMENT

For Finland:
A. E. MARTOLA

For France:
H. DE MARCILLY
J. DU SAULT

For Greece:
R. RAPHAËL
S. VENISELOS

For Hungary:
PAUL DE HEVESY

For Italy:
GIOVANNI CIRAOLO

For Japan:
While accepting in principle the provisions of Article 28,

Japan makes reservations as to the date of enforcing the interdiction provided for under letter b of the said article.

Japan understands that this interdiction does not apply to arms and signs which may have been in use or registered before it goes into effect.

The delegates of Japan sign the present Convention with the above-mentioned reservations.

ISABURO YOSHIDA
S. SHIMOMURA
S. MIURA

For Latvia:
CHARLES DUZMANS
Dr. OSKAR VOIT

For Luxembourg:
CH. G. VERMAIRE

For Mexico:
FR. CASTILLO NÁJERA

For Nicaragua:
A. SOTTILE

For Norway:
J. IRGENS
JENS MEINICH

For the Netherlands:
W. DOUDE VAN TROOSTWIJK
Dr. DIEHL
J. HARBERTS

For Persia:
ANOUCHIREVAN SEPAHBODI

For Poland:
JÓZEF G. PRACKI
W. JERZY BABECKI

For Portugal:
VASCO DE QUEVEDO
F. DE CALHEIROS E MENEZES

For Rumania:
M. B. BOERESCO
COLONEL E. VERTEJANO

For the Kingdom of the Serbs, Croats
and Slovenes:
I. CHOUMENKOVITCH

For Siam:
VARNVAIDYA

For Sweden:
K. I. WESTMAN

For Switzerland:
PAUL DINICHERT
HAUSER
ZÜBLIN
DE LA HARPE
SCHINDLER

For Czechoslovakia:
ZD. FIERLINGER

For Turkey:
HASSAN
Dr. ABDULKADIR
M. NUSRET
Dr. AKIL MOUKHTAR

For Uruguay:
ALFREDO DE CASTRO

For Venezuela:
C. PARRA-PÉREZ
I. M. HURTADO-MACHADO

UNIFICATION OF CERTAIN RULES RELATING TO INTERNATIONAL TRANSPORTATION BY AIR

Convention and additional protocol opened for signature at Warsaw October 12, 1929

Senate advice and consent to adherence, with a reservation, June 15, 1934 [1]

Adherence declared by the United States, with a reservation, June 27, 1934 [1]

Adherence of the United States deposited at Warsaw July 31, 1934

Entered into force February 13, 1933; for the United States October 29, 1934

Proclaimed by the President of the United States October 29, 1934

Amended by protocol of September 28, 1955; [2] *supplemented by convention of September 18, 1961* [3]

Notification of denunciation given by the United States November 15, 1965, and withdrawn May 14, 1966

49 Stat. 3000; Treaty Series 876

[TRANSLATION]

CONVENTION FOR THE UNIFICATION OF CERTAIN RULES RELATING TO INTERNATIONAL TRANSPORTATION BY AIR

The President of the German Reich, the Federal President of the Republic of Austria, His Majesty the King of the Belgians, the President of the United States of Brazil, His Majesty the King of the Bulgarians, the President of the Nationalist Government of China, His Majesty the King of Denmark and Iceland, His Majesty the King of Egypt, His Majesty the King of Spain, the Chief of State of the Republic of Estonia, the President of the Republic of Finland, the President of the French Republic, His Majesty the King of Great Britain, Ireland, and the British Dominions beyond the Seas, Emperor of India, the President of the Hellenic Republic, His Most Serene Highness the

---

[1] The U.S. reservation reads as follows: ". . . the first paragraph of Article 2 of the convention shall not apply to international transportation that may be performed by the United States of America or any territory or possession under its jurisdiction."

[2] 478 UNTS 371; S. Ex. H, 86th Cong., 1st sess. The United States did not become a party.

[3] 500 UNTS 31. The United States did not become a party.

Regent of the Kingdom of Hungary, His Majesty the King of Italy, His Majesty the Emperor of Japan, the President of the Republic of Latvia, Her Royal Highness the Grand Duchess of Luxemburg, the President of the United Mexican States, His Majesty the King of Norway, Her Majesty the Queen of the Netherlands, the President of the Republic of Poland, His Majesty the King of Rumania, His Majesty the King of Sweden, the Swiss Federal Council, the President of the Czechoslovak Republic, the Central Executive Committee of the Union of Soviet Socialist Republics, the President of the United States of Venezuela, His Majesty the King of Yugoslavia:

Having recognized the advantage of regulating in a uniform manner the conditions of international transportation by air in respect of the documents used for such transportation and of the liability of the carrier,

Have nominated to this end their respective Plenipotentiaries, who, being thereto duly authorized, have concluded and signed the following convention:

CHAPTER I. SCOPE—DEFINITIONS

Article 1

(1) This convention shall apply to all international transportation of persons, baggage, or goods performed by aircraft for hire. It shall apply equally to gratuitous transportation by aircraft performed by an air transportation enterprise.

(2) For the purposes of this convention the expression "international transportation" shall mean any transportation in which, according to the contract made by the parties, the place of departure and the place of destination, whether or not there be a break in the transportation or a transshipment, are situated either within the territories of two High Contracting Parties, or within the territory of a single High Contracting Party, if there is an agreed stopping place within a territory subject to the sovereignty, suzerainty, mandate or authority of another power, even though that power is not a party to this convention. Transportation without such an agreed stopping place between territories subject to the sovereignty, suzerainty, mandate, or authority of the same High Contracting Party shall not be deemed to be international for the purposes of this convention.

(3) Transportation to be performed by several successive air carriers shall be deemed, for the purposes of this convention, to be one undivided transportation, if it has been regarded by the parties as a single operation, whether it has been agreed upon under the form of a single contract or of a series of contracts, and it shall not lose its international character merely because one contract or a series of contracts is to be performed entirely within a territory subject to the sovereignty, suzerainty, mandate, or authority of the same High Contracting Party.

Article 2

(1) This convention shall apply to transportation performed by the state or by legal entities constituted under public law provided it falls within the conditions laid down in article 1.[4]

(2) This convention shall not apply to transportation performed under the terms of any international postal convention.

CHAPTER II. TRANSPORTATION DOCUMENTS

SECTION I. PASSENGER TICKET

Article 3

(1) For the transportation of passengers the carrier must deliver a passenger ticket which shall contain the following particulars:

(a) The place and date of issue;

(b) The place of departure and of destination;

(c) The agreed stopping places, provided that the carrier may reserve the right to alter the stopping places in case of necessity, and that if he exercises that right, the alteration shall not have the effect of depriving the transportation of its international character;

(d) The name and address of the carrier or carriers;

(e) A statement that the transportation is subject to the rules relating to liability established by this convention.

(2) The absence, irregularity, or loss of the passenger ticket shall not affect the existence or the validity of the contract of transportation, which shall none the less be subject to the rules of this convention. Nevertheless, if the carrier accepts a passenger without a passenger ticket having been delivered he shall not be entitled to avail himself of those provisions of this convention which exclude or limit his liability.

SECTION II. BAGGAGE CHECK

Article 4

(1) For the transportation of baggage, other than small personal objects of which the passenger takes charge himself, the carrier must deliver a baggage check.

(2) The baggage check shall be made out in duplicate, one part for the passenger and the other part for the carrier.

(3) The baggage check shall contain the following particulars:

(a) The place and date of issue;

(b) The place of departure and of destination;

---

[4] For U.S. reservation, see footnote 1, p. 983.

(*c*) The name and address of the carrier or carriers;

(*d*) The number of the passenger ticket;

(*e*) A statement that delivery of the baggage will be made to the bearer of the baggage check;

(*f*) The number and weight of the packages;

(*g*) The amount of the value declared in accordance with article 22 (2);

(*h*) A statement that the transportation is subject to the rules relating to liability established by this convention.

(4) The absence, irregularity, or loss of the baggage check shall not affect the existence or the validity of the contract of transportation which shall none the less be subject to the rules of this convention. Nevertheless, if the carrier accepts baggage without a baggage check having been delivered, or if the baggage check does not contain the particulars set out at (*d*), (*f*), and (*h*) above, the carrier shall not be entitled to avail himself of those provisions of the convention which exclude or limit his liability.

SECTION III. AIR WAYBILL

Article 5

(1) Every carrier of goods has the right to require the consignor to make out and hand over to him a document called an "air waybill"; every consignor has the right to require the carrier to accept this document.

(2) The absence, irregularity, or loss of this document shall not affect the existence or the validity of the contract of transportation which shall, subject to the provisions of article 9, be none the less governed by the rules of this convention.

Article 6

(1) The air waybill shall be made out by the consignor in three original parts and be handed over with the goods.

(2) The first part shall be marked "for the carrier", and shall be signed by the consignor. The second part shall be marked "for the consignee"; it shall be signed by the consignor and by the carrier and shall accompany the goods. The third part shall be signed by the carrier and handed by him to the consignor after the goods have been accepted.

(3) The carrier shall sign on acceptance of the goods.

(4) The signature of the carrier may be stamped; that of the consignor may be printed or stamped.

(5) If, at the request of the consignor, the carrier makes out the air waybill, he shall be deemed, subject to proof to the contrary, to have done so on behalf of the consignor.

Article 7

The carrier of goods has the right to require the consignor to make out separate waybills when there is more than one package.

Article 8

The air waybill shall contain the following particulars:

(a) The place and date of its execution;

(b) The place of departure and of destination;

(c) The agreed stopping places, provided that the carrier may reserve the right to alter the stopping places in case of necessity, and that if he exercises that right the alteration shall not have the effect of depriving the transportation of its international character;

(d) The name and address of the consignor;

(e) The name and address of the first carrier;

(f) The name and address of the consignee, if the case so requires;

(g) The nature of the goods;

(h) The number of packages, the method of packing, and the particular marks or numbers upon them;

(i) The weight, the quantity, the volume, or dimensions of the goods;

(j) The apparent condition of the goods and of the packing;

(k) The freight, if it has been agreed upon, the date and place of payment, and the person who is to pay it;

(l) If the goods are sent for payment on delivery, the price of the goods, and, if the case so requires, the amount of the expenses incurred;

(m) The amount of the value declared in accordance with article 22 (2);

(n) The number of parts of the air waybill;

(o) The documents handed to the carrier to accompany the air waybill;

(p) The time fixed for the completion of the transportation and a brief note of the route to be followed, if these matters have been agreed upon;

(q) A statement that the transportation is subject to the rules relating to liability established by this convention.

Article 9

If the carrier accepts goods without an air waybill having been made out, or if the air waybill does not contain all the particulars set out in article 8 (a) to (i), inclusive, and (q), the carrier shall not be entitled to avail himself of the provisions of this convention which exclude or limit his liability.

Article 10

(1) The consignor shall be responsible for the correctness of the particulars and statements relating to the goods which he inserts in the air waybill.

(2) The consignor shall be liable for all damages suffered by the carrier or any other person by reason of the irregularity, incorrectness or incompleteness of the said particulars and statements.

Article 11

(1) The air waybill shall be *prima facie* evidence of the conclusion of the contract, of the receipt of the goods and of the conditions of transportation.

(2) The statements in the air waybill relating to the weight, dimensions, and packing of the goods, as well as those relating to the number of packages, shall be *prima facie* evidence of the facts stated; those relating to the quantity, volume, and condition of the goods shall not constitute evidence against the carrier except so far as they both have been, and are stated in the air waybill to have been, checked by him in the presence of the consignor, or relate to the apparent condition of the goods.

Article 12

(1) Subject to his liability to carry out all his obligations under the contract of transportation, the consignor shall have the right to dispose of the goods by withdrawing them at the airport of departure or destination, or by stopping them in the course of the journey on any landing, or by calling for them to be delivered at the place of destination, or in the course of the journey to a person other than the consignee named in the air waybill, or by requiring them to be returned to the airport of departure. He must not exercise this right of disposition in such a way as to prejudice the carrier or other consignors, and he must repay any expenses occasioned by the exercise of this right.

(2) If it is impossible to carry out the orders of the consignor the carrier must so inform him forthwith.

(3) If the carrier obeys the orders of the consignor for the disposition of the goods without requiring the production of the part of the air waybill delivered to the latter, he will be liable, without prejudice to his right of recovery from the consignor, for any damage which may be caused thereby to any person who is lawfully in possession of that part of the air waybill.

(4) The right conferred on the consignor shall cease at the moment when that of the consignee begins in accordance with article 13, below. Nevertheless, if the consignee declines to accept the waybill or the goods, or if he cannot be communicated with, the consignor shall resume his right of disposition.

Article 13

(1) Except in the circumstances set out in the preceding article, the consignee shall be entitled, on arrival of the goods at the place of destination, to require the carrier to hand over to him the air waybill and to deliver the goods to him, on payment of the charges due and on complying with the conditions of transportation set out in the air waybill.

(2) Unless it is otherwise agreed, it shall be the duty of the carrier to give notice to the consignee as soon as the goods arrive.

(3) If the carrier admits the loss of the goods, or if the goods have not arrived at the expiration of seven days after the date on which they ought to have arrived, the consignee shall be entitled to put into force against the carrier the rights which flow from the contract of transportation.

Article 14

The consignor and the consignee can respectively enforce all the rights given them by articles 12 and 13, each in his own name, whether he is acting in his own interest or in the interest of another, provided that he carries out the obligations imposed by the contract.

Article 15

(1) Articles 12, 13, and 14 shall not affect either the relations of the consignor and the consignee with each other or the relations of third parties whose rights are derived either from the consignor or from the consignee.

(2) The provisions of articles 12, 13, and 14 can only be varied by express provision in the air waybill.

Article 16

(1) The consignor must furnish such information and attach to the air waybill such documents as are necessary to meet the formalities of customs, octroi, or police before the goods can be delivered to the consignee. The consignor shall be liable to the carrier for any damage occasioned by the absence, insufficiency, or irregularity of any such information or documents, unless the damage is due to the fault of the carrier or his agents.

(2) The carrier is under no obligation to enquire into the correctness or sufficiency of such information or documents.

CHAPTER III. LIABILITY OF THE CARRIER

Article 17

The carrier shall be liable for damage sustained in the event of the death or wounding of a passenger or any other bodily injury suffered by a passenger, if the accident which caused the damage so sustained took place on board the aircraft or in the course of any of the operations of embarking or disembarking.

Article 18

(1) The carrier shall be liable for damage sustained in the event of the destruction or loss of, or of damage to, any checked baggage or any goods, if the occurrence which caused the damage so sustained took place during the transportation by air.

(2) The transportation by air within the meaning of the preceding paragraph shall comprise the period during which the baggage or goods are in

charge of the carrier, whether in an airport or on board an aircraft, or, in the case of a landing outside an airport, in any place whatsoever.

(3) The period of the transportation by air shall not extend to any transportation by land, by sea, or by river performed outside an airport. If, however, such transportation takes place in the performance of a contract for transportation by air, for the purpose of loading, delivery or transshipment, any damage is presumed, subject to proof to the contrary, to have been the result of an event which took place during the transportation by air.

Article 19

The carrier shall be liable for damage occasioned by delay in the transportation by air of passengers, baggage, or goods.

Article 20

(1) The carrier shall not be liable if he proves that he and his agents have taken all necessary measures to avoid the damage or that it was impossible for him or them to take such measures.

(2) In the transportation of goods and baggage the carrier shall not be liable if he proves that the damage was occasioned by an error in piloting, in the handling of the aircraft, or in navigation and that, in all other respects, he and his agents have taken all necessary measures to avoid the damage.

Article 21

If the carrier proves that the damage was caused by or contributed to by the negligence of the injured person the court may, in accordance with the provisions of its own law, exonerate the carrier wholly or partly from his liability.

Article 22

(1) In the transportation of passengers the liability of the carrier for each passenger shall be limited to the sum of 125,000 francs. Where, in accordance with the law of the court to which the case is submitted, damages may be awarded in the form of periodical payments, the equivalent capital value of the said payments shall not exceed 125,000 francs. Nevertheless, by special contract, the carrier and the passenger may agree to a higher limit of liability.

(2) In the transportation of checked baggage and of goods, the liability of the carrier shall be limited to a sum of 250 francs per kilogram, unless the consignor has made, at the time when the package was handed over to the carrier, a special declaration of the value at delivery and has paid a supplementary sum if the case so requires. In that case the carrier will be liable to pay a sum not exceeding the declared sum, unless he proves that that sum is greater than the actual value to the consignor at delivery.

(3) As regards objects of which the passenger takes charge himself the liability of the carrier shall be limited to 5,000 francs per passenger.

(4) The sums mentioned above shall be deemed to refer to the French franc consisting of 65½ milligrams of gold at the standard of fineness of nine hundred thousandths. These sums may be converted into any national currency in round figures.

Article 23

Any provision tending to relieve the carrier of liability or to fix a lower limit than that which is laid down in this convention shall be null and void, but the nullity of any such provision shall not involve the nullity of the whole contract, which shall remain subject to the provisions of this convention.

Article 24

(1) In the cases covered by articles 18 and 19 any action for damages, however founded, can only be brought subject to the conditions and limits set out in this convention.

(2) In the cases covered by article 17 the provisions of the preceding paragraph shall also apply, without prejudice to the questions as to who are the persons who have the right to bring suit and what are their respective rights.

Article 25

(1) The carrier shall not be entitled to avail himself of the provisions of this convention which exclude or limit his liability, if the damage is caused by his wilful misconduct or by such default on his part as, in accordance with the law of the court to which the case is submitted, is considered to be equivalent to wilful misconduct.

(2) Similarly the carrier shall not be entitled to avail himself of the said provisions, if the damage is caused under the same circumstances by any agent of the carrier acting within the scope of his employment.

Article 26

(1) Receipt by the person entitled to the delivery of baggage or goods without complaint shall be *prima facie* evidence that the same have been delivered in good condition and in accordance with the document of transportation.

(2) In case of damage, the person entitled to delivery must complain to the carrier forthwith after the discovery of the damage, and, at the latest, within 3 days from the date of receipt in the case of baggage and 7 days from the date of receipt in the case of goods. In case of delay the complaint must be made at the latest within 14 days from the date on which the baggage or goods have been placed at his disposal.

(3) Every complaint must be made in writing upon the document of transportation or by separate notice in writing dispatched within the times aforesaid.

(4) Failing complaint within the times aforesaid, no action shall lie against the carrier, save in the case of fraud on his part.

Article 27

In the case of the death of the person liable, an action for damages lies in accordance with the terms of this convention against those legally representing his estate.

Article 28

(1) An action for damages must be brought, at the option of the plaintiff, in the territory of one of the High Contracting Parties, either before the court of the domicile of the carrier or of his principal place of business, or where he has a place of business through which the contract has been made, or before the court at the place of destination.

(2) Questions of procedure shall be governed by the law of the court to which the case is submitted.

Article 29

(1) The right to damages shall be extinguished if an action is not brought within 2 years, reckoned from the date of arrival at the destination, or from the date on which the aircraft ought to have arrived, or from the date on which the transportation stopped.

(2) The method of calculating the period of limitation shall be determined by the law of the court to which the case is submitted.

Article 30

(1) In the case of transportation to be performed by various successive carriers and falling within the definition set out in the third paragraph of article 1, each carrier who accepts passengers, baggage or goods shall be subject to the rules set out in this convention, and shall be deemed to be one of the contracting parties to the contract of transportation insofar as the contract deals with that part of the transportation which is performed under his supervision.

(2) In the case of transportation of this nature, the passenger or his representative can take action only against the carrier who performed the transportation during which the accident or the delay occurred, save in the case where, by express agreement, the first carrier has assumed liability for the whole journey.

(3) As regards baggage or goods, the passenger or consignor shall have a right of action against the first carrier, and the passenger or consignee who is entitled to delivery shall have a right of action against the last carrier,

and further, each may take action against the carrier who performed the transportation during which the destruction, loss, damage, or delay took place. These carriers shall be jointly and severally liable to the passenger or to the consignor or consignee.

CHAPTER IV. PROVISIONS RELATING TO COMBINED TRANSPORTATION

Article 31

(1) In the case of combined transportation performed partly by air and partly by any other mode of transportation, the provisions of this convention shall apply only to the transportation by air, provided that the transportation by air falls within the terms of article 1.

(2) Nothing in this convention shall prevent the parties in the case of combined transportation from inserting in the document of air transportation conditions relating to other modes of transportation, provided that the provisions of this convention are observed as regards the transportation by air.

CHAPTER V. GENERAL AND FINAL PROVISIONS

Article 32

Any clause contained in the contract and all special agreements entered into before the damage occurred by which the parties purport to infringe the rules laid down by this convention, whether by deciding the law to be applied, or by altering the rules as to jurisdiction, shall be null and void. Nevertheless for the transportation of goods arbitration clauses shall be allowed, subject to this convention, if the arbitration is to take place within one of the jurisdictions referred to in the first paragraph of article 28.

Article 33

Nothing contained in this convention shall prevent the carrier either from refusing to enter into any contract of transportation or from making regulations which do not conflict with the provisions of this convention.

Article 34

This convention shall not apply to international transportation by air performed by way of experimental trial by air navigation enterprises with the view to the establishment of regular lines of air navigation, nor shall it apply to transportation performed in extraordinary circumstances outside the normal scope of an air carrier's business.

Article 35

The expression "days" when used in this convention means current days, not working days.

Article 36

This convention is drawn up in French in a single copy which shall remain deposited in the archives of the Ministry for Foreign Affairs of Poland and of which one duly certified copy shall be sent by the Polish Government to the Government of each of the High Contracting Parties.

Article 37

(1) This convention shall be ratified. The instruments of ratification shall be deposited in the archives of the Ministry for Foreign Affairs of Poland, which shall give notice of the deposit to the Government of each of the High Contracting Parties.

(2) As soon as this convention shall have been ratified by five of the High Contracting Parties it shall come into force as between them on the ninetieth day after the deposit of the fifth ratification. Thereafter it shall come into force between the High Contracting Parties which shall have ratified and the High Contracting Party which deposits its instrument of ratification on the ninetieth day after the deposit.

(3) It shall be the duty of the Government of the Republic of Poland to notify the Government of each of the High Contracting Parties of the date on which this convention comes into force as well as the date of the deposit of each ratification.

Article 38

(1) This convention shall, after it has come into force, remain open for adherence by any state.

(2) The adherence shall be effected by a notification addressed to the Government of the Republic of Poland, which shall inform the Government of each of the High Contracting Parties thereof.

(3) The adherence shall take effect as from the ninetieth day after the notification made to the Government of the Republic of Poland.

Article 39

(1) Any one of the High Contracting Parties may denounce this convention by a notification addressed to the Government of the Republic of Poland, which shall at once inform the Government of each of the High Contracting Parties.

(2) Denunciation shall take effect six months after the notification of denunciation, and shall operate only as regards the party which shall have proceeded to denunciation.

Article 40

(1) Any High Contracting Party may, at the time of signature or of deposit of ratification or of adherence, declare that the acceptance which

it gives to this convention does not apply to all or any of its colonies, protectorates, territories under mandate, or any other territory subject to its sovereignty or its authority, or any other territory under its suzerainty.

(2) Accordingly any High Contracting Party may subsequently adhere separately in the name of all or any of its colonies, protectorates, territories under mandate, or any other territory subject to its sovereignty or to its authority or any other territory under its suzerainty which have been thus excluded by its original declaration.

(3) Any High Contracting Party may denounce this convention, in accordance with its provisions, separately or for all or any of its colonies, protectorates, territories under mandate, or any other territory subject to its sovereignty or to its authority, or any other territory under its suzerainty.

Article 41

Any High Contracting Party shall be entitled not earlier than two years after the coming into force of this convention to call for the assembling of a new international conference in order to consider any improvements which may be made in this convention. To this end it will communicate with the Government of the French Republic which will take the necessary measures to make preparations for such conference.

This convention, done at Warsaw on October 12, 1929, shall remain open for signature until January 31, 1930.

For Germany:
  R. RICHTER
  Dr. A. WEGERDT
  Dr. E. ALBRECHT
  Dr. OTTO RIESE

For Austria:
  STROBELE
  REINOEHL

For Belgium:
  BERNARD DE L'ESCAILLE

For the United States of Brazil:
  ALCIBIADES PEÇANHA

For Bulgaria:

For China:

For Denmark:
  L. INGERSLEV
  KNUD GREGERSEN

For Egypt:

For Spain:
  SILVIO FERNANDEZ-VALLIN

For Estonia:

For Finland:

For France:
  PIERRE ÉTIENNE FLANDIN
  GEORGES RIPERT

For Great Britain and Northern Ireland:
  A. H. DENNIS
  ORME CLARKE
  R. L. MEGARRY

For the Commonwealth of Australia:
  A. H. DENNIS
  ORME CLARKE
  R. L. MEGARRY

For the Union of South Africa:
  A. H. DENNIS
  ORME CLARKE
  R. L. MEGARRY

For the Hellenic Republic:
  G. C. LAGOUDAKIS

For Hungary:

For Italy:
  A. GIANNINI

For Japan:
  KAZUO NISHIKAWA

For Latvia:
  M. NUKŠA

For Luxemburg:
  E. ARENDT

For Mexico:

For Norway:
N. CHR. DITLEFF

For the Netherlands:
W. B. ENGELBRECHT

For Poland:
AUGUSTE ZALESKI
ALFONS KÜHN

For Rumania:
G. CRETZIANO

For Sweden:

For Switzerland:
EDM. PITTARD
Dr. F. HESS

For Czechoslovakia:
Dr. V. GIRSA

For the Union of Soviet Socialist Republics:
KOTZUBINSKY

For Venezuela:

For Yugoslavia:
IVO DE GIULLI

ADDITIONAL PROTOCOL WITH REFERENCE TO ARTICLE 2

The High Contracting Parties reserve to themselves the right to declare at the time of ratification or of adherence that the first paragraph of article 2 of this convention shall not apply to international transportation by air performed directly by the state, its colonies, protectorates, or mandated territories, or by any other territory under its sovereignty, suzerainty, or authority.

For Germany:
R. RICHTER
Dr. A. WEGERDT
Dr. E. ALBRECHT
Dr. OTTO RIESE

For Austria:
STROBELE
REINOEHL

For Belgium:
BERNARD DE L'ESCAILLE

For the United States of Brazil:
ALCIBIADES PEÇANHA

For Bulgaria:

For China:

For Denmark:
L. INGERSLEV
KNUD GREGERSEN

For Egypt:

For Spain:
SILVIO FERNANDEZ-VALLIN

For Estonia:

For Finland:

For France:
PIERRE ÉTIENNE FLANDIN
GEORGES RIPERT

For Great Britain and Northern Ireland:
A. H. DENNIS
ORME CLARKE
R. L. MEGARRY

For the Commonwealth of Australia:
A. H. DENNIS
ORME CLARKE
R. L. MEGARRY

For the Union of South Africa:
A. H. DENNIS
ORME CLARKE
R. L. MEGARRY

For the Hellenic Republic:
G. C. LAGOUDAKIS

For Hungary:

For Italy:
A. GIANNINI

For Japan:
KAZUO NISHIKAWA

For Latvia:
M. NUKŠA

For Luxemburg:
E. ARENDT

For Mexico:

For Norway:
N. CHR. DITLEFF

For the Netherlands:
W. B. ENGELBRECHT

For Poland:
AUGUSTE ZALESKI
ALFONS KÜHN

For Rumania:
G. CRETZIANO

For Sweden:

For Switzerland:
 EDM. PITTARD
 Dr. F. HESS

For Czechoslovakia:
 Dr. V. GIRSA

For the Union of Soviet Socialist Republics:
 KOTZUBINSKY

For Venezuela:

For Yugoslavia:
 IVO DE GIULLI

RIGHTS OF THE UNITED STATES AND OF ITS NATIONALS IN IRAQ

Convention, with schedules and protocol, signed at London January 9,
1930; exchanges of notes among Iraq, the United Kingdom, and
the United States January 9, 1930
Senate advice and consent to ratification April 22, 1930
Ratified by the President of the United States April 28, 1930
Ratifications exchanged at London February 24, 1931
Entered into force February 24, 1931
Proclaimed by the President of the United States March 11, 1931
Terminated, with exception of article 7, October 3, 1932, upon admis-
sion of Iraq to the League of Nations and termination of special
relations between the United Kingdom and Iraq; provisions of
article 7 concerning commerce and navigation terminated June 19,
1940, in accordance with terms of article VI of treaty of Decem-
ber 3, 1938, between the United States and Iraq [1]

47 Stat. 1817; Treaty Series 835

(i.) Whereas in virtue of the Treaty of Peace concluded with the Allied Powers and signed at Lausanne on the 24th day of July, 1923, and in virtue of the Treaty concluded with His Britannic Majesty and His Majesty the King of Iraq, signed at Angora on the 5th day of June, 1926, Turkey has renounced all rights and titles over the territory of Iraq; and

(ii.) Whereas by their decision of the 27th day of September, 1924, which is set forth in the first schedule hereto, the Council of the League of Nations agreed that, in so far as concerns Iraq, effect had been given to the provisions of article 22 of the Covenant of the League of Nations in the Treaty of Versailles [2] by the communication received by them from His Britannic Majesty's Government on that date; and

(iii.) Whereas the Treaty of Alliance referred to in the aforesaid decision of the Council of the League of Nations, and set forth in the second schedule hereto, entered into force on the 19th day of December, 1924; and

(iv.) Whereas, with the object of extending the duration of the aforesaid Treaty of Alliance, a new Treaty between His Britannic Majesty and His Majesty the King of Iraq was signed at Baghdad on the 13th day of Janu-

---
[1] TS 960, *post.*
[2] *Ante,* p. 55.

998

ary, 1926, as set forth in the third schedule hereto, and hereinafter referred to as the Treaty of 1926; and

(v.) Whereas on the 2nd day of March, 1926, a letter in the terms set forth in the fourth schedule hereto was addressed by His Britannic Majesty's Government to the League of Nations; and

(vi.) Whereas on the 11th day of March, 1926, the Council of the League of Nations recorded a resolution taking note of the Treaty of 1926; and

(vii.) Whereas the Treaty of 1926 entered into force on the 30th day of March, 1926; and

(viii.) Whereas the United States of America, by participating in the war against Germany, contributed to her defeat and the defeat of her Allies, and to the renunciation of the rights and titles of her Allies in the territory transferred by them, but has not ratified the Covenant of the League of Nations embodied in the Treaty of Versailles; and

(ix.) Whereas the United States of America recognises Iraq as an independent State; and

(x.) Whereas the President of the United States and His Britannic Majesty and His Majesty the King of Iraq desire to reach a definite understanding with respect to the rights of the United States and of its nationals in Iraq;

(xi.) The President of the United States of America of the one part and His Britannic Majesty and His Majesty the King of Iraq of the other part have decided to conclude a Convention to this effect, and have named as their plenipotentiaries:—

The President of the United States of America;

His Excellency General Charles G. Dawes, Ambassador Extraordinary and Plenipotentiary of the United States at London;

His Majesty the King of Great Britain, Ireland and the British Dominions beyond the Seas, Emperor of India;

for Great Britain and Northern Ireland;

The Right Honourable Arthur Henderson, M.P., His Majesty's Principal Secretary of State for Foreign Affairs;

His Majesty the King of Iraq;

Ja'far Pasha El Askeri, C.M.G., His Majesty's Envoy Extraordinary and Minister Plenipotentiary at London;

who, after having communicated to each other their respective full powers, found in good and due form, have agreed as follows:

ARTICLE 1

Subject to the provisions of the present Convention, the United States consents to the régime established in virtue of the decisions of the Council of the League of Nations of the 27th day of September, 1924, and of the 11th day of March, 1926, the Treaty of Alliance (as defined in the said decision of the 27th day of September, 1924), and the Treaty of 1926, and recognises the special relations existing between His Britannic Majesty and His Majesty the King of Iraq as defined in those instruments.

ARTICLE 2

The United States and its nationals shall have and enjoy all the rights and benefits secured under the terms of the aforesaid decisions and treaties to members of the League of Nations and their nationals, notwithstanding the fact that the United States is not a member of the League of Nations.

ARTICLE 3

Vested American property rights in Iraq shall be respected and in no way impaired.

ARTICLE 4

Subject to the provisions of any local laws for the maintenance of public order and public morals, and to any general educational requirements prescribed by law in Iraq, the nationals of the United States will be permitted freely to establish and maintain educational, philanthropic and religious institutions in Iraq, to receive voluntary applicants and to teach in the English language.

ARTICLE 5

Negotiations shall be entered into as soon as possible for the purpose of concluding an Extradition Treaty between the United States and Iraq in accordance with the usages prevailing among friendly States.[3]

ARTICLE 6

No modification of the special relations existing between His Britannic Majesty and His Majesty the King of Iraq, as defined in article 1 (other than the termination of such special relations as contemplated in article 7 of the present Convention) shall make any change in the rights of the United States as defined in this Convention, unless such change has been assented to by the Government of the United States.

ARTICLE 7

The present Convention shall be ratified in accordance with the respective constitutional methods of the High Contracting Parties. The ratifications shall be exchanged in London as soon as practicable. The present Convention shall take effect on the date of the exchange of ratifications, and shall cease to have effect on the termination of the special relations existing between His Britannic Majesty and His Majesty the King of Iraq in accordance with the Treaty of Alliance and the Treaty of 1926.

On the termination of the said special relations, negotiations shall be en-

---

[3] An extradition treaty between the United States and Iraq was signed at Baghdad June 7, 1934 (TS 907, *post*).

tered into between the United States and Iraq for the conclusion of a treaty in regard to their future relations and the rights of the nationals of each country in the territories of the other. Pending the conclusion of such an agreement, the nationals, vessels, goods and aircraft of the United States and all goods in transit across Iraq, originating in or destined for the United States, shall receive in Iraq the most-favoured-nation treatment; provided that the benefit of this provision cannot be claimed in respect of any matter in regard to which the nationals, vessels, goods and aircraft of Iraq, and all goods in transit across the United States, originating in or destined for Iraq, do not receive in the United States the most-favoured-nation treatment, it being understood that Iraq shall not be entitled to claim the treatment which is accorded by the United States to the commerce of Cuba under the provisions of the Commercial Convention concluded by the United States and Cuba on the 11th day of December, 1902,[4] or any other commercial convention which may hereafter be concluded by the United States with Cuba or to the commerce of the United States with any of its dependencies and the Panamá Canal Zone under existing or future laws, and that the United States shall not be entitled to claim any special treatment which may be accorded by Iraq to the nationals or commerce of neighbouring States exclusively.

In witness whereof, the undersigned have signed the present Convention, and have thereunto affixed their seals.

Done in triplicate in English and Arabic, of which, in case of divergence, the English text shall prevail, at London, this 9th day of January, 1930.

CHARLES G. DAWES   [SEAL]
ARTHUR HENDERSON   [SEAL]
JA'FAR EL ASKERI   [SEAL]

SCHEDULE I

DECISION OF THE COUNCIL OF THE LEAGUE OF NATIONS DATED THE 27TH DAY OF SEPTEMBER, 1924, RELATING TO THE APPLICATION TO IRAQ OF THE PRINCIPLES OF ARTICLE 22 OF THE COVENANT

The Council of the League of Nations,

Having regard to article 16 of the Treaty of Peace signed at Lausanne on the 24th July, 1923;

Having regard to article 22 of the Covenant of the League of Nations;

In view of the communication which has been made by the Government of His Britannic Majesty to the Council of the League of Nations on the 27th September, 1924, in the following terms:

"Whereas the territory of Iraq, which formerly constituted a part of the Turkish Empire passed into the occupation of the military forces of His Britannic Majesty in the course of the recent war, and

"Whereas it was intended by the Principal Allied Powers that the territory of Iraq should until such time as it might be able to stand alone be entrusted to a mandatory charged with the duty of rendering administrative advice and assistance to the population

---

[4] TS 427, *post.*

in accordance with the provisions of article 22 (paragraph 4) of the Covenant, and that this Mandate should be conferred on His Britannic Majesty; and

"Whereas His Britannic Majesty agreed to accept the Mandate for Iraq; and

"Whereas His Britannic Majesty has, in view of the rapid progress of Iraq, recognised an independent Government therein and has concluded with the King of Irak a treaty with Protocol and subsidiary agreements, as set forth in the Schedule hereto, and hereinafter referred to as the Treaty of Alliance; and

"Whereas the purpose of the said Treaty of Alliance is to ensure the complete observance and execution in Iraq of the principles which the acceptance of the Mandate was intended to secure;

"The Government of His Britannic Majesty is willing to agree as follows:

"I.

"So long as the Treaty of Alliance is in force, His Majesty's Government will assume, towards all Members of the League of Nations who accept the provisions of this arrangement and the benefits of the said Treaty, responsibility for the fulfilment by Iraq of the provisions of the said Treaty of Alliance.

"II.

"During the currency of the Treaty of Alliance, the Government of His Britannic Majesty, in consultation with His Majesty the King of Iraq, will take such steps as may be necessary for the conclusion of special extradition agreements on behalf of Iraq. Copies of all such agreements shall be communicated to the Council of the League.

"III.

"An annual report, to the satisfaction of the Council of the League, will be made to the Council as to the measures taken in Iraq during the year to carry out the provisions of the Treaty of Alliance. Copies of all laws and regulations promulgated in Iraq during the year will be attached to the said report.

"IV.

"No modifications of the terms of the Treaty of Alliance will be agreed to by His Britannic Majesty's Government without the consent of the Council of the League.

"V.

"If any dispute should arise between the Government of His Britannic Majesty and that of another Member of the League as to whether the provisions of the Treaty of Alliance or of the present decision are being fulfilled in Iraq, or as to their interpretation or application, such dispute, if it cannot be settled by negotiation, shall be submitted to the Permanent Court of International Justice provided for by Article 14 of the Covenant of the League.

"VI.

"In the event of Iraq being admitted to the League of Nations, the obligations hereby assumed by His Britannic Majesty's Government shall terminate.

"VII.

"On the conclusion of the period for which the Treaty of Alliance has been concluded, the Council of the League of Nations shall, if Iraq has not been admitted to the League, be invited to decide what further measures are required to give effect to article 22 of the Covenant."

Accepts the undertakings of the Government of His Britannic Majesty; and

Approves the terms of the above communication as giving effect to the provisions of article 22 of the Covenant; and

Decides that the privileges and immunities, including the benefis of consular jurisdiction and protection formerly enjoyed by capitulation or usage in the Ottoman Empire, will not be required for the protection of foreigners in Iraq so long as the Treaty of Alliance is in force.

The present instrument shall be deposited in original in the archives of the League of Nations, and certified copies shall be forwarded by the Secretary-General of the League of Nations to all Members of the League.

Done at Geneva, on the twenty-seventh day of September, one thousand nine hundred and twenty-four.

Schedule II

TREATY OF ALLIANCE BETWEEN GREAT BRITAIN AND IRAQ OF THE 10TH DAY OF OCTOBER, 1922; PROTOCOL OF THE 30TH DAY OF APRIL, 1923; AND SUBSIDIARY AGREEMENTS (BRITISH OFFICIALS, MILITARY, JUDICIAL AND FINANCIAL) OF THE 25TH DAY OF MARCH, 1924

No. 1

Treaty between His Britannic Majesty and His Majesty the King of Iraq

His Britannic Majesty of the one part, and His Majesty the King of Iraq of the other part;

Whereas His Britannic Majesty has recognised Feisal Ibn Hussein as constitutional King of Iraq; and

Whereas His Majesty the King of Iraq considers that it is to the interests of Iraq and will conduce to its rapid advancement that he should conclude a treaty with His Britannic Majesty on the basis of alliance; and

Whereas His Britannic Majesty is satisfied that the relations between himself and His Majesty the King of Iraq can now be better defined by such a treaty of alliance than by any other means:

For this purpose the High Contracting Parties have appointed as their plenipotentiaries:

His Majesty the King of the United Kingdom of Great Britain and Ireland and of the British Dominions beyond the Seas, Emperor of India:

Sir Percy Zachariah Cox, G.C.M.G., G.C.I.E., K.C.S.I., High Commissioner and Consul-General of His Britannic Majesty in Iraq;

His Majesty the King of Iraq:

His Highness Sir Saiyid 'Abd-ur-Rahman, G.B.E., Prime Minister and Naqib-al-Ashraf, Bagdad;

Who, having communicated their full powers, found in good and due order, have agreed as follows:

Article 1

At the request of His Majesty the King of Iraq, His Britannic Majesty undertakes, subject to the provisions of this treaty, to provide the State of

Iraq with such advice and assistance as may be required during the period of the present treaty, without prejudice to her national sovereignty. His Britannic Majesty shall be represented in Iraq by a High Commissioner and Consul-General assisted by the necessary staff.

ARTICLE 2

His Majesty the King of Iraq undertakes that for the period of the present treaty no gazetted official of other than Iraq nationality shall be appointed in Iraq without the concurrence of His Britannic Majesty. A separate agreement shall regulate the numbers and conditions of employment of British officials so appointed in the Iraq Government.

ARTICLE 3

His Majesty the King of Iraq agrees to frame an Organic Law for presentation to the Constituent Assembly of Iraq, and to give effect to the said law, which shall contain nothing contrary to the provisions of the present treaty and shall take account of the rights, wishes and interests of all populations inhabiting Iraq. This Organic Law shall ensure to all complete freedom of conscience and the free exercise of all forms of worship, subject only to the maintenance of public order and morals. It shall provide that no discrimination of any kind shall be made between the inhabitants of Iraq on the ground of race, religion or language, and shall secure that the right of each community to maintain its own schools for the education of its own members in its own language, while conforming to such educational requirements of a general nature as the Government of Iraq may impose, shall not be denied or impaired. It shall prescribe the constitutional procedure, whether legislative or executive, by which decisions will be taken on all matters of importance, including those involving questions of fiscal, financial and military policy.

ARTICLE 4

Without prejudice to the provisions of articles 17 and 18 of this treaty, His Majesty the King of Iraq agrees to be guided by the advice of His Britannic Majesty tendered through the High Commissioner on all important matters affecting the international and financial obligations and interests of His Britannic Majesty for the whole period of this treaty. His Majesty the King of Iraq will fully consult the High Commissioner on what is conducive to a sound financial and fiscal policy, and will ensure the stability and good organisation of the finances of the Iraq Government so long as that Government is under financial obligations to the Government of His Britannic Majesty.

ARTICLE 5

His Majesty the King of Iraq shall have the right of representation in London and in such other capitals and places as may be agreed upon by the High Contracting Parties. Where His Majesty the King of Iraq is not represented, he agrees to entrust the protection of Iraq nationals to His Britannic Majesty. His Majesty the King of Iraq shall himself issue exequaturs to representatives of foreign Powers in Iraq after His Britannic Majesty has agreed to their appointment.

ARTICLE 6

His Britannic Majesty undertakes to use his good offices to secure the admission of Iraq to membership of the League of Nations as soon as possible.

ARTICLE 7

His Britannic Majesty undertakes to provide such support and assistance to the armed forces of His Majesty the King of Iraq as may from time to time be agreed by the High Contracting Parties. A separate agreement regulating the extent and conditions of such support and assistance shall be concluded between the High Contracting Parties and communicated to the Council of the League of Nations.

ARTICLE 8

No territory in Iraq shall be ceded or leased or in any way placed under the control of any foreign Power; this shall not prevent His Majesty the King of Iraq from making such arrangements as may be necessary for the accommodation of foreign representatives and for the fulfilment of the provisions of the preceding article.

ARTICLE 9

His Majesty the King of Iraq undertakes that he will accept and give effect to such reasonable provisions as His Britannic Majesty may consider necessary in judicial matters to safeguard the interests of foreigners in consequence of the non-application of the immunities and privileges enjoyed by them under capitulation or usage. These provisions shall be embodied in a separate agreement, which shall be communicated to the Council of the League of Nations.

ARTICLE 10

The High Contracting Parties agree to conclude separate agreements to secure the execution of any treaties, agreements or undertakings which His Britannic Majesty is under obligation to see carried out in respect of Iraq. His Majesty the King of Iraq undertakes to bring in any legislation necessary to ensure the execution of these agreements. Such agreements shall be communicated to the Council of the League of Nations.

ARTICLE 11

There shall be no discrimination in Iraq against the nationals of any State, member of the League of Nations, or of any State to which His Britannic Majesty has agreed by treaty that the same rights should be ensured as it would enjoy if it were a member of the said League (including companies incorporated under the laws of such State), as compared with British nationals or those of any foreign State in matters concerning taxation, commerce or navigation, the exercise of industries or professions, or in the treatment of merchant vessels or civil aircraft. Nor shall there be any discrimination in Iraq against goods originating in or destined for any of the said States. There shall be freedom of transit under equitable conditions across Iraq territory.

Article 12

No measure shall be taken in Iraq to obstruct or interfere with missionary enterprise or to discriminate against any missionary on the ground of his religious belief or nationality, provided that such enterprise is not prejudicial to public order and good government.

Article 13

His Majesty the King of Iraq undertakes to co-operate, in so far as social, religious and other conditions may permit, in the execution of any common policy adopted by the League of Nations for preventing and combating disease, including diseases of plants and animals.

Article 14

His Majesty the King of Iraq undertakes to secure the enactment, within twelve months of the coming into force of this treaty, and to ensure the execution of a Law of Antiquities based on the rules annexed to article 421 of the Treaty of Peace signed at Sèvres on the 10th August, 1920. This law shall replace the former Ottoman Law of Antiquities, and shall ensure equality of treatment in the matter of archaeological research to the nationals of all States members of the League of Nations, and of any State to which His Britannic Majesty has agreed by treaty that the same rights should be ensured as it would enjoy if it were a member of the said League.

Article 15

A separate agreement shall regulate the financial relations between the High Contracting Parties. It shall provide, on the one hand, for the transfer by His Britannic Majesty's Government to the Government of Iraq of such works of public utility as may be agreed upon, and for the rendering by His Britannic Majesty's Government of such financial assistance as may from time to time be considered necessary for Iraq, and, on the other hand, for the progressive liquidation by the Government of Iraq of all liabilities thus incurred. Such agreement shall be communicated to the Council of the League of Nations.

ARTICLE 16

So far as is consistent with his international obligations, His Britannic Majesty undertakes to place no obstacle in the way of the association of the State of Iraq for customs or other purposes with such neighbouring Arab States as may desire it.

ARTICLE 17

Any difference that may arise between the High Contracting Parties as to the interpretation of the provisions of this treaty, shall be referred to the Permanent Court of International Justice provided for by article 14 of the Covenant of the League of Nations.[5] In such case, should there be any discrepancy between the English and Arabic texts of this treaty, the English shall be taken as the authoritative version.

ARTICLE 18

This treaty shall come into force as soon as it has been ratified by the High Contracting Parties after its acceptance by the Constituent Assembly, and shall remain in force for twenty years, at the end of which period the situation shall be examined, and if the High Contracting Parties are of opinion that the treaty is no longer required it shall be terminated. Termination shall be subject to confirmation by the League of Nations unless before that date article 6 of this treaty has come into effect, in which case notice of termination shall be communicated to the Council of the League of Nations. Nothing shall prevent the High Contracting Parties from reviewing from time to time the provisions of this treaty, and those of the separate agreements arising out of articles 7, 10 and 15, with a view to any revision which may seem desirable in the circumstances then existing, and any modification which may be agreed upon by the High Contracting Parties shall be communicated to the Council of the League of Nations.

The ratifications shall be exchanged at Bagdad.

The present treaty has been drawn up in English and Arabic. One copy in each language will remain deposited in the archives of the Iraq Government, and one copy in each language in those of the Government of His Britannic Majesty.

In witness of which the respective plenipotentiaries have signed the present treaty and have affixed thereto their seals. Done at Bagdad in duplicate this tenth day of October, one thousand nine hundred and twenty-two of the Christian Era, corresponding with the nineteenth day of Sa'far, one thousand three hundred and forty-one, Hijrah.

P. Z. Cox,
*His Britannic Majesty's High
Commissioner in Iraq.*

'Abd-Ur-Rahman,
*Naqib-al-Ashraf of Bagdad and Prime
Minister of the Iraq Government.*

---

[5] *Ante*, p. 52.

No. 2

Protocol to the Treaty of Alliance between Great Britain and Iraq of October 10, 1922

We, the undersigned plenipotentiaries of His Britannic Majesty and of His Majesty the King of Iraq respectively, having been duly authorised, met together this 30th day of April, 1923, corresponding to the 14th Ramazan, 1341, in order to sign the following protocol to the Treaty of Alliance concluded between their Majesties aforesaid on the 10th October, 1922, corresponding to the 19th Sa'far, 1341, Hijrah, subject to ratification.

PROTOCOL

It is understood between the High Contracting Parties that, notwithstanding the provisions of article 18, the present treaty shall terminate upon Iraq becoming a member of the League of Nations, and in any case not later than four years from the ratification of peace with Turkey. Nothing in this protocol shall prevent a fresh agreement from being concluded with a view to regulate the subsequent relations between the High Contracting Parties; and negotiations for that object shall be entered into between them before the expiration of the above period.

In witness of which the respective plenipotentiaries have affixed their signatures thereto. Done at Bagdad in duplicate this 30th day of April, 1923, of the Christian era, corresponding with the 14th day of Ramazan, 1341, Hijrah.

P. Z. COX,
His Britannic Majesty's High Commissioner in Iraq.

ABDUL MUHSIN-AL-SA'ADUN,
Prime Minister of the Iraq Government.

No. 3

British Officials Agreement made under Article 2 of the Treaty of Alliance between Great Britain and Iraq of October 10, 1922

We, the undersigned plenipotentiaries of His Britannic Majesty and of His Majesty the King of Iraq respectively, having been duly authorised, met together this 25th day of March, 1924, corresponding to the 19th day of Sha'ban, 1342, in order to sign the following agreement subsidiary to article 2 of the Treaty of Alliance concluded between their Majesties aforesaid on the 10th day of October, 1922, corresponding to the 19th day of Sa'far, 1341, Hijrah, subject to ratification.

THE AGREEMENT

Whereas a treaty of alliance between His Britannic Majesty and his Majesty the King of Iraq was signed at Bagdad on the 10th day of October, 1922, corresponding with the 19th day of Sa'far, 1341, Hijrah, and a protocol to the said treaty was signed at Bagdad on the 30th day of April, 1923, corresponding with the 14th day of Ramazan, 1341, Hijrah; and

Whereas by article 2 of the said treaty His Majesty the King of Iraq undertakes that for the period of the same treaty no gazetted official of other than Iraq nationality shall be appointed in Iraq without the concurrence of His Britannic Majesty; and

Whereas by the same article it is provided that a separate agreement regulating the numbers and conditions of employment of British officials so appointed in the Iraq Government shall be concluded between the High Contracting Parties:

Now therefore it is agreed as follows:

ARTICLE 1

The Iraq Government agrees to appoint a British official approved by the High Commissioner as and when it may be requested to do so to any of the posts enumerated in schedule 1 hereto annexed.

ARTICLE 2

The Iraq Government agrees that any British official appointed to serve the Iraq Government in any of the posts reserved under article 1 of this agreement, or in any of the posts enumerated in schedule 2, shall be given a contract on the pay and grading prescribed for it in the said schedule and embodying the terms and conditions of service set forth in schedule 3, save and except that British officers seconded or appointed to serve under the Ministry of Defence of the Iraq Government shall be given contracts on the pay and grading prescribed in schedule 4, and embodying the terms and conditions of service prescribed in schedule 4.

ARTICLE 3

Subject to the provisions of article 2 of the Treaty of Alliance, nothing in this agreement shall prevent the Iraq Government from engaging British technical or scientific experts or British clerical and subordinate staff on special contracts.

ARTICLE 4

The Iraq Government undertakes that the obligations accepted by them under any contract of employment signed and issued in accordance with this agreement prior to the termination of the Treaty of Alliance, including the payment of contributions to the provident fund as prescribed in schedule 3 of this agreement, shall continue in force during the continuance of such contract and on its termination, notwithstanding the prior termination of the said Treaty of Alliance.

ARTICLE 5

For the purpose of contracts of employment entered into before the termination of the Treaty of Alliance, but continuing in force after such termination as provided in article 4 of this agreement, a revision of such clauses in schedules 3 and 4 of this agreement as contain a reference to His Britannic Majesty's High Commissioner or to the Disciplinary Board constituted under clause 17 of schedule 3 shall be undertaken in connexion with the negotiations for the conclusion of a fresh agreement between the High Contracting Parties provided for in the protocol to the Treaty of Alliance.

ARTICLE 6

All British officials appointed to posts in the Iraq Government under the terms of this agreement, shall be in the service of the Iraq Government and responsible to that Government and not to the High Commissioner.

SCHEDULE 1

Advisers to the Ministries of Interior, Finance, Justice, Defence and Communications and Works.

Directors or Inspectors-General of Irrigation, Public Works, Agriculture, Tapu, Surveys and Veterinary Services.

Director or Assistant Director of Audit, Inspectors-General of Police, Posts and Telegraphs, Health, Education, Customs and Excise.

President of Court of Appeal.

SCHEDULE 2

GRADE I

Advisers to Ministries of Interior, Finance, and Justice.

Pay....................Rs. 2,500—100—3,500, provided that these rates may be exceeded if the Iraq Government is unable to obtain suitable officials except on a higher rate of pay.

GRADE II

(i.) Adviser to the Ministry of Communications and Works.
President of the Court of Appeal.
Inspector-General of Posts and Telegraphs.
Inspector-General of Police.
Inspector-General of Health.
Inspector-General of Education.
Inspector-General of Customs and Excise.
Director of Irrigation.
Director of Public Works.
Director of Audit.
Director of Agriculture.
Assistant Adviser to the Ministry of the Interior.
Assistant Adviser to the Ministry of Finance.
Revenue Secretary to the Ministry of Finance.

Pay....................Rs. 1,800—100—2,800.

NOTE.—(i.) This post may be on special short-term contract ex-grade, or may be combined with the post of Director of Irrigation or Public Works, whichever of the two is senior. If so combined or on ordinary contract, the starting pay will be Rs. 2,200.

GRADE III

Senior Administrative Inspectors.
Senior Finance Inspectors.
Senior Police Inspectors.
Deputy Inspector-General, C.I.D.

(i.) Judges, Court of First Instance.
Secretary to the Ministry of Communications and Works.
Director of Tapu.
Director of Veterinary Services.
Superintending Engineers.

(ii.) Health Specialists.
Directors of Hospitals and Institutes.
Chief Medical Officers in Mosul and Kirkuk.
Medical Officers of Health in Bagdad and Basrah.

Pay....................Rs. 1,500—75—1,800—100—2,300.

NOTE.—(i.) If appointed without knowledge of Arabic and local legal experience, to start at Rs. 1,350 and be on probation for two years.

(ii.) If allowed to take private practice, to start at Rs. 1,200, and, in the case of future appointments of Health Specialists, if they are allowed to take private practice, they may be placed in another Grade.

GRADE IV (a)

Collectors of Customs.
Director of Surveys.
Chief Agricultural Research Officer.
Chief Agricultural Inspector.
Executive Engineers, P.W.D.
Electrical Specialist.
Government Architect.

Executive Engineers, Irrigation.
Inspector of Posts.
Senior Executive Engineer, Telegraphs.
Inspectors of Education.
Qualified Medical Officers not in Grade III.

Pay................Rs. 1,200—75—1,800.

GRADE IV (b)

(i.) Junior Administrative Inspectors.
Junior Finance Inspectors.
Junior Police Inspectors (1st class).
Junior Executive Engineers, Telegraphs.
Agricultural Officers.

(ii.) Deputy Collectors of Customs.
Assistant Director of Public Health (Personnel and Accounts Section).

Pay..................Rs. 900—50—1,200—75—1,800.

NOTE.—(i.) Increments of Rs. 75 throughout.
(ii.) Not to rise beyond Rs. 1,500 in this grade unless they pass a departmental test qualifying them for post of Collector and no such post is vacant.

GRADE V

Assistant Collectors of Customs.
Assistant Irrigation Officers.
Assistant Engineers, P.W.D.
Junior Police Inspectors (2nd class).
Survey Officers.
Other Officials in Departments of Posts and Telegraphs.
Veterinary Officers.
Superintendent of Medical Stores.

Pay................Rs. 800—50—1,300.

General Note

(i.) An official already in the service of the Iraq Government, who is appointed to any post mentioned in this schedule and similar in grade to that in which he is serving at the time of such appointment, shall be placed in the grade prescribed for the post at such a point as will give him a total salary not less than the salary which he is drawing at the time of signing the new contract. In calculating such salary regard shall be had to the number of months which he has served towards the new increment due under his old contract.

(ii.) Junior Administrative Inspectors shall be placed at such a point in Grade IV as shall give them the salary nearest (either above or below) to their present salary plus Rs. 200, their position as regards increments being taken into account as above.

(iii.) In order to enable them to meet the extra expense which will be involved by the payment of rent, lighting and conservancy charges, married officers (other than Junior Administrative Inspectors) stationed in Bagdad, Basrah or Mosul, and drawing pay at the rate of less than Rs. 1,500 per mensem, shall be granted a p rsonal allowance, to be absorbed in future increments, of Rs. 150 or such portion of Rs. 150 as shall together with their salary amount to Rs. 1,500 per mensem in all.

SCHEDULE 3

REGULATIONS RELATING TO THE SERVICE OF BRITISH OFFICIALS IN IRAQ

Period of Service

1.—(1.) Every official whom it is desired to employ in the Iraq Government will be required to enter into an agreement to serve the Iraq Government for a definite period, to be specified in his agreement, of five, ten or fifteen years.

(2.) Such period of service will commence on the date on which he embarks to take up his appointment, or in the case of an official already serving in Iraq, on a date to be fixed in his contract, and shall not be considered to be interrupted by any local, sick or ordinary leave granted in accordance with these regulations.

(3.) Except in the case of officials who before the commencement of such period of service have served not less than one year in the Iraq Government and whose retention in the posts in which they are specialised has been asked for by the Iraq Government, the first year (or, in the case of officials referred to in Note (i) under Grade III in schedule 2, the first two years) of such period of service shall be probationary and the official's contract may be terminated at the end of the first or second year, as the case may be, by three months' notice in writing, and when such notice is given the High Commissioner shall be given an opportunity to give his opinion regarding the official concerned. On such termination of his contract, the official shall be entitled to any leave or leave gratuity which he has earned and a free passage to England for himself. He shall receive from the Provident Fund only the amount of such contributions as he had made thereto.

Salary

2.—(i.) The salary of an official, together with the increment to it, will be that provided for his office in schedule 2, provided that—

(a.) In the case of officials already serving under the Iraq Government and (b) in the case of new appointments of officials with special experience or qualifications, the initial salary of an official may be fixed by his contract at a point in the grade of his office higher than the initial salary of the grade.

Half Salary during Voyage on Appointment

(ii.) On being appointed an official will be entitled to half salary from the date of his embarkation to take up his new appointment to the date of his arrival in Iraq and to full salary from the date of his arrival in Iraq.

(iii.) For the purpose of this and the succeeding regulations the term "salary" means the salary attached to the office held by the official and does not include a personal allowance or other payment made to the official.

The term "emoluments" means and includes all payments made to an official including salary and allowances of every kind.

Currency of Payment in Iraq

3.—(1.) Subject to clause 16 of these regulations, emoluments paid in Iraq will be paid in rupees.

(2.) An official, on giving three months' notice, shall have the option of drawing one-third of his salary in London at the fixed conversion rate of Rs. 15 to £1, or in the event of the currency being altered at the par rate of exchange.

An official who shall have availed himself on this option may, by giving three months' notice, cancel the arrangement and draw his salary in rupees in Iraq.

Passages of Officials

4.—A.—(1.) An official will, on first appointment, be allowed a free first-class passage out to Iraq subject to his executing an agreement under which he will be bound to refund the cost thereof in the event of his relinquishing the appointment within three years from the date of his arrival in Iraq in order to take up other employment in Iraq, or within one year from the date of such arrival for any other reason than bodily or mental infirmity.

(2.) He will also, on the termination of his service, be allowed a free passage to England: provided that if the Government terminate his contract under clause 18 of these regulations for misconduct or insubordination, or the official himself terminates it for any reason other than bodily or mental infirmity, the allowance of this passage shall be at the discretion of the Disciplinary Board constituted under clause 17.

(3.) During the currency of his agreement an official will be further allowed a free passage from Iraq to England and back, once if his contract is for five years' service, twice if it is for ten years' service, and three times if it is for fifteen years' service.

(4.) The Government may provide the passage allowed under this regulation on any ship of a recognised line which carries first-class passengers between England and Iraq. If the official elects to proceed by a different route, he shall receive the actual cost of the passage chosen by him or the value of the passage chosen by Government, whichever is less.

Wives of British Officials

B.—(1.) The wife of an official already married at the commencement of his contract shall be allowed two free first-class single passages either way between England and Iraq when the contract of the official is for five years' service, three such passages when the contract is for ten years', and four such passages when it is for fifteen years' service.

(2.) When the official marries during the period of his contract, his wife shall be allowed two free single passages either way for the next five years remaining to be served by the official under his contract at the time of the marriage, and one free single passage either way for every subsequent five years remaining to be served. A period of less than five years shall not be taken into consideration in deciding to what free passage a wife may be entitled under these regulations.

(3.) Passages allowed to wives shall be provided under the same conditions as those allowed to officials under 4(A) of these regulations.

Quarters

5. In the case of an official occupying a house which is the property of the Government, an official who is occupying a house by himself shall pay rent at the rate of 8 per cent. of his salary, and an official who is sharing a house with another official shall pay rent at the rate of 4 per cent. of his salary provided that the payment made by the official or officials occupying the house shall in no case exceed a fair rent for the house calculated on the basis of the actual rents of privately-owned houses in the locality. Rent will be paid on the same principle by officials occupying houses which are not the property of the Government, provided that the payment made by the official or officials occupying the house shall in no case exceed the actual rent of the house. Should such payment be less than the rent of the house, then, in order to assist the official in paying the balance of the rent, the Government shall give such officials an allowance in aid as follows:

In Basrah and Bagdad:
Married officials not exceeding 12 per cent. of their salary.
Unmarried officials not exceeding 6 per cent. of their salary.

In other stations:
Married officials not exceeding 8 per cent. of their salary.
Unmarried officials not exceeding 4 per cent. of their salary.

These allowances in aid shall be subject to revision every year in accordance with the actual fluctuations of rents.

For the purposes of this clause the term "salary" shall be deemed to include personal allowance, if any.

Equipment of Quarters

6. The Government shall, if possible, equip all Government houses occupied by officials with such electric lights, fans and water as may be recommended by the Directorate of Health Services.

Local Leave

7. An official may at the discretion of the Government be allowed local leave not exceeding twenty-one days in each calendar year. Such leave shall not be cumulative, and shall not be combined with ordinary leave.

Ordinary Leave

8.—(i.) An official will earn ordinary leave at the rate of one day's leave for every five days of effective service. No leave other than local leave shall count as effective service.

(ii.) Ordinary leave shall be cumulative.

(iii.) Subject to the exigencies of the service, an official may be granted the ordinary leave due to him at any time he desires, and may claim the right to take the leave due to him if under a fifteen years' contract three times; if under a ten years' contract, twice; and if under a five years' contract, once.

(iv.) An official on the expiry of his service, or on the termination of his contract by the Government for any reason other than insubordination or misconduct, shall receive a gratuity in respect of ordinary leave which is due to him and which owing to the exigencies of the service he has been unable to take. This gratuity shall be calculated at the rate of one day's leave allowance for every day of leave due subject to maximum of nine months.

(v.) When on ordinary leave an official shall be entitled to full salary.

Sick Leave

9.— (i.) Short periods of absence from duty owing to sickness not exceeding ten consecutive days will be allowed in Iraq on full salary. Any absence extending beyond that period will be counted as sick leave.

(ii.) The aggregate amount of sick leave which an official may be allowed shall be as follows: —

If he is on a five years' contract . . . . 1 year.
If he is on a ten years' contract . . . . 2 years.
If he is on a fifteen years' contract . . . . 3 years.

(iii.) If these aggregate amounts are exceeded the Government shall have the option of terminating the contract without compensation.

(iv.) On each occasion of taking sick leave an official shall receive full salary for a period up to six months and thereafter such leave as is due to him up to a further six months. If no leave or insufficient leave is due to him to cover the second six months he may complete the period by additional sick leave on half-pay. At the end of this period of twelve months the Government shall have the right to terminate without compensation the service of an official who is on a five years' contract, and in other cases, i.e., if the official is on more than five years' contract, a medical board shall assemble, and, if it is considered that the official is unlikely to be fit to return to duty within the limits laid down in sub-clause (2) above, Government shall have the right to terminate the contract without compensation.

(v.) Nothing in this clause shall in any way modify the obligations of the Iraq Government to pay an officer of the Imperial forces or Indian army on return from his employment until he is fit for duty in the Imperial or Indian establishment as the case may be, subject to the maximum period of sick leave with full pay of his substantive rank provided in the regulations of the service concerned.

Medical Attendance

10. In Iraq an official will be entitled to free medical treatment, but this privilege does not extend to his family.

Compensation in case of Termination by Government

11. In the case of an official whose services are terminated by Government other than for reasons stated in clauses 1, sub-clause (3), 9, 14 and 18, Government shall pay into the Provident Fund on his behalf, and he shall receive from that fund, in addition to the sum already due to him therefrom, a sum equal to the combined contributions of Government and the official which would have fallen due in respect of the balance of his contract.

Special Compensation for Death, &c., due to Local Disturbances, &c.

12. Special compensation, which shall not be less favourable in the case of an officer of the Imperial forces or Indian army than that to which he would be entitled under the regulations of his parent service, under rules to be laid down hereafter, will be granted in the case of death, injury or loss of property, &c., due to war or local disturbances, or in the case of permanent disability certified by a medical board to have arisen out of the special circumstances of his employment. In the case of loss of property, no compensation will be paid unless it can be reasonably shown that it was impossible to insure such property or that insurance could only have been effected at an exorbitant premium. In any case compensation will be paid only in respect of articles considered necessary and indispensable, and the Government will take no responsibility for the loss, theft, or destruction of valuables, such as jewelery, works of art, &c.

Provident Fund

13. A Provident Fund shall be instituted to which Government and the officials shall contribute as follows:—

(i.) Every official shall contribute to the Provident Fund monthly by the deduction from his salary bill of one-twelfth of his pay.

(ii.) The Government shall contribute monthly in respect of each official a sum equal to twice the official's contribution during the preceding month.

(iii.) Sums deducted on this account from the salary bills of officials, together with the sums due from Government, shall be transmitted monthly to such person or persons as may be appointed Treasurer of the fund by His Britannic Majesty's Government, and the fund will be administered by trustees approved, and in accordance with rules laid down by His Britannic Majesty's Government.

(iv.) Every official, except officials on whose behalf the Government has paid or accepted liability for pension contribution up to the date of commencement of service under the new conditions, shall contribute to the fund in respect of service between the 11th November, 1920, and the date on which these conditions of service become applicable to him a sum equal to one-twelfth of his aggregate pay during such period.

(v.) Government shall contribute a like amount to that contributed by the official in respect of pre-contract service referred to in sub-clause (iv).

(vi.) In the case of officials who are lent or transferred to the Iraq Government by other Governments and who continue to qualify for the pension payable by their parent service on condition that their pension contributions continue to be paid, such pension contributions (except in so far as they are payable by the official himself under the rules of his parent service) shall continue to be paid by the Iraq Government.

The first five sub-clauses of this clause shall not apply in the case of such officials.

Languages

14. An official will be required to comply with the provisions of such regulations relating to language examinations as may be drawn up by a Disciplinary Board constituted under clause 17 of this schedule and approved by the High Commissioner. Such regulations may provide for the stoppage of promotion in the event of failure to pass an examination prescribed as compulsory, and may further provide for termination of the official's contract without compensation in the event of repeated failures.

Travelling Allowances: Acting Allowances

15. Traveling and transport allowances within Iraq and acting allowances shall be admissible in accordance with rules applicable to local officials.

Currency

16. In the event of the currency being altered, the rupee emoluments shall thereafter be payable in the new currency at the current rate of exchange except as provided in clause 3(2) of this schedule.

Discipline

17. Officials will, for the purposes of discipline, be under the supervision of a Board composed as follows:

PRESIDENT:

The Prime Minister.

MEMBERS:

A representative of his Excellency the High Commissioner, three Ministers and three senior British officials nominated by His Majesty the King.

The findings of the Board shall be subject to the approval of His Majesty the King. Before such approval is given, his Excellency the High Commissioner shall be given an opportunity of expressing his opinion on such findings.

Termination for Insubordination, &c

18. The Government has the right, subject to the approval of the Disciplinary Board as constituted under clause 17, to terminate without compensation the services of an official who has been guilty of misconduct and insubordination, and to receive back from the

Provident Fund the whole or part, as may be decided by the said Board, of the amount contributed by Government to his credit in the Provident Fund.

Termination of Contract by Official

19. An official will be entitled to terminate his contract during its currency by giving six months' notice in writing to the head of his Department, but should he do so it shall be put before the Disciplinary Board as constituted under clause 17 to decide in the circumstances whether he should receive his free passage home, any or all of the leave due to him, or more than half only of the amount standing to his credit in the Provident Fund at the time of his resignation.

20. In the case of any seconded officer of the Imperial forces or Indian army, if, on the termination of his contract otherwise than under clauses 18 and 19, he cannot be absorbed within the authorized establishment, the Iraq Government shall be liable for his pay and allowances at normal British rates for the period during which he is awaiting absorption.

Arbitration

21. If any question arises under the agreement entered into by an official whether as regards its interpretation or in any other respect, it shall be referred to the Disciplinary Board, whose decision, after the approval of His Majesty the King as provided in clause 17, shall be final.

SCHEDULE 4

REGULATIONS RELATING TO THE SERVICE OF BRITISH OFFICERS EMPLOYED UNDER THE MINISTRY OF DEFENCE OF THE IRAQ GOVERNMENT

Period of Service

1.—(1.) An officer will be required on appointment to enter into an agreement to serve the Iraq Government for a period of three years, extendable, if both parties agree and, in the case of an officer of the Imperial forces or Indian army, subject to the approval of His Britannic Majesty's Government or the Government of India, as the case may be, to five, seven and ten years by successive renewals.

(2.) Such period of service will commence on the date on which he embarks to take up his appointment, or in the case of an officer already serving in Iraq on a date to be fixed in his contract, and shall not be considered to be interrupted by any local, sick, or ordinary leave granted in accordance with these regulations.

Salary

2.—(1.) The salary of an officer together with the increment attached to it will be that provided for his office in the table of grades annexed to this schedule.

Half Salary during Voyage on Appointment

(2.) An officer proceeding to Iraq to take up an appointment under the Government of Iraq will be entitled to the full pay of his Iraq appointment from the date of arrival in Iraq and for the period from the date of embarkation to the date of his arrival in Iraq, (a) if an officer of the Imperial forces, to half-pay of his Iraq appointment or to his British regimental pay (without allowances) of his substantive rank, whichever is the greater; (b) if an officer of the Indian army, to half the pay of his Iraq appointment or to the pay of his substantive rank without staff pay if proceeding from India to Iraq, or if not so proceeding the British regimental pay of his substantive rank, whichever is the greater; (c) in all other cases to half the pay of his Iraq appointment.

Currency of Payment in Iraq

3.—(1.) Subject to clause 16 of these regulations, emoluments paid in Iraq will be paid in rupees.

(2.) An officer, on giving three months' notice, shall have the option of drawing one-third of his salary in London at the fixed conversion rate of Rs. 15 to £1, or, in the event of the currency being altered, at the par rate of exchange.

An officer who shall have availed himself of this option may, by giving three months' notice, cancel the arrangement and draw his salary in rupees in Iraq.

Passages of Officers

4.—A (1.) An officer will, on first appointment, be allowed a free first-class passage out to Iraq subject to his executing an agreement under which he will be bound to refund the cost thereof in the event of his relinquishing the appointment within three years from the date of his arrival in Iraq in order to take up other employment in Iraq, or within one year from date of such arrival for any other reason except bodily or mental infirmity.

(2.) He will also on the termination of his service be allowed a free first-class passage to England; provided that, if the Government terminates his service under clause 18 of these regulations for misconduct or insubordination, or if the officer terminates it for any other reason than bodily or mental infirmity, the allowance of this passage shall be at the discretion of the Government.

(3.) During the currency of his agreement an officer will be further allowed a free return first-class passage from Iraq to England and back, once on a three or five years' contract and once again if the contract is extended beyond five years.

If an officer who has already taken the free return passage or passages to England granted under this sub-clause or who is not entitled to any such free return passage, is sent to England on the ground of ill-health, a similar free return passage to England and back shall be granted to him.

(4.) The Government may provide the passage allowed under this regulation on any ship of a recognised line which carries first-class passengers between England and Iraq or on a British Government transport.

If the officer elects to proceed by a different route, line or class, or to a destination other than the United Kingdom, he shall receive the actual cost of the passage he takes or the value of the passage allowed under this regulation, whichever is the less.

Wives of Officers

B (1.) The wife of an officer already married at the commencement of his contract shall be allowed two free first-class single passages either way between England and Iraq if the officer's contract is for three or five years' service and one further single passage if the officer's contract is extended beyond five years.

(2.) When the officer marries during the period of his contract, the wife shall be allowed two free first-class single passages either way if and when the officer's contract is extended.

(3.) Passages allowed to wives shall be provided under the same conditions as those allowed to officers under 4A of these regulations.

Quarters

5. In the case of an officer occupying a house which is the property of the Government, rent will be charged on the following principle:

An officer who is occupying a house by himself shall pay rent at the rate of 8 per cent. of his salary and an officer who is sharing a house with another officer shall pay rent at the rate of 4 per cent. of his salary, provided that the payment made by the officer or officers occupying the house shall in no case exceed a fair rent for the house calculated on the basis of the actual rents of privately-owned houses in the locality. Rent will be paid on the same principle by officers occupying houses which are not the property of the Government, provided that the payment made by the officer or officers occupying the house shall in no case exceed the actual rent of the house. Should such payment be less than the rent of the house, then, in order to assist the officer in paying the balance of the rent, the Government shall give such officers an allowance in aid as follows:

In Basrah and Bagdad—
Married officers, not exceeding 12 per cent. of their salary.
Unmarried officers, not exceeding 6 per cent. of their salary.
In other stations—
Married officers, not exceeding 8 per cent. of their salary.
Unmarried officers, not exceeding 4 per cent. of their salary.

These allowances in aid shall be subject to revision every year in accordance with the actual fluctuations of rents.

Equipment of Quarters

6. The Government shall, if possible, equip all Government houses occupied by officers with such electric light, fans and water as may be recommended by the Directorate of Health Services.

Local Leave

7. An officer may, at the discretion of the Government, be allowed local leave not exceeding twenty-one days in each calendar year. Such leave shall not be cumulative and shall not be combined with ordinary leave. When on local leave an officer shall be entitled to full salary.

Ordinary Leave

8.—(1.) An officer shall earn one day's ordinary leave for each five days of effective service. No leave other than local leave shall count as effective service. The period spent on voyages other than on first appointment shall be reckoned as ordinary leave.

(2.) Ordinary leave shall be cumulative.

(3.) Subject to the exigencies of the service, an officer may be granted ordinary leave at any time and may claim the right to take such leave as may be due to him—

In a three years' contract—Once.
In a five years' contract—Once.
In a seven years' contract—Twice.
In a ten years' contract—Twice.

(4.) When on ordinary leave an officer shall be entitled to full salary.

(5.) An officer on the expiry of his period of service, or on the termination of his contract by the Government for any reason other than insubordination or misconduct, shall receive pay in lieu of any ordinary leave which is due to him and which owing to the exigencies of the service he has been unable to take. The amount so issued shall not in any case exceed nine months' salary.

9.—(1.) Short periods of absence from duty owing to sickness, not exceeding ten consecutive days, will be allowed in Iraq on full salary. Any such absence extending beyond that period will be counted as sick leave.

(2.) The aggregate amount of sick leave which an officer may be allowed on a three years' contract shall be eight months.

(3.) If this aggregate amount is exceeded the Government shall have the right of terminating the contract without further notice.

(4.) On each occasion of taking sick leave an officer shall receive full salary for a period up to four months and, thereafter, such leave as is due to him up to a further four months. If no leave or insufficient leave is due to him to cover the second four months he may complete the period by additional sick leave on half-pay.

At the end of this period of eight months the Government shall have the right to terminate his contract without further notice or compensation.

(5.) If his original contract or his contract as extended under clause 1 hereof exceeds three years, he shall come under the regulations as to sick leave laid down for civilian officials under clause 9 of schedule 3.

(6.) Nothing in this clause shall in any way modify the obligations of the Iraq Government to pay an officer of the Imperial forces or Indian army on return from his employment until he is fit for duty in the Imperial or Indian establishment, as the case may be, subject to the maximum period of sick leave with full pay of his substantive rank and allowances as ordinarily issuable as provided in the regulations of the service concerned.

Medical Attendance

10. In Iraq an officer will be entitled to free medical treatment, but this privilege shall not extend to his family.

Termination of Contract by Government

11. In cases other than those provided for in clauses 9, 14 and 18, the Government shall have the right to terminate an officer's contract on giving him three months' notice in writing. Such notice shall only be given with the consent of the senior British officer attached to the Ministry of Defence.

11A. Where an officer of the Imperial forces or Indian army cannot be absorbed within the authorised establishment on termination of his service under the Iraq Government, that Government shall be liable for his pay and allowances under the regulations of the service concerned for the period during which he is awaiting absorption.

Special Compensation for Death, &c., due to Local Disturbances, &c.

12. Special compensation, which shall not be less favourable in the case of an officer of the Imperial forces or Indian army than that to which he would be entitled under the regulations of his parent service, will be granted under rules to be laid down hereafter by agreement between the High Contracting Parties in the case of death, injury and loss of property, &c., due to war or local disturbances, or in the case of permanent disability certified by a medical board to have arisen out of the circumstances of his employment. In the case of loss of property, no compensation will be paid unless it can be reasonably shown that it was impossible to insure such property, or that insurance could only have been effected at an exorbitant premium. In any case compensation will be paid only in respect of articles considered necessary and indispensable and the Government will take no responsibility for the loss, theft or destruction of valuables, such as jewellery, works of art, &c.

Gratuity

13. On the expiry or termination of his contract, except under clauses 14 and 18, an officer shall be entitled in addition to any sums payable under clause 8(5) to a gratuity of one month's pay at the rate he is then drawing for every completed year of service, fractions of a year to be reckoned at the rate of one day's pay for twelve days' service.

In the case of officers who are lent or transferred to the Iraq Government by other Governments and who would continue to qualify for the pension payable by their parent service on condition that their pension contributions continue to be paid, such pension contributions (except in so far as they are payable by the officer himself under the rules of his parent service) shall continue to be paid by the Iraq Government.

Such officers will not be eligible for payment of a gratuity under this clause.

Languages

14. An officer will be required to comply with the provisions of such regulations relating to language examinations as may be drawn up by the Ministry of Defence and approved by the High Commissioner.

Such regulations may provide for the stoppage of promotion in the Iraq service in the event of failure to pass any examination prescribed as compulsory and may further provide for the termination of the officer's contract without compensation in the event of repeated failures.

Travelling Allowances.   Acting Allowances

15. Travelling and transport allowances within Iraq and acting allowances shall be admissible in accordance with rules applicable to local officers.

Currency

16. In the event of the currency being altered the rupee emoluments shall thereafter be payable in the new currency at the current rate of exchange, except as provided in clause 3(2) of this schedule.

Discipline

17. Officers will for the purpose of discipline be under the senior British officer employed under the Ministry of Defence, who will himself for disciplinary purposes be under the High Commissioner.

Termination for Insubordination, &c.

18. The Government has the right, subject to the concurrence of the High Commissioner, to terminate without compensation the services of an officer who has been guilty of insubordination or misconduct.

Termination of Contract by Officer

19. An officer will be entitled to terminate his contract on giving three months' notice in writing to the Minister of Defence, but in that case he will not be entitled to a free passage

home unless he has completed at least eighteen months' service in the country since joining or since his last return from leave. He will be entitled to receive the gratuity due to him under clause 13, but not to any leave or gratuity in lieu of leave.

Arbitration

20. If any question arises under the agreement entered into by an officer, whether as regards its meaning or in any other respect, it shall be referred to the High Commissioner, whose decision shall be final.

GRADES

GRADE I

Adviser or Under-Secretary of State to the Ministry of Defence:—

Rs.

Pay.. 2,500—100—3,500

GRADE II

Senior officers, whether in headquarters or liaison officers, with a rank not lower than that of Major, except in the case of officers already employed in such senior posts:—

Rs.

Pay.. 1,500—75—1,800
1,800—100—2,300

GRADE III

Junior (A'wan) officers:—

Rs.

Pay.. 900—50—1,200
1,200—75—1,800

REMARKS

If the officer under grade III holds the rank of Captain, his salary shall commence at Rs. 1,200, and if he holds the rank of full Lieutenant or has more than seven years' service to his credit, his salary shall commence at Rs. 1,000.

General Note

(i.) An officer already in the service of the Iraq Government who is appointed to any post mentioned in this schedule and similar in grade to that in which he is serving at the time of such appointment shall be placed in the grade prescribed for the post at such a point as will give him a total salary not less than the salary which he is drawing at the time of signing the new contract. In calculating such salary regard shall be had to the number of months which he has served towards the new increment due under his old contract.

(ii.) In order to enable them to meet the extra expense which will be involved by payment of rent, lighting and conservancy charges, married officers stationed in Bagdad, Basrah or Mosul, and drawing pay at the rate of less than Rs. 1,500 per mensem shall be granted a personal allowance, to be absorbed in future increments, of Rs. 150, or such portion of Rs. 150 as shall bring their salary up to Rs. 1,500 per mensem.

In witness of which the respective plenipotentiaries have affixed their signatures thereto. Done at Bagdad in duplicate this 25th day of March, 1924, of the Christian era, corresponding with the 19th day of Sha'ban, 1342, Hijrah.

H. DOBBS,
*His Britannic Majesty's High
Commissioner for Iraq.*

JA'FAR AL 'ASKARI,
*Prime Minister of the Iraq
Government.*

No. 4

Military Agreement made under Article 7 of the Treaty of Alliance between Great Britain and Iraq of October 10, 1922

We, the undersigned plenipotentiaries of His Britannic Majesty and of His Majesty the King of Iraq respectively, having been duly authorised, met together this 25th day of March, 1924, corresponding to the 19th day of Sha'ban, 1342, in order to sign the following agreement subsidiary to article 7 of the treaty of alliance concluded between Their Majesties aforesaid on the 10th day of October, 1922, corresponding to the 19th day of Sa'far, 1341, Hijrah, subject to ratification.

THE AGREEMENT

Whereas a treaty of alliance between His Britannic Majesty and His Majesty the King of Iraq was signed at Bagdad on the 10th day of October, 1922, corresponding with the 19th day of Sa'far, 1341, Hijrah, and a protocol to the same treaty was signed at Bagdad on the 30th day of April, 1923, corresponding with the 14th day of Ramazan, 1341, Hijrah; and

Whereas by article 7 of the said treaty His Britannic Majesty undertakes to provide such support and assistance to the armed forces of His Majesty the King of Iraq as may from time to time be agreed by the High Contracting Parties; and

Whereas by the same article it is provided that a separate agreement regulating the extent and conditions of such support and assistance shall be concluded between the High Contracting Parties and communicated to the Council of the League of Nations; and

Whereas by article 18 of the same treaty it is provided that nothing shall prevent the High Contracting Parties from reviewing from time to time the provisions of the separate agreement referred to above with a view to any revision which may seem desirable in the circumstances then existing, any modifications which may be agreed upon by the High Contracting Parties being communicated to the Council of the League of Nations:

Now therefore it is agreed as follows:

ARTICLE 1

The two Governments hereby recognize the principle that the Government of Iraq shall at the earliest possible date, provided it shall not be later than four years from the date of the conclusion of this agreement, accept full responsibility both for the maintenance of internal order and for the defence of Iraq from external aggression. With this end in view, it is agreed that the material support and assistance now being rendered by His Britannic Majesty's Government to the Government of Iraq shall be progressively reduced with all possible expedition.

ARTICLE 2

Such support and assistance as may for a time be provided by the Government of His Britannic Majesty shall take the form of the presence in Iraq either of an Imperial garrison or of local forces maintained by His Britannic Majesty's Government and of the granting of facilities in the following matters, the cost of which will be met by the Iraq Government:

1. Military and aeronautical instruction of Iraq officers in the United Kingdom so far as this may be possible.

2. The provision in sufficient quantities of arms, ammunition, equipment and aeroplanes of the latest available pattern for the Iraq army.

3. The provision of British officials whenever they may be required by the Iraq Government within the period of the Treaty.

Such support and assistance shall in no case take the form of a contribution by His Britannic Majesty's Government to the cost of the Iraq army or other local forces maintained and controlled by the Government of Iraq, and similarly the Government of Iraq shall not contribute to the cost of the Imperial garrison or forces maintained and controlled by His Britannic Majesty's Government.

ARTICLE 3

So long as the presence of an Imperial garrison or the maintenance of local forces under the control of His Britannic Majesty's Government is necessary in order to assist the Government of Iraq in attaining the full responsibility accepted in principle under article 1 of this agreement, the following provisions shall regulate the military relations to be maintained between the two Governments in Iraq.

ARTICLE 4

The Iraq Government undertake to devote not less than 25 percent. of the annual revenue of Iraq as defined in article 4 of the separate agreement regulating the financial relations between the two Governments, to the maintenance of the regular army and other local forces controlled by them, and in so far as their financial capacity permits, progressively to increase the strength of their permanent regular army of various arms in accordance with the programme prescribed in the schedule hereto annexed and to form a reserve army. The British Government shall equip the units of these forces, as and when they are completed, in accordance with the provisions of article 2 of this agreement.

ARTICLE 5

The strength and composition of the Imperial garrison and of the local forces under the control of His Britannic Majesty's Government shall be reviewed each year with a view to the progressive reduction provided for in article 3 of the financial agreement referred to in the preceding article.

ARTICLE 6

The Iraq army shall, subject to the provisions of the Iraq Constitutional Law, be commanded by His Majesty the King of Iraq. The Officer Commanding the British Forces in Iraq shall not intervene in matters relating to the Iraq army except as provided in articles 7 and 9 of this agreement.

ARTICLE 7

The Iraq Government undertake to grant the Officer Commanding the British Forces in Iraq authority to carry out such inspections of the Iraq army and other local forces as he may consider necessary in order that he may test their efficiency and to submit to His Majesty the King of Iraq, through the High Commissioner, his recommendations as to such steps as he considers necessary for their improvement, and they agree to give full consideration to the wishes of the High Commissioner regarding the movements and disposition of the Iraq army, and to provide such protection for aerodromes and landing grounds as the High Commissioner, at the instance of the Air Officer Commanding, may require. The Iraq Government shall not be entitled to assistance from His Britannic Majesty's Government as contemplated in article 8 should they fail to give effect to any recommendation of the High Commissioner regarding the movements and dispositions of the Iraq army given in virtue of this article.

ARTICLE 8

The Iraq army shall only be employed in the interests of Iraq and the two Governments hereby agree that neither Government shall undertake any military operations for the maintenance of internal order or for the defence of Iraq from external aggression without previous consultation and agreement with the other Government. The Iraq Government shall not be entitled to the assistance of any forces maintained or controlled by His Britannic Majesty's Government against or for the suppression of any external aggression or any civil disturbance or armed rising, which shall, in the opinion of the High Commissioner, have been provoked or occasioned by action taken or policy pursued by the Iraq Government contrary to the advice or express wishes of His Britannic Majesty's Government.

ARTICLE 9

In the event of operations being undertaken in which forces maintained or controlled by His Britannic Majesty's Government are to take part, the command of the combined forces shall, subject to any special arrangement which may be accepted by both parties, be vested in a British military commander selected for the purpose.

ARTICLE 10

The Iraq Government undertake to recognise and, if necessary, to secure by legislation or otherwise, the following powers and immunities for any armed forces maintained or controlled by His Britannic Majesty's Government in Iraq, such armed forces to be regarded as including civilian officials and Indian public followers attached to and inhabitants of Iraq serving with the air and military forces:

(a.) The right to require from the Iraq Government such action according to law as may be necessary in the detection and arrest of persons accused of offences committed against such armed forces or any members thereof and to secure the trial of persons so accused. It is understood that the right to secure the trial of such accused persons shall include the right to secure their trial by a British Judge of the Iraq Courts or by a Special Court composed of two British Judges of the Iraq Courts and one Iraqi Judge. Appeals either from the Ordinary Courts or from the Special Court shall lie to the Iraq Court of Appeal, which shall in such cases have a majority of British Judges. Trial before the Special Court shall only take place in circumstances which are certified in writing by the High Commissioner and the Air Officer Commanding to be of such exceptional urgency or importance as to render trial by the Ordinary Courts undesirable. Such certificate may specify the date and place of assembly of the Court in which event members of the Court shall proceed if necessary by air with such despatch as is needful for the Court to assemble at such date and place.

(b.) The right to exercise over all members of the said forces the control and jurisdiction provided by the British, Indian or other military law, to which the members of such forces are subject.

(c.) The right voluntarily to enlist inhabitants of Iraq under the Army and Air Force Acts or otherwise, it being understood that the Iraq Government undertakes for its part when called upon by the Air Officer Commanding or any person authorised by him in that behalf, to give all the assistance necessary to effect such enlistment and to remove as far as possible causes tending to prevent such enlistment.

(d.) Immunity from arrest, search, imprisonment or trial by the civil power in Iraq in respect of criminal offences for all enrolled and enlisted members of the said forces: provided that inhabitants of Iraq being members of such forces shall be ordinarily subject to the jurisdiction of the Iraq Courts and shall only enjoy such immunity in respect of acts certified by the High Commissioner or the Air Officer Commanding to be done in the performance of military or other official duties. Nothing in this sub-clause shall prevent the forcible detention by the civil power of any member of the said forces who has just committed, or is in the act of committing an offence which involves danger to life. If the member so arrested is not an inhabitant of Iraq, he shall be forthwith handed over to the Air Force or Military authorities.

(e.) Immunity from civil process in respect of any act done or omission or default made in good faith by any member of such forces when acting in performance of his military or official duties; the certificate of the High Commissioner or Air Officer Commanding that an act or omission or default was done or made in good faith in performance of such duties to be conclusive. The immunity provided by this sub-clause shall not debar persons who have incurred material damage on account of the said acts or omissions or defaults from claiming compensation otherwise than by civil process.

(f.) All such immunities and privileges in respect of civil process as are granted by the Air Force Act, the Army Act and the Indian Army Act to persons subject to such Acts, and immunity from imprisonment on the order of a Civil Court in respect of any civil action tried by such court.

ARTICLE 11

The Iraq Government undertake to introduce legislation providing for the arrest and punishment of any person who is acting or conspiring in such a way as to endanger or obstruct the said armed forces or attempting or conspiring to cause mutiny or disaffection among the said forces, or to bring the said forces into hatred or contempt, and to take action according to law against any person who is certified by the High Commissioner to be to the best of his belief so acting, attempting or conspiring, and in the case of persons of other than Iraq nationality so acting, attempting or conspiring or being likely so to act, attempt or conspire, to take such preventive steps according to law as the High Commissioner may consider desirable and practicable.

ARTICLE 12

The Iraq Government agree that, in the event of the said forces undertaking military operations in Iraq for the purpose of assisting the Iraq Government to repel external aggression or to suppress civil commotion, the King of Iraq will, on the request of the High Commissioner, proclaim martial law in all such parts of Iraq as may be affected by such aggression or commotion, and entrust its administration to the Air Officer Commanding or such other officer or officers as the Air Officer Commanding may appoint, and will further secure the passing of the necessary measure of indemnification for all acts done by the armed forces under martial law upon the subsequent re-establishment of civil government.

ARTICLE 13

The Iraq Government undertake to provide every facility for the movement of His Britannic Majesty's forces (including the use of wireless telegraph and land-line telegraphic and telephonic services and the right to lay land-lines), and for the carriage and storage of fuel and supplies for such forces on the roads, railways and waterways and in the ports of Iraq.

ARTICLE 14

The Iraq Government undertake to recognise and to secure by licence or legislation the right of His Britannic Majesty's forces to establish and work at the expense of His Britannic Majesty's Government a system of wireless telegraphs for the transmission and reception of external and internal messages on British Government service.

No payment either by way of charge or compensation for loss of traffic shall be made to the Iraq Government in respect of such messages.

His Britannic Majesty's Government undertake that no messages other than on British Government service shall be transmitted by the said system except by agreement with the Iraq Government, which agreement shall provide for compensation for loss of such traffic by the Iraq Government's Department of Posts and Telegraphs unless such messages are transmitted at the request of the Iraq Government, in which case His Britannic Majesty's Government shall be entitled to payment for the transmission of such messages.

Any compensation which may be due to the Iraq Government shall be in the form of a reduction of the debt due by the Iraq Government in respect of the telegraph system transferred to it by His Britannic Majesty's Government.

ARTICLE 15

The Iraq Government undertake at all times on the request of the High Commissioner so to restrict the working and method of transmission of the wireless telegraph station at Basrah and so to define its wave-length as to obviate interference with British Government stations, and further undertake, in the event of an emergency arising, to hand over the said station on the request of the High Commissioner to His Britannic Majesty's forces for the transmission of messages on the service of His Britannic Majesty's Government, subject to the payment of compensation for the loss of other traffic.

Furthermore, the Iraq Government agree that the above undertakings shall hold good notwithstanding the disposal of the wireless telegraph station at Basrah by sale or otherwise and that, in the event of their deciding to discontinue the use of the station, three months' notice of such intention shall be given to His Britannic Majesty's Government, who shall be given an opportunity of taking over the station before dismantlement, and of operating it for the remainder of the period of the treaty.

The terms of this article shall apply equally to any other permanent wireless telegraph installation which may be established by the Iraq Government during the period of this agreement.

SCHEDULE

PROGRAMME OF EXPANSION

1924–25.   1 Pack Battery.
           2 Battalions Infantry.
           1 Company Engineers.
           First Line Transport for all existing units.
           Expansion of Bagdad Training Centre, including initiation of a Cadets'
               College.
1925–26.   Air Unit to be initiated as recommended by Air Headquarters, subject to
               satisfactory progress being made in the strength and efficiency of the local
               ground forces in Iraq.
           2 Pack Batteries.
           1 Cavalry Regiment.
           3 Infantry Battalions.
           2 Transport Companies.
           1 Field Ambulance.
           Ammunition Column.
           Formation of Infantry Training Depots.
           Formation of Artillery and Cavalry Depots.
1926–27.   2 Field Batteries.
           3 Infantry Battalions.
           1 Company Engineers.
           1 Skeleton Company Engineers.
           1 Signal Company.
           1 Field Ambulance.
1927–28.   1 Field Battery.
           1 Pack Battery.
           3 Infantry Battalions.
           2 Transport Companies.
           1 Field Ambulance.

In witness of which the respective plenipotentiaries have affixed their signatures thereto. Done at Bagdad in duplicate this 25th day of March, 1924, of the Christian era, corresponding with the 19th day of Sha'ban, 1342, Hijrah.

H. DOBBS,
*His Britannic Majesty's High
Commissioner for Iraq.*

JA'FAR AL 'ASKARI,
*Prime Minister of the Iraq
Government.*

No. 5

*Judicial Agreement made under Article 9 of the Treaty of Alliance between
Great Britain and Iraq of October 10, 1922*

We, the undersigned plenipotentiaries of His Britannic Majesty and of His Majesty the King of Iraq respectively, having been duly authorised, met together this 25th day of March, 1924, corresponding to the 19th day of Sha'ban, 1342, in order to sign the following agreement subsidiary to article 9 of the treaty of alliance concluded between Their Majesties aforesaid on the 10th day of October, 1922, corresponding to the 19th day of Sa'far, 1341, Hijrah, subject to ratification.

THE AGREEMENT

WHEREAS a treaty of alliance between His Britannic Majesty and His Majesty the King of Iraq was signed at Bagdad on the 10th of October, 1922, corresponding with the 19th day of Sa'far, 1341, Hijrah, and a protocol to the same treaty was signed at Bagdad on the 30th day of April, 1923, corresponding with the 14th day of Ramazan, 1341, Hijrah; and

WHEREAS by article 9 of the said treaty His Majesty the King of Iraq undertakes that he will accept and give effect to such reasonable provisions as His Britannic Majesty may consider necessary in judicial matters to safeguard the interests of foreigners in consequence of the non-application of the immunities and privileges enjoyed by them under capitulation or usage, and that such provisions shall be embodied in a separate agreement which shall be communicated to the Council of the League of Nations:

Now THEREFORE it is agreed as follows:

ARTICLE 1

The expression "foreigners" means the nationals of any European or American State which formerly benefited by capitulations in Turkey and did not renounce the same by an agreement signed before the 24th July, 1923, and of any Asiatic State which is now permanently represented on the Council of the League of Nations, and includes corporations constituted under the laws of such States, and religious or charitable bodies or institutions wholly or mainly composed of nationals of such States.

Nothing in this article shall prevent the conclusion by His Majesty the King of Iraq in agreement with His Britannic Majesty of a special convention with any State providing for the extension of the benefits of this agreement to nationals and persons enjoying the protection of that State or for the non-application of this agreement to nationals of that State.

ARTICLE 2

His Majesty the King of Iraq undertakes to employ British legal experts in the Courts and to grant them judicial powers under the laws of Iraq and that the procedure now observed in the Courts in regard to the investigation of offences and the trial of cases and other matters in which foreigners are concerned shall continue and be put into force by law, that is to say:

(a.) That foreigners accused of an offence (other than a contravention) which is within the jurisdiction of a Magistrate may claim to be tried by a British Magistrate.

(b.) That foreigners accused of an offence which is beyond the jurisdiction of a Magistrate may claim that the interrogation during the preliminary investigation shall be undertaken and that the orders as to their release on bail and as to their committal for trial shall be made by a British Magistrate.

(c.) That foreigners committed for trial may claim that their trial shall be held before a Court which includes at least one British Judge, who shall preside.

(d.) That in civil actions over 750 rupees in value, foreigners who are parties to the cause may claim that the final judgment in a Court of First Instance shall be given, and that appeals or applications for revisions shall be heard by a Court presided over by a British Judge and composed so as to include one British Judge in a Court of three or less than three, two British Judges in a Court of four or five, and three British Judges in a Court of more than five.

(e.) That in criminal cases foreigners may claim that their appeal or application for revision shall be heard by a Court presided over by a British Judge and composed as prescribed by the preceding paragraph, or if all the parties joining in such appeal or application are foreigners and agree to that course, by a British Judge sitting alone.

(f.) A foreigner who is a party to the proceedings and has not sufficient knowledge of Arabic to understand them may claim that all proceedings shall be translated in English and the Magistrate shall so order if he considers the claim to be well grounded.

(*g.*) That in the towns of Bagdad and Basrah and their environs and in all other places where a British Judge or Magistrate having jurisdiction for that purpose is available the house of a foreigner shall not be entered by any judicial or administrative authority except on a warrant issued by a British Judge or Magistrate.

Where no British Judge or Magistrate is available as above and in all cases where the police are by law allowed to enter houses without search warrant, the house of a foreigner shall not be entered without a report of such entry being immediately made to the nearest British Judge or Magistrate.

Article 3

His Majesty the King of Iraq undertakes that every law affecting the jurisdiction, constitution or procedure of Courts or the appointment and discharge of Judges shall, before being presented to the legislature, be submitted in draft to the High Commissioner for his views and advice on such of its provisions as concern the interests of foreigners.

Article 4

In matters relating to the personal status of foreigners or in other matters of a civil and commercial nature in which it is customary by international usage to apply the law of another country, such law shall be applied in manner to be prescribed by law. Without prejudice to the provisions of any law relating to the jurisdiction of religious courts, or to such powers of Consuls in regard to the administration of estates of their nationals as may be recognized under agreements concluded by the Government of Iraq, cases relating to the personal status of foreigners will be dealt with by the Civil Court, subject to the conditions of this agreement. In questions of marriage, divorce, maintenance, dowry, guardianship of infants and succession of movable property, the President of the Court hearing the case, or, in case of appeal or revision, the President of the Court of Appeal and Revision hearing the case may invite the Consul or representative of the Consulate of the foreigner concerned to sit as an expert for the purpose of advising upon the personal law concerned.

Article 5

His Majesty the King of Iraq agrees to submit beforehand to the High Commissioner for his concurrence the appointment of all British Presidents and members of Courts of Appeal and Revision as well as the termination of the appointment of any British Judge or Magistrate.

Article 6.

The provisions of this agreement shall remain in force for the period of the treaty and shall cease to have effect after the expiration of that period.

In witness of which the respective plenipotentiaries have affixed their signatures thereto. Done at Bagdad in duplicate this 25th day of March, 1924, of the Christian era, corresponding with the 19th day of Sha'ban, 1342, Hijrah.

H. Dobbs,
*His Britannic Majesty's High
Commissioner for Iraq.*

Ja'far Al 'Askari,
*Prime Minister of the Iraq
Government.*

No. 6

Financial Agreement made under Article 15 of the Treaty of Alliance between Great Britain and Iraq of October 10, 1922

We, the undersigned plenipotentiaries of His Britannic Majesty and of His Majesty the King of Iraq respectively, having been duly authorised, met together this 25th day of March, 1924, corresponding to the 19th day of

Sha'ban, 1342, in order to sign the following agreement subsidiary to article 15 of the treaty of alliance concluded between Their Majesties aforesaid on the 10th day of October, 1922, corresponding to the 19th day of Sa'far, 1341, Hijrah, subject to ratification.

THE AGREEMENT

WHEREAS a treaty of alliance between His Britannic Majesty and His Majesty the King of Iraq was signed at Bagdad on the 10th day of October, 1922, corresponding with the 19th day of Sa'far, 1341, Hijrah, and a protocol to the same treaty was signed at Bagdad on the 30th day of April, 1923, corresponding with the 14th day of Ramazan, 1341, Hijrah; and

WHEREAS by article 15 of the said treaty it is provided that a separate agreement shall regulate the financial relations between the High Contracting Parties, which shall provide, on the one hand, for the transfer by His Britannic Majesty's Government to the Government of Iraq of such works of public utility as may be agreed upon, and for the rendering by His Britannic Majesty's Government of such financial assistance as may from time to time be considered necessary for Iraq, and, on the other hand, for the progressive liquidation by the Government of Iraq of all liabilities thus incurred, and that such agreement shall be communicated to the Council of the League of Nations; and

WHEREAS by article 4 of the same treaty His Majesty the King of Iraq undertakes that he will fully consult the High Commissioner on what is conducive to a sound financial and fiscal policy, and will ensure the stability and good organisation of the finances of the Iraq Government so long as that Government is under financial obligations to the Government of His Britannic Majesty; and

WHEREAS by article 18 of the same treaty it is provided that nothing shall prevent the High Contracting Parties from reviewing from time to time the provisions of the separate agreement referred to above with a view to any revision which may seem desirable in the circumstances then existing, any modifications which may be agreed upon by the High Contracting Parties being communicated to the Council of the League of Nations:

Now THEREFORE it is agreed as follows:

ARTICLE 1

The two Governments hereby recognise the principle that the entire cost of the civil administration of Iraq shall be borne on Iraq revenues, and that the Government of Iraq shall, at the earliest possible date, accept full financial responsibility for the maintenance of internal order, and for the defence of Iraq from external aggression.

ARTICLE 2

Such financial assistance as may for a time be provided by the Government of His Britannic Majesty shall take the form of the maintenance in Iraq, at the expense of His Britannic Majesty's Government, of an Imperial garrison or of local forces controlled by His Britannic Majesty's Government, but shall in no case take the form of a contribution by His Britannic Majesty's Government to the cost of the Iraq army or local forces maintained and controlled by the Government of Iraq.

ARTICLE 3

The financial assistance to be provided for the aforesaid purposes shall be progressively reduced as His Britannic Majesty's Government may determine in each financial year, and shall in any case terminate within a period not exceeding four years from the date of the ratification of peace with Turkey.

ARTICLE 4

The Government of Iraq undertake to devote not less than 25 per cent. of the revenues of Iraq towards the cost of the defence and security of Iraq.

For the purpose of this article the revenue of Iraq shall be regarded as the gross receipts in all cases under each head of revenue service with the exception of the commercial services, other than Posts, Telegraphs and Telephones, of which the net revenues shall be included.

ARTICLE 5

His Britannic Majesty's Government agree to the transfer to the Government of Iraq, and the Government of Iraq agree to accept the transfer, of the undermentioned works of public utility at the valuation shown against each of the works specified:

	Rs.
Irrigation	62, 12, 040
Roads	3, 20, 000
Bridges	11, 17, 500
Posts, Telegraphs and Telephones	17, 60, 000
Total	94, 09, 540

ARTICLE 6

The Government of Iraq accept the liability to repay to His Britannic Majesty's Government the full value of the works specified in the preceding article, representing a total sum of Rs. 94,09,540.

ARTICLE 7

The sum of Rs. 94,09,540 shall constitute a debt to be repaid by means of a terminable annuity, calculated so as to repay the capital sum, with interest at 5 per cent. per annum, within twenty years from the conclusion of this agreement.

The Government of Iraq further agree that, if from any cause the whole or part of the annuity payable in any year shall remain unpaid at the close of that year, the amount so outstanding shall be added to the total debt and converted into an annuity terminable within twenty years from the conclusion of this agreement, with interest at 5 per cent. per annum. The annuity payments required under this article shall be a first charge on the general revenues of Iraq, and no prior charge shall be set up without the consent of His Britannic Majesty's Government.

ARTICLE 8

His Britannic Majesty's Government hereby transfer to the Government of Iraq as from the 1st day of April, 1923, and for a period not exceeding four years from the ratification of the Treaty of Alliance, the management and administration of the Iraq railway system, which shall remain the property of His Britannic Majesty's Government, and the Government of Iraq hereby accept the responsibility for administering and managing the said system. So long as the railways are administered and managed by the Iraq Government, all receipts of the Iraq railways will be kept separate from the general revenues of Iraq and will be used solely for meeting (a) current expenditures of the railway, and (b) in so far as there may be any surplus of receipts over such current expenditure, the cost of further capital works undertaken with the approval of the High Commissioner, or the payment of interest on money borrowed for the purpose of such capital works. So long as the railways are administered or managed by the Government of Iraq, His Britannic Majesty's Government will do everything in their power to obtain for that Government any advice or assistance which they may require, the cost of such advice or assistance being charged as a part of the current expenses of the railways. His Britannic Majesty's Government will not sell the railways to any private purchaser within the period of four years from the ratification of the treaty except with the concurrence of the Iraq Government, which shall not be unreasonably withheld, and the Iraq Government shall not within the same period lease the railways to any private lessee without the concurrence of His Britannic Majesty's Government. In the event of the Government of Iraq desiring within the said period to acquire the ownership of the railways, whether for the purpose of selling or leasing them to any private purchaser or lessee or otherwise, His Britannic Majesty's Government shall state the terms upon which they will be prepared to transfer such ownership, and the transfer shall be made upon terms to be mutually agreed. In default of agreement as to such terms, the matter shall be referred to three arbitrators, of whom one shall be appointed by His Britannic Majesty's Government and one by the Government of Iraq. The third arbitrator shall be chosen by the other two arbitrators by agreement, or failing such agreement, by the President of the Permanent Court of International Justice. The arbitrators shall take into consideration the expenses incurred by His Britannic Majesty's Government in the construction, equipment and maintenance of the railways, and the past, actual and prospective value of the railways to the Government and people of Iraq, and shall decide what payment ought to be made by the Government of Iraq to His Britannic Majesty's Government for the transfer of ownership, and in what manner and at what dates, having regard to the general financial resources and liabilities of Iraq, such payment ought to be made. His Britannic Majesty's Government and the Government of Iraq undertake to accept and to give effect to the decision of the arbitrators.

His Britannic Majesty's Government and the Government of Iraq agree that on the expiry of the period of four years from the ratification of the Treaty of Alliance, the ownership of the railway system shall in default of prior sale or transfer be forthwith transferred to the Iraq Government on terms to be mutually agreed, or failing such agreement, to be decided by arbitration as hereinbefore provided.

Article 9

The Government of Iraq agree not to dispose by sale or in any other manner of any of the works specified in articles 5, 6, 7 and 8 without the prior consent of His Britannic Majesty's Government, until such time as repayment of the value of all the said works has been completed. Should any of the said works be so disposed of with the concurrence of His Britannic Majesty's Government, the outstanding debt to His Britannic Majesty's Government in respect of the work or works so disposed of shall simultaneously be liquidated by the Iraq Government. The negotiations for such disposal shall be conducted by the High Commissioner, and shall be subject to the approval of His Britannic Majesty's Government.

Article 10

His Britannic Majesty's Government and the Government of Iraq agree that the Port of Basrah shall be transferred to a Port Trust, and that the conditions of this transfer shall be dealt with separately, and shall include the following:

1. Port receipts and expenditure shall be excluded from Iraq General Accounts, and a Port Trust shall be set up with the authority of the Iraq Government, and subject to the approval of His Britannic Majesty's Government, to administer the port.

2. The valuation of Rs. 72,19,000 shall be treated as a debt of the Port Trust to His Britannic Majesty's Government. The terms and conditions on which the Port Trust shall operate shall be subject to the approval of His Britannic Majesty's Government, and shall be dealt with by separate arrangement in consultation with the Government of Iraq, who hereby agree to facilitate the negotiations for the establishment of the Port Trust, and to secure the position in Iraq of the said Port Trust by such legislation as may be necessary.

Article 11

1. The Government of Iraq agree that all lands and buildings, the property of the Iraq Government now in the occupation of His Britannic Majesty's Government for military and other purposes, shall remain in the undisturbed occupation of His Britannic Majesty's Government until such time as they are no longer required: provided that after the termination of the Anglo-Iraq Treaty and subject to the provisions of any further treaty or agreement which may be concluded in pursuance of the protocol to the said treaty, His Britannic Majesty's Government shall not retain such land or buildings for a period longer than may be reasonably necessary for the sale or disposal of any buildings or works, the property of His Britannic Majesty's Government, situate thereon.

2. The Iraq Government agree to transfer to his Britannic Majesty's Government, free of charge, waste Government land required for military and other purposes by His Britannic Majesty's Government, and such land as well as the buildings thereon, or to be erected thereon, shall remain the property of His Britannic Majesty's Government for so long as such land and buildings are required by His Britannic Majesty's Government, provided that after the termination of the Anglo-Iraq Treaty, and subject to the provisions of any further treaty or agreement which may be concluded in pursuance of the protocol to the said treaty, His Britannic Majesty's Government shall not require the transfer of any

further waste Government land for military purposes, and shall not retain any such land already so transferred for military purposes for a period longer than may be reasonably necessary for the disposal of such land and the buildings thereon as provided in sub-clause 5 of this article.

3. Privately-owned land or buildings required at any time before the termination of the Anglo-Iraq Treaty by His Britannic Majesty's Government for military and other purposes shall at the request of His Britannic Majesty's Government be acquired or leased by the Iraq Government under such Expropriation Law as may from time to time be in force, and the Iraq Government shall receive the purchase price or rental from His Britannic Majesty's Government. The Iraq Government agree to promulgate such legislation as may be necessary for the compulsory acquisition or leasing of any privately-owned land or buildings required by His Britannic Majesty's Government for military and other purposes, and any such legislation shall, in the case of land compulsorily leased on behalf of His Britannic Majesty's Government, empower His Britannic Majesty's Government on or before the expiration of such lease to remove any works or buildings erected on such land by His Britannic Majesty's Government, and shall further provide that, where the land or building is to be acquired or leased on behalf of His Britannic Majesty's Government, a representative of His Britannic Majesty's Government to be selected by the High Commissioner shall serve in any Assessment Board constituted under such laws. As regards privately-owned land of which ownership is acquired under this sub-clause by His Britannic Majesty's Government for military purposes, the Iraq Government shall have the right, at the termination of the treaty, to purchase by agreement or arbitration the land and the buildings thereon. As regards privately-owned land of which the leasehold is obtained under this sub-clause by His Britannic Majesty's Government for military purposes, the period of the lease shall be for the period of the treaty, but shall be extended after the termination of the treaty at the request of His Britannic Majesty's Government for such time as may be reasonably necessary to enable His Britannic Majesty's Government to dispose of the buildings thereon.

4. The Iraq Government shall place no obstacle in the way of His Britannic Majesty's Government purchasing by agreement privately-owned land or buildings.

5. His Britannic Majesty's Government shall have full power to sell land acquired by them prior to the conclusion of this agreement, and to be acquired under paragraphs 3 and 4 of this article, together with the buildings thereon, and to appropriate for their own use the proceeds of such sale, if at any time such land is no longer required by His Britannic Majesty's Government. His Britannic Majesty's Government shall have full power to dispose of land, together with the buildings thereon, transferred to them under paragraph 2 of this article, subject to payment to the Government of Iraq of the sale or rental value of the site, such value to be determined, where possible, by reference to the market value of similar land in the neighbourhood or by agreement between the two Governments.

ARTICLE 12

The Iraq Government undertake that, notwithstanding the termination of the treaty of alliance, the financial obligations accepted by them in articles 5–11 of this agreement shall continue in force until repayment of all sums due by them to His Britannic Majesty's Government under this agreement has been completed, and shall be faithfully fulfilled. They further agree that until the completion of such repayment no prior charge on the general revenues of Iraq shall be created in order to secure a loan or for any similar purpose without the prior consent of His Britannic Majesty's Government. Such consent shall not be withheld if His Britannic Majesty's Government are satisfied that the object for which such prior charge is to be created is one which will tend to secure the sound financial development of Iraq, and will not impair the capacity of the Iraq Government to discharge their liabilities to His Britannic Majesty's Government.

ARTICLE 13

The ordinary expenses of civil government and administration and the salaries and expenses of the High Commissioner and his staff will be borne entirely by the Government of Iraq. His Britannic Majesty's Government will invite Parliament to make a contribution amounting to half of the expenditure approved by the Secretary of State upon salaries and other expenses of the High Commissioner and his staff. The Government of Iraq will provide quarters for the accommodation of members of the staff of the High Commissioner, subject to the payment of reasonable rent by the officers concerned.

ARTICLE 14

1. The Government of Iraq agree that the following articles shall be exempt from customs duties on import or export:

(*a.*) All articles for the personal use of the High Commissioner.

(*b.*) All articles for the official use of the High Commissioner and his staff and of the Imperial and other forces or services maintained in Iraq at the expense of His Britannic Majesty's Government, all articles imported by or consigned to the Navy, Army and Air Force Institute or any other official canteen for His Britannic Majesty's forces, and all personal effects introduced on arrival in Iraq by members of the High Commissioner's staff and of such forces or services: provided that if any articles imported or introduced under this exemption are disposed of to other parties than those entitled to this exemption, the customs duty then in force shall be paid by the person, service, force or institute making such disposal.

(*c.*) All imported articles addressed to individual members or recognised messes of His Britannic Majesty's forces on production of a certificate that they are for the use of the individual or mess concerned.

(*d.*) All articles exported by members of His Brittanic Majesty's forces on production of a certificate that they are not exported for sale.

2. Duty shall be paid on all articles not imported directly by the authorities, forces and services detailed above, but the Iraq Government agree to grant a rebate of the duty so paid on production of a certificate from a competent authority that the articles on which duty has been paid have been delivered to and received for the official use of the High Commissioner and his staff and of the Imperial and other forces maintained in Iraq at the expense of his Brittanic Majesty's Government.

ARTICLE 15

The Government of Iraq agree not to levy any tax on the forces or services of His Britannic Majesty's Government in respect of offices, buildings, land or premises occupied by such forces or services for official purposes.

ARTICLE 16

The Government of Iraq undertake to provide for the due payment of all sums which may be payable to officials of British nationality in the employment of the Iraq Government in accordance with the provisions of the terms of the contracts of those officials, and this undertaking shall continue in force during the continuance and on the termination of such contracts.

ARTICLE 17

The Government of Iraq recognise their liability to meet as they fall due all sums or charges in respect of the Ottoman Public Debt which may be assigned to the Government of Iraq under the Treaty of Peace with Turkey.

ARTICLE 18

The forces and services of His Britannic Majesty's Government, including the Navy, Army and Air Force Institute or any other official canteen of His Britannic Majesty's forces, shall pay at most-favoured rates for all services rendered by Departments of the Iraq Government.

ARTICLE 19

His Britannic Majesty's Government agree to contribute towards the cost of upkeep and maintenance of roads and bridges used for traffic by His Britannic Majesty's forces. The expenses incurred by His Britannic Majesty's Government on public roads and bridges shall be taken into account in assessing such contribution.

In witness of which the respective plenipotentiaries have affixed their signatures thereto. Done at Bagdad in duplicate this 25th day of March, 1924, of the Christian era, corresponding with the 19th day of Sha'ban, 1342, Hijrah.

H. DOBBS,
His Britannic Majesty's High
Commissioner for Iraq.

JA'FAR AL 'ASKARI,
Prime Minister of the Iraq
Government.

SCHEDULE III

ANGLO-IRAQ TREATY OF THE 13TH DAY OF JANUARY, 1926

His Majesty the King of the United Kingdom of Great Britain and Ireland and of the British Dominions beyond the Seas, Emperor of India, of the one part; and His Majesty the King of Iraq, of the other part:

Anxious to give full effect to the stipulations in the decision of the Council of the League of Nations dated the 16th day of December, 1925, fixing the frontier between Turkey and Iraq in pursuance of article 3 of the Peace Treaty signed at Lausanne on the 24th day of July, 1923, to the effect that the relations between the high contracting parties now defined by the Treaty of Alliance and by the undertaking of His Britannic Majesty's Government approved by the Council of the League of Nations on the 27th day of September, 1924, should be continued for a period of twenty-five years, unless Iraq is, in conformity with article 1 of the Convenant of the League of Nations, admitted as a member of the League before the expiration of that period:

Bearing in mind the intention which the high contracting parties have mutually expressed in the protocol of the 30th day of April, 1923, to conclude a fresh agreement regulating subsequent relations between them:

Have decided by means of a new treaty to ensure due fulfilment of the said stipulations and have for this purpose named as their plenipotentiaries:

His Majesty the King of the United Kingdom of Great Britain and Ireland and of the British Dominions beyond the Seas, Emperor of India, Bernard Henry Bourdillon, Esquire, C.M.G., Acting High Commissioner of His Britannic Majesty in Iraq;

His Majesty the King of Iraq, Abdul Muhsin Beg al-Sa'dun, Prime Minister of the Iraq Government and Minister for Foreign Affairs;

Who, having communicated their full powers, found in good and due form, have agreed as follows:

ARTICLE 1

The provisions contained in article 18 of the treaty between the high contracting parties signed at Bagdad on the 10th day of October, 1922, of the Christian Era, corresponding with the 19th day of Safar, 1340, Hijrah, and in the protocol signed on the 30th day of April, 1923, of the Christian Era, corresponding with the 14th day of Ramazan, 1341, Hijrah, in so far as they relate to the duration of the said treaty are hereby abrogated, and the said treaty shall remain in force for a period of twenty-five years from the 16th day of December, 1925, unless before the expiration of that period Iraq shall have become a member of the League of Nations.

The various agreements between the high contracting parties subsidiary to the said treaty of the 10th day of October, 1922, shall, in so far as their duration is made dependent on that of the said treaty, likewise remain in force for the period laid down in the present treaty, but in other respects their provisions shall not be affected.

ARTICLE 2

The high contracting parties agree, immediately after the ratification of the present treaty and its approval by the Council of the League of Nations, to continue active consideration of the questions which have already been under discussion between them in regard to the revision of the agreements arising out of articles 7 and 15 of the treaty of October 10th, 1922.

ARTICLE 3

Without prejudice to the provisions of article 6 of the treaty of October 10th, 1922, in regard to the admission of Iraq into the League of Nations or the provisions of article 18 of the said treaty which permit the revision at any time, subject to the consent of the Council of the League of Nations, of the provisions of the said treaty or of certain of the agreements subsidiary thereto, His Britannic Majesty undertakes that, at the time when the treaty of October 10th, 1922, would have expired under the protocol of April 30th, 1923, and at subsequent successive intervals of four years until the expiry of the period of twenty-five years mentioned in the present treaty or until the admission of Iraq into the League of Nations, he will take into active consideration the following two questions, namely:

(1.) The question whether it is possible for him to press for the admission of Iraq into the League of Nations.

(2.) If it is not so possible, the question of the amendment, on account of the progress made by the Kingdom of Iraq or for any other reason, of the agreements referred to in article 18 of the treaty of October 10th, 1922.

The present treaty, in English and Arabic, of which in case of divergence the English text will prevail, shall be ratified and ratifications shall be exchanged as soon as possible.

In witness whereof the above-named plenipotentiaries have signed the present treaty and have affixed thereunto their seals.

Done at Bagdad the Thirteenth day of January, one thousand nine hundred and twenty-six of the Christian Era, corresponding to the Twenty-eighth day of Jamadi-al-Ukhra, one thousand three hundred and forty-four, Hijrah, in three copies, of which one shall be deposited in the archives of the League of Nations at Geneva and one shall be retained by each of the high contracting parties.

B. H. BOURDILLON,   [SEAL]   ABDUL MUHSIN AL-SA'DUN,   [SEAL]
  His Britannic Majesty's Acting High   *Prime Minister of the Iraq Government*
    Commissioner in Iraq.   *and Minister for Foreign Affairs.*

SCHEDULE IV

LETTER FROM HIS BRITANNIC MAJESTY'S GOVERNMENT TO THE SECRETARY-GENERAL OF THE LEAGUE OF NATIONS, OF THE 2ND DAY OF MARCH, 1926

FOREIGN OFFICE, *March 2, 1926.*

SIR,

In compliance with the invitation conveyed in article 2 of the decision recorded by the Council of the League of Nations on the 16th December, 1925, I am directed by Secretary Sir Austen Chamberlain to transmit to you herewith, for submission to the Council, the text of a new treaty between Great Britain and Iraq which was signed at Bagdad on the 13th January, 1926.

2. By a decision dated the 27th September, 1924, the Council accepted the terms of the Treaty of Alliance between Great Britain and Iraq supplemented by certain undertakings given by His Majesty's Government, as giving effect, in respect of Iraq, to the provisions of article 22 of the Covenant of the League of Nations. By article 2 of their decision of December last the Council made the further condition that the régime established by the aforesaid Treaty of Alliance and undertakings should be continued for a specified period. The requisite extension of the duration of the Treaty of Alliance is provided for by article 1 of the new treaty. In submitting this treaty to the Council, His Majesty's Government declare that so long as it remains in force they will regard as binding the undertakings given by them to the Council in September 1924, and will continue to act in conformity therewith.

3. His Majesty's Government are thus in a position to inform the Council that the stipulations of article 2 of the decision of December 1925 have been fulfilled, and that the necessary steps have been taken to ensure the continuance for twenty-five years of the present régime as approved by the Council in September 1924, unless Iraq is, in conformity with article 1 of the Covenant, admitted as a Member of the League before the expiration of that period.

4. Provision for periodical review of the question of the admission of Iraq to the League of Nations is made in article 3 of the new treaty.

5. By article 4 of their undertakings, approved by the Council in September 1924, His Majesty's Government engaged that they would agree to no

modification of the Treaty of Alliance without the consent of the Council of the League. They hereby give a similar undertaking in regard to the treaty of the 13th January, 1926. This undertaking will apply to any proposals that may be made, as a result of the discussions contemplated in articles 2 and 3 of the new treaty, for the revision or amendment of the agreements subsidiary to the treaty of the 10th October, 1922.

6. In the light of these explanations, His Majesty's Government request that the Council may now be moved to take action, as contemplated in article 2 of their decision of December last, to declare that their decision in regard to the Turco-Iraq frontier has become definitive.

7. The treaty of the 13th January, 1926, has now been approved by the British House of Commons and by the Chamber of Deputies and Senate of Iraq.

8. With reference to article 3 of the Council's decision of December last, I am to enclose, for the information of the Council, a memorandum dealing with the administration of the Kurdish districts in Iraq.

I am, &c.

LANCELOT OLIPHANT

PROTOCOL

On the signature this day of the Convention between His Britannic Majesty and His Majesty the King of Iraq, respectively, of the one part, and the President of the United States of America of the other part, the undersigned Plenipotentiaries, duly authorized thereto, have agreed as follows:

(1.) It is understood by the High Contracting Parties that the term "exercise of industries" as employed in article XI of the Anglo-Iraq Treaty of Alliance signed the 10th October, 1922, covers the granting and operation of concessions.

(2.) With reference to article 4 of the Convention signed this day, it is understood by the High Contracting Parties that the Iraq Government will not interfere in matters concerning the curriculum, such as the time-table, discipline and purely internal administration in schools established or maintained by nationals of the United States of America in Iraq.[6]

(3.) It is understood that upon the entry into force of the Convention signed this day and during the period of the special relations existing between His Britannic Majesty and His Majesty the King of Iraq, defined in article I of the said Convention, there will be a suspension of the capitulatory régime in Iraq so far as the rights of the United States and its nationals are concerned, and that such rights will be exercised in conformity with the decision of the Council of the League of Nations dated the 27th September, 1924.

---

[6] For an exchange of notes between the United States and Iraq relating to art. 2, see p. 1038.

(4.) It is understood that article 3 of the Convention signed this day does not prohibit the Iraq Government from expropriating American property for public purposes under normal expropriation laws of general application, and subject to the previous provision for just and reasonable compensation.

The present Protocol shall be deemed an integral part of the Convention signed this day and shall be ratified at the same time as that Convention.

In witness whereof, the respective Plenipotentiaries have signed the present Protocol and have affixed there to their seals.

Done in triplicate in English and Arabic, of which, in case of divergence, the English text shall prevail, at London, this 9th day of January, 1930.

CHARLES G. DAWES   [SEAL]
ARTHUR HENDERSON   [SEAL]
JA'FAR EL ASKERI   [SEAL]

EXCHANGES OF NOTES

The British Secretary of State for Foreign Affairs to the American Ambassador

FOREIGN OFFICE, S.W.1.
9th January, 1930.

YOUR EXCELLENCY,

On the signature this day of the Convention between His Britannic Majesty and His Majesty the King of Iraq respectively of the one part, and the President of the United States of America of the other part, I have the honour to inform Your Excellency that His Majesty's Government in the United Kingdom of Great Britain and Northern Ireland agree to furnish to the Government of the United States a duplicate of the Annual Report to be made in accordance with the terms of the Decision of the Council of the League of Nations on the 27th day of September 1924.

I have the honour to be, with the highest consideration,

Your Excellency's obedient Servant,

ARTHUR HENDERSON

HIS EXCELLENCY
    GENERAL CHARLES G. DAWES, C.B.,
        etc., etc., etc.,

The American Ambassador to the British Secretary of State for Foreign Affairs

No. 372.   EMBASSY OF THE UNITED STATES OF AMERICA

LONDON, *January 9, 1930.*

SIR:

On the signature this day of the Convention between the President of the United States of America of the one part, and His Britannic Majesty and His Majesty the King of Iraq of the other part, I have the honor to take note of your declaration that His Majesty's Government in the United Kingdom of Great Britain and Northern Ireland agree to furnish the United States Government with a duplicate of the Annual Report to be made in accordance with the terms of the Decision of the Council of the League of Nations on the 27th day of September, 1924.

I have the honor to be,
With the highest consideration, Sir,
Your most obedient, humble servant,

CHARLES G. DAWES

THE RIGHT HON^{BLE}
ARTHUR HENDERSON, P.C.,
etc., etc., etc.,
The Foreign Office.

The Minister of Iraq at London to the American Ambassador

IRAQ LEGATION 51, QUEEN'S GATE GARDENS, S. W. 7.
January, 9th., 1930.

YOUR EXCELLENCY,

I have the honour to bring to your notice a point connected with Article 2 of the Protocol attached to the Tripartite Convention between the United States of America, The United Kingdom and Iraq. Article 2 of the Protocol provides that the Government of Iraq shall not interfere in matters concerning the curriculum, such as the time-tables, discipline and purely internal administration in schools established or maintained by nationals of the United States of America in Iraq. The Iraq Government interpret this Article as not preventing the enforcement on the said schools of Article 28 of the Public Instruction Law of 1929 the translation of which runs:

It is obligatory to teach the Arabic language and the history and geography of Iraq and the history of the Arabs in accordance with the programme of the Ministry of Education in all non-technical private schools both primary and secondary. The hours devoted to the Arabic language must not be less than five hours a week in primary classes and three hours a week in secondary classes.

I have therefore been instructed by my Government to inform Your Excellency that the Iraq Government consider that Article 2 of the said Protocol shall not override the provisions of Article 28 of the above mentioned Law.

I have the honour to be, Sir
Your obedient servant,

JA'FAR EL ASKERI
The Iraq Plenipotentiary

HIS EXCELLENCY,
THE UNITED STATES PLENIPOTENTIARY

The American Ambassador to the Minister of Iraq at London

EMBASSY OF THE UNITED STATES OF AMERICA
LONDON, *January 9, 1930.*

YOUR EXCELLENCY:

I have the honor to acknowledge the receipt of Your Excellency's note of today's date, which reads as follows:

"I have the honour to bring to your notice a point connected with Article 2 of the Protocol attached to the Tripartite Convention between the United States of America, the United Kingdom and Iraq. Article 2 of the Protocol provides that the Government of Iraq shall not interfere in matters concerning the curriculum, such as the time-tables, discipline and purely internal administration in schools established or maintained by nationals of the United States of America in Iraq. The Iraq Government interprets this Article as not preventing the enforcement on the said schools of Article 28 of the Public Instruction Law of 1929, the translation of which runs:

It is obligatory to teach the Arabic language and the history and geography of Iraq and the history of the Arabs in accordance with the programme of the Ministry of Education in all non-technical private schools, both primary and secondary. The hours devoted to the Arabic language must be not less than five hours a week in primary classes and three hours a week in secondary classes.

"I have therefore been instructed by my Government to inform Your Excellency that the Iraq Government consider that Article 2 of the said Protocol shall not override the provisions of Article 28 of the above mentioned Law."

In taking note of this communication I avail myself of this opportunity to renew to Your Excellency the assurance of my high consideration.

I have the honor to be, Excellency,
Your most obedient servant,

CHARLES G. DAWES.

HIS EXCELLENCY
JA'FAR PASHA EL-ASKERI, C.M.G.,
etc., etc., etc.,
The Legation of Iraq,
London.

CHINESE COURTS IN THE INTERNATIONAL SETTLEMENT AT SHANGHAI

Agreement, with attached notes and a unilateral declaration by non-Chinese signatories regarding guaranteed rights, signed at Nanking February 17, 1930

Entered into force April 1, 1930

Agreement extended by exchange of notes of February 8, 1933,[1] for a period of three years from April 1, 1933, and "thereafter . . . until . . . denounced;" declaration renewed by unilateral declaration of February 8, 1933[1]

Terminated May 20, 1943, as between the United States and China by treaty of January 11, 1943[2]

47 Stat. 2713; Executive Agreement Series 37

AGREEMENT RELATING TO THE CHINESE COURTS IN THE INTERNATIONAL SETTLEMENT AT SHANGHAI

ARTICLE I

From the date on which the present Agreement comes into force, all former rules, agreements, exchanges of notes *et cetera* having special reference to the establishment of a Chinese court in the International Settlement at Shanghai shall be abolished.

ARTICLE II

The Chinese Government shall, in accordance with Chinese laws and regulations relating to the judiciary and subject to the terms of the present Agreement, establish in the International Settlement at Shanghai a District Court (Ti Fang Fa Yuan) and a Branch High Court (Kao Teng Fa Yuan Fen Yuan). All Chinese laws and regulations, substantive as well as procedural, which are now in force, or which may hereafter be duly enacted and promulgated shall be applicable in the Courts, due account being taken of the Land Regulations and Bye-Laws of the International Settlement,

---

[1] EAS 45, *post,* vol. 3.
[2] TS 984, *post.*

which are applicable pending their adoption and promulgation by the Chinese Government, and of the terms of the present Agreement.

Judgments, decisions and rulings of the Branch High Court are subject to appeal, according to Chinese law, to the Supreme Court of China.

ARTICLE III

The former practice of Consular deputies or Consular officials appearing to watch proceedings or to sit jointly in the Chinese court now functioning in the International Settlement shall be discontinued in the Courts established under the present Agreement.

ARTICLE IV

When any person is arrested by the municipal or judicial police, he shall, within twenty-four hours, exclusive of holidays, be sent to the Courts established under the present Agreement to be dealt with, failing which he shall be released.

ARTICLE V

The Courts established under the present Agreement shall each have a certain number of procurators to be appointed by the Chinese Government, who shall hold inquests and autopsies (Chien Yen) within the jurisdiction of these Courts and shall otherwise perform their functions in accordance with Chinese law in all cases involving the application of Articles 103 to 186 of the Chinese Criminal Code, except where the Municipal Police of the International Settlement or the party concerned has already initiated prosecution, provided that all preliminary investigations conducted by the procurator shall be held publicly and counsel for the accused shall have the right to be present and heard.

In other cases arising within the jurisdiction of the Courts, the Municipal Police or the party concerned shall prosecute. The procurator shall have the right to express his views in court in all criminal cases in which the prosecution is initiated by the Municipal Police or the party concerned.

ARTICLE VI

All judicial processes, such as summonses, warrants, orders, *et cetera*, shall be valid only after they have been signed by a judge of the Courts established under the present Agreement, whereupon they shall be served or executed by the judicial police or, as provided below, by the process-servers thereof.

No person found in the International Settlement shall be handed over to the extra-Settlement authorities without a preliminary investigation in court at which counsel for the accused shall have the right to be present and heard, except in the case of requests emanating from other modern law courts when the accused may be handed over after his identity has been established by the Court.

All judgments, decisions and rulings of the Courts shall be executed as soon as they become final as a result of the judicial procedure in force in the said Courts. Whenever necessary, the Municipal Police shall render any assistance within their power as may be requested of them.

The process-servers of the Courts shall be appointed by the Presidents of the Courts respectively and their duties shall be to serve all summonses and deliver other documents of the Courts in connection with civil cases. For the execution of judgments in civil cases, the process-servers shall be accompanied by the judicial police. The officers and members of the judicial police of the Courts shall be appointed by the President of the Branch High Court upon the recommendation of the Municipal Council and shall be subject to dismissal by the President of that Court upon cause shown. Their services will also be terminated by the President at the request of the Municipal Council upon cause shown. They shall wear the uniform designed by the Chinese judicial authorities, and shall be subject to the orders and direction of the Courts and faithful to their duties.

Article VII

The House of Detention for civil cases and the Women's Prison attached to the Chinese court now functioning in the International Settlement at Shanghai shall be transferred from that court to the Courts established under the present Agreement and shall be supervised and administered by the Chinese authorities.

All prisoners now serving sentences in the prisons attached to the Chinese court now functioning in the International Settlement and those sentenced by the Courts established under the present Agreement shall, at the discretion of the said Courts, serve their sentences either in such prisons in the Settlement or in Chinese prisons outside the Settlement, except that offenders against the Police Offences Code and the Land Regulations and Bye-Laws and persons under arrest awaiting trial shall serve their periods of detention in the Settlement. The prisons in the Settlement shall be operated, as far as practicable, in conformity with Chinese prison regulations and shall be subject to inspection, from time to time, by officers appointed by the Chinese judicial authorities.

Persons sentenced to death by the Courts established under the present Agreement shall be sent to the Chinese authorities outside of the Settlement for execution of such sentence.

Article VIII

Foreign lawyers duly qualified will be admitted to practice in the Courts established under the present Agreement in all cases in which a foreigner is a party, provided such foreign lawyer can only represent the foreign party concerned. The Municipal Council may also be represented in the same manner by duly qualified lawyers, Chinese or foreign, in any proceedings in which the Council is complainant or plaintiff or the Municipal Police is the prosecutor.

In other cases or proceedings in which the Council considers the interests of the Settlement to be involved, it may be represented by a duly qualified lawyer, Chinese or foreign, who may submit to the Court his views in writing during the proceedings and who may, if he deems necessary, file a petition in intervention in accordance with the provisions of the Code of Civil Procedure.

Foreign lawyers who are entitled to practice under this Article in the above-mentioned Courts shall apply to the Ministry of Justice for lawyers' certificates and shall be subject to Chinese laws and regulations applicable to lawyers, including those governing their disciplinary punishment.

ARTICLE IX

Four permanent representatives shall be appointed, two by the Chinese Government and two by the Governments of the other Powers signatory to the present Agreement, who together shall seek to reconcile such differences of opinion regarding the interpretation or application of the present Agreement as may be referred to them by the President of the Branch High Court or by the authorities of the signatory foreign Powers, provided that their Report shall have no binding force upon either party except by mutual consent, it being understood that no judgments, decisions, rulings or orders of the Courts, as such, shall be referred to the aforesaid representatives for consideration.

ARTICLE X

The present Agreement and the attached Notes shall enter into effect on April 1st, 1930 and shall continue in force for a period of three years from that date, provided that they may be extended for an additional period upon mutual consent of the parties thereto.

NANKING,
   February 17, 19th Year R.C. (1930).

HSU MO
   on behalf of the Minister for Foreign Affairs

J. DE PINTO DIAZ
   on behalf of the Brazilian Chargé d'Affaires

In the name of the American Minister,
JOSEPH E. JACOBS

W. MEYRICK HEWLETT
   on behalf of His Britannic Majesty's Minister

L. GRONVOLD
   on behalf of the Norwegian Chargé d'Affaires

F. E. H. GROENMAN
   on behalf of the Netherlands chargé d'affaires

In the name of the French Minister:
E. KOECHLIN

[SEAL OF THE MINISTRY OF FOREIGN AFFAIRS]

ATTACHED NOTES

The Foreign Signatories to the Chinese Minister for Foreign Affairs

NANKING, *February 17, 1930.*

SIR,

With reference to the Agreement which we have signed to-day concerning the establishment of a District Court and a Branch High Court in the International Settlement at Shanghai, we have the honour to request your confirmation of our understanding on the following points:

1. It is understood that the Courts established under the present Agreement shall exercise jurisdiction over civil and criminal cases as well as police offences and inquests in the International Settlement at Shanghai, provided that the jurisdiction of the said courts over persons shall be the same as that of other Chinese Courts and provided that their territorial jurisdiction shall be the same as that of the Chinese court now functioning in the International Settlement at Shanghai, except (*a*) mixed criminal cases arising on private foreign property outside the limits of the Settlement and (*b*) mixed civil cases arising in areas surrounding the Settlement.

2. It is understood that the present practice regarding the respective jurisdictions of the Chinese court now functioning in the International Settlement and the Court existing in the French Concession shall be followed, pending a definite arrangement between the Chinese Government and the authorities concerned.

3. It is understood that as far as practicable Chinese shall be recommended by the Municipal Council to serve as officers and members of the judicial police of the Courts established under the present Agreement. It is further understood that among the officers of the judicial police appointed by the President of the Branch High Court under Article VI of the present Agreement, there will be one to be designated by the Municipal Council, to whom will be allotted by the President an office on the Court premises and who will make an entry of all judicial processes of the Courts, such as summonses, warrants, orders and judgments, for the purpose of service or execution in accordance with the provisions of the above-mentioned Article.

4. It is understood that the establishment of the Courts provided for in the present Agreement in no way affects the validity of judgments rendered by the Chinese court now functioning in the International Settlement and its predecessor, and that such judgments shall be considered as final and valid except where an appeal has been lawfully taken or reserved. It is further understood that the judgments of the Courts established under the present Agreement shall be on the same footing as regards validity as the judgments of all other Chinese Courts.

5. It is understood that the present Agreement does not in any way affect or prejudice any future negotiations regarding the status of extra-Settlement roads.

6. It is understood that the sum of sixty thousand dollars ($60,000) now on deposit with the Bank of China to the credit of the present Chinese court in the International Settlement shall be maintained by the Chinese Government to the credit of the new Courts established under the present Agreement.

7. It is agreed that in accordance with Chinese law, there shall be maintained by the Courts established under the present Agreement, a storage room for articles confiscated by the Courts, which remain the property of the Chinese Government, it being understood that confiscated opium and instruments for the smoking and preparation thereof shall be burned publicly in the International Settlement every three months and that the Municipal Council may present to the Presidents of the Courts for transmission to the Ministry of Justice such suggestions as it may desire to make regarding the disposal of confiscated arms.

8. It is understood that upon the coming into force of the present Agreement, all cases pending in the Chinese court now functioning in the International Settlement shall be dealt with in the Courts established under the present Agreement in accordance with the procedure in force in the latter Courts, provided that the proceedings in mixed cases shall, as far as practicable, be continued from the point where they are taken over and concluded within a period of twelve months which period may be extended at the discretion of the Courts when the circumstances in any case so warrant.

We avail ourselves of this opportunity to renew to Your Excellency the assurance of our highest consideration.

J. DE PINTO DIAZ
on behalf of the Brazilian Chargé
d'Affaires

L. GRONVOLD
on behalf of the Norwegian Chargé
d'Affaires

In the name of the American Minister,
JOSEPH E. JACOBS

F. E. H. GROENMAN
on behalf of the Netherlands Chargé
d'affaires

W. MEYRICK HEWLETT
on behalf of His Britannic Majesty's
Minister

In the name of the French Minister:
E. KOECHLIN

HIS EXCELLENCY,
    DR. CHENGTING T. WANG,
        Minister for Foreign Affairs,
        Nanking.

The Chinese Minister for Foreign Affairs to Each of the Foreign Signatories

[TRANSLATION]

NANKING, *February 17, 1930.*

SIR,

I have the honour to acknowledge the receipt of your Note referring to the Agreement which we have signed to-day concerning the establishment of a District Court and a Branch High Court in the International Settlement at Shanghai, in which you request my confirmation of the following points:

"1. It is understood that the Courts established under the present Agreement shall exercise jurisdiction over civil and criminal cases as well as police offences and inquests in the International Settlement at Shanghai, provided that the jurisdiction of the said Courts over persons shall be the same as that of other Chinese Courts and provided that their territorial jurisdiction shall be the same as that of the Chinese court now functioning in the International Settlement at Shanghai, except (*a*) mixed criminal cases arising on private foreign property outside the limits of the Settlement and (*b*) mixed civil cases arising in areas surrounding the Settlement.

"2. It is understood that the present practice regarding the respective jurisdictions of the Chinese court now functioning in the International Settlement and the Court existing in the French Concession shall be followed, pending a definite arrangement between the Chinese Government and the authorities concerned.

"3. It is understood that as far as practicable Chinese shall be recommended by the Municipal Council to serve as officers and members of the judicial police of the Courts established under the present Agreement. It is further understood that among the officers of the judicial police appointed by the President of the Branch High Court under Article VI of the present Agreement, there will be one to be designated by the Municipal Council, to whom will be allotted by the President an office on the Court premises and who will make an entry of all judicial processes of the Courts, such as summonses, warrants, orders and judgments, for the purpose of service or execution in accordance with the provisions of the above-mentioned Article.

"4. It is understood that the establishment of the Courts provided for in the present Agreement in no way affects the validity of judgments rendered by the Chinese court now functioning in the International Settlement and its predecessor, and that such judgments shall be considered as final and valid except where an appeal has been lawfully taken or reserved. It is further understood that the judgments of the Courts established under the present Agreement shall be on the same footing as regards validity as the judgments of all other Chinese Courts.

"5. It is understood that the present Agreement does not in any way affect or prejudice any future negotiations regarding the status of extra-Settlement roads.

"6. It is understood that the sum of sixty thousand dollars ($60,000) now on deposit with the Bank of China to the credit of the present Chinese court in the International Settlement shall be maintained by the Chinese Government to the credit of the new Courts established under the present Agreement.

"7. It is agreed that in accordance with Chinese law, there shall be maintained by the Courts established under the present Agreement, a storage room for articles confiscated by the Courts, which remain the property of the Chinese Government, it being understood that confiscated opium and instruments for the smoking and preparation thereof shall be burned publicly in the International Settlement every three months and that the Municipal Council may present to the Presidents of the Courts for transmission to the Ministry of Justice such suggestions as it may desire to make regarding the disposal of confiscated arms.

"8. It is understood that upon the coming into force of the present Agreement, all cases pending in the Chinese court now functioning in the International Settlement shall be dealt with in the Courts established under the present Agreement in accordance with the procedure in force in the latter Courts, provided that the proceedings in mixed cases shall, as far as practicable, be continued from the point where they are taken over and concluded within a period of twelve months which period may be extended at the discretion of the Courts when the circumstances in any case so warrant."

In reply I have the honour to confirm the understanding of the points as quoted above.

I avail myself of this opportunity to renew to Your Excellency the assurance of my highest consideration.

Hsu Mo
on behalf of the Minister for Foreign Affairs

His Excellency
Mr. Nelson T. Johnson,
*American Minister to China,
Nanking.*

UNILATERAL DECLARATION REGARDING GUARANTEED RIGHTS

The Foreign Signatories to the Chinese Minister for Foreign Affairs

NANKING, CHINA. *February 17, 1930.*

EXCELLENCY:

With reference to the Agreement which we have signed today establishing a new Chinese judicial system in the International Settlement at Shanghai, we desire to point out that such Agreement cannot in any way affect or invalidate rights guaranteed to the Powers concerned and to their nationals under existing treaties between such Powers and China and we accordingly reserve our full rights in this regard.

We further reserve the right to object to the enforcement in the International Settlement of any future Chinese laws that affect or in any way invalidate the Land Regulations or Bye-Laws of the International Settlement or that may be considered prejudicial to the maintenance of peace and order within this area.

We avail ourselves of this opportunity to renew to Your Excellency the assurance of our highest consideration.

J. DE PINTO DIAZ
    on behalf of the Brazilian Chargé d'Affaires

In the name of the American Minister,
JOSEPH E. JACOBS

W. MEYRICK HEWLETT
    on behalf of His Britannic Majesty's
    Minister

L. GRONVOLD
    on behalf of the Norwegian Chargé
    d'Affaires

F. E. H. GROENMAN
    on behalf of the Netherlands chargé
    d'affaires

In the name of the French Minister:
E. KOECHLIN

HIS EXCELLENCY
    DR. C. T. WANG,
        Minister for Foreign Affairs,
        Nanking, China.

MILITARY OBLIGATIONS IN CERTAIN CASES OF DOUBLE NATIONALITY

Protocol opened for signature at The Hague April 12, 1930, and signed for the United States December 31, 1930
Senate advice and consent to ratification June 18, 1932
Ratified by the President of the United States July 5, 1932
Ratification of the United States deposited with the Secretary-General of the League of Nations August 3, 1932
Proclaimed by the President of the United States April 26, 1937
Entered into force May 25, 1937

50 Stat. 1317; Treaty Series 913

PROTOCAL RELATING TO MILITARY OBLIGATIONS IN CERTAIN CASES OF DOUBLE NATIONALITY

The undersigned plenipotentiaries, on behalf of their respective Governments,

With a view to determining in certain cases the position as regards their military obligations of persons possessing two or more nationalities,

Have agreed as follows:

Article 1

A person possessing two or more nationalities who habitually resides in one of the countries whose nationality he possesses, and who is in fact most closely connected with that country, shall be exempt from all military obligations in the other country or countries.

This exemption may involve the loss of the nationality of the other country or countries.

Article 2

Without prejudice to the provisions of Article 1 of the present Protocol, if a person possesses the nationality of two or more States and, under the law of any one of such States, has the right, on attaining his majority, to renounce or decline the nationality of that State, he shall be exempt from military service in such State during his minority.

1049

Article 3

A person who has lost the nationality of a State under the law of that State and has acquired another nationality, shall be exempt from military obligations in the State of which he has lost the nationality.

Article 4

The High Contracting Parties agree to apply the principles and rules contained in the preceding articles in their relations with each other, as from the date of the entry into force of the present Protocol.

The inclusion of the above-mentioned principles and rules in the said articles shall in no way be deemed to prejudice the question whether they do or do not already form part of international law.

It is understood that, in so far as any point is not covered by any of the provisions of the preceding articles, the existing principles and rules of international law shall remain in force.

Article 5

Nothing in the present Protocol shall affect the provisions of any treaty, convention or agreement in force between any of the High Contracting Parties relating to nationality or matters connected therewith.

Article 6

Any High Contracting Party may, when signing or ratifying the present Protocol or acceding thereto, append an express reservation excluding any one or more of the provisions of Articles 1 to 3 and 7.

The provisions thus excluded cannot be applied against the High Contracting Party who has made the reservation nor relied on by that Party against any other High Contracting Party.

Article 7

If there should arise between the High Contracting Parties a dispute of any kind relating to the interpretation or application of the present Protocol and if such dispute cannot be satisfactorily settled by diplomacy, it shall be settled in accordance with any applicable agreements in force between the Parties providing for the settlement of international disputes.

In case there is no such agreement in force between the Parties, the dispute shall be referred to arbitration or judicial settlement, in accordance with the constitutional procedure of each of the Parties to the dispute. In the absence of agreement on the choice of another tribunal, the dispute shall be referred to the Permanent Court of International Justice, if all the Parties to the dispute are Parties to the Protocol of the 16th December, 1920,[1] relating to the Statute of that Court, and if any of the Parties to the dispute is not a Party

---

[1] 6 LNTS 379; IV Trenwith 5645. The United States did not become a party.

to the Protocol of the 16th December, 1920, the dispute shall be referred to an arbitral tribunal constituted in accordance with the Hague Convention of the 18th October, 1907, for the Pacific Settlement of International Conflicts.[2]

Article 8

The present Protocol shall remain open until the 31st December, 1930, for signature on behalf of any Member of the League of Nations or of any non-Member State invited to the First Codification Conference or to which the Council of the League of Nations has communicated a copy of the Protocol for this purpose.

Article 9

The present Protocol is subject to ratification. Ratifications shall be deposited with the Secretariat of the League of Nations.

The Secretary-General shall give notice of the deposit of each ratification to the Members of the League of Nations and to the non-Member States mentioned in Article 8, indicating the date of its deposit.

Article 10

As from January 1st, 1931, any Member of the League of Nations and any non-Member State mentioned in Article 8 on whose behalf the Protocol has not been signed before that date may accede thereto.

Accession shall be effected by an instrument deposited with the Secretariat of the League of Nations. The Secretary-General of the League of Nations shall give notice of each accession to the Members of the League of Nations and to the non-Member States mentioned in Article 8, indicating the date of the deposit of the instrument.

Article 11

A procès-verbal shall be drawn up by the Secretary-General of the League of Nations as soon as ratifications or accessions on behalf of ten Members of the League of Nations or non-Member States have been deposited.[3]

A certified copy of this procès-verbal shall be sent by the Secretary-General to each Member of the League of Nations and to each non-Member State mentioned in Article 8.

Article 12

The present Protocol shall enter into force on the 90th day after the date of the procès-verbal mentioned in Article 11 as regards all Members of the League of Nations or non-Member States on whose behalf ratifications or accessions have been deposited on the date of the procès-verbal.

---

[2] TS 536, *ante,* vol. 1, p. 577.

[3] For text of procès-verbal of deposit done at Geneva Feb. 24, 1937, see 50 Stat. 1330 or p. 14 of TS 913.

As regards any Member of the League or non-Member State on whose behalf a ratification or accession is subsequently deposited, the Protocol shall enter into force on the 90th day after the date of the deposit of a ratification or accession on its behalf.

Article 13

As from January 1st, 1936, any Member of the League of Nations or any non-Member State in regard to which the present Protocol is then in force, may address to the Secretary-General of the League of Nations a request for the revision of any or all of the provisions of this Protocol. If such a request, after being communicated to the other Members of the League and non-Member States in regard to which the Protocol is then in force, is supported within one year by at least nine of them, the Council of the League of Nations shall decide, after consultation with the Members of the League of Nations and the non-Member States mentioned in Article 8, whether a conference should be specially convoked for that purpose or whether such revision should be considered at the next conference for the codification of international law.

The High Contracting Parties agree that, if the present Protocol is revised, the new Agreement may provide that upon its entry into force some or all of the provisions of the present Protocol shall be abrogated in respect of all of the Parties to the present Protocol.

Article 14

The present Protocol may be denounced.

Denunciation shall be effected by a notification in writing addressed to the Secretary-General of the League of Nations, who shall inform all Members of the League of Nations and the non-Member States mentioned in Article 8.

Each denunciation shall take effect one year after the receipt by the Secretary-General of the notification but only as regards the Member of the League or non-Member State on whose behalf it has been notified.

Article 15

1. Any High Contracting Party may, at the time of signature, ratification or accession, declare that, in accepting the present Protocol, he does not assume any obligations in respect of all or any of his colonies, protectorates, overseas territories or territories under suzerainty or mandate, or in respect of certain parts of the population of the said territories; and the present Protocol shall not apply to any territories or to the parts of their population named in such declaration.

2. Any High Contracting Party may give notice to the Secretary-General of the League of Nations at any time subsequently that he desires that the Protocol shall apply to all or any of his territories or to the parts of their population which have been made the subject of a declaration under the

preceding paragraph, and the Protocol shall apply to all the territories or the parts of their population named in such notice six months after its receipt by the Secretary-General of the League of Nations.

3. Any High Contracting Party may, at any time, declare that he desires that the present Protocol shall cease to apply to all or any of his colonies, protectorates, overseas territories or territories under suzerainty or mandate, or in respect of certain parts of the population of the said territories, and the Protocol shall cease to apply to the territories or to the parts of their population named in such declaration one year after its receipt by the Secretary-General of the League of Nations.

4. Any High Contracting Party may make the reservations provided for in Article 6 in respect of all or any of his colonies, protectorates, overseas territories or territories under suzerainty or mandate, or in respect of certain parts of the population of these territories, at the time of signature, ratification or accession to the Protocol or at the time of making a notification under the second paragraph of this article.

5. The Secretary-General of the League of Nations shall communicate to all the Members of the League of Nations and the non-Member States mentioned in Article 8 all declarations and notices received in virtue of this article.

Article 16

The present Protocol shall be registered by the Secretary-General of the League of Nations as soon as it has entered into force.

Article 17

The French and English texts of the present Protocol shall both be authoritative.

In faith whereof the Plenipotentiaries have signed the present Protocol.

Done at The Hague on the twelfth day of April, one thousand nine hundred and thirty, in a single copy, which shall be deposited in the archives of the Secretariat of the League of Nations and of which certified true copies shall be transmitted by the Secretary-General to all the Members of the League of Nations and all the non-Member States invited to the First Conference for the Codification of International Law.

Germany:
  GÖPPERT
  HERING
United States of America:
  HUGH R. WILSON
Austria:
  LEITMAIER
Belgium:
  J. DE RUELLE
  Subject to accession later for the Colony of the Congo and the mandated territories [translation].

Great Britain and Northern Ireland and all parts of the British Empire which are not separate Members of the League of Nations:
  MAURICE GWYER
  OSCAR F. DOWSON
Canada:
  PHILIPPE ROY

Irish Free State:
  JOHN J. HEARNE

India:
In accordance with the provisions of Article 15 of this Protocol I declare that His Britannic Majesty does not assume any obligation in respect of the territories in India of any Prince or Chief under His suzerainty or the population of the said territories.
BASANTA KUMAR MULLICK

Chile:
MIGUEL CRUCHAGA
ALEJANDRO ALVAREZ
H. MARCHANT

Colombia:
A. J. RESTREPO
FRANCISCO JOSÉ URRUTIA

Cuba:
Ad referendum.
DIAZ DE VILLAR
CARLOS DE ARMENTEROS

Denmark:
F. MARTENSEN-LARSEN
V. LORCK.

Egypt:
A. BADAOUI
M. SID AHMED

Spain:
A. GOICOECHEA

France:
PAUL MATTER
A. KAMMERER

Greece:
Ad referendum.
N. POLITIS
MEGALOS CALOYANNI
JEAN SPIROPOULOS

Luxemburg:
CONRAD STUMPER

Mexico:
EDUARDO SUAREZ

The Netherlands:
v. EYSINGA.
J. KOSTERS.
1. Exclude from acceptance Article 3;
2. Do not intend to assume any obligation as regards Netherlands Indies, Surinam and Curaçao [translation].[4]

Peru:
M. H. CORNEJO

Portugal:
JOSÉ CAEIRO DA MATTA
JOSÉ MARIA VILHENA BARBOSA DE MAGALHAES.
Prof. DOUTOR J. LOBO D'AVILA LIMA

Salvador:
J. GUSTAVO GUERRERO

Sweden:
K. J. WESTMAN
Subject to ratification by His Majesty the King of Sweden with the approval of the Riksdag [translation].

Uruguay:
E. E. BUERO

---

[4] The Netherlands Government, upon deposit of ratification Apr. 2, 1937, withdrew its reservation regarding art. 3. The ratification also included the Netherlands Indies, Surinam, and Curaçao.

LIMITATION AND REDUCTION OF NAVAL ARMAMENT (LONDON NAVAL TREATY)

Treaty signed at London April 22, 1930; exchanges of notes relating to interpretation of article 19 dated May 21, May 24, and June 5, 1930

Senate advice and consent to ratification, with understandings, July 21, 1930 [1]

Ratified by the President of the United States, with understandings, July 22, 1930 [1]

Ratifications deposited at London October 27, 1930

Entered into force December 31, 1930

Proclaimed by the President of the United States January 1, 1931

Expired December 31, 1936, with the exception of Part IV [2]

46 Stat. 2858; Treaty Series 830

The President of the United States of America, the President of the French Republic, His Majesty the King of Great Britain, Ireland and the British Dominions beyond the Seas, Emperor of India, His Majesty the King of Italy, and His Majesty the Emperor of Japan,

Desiring to prevent the dangers and reduce the burdens inherent in competitive armaments, and

Desiring to carry forward the work begun by the Washington Naval Conference and to facilitate the progressive realization of general limitation and reduction of armaments,

Have resolved to conclude a Treaty for the limitation and reduction of naval armament, and have accordingly appointed as their Plenipotentiaries:

---

[1] The U.S. understandings read as follows:

"Subject to the distinct and explicit understandings that there are no secret files, documents, letters, understandings or agreements which in any way, directly or indirectly, modify, change, add to, or take from any of the stipulations, agreements or statements in the said treaty; and that, excepting the agreement brought about through the exchange of notes between the Governments of the United States, Great Britain and Japan, having reference to Article 19, there is no agreement, secret or otherwise, expressed or implied, between any of the parties to the said treaty as to any construction that shall hereafter be given to any statement or provision contained therein."

[2] See arts. 22 and 23, pp. 1070 and 1071.

The President of the United States of America:
Henry L. Stimson, Secretary of State;
Charles G. Dawes, Ambassador to the Court of St. James;
Charles Francis Adams, Secretary of the Navy;
Joseph T. Robinson, Senator from the State of Arkansas;
David A. Reed, Senator from the State of Pennsylvania;
Hugh Gibson, Ambassador to Belgium;
Dwight W. Morrow, Ambassador to Mexico;

The President of the French Republic:
Mr. André Tardieu, Deputy, President of the Council of Ministers, Minister of the Interior;
Mr. Aristide Briand, Deputy, Minister for Foreign Affairs;
Mr. Jacques-Louis Dumesnil, Deputy, Minister of Marine;
Mr. François Piétri, Deputy, Minister of the Colonies;
Mr. Aimé-Joseph de Fleuriau, Ambassador of the French Republic at the Court of St. James;

His Majesty the King of Great Britain, Ireland and the British Dominions beyond the Seas, Emperor of India:

For Great Britain and Northern Ireland and all parts of the British Empire which are not separate Members of the League of Nations:
The Right Honourable James Ramsay MacDonald, M.P., First Lord of His Treasury and Prime Minister;
The Right Honourable Arthur Henderson, M.P., His Principal Secretary of State for Foreign Affairs;
The Right Honourable Albert Victor Alexander, M.P., First Lord of His Admiralty;
The Right Honourable William Wedgwood Benn, D.S.O., D.F.C., M.P., His Principal Secretary of State for India;

For the Dominion of Canada:
Colonel The Honourable James Layton Ralston, C.M.G., D.S.O., K.C., a Member of His Privy Council for Canada, His Minister for National Defence;
The Honourable Philippe Roy, a Member of His Privy Council for Canada, His Envoy Extraordinary and Minister Plenipotentiary in France for the Dominion of Canada;

For the Commonwealth of Australia:
The Honourable James Edward Fenton, His Minister for Trade and Customs;

For the Dominion of New Zealand:
Thomas Mason Wilford, Esquire, K.C., High Commissioner for the Dominion of New Zealand in London;

For the Union of South Africa:
Charles Theodore te Water, Esquire, High Commissioner for the Union of South Africa in London;

For the Irish Free State:
Timothy Aloysius Smiddy, Esquire, High Commissioner for the Irish Free State in London;

For India:
Sir Atul Chandra Chatterjee, K.C.I.E., High Commissioner for India in London;

His Majesty the King of Italy:
The Honourable Dino Grandi, Deputy, His Minister Secretary of State for Foreign Affairs;
Admiral of Division The Honourable Giuseppe Sirianni, Senator of the Kingdom, His Minister Secretary of State for Marine;
Mr. Antonio Chiaramonte-Bordonaro, His Ambassador Extraordinary and Plenipotentiary at the Court of St. James;
Admiral The Honourable Baron Afredo Acton, Senator of the Kingdom;

His Majesty the Emperor of Japan:
Mr. Reijiro Wakatsuki, Member of the House of Peers;
Admiral Takeshi Takarabe, Minister for the Navy;
Mr. Tsuneo Matsudaira, His Ambassador Extraordinary and Plenipotentiary at the Court of St. James;
Mr. Matsuzo Nagaï, His Ambassador Extraordinary and Plenipotentiary to His Majesty the King of the Belgians;

Who, having communicated to one another their full powers, found in good and due form, have agreed as follows:

PART I

ARTICLE 1

The High Contracting Parties agree not to exercise their rights to lay down the keels of capital ship replacement tonnage during the years 1931–1936 inclusive as provided in Chapter II, Part 3 of the Treaty for the Limitation of Naval Armament signed between them at Washington on the 6th February, 1922,[3] and referred to in the present Treaty as the Washington Treaty.

This provision is without prejudice to the disposition relating to the replacement of ships accidentally lost or destroyed contained in Chapter II, Part 3, Section I, paragraph (c) of the said Treaty.

---

[3] TS 671, *ante,* p. 361.

France and Italy may, however, build the replacement tonnage which they were entitled to lay down in 1927 and 1929 in accordance with the provisions of the said Treaty.

ARTICLE 2

1. The United States, the United Kingdom of Great Britain and Northern Ireland and Japan shall dispose of the following capital ships as provided in this Article:

United States:
  "Florida".
  "Utah".
  "Arkansas" or "Wyoming".
United Kingdom:
  "Benbow".
  "Iron Duke".
  "Marlborough".
  "Emperor of India".
  "Tiger".
Japan:
  "Hiyei".

(*a*) Subject to the provisions of sub-paragraph (*b*), the above ships, unless converted to target use exclusively in accordance with Chapter II, Part 2, paragraph II (*c*) of the Washington Treaty, shall be scrapped in the following manner:

One of the ships to be scrapped by the United States, and two of those to be scrapped by the United Kingdom shall be rendered unfit for warlike service, in accordance with Chapter II, Part 2, paragraph III (*b*) of the Washington Treaty, within twelve months from the coming into force of the present Treaty. These ships shall be finally scrapped, in accordance with paragraph II (*a*) or (*b*) of the said Part 2, within twenty-four months from the said coming into force. In the case of the second of the ships to be scrapped by the United States, and of the third and fourth of the ships to be scrapped by the United Kingdom, the said periods shall be eighteen and thirty months respectively from the coming into force of the present Treaty.

(*b*) Of the ships to be disposed of under this Article, the following may be retained for training purposes:

by the United States: "Arkansas" or "Wyoming".
by the United Kingdom: "Iron Duke".
by Japan: "Hiyei".

These ships shall be reduced to the condition prescribed in Section V of Annex II to Part II of the present Treaty. The work of reducing these vessels to the required condition shall begin, in the case of the United States and the

United Kingdom, within twelve months, and in the case of Japan within eighteen months from the coming into force of the present Treaty; the work shall be completed within six months of the expiration of the above-mentioned periods.

Any of these ships which are not retained for training purposes shall be rendered unfit for warlike service within eighteen months, and finally scrapped within thirty months, of the coming into force of the present Treaty.

2. Subject to any disposal of capital ships which might be necessitated, in accordance with the Washington Treaty, by the building by France or Italy of the replacement tonnage referred to in Article 1 of the present Treaty, all existing capital ships mentioned in Chapter II, Part 3, Section II of the Washington Treaty and not designated above to be disposed of may be retained during the term of the present Treaty.

3. The right of replacement is not lost by delay in laying down replacement tonnage, and the old vessel may be retained until replaced even though due for scrapping under Chapter II, Part 3, Section II, of the Washington Treaty.

ARTICLE 3

1. For the purposes of the Washington Treaty, the definition of an aircraft carrier given in Chapter II, Part 4 of the said Treaty is hereby replaced by the following definition:

The expression "aircraft carrier" includes any surface vessel of war, whatever its displacement, designed for the specific and exclusive purpose of carrying aircraft and so constructed that aircraft can be launched therefrom and landed thereon.

2. The fitting of a landing-on or flying-off platform or deck on a capital ship, cruiser or destroyer, provided such vessel was not designed or adapted exclusively as an aircraft carrier, shall not cause any vessel so fitted to be charged against or classified in the category of aircraft carriers.

3. No capital ship in existence on the 1st April, 1930, shall be fitted with a landing-on platform or deck.

ARTICLE 4

1. No aircraft carrier of 10,000 tons (10,160 metric tons) or less standard displacement mounting a gun above 6.1-inch (155 mm.) calibre shall be acquired by or constructed by or for any of the High Contracting Parties.

2. As from the coming into force of the present Treaty in respect of all the High Contracting Parties, no aircraft carrier of 10,000 tons (10,160 metric tons) or less standard displacement mounting a gun above 6.1-inch (155 mm.) calibre shall be constructed within the jurisdiction of any of the High Contracting Parties.

ARTICLE 5

An aircraft carrier must not be designed and constructed for carrying a more powerful armament than that authorised by Article IX or Article X of the Washington Treaty, or by Article 4 of the present Treaty, as the case may be.

Wherever in the said Articles IX and X the calibre of 6 inches (152 mm.) is mentioned, the calibre of 6.1 inches (155 mm.) is substituted therefor.

PART II

ARTICLE 6

1. The rules for determining standard displacement prescribed in Chapter II, Part 4 of the Washington Treaty shall apply to all surface vessels of war of each of the High Contracting Parties.

2. The standard displacement of a submarine is the surface displacement of the vessel complete (exclusive of the water in non-watertight structure) fully manned, engined, and equipped ready for sea, including all armament and ammunition, equipment, outfit, provisions for crew, miscellaneous stores, and implements of every description that are intended to be carried in war, but without fuel, lubricating oil, fresh water or ballast water of any kind on board.

3. Each naval combatant vessel shall be rated at its displacement tonnage when in the standard condition. The word "ton", except in the expression "metric tons", shall be understood to be the ton of 2,240 pounds (1,016 kilos.).

ARTICLE 7

1. No submarine the standard displacement of which exceeds 2,000 tons (2,032 metric tons) or with a gun above 5.1-inch (130 mm.) calibre shall be acquired by or constructed by or for any of the High Contracting Parties.

2. Each of the High Contracting Parties may, however, retain, build or acquire a maximum number of three submarines of a standard displacement not exceeding 2,800 tons (2,845 metric tons); these submarines may carry guns not above 6.1-inch (155 mm.) calibre. Within this number, France may retain one unit, already launched, of 2,880 tons (2,926 metric tons), with guns the calibre of which is 8 inches (203 mm.).

3. The High Contracting Parties may retain the submarines which they possessed on the 1st April, 1930, having a standard displacement not in excess of 2,000 tons (2,032 metric tons) and armed with guns above 5.1-inch (130 mm.) calibre.

4. As from the coming into force of the present Treaty in respect of all the High Contracting Parties, no submarine the standard displacement of which exceeds 2,000 tons (2,032 metric tons) or with a gun above 5.1-inch (130 mm.) calibre shall be constructed within the jurisdiction of any of the High Contracting Parties, except as provided in paragraph 2 of this Article.

ARTICLE 8

Subject to any special agreements which may submit them to limitation, the following vessels are exempt from limitation:

(*a*) naval surface combatant vessels of 600 tons (610 metric tons) standard displacement and under;

(*b*) naval surface combatant vessels exceeding 600 tons (610 metric tons), but not exceeding 2,000 tons (2,032 metric tons) standard displacement, provided they have none of the following characteristics:

(1) mount a gun above 6.1-inch (155 mm.) calibre;
(2) mount more than four guns above 3-inch (76 mm.) calibre;
(3) are designed or fitted to launch torpedoes;
(4) are designed for a speed greater than twenty knots.

(*c*) naval surface vessels not specifically built as fighting ships which are employed on fleet duties or as troop transports or in some other way than as fighting ships, provided they have none of the following characteristics:

(1) mount a gun above 6.1-inch (155 mm.) calibre;
(2) mount more than four guns above 3-inch (76 mm.) calibre;
(3) are designed or fitted to launch torpedoes;
(4) are designed for a speed greater than twenty knots;
(5) are protected by armour plate;
(6) are designed or fitted to launch mines;
(7) are fitted to receive aircraft on board from the air;
(8) mount more than one aircraft-launching apparatus on the centre line; or two, one on each broadside;
(9) if fitted with any means of launching aircraft into the air, are designed or adapted to operate at sea more than three aircraft.

ARTICLE 9

The rules as to replacement contained in Annex I to this Part II are applicable to vessels of war not exceeding 10,000 tons (10,160 metric tons) standard displacement, with the exception of aircraft carriers, whose replacement is governed by the provisions of the Washington Treaty.

ARTICLE 10

Within one month after the date of laying down and the date of completion respectively of each vessel of war, other than capital ships, aircraft carriers and the vessels exempt from limitation under Article 8, laid down or completed by or for them after the coming into force of the present Treaty, the High Contracting Parties shall communicate to each of the other High Contracting Parties the information detailed below:

(*a*) the date of laying the keel and the following particulars:

classification of the vessel;

standard displacement in tons and metric tons;

principal dimensions, namely: length at water-line, extreme beam at or below water-line;

mean draft at standard displacement;

calibre of the largest gun.

(*b*) the date of completion together with the foregoing particulars relating to the vessel at that date.

The information to be given in the case of capital ships and aircraft carriers is governed by the Washington Treaty.

ARTICLE 11

Subject to the provisions of Article 2 of the present Treaty, the rules for disposal contained in Annex II to this Part II shall be applied to all vessels of war to be disposed of under the said Treaty, and to aircraft carriers as defined in Article 3.

ARTICLE 12

1. Subject to any supplementary agreements which may modify, as between the High Contracting Parties concerned, the lists in Annex III to this Part II, the special vessels shown therein may be retained and their tonnage shall not be included in the tonnage subject to limitation.

2. Any other vessel constructed, adapted or acquired to serve the purposes for which these special vessels are retained shall be charged against the tonnage of the appropriate combatant category, according to the characteristics of the vessel, unless such vessel conforms to the characteristics of vessels exempt from limitation under Article 8.

3. Japan may, however, replace the minelayers "Aso" and "Tokiwa" by two new minelayers before the 31st December, 1936. The standard displacement of each of the new vessels shall not exceed 5,000 tons (5,080 metric tons); their speed shall not exceed twenty knots, and their other characteristics shall conform to the provisions of paragraph (*b*) of Article 8. The new vessels shall be regarded as special vessels and their tonnage shall not be chargeable to the tonnage of any combatant category. The "Aso" and "Tokiwa" shall be disposed of in accordance with Section I or II of Annex II to this Part II, on completion of the replacement vessels.

4. The "Asama", "Yakumo", "Izumo", "Iwate" and "Kasuga" shall be disposed of in accordance with Section I or II of Annex II to this Part II when the first three vessels of the "Kuma" class have been replaced by new vessels. These three vessels of the "Kuma" class shall be reduced to the condition prescribed in Section V, sub-paragraph (*b*)2 of Annex II to this Part II, and are to be used for training ships, and their tonnage shall not thereafter be included in the tonnage subject to limitation.

ARTICLE 13

Existing ships of various types, which, prior to the 1st April, 1930, have been used as stationary training establishments or hulks, may be retained in a non-seagoing condition.

ANNEX I

Rules for replacement

SECTION I. Except as provided in Section III of this Annex and Part III of the present Treaty, a vessel shall not be replaced before it becomes "over-age". A vessel shall be deemed to be "over-age" when the following number of years have elapsed since the date of its completion:

(*a*) For a surface vessel exceeding 3,000 tons (3,048 metric tons) but not exceeding 10,000 tons (10,160 metric tons) standard displacement:

(i) if laid down before the 1st January, 1920: 16 years;
(ii) if laid down after the 31st December, 1919: 20 years.

(*b*) For a surface vessel not exceeding 3,000 tons (3,048 metric tons) standard displacement:

(i) if laid down before the 1st January, 1921: 12 years;
(ii) if laid down after the 31st December, 1920: 16 years.

(*c*) For a submarine: 13 years.

The keels of replacement tonnage shall not be laid down more than three years before the year in which the vessel to be replaced becomes "over-age"; but this period is reduced to two years in the case of any replacement surface vessel not exceeding 3,000 tons (3,048 metric tons) standard displacement.

The right of replacement is not lost by delay in laying down replacement tonnage.

SECTION II. Except as otherwise provided in the present Treaty, the vessel or vessels, whose retention would cause the maximum tonnage permitted in the category to be exceeded, shall, on the completion or acquisition of replacement tonnage, be disposed of in accordance with Annex II to this Part II.

SECTION III. In the event of loss or accidental destruction a vessel may be immediately replaced.

ANNEX II

Rules for disposal of Vessels of War

The present Treaty provides for the disposal of vessels of war in the following ways:

(i) by scrapping (sinking or breaking up);
(ii) by converting the vessel to a hulk;
(iii) by converting the vessel to target use exclusively;
(iv) by retaining the vessel exclusively for experimental purposes;
(v) by retaining the vessel exclusively for training purposes.

Any vessel of war to be disposed of, other than a capital ship, may either be scrapped or converted to a hulk at the option of the High Contracting Party concerned.

Vessels, other than capital ships, which have been retained for target, experimental or training purposes, shall finally be scrapped or converted to hulks.

SECTION I. *Vessels to be scrapped*

(*a*) A vessel to be disposed of by scrapping, by reason of its replacement, must be rendered incapable of warlike service within six months of the date of the completion of its successor, or of the first of its successors if there are more than one. If, however, the completion of the new vessel or vessels be delayed, the work of rendering the old vessel incapable of warlike service shall, nevertheless, be completed within four and a half years from the date of laying the keel of the new vessel, or of the first of the new vessels; but should the new vessel, or any of the new vessels, be a surface vessel not exceeding 3,000 tons (3,048 metric tons) standard displacement, this period is reduced to three and a half years.

(b) A vessel to be scrapped shall be considered incapable of warlike service when there shall have been removed and landed or else destroyed in the ship:

(1) all guns and essential parts of guns, fire control tops and revolving parts of all barbettes and turrets;

(2) all hydraulic or electric machinery for operating turrets;

(3) all fire control instruments and rangefinders;

(4) all ammunition, explosives, mines and mine rails;

(5) all torpedoes, war heads, torpedo tubes and training racks;

(6) all wireless telegraphy installations;

(7) all main propelling machinery, or alternatively the armoured conning tower and all side armour plate;

(8) all aircraft cranes, derricks, lifts and launching apparatus. All landing-on or flying-off platforms and decks, or alternatively all main propelling machinery;

(9) in addition, in the case of submarines, all main storage batteries, air compressor plants and ballast pumps.

(c) Scrapping shall be finally effected in either of the following ways within twelve months of the date on which the work of rendering the vessel incapable of warlike service is due for completion:

(1) permanent sinking of the vessel;

(2) breaking the vessel up; this shall always include the destruction or removal of all machinery, boilers and armour, and all deck, side and bottom plating.

Section II. *Vessels to be converted to hulks*

A vessel to be disposed of by conversion to a hulk shall be considered finally disposed of when the conditions prescribed in Section I, paragraph (b), have been complied with, omitting subparagraphs (6), (7) and (8), and when the following have been effected:

(1) mutilation beyond repair of all propeller shafts, thrust blocks, turbine gearing or main propelling motors, and turbines or cylinders of main engines;

(2) removal of propeller brackets;

(3) removal and breaking up of all aircraft lifts, and the removal of all aircraft cranes, derricks and launching apparatus.

The vessel must be put in the above condition within the same limits of time as provided in Section I for rendering a vessel incapable of warlike service.

Section III. *Vessels to be converted to target use*

(a) A vessel to be disposed of by conversion to target use exclusively shall be considered incapable of warlike service when there have been removed and landed, or rendered unserviceable on board, the following:

(1) all guns;

(2) all fire control tops and instruments and main fire control communication wiring;

(3) all machinery for operating gun mountings or turrets;

(4) all ammunition, explosives, mines, torpedoes and torpedo tubes;

(5) all aviation facilities and accessories.

The vessel must be put into the above condition within the same limits of time as provided in Section I for rendering a vessel incapable of warlike service.

(b) In addition to the rights already possessed by each High Contracting Party under the Washington Treaty, each High Contracting Party is permitted to retain, for target use exclusively, at any one time:

(1) not more than three vessels (cruisers or destroyers), but of these three vessels only one may exceed 3,000 tons (3,048 metric tons) standard displacement;

(2) one submarine.

(c) On retaining a vessel for target use, the High Contracting Party concerned undertakes not to recondition if for warlike service.

SECTION IV. *Vessels retained for experimental purposes*

(a) A vessel to be disposed of by conversion to experimental purposes exclusively shall be dealt with in accordance with the provisions of Section III (a) of this Annex.

(b) Without prejudice to the general rules, and provided that due notice be given to the other High Contracting Parties, reasonable variation from the conditions prescribed in Section III (a) of this Annex, in so far as may be necessary for the purposes of a special experiment, may be permitted as a temporary measure.

Any High Contracting Party taking advantage of this provision is required to furnish full details of any such variations and the period for which they will be required.

(c) Each High Contracting Party is permitted to retain for experimental purposes exclusively at any one time:

(1) not more than two vessels (cruisers or destroyers), but of these two vessels only one may exceed 3,000 tons (3,048 metric tons) standard displacement;

(2) one submarine.

(d) The United Kingdom is allowed to retain, in their present conditions, the monitor "Roberts", the main armament guns and mountings of which have been mutilated, and the seaplane carrier "Ark Royal", until no longer required for experimental purposes. The retention of these two vessels is without prejudice to the retention of vessels permitted under (c) above.

(e) On retaining a vessel for experimental purposes the High Contracting Party concerned undertakes not to recondition it for warlike service.

SECTION V. *Vessels retained for training purposes*

(a) In addition to the rights already possessed by any High Contracting Party under the Washington Treaty, each High Contracting Party is permitted to retain for training purposes exclusively the following vessels:

United States: 1 capital ship ("Arkansas" or "Wyoming");

France: 2 surface vessels, one of which may exceed 3,000 tons (3,048 metric tons) standard displacement;

United Kingdom: 1 capital ship ("Iron Duke");

Italy: 2 surface vessels, one of which may exceed 3,000 tons (3,048 metric tons) standard displacement;

Japan: 1 capital ship ("Hiyei"), 3 cruisers ("Kuma" class).

(b) Vessels retained for training purposes under the provisions of paragraph (a) shall, within six months of the date on which they are required to be disposed of, be dealt with as follows:

1. *Capital Ships*

The following is to be carried out:

(1) removal of main armament guns, revolving parts of all barbettes and turrets; machinery for operating turrets; but three turrets with their armament may be retained in each ship;

(2) removal of all ammunition and explosives in excess of the quantity required for target practice training for the guns remaining on board;

(3) removal of conning tower and the side armour belt between the foremost and aftermost barbettes;

(4) removal or mutilation of all torpedo tubes;

(5) removal or mutilation on board of all boilers in excess of the number required for a maximum speed of eighteen knots.

2. Other surface vessels retained by France, Italy and Japan

The following is to be carried out:

(1) removal of one half of the guns, but four guns of main calibre may be retained on each vessel;

(2) removal of all torpedo tubes;

(3) removal of all aviation facilities and accessories;

(4) removal of one half of the boilers.

(*c*) The High Contracting Party concerned undertakes that vessels retained in accordance with the provisions of this Section shall not be used for any combatant purpose.

ANNEX III

Special vessels

UNITED STATES

Name and type of vessel	Displacement Tons
Aroostok—Minelayer	4,950
Oglala—Minelayer	4,950
Baltimore—Minelayer	4,413
San Francisco—Minelayer	4,083
Cheyenne—Monitor	2,800
Helena—Gunboat	1,392
Isabel—Yacht	938
Niagara—Yacht	2,600
Bridgeport—Destroyer tender	11,750
Dobbin—Destroyer tender	12,450
Melville—Destroyer tender	7,150
Whitney—Destroyer tender	12,450
Holland—Submarine tender	11,570
Henderson—Naval transport	10,000
	91,496

FRANCE

Name and type of vessel	Displacement Tons
Castor—Minelayer	3,150
Pollux—Minelayer	2,461
Commandant-Teste—Seaplane carrier	10,000
Aisne — Despatch vessel	600
Marne " "	600
Ancre " "	604
Scarpe " "	604
Suippe " "	604
Dunkerque " "	644
Laffaux " "	644
Bapaume " "	644
Nancy " "	644
Calais " "	644
Lassigny " "	644
Les Eparges " "	644
Remiremont " "	644
Tahure " "	644
Toul " "	644
Épinal " "	644
Liévin " "	644
(—)—Netlayer	2,293
	28,644

BRITISH COMMONWEALTH OF NATIONS

Name and type of vessel	Displacement Tons
Adventure—Minelayer	6, 740
(United Kingdom)	
Albatross—Seaplane carrier	5, 000
(Australia)	
Erebus—Monitor	7, 200
(United Kingdom)	
Terror—Monitor	7, 200
(United Kingdom)	
Marshal Soult—Monitor	6, 400
(United Kingdom)	
Clive—Sloop	2, 021
(India)	
Medway—Submarine depot ship	15, 000
(United Kingdom)	
	49, 561

ITALY

Name and type of vessel	Displacement Tons
Miraglia—Seaplane carrier	4, 880
Faà di Bruno—Monitor	2, 800
Monte Grappa—Monitor	605
Montello—Monitor	605
Monte Cengio—Ex-monitor	500
Monte Novegno—Ex-monitor	500
Campania—Sloop	2, 070
	11, 960

JAPAN

Name and type of vessel	Displacement Tons
Aso—Minelayer	7, 180
Tokiwa "	9, 240
Asama—Old cruiser	9, 240
Yakumo " "	9, 010
Izumo " "	9, 180
Iwate " "	9, 180
Kasuga " "	7, 080
Yodo—Gunboat	1, 320
	61, 430

PART III

The President of the United States of America, His Majesty the King of Great Britain, Ireland and the British Dominions beyond the Seas, Emperor of India, and His Majesty the Emperor of Japan, have agreed as between themselves to the provisions of this Part III:

ARTICLE 14

The naval combatant vessels of the United States, the British Commonwealth of Nations and Japan, other than capital ships, aircraft carriers and all vessels exempt from limitation under Article 8, shall be limited during the term of the present Treaty as provided in this Part III, and, in the case of special vessels, as provided in Article 12.

ARTICLE 15

For the purpose of this Part III the definition of the cruiser and destroyer categories shall be as follows:

Cruisers

Surface vessels of war, other than capital ships or aircraft carriers, the standard displacement of which exceeds 1,850 tons (1,880 metric tons), or with a gun above 5.1 inch (130 mm.) calibre.

The cruiser category is divided into two sub-categories, as follows:

(*a*) cruisers carrying a gun above 6.1-inch (155 mm.) calibre;
(*b*) cruisers carrying a gun not above 6.1-inch (155 mm.) calibre.

Destroyers

Surface vessels of war the standard displacement of which does not exceed 1,850 tons (1,880 metric tons), and with a gun not above 5.1-inch (130 mm.) calibre.

ARTICLE 16

1. The completed tonnage in the cruiser, destroyer and submarine categories which is not to be exceeded on the 31st December, 1936, is given in the following table:

Categories	United States	British Common-wealth of Nations	Japan
Cruisers:			
(*a*) with guns of more than 6.1-inch (155 mm.) calibre.	180,000 tons (182,880 metric tons)	146,800 tons (149,149 metric tons)	108,400 tons (110,134 metric tons)
(*b*) with guns of 6.1-inch (155 mm.) calibre or less.	143,500 tons (145,796 metric tons)	192,200 tons (195,275 metric tons)	100,450 tons (102,057 metric tons)
Destroyers.............	150,000 tons (152,400 metric tons)	150,000 tons (152,400 metric tons)	105,500 tons (107,188 metric tons)
Submarines.............	52,700 tons (53,543 metric tons)	52,700 tons (53,543 metric tons)	52,700 tons (53,543 metric tons)

2. Vessels which cause the total tonnage in any category to exceed the figures given in the foregoing table shall be disposed of gradually during the period ending on the 31st December, 1936.

3. The maximum number of cruisers of sub-category (*a*) shall be as follows: for the United States, eighteen; for the British Commonwealth of Nations, fifteen; for Japan, twelve.

4. In the destroyer category not more than sixteen per cent. of the allowed total tonnage shall be employed in vessels of over 1,500 tons (1,524 metric tons) standard displacement. Destroyers completed or under construction on the 1st April, 1930, in excess of this percentage may be retained, but no

other destroyers exceeding 1,500 tons (1,524 metric tons) standard displacement shall be constructed or acquired until a reduction to such sixteen per cent. has been effected.

5. Not more than twenty-five per cent. of the allowed total tonnage in the cruiser category may be fitted with a landing-on platform or deck for aircraft.

6. It is understood that the submarines referred to in paragraphs 2 and 3 of Article 7 will be counted as part of the total submarine tonnage of the High Contracting Party concerned.

7. The tonnage of any vessels retained under Article 13 or disposed of in accordance with Annex II to Part II of the present Treaty shall not be included in the tonnage subject to limitation.

ARTICLE 17

A transfer not exceeding ten percent of the allowed total tonnage of the category or sub-category into which the transfer is to be made shall be permitted between cruisers of sub-category (b) and destroyers.

ARTICLE 18

The United States contemplates the completion by 1935 of fifteen cruisers of sub-category (a) of an aggregate tonnage of 150,000 tons (152,400 metric tons). For each of the three remaining cruisers of sub-category (a) which it is entitled to construct the United States may elect to substitute 15,166 tons (15,409 metric tons) of cruisers of sub-category (b). In case the United States shall construct one or more of such three remaining cruisers of sub-category (a), the sixteenth unit will not be laid down before 1933 and will not be completed before 1936; the seventeenth will not be laid down before 1934 and will not be completed before 1937; the eighteenth will not be laid down before 1935 and will not be completed before 1938.

ARTICLE 19 [4]

Except as provided in Article 20, the tonnage laid down in any category subject to limitation in accordance with Article 16 shall not exceed the amount necessary to reach the maximum allowed tonnage of the category, or to replace vessels that become "over-age" before the 31st December, 1936. Nevertheless, replacement tonnage may be laid down for cruisers and submarines that become "over-age" in 1937, 1938 and 1939, and for destroyers that become "over-age" in 1937 and 1938.

ARTICLE 20

Notwithstanding the rules for replacement contained in Annex I to Part II:

(a) The "Frobisher" and "Effingham" (United Kingdom) may be disposed of during the year 1936. Apart from the cruisers under construction on the 1st April, 1930, the total replacement tonnage of cruisers to be completed,

---

[4] For U.S. understandings, see footnote 1, p. 1055; for exchanges of notes relating to interpretation of art. 19, see p. 1072.

in the case of the British Commonwealth of Nations, prior to the 31st December, 1936, shall not exceed 91,000 tons (92,456 metric tons).

(b) Japan may replace the "Tama" by new construction to be completed during the year 1936.

(c) In addition to replacing destroyers becoming "over-age" before the 31st December, 1936, Japan may lay down, in each of the years 1935 and 1936, not more than 5,200 tons (5,283 metric tons) to replace part of the vessels that become "over-age" in 1938 and 1939.

(d) Japan may anticipate replacement during the term of the present Treaty by laying down not more than 19,200 tons (19,507 metric tons) of submarine tonnage, of which not more than 12,000 tons (12,192 metric tons) shall be completed by the 31st December, 1936.

ARTICLE 21

If, during the term of the present Treaty, the requirements of the national security of any High Contracting Party in respect of vessels of war limited by Part III of the present Treaty are in the opinion of that Party materially affected by new construction of any Power other than those who have joined in Part III of this Treaty, that High Contracting Party will notify the other Parties to Part III as to the increase required to be made in its own tonnages within one or more of the categories of such vessels of war, specifying particularly the proposed increases and the reasons therefor, and shall be entitled to make such increase. Thereupon the other Parties to Part III of this Treaty shall be entitled to make a proportionate increase in the category or categories specified; and the said other Parties shall promptly advise with each other through diplomatic channels as to the situation thus presented.

PART IV [5]

ARTICLE 22

The following are accepted as established rules of International Law:

(1) In their action with regard to merchant ships, submarines must conform to the rules of International Law to which surface vessels are subject.

(2) In particular, except in the case of persistent refusal to stop on being duly summoned, or of active resistance to visit or search, a warship, whether surface vessel or submarine, may not sink or render incapable of navigation a merchant vessel without having first placed passengers, crew and ship's papers in a place of safety. For this purpose the ship's boats are not regarded as a place of safety unless the safety of the passengers and crew is assured, in the existing sea and weather conditions, by the proximity of land, or the presence of another vessel which is in a position to take them on board.

The High Contracting Parties invite all other Powers to express their assent to the above rules.

---

[5] See also procès-verbal signed at London Nov. 6, 1936, relating to the rules of submarine warfare, *post,* vol. 3.

PART V

ARTICLE 23

The present Treaty shall remain in force until the 31st December, 1936, subject to the following exceptions:

(1) Part IV shall remain in force without limit of time;

(2) the provisions of Articles 3, 4 and 5, and of Article 11 and Annex II to Part II so far as they relate to aircraft carriers, shall remain in force for the same period as the Washington Treaty.

Unless the High Contracting Parties should agree otherwise by reason of a more general agreement limiting naval armaments, to which they all become parties, they shall meet in conference in 1935 to frame a new treaty to replace and to carry out the purposes of the present Treaty, it being understood that none of the provisions of the present Treaty shall prejudice the attitude of any of the High Contracting Parties at the conference agreed to.

ARTICLE 24

1. The present Treaty shall be ratified by the High Contracting Parties in accordance with their respective constitutional methods and the ratifications shall be deposited at London as soon as possible. Certified copies of all the *procès-verbaux* of the deposit of ratifications will be transmitted to the Governments of all the High Contracting Parties.

2. As soon as the ratifications of the United States of America, of His Majesty the King of Great Britain, Ireland and the British Dominions beyond the Seas, Emperor of India, in respect of each and all of the Members of the British Commonwealth of Nations as enumerated in the preamble of the present Treaty, and of His Majesty the Emperor of Japan have been deposited, the Treaty shall come into force in respect of the said High Contracting Parties.

3. On the date of the coming into force referred to in the preceding paragraph, Parts I, II, IV and V of the present Treaty will come into force in respect of the French Republic and the Kingdom of Italy if their ratifications have been deposited at that date; otherwise these Parts will come into force in respect of each of those Powers on the deposit of its ratification.

4. The rights and obligations resulting from Part III of the present Treaty are limited to the High Contracting Parties mentioned in paragraph 2 of this Article. The High Contracting Parties will agree as to the date on which, and the conditions under which, the obligations assumed under the said Part III by the High Contracting Parties mentioned in paragraph 2 of this Article will bind them in relation to France and Italy; such agreement will determine at the same time the corresponding obligations of France and Italy in relation to the other High Contracting Parties.

ARTICLE 25

After the deposit of the ratifications of all the High Contracting Parties, His Majesty's Government in the United Kingdom of Great Britain and Northern Ireland will communicate the provisions inserted in Part IV of the present Treaty to all Powers which are not signatories of the said Treaty, inviting them to accede thereto definitely and without limit of time.

Such accession shall be effected by a declaration addressed to His Majesty's Government in the United Kingdom of Great Britain and Northern Ireland.

ARTICLE 26

The present Treaty, of which the French and English texts are both authentic, shall remain deposited in the archives of His Majesty's Government in the United Kingdom of Great Britain and Northern Ireland. Duly certified copies thereof shall be transmitted to the Governments of all the High Contracting Parties.

In faith whereof the above-named Plenipotentiaries have signed the present Treaty and have affixed thereto their seals.

Done at London, the twenty-second day of April, nineteen hundred and thirty.

[For the United States:]
  HENRY L. STIMSON
  CHARLES G. DAWES
  CHARLES F. ADAMS
  JOSEPH T. ROBINSON
  DAVID A. REED
  HUGH GIBSON
  DWIGHT W. MORROW

[For France:]
  ARISTIDE BRIAND
  J. L. DUMESNIL
  A. DE FLEURIAU

[For the United Kingdom:]
  J. RAMSAY MACDONALD
  ARTHUR HENDERSON
  A. V. ALEXANDER
  W. WEDGWOOD BENN

[For the Dominion of Canada:]
  PHILIPPE ROY

[For the Commonwealth of Australia:]
  JAMES E. FENTON

[For the Dominion of New Zealand:]
  T. M. WILFORD
  C. T. TE WATER

[For the Irish Free State:]
  T. A. SMIDDY

[For India:]
  ATUL C. CHATTERJEE

[For Italy:]
  G. SIRIANNI
  A. C. BORDONARO
  ALFREDO ACTON

[For Japan:]
  R. WAKATSUKI
  TAKESHI TAKARABE
  T. MATSUDAIRA
  M. NAGAI

EXCHANGES OF NOTES

The American Ambassador to the Japanese Minister for Foreign Affairs

No. 49.   EMBASSY OF THE UNITED STATES OF AMERICA,
TOKYO, *May 21, 1930.*

EXCELLENCY:

I have the honor, by direction of my Government, to state that it is the understanding of the Government of the United States that the word "category" in Article 19 of the London Naval Treaty of 1930 means "category" or "subcategory". The Government of the United States declares that it interprets the Treaty to mean that vessels becoming over age in either sub-category "A" or subcategory "B" of the cruiser categories (Article 16) shall be replaceable only in that subcategory.

The American Government will be most happy to have the confirmation of this understanding from the Japanese Government.

I avail myself of this opportunity to renew to Your Excellency the assurances of my highest consideration.

W. R. CASTLE, JR.

HIS EXCELLENCY
 BARON KIJURO SHIDEHARA,
  His Imperial Japanese Majesty's Minister
  for Foreign Affairs, etc., etc., etc.

———— ————

The Japanese Minister for Foreign Affairs to the American Ambassador

[TRANSLATION]

No. 66/T1   DEPARTMENT OF FOREIGN AFFAIRS,
          TOKYO, *May 24, 1930.*

EXCELLENCY:

I have the honor to acknowledge receipt of your Note dated May 21, 1930, relative to the interpretation of the term "category" appearing in Article 19 of the London Naval Treaty of 1930.

The Imperial Government understands the word "category" appearing in Article 19 of the above-mentioned treaty to mean "category" or "sub-category;" thus, it interprets this treaty in the sense that ships belonging to either sub-category (*a*) or sub-category (*b*) of the cruiser category (Article 16) which shall become over age may be replaced only within that sub-category.

I avail myself of this opportunity to renew to Your Excellency the assurances of my highest consideration.

BARON KIJURO SHIDEHARA,
Minister for Foreign Affairs.
[SEAL]

HIS EXCELLENCY
 W. R. CASTLE, JR.,
  Ambassador Extraordinary and Plenipotentiary
  of the United States of America.

The American Ambassador to the British Secretary of State for Foreign Affairs

No. 611.   EMBASSY OF THE UNITED STATES OF AMERICA
                                LONDON, *June 5, 1930.*

SIR:

It is the understanding of the Government of the United States that the word "category" in Article 19 of the London Naval Treaty of 1930 means category or sub-category. The Government of the United States declares that it interprets the Treaty to mean that vessels becoming over-age of either sub-category A or sub-category B of the cruiser categories (Article 16) shall be replaceable only in that sub-category.

I have the honor to state that my Government would be most happy to have a note of confirmation as to whether this interpretation is shared by His Majesty's Government.

I have the honor to be, with the highest consideration, Sir,
            Your most obedient, humble Servant,
                                (For the Ambassador)
                                        RAY ATHERTON
                                        Counselor of Embassy.

THE RIGHT HON^BLE
    ARTHUR HENDERSON, M. P., etc., etc., etc.,
        Foreign Office, S. W. 1.

––––––

The British Secretary of State for Foreign Affairs to the American Ambassador

A 3861/1/45.   FOREIGN OFFICE, S. W. 1.
                                June 5th, 1930.

YOUR EXCELLENCY,

In the note No. 611 which Your Excellency was so good as to address to me on June 5th you stated that it was the understanding of the Government of the United States that the word "category" in Article 19 of the London Naval Treaty, 1930, meant category or sub-category. Your Excellency added that the Government of the United States declared that it interpreted the Treaty to mean that vessels becoming over-age of either sub-category A or sub-category B of the cruiser categories (Article 16) shall be replaceable only in that sub-category.

2. His Majesty's Government in the United Kingdom note the above understanding and interpretation of the London Naval Treaty of 1930 and concur therein. His Majesty's Government in the United Kingdom do so without prejudice to Article 20(a) of that Treaty under which they understand that the tonnage to be scrapped and replaced in the case of the British Commonwealth of Nations by the 91,000 tons of 6″ cruiser tonnage which

may be completed before 31st December, 1936, comprises partly 6″ gun cruiser tonnage and partly cruiser tonnage of the 7.5″ gun "Effingham" class.

I have the honour to be, with the highest consideration,

Your Excellency's obedient Servant,

(For the Secretary of State)

ROBERT VANSITTART

HIS EXCELLENCY

GENERAL CHARLES G. DAWES, C. B.,

&c., &c., &c.

LOAD LINES

*Convention and final protocol signed at London July 5, 1930, with
annexes; final act of the International Load Line Conference,
July 5, 1930* [1]
Senate advice and consent to ratification, February 27, 1931
Ratified by the President of the United States May 1, 1931
Ratification of the United States deposited at London June 10, 1931
Entered into force January 1, 1933
*Proclaimed by the President of the United States, with a declaration,
January 5, 1933* [2]
Modified and amended August 23, 1938, [3] *July 13, 1957,* [4] *and August 7,
1959* [5]
Superseded by convention of April 5, 1966, [6] *as between contracting
parties to the later convention, to the extent that their provisions
conflict*

47 Stat. 2228; Treaty Series 858

International Load Line Convention

PREAMBLE

THE Governments of Germany, the Commonwealth of Australia, Belgium,
Canada, Chile, Cuba, Denmark, the Free City of Danzig, Spain, the Irish
Free State, the United States of America, Finland, France, the United King-
dom of Great Britain and Northern Ireland, Greece, India, Iceland, Italy,
Japan, Latvia, Mexico, Norway, New Zealand, Paraguay, the Netherlands,
Peru, Poland, Portugal, Sweden, and the Union of Socialist Soviet Republics;
desiring to promote safety of life and property at sea by establishing in com-
mon agreement uniform principles and rules with regard to the limits to which
ships on international voyages may be loaded, have resolved to conclude a
Convention for that purpose and have appointed as their Plenipotentiaries:

The Government of Germany:

Mr. Gustav Koenigs, Ministerialdirigent in the Reichsverkehrsministerium,
Geheimer Regierungsrat, Berlin.

Mr. Arthur Werner, Ministerialrat in the Reichsverkehrsministerium,
Geheimer Justizrat, Berlin.

---

[1] For exchanges of notes relating to modifications of the French text of the rules contained in annex I, see 47 Stat. 2394 or p. 187 of TS 858.

[2] For text of U.S. declaration, made at time of signing and maintained in the President's
proclamation, see p. 1148.

[3] TS 942, *post*, vol. 3.

[4] 10 UST 1271; TIAS 4266.

[5] 11 UST 1992; TIAS 4550.

[6] 18 UST 1857; TIAS 6331.

Professor Walter Laas, Director of the "Germanischer Lloyd" Classification Society, Berlin.

Mr. Karl Sturm, Verwaltungsdirector of the See-Berufsgenossenschaft, Hamburg.

The Government of the Commonwealth of Australia:

Captain Henry Priaulx Cayley, Royal Australian Navy, Commonwealth Naval Representative in London.

Mr. Vincent Cyril Duffy, Australia House.

The Government of Belgium:

Mr. Raoul F. Grimard, Naval Engineer, Technical Adviser to the Central Naval Department.

The Government of Canada:

Mr. Alexander Johnston, Deputy Minister of Marine.

The Government of Chile:

Lieut.-Commander Constructor Oscar Bunster, Member of the Chilian Naval Commission in London.

The Government of Cuba:

Mr. Guillermo Patterson, Cuban Minister in London.

The Government of Denmark:

Mr. Emil Krogh, Assistant Secretary in the Ministry of Shipping and Fisheries.

Mr. Aage H. Larsen, Naval Architect and Engineer in Chief to the Ministry of Shipping and Fisheries.

Mr. J. A. Körbing, Director of the "Forenede Dampskibsselskab," Copenhagen.

Captain H. P. Hagelberg, Chairman of the Association of Danish Shipmasters.

Mr. Erik Jacobsen, Trade Union Manager.

The Government of the Free City of Danzig:

Mr. Alphonse Poklewski-Koziell, Commercial Counsellor, Polish Legation, London.

Mr. Waldemar Sieg, Commercial Counsellor.

The Government of Spain:

Mr. Octaviano Martinez-Barca, Engineer, Spanish Navy.

The Government of the Irish Free State:

Mr. J. W. Dulanty, Commissioner for Trade for the Irish Free State in Great Britain.

Mr. T. J. Hegarty, Ship Surveyor, Transport and Marine Branch, Department of Industry and Commerce.

The Government of the United States of America:

Mr. Herbert B. Walker, President of the American Steamship Owners' Association.

Mr. David Arnott, Chief Surveyor, American Bureau of Shipping.

Mr. Laurens Prior, Bureau of Navigation, Department of Commerce.

Mr. Howard C. Towle, National Council of American Shipbuilders.

Mr. Samuel D. McComb, Marine Office of America.

Captain Albert F. Pillsbury, Pillsbury and Curtis, San Francisco.

Mr. Robert F. Hand, Vice-President Standard Shipping Company, New York.

Mr. James Kennedy, General Manager, Marine Department, Gulf Refining Company, New York.

Mr. H. W. Warley, Vice-President Ore Steamship Corporation, New York.

Rear-Admiral John G. Tawresey, C.C., United States Navy (Retired). United States Shipping Board.

The Government of Finland:

Mr. A. H. Saastamoinen, Finnish Minister in London.

Commander Birger Brandt, Finnish Shipmasters' Association.

The Government of France:

Mr. André Maurice Haarbleicher, Naval Construction Corps, Director of the Departments of the Mercantile Fleet and of Naval Material at the Ministry of the Mercantile Marine.

Mr. René Hippolyte Joseph Lindemann, Assistant Director of the Department of Marine Labour and of the Accountants' Department at the Ministry of the Mercantile Marine.

Mr. Jean Henri Théophile Marie, Naval Construction Corps, Assistant to the Director of the Departments of the Mercantile Fleet and of Naval Material at the Ministry of the Mercantile Marine.

Mr. A.H.A. de Berlhe, Deputy Manager of the Bureau Veritas.

The Government of the United Kingdom of Great Britain and Northern Ireland:

Sir Henry F. Oliver, Admiral of the Fleet, Royal Navy.

Captain F. W. Bate, Professional Officer, Mercantile Marine Department, Board of Trade.

Mr. A. J. Daniel, Principal Ship Surveyor, Board of Trade.

Captain J. T. Edwards, Master Mariner (Retired).

Sir Ernest W. Glover, Chamber of Shipping of the United Kingdom.

Sir Norman Hill, Chairman, Merchant Shipping Advisory Committee, Board of Trade.

Sir Charles Hipwood, Board of Trade.

Mr. J. Foster King, Chief Surveyor to the British Corporation Register of Shipping and Aircraft.

Dr. J. Montgomerie, Chief Ship Surveyor to Lloyd's Register of Shipping.

Sir Charles J. O. Sanders, Chairman, Load-Line Committee, 1927–1929.

Mr. William Robert Spence, General Secretary, National Union of Seamen.

Captain A. Spencer, Master Mariner (Retired).

The Government of Greece:

Mr. Nicolas G. Lely, Consul-General for Greece in London.

The Government of India:

Sir Geoffrey L. Corbett, Late Secretary to the Government of India, Commerce Department.

Mr. Nowrojee Dadabhoy Allbless, Chairman of Scindia Steamships (London) Ltd.

Captain Kavas Ookerjee, Marine Superintendent, Scindia Steam Navigation Company, Ltd., Bombay.

Engineer-Commander John Sutherland Page, Royal Indian Marine, late Principal Engineer and Ship Surveyor, Government of Bengal.

The Government of Iceland:

Mr. Emil Krogh, Assistant Secretary to the Danish Ministry of Shipping and Fisheries.

Mr. Aage H. Larsen, Naval Architect and Engineer in Chief to the Danish Ministry of Shipping and Fisheries.

Mr. J. A. Körbing, Director of the "Forenede Dampskibsselskab," Copenhagen.

Captain H. P. Hagelberg, Chairman of the Association of Danish Shipmasters.

Mr. Erik Jacobsen, Trade Union Manager, Denmark.

The Government of Italy:

General Giulio Ingianni, General Director of the Mercantile Marine.

Admiral Giuseppe Cantù, Admiral of Division, Technical Inspector of the Mercantile Marine.

Professor Torquato Giannini, Counsellor for Emigration in the Italian Foreign Office.

The Government of Japan:

Mr. Shoichi Nakayama, First Class Secretary of Embassy, London.

Mr. Sukefumi Iwai, Expert in the Local Administration Office of Communications.

The Government of Latvia:

Mr. Arturs Ozols, Director of the Marine Department.

Captain Andrejs Lonfelds, Latvian Shipowners' Society.

The Government of Mexico:

Mr. Gustavo Luders de Negri, Consul-General for Mexico in London.

The Government of Norway:

Mr. Erling Bryn, Director of the Department of Shipping, Ministry of Commerce and Navigation.

Mr. Johan Schönheyder, Surveyor-in-Chief in the Ministry of Commerce and Navigation.

Dr. J. Bruhn, Director of the Norwegian Veritas.

Mr. J. Hysing Olsen, Shipowner.

Mr. Eivind Tonnesen, Managing Director of the Norwegian Shipmasters' Association.

Mr. A. Birkeland, President of the Norwegian Sailors' and Firemen's Union.

The Government of New Zealand:

Sir Thomas Mason Wilford, High Commissioner for New Zealand in London.

Sir Charles Holdsworth, Managing Director of the Union Steamship Company of New Zealand, Ltd.

The Government of Paraguay:

Dr. Horacio Carisimo, Chargé d'Affaires in London.

The Government of the Netherlands:

Vice-Admiral (retired) C. Fock, Inspector-General of Navigation, Chairman of the Freeboard Assigning Commission.

Mr. A. van Driel, Naval Architect, Adviser on Naval Architecture to the Shipping Inspection Service, Member and Secretary of the Freeboard Assigning Commission.

Mr. J. Brautigam, Chairman of the Netherlands Union of Transport Workers, Member of the Second Chamber of the States-General.

Mr. J. W. Langeler, Inspector of Shipping, Dutch East Indies.

Mr. J. Rypperda Wierdsma, Chairman of the Holland-America Line.

Captain G. L. Heeris, Secretary of the Netherlands Shipowners' Association.

The Government of Peru:

Captain Manuel D. Faura, Naval Attaché in London.

The Government of Poland:

Mr. Alphonse Poklewski-Koziell, Commercial Counsellor, Polish Embassy, London.

Mr. Boguslaw Bagniewski, Counsellor, Ministry of Industry and Trade, Warsaw.

The Government of Portugal:

Mr. Thomaz Ribeiro de Mello, Minister Plenipotentiary; Head of the Economic Section of the Portuguese Ministry of Foreign Affairs.

Captain Carlos Theodoro da Costa, Naval Architect.

The Government of Sweden:

Baron Erik Kule Palmstierna, Swedish Minister in London.

Mr. Per Axel Lindblad, Assistant Under-Secretary in the Board of Trade.

Captain Erik Axel Fredrik Eggert, Maritime Expert to the Social Board.

The Government of the Union of Socialist Soviet Republics:

Mr. Dimitri Bogomoloff, Counsellor of the Soviet Embassy in London.

Who, having communicated their full powers, found in good and due form, have agreed as follows:

CHAPTER I. PRELIMINARY

ARTICLE 1

General Obligation of Convention

So that the load lines prescribed by this Convention shall be observed, the Contracting Governments undertake to give effect to the provisions of this Convention, to promulgate all regulations, and to take all other steps which may be necessary to give this Convention full and complete effect.

The provisions of this Convention are completed by Annexes, which have the same force and take effect at the same time as this Convention. Every reference to this Convention implies at the same time a reference to the Rules annexed thereto.

ARTICLE 2

Scope of Convention

1. This Convention applies to all ships engaged on international voyages, which belong to countries the Governments of which are Contracting Governments, or to territories to which this Convention is applied under Article 21, except—

(a) ships of war; ships solely engaged in fishing; pleasure yachts and ships not carrying cargo or passengers;

(b) ships of less than 150 tons gross.

2. Ships when engaged on international voyages between the near neighbouring ports of two or more countries may be exempted by the Administration to which such ships belong from the provisions of this Convention, so long as they shall remain in such trades, if the Governments of the countries in which such ports are situated shall be satisfied that the sheltered nature and conditions of such voyages between such ports make it unreasonable or impracticable to apply the provisions of this Convention to ships engaged in such trades.

3. All agreements and arrangements relating to load line or matters appertaining thereto at present in force between Contracting Governments

shall continue to have full and complete effect during the terms thereof as regards—

(*a*) ships to which this Convention does not apply;

(*b*) ships to which this Convention applies in respect of matters for which it has not expressly provided.

To the extent, however, that such agreements or arrangements conflict with the provisions of this Convention, the provisions of this Convention shall prevail.

Subject to any such agreement or arrangement—

(*a*) all ships to which this Convention does not apply; and

(*b*) all matters which are not expressly provided for in this Convention;

shall remain subject to the legislation of each Contracting Government to the same extent as if this Convention had not been made.

ARTICLE 3

Definitions

In this Convention, unless expressly provided otherwise—

(*a*) a ship is regarded as belonging to a country if it is registered by the Government of that country;

(*b*) the expression "Administration" means the Government of the country to which the ship belongs;

(*c*) an "international voyage" is a voyage from a country to which this Convention applies to a port outside such country, or conversely, and for this purpose, every colony, overseas territory, protectorate or territory under suzerainty or mandate is regarded as a separate country;

(*d*) the expression "Rules" means the Rules contained in Annexes I, II and III;

(*e*) a "new ship" is a ship, the keel of which is laid on or after the 1st July, 1932, all other ships being regarded as existing ships.

(*f*) the expression "steamer" includes any vessel propelled by machinery.

ARTICLE 4

Cases of "Force Majeure"

No ship, which is not subject to the provisions of this Convention at the time of its departure on any voyage, shall become subject to the provisions of this Convention on account of any deviation from its intended voyage due to stress of weather or any other cause of *force majeure*.

In applying the provisions of this Convention, the Administration shall give due consideration to any deviation or delay caused to any ship owing to stress of weather or to any other cause of *force majeure*.

CHAPTER II. LOAD LINE: SURVEY AND MARKING

ARTICLE 5

General Provisions

No ship to which this Convention applies shall proceed to sea on an international voyage after the date on which this Convention comes into force, unless the ship, being—

A—a new ship,

(*a*) has been surveyed in accordance with the provisions of Annex I;
(*b*) complies with the provisions of Part II of Annex I; and
(*c*) has been marked in accordance with the provisions of this Convention.

B—an existing ship,

(*a*) has been surveyed and marked (whether before or after this Convention comes into force) in accordance with the conditions prescribed either in paragraph A of this Article or in one of the sets of Rules for the Assignment of Load Line particularised in Annex IV; and

(*b*) complies with the provisions of Part II of Annex I in principle, and also in detail, so far as is reasonable and practicable, having regard to the efficiency of (i) the protection of openings; (ii) guard rails; (iii) freeing ports, and (iv) means of access to crews' quarters provided by the existing arrangements, fittings and appliances on the ship.

ARTICLE 6

Provisions for Steamers carrying Timber Deck Cargoes

1. A steamer which has been surveyed and marked under Article 5 shall be entitled to be surveyed and marked with a timber load line under Part V of Annex I if, being—

A—a new ship, it complies with the conditions and provisions prescribed in Part V of Annex I;

B—an existing ship, it complies with the conditions and provisions of Part V of Annex I other than Rule LXXX, and also in principle, so far as is reasonable and practicable, with the conditions and provisions prescribed by Rule LXXX provided that in assigning a timber load line to an existing ship the Administration shall make such addition to the freeboard as shall be reasonable having regard to the extent to which such ship falls short of full compliance with the conditions and provisions prescribed in Rule LXXX.

2. A steamer when using the timber load line shall comply with Rules LXXXIV, LXXXV, LXXXVI, LXXXVIII and LXXXIX.

ARTICLE 7

Provisions for Tankers

A steamer which has been surveyed under Article 5 shall be entitled to be surveyed and marked as a tanker under Part VI of Annex I if, being—

A—a new ship, it complies with the conditions and provisions prescribed in Part VI of Annex I;

B—an existing ship, it complies with the conditions and provisions in Rules XCIII, XCVI, XCVII, XCVIII and XCIX, and also in principle so far as is reasonable and practicable with Rules XCIV, XCV and C, provided that in assigning a tanker load line to an existing ship the Administration shall make such addition to the freeboard as shall be reasonable having regard to the extent to which such ship falls short of full compliance with the conditions and provisions prescribed in Rules XCIV, XCV and C.

ARTICLE 8

Provisions for Ships of Special Types

For steamers over 300 feet in length, possessing constructional features similar to those of a tanker which afford extra invulnerability against the sea, a reduction in freeboard may be granted.

The amount of such reduction shall be determined by the Administration in relation to the freeboard assigned to tankers, having regard to the degree of compliance with the conditions of assignment laid down for these ships, and the degree of subdivision provided.

The freeboard assigned to such a ship shall in no case be less than would be assigned to the ship as a tanker.

ARTICLE 9

Survey

The survey and marking of ships for the purpose of this Convention shall be carried out by officers of the country to which the ships belong, provided that the Government of each country may entrust the survey and marking of its ships either to Surveyors nominated for this purpose, or to organizations recognized by it. In every case the Government concerned fully guarantees the completeness and efficiency of the survey and marking.

ARTICLE 10

Zones and Seasonal Areas

A ship to which this Convention applies shall conform to the conditions applicable to the zones and seasonal areas described in Annex II to this Convention.

A port standing on the boundary line between two zones shall be regarded as within the zone from or into which the ship arrives or departs.

CHAPTER III. CERTIFICATES

ARTICLE 11

Issue of Certificates

A certificate, called "International Load Line Certificate," shall be issued to every ship which has been surveyed and marked in accordance with this Convention, but not otherwise.

An International Load Line Certificate shall be issued either by the Government of the country to which the ship belongs or by any person or organisation duly authorised by that Government, and in every case the Government assumes full responsibility for the certificate.

ARTICLE 12

Issue of Certificates by another Government

The Government of a country to which this Convention applies may, at the request of the Government of any other country to which this Convention applies, cause any ship which belongs to the last-mentioned country, or (in the case of an unregistered ship) which is to be registered by the Government of that country, to be surveyed and marked, and, if satisfied that the requirements of this Convention are complied with, issue an International Load Line Certificate to such ship, under its own responsibility. Any certificate so issued must contain a statement to the effect that it has been issued at the request of the Government of the country to which the ship belongs, or of the Government by whom the ship is to be registered, as the case may be, and it shall have the same force and receive the same recognition as a certificate issued under Article 11 of this Convention.

ARTICLE 13

Form of Certificate

The International Load Line Certificates shall be drawn up in the official language or languages of the country by which they are issued.

The form of the certificate shall be that of the model given in Annex III, subject to such modifications as may, in accordance with Rule LXXVIII, be made in the case of ships carrying timber deck cargoes.

ARTICLE 14

Duration of Certificates

1. An International Load Line Certificate shall, unless it is renewed in accordance with the provisions of paragraph 2 of this Article, expire at the

end of such period as may be specified therein by the Administration which issues it: but the period so specified shall not exceed five years from the date of issue.

2. An International Load Line Certificate may be renewed from time to time by the Administration which issued it for such period (not exceeding five years on any occasion) as the Administration thinks fit, after a survey not less effective than the survey required by this Convention before the issue of the certificate, and any such renewal shall be endorsed on the certificate.

3. An Administration shall cancel any International Load Line Certificate issued to a ship belonging to its country:

A. If material alterations have taken place in the hull and superstructures of the ship which affect the calculations of freeboard.

B. If the fittings and appliances for the (i) protection of openings, (ii) guard rails, (iii) freeing ports and (iv) means of access to crews' quarters are not maintained in as effective a condition as they were in when the certificate was issued.

C. If the ship is not inspected periodically at such times and under such conditions as the Administration may think necessary for the purpose of securing that the hull and superstructures referred to in Condition A are not altered and that the fittings and appliances referred to in Condition B are maintained as therein provided throughout the duration of the certificate.

ARTICLE 15

Acceptance of Certificates

International Load Line Certificates issued under the authority of a Contracting Government shall be accepted by the other Contracting Governments as having the same force as the certificates issued by them to ships belonging to their respective countries.

ARTICLE 16

Control

1. A ship to which this Convention applies, when in a port of a country to which it does not belong, is in any case subject to control with respect to load line as follows: An officer duly authorised by the Government of that country may take such steps as may be necessary for the purpose of seeing that there is on board a valid International Load Line Certificate. If there is such a certificate on board the ship, such control shall be limited to the purpose of securing—

(a) that the ship is not loaded beyond the limits allowed by the certificate;

(b) that the position of the load line on the ship corresponds with the certificate; and

(c) that the ship has not been so materially altered in respect to the matters dealt with in conditions A and B (set out in paragraph 3 of Article 14) that the ship is manifestly unfit to proceed to sea without danger to human life.

2. Only officers possessing the necessary technical qualifications shall be authorised to exercise control as aforesaid, and if such control is exercised under (c) above, it shall only be exercised in so far as may be necessary to secure that the ship shall be made fit to proceed to sea without danger to human life.

3. If control under this Article appears likely to result in legal proceedings being taken against the ship, or in the ship being detained, the Consul of the country to which the ship belongs shall be informed as soon as possible of the circumstances of the case.

ARTICLE 17

Privileges

The privileges of this Convention may not be claimed in favour of any ship unless it holds a valid International Load Line Certificate.

CHAPTER IV. GENERAL PROVISIONS

ARTICLE 18

Equivalents

Where in this Convention it is provided that a particular fitting, or appliance, or type thereof, shall be fitted or carried in a ship, or that any particular arrangement shall be adopted, any Administration may accept in substitution therefor any other fitting, or appliance, or type thereof, or any other arrangement, provided that such Administration shall have been satisfied that the fitting, or appliance, or type thereof, or the arrangement substituted is in the circumstances at least as effective as that specified in this Convention.

Any Administration which so accepts a new fitting, or appliance, or type thereof, or new arrangement shall communicate the fact to the other Administrations, and, upon request, the particulars thereof.

ARTICLE 19

Laws, Regulations, Reports

The Contracting Governments undertake to communicate to each other—

(1) the text of laws, decrees, regulations and decisions of general application which shall have been promulgated on the various matters within the scope of this Convention;

(2) all available official reports or official summaries of reports in so far as they show the results of the provisions of this Convention, provided always that such reports or summaries are not of a confidential nature.

The Government of the United Kingdom of Great Britain and Northern Ireland is invited to serve as an intermediary for collecting all this information and for bringing it to the knowledge of the other Contracting Governments.

ARTICLE 20

Modifications, Future Conferences

1. Modifications of this Convention which may be deemed useful or necessary improvements may at any time be proposed by any Contracting Government to the Government of the United Kingdom of Great Britain and Northern Ireland, and such proposals shall be communicated by the latter to all the other Contracting Governments, and if any such modifications are accepted by all the Contracting Governments (including Governments which have deposited ratifications or accessions which have not yet become effective) this Convention shall be modified accordingly.

2. Conferences for the purpose of revising this Convention shall be held at such times and places as may be agreed upon by the Contracting Governments.

A Conference for this purpose shall be convoked by the Government of the United Kingdom of Great Britain and Northern Ireland whenever, after this Convention has been in force for five years, one-third of the Contracting Governments express a desire to that effect.

CHAPTER V. FINAL PROVISIONS

ARTICLE 21

Application to Colonies

1. A Contracting Government may, at the time of signature, ratification, accession or thereafter, by a notification in writing addressed to the Government of the United Kingdom of Great Britain and Northern Ireland, declare its desire that this Convention shall apply to all or any of its Colonies, overseas territories, protectorates or territories under suzerainty or mandate, and this Convention shall apply to all the territories named in such notification, two months after the date of the receipt thereof, but, failing such notification, this Convention will not apply to any such territories.

2. A Contracting Government may at any time by a notification in writing addressed to the Government of the United Kingdom of Great Britain and Northern Ireland express its desire that this Convention shall cease to apply to all or any of its colonies, overseas territories, protectorates or territories under

suzerainty or mandate to which this Convention shall have, under the provisions of the preceding paragraph, been applicable for a period of not less than five years, and in such case the Convention shall cease to apply twelve months after the date of the receipt of such notification by the Government of the United Kingdom of Great Britain and Northern Ireland to all territories mentioned therein.

3. The Government of the United Kingdom of Great Britain and Northern Ireland shall inform all the other Contracting Governments of the application of this Convention to any Colony, overseas territory, protectorate or territory under suzerainty or mandate under the provisions of paragraph 1 of this Article, and of the cessation of any such application under the provisions of paragraph 2, stating in each case the date from which this Convention has become or will cease to be applicable.

Article 22

Authentic Texts, Ratification

This Convention, of which both the English and French texts shall be authentic, shall be ratified.

The instruments of ratification shall be deposited in the archives of the Government of the United Kingdom of Great Britain and Northern Ireland, which will notify all the other signatory or acceding Governments of all ratifications desposited and the date of their deposit.

Article 23

Accession

A Government (other than the Government of a territory to which Article 21 applies) on behalf of which this Convention has not been signed, shall be allowed to accede thereto at any time after the Convention has come into force. Accessions shall be effected by means of notification in writing addressed to the Government of the United Kingdom of Great Britain and Northern Ireland, and shall take effect three months after their receipt.

The Government of the United Kingdom of Great Britain and Northern Ireland shall inform all signatory and acceding Governments of all accessions received and of the date of their receipt.

Article 24

Date of Coming in Force

This Convention shall come into force on the 1st July, 1932, as between the Governments which have deposited their ratifications by that date, and provided that at least five ratifications have been deposited with the Government of the United Kingdom of Great Britain and Northern Ireland. Should five ratifications not have been deposited by that date, this Convention shall come into force three months after the date on which the fifth ratification is deposited. Ratifications deposited after the date on which this Convention has come into force shall take effect three months after the date of their deposit.

ARTICLE 25

Denunciation

This Convention may be denounced on behalf of any Contracting Government at any time after the expiration of five years from the date on which the Convention comes into force in so far as that Government is concerned. Denunciation shall be effected by a notification in writing addressed to the Government of the United Kingdom of Great Britain and Northern Ireland, which will notify all the other contracting Governments of all denunciations received and of the date of their receipt.

A denunciation shall take effect twelve months after the date on which notification thereof is received by the Government of the United Kingdom of Great Britain and Northern Ireland.

In faith whereof, the Plenipotentiaries have signed hereafter.

Done at London this fifth day of July, 1930, in a single copy, which shall remain deposited in the archives of the Government of the United Kingdom of Great Britain and Northern Ireland, which shall transmit certified true copies thereof to all signatory Governments.

[For Germany:]
GUSTAV KOENIGS
WALTER LAAS
KARL STURM

[For Australia:]
H. P. CAYLEY
V. C. DUFFY

[For Belgium:]
R. GRIMARD

[For Canada:]
A. JOHNSTON

[For Chile:]
OSCAR BUNSTER

[For Cuba:]
GUILLERMO PATTERSON

[For Denmark:]
EMIL KROGH
AAGE H. LARSEN
H. P. HAGELBERG

[For Spain:]
OCTAVIANO M. BARCA

[For the Irish Free State:]
SEAN DULCHAONTIGH
T. J. HEGARTY

[For the United States:]
HERBERT B. WALKER
DAVID ARNOTT
LAURENS PRIOR
HOWARD C. TOWLE
ALBERT F. PILLSBURY
ROBERT F. HAND
JAS. KENNEDY
H. W. WARLEY
JOHN G. TAWRESEY

[For Sweden:]
E. PALMSTIERNA
E. EGGERT

[For Finland:]
A. H. SAASTAMOINEN
B. BRANDT

[For France:]
JEAN MARIE
A. DE BERLHE

[For the United Kingdom:]
H. F. OLIVER
F. W. BATE
ALFRED J. DANIEL
JOHN T. EDWARDS
ERNEST W. GLOVER
NORMAN HILL

C. Hipwood
J. Foster King
J. Montgomerie
Charles J. O. Sanders
W. R. Spence
A. Spencer

[For Greece:]
N. G. Lely

[For India:]
G. L. Corbett
Nowrojee Dadabhoy Allbless
Kavas Ookerjee
J. S. Page

[For Iceland:]
Emil Krogh
Aage H. Larsen
H. P. Hagelberg

[For Italy:]
Giulio Ingianni
Giuseppe Cantù

[For Japan:]
S. Nakayama
S. Iwai

[For Latvia:]
A. Ozols

[For Mexico:]
G. Luders de Negri

[For Norway:]
E. Bryn
J. Schönheyder

[For New Zealand:]
Thomas M. Wilford
C. Holdsworth

[For the Netherlands:]
C. Fock
A. van Driel
Joh. Brautigam
Langeler
J. R. Wierdsma

[For Peru:]
M. D. Faura

[For Poland:]
A. Poklewski-Koziell
B. Bagniewski

[For Portugal:]
Thomaz Ribeiro de Mello
Carlos Theodoro da Costa

[For the Union of Soviet Socialist
Republics:]
D. Bogomoloff

[For Paraguay:]
S. Horacio Carísimo

[For Italy:]
T. C. Giannini

Final Protocol

At the moment of signing the International Load Line Convention concluded this day, the under-mentioned Plenipotentiaries have agreed on the following:

I

Ships engaged solely on voyages on the Great Lakes of North America and ships engaged in other inland waters are to be regarded as outside the scope of the Convention.

II

This Convention is not applied to the existing ships of the United States of America and of France of the lumber schooner type propelled by power, with or without sails, or by sails alone.

III

The Government of the United Kingdom of Great Britain and Northern Ireland shall convoke a Conference of the Contracting Governments of the countries to which tankers belong, upon request of the United States of America, at any time within the five-year period mentioned in Article 20, for the purpose of discussing matters relating to tanker freeboard.

The Contracting Governments will not raise any objection to the provisions contained in this Convention in regard to tanker load line being altered as may be determined at such Conference, provided that the conclusions then reached are communicated forthwith to the Governments signatory to the present Convention and that no objection is received by the Government of the United Kingdom of Great Britain and Northern Ireland within six months of the despatch of such communication.

In Witness whereof the Plenipotentiaries have drawn up this Final Protocol which shall have the same force and the same validity as if the provisions thereof had been inserted in the text of the Convention to which it belongs.

Done at London this fifth day of July, 1930, in a single copy which shall be deposited in the archives of the Government of the United Kingdom of Great Britain and Northern Ireland, which shall transmit certified true copies thereof to all signatory Governments.

[For Germany:]
GUSTAV KOENIGS
WALTER LAAS
KARL STURM

[For Australia:]
H. P. CAYLEY
V. C. DUFFY

[For Belgium:]
R. GRIMARD

[For Canada:]
A. JOHNSTON

[For Chile:]
OSCAR BUNSTER

[For Cuba:]
GUILLERMO PATTERSON

[For Denmark:]
EMIL KROGH
AAGE H. LARSEN
H. P. HAGELBERG

[For Spain:]
OCTAVIANO M. BARCA

[For the Irish Free State:]
SEAN DULCHAONTIGH
T. J. HEGARTY

[For the United States:]
HERBERT B. WALKER
DAVID ARNOTT
LAURENS PRIOR
HOWARD C. TOWLE
ALBERT F. PILLSBURY
ROBERT F. HAND
JAS. KENNEDY
H. W. WARLEY
JOHN G. TAWRESEY

[For Sweden:]
E. PALMSTIERNA
E. EGGERT

[For Finland:]
A. H. SAASTAMOINEN
B. BRANDT

[For France:]
JEAN MARIE
A. DE BERLHE

[For the United Kingdom:]
H. F. OLIVER
F. W. BATE
ALFRED J. DANIEL
JOHN T. EDWARDS
ERNEST W. GLOVER
NORMAN HILL
C. HIPWOOD
J. FOSTER KING
J. MONTGOMERIE
CHARLES J. O. SANDERS
W. R. SPENCE
A. SPENCER

[For Greece:]
N. G. LELY

[For India:]
G. L. CORBETT
NOWROJEE DADABHOY ALLBLESS
KAVAS OOKERJEE
J. S. PAGE

[For Iceland:]
EMIL KROGH
AAGE H. LARSEN
H. P. HAGELBERG

[For Italy:]
GIULIO INGIANNI
GIUSEPPE CANTÙ

[For Japan:]
  S. Nakayama
  S. Iwai
[For Latvia:]
  A. Ozols
[For Mexico:]
  G. Luders de Negri
[For Norway:]
  E. Bryn
  J. Schönheyder
[For New Zealand:]
  Thomas M. Wilford
  C. Holdsworth
[For the Netherlands:]
  C. Fock
  A. van Driel
  Joh. Brautigam

Langeler
J. R. Wierdsma
[For Peru:]
  M. D. Faura
[For Poland:]
  A. Poklewski-Koziell
  B. Bagniewski
[For Portugal:]
  Thomaz Ribeiro de Mello
  Carlos Theodoro da Costa
[For the Union of Soviet Socialist Republics:]
  D. Bogomoloff
[For Paraguay:]
  S. Horacio Carísimo
[For Italy:]
  T. C. Giannini

Annex I

RULES FOR DETERMINING MAXIMUM LOAD LINES OF MERCHANT SHIPS

PART I. GENERAL

The Rules necessarily assume that the nature and stowage of the cargo, ballast, &c., are such as to secure sufficient stability for the ship.

Rule I. *Definitions*

Steamer.—The term "steamer" includes all ships having sufficient means for mechanical propulsion, except where provided with sufficient sail area for navigation under sails alone.

A ship fitted with mechanical means of propulsion and with sail area insufficient for navigation under sails alone may be assigned a load line under Part III of these Rules.

A lighter, barge or other ship without independent means of propulsion, when towed, is to be assigned a load line under Part III of these Rules.

Sailing Ship.—The term "sailing ship" includes all ships provided with sufficient sail area for navigation under sails alone, whether or not fitted with mechanical means of propulsion.

Flush Deck Ship.—A flush deck ship is one which has no superstructure on the freeboard deck.

Superstructure.—A superstructure is a decked structure on the freeboard deck extending from side to side of the ship. A raised quarter deck is considered a superstructure.

Freeboard.—The freeboard assigned is the distance measured vertically downwards at the side of the ship amidships from the upper edge of the deck line to the upper edge of the load line mark.

Freeboard Deck.—The freeboard deck is the deck from which the freeboard is measured, and is the uppermost complete deck having permanent means of closing all openings in weather portions of the deck in accordance with Rules VIII to XVI. It is the upper deck in flush deck ships and ships with detached superstructures.

In ships having discontinuous freeboard decks within superstructures which are not intact, or which are not fitted with Class 1 closing appliances, the lowest line of the deck below the superstructure deck is taken as the freeboard deck.

Amidships.—Amidships is the middle of the length of the summer load water-line, as defined in Rule XXXII.

Rule II. *Deck Line*

The deck line is a horizontal line twelve inches in length and one inch in breadth. It is to be marked amidships on each side of the ship, and its upper edge is to pass through the point where the continuation outwards of the upper surface of the freeboard deck intersects the outer surface of the shell. (See figure 1.) Where the deck is partly sheathed amidships, the upper edge of the deck line is to pass through the point where the continuation outwards of the upper surface of the actual sheathing at amidships intersects the outer surface of the shell.

Rule III. *Load Line Disc*

The load line disc is twelve inches in diameter and is intersected by a horizontal line eighteen inches in length and one inch in breadth, the upper edge of which passes through the centre of the disc. The disc is to be marked amidships below the deck line.

Rule IV. *Lines to be used in connection with the Disc*

The lines which indicate the maximum load line in different circumstances and in different seasons (see Annex II) are to be horizontal lines, nine inches in length and one inch in breadth, which extend from, and are at right angles to, a vertical line marked 21 inches forward of the centre of the disc (see figure 1).

The following are the lines to be used:

Summer Load Line. The Summer load line is indicated by the upper edge of the line which passes through the centre of the disc and also by a line marked S.

Winter Load Line. The Winter load line is indicated by the upper edge of a line marked W.

Winter North Atlantic Load Line. The Winter North Atlantic load line is indicated by the upper edge of a line marked WNA.

Tropical Load Line. The Tropical Load Line is indicated by the upper edge of a line marked T.

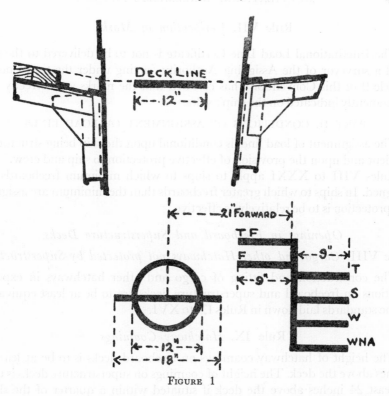

FIGURE 1

Fresh Water Load Lines. The Fresh Water load line in Summer is indicated by the upper edge of a line marked F. The difference between the Fresh Water load line in summer and the Summer load line is the allowance to be made for loading in Fresh Water at the other load lines. The Tropical Fresh Water load line is indicated by the upper edge of a line marked T.F.[7]

Rule V. *Mark of Assigning Authority*

The Authority by whom the load lines are assigned may be indicated by letters measuring about 4½ inches by 3 inches marked alongside the disc and above the centre line.

Rule VI. *Details of Marking*

The disc, lines and letters are to be painted in white or yellow on a dark ground or in black on a light ground. They are also to be carefully cut in or centre-punched on the sides of iron and steel ships, and on wood ships they are to be cut into the planking for at least one-eight of an inch. The marks are to be plainly visible, and, if necessary, special arrangements are to be made for this purpose.

---

[7] Where sea-going steamers navigate a river or inland water, deeper loading is permitted corresponding to the weight of fuel, &c., required for consumption between the point of departure and the open sea. [Footnote in original.]

Rule VII. *Verification of Marks*

The International Load Line Certificate is not to be delivered to the ship until a surveyor of the Assigning Authority (acting under the provisions of Article 9 of this Convention) has certified that the marks are correctly and permanently indicated on the ship's sides.

PART II. CONDITIONS OF ASSIGNMENT OF LOAD LINES

The assignment of load lines is conditional upon the ship being structurally efficient and upon the provision of effective protection to ship and crew.

Rules VIII to XXXI apply to ships to which minimum freeboards are assigned. In ships to which greater freeboards than the minimum are assigned, the protection is to be relatively as effective.

Openings in Freeboard and Superstructure Decks

Rule VIII. *Cargo and other Hatchways not protected by Superstructures*

The construction and fitting of cargo and other hatchways in exposed positions on freeboard and superstructure decks are to be at least equivalent to the standards laid down in Rules IX to XVI.

Rule IX. *Hatchway Coamings*

The height of hatchway coamings on freeboard decks is to be at least 24 inches above the deck. The height of coamings on superstructure decks is to be at least 24 inches above the deck if situated within a quarter of the ship's length from the stem, and at least 18 inches if situated elsewhere.

Coamings are to be of steel, are to be substantially constructed and, where required to be 24 inches high, are to be fitted with an efficient horizontal stiffener placed not lower than 10 inches below the upper edge, and fitted with efficient brackets or stays from the stiffener to the deck, at intervals of not more than 10 feet. Where end coamings are protected, these requirements may be modified.

Rule X. *Hatchway Covers*

Covers to exposed hatchways are to be efficient, and where they are made of wood, the finished thickness is to be at least $2\frac{3}{8}$ inches in association with a span of not more than 5 feet. The width of each bearing surface for these hatchway covers is to be at least $2\frac{1}{2}$ inches.

Rule XI. *Hatchway Beams and Fore-and-Afters*

Where wood hatchway covers are fitted the hatchway beams and fore-and-afters are to be of the scantlings and spacing given in Table 1 where coamings 24 inches high are required, and as given in Table 2 where coamings 18 inches high are required. Angle bar mountings on the upper edge are to extend continuously for the full length of each beam. Wood fore-and-afters are to be steel shod at all bearing surfaces.

TABLE 1

(Coamings 24 inches in height)

HATCHWAY BEAMS AND FORE-AND-AFTERS for Ships 200 feet or more in length*

HATCHWAY BEAMS

Breadth of Hatchway.	Mounting.	Beams with Fore-and-Afters. Spacing Centre to Centre.			Beams without Fore-and-Afters. Spacing Centre to Centre.	
		6' 0"	8' 0"	10' 0"	4' 0"	5' 0"
	ins. ins. ins.	ins. ins.	ins. ins.	ins. ins.	ins. ins.	ins. ins.
10' 0"	3 × 3 × .40A	11 × .30P	12 × .32P	14 × .34P	9 × .46BP	10 × .50BP
12' 0"	3 × 3 × .40A	12 × .32P	14 × .34P	17 × .36P	11 × .50BP	12 × .50BP
14' 0"	3 × 3 × .42A	14 × .34P	17 × .36P	20 × .38P	12 × .50BP	12 × .32P
16' 0"	3½ × 3 × .42A	16 × .36P	19 × .38P	22 × .38P	12 × .32P	14 × .34P
18' 0"	4 × 3 × .44A	18 × .36P	21 × .38P	25 × .40P	14 × .34P	16 × .36P
20' 0"	4 × 3 × .44A	20 × .38P	24 × .40P	28 × .42P	15 × .34P	18 × .36P
22' 0"	4½ × 3 × .46A	22 × .38P	26 × .42P	30 × .44P	16 × .36P	19 × .36P
24' 0"	5 × 3½ × .46A	23 × .40P	28 × .42P	32 × .44P	17 × .36P	20 × .38P
26' 0"	5½ × 3½ × .48A	24 × .40P	29 × .42P	34 × .46P	18 × .36P	21 × .38P
28' 0"	6 × 3½ × .50A	25 × .40P	31 × .44P	36 × .48P	19 × .38P	22 × .38P
30' 0"	6 × 3½ × .52A	26 × .42P	32 × .44P	38 × .48P	20 × .38P	23 × .40P

*In ships not exceeding 100 feet in length, the depths of beams which are formed of plates and angles may be 60 per cent. of the depths given above; the depths of beams and steel fore-and-afters formed of bulb angle or bulb plate section may be 80 per cent. of the depths given above; the thickness of plates, bulb angles and bulb plates should correspond to the thickness tabulated for the reduced depths with a minimum thickness of .30 inch; the depths and breadths of wood fore-and-afters may be 80 per cent. of those given in the tables for side fore-and-afters, but the centre fore-and-afters must be not less than 6½ inches wide. In ships between 100 feet and 200 feet in length, the sizes of the beams and fore-and-afters are to be determined by linear interpolation. [Footnote in original.]

FORE-AND-AFTERS

Length of Fore-and-Afters.	Mounting.	Bulb Plate. Centre Fore-and-Afters. Spacing Centre to Centre.			Bulb Angle. Side Fore-and-Afters. Spacing Centre to Centre.		
		3' 0''	4' 0''	5' 0''	3' 0''	4' 0''	5' 0''
	ins. × ins. = ins.	ins. × ins.	ins. × ins.	ins. × ins.	ins. × ins. × ins.	ins. × ins. × ins.	ins. × ins. × ins.
6' 0''	2½ × 2½ × .36	6 × .36	6½ × .38	7 × .38	6 × 3 × .36	6½ × 3½ × .38	7 × 3½ × .38
8' 0''	2½ × 2½ × .38	7 × .42	8 × .44	9 × .44	7 × 3½ × .42	8 × 3 × .44	9 × 3½ × .44
10' 0''	2½ × 2½ × .40	8 × .50	9½ × .50	11 × .50	8 × 3½ × .50	9½ × 3½ × .50	11 × 3½ × .50

	Wood Centre Fore-and-Afters. Spacing Centre to Centre.						Wood Side Fore-and-Afters. Spacing Centre to Centre.					
	3' 0''		4' 0''		5' 0''		3' 0''		4' 0''		5' 0''	
	D	B	D	B	D	B	D	B	D	B	D	B
	ins.	ins.	ins.	ins.	ins.	ins.	ins.	ins.	ins.	ins.	ins.	ins.
6' 0''	5½	7	6	6½	6½	7	5½	5½	6	6	6½	6
8' 0''	6½	7	7½	8	8	8	6½	6½	7½	7	8	7
10' 0''	8	8	8½	9	9	9	7	7	8½	8	9	9

A=Plain angle. BP=Bulb plate. P=Plate. D=Depth. B=Breadth.

Depths for hatchway beams are at the middle of the length and are measured from the top mounting to the lower edge. Depths for fore-and-afters are measured from the underside of the hatch covers to the lower edge. Sizes for intermediate lengths and spacing are obtained by interpolation. Where plates are specified, two angles, of the sizes given for mountings, are to be fitted at the upper and at the lower part of the beam. Where bulb plates are specified, two angles, of the size given for mountings, are to be fitted at the upper part of the beam or fore-and-after. Where bulb angles are specified, one angle, of the size given for mountings, is to be fitted at the upper part of the section. Where the specified flanges of an angle are of different dimensions, the larger flange is to be horizontal.

TABLE 2

(Coaming 18 inches in height)

HATCHWAY BEAMS AND FORE-AND-AFTERS FOR SHIPS 200 FEET OR MORE IN LENGTH*

HATCHWAY BEAMS

Breadth of Hatchway.	Mounting.	Beams with Fore-and-Afters. Spacing Centre to Centre.			Beams without Fore-and-Afters. Spacing Centre to Centre.	
		6' 0''	8' 0''	10' 0''	4' 0''	5' 0''
ins.	ins. × ins. × ins.	ins. × ins.	ins. × ins.	ins. × ins.	ins. × ins.	ins. × ins.
10' 0''	3 × 3 × .40A	9½ × .46BP	10½ × .50BP	11½ × .52BP	8 × .40BP	9 × .44BP
12' 0''	3 × 3 × .40A	11 × .50BP	11 × .30P	13 × .34P	9 × .44BP	10 × .50BP
14' 0''	3 × 3 × .42A	11 × .30P	13 × .32P	15 × .34P	10 × .50BP	11½ × .50BP
16' 0''	3½ × 3 × .42A	12 × .32P	15 × .34P	17 × .36P	11 × .30P	11 × .30P
18' 0''	4 × 3 × .44A	14 × .34P	17 × .36P	19 × .38P	11 × .30P	12 × .32P
20' 0''	4 × 3 × .44A	16 × .36P	19 × .38P	21 × .38P	12 × .32P	13 × .34P
22' 0''	4½ × 3 × .46A	17 × .36P	20 × .38P	23 × .40P	12½ × .32P	14 × .34P
24' 0''	5 × 3½ × .46A	18 × .36P	21 × .38P	25 × .40P	13 × .34P	14½ × .34P
26' 0''	5½ × 3½ × .48A	19 × .38P	22 × .38P	26 × .42P	13½ × .34P	15 × .34P
28' 0''	6 × 3½ × .50A	20 × .38P	23 × .40P	27 × .42P	14 × .34P	16 × .36P
30' 0''	6 × 3½ × .52A	21 × .38P	24 × .40P	28 × .42P	15 × .34P	17 × .36P

* In ships not exceeding 100 feet in length, the depths of beams which are formed of plates and angles may be 60 percent. of the depths given above; the depths of beams and steel fore-and-afters formed of bulb angle or bulb plate section may be 80 percent. of the depths given above; the thickness of plates, bulb angles and bulb plates should correspond to the thickness tabulated for the reduced depths with a minimum thickness of .30 inch; the depths and breadths of wood fore-and-afters may be 80 per cent of those given in the tables for side fore-and-afters, but the centre fore-and-afters must be not less than 6½ inches wide. In ships between 100 feet and 200 feet in length, the sizes of the beams and fore-and-afters are to be determined by linear interpolation. [Footnote in original.]

FORE-AND-AFTERS

Length of Fore-and-Afters.	Mounting.			Bulb Plate. Centre Fore-and-Afters. Spacing Centre to Centre.						Bulb Angle. Side Fore-and-Afters. Spacing Centre to Centre.		
				3' 0"		4' 0"		5' 0"		3' 0"	4' 0"	5' 0"
	ins.	ins.	ins.	ins.	ins.	ins.	ins.	ins.	ins.	ins.	ins.	ins.
6' 0"	2½ ×	2½ ×	.36	5 ×	.34	5½ ×	.34	6 ×	.36	5 × 3 × .34	5½ × 3 × .34	6 × 3 × .36
8' 0"	2½ ×	2½ ×	.38	6 ×	.38	7 ×	.40	7½ ×	.42	6 × 3 × .38	7 × 3 × .40	7½ × 3½ × .42
10' 0"	2½ ×	2½ ×	.40	7 ×	.44	8 ×	.46	9 ×	.50	7 × 3 × .44	8 × 3½ × .46	9 × 3½ × .50

	Wood Centre Fore-and-Afters. Spacing Centre to Centre.						Wood Side Fore-and-Afters. Spacing Centre to Centre.					
	3' 0"		4' 0"		5' 0"		3' 0"		4' 0"		5' 0"	
	D	B	D	B	D	B	D	B	D	B	D	B
	ins.	ins.	ins.	ins.	ins.	ins.	ins.	ins.	ins.	ins.	ins.	ins.
6' 0"	5	7	5½	7	6	7	5	5	5½	5	6	5
8' 0"	6	7	6½	7	7	7	5	5	6½	6	7	6
10' 0"	7	7	7½	7	8	7	6	6	7½	7	8	7

A=Plain angle.   BP=Bulb plate.   P=Plate.   D=Depth.   B=Breadth.

Depths for hatchway beams are at the middle of the length and are measured from the top mounting to the lower edge. Depths for fore-and-afters are measured from the under side of the hatch covers to the lower edge. Sizes for intermediate lengths and spacing are obtained by interpolation. Where plates are specified, two angles, of the sizes given for mountings, are to be fitted at the upper and at the lower part of the beam. Where bulb plates are specified, two angles, of the size given for mountings, are to be fitted at the upper part of the beam or fore-and-after. Where bulb angles are specified, one angle, of the size given for mountings, is to be fitted at the upper part of the section. Where the specified flanges of an angle are of different dimensions, the larger flange is to be horizontal.

Rule XII. *Carriers or Sockets*

Carriers or sockets for hatchway beams and fore-and-afters are to be of steel at least ½ inch thick, and are to have a width of bearing surface of at least 3 inches.

Rule XIII. *Cleats*

Strong cleats at least 2½ inches wide are to be fitted at intervals of not more than 2 feet from centre to centre; the end cleats are to be placed not more than 6 inches from each corner of the hatchway.

Rule XIV. *Battens and Wedges*

Battens and wedges are to be efficient and in good condition.

Rule XV. *Tarpaulins*

At least two tarpaulins in good condition, thoroughly waterproofed and of ample strength, are to be provided for each hatchway in an exposed position on freeboard and superstructure decks. The material is to be guaranteed free from jute, and of the standard weight and quality laid down by each Administration.

Rule XVI. *Security of Hatchway Covers*

At all hatchways in exposed positions on freeboard and superstructure decks ring bolts or other fittings for lashings are to be provided.

Where the breadth of the hatchway exceeds 60 per cent. of the breadth of the deck in way of the hatchway, and the coamings are required to be 24 inches high, fittings for special lashings are to be provided for securing the hatchway covers after the tarpaulins are battened down.

Rule XVII. *Cargo and other Hatchways in the Freeboard Deck within Superstructures which are fitted with Closing Appliances less efficient than Class 1*

The construction and fitting of such hatchways are to be at least equivalent to the standards laid down in Rule XVIII.

Rule XVIII. *Hatchway Coamings and Closing Arrangements*

Cargo, coaling and other hatchways in the freeboard deck within superstructures which are fitted with Class 2 closing appliances are to have coamings at least 9 inches in height and closing arrangements as effective as those required for exposed cargo hatchways whose coamings are 18 inches high.

Where the closing appliances are less efficient than Class 2, the hatchways are to have coamings at least 18 inches in height, and are to have fittings and closing arrangements as effective as those required for exposed cargo hatchways.

Rule XIX. *Machinery Space Openings in Exposed Positions on Freeboard and Raised Quarter Decks*

Such openings are to be properly framed and efficiently enclosed by steel casings of ample strength, and where the casings are not protected by other structures their strength is to be specially considered. Doors in such casings are to be of steel, efficiently stiffened, permanently attached, and capable of being closed and secured from both sides. The sills of openings are to be at least 24 inches above the freeboard deck and at least 18 inches above the raised quarter deck.

Fiddley, funnel, and ventilator coamings are to be as high above the deck as is reasonable and practicable. Fiddley openings are to have strong steel covers permanently attached in their proper positions.

Rule XX. *Machinery Space Openings in Exposed Positions on Super-structure Decks other than Raised Quarter Decks*

Such openings are to be properly framed and efficiently enclosed by strong steel casings. Doors in such cases are to be strongly constructed, permanently attached, and capable of being closed and secured from both sides. The sills of the openings are to be at least 15 inches above superstructure decks.

Fiddley, funnel and ventilator coamings are to be as high above the deck as is reasonable and practicable. Fiddley openings are to have strong steel covers permanently attached in their proper positions.

Rule XXI. *Machinery Space Openings in the Freeboard Deck within Super-structures which are fitted with Closing Appliances less efficient than Class* 1

Such openings are to be properly framed and efficiently enclosed by steel casings. Doors in such casings are to be strongly constructed, permanently attached, and capable of being securely closed. The sills of the openings are to be at least 9 inches above the deck where the superstructures are closed by Class 2 closing appliances, and at least 15 inches above the deck where the closing appliances are less efficient than Class 2.

Rule XXII. *Flush Bunker Scuttles*

Flush bunker scuttles may be fitted in superstructure decks, and where so fitted are to be of iron or steel, of substantial construction, with screw or bay-onet joints. Where a scuttle is not secured by hinges, a permanent chain at-tachment is to be provided. The position of flush bunker scuttles in small ships in special trades is to be dealt with by each Assigning Authority.

Rule XXIII. *Companionways*

Companionways in exposed positions on freeboard decks and on decks of enclosed superstructures are to be of substantial construction. The sills of the doorways are to be of the heights specified for hatchway coamings (see Rules IX and XVIII). The doors are to be strongly constructed and capable of being closed and secured from both sides. Where the companionway is situated within a quarter of the ship's length from the stem, it is to be of steel and riveted to the deck plating.

Rule XXIV. *Ventilators in Exposed Positions on Freeboard and Superstructure Decks*

Such ventilators to spaces below freeboard decks or decks of superstructures which are intact or fitted with Class 1 closing appliances are to have coamings of steel, substantially constructed, and efficiently connected to the deck by rivets spaced four diameters apart centre to centre, or by equally effective means. The deck plating at the base of the coaming is to be efficiently stiffened between the deck beams. The ventilator openings are to be provided with efficient closing arrangements.

Where such ventilators are situated on the freeboard deck, or on the superstructure deck within a quarter of the ship's length from the stem, and the closing arrangements are of a temporary character, the coamings are to be at least 36 inches in height; in other exposed positions on the superstructure deck they are to be at least 30 inches in height. Where the coaming of any ventilator exceeds 36 inches in height, it is to be specially supported and secured.

Rule XXV. *Air Pipes*

Where the air pipes to ballast and other tanks extend above freeboard or superstructure decks, the exposed parts of the pipes are to be of substantial construction; the height from the deck to the opening is to be at least 36 inches in wells on freeboard decks, 30 inches on raised quarter decks, and 18 inches on other superstructure decks. Satisfactory means are to be provided for closing the openings of the air pipes.

Openings in the Sides of Ships

Rule XXVI. *Gangway, Cargo and Coaling Ports, &c.*

Openings in the sides of ships below the freeboard deck are to be fitted with watertight doors or covers which, with their securing appliances, are to be of sufficient strength.

Rule XXVII. *Scuppers and Sanitary Discharge Pipes*

Discharges led through the ship's sides from spaces below the freeboard deck are to be fitted with efficient and accessible means for preventing water from passing inboard. Each separate discharge may have an automatic non-return valve with a positive means of closing it from a position above the freeboard deck, or two automatic non-return valves without positive means of closing, provided the upper valve is situated so that it is always accessible for examination under service conditions. The positive action valve is to be readily accessible and is to be provided with means for showing whether the valve is open or closed. Cast iron is not to be accepted for such valves where attached to the sides of the ship.

Conditional upon the type and the location of the inboard ends of such openings, similar provisions may be prescribed by the Assigning Authority as to discharges from spaces within enclosed superstructures.

Where scuppers are fitted in superstructures not fitted with Class 1 closing appliances they are to have efficient means for preventing the accidental admission of water below the freeboard deck.

Rule XXVIII. *Side Scuttles*

Side scuttles to spaces below the freeboard deck or to spaces below the superstructure deck of superstructures closed by Class 1 or Class 2 closing appliances are to be fitted with efficient inside deadlights permanently attached in their proper positions so that they can be effectively closed and secured watertight.

Where, however, such spaces in superstructures are appropriated to passengers other than steerage passengers or to crew, the side scuttles may have portable deadlights stowed adjacent to the side scuttles, provided they are readily accessible at all times on service.

The side scuttles and deadlights are to be of substantial and approved construction.

Rule XXIX. *Guard Rails*

Efficient guard rails or bulwarks are to be fitted on all exposed portions of freeboard and superstructure decks.

Rule XXX. *Freeing Ports*

Where bulwarks on the weather portions of freeboard or superstructure decks form "wells," ample provision is to be made for rapidly freeing the decks of water and for draining them. The minimum freeing port area on each side of the ship for each well on the freeboard deck and on the raised quarter-deck is to be that given by the following scale; the minimum area for each well on any other superstructure deck is to be one-half the area given by the scale. Where the length of the well exceeds .7 L, the scale may be modified.

SCALE of Freeing Port Area

Length of Bulwarks in "Well" in Feet.	Freeing Port Area on each side in Square Feet.
15	8. 0
20	8. 5
25	9. 0
30	9. 5
35	10. 0
40	10. 5
45	11. 0
50	11. 5
55	12. 0
60	12. 5
65	13. 0
Above 65	1 square foot for each additional 5 feet length of bulwark.

The lower edges of the freeing ports are to be as near the deck as practicable and preferably not higher than the upper edge of the gunwale bar. Two-thirds of the freeing port area required is to be provided in the midship half of the well. In ships with less than the standard sheer the freeing port area is to be suitably increased.

All such openings in the bulwarks are to be protected by rails or bars spaced about 9 inches apart. If shutters are fitted to freeing ports, ample clearance is to be provided to prevent jamming. Hinges are to have brass pins.

Rule XXXI. *Protection of Crew*

Gangways, lifelines or other satisfactory means are to be provided for the protection of the crew in getting to and from their quarters. The strength of houses for the accommodation of crew on flush deck steamers is to be equivalent to that required for superstructure bulkheads.

PART III. LOAD LINE FOR STEAMERS

Rule XXXII. *Length* (L)

The length used with the Rules and Freeboard Table is the length in feet on the summer load water-line from the foreside of the stem to the afterside of the rudder post. Where there is no rudder post, the length is measured from the foreside of the stem to the axis of the rudder stock. For ships with cruiser sterns, the length is to be taken as 96 per cent. of the total length on the designed summer load water-line or as the length from the fore side of the stem to the axis of the rudder stock if that be the greater.

Rule XXXIII. *Breadth* (B)

The breadth is the maximum breadth in feet amidships to the moulded line of the frame in iron or steel ships, and to the outside of the planking in wood or composite ships.

Rule XXXIV. *Moulded Depth*

The moulded depth is the vertical distance in feet, measured amidships, from the top of the keel to the top of the freeboard deck beam at side. In wood and composite ships the distance is measured from the lower edge of the keel rabbet. Where the form at the lower part of the midship section is of a hollow character, or where thick garboards are fitted, the depth is measured from the point where the line of the flat of the bottom continued inwards cuts the side of the keel.

Rule XXXV. *Depth for Freeboard* (D)

The depth used with the Freeboard Table is the moulded depth plus the thickness of stringer plate, or plus $\dfrac{T(L-S)}{L}$ if that be greater, where—

T is the mean thickness of the exposed deck clear of deck openings, and

S is the total length of superstructures as defined in Rule XL.

Where the topsides are of unusual form, D is the depth of a midship section having vertical topsides, standard round of beam and area of topside section equal to that in the actual midship section. Where there is a step or break in the topsides (*e.g.*, as in the Turret Deck ship) 70 per cent. of the area above the step or break is included in the area used to determine the equivalent section.

In a ship without an enclosed superstructure covering at least .6 L amidships, without a complete trunk or without a combination of intact partial superstructures and trunk extending all fore and aft, where D is less than $\dfrac{L}{15}$, the depth used with the Table is not to be taken as less than $\dfrac{L}{15}$.

Rule XXXVI. *Coefficient of Fineness* (c)

The coefficient of fineness used with the Freeboard Table is given by—

$$c = \frac{35\Delta}{\text{L.B.}d_1},$$

where Δ is the ship's moulded displacement in tons (excluding bossing) at a mean moulded draught d_1 which is 85 per cent. of the moulded depth.

The coefficient c is not to be taken as less than .68.

Rule XXXVII. *Strength*

The Assigning Authority is to be satisfied with the structural strength of ships to which freeboards are assigned.

Ships which comply with the highest standard of the rules of a Classification Society recognised by the Administration, shall be regarded as having sufficient strength for the minimum freeboards allowed under the Rules.

Ships which do not comply with the highest standard of the rules of a Classification Society recognised by the Administration, shall be assigned such increased freeboards as shall be determined by the Assigning Authority, and for guidance the following strength moduli are formulated:—

Material.—The strength moduli are based on the assumption that the structure is built of mild steel, manufactured by the open hearth process (acid or basic), and having a tensile strength of 26 to 32 tons per square inch, and an elongation of at least 16 per cent. on a length of 8 inches.

Strength Deck.—The strength deck is the uppermost deck which is incorporated into and forms an integral part of the longitudinal girder within the half-length amidships.

Depth to Strength Deck (Ds).—The depth to strength deck is the vertical distance in feet amidships from the top of the keel to the top of the strength deck beam at side.

Draught (d).—The draught is the vertical distance in feet amidships from the top of the keel to the centre of the disc.

Longitudinal Modulus.—The longitudinal modulus $\dfrac{I}{y}$ is the moment of inertia I of the midship section about the neutral axis divided by the distance y measured from the neutral axis to the top of the strength deck beam at side, calculated in way of openings but without deductions for rivet holes. Areas are measured in square inches and distances in feet.

Below the strength deck, all continuous longitudinal members other than such parts of under deck girders as are required entirely for supporting purposes, are included. Above the strength deck, the gunwale angle bar and the extension of the sheerstrake are the only members included.

The required longitudinal modulus for effective material is expressed by f.d.B., where f is the factor obtained from the following table:

L.	f.	L.	f.
100	1. 80	360	9. 40
120	2. 00	380	10. 30
140	2. 35	400	11. 20
160	2. 70	420	12. 15
180	3. 15	440	13. 10
200	3. 60	460	14. 15
220	4. 20	480	15. 15
240	4. 80	500	16. 25
260	5. 45	520	17. 35
280	6. 20	540	18. 45
300	6. 95	560	19. 60
320	7. 70	580	20. 80
340	8. 55	600	22. 00

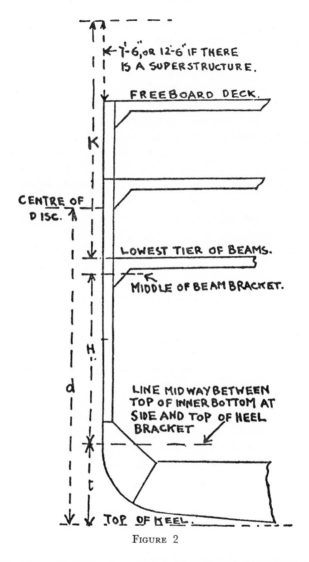

FIGURE 2

For intermediate lengths, the value of f is determined by interpolation.
This formula applies where L does not exceed 600 feet; B is between $\frac{L}{10}+5$ and $\frac{L}{10}+20$, both inclusive, and $\frac{L}{Ds}$ is between 10 and 13.5, both inclusive.

Frame.—For the purpose of the frame modulus, the frame is regarded as composed of a frame angle and a reverse angle each of the same size and thickness.

Frame Modulus.—The modulus $\frac{I}{y}$ of the midship frame below the lowest tier of beams is the moment of inertia I of the frame section about the neutral axis divided by the distance y measured from the neutral axis to the extremity of the frame section, calculated without deduction for rivet and bolt holes. The modulus is measured in inch units.

The required frame modulus is expressed by $\dfrac{s(d-t)(f_1+f_2),}{1,000}$ where—

s is the frame spacing in inches.

t is the vertical distance in feet measured at amidships from the top of the keel to a point midway between the top of the inner bottom at side and the top of the heel bracket (see Figure 2); where there is no double bottom, t is measured to a point midway between the top of the floor at centre and the top of the floor at side.

f_1 is a coefficient depending on H, which, in ships fitted with double bottoms, is the vertical distance in feet from the middle of the beam bracket of the lowest tier of beams at side to a point midway between the top of the inner bottom at side and the top of the heel bracket (see Figure 2). Where there is no double bottom, H is measured to a point midway between the top of the floor at centre and the top of the floor at side. Where the frame obtains additional strength from the form of the ship, due allowance is made in the value of f_1.

f_2 is a coefficient depending on K, which is the vertical distance in feet from the top of the lowest tier of beams at side to a point 7 feet 6 inches above the freeboard deck at side, or, if there is a superstructure, to a point 12 feet 6 inches above the freeboard deck at side (see Figure 2). The values of f_1 and f_2 are obtained from the following tables:—

H in feet.....	0	7	9	11	13	15	17	19	21	23	25
f_1........................	9	11	12. 5	15	19	24	29. 5	36	43	51	59

K in feet............	0	5	10	15	20	25	30	35	40
f_2....................	0	0. 5	1. 0	2. 0	3. 0	4. 5	6. 5	9. 0	12. 0

Intermediate values are obtained by interpolation.

This formula applies where D is between 15 feet and 60 feet, both inclusive, B is between $\dfrac{L}{10}+5$ and $\dfrac{L}{10}+20$, both inclusive, $\dfrac{L}{Ds}$ is between 10 and 13.5, both inclusive; and the horizontal distance from the outside of the frame to the centre of the first row of pillars does not exceed 20 feet.

In single deck ships of ordinary form, where H does not exceed 18 feet, the frame modulus determined by the preceding method is multiplied by the factor f_3 where

$$f_3 = .50 + .05 \ (H-8).$$

Where the horizontal distance from the outside of the frame to the centre of the first row of pillars exceeds 20 feet, the Assigning Authority is to be satisfied that sufficient additional strength is provided.

Superstructures

Rule XXXVIII. *Height of Superstructure*

The height of a superstructure is the least vertical height measured from the top of the superstructure deck to the top of the freeboard deck beams minus the difference between D and the moulded depth (*see* Rules XXXIV and XXXV).

Rule XXXIX. *Standard Height of Superstructure*

The standard height of a raised quarter deck is 3 feet for ships up to and including 100 feet in length, 4 feet for ships 250 feet in length and 6 feet for ships 400 feet in length and above. The standard height of any other super-structure is 6 feet for ships up to and including 250 feet in length and 7 feet 6 inches for ships 400 feet in length and above. The standard height at inter-mediate lengths is obtained by interpolation.

Rule XL. *Length of Superstructure* (S)

The length of a superstructure is the mean covered length of the parts of the superstructure which extend to the sides of the ship and lie within lines drawn perpendicular to the extremities of the Summer load water-line, as defined in Rule XXXII.

Rule XLI. *Enclosed Superstructure*

A detached superstructure is regarded as enclosed only where—

(*a*) the enclosing bulkheads are of efficient construction (*see* Rule XLII);
(*b*) the access openings in these bulkheads are fitted with Class 1 or Class 2 closing appliances (*see* Rules XLIII and XLIV);
(*c*) all other openings in sides or ends of the superstructure are fitted with efficient weathertight means of closing; and
(*d*) independent means of access to crew, machinery, bunker and other working spaces within bridges and poops are at all times available when the bulkhead openings are closed.

Rule XLII. *Superstructure Bulkheads*

Bulkheads at exposed ends of poops, bridges and forecastles are deemed to be of efficient construction where the Assigning Authority is satisfied that, in the circumstances, they are equivalent to the following standard for ships with minimum freeboards under which standard the stiffeners and plating are of the scantlings given in Table 3, the stiffeners are spaced 30 inches apart, the stiffeners on poop and bridge front bulkheads have efficient end connections, and those on after bulkheads of bridges and forecastles extend for the whole distance between the margin angles of the bulkheads.

TABLE 3

Exposed Bulkheads of Superstructures of Standard Height

Bridge Front Bulkheads. Unprotected Bulkheads of Poops .4 L or more in Length.		Bulkheads of Poops Partially Protected or less in Length than .4 L.		After Bulkheads of Bridges and Forecastles.	
Length of Ship.	Bulb Angle Stiffeners.	Length of Ship.	Plain Angle Stiffeners.	Length of Ship.	Plain Angle Stiffeners.
Feet.	Inches.	Feet.	Inches.	Feet.	Inches.
Under 160	5½×3 ×.30	Under 150	3 ×2½×.30	Under 150	2½×2½×.26
160	6 ×3 ×.32	150	3½×2½×.32	150	3 ×2½×.28
200	6½×3 ×.34	200	4 ×3 ×.34	250	3½×3 ×.30
240	7 ×3 ×.36	250	4½×3 ×.36	350	4 ×3 ×.32
280	7½×3 ×.38	300	5 ×3 ×.38		
320	8 ×3 ×.40	350	5½×3 ×.42		
360	8½×3 ×.42	400	6 ×3 ×.44		
400	9 ×3 ×.44	450	6½×3½×.46		
440	9½×3½×.46	500	7 ×3½×.48		
480	10 ×3½×.48	550	7 ×3½×.50		
520	10½×3½×.50				
560	11 ×3½×.52				

Length of Ship.	Bulkhead Plating.	Length of Ship.	Bulkhead Plating.	Length of Ship.	Bulkhead Plating.
Feet.	Inch.	Feet.	Inch.	Feet.	Inch.
200 and under	.3	160 and under	.24	160 and under	.20
380 and above	.44	400 and above	.38	400 and above	.30

For ships intermediate in length the thicknesses of bulkhead plating are obtained by interpolation.

Appliances for Closing Access Openings in Bulkheads at ends of Detached Superstructures

Rule XLIII. Class 1 Closing Appliances

These appliances are of iron and steel, are in all cases permanently and strongly attached to the bulkhead, are framed, stiffened and fitted so that the whole structure is of equivalent strength to the unpierced bulkhead, and are weathertight when closed. The means for securing these appliances are permanently attached to the bulkhead or to the appliances, and the latter are so arranged that they can be closed and secured from both sides of the bulkhead or from the deck above. The sills of the access openings are at least 15 inches above the deck.

Rule XLIV. *Class 2 Closing Appliances*

These appliances are (*a*) strongly framed hard wood hinged doors, which are not more than 30 inches wide nor less than 2 inches thick; or (*b*) shifting boards fitted for the full height of the opening in channels riveted to the bulkhead, the shifting boards being at least 2 inches thick where the width of opening is 30 inches or less, and increased in thickness at the rate of 1 inch for each additional 15 inches of width, or (*c*) portable plates of equal efficiency.

Temporary Appliances for Closing Openings in Superstructure Decks

Rule XLV

Temporary closing appliances for middle line openings in the deck of an enclosed superstructure consist of—

(*a*) a steel coaming not less than 9 inches in height efficiently riveted to the deck;

(*b*) hatchway covers as required by Rule X, secured by hemp lashings; and

(*c*) hatchway supports as required by Rules XI and XII and Table 1 or 2.

Effective Length of Detached Superstructures

Rule XLVI. *General*

Where exposed bulkheads at the ends of poops, bridges, and forecastles are not of efficient construction (*see* Rule XLII) they are considered as non-existent.

Where in the side plating of a superstructure there is an opening not provided with permanent means of closing, the part of the superstructure in way of the opening is regarded as having no effective length.

Where the height of a superstructure is less than the standard its length is reduced in the ratio of the actual to the standard height. Where the height exceeds the standard, no increase is made in the length of the superstructure.

Rule XLVII. *Poop*

Where there is an efficient bulkhead and the access openings are fitted with Class 1 closing appliances, the length to the bulkhead is effective. Where the access openings in an efficient bulkhead are fitted with Class 2 closing appliances and the length to the bulkhead is .5 L or less, 100 per cent. of that length is effective; where the length is .7 L or more, 90 per cent. of that length is effective; where the length is between .5 L and .7 L, an intermediate percentage of that length is effective; where an allowance is given for an efficient adjacent trunk (*see* Rule LI), 90 per cent. of the length to the bulkhead is to be taken as effective. 50 per cent. of the length of an open poop or of an open extension beyond an efficient bulkhead is effective.

Rule XLVIII. *Raised Quarter Deck*

Where there is an efficient intact bulkhead, the length to the bulkhead is effective. Where the bulkhead is not intact, the superstructure is considered as a poop of less than standard height.

Rule XLIX. *Bridge*

Where there is an efficient bulkhead at each end, and the access openings in the bulkheads are fitted with Class 1 closing appliances, the length between the bulkheads is effective.

Where the access openings in the forward bulkhead are fitted with Class 1 closing appliances and the access openings in the after bulkhead with Class 2 closing appliances, the length between the bulkheads is effective; where an allowance is given for an efficient trunk, adjacent to the after bulkhead (*see* Rule LI), 90 per cent. of the length is effective. Where the access openings in both bulkheads are fitted with Class 2 closing appliances, 90 per cent. of the length between the bulkheads is effective. Where the access openings in the forward bulkhead are fitted with Class 1 or Class 2 closing appliances and the access openings in the after bulkhead have no closing appliances, 75 per cent. of the length between the bulkheads is effective. Where the access openings in both bulkheads have no closing appliances, 50 per cent. of the length is effective. 75 per cent. of the length of an open extension beyond the after bulkhead, and 50 per cent. of that beyond the forward bulkhead, are effective.

Rule L. *Forecastle*

Where there is an efficient bulkhead and the access openings are fitted with Class 1 or Class 2 closing appliances, the length to the bulkhead is effective. Where no closing appliances are fitted and the sheer forward of amidships is not less than the standard sheer, 100 per cent. of the length of the forecastle forward of .1 L from the forward perpendicular is effective; where the sheer forward is half the standard sheer or less, 50 per cent. of that length is effective; and where the sheer forward is intermediate between the standard and half the standard sheer, an intermediate percentage of that length is effective. 50 per cent. of the length of an open extension beyond the bulkhead or beyond .1 L from the forward perpendicular is effective.

Rule LI. *Trunk*

A trunk or similar structure which does not extend to the sides of the ship is regarded as efficient provided that—

(*a*) the trunk is at least as strong as a superstructure;

(*b*) the hatchways are in the trunk deck, and comply with the requirements of Rules VIII to XVI, and the width of the trunk deck stringer provides a satisfactory gangway and sufficient lateral stiffness;

(*c*) a permanent working platform fore and aft fitted with guard rails is provided by the trunk deck, or by detached trunks connected to other superstructures by efficient permanent gangways;

(*d*) ventilators are protected by the trunk, by watertight covers or by equivalent means;

(*e*) open rails are fitted on the weather portions of the freeboard deck in way of the trunk for at least half their length;

(*f*) the machinery casings are protected by the trunk, by a superstructure of standard height, or by a deck house of the same height and of equivalent strength.

Where access openings in poop and bridge bulkheads are fitted with Class 1 closing appliances, 100 per cent. of the length of an efficient trunk reduced in the ratio of its mean breadth to B is added to the effective length of the superstructures. Where the access openings in these bulkheads are not fitted with Class 1 closing appliances 90 per cent. is added.

The standard height of a trunk is the standard height of a bridge.

Where the height of the trunk is less than the standard height of a bridge, the addition is reduced in the ratio of the actual to the standard height; where the height of hatchway coamings on the trunk deck is less than the standard height of coamings (*see* Rule IX), a reduction from the actual height of trunk is to be made which corresponds to the difference between the actual and the standard height of coamings.

Effective Length of Enclosed Superstructures with Middle Line Openings

Rule LII. *Enclosed Superstructure with Middle Line Openings in the deck not Provided with Permanent Means of Closing*

Where there is an enclosed superstructure with one or more middle line openings in the deck not provided with permanent means of closing (*see* Rules VIII to XVI), the effective length of the superstructure is determined as follows:—

(1) Where efficient temporary closing appliances are not provided for the middle line deck openings (*see* Rule XLV), or the breadth of opening is 80 per cent. or more of the breadth B_1, of the superstructure deck at the middle of the opening, the ship is considered as having an open well in way of each opening, and freeing ports are to be provided in way of this well. The effective length of superstructure between openings is governed by Rules XLVII, XLIX, and L.

(2) Where efficient temporary closing appliances are provided for middle line deck openings and the breadth of opening is less than .8 B_1,

the effective length is governed by Rules XLVII, XLIX, and L, except that where access openings in 'tween deck bulkheads are closed by Class 2 closing appliances, they are regarded as being closed by Class 1 closing appliances in determining the effective length. The total effective length is obtained by adding to the length determined by (1) the difference between this length and the length of the ship modified in the ratio of—

$$\frac{B_1-b}{B_1} \text{ where } b=\text{breadth of deck opening};$$

where $\dfrac{B_1-b}{B_1}$ is greater than .5 it is taken as .5.

Deductions for Superstructures

Rule LIII. Deductions for Superstructures

Where the effective length of superstructures is 1.0 L, the deduction from the freeboard is 14 inches at 80 feet length of ship, 34 inches at 280 feet length, and 42 inches at 400 feet length and above; deductions at intermediate lengths are obtained by interpolation. Where the total effective length of superstructures is less than 1.0 L the deduction is a percentage obtained from the following Table:

Superstructures.	Total Effective Length of Superstructure (E).											Line.
	0.	.1 L.	.2 L.	.3 L.	.4 L.	.5 L.	.6 L.	.7 L.	.8 L.	.9 L.	1.0 L.	
	Per cent.	Per cent.	Per cent.	Per cent.	Per cent.	Per cent.	Per cent.	Per cent.	Per cent.	Per cent.	Per cent.	
All types with forecastle and without detached bridge.	0	5	10	15	23. 5	32	46	63	75. 3	87. 7	100	A
All types with forecastle and detached bridge*.	0	6. 3	12. 7	19	27. 5	36	46	63	75. 3	87. 7	100	B

*Where the effective length of a detached bridge is less than .2 L the percentages are obtained by interpolation between lines B and A.

Where no forecastle is fitted the above percentages are reduced by 5.

Percentages for intermediate lengths of superstructures are obtained by interpolation. [Footnote in original.]

Sheer

Rule LIV. *General*

The sheer is measured from the deck at side to a line of reference drawn parallel to the keel through the sheer line at amidships.

In ships designed to trim by the stern in service, the sheer may be measured in relation to the load line, provided an additional mark is placed at .25 L forward of amidships, to indicate the assigned load line. This mark is to be similar to the load line disc amidships.

In flush deck ships and in ships with detached superstructures the sheer is measured at the freeboard deck.

In ships with topsides of unusual form in which there is a step or break in the topsides, the sheer is considered in relation to the equivalent depth amidships (*see* Rule XXXV).

In ships with a superstructure of standard height which extends over the whole length of the freeboard deck, the sheer is measured at the superstructure deck; where the height exceeds the standard, the sheer may be considered in relation to the standard height.

Where a superstructure is intact or access openings in its enclosing bulkheads are fitted with Class 1 closing appliances, and the superstructure deck has at least the same sheer as the exposed freeboard deck, the sheer of the enclosed portion of the freeboard deck is not taken into account.

Rule LV. *Standard Sheer Profile*

The ordinates (in inches) of the standard sheer profile are given in the following table, where L is the number of feet in the length of the ship:

Station.	Ordinate.	Factor.
A.P.	$.1\ L + 10$	1
1/6 L from A.P.	$.0445\ L + 4.45$	4
1/3 L from A.P.	$.011\ L + 1.1$	2
Amidships.	0	4
1/3 L from F.P.	$.022\ L + 2.2$	2
1/6 L from F.P.	$.089\ L + 8.9$	4
F.P.	$.2\ L + 20$	1

A.P.=After end of Summer load water-line.   F.P.=Fore end of Summer load water-line.

Rule LVI. *Measurement of Variations from Standard Sheer Profile*

Where the sheer profile differs from the standard, the seven ordinates of each profile are multiplied by the appropriate factors given in the table of ordinates. The difference between the sums of the respective products, divided by 18, measures the deficiency or excess of sheer. Where the after half of the sheer profile is greater than the standard and the forward half is less than the standard, no credit is allowed for the part in excess and the deficiency only is measured.

Where the forward half of the sheer profile exceeds the standard, and the after portion of the sheer profile is not less than 75 per cent. of the standard, credit is allowed for the part in excess; where the after part is less than 50 per cent. of the standard no credit is given for the excess sheer forward. Where the after sheer is between 50 per cent. and 75 per cent. of the standard, intermediate allowances may be granted for excess sheer forward.

Rule LVII. *Correction for Variations from Standard Sheer Profile*

The correction for sheer is the deficiency or excess of sheer (*see* Rule LVI), multiplied by $.75-\dfrac{S}{2L}$, where S is the total length of superstructure, as defined in Rule XL.

Rule LVIII. *Addition for Deficiency in Sheer*

Where the sheer is less than the standard, the correction for deficiency in sheer (*see* Rule LVII) is added to the freeboard.

Rule LIX. *Deduction for Excess Sheer*

In flush deck ships and in ships where an enclosed superstructure covers .1 L before and .1 L abaft amidships, the correction for excess of sheer (*see* Rule LVII) is deducted from the freeboard; in ships with detached superstructures where no enclosed superstructure covers amidships, no deduction is made from the freeboard; where an enclosed superstructure covers less than .1 L before and .1 L abaft amidships, the deduction is obtained by interpolation. The maximum deduction for excess sheer is $1\frac{1}{2}$ inches at 100 feet and increases at the rate of $1\frac{1}{2}$ inches for each additional 100 feet in the length of the ship.

Round of Beam

Rule LX. *Standard Round of Beam*

The standard round of beam of the freeboard deck is one-fiftieth of the breadth of the ship.

Rule LXI. *Round of Beam Correction*

Where the round of beam of the freeboard deck is greater or less than the standard, the freeboard is decreased or increased respectively by one-fourth of the difference between the actual and the standard round of beam, multiplied by the proportion of the length of the freeboard deck not covered by enclosed superstructures. Twice the standard round of beam is the maximum for which allowance is given.

Minimum Freeboards

Rule LXII. *Summer Freeboard*

The minimum freeboard in Summer is the freeboard derived from the Freeboard Table after corrections for departures from the standards and after deduction for superstructures.

The freeboard in salt water measured from the intersection of the upper surface of the freeboard deck with the outer surface of the shell is not to be less than 2 inches.

Rule LXIII. *Tropical Freeboard*

The minimum freeboard in the Tropical Zone is the freeboard obtained by a deduction from the Summer freeboard of $\frac{1}{4}$ inch per foot of Summer draught measured from the top of the keel to the centre of the disc.

The freeboard in salt water measured from the intersection of the upper surface of the freeboard deck with the outer surface of the shell is not to be less than 2 inches.

Rule LXIV. *Winter Freeboard*

The minimum freeboard in Winter is the freeboard obtained by an addition to the Summer freeboard of $\frac{1}{4}$ inch per foot of Summer draught, measured from the top of the keel to the centre of the disc.

Rule LXV. *Winter North Atlantic Freeboard*

The minimum freeboard for ships not exceeding 330 feet in length on voyages across the North Atlantic, North of latitude 36° N., during the winter months, is the Winter freeboard plus two inches; for ships over 330 feet in length it is the Winter freeboard.

Rule LXVI. *Fresh Water Freeboard*

The minimum freeboard in fresh water of unit density is the freeboard obtained by deducting from the minimum freeboard in salt water $\dfrac{\Delta}{40\,T}$ inches,

where
   Δ = displacement in salt water in tons at the Summer load water-line, and
   T = tons per inch immersion in salt water at the Summer load water-line.

Where the displacement at the Summer load water-line cannot be certified, the deduction is to be $\frac{1}{4}$ inch per foot of Summer draught, measured from the top of the keel to the centre of the disc.

Rule LXVII. *Freeboard Table for Steamers*

Basic Minimum Summer Freeboards for Steamers which Comply with the Standards Laid Down in the Rules.

L.	Freeboard.	L.	Freeboard.	L.	Freeboard.	L.	Freeboard.
(Feet.)	(Inches.)	(Feet.)	(Inches.)	(Feet.)	(Inches.)	(Feet.)	(Inches.)
80	8.0	250	32.3	420	77.8	590	127.0
90	9.0	260	34.4	430	80.9	600	129.5
100	10.0	270	36.5	440	84.0	610	132.0
110	11.0	280	38.7	450	87.1	620	134.4
120	12.0	290	41.0	460	90.2	630	136.8
130	13.0	300	43.4	470	93.3	640	139.1
140	14.2	310	45.9	480	96.3	650	141.4
150	15.5	320	48.4	490	99.3	660	143.7
160	16.9	330	51.0	500	102.3	670	145.9
170	18.3	340	53.7	510	105.2	680	148.1
180	19.8	350	56.5	520	108.1	690	150.2
190	21.4	360	59.4	530	110.9	700	152.3
200	23.1	370	62.4	540	113.7	710	154.4
210	24.8	380	65.4	550	116.4	720	156.4
220	26.6	390	68.4	560	119.1	730	158.5
230	28.5	400	71.5	570	121.8	740	160.5
240	30.3	410	74.6	580	124.4	750	162.5

(i) The minimum freeboards for flush deck steamers are obtained by an addition to the above Table at the rate of $1\frac{1}{2}$ inches for every 100 feet of length.

(ii) The freeboards at intermediate lengths are obtained by interpolation.

(iii) Where c exceeds .68, the freeboard is multiplied by the factor $\dfrac{c+.68}{1.36}$.

(iv) Where D exceeds $\dfrac{L}{15}$ the freeboard is increased by $\left\{D-\dfrac{L}{15}\right\}R$ inches, where R is $\dfrac{L}{130}$ at lengths less than 390 feet, and 3 at 390 feet length and above.

In a ship with an enclosed superstructure covering at least .6 L amidships, with a complete trunk, or with a combination of intact partial superstructures and trunk which extends all fore and aft, where D is less than $\dfrac{L}{15}$, the freeboard is reduced at the above rate. Where the height of superstructures or trunk is less than the standard height, the reduction is in the ratio of the actual to the standard height.

(v) Where the actual depth to the surface of the freeboard deck amidships is greater or less than D, the difference between the depths (in inches) is added to or deducted from the freeboard.

PART IV. LOAD LINES FOR SAILING SHIPS

Rule LXVIII. *Lines to be Used in Connection with the Disc*

Winter and Tropical load lines are not marked on sailing ships. The maximum load line to which sailing ships may be laden in salt water in Winter and in the Tropical Zone is the centre of the disc (*see* Figure 3).

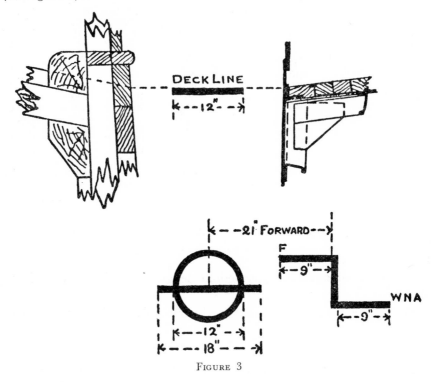

FIGURE 3

Rule LXIX. *Conditions of Assignment of Load Line*

The conditions of assignment are those contained in Part II of these Rules.

Rule LXX. *Computation of Freeboard*

Freeboards are computed from the Freeboard Table for Sailing Ships in the same manner as the freeboards for steamers are computed from the Freeboard Table for Steamers, except as follows:

Rule LXXI. *Depth for Freeboard* (D)

In sailing ships having a greater rate of rise of floor than $1\frac{1}{2}$ inches per foot, the vertical distance from the top of keel (Rule XXXIV), is reduced by half the difference between the total rise of floor at the half-breadth of the ship and the total rise at $1\frac{1}{2}$ inches per foot. $2\frac{1}{2}$ inches per foot of half-breadth is the maximum rate of rise for which a deduction is made.

Where the form at the lower part of the midship section is of a hollow character, or thick garboards are fitted, the depth is measured from the point where the line of the flat of the bottom continued inwards cuts the side of the keel.

The depth used with the Freeboard Table is to be taken as not less than $\frac{L}{12}$.

Rule LXXII. *Coefficient of fineness* (c)

The coefficient used with the Freeboard Table is to be taken as not less than .62 and not greater than .72.

Rule LXXIII. *Superstructures in Wood Ships*

In wood ships the construction and closing arrangements of superstructures for which deductions are made from the freeboard are to be to the satisfaction of the Assigning Authority.

Rule LXXIV. *Deductions for Superstructures*

Where the effective length of superstructures is 1.0 L, the deduction from the freeboard is 3 inches at 80 feet length of ship, and 28 inches at 330 feet length and above; deductions at intermediate lengths are obtained by interpolation. Where the total effective length of superstructures is less than 1.0 L, the deduction is a percentage obtained from the following Table:

Type of Super-structures.	Total Effective Length of Superstructures (E).											Line.
	0	.1 L	.2 L	.3 L	.4 L	.5 L	.6 L	.7 L	.8 L	.9 L	1.0 L	
	%	%	%	%	%	%	%	%	%	%	%	
All types without Bridge.............	0	7	13	17	23. 5	30	$47\frac{1}{2}$	70	80	90	100	A
All types with Bridge*.	0	7	14. 7	22	32	42	56	70	80	90	100	B

*Where the effective length of Bridge is less than .2 L, the percentages are obtained by interpolation between lines B and A. Percentages for intermediate lengths of superstructures are obtained by interpolation. [Footnote in original.]

Rule LXXV. *Minimum Freeboards*

No addition to the freeboard is required for Winter freeboard, nor is a deduction permitted for Tropical freeboard.

An increase in freeboard of 3 inches is made for voyages across the North Atlantic North of latitude 36° N. during the winter months.

In computing the fresh water freeboard for a wood ship, the draught is measured from the lower edge of the rabbet of keel to the centre of the disc.

Rule LXXVI. *Freeboard Table for Sailing Ships*

Minimum Summer, Winter, and Tropical Freeboards for Iron and Steel Flush Deck Sailing Ships, which comply with the Standards laid down in the Rules

L.	Freeboard	L.	Freeboard	L.	Freeboard	L.	Freeboard
Feet.	Inches.	Feet.	Inches.	Feet.	Inches.	Feet.	Inches.
80	9. 2	140	21. 3	200	35. 4	270	53. 5
90	11. 0	150	23. 5	210	37. 9	280	56. 3
100	12. 9	160	25. 8	220	40. 4	290	59. 1
110	14. 9	170	28. 2	230	42. 9	300	61. 9
120	17. 0	180	30. 6	240	45. 5	310	64. 7
130	19. 1	190	33. 0	250	48. 1	320	67. 6
				260	50. 8	330	70. 5

(i) The freeboards at intermediate lengths are obtained by interpolation.

(ii) Where c exceeds .62, the freeboard is multiplied by the factor

$$\frac{c+.62}{1.24}$$

(iii) Where D exceeds $\frac{L}{12}$ the freeboard is increased by

$$\left\{D-\frac{L}{12}\right\}\times\left\{1+\frac{L}{250}\right\}\text{inches.}$$

(iv) Where the actual depth to the surface of the freeboard deck amidships is greater or less than D, the difference between the depths (in inches) is added to or deducted from the freeboard.

Rule LXXVII. *Freeboard for Wood Sailing Ships*

The freeboard for a wood sailing ship is the final freeboard the ship would obtain if she were of iron and steel, with the addition of such penalties as the Assigning Authority may determine, having regard to the classification, construction, age and condition of the ship.

Wood ships of primitive build such as dhows, junks, prahus, &c., are to be dealt with by the Administration so far as is reasonable and practicable under the Rules for Sailing Ships.

PART V. LOAD LINES FOR STEAMERS CARRYING TIMBER DECK CARGOES

Definitions

Timber Deck Cargo.—The term "timber deck cargo" means a cargo of timber carried on an uncovered part of a freeboard or superstructure deck. The term does not include wood pulp or similar cargo.

Timber Load Line.—A timber load line is a special load line to be used only when the ship is carrying a timber deck cargo in compliance with the following conditions and regulations:

Rule LXXVIII. *Marks on the Ship's Sides*

Timber Load Lines.—The lines which indicate the maximum timber load lines in different circumstances and at different seasons are to be horizontal lines, 9 inches in length and 1 inch in breadth, which extend from, and are at right angles to, a vertical line marked 21 inches abaft the centre of the disc (*see* Figure 4). They are to be marked and verified similarly to the ordinary load lines (see Rules V to VII).

The Summer Timber Load Line is indicated by the upper edge of a line marked LS.

The Winter Timber Load Line is indicated by the upper edge of a line marked LW.

The Winter North Atlantic Timber Load Line is indicated by the upper edge of a line marked LWNA.

The Tropical Timber Load Line is indicated by the upper edge of a line marked LT.

The Fresh Water Timber Load Line in Summer is indicated by the upper edge of a line marked LF. The difference between the Fresh Water Timber load line in Summer and the Summer Timber load line is the allowance to be made for loading in fresh water at the other Timber load lines. The Fresh

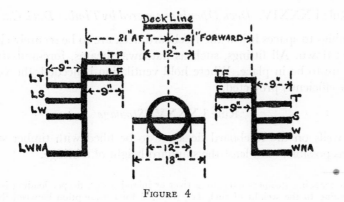

FIGURE 4

Water Timber load line in the Tropical Zone is indicated by the upper edge of a line marked LTF.[8]

Supplementary Conditions of Assignment and Regulations for Deeper Loading

Rule LXXIX. *Construction of Ship*

The structure of the ship is to be of sufficient strength for the deeper draught allowed and for the weight of the deck cargo.

Rule LXXX. *Superstructures*

The ship is to have a forecastle of at least standard height and at least 7 per cent. of the length of the ship, and, in addition, a poop, or a raised quarter deck with a strong steel hood or deck house fitted aft.

Rule LXXXI. *Machinery Casings*

Machinery casings on the freeboard deck are to be protected by a superstructure of at least standard height, unless the machinery casings are of sufficient strength and height to permit of the carriage of timber alongside.

Rule LXXXII. *Double Bottom Tanks*

Double bottom tanks where fitted within the midship half length of the ship are to have adequate longitudinal subdivision.

Rule LXXXIII. *Bulwarks*

The ship must be fitted either with permanent bulwarks at least 3 feet 3 inches high, specially stiffened on the upper edge and supported by strong bulwark stays attached to the deck in the way of the beams and provided with necessary freeing ports, or with efficient rails of the same height as the above and of specially strong construction.

Rule LXXXIV. *Deck Openings covered by Timber Deck Cargo*

Openings to spaces below the freeboard deck are to be securely closed and battened down. All fittings, such as hatchway beams, fore-and-afters, and covers, are to be in place. Where hold ventilation is needed, the ventilators are to be efficiently protected.

Rule LXXXV. *Stowage*

The wells on the freeboard deck are to be filled with timber stowed as solidly as possible, to at least the standard height of a bridge.

---

[8] Where seagoing steamers navigate a river or inland water, deeper loading is permitted corresponding to the weight of fuel, &c., required for consumption between the point of departure and the open sea. [Footnote in original.]

On a ship within a seasonal winter zone in winter, the height of the deck cargo above the freeboard deck is not to exceed one-third of the extreme breadth of the ship.

All timber deck cargo is to be compactly stowed, lashed and secured. It must not interfere in any way with the navigation and necessary work of the ship, or with the provision of a safe margin of stability at all stages of the voyage, regard being given to additions of weight, such as those due to absorption of water and to losses of weight such as those due to consumption of fuel and stores.

Rule LXXXVI. *Protection of Crew, Access to Machinery Space, &c.*

Safe and satisfactory access to the quarters of the crew, to the machinery space and to all other parts used in the necessary work of the ship, is to be available at all times. Deck cargo in way of openings which give access to such parts is to be so stowed that the openings can be properly closed and secured against the admission of water. Efficient protection for the crew in the form of guard rails or life lines, spaced not more than 12 inches apart vertically, is to be provided on each side of the deck cargo to a height of at least 4 feet above the cargo. The cargo is to be made sufficiently level for gangway purposes.

Rule LXXXVII. *Steering Arrangements*

Steering arrangements are to be effectively protected from damage by cargo, and, as far as practicable, are to be accessible. Efficient provision is to be made for steering in the event of a breakdown in the main steering arrangements.

Rule LXXXVIII. *Uprights*

Uprights when required by the nature of the timber are to be of adequate strength and may be of wood or metal; the spacing is to be suitable for the length and character of timber carried, but is not to exceed 10 feet. Strong angles or metal sockets efficiently secured to the stringer plate or equally efficient means are to be provided for securing the uprights.

Rule LXXXIX. *Lashings*

Timber deck cargo is to be efficiently secured throughout its length by independent overall lashings spaced not more than 10 feet apart.

Eye plates for these lashings are to be riveted to the sheerstrake at intervals of not more than 10 feet, the distance from an end bulkhead of a superstructure to the first eye plate being not more than 6 feet 6 inches. Additional eye plates may be fitted on the stringer plate.

Overall lashings are to be in good condition and are to be not less than ¾ inch close link chain or flexible wire rope of equivalent strength, fitted with sliphooks and stretching screws, which are to be accessible at all times. Wire rope lashings are to have a short length of long link chain to permit the length of lashings to be regulated.

When timber is in lengths less than 12 feet, the spacing of the lashings is to be reduced to suit the length of timber or other suitable provision made.

When the spacing of the lashings is 5 feet or less, the size of the lashing may be reduced, but not less than $\frac{1}{2}$ inch chain or equivalent wire rope is to be used.

All fittings required for securing the lashings are to be of strength corresponding to the strength of the lashings.

On superstructure decks, uprights, where fitted, are to be about 10 feet apart and are to be secured by athwartship lashings of ample strength.

Rule XC. *Plans*

Plans showing the fittings and arrangements for stowing and securing timber deck cargoes in compliance with the foregoing conditions and regulations are to be submitted to the Assigning Authority.

Freeboard

Rule XCI. *Computation of Freeboard*

Where the Assigning Authority is satisfied that the ship is suitable and that the conditions and arrangements are at least equal to the foregoing requirements for the carriage of timber deck cargo, the Summer freeboards computed in accordance with the Rules and Tables in Part III may be modified to give special timber freeboards, by substituting the following percentages for those in Rule LIII:

Total Effective Length of Superstructures

	0	.1 L	.2 L	.3 L	.4 L	.5 L	.6 L	.7 L	.8 L	.9 L	1.0 L
All types.....	% 20	% 30.75	% 41.5	% 52.25	% 63	% 69.25	% 75.5	% 81.5	% 87.5	% 93.75	% 100

The Winter Timber freeboard is to be obtained by adding to the Summer Timber freeboard one-third of an inch per foot of the moulded Summer Timber draught.

The Winter North Atlantic Timber freeboards are the Winter North Atlantic freeboards prescribed in Rule LXV.

The Tropical Timber freeboard is to be obtained by deducting from the Summer Timber freeboard one-quarter of an inch per foot of the moulded Summer Timber draught.

PART VI. LOAD LINES FOR TANKERS

Definition

Tanker. The term "tanker" includes all steamers specially constructed for the carriage of liquid cargoes in bulk.

Rule XCII. *Marks on the Ship's Sides*

The marks on the ship's sides are to be as provided in the figure in Rule IV.

Supplementary Conditions of Assignment for Deeper Loading

Rule XCIII. *Construction of Ship*

The structure of the ship is to be of sufficient strength for the increased draught corresponding to the freeboard assigned.

Rule XCIV. *Forecastle*

The ship is to have a forecastle of which the length is not less than 7 per cent. of the length of the ship and the height is not less than the standard height.

Rule XCV. *Machinery Casings*

The openings in machinery casings on the freeboard deck are to be fitted with steel doors. The casings are to be protected by an enclosed poop or bridge of at least standard height, or by a deck house of equal height and of equivalent strength. The bulkheads at the ends of these structures are to be of the scantlings required for bridge front bulkheads. All entrances to the structures from the freeboard deck are to be fitted with effective closing appliances and the sills are to be at least 18 inches above the deck. Exposed machinery casings on the superstructure deck are to be of substantial construction, and all openings in them are to be fitted with steel closing appliances permanently attached to the casings and capable of being closed and secured from both sides; the sills of such openings are to be at least 15 inches above the deck. Fiddley openings are to be as high above the superstructure deck as is reasonable and practicable and are to have strong steel covers permanently attached in their proper positions.

Rule XCVI. *Gangway*

An efficiently constructed permanent gangway of sufficient strength for its exposed position is to be fitted fore and aft at the level of the superstructure deck between the poop and midship bridge, and when crew are berthed forward, from the bridge to the forecastle, or other equivalent means of access may be provided to carry out the purpose of the gangway, such as passages below deck.

Rule XCVII. *Protection of Crew, Access to Machinery Space, &c.*

Safe and satisfactory access from the gangway level to the quarters of the crew, the machinery space and all other parts used in the necessary work of the ship, is to be available at all times. This rule does not apply to pump rooms entered from the freeboard deck, when fitted with Class 1 closing appliances.

Rule XCVIII. *Hatchways*

All hatchways on the freeboard deck and on the deck of expansion trunks are to be closed watertight by efficient steel covers.

Rule XCIX. *Ventilators*

Ventilators to spaces below the freeboard deck are to be of ample strength or are to be protected by superstructures or equally efficient means.

Rule C. *Freeing Arrangements*

Ships with bulwarks are to have open rails fitted for at least half the length of the exposed portion of the weather deck or other effective freeing arrangements. The upper edge of the sheerstrake is to be kept as low as practicable, and preferably not higher than the upper edge of the gunwhale bar.

Where superstructures are connected by trunks, open rails are to be fitted for the whole length of the weather portions of the freeboard deck.

Rule CI. *Plans*

Plans showing proposed fittings and arrangements are to be submitted to the Assigning Authority for approval.

Freeboards

Rule CII. *Computation of Freeboard*

When the Assigning Authority is satisfied that the foregoing requirements are fulfilled, the Summer freeboard may be computed from the Table for Tankers; all corrections except those for flush-deck steamers, detached superstructures, excess sheer, and winter voyages across the North Atlantic are to be made in accordance with Part III of the Rules.

Rule CIII. *Deduction for Detached Superstructures*

When the total effective length of superstructure is less than 1.0 L, the deduction is a percentage of that for a superstructure of length 1.0 L, and is obtained from the following table:

Total Effective Length of Superstructures

	0	.1 L	.2 L	.3 L	.4 L	.5 L	.6 L	.7 L	.8 L	.9 L	1.0 L
All types.........	% 0	% 7	% 14	% 21	% 31	% 41	% 52	% 63	% 75. 3	% 87. 7	% 100

Rule CIV. *Deduction for Excess Sheer*

Where the sheer is greater than the standard, the correction for excess sheer (*see* Rule LVII of Part III, Load Lines for Steamers) is deducted from the freeboard for all tankers. Rule LIX of Part III does not apply except that the maximum deduction for excess sheer is 1½ inches at 100 feet and increases at the rate of 1½ inches for each additional 100 feet in the length of the ship.

Rule CV. *Winter North Atlantic Freeboard*

The minimum freeboard for voyages across the North Atlantic, north of latitude 36° N., during the winter months, is the Winter Freeboard plus an addition at a rate of 1 inch per 100 feet in length.

Rule CVI. *Freeboard Table for Tankers*

L in Feet.	Freeboard in Inches.	L in Feet.	Freeboard in Inches.
190	21. 5	400	62. 5
200	23. 1	410	64. 9
210	24. 7	420	67. 4
220	26. 3	430	69. 9
230	28. 0	440	72. 5
240	29. 7	450	75. 1
250	31. 5	460	77. 7
260	33. 3	470	80. 2
270	35. 2	480	82. 7
280	37. 1	490	85. 1
290	39. 1	500	87. 5
300	41. 1	510	89. 8
310	43. 1	520	92. 1
320	45. 1	530	94. 3
330	47. 1	540	96. 5
340	49. 2	550	98. 6
350	51. 3	560	100. 7
360	53. 5	570	102. 7
370	55. 7	580	104. 6
380	57. 9	590	106. 5
390	60. 2	600	108. 4

Ships above 600 feet are to be dealt with by the Administration.

Annex II [9]

BOUNDARIES OF THE ZONES AND SEASONAL AREAS

Zones

The southern boundary of the northern "Winter Seasonal" zone is a line drawn from the east coast of North America along the parallel of lat. 36° N. to Tarifa in Spain; from the east coast of Korea along the parallel of lat.

---

[9] The separate print of TS 858 contains a large map entitled "Outline of the World," at the beginning of annex II.

35° N. to the west coast of Honshiu, Japan; from the east coast of Honshiu along the parallel of lat. 35° N. to long. 150° W., and thence along a rhumb line to the west coast of Vancouver Island at lat. 50° N., Fusan (Korea) and Yokohama to be considered as being on the boundary line of the northern "Winter Seasonal" zone and the "Summer" zone.

The northern boundary of the "Tropical" zone is a line drawn from the east coast of the South America at lat. 10° N. along the parallel 10° N. to long. 20° W., thence north to lat. 20° N. and thence along the parallel of lat. 20° N. to the west coast of Africa; a line from the east coast of Africa along the parallel of lat. 8° N. to the west coast of the Malay Peninsula, following thence the coast of Malay and Siam to the east coast of Cochin China at lat. 10° N., thence along the parallel of lat. 10° N. to long. 145° E., thence north to lat. 13° N. and thence along the parallel of lat. 13° N. to the west coast of Central America, Saigon to be considered as being on the boundary line of the "Tropical" zone and the "Seasonal Tropical" area (4).

The southern boundary of the "Tropical" zone is a line drawn from the east coast of South America along the Tropic of Capricorn to the west coast of Africa; from the east coast of Africa along the parallel at lat. 20° S. to the west coast of Madagascar, thence along the west and north coast of Madagascar to long. 50° E., thence north to lat. 10° S., thence along the parallel of lat. 10° S. to long. 110° E., thence along a rhumb line to Port Darwin, Australia, thence eastwards along the coast of Australia and Wessel Island to Cape Wessel, thence along the parallel of lat. 11° S. to the west side of Cape York, from the east side of Cape York at lat. 11° S. along the parallel of lat. 11° S. to long. 150° W., thence along a rhumb line to the point lat. 26° S. long. 75° W., and thence along a rhumb line to the west coast of South America at lat. 30° S., Coquimbo, Rio de Janeiro and Port Darwin to be considered as being on the boundary line of the "Tropical" and "Summer" zones.

The following regions are to be included in the "Tropical" zone:

(1) *The Suez Canal, the Red Sea and the Gulf of Aden,* from Port Said to the meridian of 45° E., Aden and Berbera to be considered as being on the boundary line of the "Tropical" zone and the "Seasonal Tropical" area 2(b).

(2) *The Persian Gulf* to the meridian of 59° E.

The northern boundary of the southern "Winter Seasonal" zone is a line drawn from the east coast of South America along the parallel of lat. 40° S. to long. 56° W., thence along a rhumb line to the point lat. 34° S., long. 50° W., thence along the parallel of lat. 34° S. to the west coast of South Africa; from the east coast of South Africa at lat. 30° S. along a rhumb line to the west coast of Australia at lat. 35° S., thence along the south coast of Australia to Cape Arid, thence along a rhumb line to Cape Grim, Tasmania, thence along the north coast of Tasmania to Eddystone Point, thence along a rhumb line to the west coast of South Island, New Zealand, at long. 170° E., thence along the west, south and east coasts of South Island to Cape Saunders, thence along a rhumb line to the point lat. 33° S. long. 170° W.; and thence along the parallel of lat. 33° S. to the west coast of South America, Valparaiso, Cape Town and Durban to be considered as being on the boundary line of the southern "Seasonal Winter" and "Summer" zones.

Summer Zones. The remaining areas constitute the "Summer" Zones.

Seasonal Areas

The following areas are Seasonal Tropical Areas:

(1) *In the North Atlantic Ocean.*

An area bounded on the north by a line from Cape Catoche in Yucatan to Cape San Antonio in Cuba, by the South Cuban Coast to lat. 20° N. and by the parallel of lat. 20° N. to the point lat. 20° N. long. 20° W.; on the west by the coast of Central America; on the south by the north coast of South America and by parallel of lat. 10° N., and on the east by the meridian of 20° W.

Tropical: 1st November to 15th July.
Summer: 16th July to 31st October.

(2) *Arabian Sea.*

(a) *North of lat. 24° N.*

Karachi is to be considered as being on the boundary line of this area and the seasonal Tropical area (b) below.

Tropical: 1st August to 20th May.
Summer: 21st May to 31st July.

(b) *South of lat. 24° N.*

Tropical: 1st December to 20th May, and 16th September to 15th October.
Summer: 21st May to 15th September and 16th October to 30th November.

(3) *Bay of Bengal.*

Tropical: 16th December to 15th April.
Summer: 16th April to 15th December.

(4) *In the China Sea.*

An area bounded on the west and north by the coast of Indo-China and China to Hong Kong, on the east by a rhumb line to the port of Sual (Luzon Island), and by the west coast of the Islands of Luzon, Samar and Leyte to the parallel of 10° N., and on the south by the parallel of lat. 10° N.

Hong Kong and Sual to be considered as being on the boundary of the "Seasonal Tropical" and "Summer" Zones.

Tropical: 21st January to 30th April.
Summer: 1st May to 20th January.

(5) *In the North Pacific Ocean.*

(*a*) An area bounded on the north by the parallel of lat. 25° N., on the west by the meridian of 160° E., on the south by the parallel of lat. 13° N., and on the east by the meridian of 130° W.

Tropical: 1st April to 31st October.
Summer: 1st November to 31st March.

(*b*) An area bounded on the north and east by the coast of California, Mexico and Central America, on the west by the meridian of 120° W. and by a rhumb line from the point lat. 30° N., long. 120° W., to the point lat. 13° N., long. 105° W., and on the south by the parallel of lat. 13° N.

Tropical: 1st March to 30th June and 1st to 30th November.
Summer: 1st July to 31st October and 1st December to 28th/29th February.

(6) *In the South Pacific Ocean.*

(*a*) An area bounded on the north by the parallel of lat. 11° S., on the west by the east coast of Australia, on the south by the parallel of lat. 20° S., and on the east by the meridian of 175° E., together with the Gulf of Carpentaria south of lat. 11° S.

Tropical: 1st April to 30th November.
Summer: 1st December to 31st March.

(*b*) An area bounded on the west by the meridian of 150° W., on the south by the parallel of lat. 20° S., and on the north and east by the rhumb line forming the southern boundary of the "Tropical" zone.

Tropical: from 1st March to 30th November.
Summer: from 1st December to 28th/29th February.

The following are "Seasonal Winter" areas:

Northern "Seasonal Winter" Zone (between North America and Europe).

(*a*) In the area within and to the Northwards of the following line:

A line drawn south from the coast of Greenland at long. 50° W. to lat. 45° N., thence along the parallel of lat. 45° N. to the meridian of 15° W., thence north to lat. 60° N., thence along the parallel of lat. 60° N. to the west coast of Norway, Bergen to be considered as being on the boundary line of this area and area (*b*) below.

Winter from 16th October to 15th April.
Summer from 16th April to 15th October.

(*b*) An area outside area (*a*) above and north of the parallel of lat. 36° N.

Winter from 1st November to 31st March.
Summer from 1st April to 31st October.

Baltic (bounded by the parallel of latitude of the Skaw).

Winter from 1st November to 31st March.
Summer from 1st April to 31st October.

Mediterranean and Black Sea.

Winter from 16th December to 15th March.
Summer from 16th March to 15th December.

Northern "Seasonal Winter" Zone (between Asia and North America, except Sea of Japan, South of 50° N.).

Winter from 16th October to 15th April.
Summer from 16th April to 15th October.

Sea of Japan between the parallels of lat. 35° N. and 50° N.

Winter from 1st December to 28/29th February.
Summer from 1st March to 30th November.

Southern "Seasonal Winter" Zone.

Winter from 16th April to 15th October.
Summer from 16th October to 15th April.

Annex III

INTERNATIONAL LOAD LINE CERTIFICATE

Issued under the authority of the Government of .... under the provisions of the International Load Line Convention, 1930.

Distinctive Number
or Letters ......

Ship..
Port of Registry...
Gross Tonnage...

	Freeboard from deck line.	*Load Line*
Tropical..		(a).......above (b).
summer	....	(b) Upper edge of line through centre of disc.
Winter	....	(c)........ below (b).
Winter in North Atlantic.		(d).......below (b).

Allowance for fresh water for all freeboards....................................

The upper edge of the deck line from which these freeboards are measured is ....
inches above the top of the .... deck at side.

This is to Certify that this ship has been surveyed and the freeboards and load lines shown above have been assigned in accordance with the Convention.

This certificate remains in force until ....

Issued at .... on the ....

day of ....

Here follows the signature or seal and the description of the authority issuing the certificate.

Note.—Where sea-going steamers navigate a river or inland water, deeper loading is permitted corresponding to the weight of fuel, &c., required for consumption between the point of departure and the open sea.

The provisions of the Convention being fully complied with by this ship, this certificate is renewed till ....

Place .... Date ....
Signature or Seal and description of authority.

The provisions of the Convention being fully complied with by this ship, this certificate is renewed till . ...

Place .... Date ....
Signature or Seal and description of authority.

The provisions of the Convention being fully complied with by this ship, this certificate is renewed till ....

Place .... Date ....
Signature or Seal and description of authority.

Annex IV

TITLES OF LOAD LINE LAWS AND RULES REGARDED AS EQUIVALENT
TO THE BRITISH BOARD OF TRADE RULES, 1906

Australia

Part IV of the Navigation Act, 1912–1920, and Navigation (Load Line) Regulations of the 17th December, 1924.

Belgium

Loi sur la sécurité des navires (7 decembre 1920).

Chile

Reglamento para el trazado del disco marcas y linea oficial de carguio de las naves mercantes (Decree No. 1896 of the 12th November, 1919).

Denmark

Merchant Shipping (Inspection of Ships) Act of the 29th March, 1920, with later amendments.

Rules and Tables of Freeboard for Ships, dated the 30th September, 1909, as amended by Notification of the 25th July, 1918.

France

Loi du 17 avril 1907, arrêté du 5 septembre 1908. Décret du 21 septembre 1908. Autre décret du 21 septembre 1908 modifié par le décret du 1er septembre 1925. Décret du 12 mai 1927. Décret du 17 janvier 1928.

Germany

Vorschriften der See-Berufsgenossenschaft über den Freibord für Dampfer und Segelschiffe, Ausgabe 1908.

Hong Kong

Merchant Shipping Consolidation Ordinance (No. 10 of 1899), as amended by Ordinances Nos. 31 of 1901, 2 of 1903, 5 of 1905, 16 of 1906, 9 of 1909, and 6 of 1910.

Iceland

Law No. 58 of the 14th June, 1929, Sections 25–26.

India

Indian Merchant Shipping Act, 1923.

Italy

Regole e tavole per assignazione del "Bordo Libero" approved by decree dated the 1st February, 1929—VII of the Italian Minister for Communications.

Prior to 1929—British Board of Trade Rules, 1906.

Japan
   Ship Load Line Law [Law No. 2 of the 10th year of Taisho (1921)] and the Rules and Regulations relating thereto.

Netherlands
   Decree of the 22nd September, 1909 (Official Journal No. 315).

Netherlands Indies
   Netherlands Decree of the 22nd September, 1909 (Official Journal No. 315).

New Zealand
   British Board of Trade Rules, 1906.

Norway
   Norwegian Freeboard Rules and Tables of 1909.

Portugal
   Decree No. 11,210 of the 18th July, 1925, and Regulations and Instructions relating thereto.

Spain
   Reglamento para el Trazado del Disco y Marcas de Maxima Carga de los buques marchantes, 1914.

Straits Settlements
   British Board of Trade Rules, 1906.

Sweden
   Rules and Tables of Freeboard approved by decree of the 21st May, 1910.

United Kingdom
   Board of Trade Rules, 1906.

United States of America
   British Board of Trade Rules, 1906.

Union of Soviet Socialist Republics
   Rules and Regulations relating to the Load Lines of seagoing merchant vessels, published by Register of the Union of Soviet Socialist Republics, 1928.

FINAL ACT OF THE INTERNATIONAL LOAD LINE CONFERENCE, 1930

THE Governments of Germany, the Commonwealth of Australia, Belgium, Canada, Chile, Cuba, Denmark, the Free City of Danzig, Spain, the Irish Free State, the United States of America, Finland, France, the United Kingdom of Great Britain and Northern Ireland, Greece, India, Iceland, Italy, Japan, Latvia, Mexico, Norway, New Zealand, Paraguay, the Netherlands, Peru, Poland, Portugal, Sweden and the Union of Soviet Socialist Republics;

Desiring to promote safety of life and property at sea by establishing in common agreement uniform principles and rules with regard to the limits to which ships on international voyages may be loaded;

Having decided to participate in an international conference which, upon the invitation of the Government of the United Kingdom of Great Britain and Northern Ireland, was held in London;

Appointed the following delegations:

GERMANY

Delegates

Mr. Gustav Koenigs . . . . . Ministerialdirigent in the Reichsverkehrsministerium, Geheimer Regierungsrat, Berlin.

Mr. Arthur Werner . . . . . Ministerialrat in the Reichsverkehrsministerium, Geheimer Justizrat, Berlin.

Professor Walter Laas . . . . Director of the "Germanischer Lloyd" Classification Society, Berlin.

Mr. Karl Sturm . . . . . . Verwaltungsdirektor of the See-Berufsgenossenschaft, Hamburg.

Experts

Captain A. N. Elingius . . . . Inspector of the "Hamburg-Südamerika-Line," Hamburg.

Mr. Wilhelm Heberling . . . . Diplom-Ingenieur, "Germanischer Lloyd" Classification Society, Berlin.

Captain Ernst Knutzen . . . . Inspector of the "Atlantic Tank-Rhederei for Verband deutscher Kapitäne und Schiffsoffiziere," Hamburg.

Mr. Franz Köhler . . . . . . Gesamtverband, Abteilung Seeleute, Berlin.

Captain Ludwig Schmidt . . . Inspector of the "Hansa-Line," Bremen.

Captain Ludwig Schubart . . . Oberregierungsrat in the "Deutsche Seewarte," Hamburg.

Captain Conrad Soerensen . . . Inspector of the "Dampfschifffahrtsgesellschaft 1869," Flensburg.

Mr. Johann Winter . . . . . Chief Engineer, First Ship Surveyor, See-Berufsgenossenschaft, Hamburg.

THE COMMONWEALTH OF AUSTRALIA

Delegates

Captain Henry Priaulx Cayley . Royal Australian Navy, Commonwealth Naval Representative in London.

Mr. Vincent Cyril Duffy . . . Australia House.

Secretary

Paymaster Lieut.-Com. A. Freyer . Royal Australian Navy.

BELGIUM

Delegate

Mr. Raoul F. Grimard . . . . Naval Engineer, Technical Adviser to the Central Naval Department.

CANADA

Delegate

Mr. Alexander Johnston . . . . Deputy Minister of Marine.

Experts

Mr. C. F. M. Duguid . . . . . Chief Naval Architect.

Captain J. Gillies . . . . . . Canadian Pacific Steamships, Ltd.

Mr. Frank McDonnell . . . . Chairman, Board of Steamship Inspection.

Captain H. E. Nedden . . . . Canadian National Steamship Co.

Captain R. A. Goudey . . . . Canadian National Steamship Co.

Secretary

Miss Edna Stowe

CHILE

Delegate

Lieut.-Commander Constructor   Member of the Chilian Naval Commission in London.
Oscar Bunster

CUBA

Delegate

Mr. Guillermo Patterson . . . . Cuban Minister in London.

DENMARK

Delegates

Mr. Emil Krogh . . . . . . Assistant Secretary in the Ministry of Shipping and Fisheries.

Mr. Aage H. Larsen . . . . . Naval Architect and Engineer-in-Chief to the Ministry of Shipping and Fisheries.

Mr. J. A. Körbing . . . . . . Director of the "Forenede Damp-skibsselskab," Copenhagen.

Captain H. P. Hagelberg . . . Chairman of the Association of Danish Shipmasters.

Mr. Erik Jacobsen . . . . . . Trade Union Manager.

Experts

Mr. P. Villadsen . . . . . . Principal in the Ministry of Shipping and Fisheries.

Mr. Peder Fischer . . . . . . Naval Architect.

THE FREE CITY OF DANZIG

Delegates

Mr. Alphonse Poklewski-Koziell . Commercial Counsellor, Polish Legation, London.

Mr. Waldemar Sieg . . . . . Commercial Counsellor.

SPAIN

Delegate

Mr. Octaviano Martinez-Barca . Engineer, Spanish Navy.

IRISH FREE STATE

Delegates

Mr. J. W. Dulanty . . . . . Commissioner for Trade for the Irish Free State in Great Britain.

Mr. T. J. Hegarty . . . . . Ship Surveyor, Transport and Marine Branch, Department of Industry and Commerce.

UNITED STATES OF AMERICA

Delegates

Mr. Herbert B. Walker . . . . President of the American Steamship Owners' Association.

Mr. David Arnott . . . . . . Chief Surveyor, American Bureau of Shipping.

Mr. Laurens Prior . . . . . Bureau of Navigation, Department of Commerce.

Mr. Howard C. Towle . . . . National Council of American Shipbuilders.

Mr. Samuel D. McComb . . . Marine Office of America.

Captain Albert F. Pillsbury . . . Pillsbury and Curtis, San Francisco.

Mr. Robert F. Hand . . . . . Vice-President Standard Shipping Co., New York.

Mr. James Kennedy . . . . . General Manager, Marine Department, Gulf Refining Co., New York.

Mr. H. W. Warley . . . . . Vice-President Ore Steamship Corporation, New York.

Rear-Admiral John G. Tawresey . C.C., United States Navy, Retired, United States Shipping Board.

Technical Advisers

Mr. David W. Dickie . . . . Engineer and Naval Architect, Attorney-at-Law, San Francisco.

Captain P. C. Grening . . . . Director for Europe, United States Shipping Board Merchant Fleet Corporation.

Mr. G. A. Smith . . . . . . American Bureau of Shipping.

FINLAND

Delegates

Mr. A. H. Saastamoinen . . . Finnish Minister in London.

Commander Birger Brandt . . . Finnish Shipmasters' Association.

Assistant Delegate

Mr. E. Wälikangas . . . . . Finnish Legation, London.

FRANCE

Delegates

Mr. André Maurice Haarbleicher . Naval Construction Corps, Director of the Departments of the Mercantile Fleet and of Naval Material at the Ministry of the Mercantile Marine.

Mr. René Hippolyte Joseph Lindemann. Assistant Director of the Department of Marine Labour and of the Accountants' Department at the Ministry of the Mercantile Marine.

Mr. Jean Henri Theophile Marie . Naval Construction Corps, Assistant to the Director of the Departments of the Mercantile Fleet and of Naval Material at the Ministry of the Mercantile Marine.

Mr. A. H. A de Berlhe . . . . Deputy Manager of the Bureau Veritas.

Assistant to the Delegates

Mr. J. Volmat . . . . Chief Hydrographer, 2nd Class, representing the French Admiralty.

Experts

Mr. Jacques de Berlhe . . . . Engineer to the Bureau Veritas.

Mr. Brillié	Chief Consulting Engineer of the Compagnie Générale Transatlantique.
Mr. M. A. R. de Catalano . . .	Chief Superintendent of the Compagnie Générale Transatlantique.
Mr. J. R. L. Dubois	Chief Marine Superintendent of the Compagnie des Messageries Maritimes.
Mr. G. Falcoz	Chief Engineer of the Compagnie des Messageries Maritimes.
Mr. Ch. le Pelletier	Chief Engineer of the Compagnie des Chargeurs Réunis.
Mr. A. Nizery	Manager of the Compagnie des Chargeurs Réunis.
Mr. Patry	Chief Engineer of the Bureau Veritas.
Mr. J. Perrachon	Assistant Manager of the Compagnie Auxiliaire de Navigation.
Mr. Jules M. A. T. Pinczon . .	Chief Consulting Engineer of the Chantiers de Saint-Nazaire.
Mr. R. Rossigneux	Chief of the Technical Department of the Comité Central des Armateurs de France.

Secretary

Captain C. F. J. Dilly	Inspector of Navigation, Ministry of Mercantile Marine.

UNITED KINGDOM OF GREAT BRITAIN AND NORTHERN IRELAND

Delegates

Sir Henry F. Oliver	Admiral of the Fleet, Royal Navy.
Captain F. W. Bate	Professional Officer, Mercantile Marine Department, Board of Trade.
Mr. A. J. Daniel	Principal Ship Surveyor, Board of Trade.
Captain J. T. Edwards	Master Mariner, Retired.
Sir Ernest W. Glover	Chamber of Shipping of the United Kingdom.
Sir Norman Hill	Chairman, Merchant Shipping Advisory Committee, Board of Trade.
Sir Charles Hipwood	Board of Trade.
Mr. J. Foster King	Chief Surveyor to the British Corporation Register of Shipping and Aircraft.

Dr. J. Montgomerie . . . . . Chief Ship Surveyor to Lloyd's Register of Shipping.

Sir Charles J. O. Sanders . . . Chairman, Load Line Committee, 1927–1929.

Mr. William Robert Spence . . General Secretary, National Union of Seamen.

Captain A. Spencer . . . . . Master Mariner, Retired.

Secretary

Mr. A. E. Lee . . . . Board of Trade.

Assistant Secretaries

Mr. G. C. Ager . . . . . . Board of Trade.
Mr. W. Graham . . . . . . Board of Trade.
Mr. H. C. Miller . . . . . Board of Trade.
Mr. J. T. Munden . . . . . Board of Trade.
Mr. W. E. Stimpson . . . . Board of Trade.

GREECE

Delegate

Mr. Nicolas G. Lely . . . . . Consul-General for Greece in London.

Expert Advisers

Commander Basil Scarpetis . . Commander Harbour Master, Head of the Shipping Services at the Greek Consulate-General, London.

Acting Commander Evanghelos Roussos — Assistant of the Naval and Air Attaché of Greece, London.

INDIA

Delegates

Sir Geoffrey L. Corbett . . . . Late Secretary to the Government of India, Commerce Department.

Mr. Nowrojee Dadabhoy Allbless . Chairman of Scindia Steamships (London), Ltd.

Captain Kavas Ookerjee . . . Marine Superintendent, Scindia Steam Navigation Co., Ltd., Bombay.

Engineer-Commander John Sutherland Page — Royal Indian Marine. Late Principal Engineer and Ship Surveyor, Government of Bengal.

ICELAND

Delegates

Mr. Emil Krogh . . . . . . Assistant Secretary in the Danish Ministry of Shipping and Fisheries.

Mr. Aage H. Larsen . . . . Naval Architect and Engineer-in-Chief to the Danish Ministry of Shipping and Fisheries.

Mr. J. A. Körbing . . . . . Director of the "Forenede Dampskibsselskab," Copenhagen.

Captain H. P. Hagelberg . . . Chairman of the Association of Danish Shipmasters.

Mr. Erik Jacobsen . . . . . Trade Union Manager, Denmark.

Experts

Mr. P. Villadsen . . . . . . Principal in the Danish Ministry of Shipping and Fisheries.

Mr. Peder Fischer . . . . . Naval Architect.

ITALY

Delegates

General Giulio Ingianni . . . General Director of the Mercantile Marine.

Admiral Giuseppe Cantù . . . Admiral of Division, Technical Inspector of the Mercantile Marine.

Professor Torquato Giannini . . Counsellor for Emigration in the Italian Foreign Office.

Assistant Delegate

Dr. Gaetano Lampertico . . . Vice-Counsellor for Emigration in the Italian Foreign Office.

Experts

Mr. Carlo Doerfles . . . . . Naval Architect, Head of the Technical Office of the Registro Italiano Navale ed Aeronautico, Trieste.

Mr. Aroldo Palanca . . . . . Representing the Italian Shipowners' Federation.

Mr. Gino Soldà . . . . . . Naval Architect, Inspector of the Registro Italiano Navale ed Aeronautico.

Mr. Giuseppe Gasparini . . . . Naval Architect, representing the Italian General Confederation of Industry.

Captain Luigi Zino . . . . . Representing the Italian Cargo Shipowners' Federation, Genoa.

Captain Arturo Romano . . . Representing the Italian Confederation of Captains, Officers and Sea-
men.

JAPAN

Delegates

Mr. Shoichi Nakayama . . . . First-Class Secretary of Embassy.
Mr. Sukefumi Iwai . . . . . Expert in the Local Administration
Office of Communications.

Experts

Mr. Kumaichi Showno . . . . Expert in the Local Administration
Office of Communications.

Mr. Takeji Kobayashi . . . . Secretary in the Department of Communications.

Mr. Motoki Matsumura . . . . Attaché.
Captain Nagayoshi Hori . . . Temporary Staff in the Department of
Communications.

LATVIA

Delegates

Mr. Arturs Ozols . . . . . . Director of the Marine Department.
Captain Andrejs Lonfelds . . . Latvian Shipowners' Society.

MEXICO

Delegate

Mr. Gustavo Luders de Negri . . Consul-General for Mexico in London.

Secretary

Mr. Macedonio Garza . . . . Vice-Consul for Mexico, London.

NORWAY

Delegates

Mr. Erling Bryn . . . . . . Director of the Department of Shipping, Ministry of Commerce and
Navigation.

Mr. Johan Schönheyder . . . . Surveyor-in-Chief in the Ministry of
Commerce and Navigation.

Dr. J. Bruhn . . . . Director of the Norwegian Veritas.
Mr. J. Hysing Olsen . . . . . Shipowner.
Mr. Eivind Tonnesen . . . . Managing Director of the Norwegian
Shipmasters' Association.

Mr. A. Birkeland . . . . . . President of the Norwegian Sailors'
and Firemen's Union.

Adviser

Mr. E. Wettergreen . . . . . Chief of Division in the Ministry of Commerce and Navigation.

NEW ZEALAND

Delegates

Sir Thomas Mason Wilford . . High Commissioner for New Zealand in London.

Sir Charles Holdsworth . . . . Managing Director of the Union Steamship Company of New Zealand, Ltd.

PARAGUAY

Delegate

Dr. Horacio Carisimo . . . . Chargé d'Affaires in London.

NETHERLANDS

Delegates

Vice-Admiral (retired) C. Fock . Inspector-General of Navigation, Chairman of the Freeboard Assigning Commission.

Mr. A. van Driel . . . . . . Naval Architect, Adviser on Naval Architecture to the Shipping Inspection Service, Member and Secretary of the Freeboard Assigning Commission.

Mr. J. Brautigam . . . . . . Chairman of the Netherlands Union of Transport Workers, Member of the Second Chamber of the States General.

Mr. J. W. Langeler . . . . . Inspector of Shipping, Dutch East Indies.

Mr. J. Rypperda Wierdsma . . Chairman of the Holland-America Line.

Captain G. L. Heeris . . . . . Secretary of the Netherlands Shipowners' Association.

Experts

Mr. H. Keyser . . . . Assistant Director of the Royal Netherlands Meteorological Institute.

Professor N. Kal . . . . . . Professor in Naval Architecture at the Technical University, Delft.

Mr. F. Reedeker . . . . . . Master Mariner, retired.

Mr. G. de Ronde . . . . . . Master Mariner, retired.

Mr. J. Carpentier-Alting . . . . Naval Architect.

Secretary

Jonkheer O. Reuchlin . . . . Attaché to the Netherlands Legation, London.

PERU

Delegate

Captain Manuel D. Faura . . . Naval Attaché in London.

POLAND

Delegates

Mr. Alphonse Poklewski-Koziell . Commercial Counsellor, Polish Embassy, London.

Mr. Boguslaw Bagniewski . . . Counsellor, Ministry of Industry and Trade, Warsaw.

PORTUGAL

Delegates

Mr. Thomaz Ribeiro de Mello . . Head of the Economic Section of the Portuguese Ministry of Foreign Affairs.

Captain Carlos Theodoro da Costa . Naval Architect.

SWEDEN

Delegates

Baron Erik Kule Palmstierna . . Swedish Minister in London.

Mr. Per Axel Lindblad . . . . Assistant Under-Secretary in the Board of Trade.

Captain Erik Axel Fredrik Eggert . Maritime Expert to the Social Board.

Experts and Assistant Delegates

Mr. G. MacE. Böös . . . . . First Amanuensis in the Board of Trade.

Mr. A. W. Palmqvist . . . . . Controller of Tonnage, Gothenburg District.

Captain O. A. Nordborg . . . . Member of the First Chamber of Parliament, Director of the Swedish Shipowners' Association.

Captain N. P. Larsson . . . . President of the Swedish Society of Masters and Officers of the Mercantile Marine.

Mr. N. Olsson . . . . . . President of the Swedish Seamen's Union.

UNION OF SOCIALIST SOVIET REPUBLICS

Delegate

Mr. Dimitri Bogomoloff . . . . Counsellor of the Soviet Embassy in London.

Experts

Mr. P. Matveeff . . . . . . Naval Engineer.
Mr. A. A. Kaukul . . . . . Anglo-Soviet Shipping Co.

The Governments of Austria, Estonia, Hungary and Turkey appointed observers as follows:

Austria

Mr. K. Zeileissen . . . . . . Secretary to the Austrian Legation, London.

Estonia

Mr. R. A. Mollerson . . . . . Counsellor of Estonian Legation, London.

Hungary

Baron Ivan Rubido-Zichy . . . Hungarian Minister in London.

Turkey

Mehmet Ali Şevki Pasha . . . Counselor to the Turkish Embassy in London.

The League of Nations having been invited to send representatives to the Conference to act as observers, appointed the following delegation for this purpose:

Mr. Robert Haas . . . . Secretary-General of the Advisory and Technical Committee for Communications and Transit.
Mr. J. M. F. Romein . . . . Secretary of the Permanent Committee for Ports and Maritime Navigation.

Who accordingly assembled in London.

Admiral of the Fleet Sir Henry F. Oliver was appointed President of the Conference, and **Mr. A. E. Lee, Secretary-General.**

For the purposes of its work the Conference set up the following Committees, of which the under-mentioned were Presidents:

Administration Committee: Mr. Koenigs.
Main Technical Committee: Sir Charles Sanders.
Tankers Committee: Mr. Kennedy.

Timber Ships Committee: Mr. Emil Krogh.
Special Types of Ship Committee: Vice-Admiral Fock.
Zones Committee: General Ingianni.
Drafting Committee: Mr. Haarbleicher.
Credentials Committee: Mr. Nakayama.

In the course of a series of meetings between the 20th May, 1930, and
the 5th July, 1930, a Load Line Convention, dated the 5th July 1930, was
drawn up.

I

The Conference takes note of the following declarations, made by the
undermentioned delegation:

The Plenipotentiaries of the United States of America formally declare
that the signing of the International Load Line Convention by them, on
the part of the United States of America, on this date, is not to be construed
to mean that the Government of the United States of America recognizes
a régime or entity which signs or accedes to the Convention as the Government of a country when that régime or entity is not recognized by the Government of the United States of America as the Government of that country.

The Plenipotentiaries of the United States of America further declare
that the participation of the United States of America in the International
Load Line Convention signed on this date does not involve any contractual
obligation on the part of the United States of America to a country, represented by a régime or entity which the Government of the United States
of America does not recognize as the Government of that country, until
such country has a Government recognized by the Government of the United
States of America.

II

The Conference also adopts the following recommendations:

Ships of less than 150 tons gross Engaged on International Voyages

The Conference recommends that such regulations as may be made by
any of the Contracting Governments relating to ships of less than 150 tons
gross engaged on international voyages should, so far as practicable and
reasonable, be framed in accordance with the principles and rules laid down
in this Convention, and should whenever possible be made after consultation
and agreement with the Governments of the other countries concerned in
such international voyages.

Strength

As under the Rules attached to this Convention, ships which comply with
the highest standard laid down in the rules of a classification society recognised by the Administration are regarded as having sufficient strength for
the minimum freeboards allowed under the rules, the Conference recom-

mends that each Administration should request the Society or Societies which it has recognised to confer from time to time with the Societies recognised by other Administrations, with a view to securing as much uniformity as possible in the application of the standards of strength on which freeboard is based.

Annual Surveys

The Conference recommends that, if possible, each Administration should make arrangements for the periodical inspections referred to in paragraph (3) (c) of Article 14 to be held at intervals of approximately twelve months so far as concerns the maintenance of the fittings and appliances referred to in Condition B of paragraph 3 of that Article (*i.e.*, the fittings and appliances for the (i) protection of openings, (ii) guard rails, (iii) freeing ports and (iv) means of access to crews' quarters).

Information regarding Damage to Tankers

The Conference recommends that the Governments of the countries to which tankers belong shall keep records of all structural and deck damage to these ships caused by stress of weather, so that information with regard to these matters may be available.

In faith whereof the undersigned have affixed their signatures to the present Act.

Done in London this fifth day of July, 1930, in a single copy which shall be deposited in the archives of the Government of the United Kingdom of Great Britain and Northern Ireland, which shall transmit certified true copies thereof to all signatory Governments.

[For Germany:]
GUSTAV KOENIGS
WALTER LAAS
KARL STURM
WILHELM HEBERLING

[For Australia:]
H. P. CAYLEY
V. C. DUFFY

[For Belgium:]
R. GRIMARD

[For Canada:]
A. JOHNSTON
CHAS. DUGUID
FRANK McDONNELL
EDNA STOWE

[For Chile:]
OSCAR BUNSTER

[For Cuba:]
GUILLERMO PATTERSON

[For Denmark:]
EMIL KROUGH
AAGE H. LARSEN
H. P. HAGELBERG
P. VILLADSEN
P. FISCHER

[For Spain:]
OCTAVIANO M. BARCA

[For the Irish Free State:]
SEAN DULCHAONTIGH
T. J. HEGARTY

[For the United States:]
HERBERT B. WALKER
DAVID ARNOTT
LAURENS PRIOR
HOWARD C. TOWLE
ALBERT F. PILLSBURY
ROBERT F. HAND
JAS. KENNEDY
H. W. WARLEY

JOHN G. TAWRESEY
DAVID W. DICKIE
PAUL C. GRENING
GEORGE A. SMITH

[For Finland:]
A. H. SAASTAMOINEN
B. BRANDT

[For France:]
JEAN MARIE
A. DE BERLHE
J. VOLMAT
J. DE BERLHE
R. ROSSIGNEUX
CH. DILLY

[For the United Kingdom:]
H. F. OLIVER
F. W. BATE
ALFRED J. DANIEL
JOHN T. EDWARDS
ERNEST W. GLOVER
NORMAN HILL
C. HIPWOOD
J. FOSTER KING
J. MONTGOMERIE
CHARLES J. O. SANDERS
W. R. SPENCE
A. SPENCER
A. E. LEE
G. C. AGER
W. GRAHAM
H. C. MILLER
J. T. MUNDEN
W. E. STIMPSON

[For Sweden:]
E. PALMSTIERNA
E. EGGERT
GUNNAR BÖÖS

[For Greece:]
N. G. LELY
E. ROUSSOS

[For India:]
G. L. CORBETT
NOWROJEE DADABHOY ALLBLESS
KAVAS OOKERJEE
J. S. PAGE

[For Iceland:]
EMIL KROGH
AAGE H. LARSEN
H. P. HAGELBERG
P. VILLADSEN
P. FISCHER

[For Italy:]
GIULIO INGIANNI
GIUSEPPE CANTÙ
ING. CARLO DOERFLES
G. SOLDÀ
G. GASPARINI

[For Japan:]
S. NAKAYAMA
S. IWAI
K. SHOWNO
T. KOBAYASHI
M. MATSUMURA
N. HORI

[For Latvia:]
A. OZOLS

[For Mexico:]
G. LUDERS DE NEGRI

[For Norway:]
E. BRYN
J. SCHÖNHEYDER

[For New Zealand:]
THOMAS M. WILFORD
C. HOLDSWORTH

[For the Netherlands:]
C. FOCK
A. VAN DRIEL
JOH. BRAUTIGAM
LANGELER
J. R. WIERDSMA

[For Peru:]
M. D. FAURA

[For Poland:]
A. POKLEWSKI-KOZIELL
B. BAGNIEWSKI

[For Portugal:]
THOMAZ RIBEIRO DE MELLO
CARLOS THEODORO DA COSTA

[For the Union of Soviet Socialist
    Republics:]
D. BOGOMOLOFF
P. MATVEEFF
A. KAUKUL

[For the League of Nations Permanent
    Committee for Ports and Maritime
    Navigation:]
J. M. F. ROMEIN

[For Paraguay:]
S. HORACIO CARÍSIMO

[For Italy:]
T. C. GIANNINI

[For exchanges of notes relating to modifications of the French text of the rules contained in annex I, see 47 Stat. 2394 or p. 187 of TS 858.]

INDEX

INDEX

1151

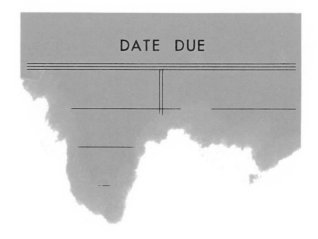

DATE DUE